D1209956

WOMANTHOLOGY

★ ★ ★

HEROIC

Womanthology.blogspot.com

IDW founded by Ted Adams, Alex Garner, Kris Oprisko, and Robbie Robbins | International Rights Representative, Christine Meyer: christine@gfloystudio.com

ISBN: 978-1-61377-147-1

14 13 12 11   1 2 3 4

Ted Adams, CEO & Publisher
Greg Goldstein, Chief Operating Officer
Robbie Robbins, EVP/Sr. Graphic Artist
Chris Ryall, Chief Creative Officer/Editor-in-Chief
Matthew Ruzicka, CPA, Chief Financial Officer
Alan Payne, VP of Sales

Become our fan on Facebook **facebook.com/idwpublishing**
Follow us on Twitter **@idwpublishing**
Check us out on YouTube **youtube.com/idwpublishing**
www.IDWPUBLISHING.com

< Renae De Liz
Renae De Liz

Female Creators-Would you be interested in being a part of an anthology made by all females, possibly published, w/profits for a cause?

17 May via web

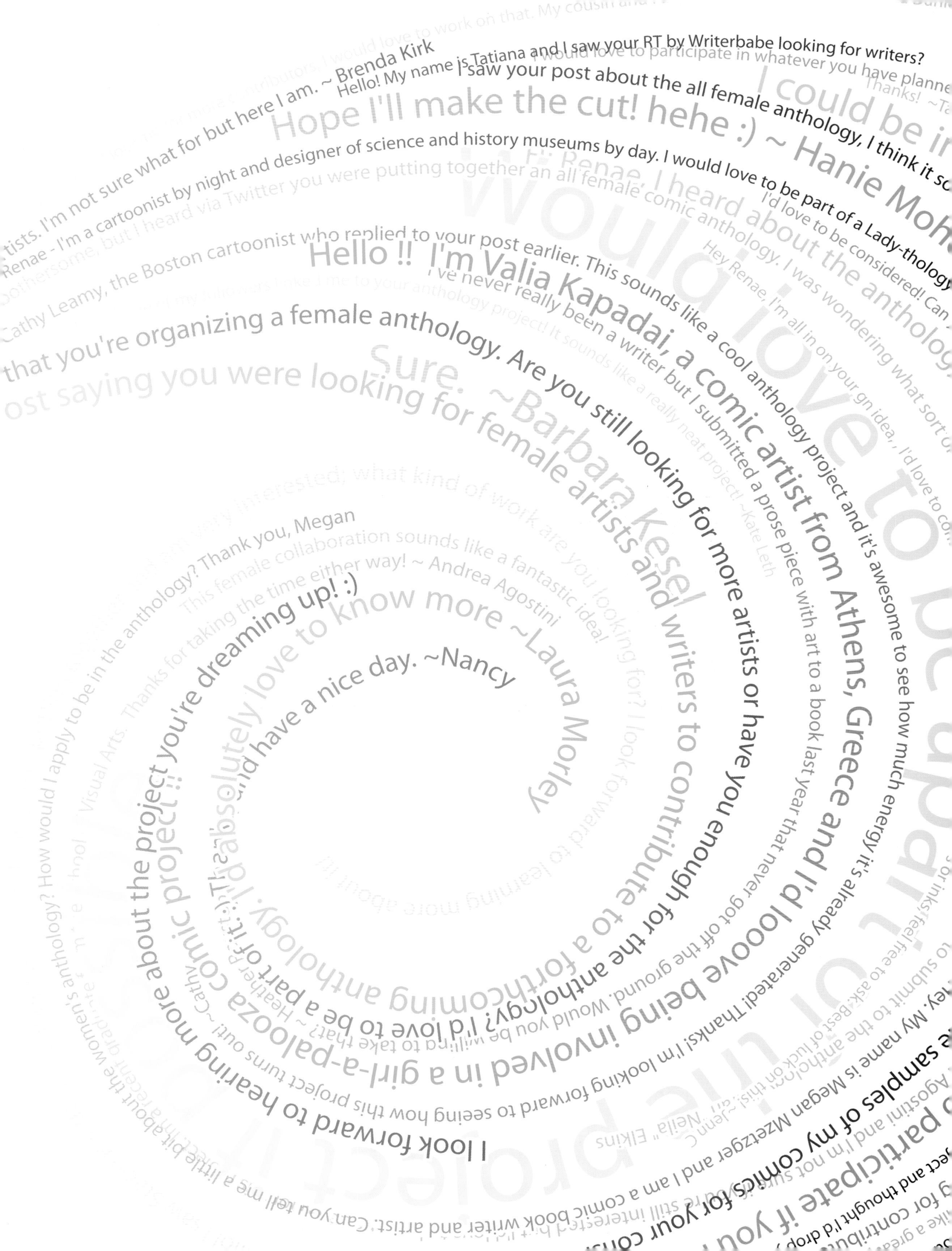

Hello! My name is Tatiana and I saw your RT by Writerbabe looking for writers?
I would love to participate in whatever you have planned
Thanks! ~Ta
I saw your post about the all female anthology, I think it so
I'm not sure what for but here I am. ~ Brenda Kirk
Hope I'll make the cut! hehe :) ~ Hanie Moh
I could be in
Renae - I'm a cartoonist by night and designer of science and history museums by day. I would love to be part of a Lady-thology
bothersome, but I heard via Twitter you were putting together an all female comic anthology. I was wondering what sort of
Hi Renae, I heard about the anthology. Can
I'd love to be considered!
would love to be apart of the project
Cathy Leamy, the Boston cartoonist who replied to your post earlier. This sounds like a cool anthology project and it's awesome to see how much energy it's already generated! Thanks! I'm looking forward to seeing how this project turns out!
Hey Renae, I'm all in on your gn idea, I'd love to co
Hello !! I'm Valia Kapadai, a comic artist from Athens, Greece and I'd looove being involved in a girl-a-palooza comic project !!
I've never really been a writer but I submitted a prose piece with art to a book last year that never got off the ground. Would you be willing to take that? ~ Heather
that you're organizing a female anthology. Are you still looking for more artists or have you enough for the anthology? I'd love to be a part of it! :) Thanks
this anthology project! It sounds like a really neat project! ~Kate Leth
ost saying you were looking for female artists and writers to contribute to a forthcoming anthology. I'd absolutely love to know more ~Laura Morley
Sure. ~Barbara Kesel
very interested; what kind of work are you looking for? I look forward to learning more about
Thank you, Megan
How would I apply to be in the anthology?
This female collaboration sounds like a fantastic idea!
Thanks for taking the time either way! ~ Andrea Agostini
the project you're dreaming up! :)
and have a nice day. ~Nancy
I look forward to hearing more about the project
Visual Arts
~Cathy
a little bit about the women's anthology?
I am a comic book writer and artist. Can you tell me
My name is Megan Mzetzger and I am a comic
samples of my comics for your cons
participate if you
Best of luck on this
Agostini and I'm not sure if you're still interested
Nella" Elkins
feel free to submit to the anthology
ect and thought I'd drop
for contribu

FOREWORD

★ ★ ☆

Welcome to *Womanthology: Heroic!*

The massive book you hold in your hand, believe it or not, started out very simply. It was originally intended to be a small anthology by a handful of women. But it was instantly clear that it wasn't going to sit back and just be a quaint little project.

On May 17th, 2011 comic book artist Renae De Liz sent a single message on Twitter.com asking if there were any female creators interested in working on a book together with proceeds going to charity. Over one hundred contributors signed up that day. At the time it was uncertain whether or not the book would even be published, however, the overwhelming amount of interest and heartfelt dedication to comics by the women could not be ignored.

June became a whirlwind of activity to get the project off the ground. A forum was established, websites were made, a name and a theme were decided upon, and the charity was picked by everyone on project. The logistics behind an anthology of this magnitude were incredibly complicated, however with the help of a few highly motivated contributors, particularly Laura Morley (now Assistant Project Manager), lists were made, writers were matched with artists, and editors were assigned to manageable groups. Professional female creators were paired with the less experienced, offering up chances for them to gain huge amounts of experience and knowledge.

The search for a publisher began and IDW Publishing stepped up right away. Having a publisher lent credibility to the project while also allowing 150 women to be published by a major company and have their work distributed all over the world. A month after its start, *Womanthology* had a publisher, but the project being for charity, funding still had to be made to meet the huge printing costs, so Renae started building the Kickstarter campaign.

The goal for a small print run was $25,000 and we had 30 days to pull in the support. The Kickstarter launched around 7pm EST on July 7th, 2011, only a month and a half since the initial idea.

There isn't a word to describe how it felt to be a part of what happened next. Brain-melted-y is close. The response was overwhelming! *Womanthology* surpassed the $25,000 mark in a mere 19 hours and in 30 days raised $109,301 with 2,001 people pledging to the project. Support flooded in from all over comics, movies, and beyond. Even high profile creators got very generously involved in spreading the word and supplying rewards for backers. It all happened so fast but as the dust settled there was no time to stop and take it in.

Production was set to a grueling two months, not only to get the book out earlier to Kickstarter backers, but also to give contributors involved the professional comics creator experience which often involves rough deadlines. Remarkably, every single creator on every single team—over 150 women—hit their deadlines spot on! Testament to how much love and passion went into seeing this project become something special.

Womanthology is a book unlike any other. As you read we hope you'll take a minute to learn about each woman who worked so hard to bring this idea to fruition and consider them for your next project. Thank you so much for picking up this book. You're doing a great thing for the creators and helping people in dire need through the great charities we've picked. Thank you!

- The Womanthology Team

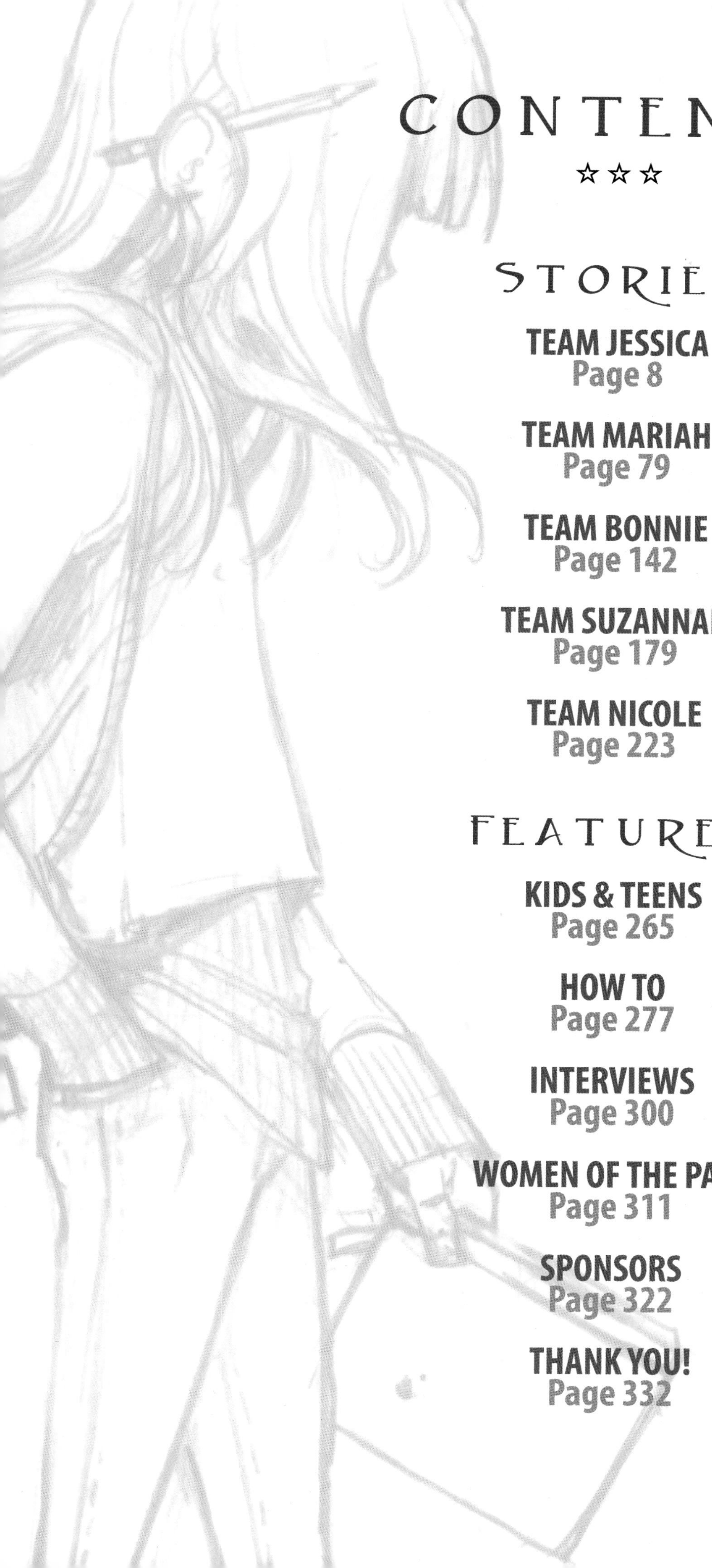

CONTENTS

☆☆☆

STORIES

FEATURES

HEROIC

☆ ☆ ☆ Heroic is the theme of this Anthology. We chose Heroic because it's a positive, strong, versatile word that can be visualized and translated in so very many different ways. All stories and artwork created in this book are each individual interpretations of that theme: Heroic.

PROJECT MANAGER - RENAE DE LIZ

Location: Cape Elizabeth, Maine
Day Job: Comic book artist, and mom of two crazy boys!

A little about yourself: Don't really know how to start! I was born in Anchorage, Alaska, and have been all over the place since—California, Oregon, Kansas, and finally Maine. I've been drawing my entire life, and absolutely adored comics and dreamt of someday being a comic artist. After high school, however, I quit drawing, thinking nothing would ever come from it, and that I'd never be good enough. Four years later, as a single mother of my son Tycen, while working one dead-end job after another, I started thinking about my dream to be a comic artist again, and decided to try and do something about it this time. I did a lot of research online, and spent the next couple years learning, meeting people, and practicing drawing, which started putting me on the right track. The biggest change came when I decided to travel outside my small town in Oregon for the first time to attend San Diego Comic Con 2005. There I got my first-ever paid art job, and also met my future husband, Ray Dillon, who was also a comic artist. One job led to the next, and has only gotten bigger and better ever since! I was able to make this my full-time job with Ray, and eventually Ray and I got married (at San Diego Comic Con 2009! ;D). We then had another little boy named Drake. And here we are! Working in comics like crazy people, chasing our kids around, and thanking our lucky stars we get to work in comics as our jobs. :) My story is full of amazing people who have been caring, understanding, supportive, and wonderful, so I like to feel my part in *Womanthology* is in huge part thanks to all of those people who have helped us along the way.

What does *Womanthology* mean to you? I feel women in comics have this unique and amazing way of portraying stories in the comics medium, and I wanted to support and showcase those visions. Similarly, from my observations over time (and from growing as a female creator myself) I know there are some challenges unique from males that a lot of female artists can go through while trying to make something of their dreams. In large part, this book is my attempt to reach out in those troublesome areas and lend a hand up through it, share knowledge, experience, and help show these amazing women just how much they can really accomplish, and that they can overcome any obstacle. To me, *Womanthology* means hope and change.

What was the best part of being on *Womanthology*: There have been some amazing stories behind the scenes that have really touched my heart, from young creators gaining newfound confidence, to some finding their first art jobs because of this, to those just so excited to be a part of this, and having so much fun. So much positivity has come from this, and I can't really explain just how happy that makes me!

Funny fact: My idea of a romantic date is a large pizza, two vanilla cupcakes, and a great co-op first person shooter video game! :)

☆ ☆ ☆

CREATOR BOX

WHAZIT?: Look at the bottom of the first page of each story to learn more about the creators that worked on that story!
SOUNDS NEAT!: Hey, thanks!
ALRIGHTY THEN: yep...

And their website links here!

 **PRO TIP**

TIPS!
BY PROFESSIONALS

SCATTERED THROUGHOUT THE BOOK WILL BE TIPS ON VARIOUS COMIC-RELATED SUBJECTS FROM VARIOUS INDUSTRY PROFESSIONALS WORKING ON WOMANTHOLOGY!

HE BOOK

TEAMS

☆ ☆ ☆ There were over 150 contributors working on this book, in which we had five editors handle their own "team" of ladies. Each team collaborated and worked hard together throughout this entire experience, so we felt they should be put together in the book as well.

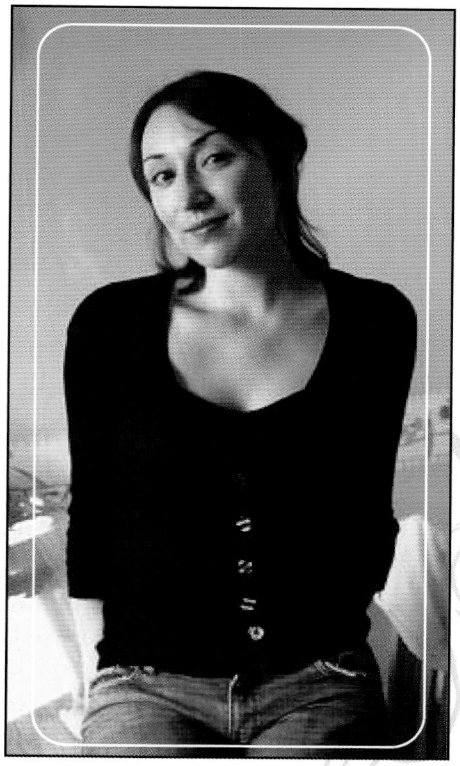

ASSISTANT PROJECT MANAGER - LAURA MORLEY

Location: Cambridge, UK
Day Job: I'm a technical writer and project manager at a software company.

A little about yourself: I'm an aspiring writer with a taste for hard-boiled noirs, old-school pulps, and heroes whose good intentions outstrip their powers. In comics, I have this awkwardly irreconcilable love for crunchy, heavy-duty, high-concept drama (*Ex Machina, Planetary*), and knockabout character comedy (*Justice League International*). After a childhood spent being bored and rustic in the Westcountry, I pursued relentlessly pragmatic, vocational studies (social anthropology, and history and philosophy of science, with side-interests in interpersonal drama and excessive coffee consumption) at Cambridge University, before dropping out of a PhD to work in publishing and web stuff. Though I write long-form fiction too, I love comics for being so collaborative: there's this electricity you get when working with others to bring a story to life, and I find it irresistible. Just now I'm finishing up a graphic novel script, and working on some minicomics; you can follow my continuing adventures at lauramorley.com

What does *Womanthology* mean to you? I heard of the project through Renae's initial call-for-submissions tweet, and replied to say I'd love both to write and to do any back-stage admin wrangling required. A project this size turns out to need quite a lot of that wrangling, and I wound up helping to organize creator teams, and acting as a first contact for contributors and Kickstarter backers. When the Kickstarter really took off, this ballooned into a big (but very rewarding) job, where a "typical" day might include collecting cameo reference photos for our artists, arranging interviews with a pro creator, helping editors chase submissions, arranging reward fulfillment, and handling publicity requests. So *Womanthology's* more than once taught me what 3 a.m. looks like by the glow of a lonely laptop screen, but it's also taught me how much you can achieve with effort and determination: how generous the comics community is (with their resources and their time); how much talent and enthusiasm there is out there; and how rewarding a sleepless night (when spent on something you love!) can really be.

What was the best part of being on *Womanthology*: It's been such a great chance to meet happy people! Comics can sometimes feel mired in negativity, and this has been a great corrective to that. From backers who've said the project inspires them and their kids, through contributors seeing their first work in print, right up to some very big-name industry figures who've helped us out of the kindness of their hearts, almost everyone I've dealt with for *Womanthology* has been positive, energised, and inspired, and it fills me with hope for this geeky world I love so much.

Funny fact: Last March I abseiled off Cambridge City Hall dressed as Batgirl, to raise funds for East Anglia Children's Hospices—check out justgiving.com/batusi :)

☆ ☆ ☆

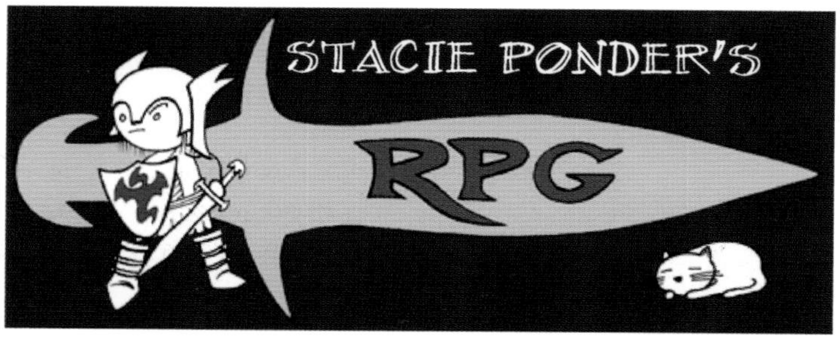
STACIE PONDER'S
RPG

THROUGHOUT THE BOOK IN THE BOTTOM BAR, YOU WILL FIND A TINY, CONTINUOUS, & HILARIOUS STORY WRITTEN & DRAWN BY ***STACIE PONDER,*** EXPANDING THE UNIVERSE SHE HAS CREATED WITH HER WEBCOMIC

HTTP://WWW.RPGCOMIC.COM
HTTP://WWW.STACIEPONDER.COM

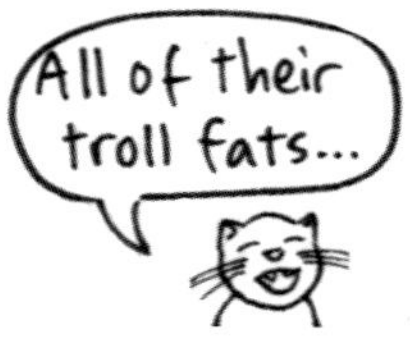
All of their troll fats...

PART ONE

TEAM JESSICA

☆ ☆ ☆ For each section of *Womanthology* a different lady took on the role of editor over the writers, pencillers, inkers, colorists, and letterers for their stories or pinups. They were in charge of making sure the creators worked as a team, had all the info they needed, and that all stories and pinups were turned in on time. This section is Jessica Hickman's.

EDITOR - JESSICA HICKMAN
Location: Minnesota
Day Job: Paper pusher/office work

A little about yourself: Born and raised in Ajo (Ah-ho), Arizona. Art graduate from Arizona State University. I now live in the frozen tundra of the Midwest with my two cats in a little studio apartment. I like to come home, sit on my sofa, watch horror films, and doodle until I fall asleep. Really, does it get any better than that? NO.

What does *Womanthology* mean to you? Well – after I suggested the idea to Renae she asked if I wanted to help out and I said sure. Then I was "promoted" to Editor (ha!). And I have learned SO MUCH. Working with various people on a project, editing stories and artwork, maintaining professionalism while representing *Womanthology*, taking accountability, making sure my teams adhere to deadlines, and on and on. All while doing my own comic for the book. It's been a very rewarding experience and I can't wait for the book to be out.

What was the best part of being on *Womanthology*: All the incredibly talented people I have met. It has been very inspiring to be surrounded by such talented creators throughout this process. Women (professionals and newcomers) who have selflessly donated their time and talent to this project. It has been a pleasure to work with all of them.

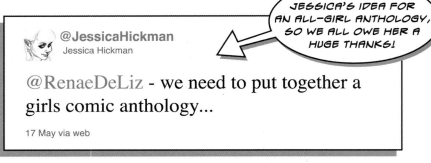

@JessicaHickman
Jessica Hickman

@RenaeDeLiz - we need to put together a girls comic anthology...

17 May via web

IT WAS JESSICA'S IDEA FOR AN ALL-GIRL ANTHOLOGY, SO WE ALL OWE HER A HUGE THANKS!

Funny fact: I did not learn to drive until I was 25 years old. I didn't have the need (or finances) for a car at the time – so I just biked everywhere while I was in college.

RACHEL DEERING
SKILLS: Editor, Letterer
LOCATION: Columbus, OH
FUN FACT: I sing in a heavy metal band!

http://twitter.com/#!/racheldeering

RACHEL DEERING IS THE MAIN LETTERER ON WOMANTHOLOGY, SO IF YOU SEE THAT NAME POPPING UP ALL OVER THE PLACE, NOW YOU'LL KNOW WHY! SHE'S ALSO A WRITER AND EDITOR IN THE BOOK! SO KEEP AN EYE OUT! =)

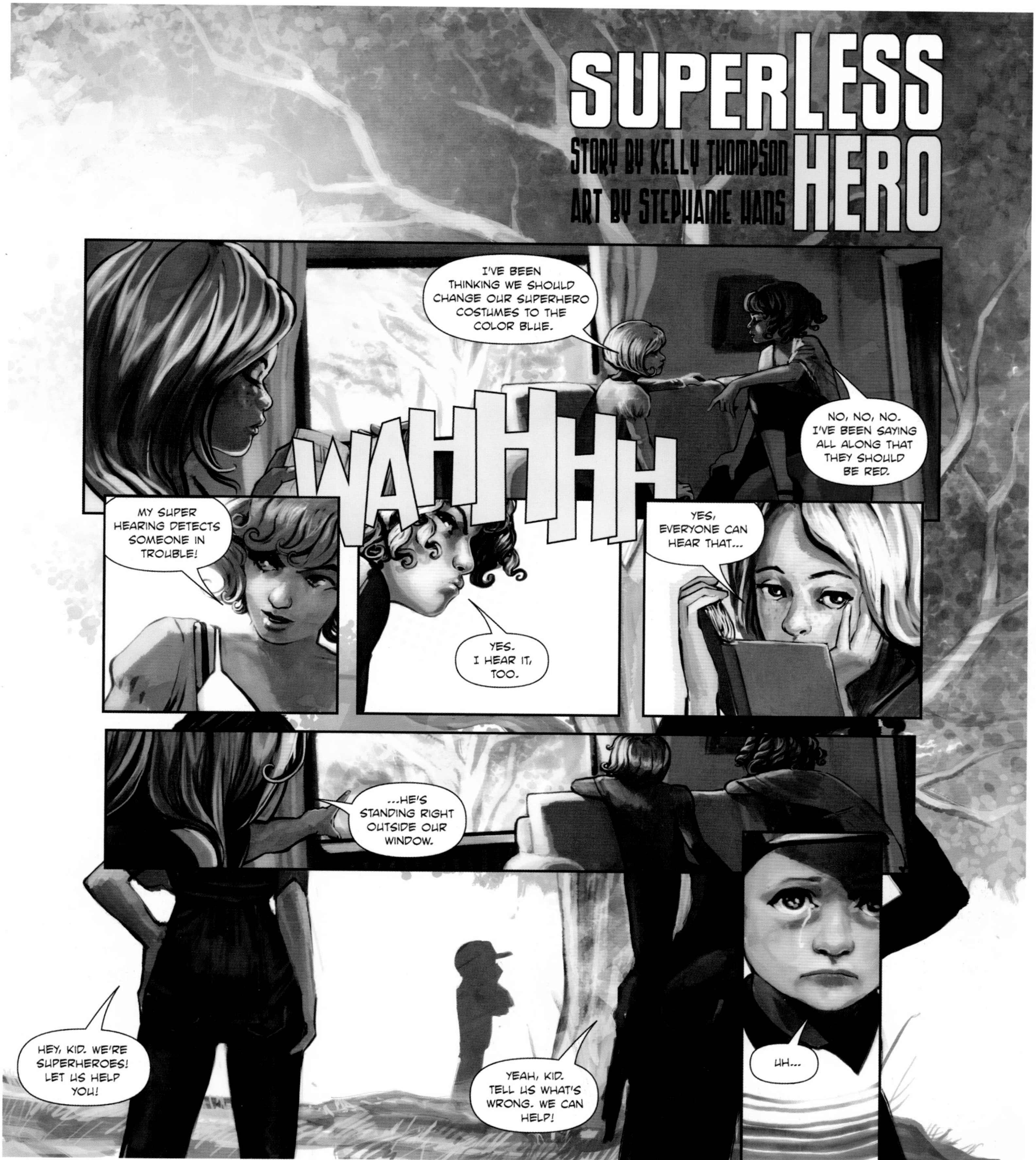
SUPERLESS HERO
STORY BY KELLY THOMPSON
ART BY STEPHANIE HANS
I'VE BEEN THINKING WE SHOULD CHANGE OUR SUPERHERO COSTUMES TO THE COLOR BLUE.
NO, NO, NO. I'VE BEEN SAYING ALL ALONG THAT THEY SHOULD BE RED.
WAHHHHH
MY SUPER HEARING DETECTS SOMEONE IN TROUBLE!
YES. I HEAR IT, TOO.
YES, EVERYONE CAN HEAR THAT...
...HE'S STANDING RIGHT OUTSIDE OUR WINDOW.
HEY, KID. WE'RE SUPERHEROES! LET US HELP YOU!
YEAH, KID. TELL US WHAT'S WRONG. WE CAN HELP!
UH...

WRITER: KELLY THOMPSON ARTIST: STEPHANIE HANS LETTERER: RACHEL DEERING

☆☆☆

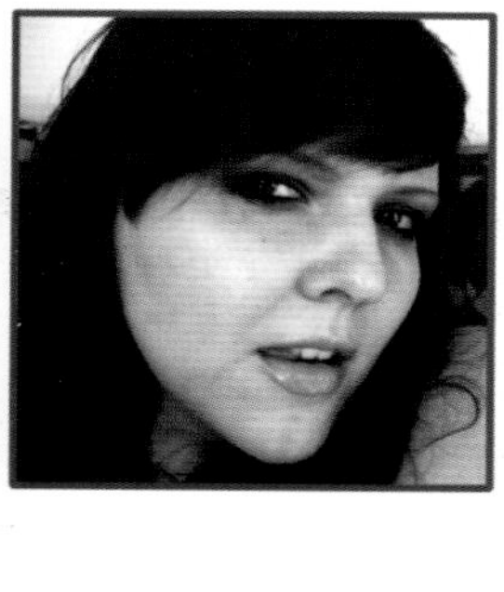

KELLY THOMPSON

SKILLS: Writer
LOCATION: NYC
FUN FACT: I love superheroes so much that I wrote a novel about them, coming soon to a bookstore near you if my agent and I have anything to say about it.

http://1979semifinalist.wordpress.com

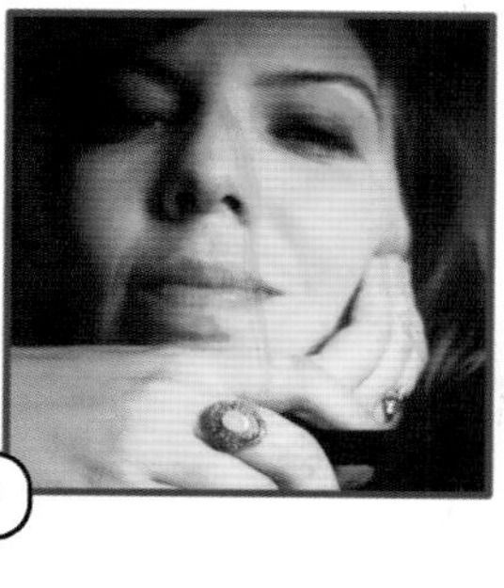

STEPHANIE HANS

SKILLS: Artist, Painter
LOCATION: France
FUN FACT: Until 26, I thought everybody was reading at least three books a month...

www.grainedepluie.com

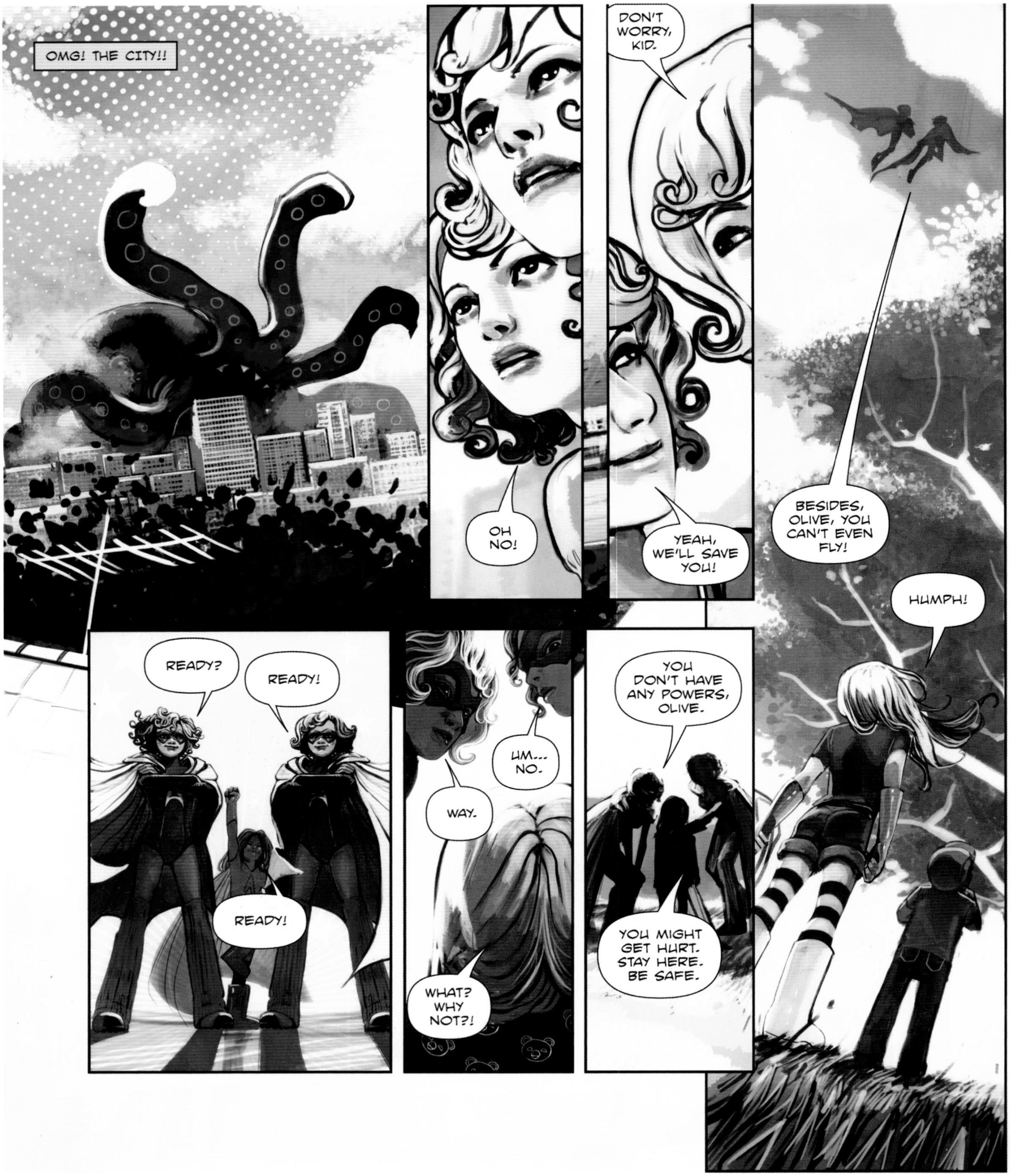
OMG! THE CITY!!
OH NO!
DON'T WORRY, KID.
YEAH, WE'LL SAVE YOU!
BESIDES, OLIVE, YOU CAN'T EVEN FLY!
HUMPH!
READY?
READY!
READY!
UM... NO.
WAY.
WHAT? WHY NOT?!
YOU DON'T HAVE ANY POWERS, OLIVE.
YOU MIGHT GET HURT. STAY HERE. BE SAFE.

☆ ☆ ☆

WOMANTHOLOGY STATISTICS

Womanthology contributors come from over 11 countries, and range in age from under 10 to over 70. *Womanthology* received press coverage as far afield as Oman, Brazil, and Wales.

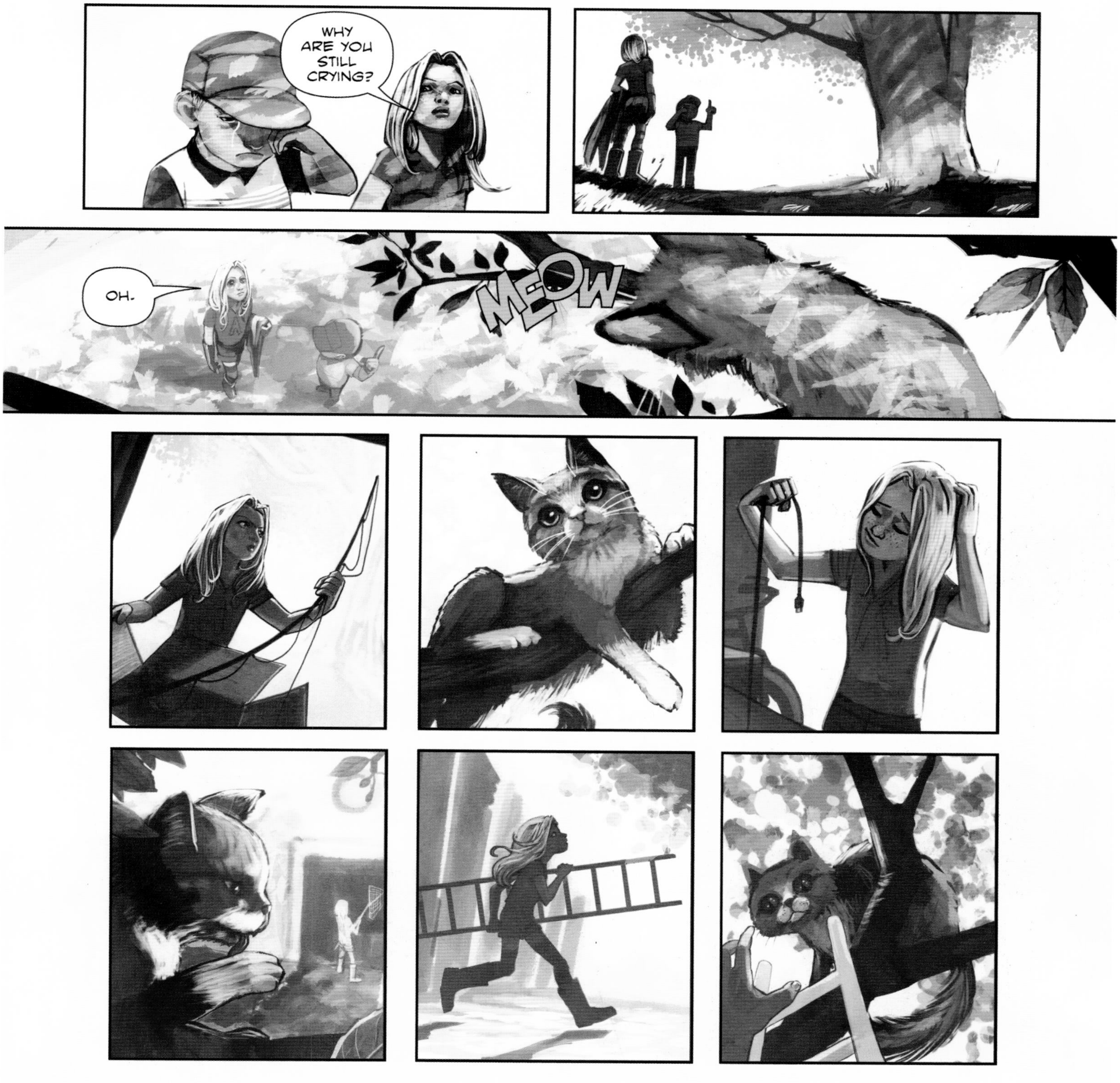
WHY ARE YOU STILL CRYING?
OH.
MEOW

☆☆☆

WOMANTHOLOGY STATISTICS

Womanthology took only 19 hours to reach its original funding target.
Womanthology is the best-funded comics project ever to feature on Kickstarter.
Womanthology is the 25th most funded Kickstarter project of any kind in history.
The *Womanthology* project received over 3,000 emails in its first six months of existence.

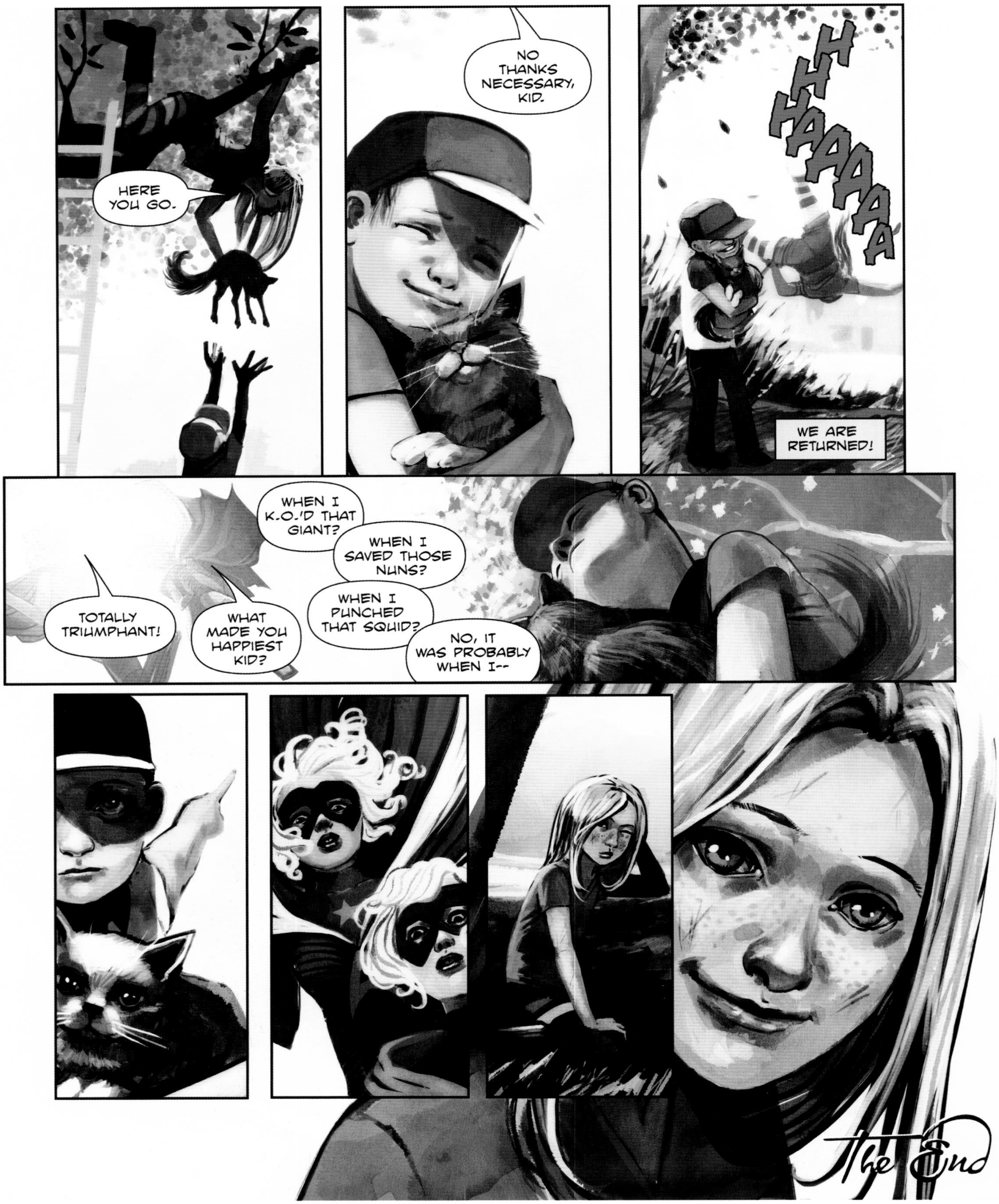
HERE YOU GO.
NO THANKS NECESSARY, KID.
HHHAAAAAAA
WE ARE RETURNED!
TOTALLY TRIUMPHANT!
WHAT MADE YOU HAPPIEST KID?
WHEN I K.O.'D THAT GIANT?
WHEN I SAVED THOSE NUNS?
WHEN I PUNCHED THAT SQUID?
NO, IT WAS PROBABLY WHEN I--
The End

☆☆☆

PRO TIP

TIME TO GROW

BY LAURA MORLEY

"DON'T GIVE UP. EVERYONE WHO CAN DRAW BEAUTIFULLY NOW WAS A BEGINNER ONCE. AND DON'T GET FRUSTRATED IF YOUR WORK DOESN'T YET LOOK THE WAY YOU WANT IT TO. PERSEVERANCE IS THE MOST IMPORTANT SKILL YOU'LL NEED, AND IT'S ONE YOU CAN START USING RIGHT NOW."

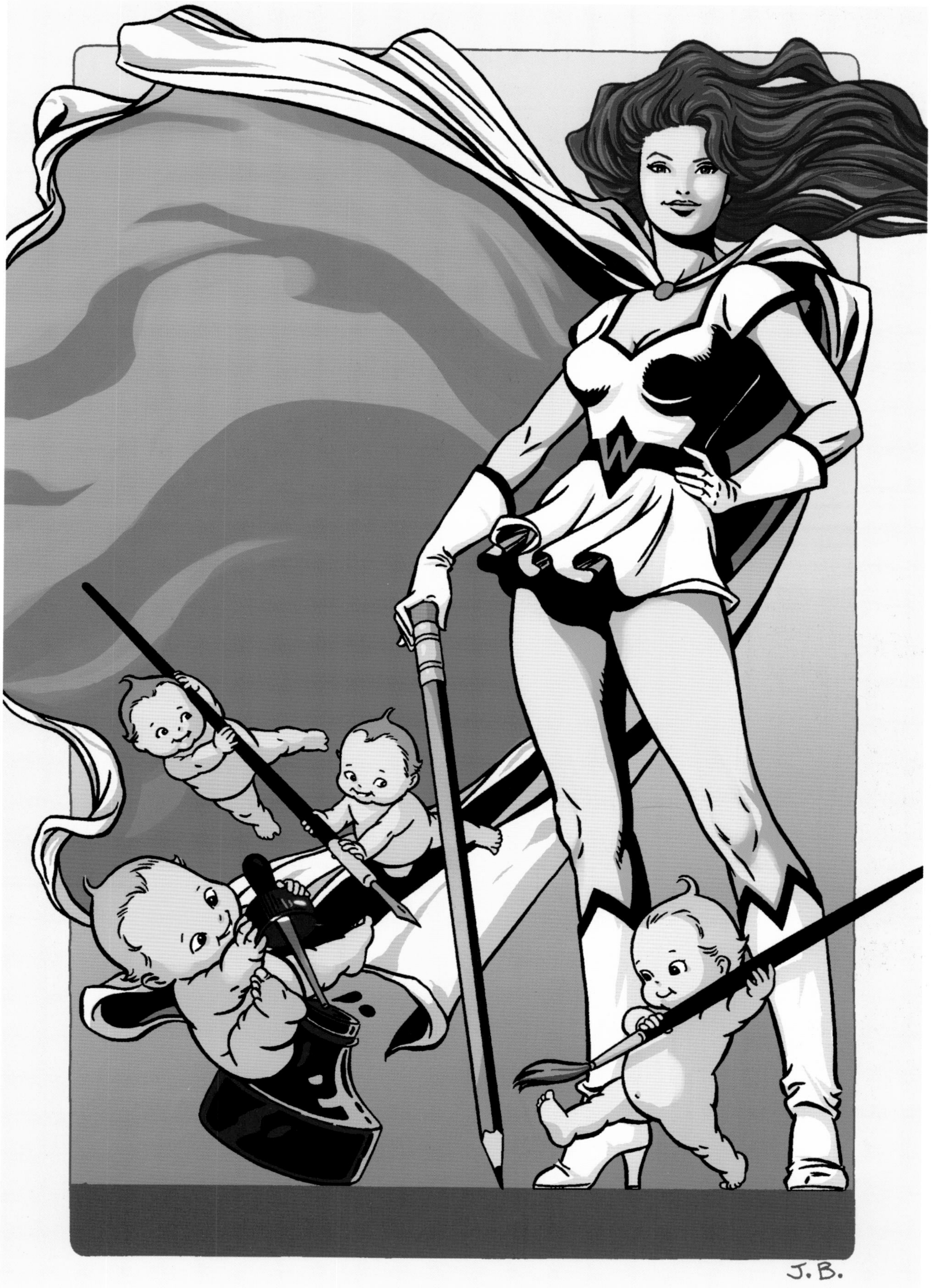
J.B.

☆☆☆

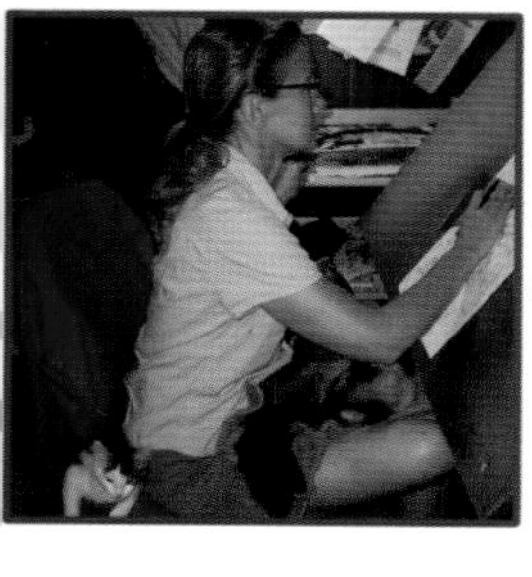

JUNE BRIGMAN

SKILLS: Penciller, Inker
LOCATION: Atlanta, Georgia
FUN FACT: I have the same birthday as Pablo Piccaso.

www.ArtWanted.com/juneart

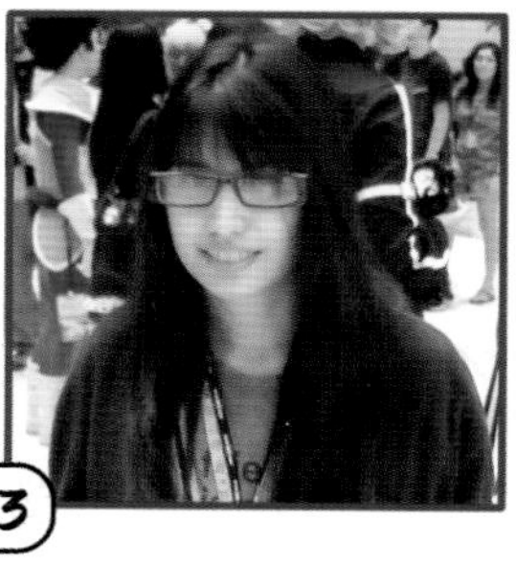

LISA KIRK

SKILLS: Colorist
LOCATION: Atlanta, Georgia
FUN FACT: Outside of art I like to spend time working on aquariums and aquascaping.

http://lisa-kirk.blogspot.com

STRENGTH & CONFIDENCE

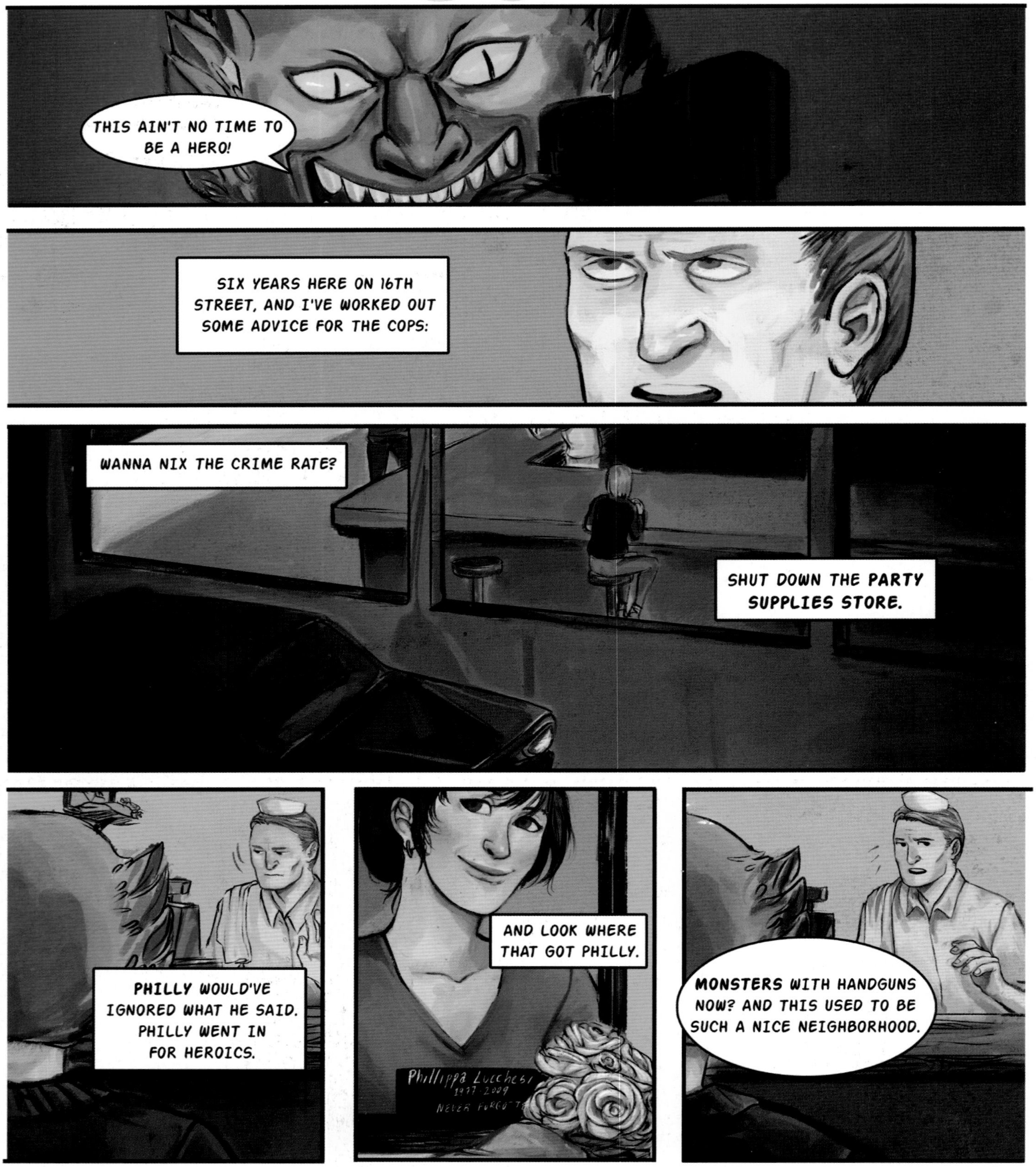

THIS AIN'T NO TIME TO BE A HERO!
SIX YEARS HERE ON 16TH STREET, AND I'VE WORKED OUT SOME ADVICE FOR THE COPS:
WANNA NIX THE CRIME RATE?
SHUT DOWN THE PARTY SUPPLIES STORE.
PHILLY WOULD'VE IGNORED WHAT HE SAID. PHILLY WENT IN FOR HEROICS.
AND LOOK WHERE THAT GOT PHILLY.
Phillippa Lucchesi
1977-2009
NEVER FORGOTTEN
MONSTERS WITH HANDGUNS NOW? AND THIS USED TO BE SUCH A NICE NEIGHBORHOOD.

WRITER: LAURA MORLEY ARTIST: THALIA DE LA TORRE

☆☆☆

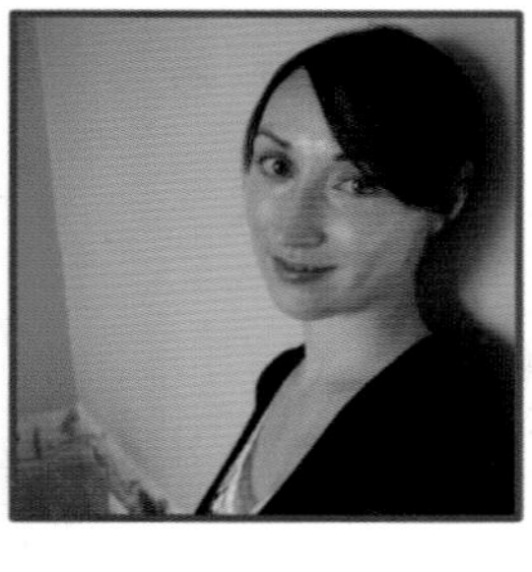

LAURA MORLEY

SKILLS: Writer
LOCATION: Cambridge, UK
FUN FACT: My first publishing credit was in an Aston Villa F.C. football fanzine.

ejne7.wordpress.com

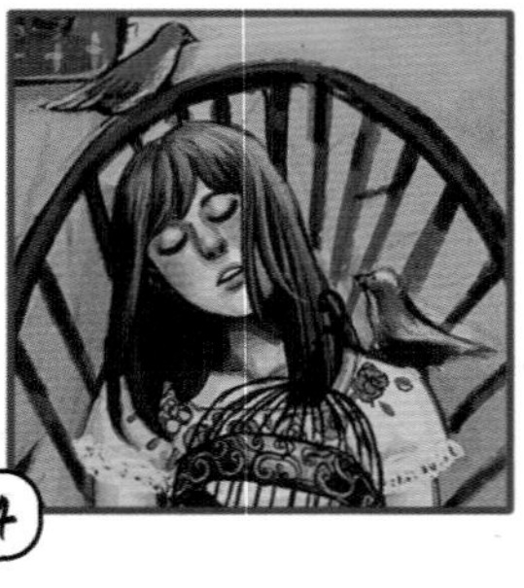

THALIA DE LA TORRE

SKILLS: Artist
LOCATION: Mexico City
FUN FACT: I can bend my arms 360 degrees :D

belivac.blogspot.com

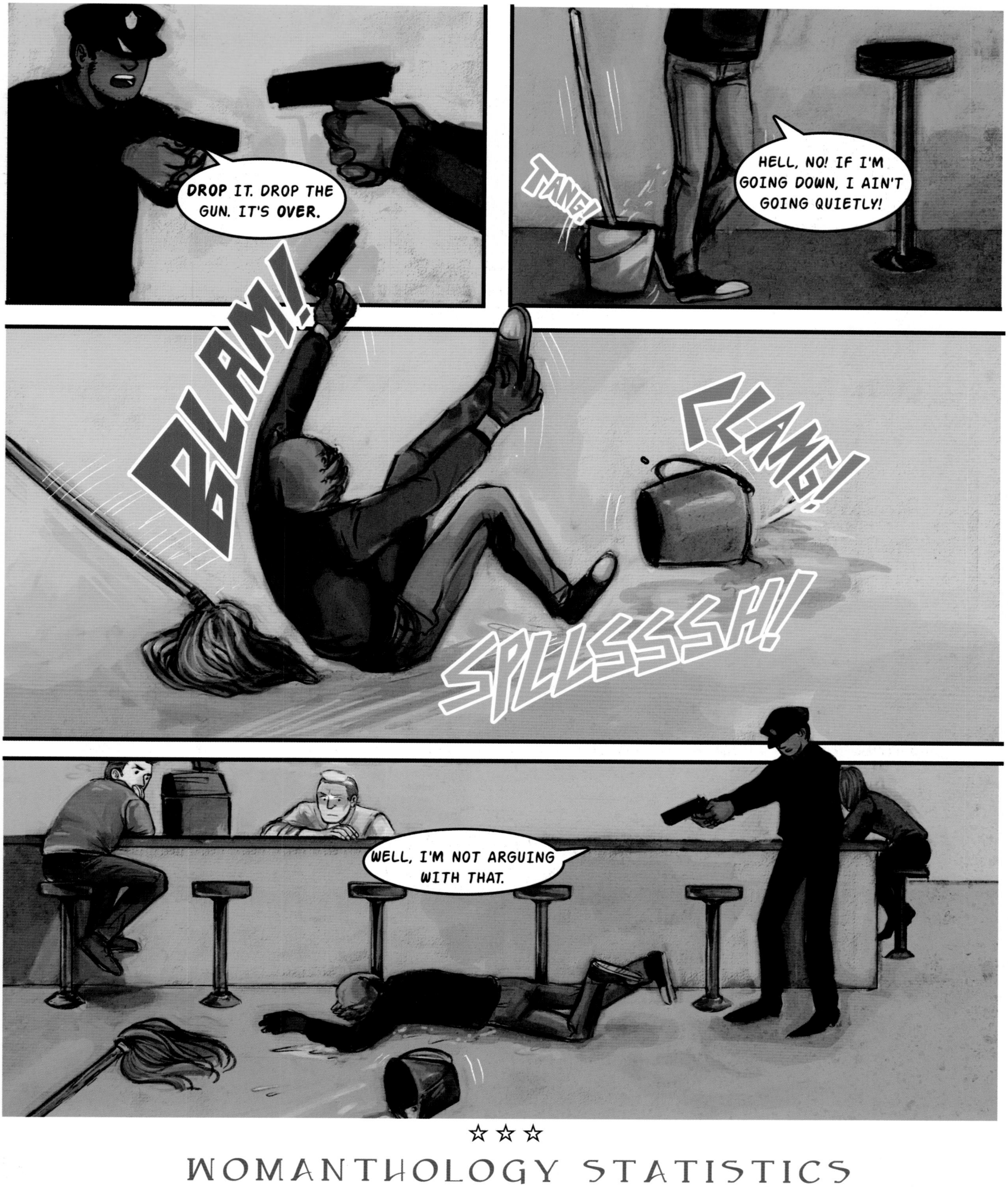
DROP IT. DROP THE GUN. IT'S OVER.
TANG!
HELL, NO! IF I'M GOING DOWN, I AIN'T GOING QUIETLY!
BLAM!
CLANG!
SPLLSSSSH!
WELL, I'M NOT ARGUING WITH THAT.

☆ ☆ ☆

WOMANTHOLOGY STATISTICS

CONTRIBUTOR ESTIMATES

168 total contributors. 56 team artists. 52 team writers. 28 solo pinup/one-page contributors. 11 colorists. Two inkers. Two letterers. 11 contributors under 18. Six feature writers or interviewees who didn't otherwise contribute. There were several people who did multiple duties but were counted only once.

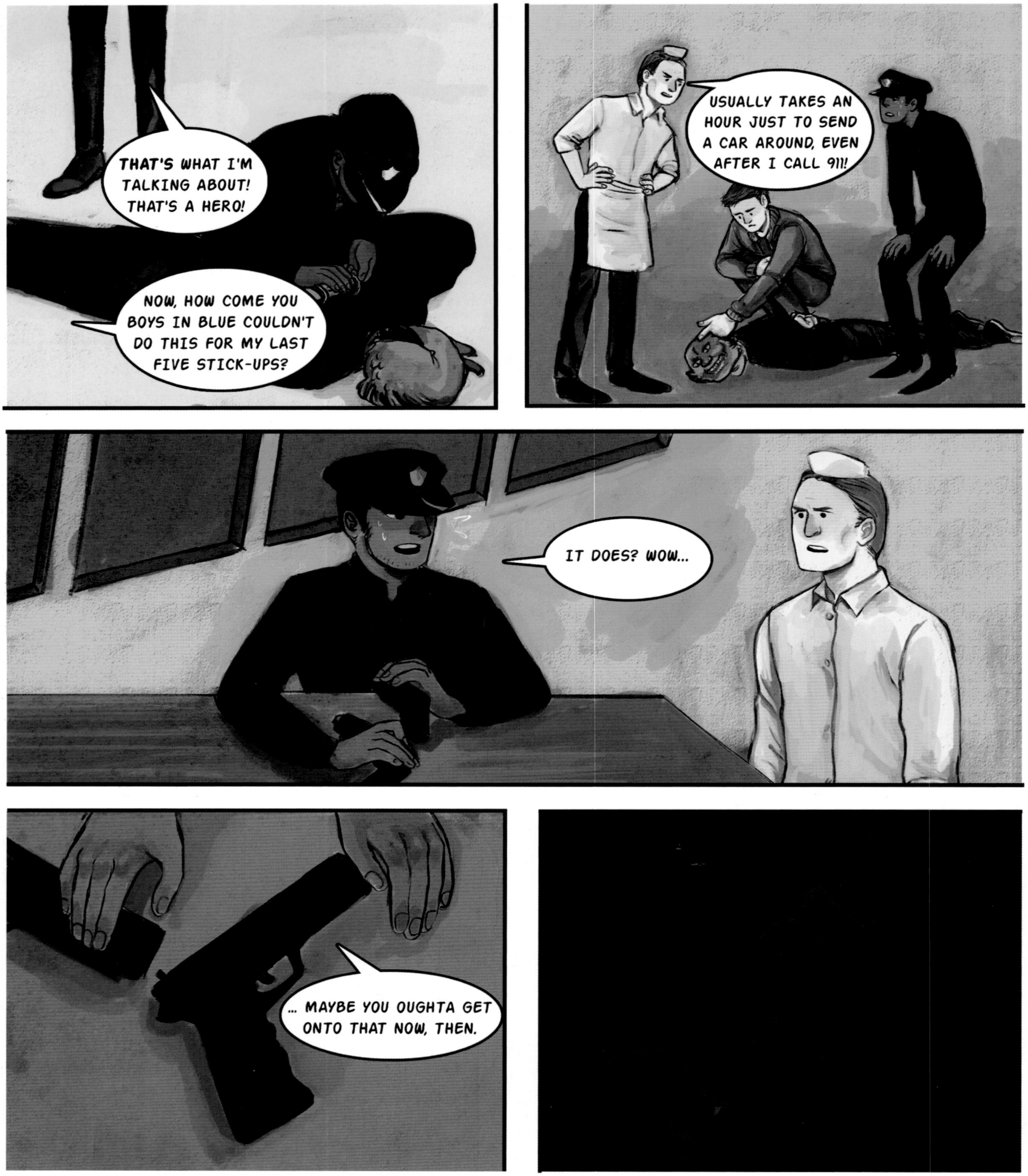
THAT'S WHAT I'M TALKING ABOUT! THAT'S A HERO!
NOW, HOW COME YOU BOYS IN BLUE COULDN'T DO THIS FOR MY LAST FIVE STICK-UPS?
USUALLY TAKES AN HOUR JUST TO SEND A CAR AROUND, EVEN AFTER I CALL 911!
IT DOES? WOW...
... MAYBE YOU OUGHTA GET ONTO THAT NOW, THEN.

☆ ☆ ☆

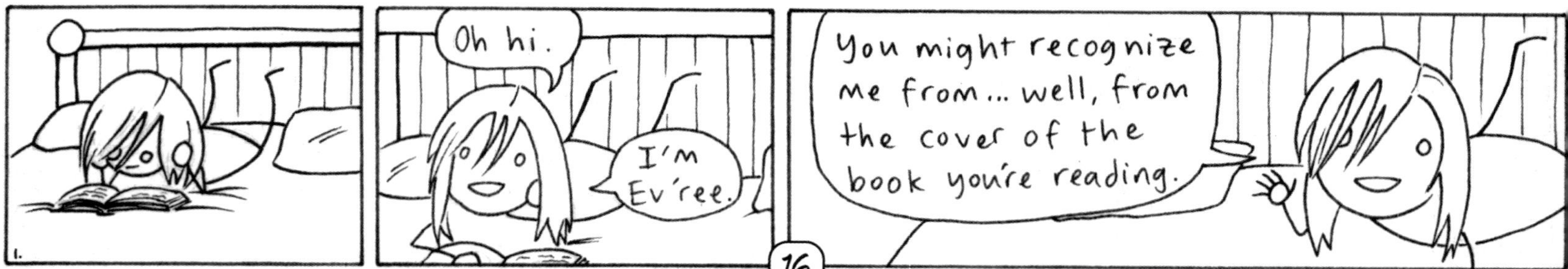
1.
Oh hi.
I'm Ev'ree.
You might recognize me from... well, from the cover of the book you're reading.

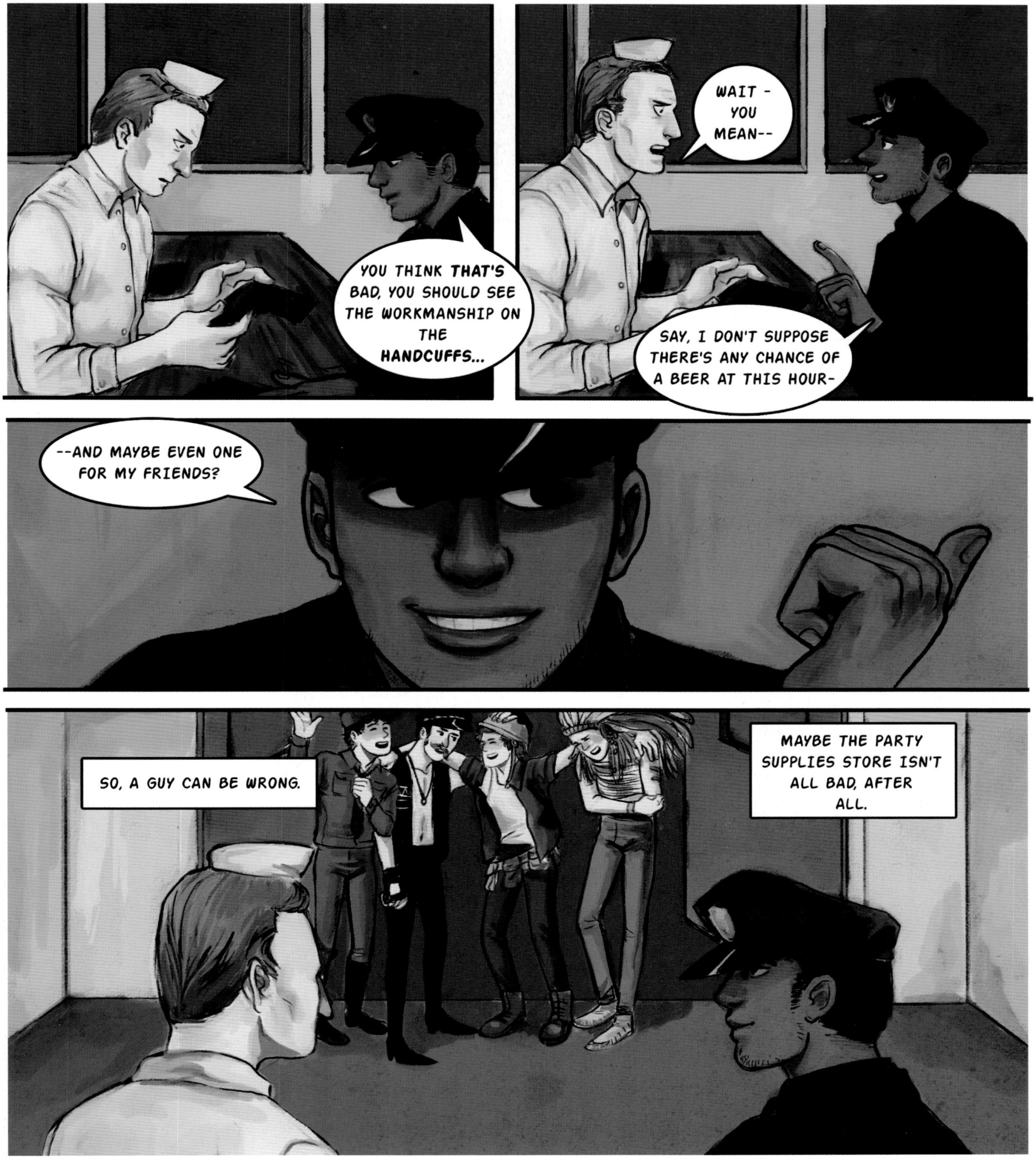
YOU THINK THAT'S BAD, YOU SHOULD SEE THE WORKMANSHIP ON THE HANDCUFFS...
WAIT - YOU MEAN--
SAY, I DON'T SUPPOSE THERE'S ANY CHANCE OF A BEER AT THIS HOUR-
--AND MAYBE EVEN ONE FOR MY FRIENDS?
SO, A GUY CAN BE WRONG.
MAYBE THE PARTY SUPPLIES STORE ISN'T ALL BAD, AFTER ALL.

☆ ☆ ☆

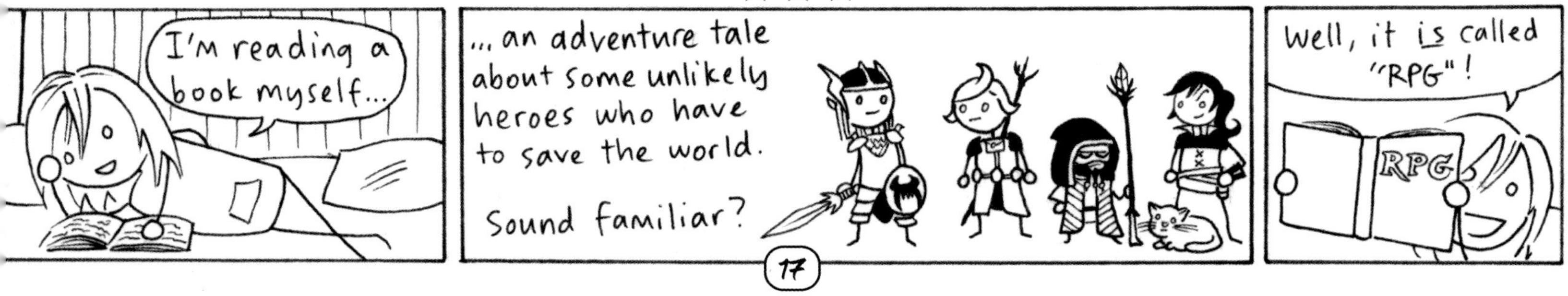
I'm reading a book myself...
... an adventure tale about some unlikely heroes who have to save the world.
Sound familiar?
Well, it is called "RPG"!
RPG

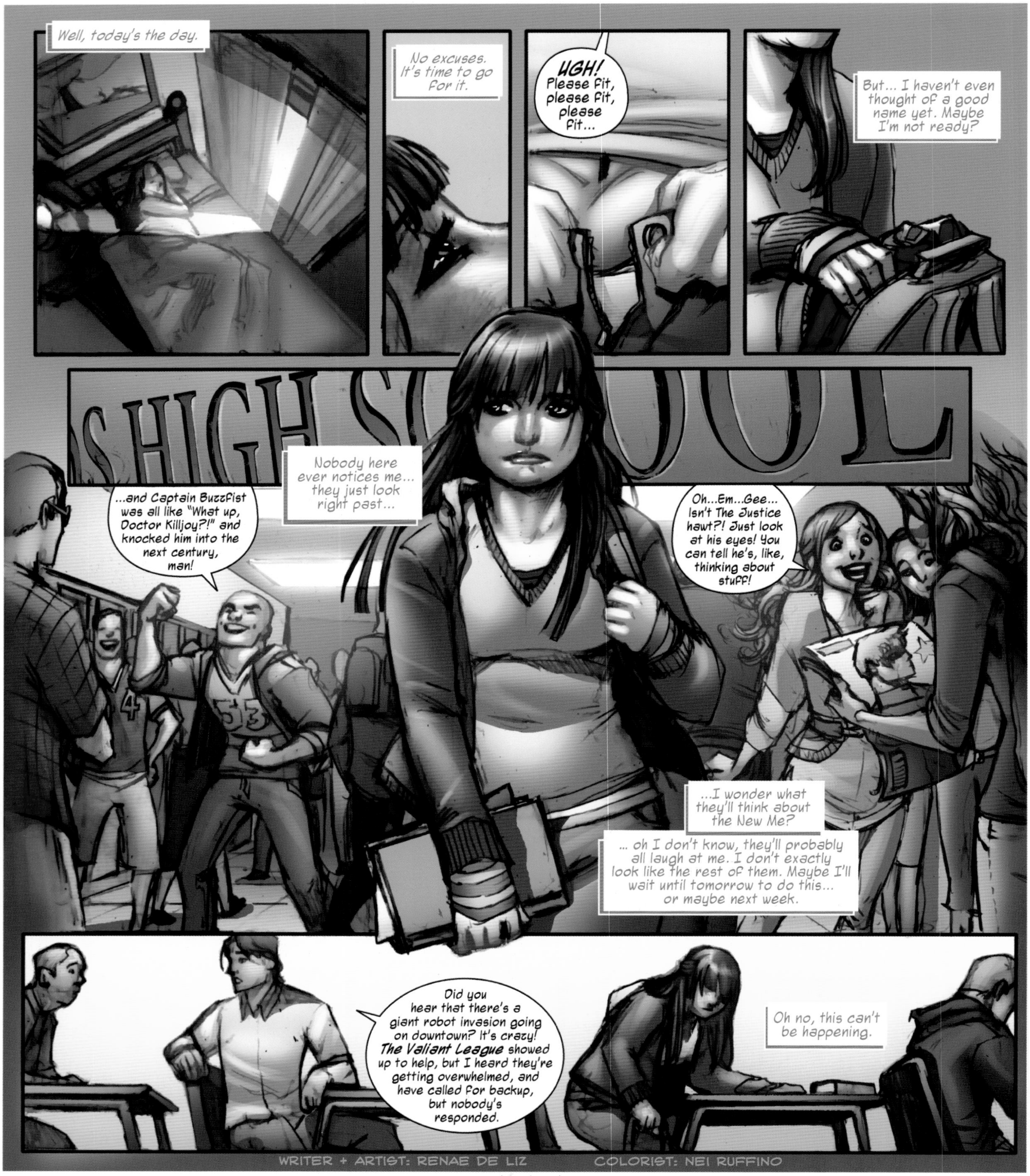
Well, today's the day.
No excuses. It's time to go for it.
UGH! Please fit, please fit, please fit...
But... I haven't even thought of a good name yet. Maybe I'm not ready?
HIGH SCHOOL
Nobody here ever notices me... they just look right past...
...and Captain Buzzfist was all like "What up, Doctor Killjoy?!" and knocked him into the next century, man!
Oh...Em...Gee... Isn't The Justice hawt?! Just look at his eyes! You can tell he's, like, thinking about stuff!
...I wonder what they'll think about the New Me?
... oh I don't know, they'll probably all laugh at me. I don't exactly look like the rest of them. Maybe I'll wait until tomorrow to do this... or maybe next week.
Did you hear that there's a giant robot invasion going on downtown? It's crazy! The Valiant League showed up to help, but I heard they're getting overwhelmed, and have called for backup, but nobody's responded.
Oh no, this can't be happening.
WRITER + ARTIST: RENAE DE LIZ COLORIST: NEI RUFFINO

☆☆☆

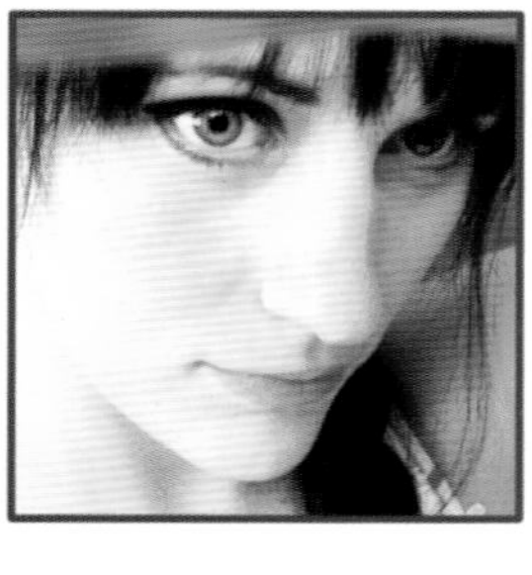

RENAE DE LIZ

SKILLS: Artist & *Womanthology* Manager
LOCATION: Cape Elizabeth, Maine
FUN FACT: Sported a wicked mullet in 4th grade while listening to homemade recordings of video game music.

http://RenaeDeLiz.blogspot.com/

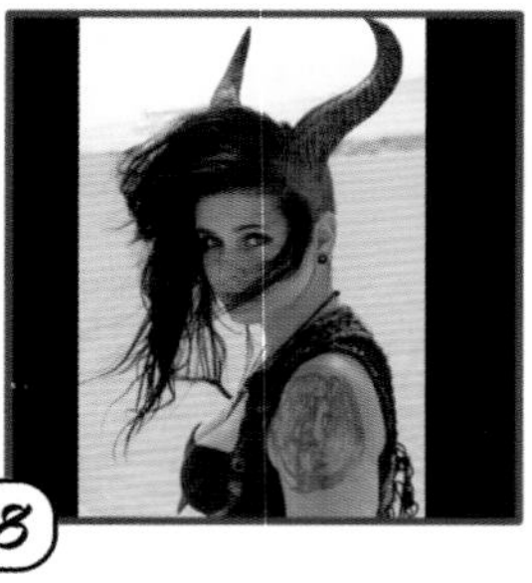

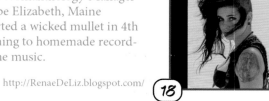

NEI RUFFINO

SKILLS: Colorist
LOCATION: USA
FUN FACT: I love the smell of vinyl :)

http://www.bakanekonei.deviantart.com

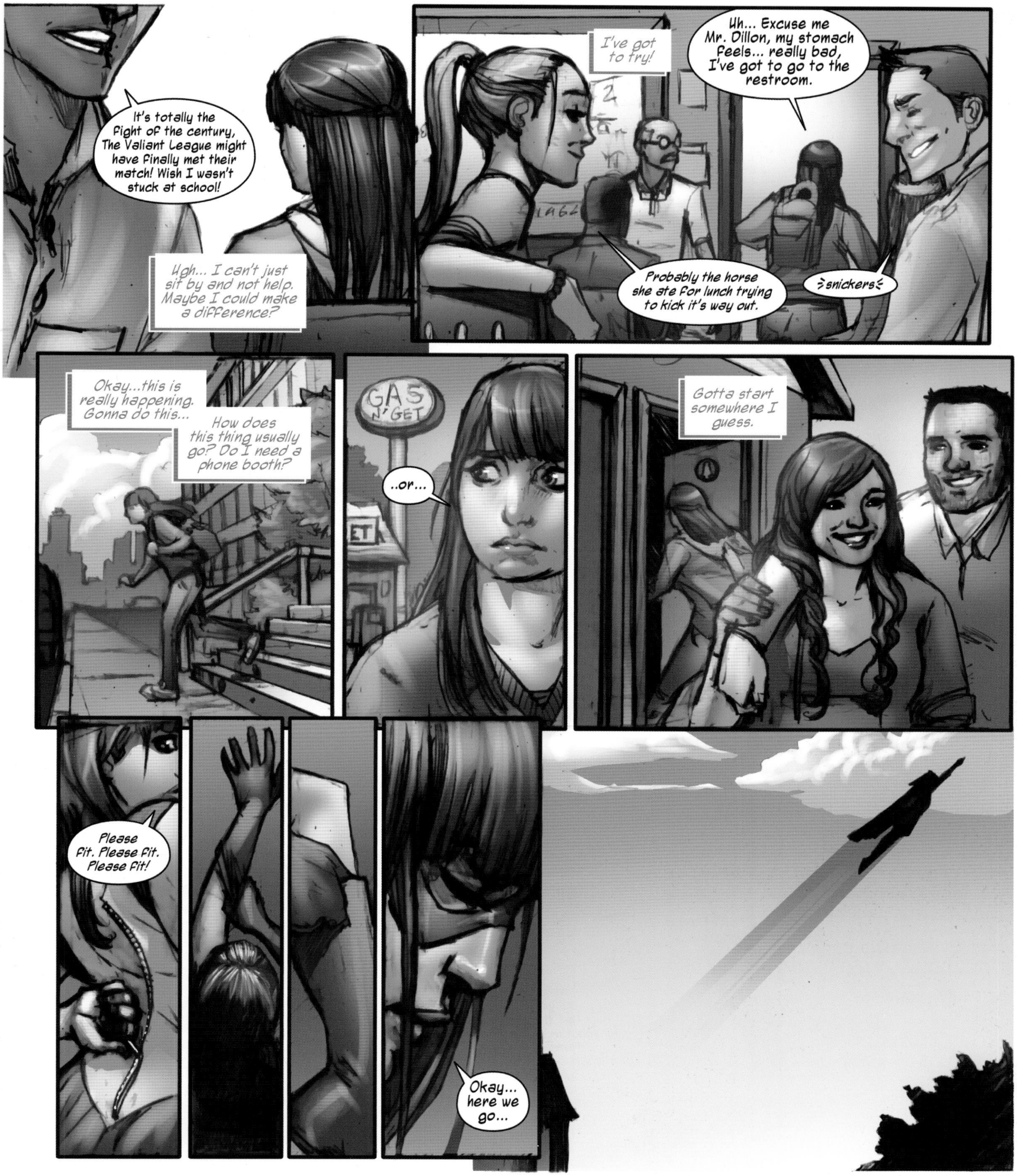
It's totally the fight of the century, The Valiant League might have finally met their match! Wish I wasn't stuck at school!
Ugh... I can't just sit by and not help. Maybe I could make a difference?
I've got to try!
Uh... Excuse me Mr. Dillon, my stomach feels... really bad, I've got to go to the restroom.
Probably the horse she ate for lunch trying to kick it's way out.
snickers
Okay...this is really happening. Gonna do this...
How does this thing usually go? Do I need a phone booth?
GAS N' GET
..or...
Gotta start somewhere I guess.
Please fit. Please fit. Please fit!
Okay... here we go...

☆ ☆ ☆

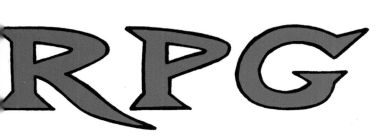

RPG

written & illustrated by
Stacie Ponder

www.stacieponder.com
www.rpgcomic.com

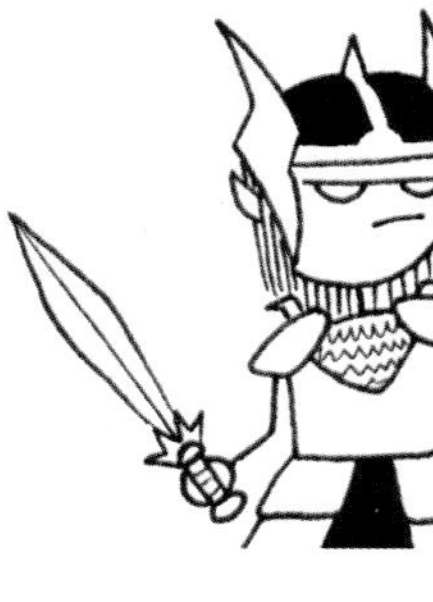

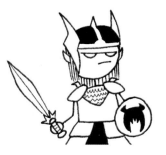

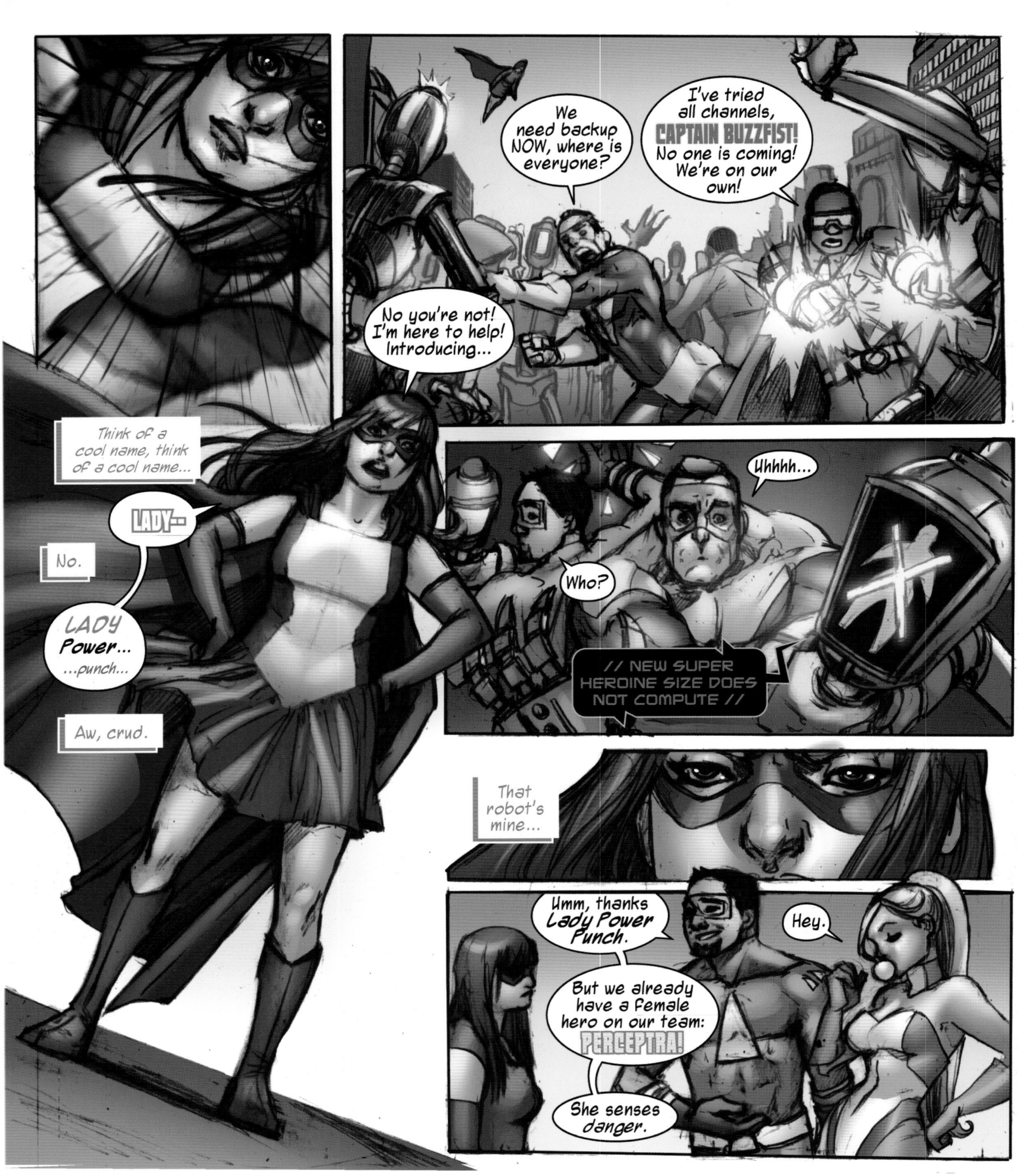
We need backup NOW, where is everyone?
I've tried all channels, CAPTAIN BUZZFIST! No one is coming! We're on our own!
No you're not! I'm here to help! Introducing...
Think of a cool name, think of a cool name...
LADY--
No.
LADY Power... ...punch...
Aw, crud.
Uhhhh...
Who?
// NEW SUPER HEROINE SIZE DOES NOT COMPUTE //
That robot's mine...
Umm, thanks Lady Power Punch.
Hey.
But we already have a female hero on our team: PERCEPTRA!
She senses danger.

☆ ☆ ☆

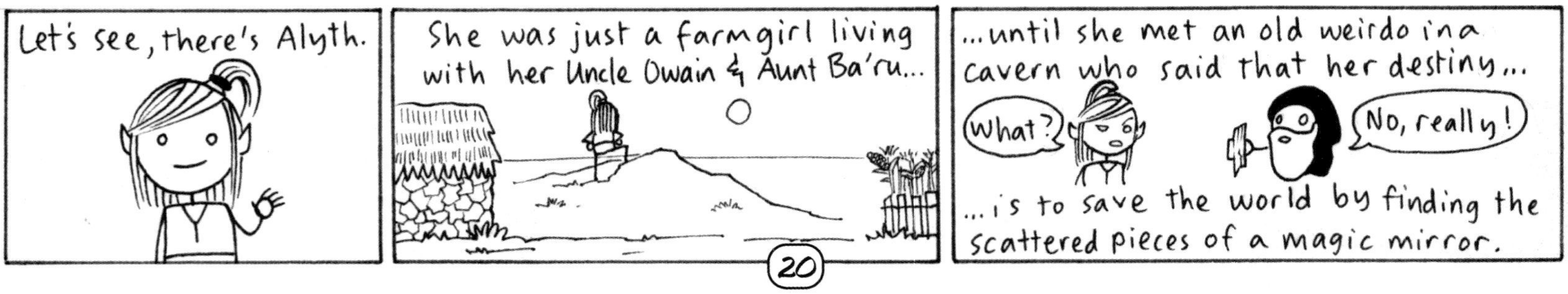
Let's see, there's Alyth.
She was just a farmgirl living with her Uncle Owain & Aunt Ba'ru...
...until she met an old weirdo in a cavern who said that her destiny...
What?
No, really!
...is to save the world by finding the scattered pieces of a magic mirror.

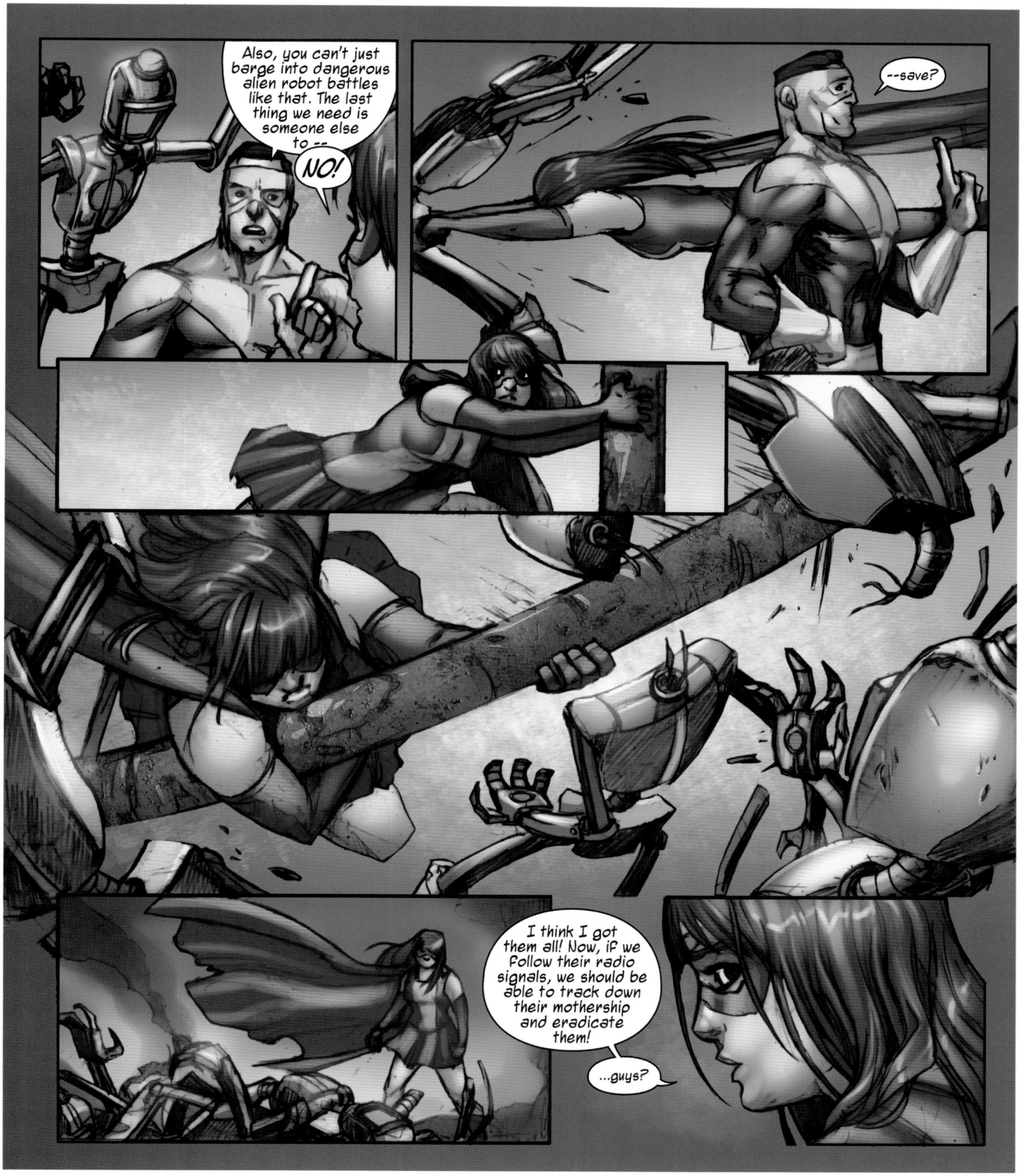
Also, you can't just barge into dangerous alien robot battles like that. The last thing we need is someone else to --
NO!
--save?
I think I got them all! Now, if we follow their radio signals, we should be able to track down their mothership and eradicate them!
...guys?

☆ ☆ ☆

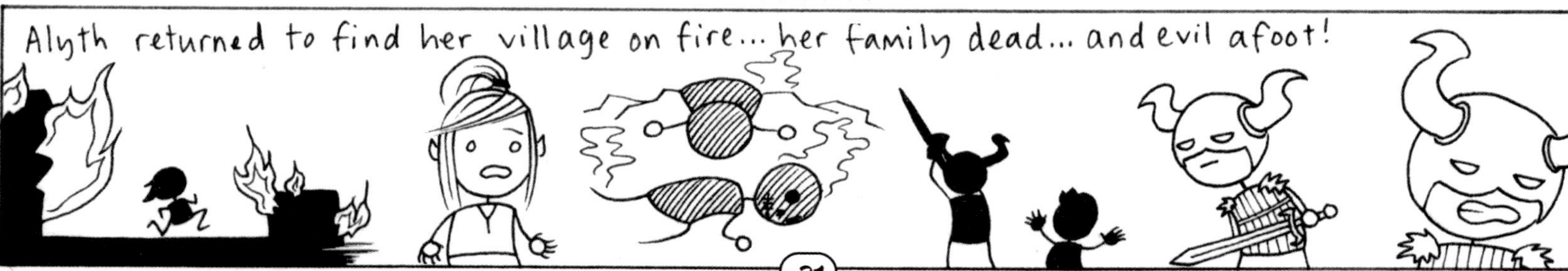
Alyth returned to find her village on fire... her family dead... and evil afoot!

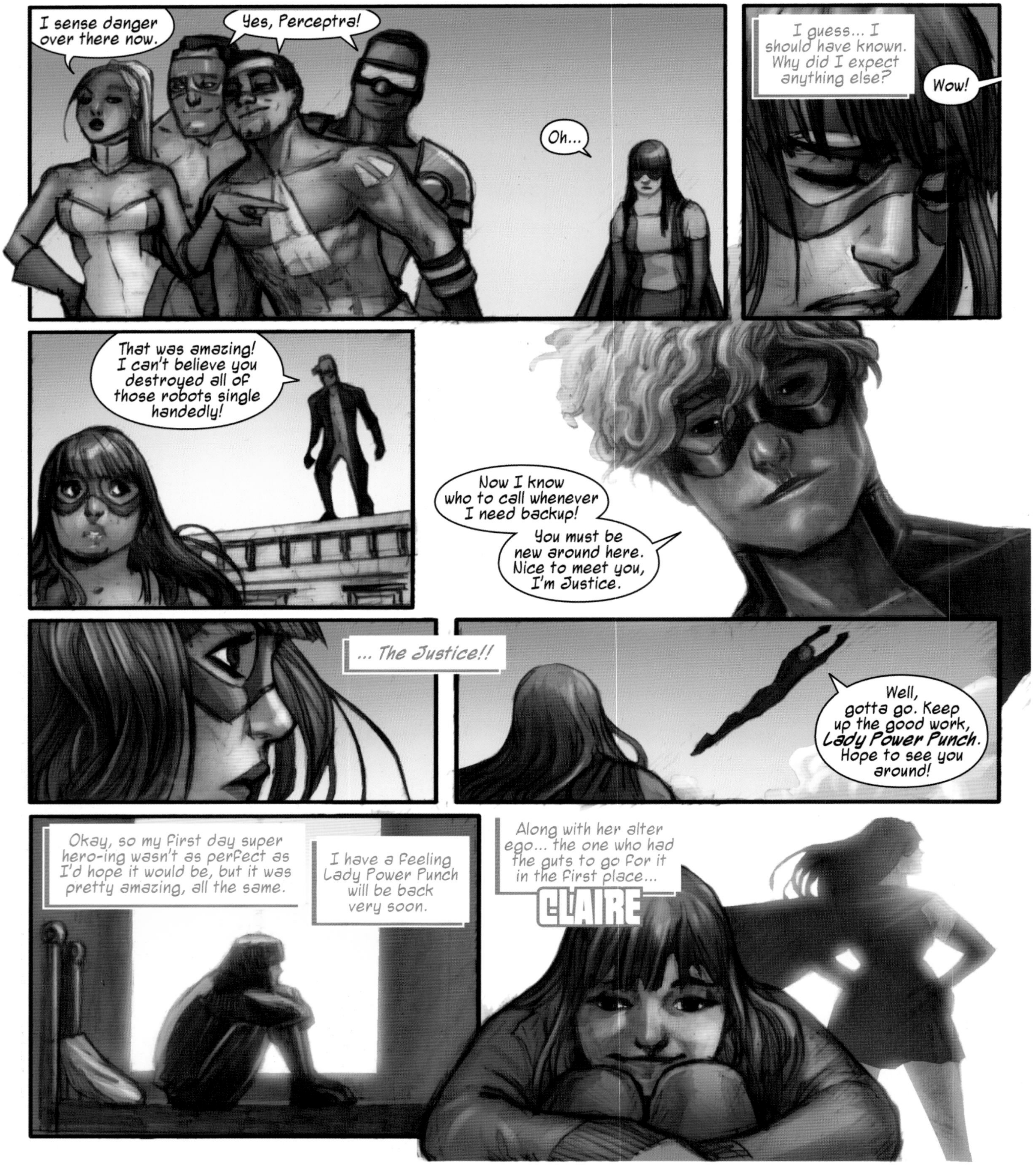

I sense danger over there now.
Yes, Perceptra!
Oh...
I guess... I should have known. Why did I expect anything else?
Wow!
That was amazing! I can't believe you destroyed all of those robots single handedly!
Now I know who to call whenever I need backup!
You must be new around here. Nice to meet you, I'm Justice.
... The Justice!!
Well, gotta go. Keep up the good work, Lady Power Punch. Hope to see you around!
Okay, so my first day super hero-ing wasn't as perfect as I'd hope it would be, but it was pretty amazing, all the same.
I have a feeling Lady Power Punch will be back very soon.
Along with her alter ego... the one who had the guts to go for it in the first place...
CLAIRE

☆ ☆ ☆

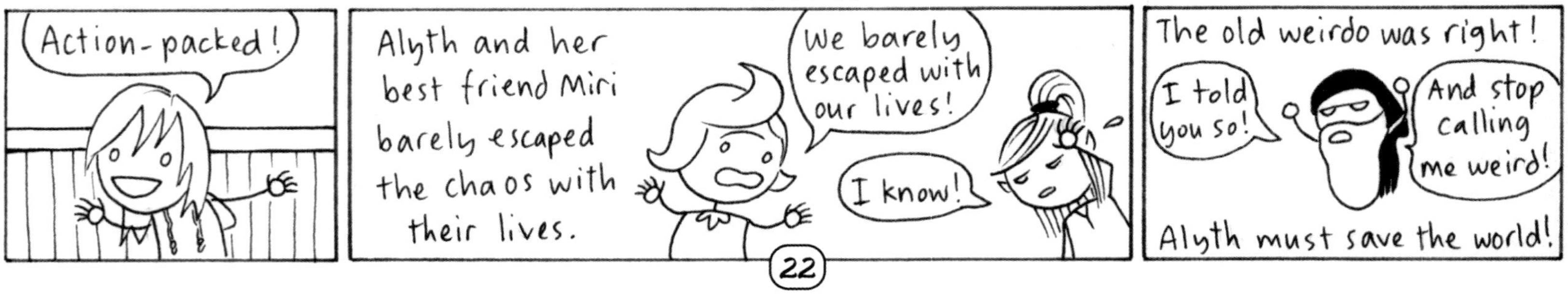

Action-packed!
Alyth and her best friend Miri barely escaped the chaos with their lives.
We barely escaped with our lives!
I know!
The old weirdo was right!
I told you so!
And stop calling me weird!
Alyth must save the world!

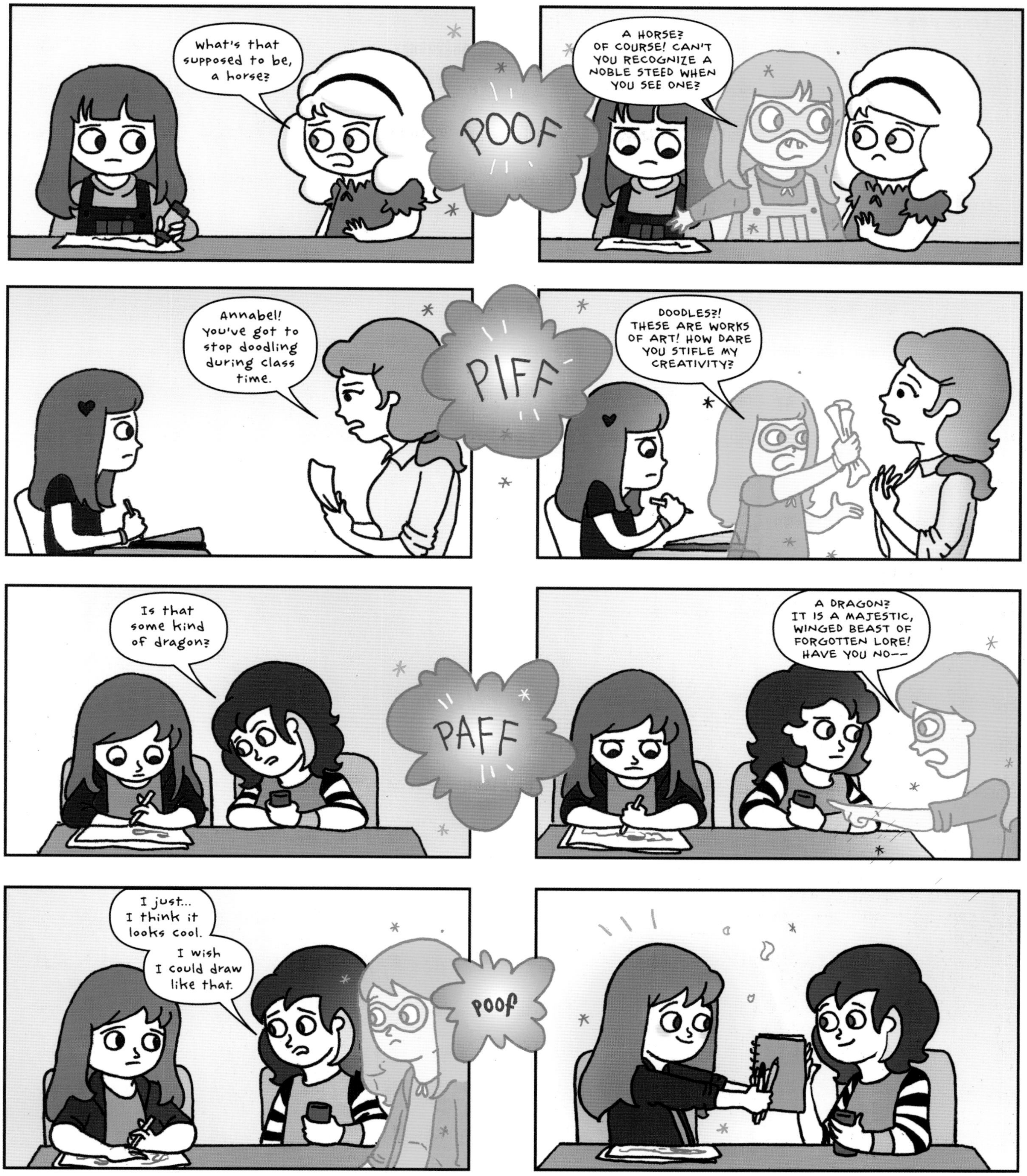
What's that supposed to be, a horse?
POOF
A HORSE? OF COURSE! CAN'T YOU RECOGNIZE A NOBLE STEED WHEN YOU SEE ONE?
Annabel! You've got to stop doodling during class time.
PIFF
DOODLES?! THESE ARE WORKS OF ART! HOW DARE YOU STIFLE MY CREATIVITY?
Is that some kind of dragon?
PAFF
A DRAGON? IT IS A MAJESTIC, WINGED BEAST OF FORGOTTEN LORE! HAVE YOU NO--
I just... I think it looks cool.
I wish I could draw like that.
poof

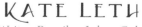

writer & ARTist: Kate Leth Letterer: Rachel Deering

☆☆☆

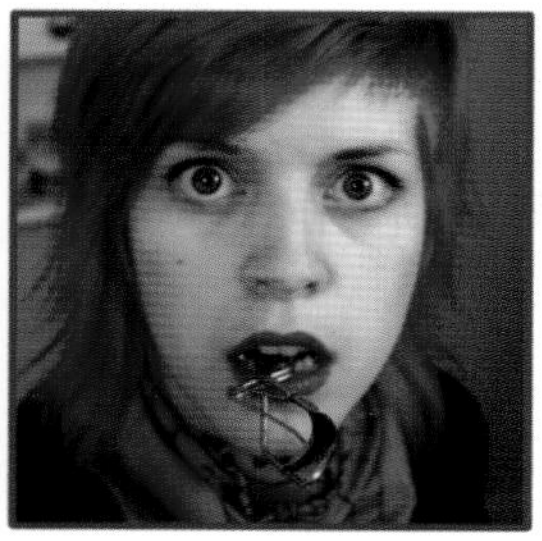

KATE LETH

SKILLS: Writer, Penciler, Inker, Colourist
LOCATION: Halifax, Nova Scotia, Canada
FUN FACT: I am a comics artist that works in a comic store. I have a cat named Leeloo.

kateordiecomics.com

PRO TIP WRITING BY BARBARA RANDALL KESEL

"DON'T TAKE ANY ONE CRITICISM AS GOSPEL, BUT IF YOU KEEP HEARING THE SAME CRITICISM, PAY ATTENTION. THEN FIX IT OR DEFY IT, BECAUSE YOUR STYLE COMES FROM EVERYTHING YOU DO 'WRONG' CONSISTENTLY."

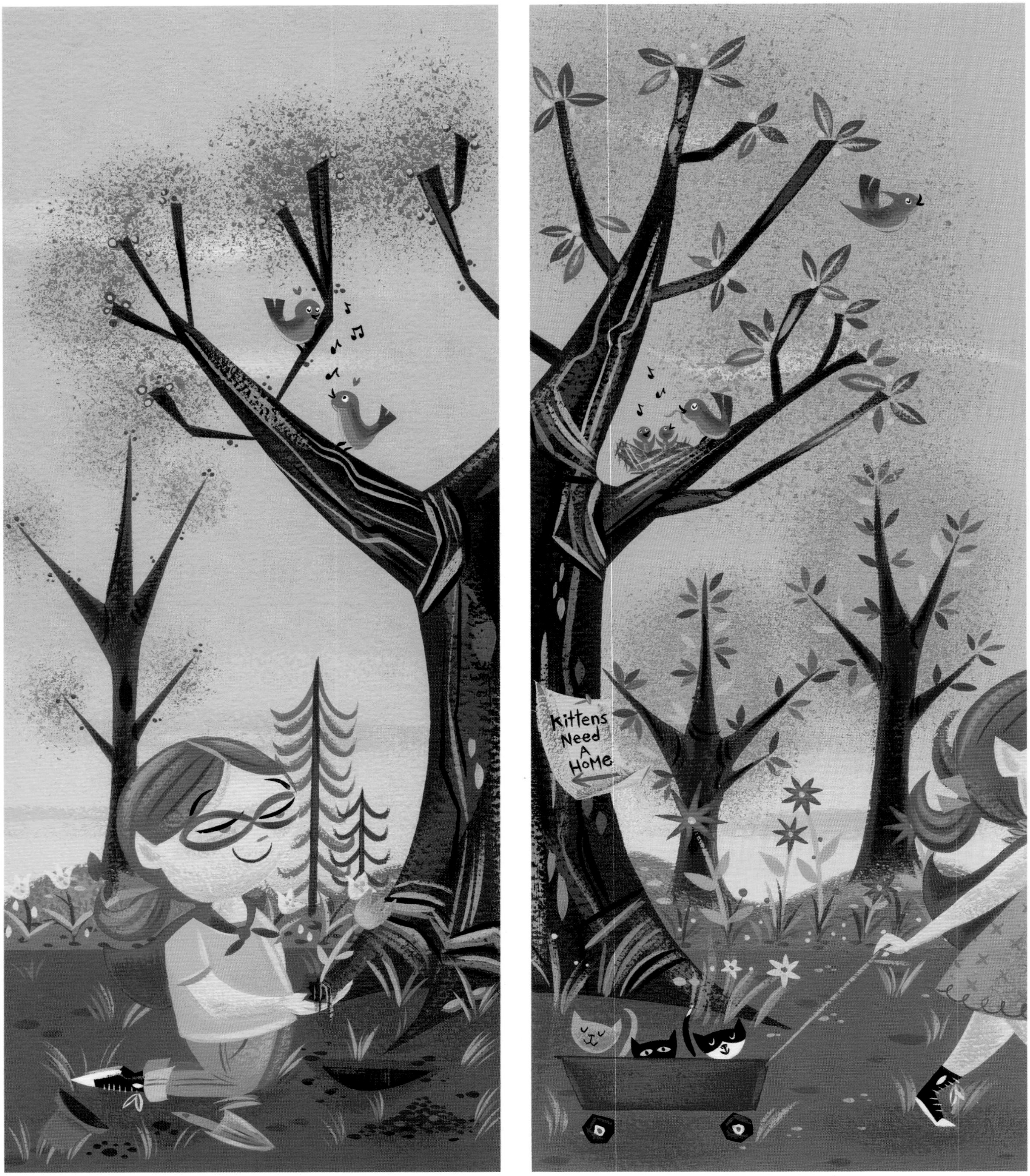
Kittens Need A Home

☆☆☆

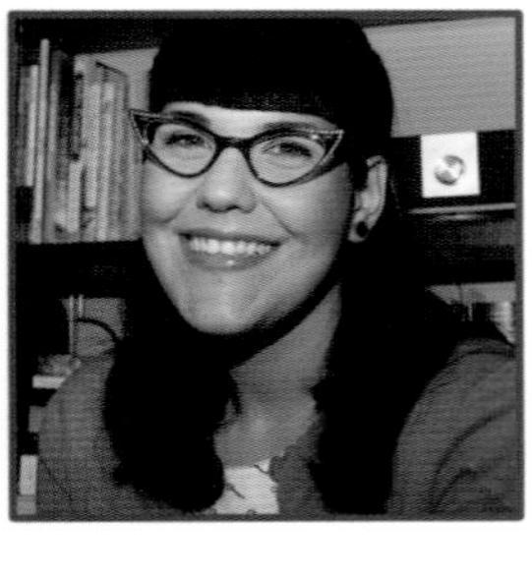

STEPHANIE BUSCEMA

SKILLS: Artist
LOCATION: New York

www.stephaniebuscema.com

PRO TIP

DRAWING
BY RENAE DE LIZ

"IF WHAT YOU'RE GOING FOR IS YOUR OWN UNIQUE STYLE, TRY NOT TO 'STUDY' OTHER PEOPLE'S ARTWORK TOO MUCH, OTHERWISE YOU'LL ONLY END UP DRAWING IN SOMEONE ELSE'S STYLE. IT MAY BE THE ROUGHER ROAD TO LEARN EVERYTHING BY YOURSELF, BUT IN THE END YOU'D HAVE A STYLE THAT YOU CAN BE PROUD TO CALL YOUR OWN."

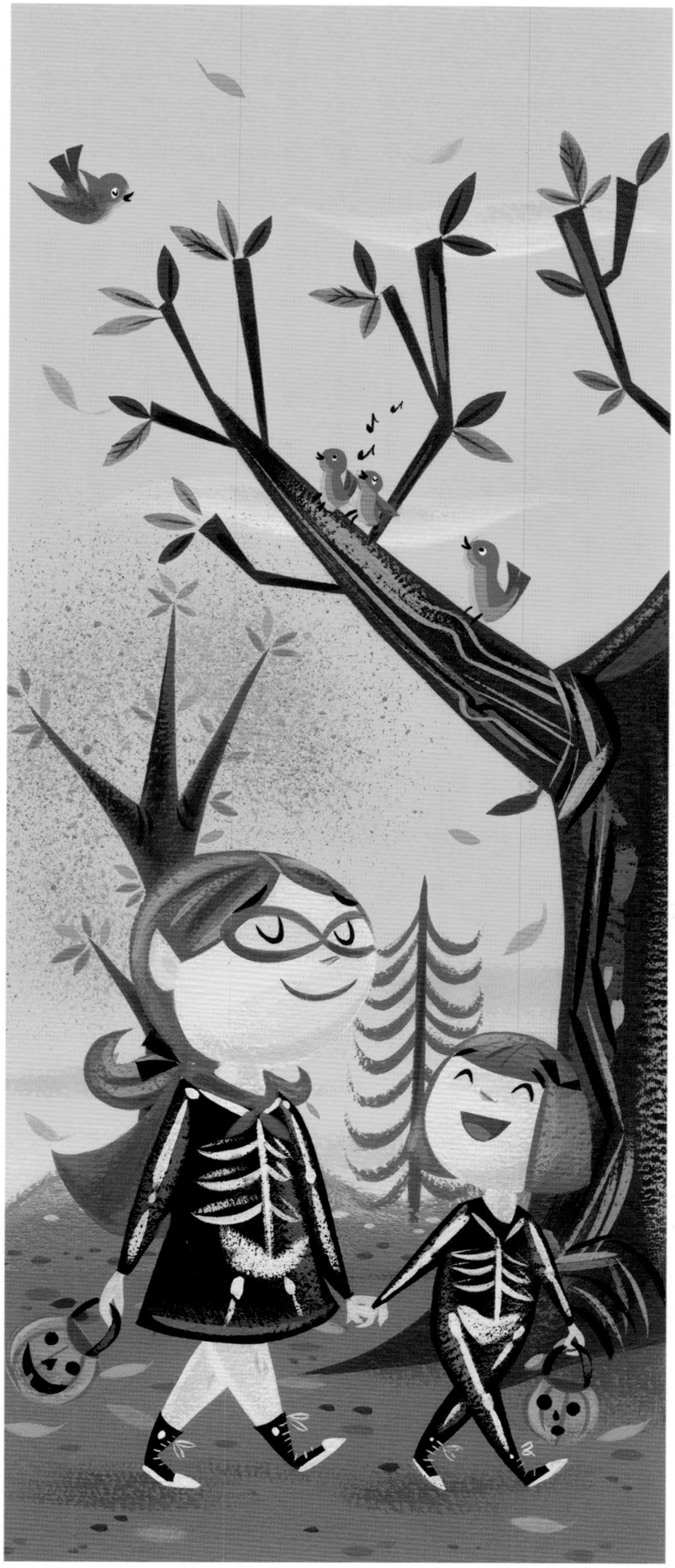

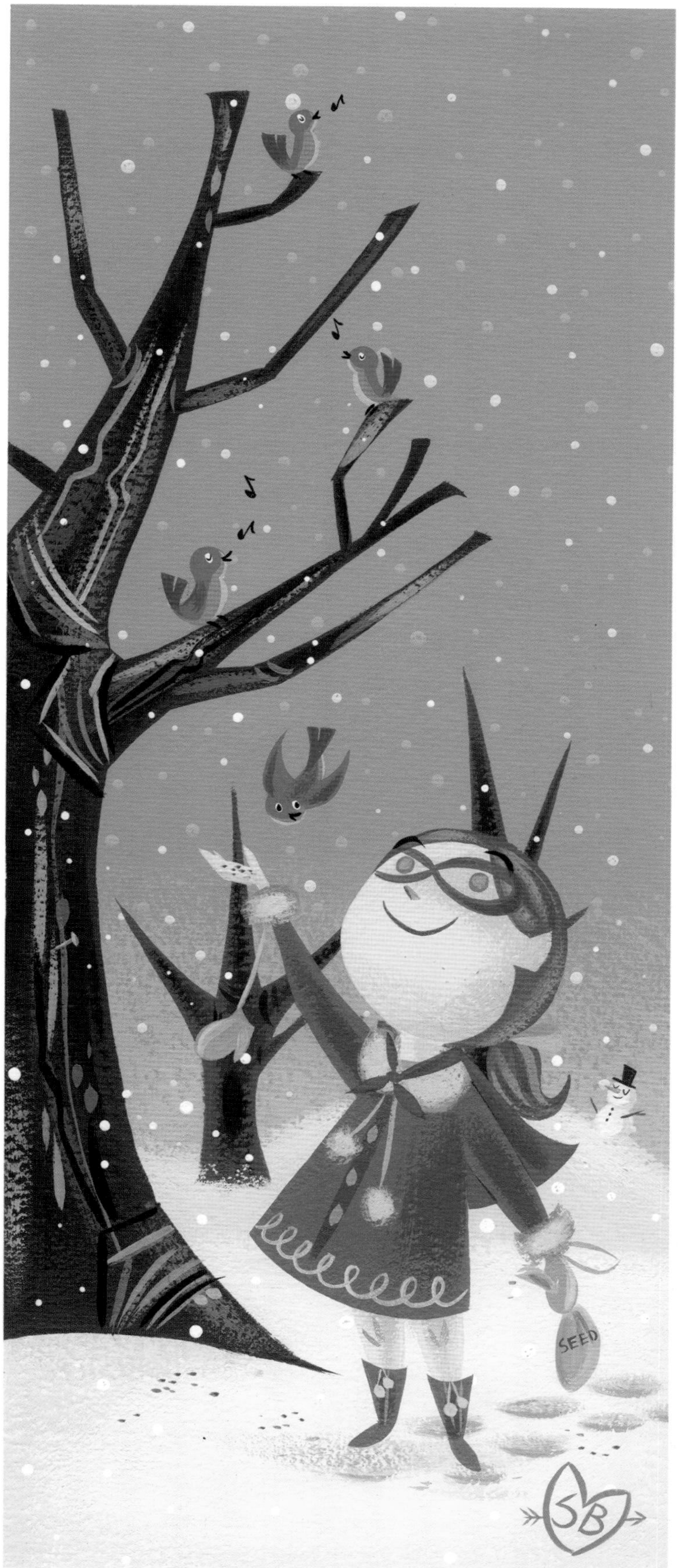
SEED

☆ ☆ ☆

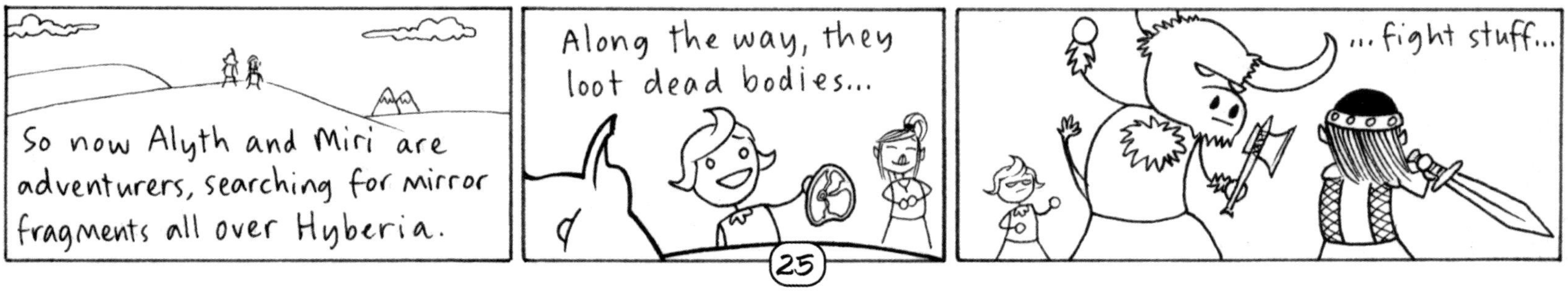
So now Alyth and Miri are adventurers, searching for mirror fragments all over Hyberia.
Along the way, they loot dead bodies...
...fight stuff...

THE wraiths OF roseland

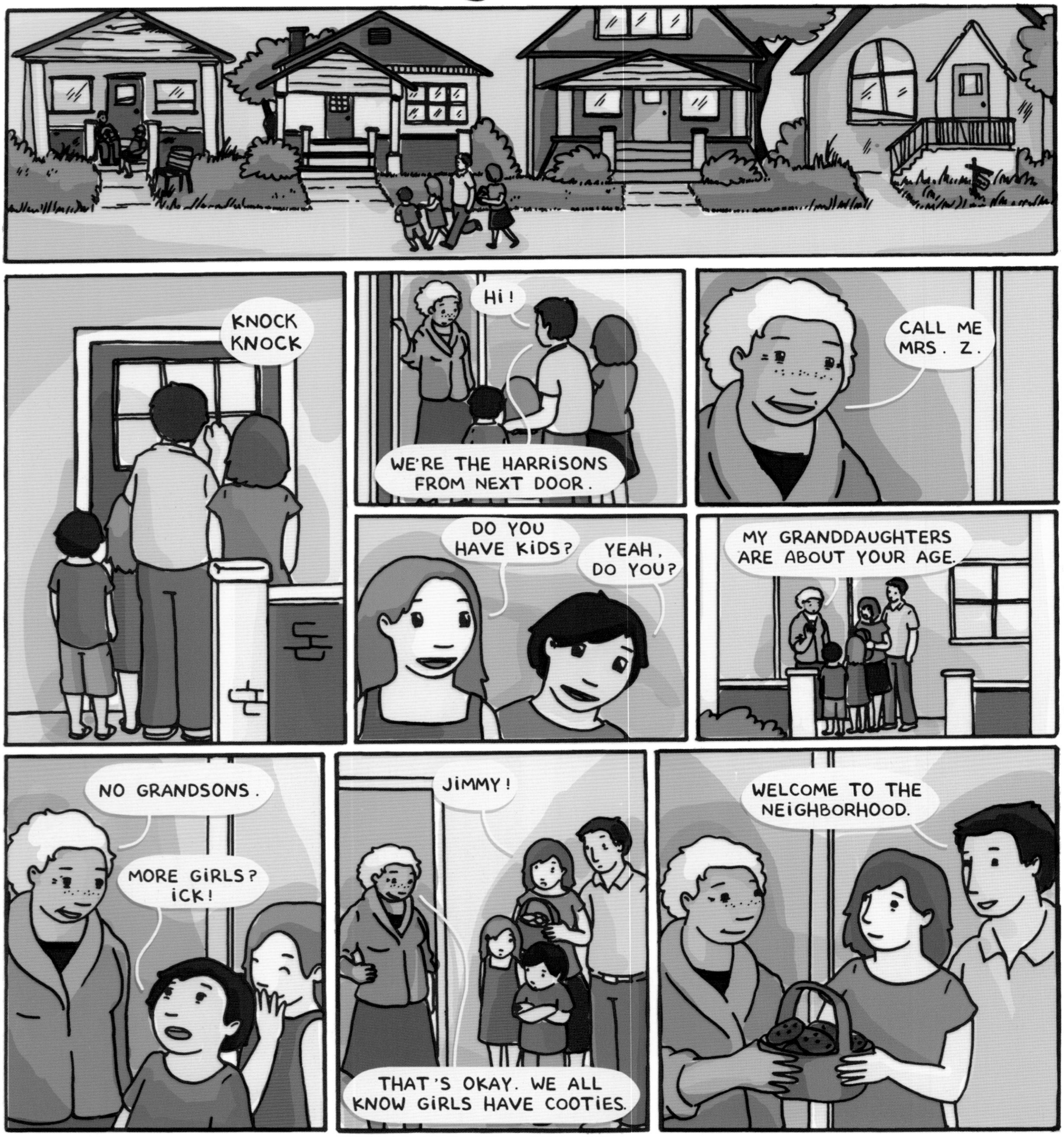

KNOCK KNOCK
HI!
WE'RE THE HARRISONS FROM NEXT DOOR.
CALL ME MRS. Z.
DO YOU HAVE KIDS?
YEAH, DO YOU?
MY GRANDDAUGHTERS ARE ABOUT YOUR AGE.
NO GRANDSONS.
MORE GIRLS? ICK!
JIMMY!
THAT'S OKAY. WE ALL KNOW GIRLS HAVE COOTIES.
WELCOME TO THE NEIGHBORHOOD.

☆ ☆ ☆

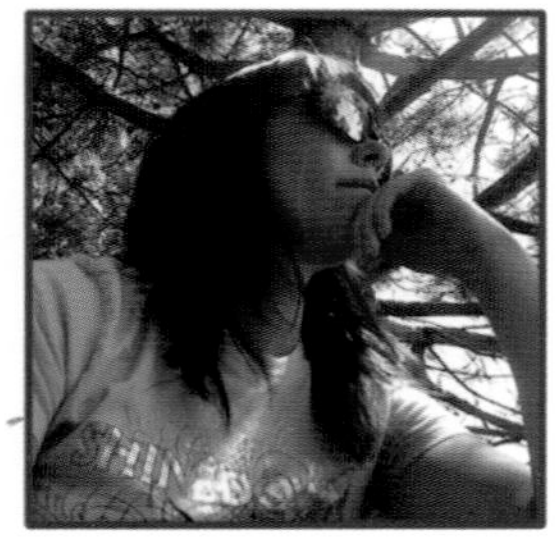

MARTEL SARDINA

SKILLS: Writer
LOCATION: Chicago, IL
FUN FACT: I love dachshunds!

www.martelsardina.com

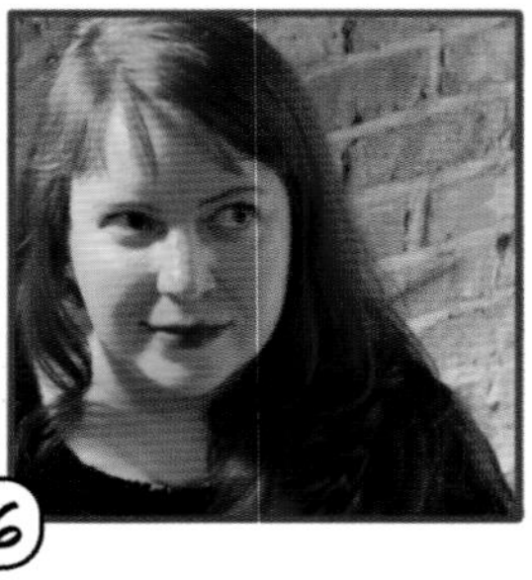

SARAH BECAN

SKILLS: Penciller, Inker, Colorist, and Letterer
LOCATION: Chicago, IL
FUN FACT: I play the accordion.

www.sarahbecan.com

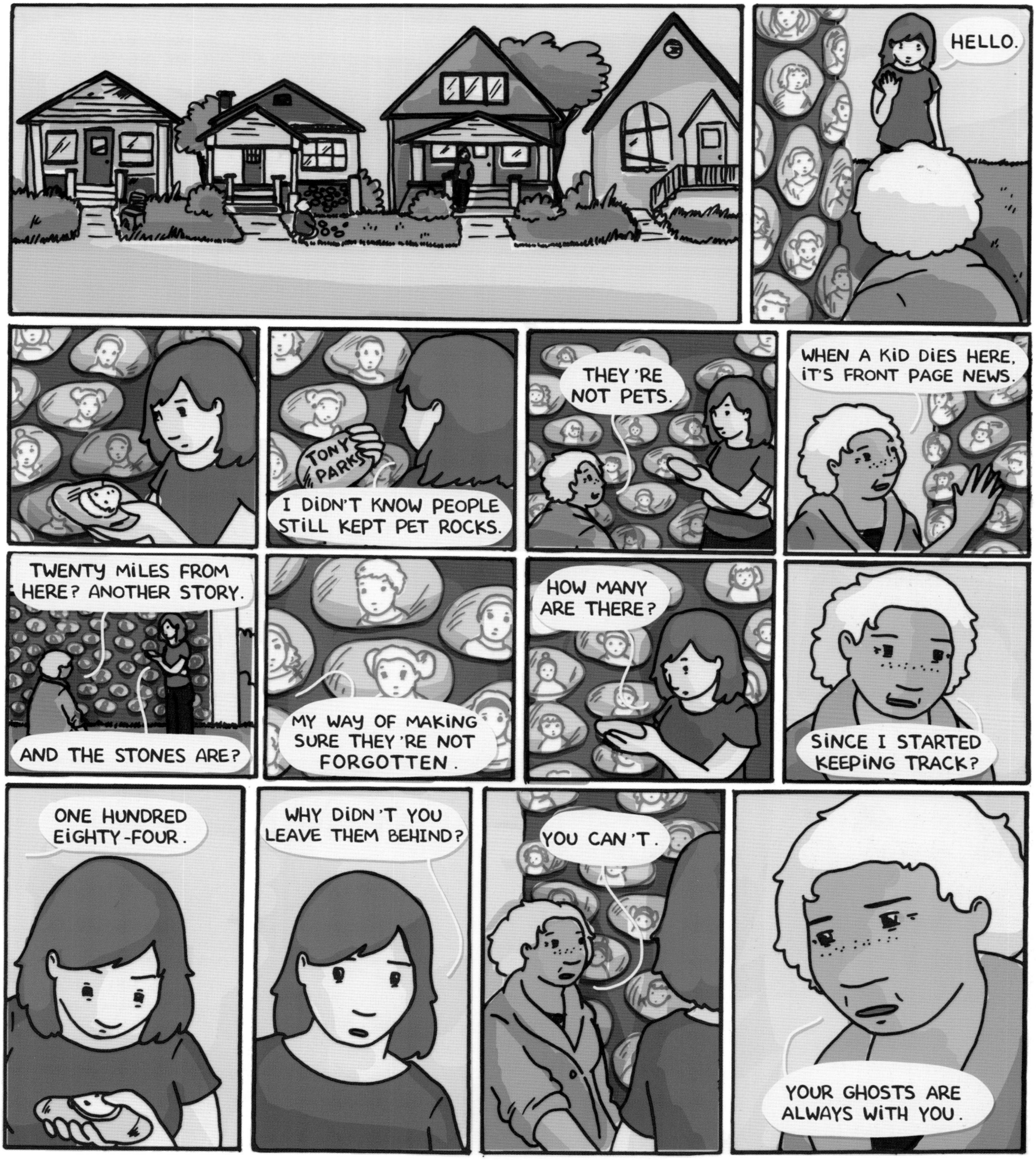

HELLO.
TONY PARKS
I DIDN'T KNOW PEOPLE STILL KEPT PET ROCKS.
THEY'RE NOT PETS.
WHEN A KID DIES HERE, IT'S FRONT PAGE NEWS.
TWENTY MILES FROM HERE? ANOTHER STORY.
AND THE STONES ARE?
MY WAY OF MAKING SURE THEY'RE NOT FORGOTTEN.
HOW MANY ARE THERE?
SINCE I STARTED KEEPING TRACK?
ONE HUNDRED EIGHTY-FOUR.
WHY DIDN'T YOU LEAVE THEM BEHIND?
YOU CAN'T.
YOUR GHOSTS ARE ALWAYS WITH YOU.

☆ ☆ ☆

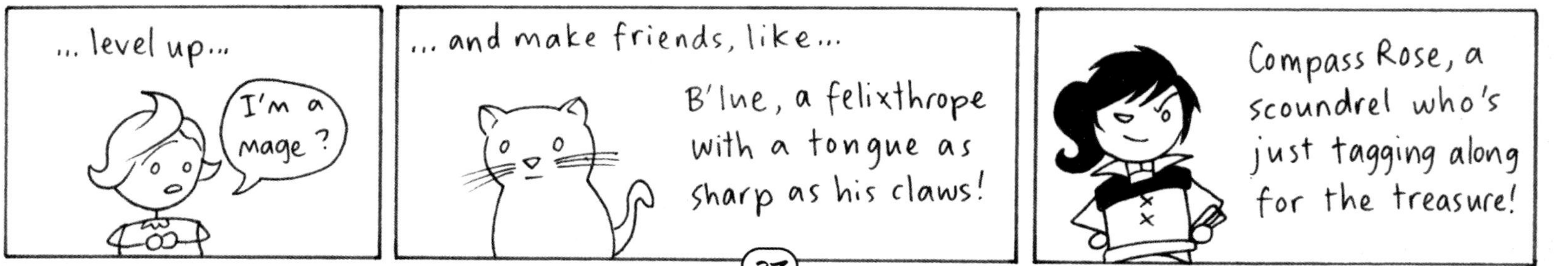

... level up...
I'm a mage?
... and make friends, like...
B'lue, a felixthrope with a tongue as sharp as his claws!
Compass Rose, a scoundrel who's just tagging along for the treasure!

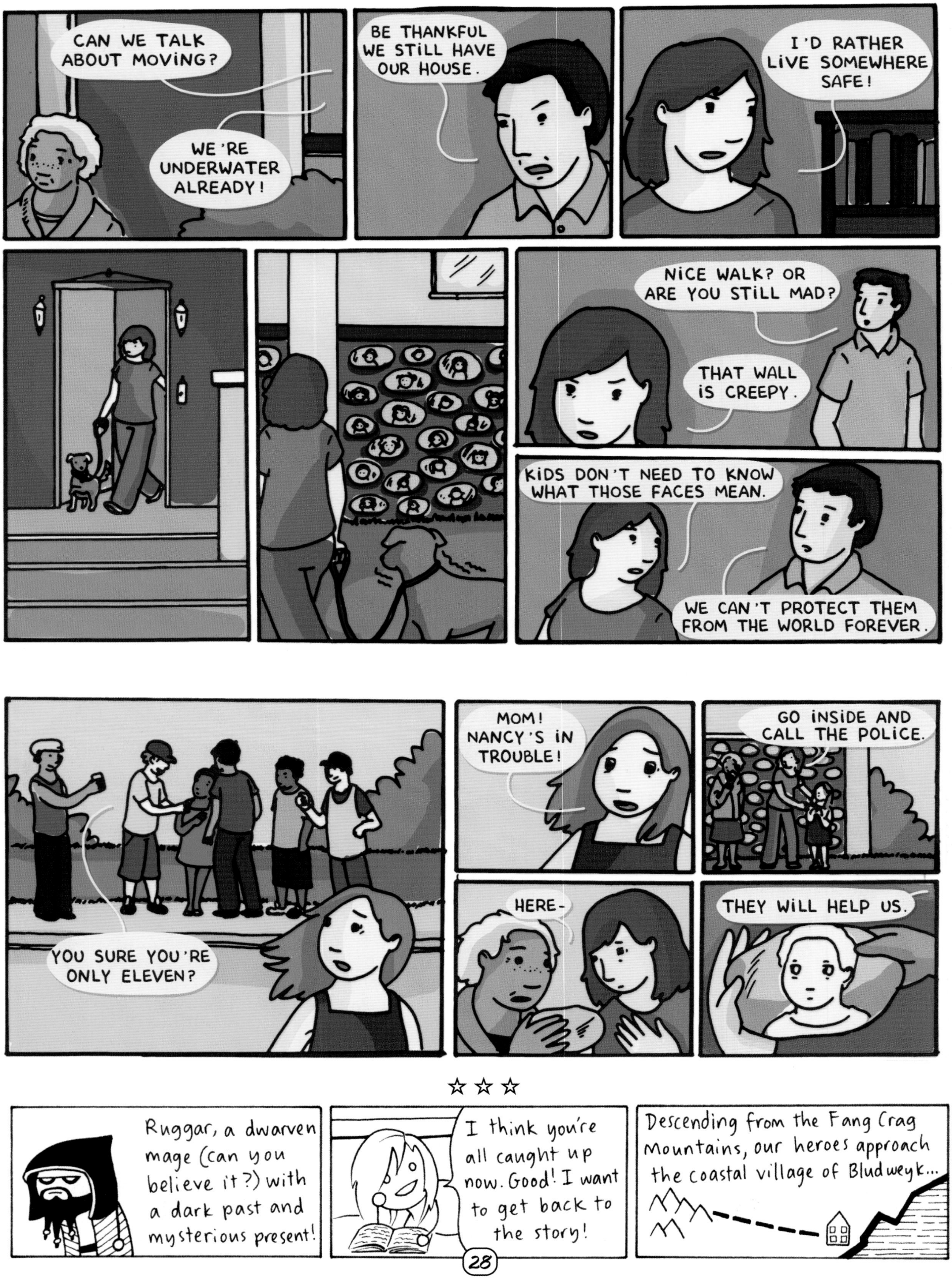
CAN WE TALK ABOUT MOVING?
WE'RE UNDERWATER ALREADY!
BE THANKFUL WE STILL HAVE OUR HOUSE.
I'D RATHER LIVE SOMEWHERE SAFE!
NICE WALK? OR ARE YOU STILL MAD?
THAT WALL IS CREEPY.
KIDS DON'T NEED TO KNOW WHAT THOSE FACES MEAN.
WE CAN'T PROTECT THEM FROM THE WORLD FOREVER.
YOU SURE YOU'RE ONLY ELEVEN?
MOM! NANCY'S IN TROUBLE!
GO INSIDE AND CALL THE POLICE.
HERE-
THEY WILL HELP US.
☆ ☆ ☆
Ruggar, a dwarven mage (can you believe it?) with a dark past and mysterious present!
I think you're all caught up now. Good! I want to get back to the story!
Descending from the Fang Crag Mountains, our heroes approach the coastal village of Bludweyk...

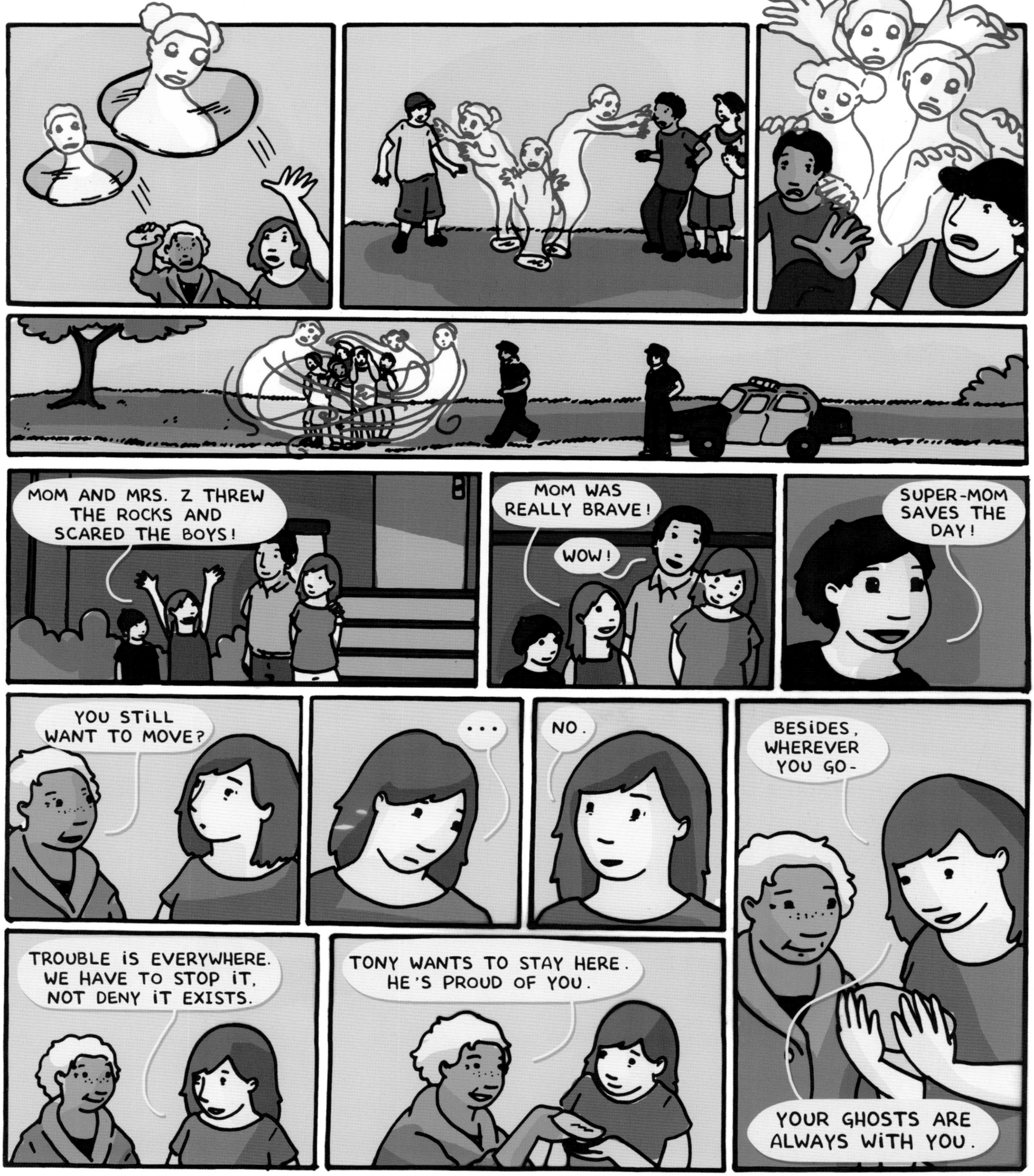
MOM AND MRS. Z THREW THE ROCKS AND SCARED THE BOYS!
MOM WAS REALLY BRAVE!
WOW!
SUPER-MOM SAVES THE DAY!
YOU STILL WANT TO MOVE?
...
NO.
BESIDES, WHEREVER YOU GO-
TROUBLE IS EVERYWHERE. WE HAVE TO STOP IT, NOT DENY IT EXISTS.
TONY WANTS TO STAY HERE. HE'S PROUD OF YOU.
YOUR GHOSTS ARE ALWAYS WITH YOU.

☆ ☆ ☆

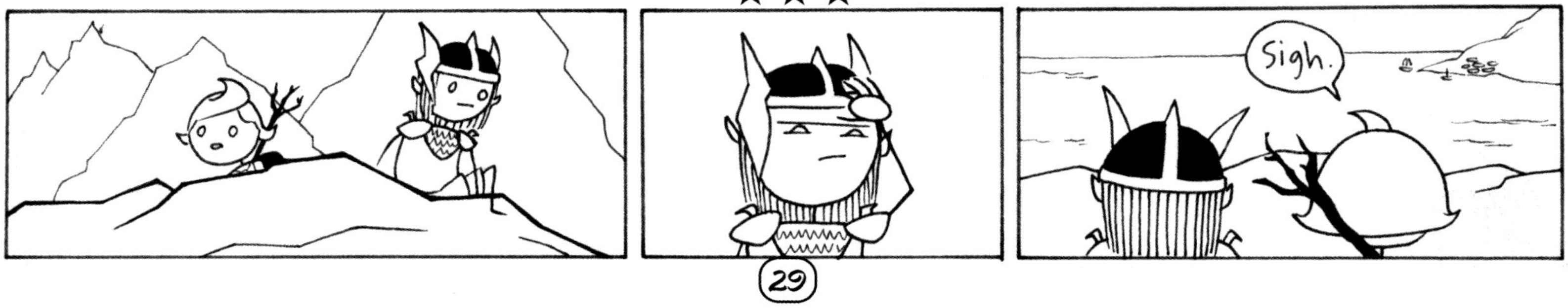
Sigh.

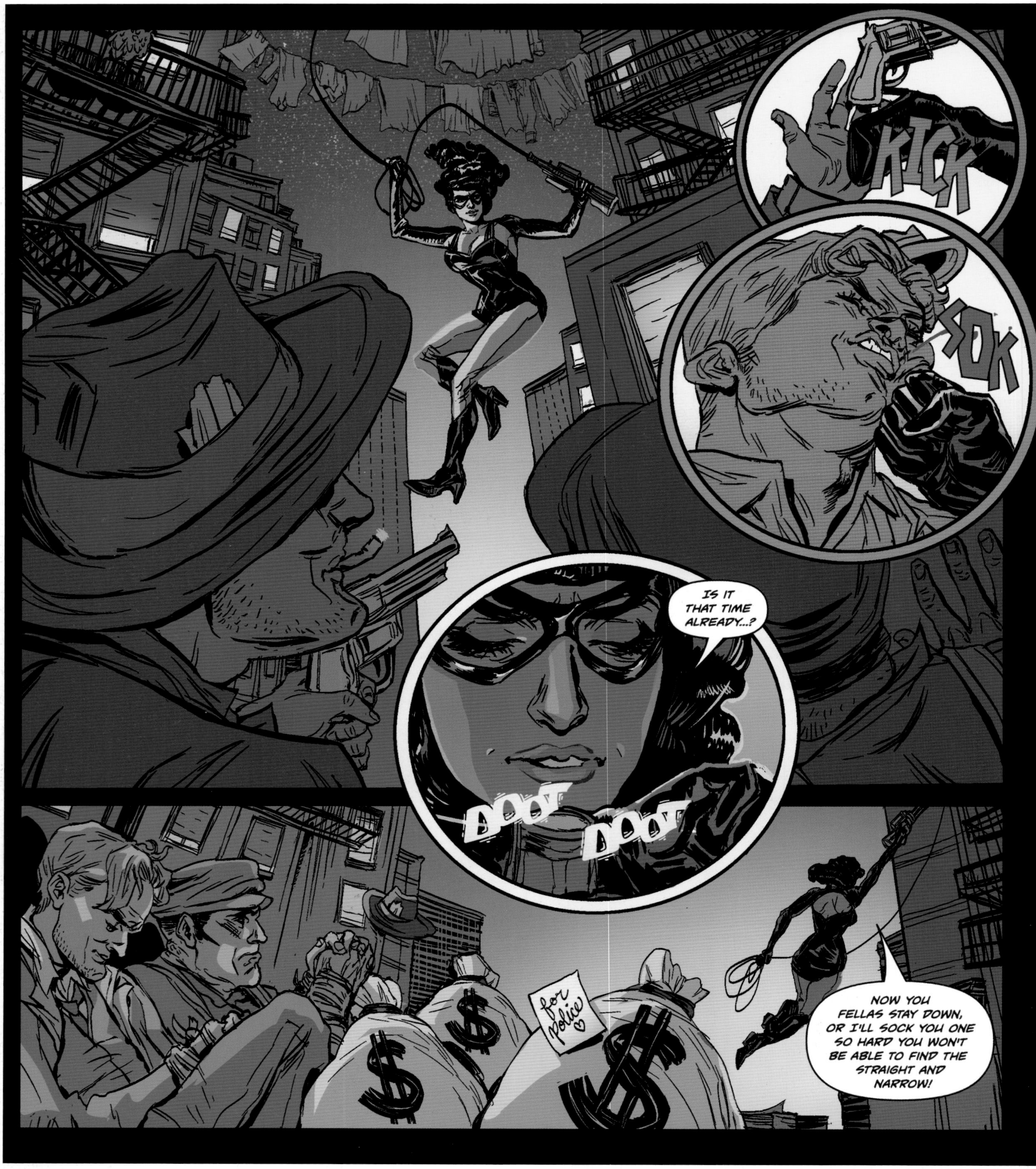
KICK
SOK
IS IT THAT TIME ALREADY...?
DOOT
DOOT
for police
NOW YOU FELLAS STAY DOWN, OR I'LL SOCK YOU ONE SO HARD YOU WON'T BE ABLE TO FIND THE STRAIGHT AND NARROW!

☆ ☆ ☆

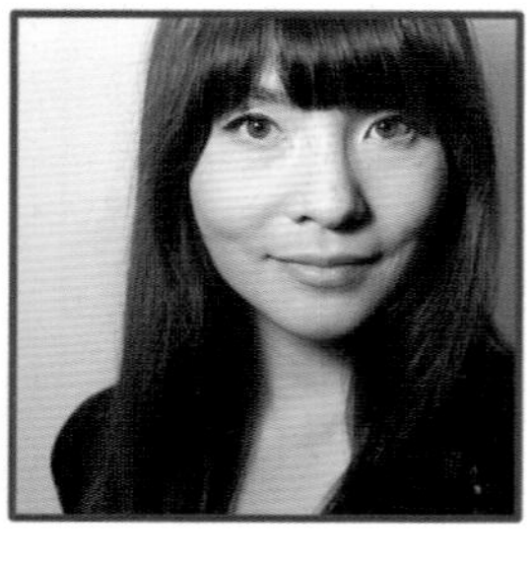

MING DOYLE

SKILLS: Penciller, Inker, Writer
LOCATION: Boston, MA
FUN FACT: Retro futuristic enthusiast.

http://www.mingdoyle.com

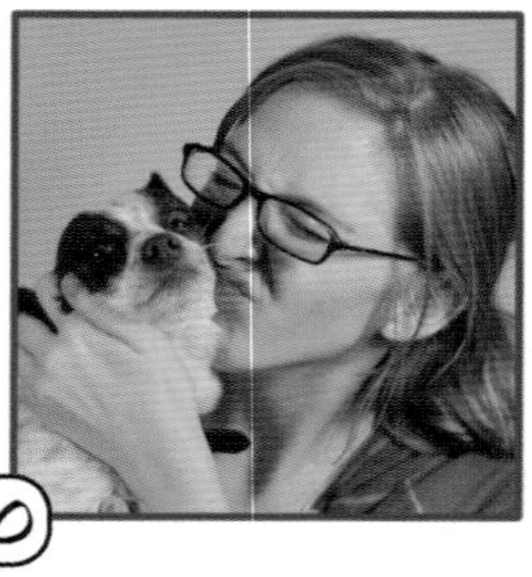

JORDIE BELLAIRE

SKILLS: Colorist
LOCATION: Brooklyn or Dublin
FUN FACT: Cappuccino admirer.

http://jordiecolorsthings.tumblr.com

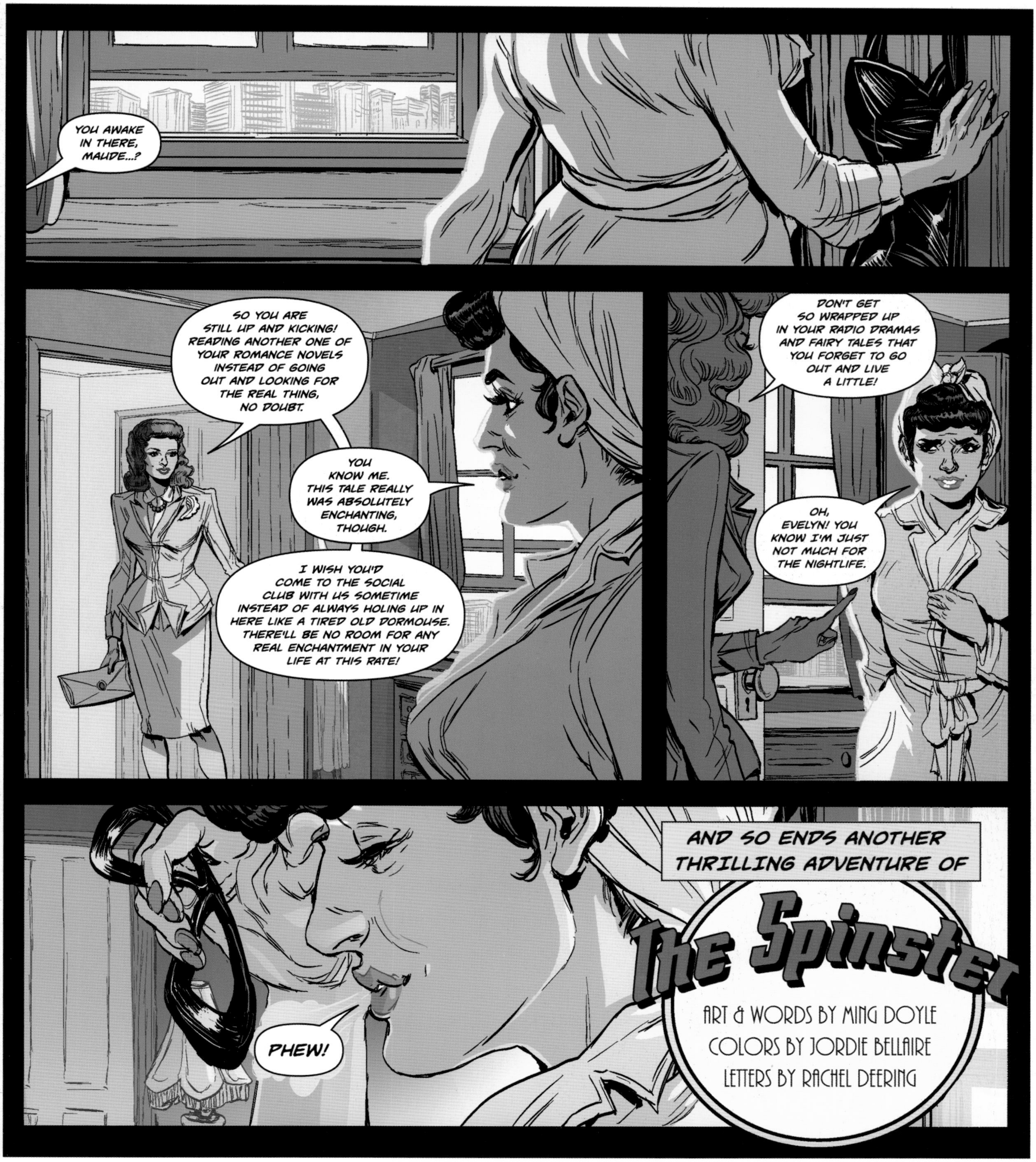
YOU AWAKE IN THERE, MAUDE...?
SO YOU ARE STILL UP AND KICKING! READING ANOTHER ONE OF YOUR ROMANCE NOVELS INSTEAD OF GOING OUT AND LOOKING FOR THE REAL THING, NO DOUBT.
YOU KNOW ME. THIS TALE REALLY WAS ABSOLUTELY ENCHANTING, THOUGH.
I WISH YOU'D COME TO THE SOCIAL CLUB WITH US SOMETIME INSTEAD OF ALWAYS HOLING UP IN HERE LIKE A TIRED OLD DORMOUSE. THERE'LL BE NO ROOM FOR ANY REAL ENCHANTMENT IN YOUR LIFE AT THIS RATE!
DON'T GET SO WRAPPED UP IN YOUR RADIO DRAMAS AND FAIRY TALES THAT YOU FORGET TO GO OUT AND LIVE A LITTLE!
OH, EVELYN! YOU KNOW I'M JUST NOT MUCH FOR THE NIGHTLIFE.
AND SO ENDS ANOTHER THRILLING ADVENTURE OF
The Spinster
ART & WORDS BY MING DOYLE
COLORS BY JORDIE BELLAIRE
LETTERS BY RACHEL DEERING
PHEW!

☆ ☆ ☆

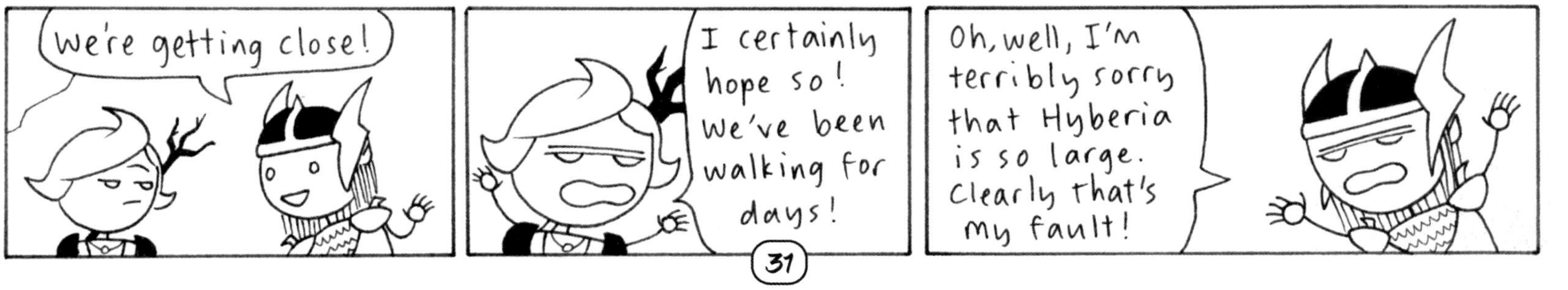
We're getting close!
I certainly hope so! We've been walking for days!
Oh, well, I'm terribly sorry that Hyberia is so large. Clearly that's my fault!

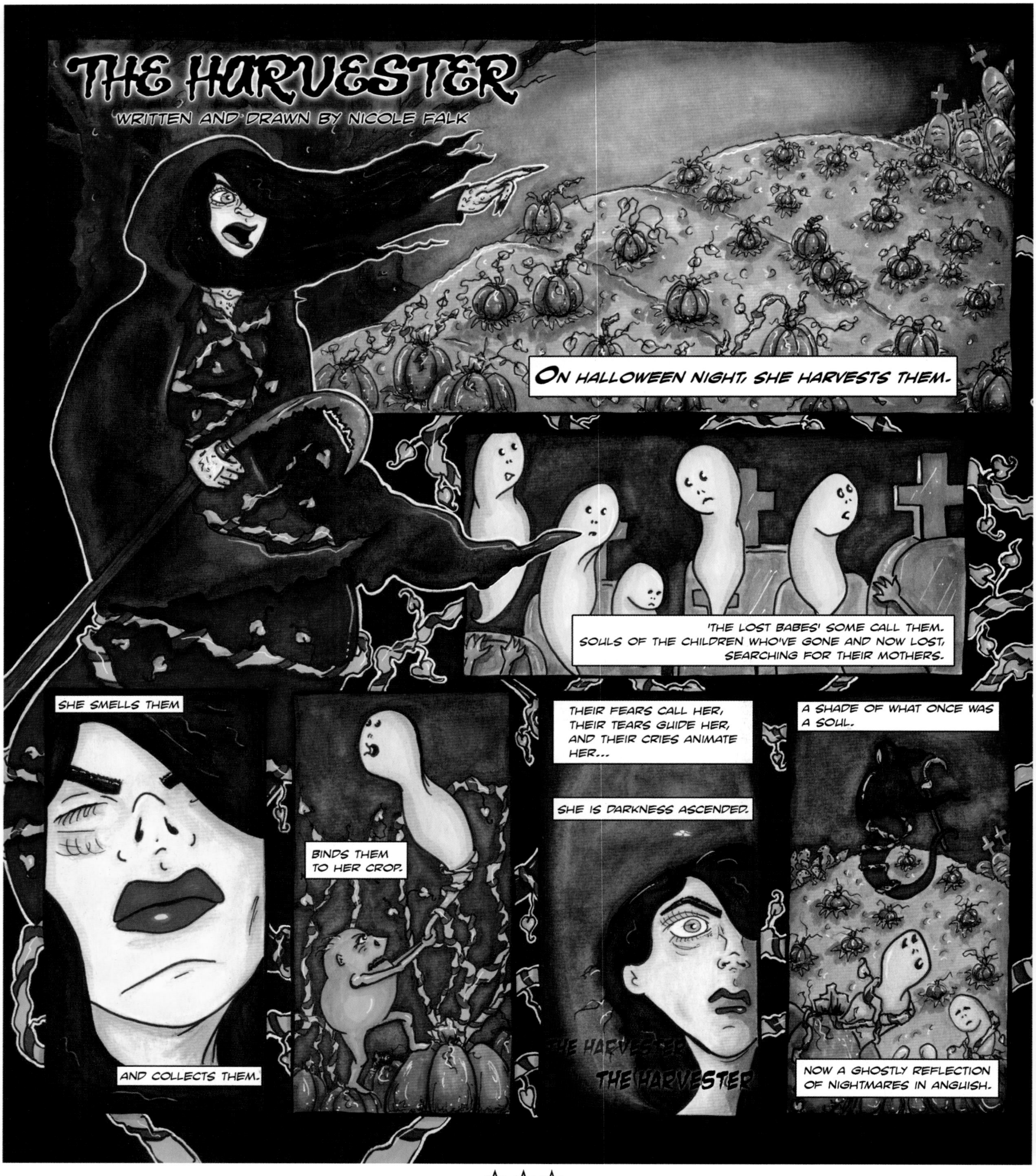
THE HARVESTER
WRITTEN AND DRAWN BY NICOLE FALK
ON HALLOWEEN NIGHT, SHE HARVESTS THEM.
'THE LOST BABES' SOME CALL THEM. SOULS OF THE CHILDREN WHO'VE GONE AND NOW LOST, SEARCHING FOR THEIR MOTHERS.
SHE SMELLS THEM
AND COLLECTS THEM.
BINDS THEM TO HER CROP.
THEIR FEARS CALL HER, THEIR TEARS GUIDE HER, AND THEIR CRIES ANIMATE HER...
SHE IS DARKNESS ASCENDED.
THE HARVESTER
A SHADE OF WHAT ONCE WAS A SOUL.
NOW A GHOSTLY REFLECTION OF NIGHTMARES IN ANGUISH.

☆ ☆ ☆

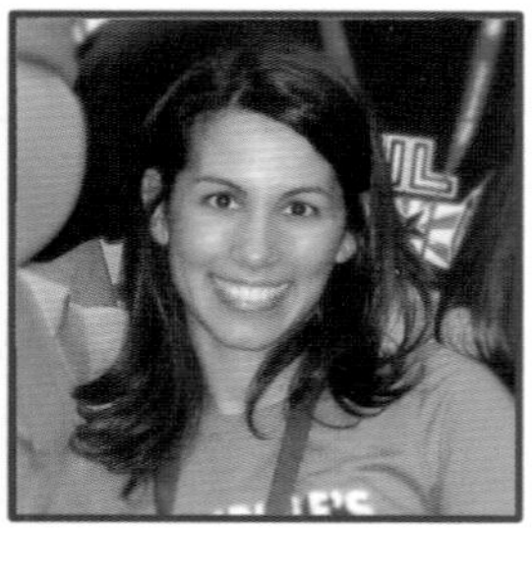

NICOLE FALK

SKILLS: Editor, Comic Creator, Writer, Artist
LOCATION: In the deep, dark woods...of New Jersey.
FUN FACT: I love halloween, spooky things, and all that goes in between.

www.nicolefalk.com

PRO TIP ETIQUETTE

BY NICOLE FALK

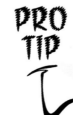

"PLEASE DO NOT SEND IN A DRAFT OF YOUR WORK TO AN EDITOR, WITH A NOTE SAYING 'YOU HAVE A FULL TIME JOB, SO YOU WON'T HAVE TIME FOR TOO MANY CORRECTIONS' OR SOMETHING ALONG THOSE LINES. #1 YOU ARE ALREADY SENDING NEGATIVE VIBES TO THE EDITOR AND IT IS CREATING TENSION FOR NO REASON. #2 EDITORS AREN'T GIVING YOU BUSY WORK, THEY ARE TRYING TO HELP YOU BRING OUT THE BEST OF YOUR OWN WORK! #3 WHAT?!"

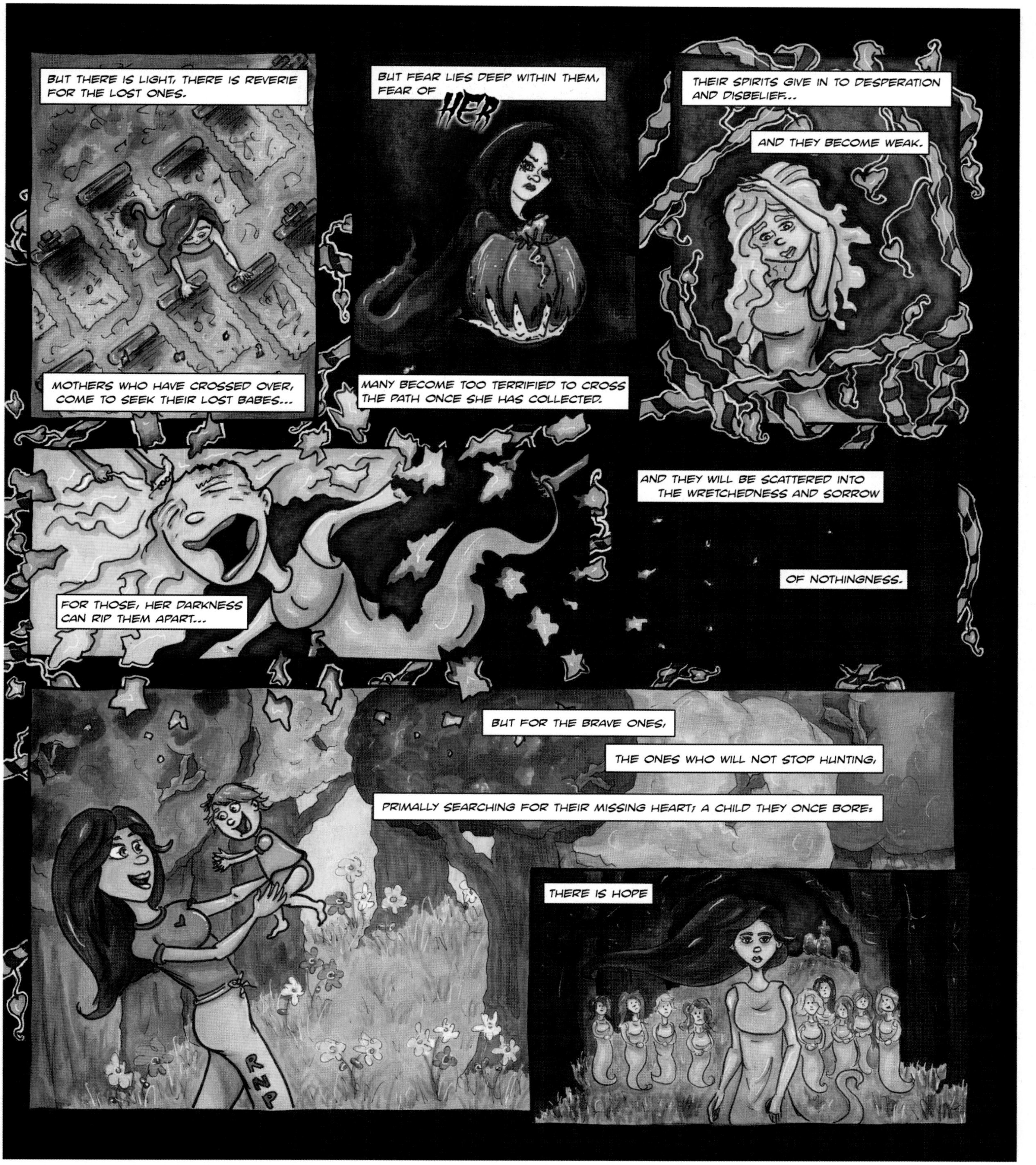
BUT THERE IS LIGHT, THERE IS REVERIE FOR THE LOST ONES.
MOTHERS WHO HAVE CROSSED OVER, COME TO SEEK THEIR LOST BABES...
BUT FEAR LIES DEEP WITHIN THEM, FEAR OF
HER
MANY BECOME TOO TERRIFIED TO CROSS THE PATH ONCE SHE HAS COLLECTED.
THEIR SPIRITS GIVE IN TO DESPERATION AND DISBELIEF...
AND THEY BECOME WEAK.
FOR THOSE, HER DARKNESS CAN RIP THEM APART...
AND THEY WILL BE SCATTERED INTO THE WRETCHEDNESS AND SORROW
OF NOTHINGNESS.
BUT FOR THE BRAVE ONES,
THE ONES WHO WILL NOT STOP HUNTING,
PRIMALLY SEARCHING FOR THEIR MISSING HEART; A CHILD THEY ONCE BORE:
RNP
THERE IS HOPE

☆ ☆ ☆

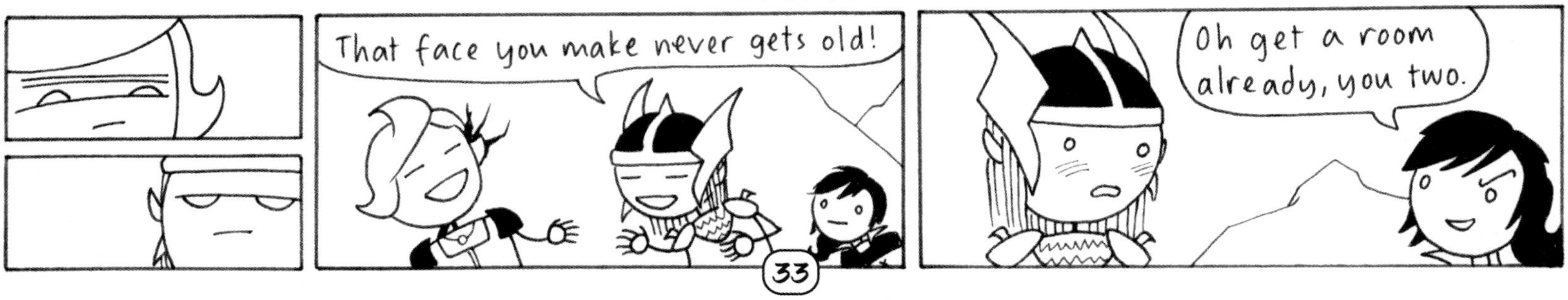
That face you make never gets old!
Oh get a room already, you two.

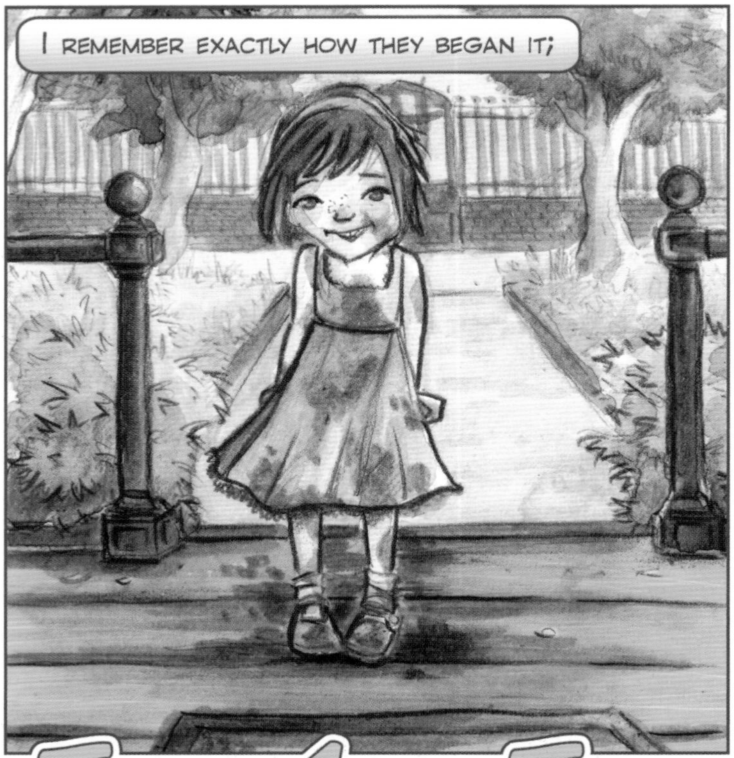
I REMEMBER EXACTLY HOW THEY BEGAN IT;

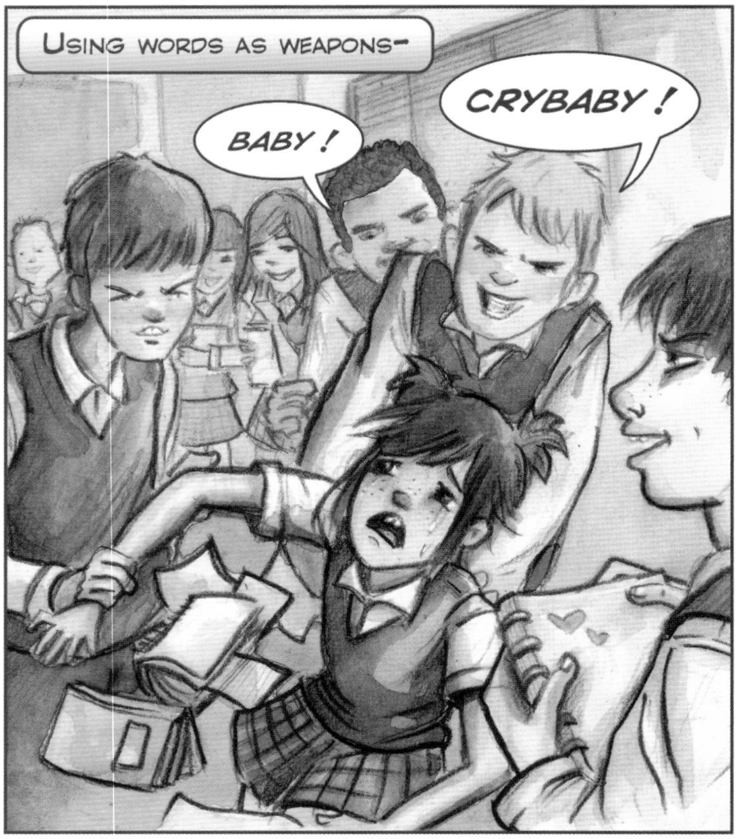
USING WORDS AS WEAPONS-
BABY!
CRYBABY!

THE ALL TOO REAL WORLD

story Amanda McMurray - Valia Kapadai art

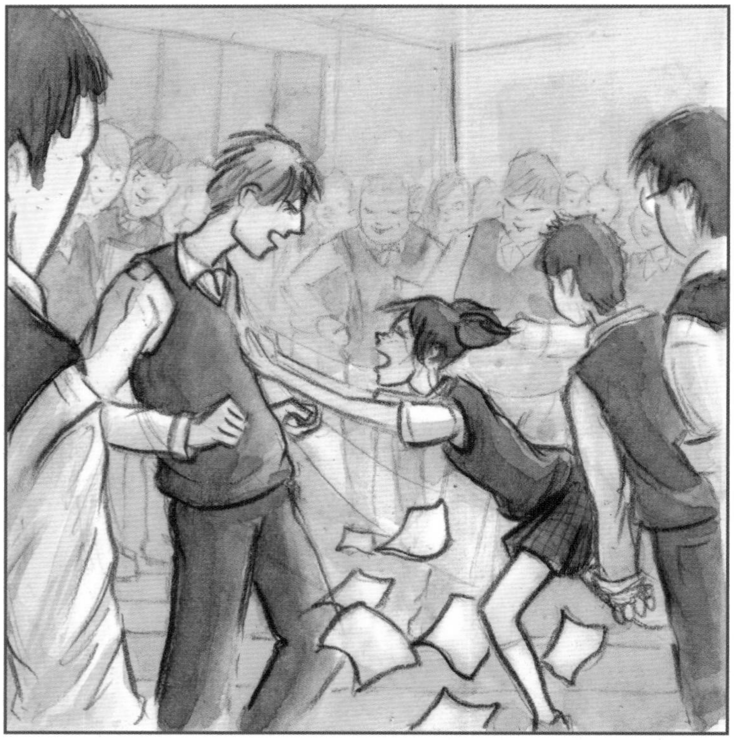

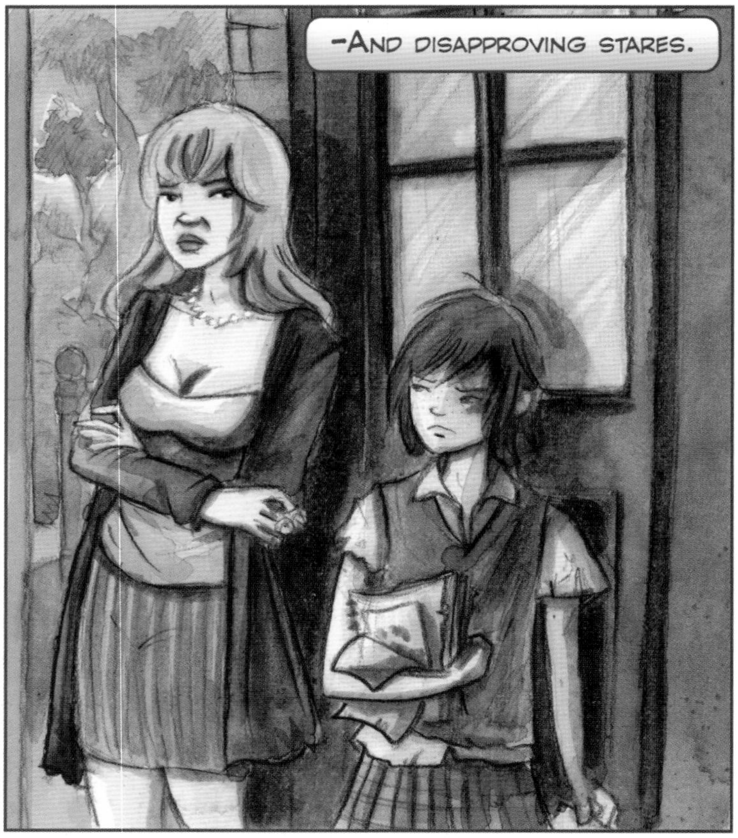
-AND DISAPPROVING STARES.

☆☆☆

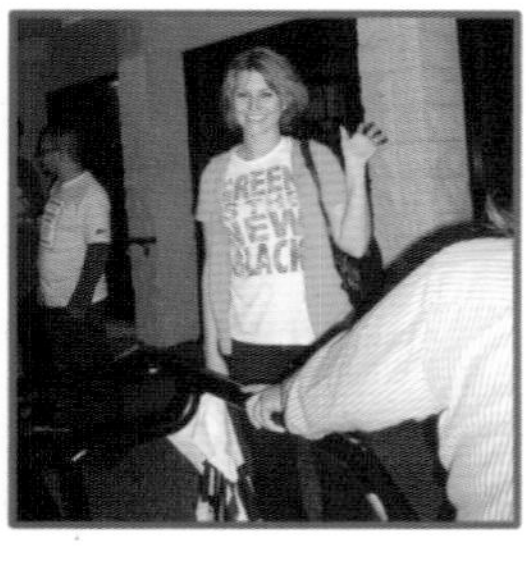

AMANDA MCMURRAY

SKILLS: Writer
LOCATION: Denver, CO
FUN FACT: I must be Clark Kent's long-lost sister because I'm so clumsy!

https://www.facebook.com/#!/mandykmcmurray

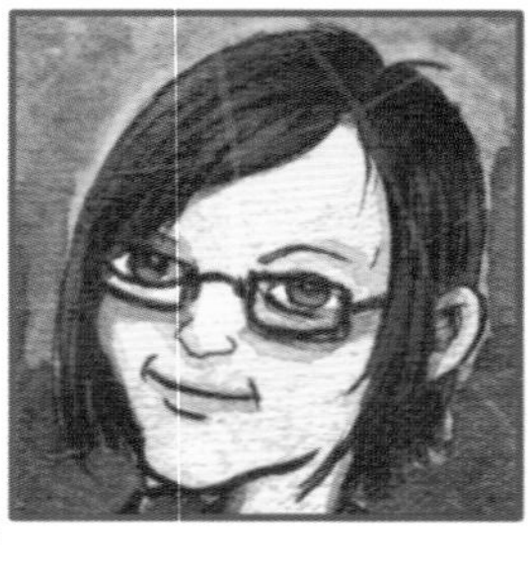

VALIA KAPADAI

SKILLS: Artist (pencils, inks, colours, letter
LOCATION: Athens, Greece
FUN FACT: I am a hopeless day-dreamer.

www.neurotic-elf.deviantart.co

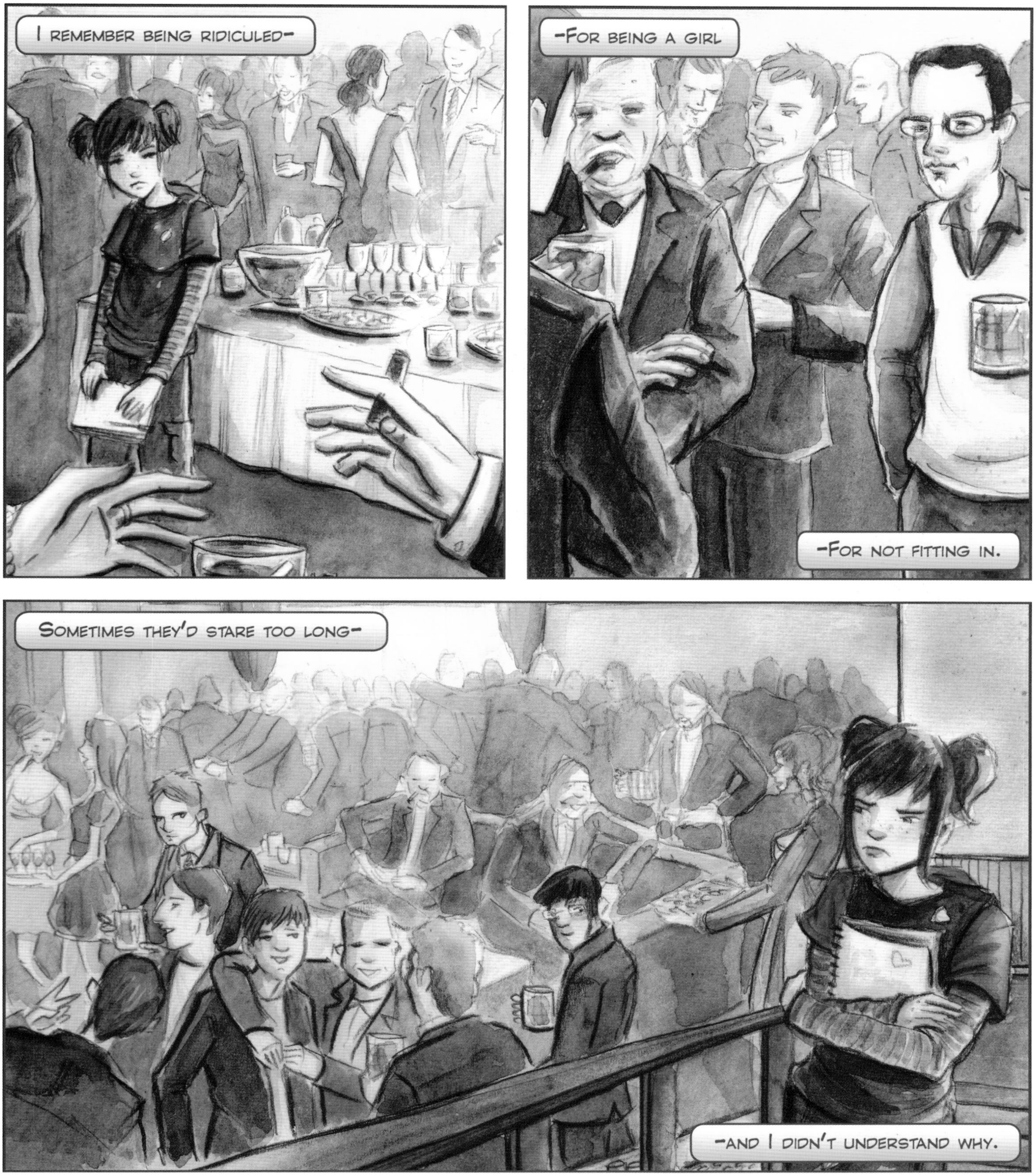
I remember being ridiculed–
–For being a girl
–For not fitting in.
Sometimes they'd stare too long–
–and I didn't understand why.

☆ ☆ ☆

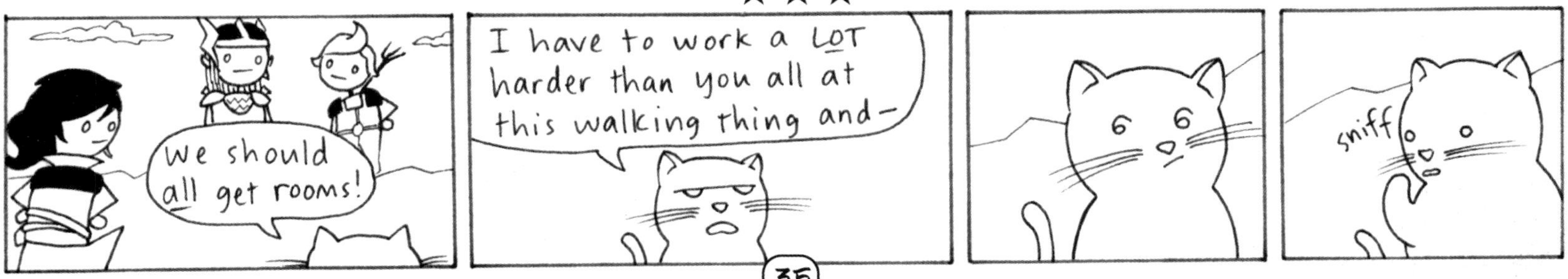
We should all get rooms!
I have to work a LOT harder than you all at this walking thing and–
sniff

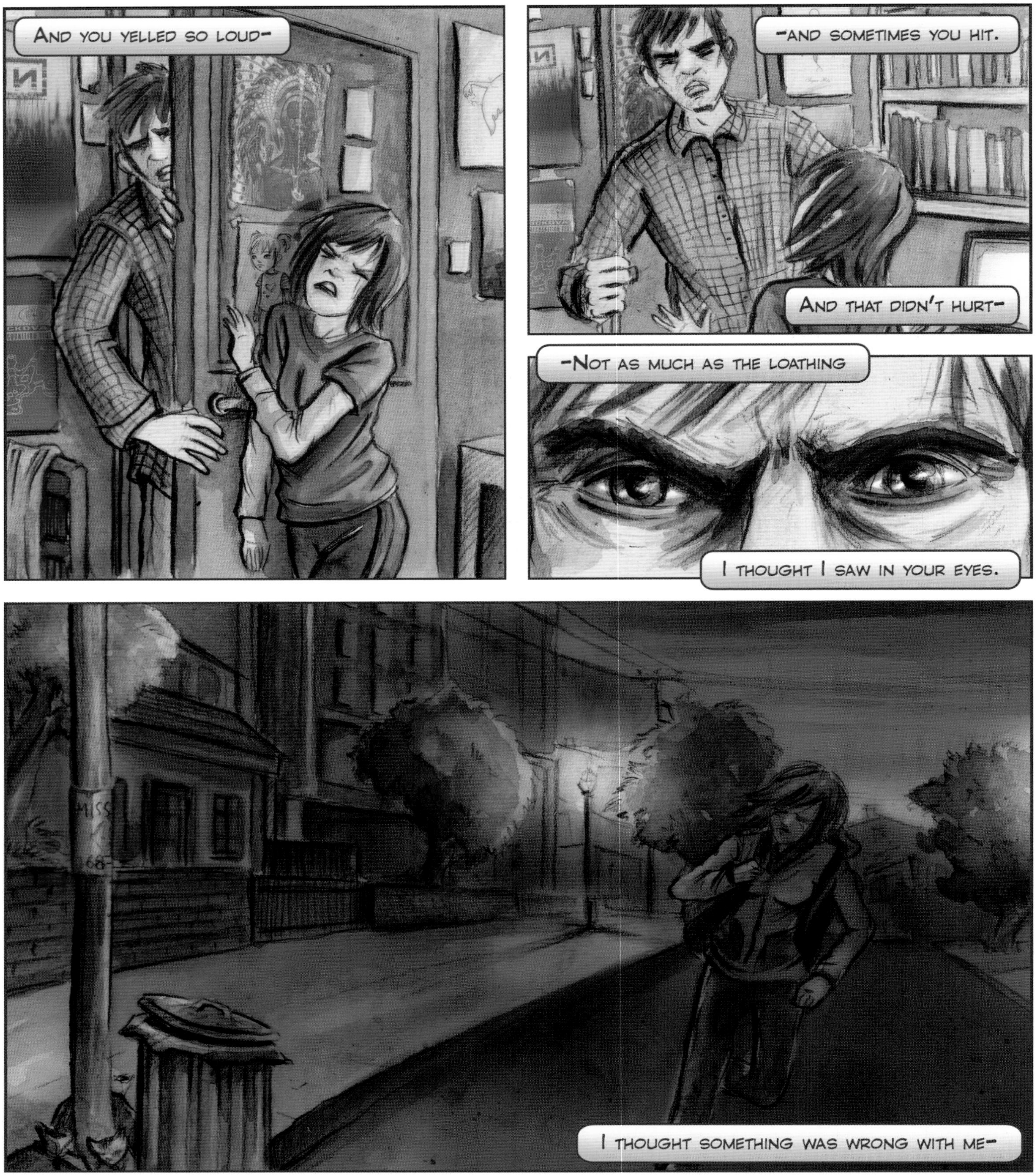
And you yelled so loud-
-and sometimes you hit.
And that didn't hurt-
-Not as much as the loathing
I thought I saw in your eyes.
I thought something was wrong with me-

☆☆☆

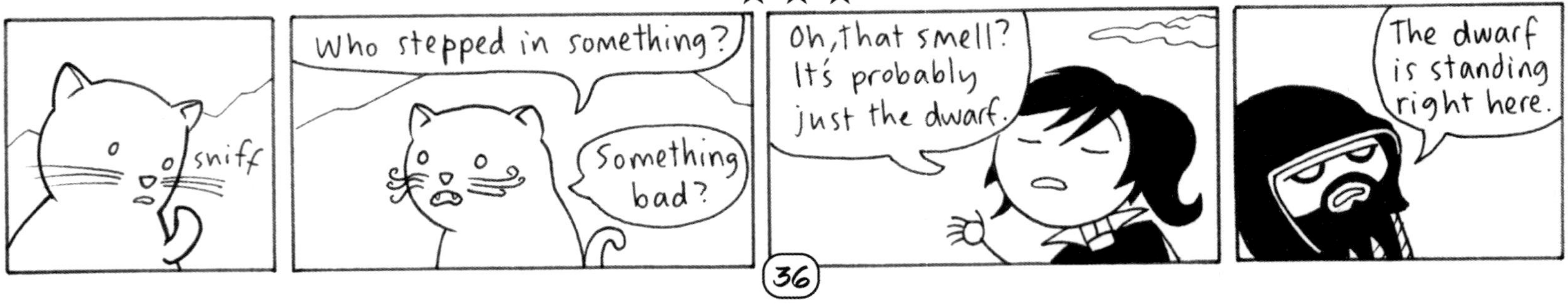
sniff
Who stepped in something?
Something bad?
Oh, that smell? It's probably just the dwarf.
The dwarf is standing right here.

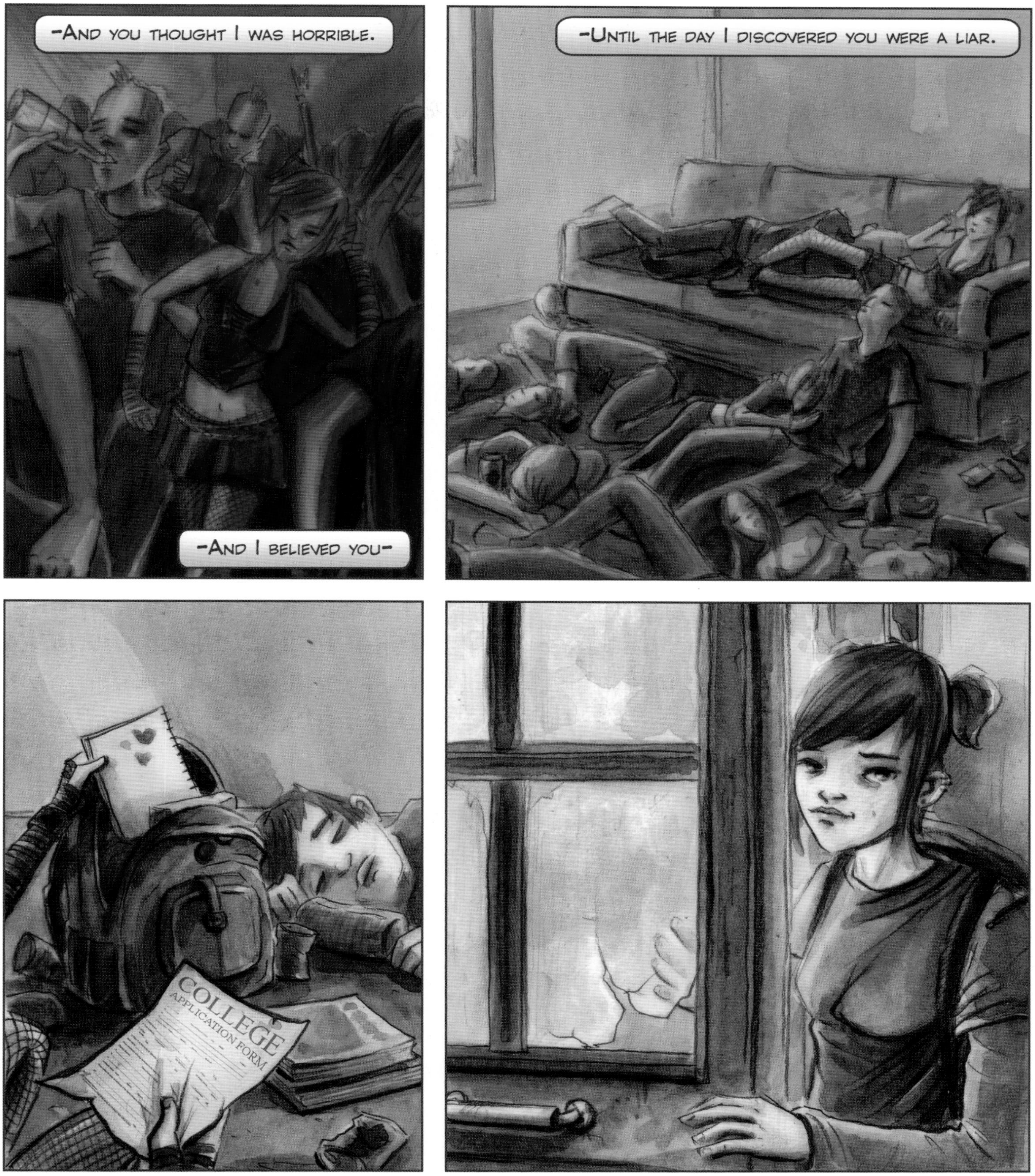
-And you thought I was horrible.
-And I believed you-
-Until the day I discovered you were a liar.
COLLEGE
APPLICATION FORM

☆ ☆ ☆

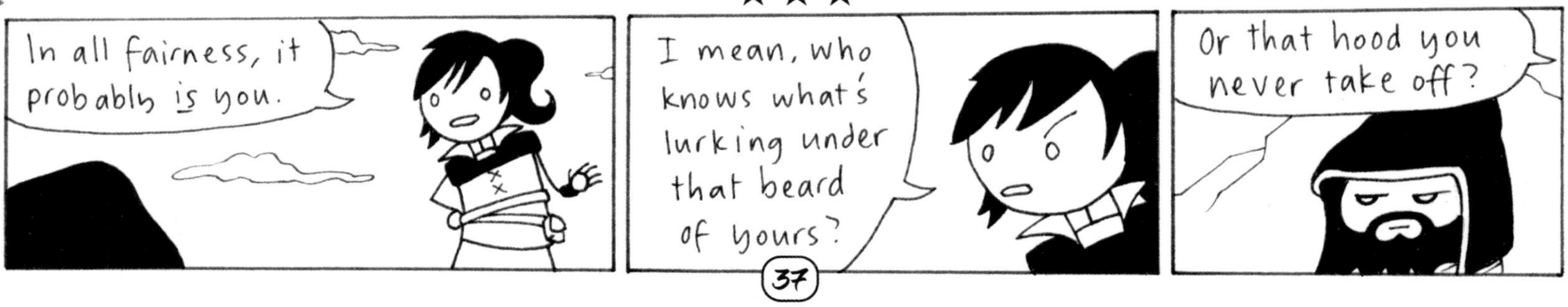
In all fairness, it probably is you.
I mean, who knows what's lurking under that beard of yours?
Or that hood you never take off?

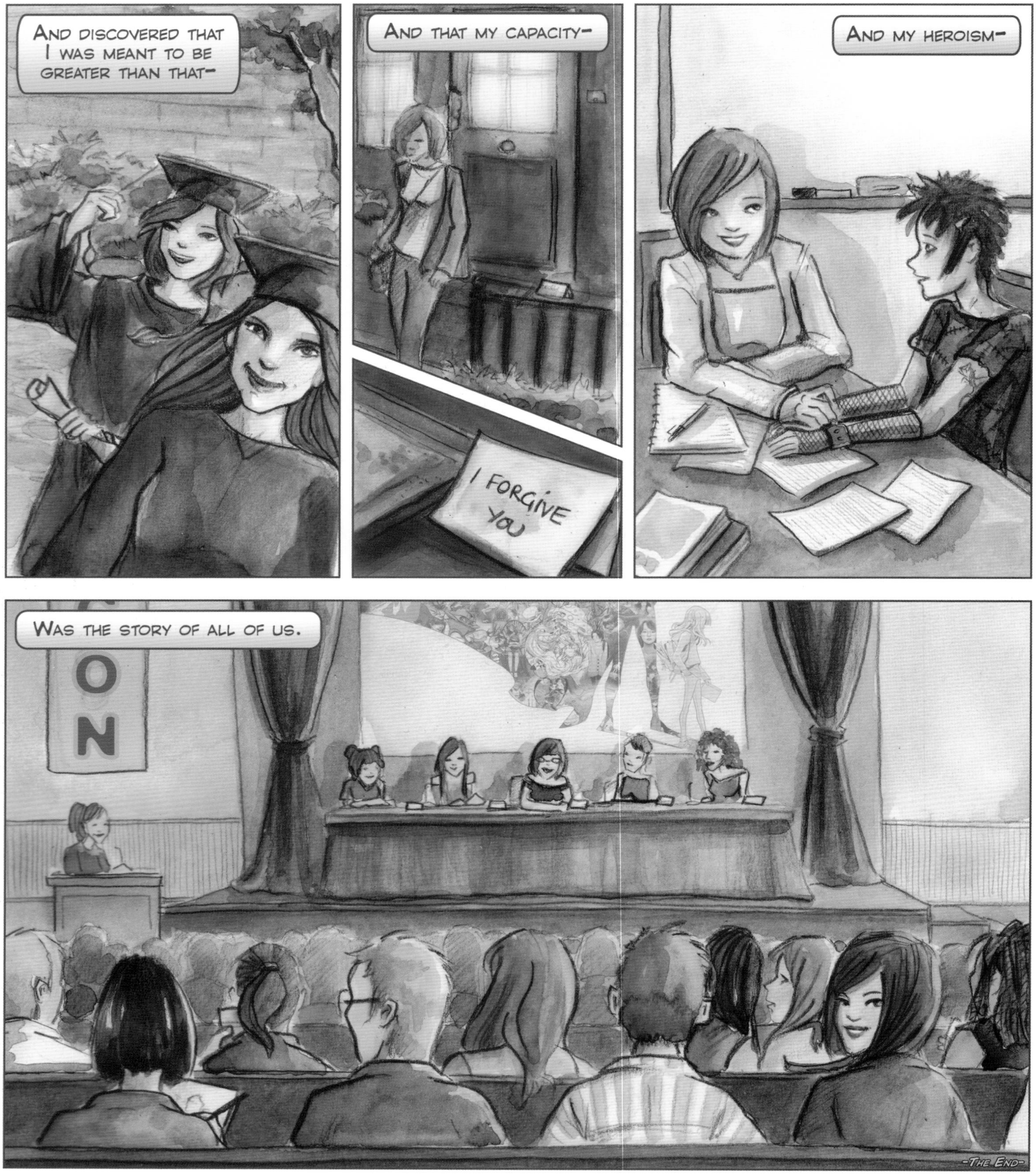
And discovered that I was meant to be greater than that–
And that my capacity–
I forgive you
And my heroism–
Was the story of all of us.
–The End–

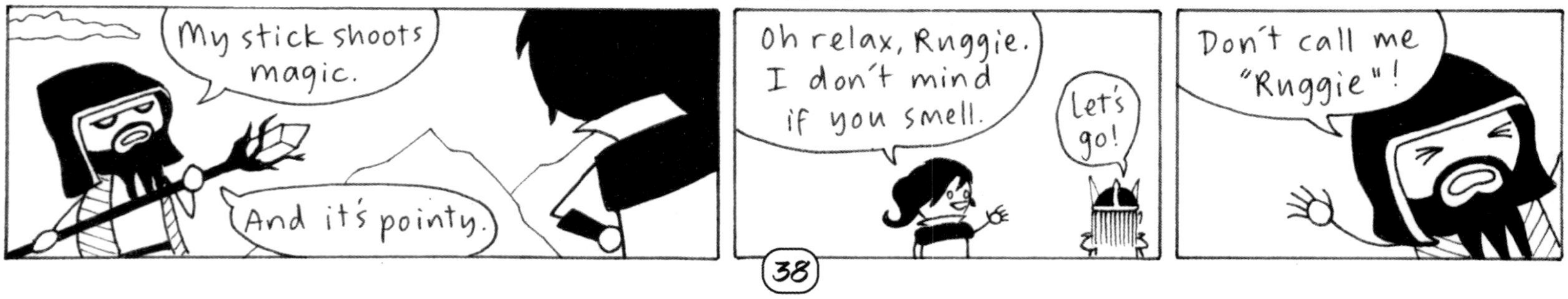
My stick shoots magic.
And it's pointy.
Oh relax, Ruggie. I don't mind if you smell.
Let's go!
Don't call me "Ruggie"!

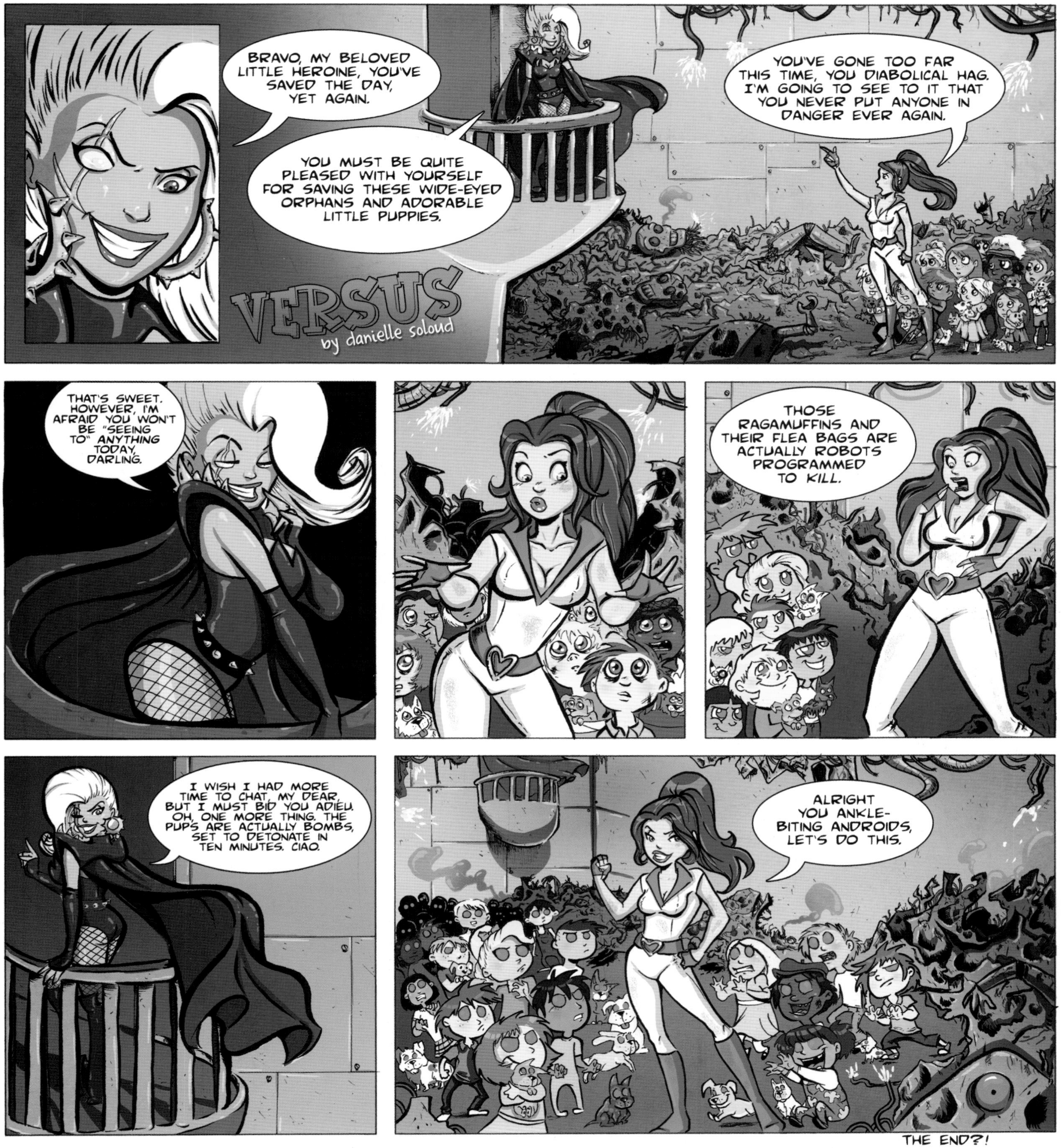
BRAVO, MY BELOVED LITTLE HEROINE, YOU'VE SAVED THE DAY, YET AGAIN.
YOU MUST BE QUITE PLEASED WITH YOURSELF FOR SAVING THESE WIDE-EYED ORPHANS AND ADORABLE LITTLE PUPPIES.
VERSUS
by danielle soloud
YOU'VE GONE TOO FAR THIS TIME, YOU DIABOLICAL HAG. I'M GOING TO SEE TO IT THAT YOU NEVER PUT ANYONE IN DANGER EVER AGAIN.
THAT'S SWEET. HOWEVER, I'M AFRAID YOU WON'T BE "SEEING TO" ANYTHING TODAY, DARLING.
THOSE RAGAMUFFINS AND THEIR FLEA BAGS ARE ACTUALLY ROBOTS PROGRAMMED TO KILL.
I WISH I HAD MORE TIME TO CHAT, MY DEAR, BUT I MUST BID YOU ADIEU. OH, ONE MORE THING. THE PUPS ARE ACTUALLY BOMBS, SET TO DETONATE IN TEN MINUTES. CIAO.
ALRIGHT YOU ANKLE-BITING ANDROIDS, LET'S DO THIS.
THE END?!

☆ ☆ ☆

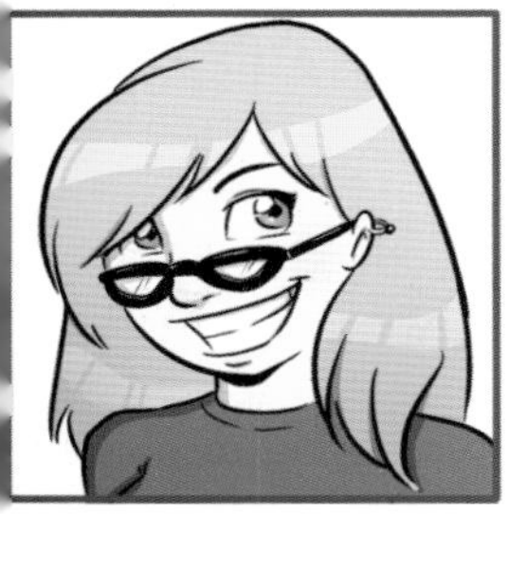

DANIELLE SOLOUD

SKILLS: Writer, Artist
LOCATION: Orlando, FL
FUN FACT: "Danielle Soloud" is actually a pseudonym that stems from my days as a hard house DJ. My real name is Danielle Gransaull.

www.DanielleSoloud.com

PRO TIP

WORK ETHIC
BY SUZANNAH ROWNTREE

"WORK HARD AND CARE ABOUT WHAT YOU DO, AND GOOD THINGS WILL COME TO YOU."

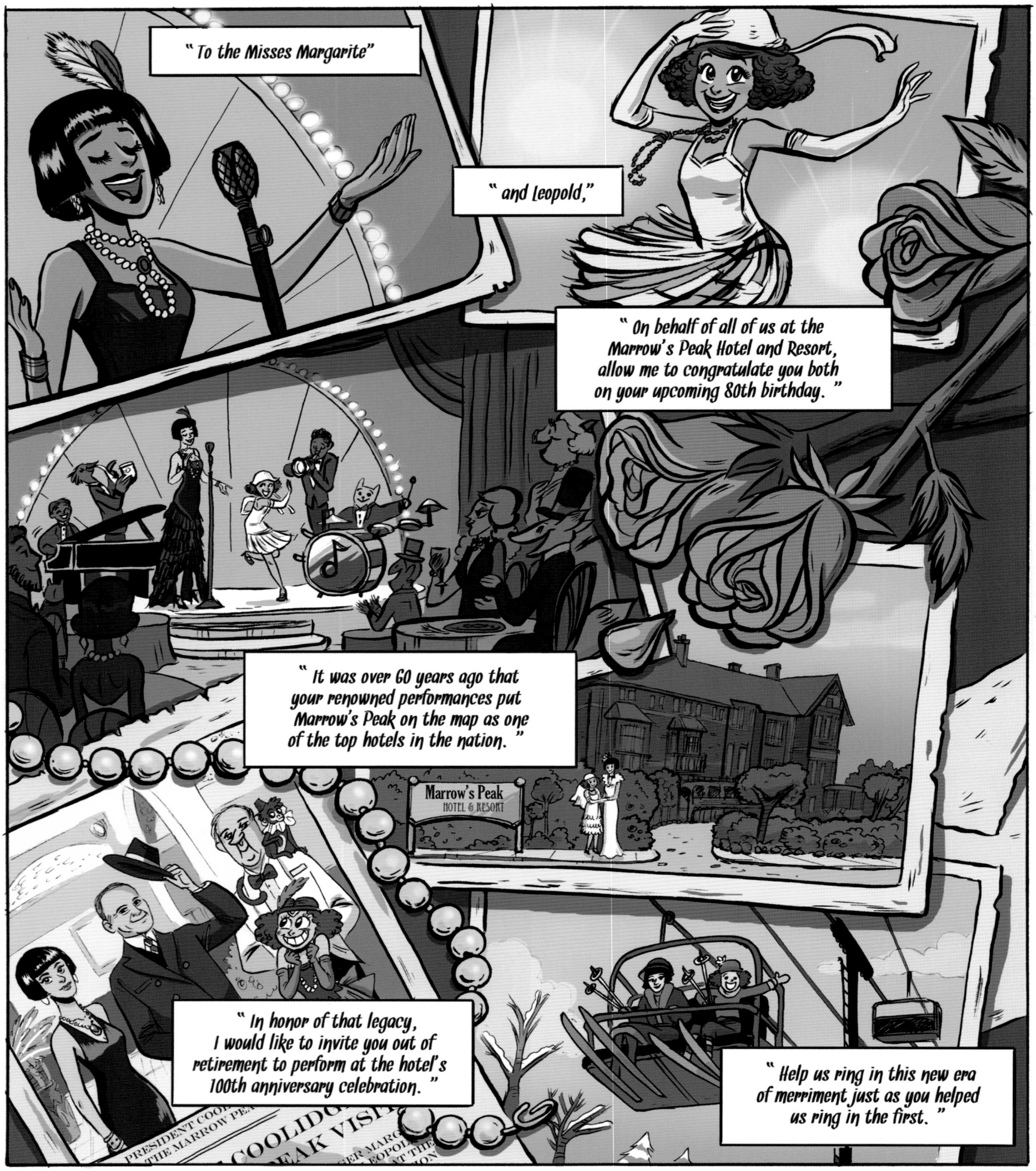
"To the Misses Margarite"
"and Leopold,"
"On behalf of all of us at the Marrow's Peak Hotel and Resort, allow me to congratulate you both on your upcoming 80th birthday."
"It was over 60 years ago that your renowned performances put Marrow's Peak on the map as one of the top hotels in the nation."
Marrow's Peak
HOTEL & RESORT
"In honor of that legacy, I would like to invite you out of retirement to perform at the hotel's 100th anniversary celebration."
"Help us ring in this new era of merriment just as you helped us ring in the first."

WRITER: JOAMETTE GIL ARTIST: KATIE SHANAHAN COLORS: KATIE SHANAHAN & MARY BELLAMY LETTERS: RACHEL DEERING

☆☆☆

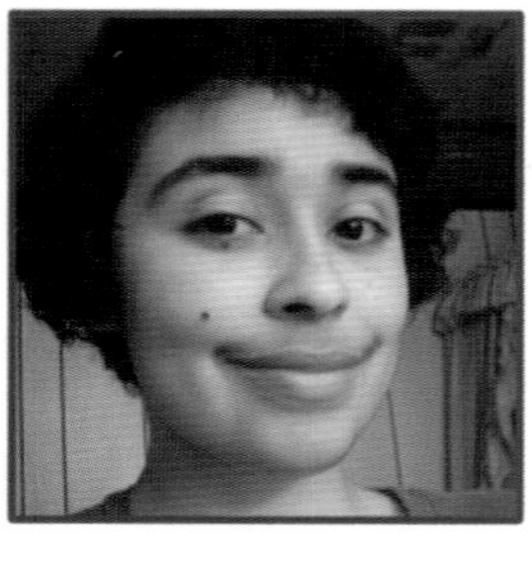

JOAMETTE GIL

SKILLS: Writer
LOCATION: Olympia, WA
FUN FACT: Went on to create *EXILE* with Brian Denham.

blackinkbird.com

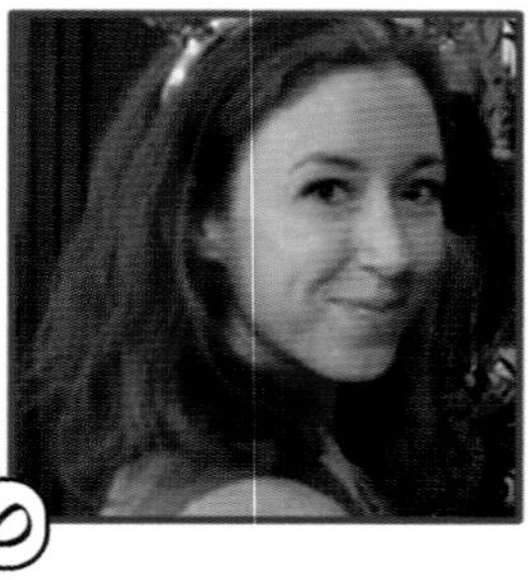

KATIE SHANAHAN

SKILLS: Pencils, Inks, Color
LOCATION: Toronto, Canada
FUN FACT: I'm a storyboard artist by day and a comic-making nut bar by night!

www.ktshy.com

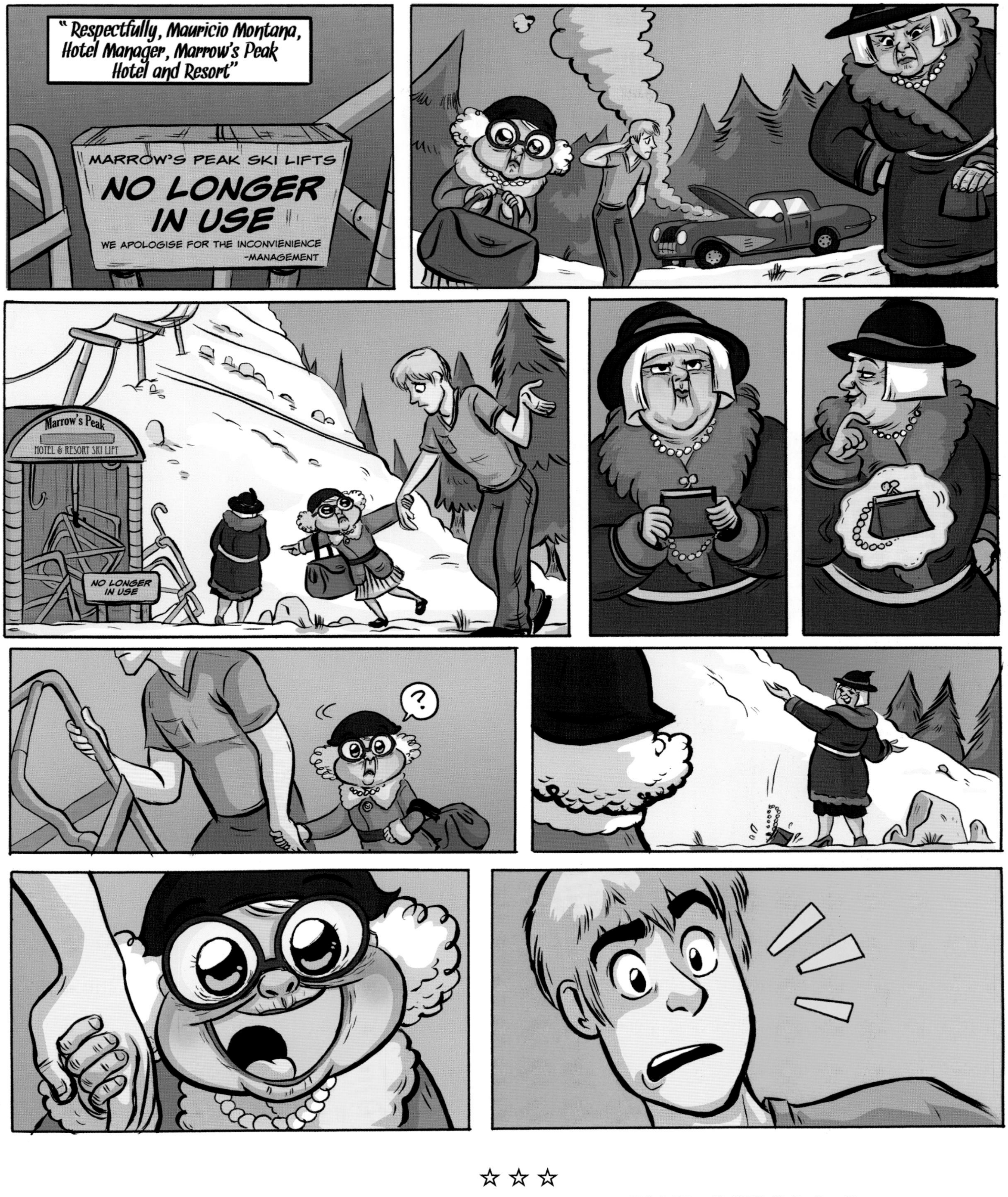
"Respectfully, Mauricio Montana, Hotel Manager, Marrow's Peak Hotel and Resort"
MARROW'S PEAK SKI LIFTS
NO LONGER IN USE
WE APOLOGISE FOR THE INCONVIENIENCE
-MANAGEMENT
Marrow's Peak
HOTEL & RESORT SKI LIFT
NO LONGER IN USE
?

☆ ☆ ☆

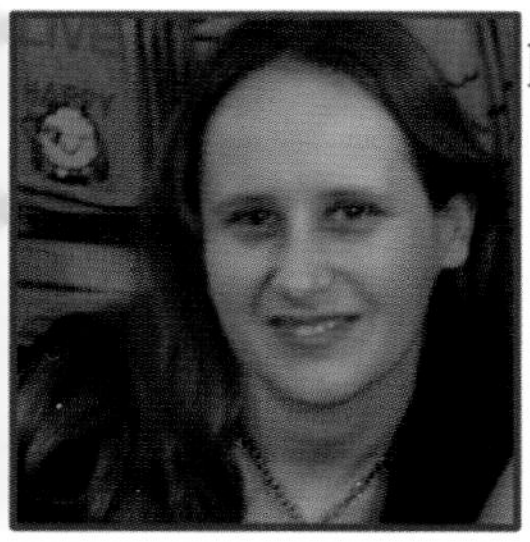

MARY "ZORILITA" BELLAMY

SKILLS: Illustrator, Colorist
LOCATION: Los Angeles, CA
FUN FACT: I am strangely good at home repair.

http://www.marybellamy.com

PRO TIP

WRITING
BY BONNIE BURTON

"WHEN WRITING COMICS BE SURE TO KEEP YOUR DIALOG SHORT, INTERESTING, AND RELEVANT TO THE FLOW OF THE STORY. YOU WANT THE IMAGES TO SPEAK FOR YOU, SO BE SURE TO GIVE AS MUCH DETAIL IN THE DESCRIPTIONS OF THE ACTIONS, THE CHARACTERS, AND THE SCENERY WHILE STILL ALLOWING YOUR ARTIST TO GIVE THEIR OWN INTERPRETATION."

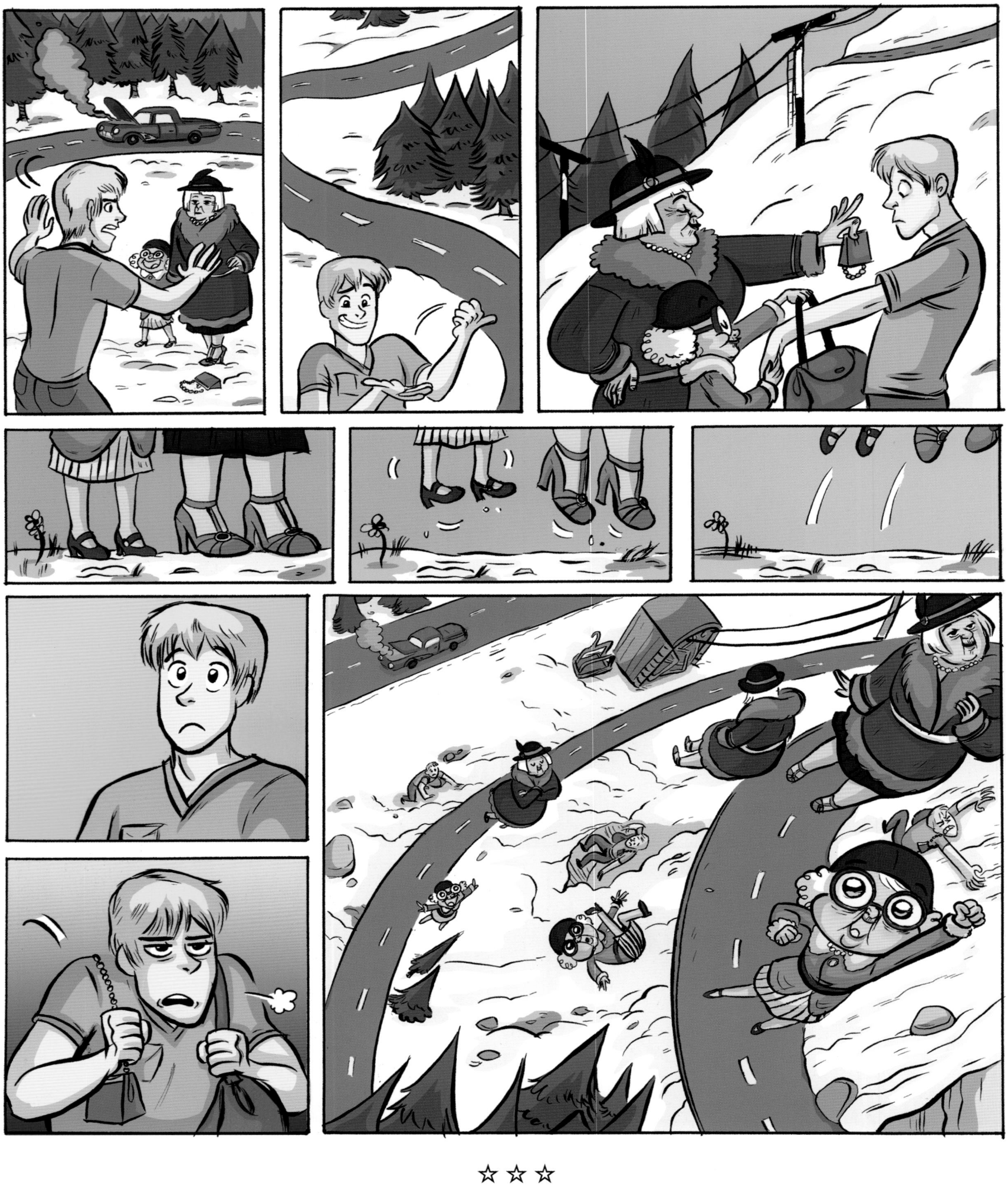

☆ ☆ ☆

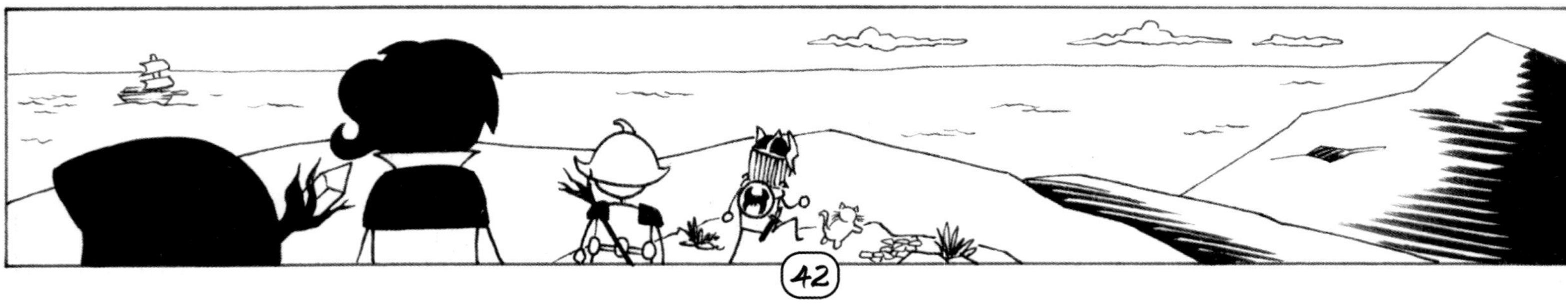

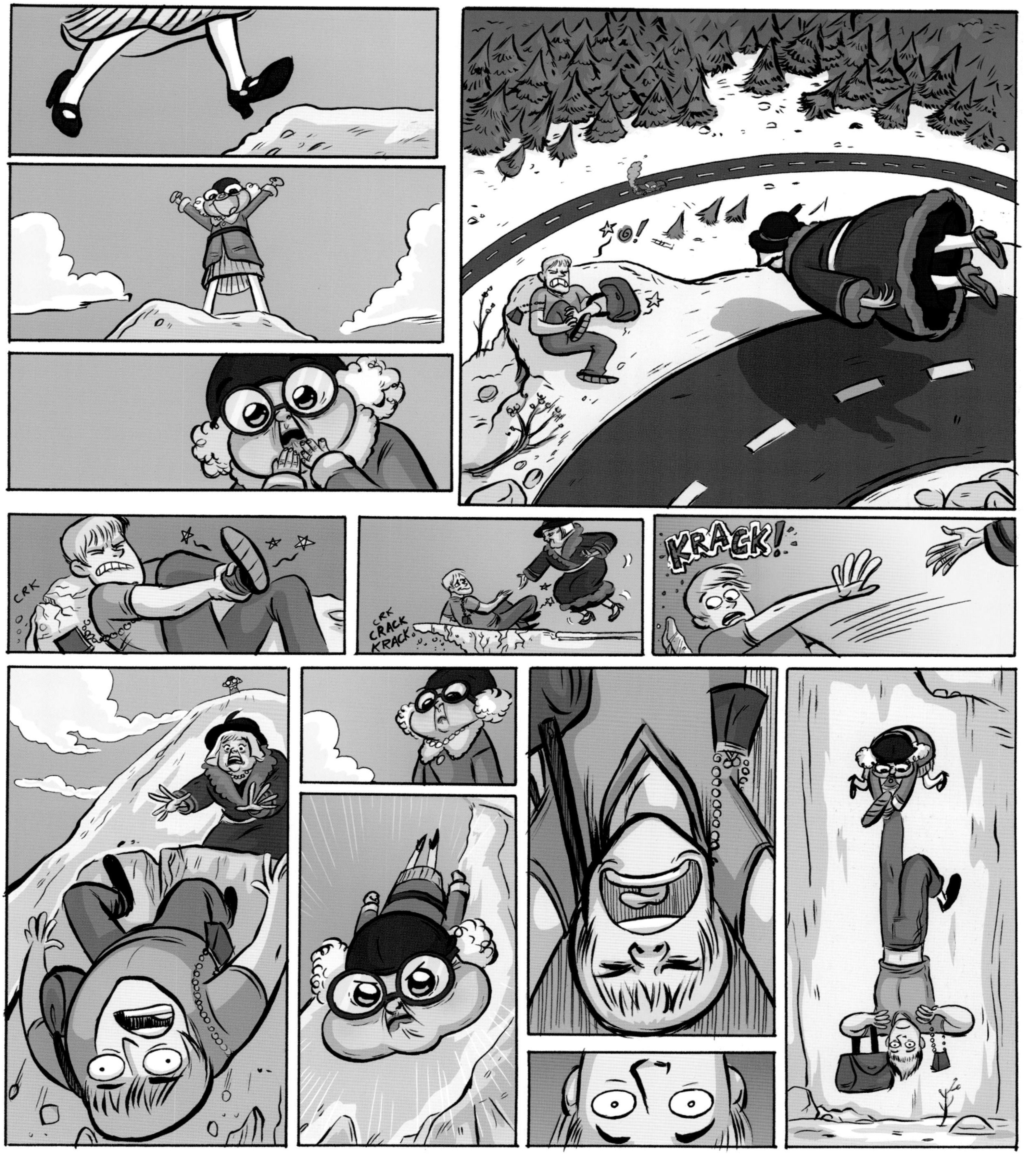
CRK
CRK
CRACK
KRACK
KRACK!

☆ ☆ ☆

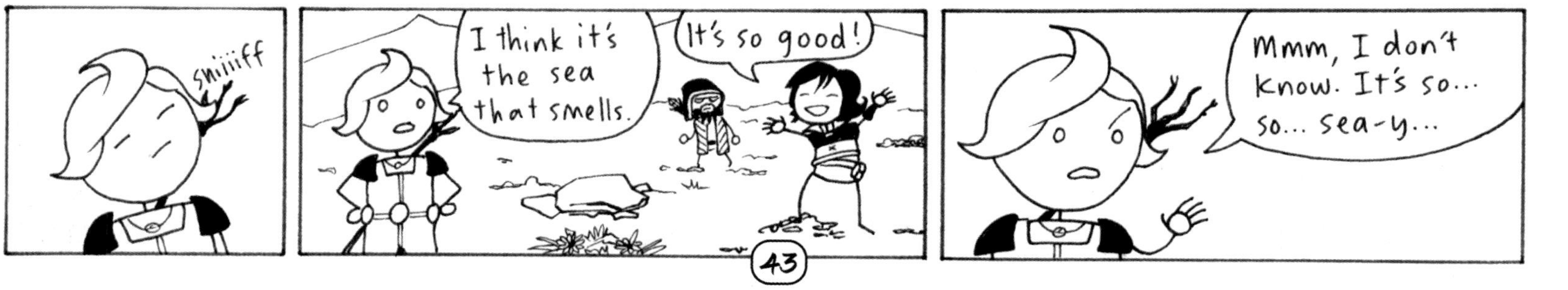
sniiiiff
I think it's the sea that smells.
It's so good!
Mmm, I don't know. It's so... so... sea-y...

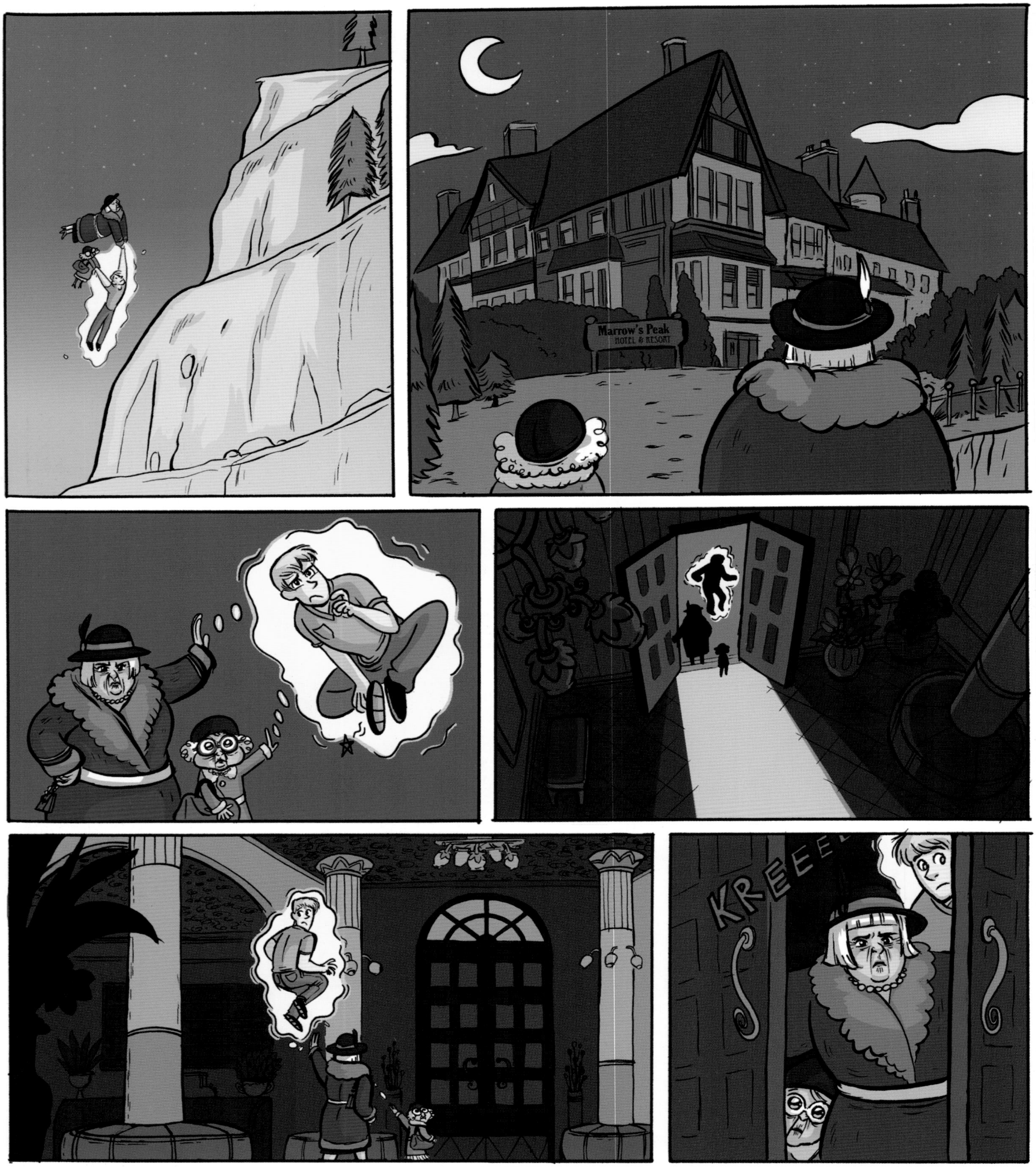

Marrow's Peak
HOTEL & RESORT
KREEE

☆ ☆ ☆

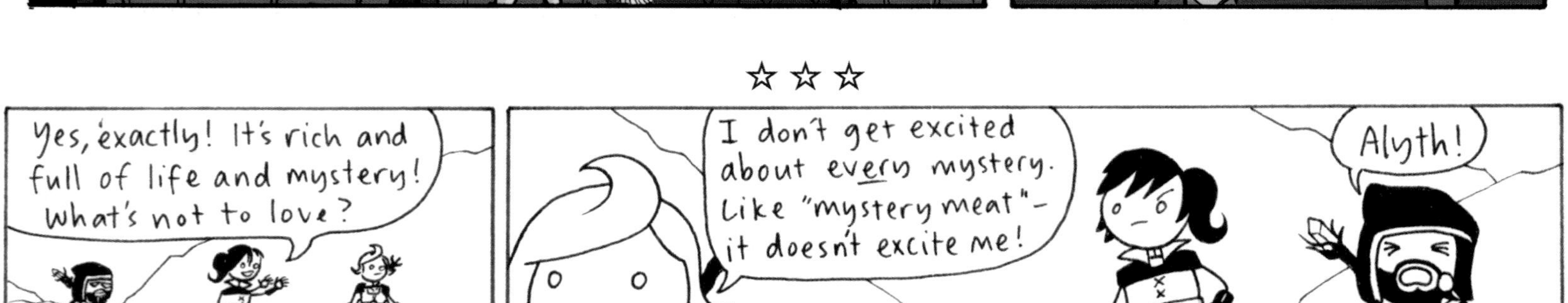

Yes, exactly! It's rich and full of life and mystery! What's not to love?
I don't get excited about every mystery. Like "mystery meat" – it doesn't excite me!
Alyth!

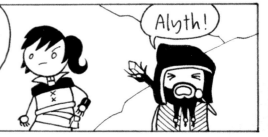

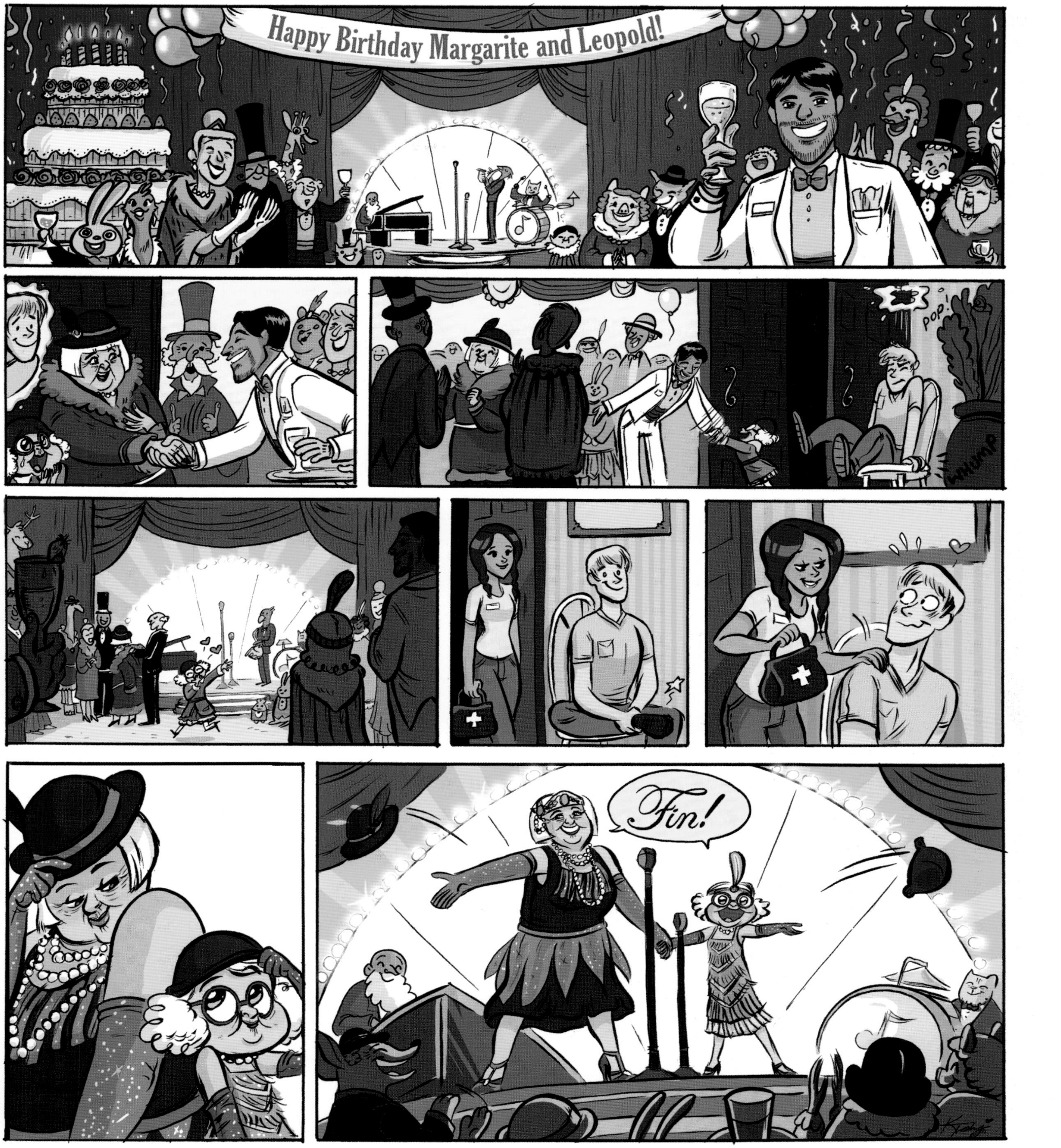
Happy Birthday Margarite and Leopold!
POP!
WHUMP
Fin!

☆ ☆ ☆

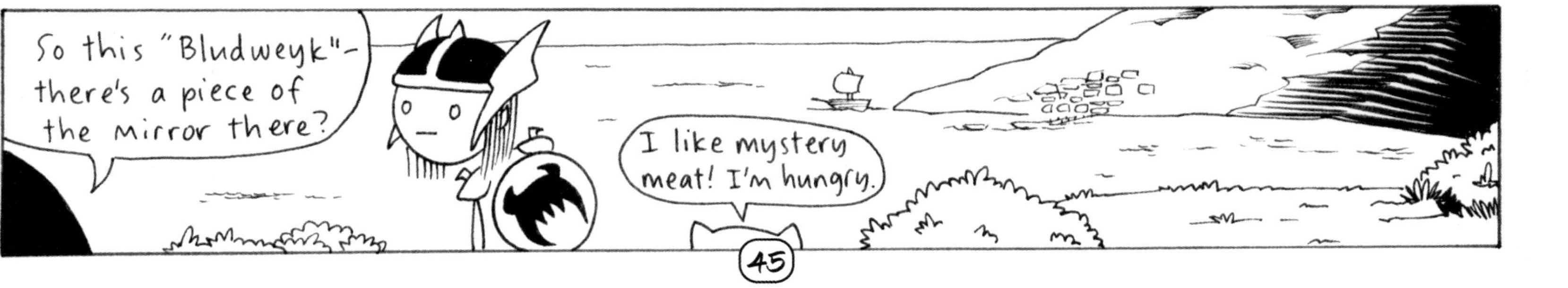
So this "Bludweyk"- there's a piece of the mirror there?
I like mystery meat! I'm hungry.

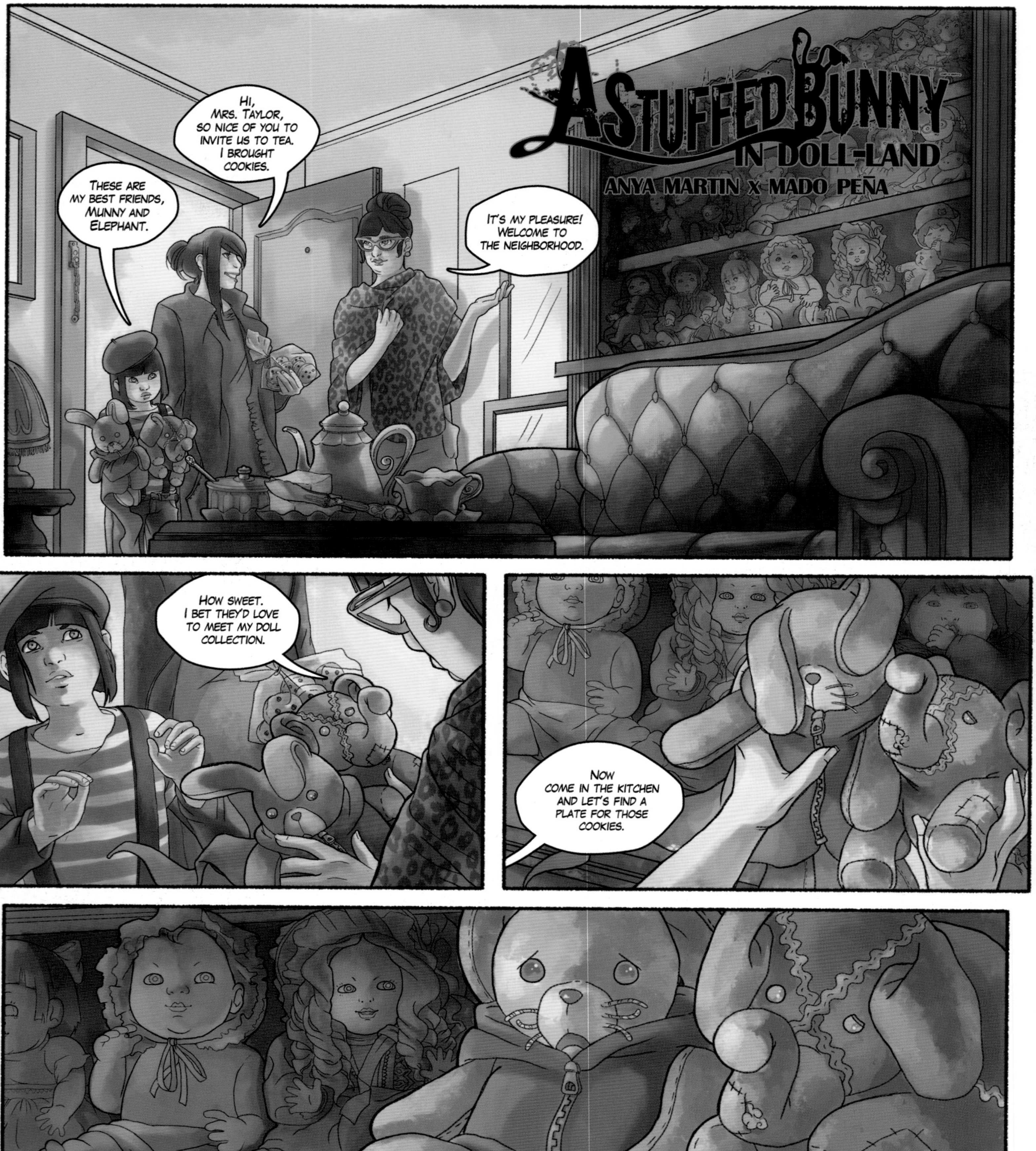

A STUFFED BUNNY
IN DOLL-LAND
ANYA MARTIN x MADO PEÑA
HI, MRS. TAYLOR, SO NICE OF YOU TO INVITE US TO TEA. I BROUGHT COOKIES.
THESE ARE MY BEST FRIENDS, MUNNY AND ELEPHANT.
IT'S MY PLEASURE! WELCOME TO THE NEIGHBORHOOD.
HOW SWEET. I BET THEY'D LOVE TO MEET MY DOLL COLLECTION.
NOW COME IN THE KITCHEN AND LET'S FIND A PLATE FOR THOSE COOKIES.

☆ ☆ ☆

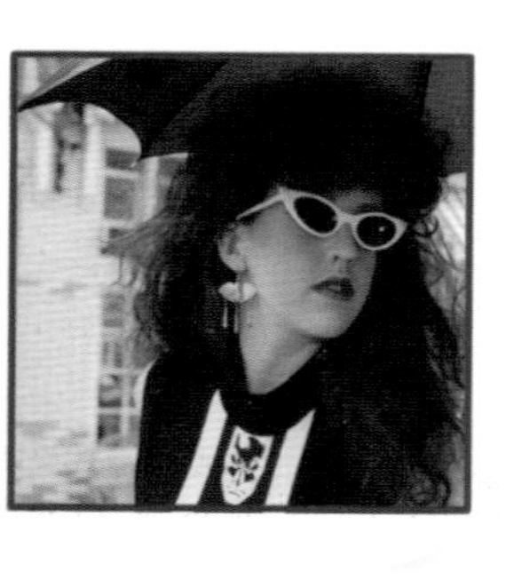

ANYA MARTIN

SKILLS: Writer
LOCATION: Atlanta, GA
FUN FACT: Used to cry and refuse to answer when anyone called me anything but Batgirl. OK, I was 3!

www.ATLRetro.com

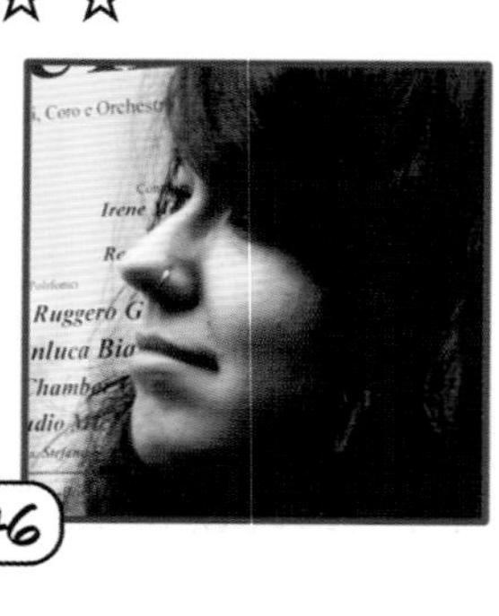

MADO PEñA

SKILLS: Penciller, Colorist, Letterer
LOCATION: Barcelona
FUN FACT: I got this all on my mind, then I had only two choices: medication or drawing it out.

http://respuestaennegro.blogspot.com

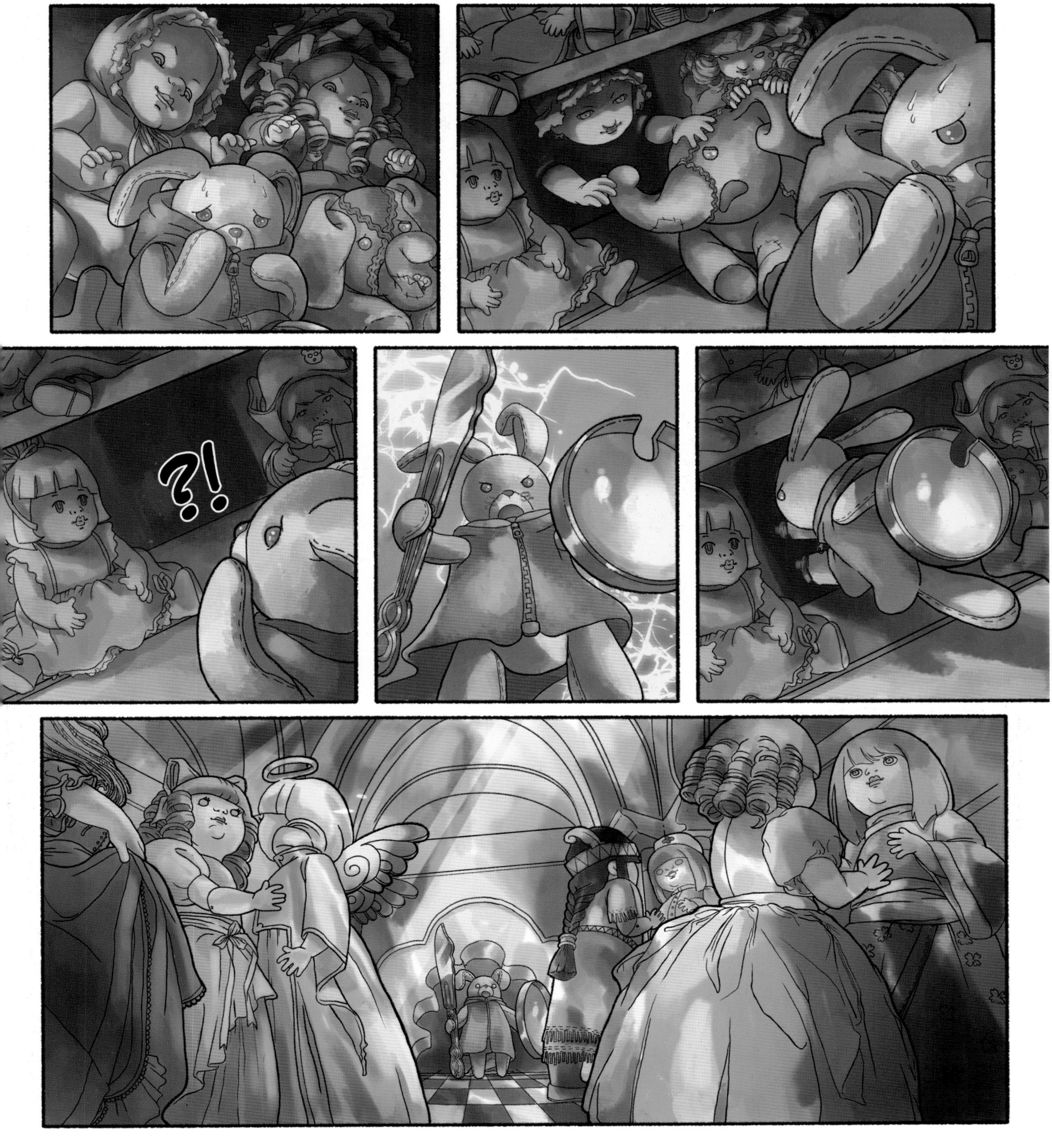
?!

☆ ☆ ☆

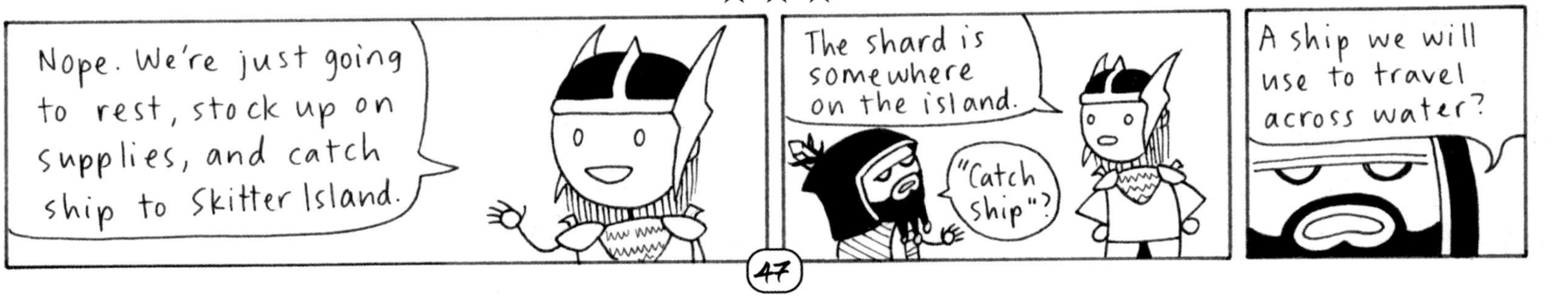
Nope. We're just going to rest, stock up on supplies, and catch ship to Skitter Island.
The shard is somewhere on the island.
"Catch ship"?
A ship we will use to travel across water?

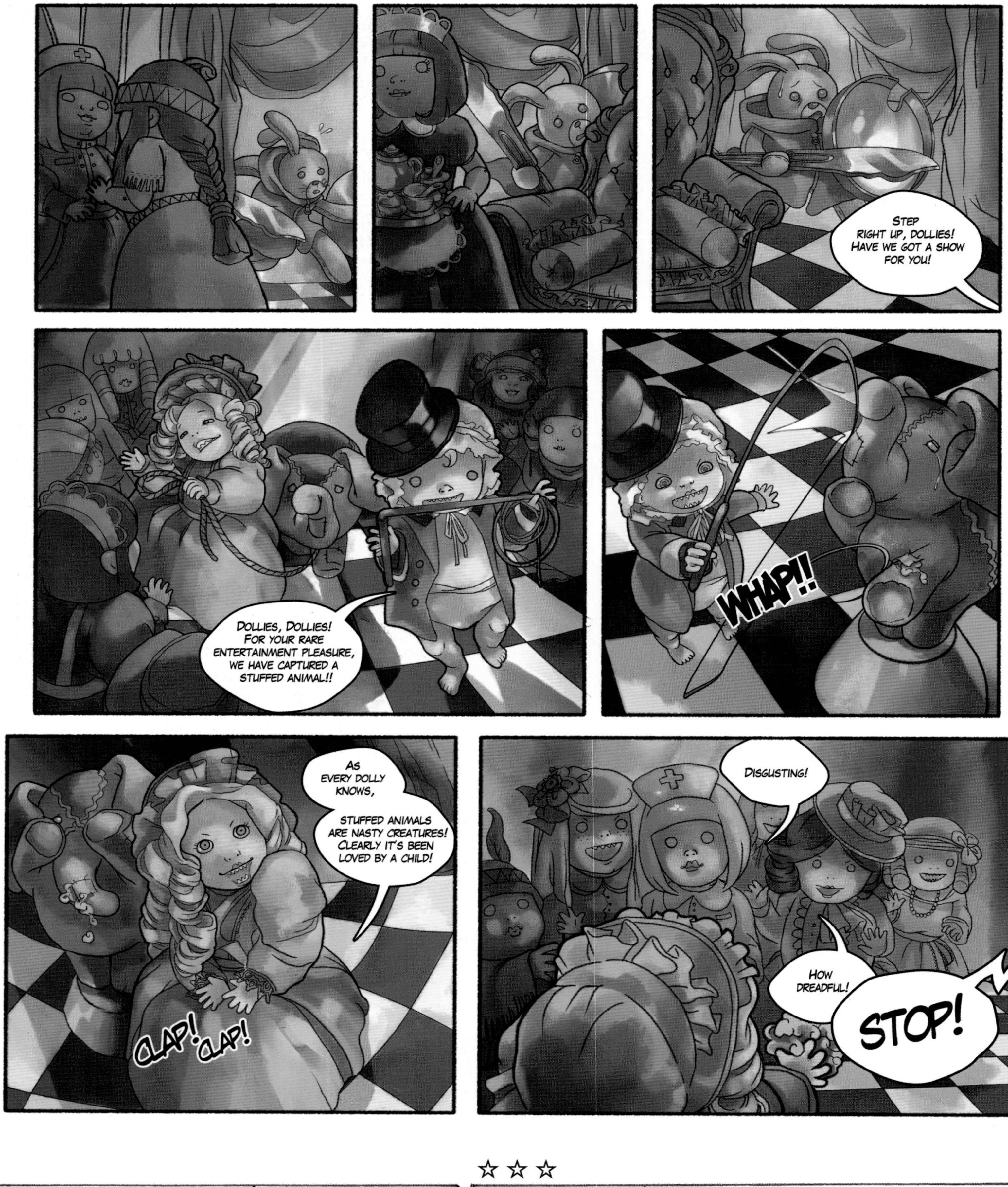

STEP RIGHT UP, DOLLIES! HAVE WE GOT A SHOW FOR YOU!
DOLLIES, DOLLIES! FOR YOUR RARE ENTERTAINMENT PLEASURE, WE HAVE CAPTURED A STUFFED ANIMAL!!
WHAP!!
AS EVERY DOLLY KNOWS,
STUFFED ANIMALS ARE NASTY CREATURES! CLEARLY IT'S BEEN LOVED BY A CHILD!
CLAP! CLAP!
DISGUSTING!
HOW DREADFUL!
STOP!

☆ ☆ ☆

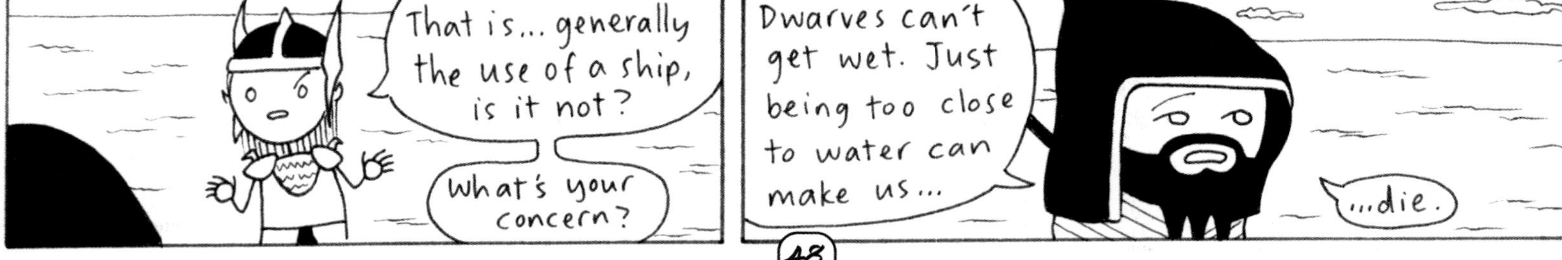

That is... generally the use of a ship, is it not?
What's your concern?
Dwarves can't get wet. Just being too close to water can make us...
...die.

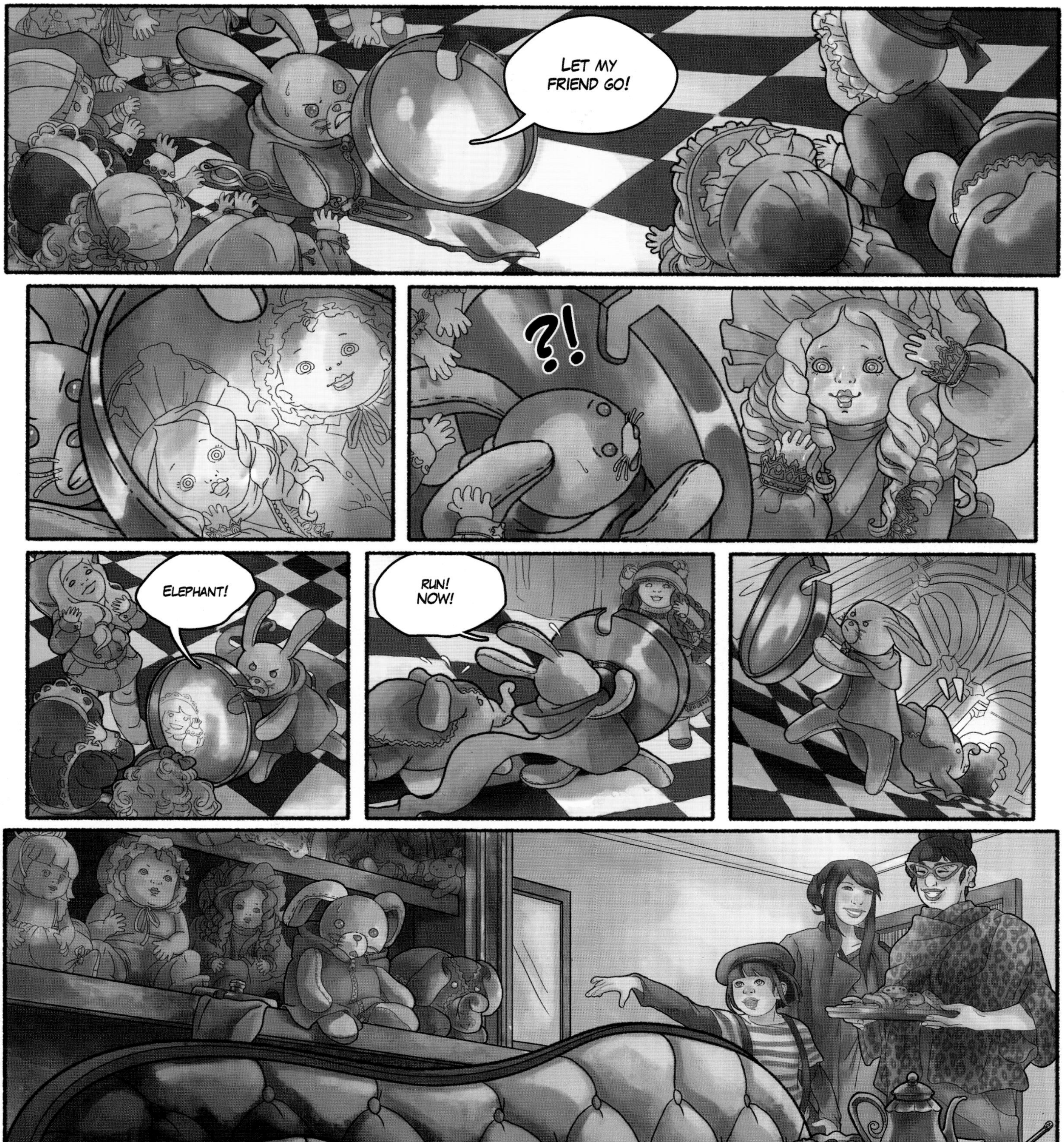
LET MY FRIEND GO!
?!
ELEPHANT!
RUN! NOW!

☆ ☆ ☆

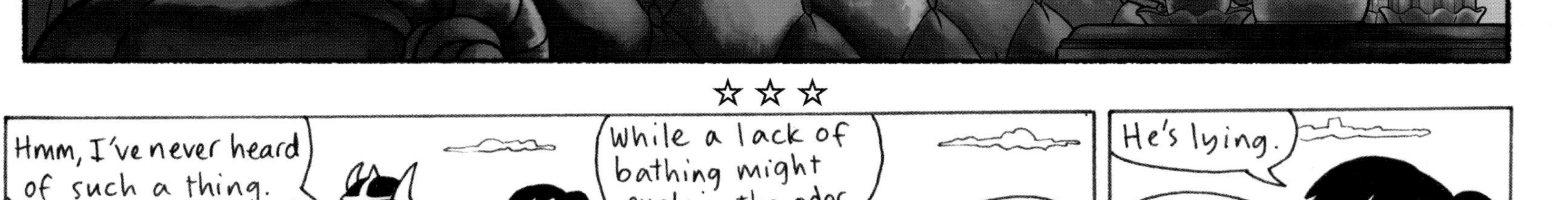
Hmm, I've never heard of such a thing.
Sure you have. I just told you!
While a lack of bathing might explain the odor...
Are you hungry?
He's lying.
He's afraid of the sea!

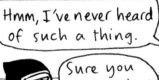

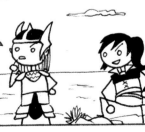

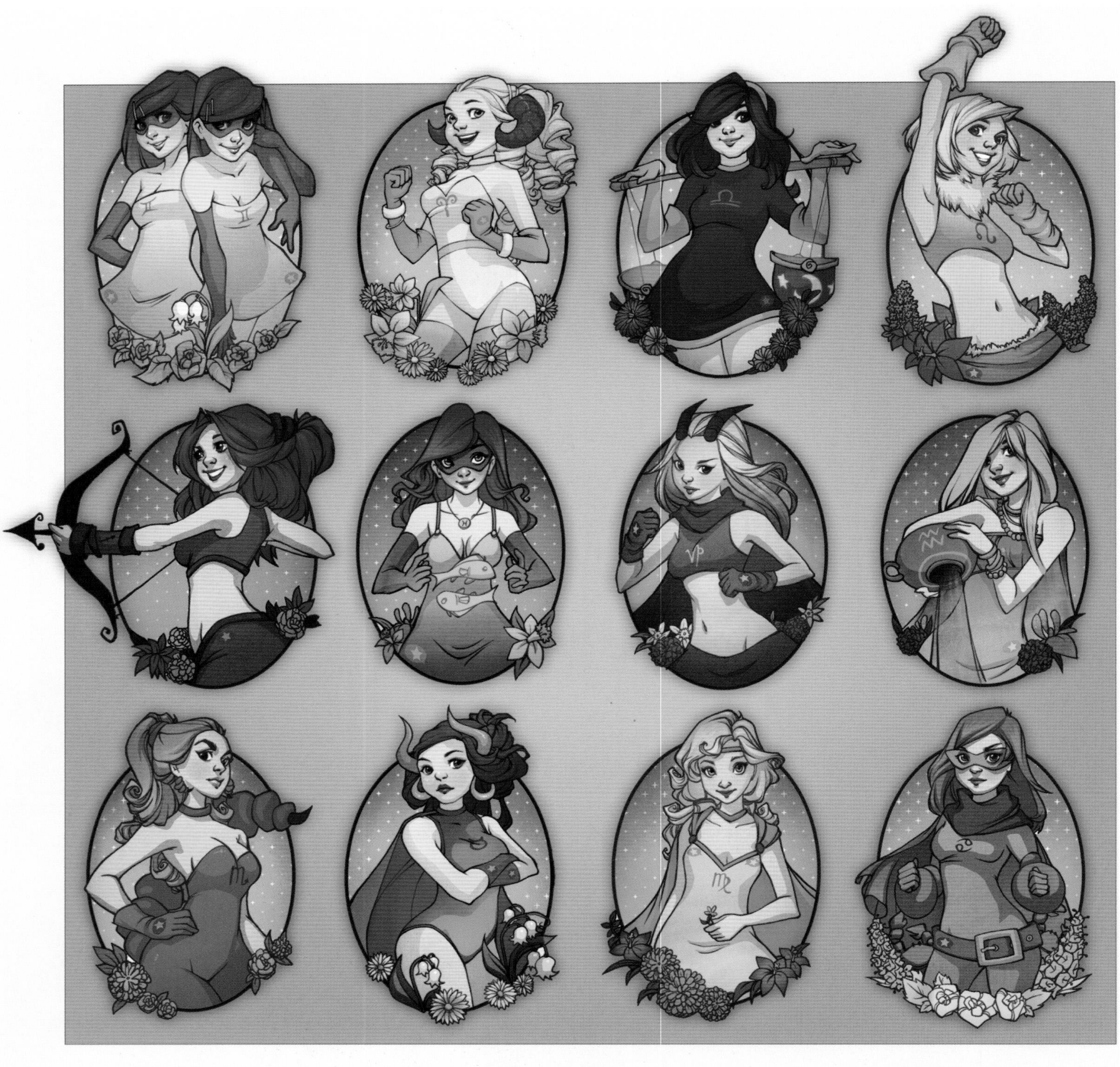

☆☆☆

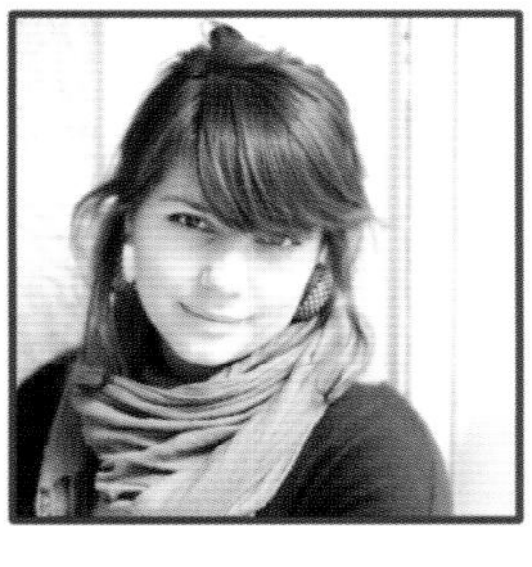

LOIS VAN BAARLE

SKILLS: Digital Painter
LOCATION: The Netherlands
FUN FACT: My favorite way of spending summer vacations back in the day was drawing non-stop.

www.loish.net

PRO TIP

LETTERING
BY RACHEL DEERING

"ALWAYS TRY TO COLOR CAPTION BOXES AND SOUND EFFECTS FROM THE PALETTE OF THE PANEL IN WHICH YOU ARE WORKING. IF THAT WON'T WORK, AT LEAST TRY TO PULL THE COLOR FROM SOMEWHERE ON THAT PAGE."

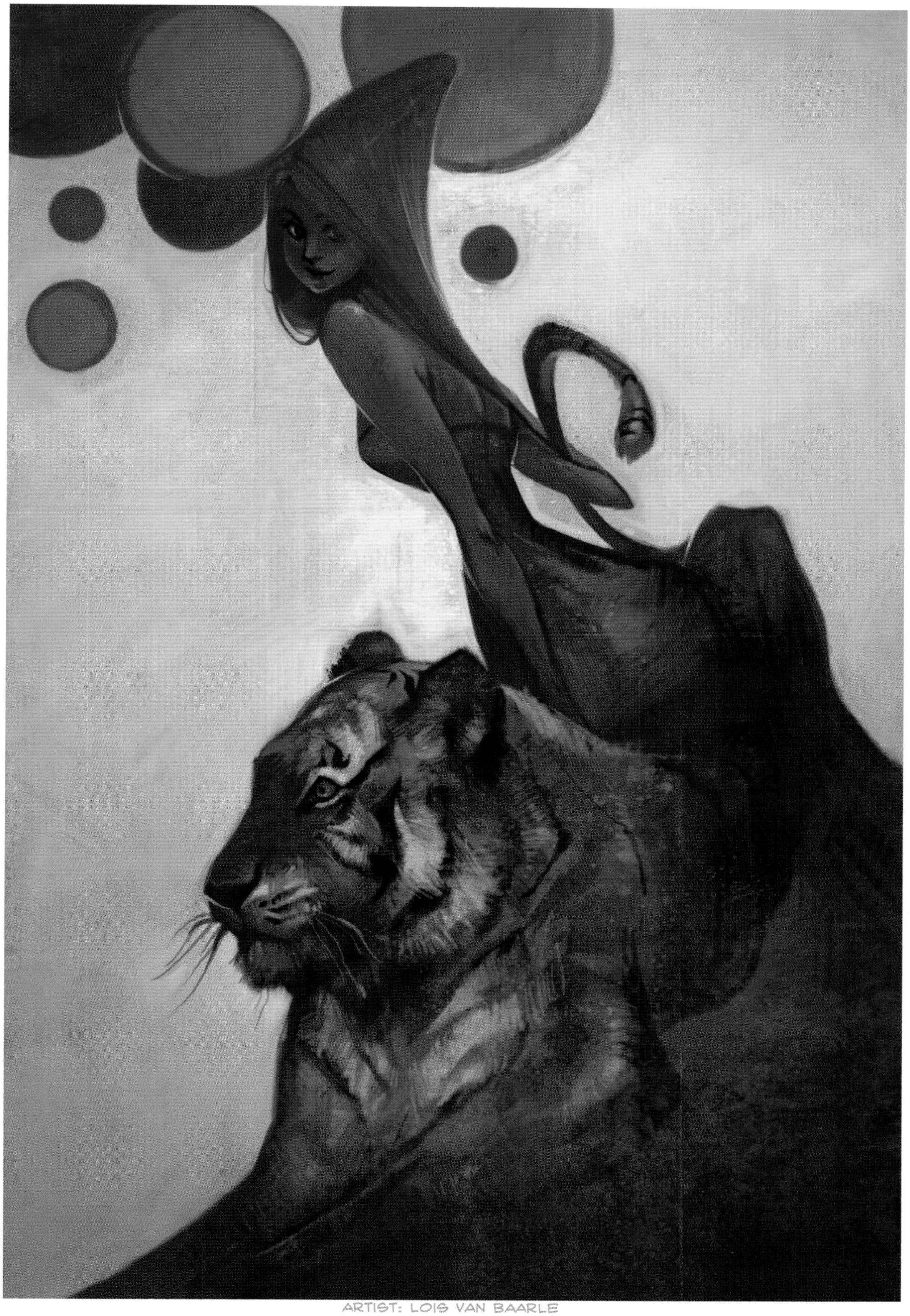

ARTIST: LOIS VAN BAARLE

☆☆☆

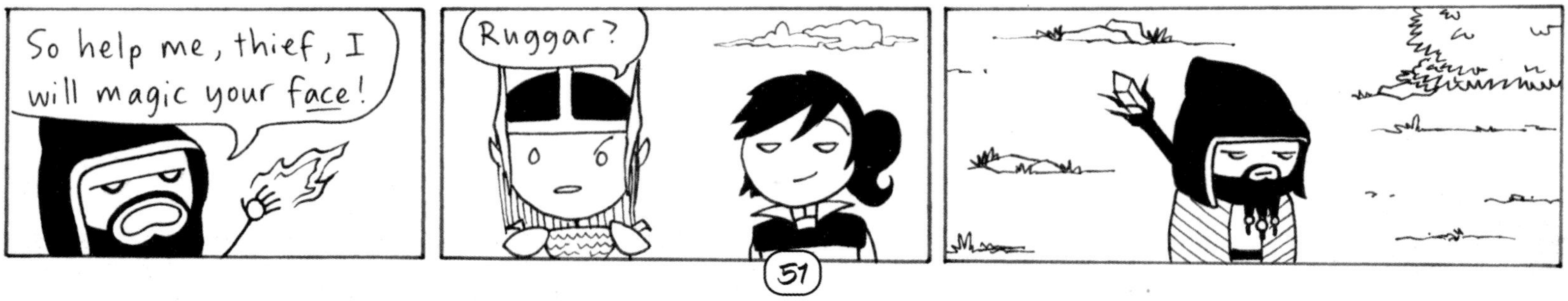
So help me, thief, I will magic your face!
Ruggar?

I'M NOT OMNi GiRL!

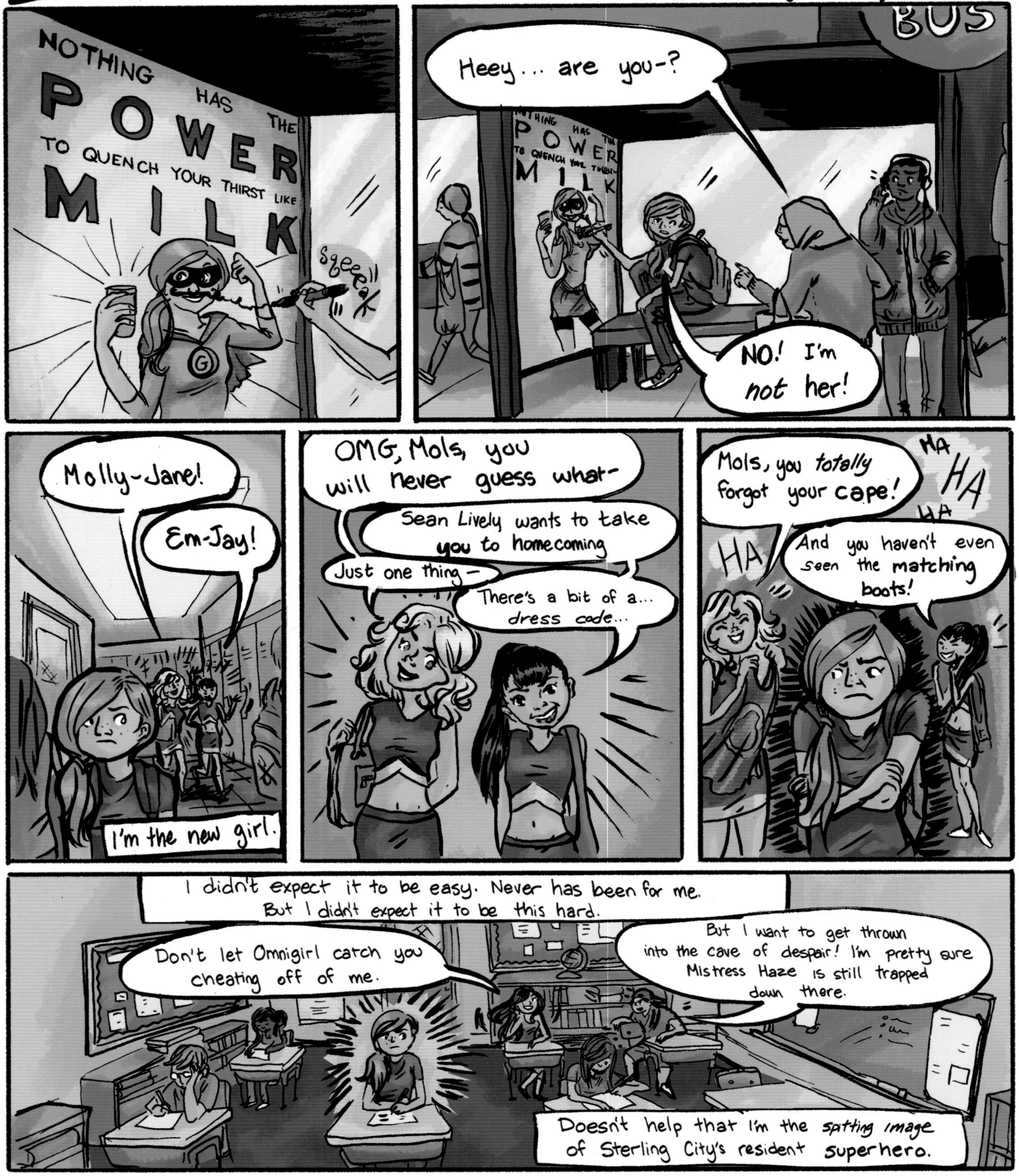

NOTHING HAS THE POWER TO QUENCH YOUR THIRST LIKE MILK
sqeeeak
G
BUS
Heey... are you-?
NO! I'm not her!
Molly-Jane!
Em-Jay!
I'm the new girl.
OMG, Mols, you will never guess what-
Sean Lively wants to take you to homecoming
Just one thing-
There's a bit of a... dress code...
Mols, you totally forgot your cape!
HA HA HA
HA
And you haven't even seen the matching boots!
I didn't expect it to be easy. Never has been for me. But I didn't expect it to be this hard.
Don't let Omnigirl catch you cheating off of me.
But I want to get thrown into the cave of despair! I'm pretty sure Mistress Haze is still trapped down there.
Doesn't help that I'm the spitting image of Sterling City's resident superhero.

☆☆☆

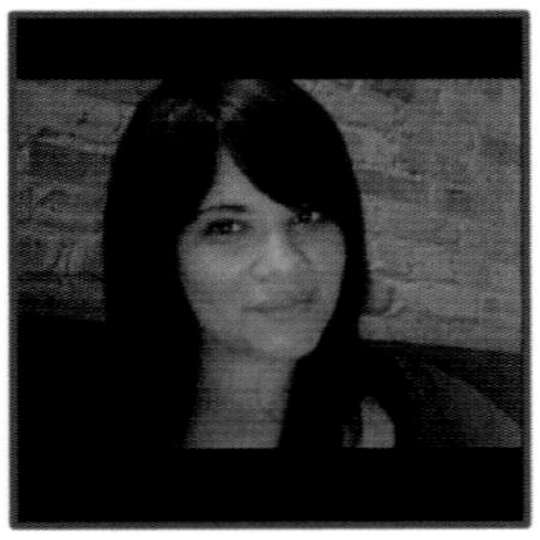

LAUREN BURKE

SKILLS: Writer
LOCATION: Chicago
FUN FACT: I collect and re-edit vintage film reels.

http://pi-jane.com/

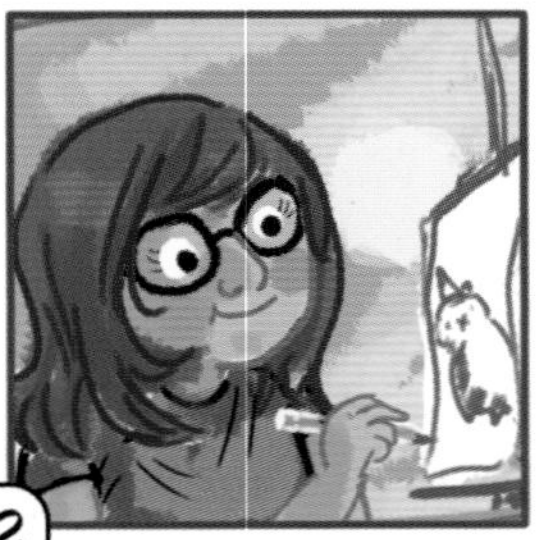

MEGAN BRENNAN

SKILLS: Penciler, Inker, Colorist, Letterer
LOCATION: New Jersey
FUN FACT: I overthink answers for questionnaires!!

http://www.Megan-Brennan.com

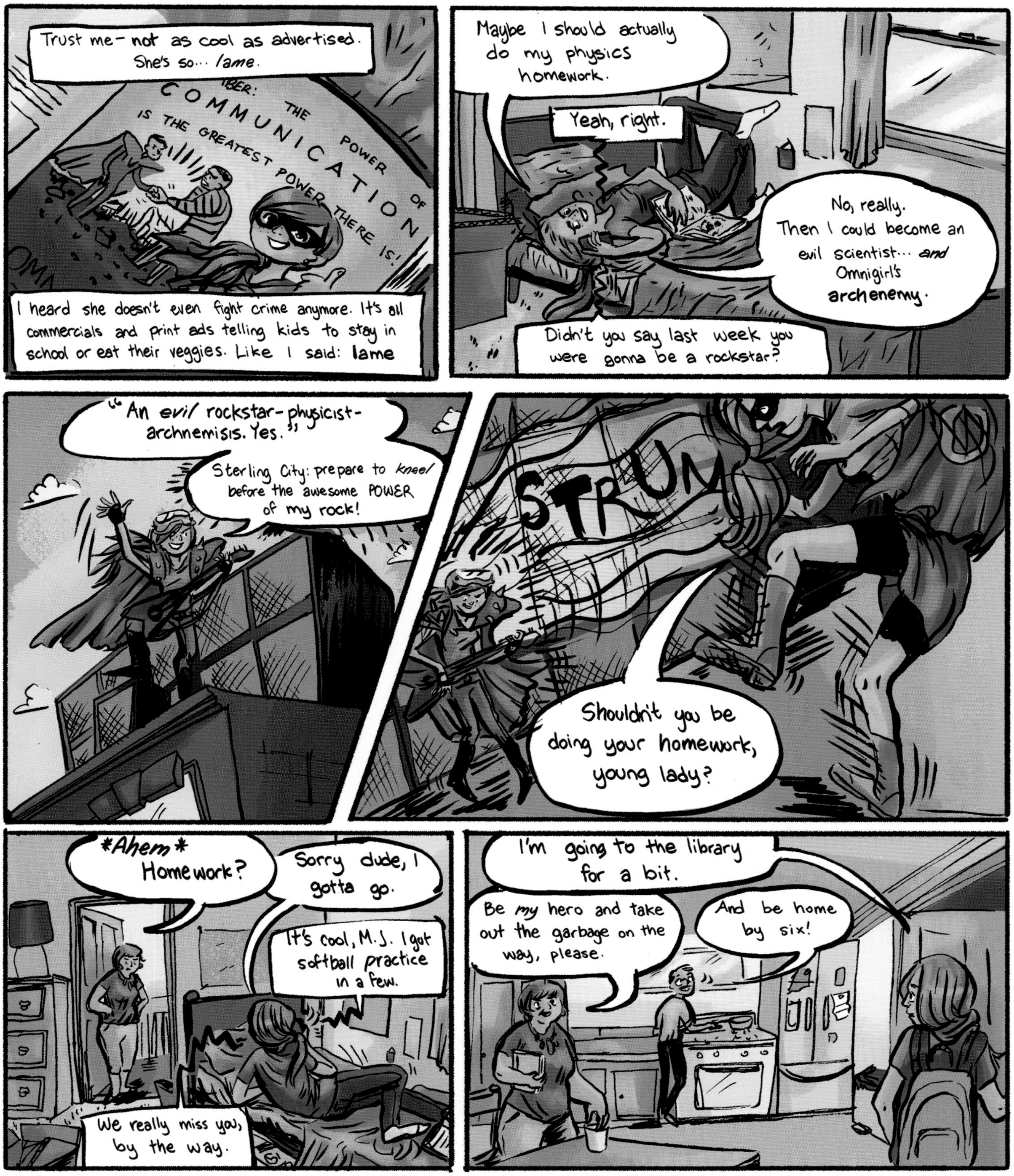
Trust me– not as cool as advertised. She's so... lame.
COMMUNICATION
THE POWER OF COMMUNICATION IS THE GREATEST POWER THERE IS!
I heard she doesn't even fight crime anymore. It's all commercials and print ads telling kids to stay in school or eat their veggies. Like I said: lame
Maybe I should actually do my physics homework.
Yeah, right.
No, really. Then I could become an evil scientist... and Omnigirl's archenemy.
Didn't you say last week you were gonna be a rockstar?
"An evil rockstar-physicist-archnemisis. Yes."
Sterling City: prepare to kneel before the awesome POWER of my rock!
STRUM
Shouldn't you be doing your homework, young lady?
Ahem Homework?
Sorry dude, I gotta go.
It's cool, M.J. I got softball practice in a few.
We really miss you, by the way.
I'm going to the library for a bit.
Be my hero and take out the garbage on the way, please.
And be home by six!

☆ ☆ ☆

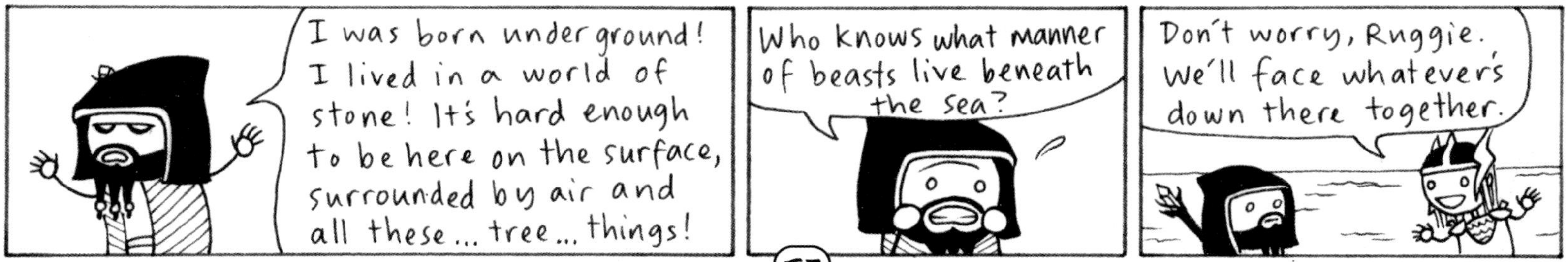
I was born underground! I lived in a world of stone! It's hard enough to be here on the surface, surrounded by air and all these... tree... things!
Who knows what manner of beasts live beneath the sea?
Don't worry, Ruggie. We'll face whatever's down there together.

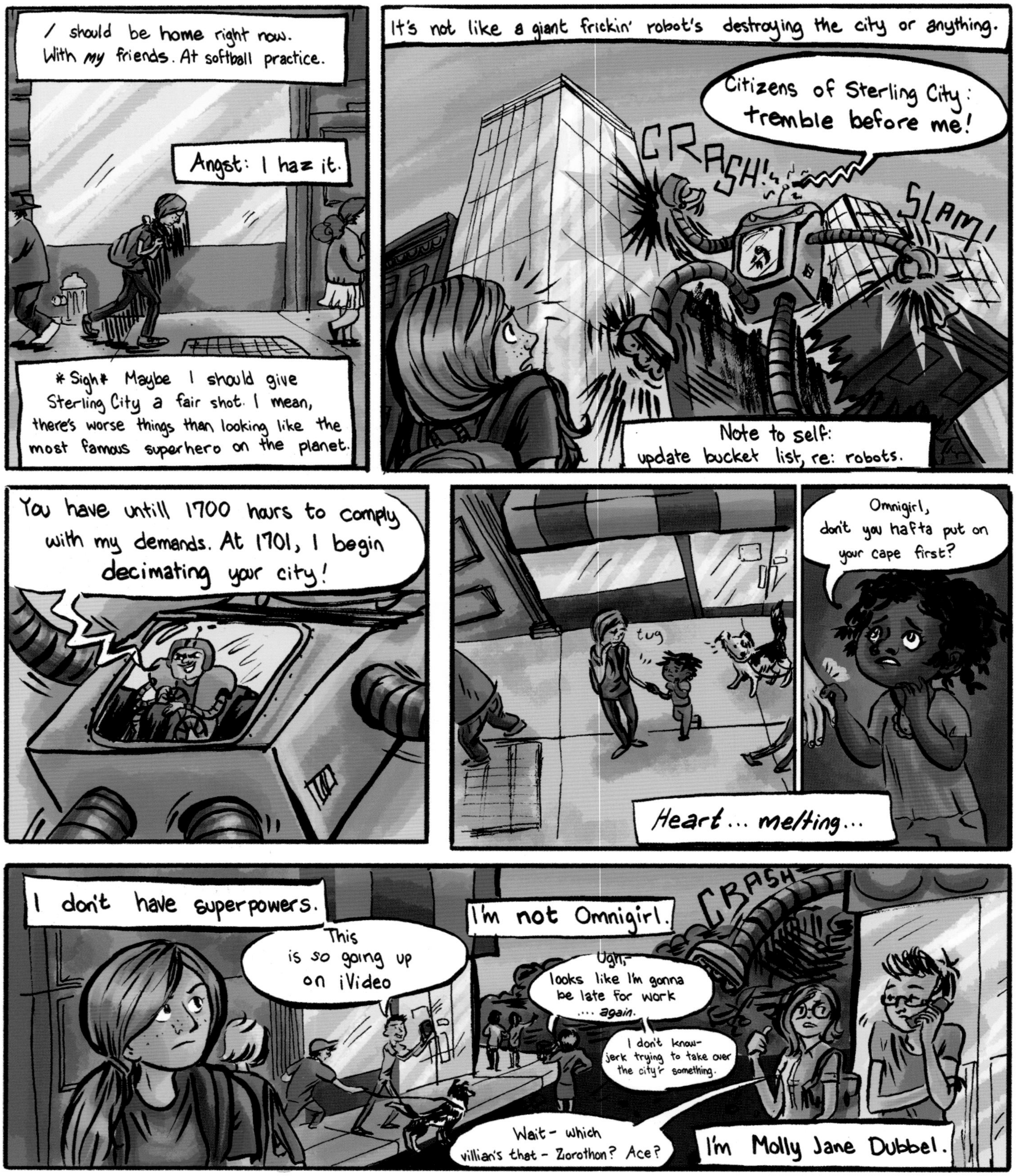
I should be home right now. With *my* friends. At softball practice.
Angst: I haz it.
Sigh Maybe I should give Sterling City a fair shot. I mean, there's worse things than looking like the most famous superhero on the planet.
It's not like a giant frickin' robot's destroying the city or anything.
Citizens of Sterling City: tremble before me!
CRASH!
SLAM!
Note to self: update bucket list, re: robots.
You have untill 1700 hours to comply with my demands. At 1701, I begin decimating your city!
tug
Omnigirl, don't you hafta put on your cape first?
Heart... melting...
I don't have superpowers.
This is so going up on iVideo
I'm not Omnigirl.
CRASH
Ugh, looks like I'm gonna be late for work .... *again*.
I don't know- jerk trying to take over the city'r something.
Wait- which villian's that - Zorothon? Ace?
I'm Molly Jane Dubbel.

☆ ☆ ☆

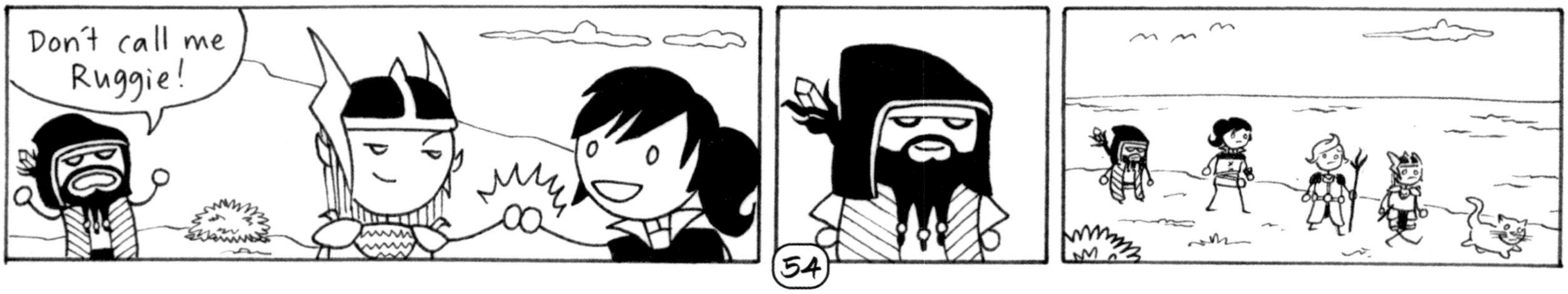
Don't call me Ruggie!

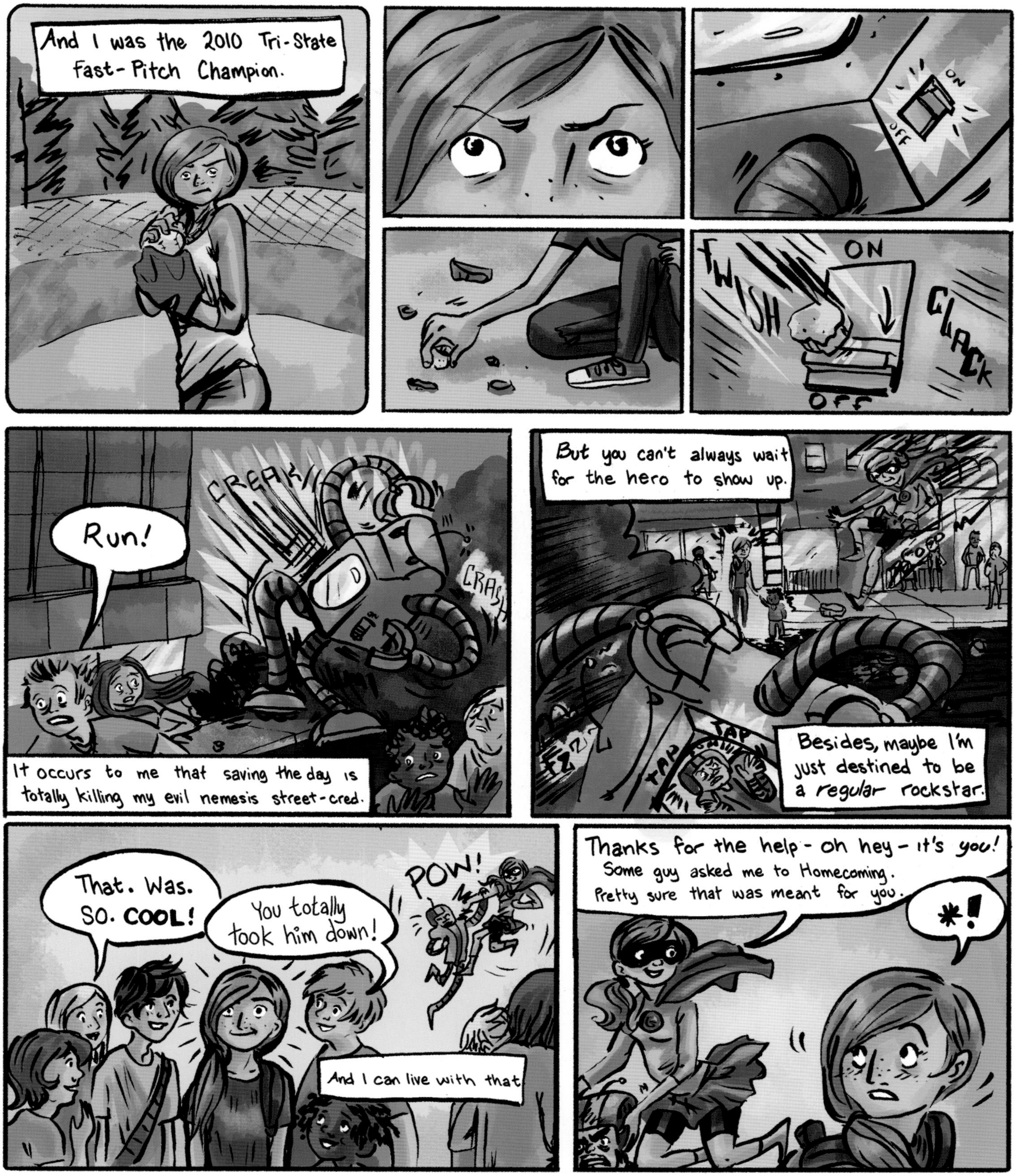

And I was the 2010 Tri-State Fast-Pitch Champion.
ON
OFF
ON
FWISH
CLACK
OFF
Run!
CREAK
CRASH
It occurs to me that saving the day is totally killing my evil nemesis street-cred.
But you can't always wait for the hero to show up.
Besides, maybe I'm just destined to be a *regular* rockstar.
That. Was. SO. **COOL!**
You totally took him down!
POW!
And I can live with that.
Thanks for the help - oh hey - it's *you!* Some guy asked me to Homecoming. Pretty sure that was meant for you.
*!

☆ ☆ ☆

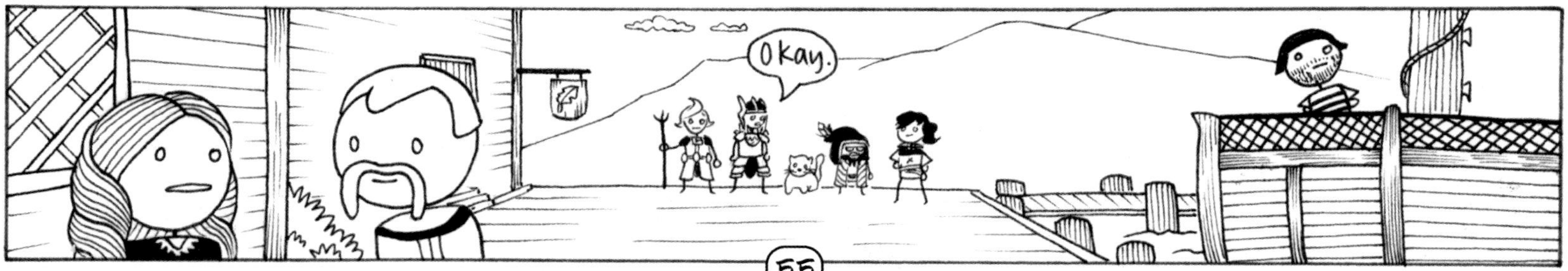

Okay.

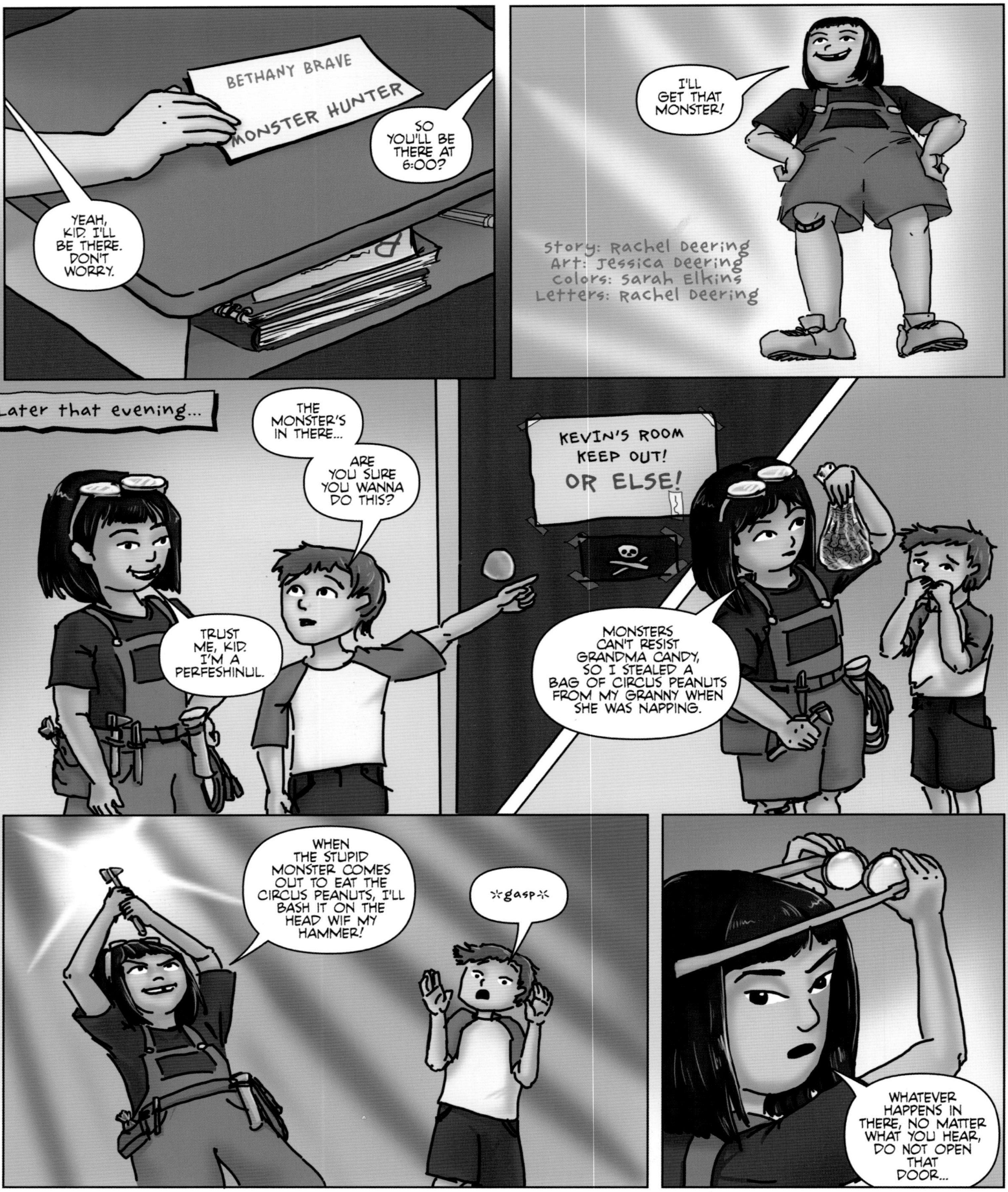
BETHANY BRAVE
MONSTER HUNTER
SO YOU'LL BE THERE AT 6:00?
YEAH, KID. I'LL BE THERE. DON'T WORRY.
I'LL GET THAT MONSTER!
Story: Rachel Deering
Art: Jessica Deering
Colors: Sarah Elkins
Letters: Rachel Deering
Later that evening...
THE MONSTER'S IN THERE...
ARE YOU SURE YOU WANNA DO THIS?
TRUST ME, KID. I'M A PERFESHINUL.
KEVIN'S ROOM
KEEP OUT!
OR ELSE!
MONSTERS CAN'T RESIST GRANDMA CANDY, SO I STEALED A BAG OF CIRCUS PEANUTS FROM MY GRANNY WHEN SHE WAS NAPPING.
WHEN THE STUPID MONSTER COMES OUT TO EAT THE CIRCUS PEANUTS, I'LL BASH IT ON THE HEAD WIF MY HAMMER!
gasp
WHATEVER HAPPENS IN THERE, NO MATTER WHAT YOU HEAR, DO NOT OPEN THAT DOOR...

☆ ☆ ☆

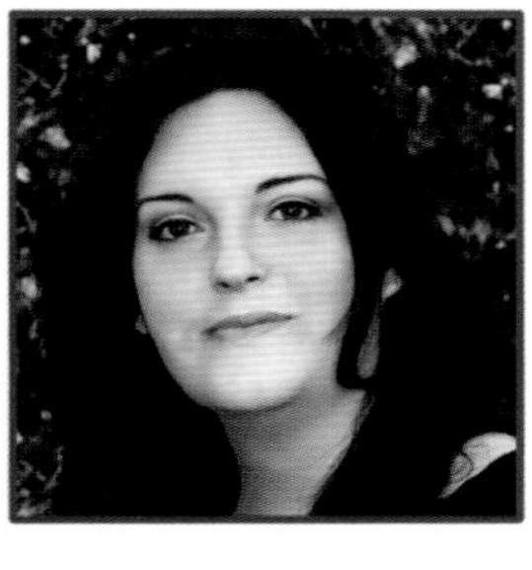

RACHEL DEERING

SKILLS: Editor, Letterer
LOCATION: Columbus, OH
FUN FACT: I sing in a heavy metal band!

http://twitter.com/#!/racheldeering

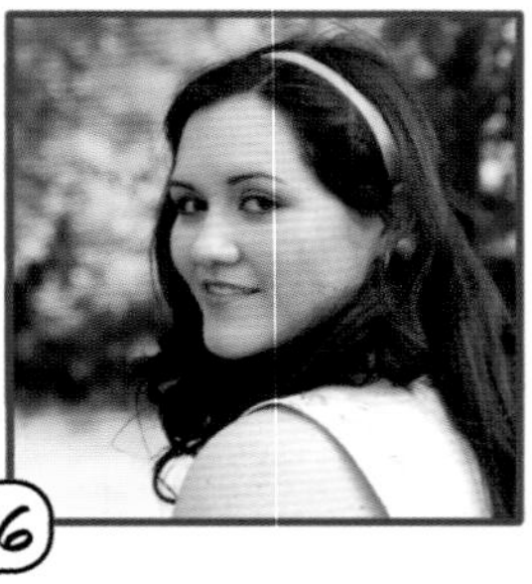

JESSICA DEERING

SKILLS: Penciller, Inker, Painter
LOCATION: Columbus, OH
FUN FACT: I can't buy anything I see in stores without trying to make it first.

paddlelikethedevil.blogspot.com

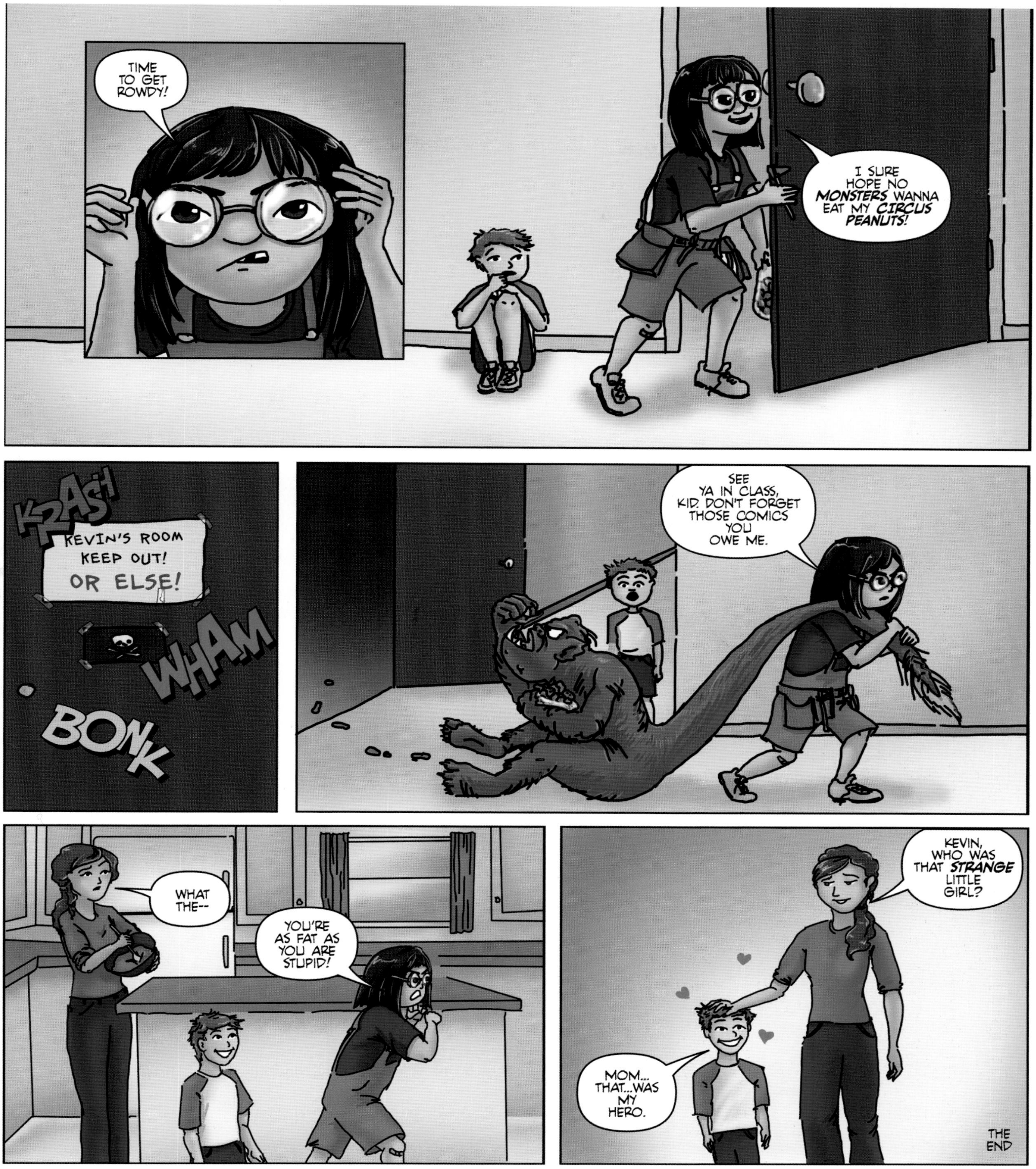
TIME TO GET ROWDY!
I SURE HOPE NO MONSTERS WANNA EAT MY CIRCUS PEANUTS!
KRASH
KEVIN'S ROOM KEEP OUT! OR ELSE!
WHAM
BONK
SEE YA IN CLASS, KID. DON'T FORGET THOSE COMICS YOU OWE ME.
WHAT THE--
YOU'RE AS FAT AS YOU ARE STUPID!
KEVIN, WHO WAS THAT STRANGE LITTLE GIRL?
MOM... THAT...WAS MY HERO.
THE END

☆ ☆ ☆

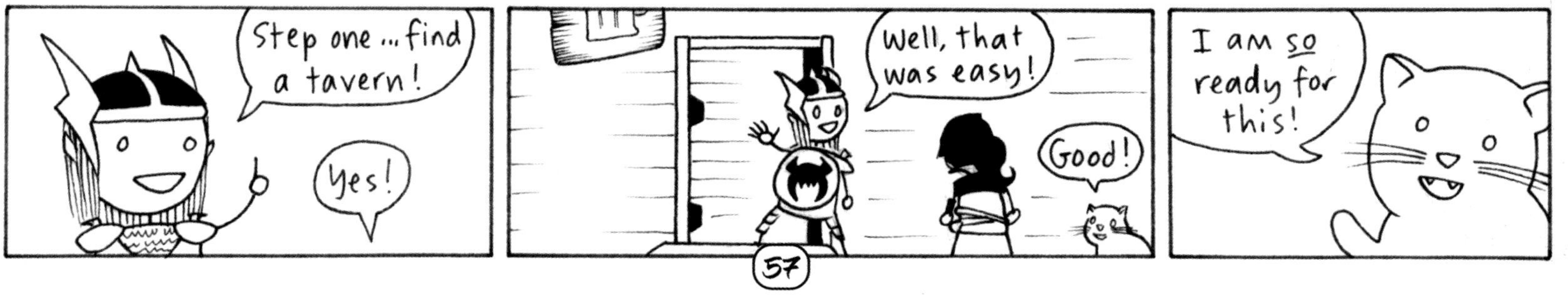
Step one ... find a tavern!
Yes!
Well, that was easy!
Good!
I am so ready for this!

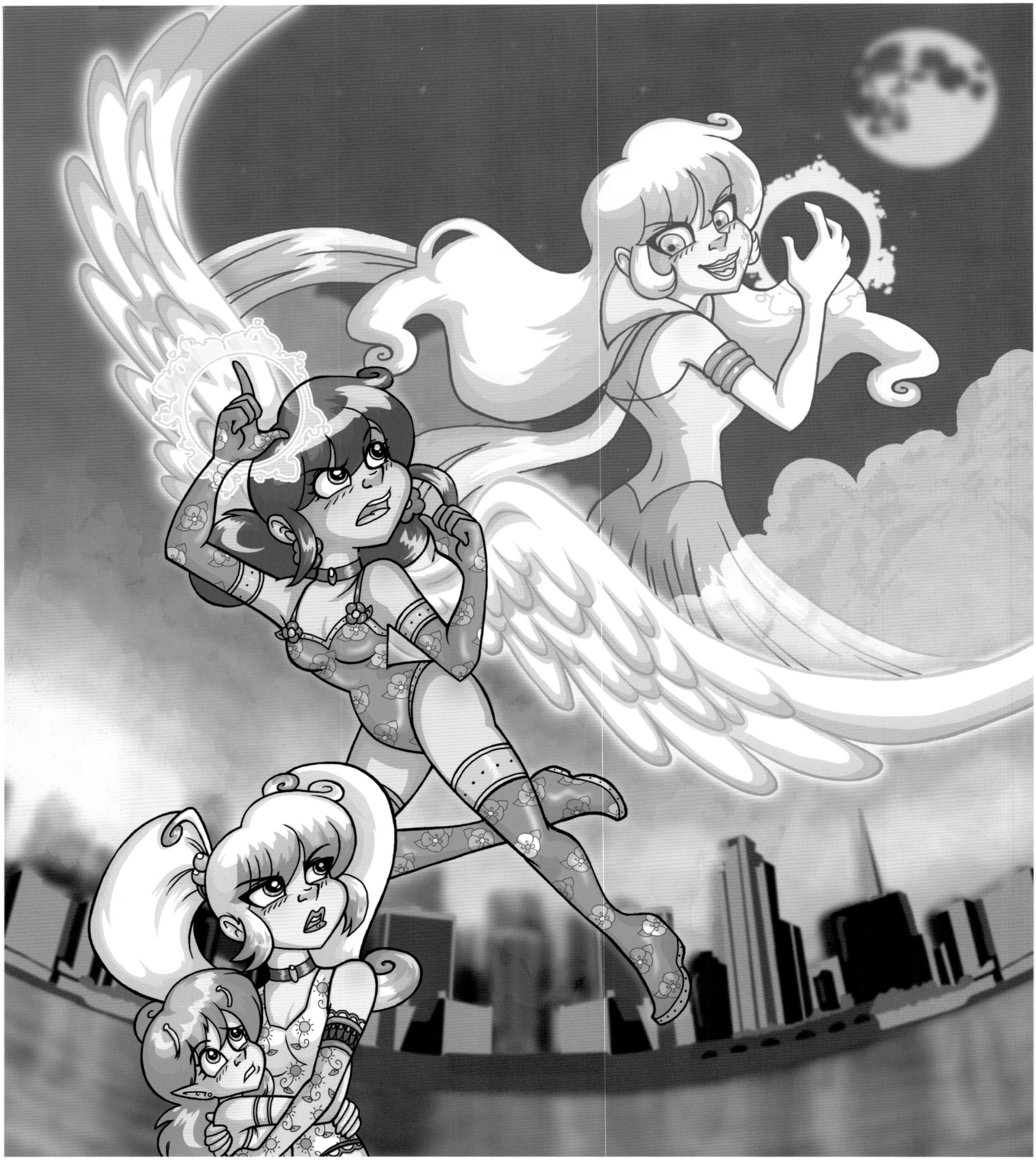

☆☆☆

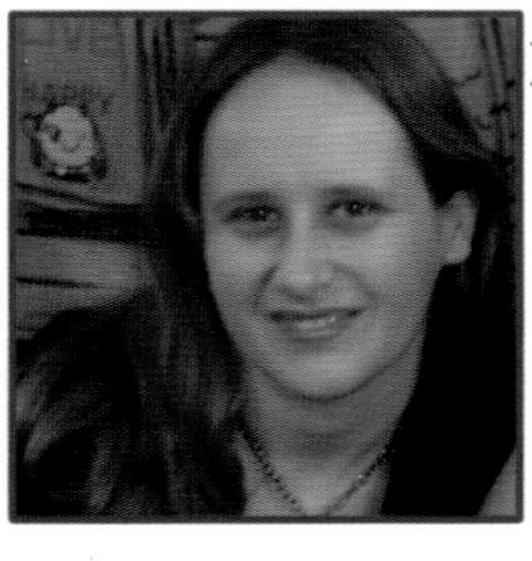

MARY "ZORILITA" BELLAMY

SKILLS: Illustrator, Colorist
LOCATION: Los Angeles, CA
FUN FACT: I am strangely good at home repair.

http://www.marybellamy.com

PRO TIP

DRAWING
BY NICOLE SIXX

"THE ONE THING I HEAR CONSTANTLY OUT OF EVERY GREAT ARTIST'S MOUTH IS IF YOU WANT TO BE AN ARTIST, JUST DRAW. EVERY DAY. EVERY DAY.

AS FOR MY OWN ADVICE, BE NICE, PRAY IF IT SUITS YOU, AND ALWAYS HAVE A PLAN."

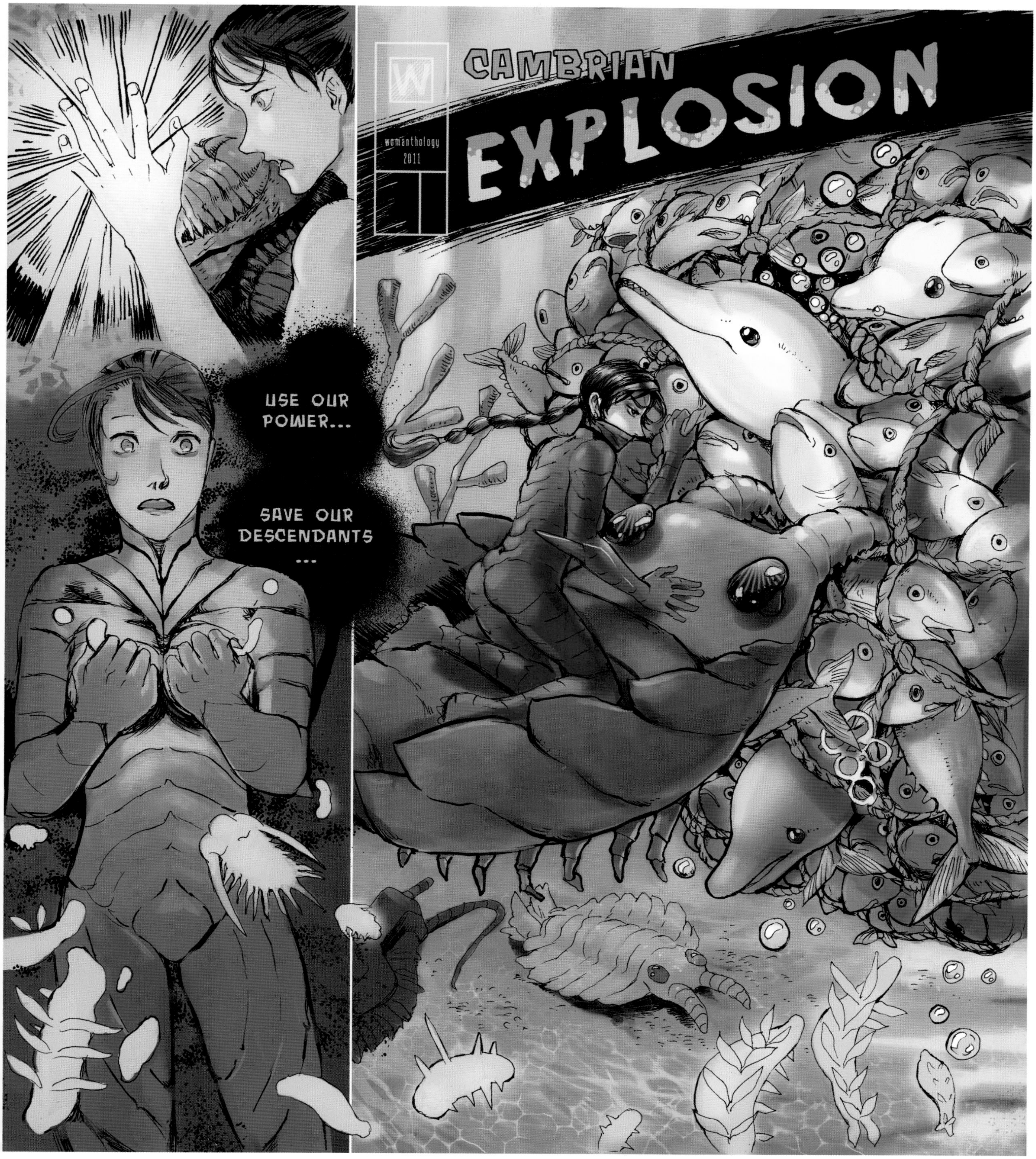
CAMBRIAN EXPLOSION
womanthology 2011
USE OUR POWER...
SAVE OUR DESCENDANTS ...

☆ ☆ ☆

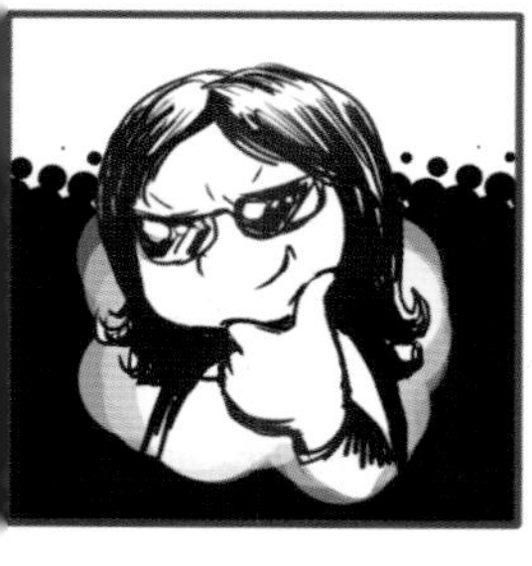

VERA L

SKILLS: Inker, Letterer, Colorist
LOCATION: San Francisco, California
FUN FACT: I like fossils.

www.tinsc.com

PRO TIP PROFESSIONALISM

BY DEVIN GRAYSON

"EVERY INDUSTRY CONTACT COUNTS! THEIR IZ KNOW ACUSE 4 KNOT SPILL-CHECKING + WREADING OVAH YOU'RE EMALES WHENE U RIGHT SOMEBODIES FOUR HULP ORE ADVISE!"

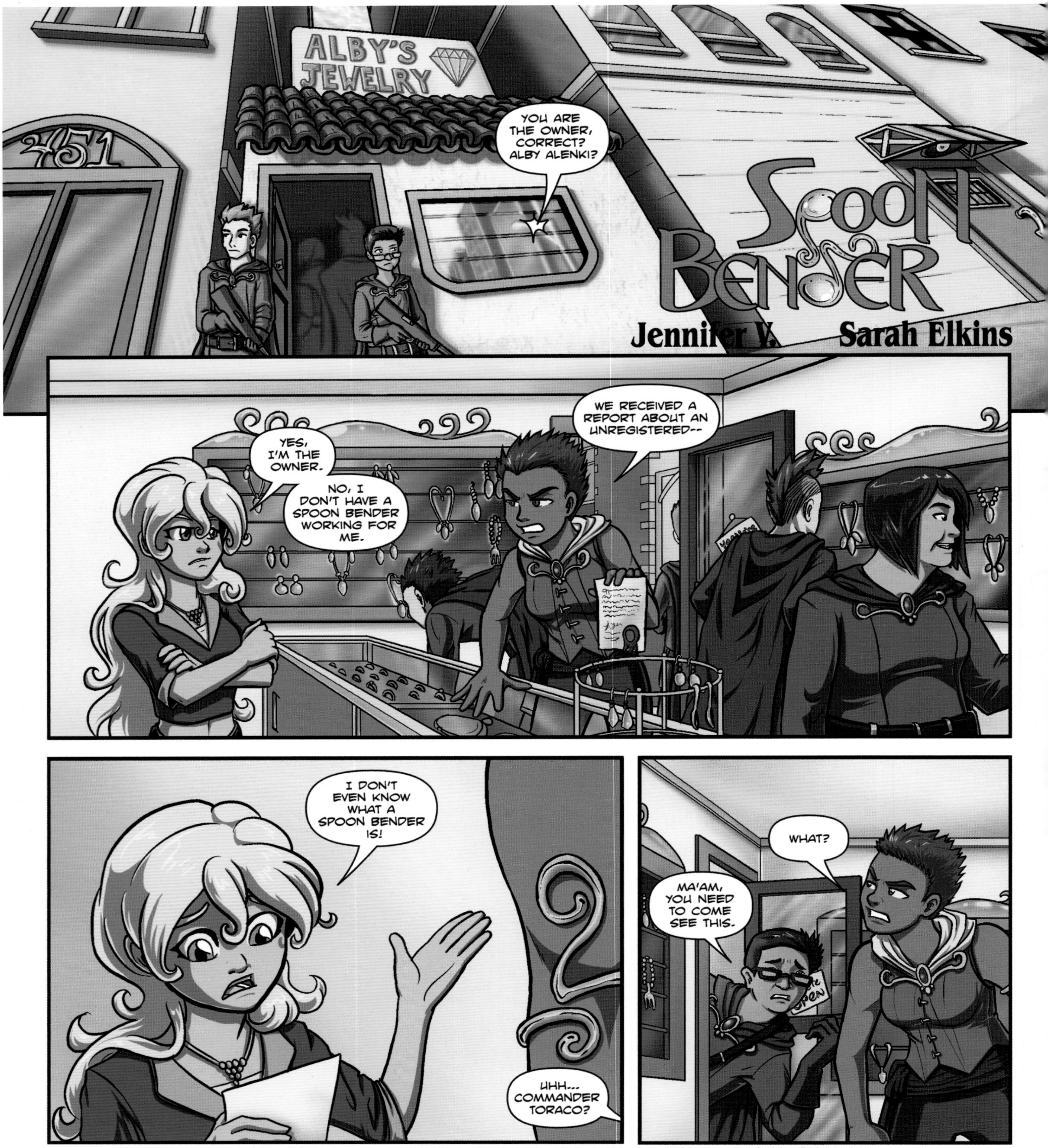
ALBY'S JEWELRY
451
YOU ARE THE OWNER, CORRECT? ALBY ALENKI?
SPOON BENDER
Jennifer V.
Sarah Elkins
YES, I'M THE OWNER.
NO, I DON'T HAVE A SPOON BENDER WORKING FOR ME.
WE RECEIVED A REPORT ABOUT AN UNREGISTERED--
I DON'T EVEN KNOW WHAT A SPOON BENDER IS!
UHH... COMMANDER TORACO?
WHAT?
MA'AM, YOU NEED TO COME SEE THIS.

WRITER: JENNIFER V ARTIST: SARAH "NEILA" ELKINS LETTERS: RACHEL DEERING

☆☆☆

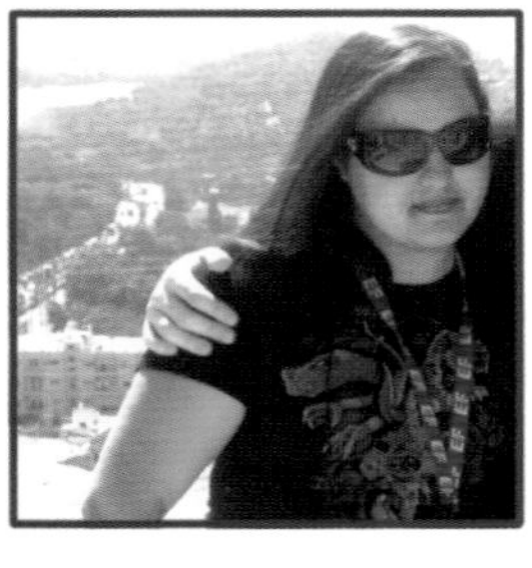

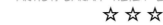

JENNIFER V

SKILLS: Writer
LOCATION: Orlando, FL
FUN FACT: The first thing I ever read was a sign that said "Hot Dogs and Hot Prizes"! I had just turned two!

www.childofdumas.deviantart.com

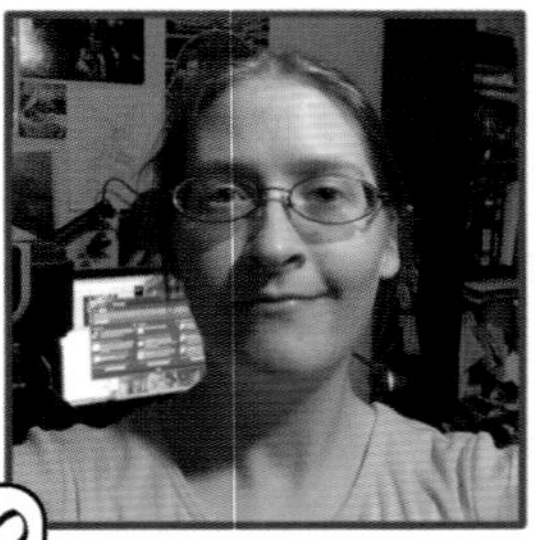

SARAH "NEILA" ELKINS

SKILLS: Penciler, Inker, Colorist
LOCATION: Texas
FUN FACT: I have a snaggle tooth that lets me make that "one fanged vampire smile" you see in Anime.

http://neilak20.deviantart.com/

BETTER BE A GOOD REASON FOR INTERRUPTING ME, SERGEANT.

I'D CALL THIS A GOOD REASON.

RRRRAAAAW!

BRING IT DOWN!

BRAK BRAK BRAK

FWOOSH

RRRAAK-GRRAAAK!

BOOM

TNK TNK TNK

WHAT THE--

I GOT THIS.

★ ★ ★

Welcome to The Crusty Mug, strangers.

All of your hams, please!

"Crusty Mug" doesn't sound very sanitary.

Hams and ales all around!

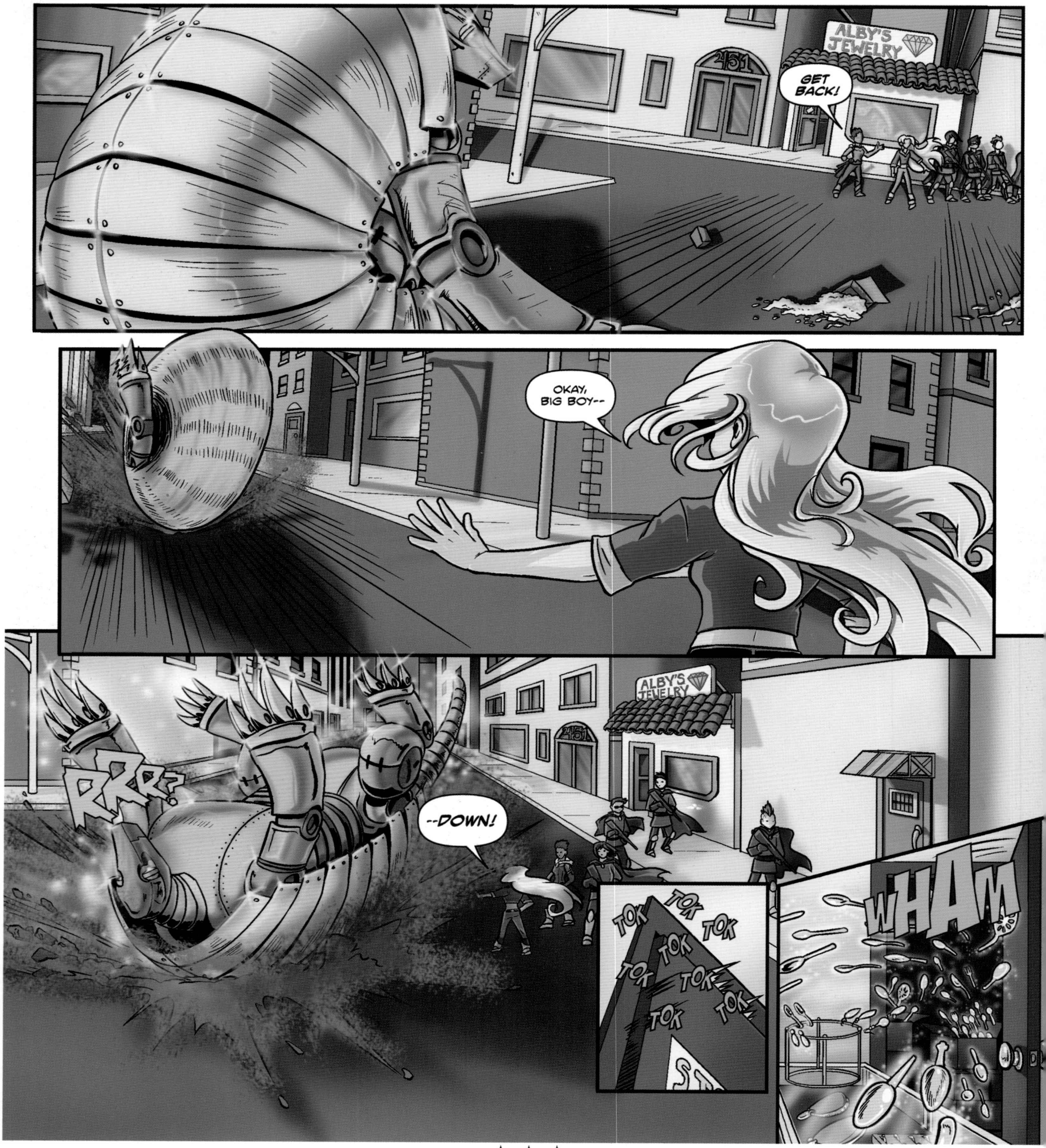
ALBY'S JEWELRY
GET BACK!
OKAY, BIG BOY--
ALBY'S JEWELRY
RRR?
--DOWN!
TOK TOK TOK TOK TOK TOK TOK TOK
WHAM

☆ ☆ ☆

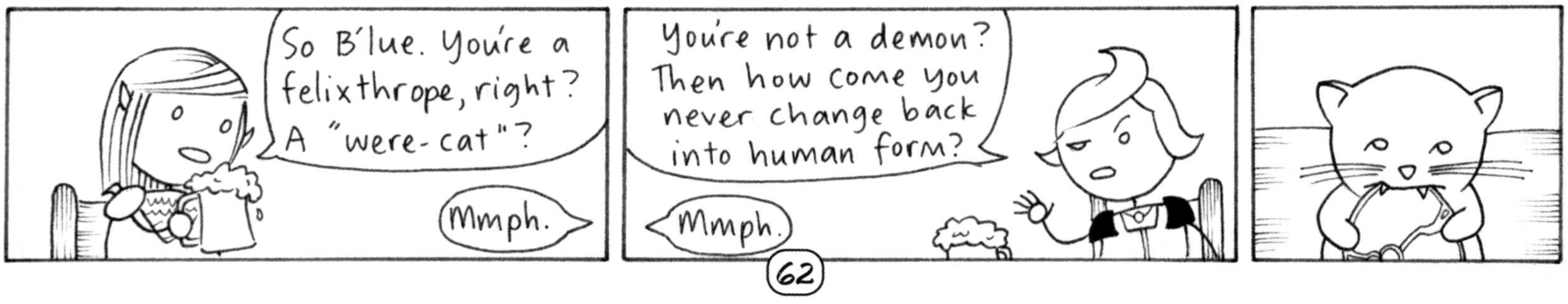
So B'lue. You're a felixthrope, right? A "were-cat"?
Mmph.
You're not a demon? Then how come you never change back into human form?
Mmph.

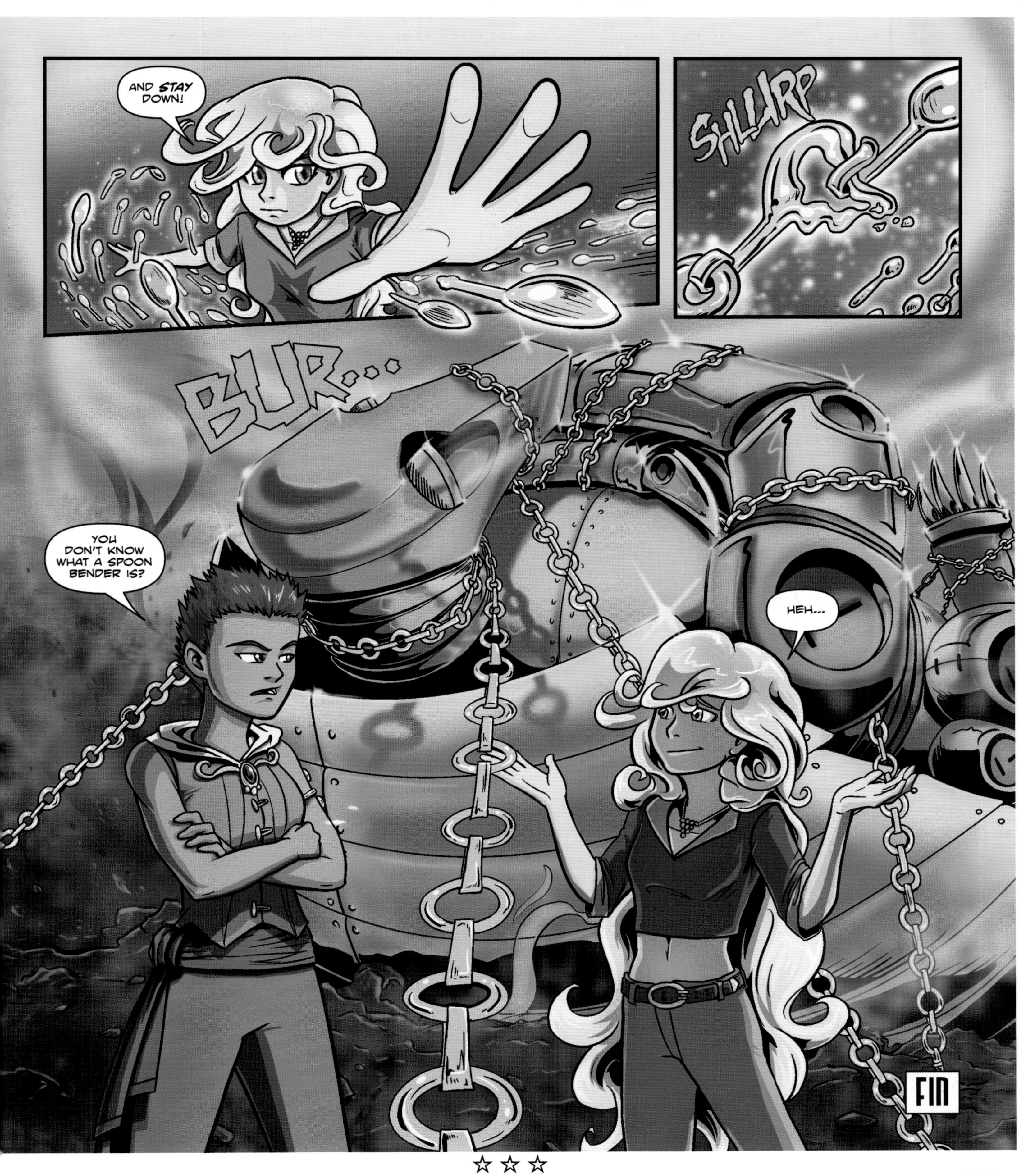
AND **STAY** DOWN!
SHLURP
BUR...
YOU DON'T KNOW WHAT A SPOON BENDER IS?
HEH...
FIN

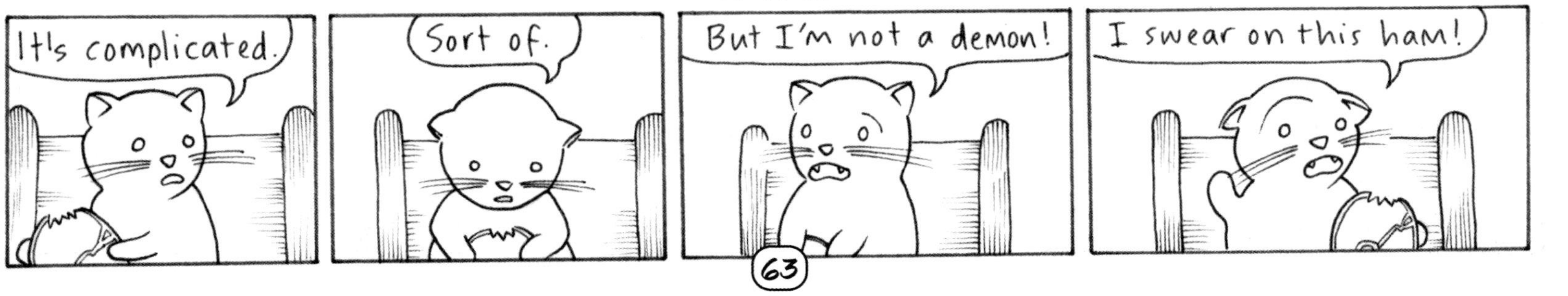
It's complicated.
Sort of.
But I'm not a demon!
I swear on this ham!

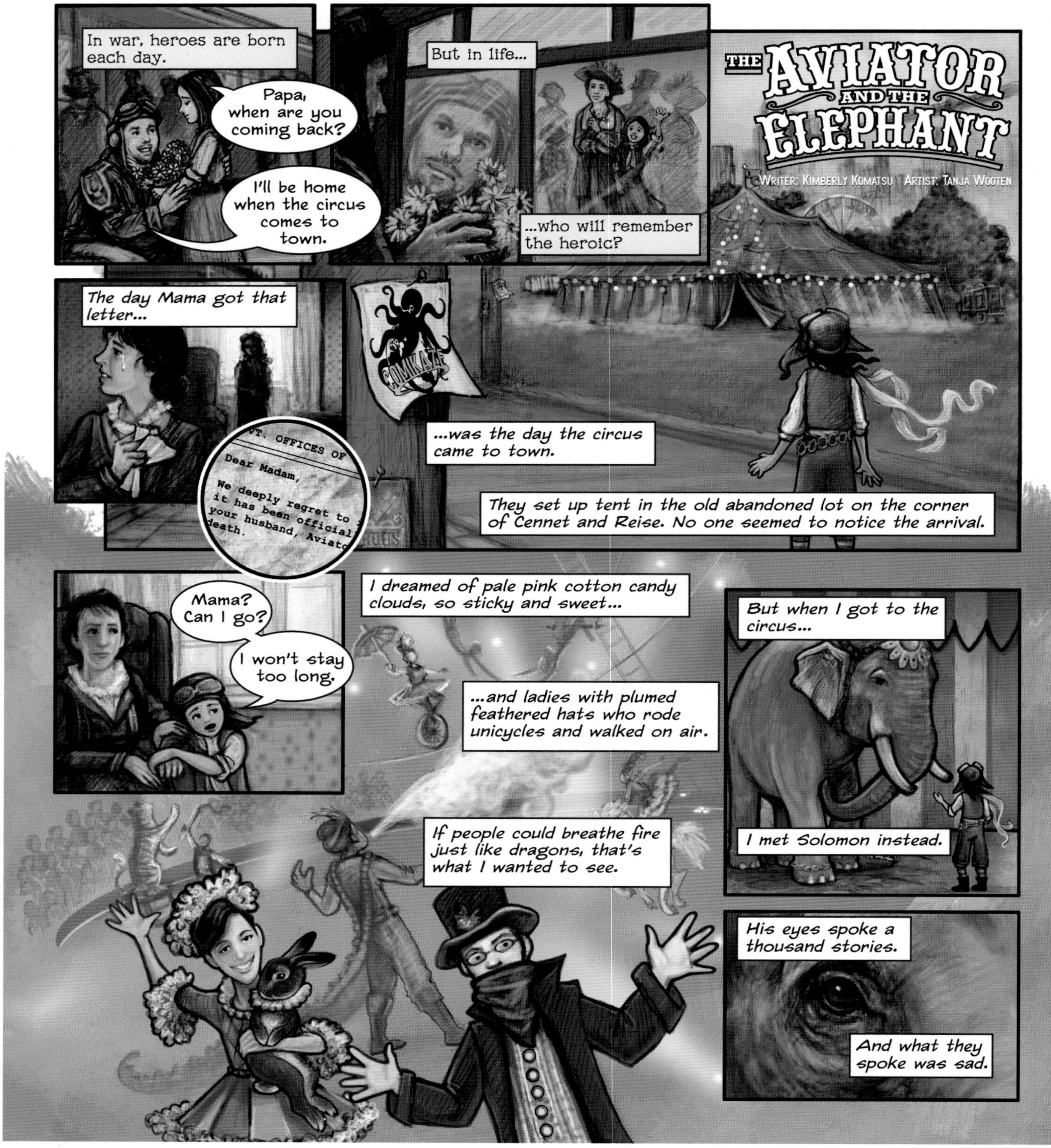
In war, heroes are born each day.
Papa, when are you coming back?
I'll be home when the circus comes to town.
But in life...
...who will remember the heroic?
THE AVIATOR AND THE ELEPHANT
WRITER: KIMBERLY KOMATSU ARTIST: TANJA WOOTEN
The day Mama got that letter...
VT. OFFICES OF
Dear Madam,
We deeply regret to
it has been official
your husband, Aviato
death.
COMIKAZE
...was the day the circus came to town.
They set up tent in the old abandoned lot on the corner of Cennet and Reise. No one seemed to notice the arrival.
Mama? Can I go?
I won't stay too long.
I dreamed of pale pink cotton candy clouds, so sticky and sweet...
...and ladies with plumed feathered hats who rode unicycles and walked on air.
If people could breathe fire just like dragons, that's what I wanted to see.
But when I got to the circus...
I met Solomon instead.
His eyes spoke a thousand stories.
And what they spoke was sad.

☆ ☆ ☆

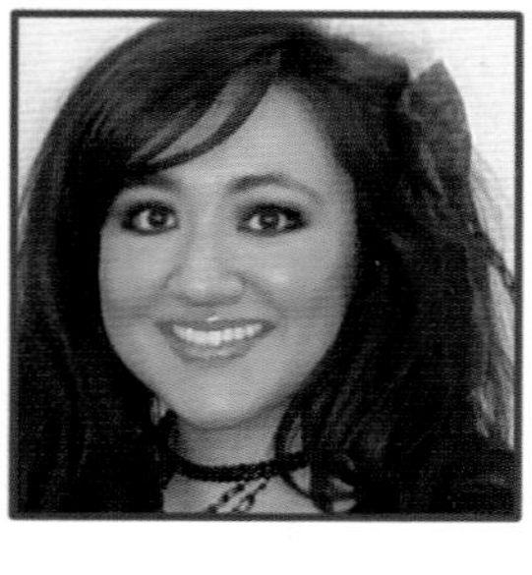

KIMBERLY KOMATSU

SKILLS: Writer
LOCATION: Los Angeles, California
FUN FACT: Storytelling word nerd, tap-dancing dreamer, lightsaber-wielding adventurer, and friend to all animals.

www.thomasgeorgebooks.com

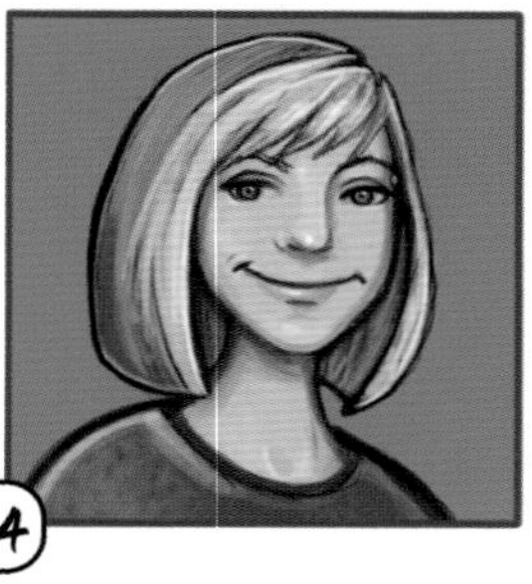

TANJA WOOTEN

SKILLS: Artist (Pencils, Inks, Colors, Letters)
LOCATION: Hot Springs, Arkansas
FUN FACT: Studied veterinary medicine before switching to art school.

www.tanjawooten.com

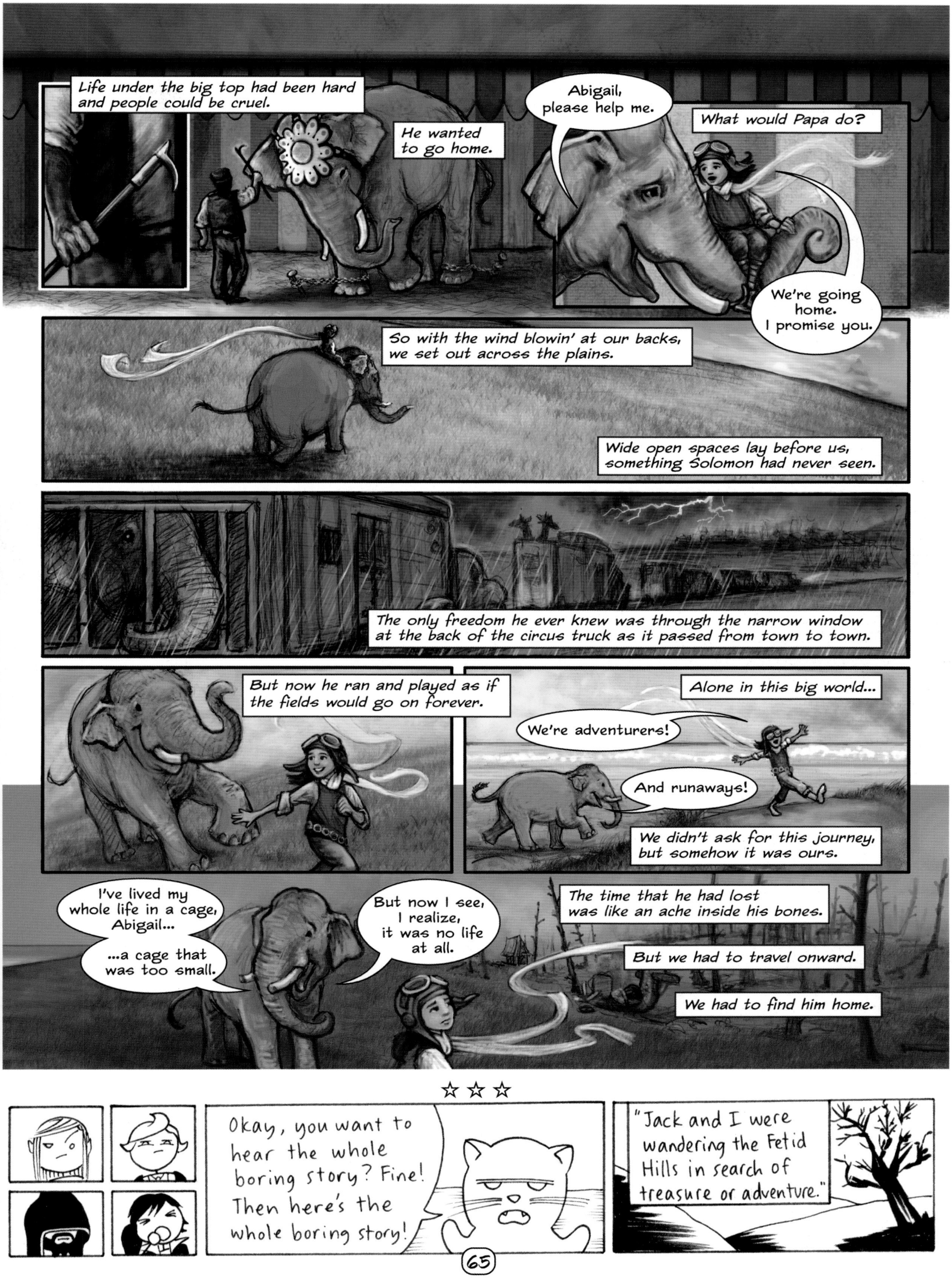
Life under the big top had been hard and people could be cruel.
He wanted to go home.
Abigail, please help me.
What would Papa do?
We're going home. I promise you.
So with the wind blowin' at our backs, we set out across the plains.
Wide open spaces lay before us, something Solomon had never seen.
The only freedom he ever knew was through the narrow window at the back of the circus truck as it passed from town to town.
But now he ran and played as if the fields would go on forever.
Alone in this big world...
We're adventurers!
And runaways!
We didn't ask for this journey, but somehow it was ours.
I've lived my whole life in a cage, Abigail...
...a cage that was too small.
But now I see, I realize, it was no life at all.
The time that he had lost was like an ache inside his bones.
But we had to travel onward.
We had to find him home.
☆☆☆
Okay, you want to hear the whole boring story? Fine! Then here's the whole boring story!
"Jack and I were wandering the Fetid Hills in search of treasure or adventure."

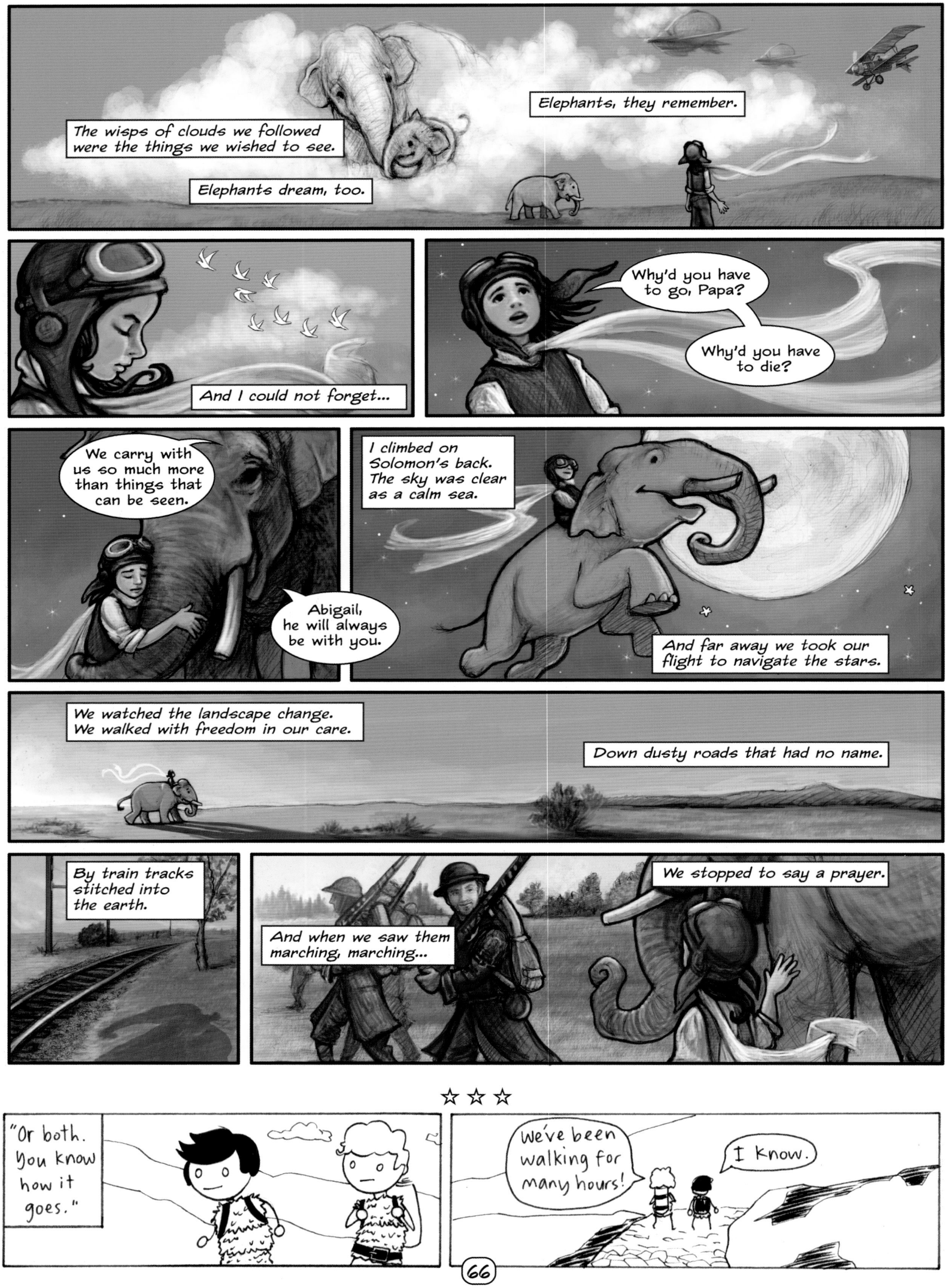

The wisps of clouds we followed were the things we wished to see.
Elephants dream, too.
Elephants, they remember.
And I could not forget...
Why'd you have to go, Papa?
Why'd you have to die?
We carry with us so much more than things that can be seen.
Abigail, he will always be with you.
I climbed on Solomon's back. The sky was clear as a calm sea.
And far away we took our flight to navigate the stars.
We watched the landscape change. We walked with freedom in our care.
Down dusty roads that had no name.
By train tracks stitched into the earth.
And when we saw them marching, marching...
We stopped to say a prayer.
☆ ☆ ☆
"Or both. You know how it goes."
We've been walking for many hours!
I know.

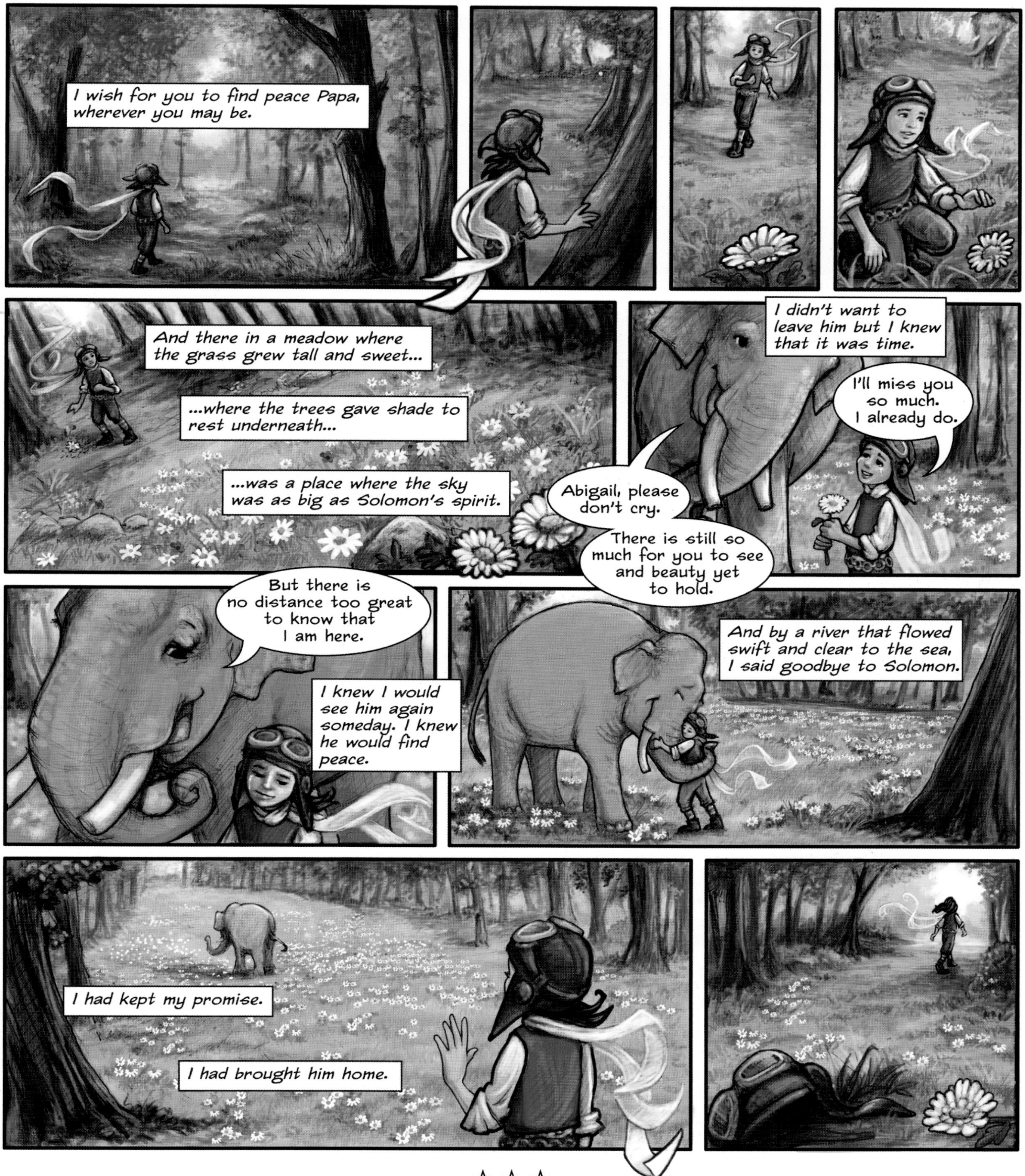
I wish for you to find peace Papa, wherever you may be.
And there in a meadow where the grass grew tall and sweet...
...where the trees gave shade to rest underneath...
...was a place where the sky was as big as Solomon's spirit.
I didn't want to leave him but I knew that it was time.
I'll miss you so much. I already do.
Abigail, please don't cry.
There is still so much for you to see and beauty yet to hold.
But there is no distance too great to know that I am here.
I knew I would see him again someday. I knew he would find peace.
And by a river that flowed swift and clear to the sea, I said goodbye to Solomon.
I had kept my promise.
I had brought him home.

☆☆☆

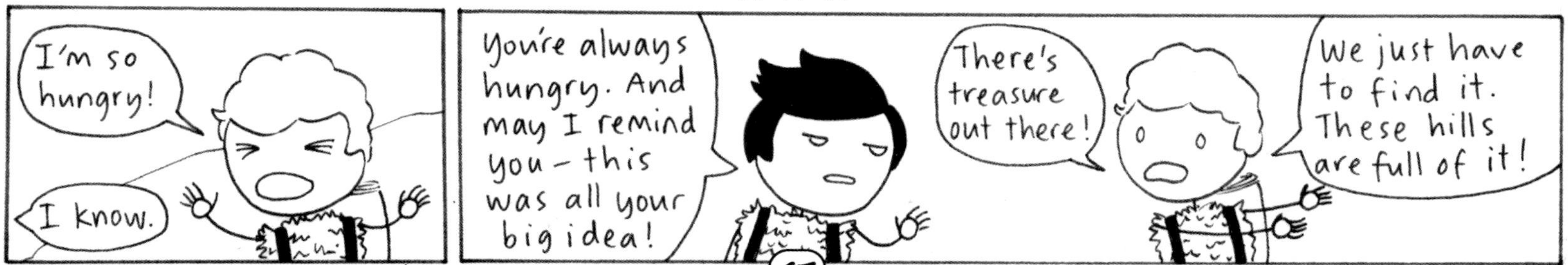
I'm so hungry!
I know.
You're always hungry. And may I remind you – this was all your big idea!
There's treasure out there!
We just have to find it. These hills are full of it!

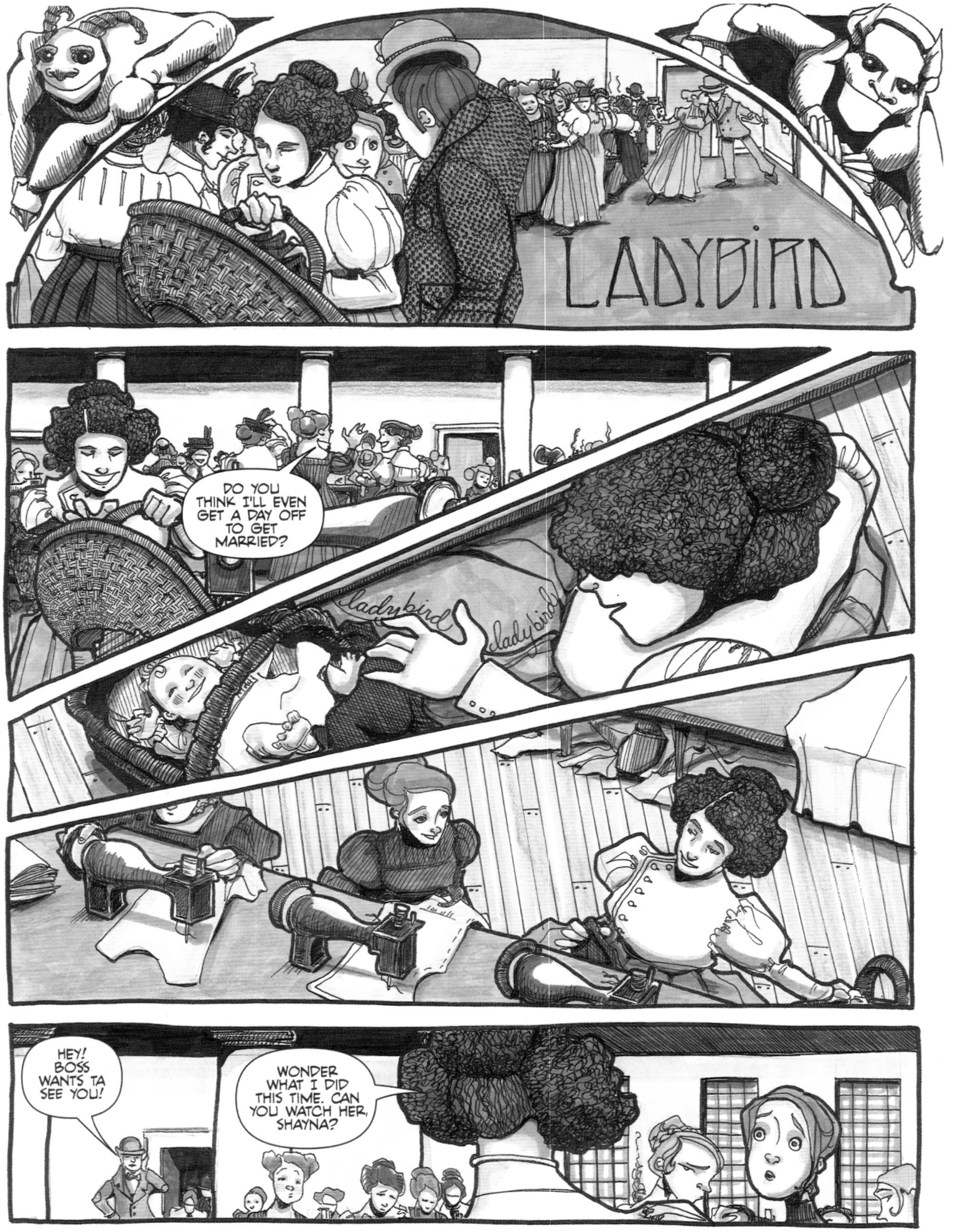
LADYBIRD
DO YOU THINK I'LL EVEN GET A DAY OFF TO GET MARRIED?
ladybird
ladybird
HEY! BOSS WANTS TA SEE YOU!
WONDER WHAT I DID THIS TIME. CAN YOU WATCH HER, SHAYNA?

WRITER: RACHEL PANDICH AND JENNA BUSCH   ARTIST: JANET LEE   LETTERS: RACHEL DEERING

☆☆☆

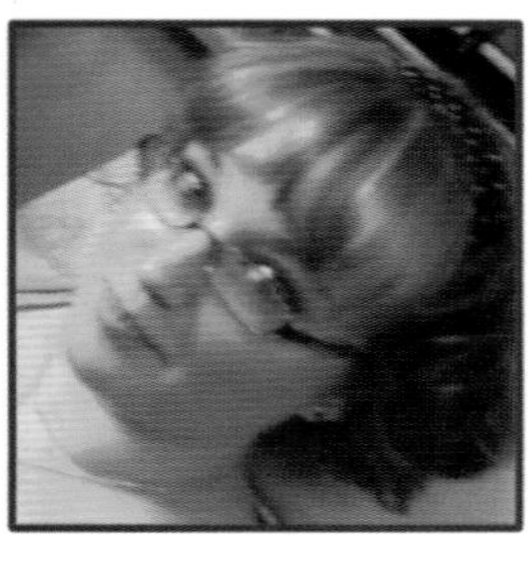

RACHEL PANDICH

SKILLS: Writer
LOCATION: Orange Park, FL
FUN FACT: I willingly pick up poo at an animal rescue farm. Ruining a dung beetle's day is fun.

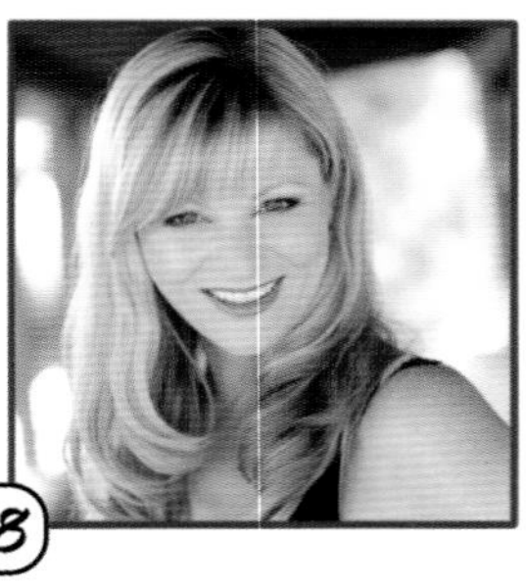

JENNA BUSCH

SKILLS: Writer-"Archetypes," Co-writer-"Ladybird
LOCATION: Los Angeles, CA
FUN FACT: I've been a musical theater actress, a makeup artist, an entertainment journalist...and I speak a little Gaelic!

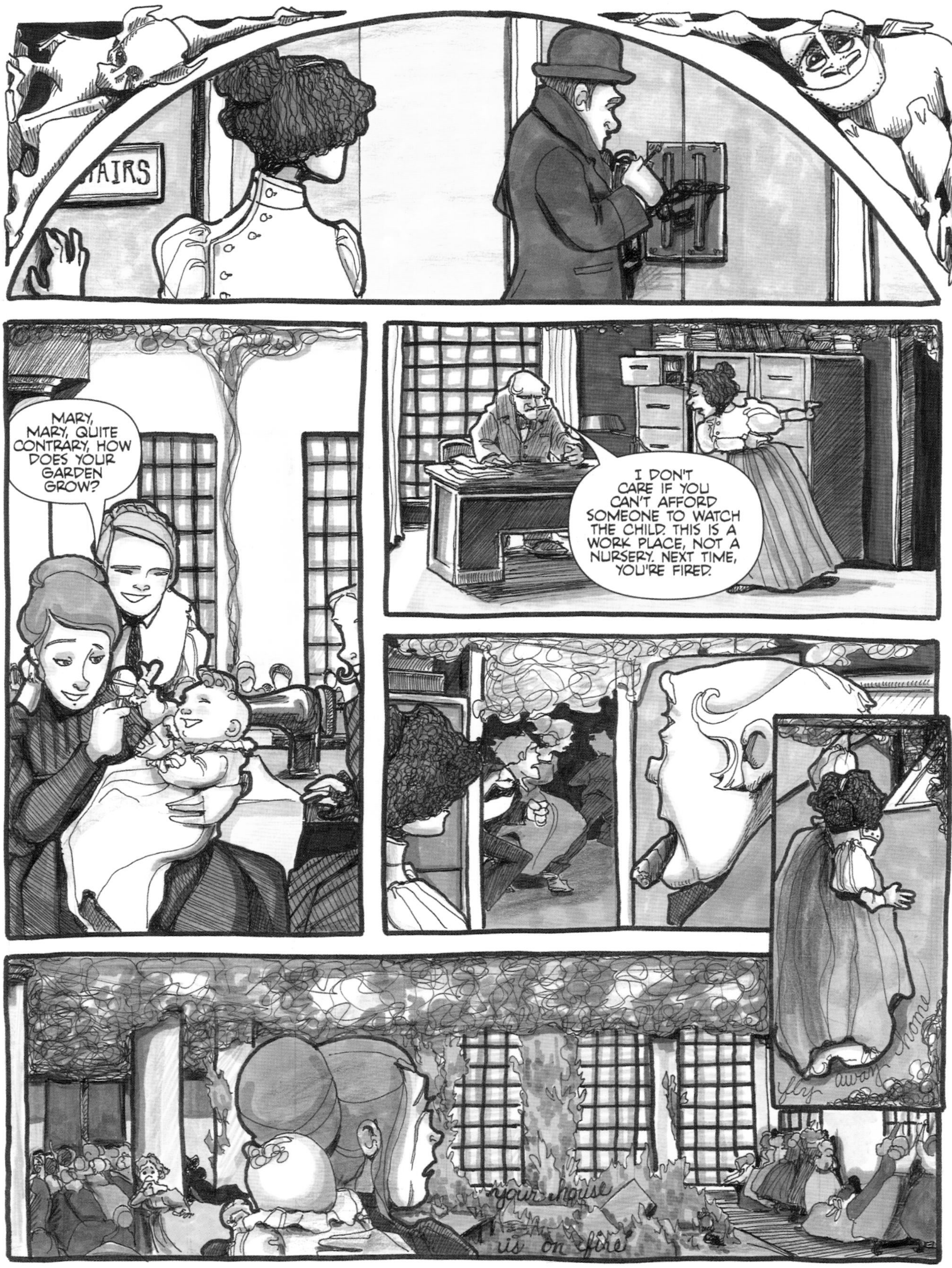
MARY, MARY, QUITE CONTRARY, HOW DOES YOUR GARDEN GROW?
I DON'T CARE IF YOU CAN'T AFFORD SOMEONE TO WATCH THE CHILD. THIS IS A WORK PLACE, NOT A NURSERY. NEXT TIME, YOU'RE FIRED.
fly away home
your house is on fire

☆☆☆

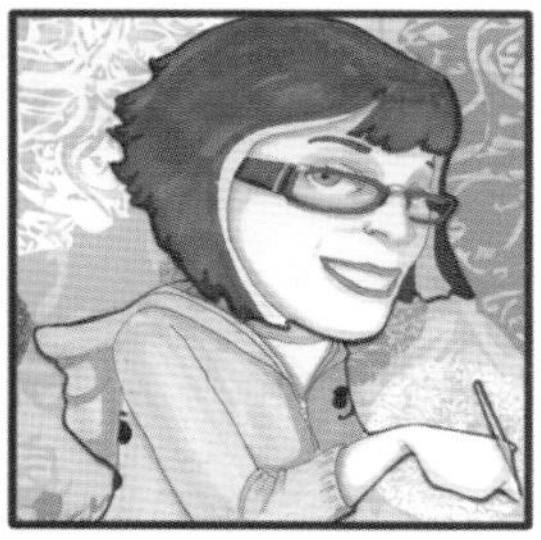

JANET LEE

SKILLS: Penciller, Inker, Colorist, *Decoupage Maven*
LOCATION: Nashville, TN
FUN FACT: I can wiggle my ears.

www.j-k-lee.com

PRO TIP

DETERMINATION
BY TRINA ROBBINS

"BE POLITE ABOUT IT, BUT DON'T TAKE NO FOR AN ANSWER. WHEN ALL THOSE MAINSTREAM PUBLISHERS AND EDITORS TOLD ME GIRLS DON'T READ COMICS AND WOMEN HAD NEVER DONE COMICS, I KNEW THEY WERE WRONG, SO I DID THE RESEARCH AND WROTE MY HISTORIES OF WOMEN CARTOONISTS, AND MY HISTORY OF GIRLS AND WOMEN'S COMICS, 'FROM GIRLS TO GRRRLZ.' NOW, WITH THE IMMENSE SUCCESS OF MANGA, EDITORS CAN NO LONGER SAY GIRLS DON'T READ COMICS."

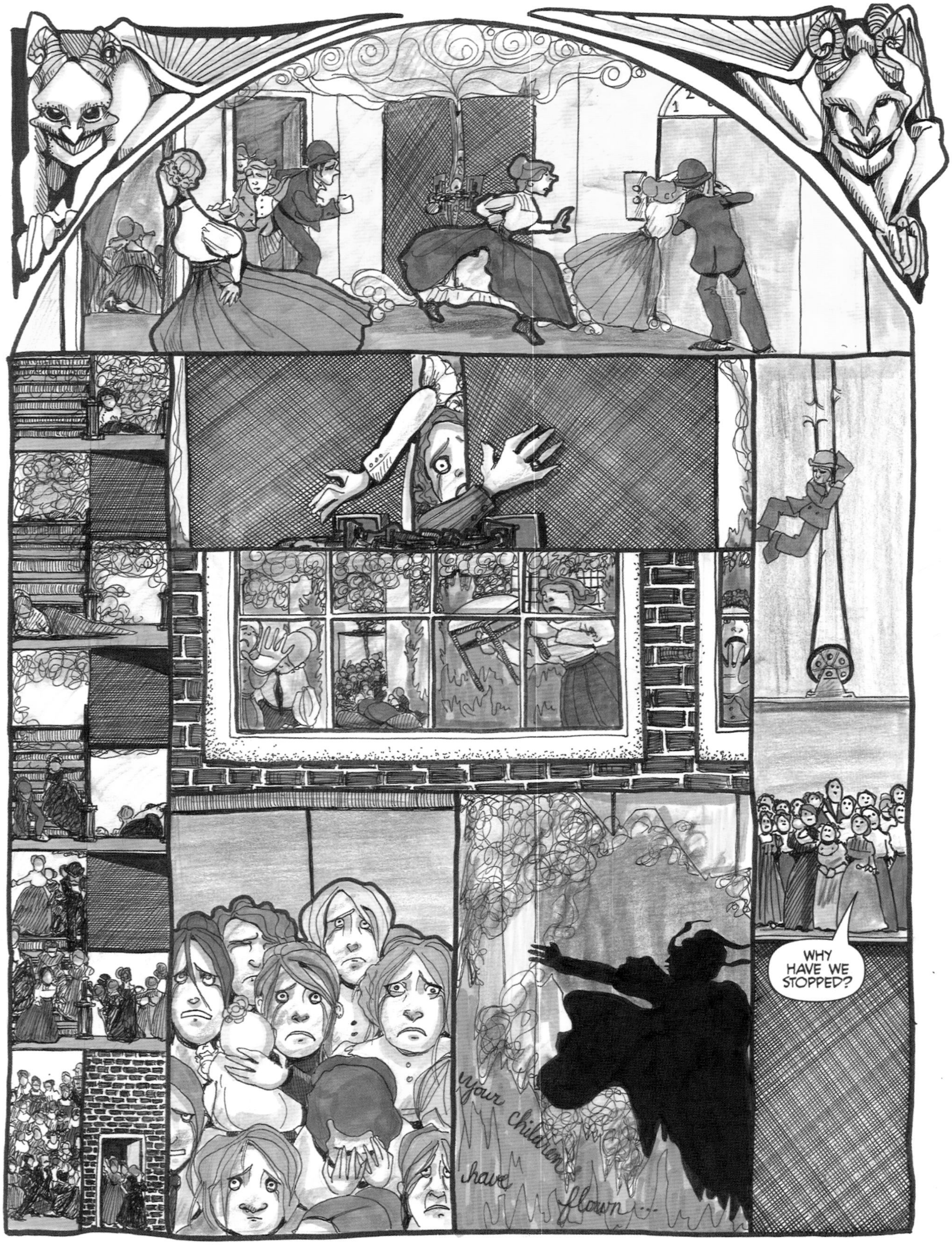
WHY HAVE WE STOPPED?
your children have flown...

☆ ☆ ☆

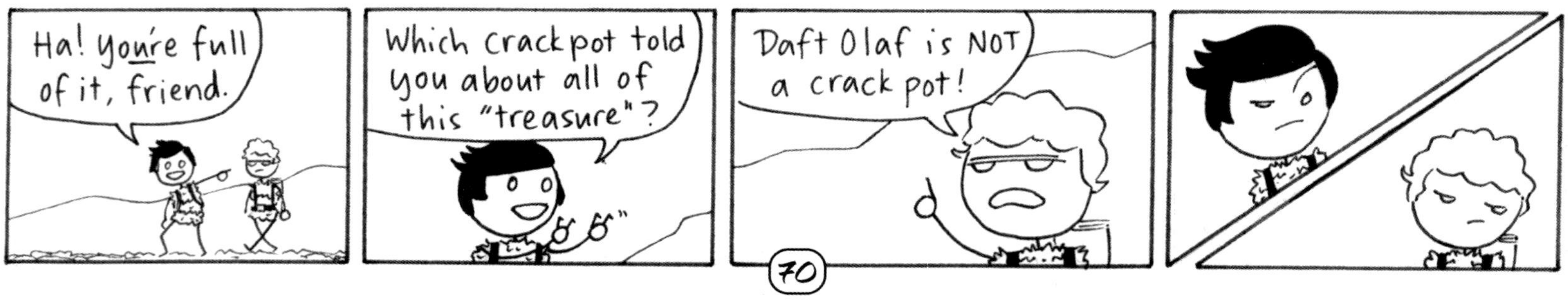
Ha! you're full of it, friend.
Which crackpot told you about all of this "treasure"?
Daft Olaf is NOT a crack pot!

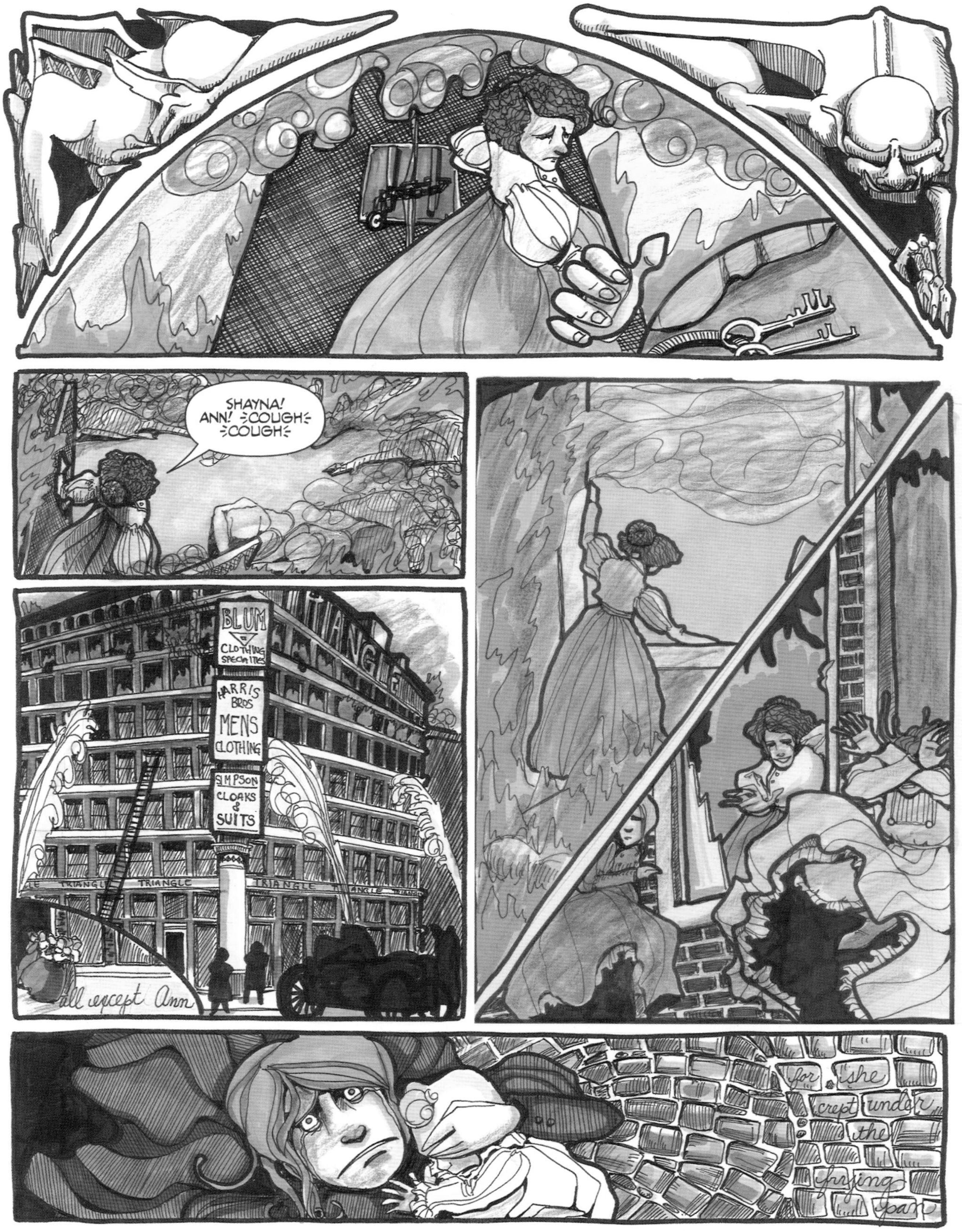
SHAYNA! ANN! COUGH COUGH
BLUM CLOTHING SPECIALTIES
HARRIS BROS MENS CLOTHING
SIMPSON CLOAKS & SUITS
TRIANGLE
all except Ann
for she crept under the frying pan

☆ ☆ ☆

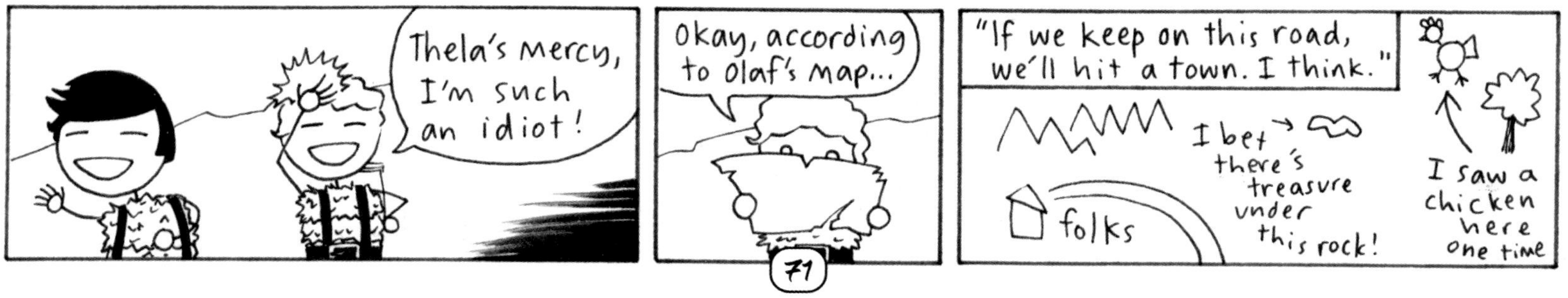
Thela's mercy, I'm such an idiot!
Okay, according to Olaf's map...
"If we keep on this road, we'll hit a town. I think."
folks
I bet there's treasure under this rock!
I saw a chicken here one time

SOLACE

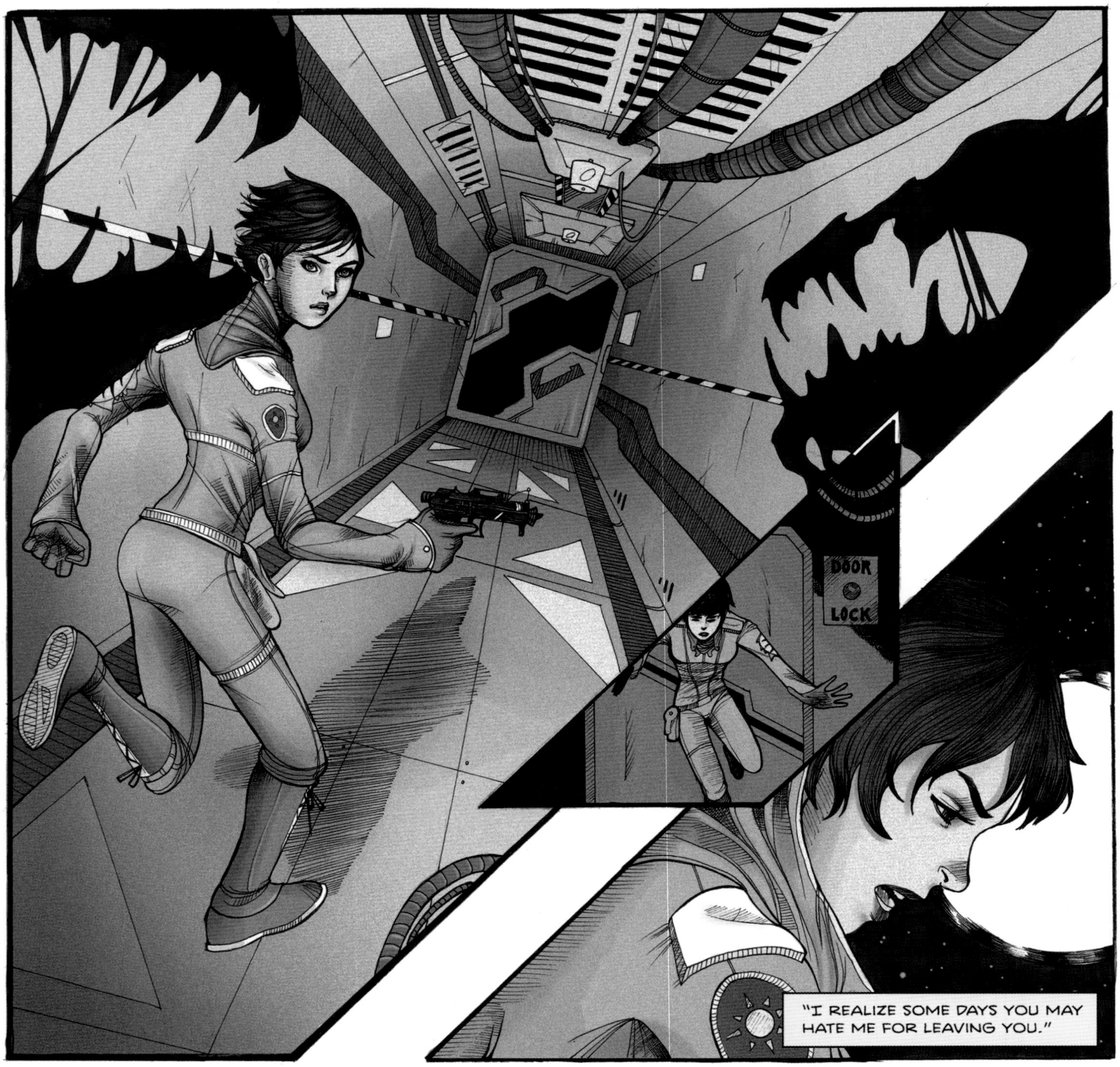
DOOR LOCK
"I REALIZE SOME DAYS YOU MAY HATE ME FOR LEAVING YOU."

WRITER: JENN CORELLA ARTIST: CHRISSIE ZULLO LETTERS: RACHEL DEERING

☆☆☆

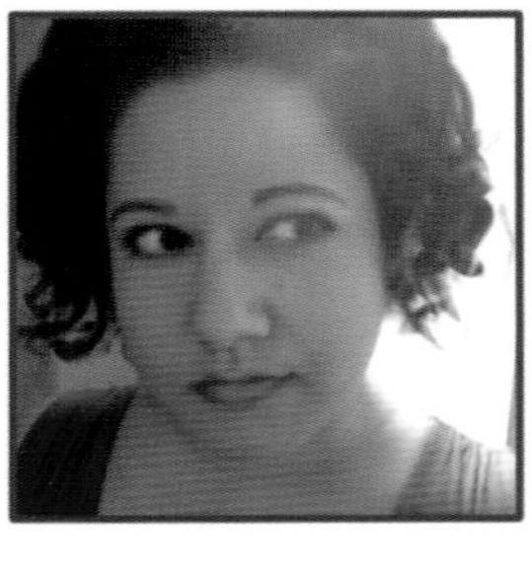

JENN CORELLA

SKILLS: Writer
LOCATION: Tucson, AZ
FUN FACT: My imagination is what drives me, and I'm proud of the dork in there.

www.jenncorella.com

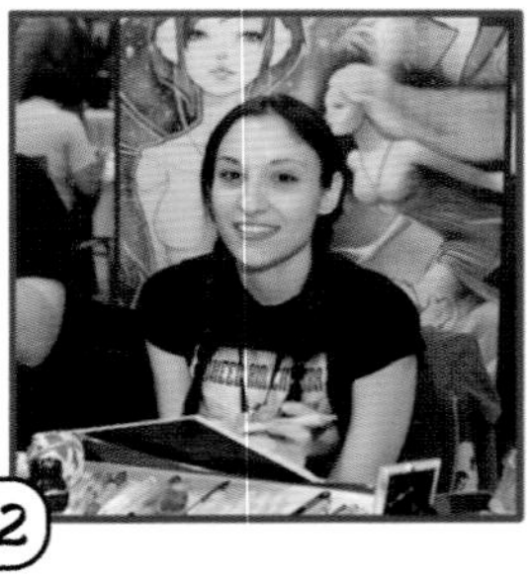

CHRISSIE ZULLO

SKILLS: Penciller, Inker, and Colorist
LOCATION: New York City, NY
FUN FACT: I have a strange affection toward the yeti.

http://chrissiez.blogspot.com

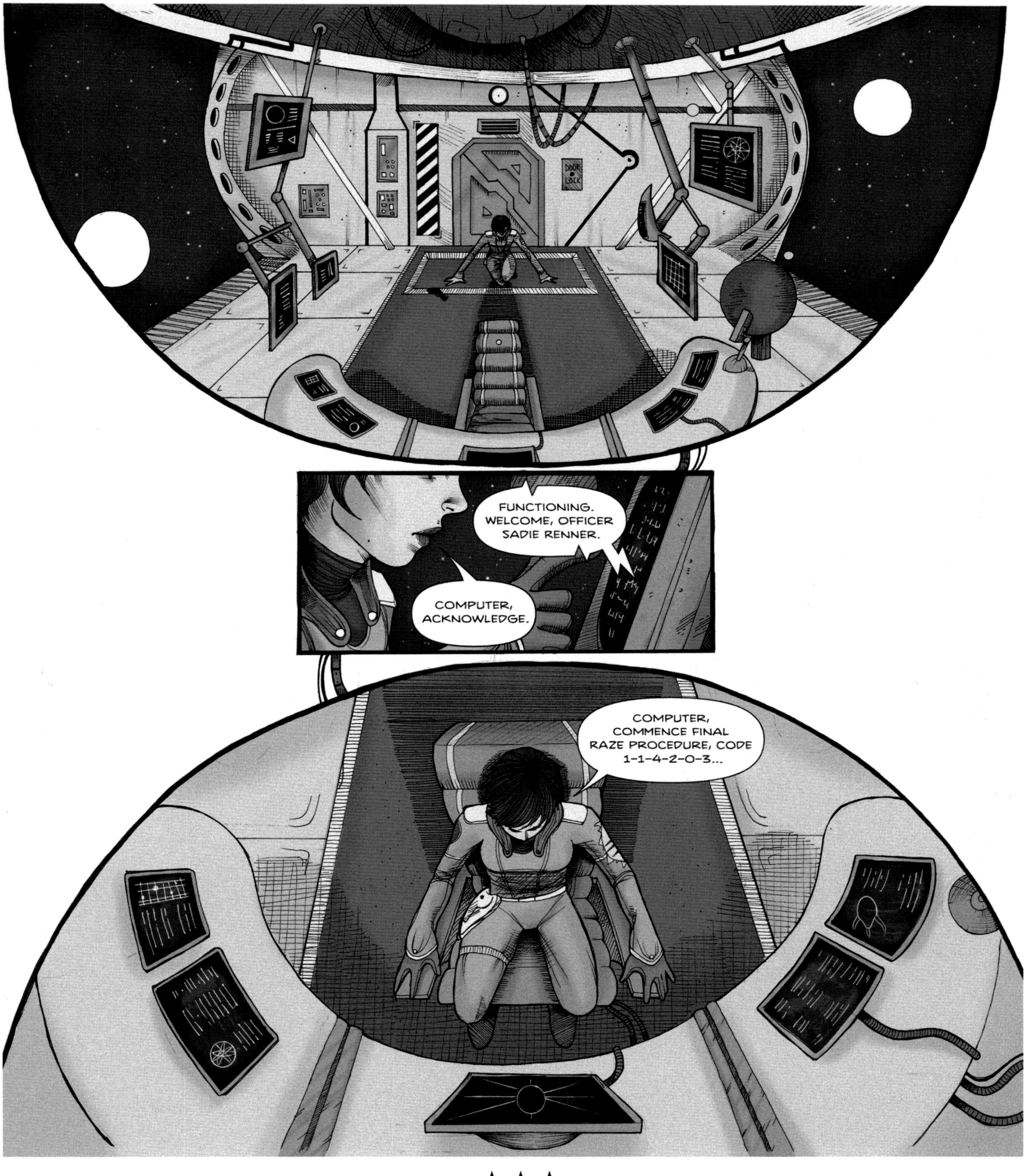
COMPUTER, ACKNOWLEDGE.
FUNCTIONING. WELCOME, OFFICER SADIE RENNER.
COMPUTER, COMMENCE FINAL RAZE PROCEDURE, CODE 1-1-4-2-0-3...

☆ ☆ ☆

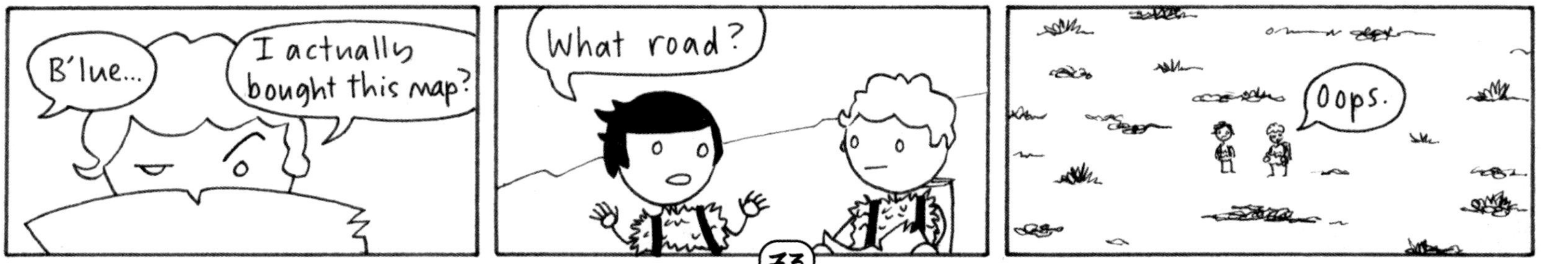
B'lue...
I actually bought this map?
What road?
Oops.

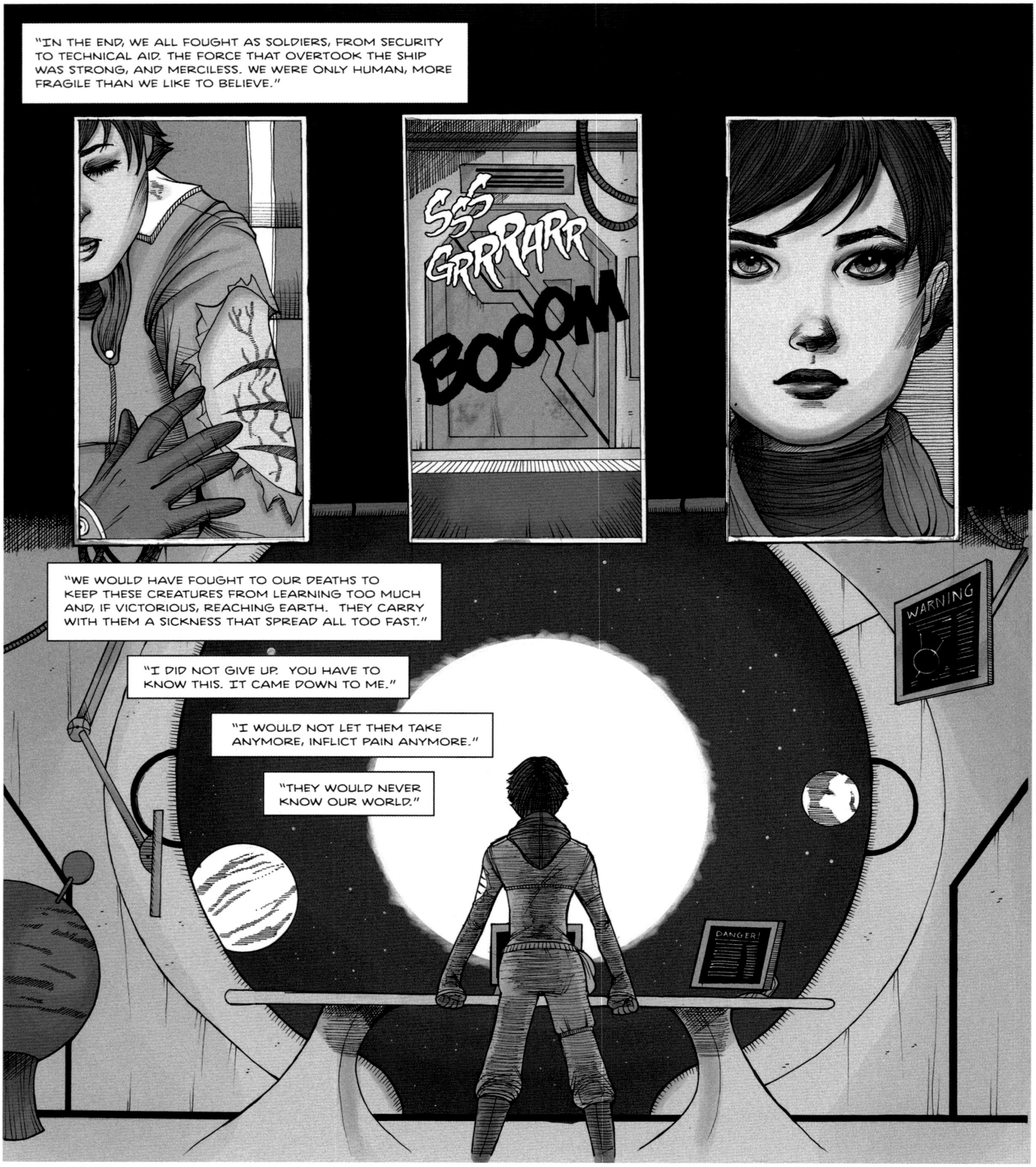
"IN THE END, WE ALL FOUGHT AS SOLDIERS, FROM SECURITY TO TECHNICAL AID. THE FORCE THAT OVERTOOK THE SHIP WAS STRONG, AND MERCILESS. WE WERE ONLY HUMAN, MORE FRAGILE THAN WE LIKE TO BELIEVE."
SSS
GRRRARR
BOOOM
"WE WOULD HAVE FOUGHT TO OUR DEATHS TO KEEP THESE CREATURES FROM LEARNING TOO MUCH AND, IF VICTORIOUS, REACHING EARTH. THEY CARRY WITH THEM A SICKNESS THAT SPREAD ALL TOO FAST."
WARNING
"I DID NOT GIVE UP. YOU HAVE TO KNOW THIS. IT CAME DOWN TO ME."
"I WOULD NOT LET THEM TAKE ANYMORE, INFLICT PAIN ANYMORE."
"THEY WOULD NEVER KNOW OUR WORLD."
DANGER!

☆ ☆ ☆

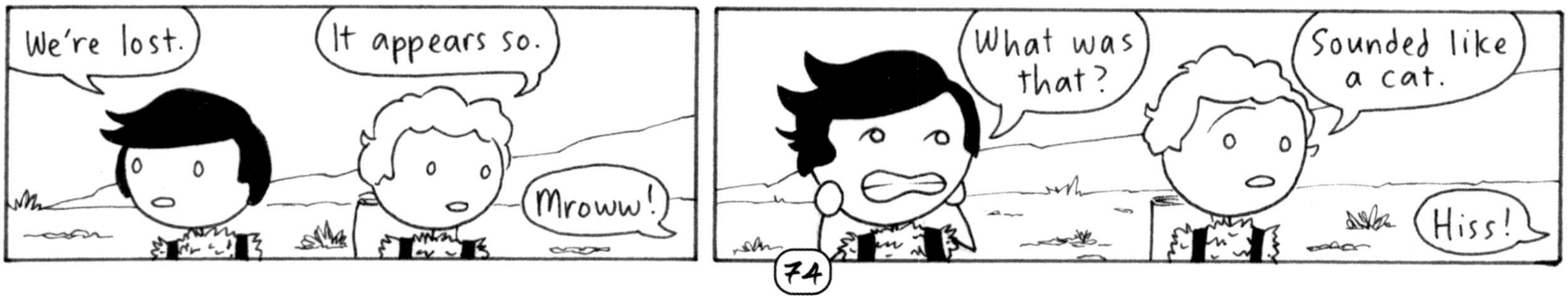
We're lost.
It appears so.
Mroww!
What was that?
Sounded like a cat.
Hiss!

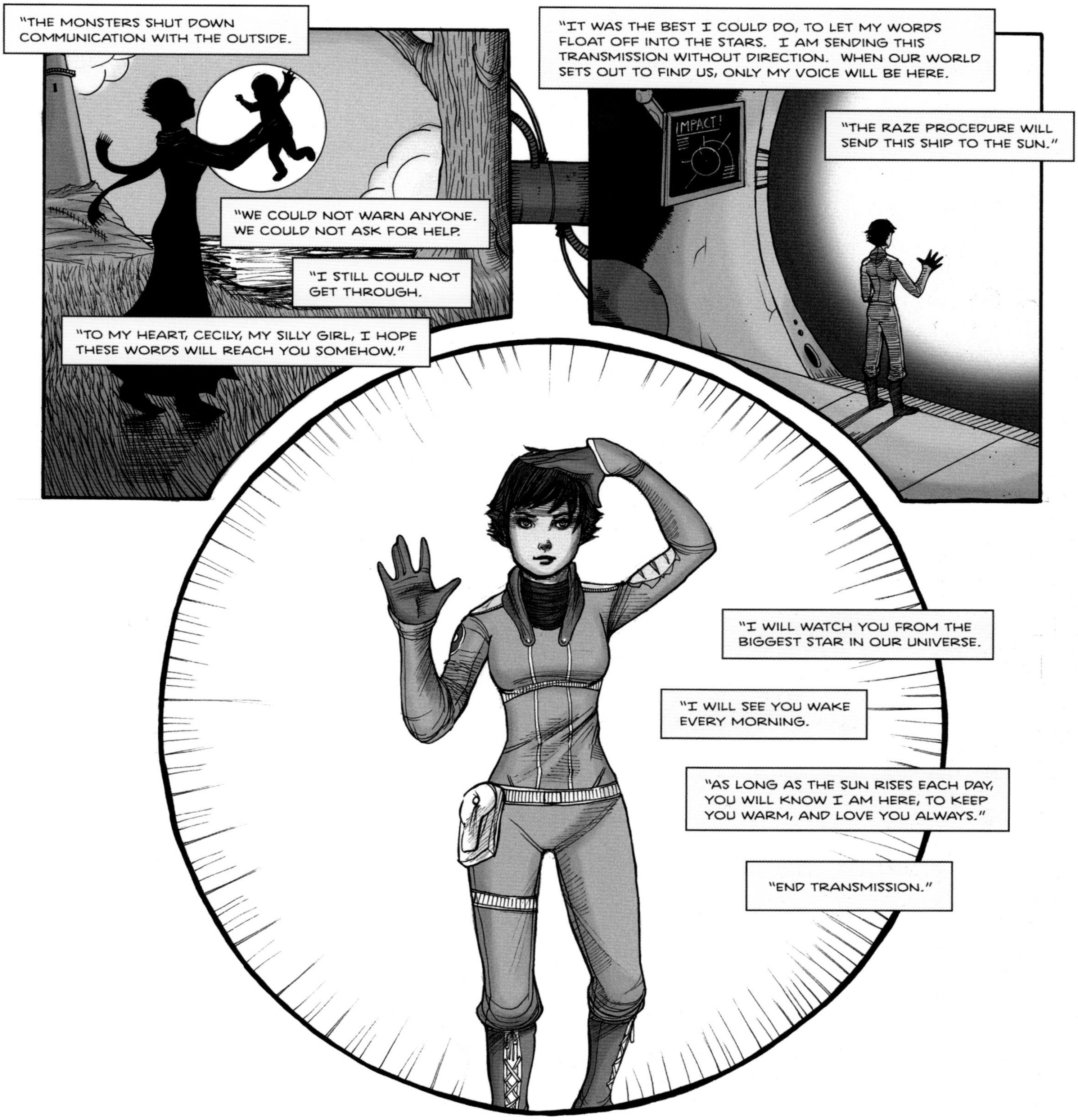
"THE MONSTERS SHUT DOWN COMMUNICATION WITH THE OUTSIDE.
"WE COULD NOT WARN ANYONE. WE COULD NOT ASK FOR HELP.
"I STILL COULD NOT GET THROUGH.
"TO MY HEART, CECILY, MY SILLY GIRL, I HOPE THESE WORDS WILL REACH YOU SOMEHOW."
"IT WAS THE BEST I COULD DO, TO LET MY WORDS FLOAT OFF INTO THE STARS. I AM SENDING THIS TRANSMISSION WITHOUT DIRECTION. WHEN OUR WORLD SETS OUT TO FIND US, ONLY MY VOICE WILL BE HERE.
IMPACT!
"THE RAZE PROCEDURE WILL SEND THIS SHIP TO THE SUN."
"I WILL WATCH YOU FROM THE BIGGEST STAR IN OUR UNIVERSE.
"I WILL SEE YOU WAKE EVERY MORNING.
"AS LONG AS THE SUN RISES EACH DAY, YOU WILL KNOW I AM HERE, TO KEEP YOU WARM, AND LOVE YOU ALWAYS."
"END TRANSMISSION."

☆ ☆ ☆

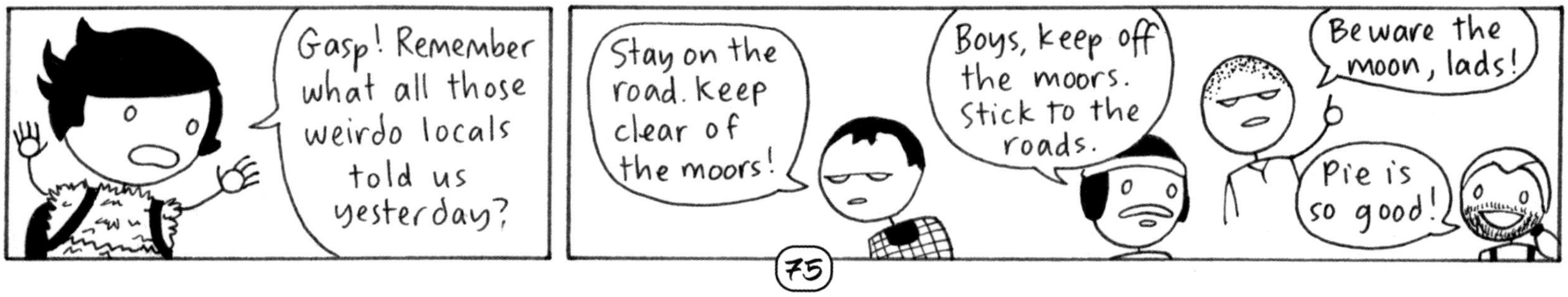
Gasp! Remember what all those weirdo locals told us yesterday?
Stay on the road. Keep clear of the moors!
Boys, keep off the moors. Stick to the roads.
Beware the moon, lads!
Pie is so good!

...THREAT CONTAINED...

...SURVIVOR...

...SAFE...

MOMMY?
END

☆ ☆ ☆

Mmm, pie Is so good!
Wait...
...are these the moors?
I don't know!
What does a moors look like?
Mew mew!

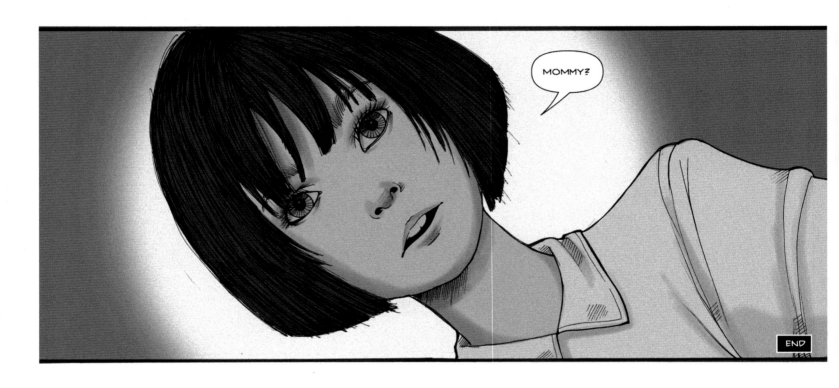

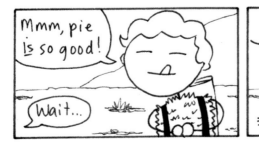

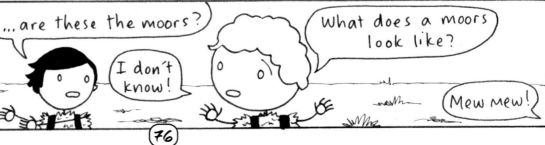

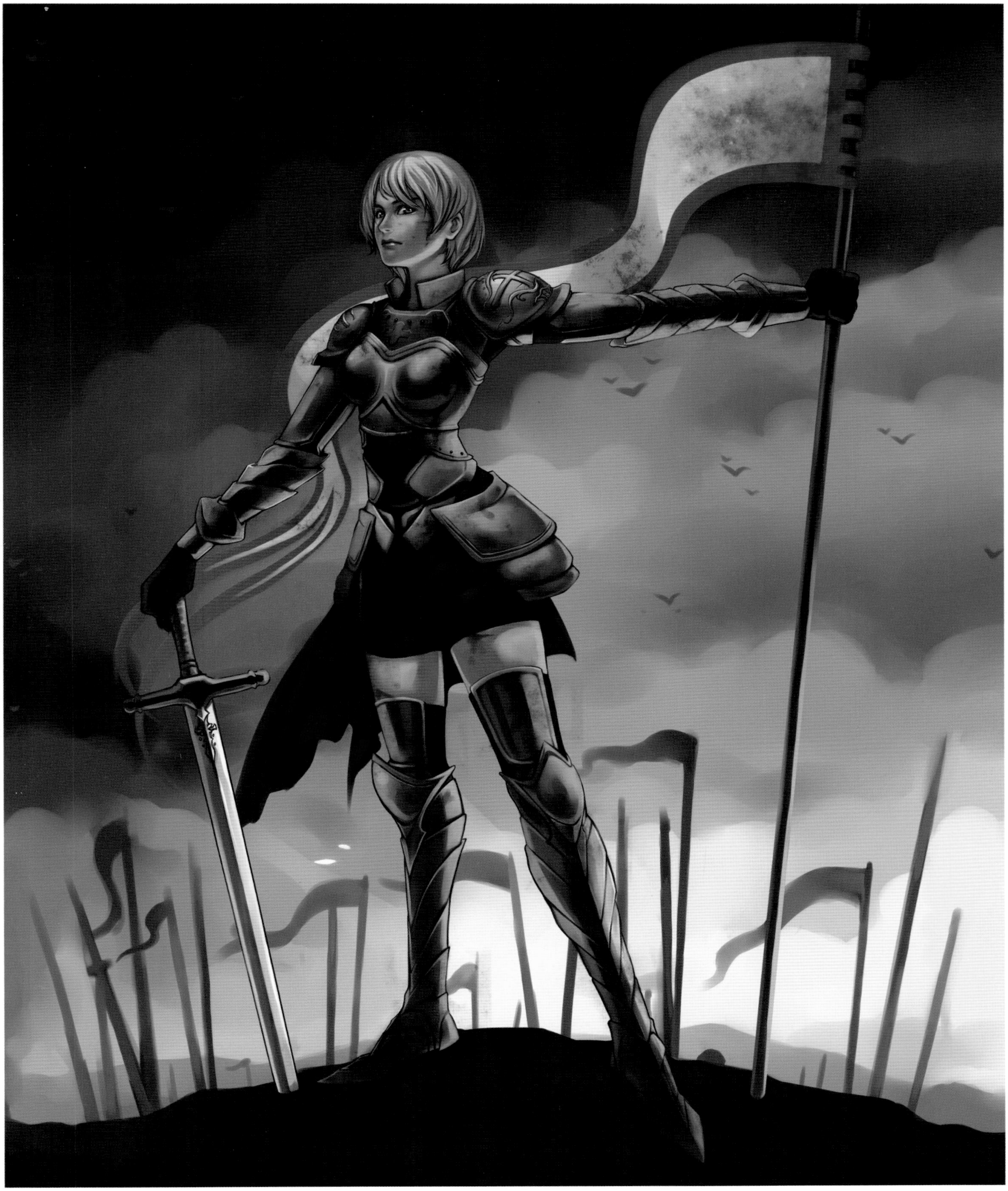

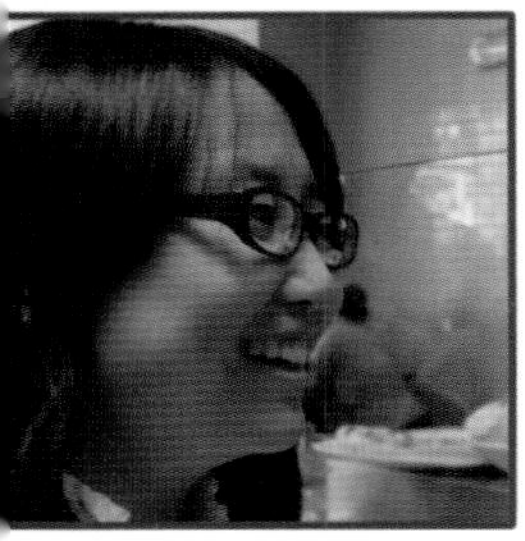

QING HAN

SKILLS: Tutorial and Pinup Artist
LOCATION: Ontario, Canada
FUN FACT: Can't work without music :D.

http://qinni.deviantart.com

☆☆☆

PRO TIP

CONVENTIONS
BY RENAE DE LIZ

"ALWAYS HAVE YOUR PORTFOLIO AND BUSINESS CARDS HANDY! HOWEVER, DON'T EVER GO IN *EXPECTING* PEOPLE TO LOOK AT YOUR WORK. MOST OF THE TIME THE SIMPLE GESTURE OF GOING UP AND INTRODUCING YOURSELF OPENS UP THE DOOR FOR SHOWING YOUR WORK TO THAT PERSON LATER ON WHEN THEY AREN'T SO BUSY AT A CONVENTION, WHICH IS MUCH BETTER FOR YOU!"

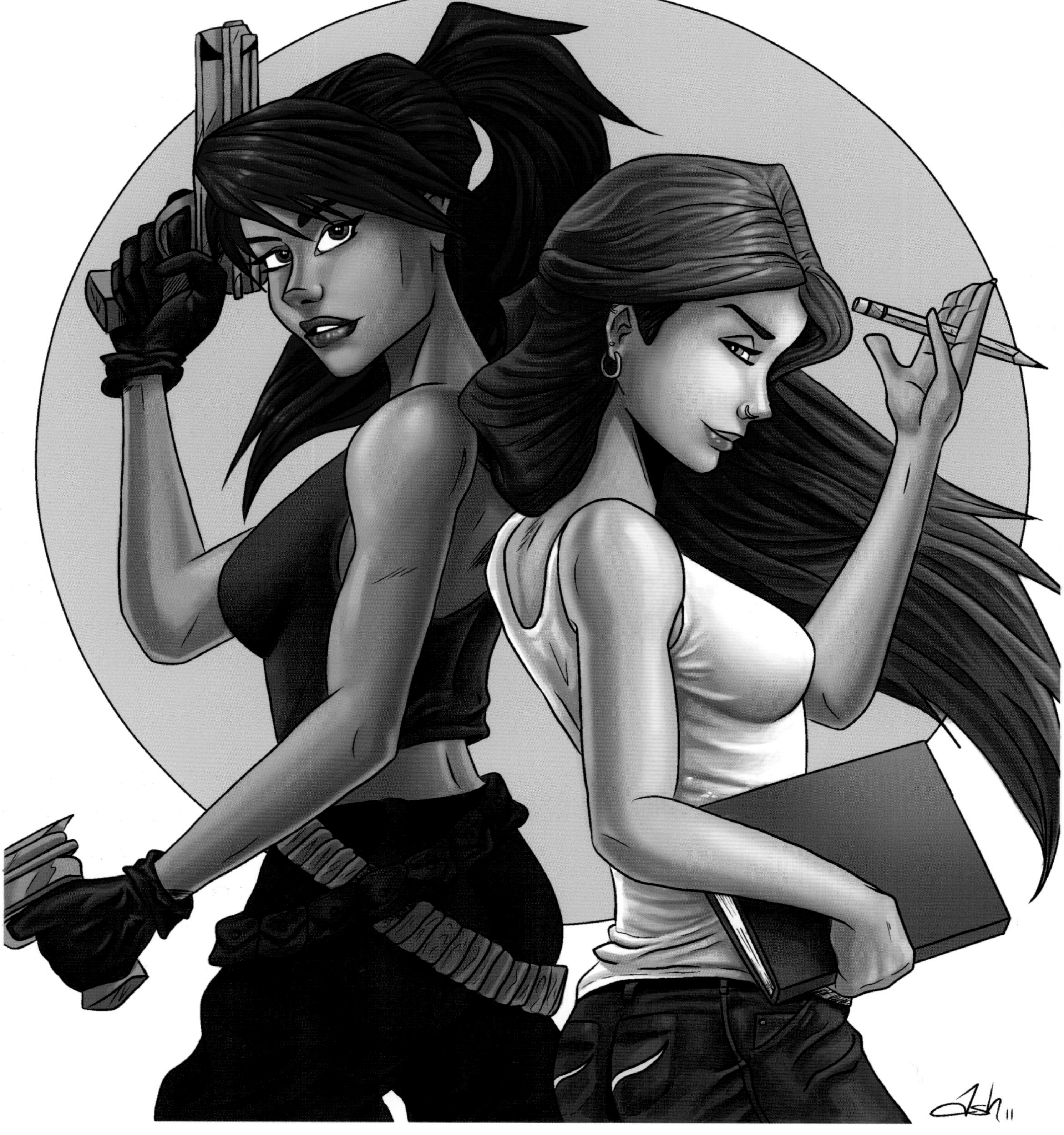

☆☆☆

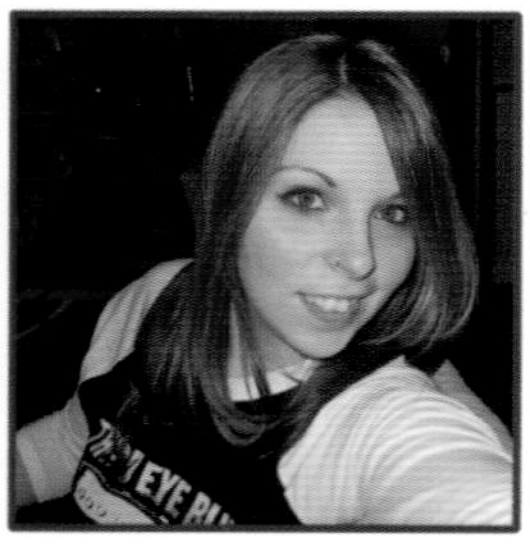

Ashlee Brienzo Lentini

SKILLS: Penciller, Inker, Colorist
LOCATION: Fairhaven/Dartmouth, Massachusetts
FUN FACT: I have successfully mastered the Art of Tripping Over Nothing.

http://haightstreetgirl.deviantart.com/

PRO TIP

OBSESSION
BY ANNIE NOCENTI

"OBSESSION. SOMETIMES I THINK THE KEY TO ALL LIFE AND ART IS OBSESSION. WHATEVER IT IS, OLD BONES, BULLFIGHTING, BATS... PUT YOUR PASSIONS INTO YOUR COMICS AND WE'LL FOLLOW YOU LIKE LAP DOGS."

PART TWO

TEAM MARIAH

☆ ☆ ☆ For each section of *Womanthology* a different lady took on the role of editor over the writers, pencillers, inkers, colorists, and letterers for their stories or pinups. They were in charge of making sure the creators worked as a team, had all the info they needed, and that all stories and pinups were turned in on time. This section is Mariah McCourt's.

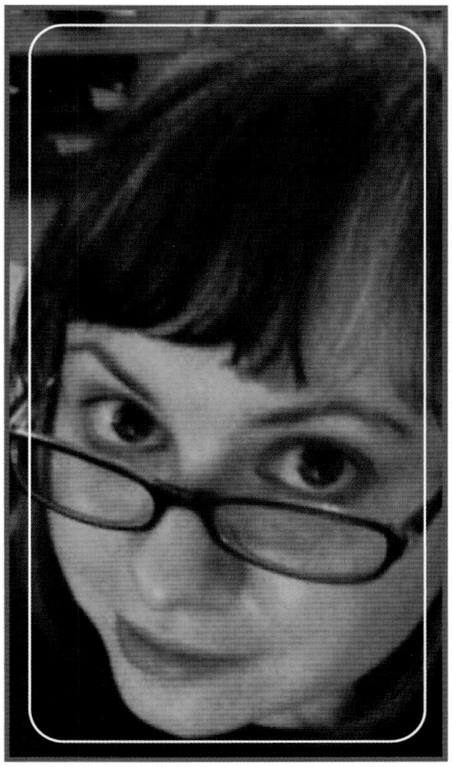

EDITOR - MARIAH MCCOURT

Location: San Francisco
Day Job: Writer/Editor

A little about yourself: I'm a feisty little writer, editor, and artist with a strange and mysterious past that involves monsters, goblins, and dragons. I love stories, I love squidly octopi, and I love cupcakes. I seem to find myself writing a lot of stories with vampires in them (*True Blood/Angel*), which is why I decided to do a zombie story for *Womanthology*. My biggest hope is that people get something meaningful out of my work. We all need that sense of connection and that's my goal in every tale I tell.

What does *Womanthology* mean to you? Helping creators break into comics is one of the things that's most rewarding about working in this industry. But it's not something I get to do very often with the types of books I edit, so working on *Womanthology*, which is entirely about giving new creators an opportunity to work with professionals and tell stories they want to tell, there was no way I could say no to that. It's been an incredibly rewarding, collaborative process, and I've loved every minute of it.

Funny fact: Ever since I was a little kid I have wanted to ride a dragon.

☆ ☆ ☆

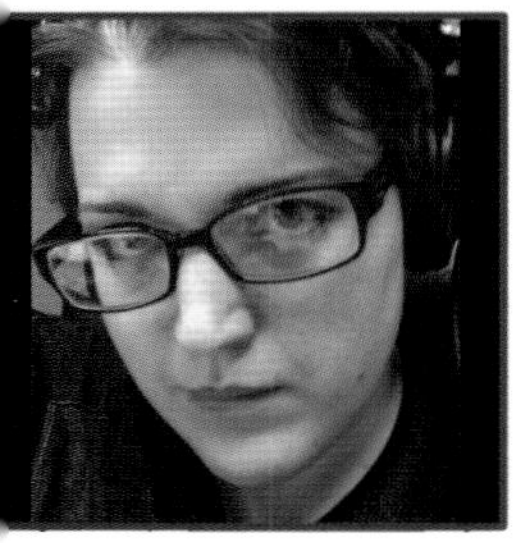

KARA LEOPARD
SKILLS: Layouts
LOCATION: College Station, TX
FUN FACT: I'm an adventure enthusiast and a social media addict.

http://artofdrkara.com

KARA LEOPARD PUT A TON OF WORK INTO GATHERING ALL THE INFO AND PHOTOS, AND DESIGNING ALL OF THESE CREATOR WRITE-UPS. THANKS, KARA!

A HUNTER DWELLS AIMLESSLY IN A SHROUDED, MYSTERIOUS WORLD...

SHE IS LONELY. HER EYES ARE AS DISTANT AND MYSTERIOUS AS THE WORLD SURROUNDING HER.

SHE SPENT HER DAYS PREYING UPON INNOCENT CREATURES...

WHILE SHE SPENT NIGHTS IDLING AWAY THE HOURS IN AN INESCAPABLE AND DESOLATE DARKNESS

HOWLLLLL!!!

WRITER: RAVEN MOORE   ARTIST: CAMILLA D'ERRICO   COLORS: ALICIA FERNANDEZ   LETTERS: RACHEL DEERING

★ ★ ☆

RAVEN MOORE

SKILLS: Writer
LOCATION: Chicago, IL
FUN FACT: Author of upcoming fantasy series *Memoria* and fashion illustration book *Life/ILLUSTRATED*.

www.thewriterbabeseries.com

CAMILLA D'ERRICO

SKILLS: Penciller
LOCATION: Vancouver
FUN FACT: Anime fan.

www.camकिlladerrico.com

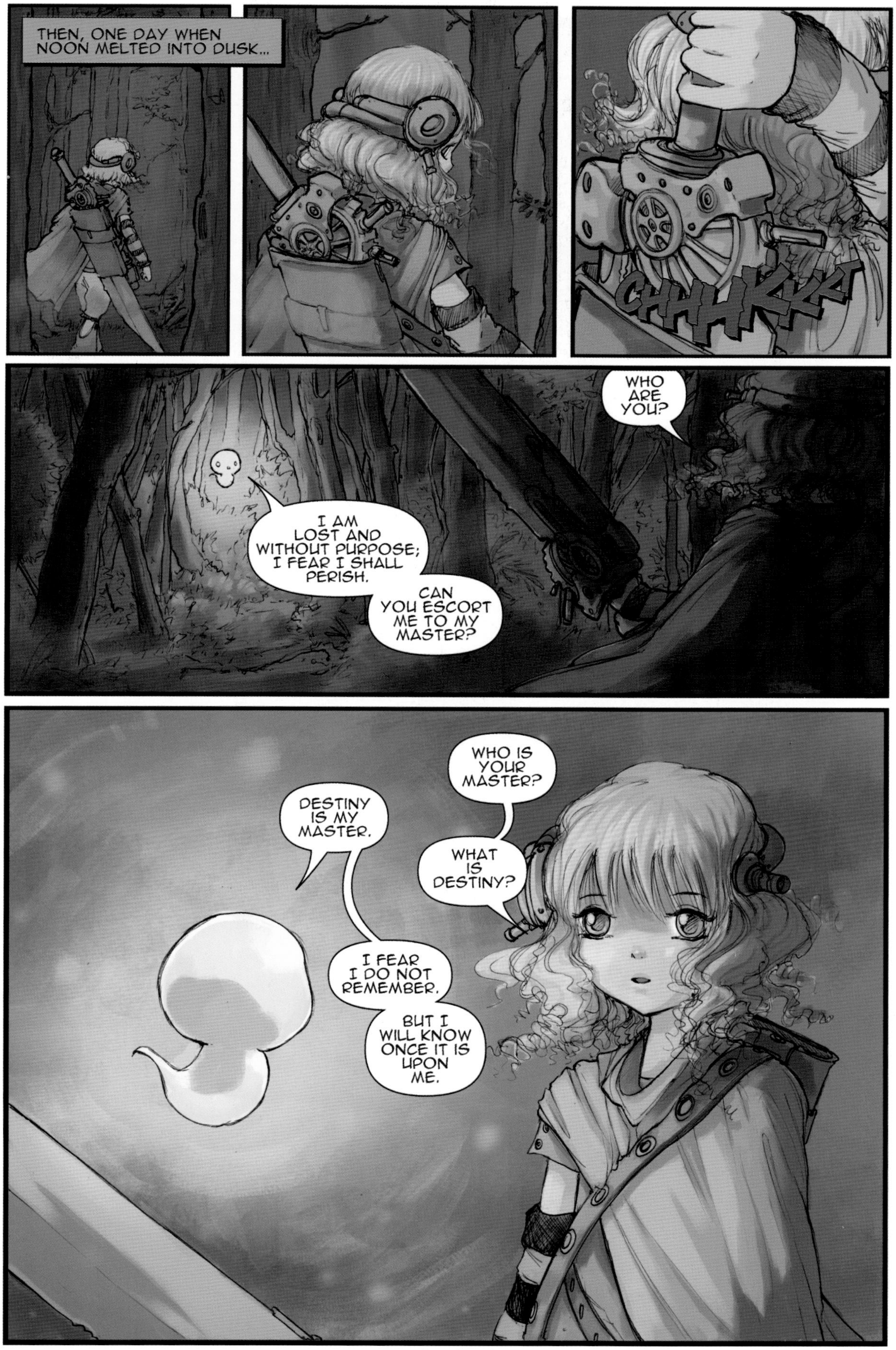
THEN, ONE DAY WHEN NOON MELTED INTO DUSK...
WHO ARE YOU?
I AM LOST AND WITHOUT PURPOSE; I FEAR I SHALL PERISH.
CAN YOU ESCORT ME TO MY MASTER?
WHO IS YOUR MASTER?
DESTINY IS MY MASTER.
WHAT IS DESTINY?
I FEAR I DO NOT REMEMBER.
BUT I WILL KNOW ONCE IT IS UPON ME.

☆ ☆ ☆

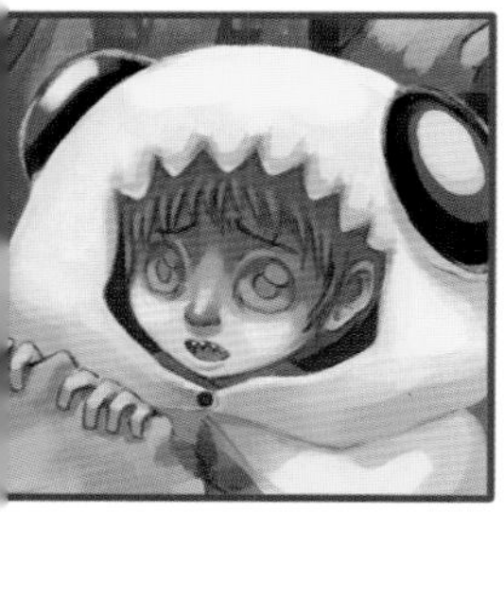

ALICIA FERNÁNDEZ

SKILLS: Penciller, Colorist, Letterer
LOCATION: Barcelona
FUN FACT: I like monsters. They don't usually taste good, but make great stories.

ohmybug.deviantart.com

PRO TIP COLORS BY KALI FONTECCHIO

"COLOR CHOICE IS SUPER IMPORTANT. I FIND THAT CHOOSING A FEW COLORS AND THEN STAYING WITHIN THAT FAMILY OF CLOSELY RELATED COLORS HELPS KEEP THINGS HARMONIOUS. IF I CHOOSE A CERTAIN TYPE OF RED, I WILL CHOOSE A SIMILAR LIGHT RED BUT ADD MORE GRAY TO SLIGHTLY OFFSET IT SO THAT IT IS NOT EXACTLY THE SAME COLOR, JUST LIGHTER. NEUTRALS ARE GREAT FOR MAKING A FEW BRIGHT COLORS POP. CONTRAST IS IMPORTANT TOO SO THAT YOUR COLORS DO NOT LOOK MUDDY. A GOOD TRICK IS TO LOOK AT IT IN PHOTOSHOP AND MAKE IT GRAYSCALE TO SEE HOW IT ALL READS TOGETHER."

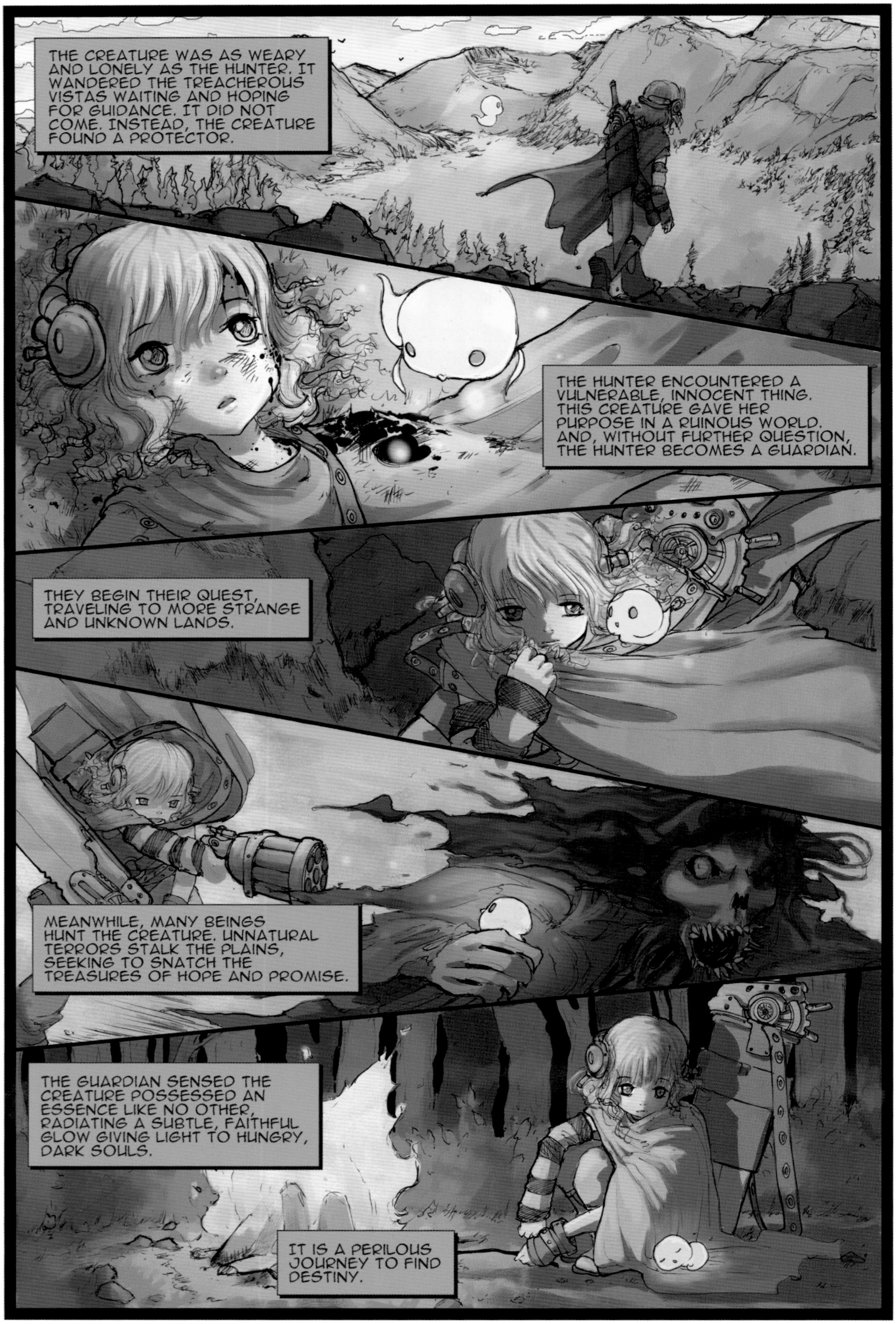
THE CREATURE WAS AS WEARY AND LONELY AS THE HUNTER. IT WANDERED THE TREACHEROUS VISTAS WAITING AND HOPING FOR GUIDANCE. IT DID NOT COME. INSTEAD, THE CREATURE FOUND A PROTECTOR.
THE HUNTER ENCOUNTERED A VULNERABLE, INNOCENT THING. THIS CREATURE GAVE HER PURPOSE IN A RUINOUS WORLD. AND, WITHOUT FURTHER QUESTION, THE HUNTER BECOMES A GUARDIAN.
THEY BEGIN THEIR QUEST, TRAVELING TO MORE STRANGE AND UNKNOWN LANDS.
MEANWHILE, MANY BEINGS HUNT THE CREATURE. UNNATURAL TERRORS STALK THE PLAINS, SEEKING TO SNATCH THE TREASURES OF HOPE AND PROMISE.
THE GUARDIAN SENSED THE CREATURE POSSESSED AN ESSENCE LIKE NO OTHER, RADIATING A SUBTLE, FAITHFUL GLOW GIVING LIGHT TO HUNGRY, DARK SOULS.
IT IS A PERILOUS JOURNEY TO FIND DESTINY.

☆☆☆

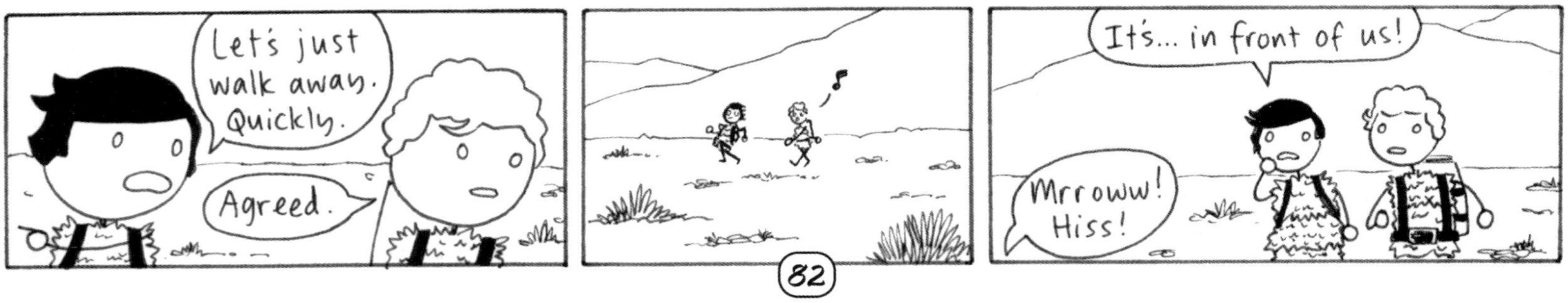
Let's just walk away. Quickly.
Agreed.
It's... in front of us!
Mrroww! Hiss!

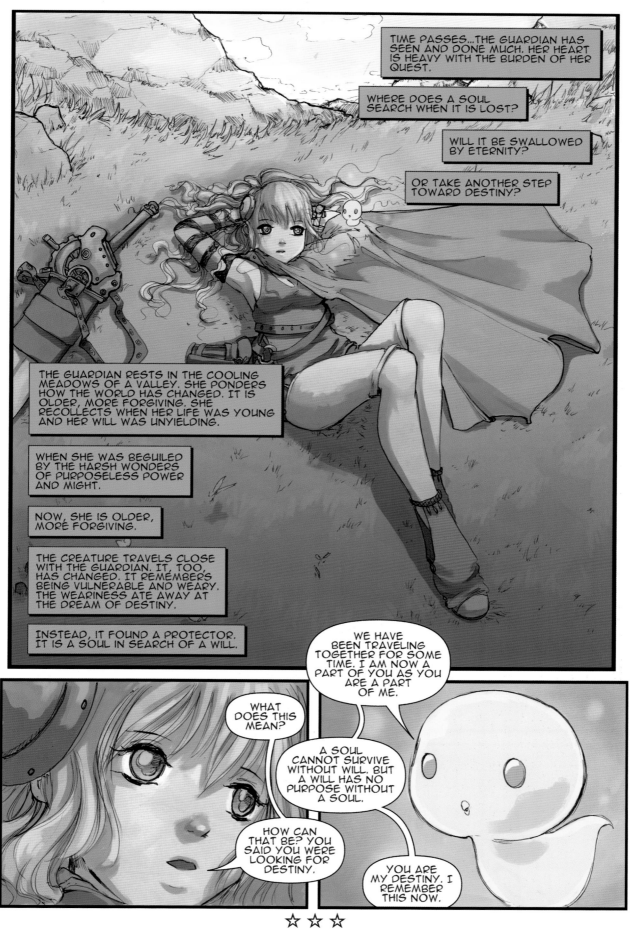

TIME PASSES...THE GUARDIAN HAS SEEN AND DONE MUCH. HER HEART IS HEAVY WITH THE BURDEN OF HER QUEST.

WHERE DOES A SOUL SEARCH WHEN IT IS LOST?

WILL IT BE SWALLOWED BY ETERNITY?

OR TAKE ANOTHER STEP TOWARD DESTINY?

THE GUARDIAN RESTS IN THE COOLING MEADOWS OF A VALLEY. SHE PONDERS HOW THE WORLD HAS CHANGED. IT IS OLDER, MORE FORGIVING. SHE RECOLLECTS WHEN HER LIFE WAS YOUNG AND HER WILL WAS UNYIELDING.

WHEN SHE WAS BEGUILED BY THE HARSH WONDERS OF PURPOSELESS POWER AND MIGHT.

NOW, SHE IS OLDER, MORE FORGIVING.

THE CREATURE TRAVELS CLOSE WITH THE GUARDIAN. IT, TOO, HAS CHANGED. IT REMEMBERS BEING VULNERABLE AND WEARY. THE WEARINESS ATE AWAY AT THE DREAM OF DESTINY.

INSTEAD, IT FOUND A PROTECTOR. IT IS A SOUL IN SEARCH OF A WILL.

WE HAVE BEEN TRAVELING TOGETHER FOR SOME TIME. I AM NOW A PART OF YOU AS YOU ARE A PART OF ME.

WHAT DOES THIS MEAN?

A SOUL CANNOT SURVIVE WITHOUT WILL. BUT A WILL HAS NO PURPOSE WITHOUT A SOUL.

HOW CAN THAT BE? YOU SAID YOU WERE LOOKING FOR DESTINY.

YOU ARE MY DESTINY. I REMEMBER THIS NOW.

★ ★ ☆

Meow!

It's moving. Circling us!

What do we do?

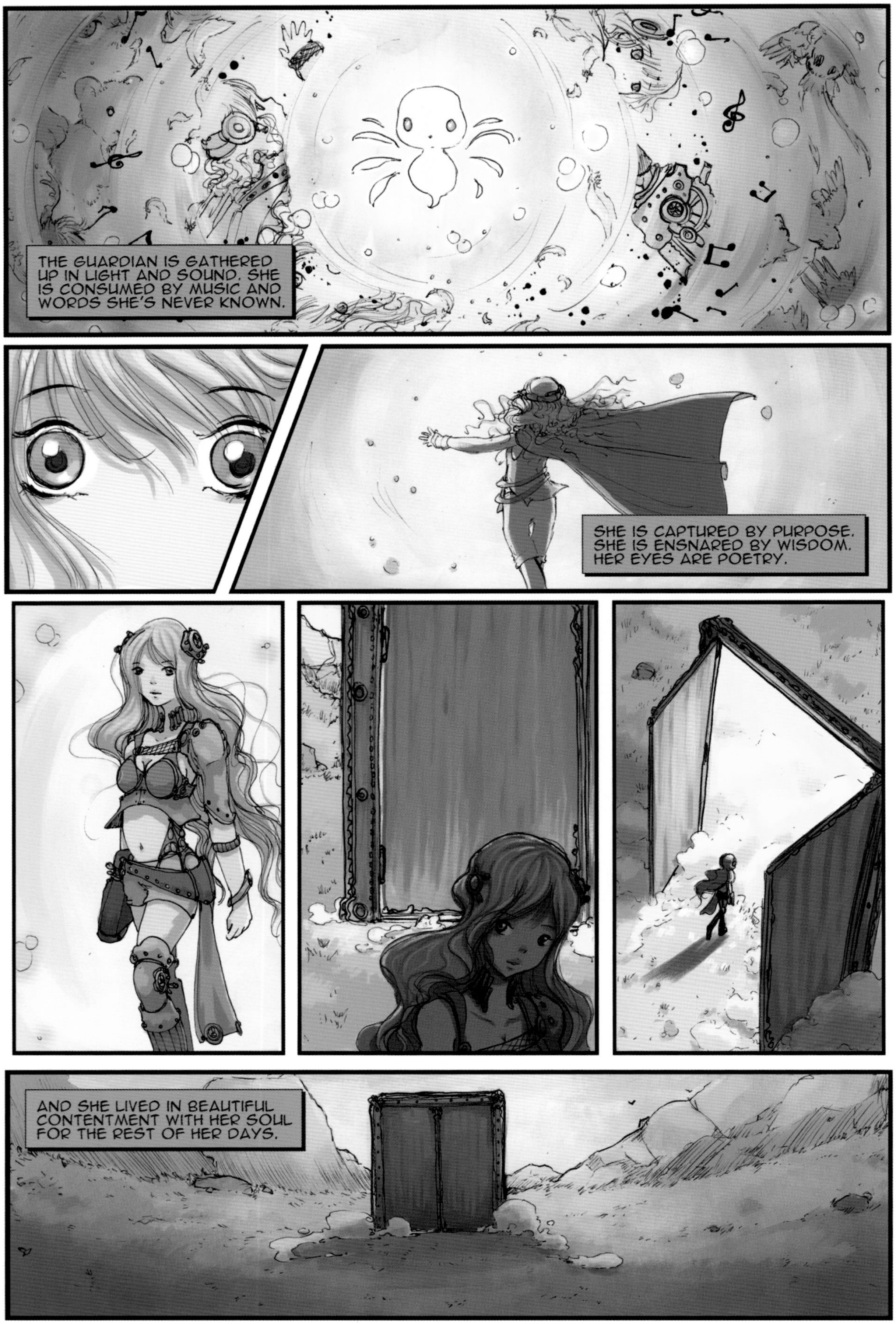
THE GUARDIAN IS GATHERED UP IN LIGHT AND SOUND. SHE IS CONSUMED BY MUSIC AND WORDS SHE'S NEVER KNOWN.
SHE IS CAPTURED BY PURPOSE. SHE IS ENSNARED BY WISDOM. HER EYES ARE POETRY.
AND SHE LIVED IN BEAUTIFUL CONTENTMENT WITH HER SOUL FOR THE REST OF HER DAYS.

☆ ☆ ☆

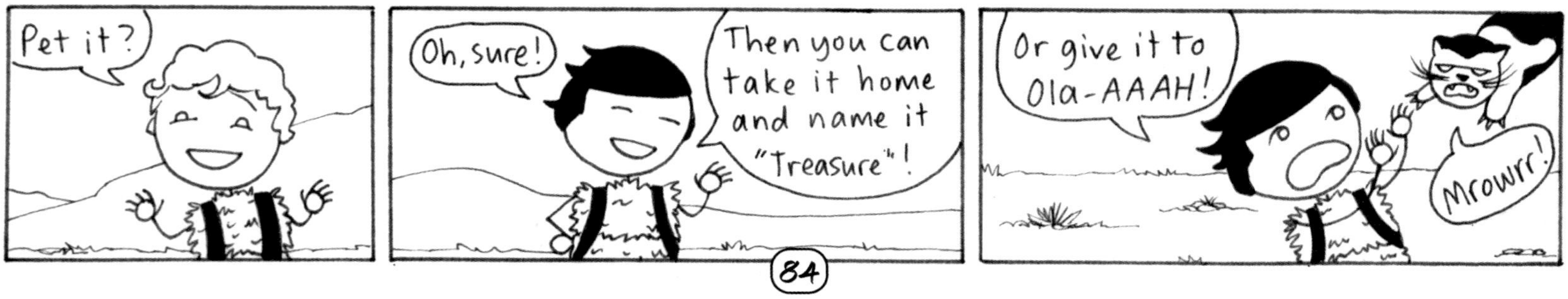
Pet it?
Oh, sure!
Then you can take it home and name it "Treasure"!
Or give it to Ola-AAAH!
Mrowrr!

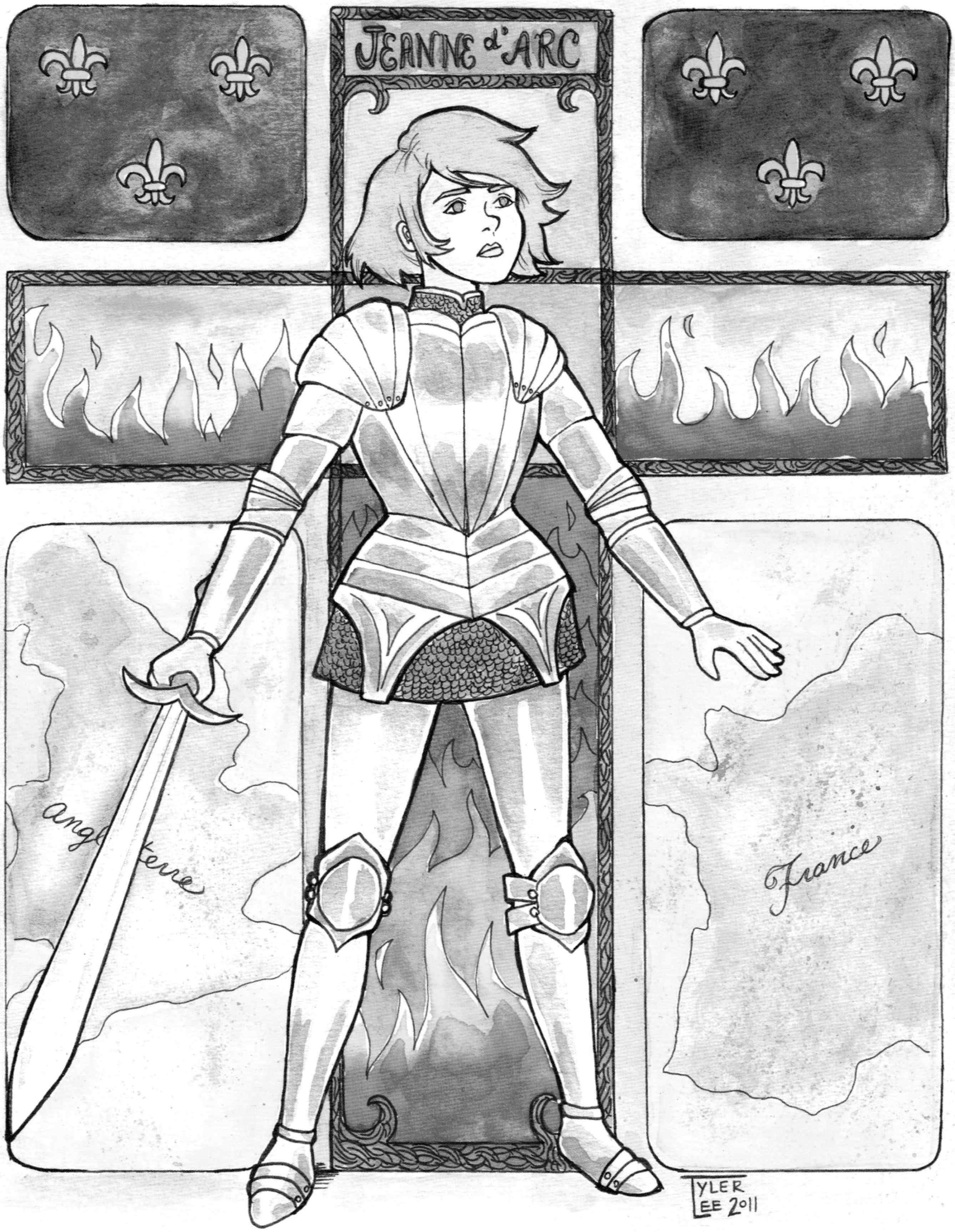
JEANNE d'ARC
angleterre
France
TYLER LEE 2011

☆ ☆ ☆

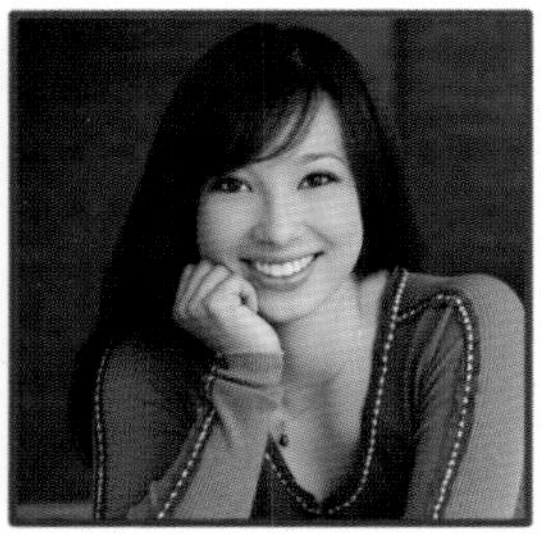

TYLER LEE

SKILLS: Penciller, Inker, Colorist
LOCATION: San Diego, CA
FUN FACT: Things I enjoy: comics, food, sleep, dinosaurs.

PRO TIP

HISTORY
BY GAIL SIMONE

"I HIGHLY RECOMMEND BUILDING UP A LIBRARY OF HISTORY BOOKS. GO TO THE CLOSE-OUT SALES TABLES AT BOOKSTORES AND BUY EVERY BOOK ON HISTORY YOU CAN. IF YOU CAN READ A GREAT BOOK ON HISTORY AND NOT COME UP WITH SOME BRILLIANT IDEAS, YOU MIGHT NOT BE CUT OUT TO BE A WRITER. ALSO, LEARN THE VALUE OF A SECOND DRAFT. READ THROUGH EVERY WORD, AND DEVELOP THE ABILITY TO CUT YOUR FAVORITE BITS IF THEY DETRACT FROM THE WHOLE."

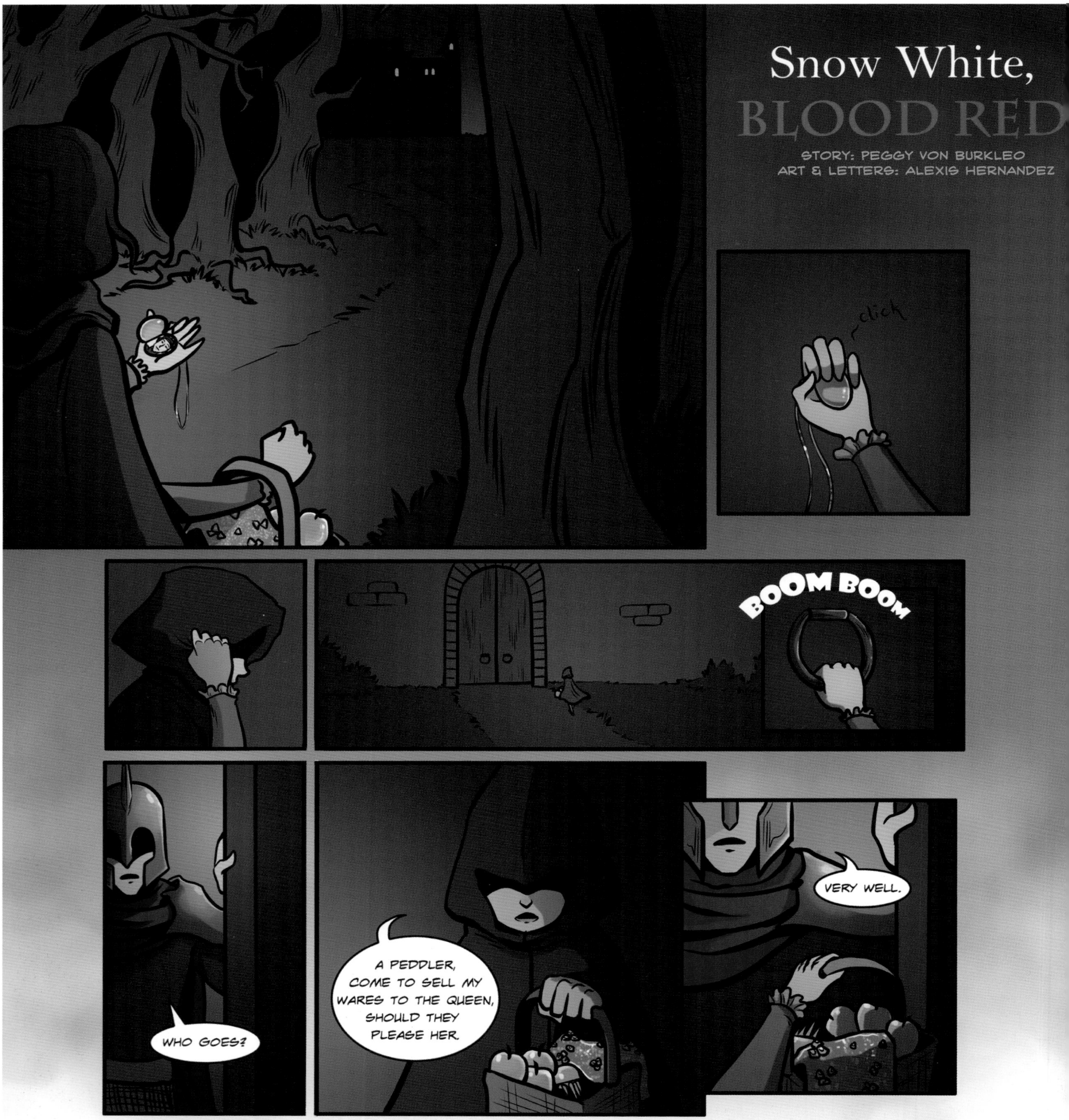

Snow White,
BLOOD RED
STORY: PEGGY VON BURKLEO
ART & LETTERS: ALEXIS HERNANDEZ
click
BOOM BOOM
WHO GOES?
A PEDDLER, COME TO SELL MY WARES TO THE QUEEN, SHOULD THEY PLEASE HER.
VERY WELL.

☆☆☆

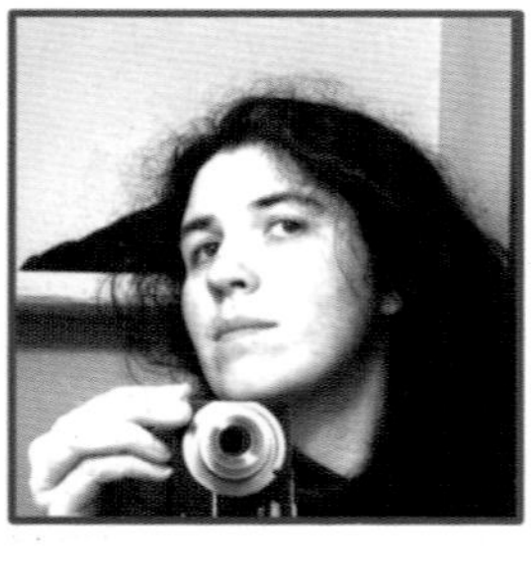

PEGGY VON BURKLEO

SKILLS: Writer
LOCATION: California
FUN FACT: I love bad jokes and puns!

http://samhainnight.com

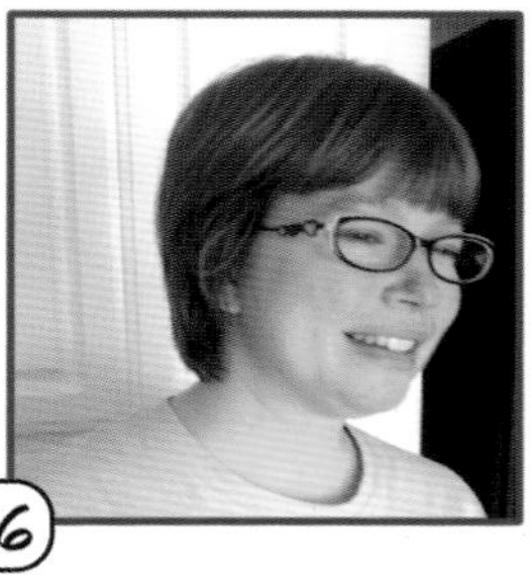

ALEXIS HERNANDEZ

SKILLS: Penciler, Inker and Colorist
LOCATION: California
FUN FACT: I used to wash dogs to pay the bills. I discovered that dogs are rarely thrilled about having a stranger bathe them. Not that I blame them, that would be weird.

www.glowingraptor.com

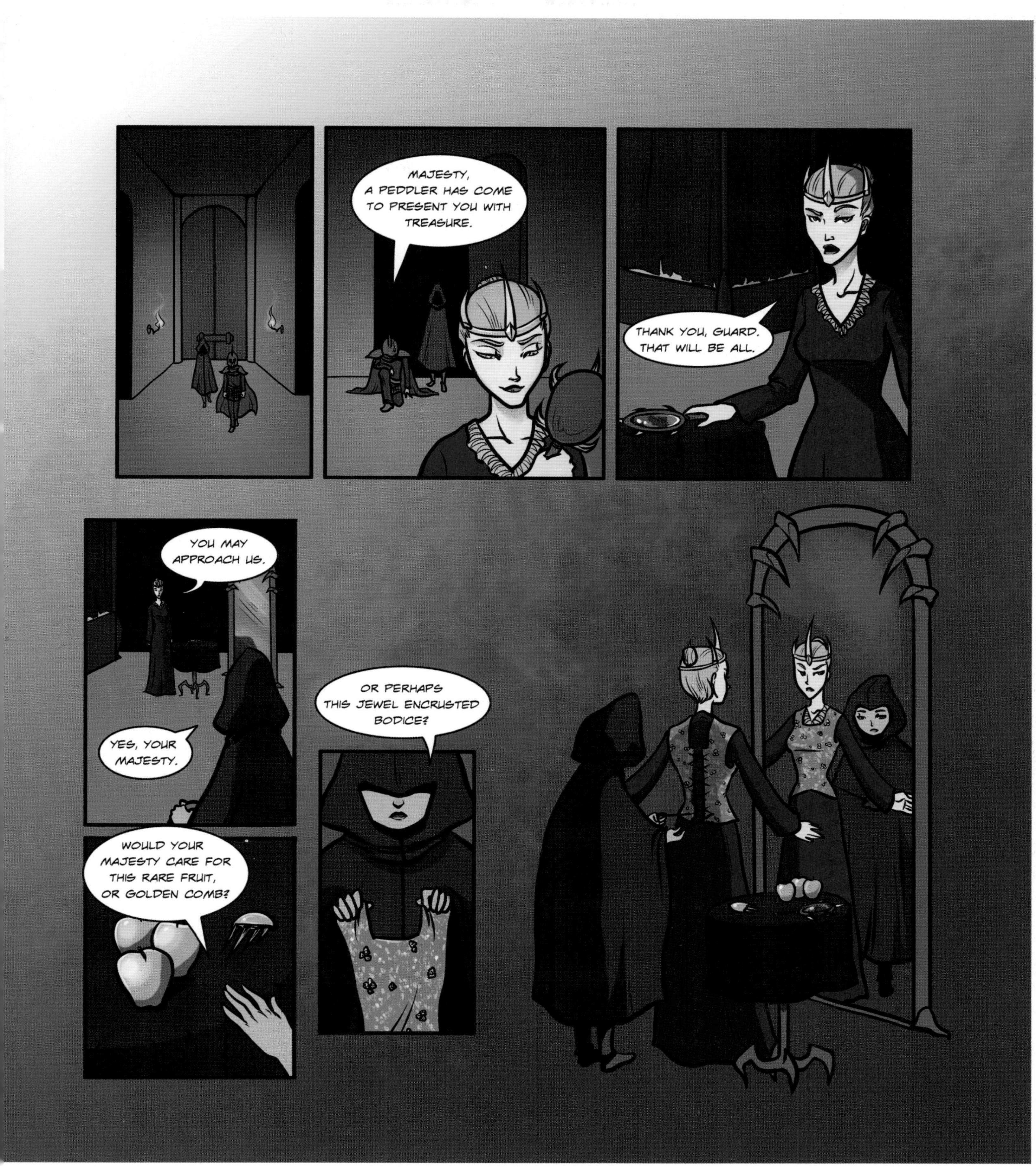
MAJESTY, A PEDDLER HAS COME TO PRESENT YOU WITH TREASURE.
THANK YOU, GUARD. THAT WILL BE ALL.
YOU MAY APPROACH US.
YES, YOUR MAJESTY.
WOULD YOUR MAJESTY CARE FOR THIS RARE FRUIT, OR GOLDEN COMB?
OR PERHAPS THIS JEWEL ENCRUSTED BODICE?

☆ ☆ ☆

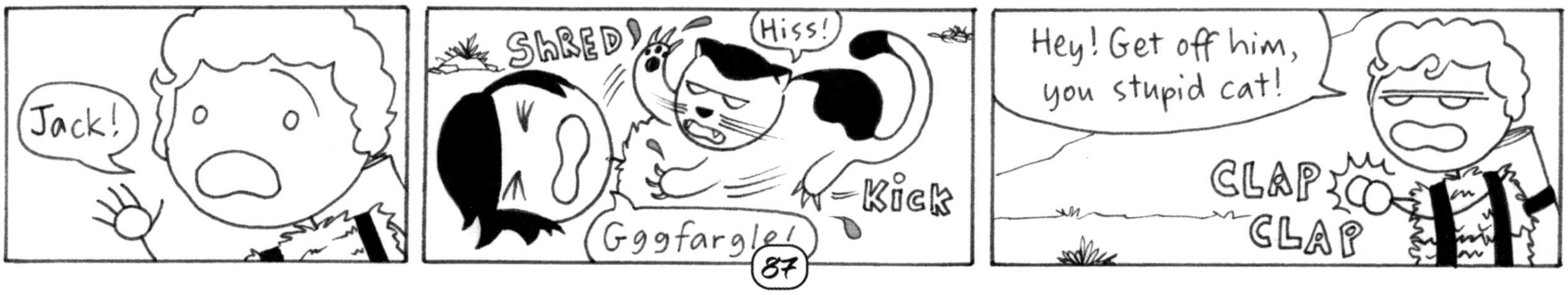
Jack!
SHRED
Hiss!
Kick
Gggfargle!
Hey! Get off him, you stupid cat!
CLAP
CLAP

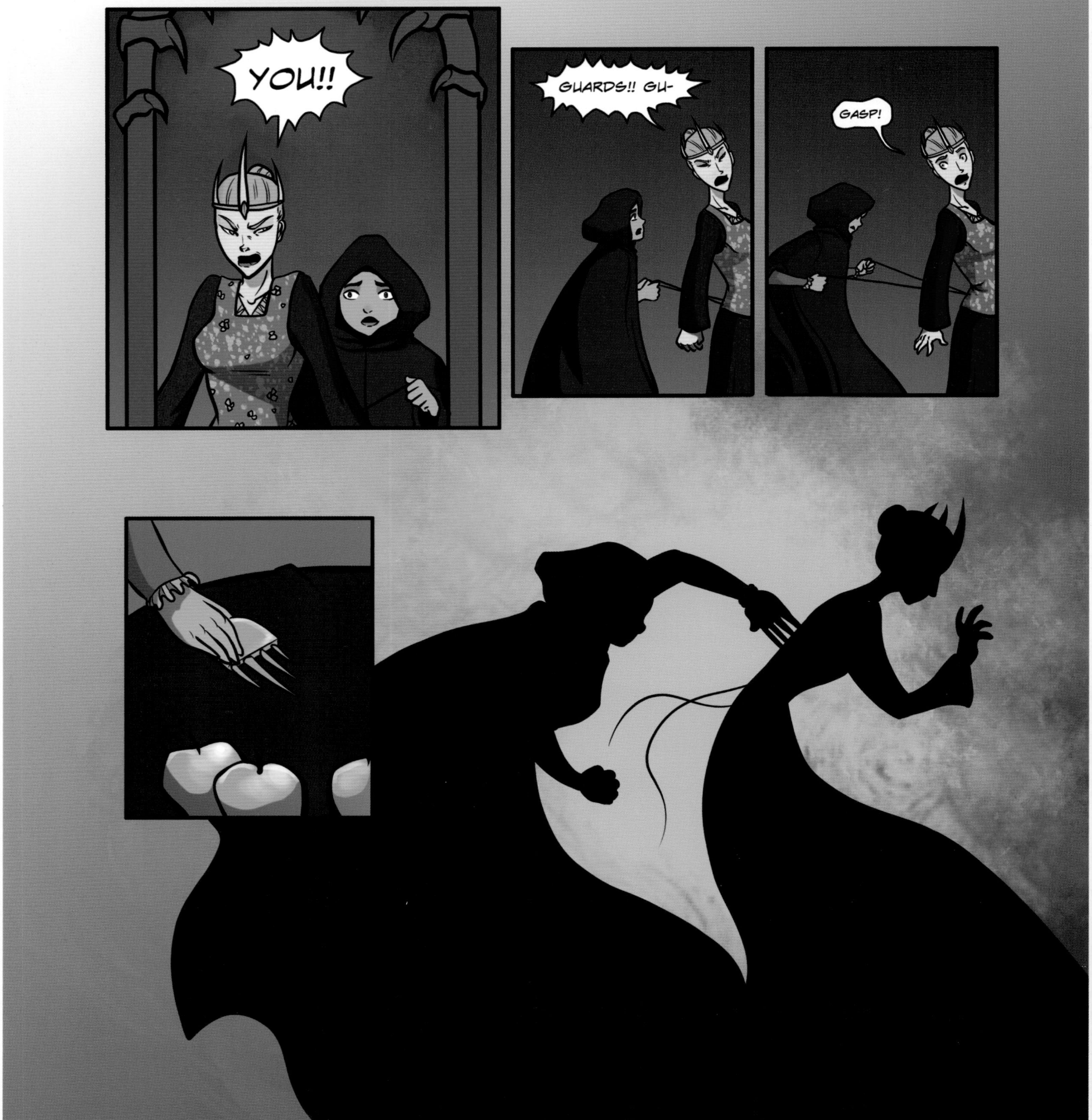
YOU!!
GUARDS!! GU-
GASP!

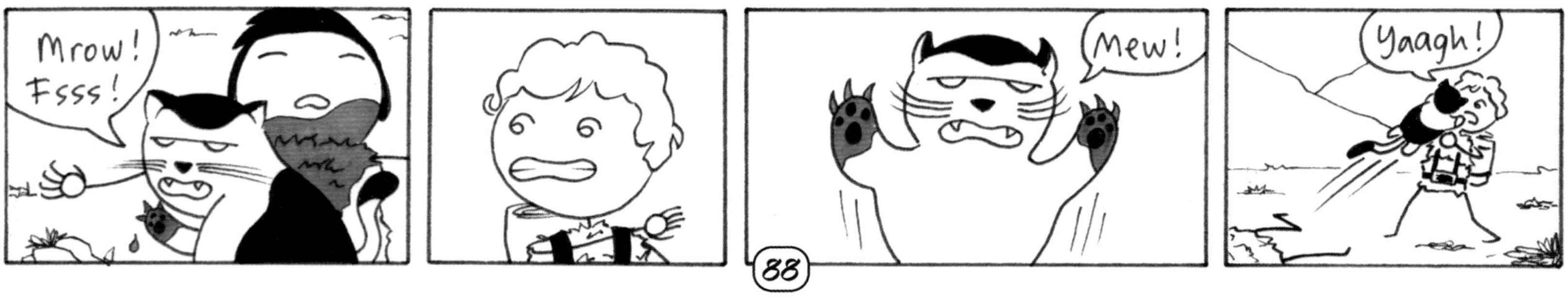
Mrow! Fsss!
Mew!
Yaagh!

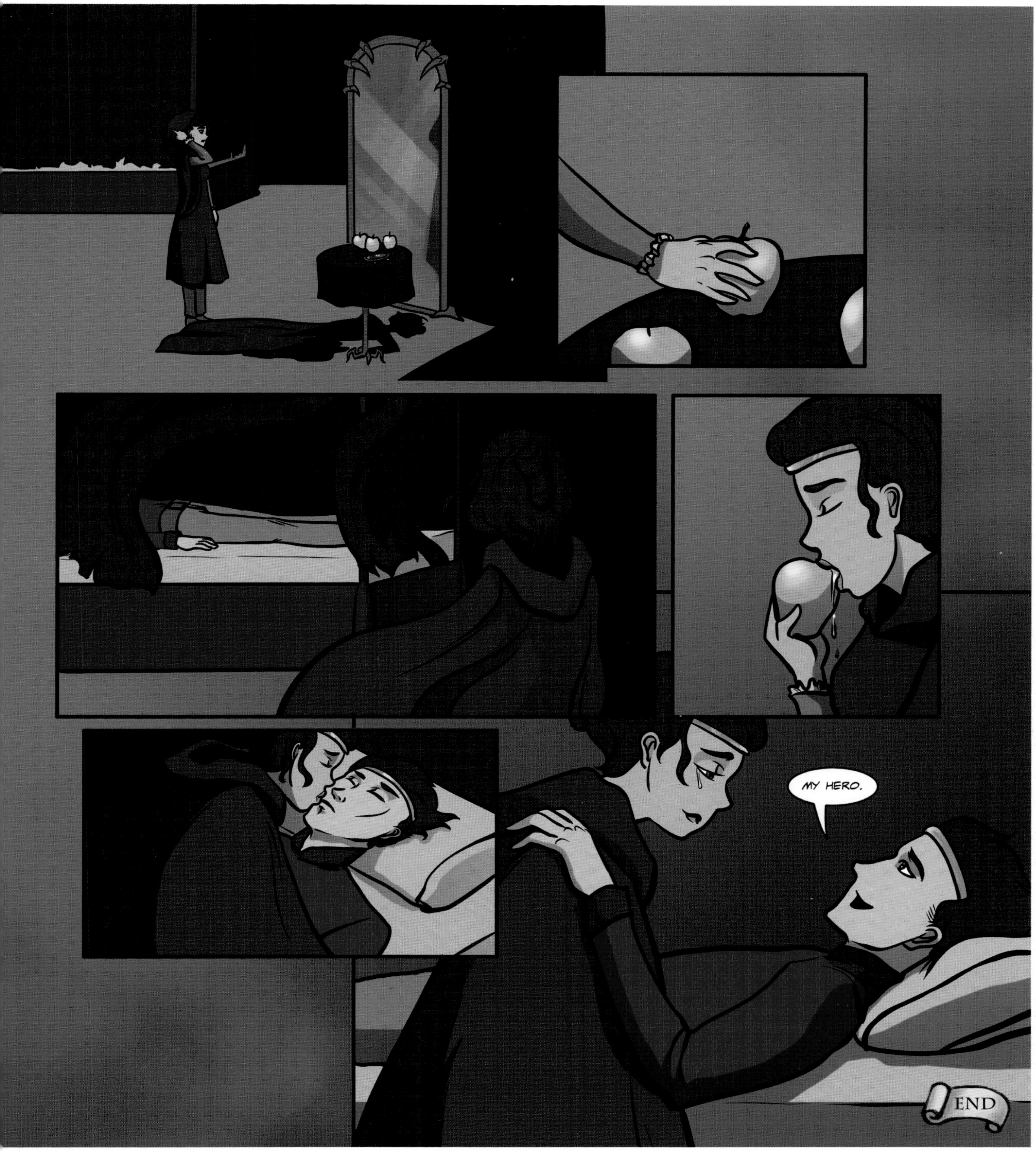
MY HERO.
END

☆ ☆ ☆

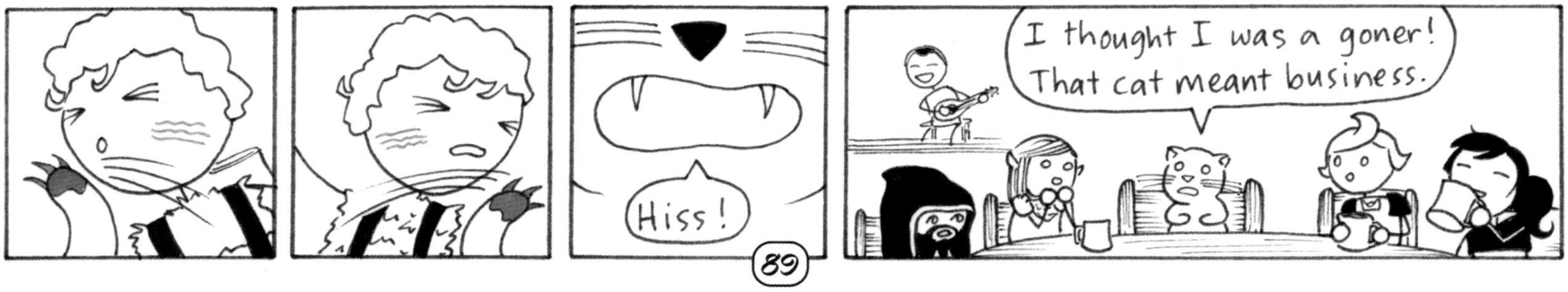
Hiss!
I thought I was a goner! That cat meant business.

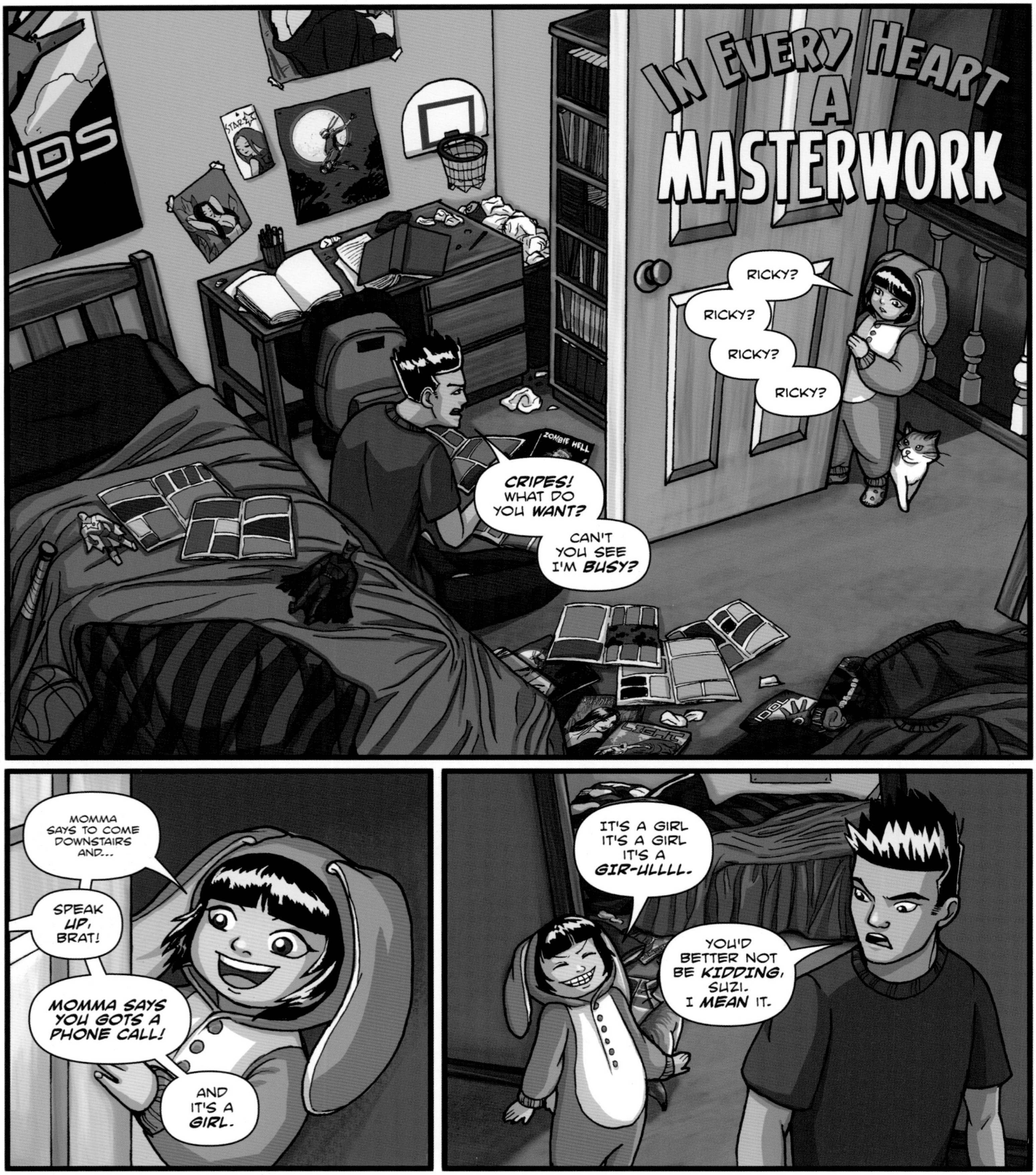
IN EVERY HEART A MASTERWORK
RICKY?
RICKY?
RICKY?
RICKY?
ZOMBIE HELL
CRIPES! WHAT DO YOU WANT?
CAN'T YOU SEE I'M BUSY?
MOMMA SAYS TO COME DOWNSTAIRS AND...
SPEAK UP, BRAT!
MOMMA SAYS YOU GOTS A PHONE CALL!
AND IT'S A GIRL.
IT'S A GIRL IT'S A GIRL IT'S A GIR-ULLLL.
YOU'D BETTER NOT BE KIDDING, SUZI. I MEAN IT.

WRITER: GAIL SIMONE ART: JEAN KANG LETTERS: RACHEL DEERING

☆ ☆ ☆

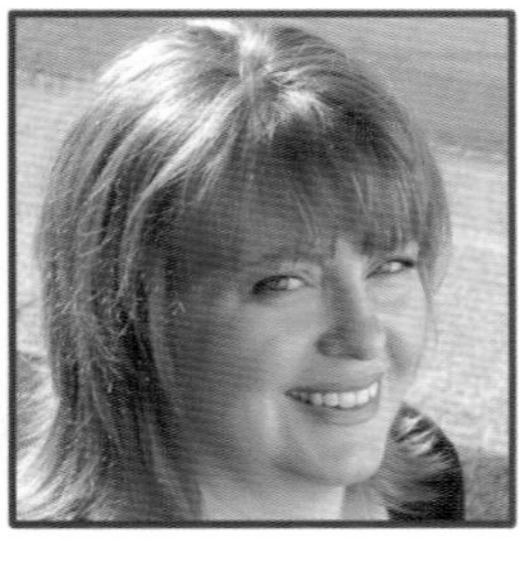

GAIL SIMONE

SKILLS: Writer
LOCATION: Oregon
FUN FACT: I am allergic to everything fun.

www.tumblr.com/tumblelog/gailsimone

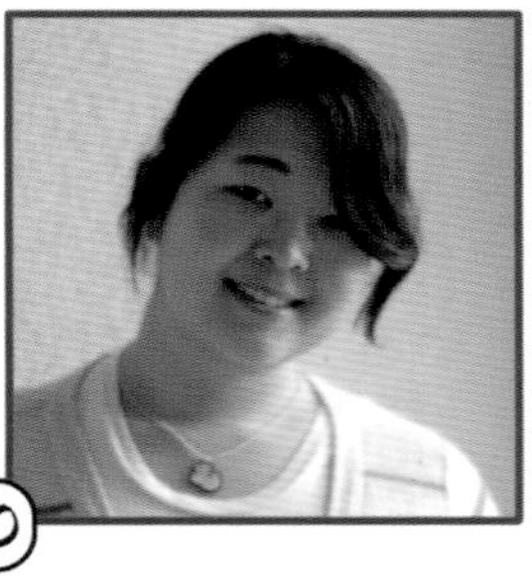

JEAN KANG

SKILLS: Penciller, Inker, Colorist
LOCATION: Los Angeles, CA
FUN FACT: I didn't get into mainstream American comics till my early 20s and now I'm completely obsessed!

www.jeandrawsstuff.co

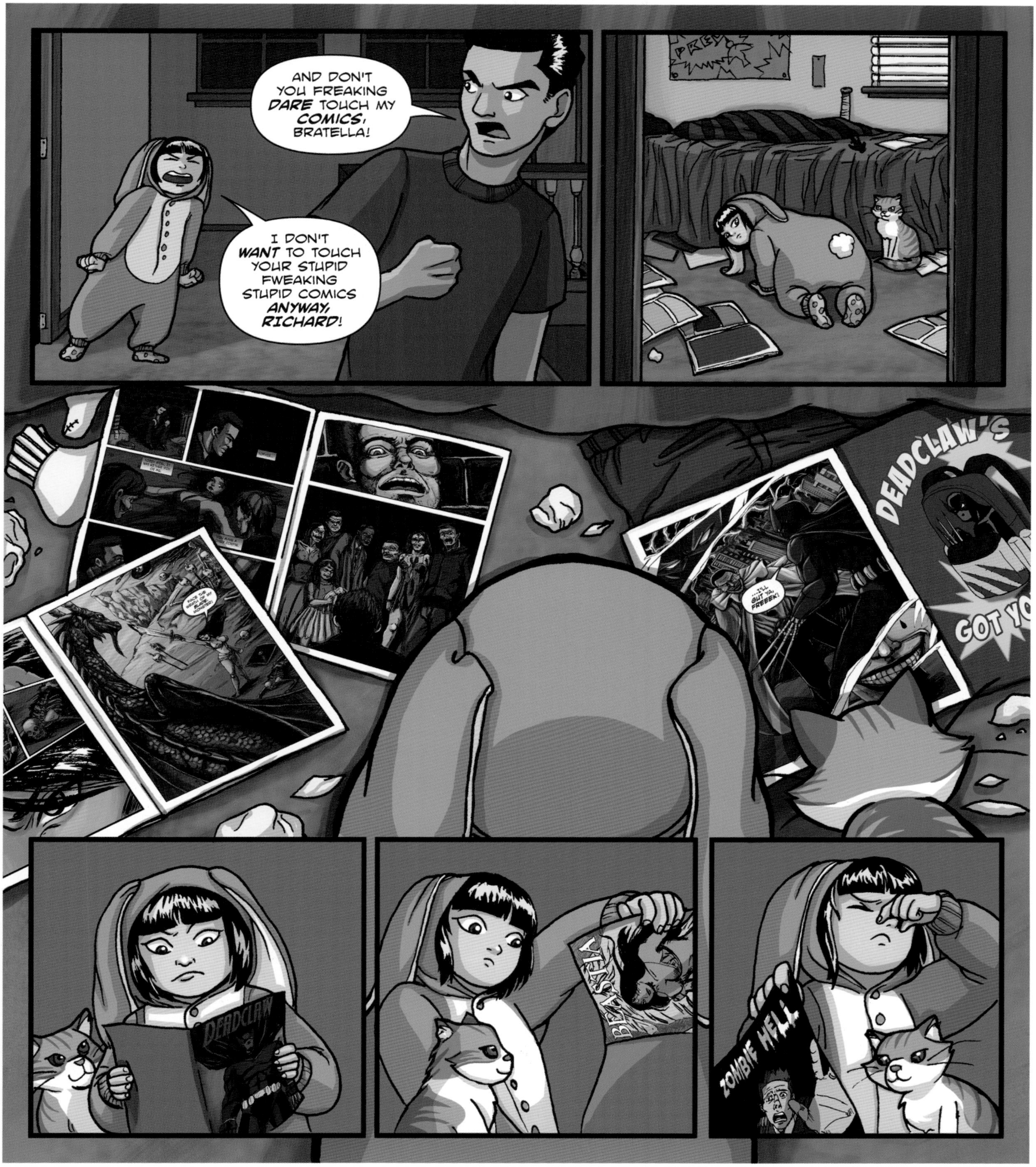
AND DON'T YOU FREAKING DARE TOUCH MY COMICS, BRATELLA!
I DON'T WANT TO TOUCH YOUR STUPID FWEAKING STUPID COMICS ANYWAY, RICHARD!
FACE THE WRATH OF MY BLADE, MONSTER!
...I'LL GUT YA, FREEEK!
DEADCLAW'S
GOT YO
DEADCLAW
ZOMBIE HELL!

☆ ☆ ☆

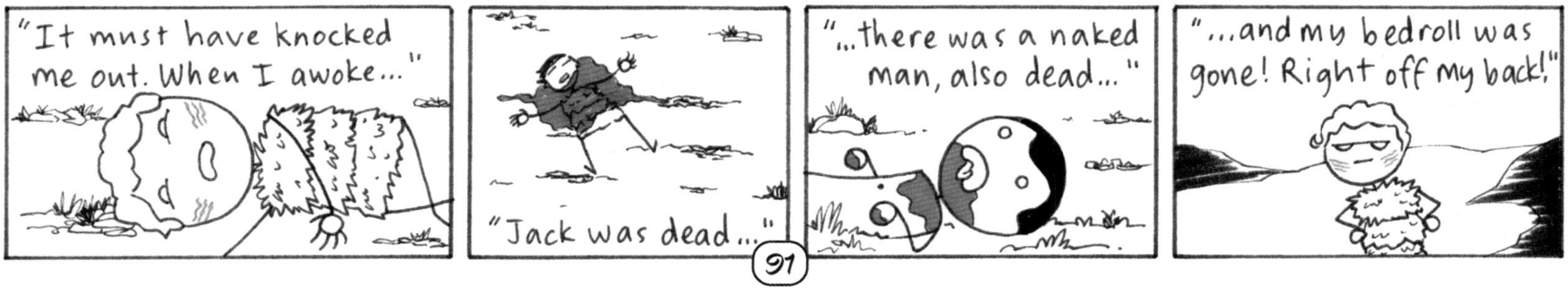
"It must have knocked me out. When I awoke..."
"Jack was dead..."
"...there was a naked man, also dead..."
"...and my bedroll was gone! Right off my back!"

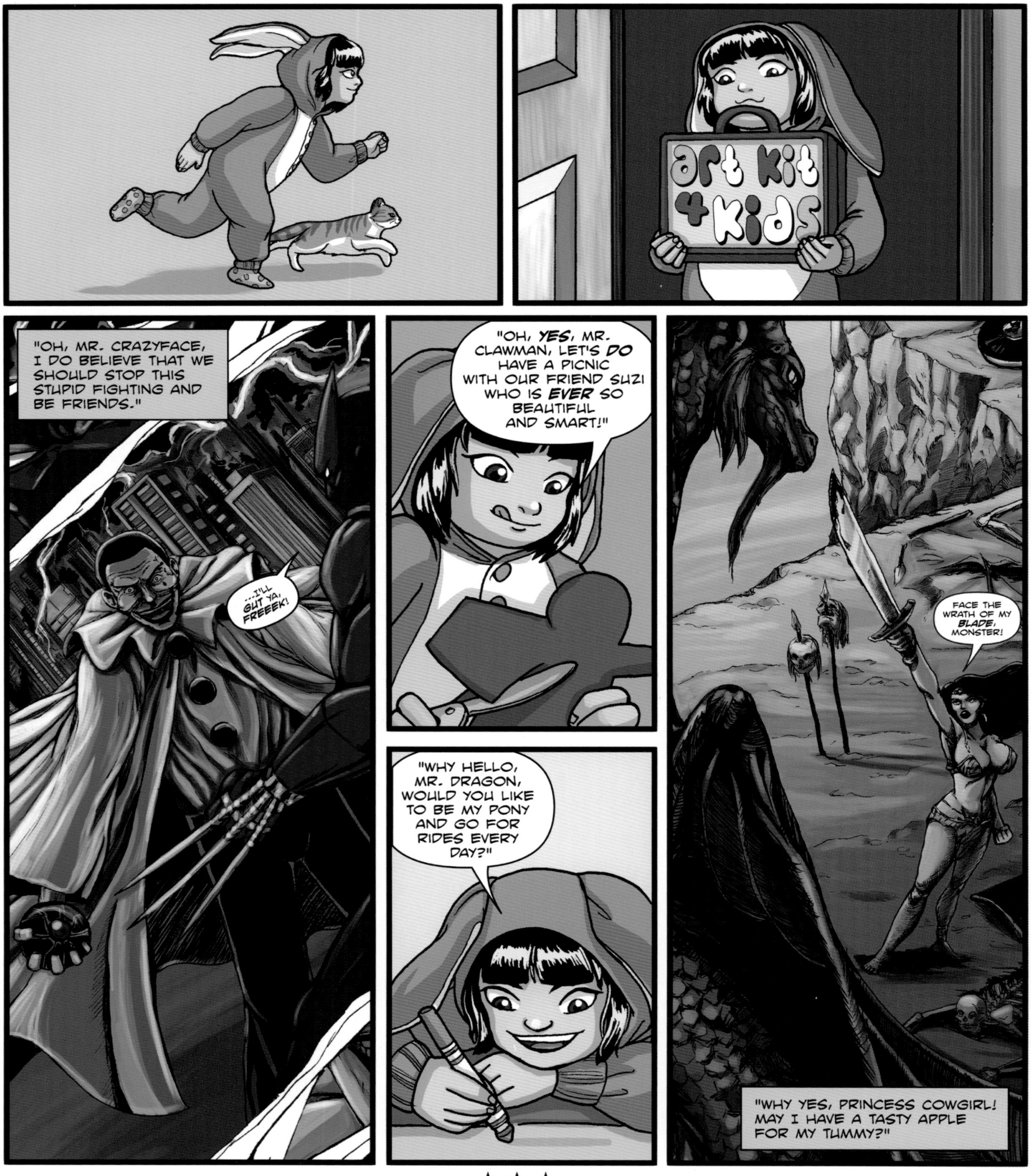
art kit 4 kids
"OH, MR. CRAZYFACE, I DO BELIEVE THAT WE SHOULD STOP THIS STUPID FIGHTING AND BE FRIENDS."
...I'LL GUT YA, FREEEK!
"OH, YES, MR. CLAWMAN, LET'S DO HAVE A PICNIC WITH OUR FRIEND SUZI WHO IS EVER SO BEAUTIFUL AND SMART!"
"WHY HELLO, MR. DRAGON, WOULD YOU LIKE TO BE MY PONY AND GO FOR RIDES EVERY DAY?"
FACE THE WRATH OF MY BLADE, MONSTER!
"WHY YES, PRINCESS COWGIRL! MAY I HAVE A TASTY APPLE FOR MY TUMMY?"

☆ ☆ ☆

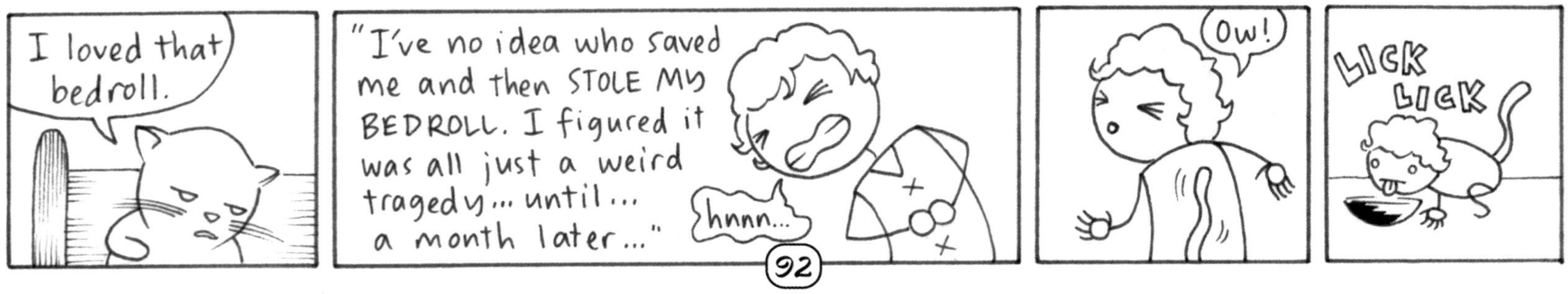
I loved that bedroll.
"I've no idea who saved me and then STOLE MY BEDROLL. I figured it was all just a weird tragedy... until... a month later..."
hnnn...
Ow!
LICK LICK

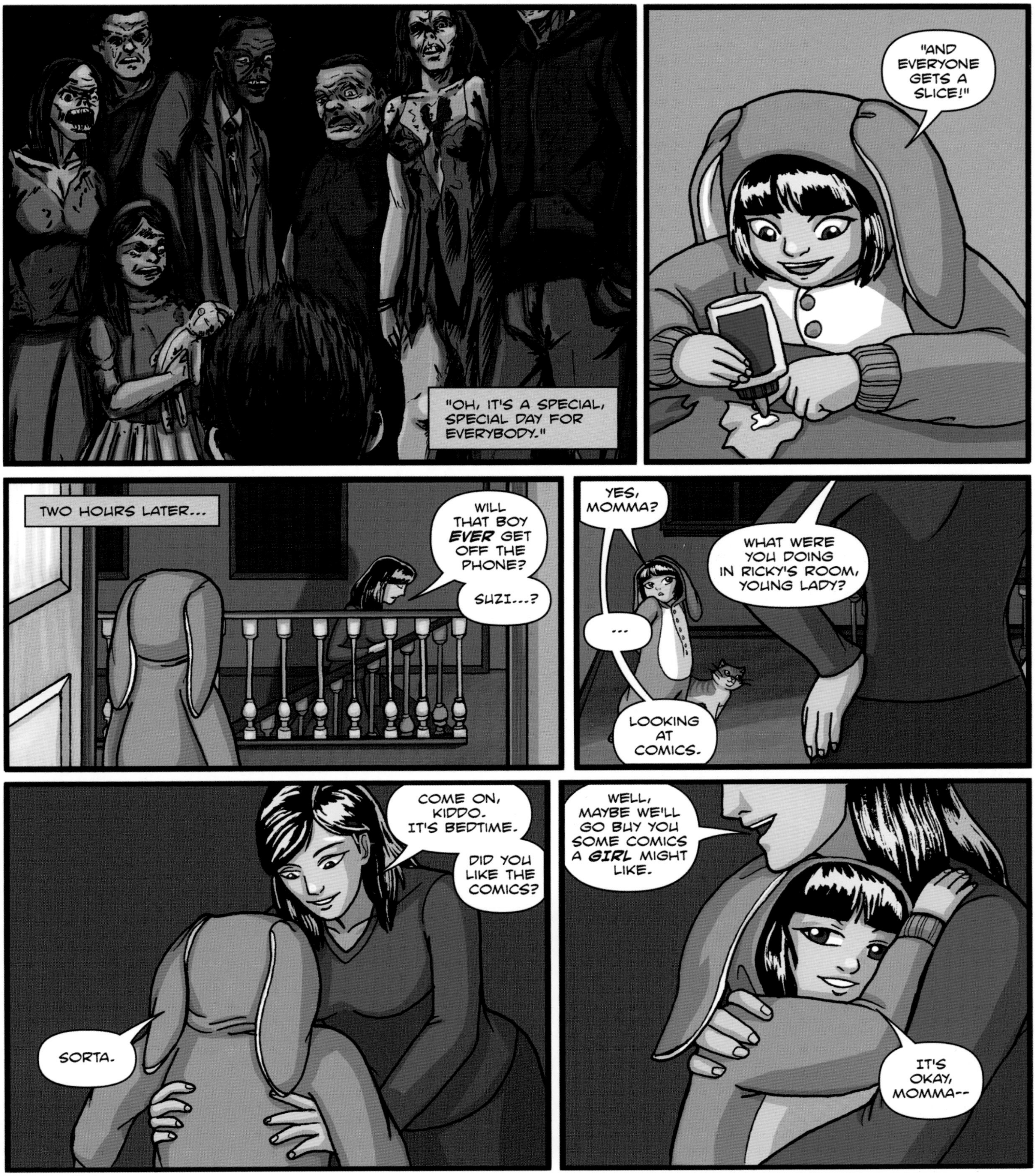
"OH, IT'S A SPECIAL, SPECIAL DAY FOR EVERYBODY."
"AND EVERYONE GETS A SLICE!"
TWO HOURS LATER...
WILL THAT BOY **EVER** GET OFF THE PHONE?
SUZI...?
YES, MOMMA?
WHAT WERE YOU DOING IN RICKY'S ROOM, YOUNG LADY?
...
LOOKING AT COMICS.
COME ON, KIDDO. IT'S BEDTIME.
DID YOU LIKE THE COMICS?
SORTA.
WELL, MAYBE WE'LL GO BUY YOU SOME COMICS A **GIRL** MIGHT LIKE.
IT'S OKAY, MOMMA--

☆ ☆ ☆

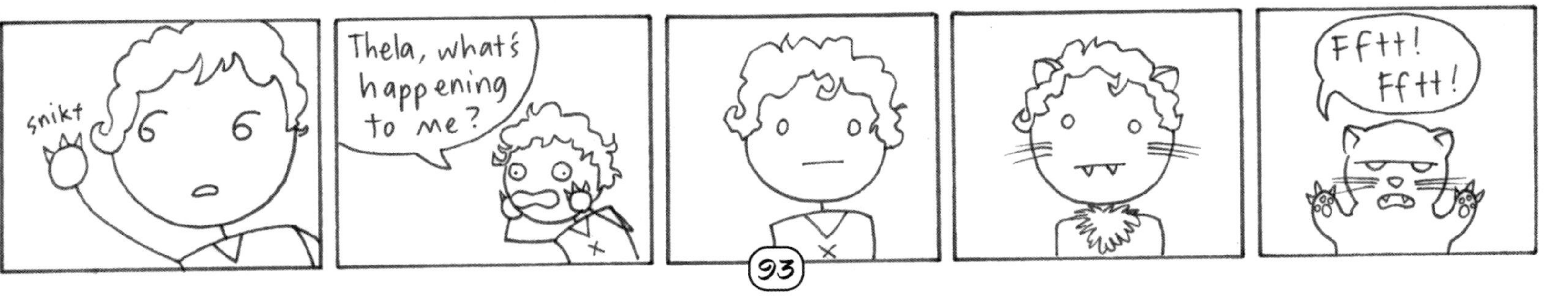
snikt
Thela, what's happening to me?
Fftt! Fftt!

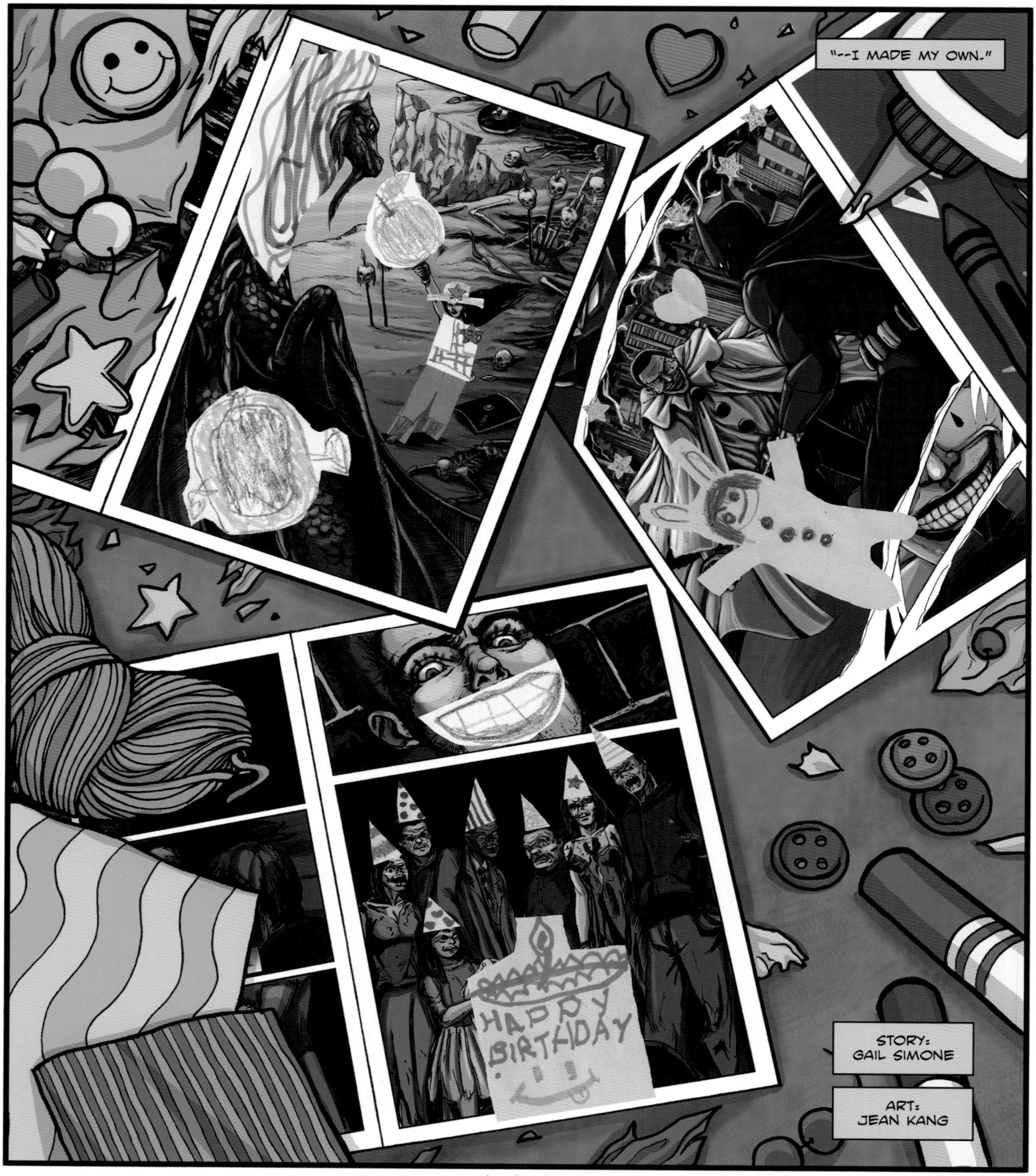
"--I MADE MY OWN."
HAPPY BIRTHDAY
STORY: GAIL SIMONE
ART: JEAN KANG

☆☆☆

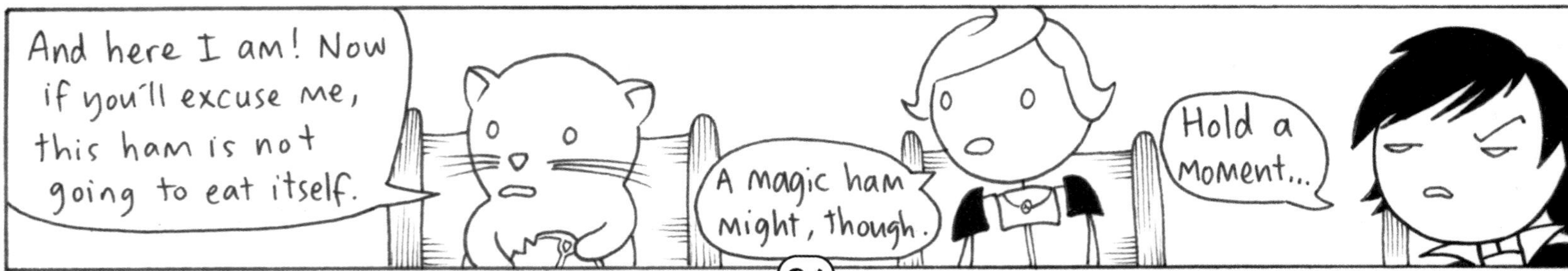
And here I am! Now if you'll excuse me, this ham is not going to eat itself.
A magic ham might, though.
Hold a moment...

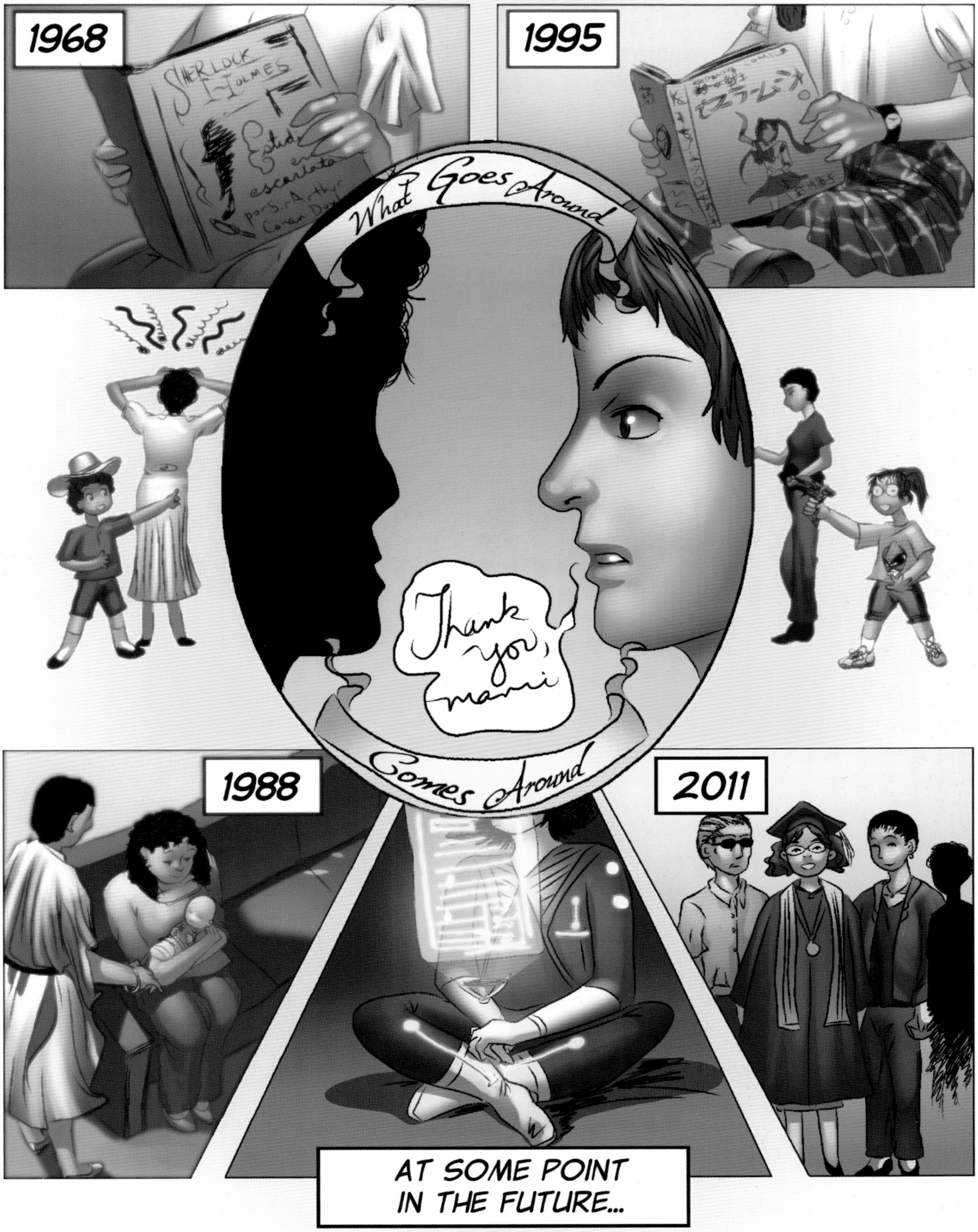
1968
1995
What Goes Around
Thank you, mami
Comes Around
1988
2011
AT SOME POINT IN THE FUTURE...

☆☆☆

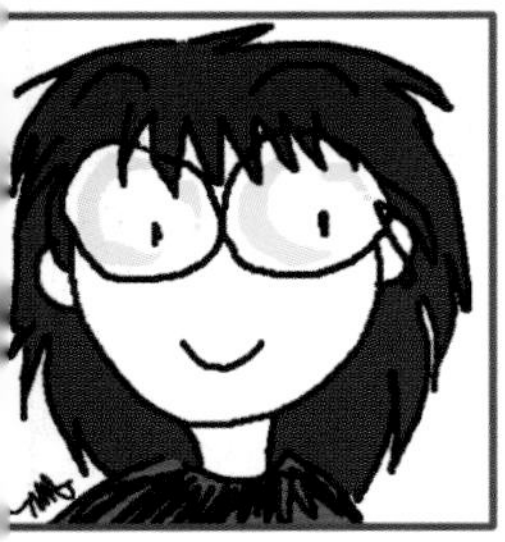

NAAN

SKILLS: Penciller, Inker, Letterer
LOCATION: Iowa
FUN FACT: I am the plainest person in existence :D

revolutionmillennium.comicdish.com

PRO TIP

GUTTERS

BY BARBARA KAALBERG

"THE SPACES BETWEEN PANELS ON A COMIC PAGE ARE CALLED 'GUTTERS.'"

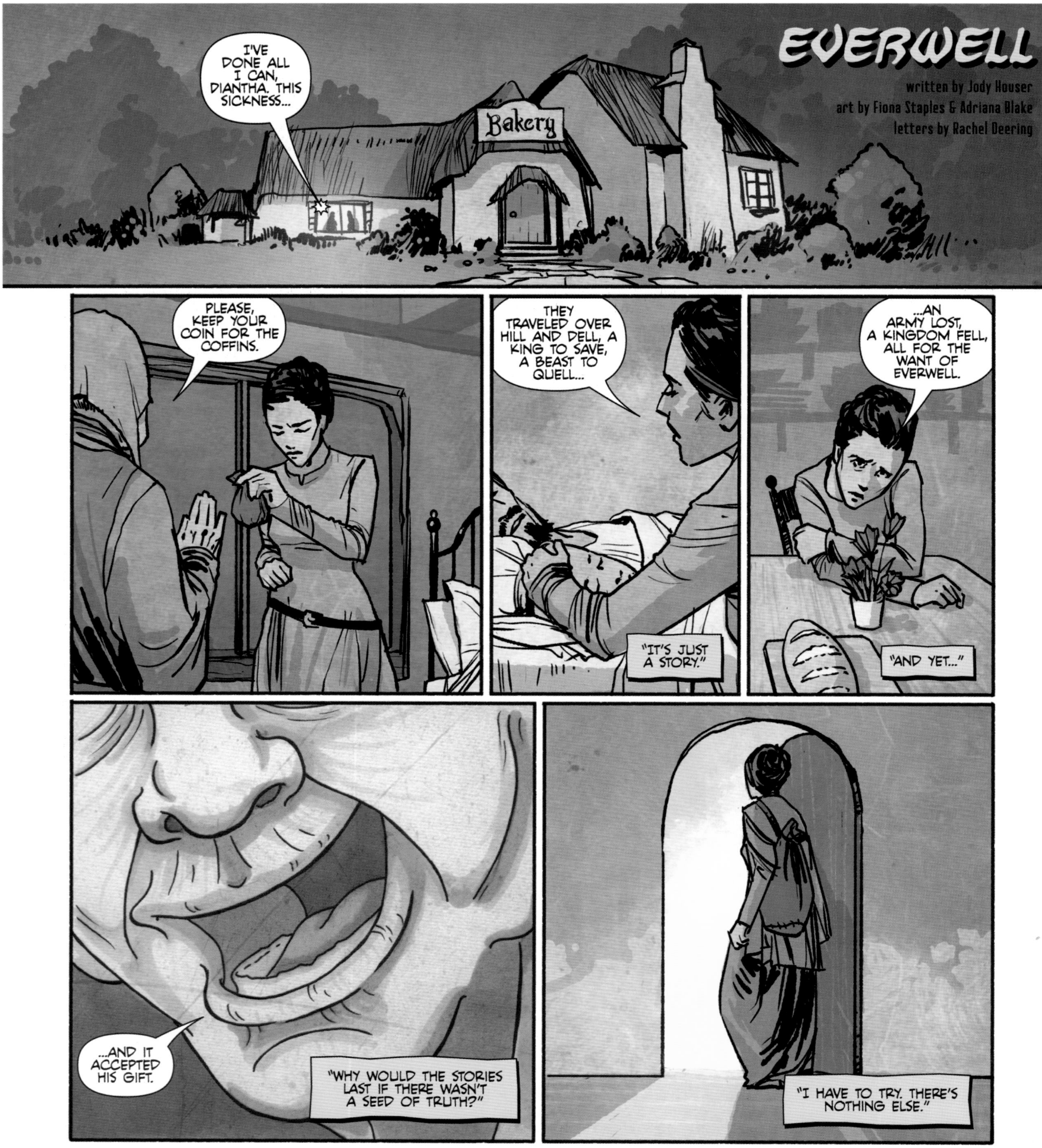
EVERWELL
written by Jody Houser
art by Fiona Staples & Adriana Blake
letters by Rachel Deering
I'VE DONE ALL I CAN, DIANTHA. THIS SICKNESS...
Bakery
PLEASE, KEEP YOUR COIN FOR THE COFFINS.
THEY TRAVELED OVER HILL AND DELL, A KING TO SAVE, A BEAST TO QUELL...
"IT'S JUST A STORY."
...AN ARMY LOST, A KINGDOM FELL, ALL FOR THE WANT OF EVERWELL.
"AND YET..."
...AND IT ACCEPTED HIS GIFT.
"WHY WOULD THE STORIES LAST IF THERE WASN'T A SEED OF TRUTH?"
"I HAVE TO TRY. THERE'S NOTHING ELSE."

☆ ☆ ☆

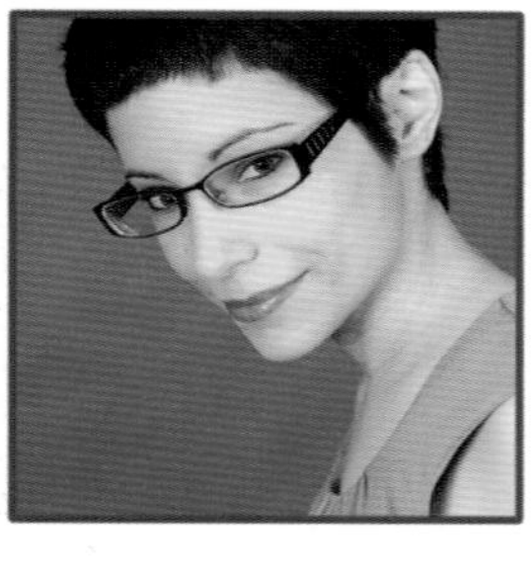

JODY HOUSER

SKILLS: Writer
LOCATION: Los Angeles
FUN FACT: I also write screenplays and create webcomics about things like bricks and cupcakes.

MindEclipse.com

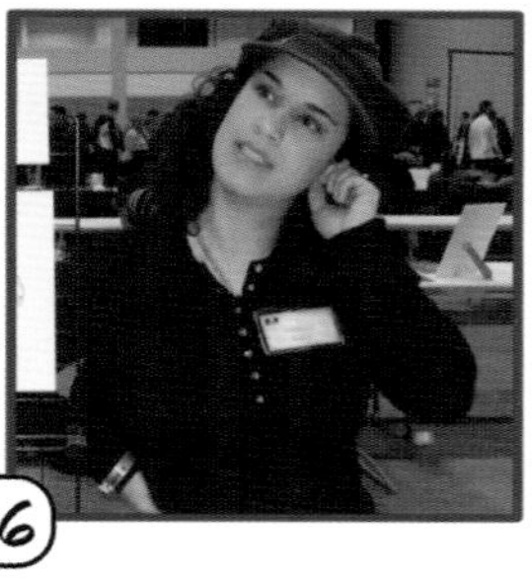

ADRIANA BLAKE

SKILLS: Penciller, Inker, and Colorist
LOCATION: Ontario, Canada
FUN FACT: Born in Venezuela, lived in the US for almost 10 years, and now living in Canada!

www.littleteacup.net

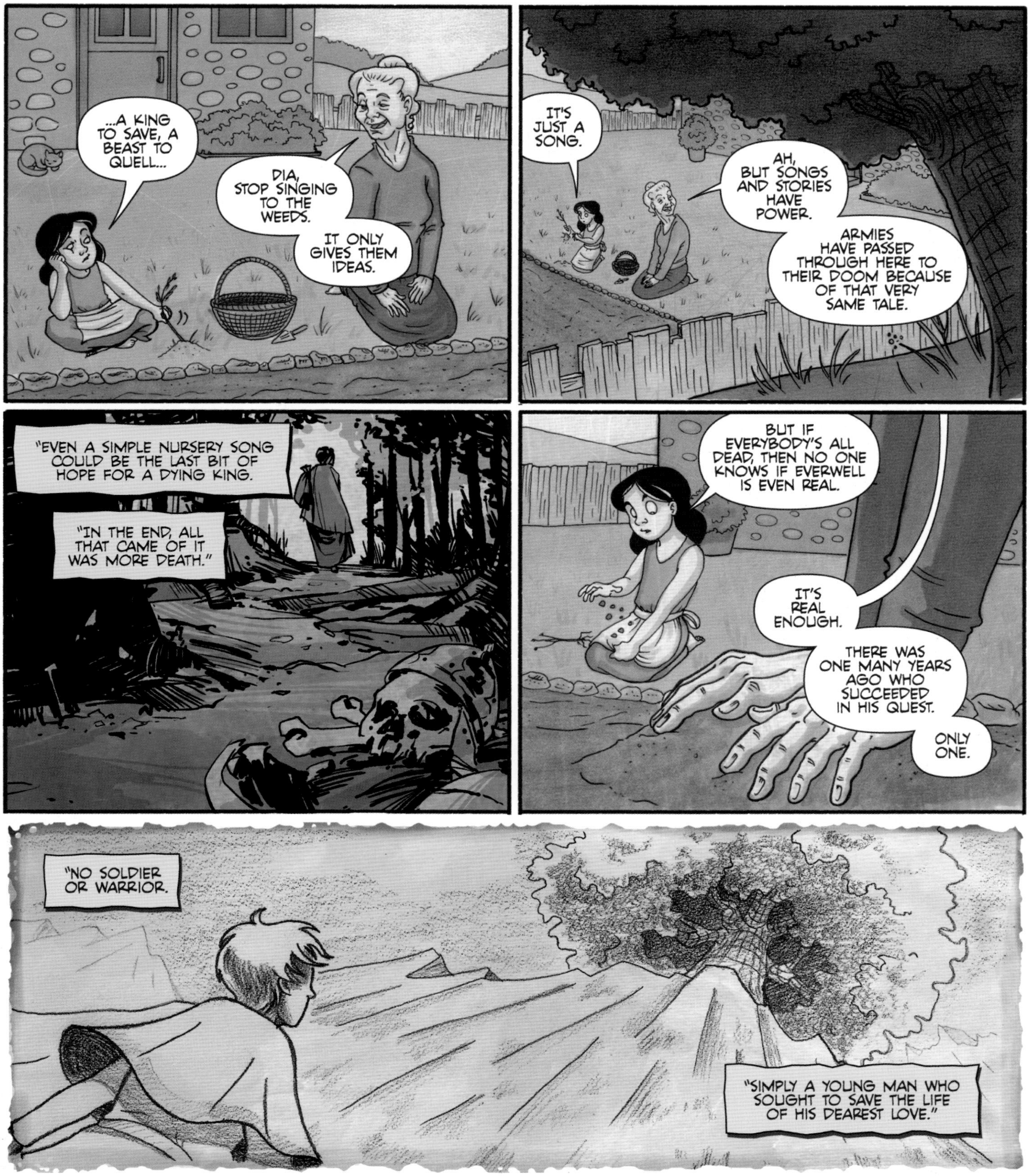
...A KING TO SAVE, A BEAST TO QUELL...
DIA, STOP SINGING TO THE WEEDS.
IT ONLY GIVES THEM IDEAS.
IT'S JUST A SONG.
AH, BUT SONGS AND STORIES HAVE POWER.
ARMIES HAVE PASSED THROUGH HERE TO THEIR DOOM BECAUSE OF THAT VERY SAME TALE.
"EVEN A SIMPLE NURSERY SONG COULD BE THE LAST BIT OF HOPE FOR A DYING KING.
"IN THE END, ALL THAT CAME OF IT WAS MORE DEATH."
BUT IF EVERYBODY'S ALL DEAD, THEN NO ONE KNOWS IF EVERWELL IS EVEN REAL.
IT'S REAL ENOUGH.
THERE WAS ONE MANY YEARS AGO WHO SUCCEEDED IN HIS QUEST.
ONLY ONE.
"NO SOLDIER OR WARRIOR.
"SIMPLY A YOUNG MAN WHO SOUGHT TO SAVE THE LIFE OF HIS DEAREST LOVE."

☆ ☆ ☆

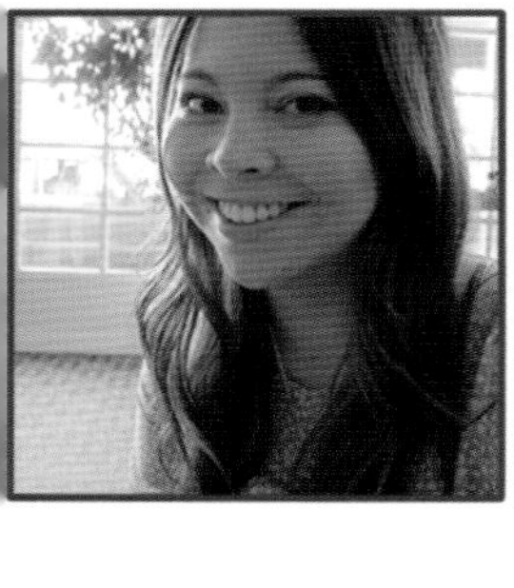

FIONA STAPLES

SKILLS: Artist
LOCATION: Canada
FUN FACT: I love dim sum and Archie comics.

www.fionastaples.com

PRO TIP

EDITORS
BY ROBIN FURTH

"GOOD EDITORS ARE WORTH THEIR WEIGHT IN GOLD! THEY CAN REALLY HELP YOU HONE YOUR WORK. IN MY EXPERIENCE, A GOOD EDITOR IS AN ARTISTIC COLLABORATOR."

SHE WAS GRAVELY ILL WHEN THE YOUNG MAN HEARD A TALE OF A CERTAIN FLOWER, MAGICAL AND VERY RARE.

A FLOWER SAID TO BE SO POTENT THAT A SINGLE PETAL COULD CURE ANY AILMENT.

"IT WAS A BRUTAL JOURNEY FOR AN ARMY WELL TRAINED AND OUTFITTED WITH SUPPLIES."

"FOR A LONE TRAVELER, IT MEANT ALMOST CERTAIN DEATH."

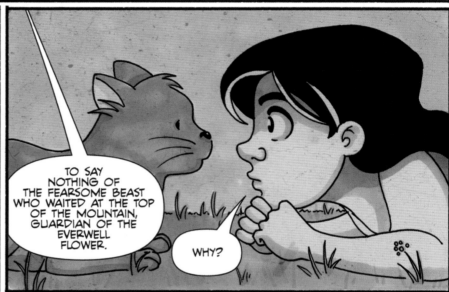

TO SAY NOTHING OF THE FEARSOME BEAST WHO WAITED AT THE TOP OF THE MOUNTAIN, GUARDIAN OF THE EVERWELL FLOWER.

WHY?

"NOT EVERYTHING HAS A WHY THAT WE CAN UNDERSTAND. IT SIMPLY DOES AS IT DOES."

DID HE... FIGHT IT?

A CREATURE THAT SLAUGHTERED ARMIES?

LOVE HADN'T MADE HIM *THAT* FOOLISH.

☆ ☆ ☆

None of that explains why you never change back to human form.

Or why you've never tried to kill any of us.

Truth.

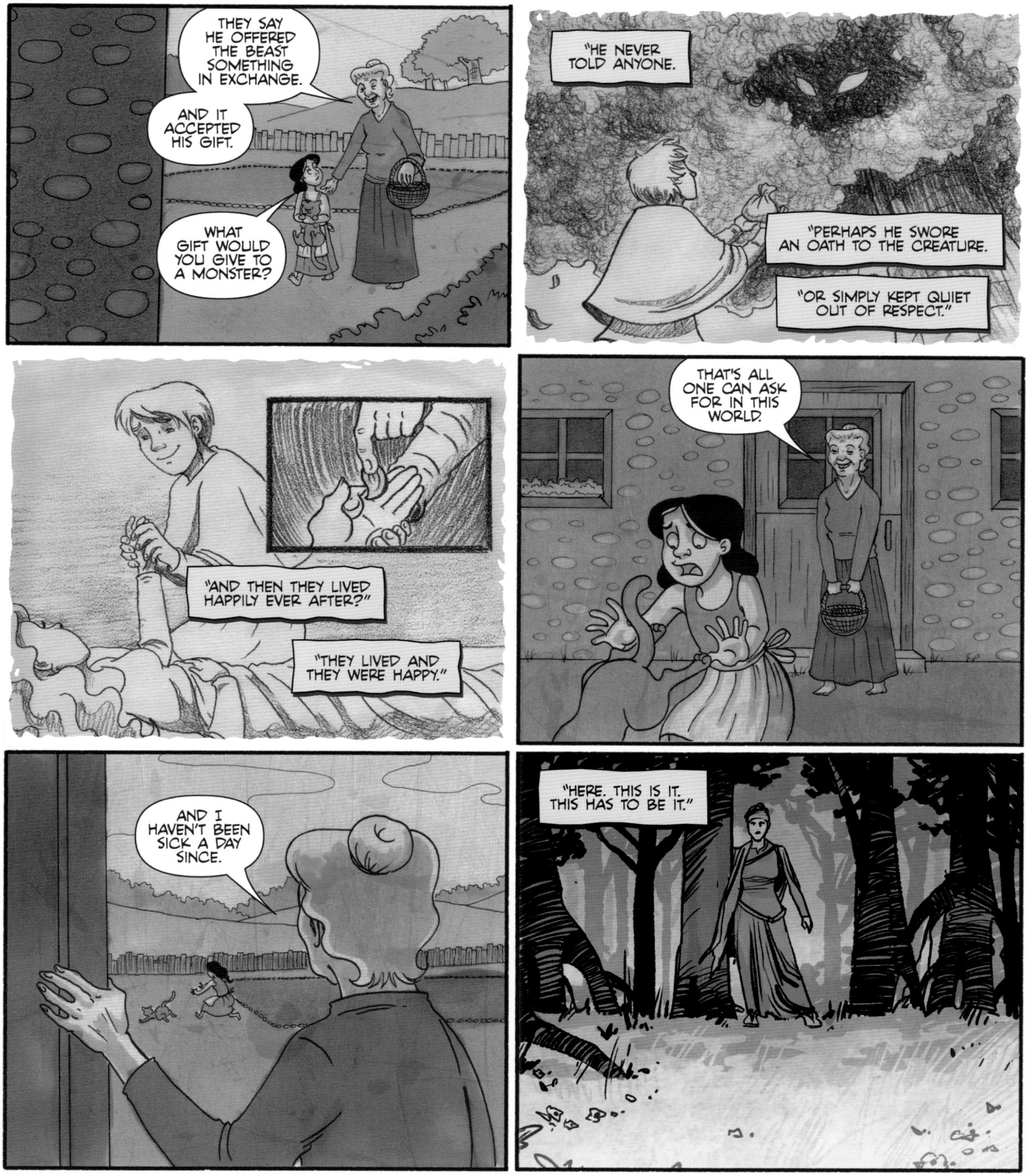
THEY SAY HE OFFERED THE BEAST SOMETHING IN EXCHANGE.
AND IT ACCEPTED HIS GIFT.
WHAT GIFT WOULD YOU GIVE TO A MONSTER?
"HE NEVER TOLD ANYONE.
"PERHAPS HE SWORE AN OATH TO THE CREATURE.
"OR SIMPLY KEPT QUIET OUT OF RESPECT."
"AND THEN THEY LIVED HAPPILY EVER AFTER?"
"THEY LIVED AND THEY WERE HAPPY."
THAT'S ALL ONE CAN ASK FOR IN THIS WORLD.
AND I HAVEN'T BEEN SICK A DAY SINCE.
"HERE. THIS IS IT. THIS HAS TO BE IT."

☆ ☆ ☆

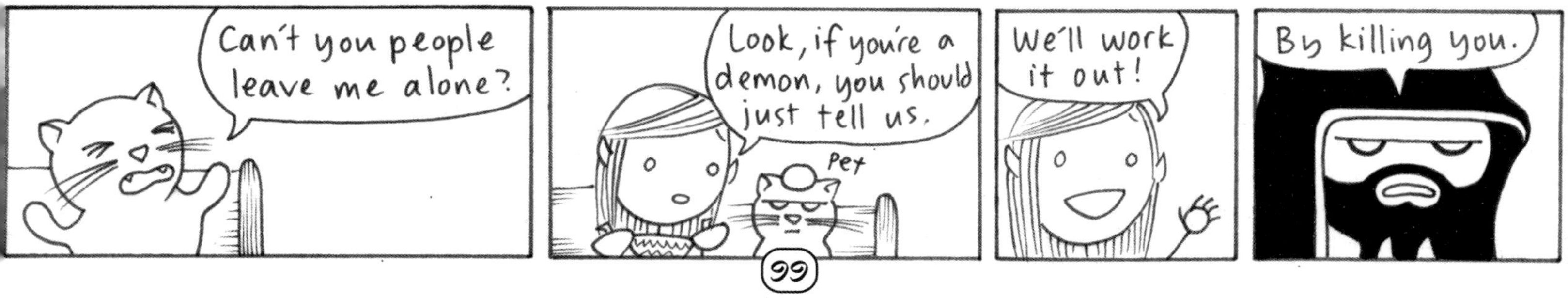
Can't you people leave me alone?
Look, if you're a demon, you should just tell us.
Pet
We'll work it out!
By killing you.

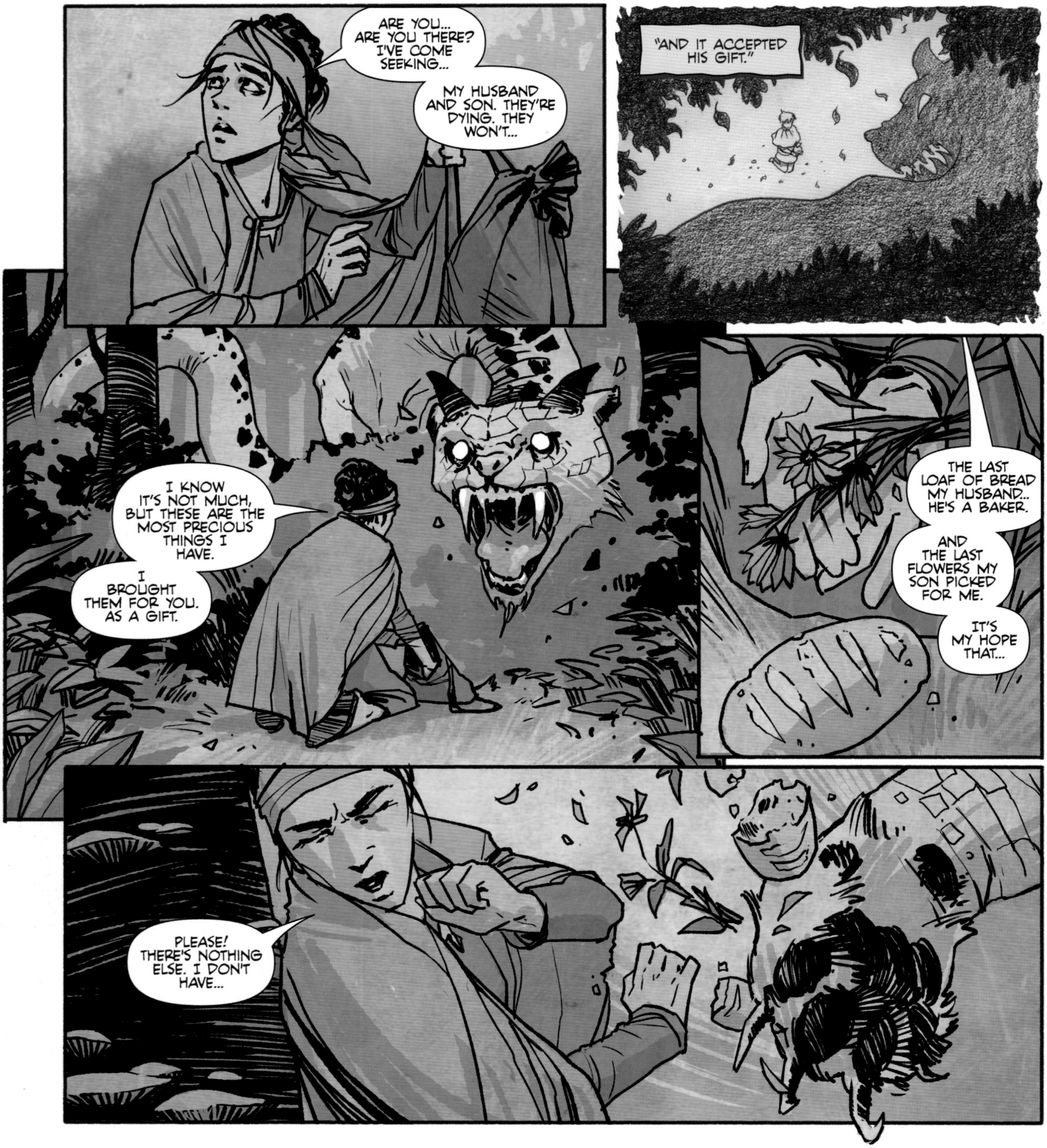
ARE YOU... ARE YOU THERE? I'VE COME SEEKING...
MY HUSBAND AND SON. THEY'RE DYING. THEY WON'T...
"AND IT ACCEPTED HIS GIFT."
I KNOW IT'S NOT MUCH, BUT THESE ARE THE MOST PRECIOUS THINGS I HAVE.
I BROUGHT THEM FOR YOU. AS A GIFT.
THE LAST LOAF OF BREAD MY HUSBAND... HE'S A BAKER.
AND THE LAST FLOWERS MY SON PICKED FOR ME.
IT'S MY HOPE THAT...
PLEASE! THERE'S NOTHING ELSE. I DON'T HAVE...

☆ ☆ ☆

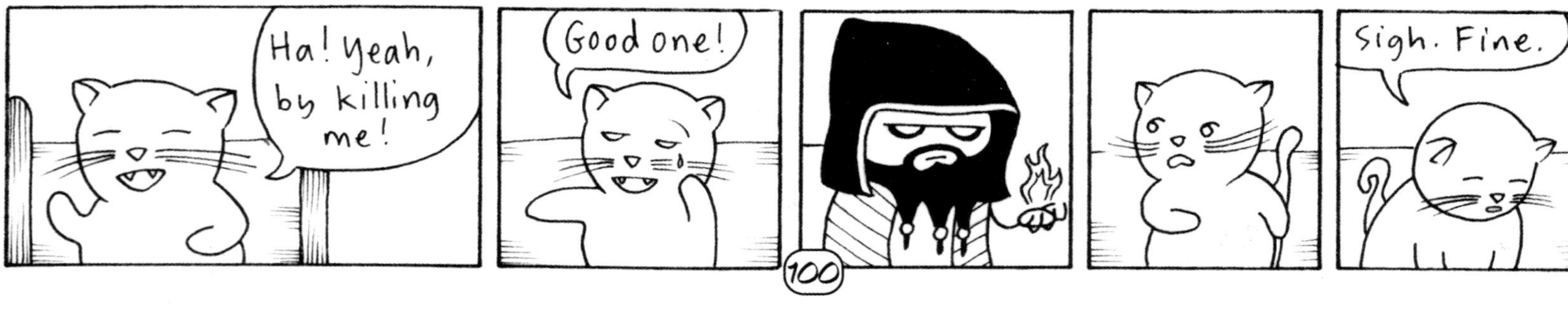
Ha! Yeah, by killing me!
Good one!
Sigh. Fine.

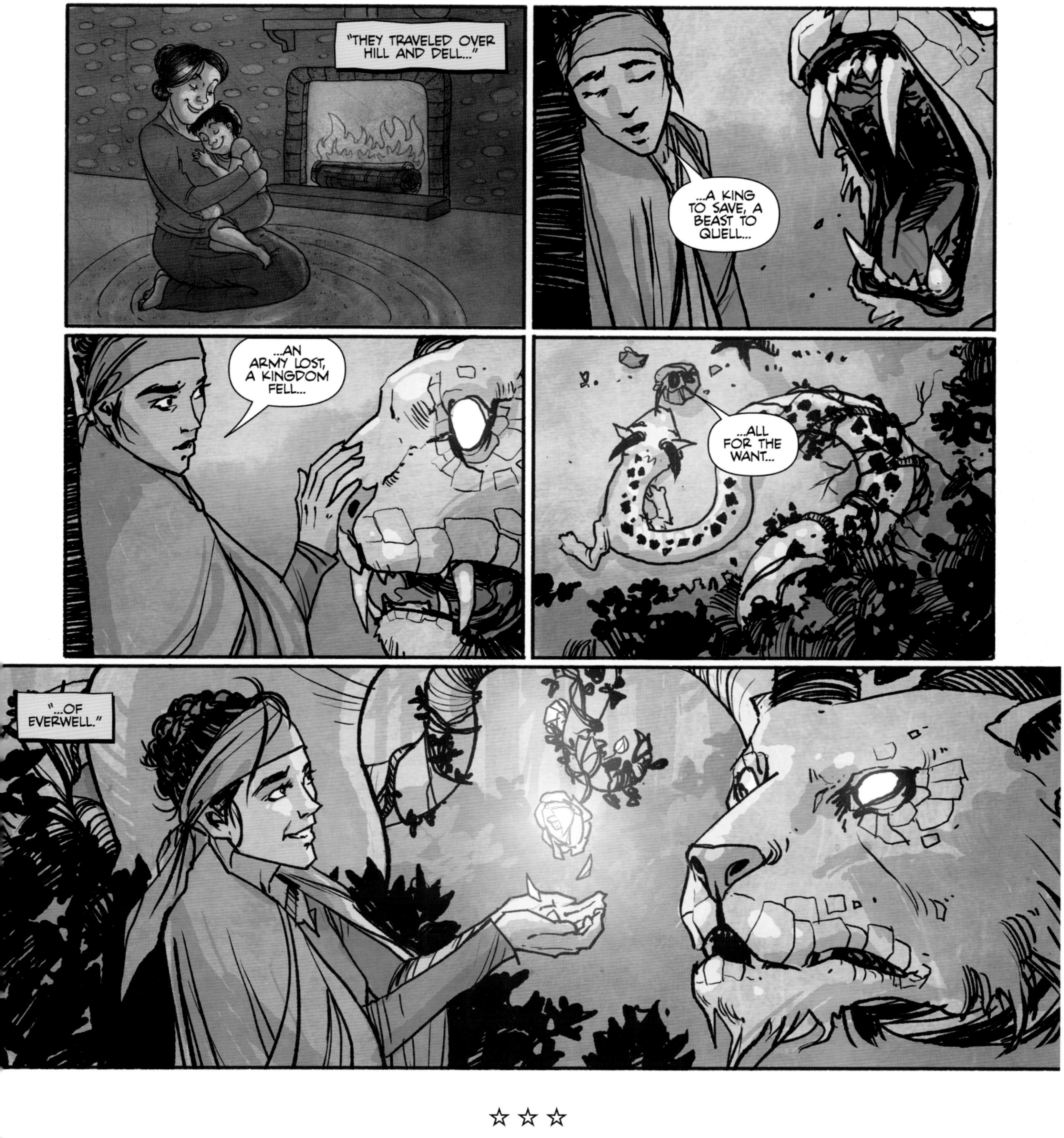
"THEY TRAVELED OVER HILL AND DELL..."
...A KING TO SAVE, A BEAST TO QUELL...
...AN ARMY LOST, A KINGDOM FELL...
...ALL FOR THE WANT...
"...OF EVERWELL."

☆ ☆ ☆

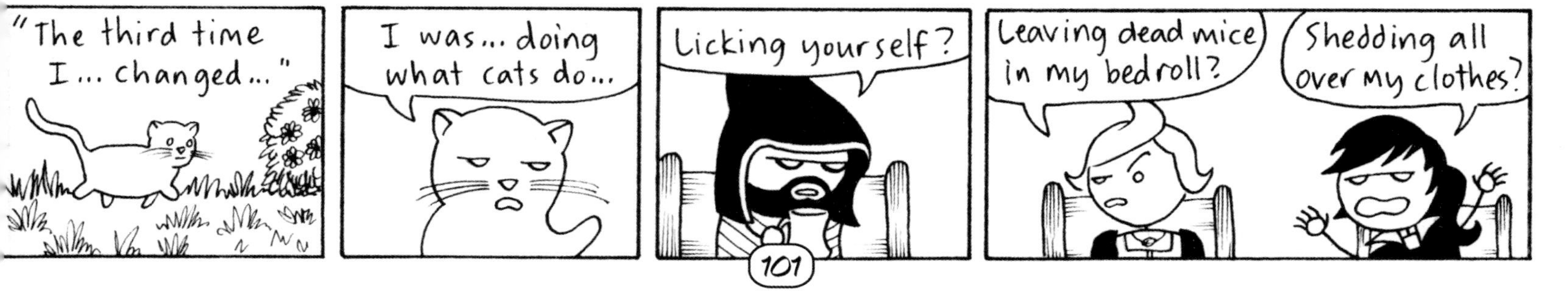
"The third time I... changed..."
I was... doing what cats do...
Licking yourself?
Leaving dead mice in my bedroll?
Shedding all over my clothes?

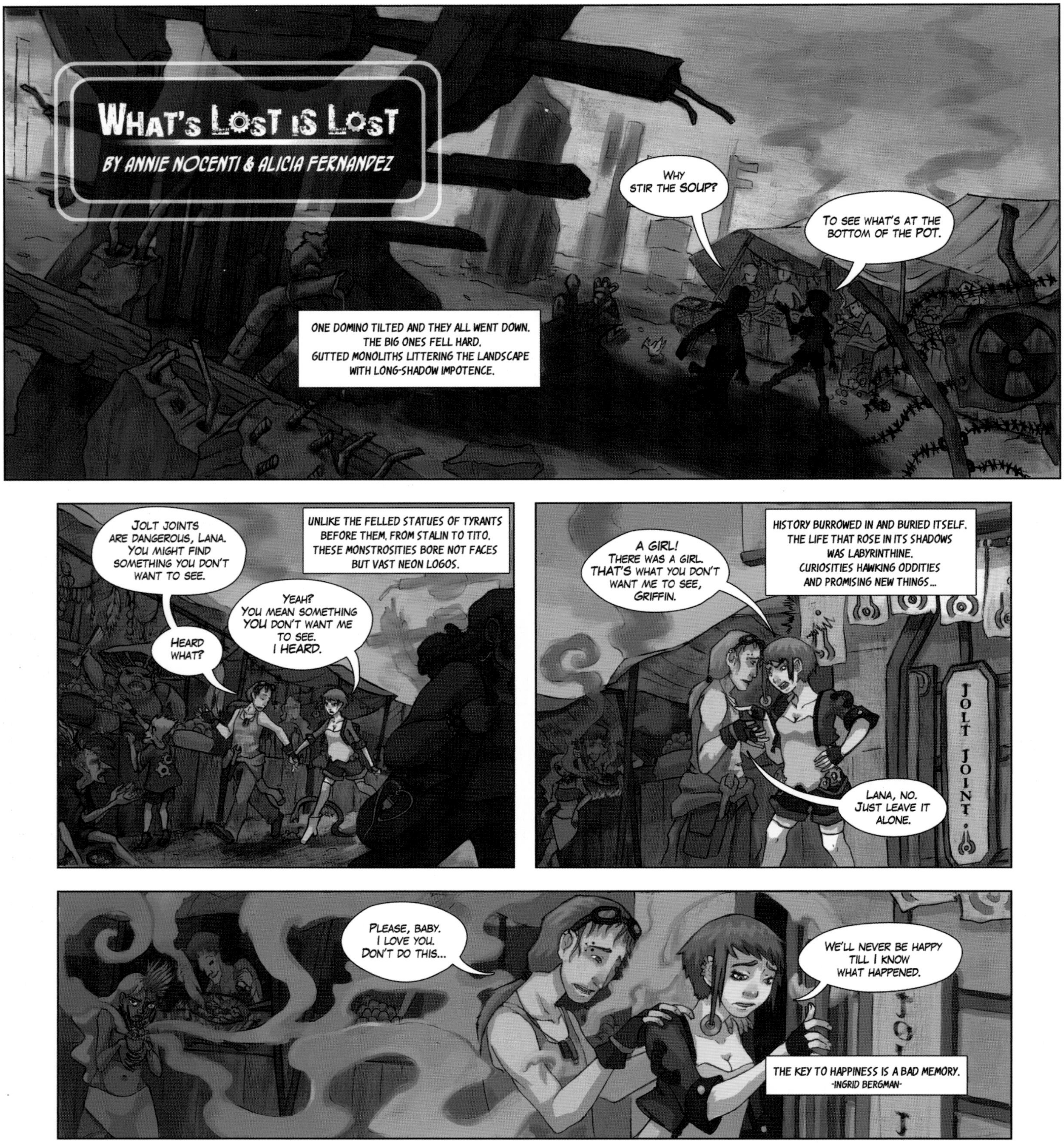
WHAT'S LOST IS LOST
BY ANNIE NOCENTI & ALICIA FERNANDEZ
WHY STIR THE SOUP?
TO SEE WHAT'S AT THE BOTTOM OF THE POT.
ONE DOMINO TILTED AND THEY ALL WENT DOWN. THE BIG ONES FELL HARD. GUTTED MONOLITHS LITTERING THE LANDSCAPE WITH LONG-SHADOW IMPOTENCE.
JOLT JOINTS ARE DANGEROUS, LANA. YOU MIGHT FIND SOMETHING YOU DON'T WANT TO SEE.
UNLIKE THE FELLED STATUES OF TYRANTS BEFORE THEM, FROM STALIN TO TITO, THESE MONSTROSITIES BORE NOT FACES BUT VAST NEON LOGOS.
YEAH? YOU MEAN SOMETHING YOU DON'T WANT ME TO SEE. I HEARD.
HEARD WHAT?
HISTORY BURROWED IN AND BURIED ITSELF. THE LIFE THAT ROSE IN ITS SHADOWS WAS LABYRINTHINE. CURIOSITIES HAWKING ODDITIES AND PROMISING NEW THINGS...
A GIRL! THERE WAS A GIRL. THAT'S WHAT YOU DON'T WANT ME TO SEE, GRIFFIN.
JOLT JOINT
LANA, NO. JUST LEAVE IT ALONE.
PLEASE, BABY. I LOVE YOU. DON'T DO THIS...
WE'LL NEVER BE HAPPY TILL I KNOW WHAT HAPPENED.
THE KEY TO HAPPINESS IS A BAD MEMORY.
-INGRID BERGMAN-

☆ ☆ ☆

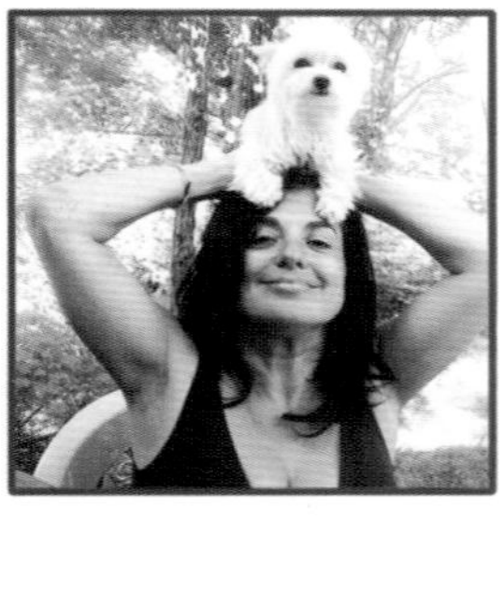

ANNIE NOCENTI

SKILLS: Writer
LOCATION: New York City
FUN FACT: That's not my dog on my head.

www.annienocenti.com

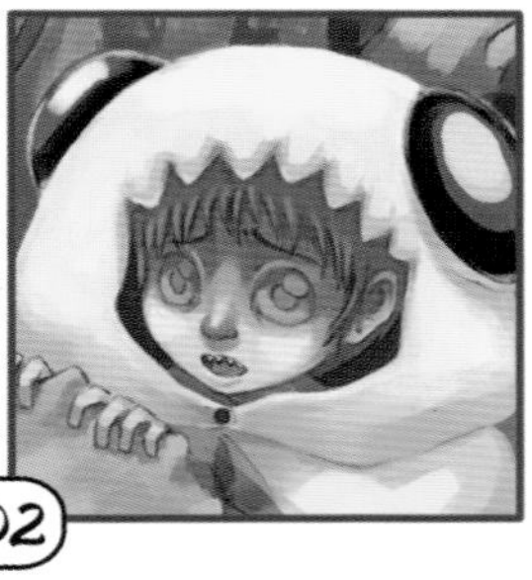

ALICIA FERNÁNDEZ

SKILLS: Penciller, Colorist, Letterer
LOCATION: Barcelona
FUN FACT: I like monsters. They don't usually taste good, but make great stories.

ohmybug.deviantart.com

MEMORY IS A LUNATIC THAT HOARDS WORTHLESS HUMILIATIONS....

ONE OF THE NEW ONES. EYES OF CUT CRYSTAL. MANNERED AS A PRAYING MANTIS.

...BUT COME IN IF YOU MUST.

LET'S GO, LANA...

NO. I HAVE TO KNOW.

CAVEAT EMPTOR. BUYER BEWARE.

I DON'T CARE. EVERYONE SAYS I'VE BEEN DIFFERENT SINCE, BUT NO ONE WILL TELL MY WHY.

IT'S LIKE THERE'S A MOVIE OF MY LIFE THAT EVERYONE HAS SEEN BUT ME.

BUT HER MIND BURIED THIS THING FOR A GOOD REASON. I'M AFRAID IF SHE SEES IT...

EITHER CHOICE...

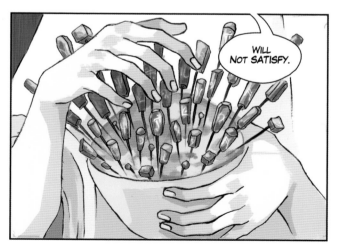

WILL NOT SATISFY.

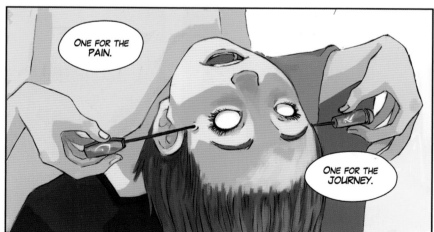

ONE FOR THE PAIN.

ONE FOR THE JOURNEY.

☆ ☆ ☆

Being so cute and soft that I want to put you in a dress and hug you and smush you and eat you?

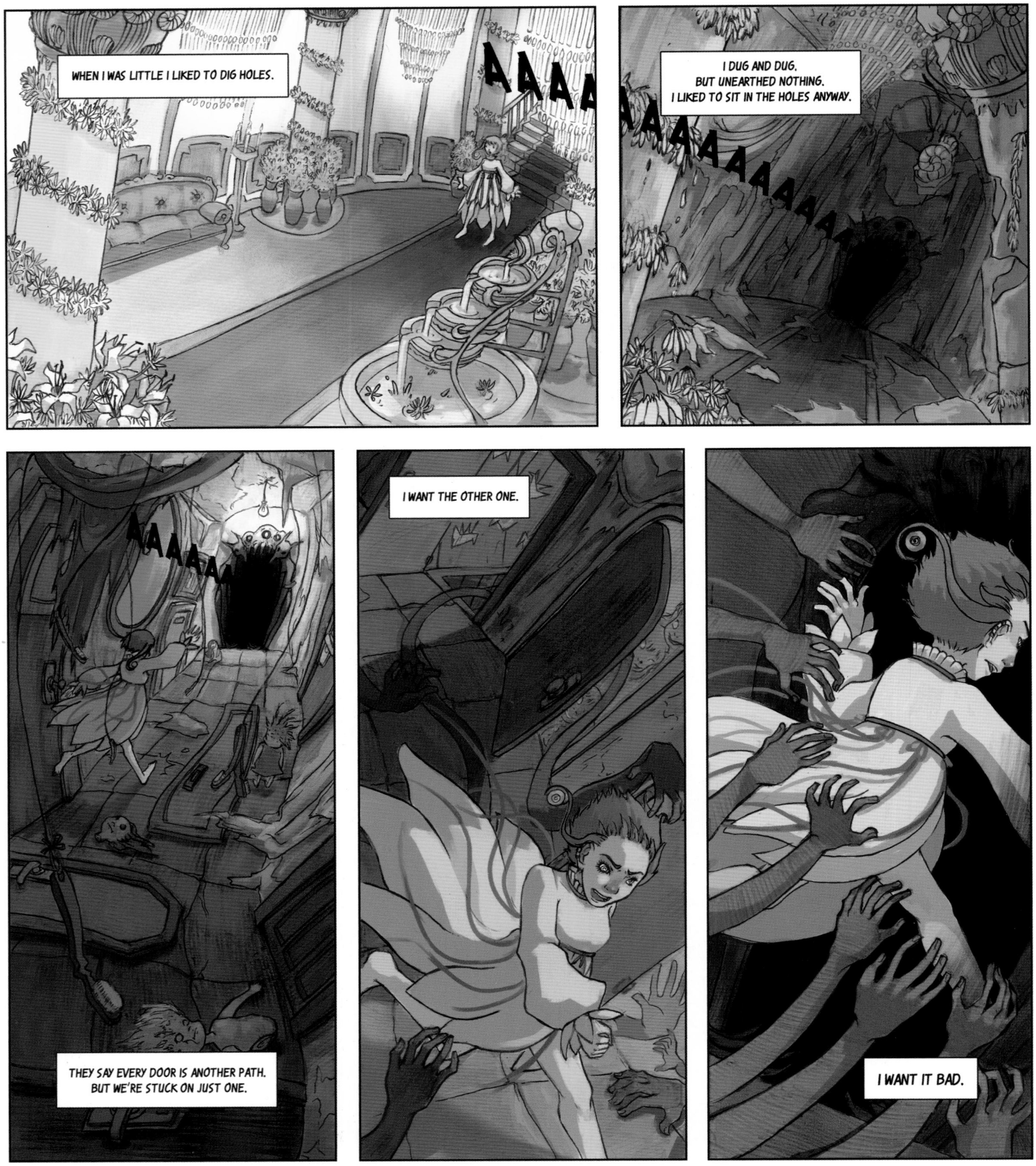
WHEN I WAS LITTLE I LIKED TO DIG HOLES.
AAAA
I DUG AND DUG,
BUT UNEARTHED NOTHING.
I LIKED TO SIT IN THE HOLES ANYWAY.
AAAAAAAAAAA
AAAAAA
THEY SAY EVERY DOOR IS ANOTHER PATH.
BUT WE'RE STUCK ON JUST ONE.
I WANT THE OTHER ONE.
I WANT IT BAD.

☆ ☆ ☆

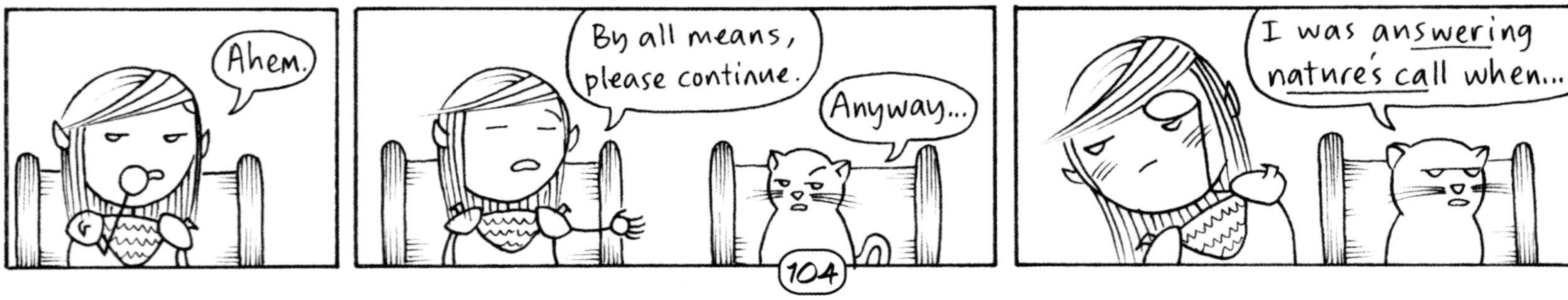
Ahem.
By all means, please continue.
Anyway...
I was answering nature's call when...

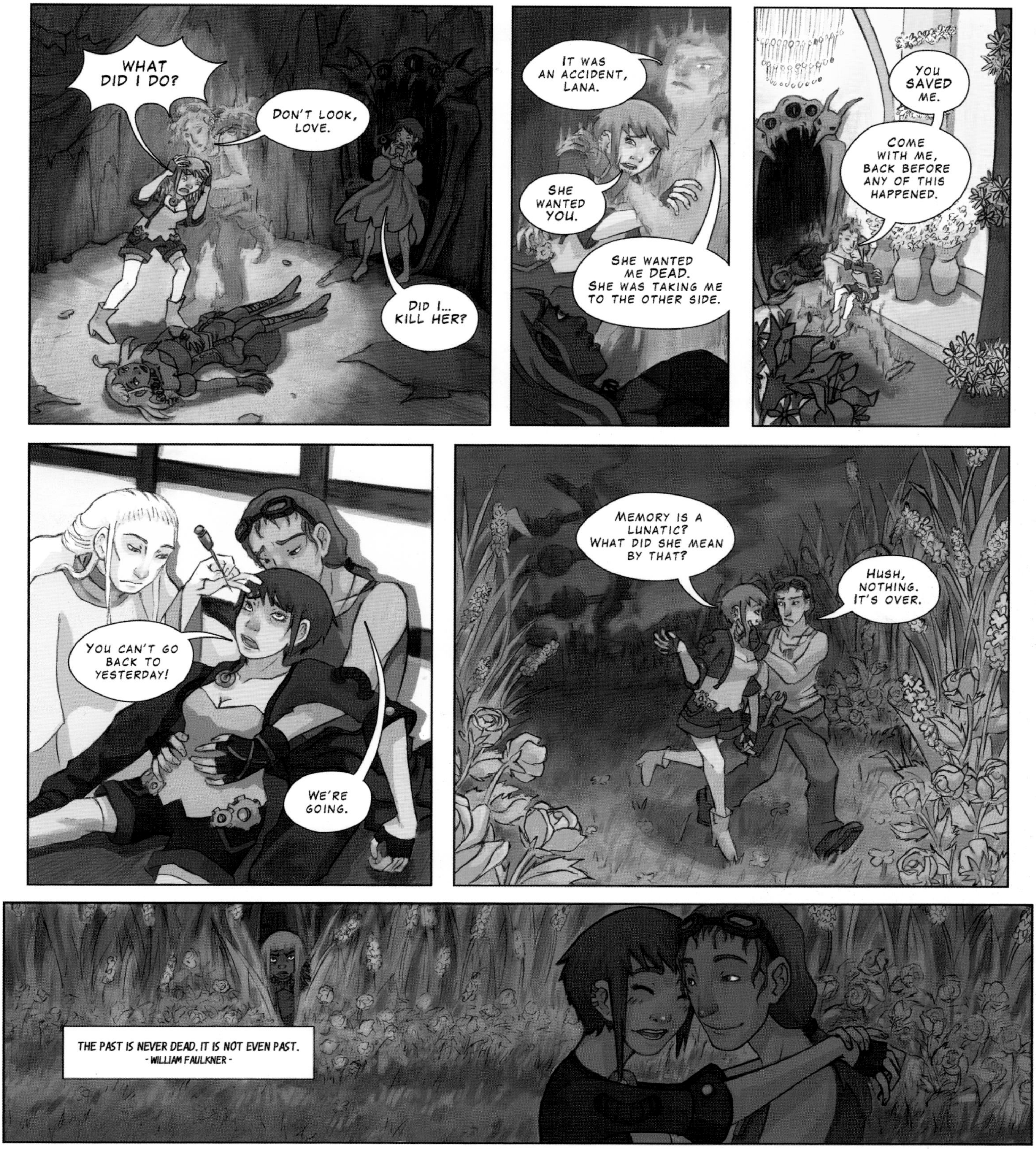
WHAT DID I DO?
DON'T LOOK, LOVE.
DID I... KILL HER?
IT WAS AN ACCIDENT, LANA.
SHE WANTED YOU.
SHE WANTED ME DEAD. SHE WAS TAKING ME TO THE OTHER SIDE.
YOU SAVED ME.
COME WITH ME, BACK BEFORE ANY OF THIS HAPPENED.
YOU CAN'T GO BACK TO YESTERDAY!
WE'RE GOING.
MEMORY IS A LUNATIC? WHAT DID SHE MEAN BY THAT?
HUSH, NOTHING. IT'S OVER.
THE PAST IS NEVER DEAD. IT IS NOT EVEN PAST.
- WILLIAM FAULKNER -

☆ ☆ ☆

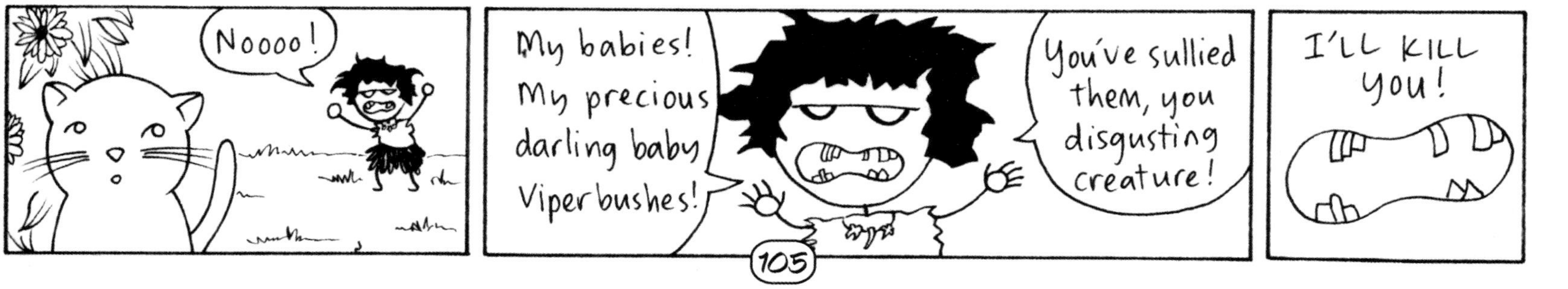
Noooo!
My babies! My precious darling baby Viperbushes!
You've sullied them, you disgusting creature!
I'LL KILL YOU!

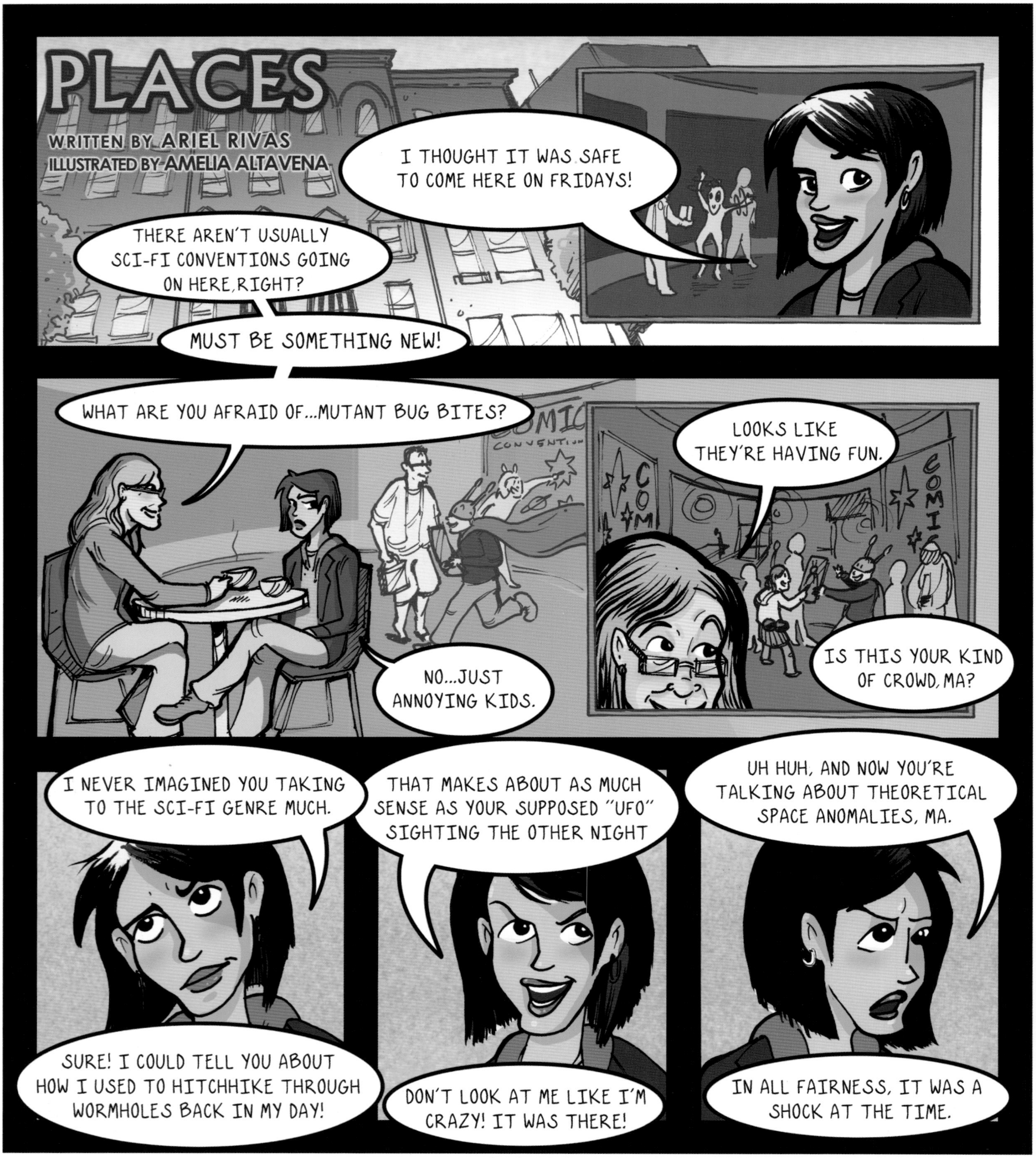
PLACES
WRITTEN BY ARIEL RIVAS
ILLUSTRATED BY AMELIA ALTAVENA
THERE AREN'T USUALLY SCI-FI CONVENTIONS GOING ON HERE, RIGHT?
I THOUGHT IT WAS SAFE TO COME HERE ON FRIDAYS!
MUST BE SOMETHING NEW!
WHAT ARE YOU AFRAID OF...MUTANT BUG BITES?
NO...JUST ANNOYING KIDS.
COMIC CONVENTION
LOOKS LIKE THEY'RE HAVING FUN.
IS THIS YOUR KIND OF CROWD, MA?
I NEVER IMAGINED YOU TAKING TO THE SCI-FI GENRE MUCH.
SURE! I COULD TELL YOU ABOUT HOW I USED TO HITCHHIKE THROUGH WORMHOLES BACK IN MY DAY!
THAT MAKES ABOUT AS MUCH SENSE AS YOUR SUPPOSED "UFO" SIGHTING THE OTHER NIGHT
DON'T LOOK AT ME LIKE I'M CRAZY! IT WAS THERE!
UH HUH, AND NOW YOU'RE TALKING ABOUT THEORETICAL SPACE ANOMALIES, MA.
IN ALL FAIRNESS, IT WAS A SHOCK AT THE TIME.

☆ ☆ ☆

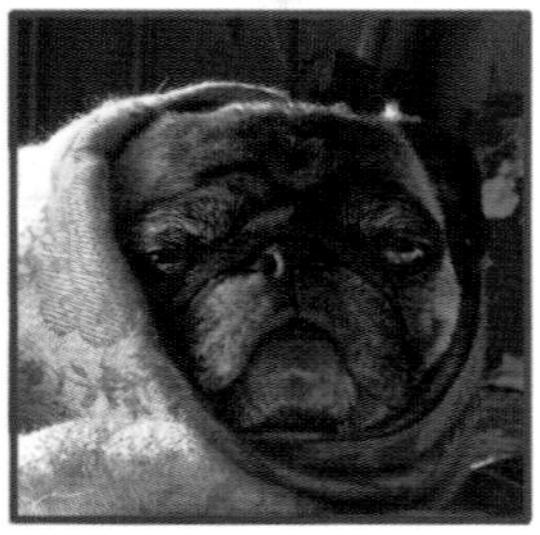

ARIEL RIVAS

SKILLS: Writer
LOCATION: Midwest, USA
FUN FACT: I collect plush pugs - also real ones. :)

http://windy-asylum.deviantart.com/

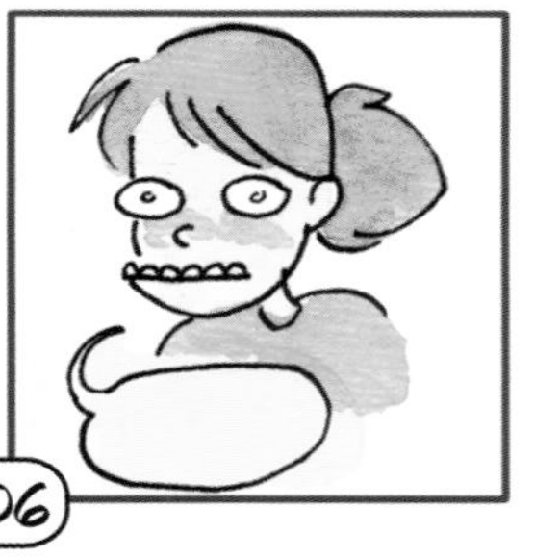

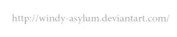

AMELIA ALTAVENA

SKILLS: Cartoonist
LOCATION: San Francisco, CA
FUN FACT: When I'm not cartooning I'm a museum exhibit designer for science centers and history museums all over the world. I also pheasant hunt, rock climb, and play ice hockey!

http://sketchfervor.com

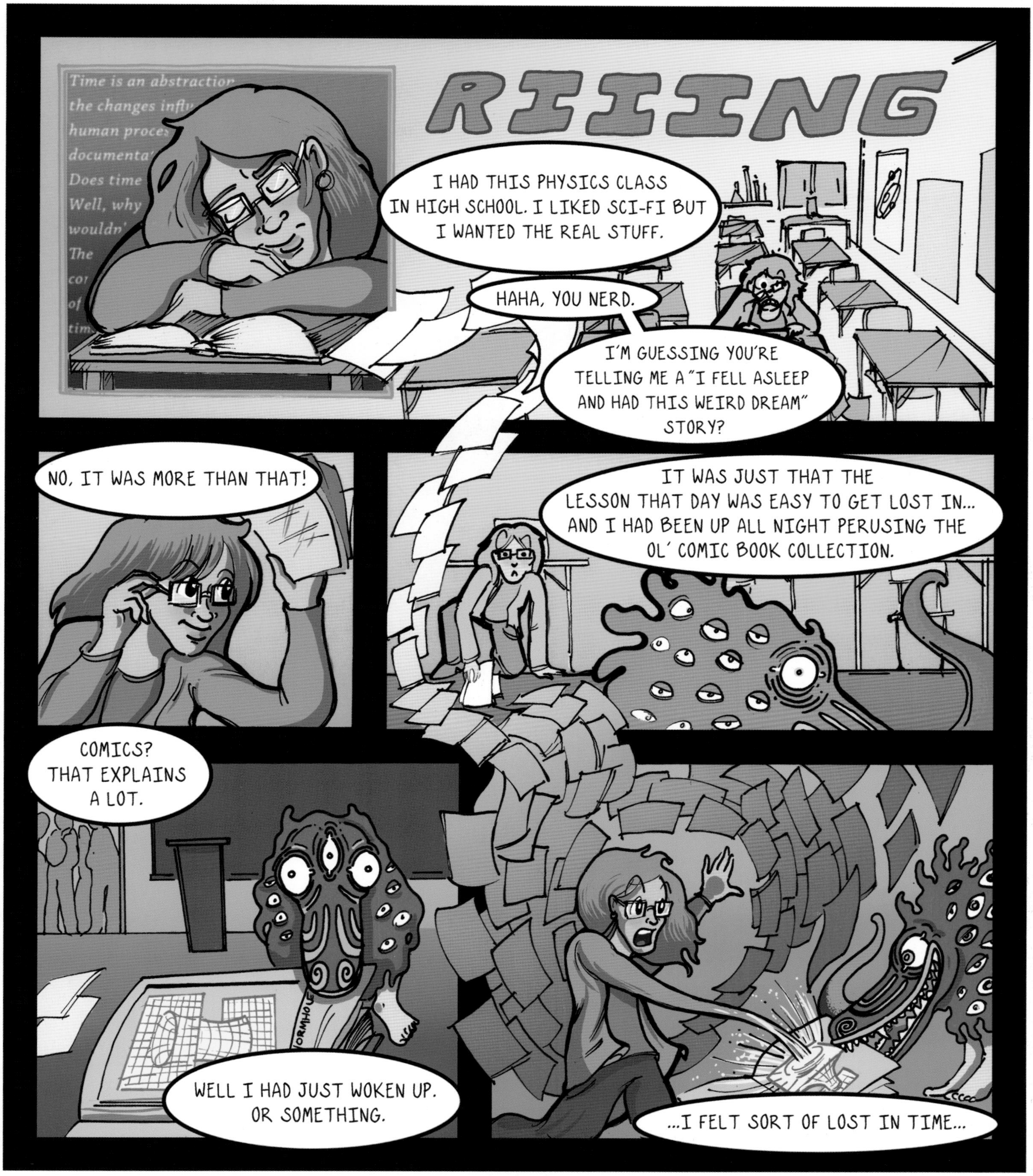
RIIIING
I HAD THIS PHYSICS CLASS IN HIGH SCHOOL. I LIKED SCI-FI BUT I WANTED THE REAL STUFF.
HAHA, YOU NERD.
I'M GUESSING YOU'RE TELLING ME A "I FELL ASLEEP AND HAD THIS WEIRD DREAM" STORY?
NO, IT WAS MORE THAN THAT!
IT WAS JUST THAT THE LESSON THAT DAY WAS EASY TO GET LOST IN... AND I HAD BEEN UP ALL NIGHT PERUSING THE OL' COMIC BOOK COLLECTION.
COMICS? THAT EXPLAINS A LOT.
WELL I HAD JUST WOKEN UP. OR SOMETHING.
...I FELT SORT OF LOST IN TIME...

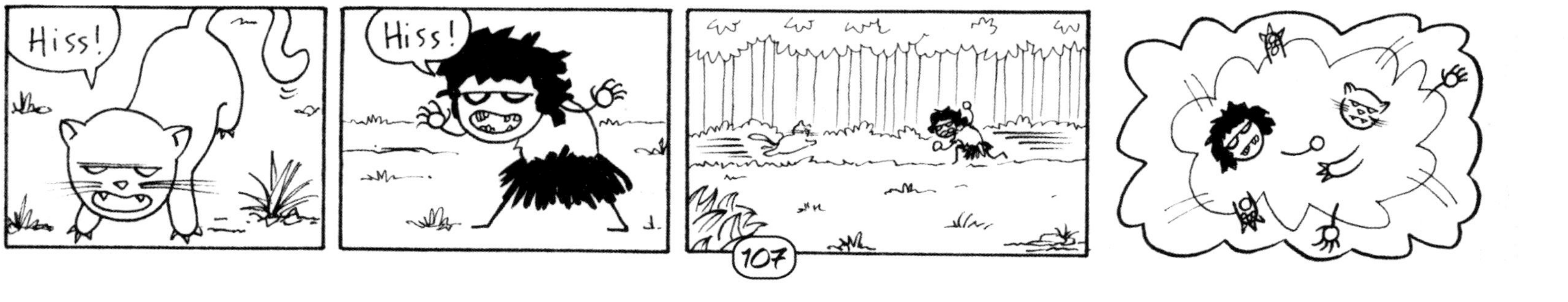
Hiss!
Hiss!

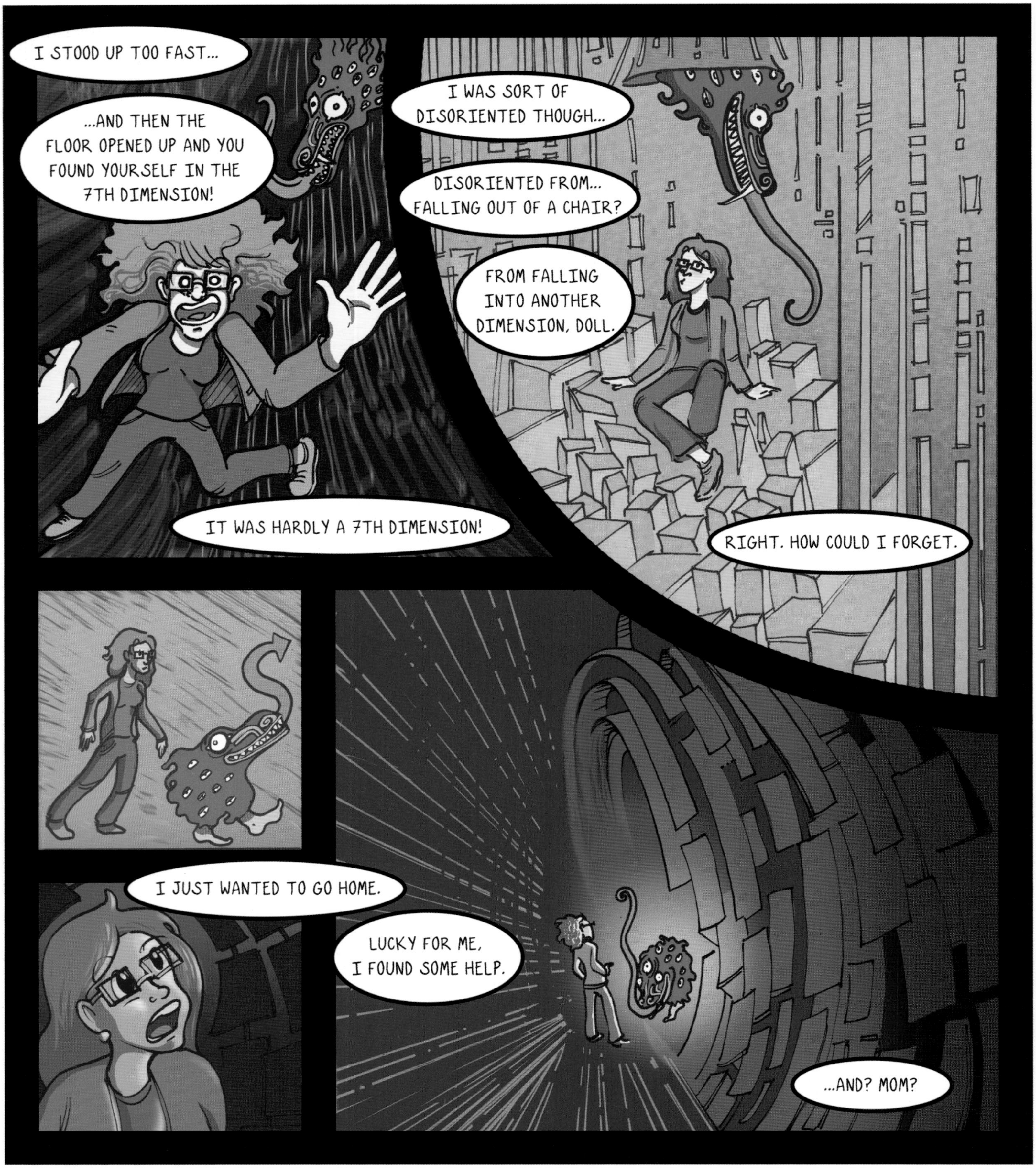
I STOOD UP TOO FAST...
...AND THEN THE FLOOR OPENED UP AND YOU FOUND YOURSELF IN THE 7TH DIMENSION!
IT WAS HARDLY A 7TH DIMENSION!
I WAS SORT OF DISORIENTED THOUGH...
DISORIENTED FROM... FALLING OUT OF A CHAIR?
FROM FALLING INTO ANOTHER DIMENSION, DOLL.
RIGHT. HOW COULD I FORGET.
I JUST WANTED TO GO HOME.
LUCKY FOR ME, I FOUND SOME HELP.
...AND? MOM?

☆☆☆

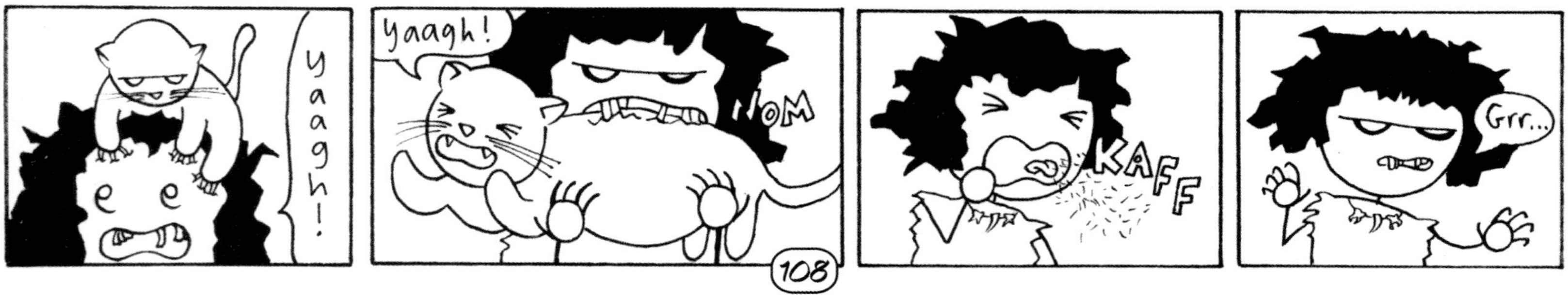
Yaagh!
Yaagh!
OM
KAFF
Grr...

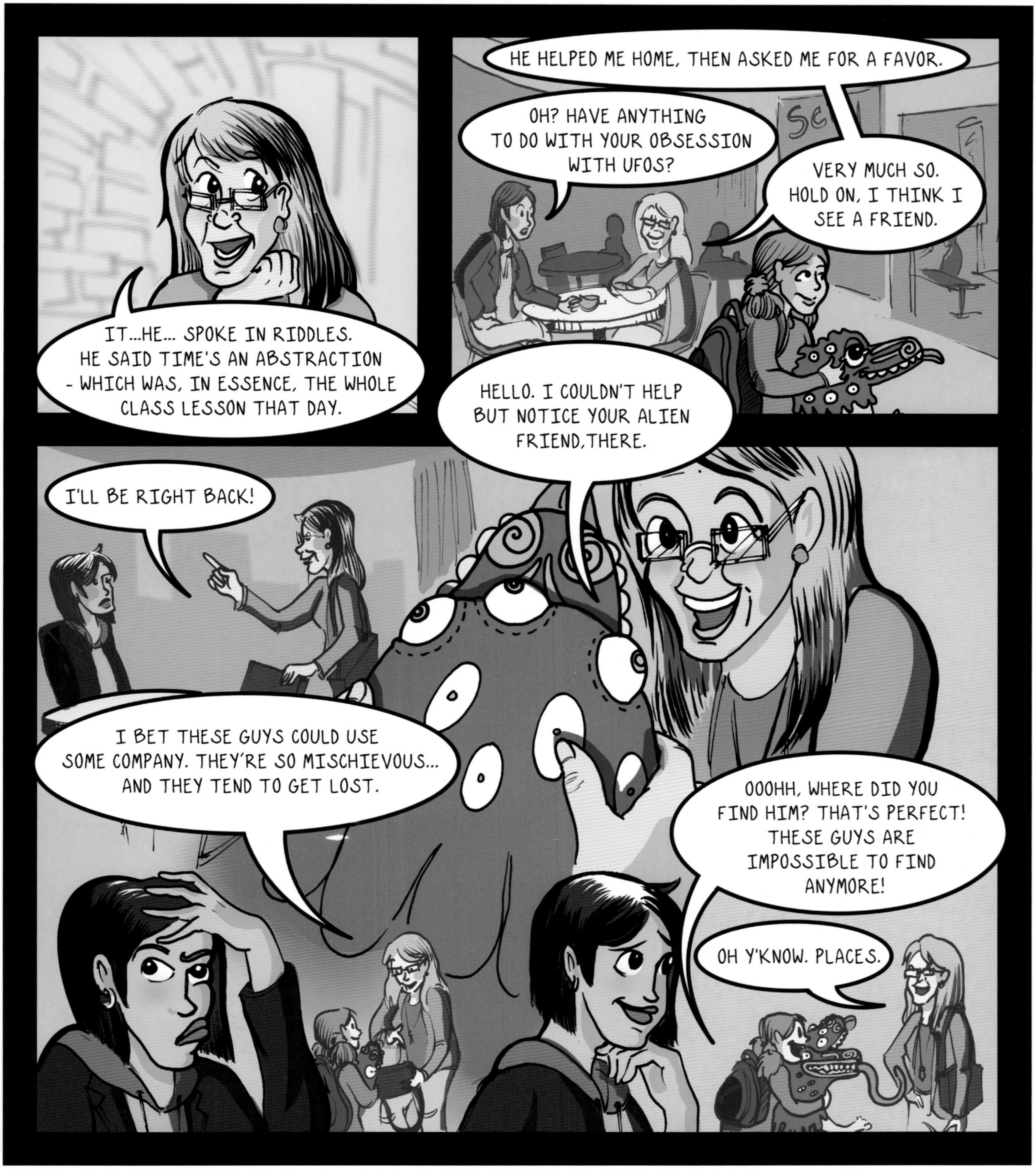
IT...HE... SPOKE IN RIDDLES. HE SAID TIME'S AN ABSTRACTION - WHICH WAS, IN ESSENCE, THE WHOLE CLASS LESSON THAT DAY.
HE HELPED ME HOME, THEN ASKED ME FOR A FAVOR.
OH? HAVE ANYTHING TO DO WITH YOUR OBSESSION WITH UFOS?
VERY MUCH SO. HOLD ON, I THINK I SEE A FRIEND.
I'LL BE RIGHT BACK!
HELLO. I COULDN'T HELP BUT NOTICE YOUR ALIEN FRIEND, THERE.
I BET THESE GUYS COULD USE SOME COMPANY. THEY'RE SO MISCHIEVOUS... AND THEY TEND TO GET LOST.
OOOHH, WHERE DID YOU FIND HIM? THAT'S PERFECT! THESE GUYS ARE IMPOSSIBLE TO FIND ANYMORE!
OH Y'KNOW. PLACES.

☆ ☆ ☆

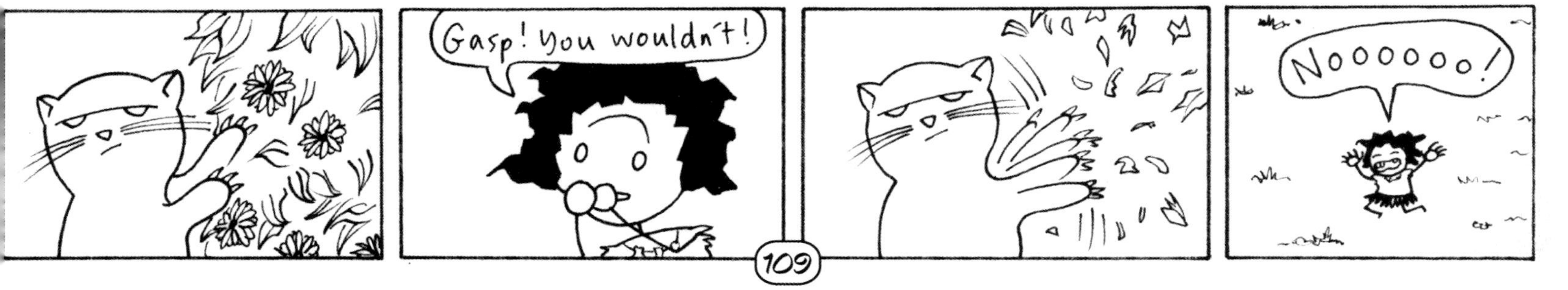
Gasp! You wouldn't!
Noooooo!

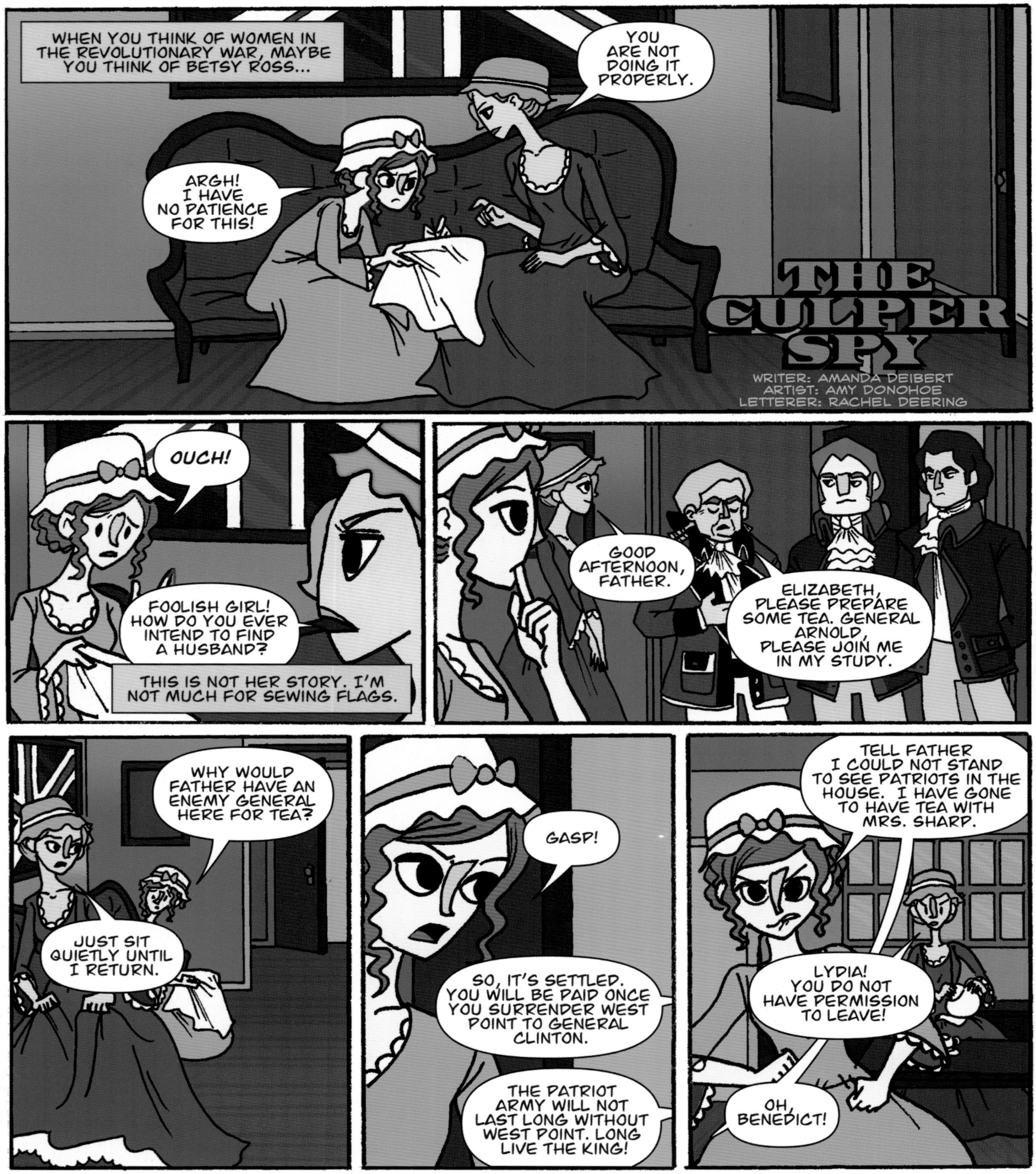
WHEN YOU THINK OF WOMEN IN THE REVOLUTIONARY WAR, MAYBE YOU THINK OF BETSY ROSS...
YOU ARE NOT DOING IT PROPERLY.
ARGH! I HAVE NO PATIENCE FOR THIS!
THE CULPER SPY
WRITER: AMANDA DEIBERT
ARTIST: AMY DONOHOE
LETTERER: RACHEL DEERING
OUCH!
FOOLISH GIRL! HOW DO YOU EVER INTEND TO FIND A HUSBAND?
THIS IS NOT HER STORY. I'M NOT MUCH FOR SEWING FLAGS.
GOOD AFTERNOON, FATHER.
ELIZABETH, PLEASE PREPARE SOME TEA. GENERAL ARNOLD, PLEASE JOIN ME IN MY STUDY.
WHY WOULD FATHER HAVE AN ENEMY GENERAL HERE FOR TEA?
JUST SIT QUIETLY UNTIL I RETURN.
GASP!
SO, IT'S SETTLED. YOU WILL BE PAID ONCE YOU SURRENDER WEST POINT TO GENERAL CLINTON.
THE PATRIOT ARMY WILL NOT LAST LONG WITHOUT WEST POINT. LONG LIVE THE KING!
TELL FATHER I COULD NOT STAND TO SEE PATRIOTS IN THE HOUSE. I HAVE GONE TO HAVE TEA WITH MRS. SHARP.
LYDIA! YOU DO NOT HAVE PERMISSION TO LEAVE!
OH, BENEDICT!

☆ ☆ ☆

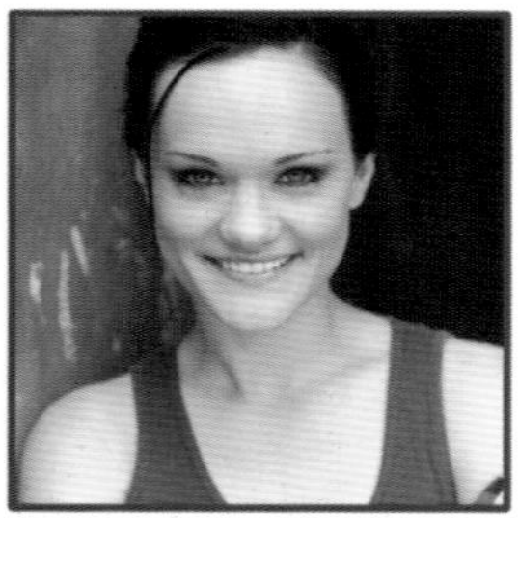

AMANDA DEIBERT

SKILLS: Writer
LOCATION: Los Angeles
FUN FACT: I live with 100,000 cats.

www.amandadeibert.com

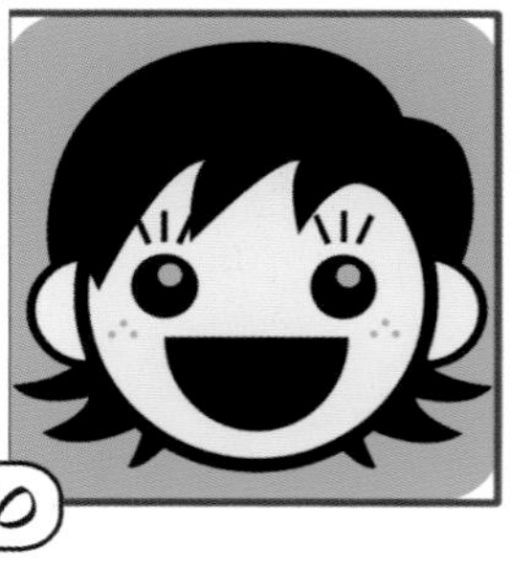

AMY DONOHOE

SKILLS: Penciller, Inker, and Colorist
LOCATION: Texarkana, TX
FUN FACT: I do stuff and like things.

www.amism.net

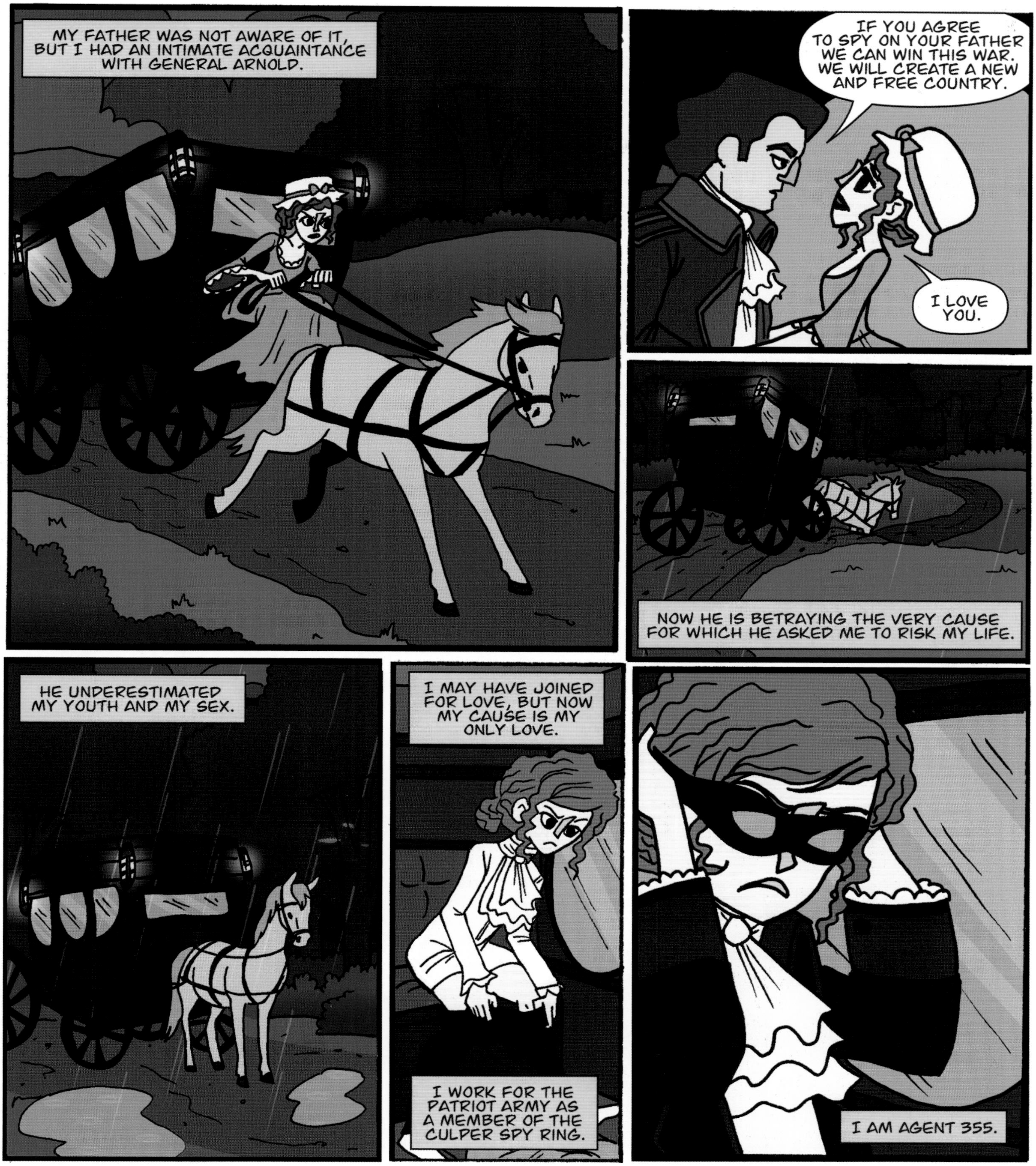
MY FATHER WAS NOT AWARE OF IT, BUT I HAD AN INTIMATE ACQUAINTANCE WITH GENERAL ARNOLD.
IF YOU AGREE TO SPY ON YOUR FATHER WE CAN WIN THIS WAR. WE WILL CREATE A NEW AND FREE COUNTRY.
I LOVE YOU.
NOW HE IS BETRAYING THE VERY CAUSE FOR WHICH HE ASKED ME TO RISK MY LIFE.
HE UNDERESTIMATED MY YOUTH AND MY SEX.
I MAY HAVE JOINED FOR LOVE, BUT NOW MY CAUSE IS MY ONLY LOVE.
I WORK FOR THE PATRIOT ARMY AS A MEMBER OF THE CULPER SPY RING.
I AM AGENT 355.

☆ ☆ ☆

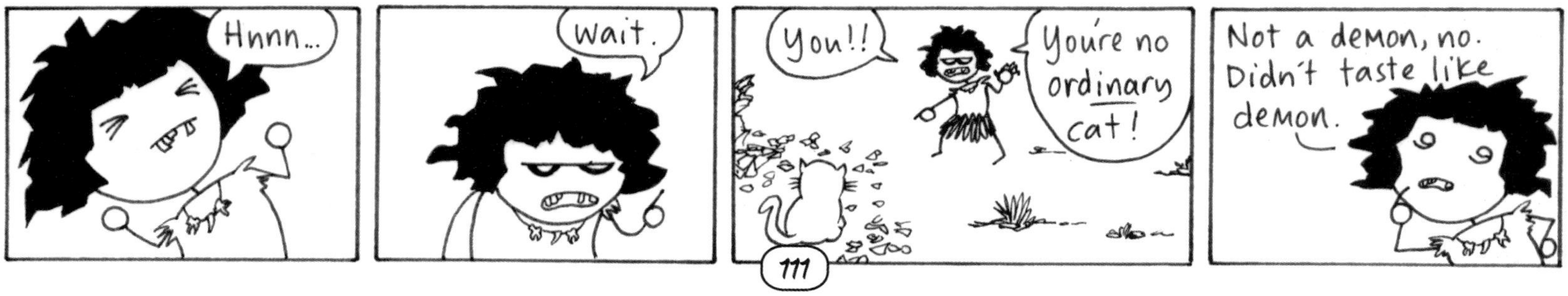
Hnnn...
wait.
You!!
You're no ordinary cat!
Not a demon, no. Didn't taste like demon.

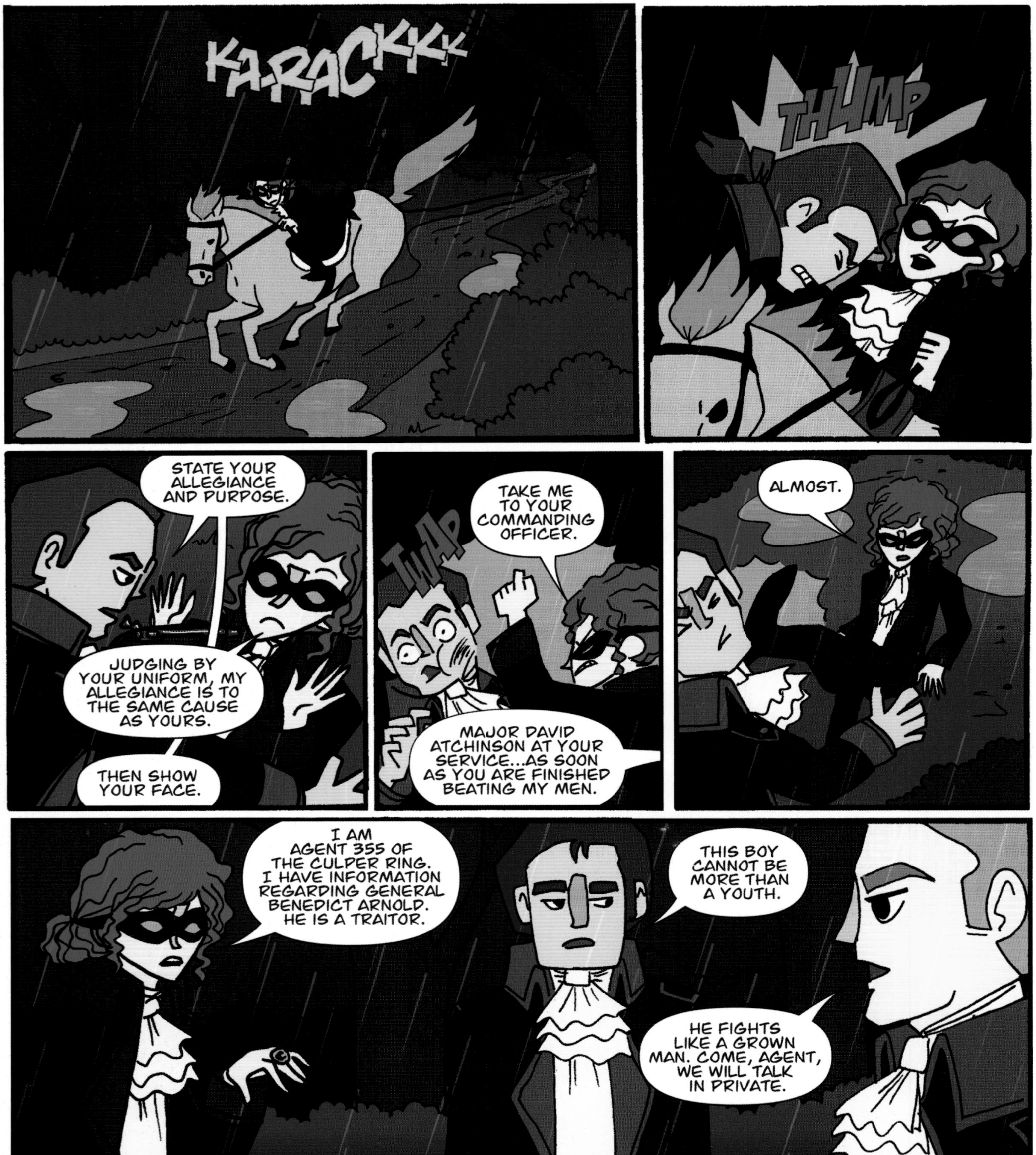
KA-RACKKK
THUMP
STATE YOUR ALLEGIANCE AND PURPOSE.
JUDGING BY YOUR UNIFORM, MY ALLEGIANCE IS TO THE SAME CAUSE AS YOURS.
THEN SHOW YOUR FACE.
TWAP
TAKE ME TO YOUR COMMANDING OFFICER.
MAJOR DAVID ATCHINSON AT YOUR SERVICE...AS SOON AS YOU ARE FINISHED BEATING MY MEN.
ALMOST.
I AM AGENT 355 OF THE CULPER RING. I HAVE INFORMATION REGARDING GENERAL BENEDICT ARNOLD. HE IS A TRAITOR.
THIS BOY CANNOT BE MORE THAN A YOUTH.
HE FIGHTS LIKE A GROWN MAN. COME, AGENT, WE WILL TALK IN PRIVATE.

☆ ☆ ☆

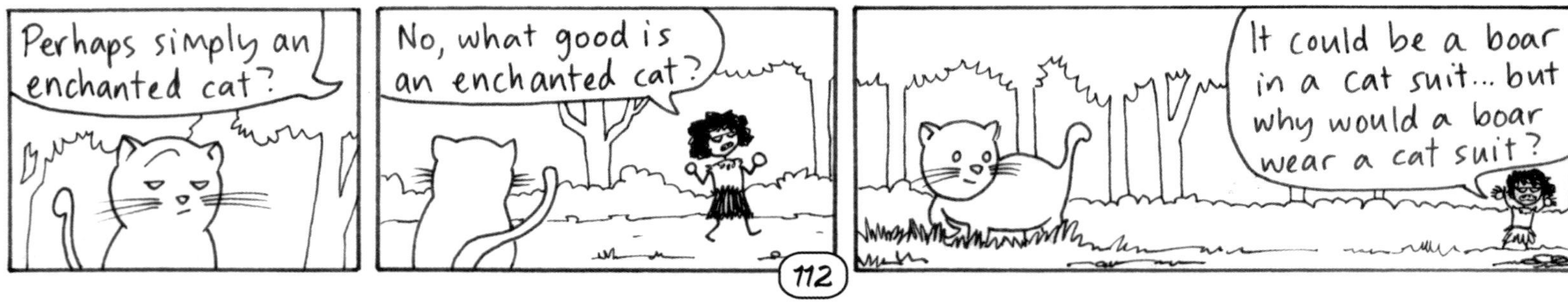
Perhaps simply an enchanted cat?
No, what good is an enchanted cat?
It could be a boar in a cat suit... but why would a boar wear a cat suit?

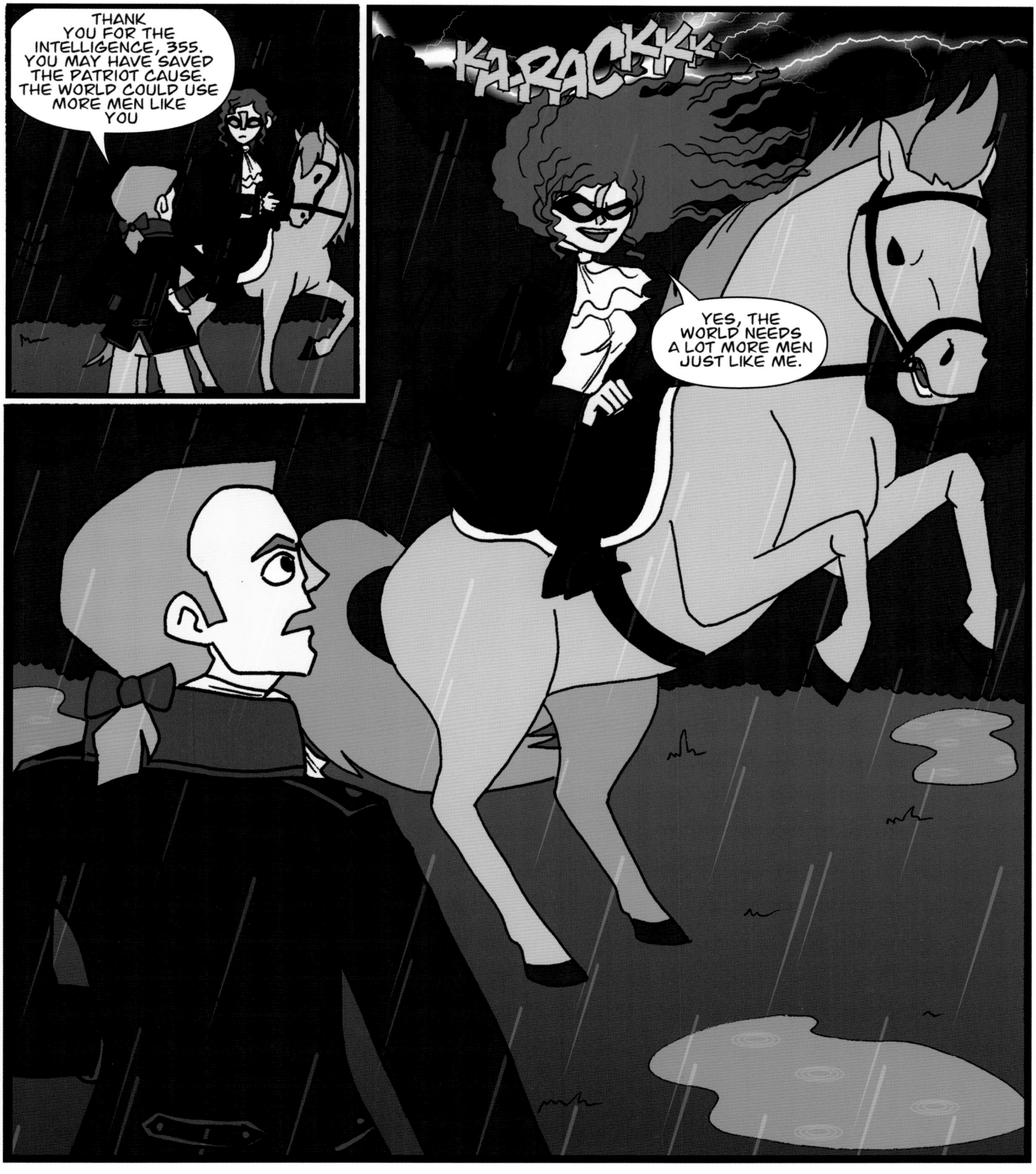
THANK YOU FOR THE INTELLIGENCE, 355. YOU MAY HAVE SAVED THE PATRIOT CAUSE. THE WORLD COULD USE MORE MEN LIKE YOU
KA-RACKK
YES, THE WORLD NEEDS A LOT MORE MEN JUST LIKE ME.

☆ ☆ ☆

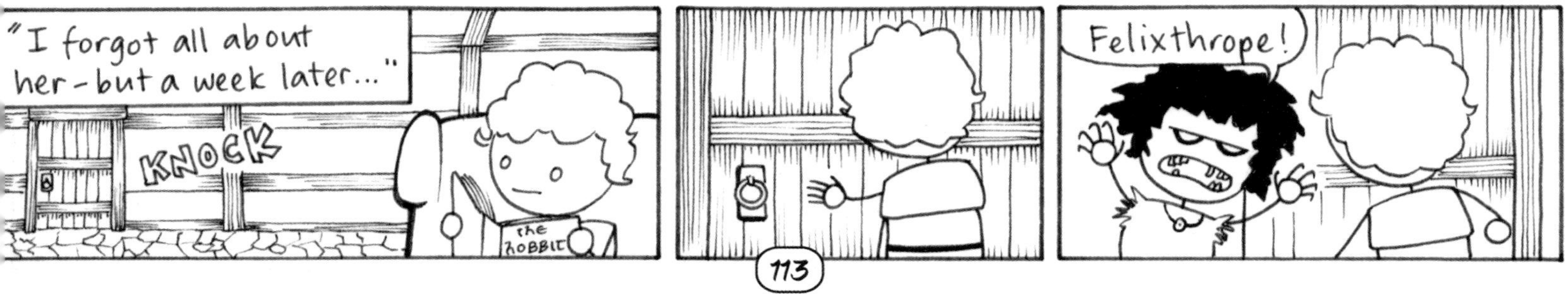
"I forgot all about her-but a week later..."
KNOCK
the Hobbit
Felixthrope!

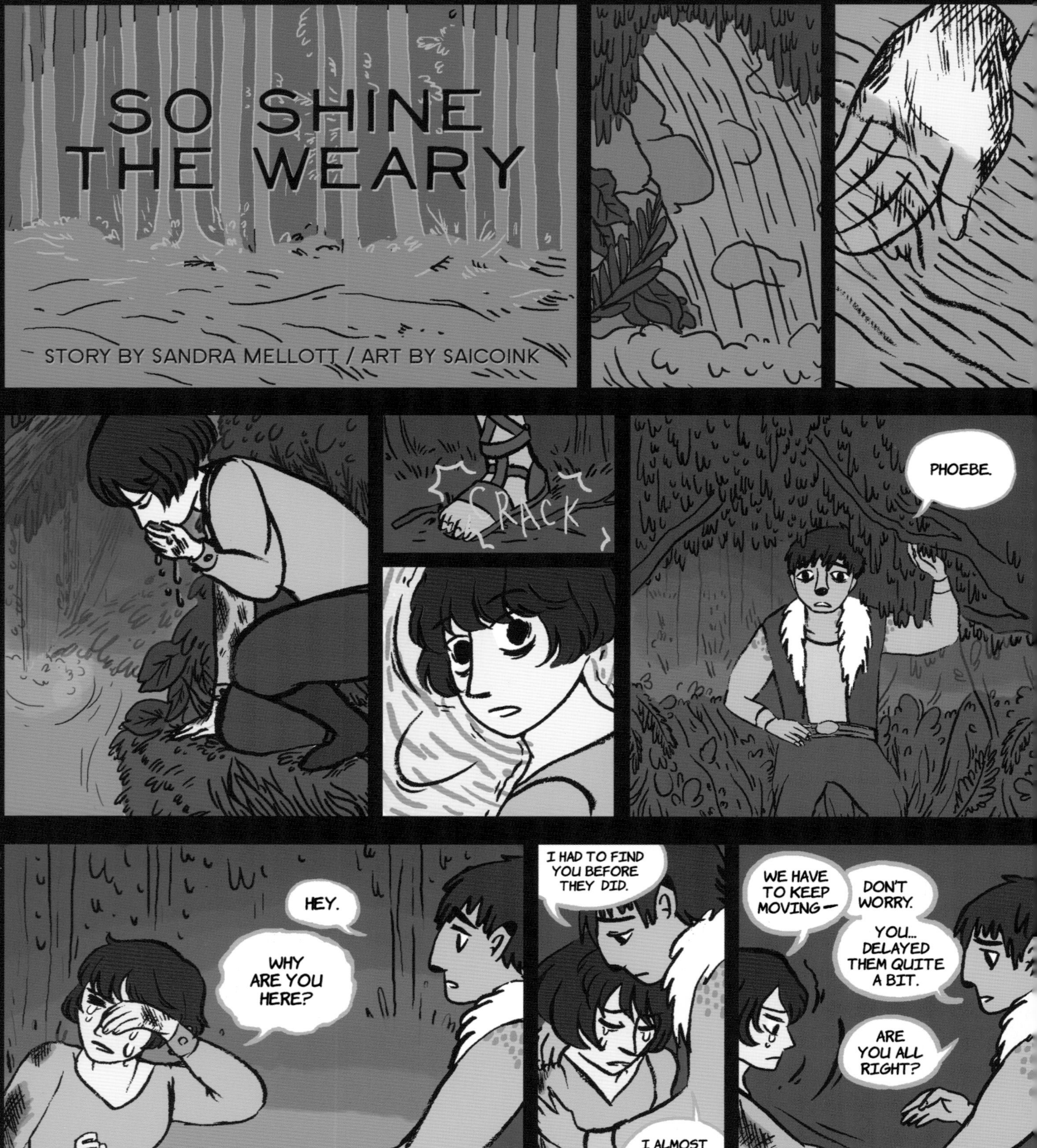
SO SHINE THE WEARY
STORY BY SANDRA MELLOTT / ART BY SAICOINK
CRACK
PHOEBE.
HEY.
WHY ARE YOU HERE?
I HAD TO FIND YOU BEFORE THEY DID.
I ALMOST LOST YOUR SCENT.
WE HAVE TO KEEP MOVING—
DON'T WORRY.
YOU... DELAYED THEM QUITE A BIT.
ARE YOU ALL RIGHT?

★ ★ ★

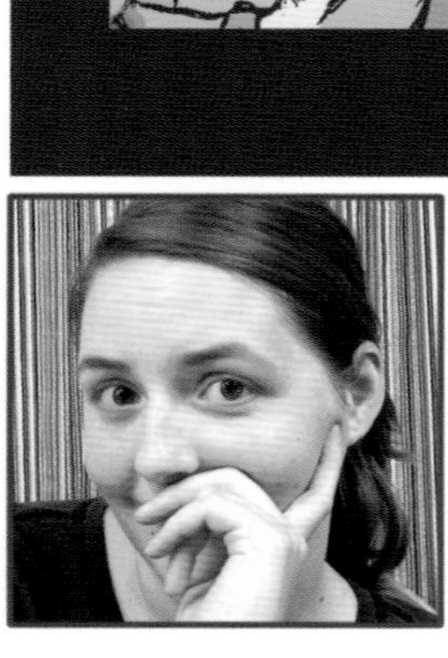

SANDRA MELLOTT

SKILLS: Writer
LOCATION: Butte, Montana
FUN FACT: I carry white-out and markers with me so that I can correct punctuation errors on signs and public postings.

whes.deviantart.com

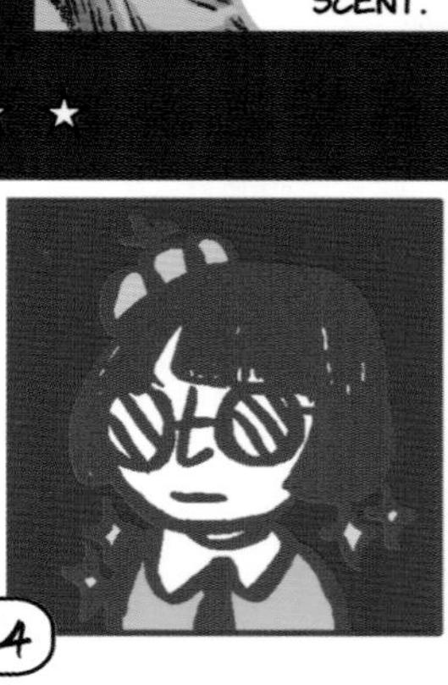

SAICOINK

SKILLS: Pencils, Inks, Colors, and Letteri
LOCATION: Canada
FUN FACT: I like to sit alone in cafes, loo ing at the window and watching the peop pass by.

http://www.saicoink.

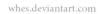

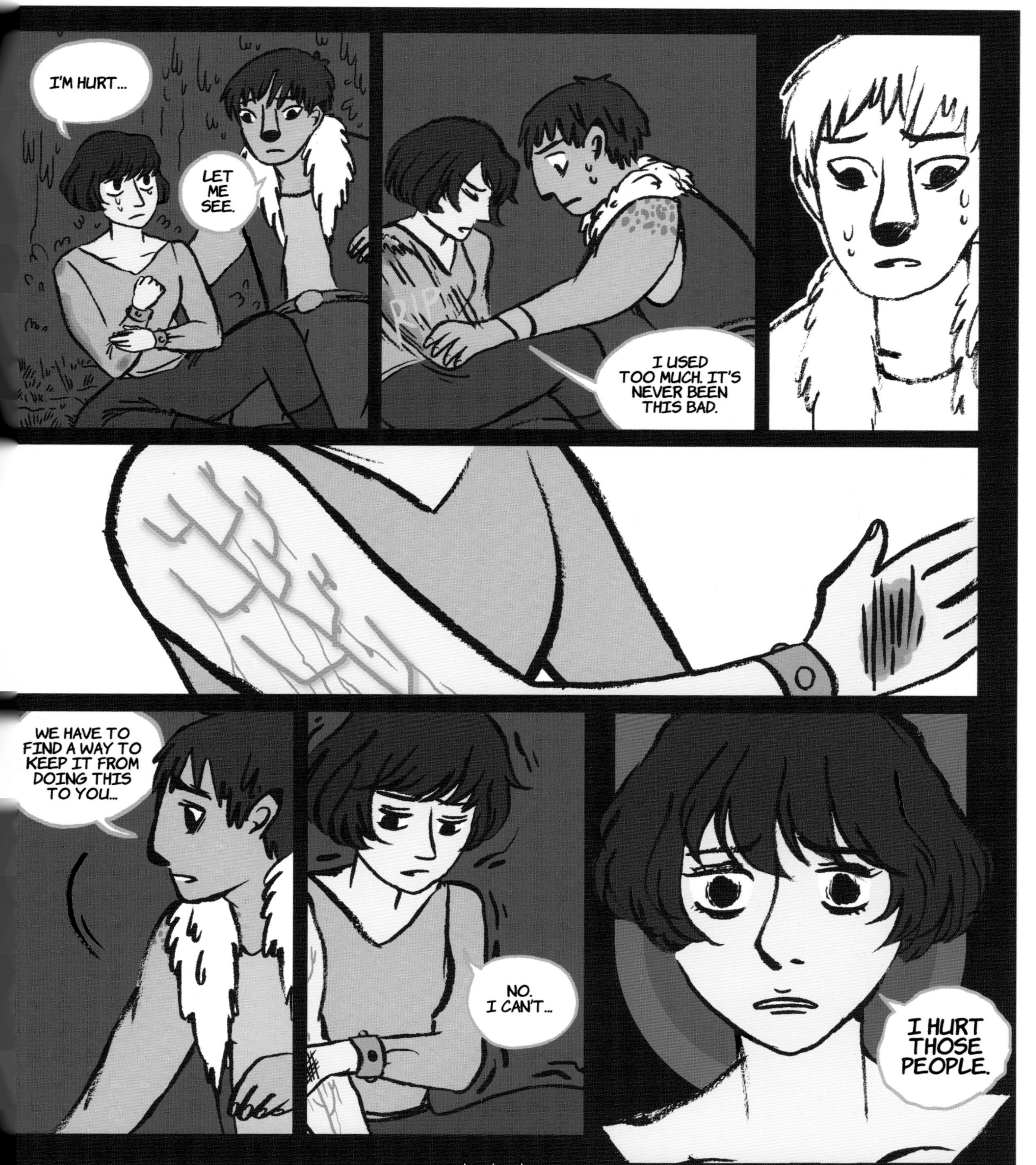
I'M HURT...
LET ME SEE.
I USED TOO MUCH. IT'S NEVER BEEN THIS BAD.
WE HAVE TO FIND A WAY TO KEEP IT FROM DOING THIS TO YOU...
NO. I CAN'T...
I HURT THOSE PEOPLE.

★ ★ ★

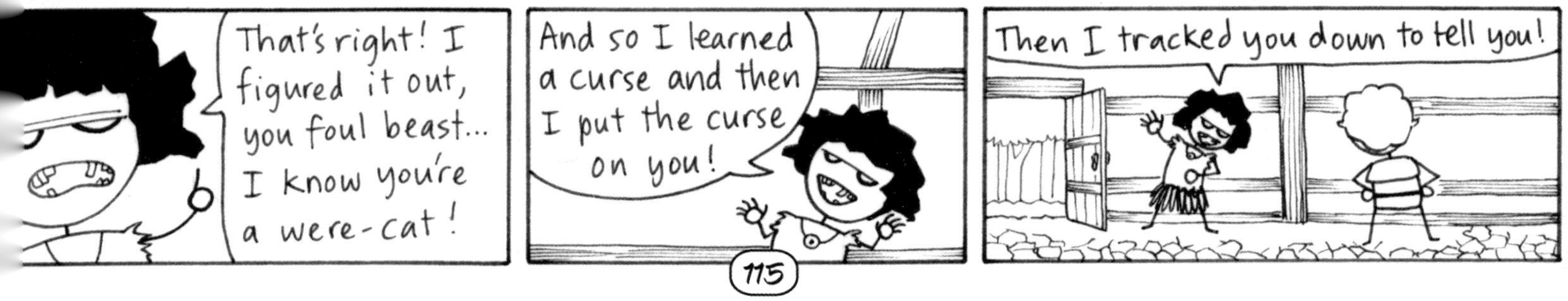
That's right! I figured it out, you foul beast... I know you're a were-cat!
And so I learned a curse and then I put the curse on you!
Then I tracked you down to tell you!

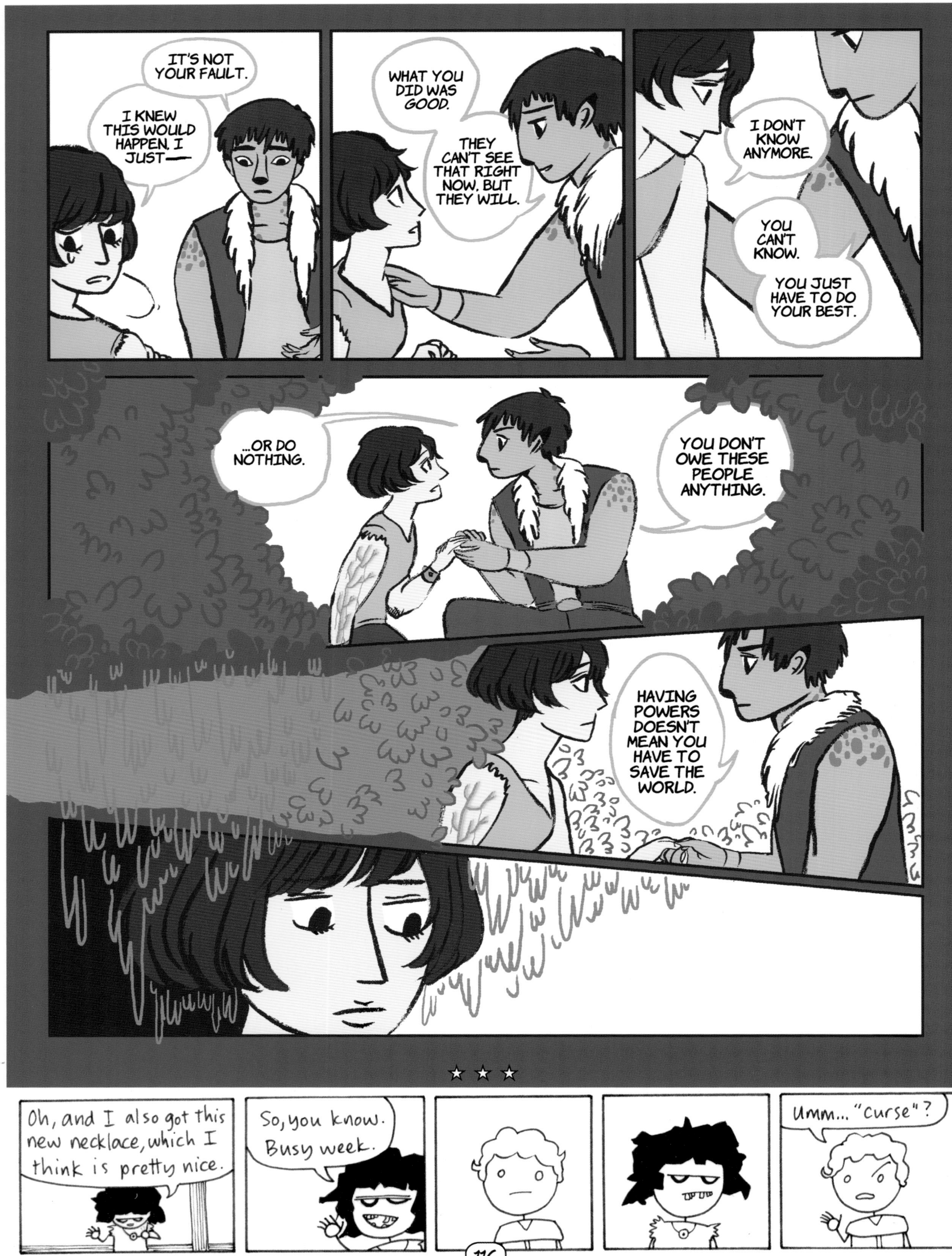
I KNEW THIS WOULD HAPPEN. I JUST—
IT'S NOT YOUR FAULT.
WHAT YOU DID WAS GOOD.
THEY CAN'T SEE THAT RIGHT NOW, BUT THEY WILL.
I DON'T KNOW ANYMORE.
YOU CAN'T KNOW.
YOU JUST HAVE TO DO YOUR BEST.
...OR DO NOTHING.
YOU DON'T OWE THESE PEOPLE ANYTHING.
HAVING POWERS DOESN'T MEAN YOU HAVE TO SAVE THE WORLD.
Oh, and I also got this new necklace, which I think is pretty nice.
So, you know. Busy week.
Umm... "curse"?

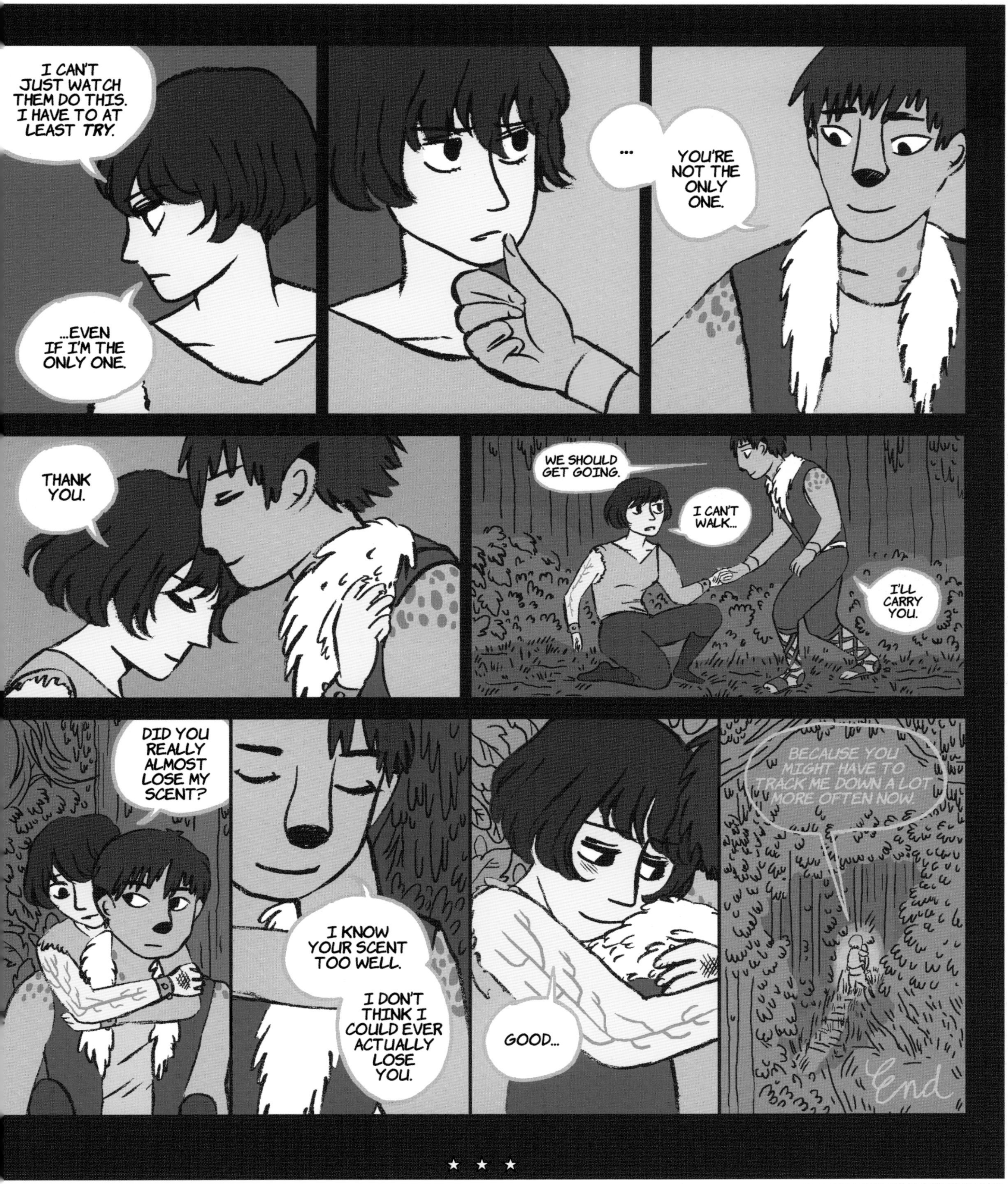
I CAN'T JUST WATCH THEM DO THIS. I HAVE TO AT LEAST TRY.
...EVEN IF I'M THE ONLY ONE.
...
YOU'RE NOT THE ONLY ONE.
THANK YOU.
WE SHOULD GET GOING.
I CAN'T WALK...
I'LL CARRY YOU.
DID YOU REALLY ALMOST LOSE MY SCENT?
I KNOW YOUR SCENT TOO WELL.
I DON'T THINK I COULD EVER ACTUALLY LOSE YOU.
GOOD...
BECAUSE YOU MIGHT HAVE TO TRACK ME DOWN A LOT MORE OFTEN NOW.
End

★ ★ ★

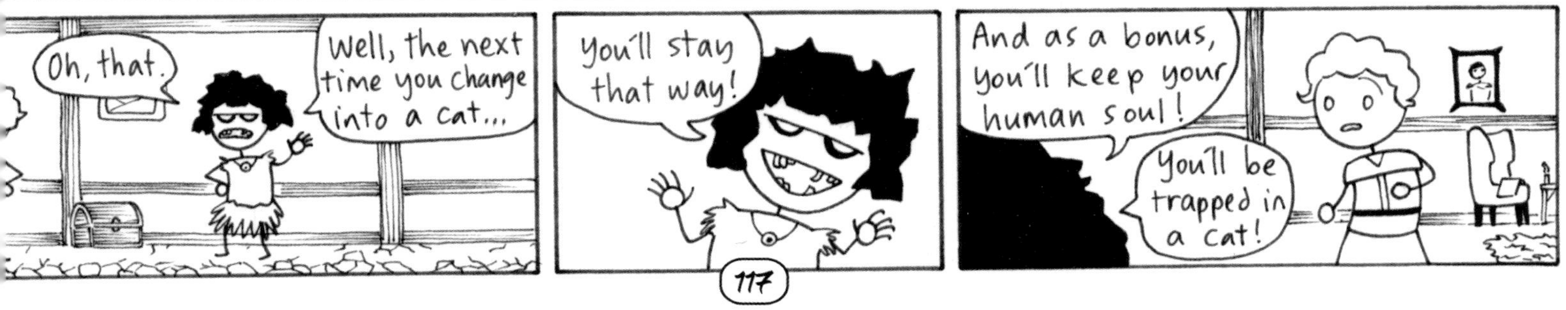
Oh, that.
Well, the next time you change into a cat...
You'll stay that way!
And as a bonus, you'll keep your human soul!
You'll be trapped in a cat!

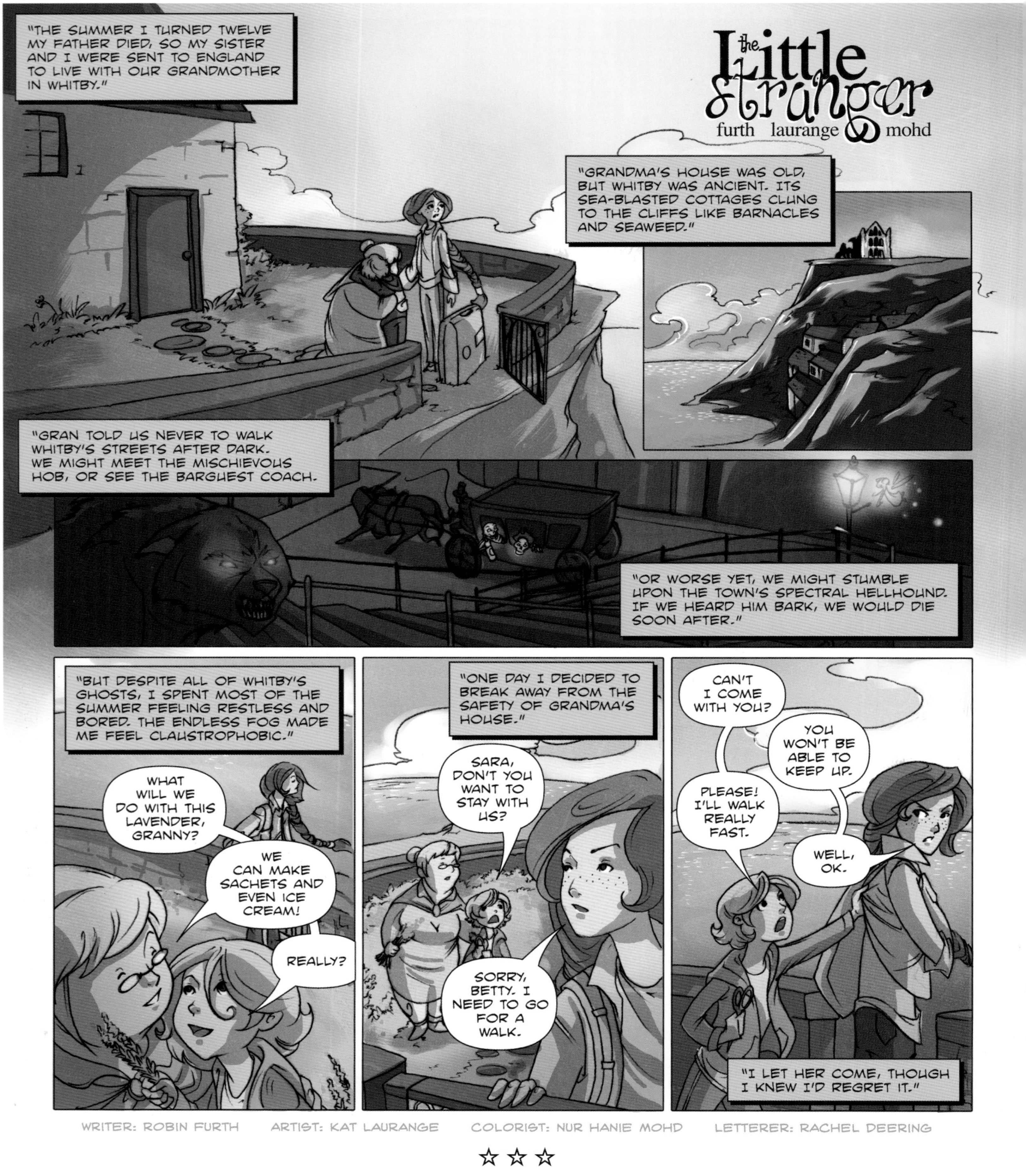
the Little Stranger
furth laurange & mohd
"THE SUMMER I TURNED TWELVE MY FATHER DIED, SO MY SISTER AND I WERE SENT TO ENGLAND TO LIVE WITH OUR GRANDMOTHER IN WHITBY."
"GRANDMA'S HOUSE WAS OLD, BUT WHITBY WAS ANCIENT. ITS SEA-BLASTED COTTAGES CLUNG TO THE CLIFFS LIKE BARNACLES AND SEAWEED."
"GRAN TOLD US NEVER TO WALK WHITBY'S STREETS AFTER DARK. WE MIGHT MEET THE MISCHIEVOUS HOB, OR SEE THE BARGUEST COACH.
"OR WORSE YET, WE MIGHT STUMBLE UPON THE TOWN'S SPECTRAL HELLHOUND. IF WE HEARD HIM BARK, WE WOULD DIE SOON AFTER."
"BUT DESPITE ALL OF WHITBY'S GHOSTS, I SPENT MOST OF THE SUMMER FEELING RESTLESS AND BORED. THE ENDLESS FOG MADE ME FEEL CLAUSTROPHOBIC."
WHAT WILL WE DO WITH THIS LAVENDER, GRANNY?
WE CAN MAKE SACHETS AND EVEN ICE CREAM!
REALLY?
"ONE DAY I DECIDED TO BREAK AWAY FROM THE SAFETY OF GRANDMA'S HOUSE."
SARA, DON'T YOU WANT TO STAY WITH US?
SORRY, BETTY. I NEED TO GO FOR A WALK.
CAN'T I COME WITH YOU?
YOU WON'T BE ABLE TO KEEP UP.
PLEASE! I'LL WALK REALLY FAST.
WELL, OK.
"I LET HER COME, THOUGH I KNEW I'D REGRET IT."

WRITER: ROBIN FURTH ARTIST: KAT LAURANGE COLORIST: NUR HANIE MOHD LETTERER: RACHEL DEERING

☆ ☆ ☆

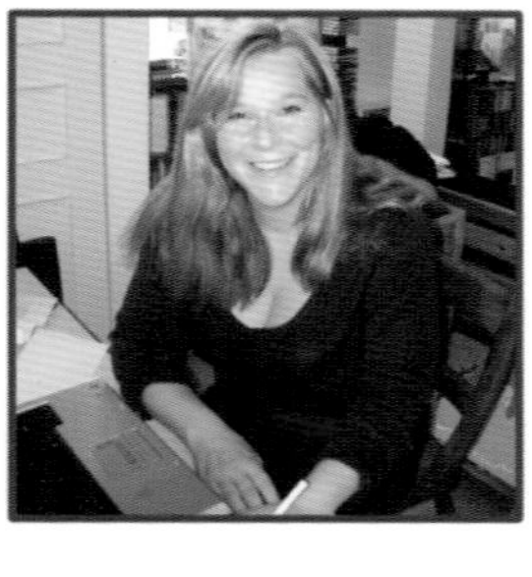

ROBIN FURTH

SKILLS: Writer
LOCATION: US/UK
FUN FACT: I've spent much of the last decade traveling around Mid-World with a wandering gunslinger!

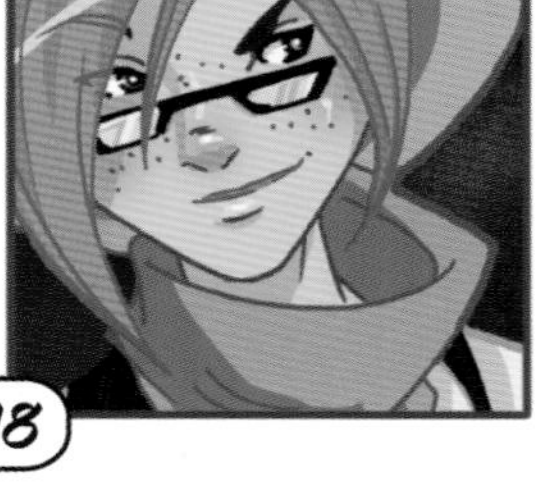

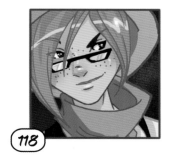

KAT LAURANGE

SKILLS: Penciller, Inker
LOCATION: Texas
FUN FACT: When I was little, I wanted to be a vet. That, or a pirate!

katlaurange.daportfolio.com

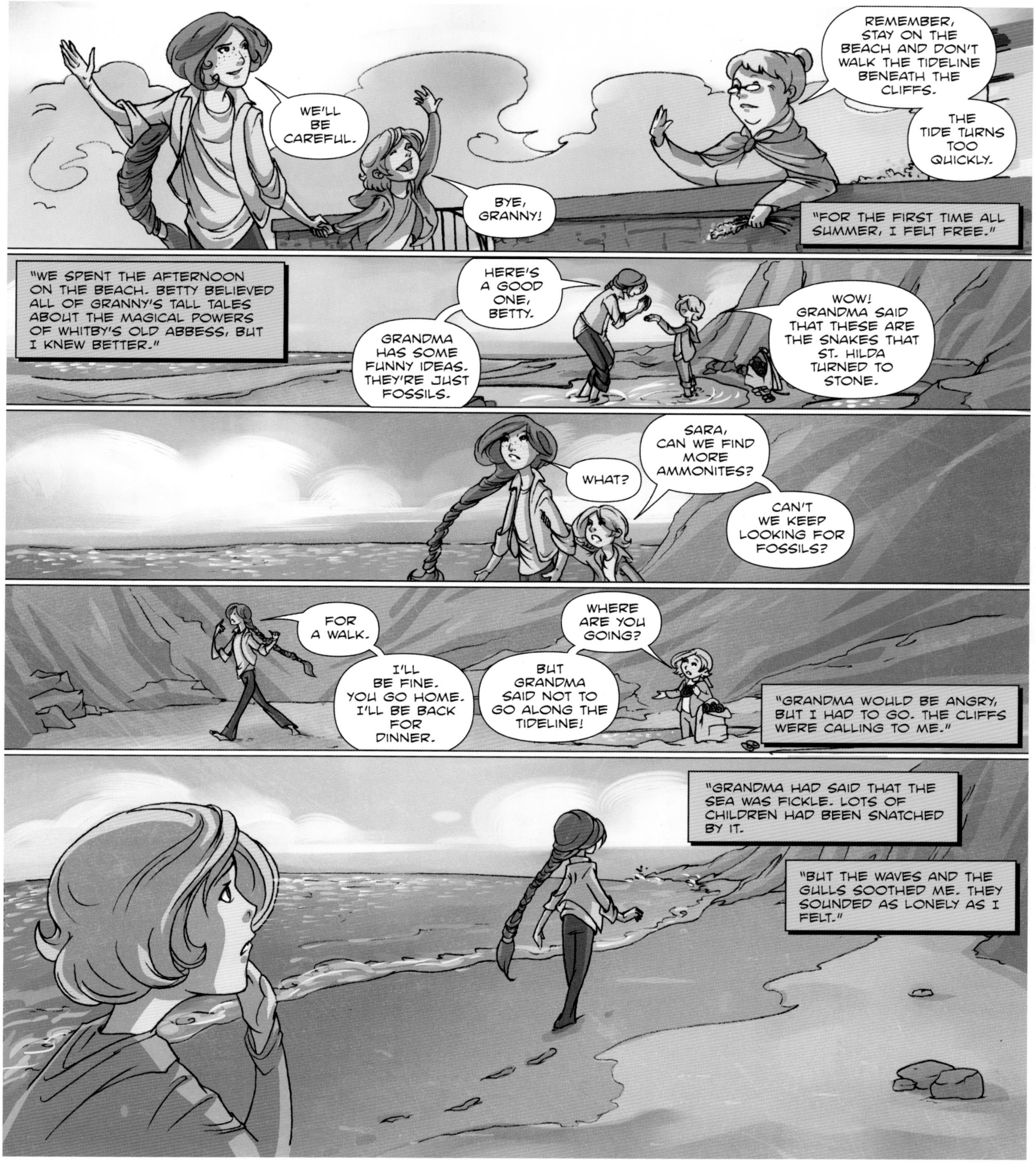
WE'LL BE CAREFUL.
BYE, GRANNY!
REMEMBER, STAY ON THE BEACH AND DON'T WALK THE TIDELINE BENEATH THE CLIFFS.
THE TIDE TURNS TOO QUICKLY.
"FOR THE FIRST TIME ALL SUMMER, I FELT FREE."
"WE SPENT THE AFTERNOON ON THE BEACH. BETTY BELIEVED ALL OF GRANNY'S TALL TALES ABOUT THE MAGICAL POWERS OF WHITBY'S OLD ABBESS, BUT I KNEW BETTER."
HERE'S A GOOD ONE, BETTY.
GRANDMA HAS SOME FUNNY IDEAS. THEY'RE JUST FOSSILS.
WOW! GRANDMA SAID THAT THESE ARE THE SNAKES THAT ST. HILDA TURNED TO STONE.
WHAT?
SARA, CAN WE FIND MORE AMMONITES?
CAN'T WE KEEP LOOKING FOR FOSSILS?
FOR A WALK.
I'LL BE FINE. YOU GO HOME. I'LL BE BACK FOR DINNER.
WHERE ARE YOU GOING?
BUT GRANDMA SAID NOT TO GO ALONG THE TIDELINE!
"GRANDMA WOULD BE ANGRY, BUT I HAD TO GO. THE CLIFFS WERE CALLING TO ME."
"GRANDMA HAD SAID THAT THE SEA WAS FICKLE. LOTS OF CHILDREN HAD BEEN SNATCHED BY IT.
"BUT THE WAVES AND THE GULLS SOOTHED ME. THEY SOUNDED AS LONELY AS I FELT."

☆☆☆

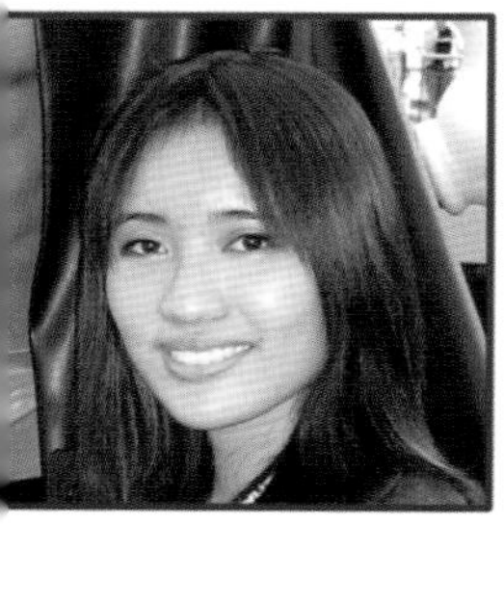

NUR HANIE MOHD

SKILLS: Penciller, Colorist, Inker, Letterer
LOCATION: Kuching, Malaysia
FUN FACT: My hand moves funny.

http://haniemohd.blogspot.com

PRO TIP

VISUAL DETAIL
BY ROBIN FURTH

"WHEN YOU WRITE YOUR SCRIPT, MAKE SURE THAT YOU INCLUDE LOTS OF VISUAL DETAIL SO THAT THE ARTIST YOU ARE WORKING WITH CAN SEE EXACTLY WHAT YOU SEE. TAKE TIME OVER EACH PANEL, MAKING SURE THAT YOU ARE CLEAR AND EXACT. REMEMBER, YOU ARE PAINTING PICTURES WITH WORDS."

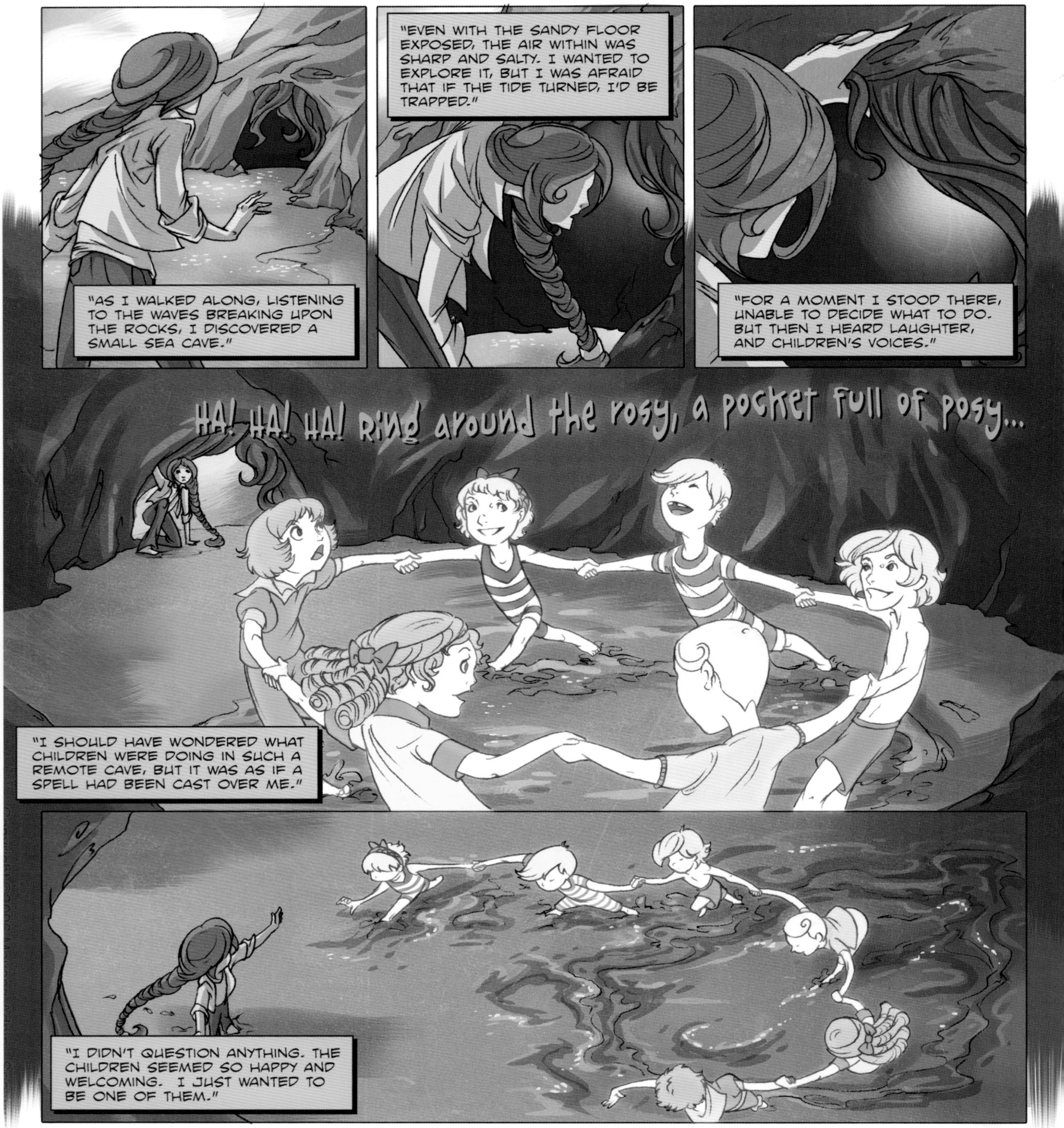
"AS I WALKED ALONG, LISTENING TO THE WAVES BREAKING UPON THE ROCKS, I DISCOVERED A SMALL SEA CAVE."
"EVEN WITH THE SANDY FLOOR EXPOSED, THE AIR WITHIN WAS SHARP AND SALTY. I WANTED TO EXPLORE IT, BUT I WAS AFRAID THAT IF THE TIDE TURNED, I'D BE TRAPPED."
"FOR A MOMENT I STOOD THERE, UNABLE TO DECIDE WHAT TO DO. BUT THEN I HEARD LAUGHTER, AND CHILDREN'S VOICES."
HA! HA! HA! Ring around the rosy, a pocket full of posy...
"I SHOULD HAVE WONDERED WHAT CHILDREN WERE DOING IN SUCH A REMOTE CAVE, BUT IT WAS AS IF A SPELL HAD BEEN CAST OVER ME."
"I DIDN'T QUESTION ANYTHING. THE CHILDREN SEEMED SO HAPPY AND WELCOMING. I JUST WANTED TO BE ONE OF THEM."

☆ ☆ ☆

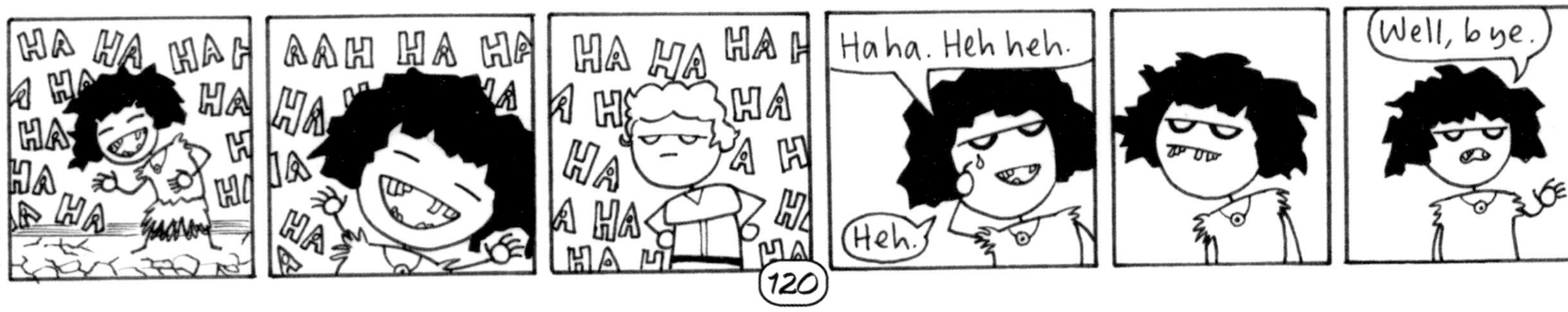
HA HA HA
AAH HA HA
HA HA HA
Haha. Heh heh.
Heh.
Well, bye.

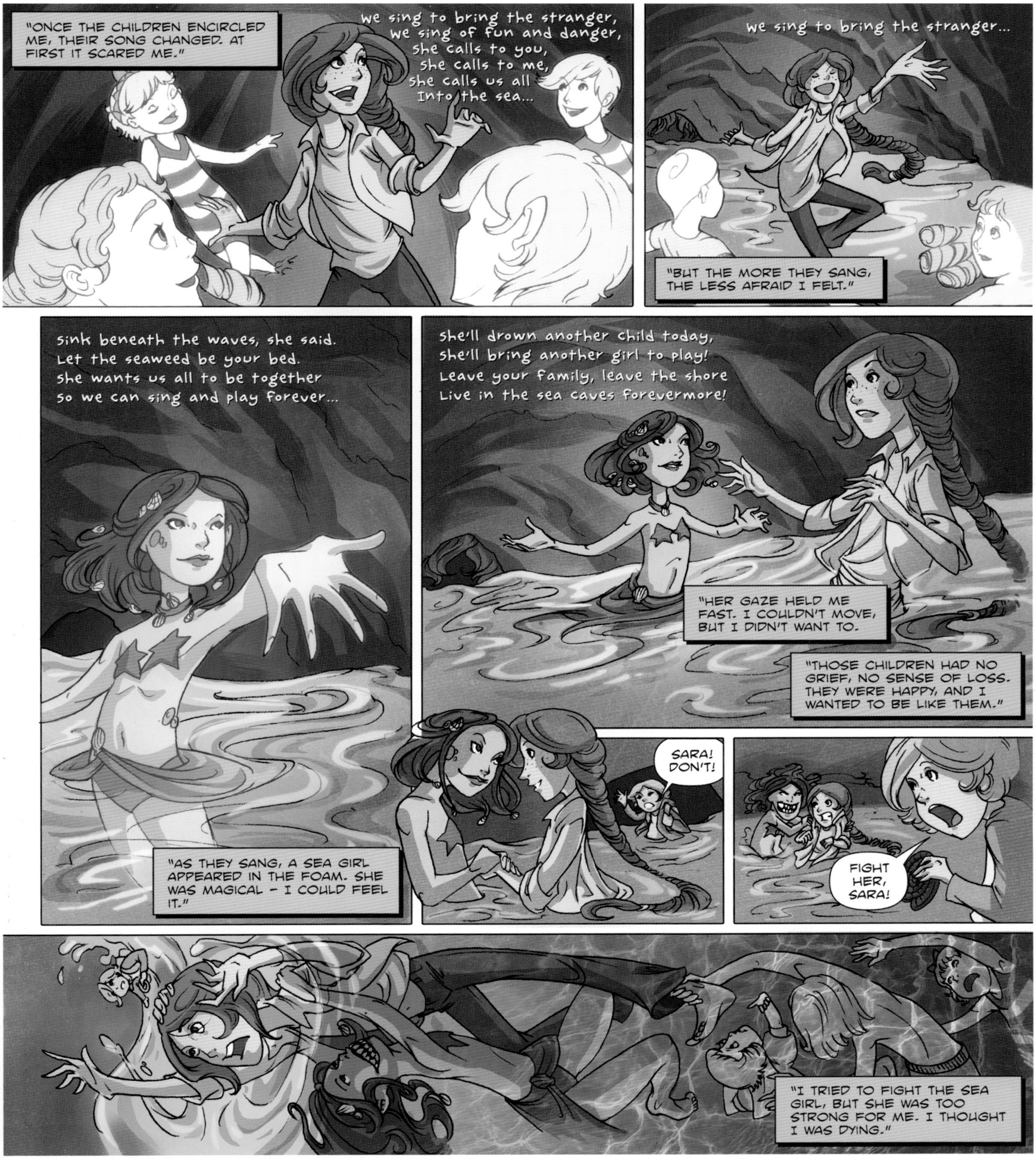
"ONCE THE CHILDREN ENCIRCLED ME, THEIR SONG CHANGED. AT FIRST IT SCARED ME."
We sing to bring the stranger, we sing of fun and danger, she calls to you, she calls to me, she calls us all into the sea...
We sing to bring the stranger...
"BUT THE MORE THEY SANG, THE LESS AFRAID I FELT."
Sink beneath the waves, she said. Let the seaweed be your bed. She wants us all to be together so we can sing and play forever...
She'll drown another child today, she'll bring another girl to play! Leave your family, leave the shore Live in the sea caves forevermore!
"HER GAZE HELD ME FAST. I COULDN'T MOVE, BUT I DIDN'T WANT TO.
"THOSE CHILDREN HAD NO GRIEF, NO SENSE OF LOSS. THEY WERE HAPPY, AND I WANTED TO BE LIKE THEM."
"AS THEY SANG, A SEA GIRL APPEARED IN THE FOAM. SHE WAS MAGICAL - I COULD FEEL IT."
SARA! DON'T!
FIGHT HER, SARA!
"I TRIED TO FIGHT THE SEA GIRL, BUT SHE WAS TOO STRONG FOR ME. I THOUGHT I WAS DYING."

☆ ☆ ☆

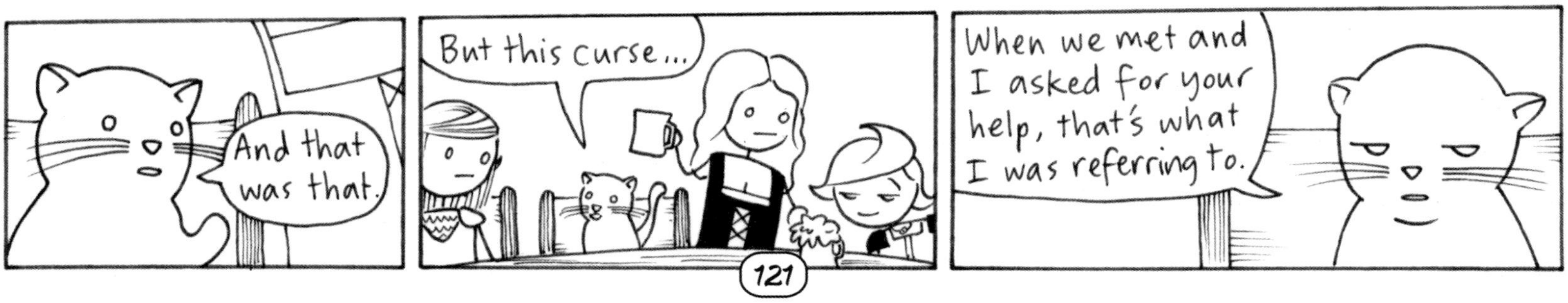
And that was that.
But this curse...
When we met and I asked for your help, that's what I was referring to.

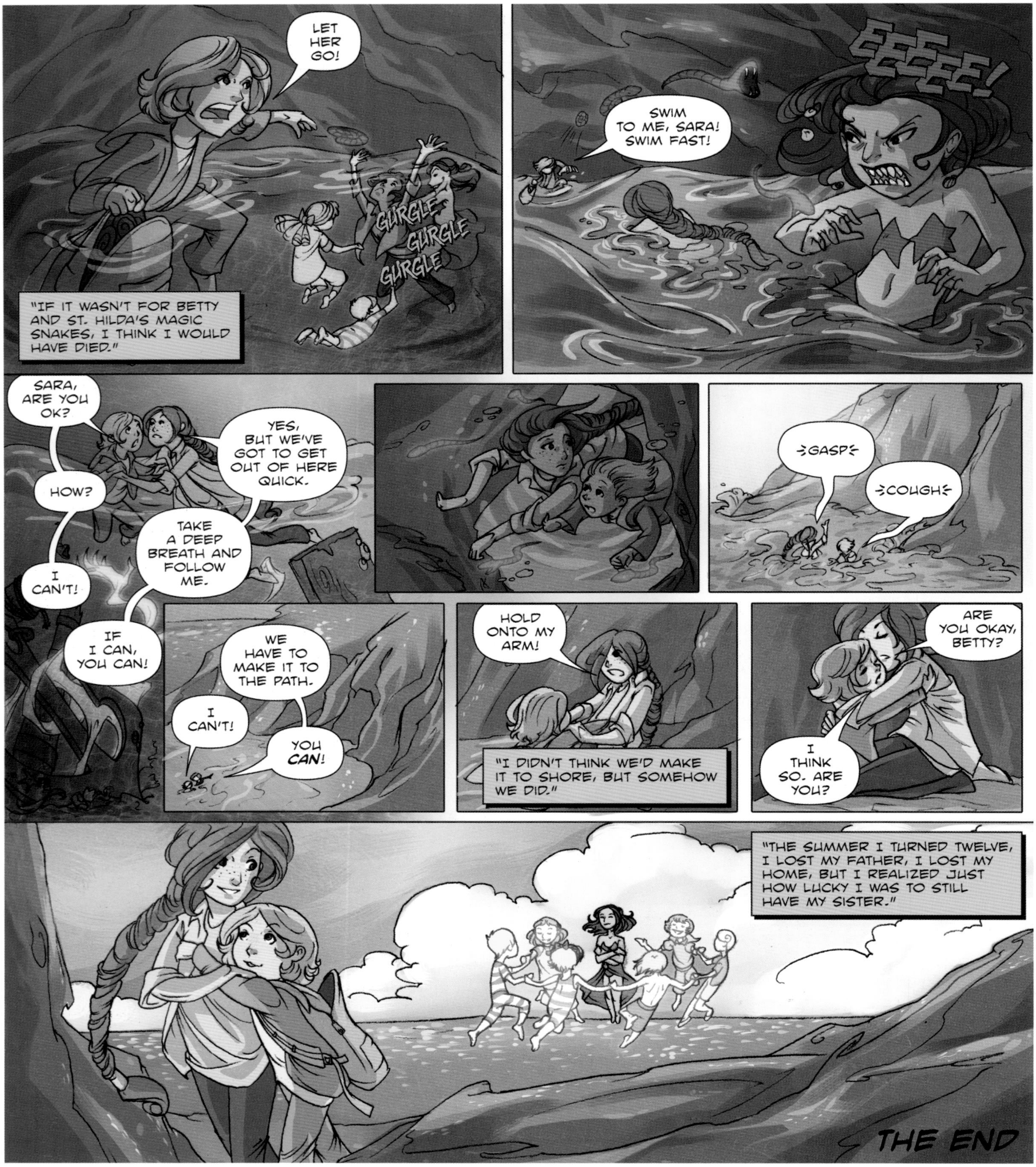
LET HER GO!
GURGLE
GURGLE
GURGLE
"IF IT WASN'T FOR BETTY AND ST. HILDA'S MAGIC SNAKES, I THINK I WOULD HAVE DIED."
EEEEE!
SWIM TO ME, SARA! SWIM FAST!
SARA, ARE YOU OK?
YES, BUT WE'VE GOT TO GET OUT OF HERE QUICK.
HOW?
TAKE A DEEP BREATH AND FOLLOW ME.
I CAN'T!
IF I CAN, YOU CAN!
GASP
COUGH
WE HAVE TO MAKE IT TO THE PATH.
I CAN'T!
YOU **CAN**!
HOLD ONTO MY ARM!
"I DIDN'T THINK WE'D MAKE IT TO SHORE, BUT SOMEHOW WE DID."
ARE YOU OKAY, BETTY?
I THINK SO. ARE YOU?
"THE SUMMER I TURNED TWELVE, I LOST MY FATHER, I LOST MY HOME, BUT I REALIZED JUST HOW LUCKY I WAS TO STILL HAVE MY SISTER."
THE END

☆ ☆ ☆

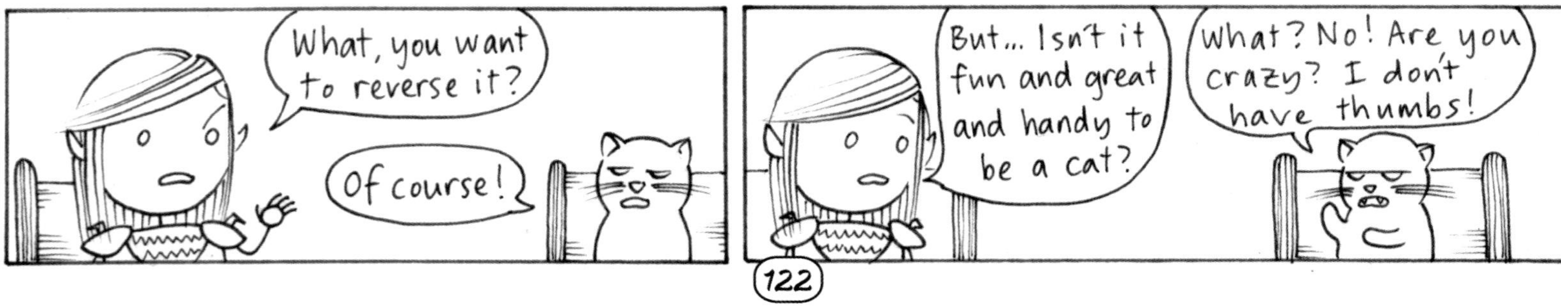
What, you want to reverse it?
Of course!
But... Isn't it fun and great and handy to be a cat?
What? No! Are you crazy? I don't have thumbs!

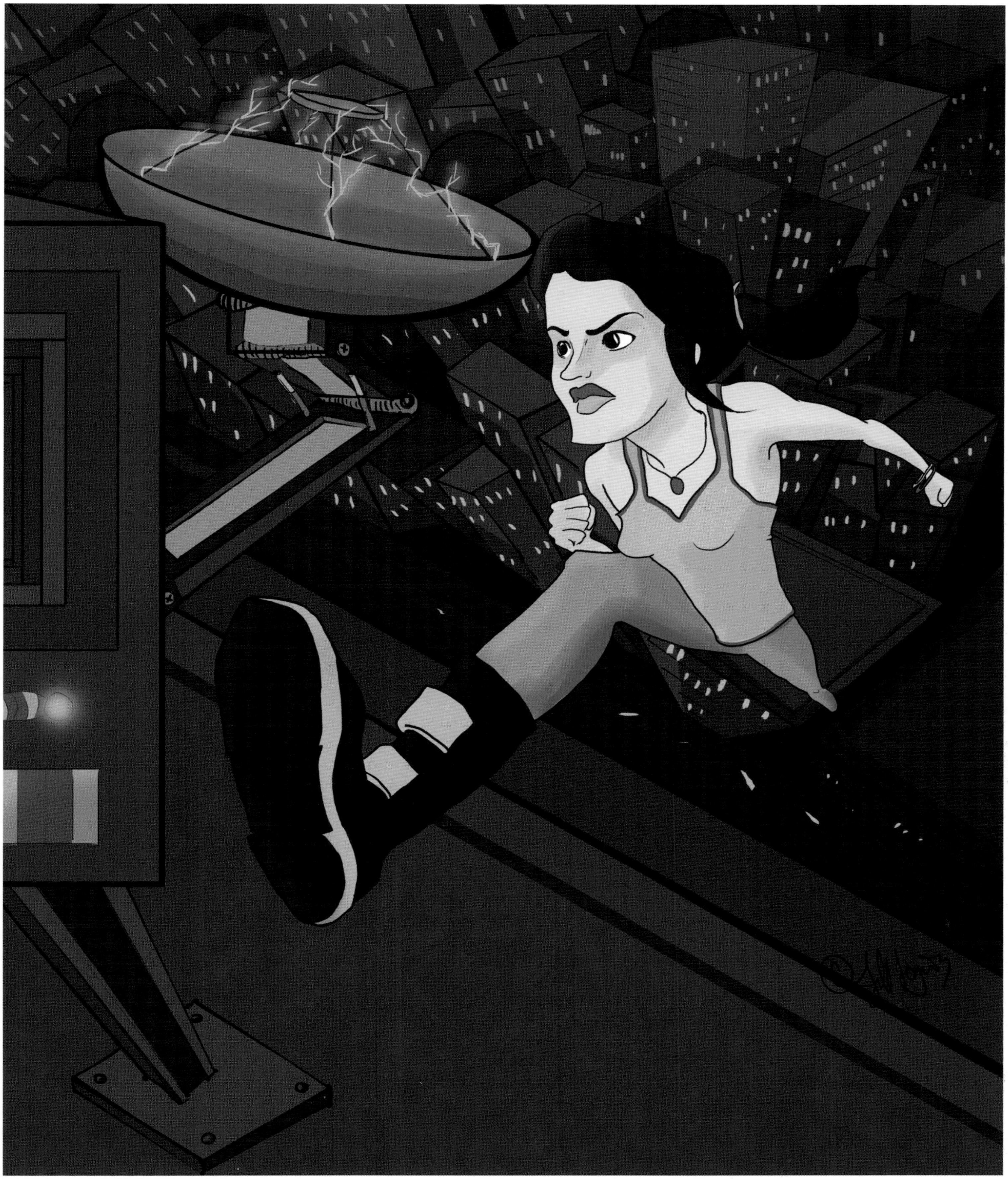

☆☆☆

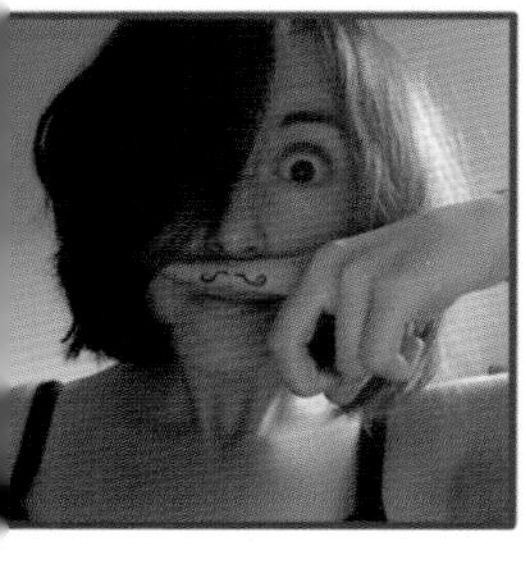

JILL FOGARTY

SKILLS: Pinup Artist
LOCATION: Halifax, Nova Scotia, Canada
FUN FACT: I have a growing collection of tiny col-erase pencils I can't seem to allow myself to throw away.

jillfogarty.blogspot.com

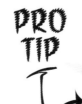

PRO TIP

PROFESSIONALISM
BY JESSICA HICKMAN

"THE COMIC INDUSTRY IS SURPRISINGLY SMALL. ONCE YOU START PUTTING YOUR ARTWORK OUT THERE, PEOPLE WILL PAY ATTENTION. AND IF YOU DO NOT CONDUCT YOURSELF IN A PROFESSIONAL MANNER ONLINE – NO MATTER HOW FEW OR HOW MANY PEOPLE ARE WATCHING YOUR WORK – THAT REPUTATION WILL FOLLOW YOU. IF YOU ARE RUDE AND DISRESPECTFUL, PEOPLE – INCLUDING EDITORS – MIGHT NOT WANT TO WORK WITH YOU ON FUTURE PROJECTS."

SHADOW-DANCERS

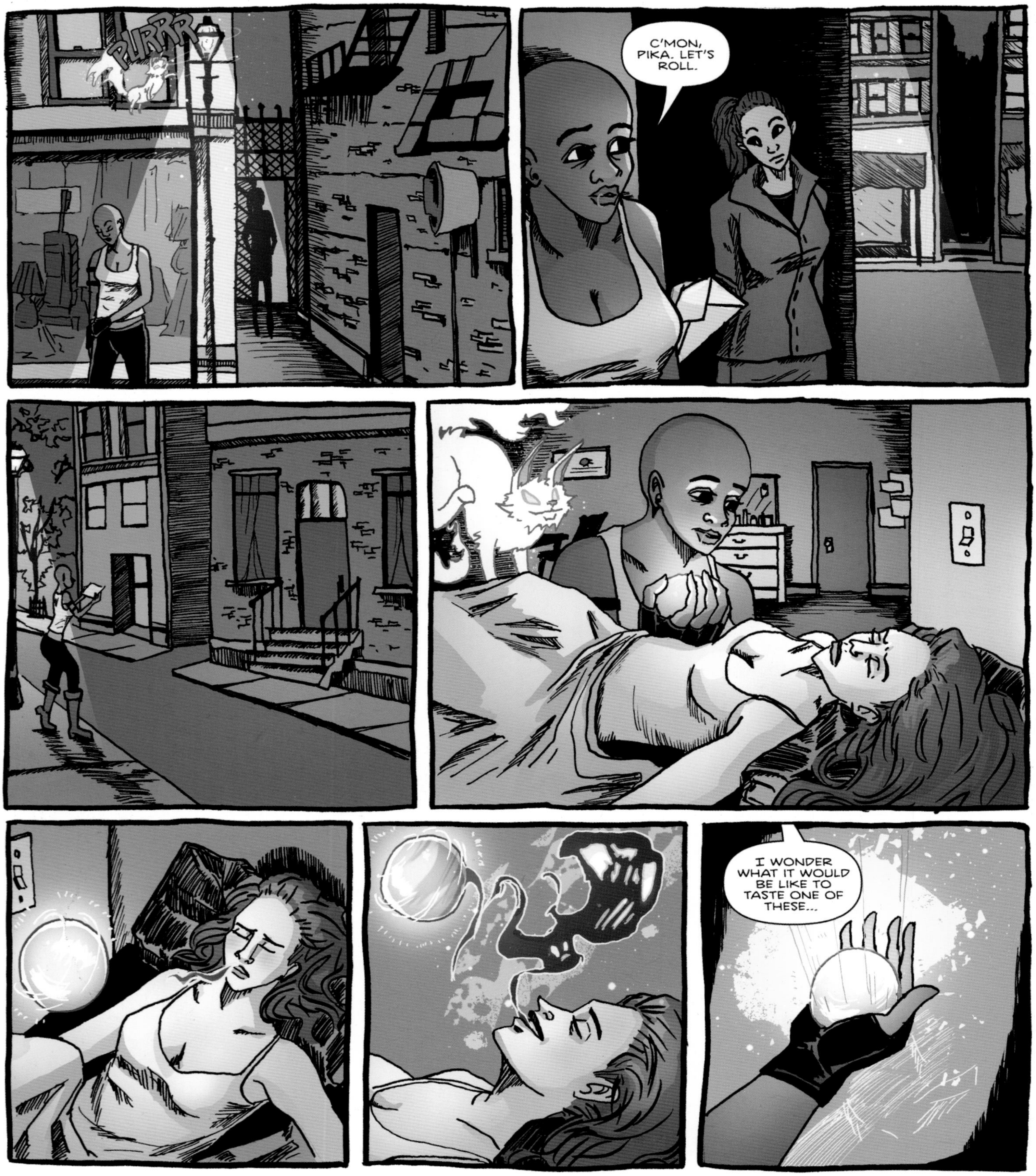
PURRR
C'MON, PIKA. LET'S ROLL.
I WONDER WHAT IT WOULD BE LIKE TO TASTE ONE OF THESE...

WRITER: TATIANA CHRISTIAN ARTIST: ANDREA AGOSTINI COLORIST: BETTIE BREITWIESER LETTERER: RACHEL DEERING

☆☆☆

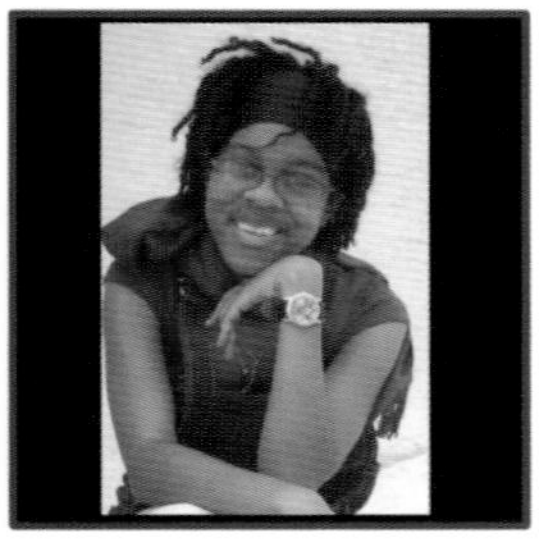

TATIANA CHRISTIAN

SKILLS: Writer; Part of Social Media Team
LOCATION: New York, New York
FUN FACT: I like to read words both upside down and backwards.

parisianfeline.wordpress.com

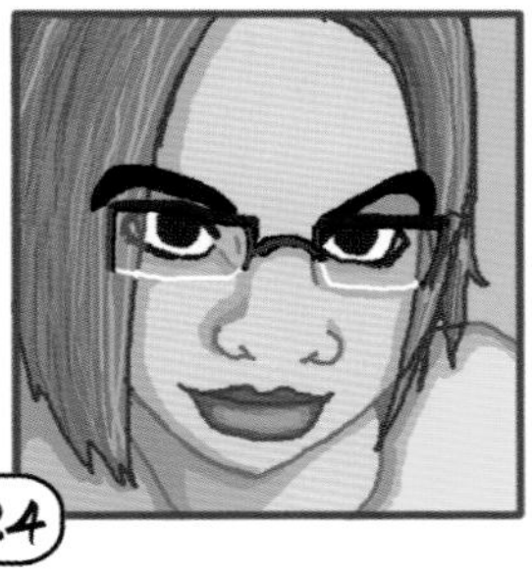

ANDREA AGOSTINI

SKILLS: Penciller, Inker
LOCATION: Taunton, Massachusetts
FUN FACT: I still wonder if I should have become a police officer instead of a cartoonist.

www.andrea-agostini.com

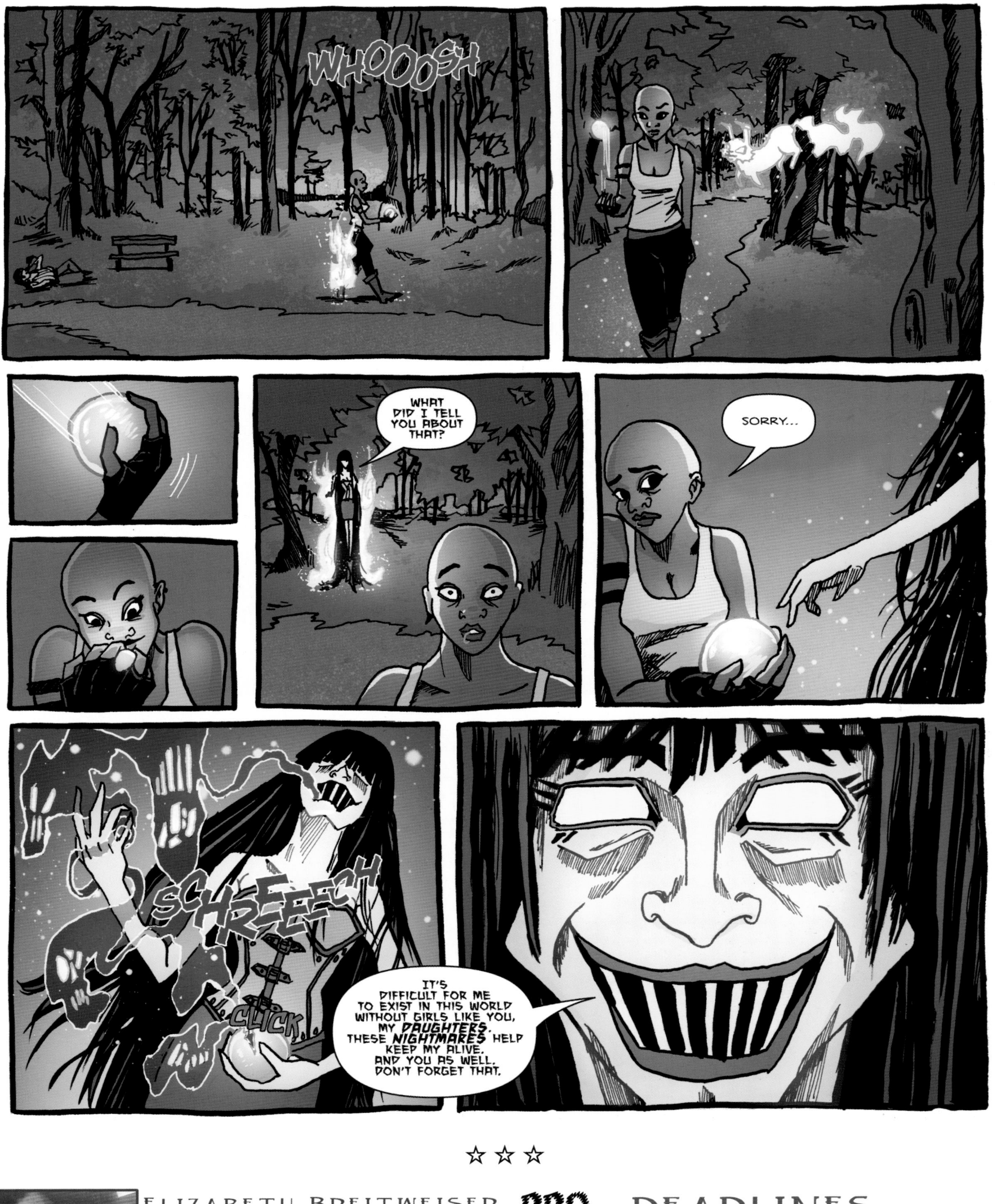
WHOOOOSH
WHAT DID I TELL YOU ABOUT THAT?
SORRY...
SCHREEEECH
CLICK
IT'S DIFFICULT FOR ME TO EXIST IN THIS WORLD WITHOUT GIRLS LIKE YOU, MY *DAUGHTERS*. THESE *NIGHTMARES* HELP KEEP MY ALIVE. AND YOU AS WELL. DON'T FORGET THAT.

☆☆☆

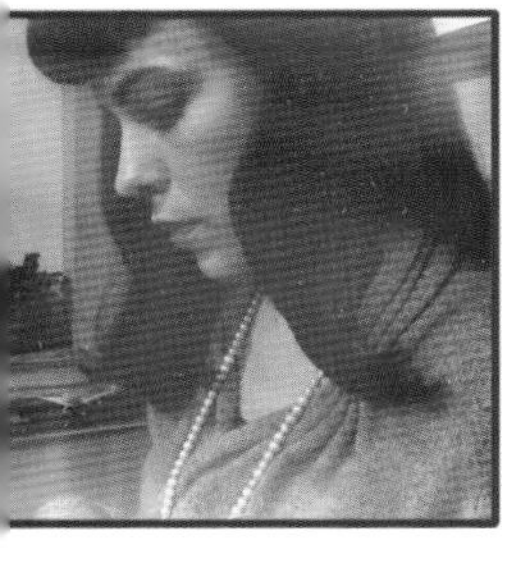

ELIZABETH BREITWEISER

SKILLS: Colorist
LOCATION: Little Rock, AR
FUN FACT: Married to illustrator Mitch Breitweiser. We're both full-time comic creators and flat-faced cat herders!

PRO TIP

DEADLINES
BY STEPHANIE HANS

"NEVER MISS A DEADLINE!"

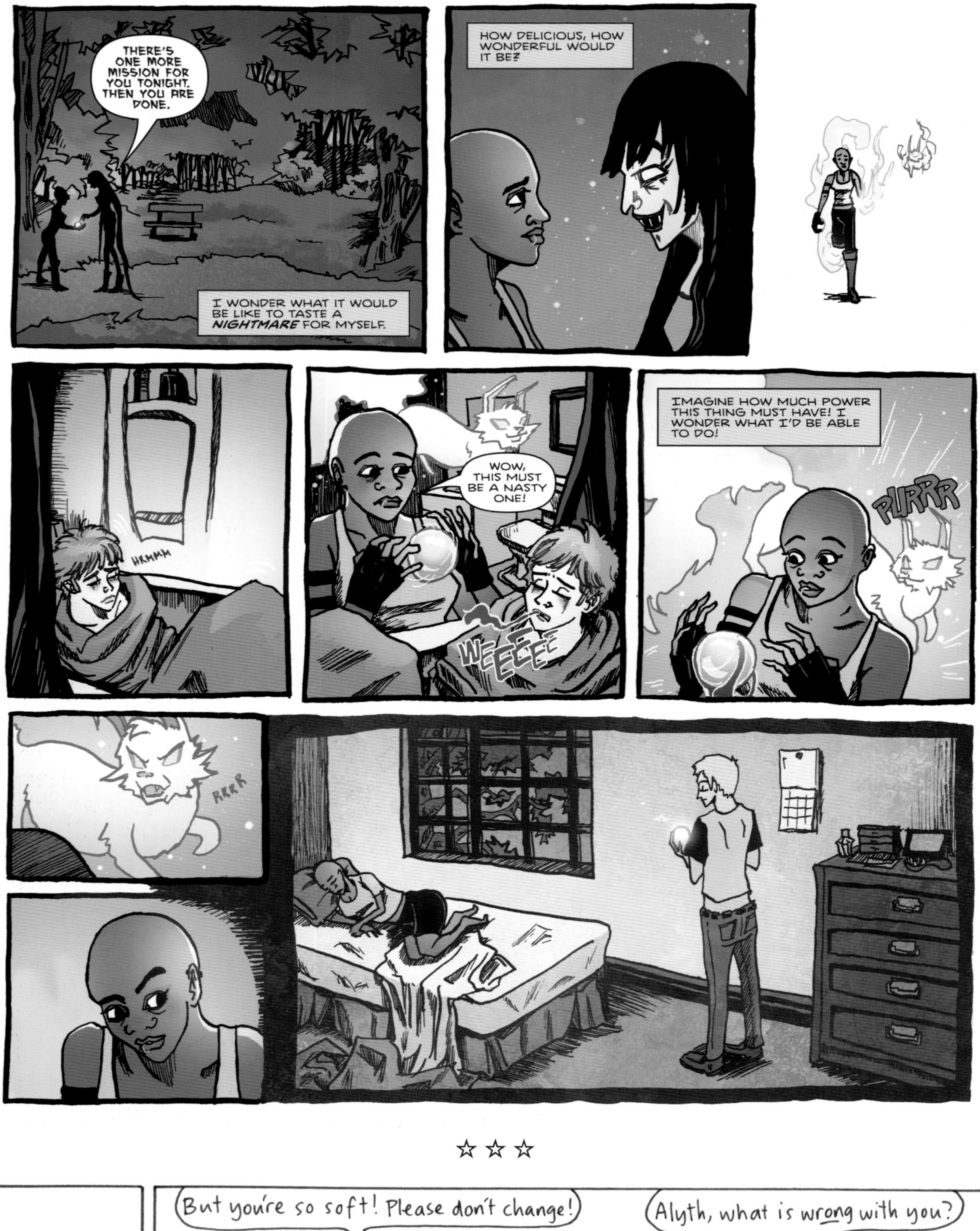
THERE'S ONE MORE MISSION FOR YOU TONIGHT. THEN YOU ARE DONE.
I WONDER WHAT IT WOULD BE LIKE TO TASTE A *NIGHTMARE* FOR MYSELF.
HOW DELICIOUS, HOW WONDERFUL WOULD IT BE?
HMMM
WOW, THIS MUST BE A NASTY ONE!
WEEEEE
IMAGINE HOW MUCH POWER THIS THING MUST HAVE! I WONDER WHAT I'D BE ABLE TO DO!
PURRR
RRRR

☆☆☆

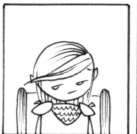

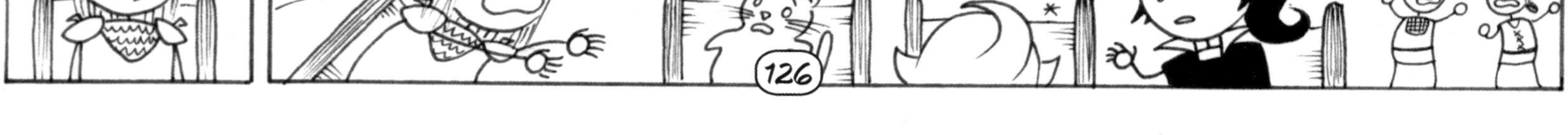
But you're so soft! Please don't change!
Aah!
Alyth, what is wrong with you?

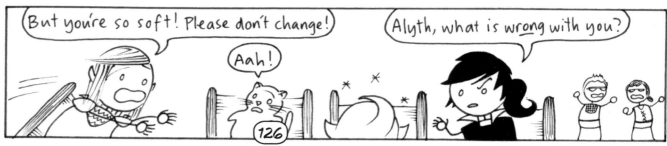

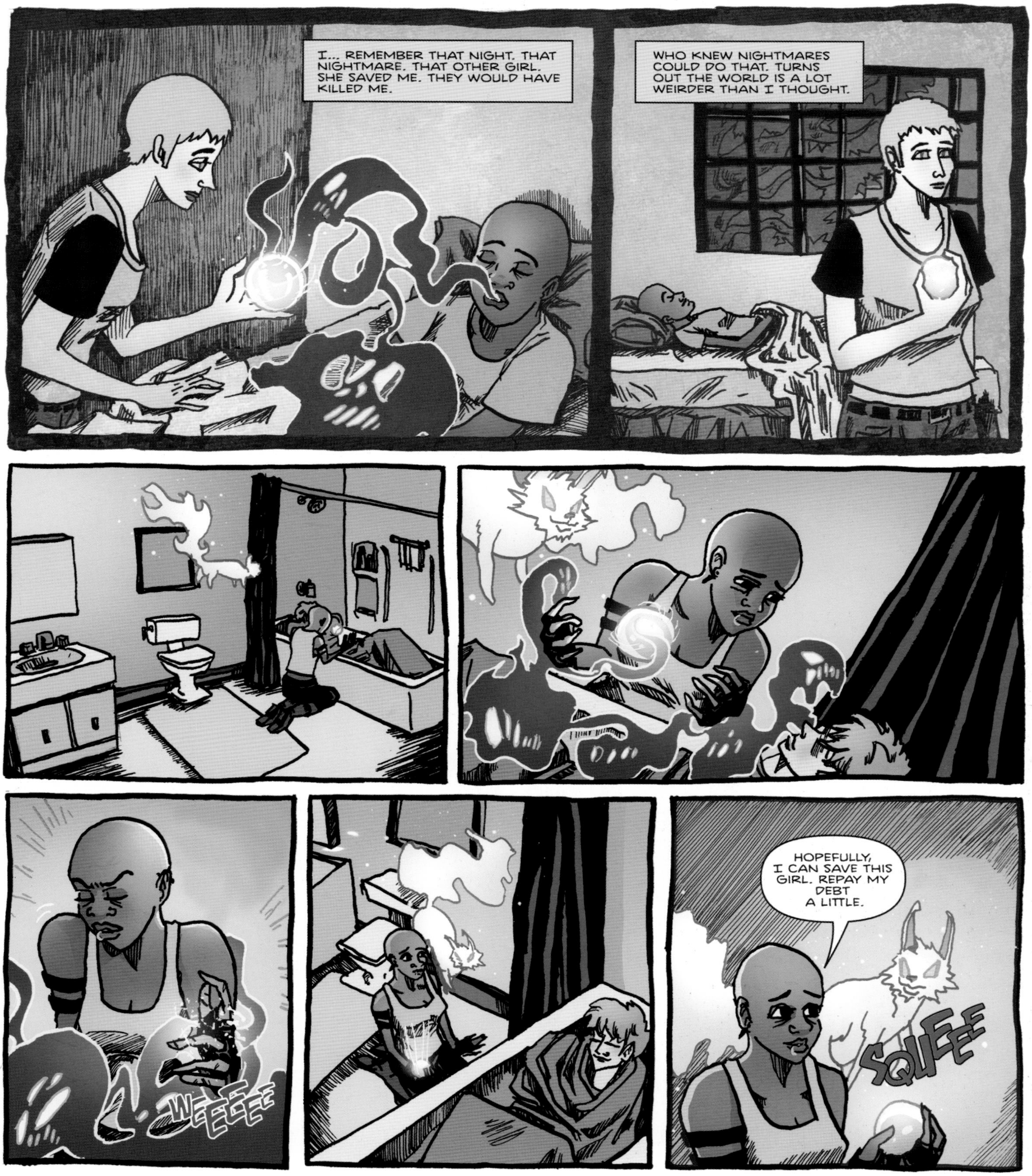
I... REMEMBER THAT NIGHT. THAT NIGHTMARE. THAT OTHER GIRL. SHE SAVED ME. THEY WOULD HAVE KILLED ME.
WHO KNEW NIGHTMARES COULD DO THAT. TURNS OUT THE WORLD IS A LOT WEIRDER THAN I THOUGHT.
WEEEEE
HOPEFULLY, I CAN SAVE THIS GIRL. REPAY MY DEBT A LITTLE.
SQUEEEE

☆ ☆ ☆

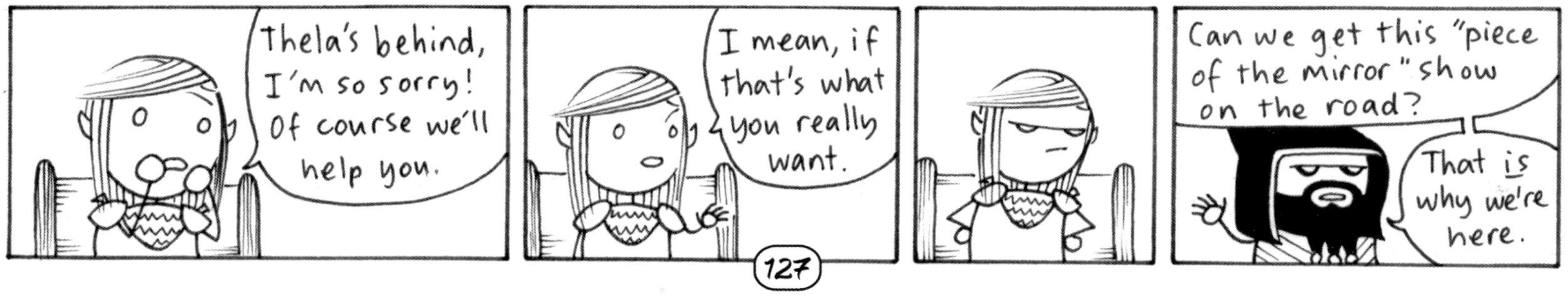
Thela's behind, I'm so sorry! Of course we'll help you.
I mean, if that's what you really want.
Can we get this "piece of the mirror" show on the road?
That is why we're here.

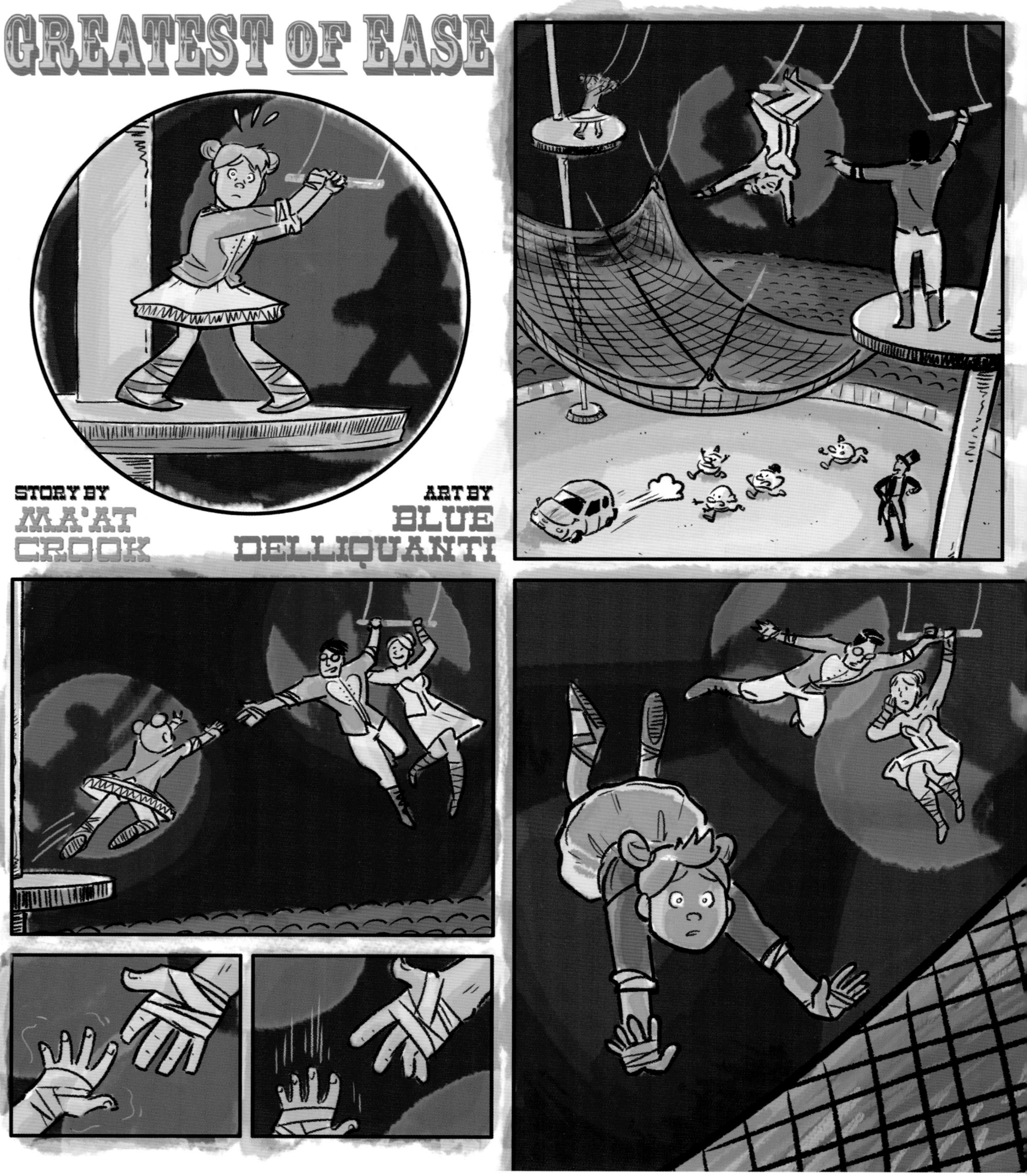
GREATEST OF EASE
STORY BY
MA'AT CROOK
ART BY
BLUE DELLIQUANTI

☆ ☆ ☆

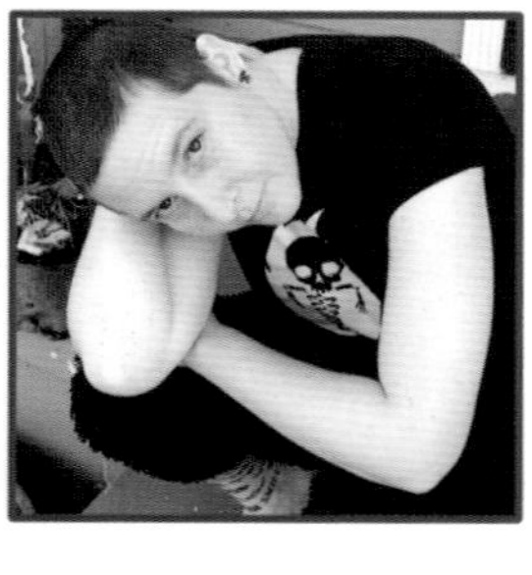

MA'AT CROOK

SKILLS: Writer
LOCATION: San Diego
FUN FACT: I used to be painfully shy, now I get paid to speak in public.

maatcrook.tumblr.com

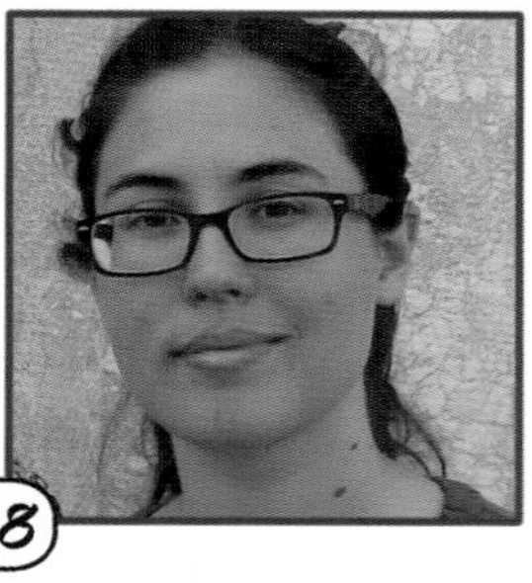

BLUE DELLIQUANT

SKILLS: Penciller, Inker, Colorist, Letterer
LOCATION: Atlanta, GA
FUN FACT: I've been to more than 10 countries!

bluedelliquanti.com

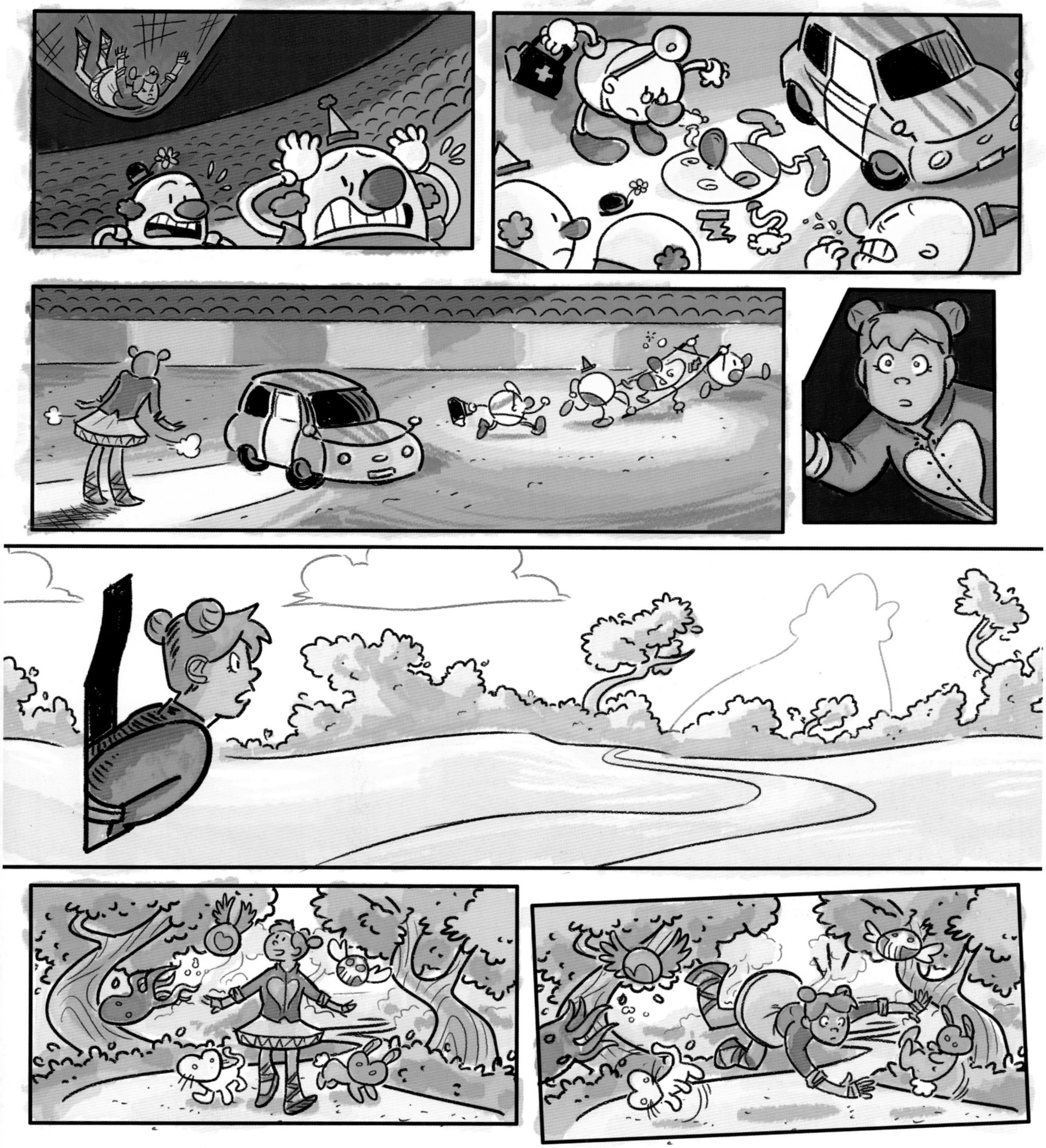

☆ ☆ ☆

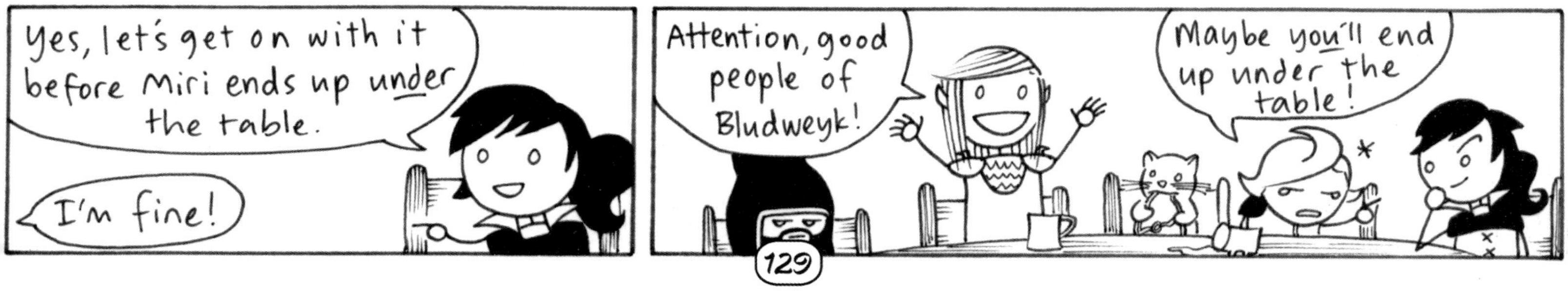
Yes, let's get on with it before Miri ends up under the table.
I'm fine!
Attention, good people of Bludweyk!
Maybe you'll end up under the table!
*

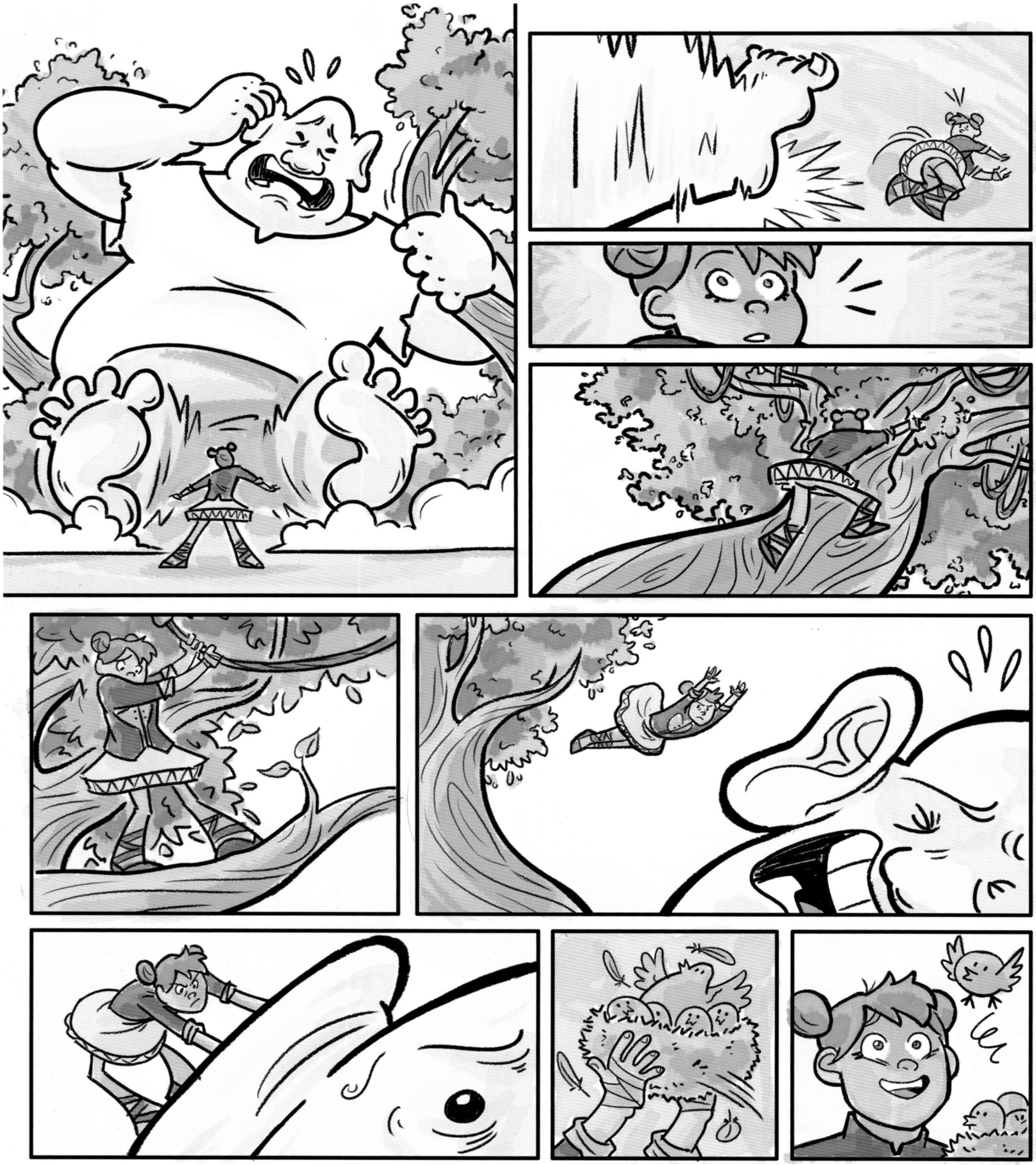

☆ ☆ ☆

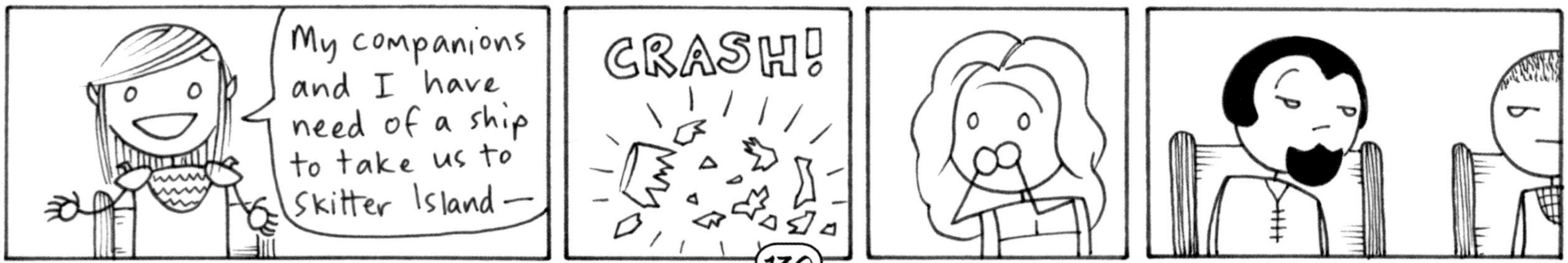
My companions and I have need of a ship to take us to Skitter Island—
CRASH!

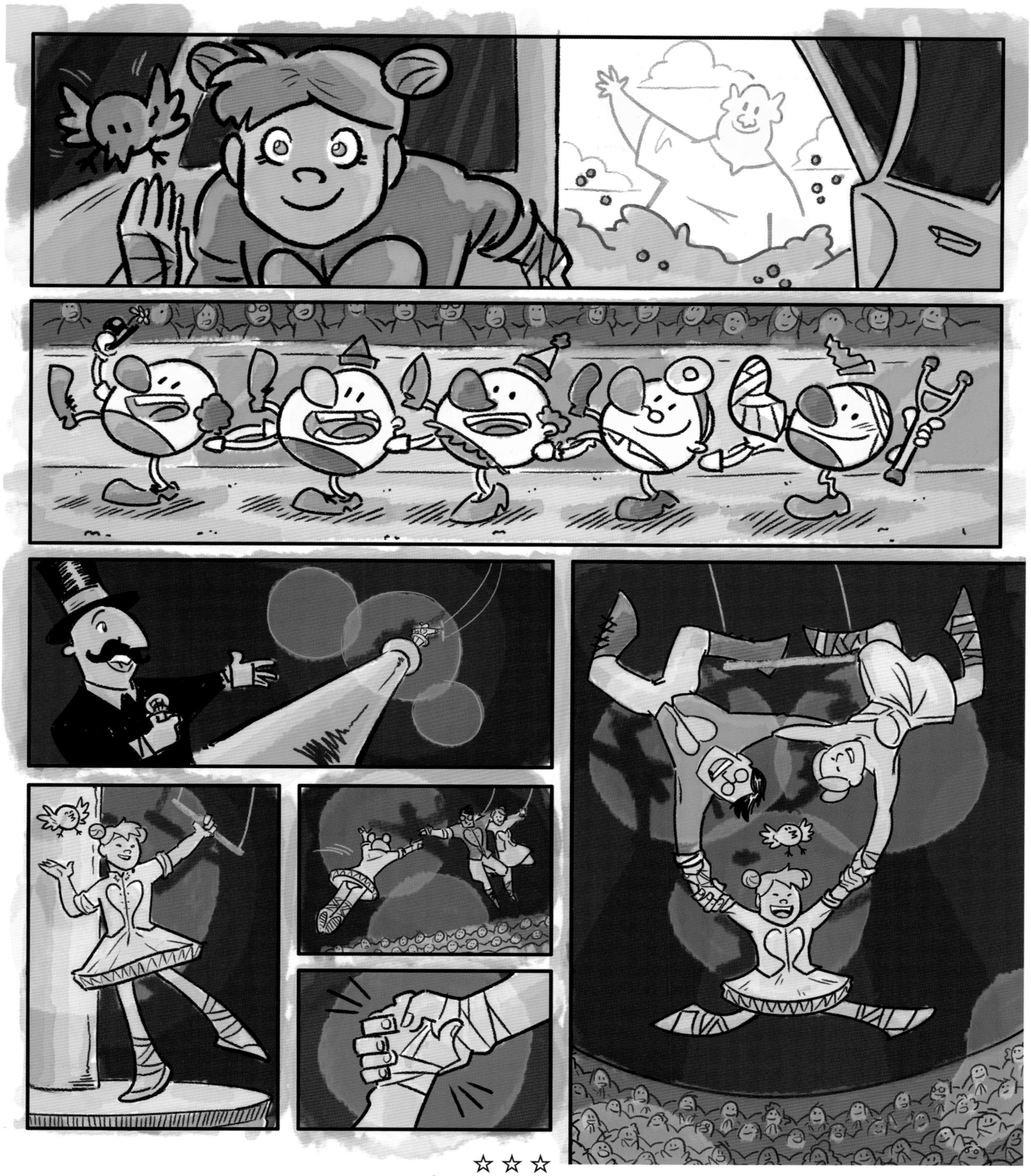

☆ ☆ ☆

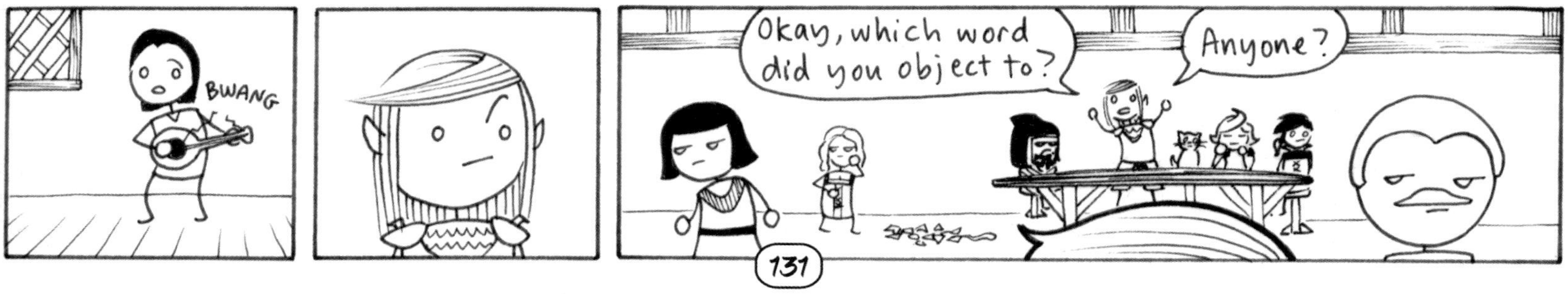
BWANG
Okay, which word did you object to?
Anyone?

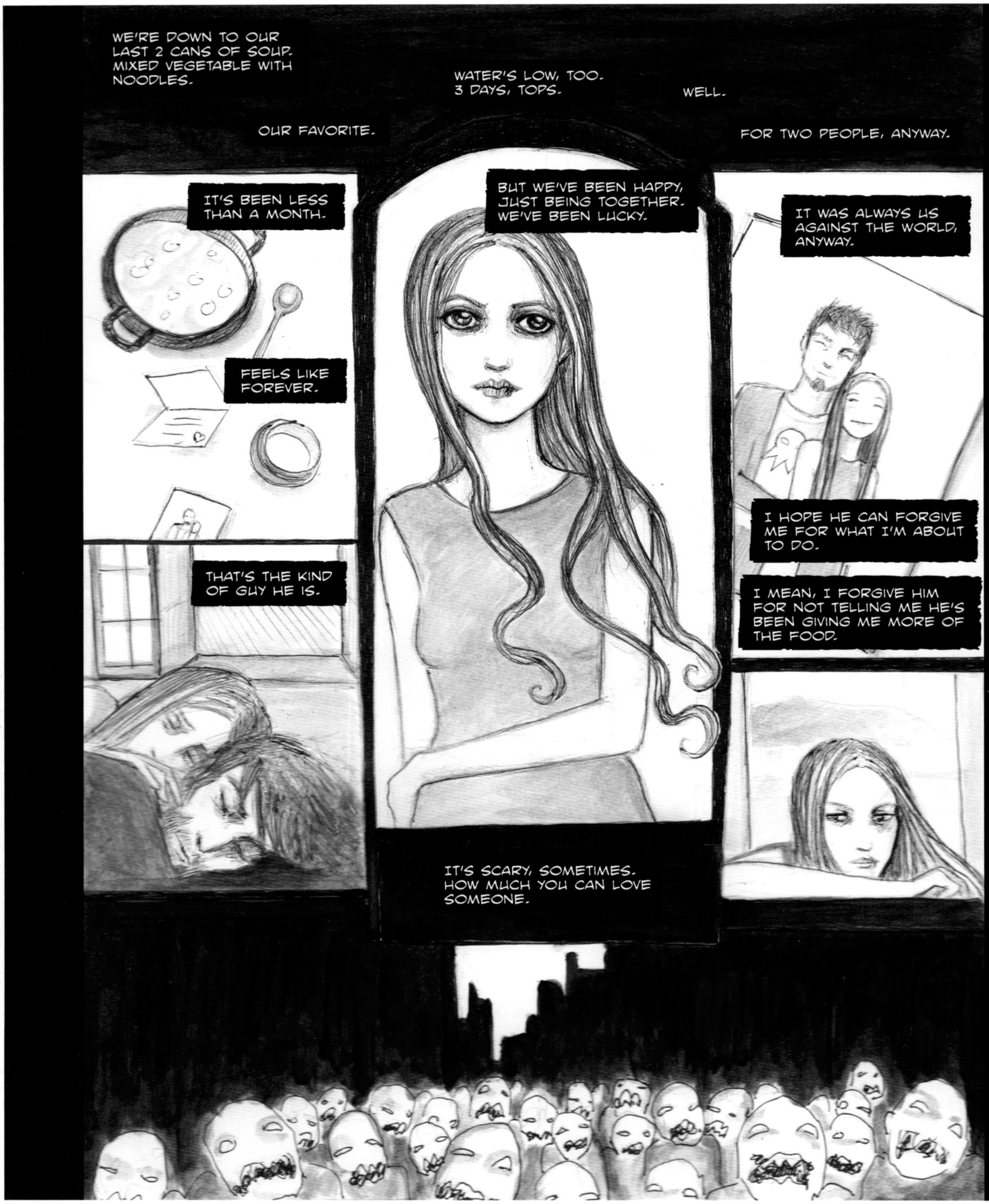

WE'RE DOWN TO OUR LAST 2 CANS OF SOUP. MIXED VEGETABLE WITH NOODLES.
OUR FAVORITE.
WATER'S LOW, TOO. 3 DAYS, TOPS.
WELL.
FOR TWO PEOPLE, ANYWAY.
IT'S BEEN LESS THAN A MONTH.
FEELS LIKE FOREVER.
THAT'S THE KIND OF GUY HE IS.
BUT WE'VE BEEN HAPPY, JUST BEING TOGETHER. WE'VE BEEN LUCKY.
IT WAS ALWAYS US AGAINST THE WORLD, ANYWAY.
I HOPE HE CAN FORGIVE ME FOR WHAT I'M ABOUT TO DO.
I MEAN, I FORGIVE HIM FOR NOT TELLING ME HE'S BEEN GIVING ME MORE OF THE FOOD.
IT'S SCARY, SOMETIMES. HOW MUCH YOU CAN LOVE SOMEONE.

writer & artist: Mariah McCourt Letterer: Rachel Deering

☆☆☆

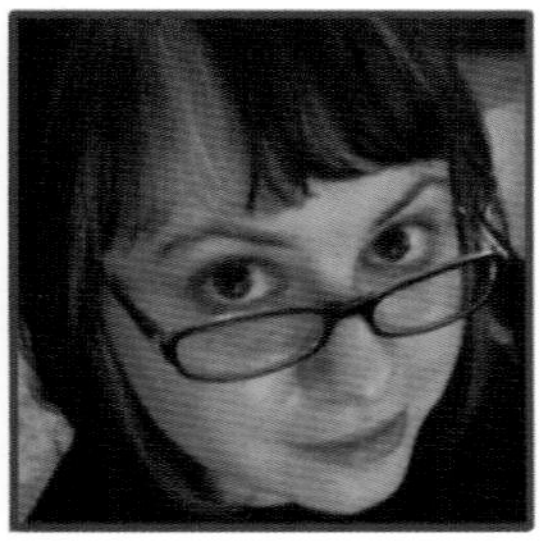

MARIAH MCCOURT

SKILLS: Writer, Artist, Editor
LOCATION: San Francisco
FUN FACT: Stories are my life.

squidygirl.blogspot.com

PRO TIP

NO APOLOGIES

BY WENDY PINI

"YOUNG WOMAN ARTIST WANTING TO BREAK INTO TH[E] COMICS INDUSTRY: PLEASE PLEASE PLEASE! WHEN YO[U] PRESENT YOUR PORTFOLIO FOR REVIEW TO AN EDITOR O[R] PUBLISHER NEVER NEVER NEVER APOLOGIZE FOR TH[E] WORK OR ADMIT IN ANY WAY THAT IT'S LESS THAN YOU[R] BEST. NEVER EXPLAIN YOUR WORK. STAND THER[E] QUIETLY, NO MATTER HOW MUCH THE SILENCE IS KILLIN[G] YOU, AND ALLOW THE EXPERIENCED PROFESSIONA[L] REVIEWING YOUR PORTFOLIO TO FORM THEIR OW[N] OPINION."

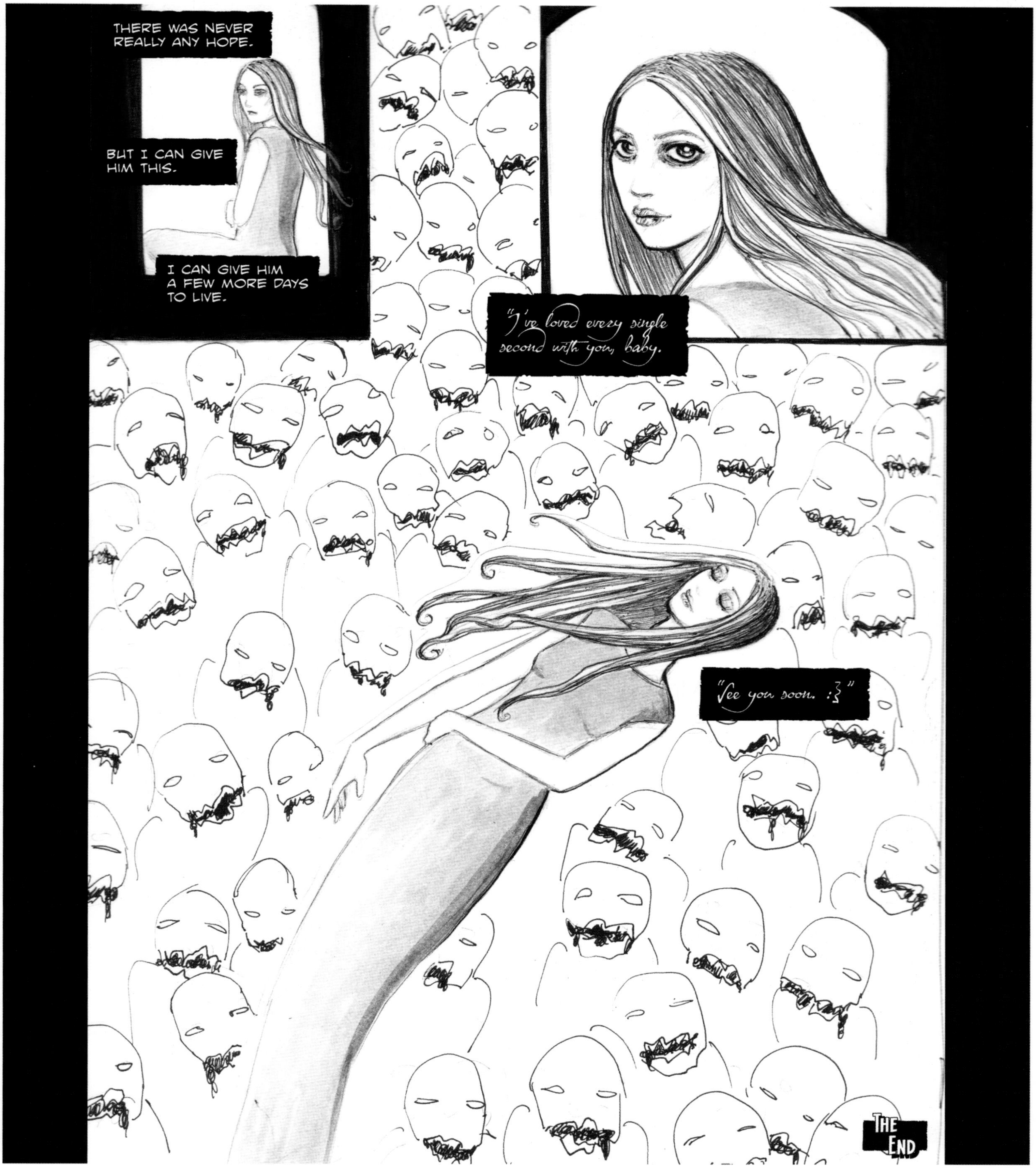
THERE WAS NEVER REALLY ANY HOPE.
BUT I CAN GIVE HIM THIS.
I CAN GIVE HIM A FEW MORE DAYS TO LIVE.
"I've loved every single second with you, baby.
"See you soon. :3"
THE END

☆ ☆ ☆

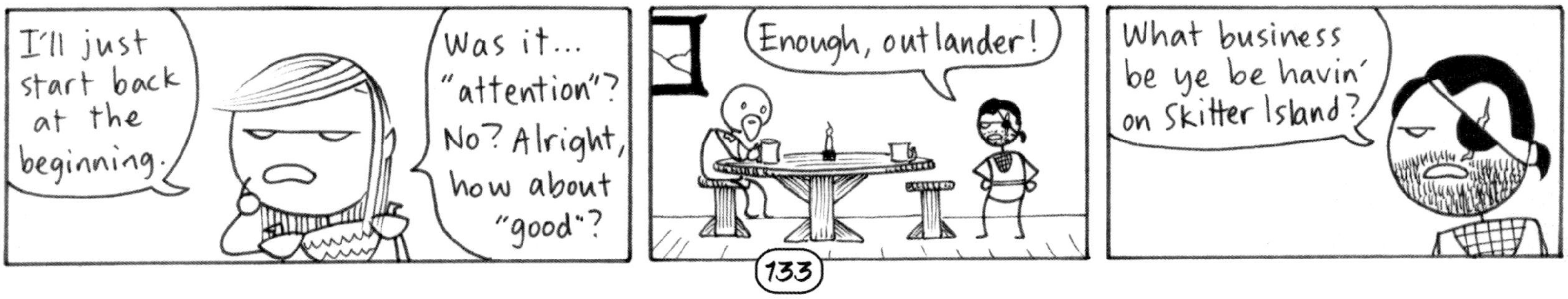
I'll just start back at the beginning.
Was it... "attention"? No? Alright, how about "good"?
Enough, outlander!
What business be ye be havin' on Skitter Island?

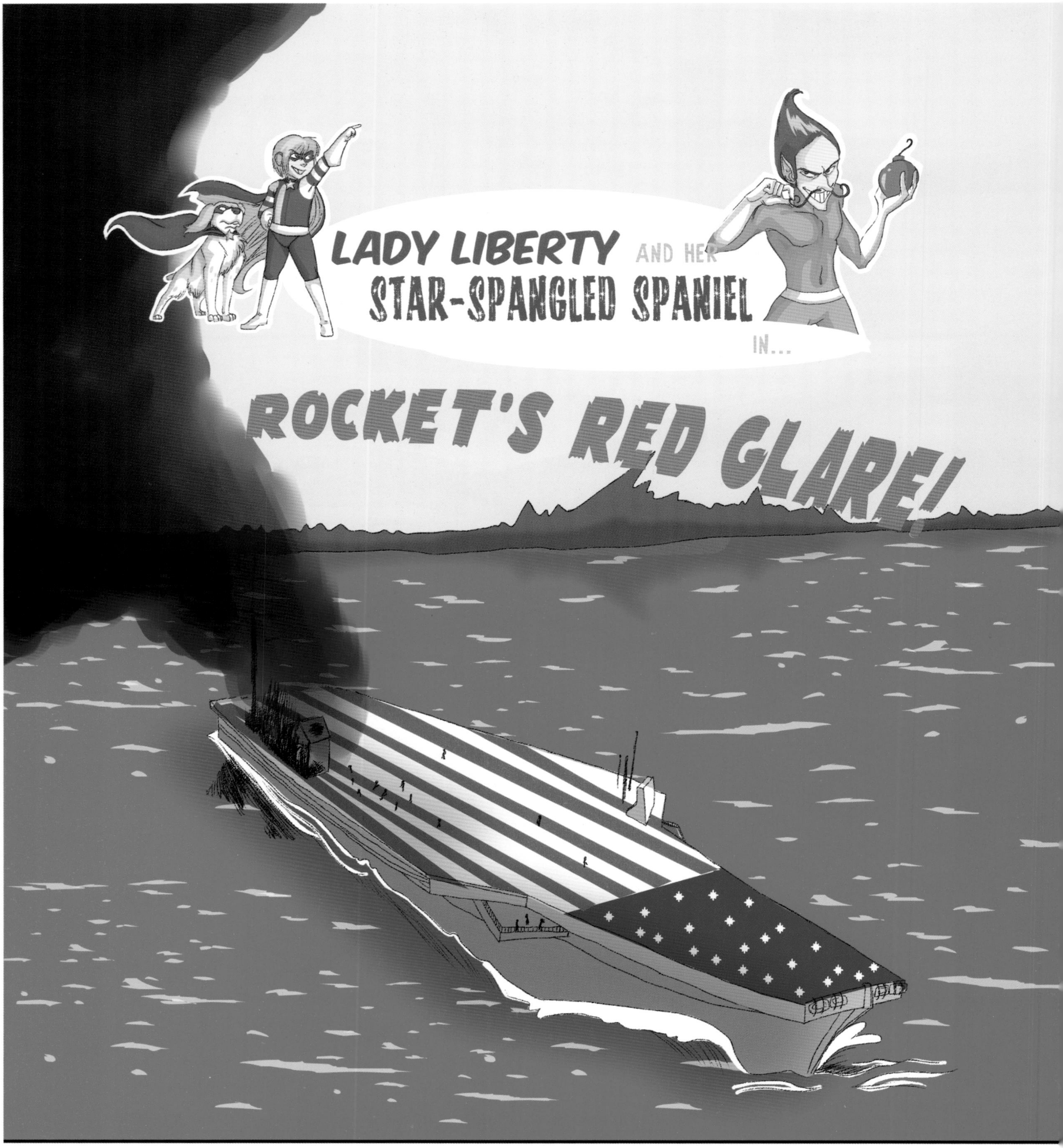
LADY LIBERTY AND HER
STAR-SPANGLED SPANIEL
IN...
ROCKET'S RED GLARE!

WRITER: SAMANTHA J. MATHIS ARTIST: CAYTLIN VILLABRANDT COLORIST: MARY BELLAMY

☆ ☆ ☆

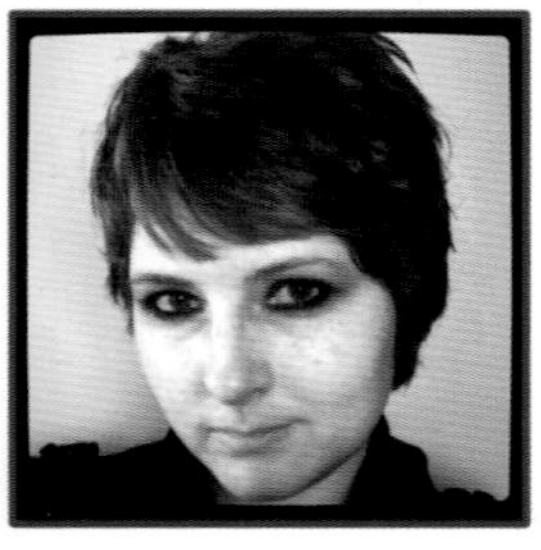

SAMANTHA J. MATHIS

SKILLS: Writer
LOCATION: Placentia, CA
FUN FACT: On top of being a writer, I'm also a seamstress and a bartender!

www.brokenglasscomic.com

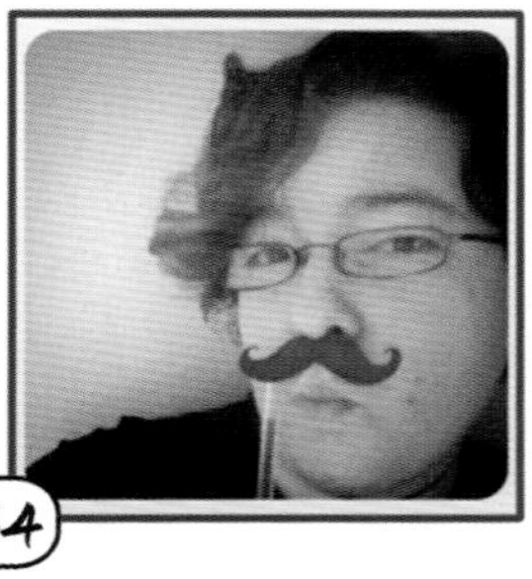

CAYTLIN VILBRANDT

SKILLS: Penciller, Inker, Letterer
LOCATION: Renton, WA
FUN FACT: I'm secretly a superhero with MAD PARTY SKILLS.

www.criticalhitdesign.com

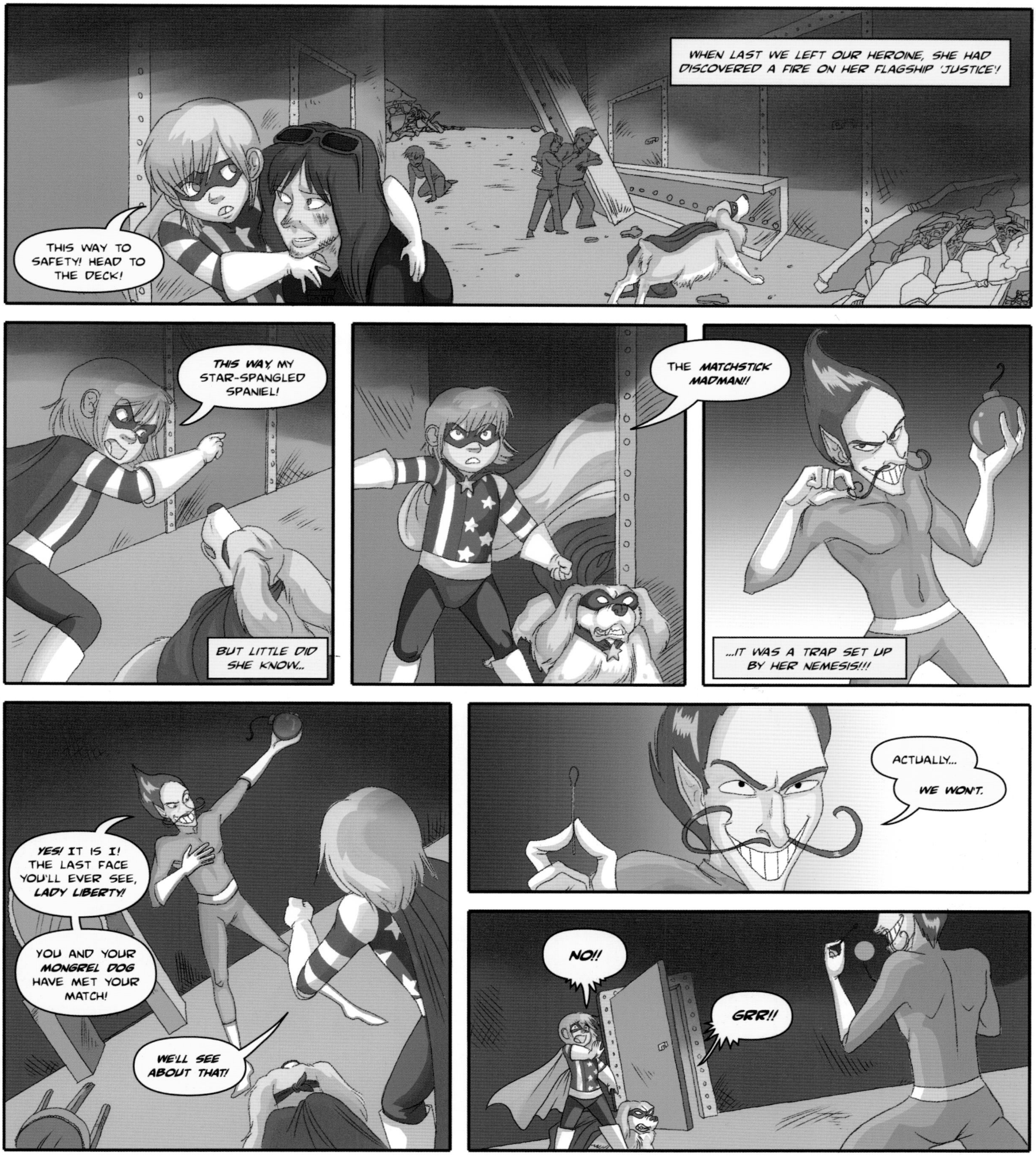
WHEN LAST WE LEFT OUR HEROINE, SHE HAD DISCOVERED A FIRE ON HER FLAGSHIP 'JUSTICE'!
THIS WAY TO SAFETY! HEAD TO THE DECK!
THIS WAY, MY STAR-SPANGLED SPANIEL!
BUT LITTLE DID SHE KNOW...
THE MATCHSTICK MADMAN!!
...IT WAS A TRAP SET UP BY HER NEMESIS!!!
YES! IT IS I! THE LAST FACE YOU'LL EVER SEE, LADY LIBERTY!
YOU AND YOUR MONGREL DOG HAVE MET YOUR MATCH!
WE'LL SEE ABOUT THAT!
ACTUALLY...
WE WON'T.
NO!!
GRR!!

☆ ☆ ☆

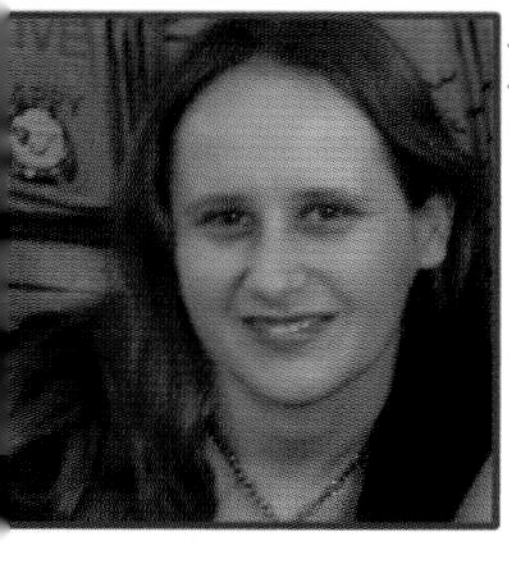

MARY "ZORILITA" BELLAMY

SKILLS: Illustrator, Colorist
LOCATION: Los Angeles, CA
FUN FACT: I am strangely good at home repair.

http://www.marybellamy.com

PRO TIP

DEDICATION
BY MARIAH MCCOURT

"COMICS IS A TOUGH FIELD. IT'S FRUSTRATING, IT'S WONDERFUL, IT'S FULL OF UPS AND DOWNS. IF YOU REALLY WANT TO BE PART OF IT, DON'T GIVE UP. BE KIND, BE PROFESSIONAL, BE FULL OF ENTHUSIASM AND JOY. AND AT THE END OF THE DAY, ALWAYS TRY TO REMEMBER, NO MATTER HOW TOUGH OR EXHAUSTING IT'S BEEN: IT'S ALSO JUST COMICS. TOMORROW YOU CAN TRY AGAIN."

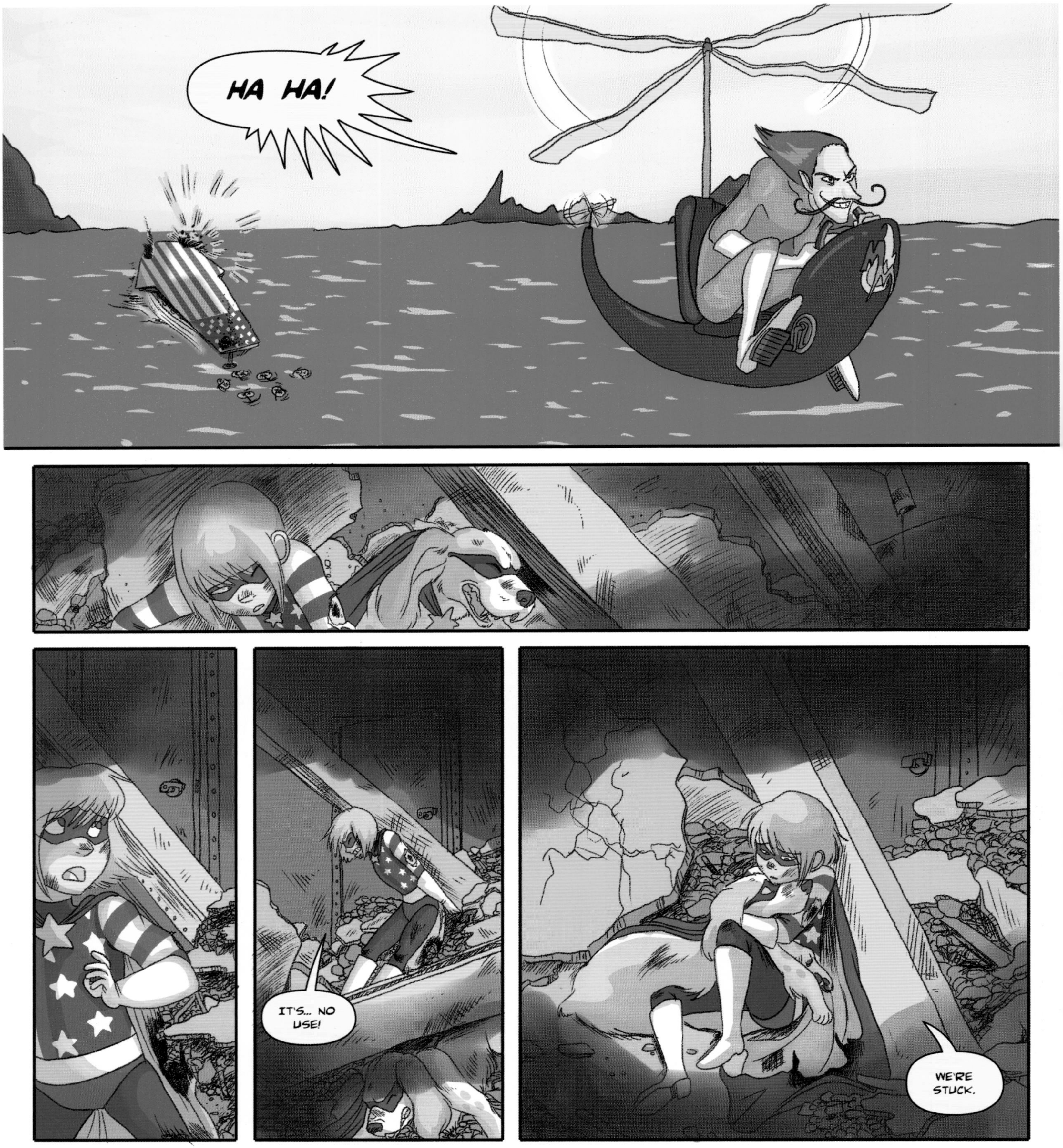
HA HA!
IT'S... NO USE!
WE'RE STUCK.

☆☆☆

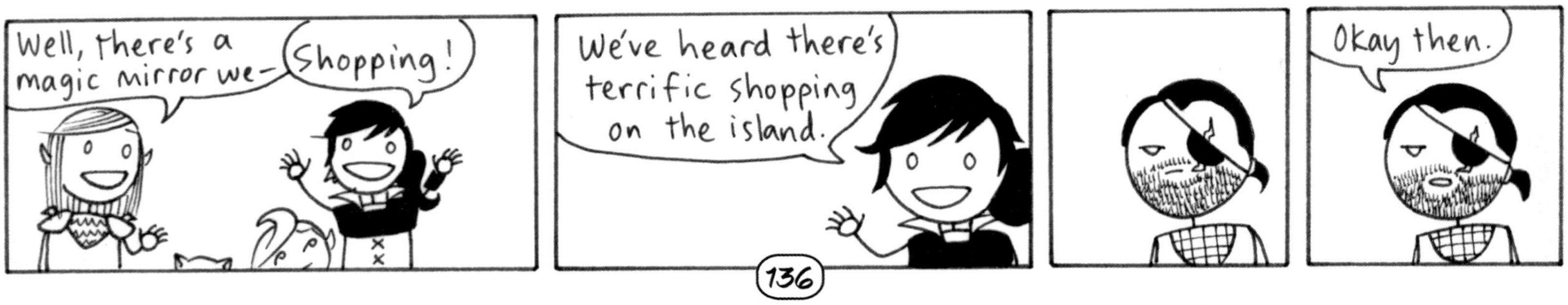
Well, there's a magic mirror we-
Shopping!
We've heard there's terrific shopping on the island.
Okay then.

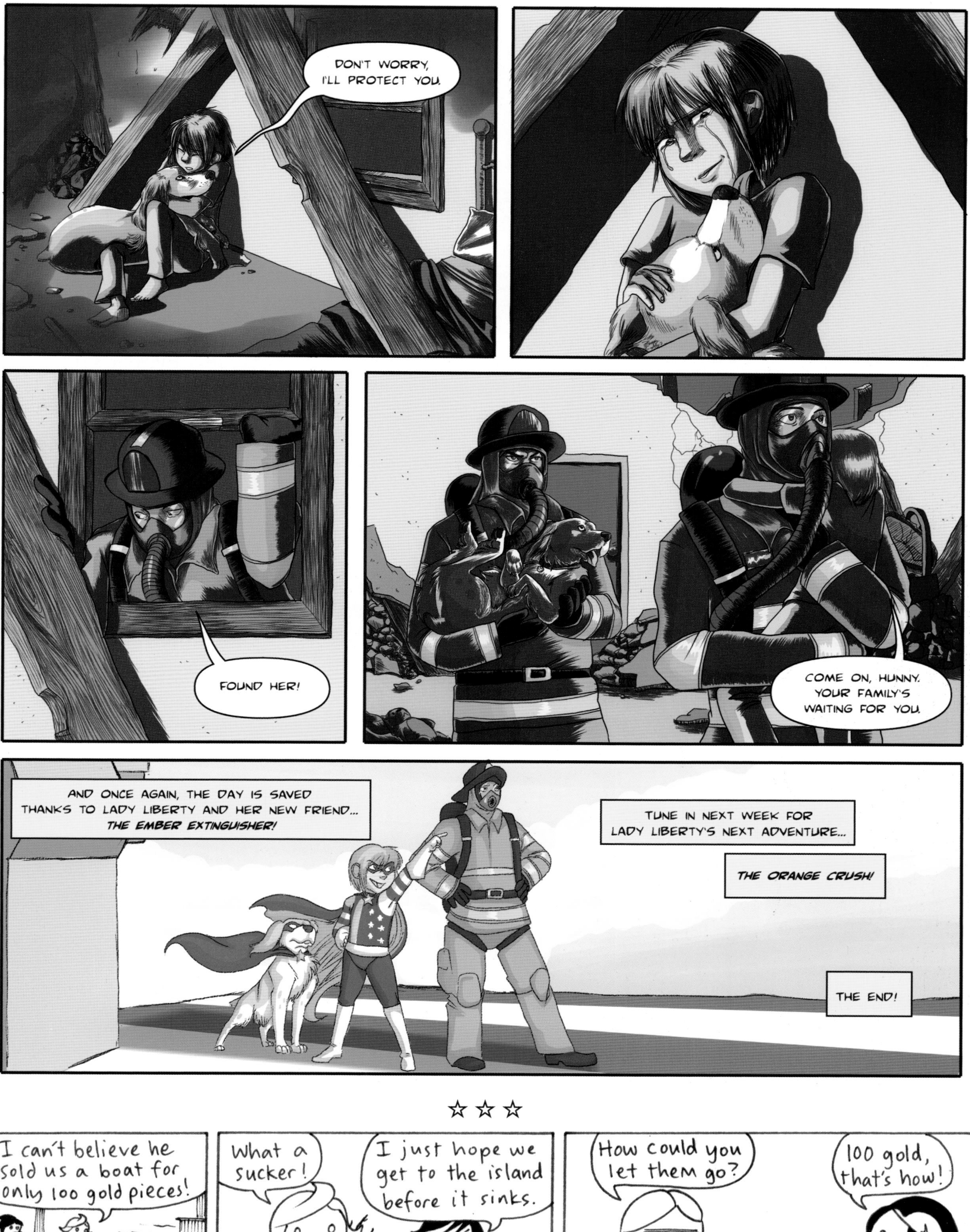

DON'T WORRY, I'LL PROTECT YOU.
FOUND HER!
COME ON, HUNNY. YOUR FAMILY'S WAITING FOR YOU.
AND ONCE AGAIN, THE DAY IS SAVED THANKS TO LADY LIBERTY AND HER NEW FRIEND... *THE EMBER EXTINGUISHER!*
TUNE IN NEXT WEEK FOR LADY LIBERTY'S NEXT ADVENTURE...
THE ORANGE CRUSH!
THE END!

☆ ☆ ☆

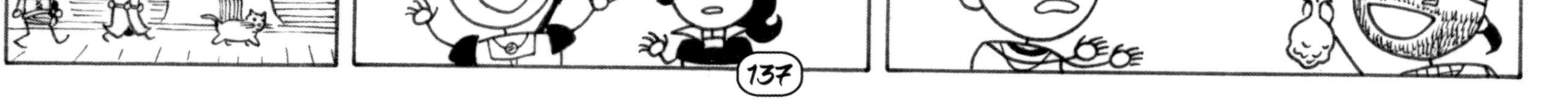

I can't believe he sold us a boat for only 100 gold pieces!
What a sucker!
I just hope we get to the island before it sinks.
How could you let them go?
100 gold, that's how!

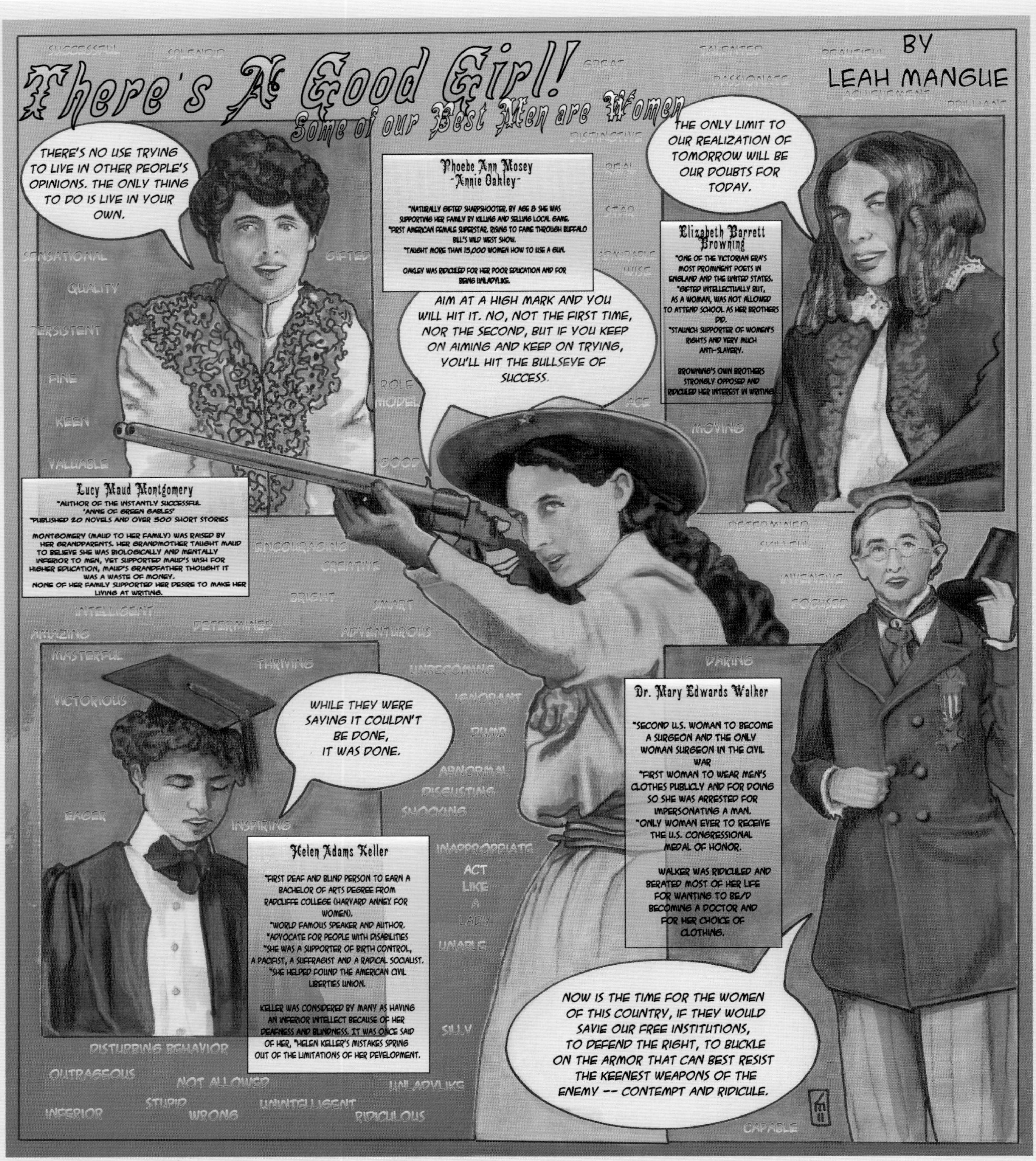
There's A Good Girl!
Some of our Best Men are Women
BY LEAH MANGUE
THERE'S NO USE TRYING TO LIVE IN OTHER PEOPLE'S OPINIONS. THE ONLY THING TO DO IS LIVE IN YOUR OWN.
Phoebe Ann Mosey -Annie Oakley-
*NATURALLY GIFTED SHARPSHOOTER. BY AGE 8 SHE WAS SUPPORTING HER FAMILY BY KILLING AND SELLING LOCAL GAME.
*FIRST AMERICAN FEMALE SUPERSTAR, RISING TO FAME THROUGH BUFFALO BILL'S WILD WEST SHOW.
*TAUGHT MORE THAN 15,000 WOMEN HOW TO USE A GUN.
OAKLEY WAS RIDICULED FOR HER POOR EDUCATION AND FOR BEING UNLADYLIKE.
THE ONLY LIMIT TO OUR REALIZATION OF TOMORROW WILL BE OUR DOUBTS FOR TODAY.
Elizabeth Barrett Browning
*ONE OF THE VICTORIAN ERA'S MOST PROMINENT POETS IN ENGLAND AND THE UNITED STATES.
*GIFTED INTELLECTUALLY BUT, AS A WOMAN, WAS NOT ALLOWED TO ATTEND SCHOOL AS HER BROTHERS DID.
*STAUNCH SUPPORTER OF WOMEN'S RIGHTS AND VERY MUCH ANTI-SLAVERY.
BROWNING'S OWN BROTHERS STRONGLY OPPOSED AND RIDICULED HER INTEREST IN WRITING.
AIM AT A HIGH MARK AND YOU WILL HIT IT. NO, NOT THE FIRST TIME, NOR THE SECOND, BUT IF YOU KEEP ON AIMING AND KEEP ON TRYING, YOU'LL HIT THE BULLSEYE OF SUCCESS.
Lucy Maud Montgomery
*AUTHOR OF THE INSTANTLY SUCCESSFUL 'ANNE OF GREEN GABLES'
*PUBLISHED 20 NOVELS AND OVER 500 SHORT STORIES
MONTGOMERY (MAUD TO HER FAMILY) WAS RAISED BY HER GRANDPARENTS. HER GRANDMOTHER TAUGHT MAUD TO BELIEVE SHE WAS BIOLOGICALLY AND MENTALLY INFERIOR TO MEN, YET SUPPORTED MAUD'S WISH FOR HIGHER EDUCATION, MAUD'S GRANDFATHER THOUGHT IT WAS A WASTE OF MONEY.
NONE OF HER FAMILY SUPPORTED HER DESIRE TO MAKE HER LIVING AT WRITING.
WHILE THEY WERE SAYING IT COULDN'T BE DONE, IT WAS DONE.
Helen Adams Keller
*FIRST DEAF AND BLIND PERSON TO EARN A BACHELOR OF ARTS DEGREE FROM RADCLIFFE COLLEGE (HARVARD ANNEX FOR WOMEN).
*WORLD FAMOUS SPEAKER AND AUTHOR.
*ADVOCATE FOR PEOPLE WITH DISABILITIES
*SHE WAS A SUPPORTER OF BIRTH CONTROL, A PACIFIST, A SUFFRAGIST AND A RADICAL SOCIALIST.
*SHE HELPED FOUND THE AMERICAN CIVIL LIBERTIES UNION.
KELLER WAS CONSIDERED BY MANY AS HAVING AN INFERIOR INTELLECT BECAUSE OF HER DEAFNESS AND BLINDNESS. IT WAS ONCE SAID OF HER, "HELEN KELLER'S MISTAKES SPRING OUT OF THE LIMITATIONS OF HER DEVELOPMENT.
Dr. Mary Edwards Walker
*SECOND U.S. WOMAN TO BECOME A SURGEON AND THE ONLY WOMAN SURGEON IN THE CIVIL WAR
*FIRST WOMAN TO WEAR MEN'S CLOTHES PUBLICLY AND FOR DOING SO SHE WAS ARRESTED FOR IMPERSONATING A MAN.
*ONLY WOMAN EVER TO RECEIVE THE U.S. CONGRESSIONAL MEDAL OF HONOR.
WALKER WAS RIDICULED AND BERATED MOST OF HER LIFE FOR WANTING TO BE/DO BECOMING A DOCTOR AND FOR HER CHOICE OF CLOTHING.
NOW IS THE TIME FOR THE WOMEN OF THIS COUNTRY, IF THEY WOULD SAVIE OUR FREE INSTITUTIONS, TO DEFEND THE RIGHT, TO BUCKLE ON THE ARMOR THAT CAN BEST RESIST THE KEENEST WEAPONS OF THE ENEMY -- CONTEMPT AND RIDICULE.
SUCCESSFUL SPLENDID GREAT TALENTED BEAUTIFUL PASSIONATE ACHIEVEMENT BRILLIANT DISTINCTIVE REAL STAR ADMIRABLE WISE SENSATIONAL GIFTED QUALITY PERSISTENT FINE KEEN VALUABLE ROLE MODEL GOOD ACE MOVING ENCOURAGING CREATIVE BRIGHT SMART INTELLIGENT DETERMINED AMAZING ADVENTUROUS DETERMINED SKILLFUL INVENTIVE FOCUSED MASTERFUL THRIVING VICTORIOUS UNBECOMING IGNORANT DUMB DARING ABNORMAL DISGUSTING SHOCKING EAGER INSPIRING INAPPROPRIATE ACT LIKE A LADY UNABLE SILLY DISTURBING BEHAVIOR OUTRAGEOUS NOT ALLOWED UNLADYLIKE INFERIOR STUPID WRONG UNINTELLIGENT RIDICULOUS CAPABLE

☆ ☆ ☆

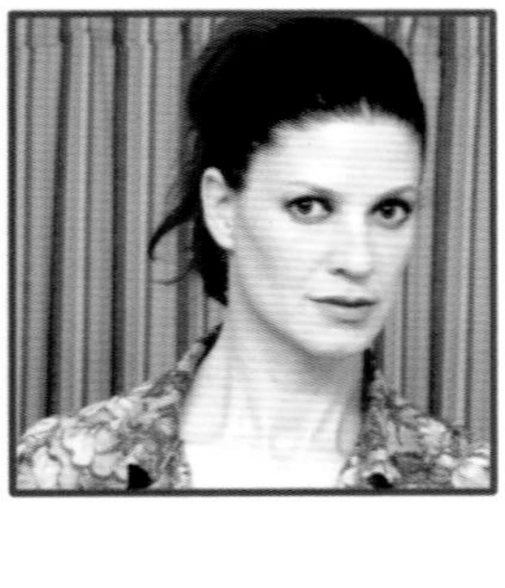

LEAH MANGUE

SKILLS: Penciller, Colorist, Inker, Letterer
LOCATION: Palm Desert, CA
FUN FACT: I am the 18th great grand-daughter of Geoffrey Chaucer.

http://www.lmangue-art.net

PRO TIP

PORTFOLIO

BY BARBARA KAALBER

"ONCE YOU'VE SHOWN A PORTFOLIO, HAVE PREPARED PACKAGE OF COPIES READY TO GIV THE INTERVIEWER. EACH PAGE SHOULD INCLUDE MINIMUM OF YOUR NAME, PHONE, AND EMAIL CASE THEY SHOULD BECOME SEPARATED."

The New Adventures of Queen Elizabeth I

By Christianne Benedict

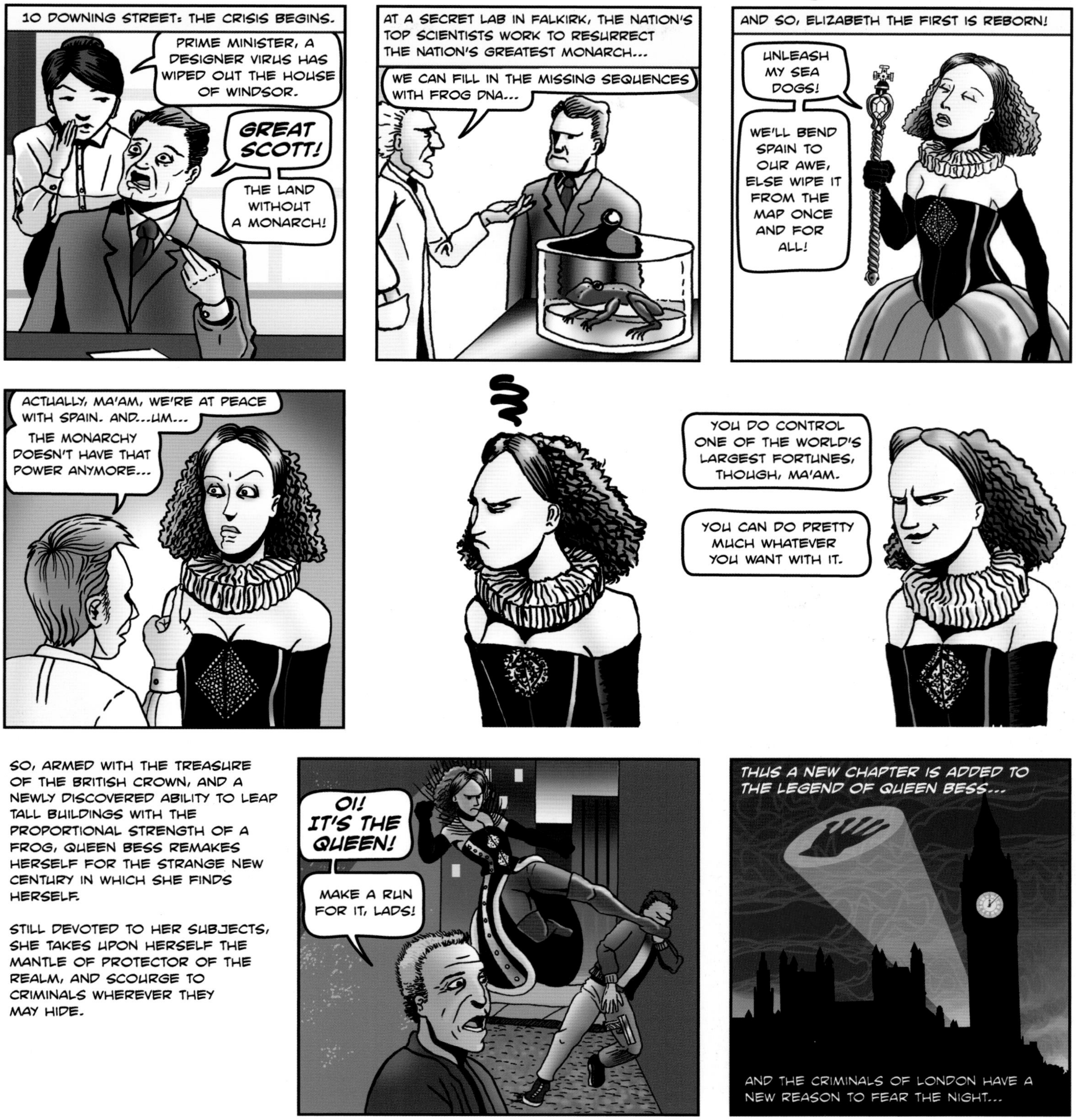

10 DOWNING STREET: THE CRISIS BEGINS.
PRIME MINISTER, A DESIGNER VIRUS HAS WIPED OUT THE HOUSE OF WINDSOR.
GREAT SCOTT!
THE LAND WITHOUT A MONARCH!
AT A SECRET LAB IN FALKIRK, THE NATION'S TOP SCIENTISTS WORK TO RESURRECT THE NATION'S GREATEST MONARCH...
WE CAN FILL IN THE MISSING SEQUENCES WITH FROG DNA...
AND SO, ELIZABETH THE FIRST IS REBORN!
UNLEASH MY SEA DOGS!
WE'LL BEND SPAIN TO OUR AWE, ELSE WIPE IT FROM THE MAP ONCE AND FOR ALL!
ACTUALLY, MA'AM, WE'RE AT PEACE WITH SPAIN. AND...UM...
THE MONARCHY DOESN'T HAVE THAT POWER ANYMORE...
YOU DO CONTROL ONE OF THE WORLD'S LARGEST FORTUNES, THOUGH, MA'AM.
YOU CAN DO PRETTY MUCH WHATEVER YOU WANT WITH IT.
SO, ARMED WITH THE TREASURE OF THE BRITISH CROWN, AND A NEWLY DISCOVERED ABILITY TO LEAP TALL BUILDINGS WITH THE PROPORTIONAL STRENGTH OF A FROG, QUEEN BESS REMAKES HERSELF FOR THE STRANGE NEW CENTURY IN WHICH SHE FINDS HERSELF.
STILL DEVOTED TO HER SUBJECTS, SHE TAKES UPON HERSELF THE MANTLE OF PROTECTOR OF THE REALM, AND SCOURGE TO CRIMINALS WHEREVER THEY MAY HIDE.
OI! IT'S THE QUEEN!
MAKE A RUN FOR IT, LADS!
THUS A NEW CHAPTER IS ADDED TO THE LEGEND OF QUEEN BESS...
AND THE CRIMINALS OF LONDON HAVE A NEW REASON TO FEAR THE NIGHT...

☆ ☆ ☆

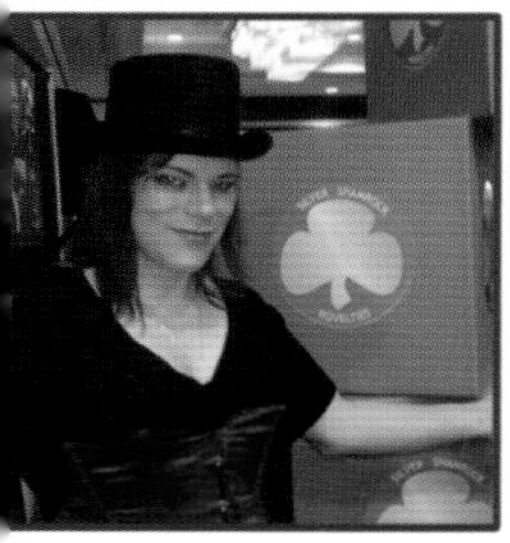

CHRISTIANNE BENEDICT

SKILLS: Writer, Penciller, Inker, Letterer, Colorist
LOCATION: Columbia, MO
FUN FACT: I once watched *Night of the Living Dead* from the safety of a fort made from couch cushions.

krelllabs.blogspot.com

PRO TIP

BE HELPFUL

BY DANI JONES

"DO YOUR BEST TO BE HELPFUL AND COURTEOUS TO OTHER ARTISTS AND PEERS. GIVE ADVICE, DON'T JUST ASK FOR IT. ENCOURAGE OTHERS, DON'T JUST FEED OFF THEIR COMPLIMENTS. HELP PROMOTE FRIENDS INSTEAD OF CONSTANTLY TRYING TO SELL YOURSELF."

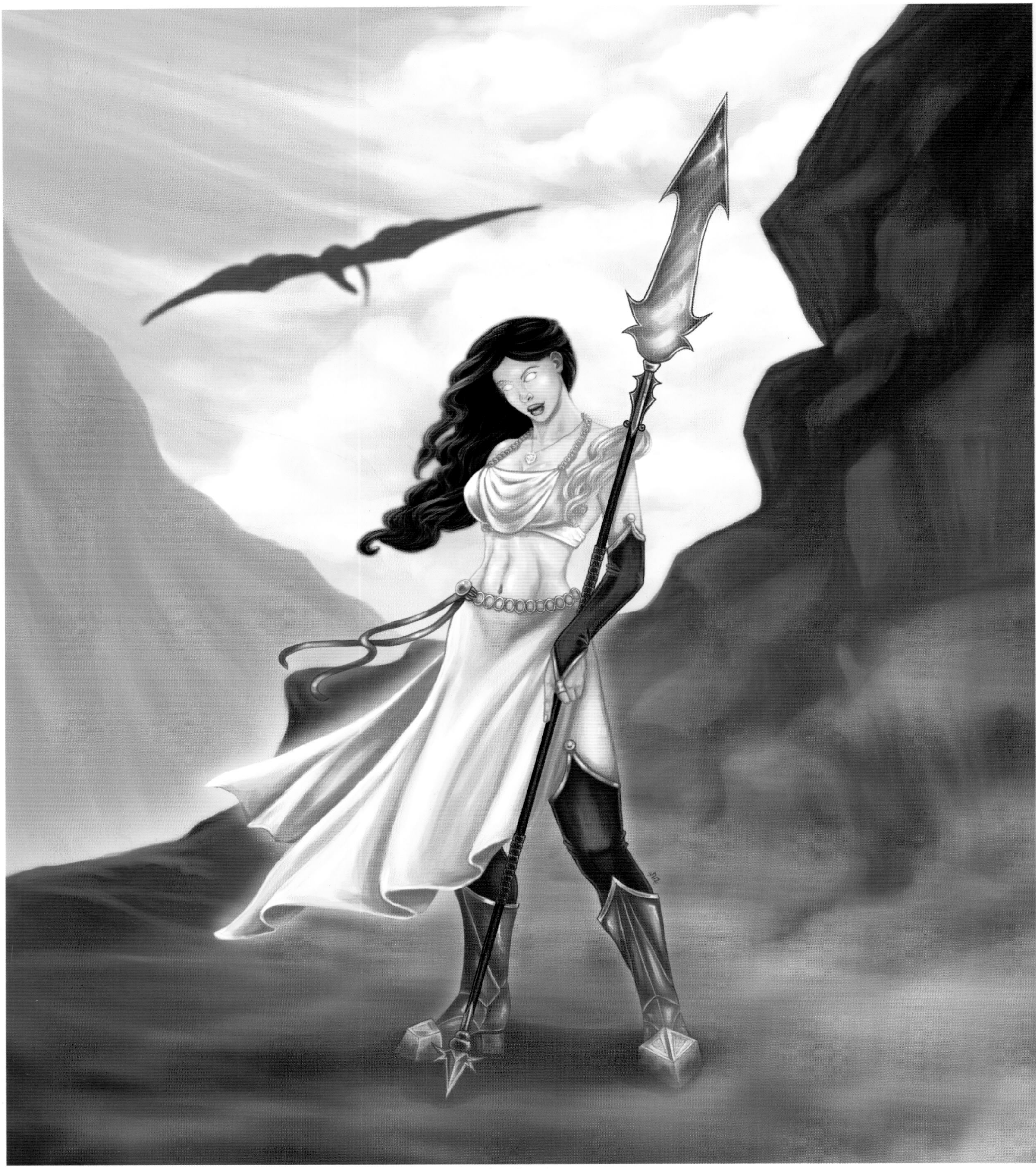

☆☆☆

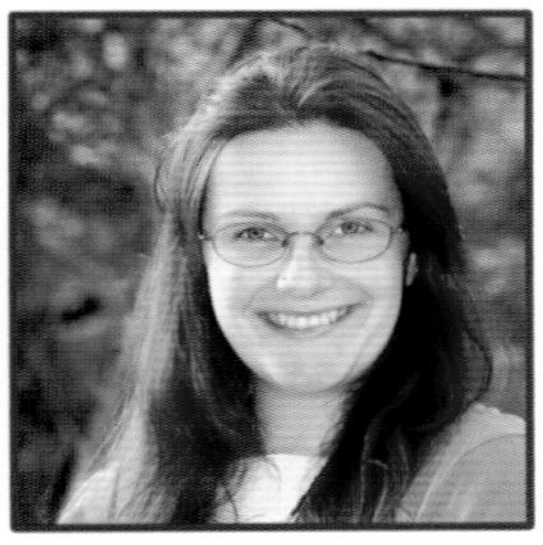

KATHRYN WHITEFORD

SKILLS: Pinup Artist

LOCATION: Australia

FUN FACT: I have very flexible eyebrows.

www.HoneyDragon.net

PRO TIP

EXPERIMENT

BY BARBARA RANDALL KESEL

"DON'T BE AFRAID TO TRY SOMETHING YOU'RE NOT SURE YOU CAN DRAW: ALL THE CAMERA SEES IS BLACK AND WHITE—NOT THE LAYERS OF INK AND WHITE PAINT IT TOOK TO GET THERE."

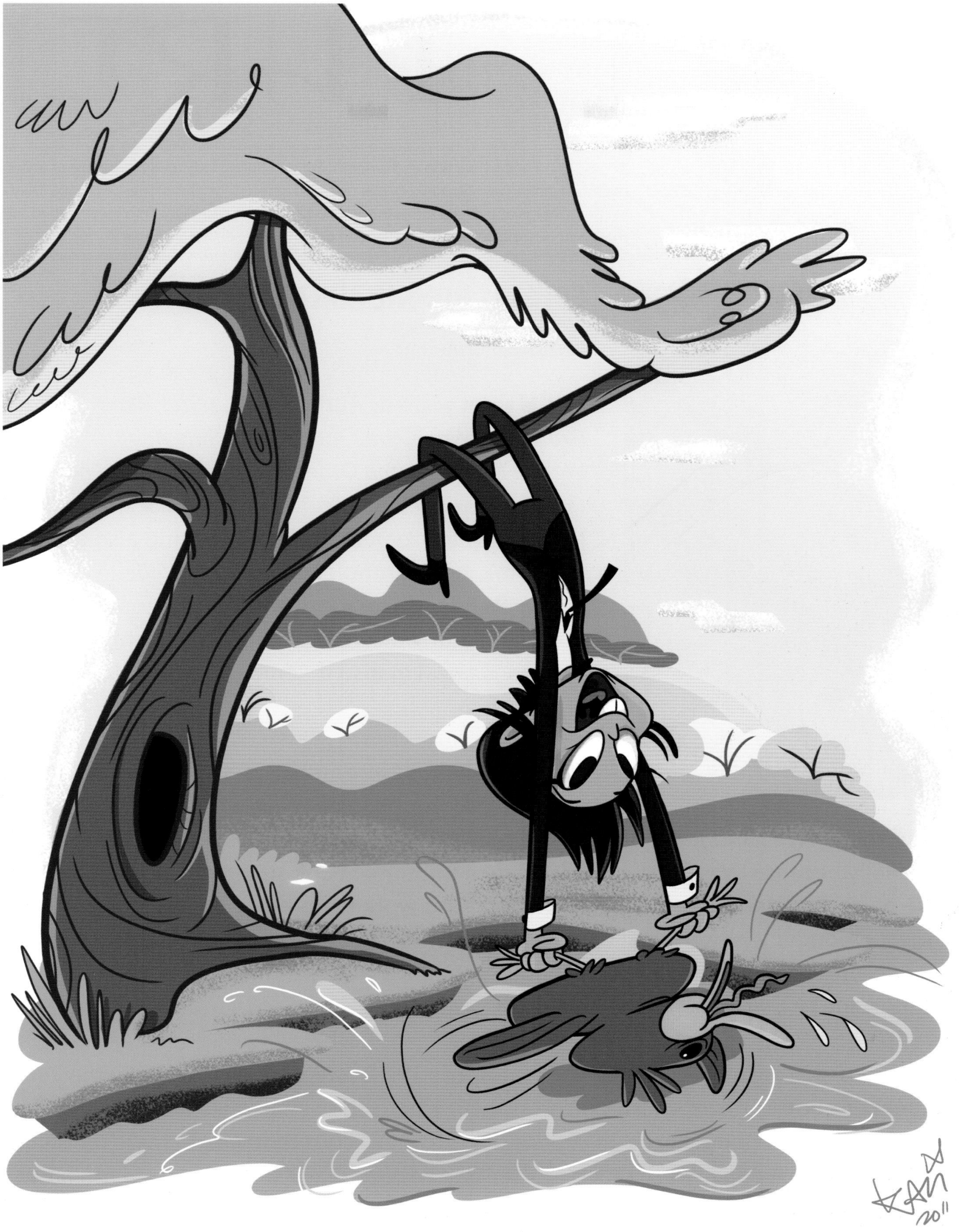

Kali 2011

☆☆☆

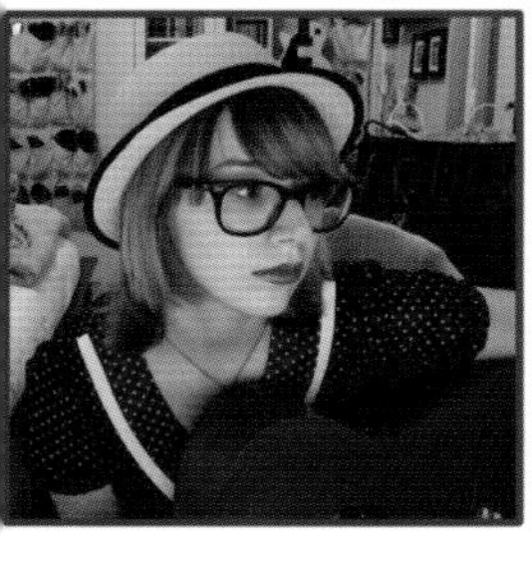

KALI FONTECCHIO

SKILLS: All?
LOCATION: Burbank, CA
FUN FACT: When I was a kid I wanted to grow up to be Bob Dylan.

kalikazoo.blogspot.com

PRO TIP

IT'S A JOB

BY RENAE DE LIZ

"PROFESSIONAL COMIC BOOK ARTISTS TYPICALLY DRAW FOR 8 HOURS A DAY LIKE A 9-5 JOB. CHALLENGE YOURSELF TO DO THAT RIGHT NOW AND YOUR WORK WILL IMPROVE VERY QUICKLY WHILE PREPARING YOU FOR A CAREER IN COMICS."

PART THREE

TEAM BONNIE

☆ ☆ ☆ For each section of *Womanthology* a different lady took on the role of editor over the writers, pencillers, inkers, colorists, and letterers for their stories or pinups. They were in charge of making sure the creators worked as a team, had all the info they needed, and that all stories and pinups were turned in on time. This section is Bonnie Burton's.

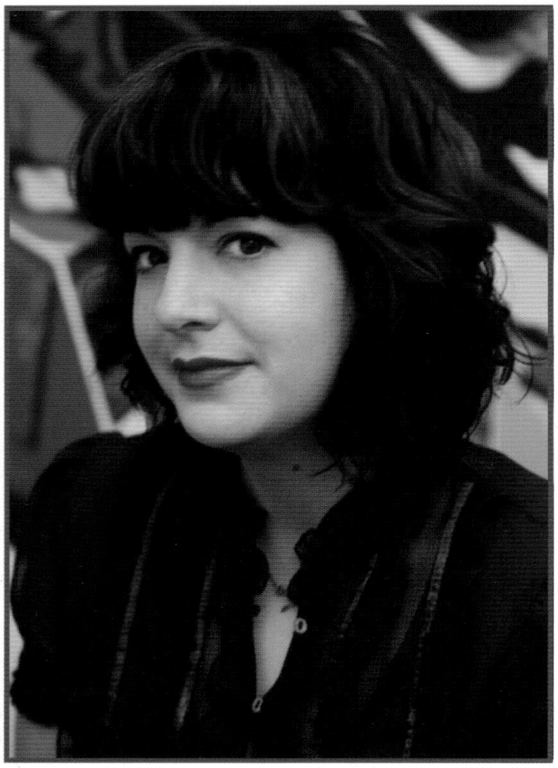

EDITOR - BONNIE BURTON

Location: San Francisco
Day Job: Editor/Author

A little about yourself: Author of *The Star Wars Craft Book*, *Draw Star Wars: The Clone Wars*, *Girls Against Girls: Why We Are Mean to Each Other and How We Can Change*, *You Can Draw Star Wars*, and *The Clone Wars: Planets in Peril*. In addition to *Womanthology* my writing also appears in the comic book anthology *The Girls' Guide to Guys' Stuff*. I've written for the magazines *Wired*, *Geek Monthly*, *Craft*, *BUST*, and *Star Wars Insider*. I have a monthly column for *SFX magazine*. I'm also a Senior Editor for Starwars.com at Lucasfilm.

What does *Womanthology* mean to you? It's important for women and young girls everywhere to be inspired to believe in themselves and make their own comics. *Womanthology* was a great experience for me personally because I've always wanted to do a full comic book story and I got to collaborate with one of my favorite artists: Jessica Hickman! Also working as an editor on the *Womanthology* project I worked with so many talented ladies who were both professionals and first-time comic book writers and artists. The fact that it's also for charity just makes the experience even more important.

Funny fact: For fun, I write TV spec scripts that are too weird to ever air, like *Buffy the Vampire Slayer* meets Count Chocula, or an episode of *CSI* where the serial killer murders his victims using craft glitter and googly eyes. In college, I wrote a TV script that was a crossover between *The X-Files* and *Murder, She Wrote* called *Mulder, She Wrote*. I really should be running a TV network.

☆ ☆ ☆

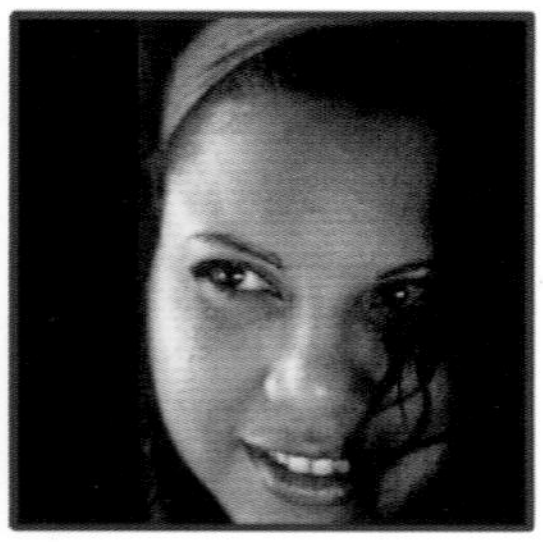

TARA-LEA ALESZCZYK

SKILLS: Editorial Coordinator
LOCATION: New Jersey
FUN FACT: Irony of ironies, I'm a horror writer who's afraid of the dark.

TARA-LEA ALESZCZYK HELPED WITH VARIOUS ORGANIZATIONAL TASKS ON THE PROJECT. THANK YOU, TARA!!

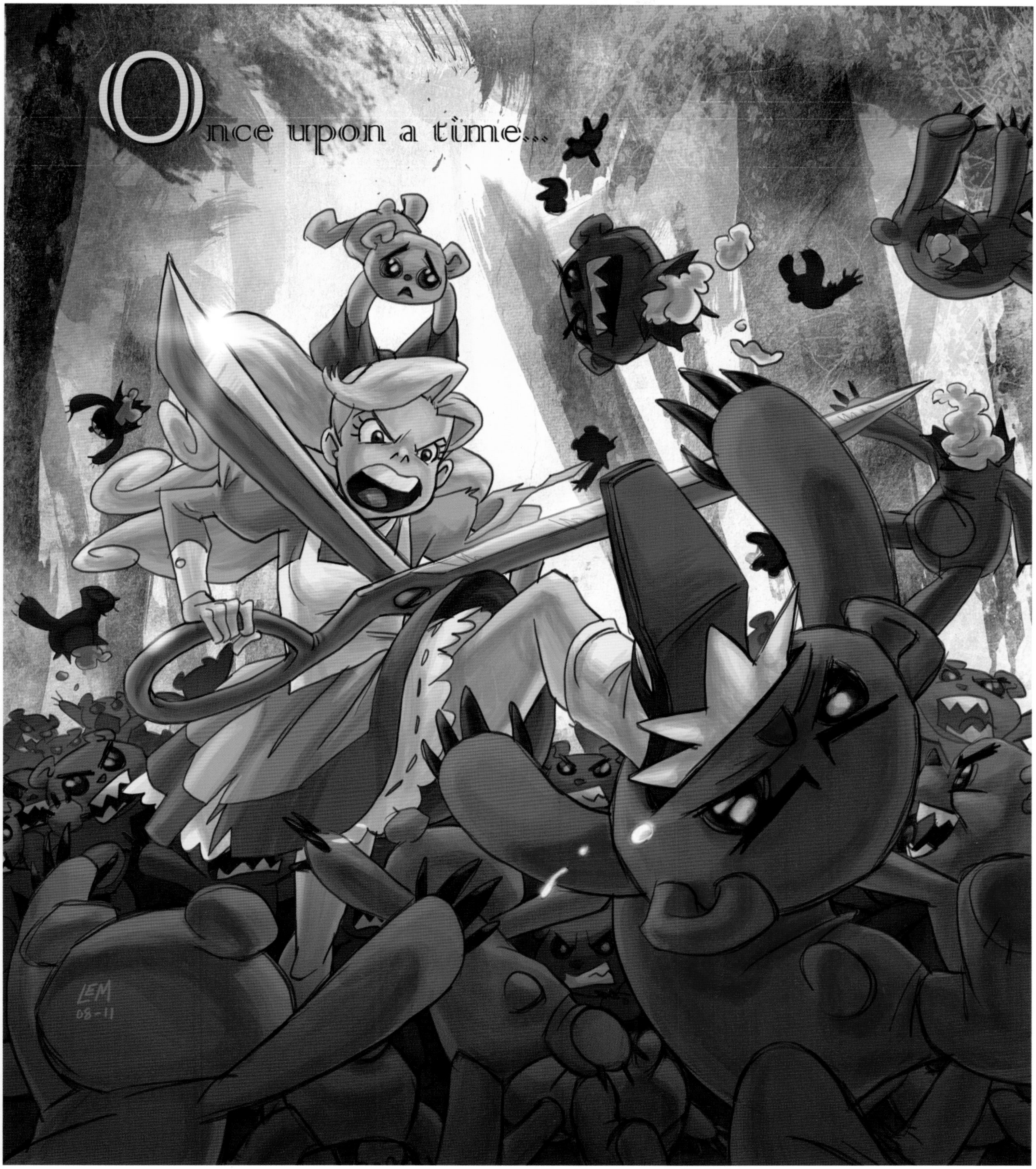
Once upon a time...
LEM
08-11

☆ ☆ ☆

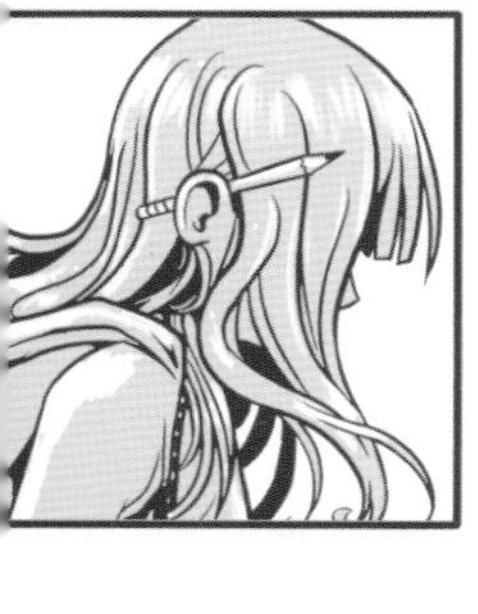

LAUREN MONTGOMERY

SKILLS: Pencils, Colors
LOCATION: Los Angeles, CA
FUN FACT: I love cheese.

www.laurenmontgomery.blogspot.com

PRO TIP

OUT LOUD

BY LAURA MORLEY

"ALWAYS READ YOUR DIALOGUE OUT LOUD. YES, YOU CAN DO FUNNY VOICES IF YOU WANT. IT'LL POINT OUT AWKWARD TURNS OF PHRASE, OVER-LONG SPEECHES, AND TIRED-OUT VERBAL TICS IN AN INSTANT."

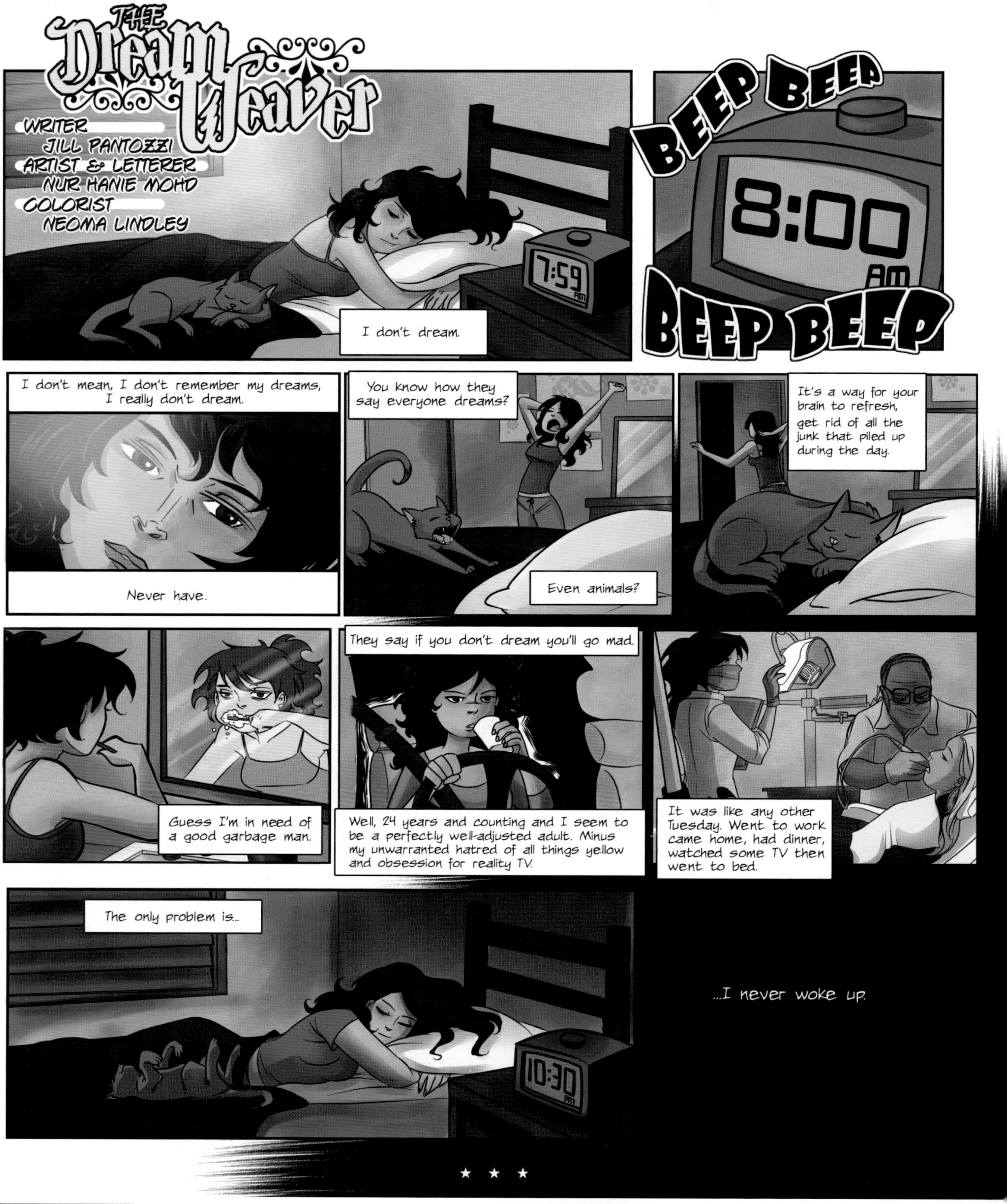
THE Dream Weaver
WRITER
JILL PANTOZZI
ARTIST & LETTERER
NUR HANIE MOHD
COLORIST
NEOMA LINDLEY
7:59 AM
I don't dream.
BEEP BEEP
8:00 AM
BEEP BEEP
I don't mean, I don't remember my dreams, I really don't dream.
Never have.
You know how they say everyone dreams?
Even animals?
It's a way for your brain to refresh, get rid of all the junk that piled up during the day.
Guess I'm in need of a good garbage man.
They say if you don't dream you'll go mad.
Well, 24 years and counting and I seem to be a perfectly well-adjusted adult. Minus my unwarranted hatred of all things yellow and obsession for reality TV.
It was like any other Tuesday. Went to work came home, had dinner, watched some TV then went to bed.
The only problem is...
10:30 PM
...I never woke up.
★ ★ ★

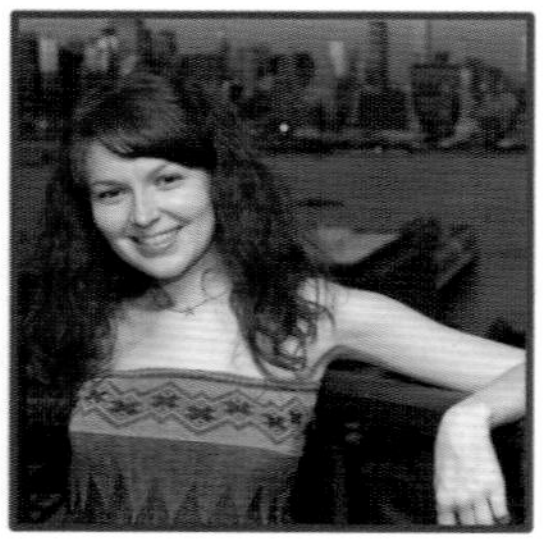

JILL PANTOZZI

SKILLS: Writer
LOCATION: New Jersey
FUN FACT: Batman is my boyfriend. Don't tell my boyfriend.

http://www.thenerdybird.com/

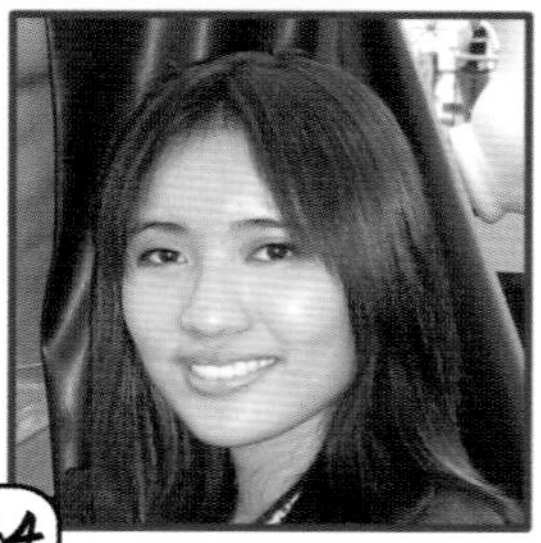

NUR HANIE MOHD

SKILLS: Penciller, Colorist, Inker, Letterer
LOCATION: Kuching, Malaysia
FUN FACT: My hand moves funny.

http://haniemohd.blogspot.com

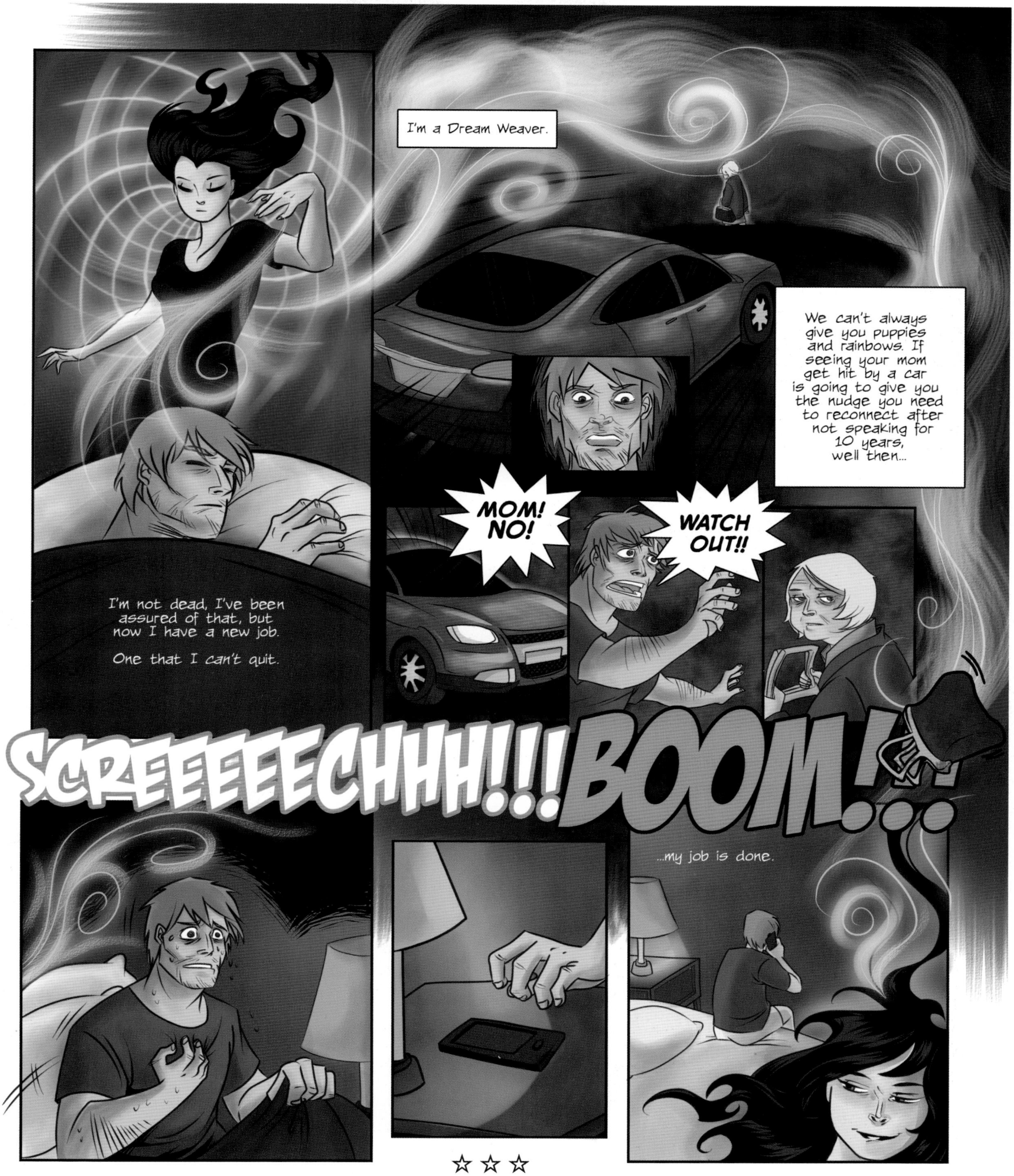
I'm a Dream Weaver.
I'm not dead, I've been assured of that, but now I have a new job.
One that I can't quit.
We can't always give you puppies and rainbows. If seeing your mom get hit by a car is going to give you the nudge you need to reconnect after not speaking for 10 years, well then...
MOM! NO!
WATCH OUT!!
SCREEEEEECHHH!!!
BOOM!!!
...my job is done.

☆☆☆

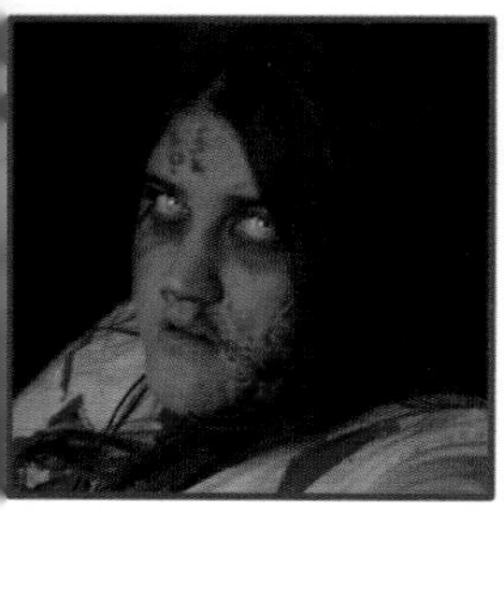

Neoma Lindley

SKILLS: Colorist
LOCATION: Sterling Heights, Michigan
FUN FACT: I am undead.

PRO TIP

Role Model
BY WENDY PINI

"BE THE ROLE MODEL YOU WISHED YOU, YOURSELF, HAD WHEN YOU WERE VERY YOUNG. TREAT YOURSELF LIKE GOLD AND OTHERS WILL, TOO."

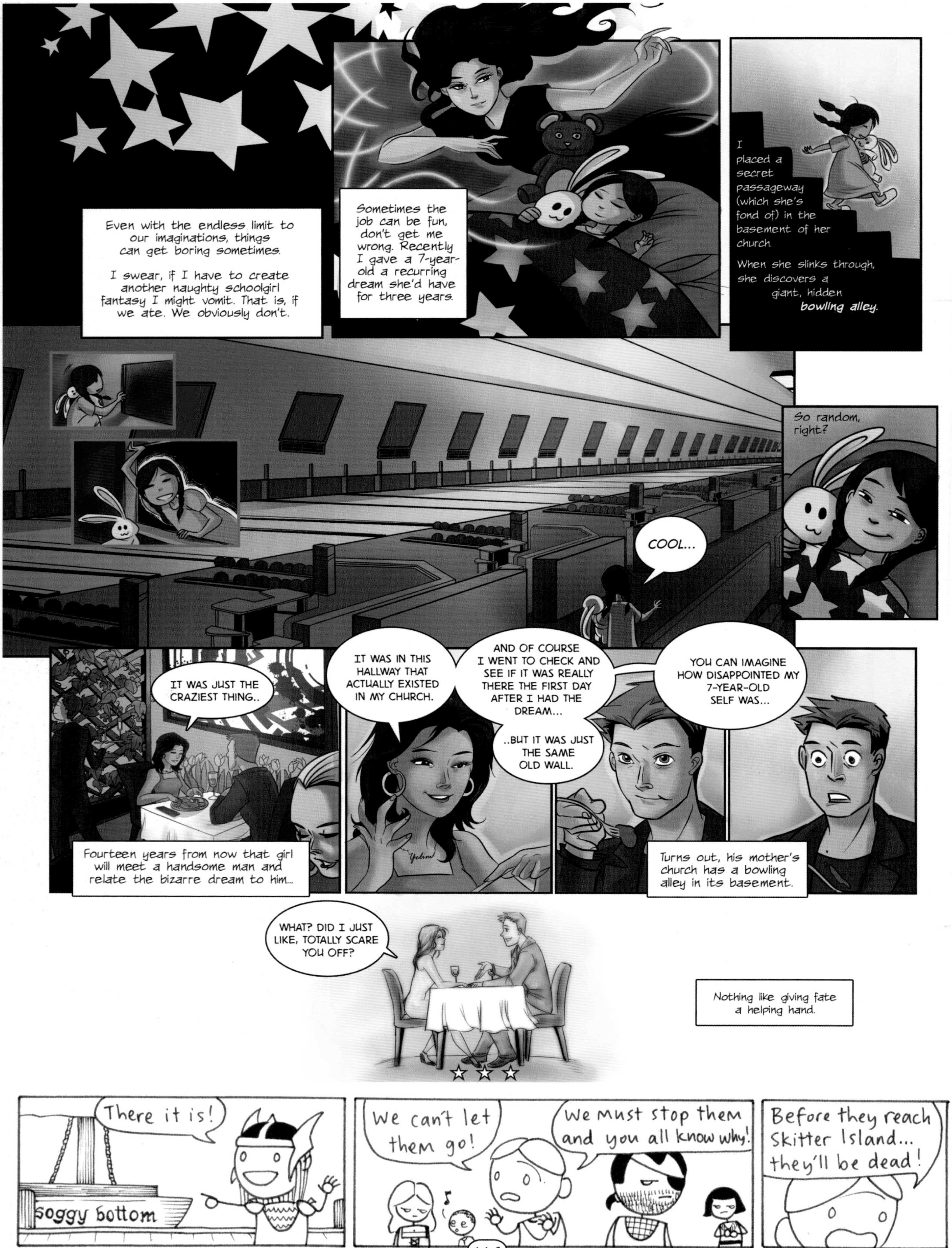
Even with the endless limit to our imaginations, things can get boring sometimes.
I swear, if I have to create another naughty schoolgirl fantasy I might vomit. That is, if we ate. We obviously don't.
Sometimes the job can be fun, don't get me wrong. Recently I gave a 7-year-old a recurring dream she'd have for three years.
I placed a secret passageway (which she's fond of) in the basement of her church.
When she slinks through, she discovers a giant, hidden bowling alley.
COOL...
So random, right?
IT WAS JUST THE CRAZIEST THING..
Fourteen years from now that girl will meet a handsome man and relate the bizarre dream to him...
IT WAS IN THIS HALLWAY THAT ACTUALLY EXISTED IN MY CHURCH.
AND OF COURSE I WENT TO CHECK AND SEE IF IT WAS REALLY THERE THE FIRST DAY AFTER I HAD THE DREAM...
..BUT IT WAS JUST THE SAME OLD WALL.
YOU CAN IMAGINE HOW DISAPPOINTED MY 7-YEAR-OLD SELF WAS...
Turns out, his mother's church has a bowling alley in its basement.
WHAT? DID I JUST LIKE, TOTALLY SCARE YOU OFF?
Nothing like giving fate a helping hand.
There it is!
soggy bottom
We can't let them go!
We must stop them and you all know why!
Before they reach Skitter Island... they'll be dead!

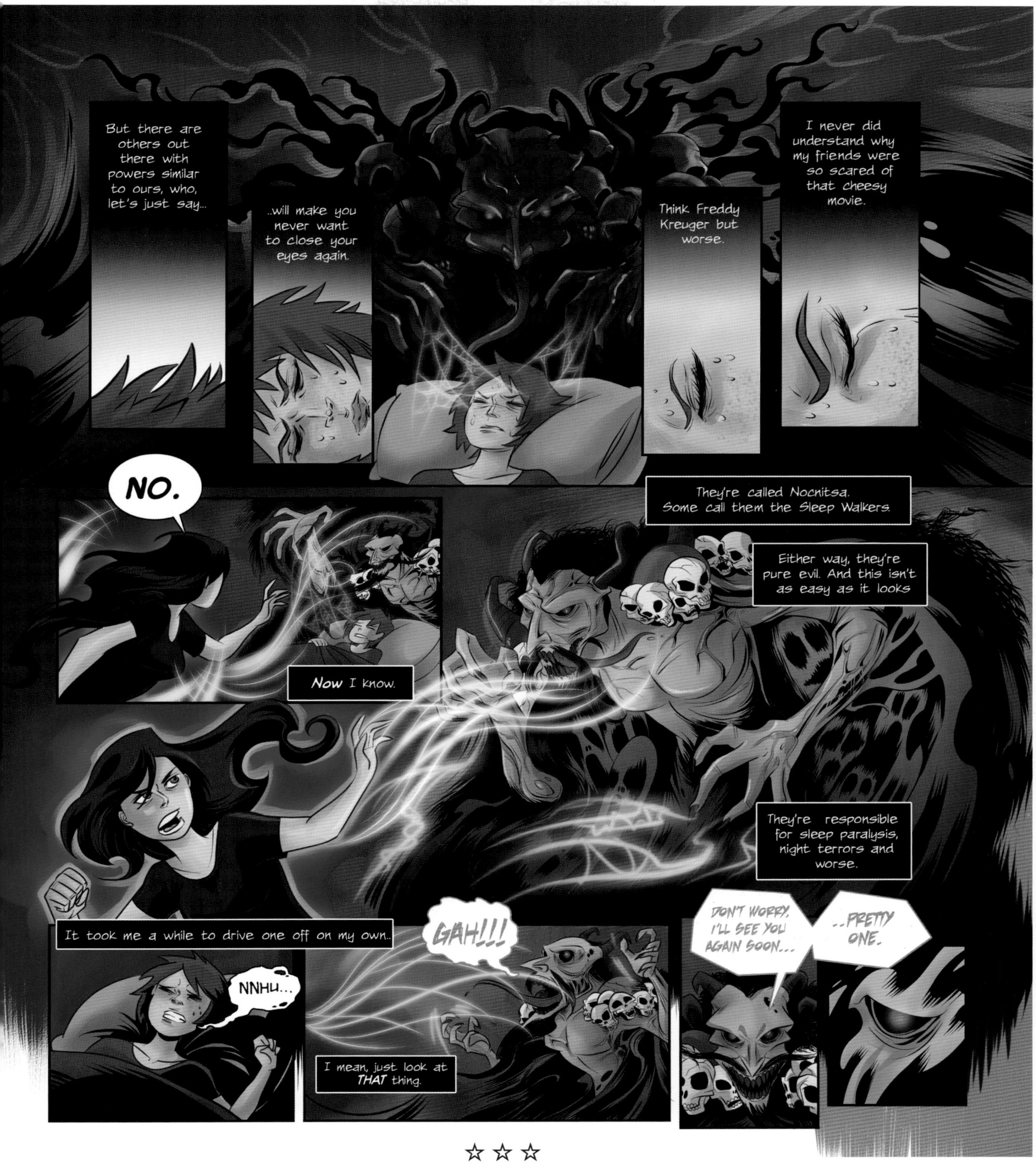

But there are others out there with powers similar to ours, who, let's just say...
...will make you never want to close your eyes again.
Think Freddy Kreuger but worse.
I never did understand why my friends were so scared of that cheesy movie.
NO.
Now I know.
They're called Nocnitsa. Some call them the Sleep Walkers.
Either way, they're pure evil. And this isn't as easy as it looks
They're responsible for sleep paralysis, night terrors and worse.
It took me a while to drive one off on my own...
NNHU...
GAH!!!
I mean, just look at THAT thing.
DON'T WORRY, I'LL SEE YOU AGAIN SOON...
...PRETTY ONE.

☆ ☆ ☆

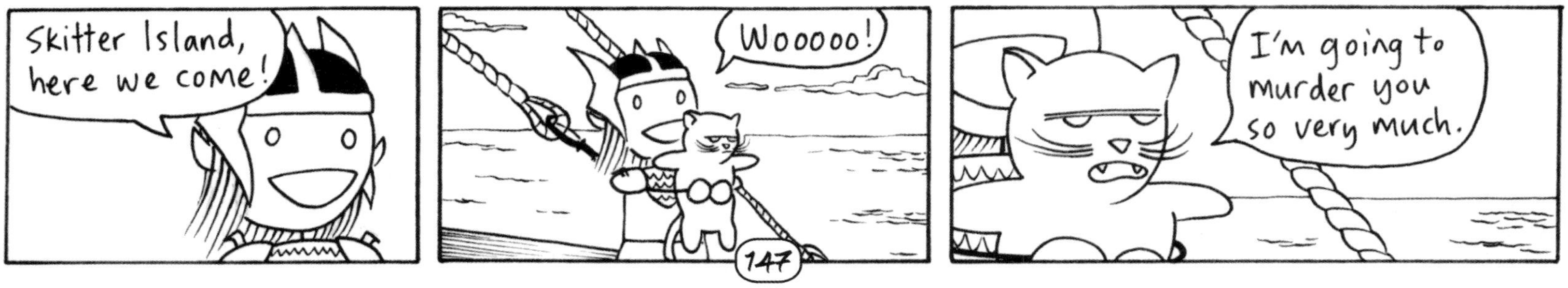

Skitter Island, here we come!
Wooooo!
I'm going to murder you so very much.

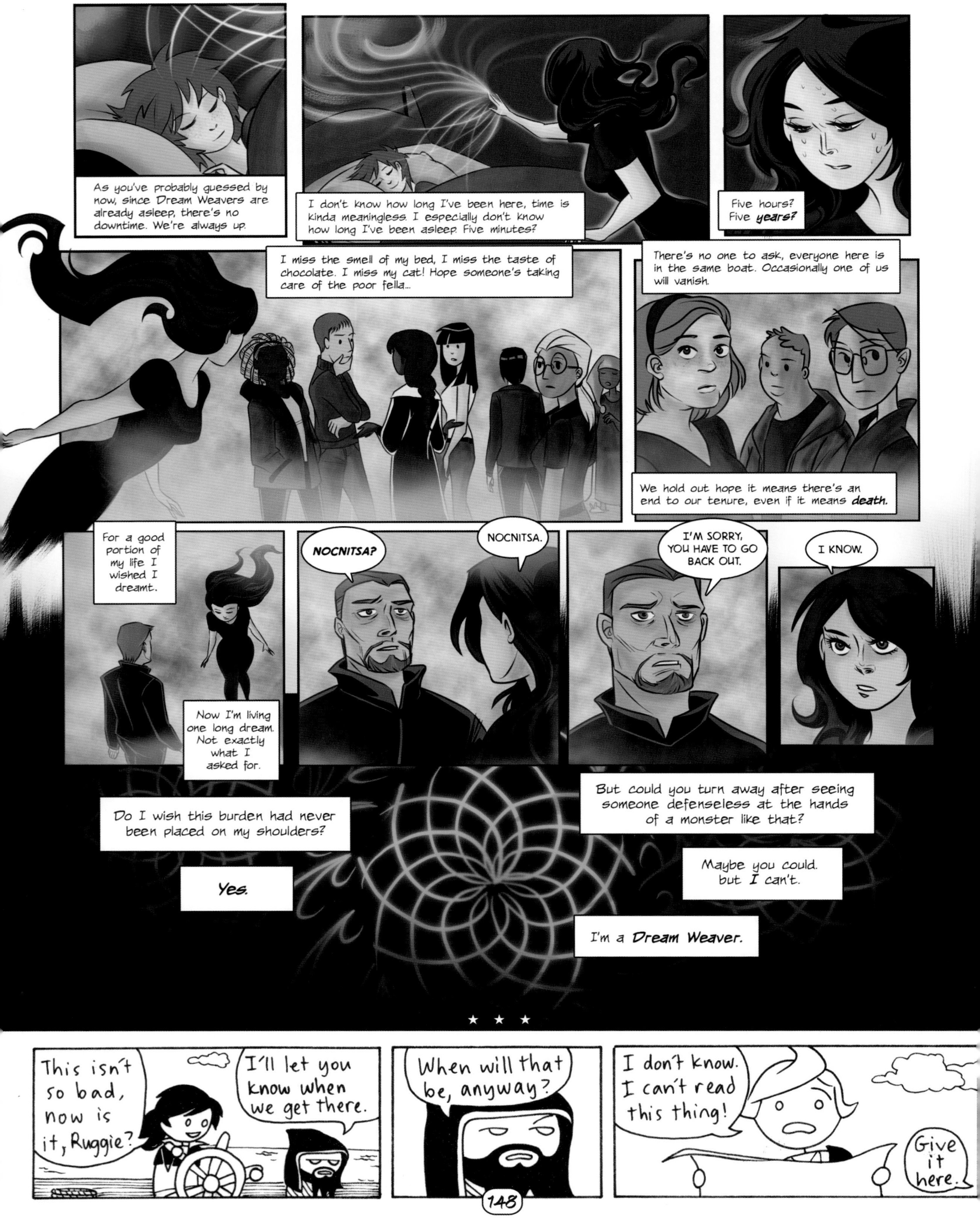
As you've probably guessed by now, since Dream Weavers are already asleep, there's no downtime. We're always up.
I don't know how long I've been here, time is kinda meaningless. I especially don't know how long I've been asleep. Five minutes?
Five hours? Five **years?**
I miss the smell of my bed, I miss the taste of chocolate. I miss my cat! Hope someone's taking care of the poor fella...
There's no one to ask, everyone here is in the same boat. Occasionally one of us will vanish.
We hold out hope it means there's an end to our tenure, even if it means **death.**
For a good portion of my life I wished I dreamt.
Now I'm living one long dream. Not exactly what I asked for.
NOCNITSA?
NOCNITSA.
I'M SORRY, YOU HAVE TO GO BACK OUT.
I KNOW.
Do I wish this burden had never been placed on my shoulders?
Yes.
But could you turn away after seeing someone defenseless at the hands of a monster like that?
Maybe you could. but ***I*** can't.
I'm a ***Dream Weaver.***
This isn't so bad, now is it, Ruggie?
I'll let you know when we get there.
When will that be, anyway?
I don't know. I can't read this thing!
Give it here.

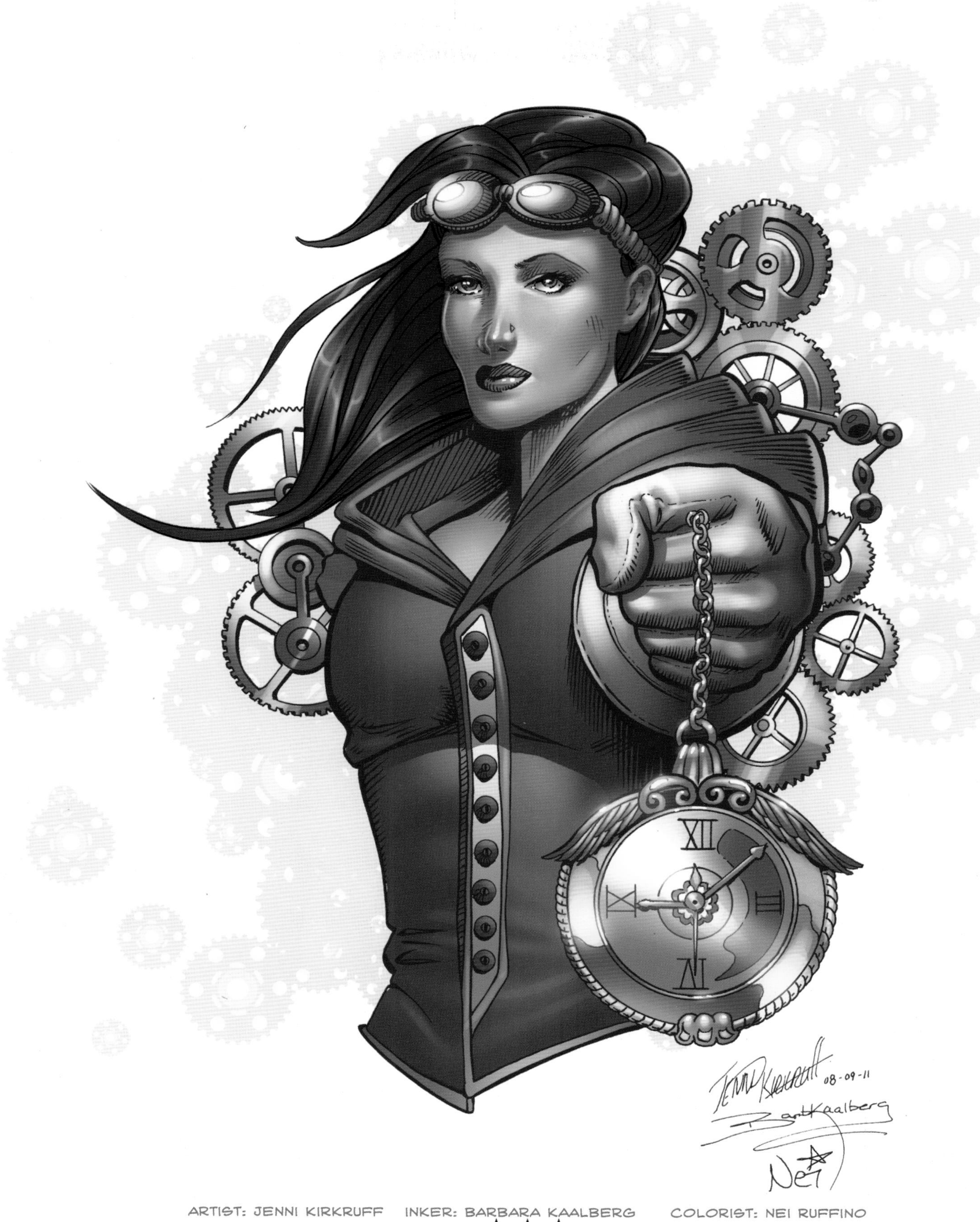

ARTIST: JENNI KIRKRUFF   INKER: BARBARA KAALBERG   COLORIST: NEI RUFFINO

☆☆☆

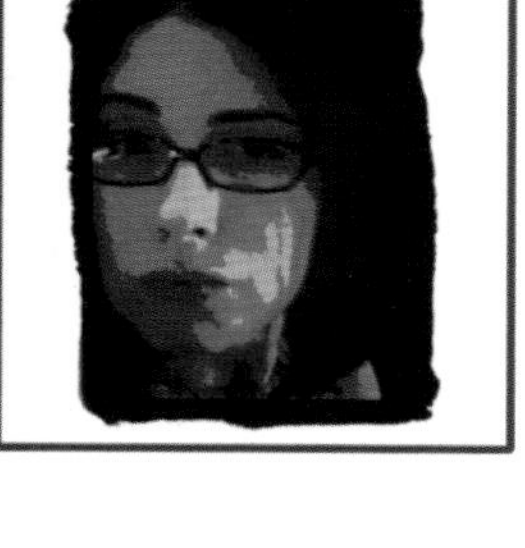

JENNI KIRKRUFF

SKILLS: Penciller
LOCATION: Harrisburg, OR
FUN FACT: Nickname is "Jester" and has been since middle school.

http://www.thejesterstoybox.com

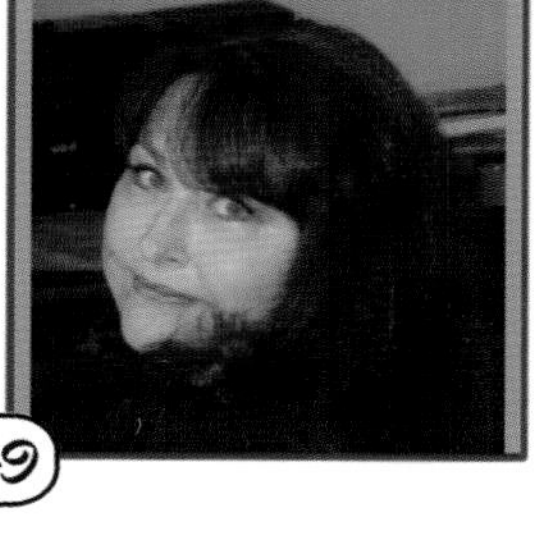

BARBARA KAALBERG

SKILLS: Inker
LOCATION: Madison, WI
FUN FACT: I started out as a fantasy painter before switching to inking.

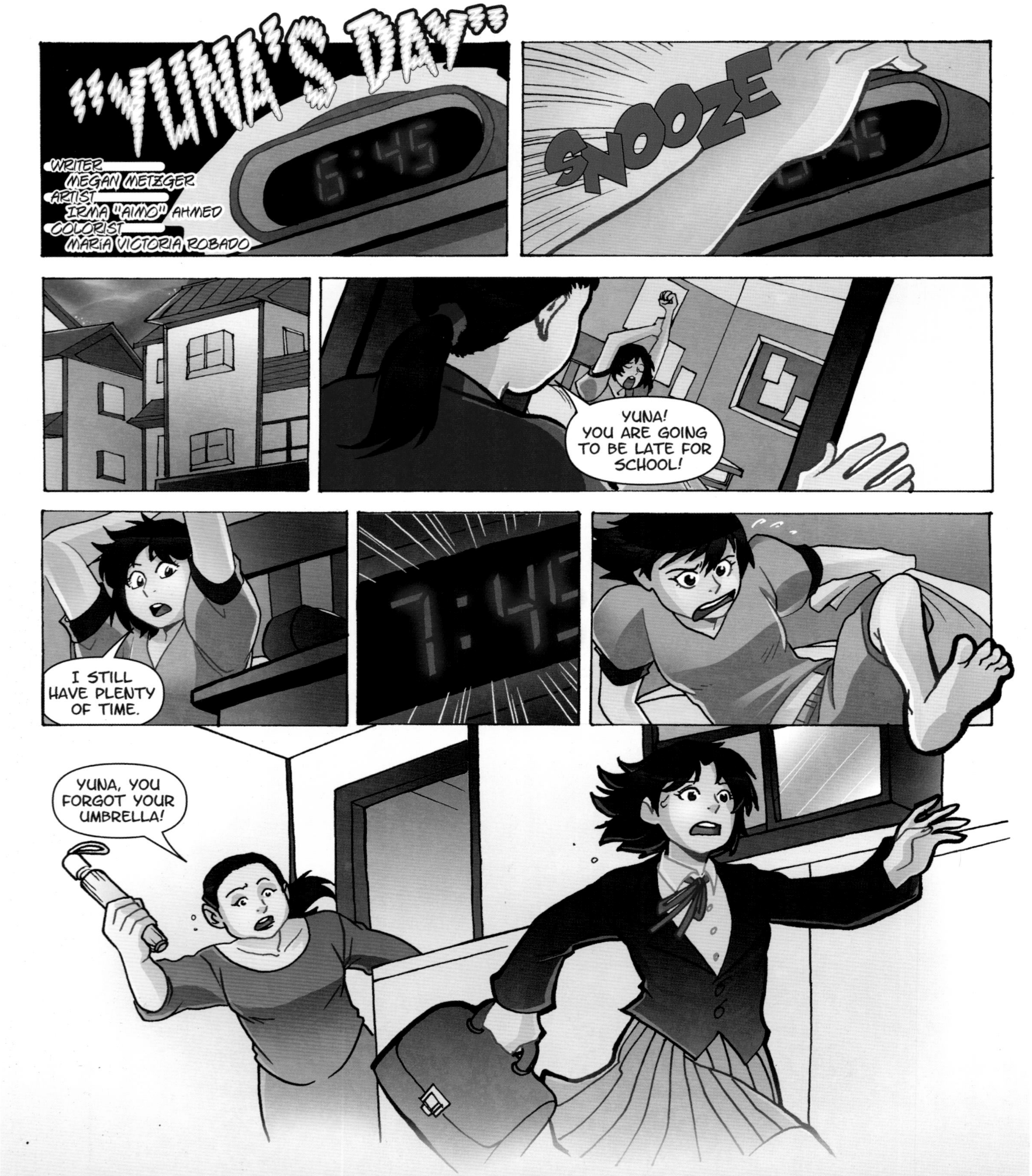
"YUNA'S DAY"
WRITER
MEGAN METZGER
ARTIST
IRMA "AIMO" AHMED
COLORIST
MARIA VICTORIA ROBADO
6:45
SNOOZE
YUNA! YOU ARE GOING TO BE LATE FOR SCHOOL!
I STILL HAVE PLENTY OF TIME.
7:45
YUNA, YOU FORGOT YOUR UMBRELLA!

WRITER: MEGAN METZGER ARTIST: IRMA "AIMO" AHMED COLORIST: MARIA VICTORIA ROBADO LETTERER: RACHEL DEERING

☆☆☆

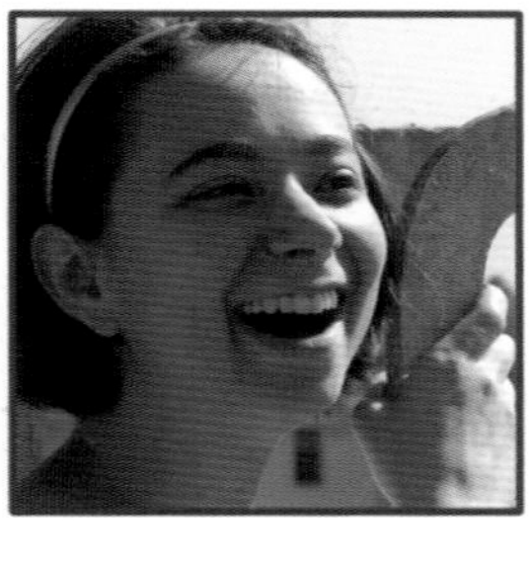

MEGAN METZGER

SKILLS: Writer
LOCATION: LA
FUN FACT: If you want my love, don't buy me diamonds – make me a sandwich!

MeganMetzger.Com

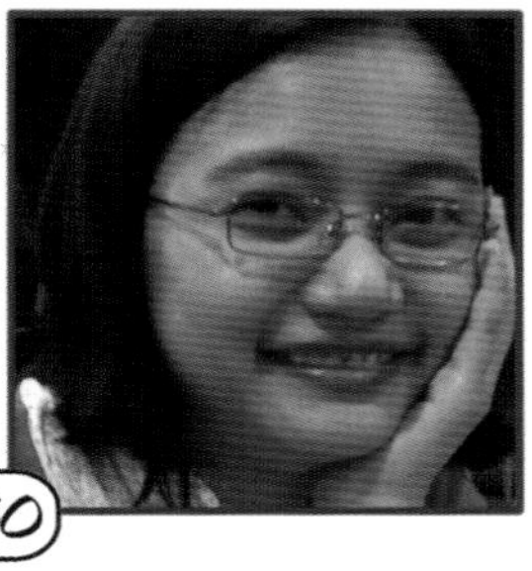

IRMA "AIMO" AHMED

SKILLS: Penciller, Inker
LOCATION: Malaysia
FUN FACT: I am a chronic Sketchbook Collector.

aimostudio.com

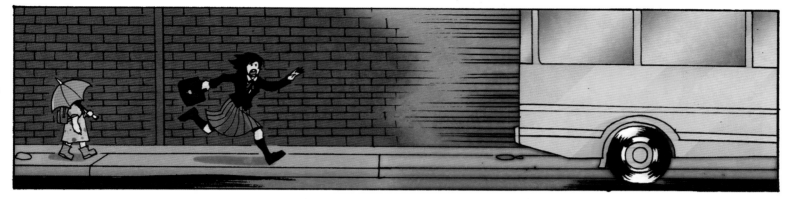

 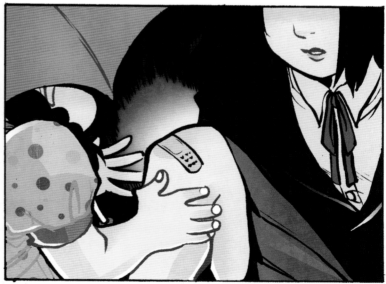

☆ ☆ ☆

DRAW
BY MARIAH MCCOURT

MARIA VICTORIA ROBADO

SKILLS: Colorist
LOCATION: Argentina
FUN FACT: I'm thinking of a way to unite Astronomy and Comics...

www.shouri.com.ar

PRO TIP

"DRAW PEOPLE. ALL THE TIME. AT THE COFFEE SHOP, ON THE TRAIN, SITTING AT THE PARK, WALKING DOWN THE STREET. DRAW THEM CONSTANTLY. WATCH HOW THEY REALLY MOVE, HOW THEY SIT, HOW CLOTHING IS WORN. WATCH THEIR FACES, HOW THEY LAUGH OR CRY OR SPEAK. DRAW OLD PEOPLE, YOUNG PEOPLE, AND EVERY ETHNICITY. DON'T EVER STOP OBSERVING THE WORLD AROUND YOU BECAUSE IT WILL INFORM EVERY FICTIONAL WORLD (OR NON-FICTIONAL WORLD) YOU'RE ASKED TO DRAW. NEVER LET YOUR WORK STAGNATE, ALWAYS SEEK TO BE BETTER AND LEARN NEW THINGS. COMICS STORYTELLING IS AN ART-FORM UNTO ITSELF, DON'T SACRIFICE CLARITY FOR STYLE. AND MOST OF ALL: HAVE FUN."

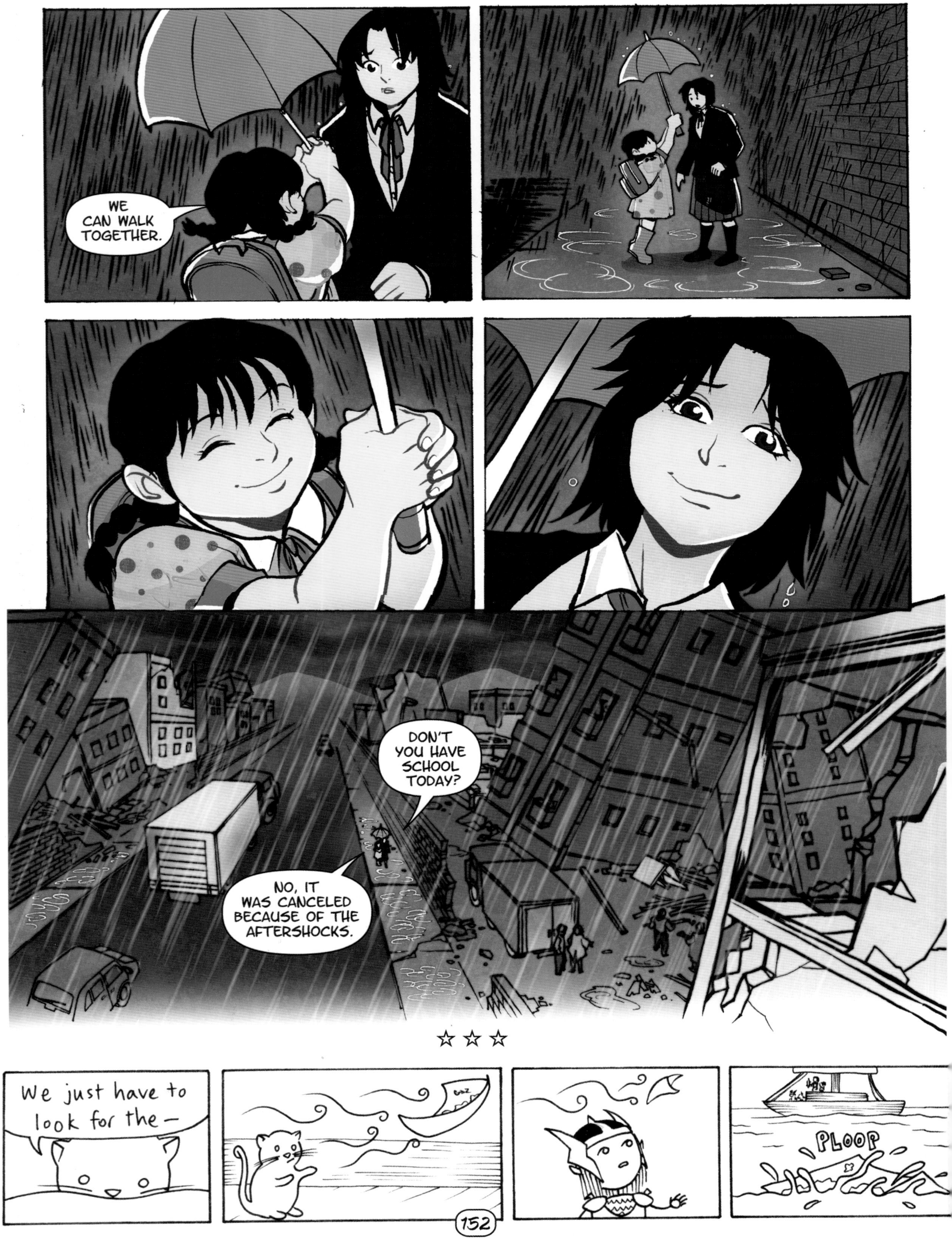
WE CAN WALK TOGETHER.
DON'T YOU HAVE SCHOOL TODAY?
NO, IT WAS CANCELED BECAUSE OF THE AFTERSHOCKS.
We just have to look for the—
PLOOP

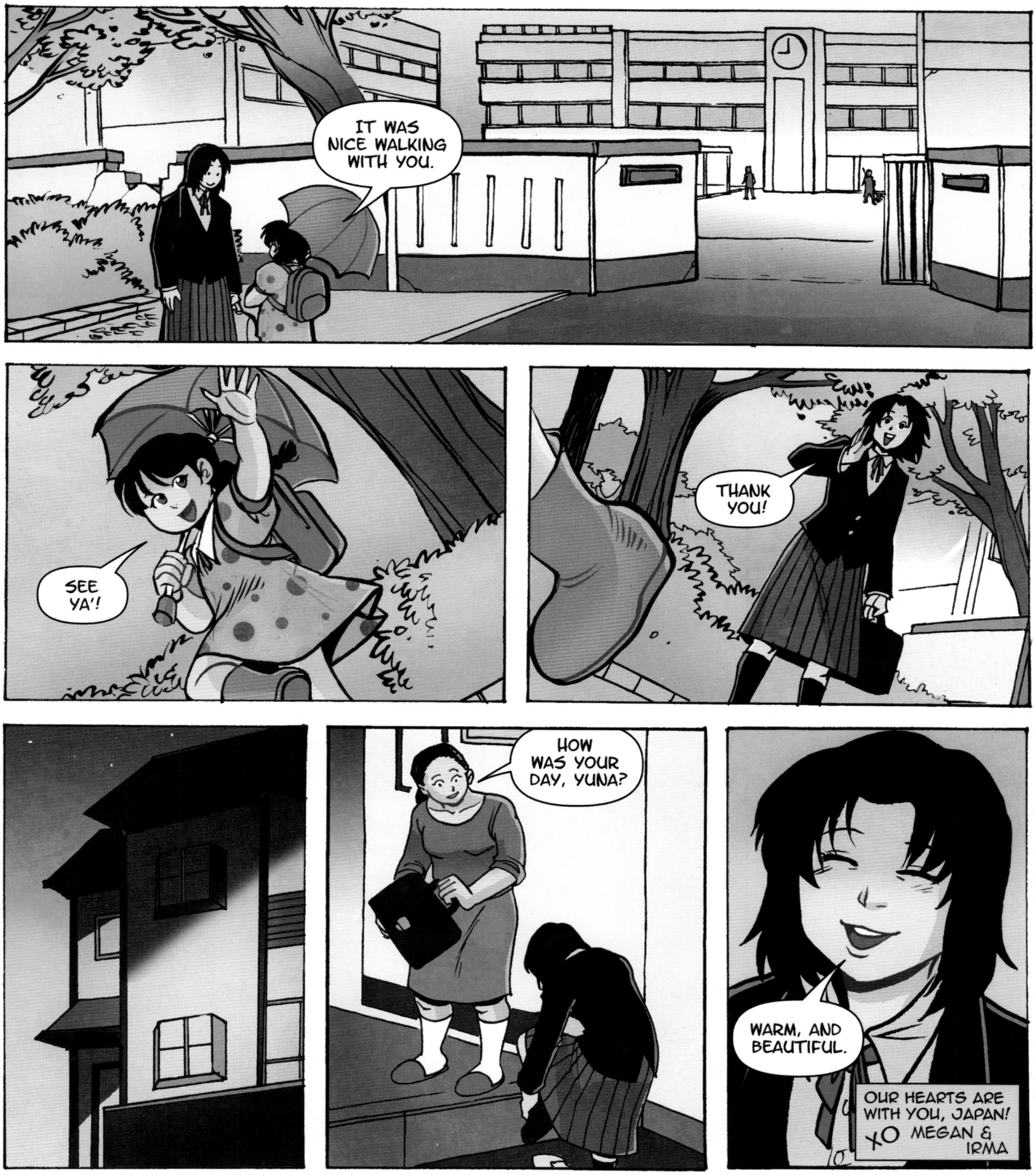
IT WAS NICE WALKING WITH YOU.
SEE YA'!
THANK YOU!
HOW WAS YOUR DAY, YUNA?
WARM, AND BEAUTIFUL.
OUR HEARTS ARE WITH YOU, JAPAN!
XO MEGAN & IRMA

☆ ☆ ☆

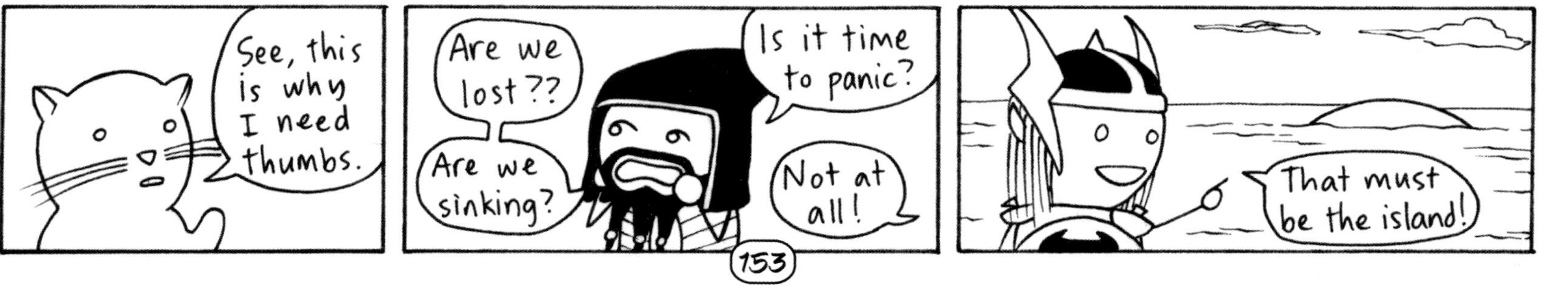
See, this is why I need thumbs.
Are we lost??
Are we sinking?
Is it time to panic?
Not at all!
That must be the island!

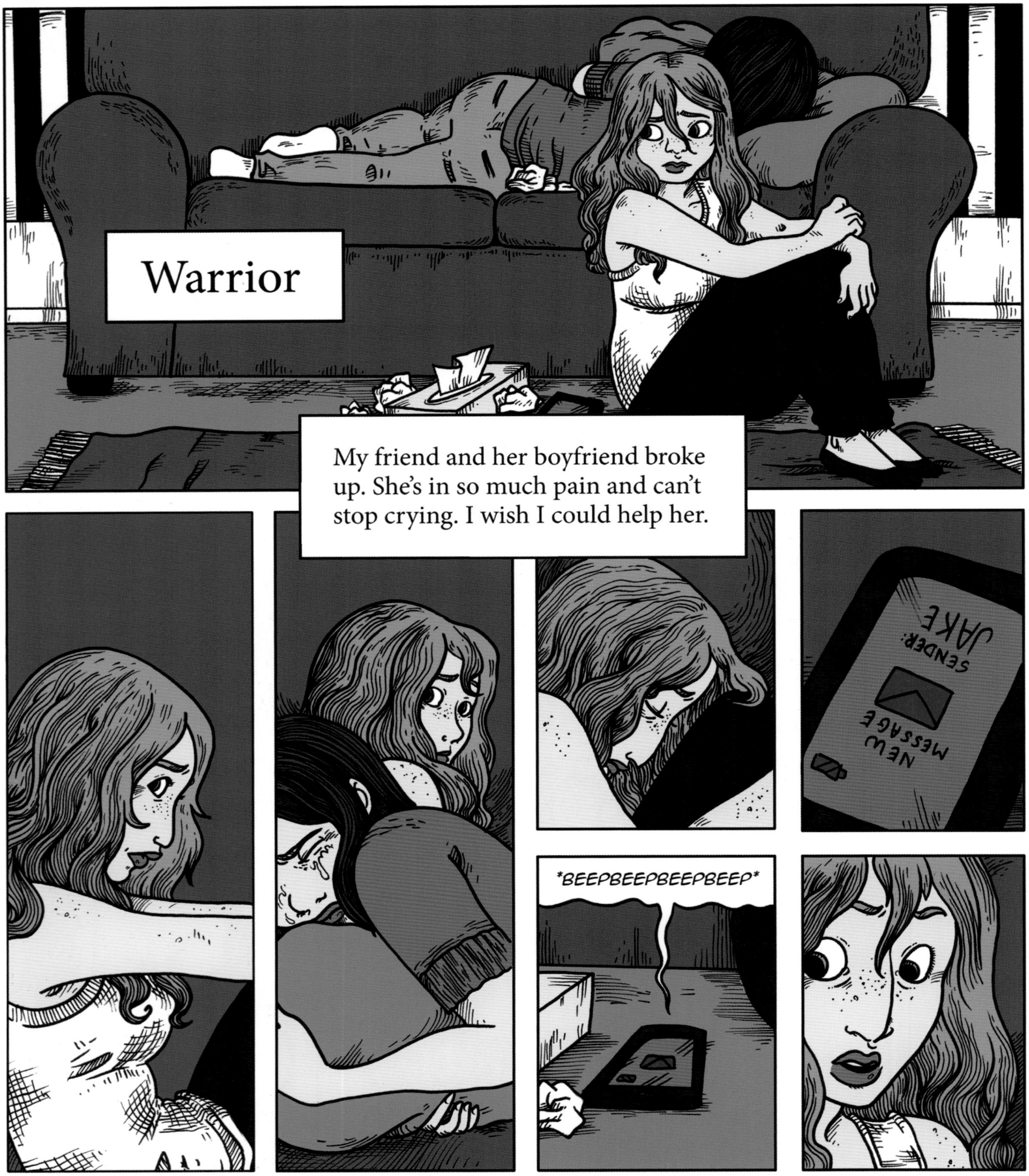
Warrior
My friend and her boyfriend broke up. She's in so much pain and can't stop crying. I wish I could help her.
NEW MESSAGE
SENDER: JAKE
BEEPBEEPBEEPBEEP

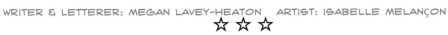

WRITER & LETTERER: MEGAN LAVEY-HEATON ARTIST: ISABELLE MELANÇON

☆☆☆

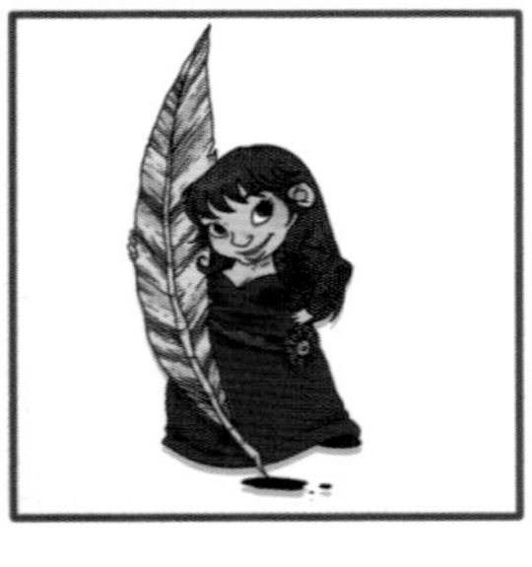

MEGAN LAVEY-HEATON

SKILLS: Writer, Letterer
LOCATION: Mechanicsburg, PA
FUN FACT: When I'm not writing comics, I'm an editor at a tech news site and a newspaper designer -- all while juggling an international marriage. And for my next parlor trick...

http://mlheaton.namesakecomic.com

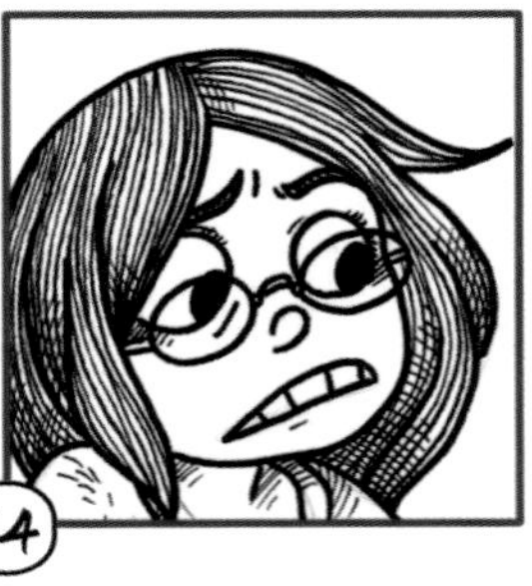

ISABELLE MELANCON

SKILLS: Sketch, Inker, Colorist
LOCATION: Canada
FUN FACT: I adore fairy tales, mythology, and cookies to an absurd degree.

www.isabellemelancon.com

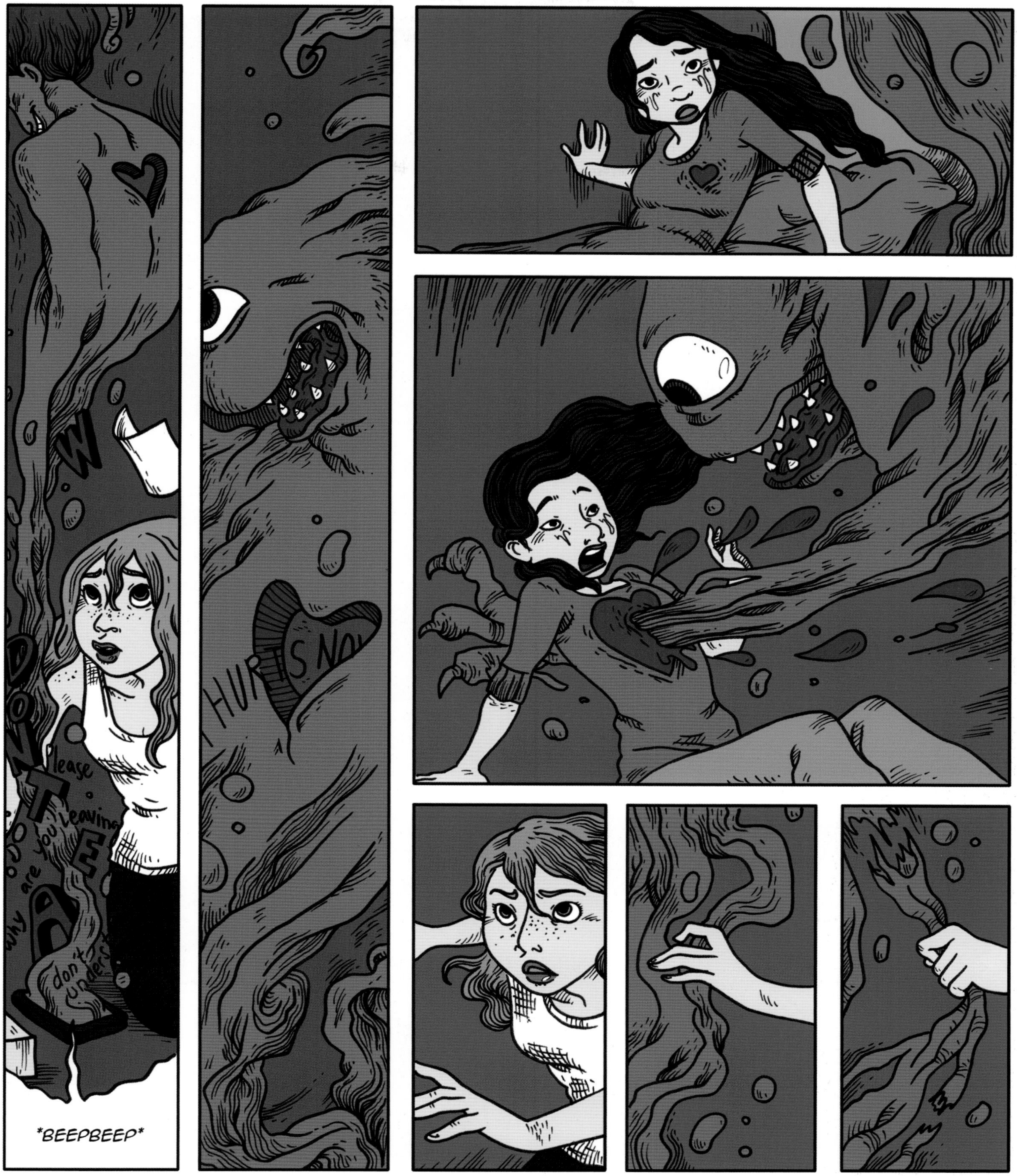
BEEPBEEP

☆ ☆ ☆

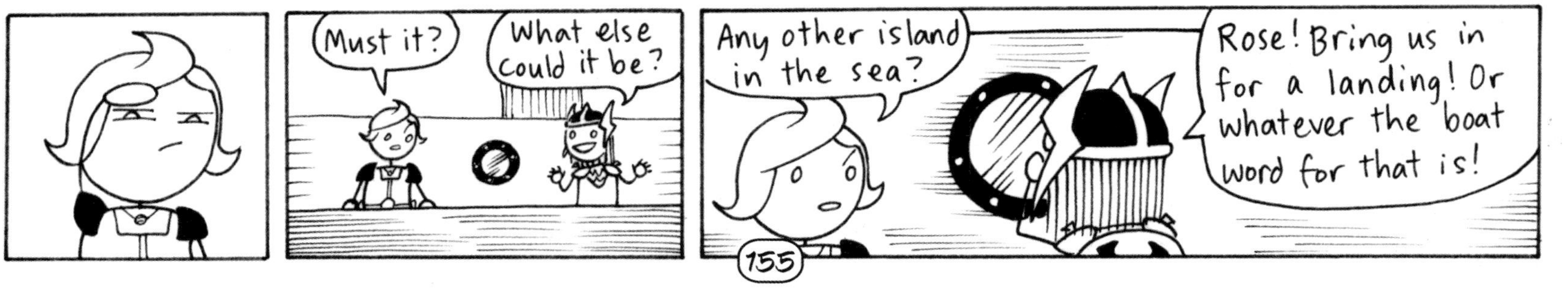
Must it?
What else could it be?
Any other island in the sea?
Rose! Bring us in for a landing! Or whatever the boat word for that is!

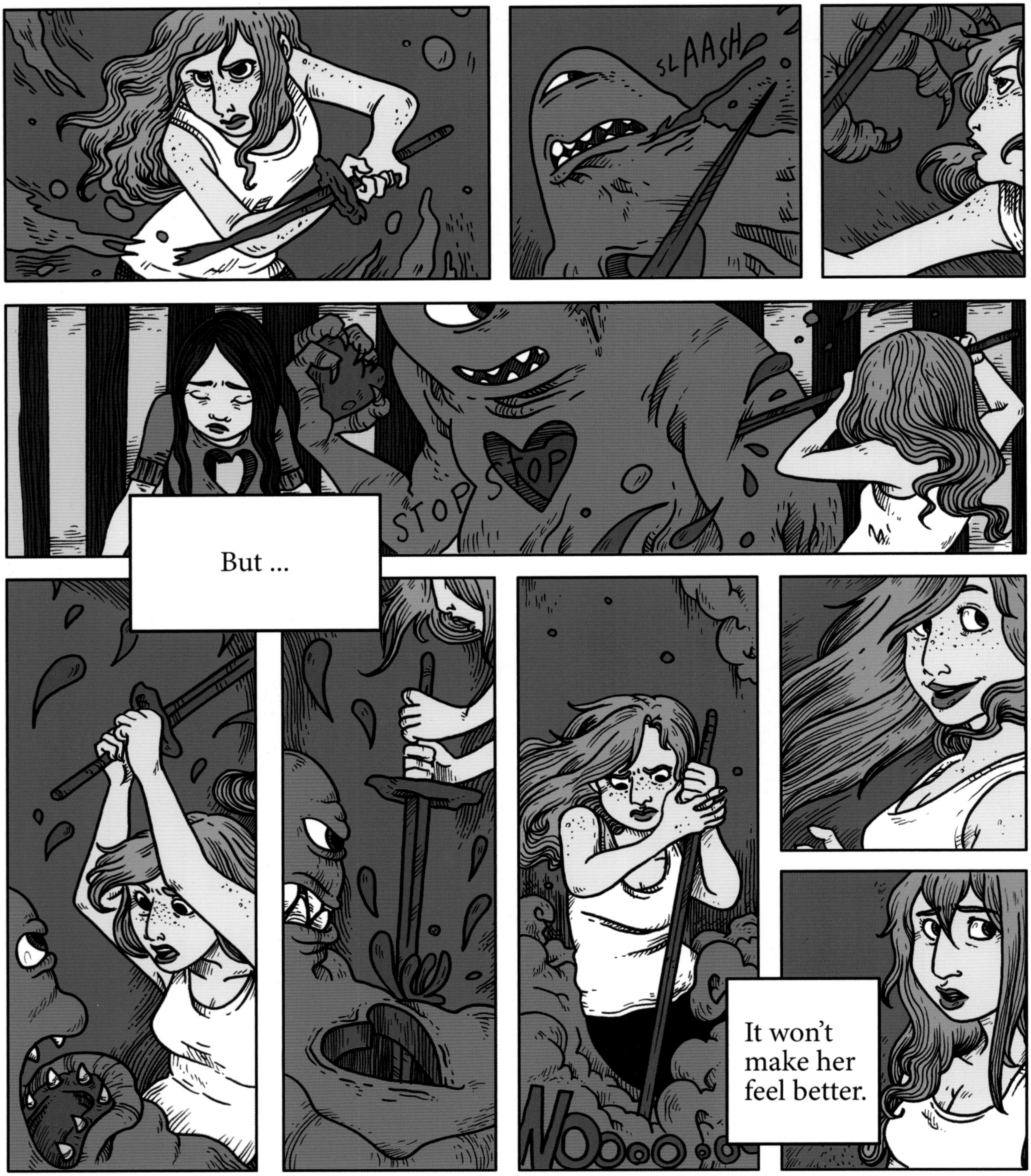
SLAASH
STOP STOP
But ...
It won't make her feel better.
NOooo..oo

☆ ☆ ☆

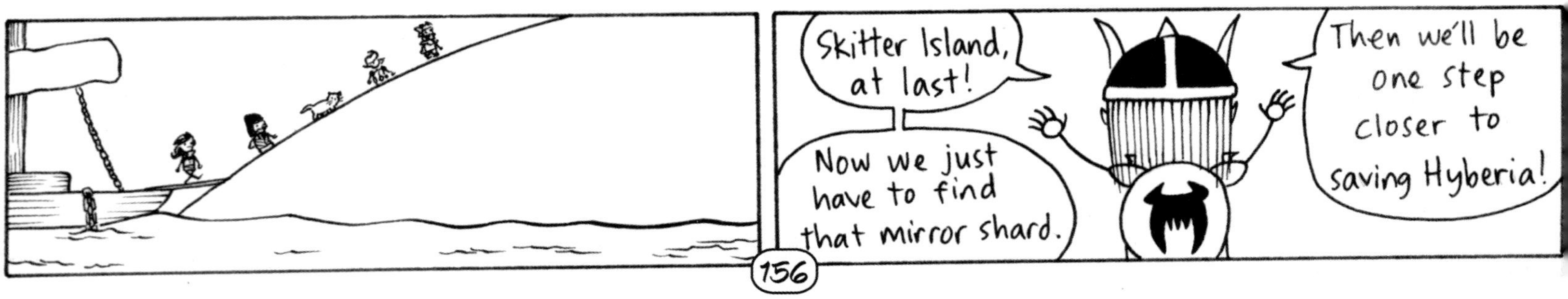
Skitter Island, at last!
Now we just have to find that mirror shard.
Then we'll be one step closer to saving Hyberia!

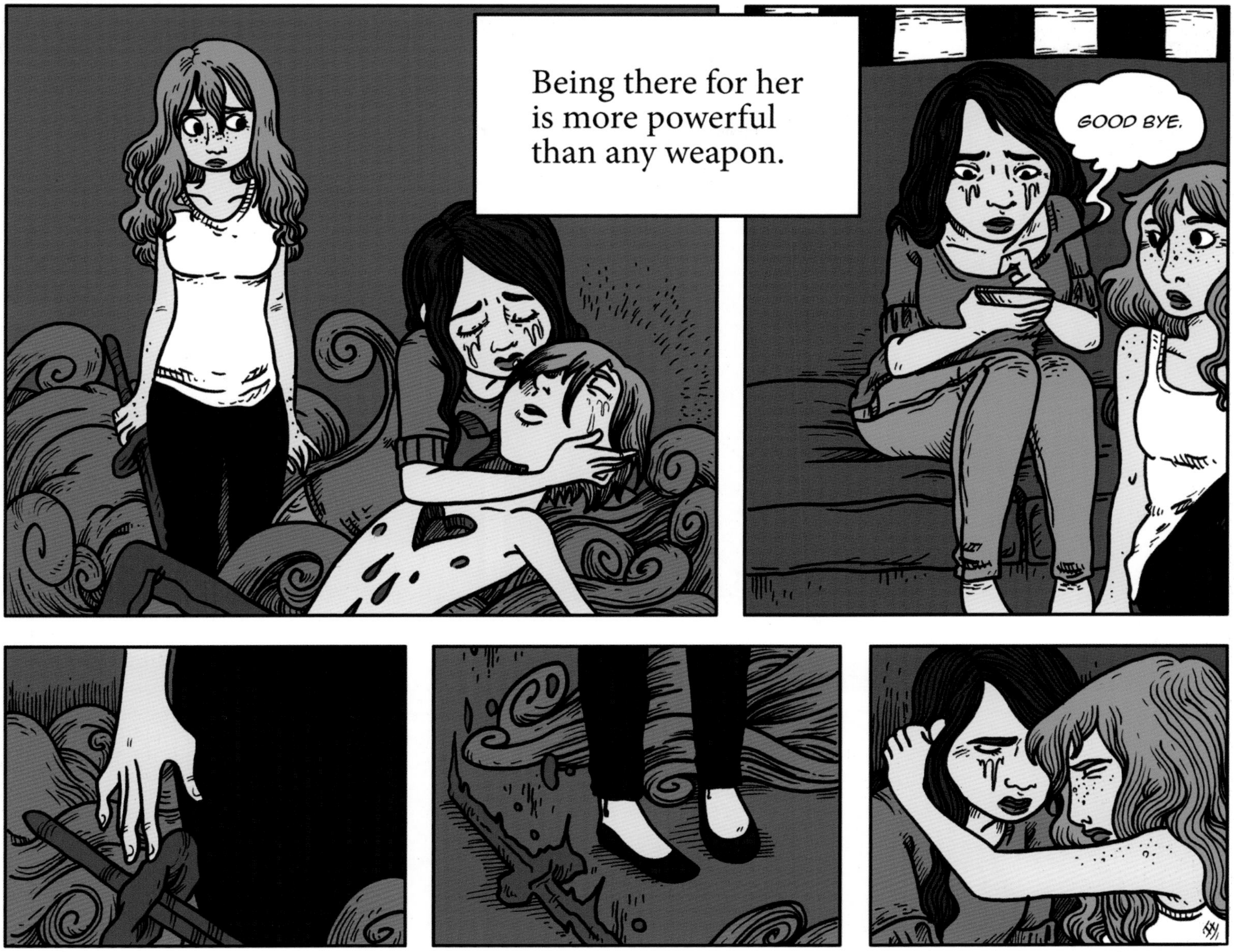
Being there for her is more powerful than any weapon.
GOOD BYE.

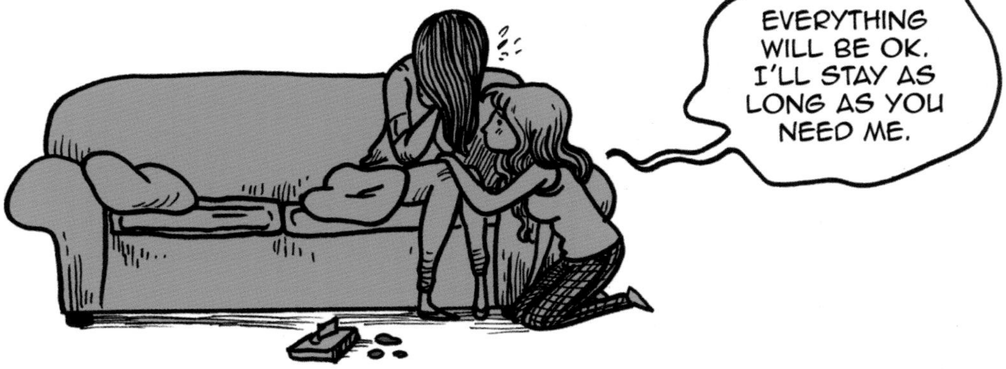
EVERYTHING WILL BE OK. I'LL STAY AS LONG AS YOU NEED ME.

☆ ☆ ☆

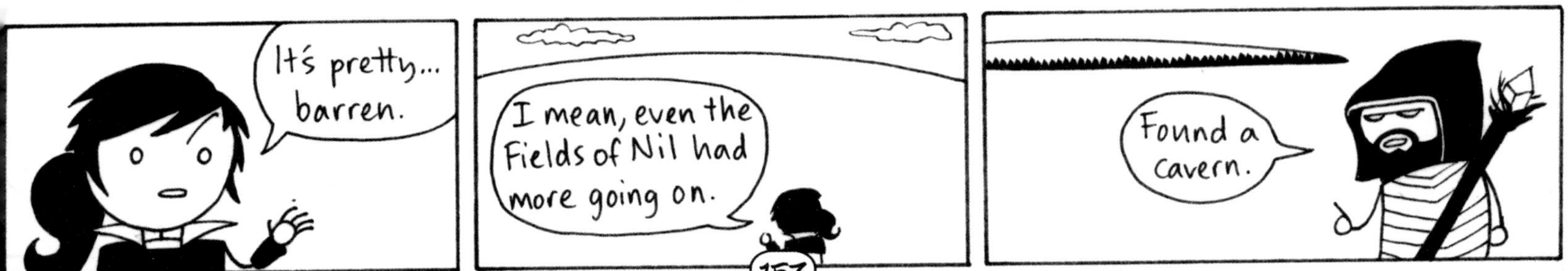
It's pretty... barren.
I mean, even the Fields of Nil had more going on.
Found a cavern.

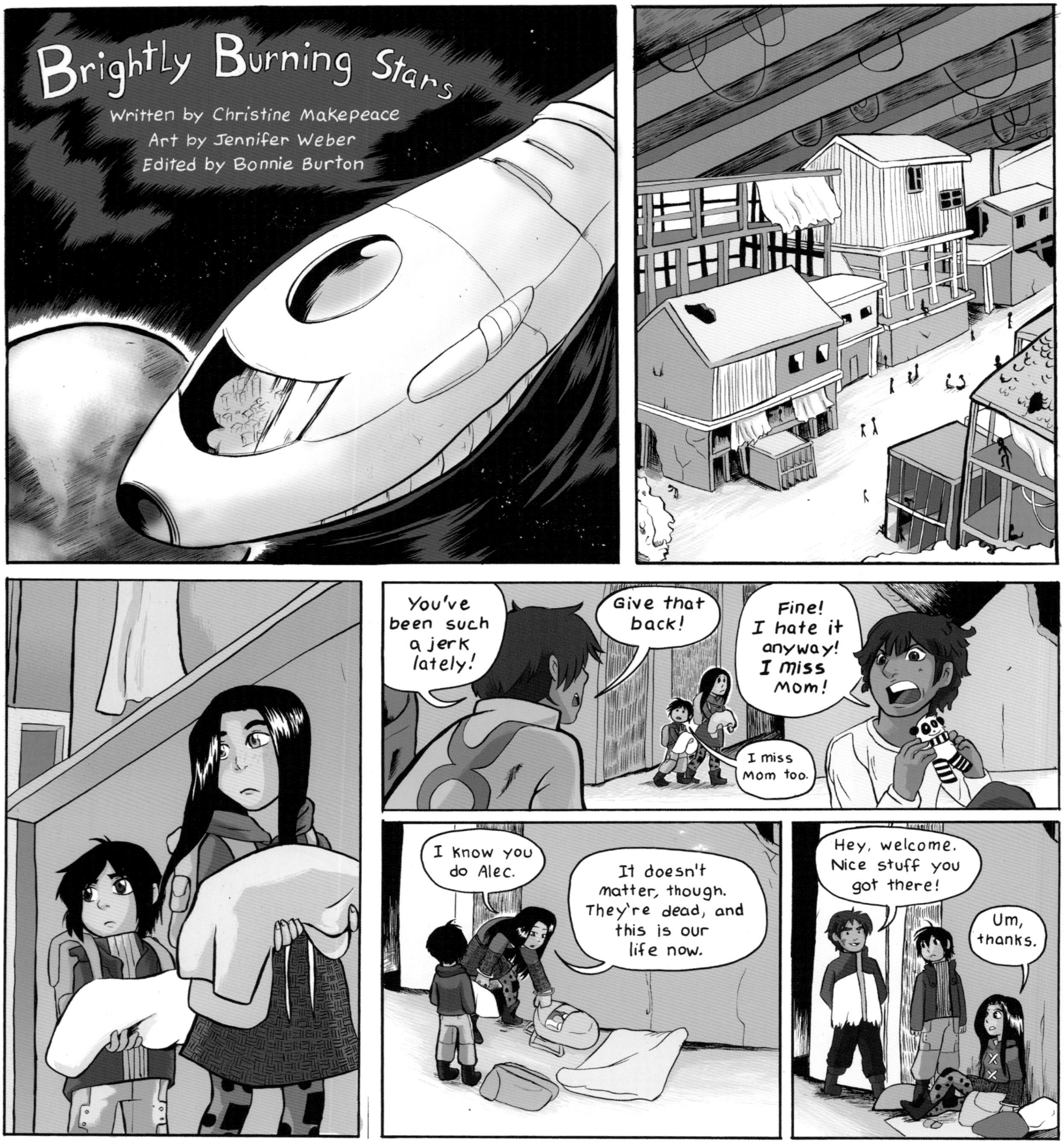
Brightly Burning Stars
Written by Christine Makepeace
Art by Jennifer Weber
Edited by Bonnie Burton
You've been such a jerk lately!
Give that back!
Fine! I hate it anyway! I miss Mom!
I miss Mom too.
I know you do Alec.
It doesn't matter, though. They're dead, and this is our life now.
Hey, welcome. Nice stuff you got there!
Um, thanks.

☆☆☆

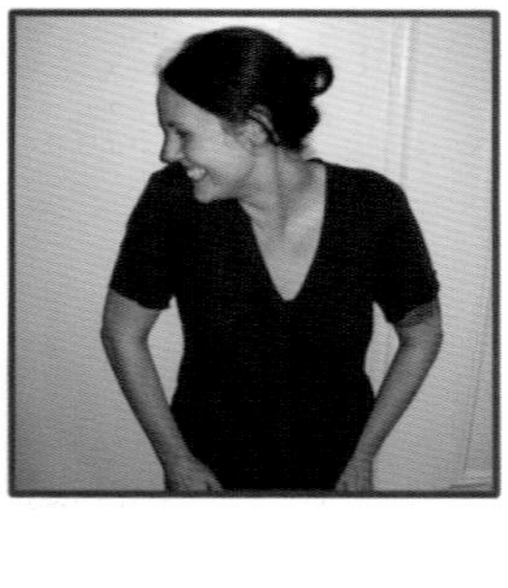

CHRISTINE MAKEPEACE

SKILLS: Writer
LOCATION: NYC
FUN FACT: In love with Kermit the Frog.

www.cmakepeace.com

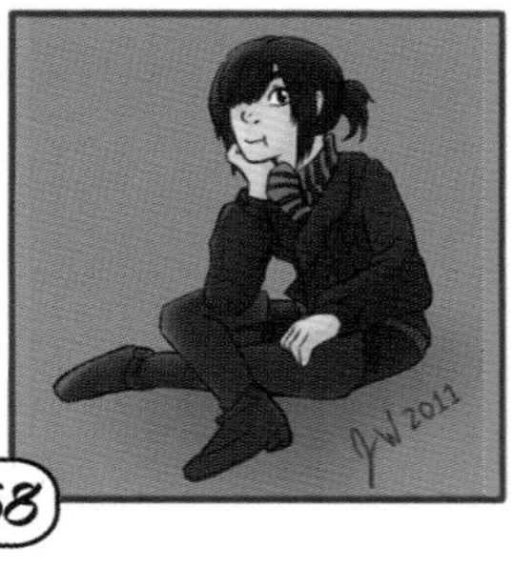

JENNIFER WEBER

SKILLS: Penciller, Inker, Colorist, Letterer
LOCATION: New York City
FUN FACT: I made Eustace's mask from *Courage the Cowardly Dog* one year for Halloween. It's life size, and hangs out in our living room.

runliljared.com

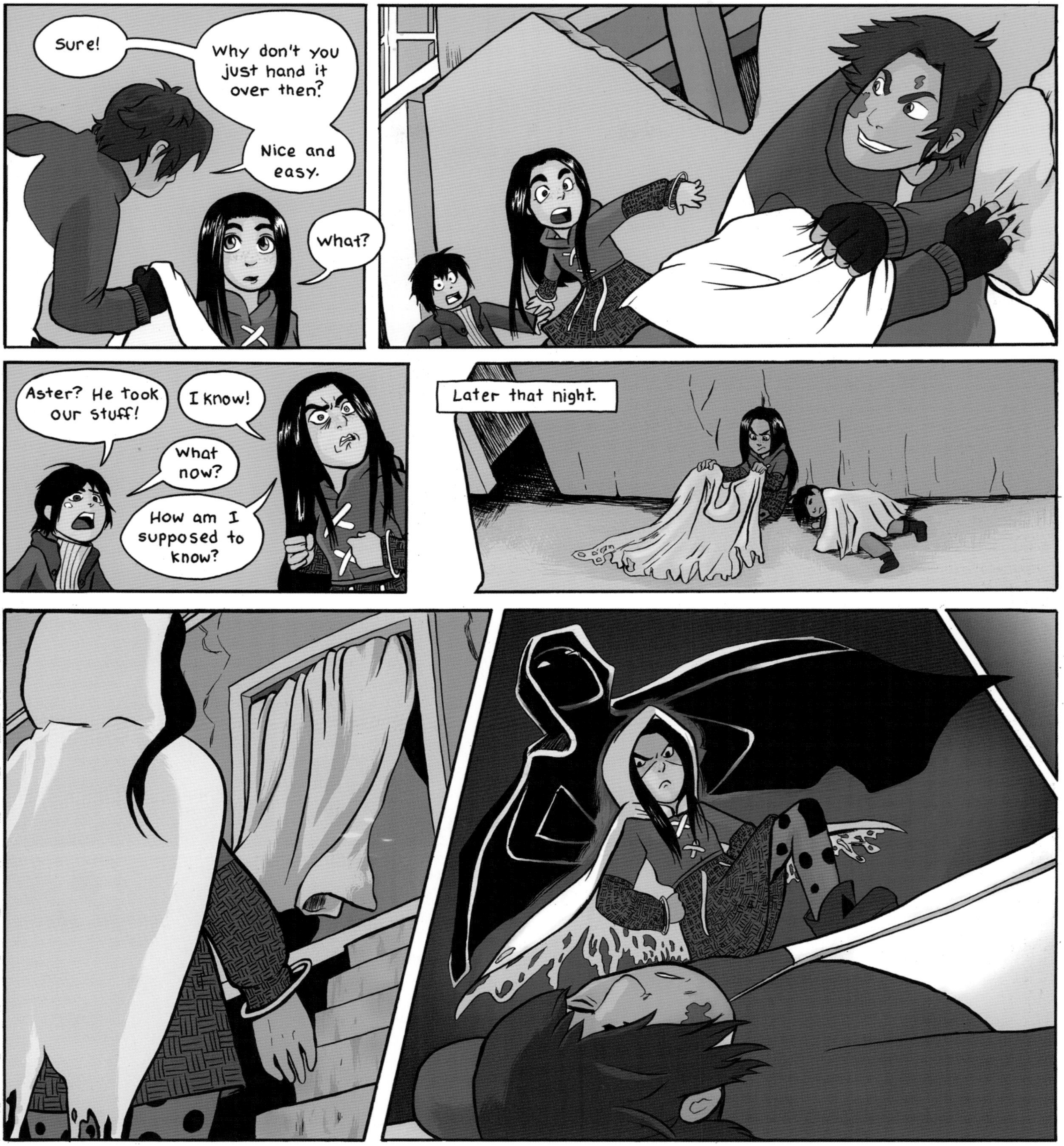
Sure!
Why don't you just hand it over then?
Nice and easy.
What?
Aster? He took our stuff!
I know!
What now?
How am I supposed to know?
Later that night.

☆ ☆ ☆

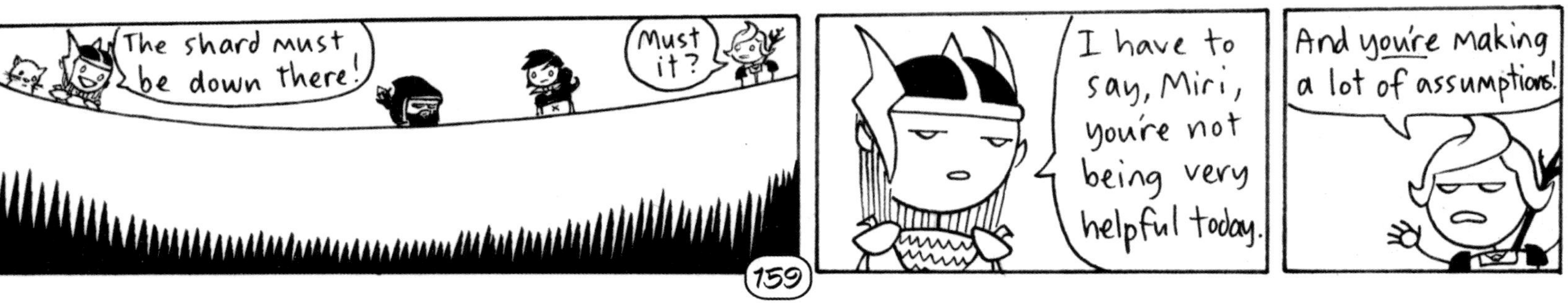
The shard must be down there!
Must it?
I have to say, Miri, you're not being very helpful today.
And you're making a lot of assumptions!

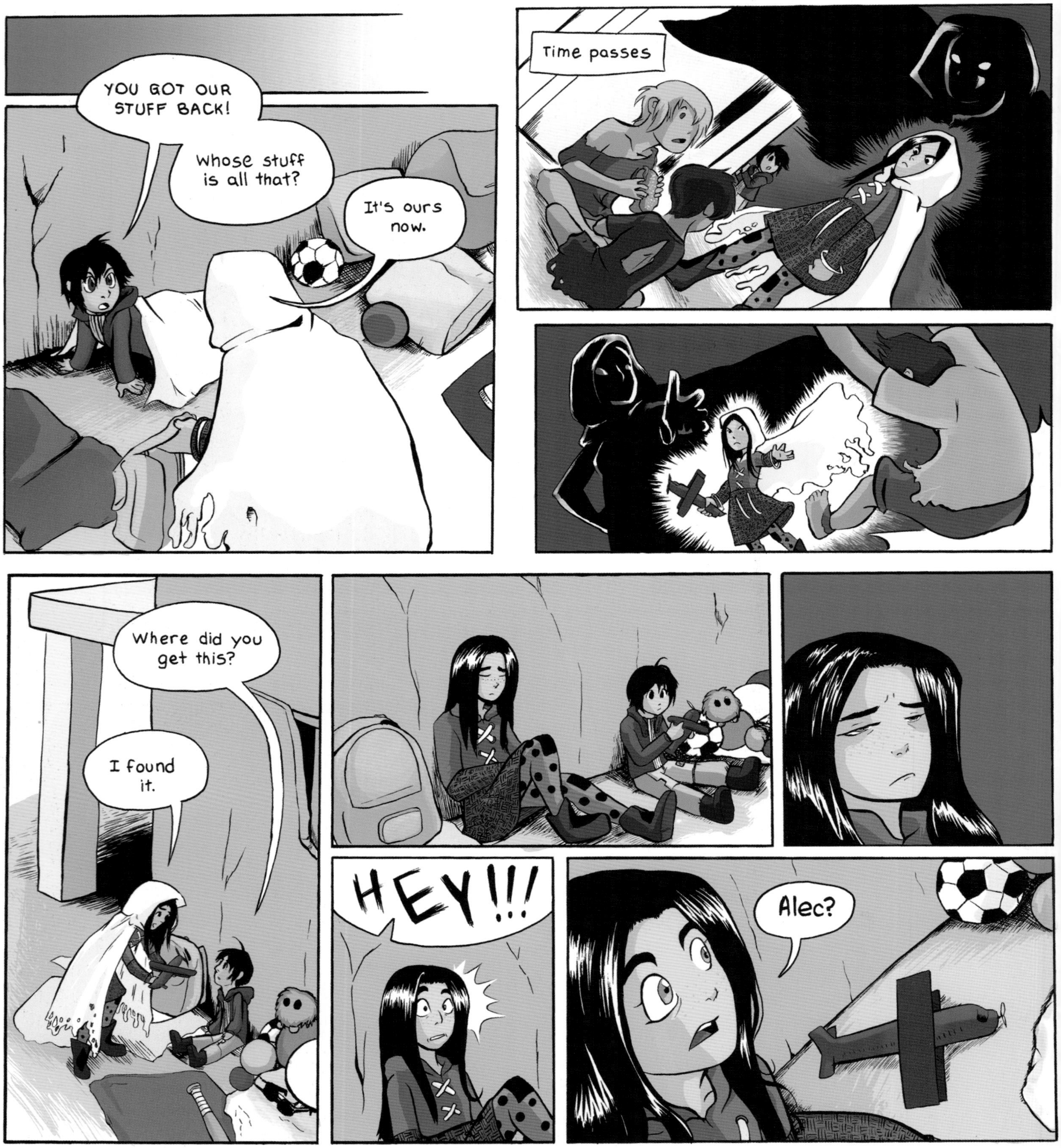
YOU GOT OUR STUFF BACK!
Whose stuff is all that?
It's ours now.
Time passes
Where did you get this?
I found it.
HEY!!!
Alec?

☆ ☆ ☆

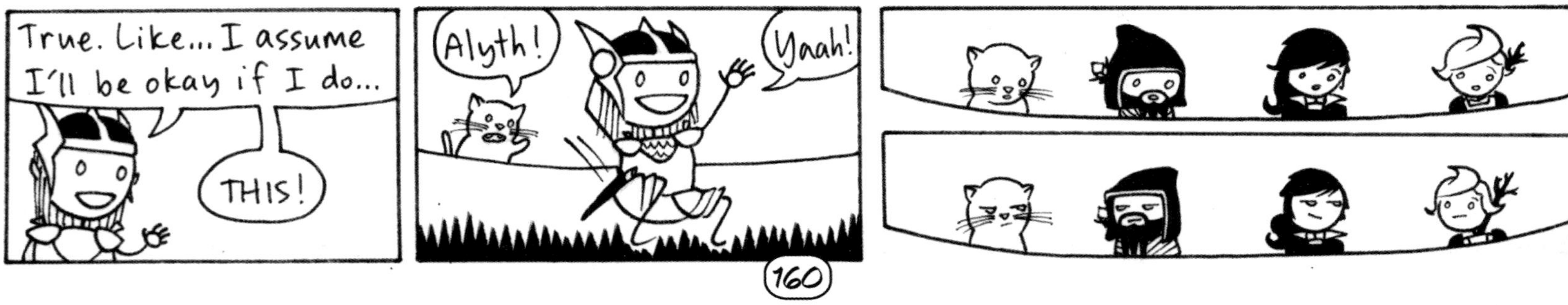
True. Like... I assume I'll be okay if I do...
THIS!
Alyth!
Yaah!

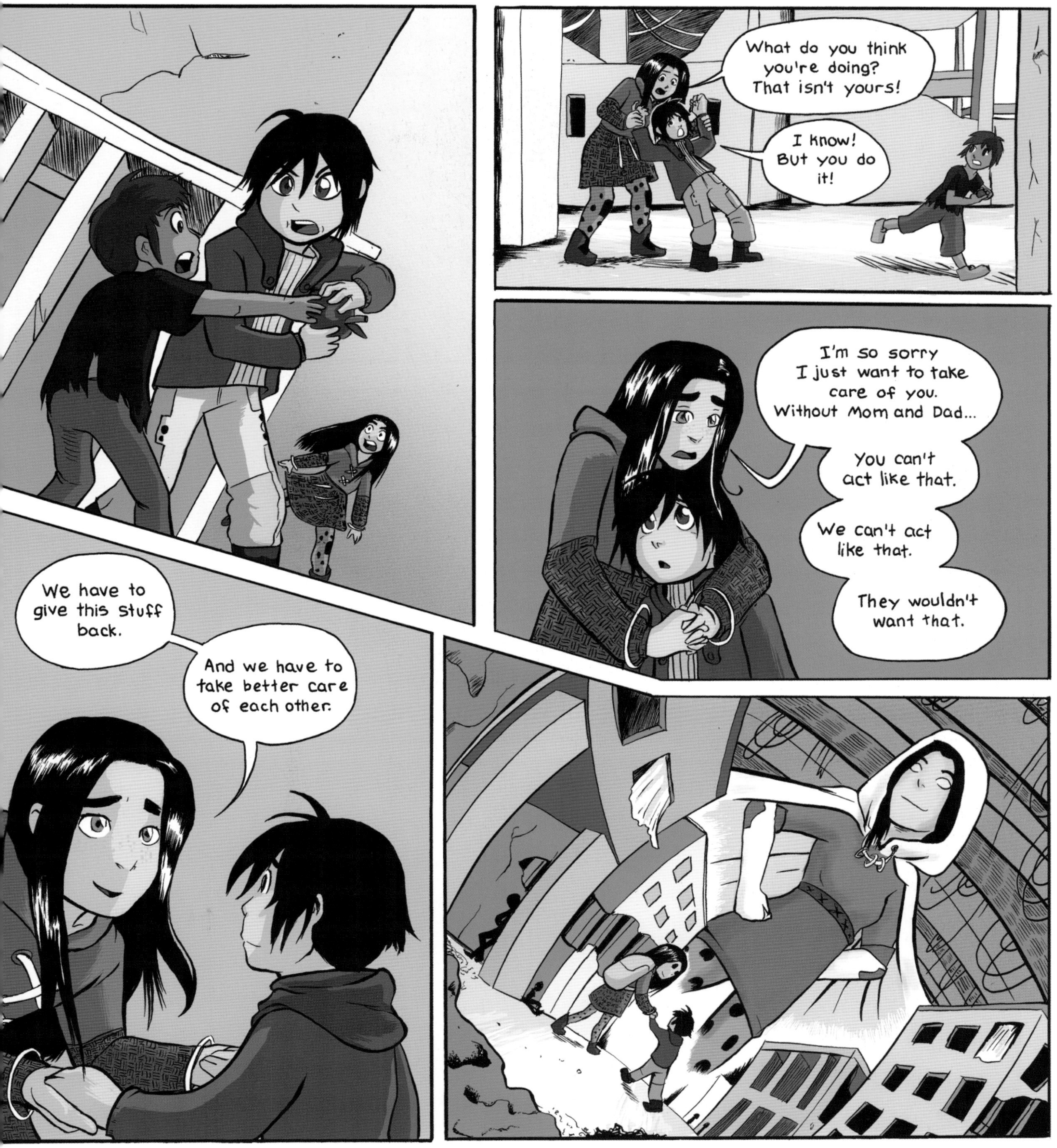
What do you think you're doing? That isn't yours!
I know! But you do it!
I'm so sorry I just want to take care of you. Without Mom and Dad...
You can't act like that.
We can't act like that.
They wouldn't want that.
We have to give this stuff back.
And we have to take better care of each other.

☆ ☆ ☆

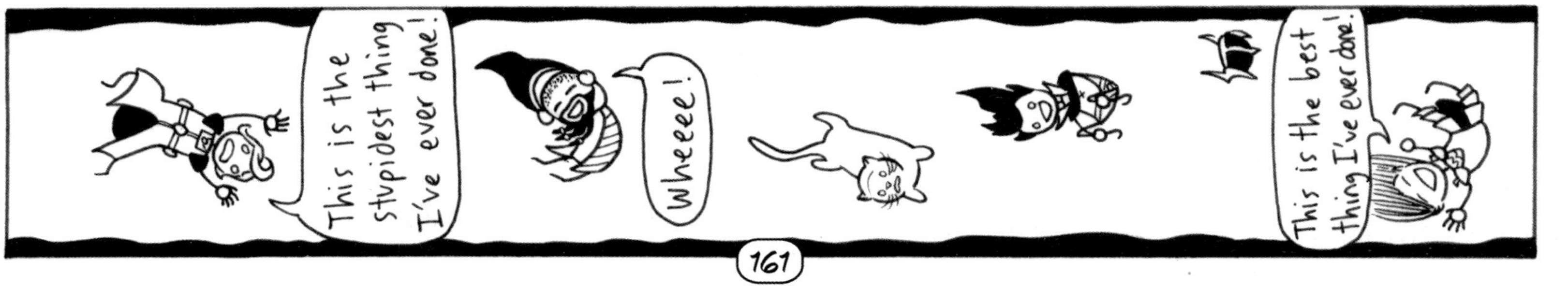
This is the stupidest thing I've ever done!
Wheeee!
This is the best thing I've ever done!

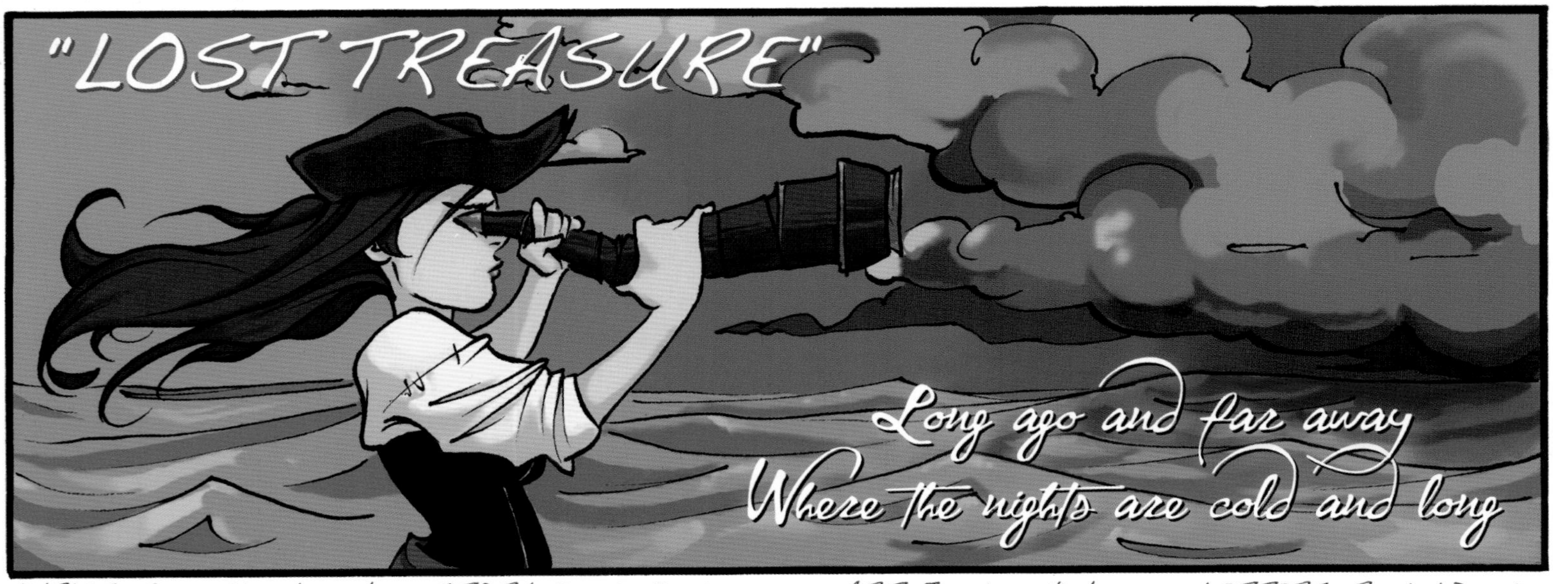
"LOST TREASURE"
Long ago and far away
Where the nights are cold and long

LYRICS: Samantha Newark STORY: Bonnie Burton ART: Jessica Hickman LETTERS: Rachel Deering

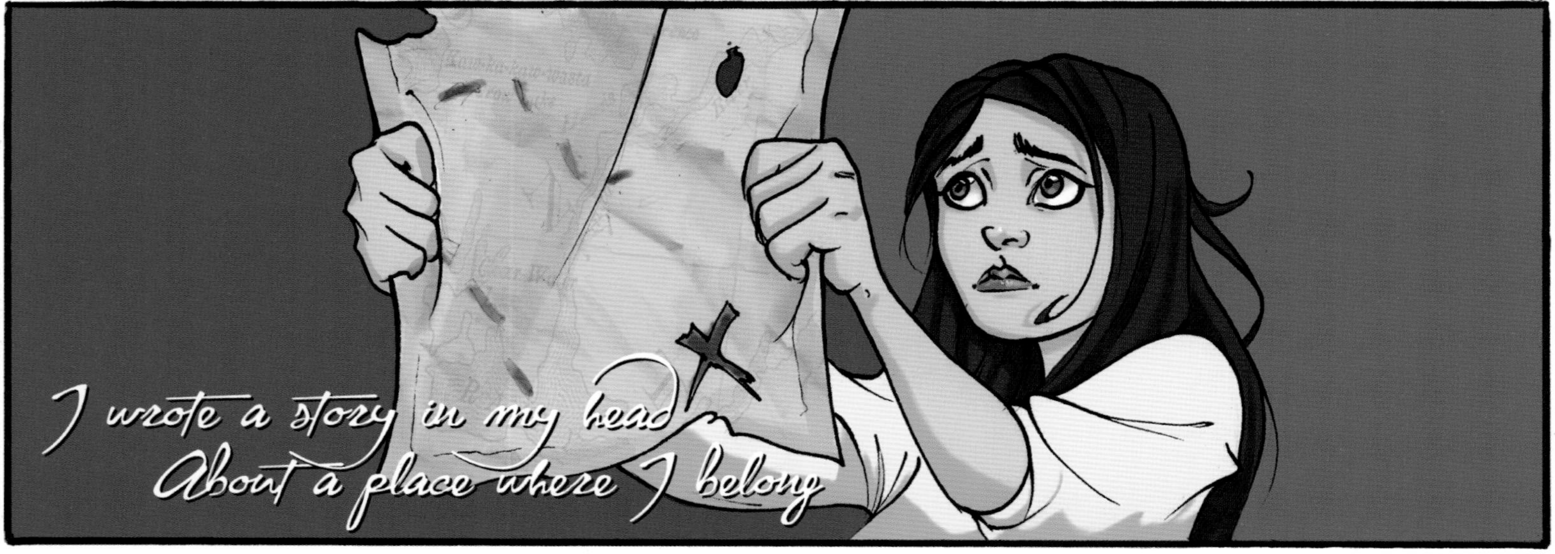
I wrote a story in my head
About a place where I belong

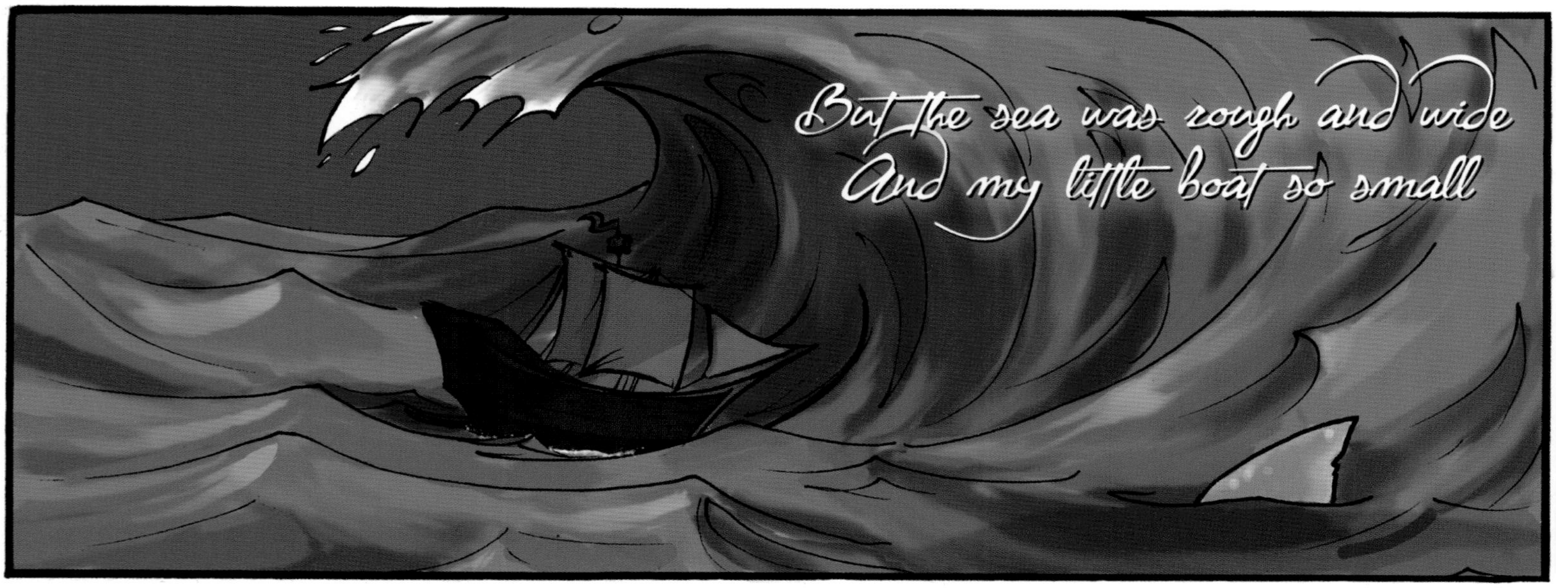
But the sea was rough and wide
And my little boat so small

☆☆☆

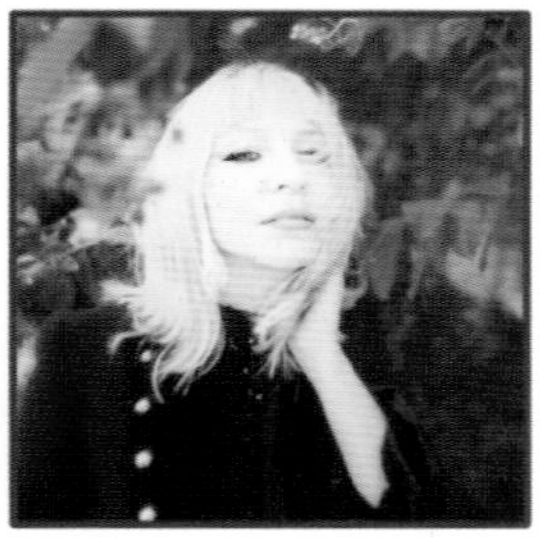

SAMANTHA NEWARK

SKILLS: Singer, Songwriter, Voice-Over Artist
LOCATION: Nashville, TN
FUN FACT: Voice of Jem and Jerrica from *JEM AND THE HOLOGRAMS* cartoon.

www.samanthanewark.com

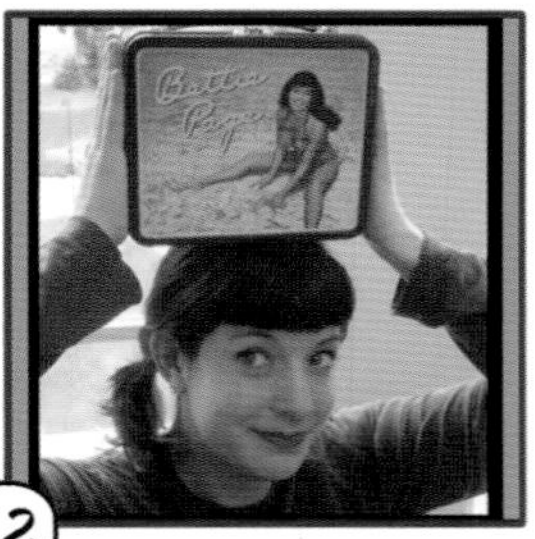

BONNIE BURTON

SKILLS: Editor, Writer
LOCATION: San Francisco, CA
FUN FACT: I put googly eyes on all the condiments in my fridge.

www.grrl.com

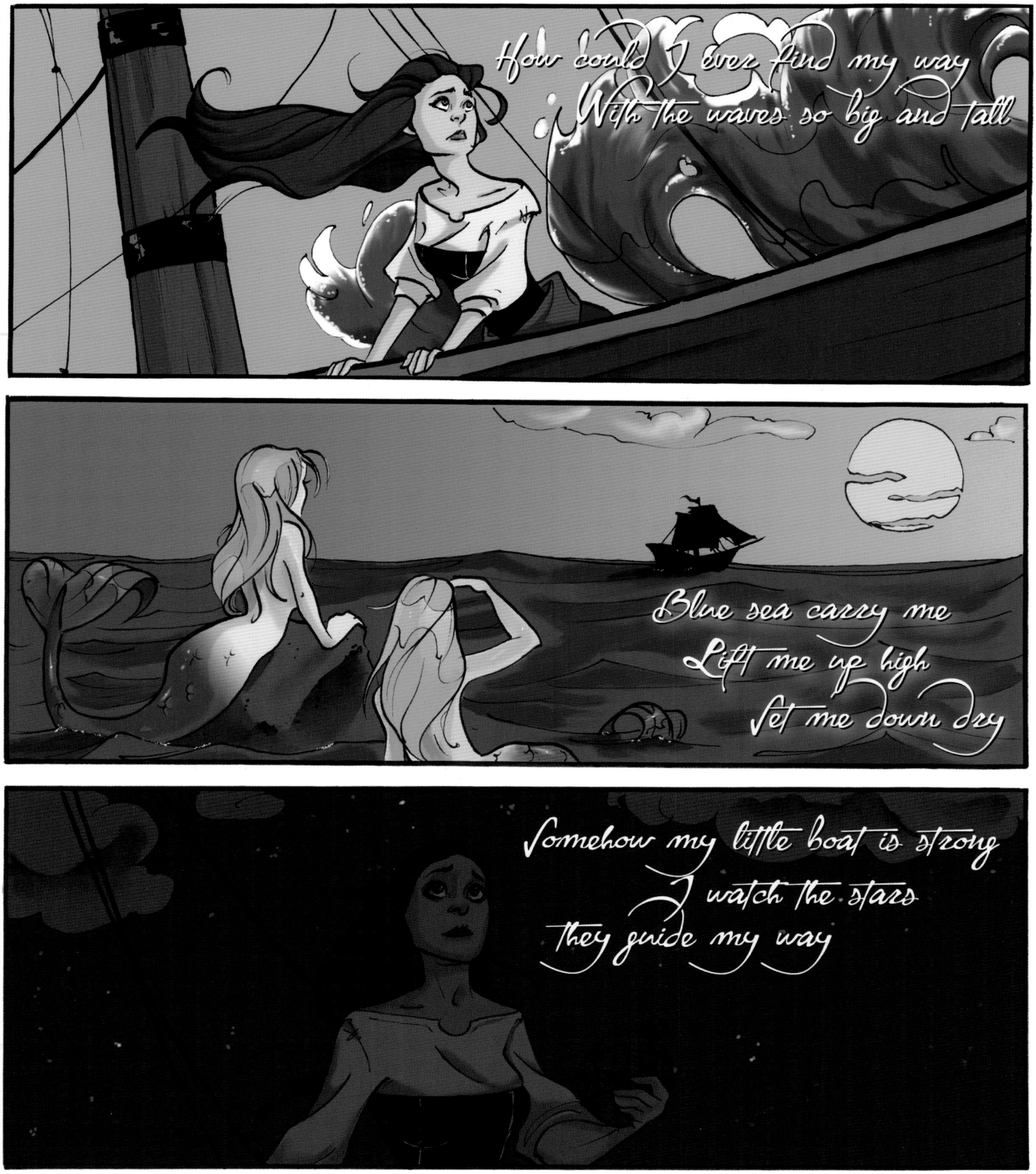
How could I ever find my way
With the waves so big and tall
Blue sea carry me
Lift me up high
Set me down dry
Somehow my little boat is strong
I watch the stars
they guide my way

☆ ☆ ☆

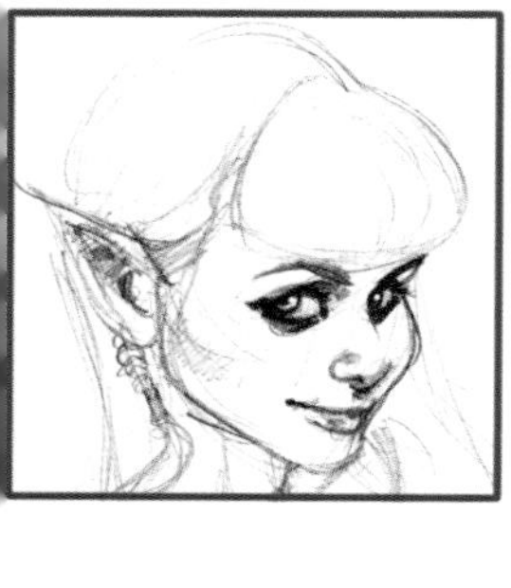

JESSICA HICKMAN

SKILLS: Penciller, Inker, Colorist
LOCATION: Minnesota
FUN FACT: Shark lover

jessicahickman.com

PRO TIP

TARGET
BY ANNIE NOCENTI

"TO USE AN OBNOXIOUS PHRASE: TARGET MARKET. LOOK AT THE WORK THAT A PUBLISHER PUTS OUT, AND SEND THEM TAILORED SAMPLES TO FIT WHAT THEY LIKE. THEY KNOW WHAT THEY WANT, WHAT SELLS FOR THEIR READERSHIP, SO DON'T SEND THEM A KIWI WHEN ALL THEY PRINT ARE APPLES. OKAY, THIS IS CYNICAL, DEMORALIZING, COWTOWING ADVICE, BUT WORTH A SHOT."

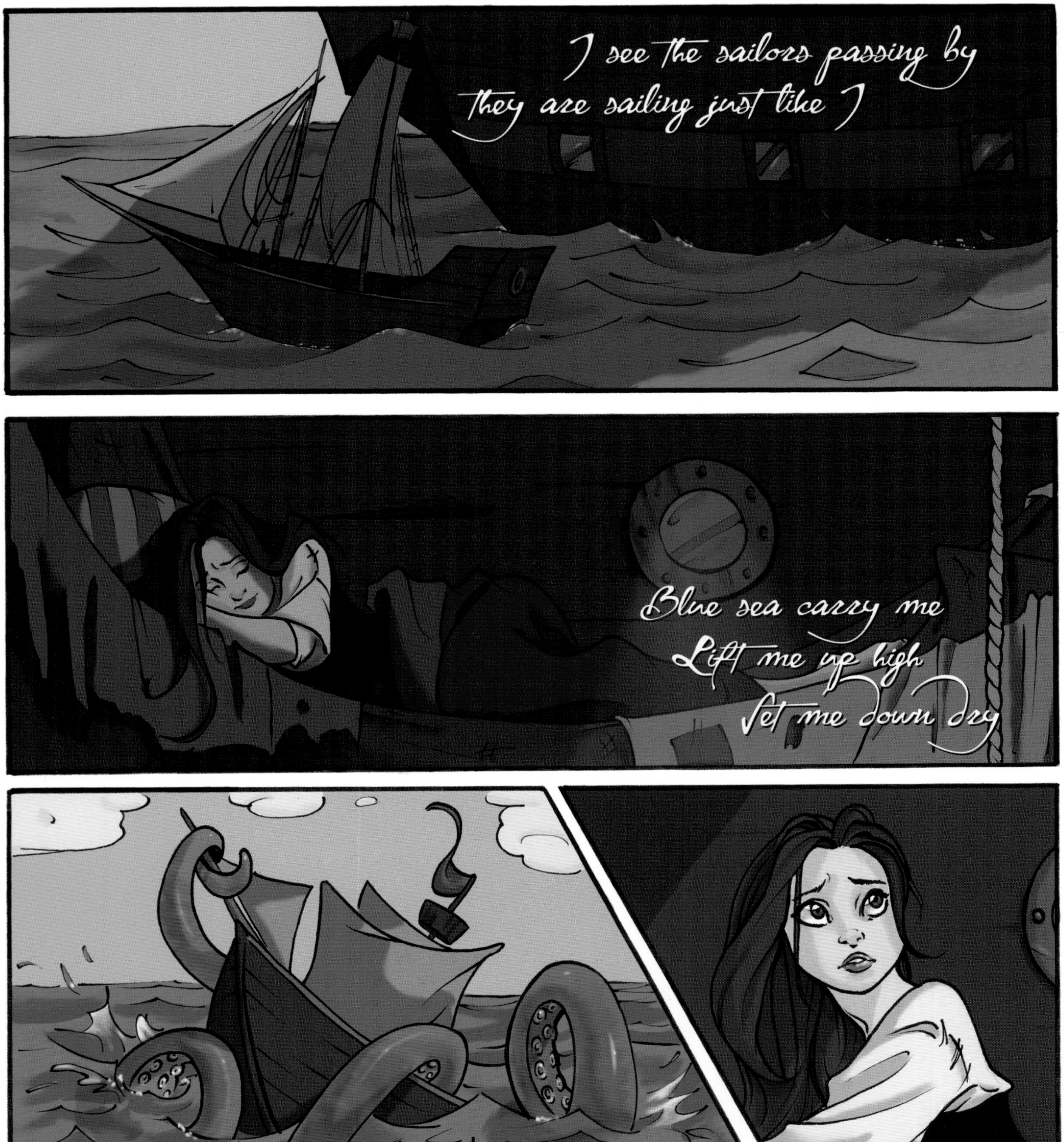
I see the sailors passing by
they are sailing just like I
Blue sea carry me
Lift me up high
Set me down dry

☆ ☆ ☆

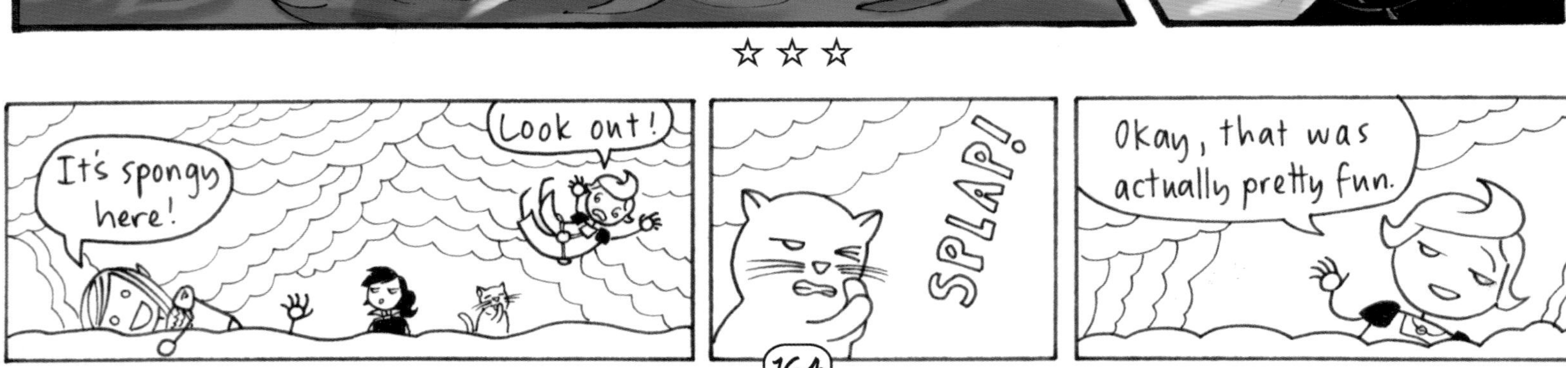
It's spongy here!
Look out!
SPLAP!
Okay, that was actually pretty fun.

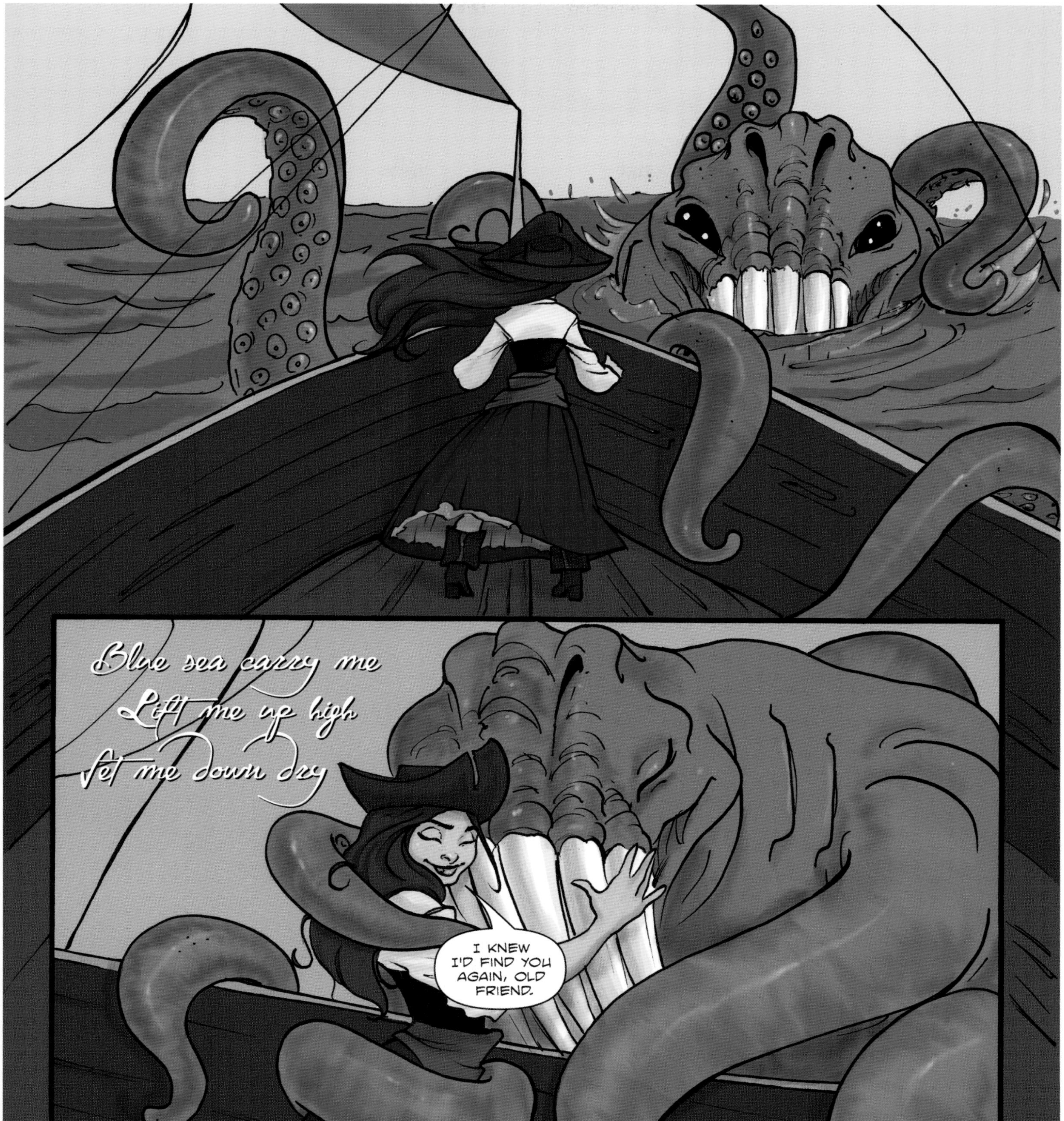
Blue sea carry me
Lift me up high
Set me down dry
I KNEW I'D FIND YOU AGAIN, OLD FRIEND.

☆ ☆ ☆

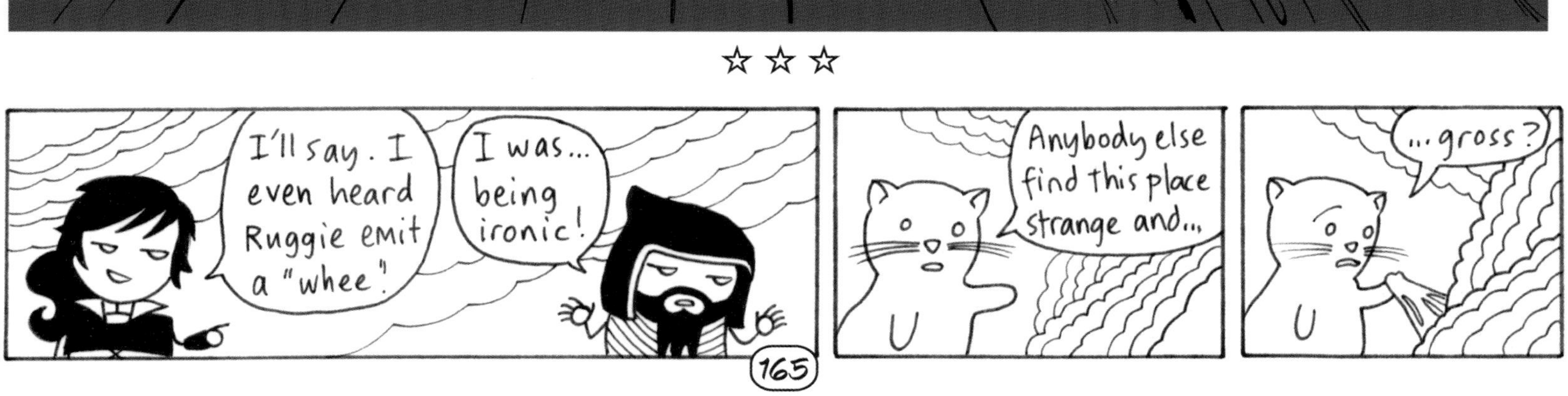
I'll say. I even heard Ruggie emit a "whee"!
I was... being ironic!
Anybody else find this place strange and...
...gross?

AND YOU WILL KNOW THEM by the RAKE of Their HATS

WRITER: HEATHER ROYSTON
ARTIST: JOLENE HOUSER
COLORS: ELLI MOKA
LETTERS: RACHEL DEERING

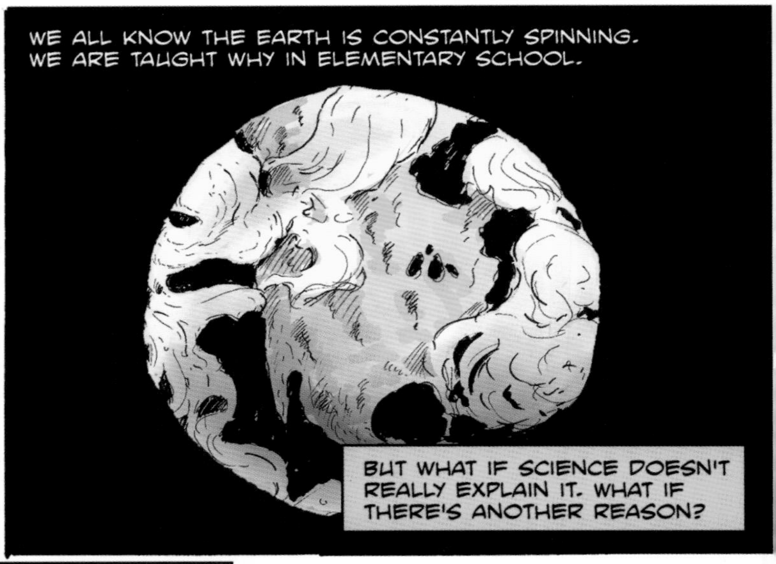
WE ALL KNOW THE EARTH IS CONSTANTLY SPINNING. WE ARE TAUGHT WHY IN ELEMENTARY SCHOOL.
BUT WHAT IF SCIENCE DOESN'T REALLY EXPLAIN IT. WHAT IF THERE'S ANOTHER REASON?

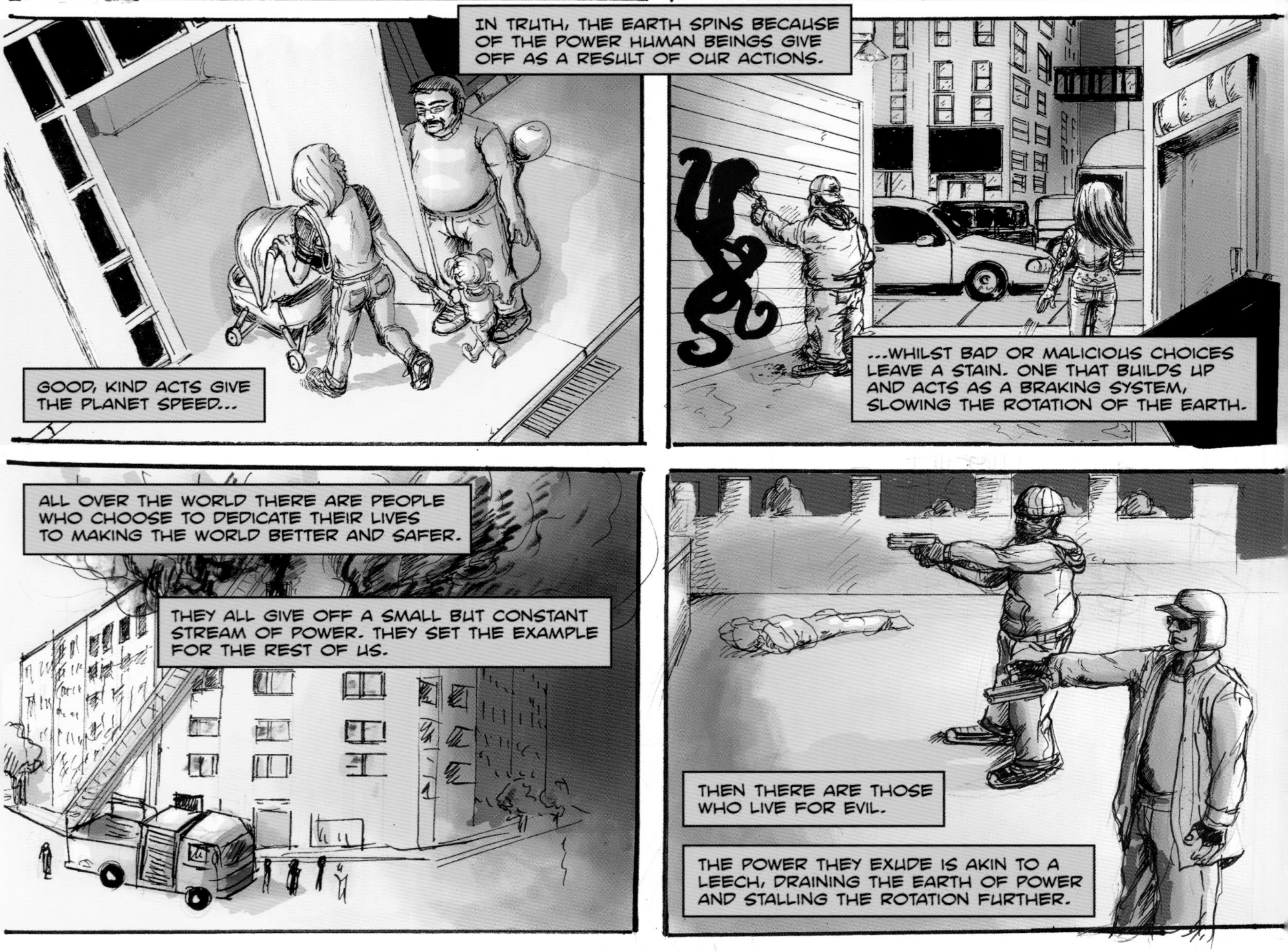
IN TRUTH, THE EARTH SPINS BECAUSE OF THE POWER HUMAN BEINGS GIVE OFF AS A RESULT OF OUR ACTIONS.
GOOD, KIND ACTS GIVE THE PLANET SPEED...
...WHILST BAD OR MALICIOUS CHOICES LEAVE A STAIN. ONE THAT BUILDS UP AND ACTS AS A BRAKING SYSTEM, SLOWING THE ROTATION OF THE EARTH.
ALL OVER THE WORLD THERE ARE PEOPLE WHO CHOOSE TO DEDICATE THEIR LIVES TO MAKING THE WORLD BETTER AND SAFER.
THEY ALL GIVE OFF A SMALL BUT CONSTANT STREAM OF POWER. THEY SET THE EXAMPLE FOR THE REST OF US.
THEN THERE ARE THOSE WHO LIVE FOR EVIL.
THE POWER THEY EXUDE IS AKIN TO A LEECH, DRAINING THE EARTH OF POWER AND STALLING THE ROTATION FURTHER.

☆ ☆ ☆

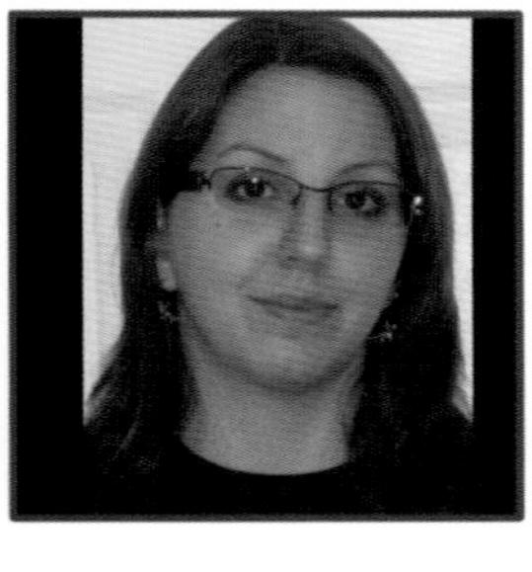

HEATHER ROYSTON

SKILLS: Writer
LOCATION: Saint Augustine, Florida
FUN FACT: I joined *Womanthology* on a whim. I had lost all interest in writing before this came along.

www.twitter.com/shalahoyden

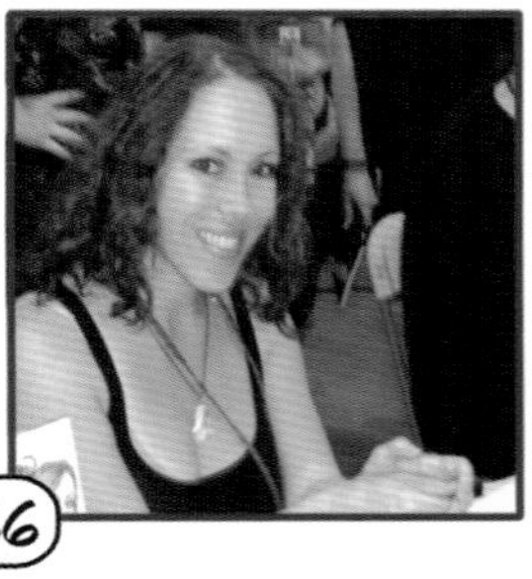

JOLENE HOUSER

SKILLS: Penciller
LOCATION: Arizona
FUN FACT: I am a vegetarian.

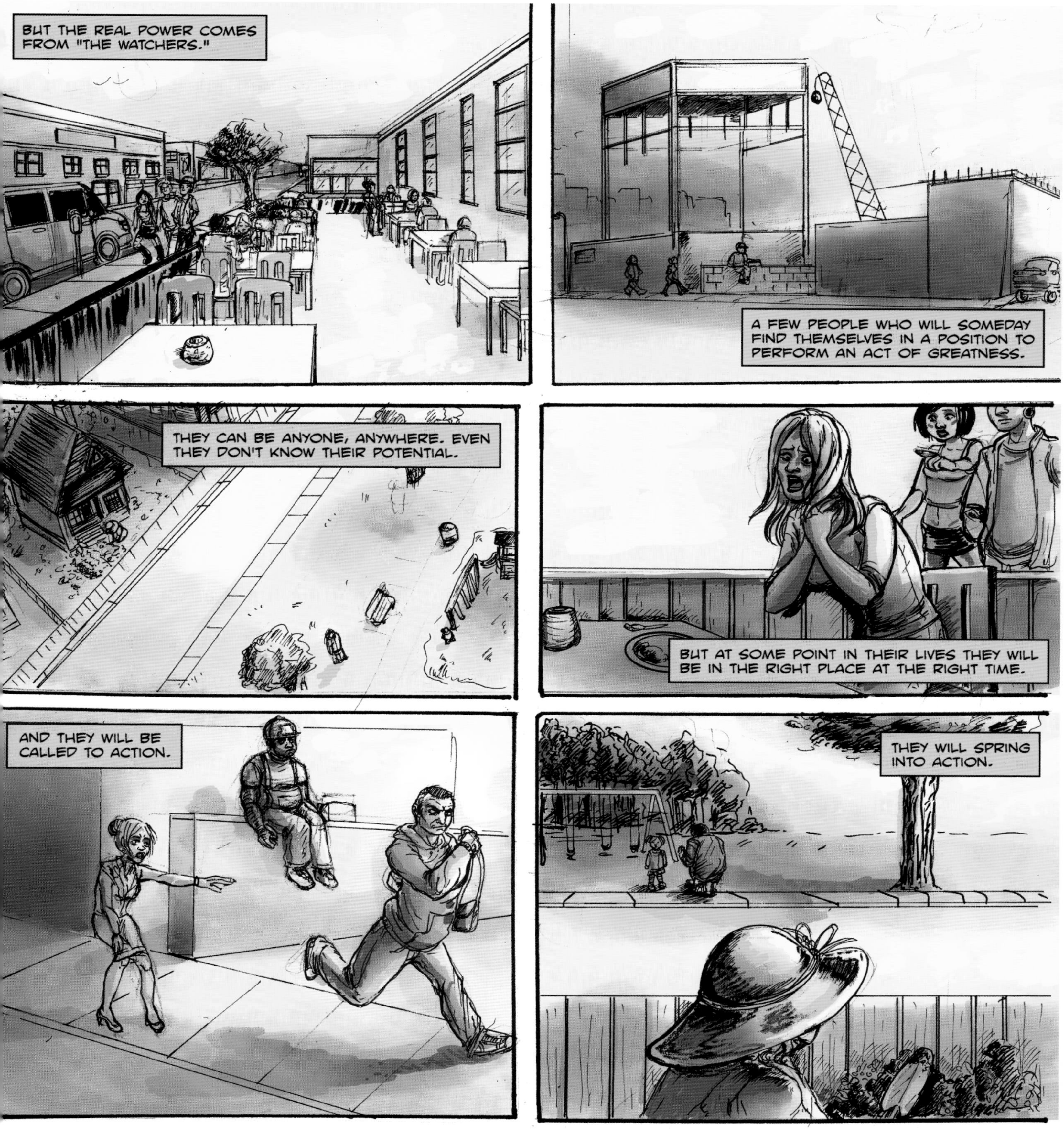
BUT THE REAL POWER COMES FROM "THE WATCHERS."
A FEW PEOPLE WHO WILL SOMEDAY FIND THEMSELVES IN A POSITION TO PERFORM AN ACT OF GREATNESS.
THEY CAN BE ANYONE, ANYWHERE. EVEN THEY DON'T KNOW THEIR POTENTIAL.
BUT AT SOME POINT IN THEIR LIVES THEY WILL BE IN THE RIGHT PLACE AT THE RIGHT TIME.
AND THEY WILL BE CALLED TO ACTION.
THEY WILL SPRING INTO ACTION.

☆☆☆

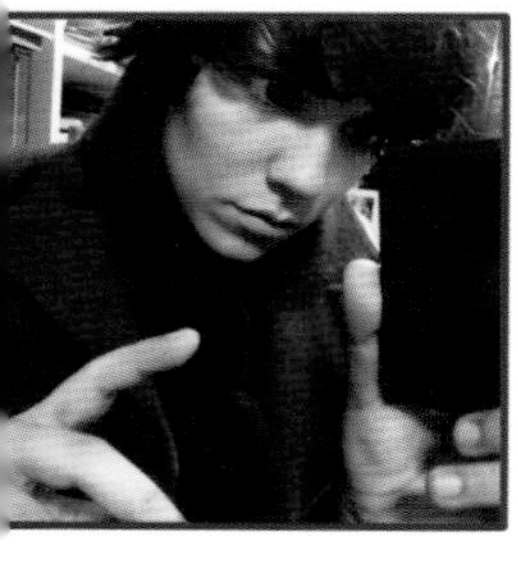

ELLI "HARRY" MOKA

SKILLS: Colorist
LOCATION: Piraeus, Greece
FUN FACT: I am a Chamelion Arched Time Lord.

http://asaph.deviantart.com/

PRO TIP

PUBLISHING
BY BONNIE BURTON

"IF YOU'RE FRUSTRATED BECAUSE YOU CAN'T SEEM TO GET YOUR FAVORITE PUBLISHER TO TAKE NOTICE OF YOUR AWESOME COMIC, PUBLISH IT YOURSELF ONLINE! SOME OF THE COOLEST COMICS TO EVER GET PICKED UP BY A PUBLISHER STARTED OUT AS WEB COMICS. PUBLISH YOUR COMIC ONCE A WEEK ON YOUR BLOG THEN PROMOTE IT ON TWITTER, FACEBOOK, GOOGLE+, COMIC FORUMS, AND WHEREVER YOU THINK YOUR POTENTIAL READERSHIP MIGHT HANG OUT!"

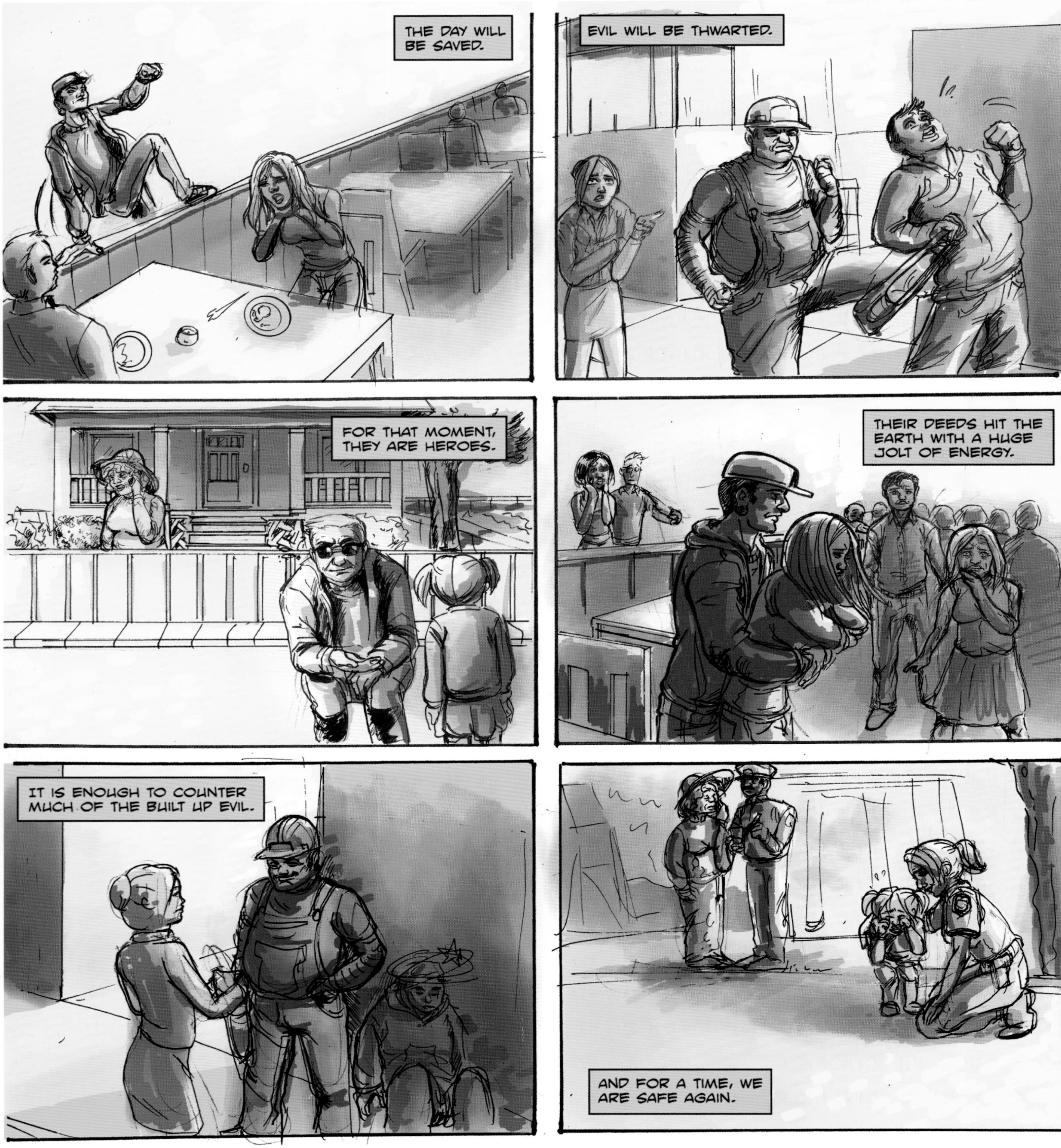
THE DAY WILL BE SAVED.
EVIL WILL BE THWARTED.
FOR THAT MOMENT, THEY ARE HEROES.
THEIR DEEDS HIT THE EARTH WITH A HUGE JOLT OF ENERGY.
IT IS ENOUGH TO COUNTER MUCH OF THE BUILT UP EVIL.
AND FOR A TIME, WE ARE SAFE AGAIN.

☆ ☆ ☆

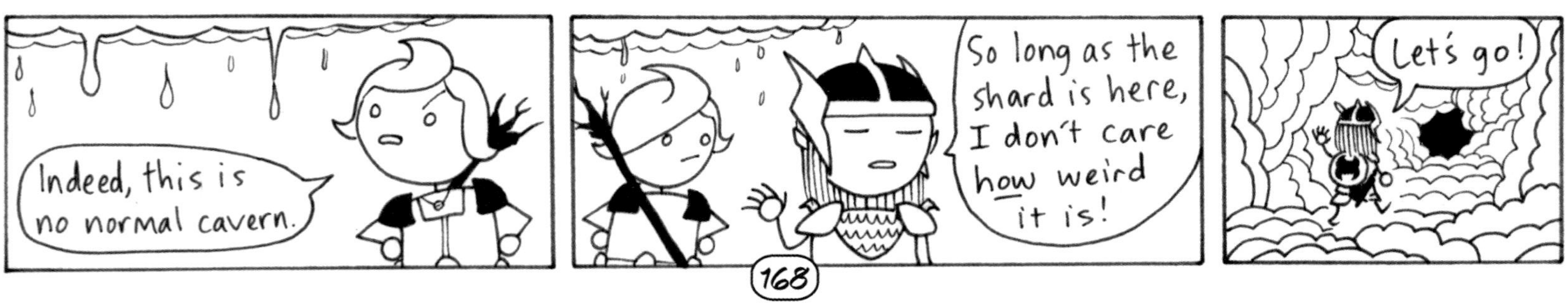
Indeed, this is no normal cavern.
So long as the shard is here, I don't care how weird it is!
Let's go!

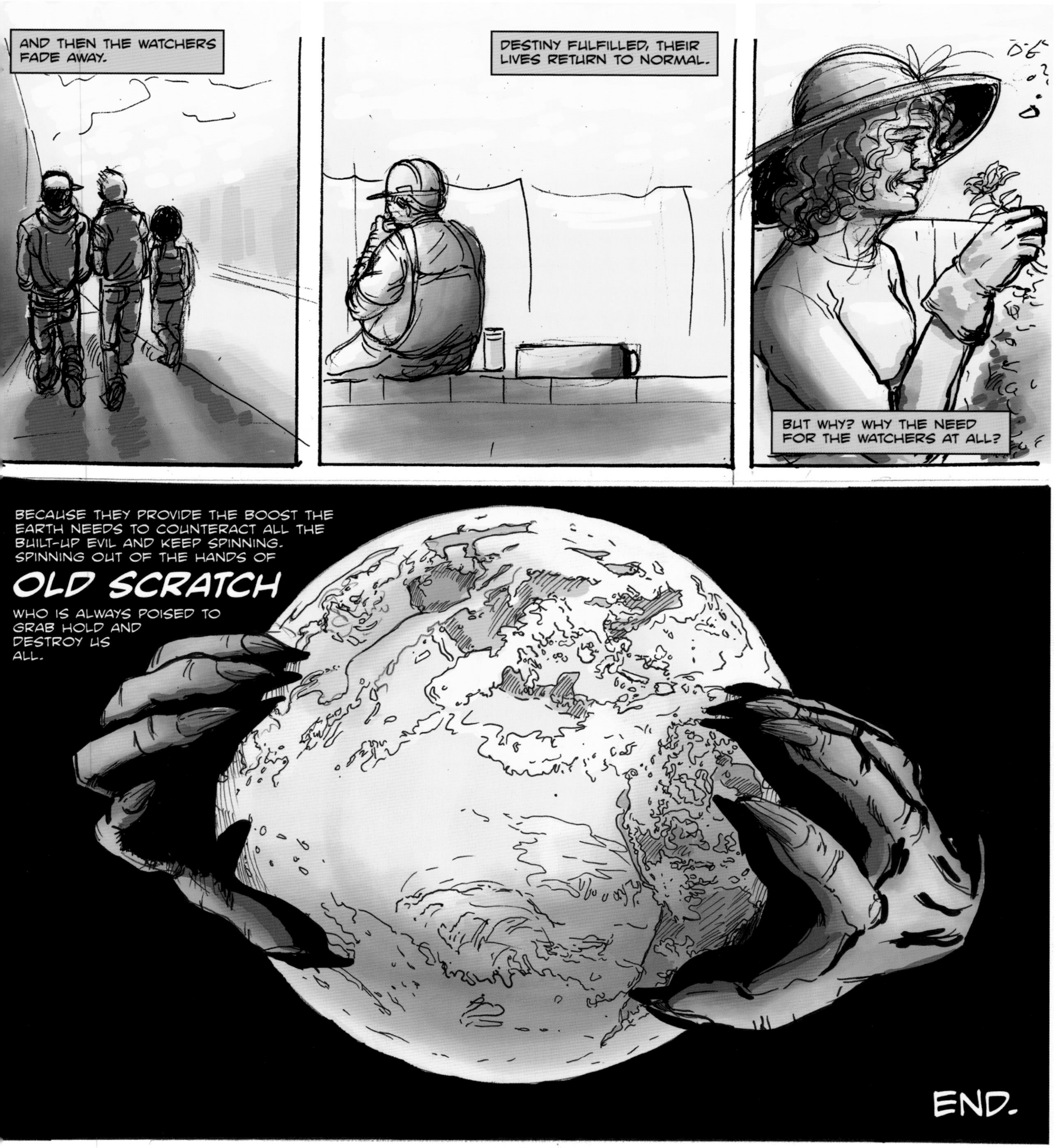
AND THEN THE WATCHERS FADE AWAY.
DESTINY FULFILLED, THEIR LIVES RETURN TO NORMAL.
BUT WHY? WHY THE NEED FOR THE WATCHERS AT ALL?
BECAUSE THEY PROVIDE THE BOOST THE EARTH NEEDS TO COUNTERACT ALL THE BUILT-UP EVIL AND KEEP SPINNING. SPINNING OUT OF THE HANDS OF
OLD SCRATCH
WHO IS ALWAYS POISED TO GRAB HOLD AND DESTROY US ALL.
END.

☆ ☆ ☆

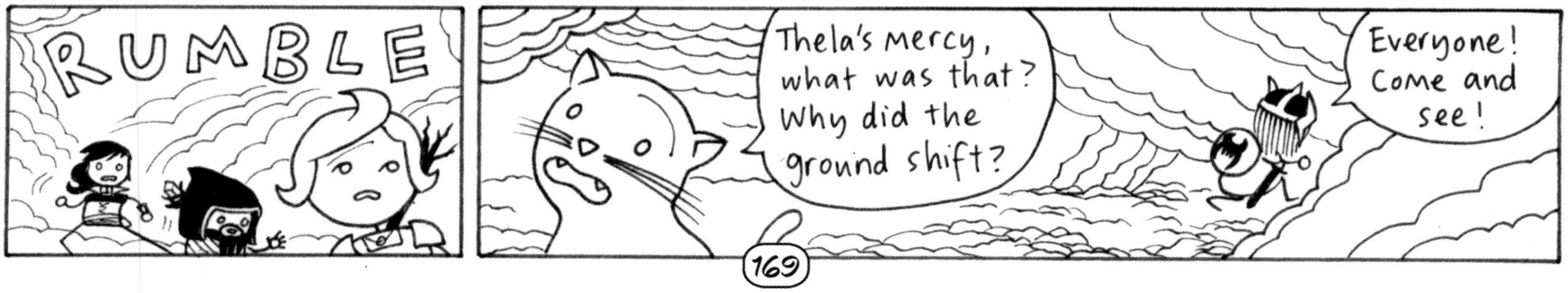
RUMBLE
Thela's mercy, what was that? Why did the ground shift?
Everyone! Come and see!

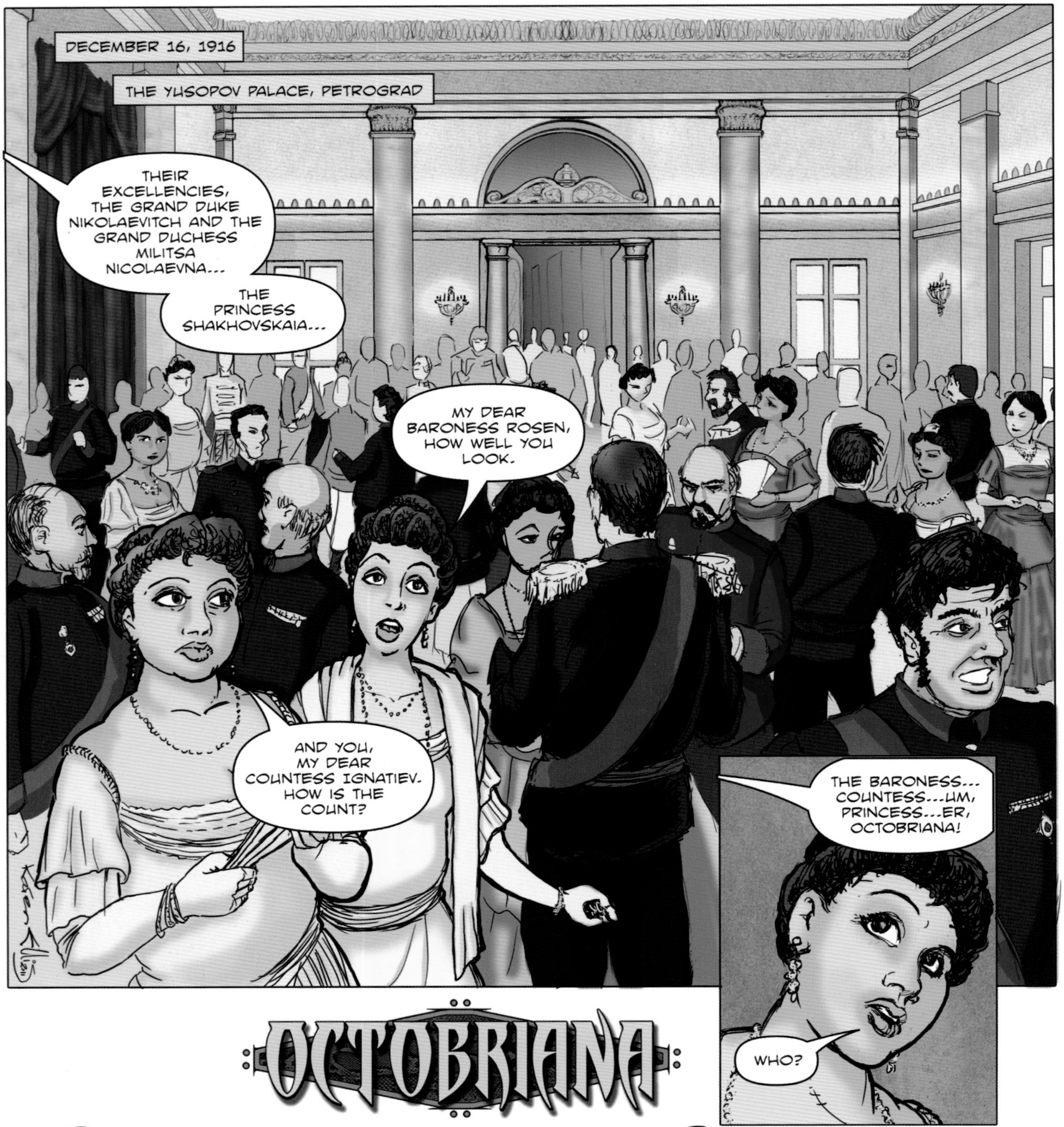
DECEMBER 16, 1916
THE YUSOPOV PALACE, PETROGRAD
THEIR EXCELLENCIES, THE GRAND DUKE NIKOLAEVITCH AND THE GRAND DUCHESS MILITSA NICOLAEVNA...
THE PRINCESS SHAKHOVSKAIA...
MY DEAR BARONESS ROSEN, HOW WELL YOU LOOK.
AND YOU, MY DEAR COUNTESS IGNATIEV. HOW IS THE COUNT?
THE BARONESS... COUNTESS...UM, PRINCESS...ER, OCTOBRIANA!
WHO?

OCTOBRIANA

How it Really Happened

TRINA ROBBINS **KAREN ELLIS**

COLORISTS: KIMBERLY ANNE BLACK (PG.1) KAREN ELLIS (PG.2-3) LETTERS: RACHEL DEERING

☆ ☆ ☆

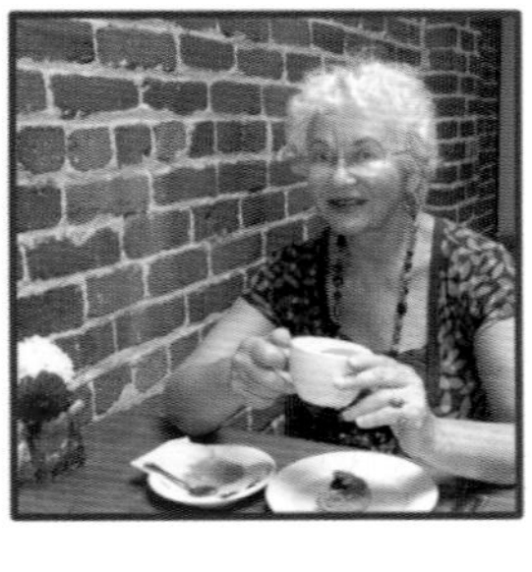

TRINA ROBBINS

SKILLS: Writer, Herstorian
LOCATION: San Francisco, CA
FUN FACT: I can tap dance and do the hula.

www.trinarobbins.com

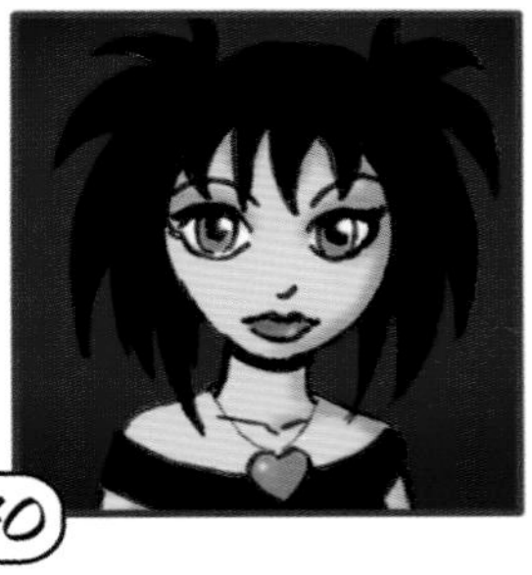

KAREN ELLIS

SKILLS: Penciller, Inker
LOCATION: Bristol, England
FUN FACT: When not drawing comics, I live the Goth dream by working in a graveyard.

http://www.planetkaren.co.uk

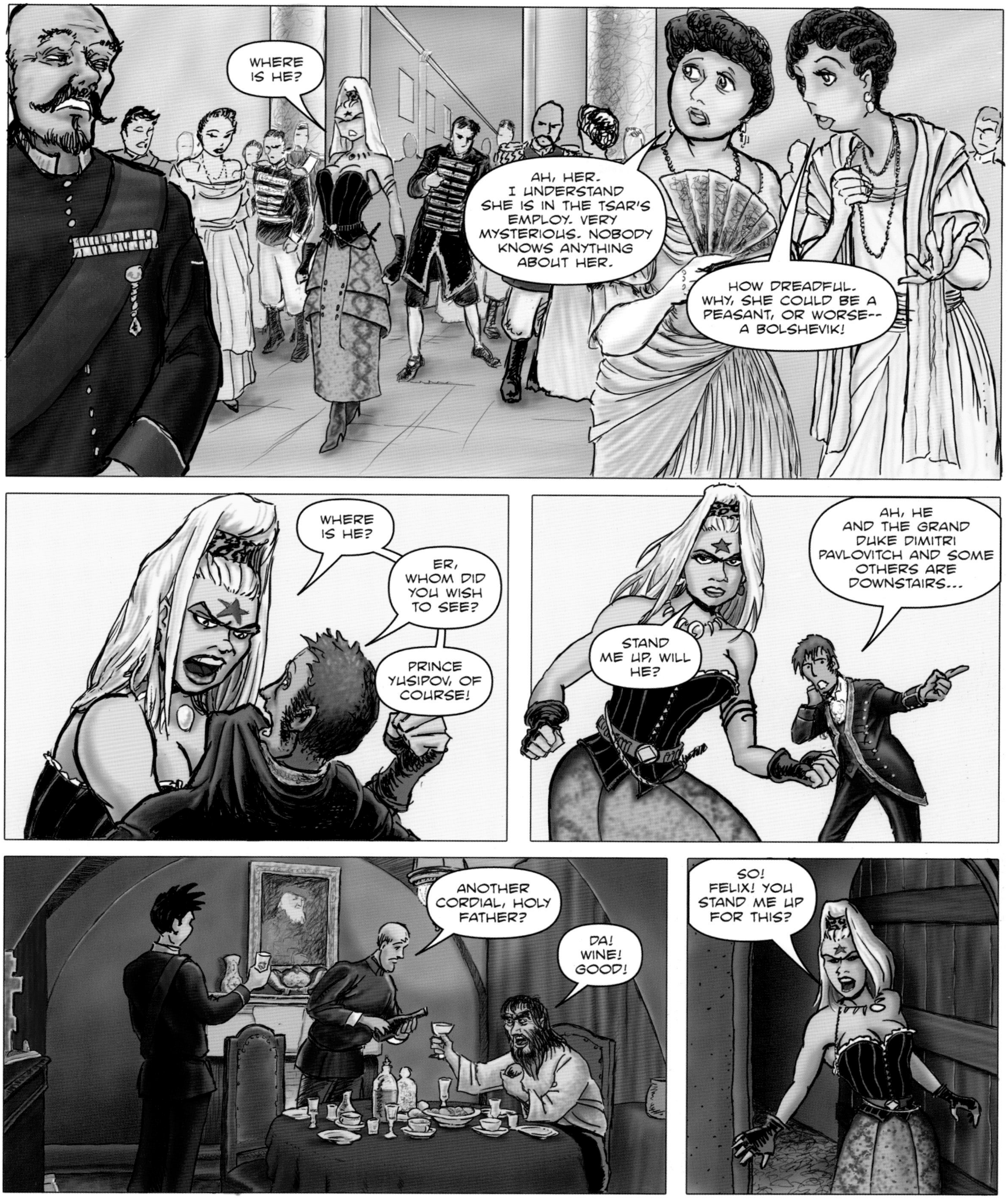
WHERE IS HE?
AH, HER. I UNDERSTAND SHE IS IN THE TSAR'S EMPLOY. VERY MYSTERIOUS. NOBODY KNOWS ANYTHING ABOUT HER.
HOW DREADFUL. WHY, SHE COULD BE A PEASANT, OR WORSE-- A BOLSHEVIK!
WHERE IS HE?
ER, WHOM DID YOU WISH TO SEE?
PRINCE YUSIPOV, OF COURSE!
AH, HE AND THE GRAND DUKE DIMITRI PAVLOVITCH AND SOME OTHERS ARE DOWNSTAIRS...
STAND ME UP, WILL HE?
ANOTHER CORDIAL, HOLY FATHER?
DA! WINE! GOOD!
SO! FELIX! YOU STAND ME UP FOR THIS?

☆ ☆ ☆

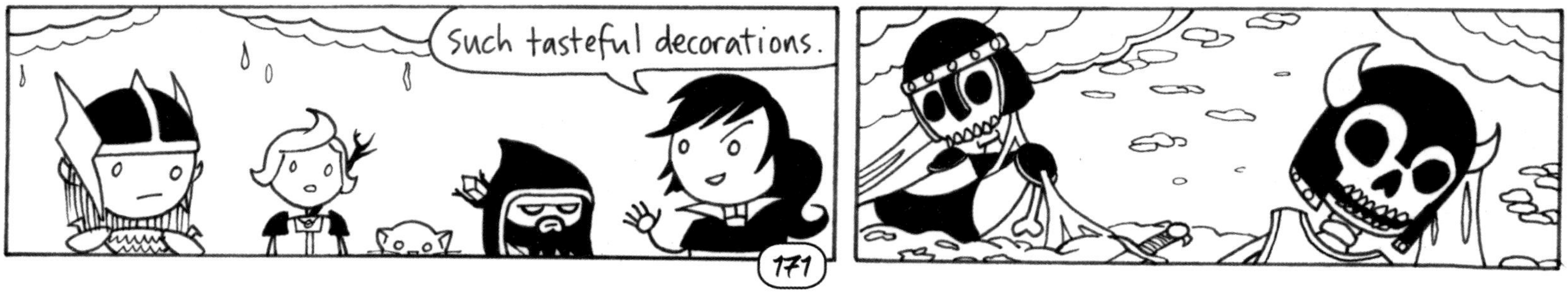
Such tasteful decorations.

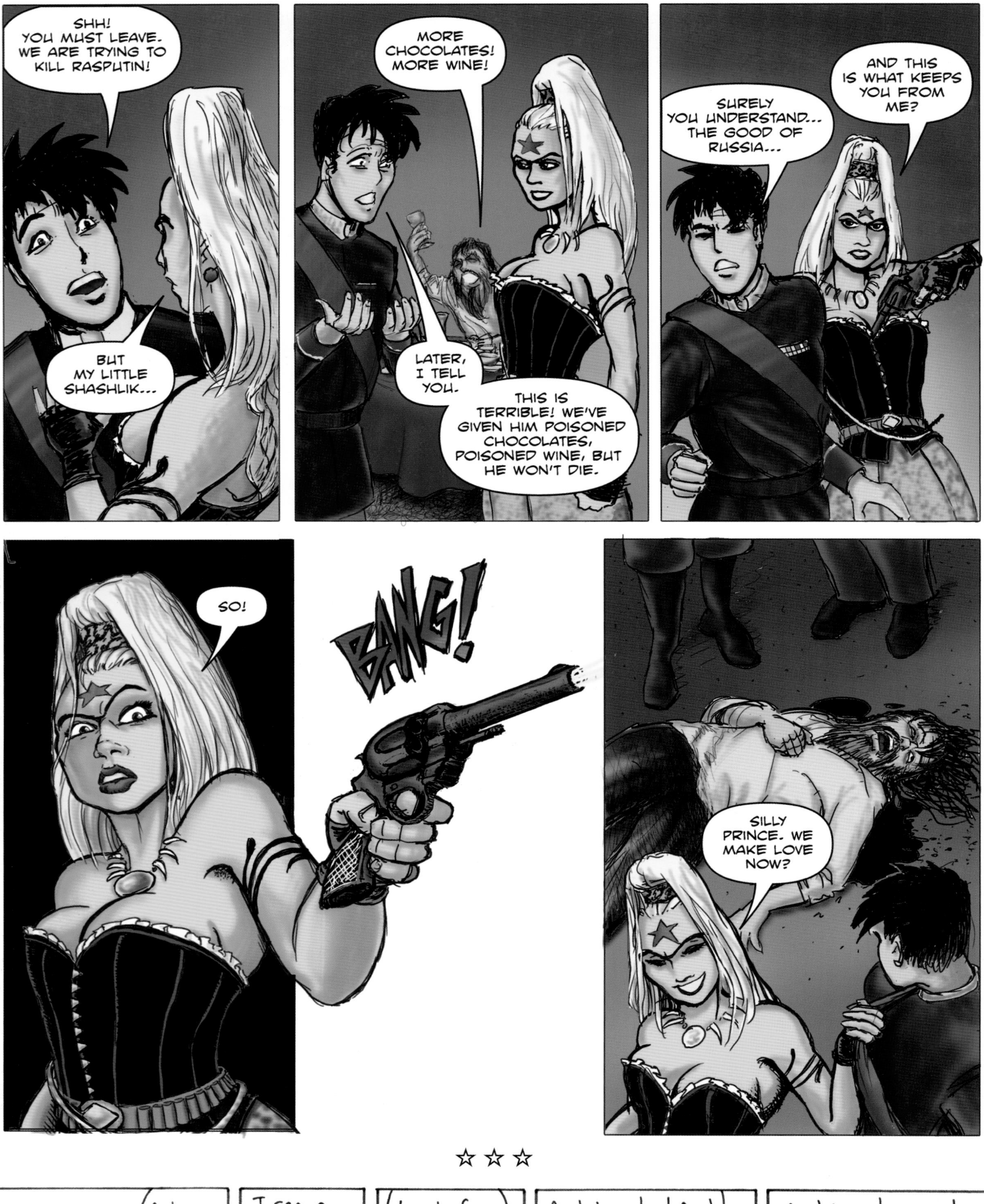
SHH! YOU MUST LEAVE. WE ARE TRYING TO KILL RASPUTIN!
BUT MY LITTLE SHASHLIK...
MORE CHOCOLATES! MORE WINE!
LATER, I TELL YOU.
THIS IS TERRIBLE! WE'VE GIVEN HIM POISONED CHOCOLATES, POISONED WINE, BUT HE WON'T DIE.
SURELY YOU UNDERSTAND... THE GOOD OF RUSSIA...
AND THIS IS WHAT KEEPS YOU FROM ME?
SO!
BANG!
SILLY PRINCE. WE MAKE LOVE NOW?

☆ ☆ ☆

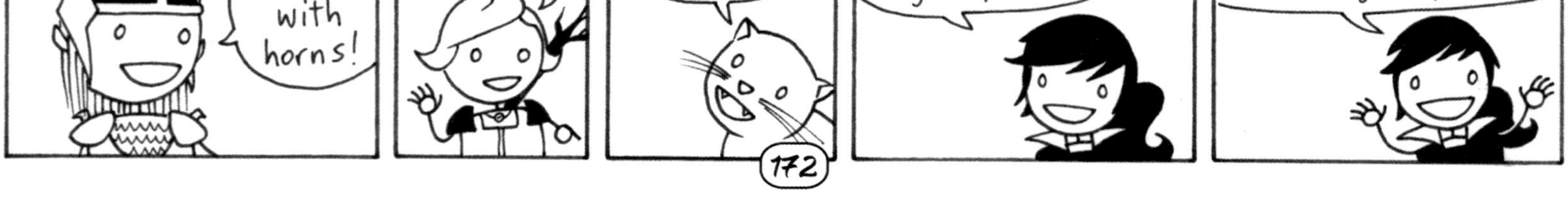
Ooh, a helmet with horns!
I see a poultice!
Look for cakes!
And jewelry! And gold pieces!
And jewelry made out of gold pieces!

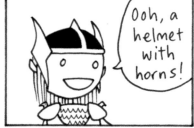

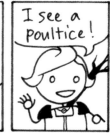

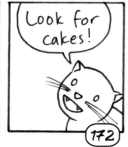

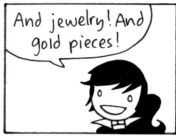

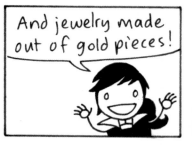

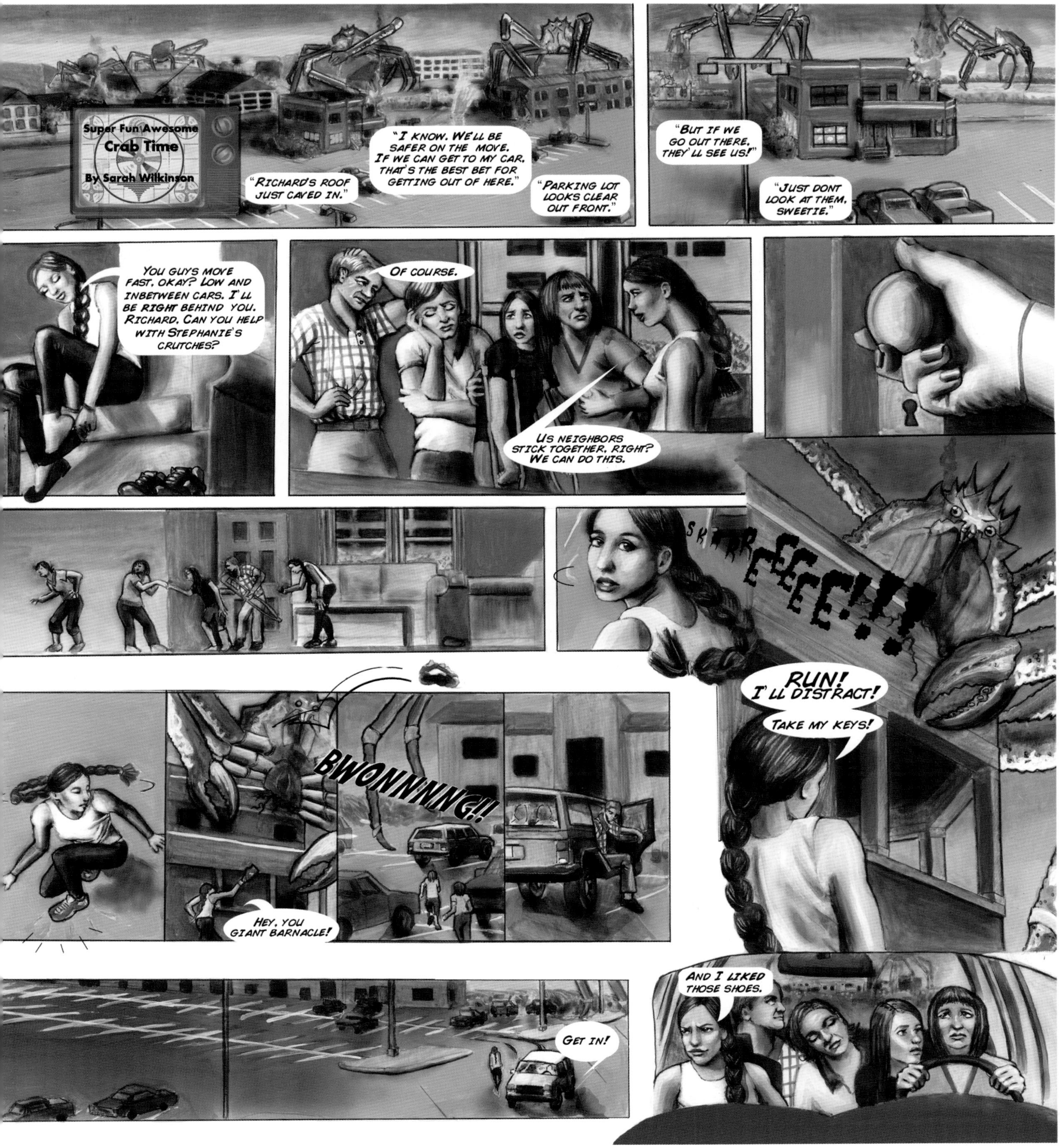

Super Fun Awesome
Crab Time
By Sarah Wilkinson
"Richard's roof just caved in."
"I know. We'll be safer on the move. If we can get to my car, that's the best bet for getting out of here."
"Parking lot looks clear out front."
"But if we go out there, they'll see us!"
"Just dont look at them, sweetie."
You guys move fast, okay? Low and inbetween cars. I'll be right behind you. Richard, can you help with Stephanie's crutches?
Of course.
Us neighbors stick together, right? We can do this.
SKRRREEEEE!!!!
Run! I'll distract!
Take my keys!
BWONNNNNG!!
Hey, you giant barnacle!
Get in!
And I liked those shoes.

☆ ☆ ☆

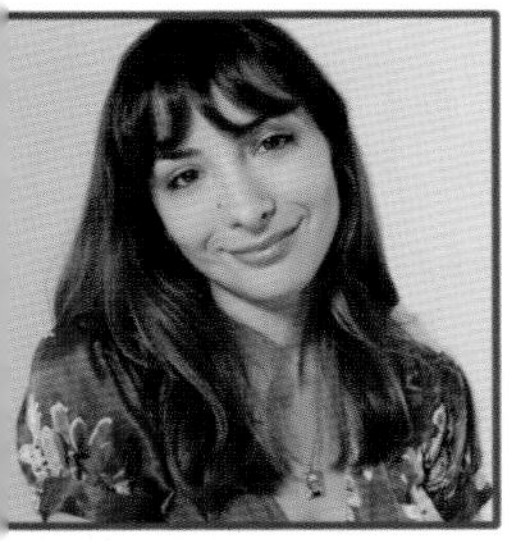

Sarah Wilkinson

SKILLS: Writer, Penciller, Colorist, Inker, Letterer
LOCATION: Detroit, MI
FUN FACT: I'm left handed, but am forced to conform to a right-handed world! Left-handed scissors are so wrong.
www.sarahwilkinson.net

PRO TIP

Social Network
by Renae De Liz

"Social sites are wonderful ways to promote yourself, but you need to balance a good mix between personal and professional. A lot of the time publishers hire people, not just the talent. So always conduct yourself in a way that is acceptable while online. You never know who's watching!"

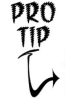

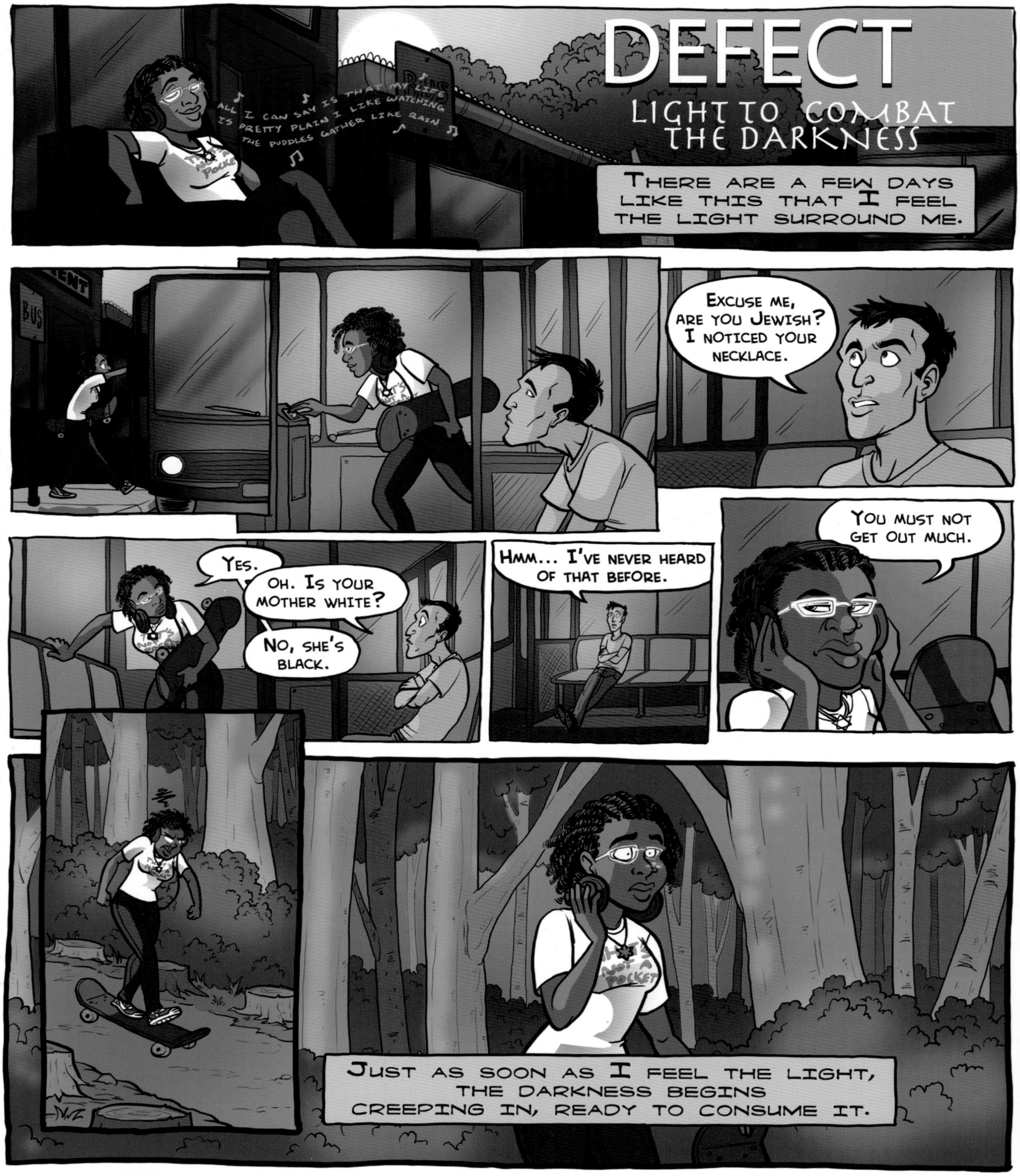
DEFECT
LIGHT TO COMBAT THE DARKNESS
ALL I CAN SAY IS THAT MY LIFE IS PRETTY PLAIN I LIKE WATCHING THE PUDDLES GATHER LIKE RAIN
BUS
THERE ARE A FEW DAYS LIKE THIS THAT I FEEL THE LIGHT SURROUND ME.
BUS
EXCUSE ME, ARE YOU JEWISH? I NOTICED YOUR NECKLACE.
YES.
OH. IS YOUR MOTHER WHITE?
NO, SHE'S BLACK.
HMM... I'VE NEVER HEARD OF THAT BEFORE.
YOU MUST NOT GET OUT MUCH.
JUST AS SOON AS I FEEL THE LIGHT, THE DARKNESS BEGINS CREEPING IN, READY TO CONSUME IT.

WRITER: TALISHA HARRISON ARTIST & LETTERER: KELLY TURNBULL COLORING: DAWN BEST

☆ ☆ ☆

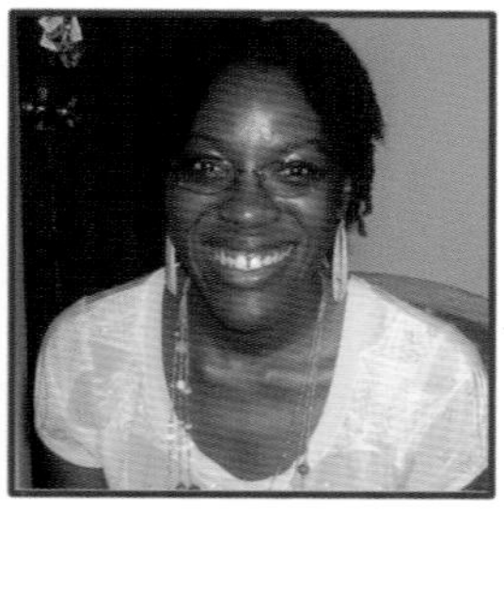

TALISHA HARRISON

SKILLS: Writer
LOCATION: Longwood, FL
FUN FACT: I have two beta fish named Mystique and Rogue.

https://www.facebook.com/pages/Tali-Adinas-Days-of-Future-Past/185249131503765

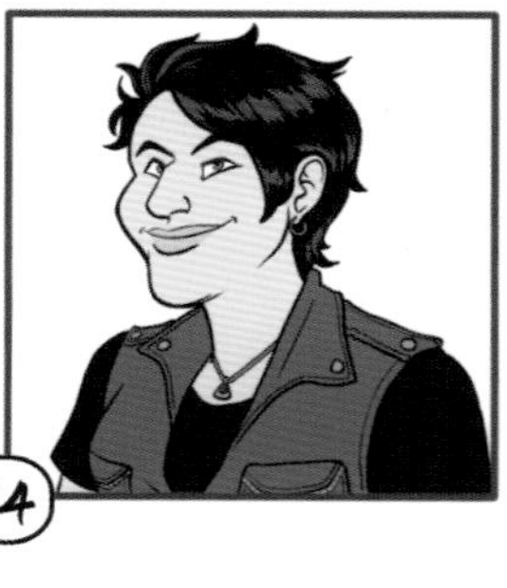

KELLY TURNBULL

SKILLS: Penciller, Inker, Letterer
LOCATION: Los Angeles
FUN FACT: I collect animal skulls I clean myself.

manlyguys.com

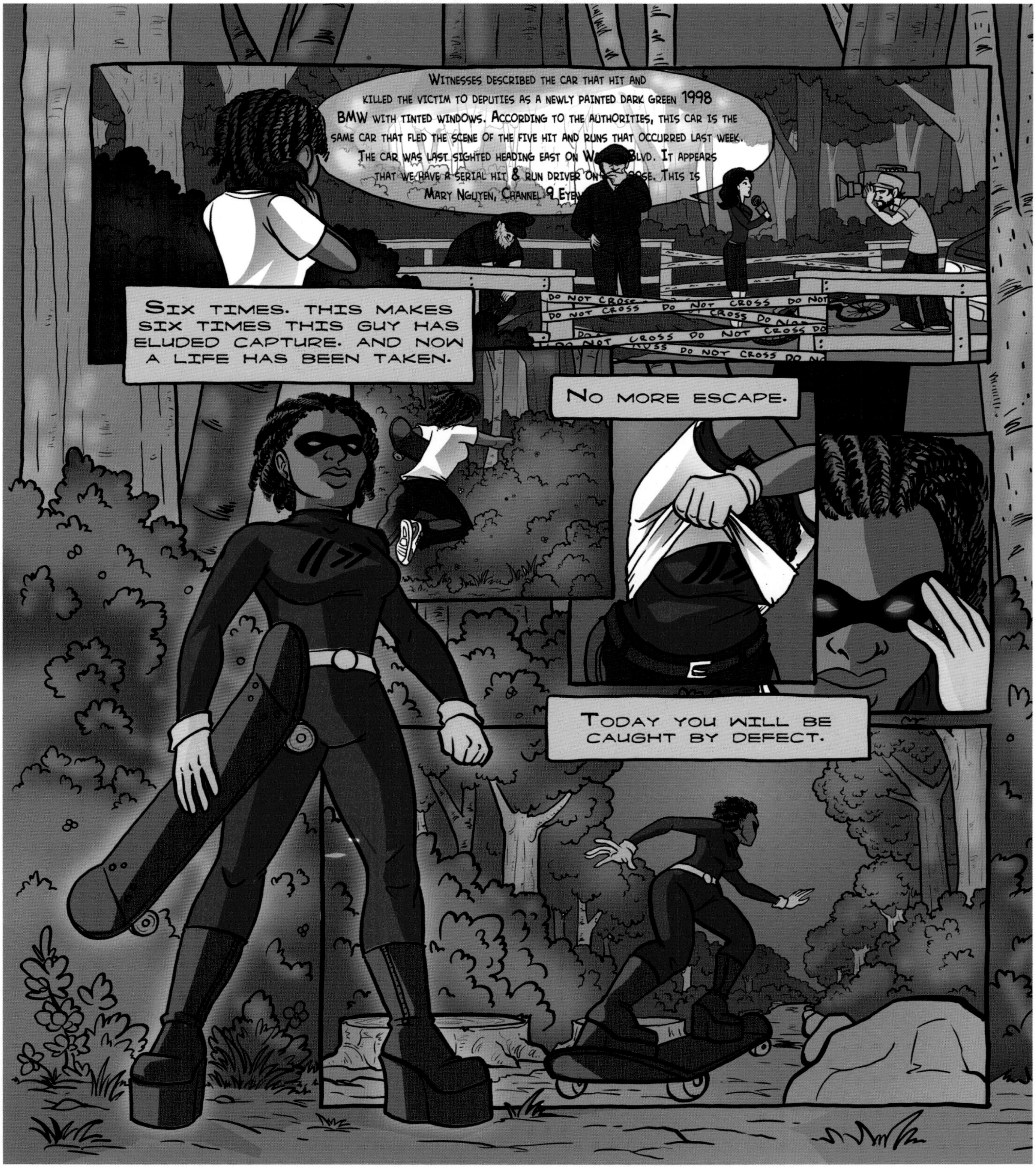
Witnesses described the car that hit and killed the victim to deputies as a newly painted dark green 1998 BMW with tinted windows. According to the authorities, this car is the same car that fled the scene of the five hit and runs that occurred last week. The car was last sighted heading east on W Blvd. It appears that we have a serial hit & run driver on ose. This is Mary Nguyen, Channel 9 Eye
DO NOT CROSS
Six times. This makes six times this guy has eluded capture. And now a life has been taken.
No more escape.
Today you will be caught by defect.

☆ ☆ ☆

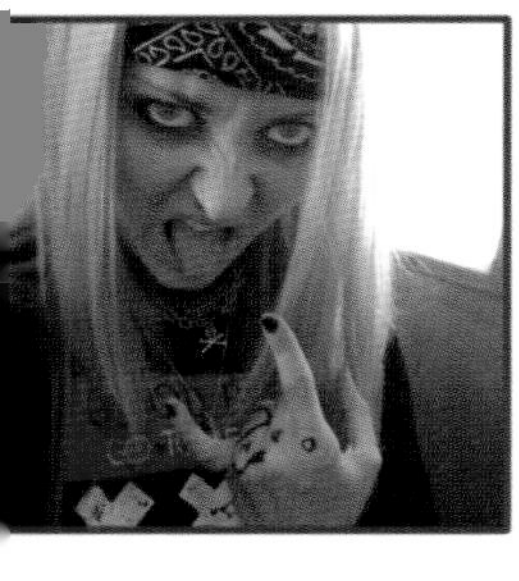

Dawn Best

SKILLS: Inker, Colorist
LOCATION: Columbus, OH
FUN FACT: Not the best artist in the world - just the busiest!

http://www.dawnbest.com

PRO TIP

NAME

BY DANI JONES

"USE A CONSISTENT NAME (PREFERABLY YOUR REAL NAME, NOT A VAGUE NICKNAME OR ALIAS) ACROSS ALL YOUR WEBSITE DOMAINS, SOCIAL NETWORK USERNAMES, AND ONLINE PROFILES. IT WILL MAKE IT EASIER FOR PEOPLE TO GET TO KNOW YOU AND REMEMBER WHO YOU ARE."

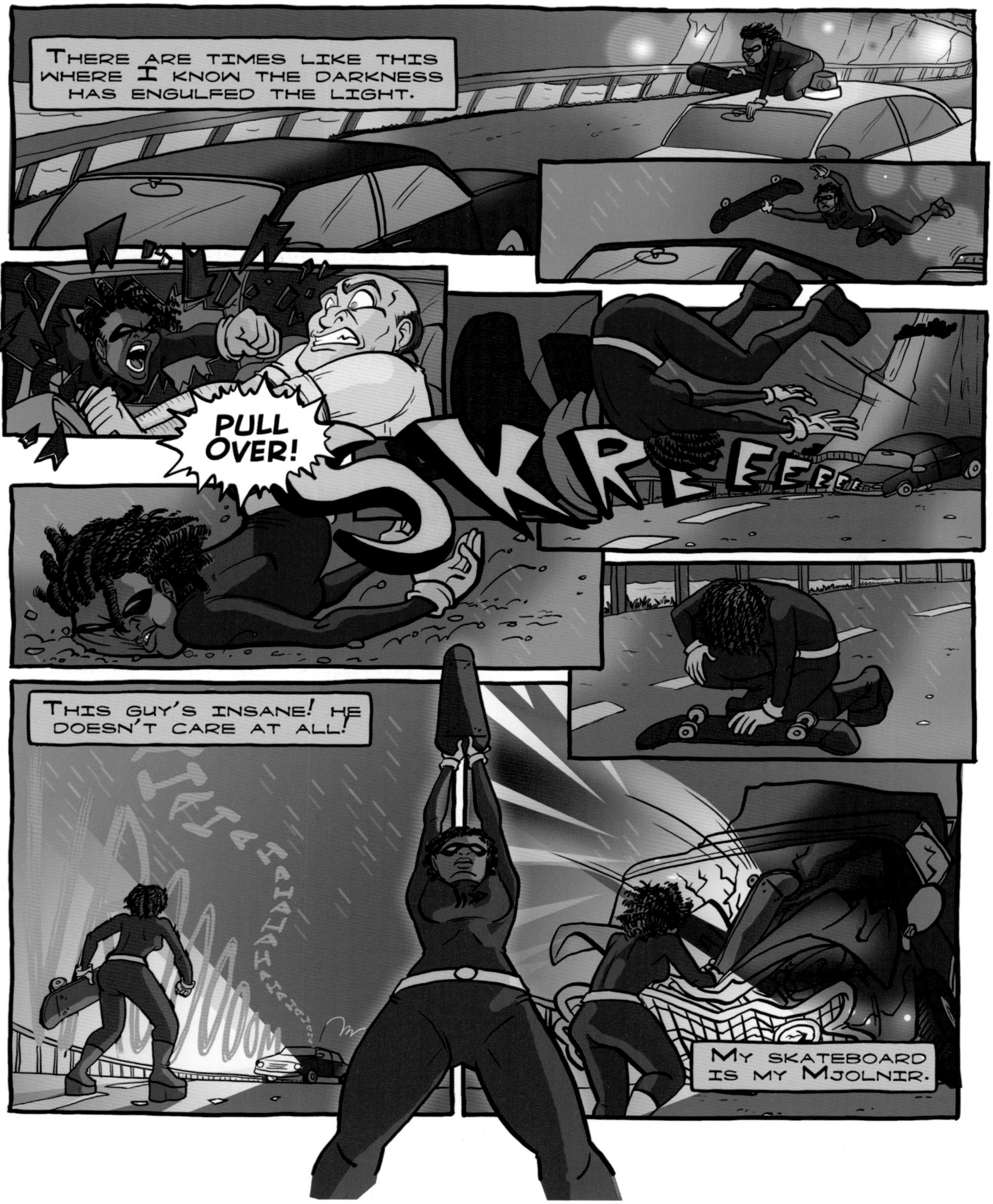
There are times like this where I know the darkness has engulfed the light.
PULL OVER!
SKREEEEE
This guy's insane! He doesn't care at all!
HAHAHAHA
My skateboard is my Mjolnir.

☆ ☆ ☆

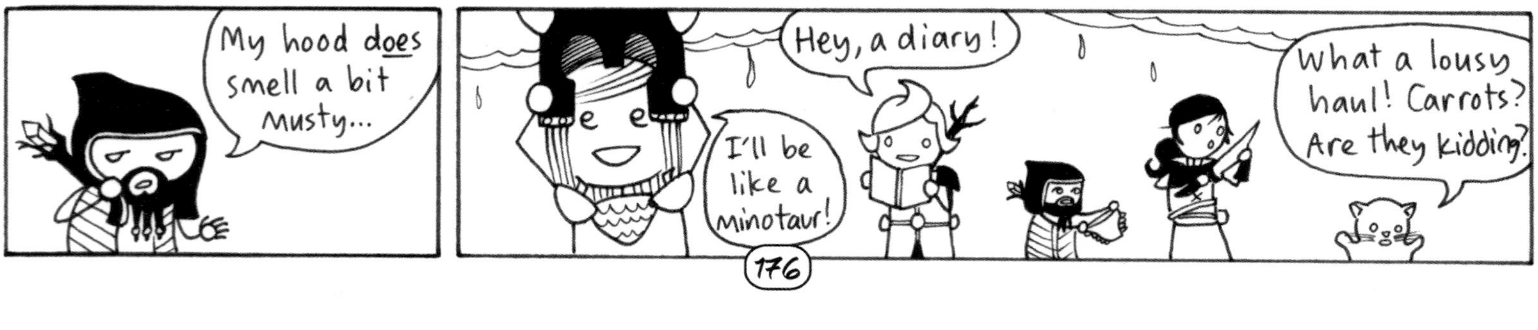
My hood does smell a bit musty...
Hey, a diary!
I'll be like a minotaur!
What a lousy haul! Carrots? Are they kidding?

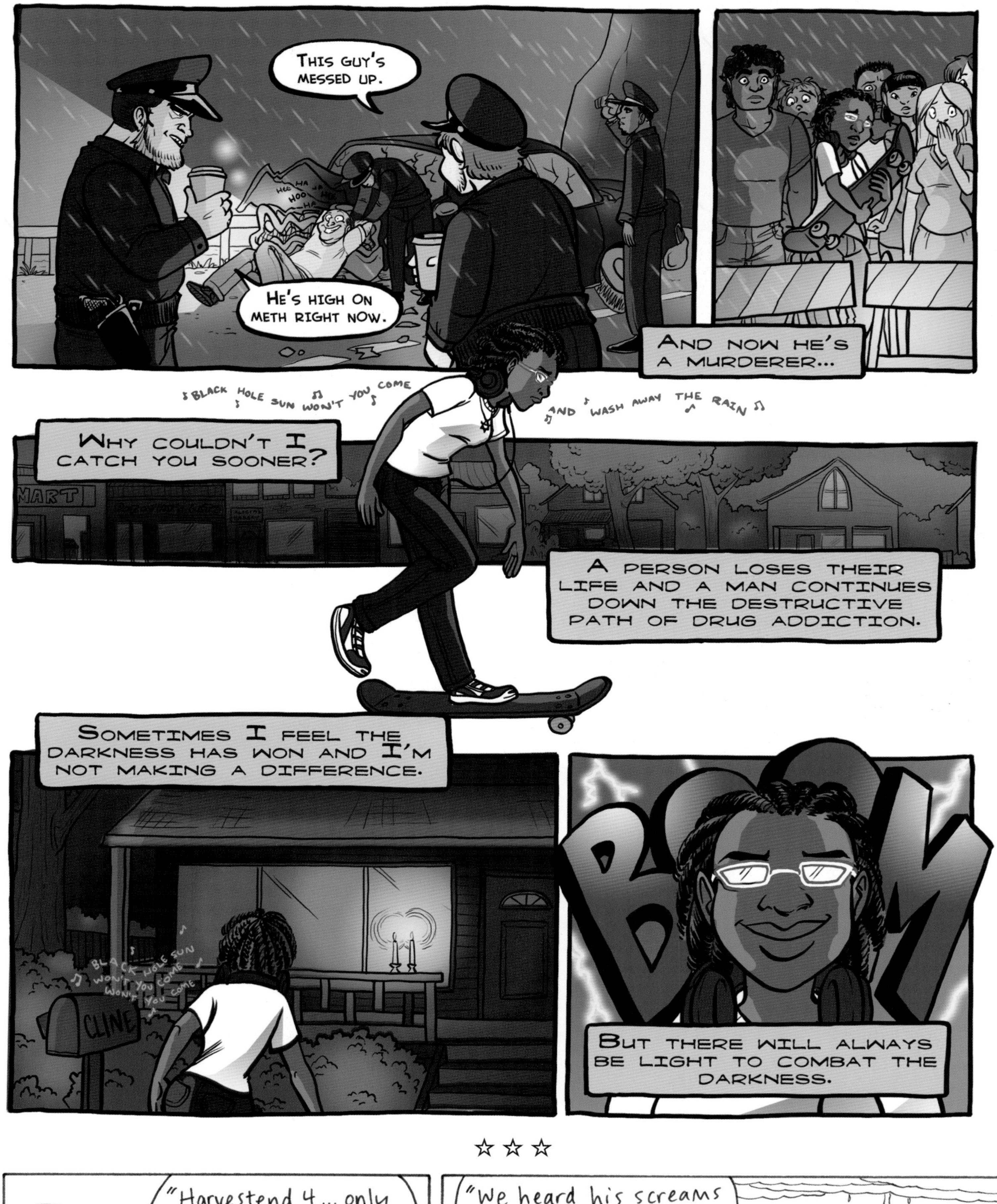
THIS GUY'S MESSED UP.
HE'S HIGH ON METH RIGHT NOW.
AND NOW HE'S A MURDERER...
BLACK HOLE SUN WON'T YOU COME
AND WASH AWAY THE RAIN
WHY COULDN'T I CATCH YOU SOONER?
MART
A PERSON LOSES THEIR LIFE AND A MAN CONTINUES DOWN THE DESTRUCTIVE PATH OF DRUG ADDICTION.
SOMETIMES I FEEL THE DARKNESS HAS WON AND I'M NOT MAKING A DIFFERENCE.
BLACK HOLE SUN WON'T YOU COME WON'T YOU COME
CLINE
BOOM
BUT THERE WILL ALWAYS BE LIGHT TO COMBAT THE DARKNESS.

☆ ☆ ☆

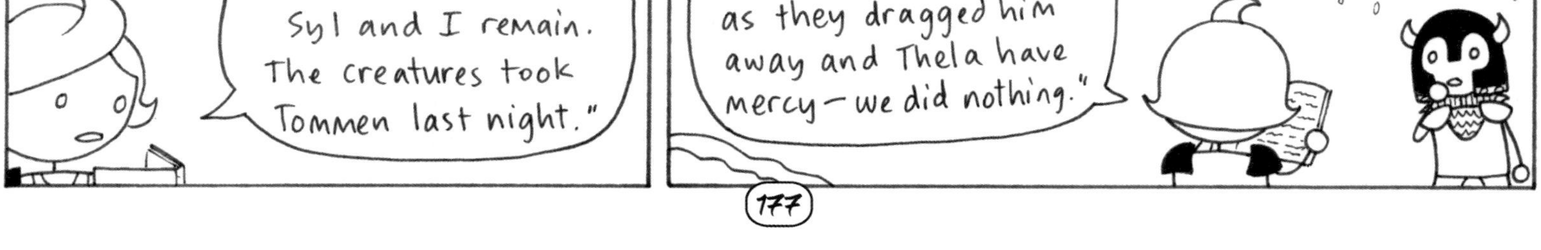
"Harvestend 4... only Syl and I remain. The creatures took Tommen last night."
"We heard his screams as they dragged him away and Thela have mercy—we did nothing."

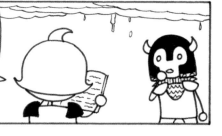

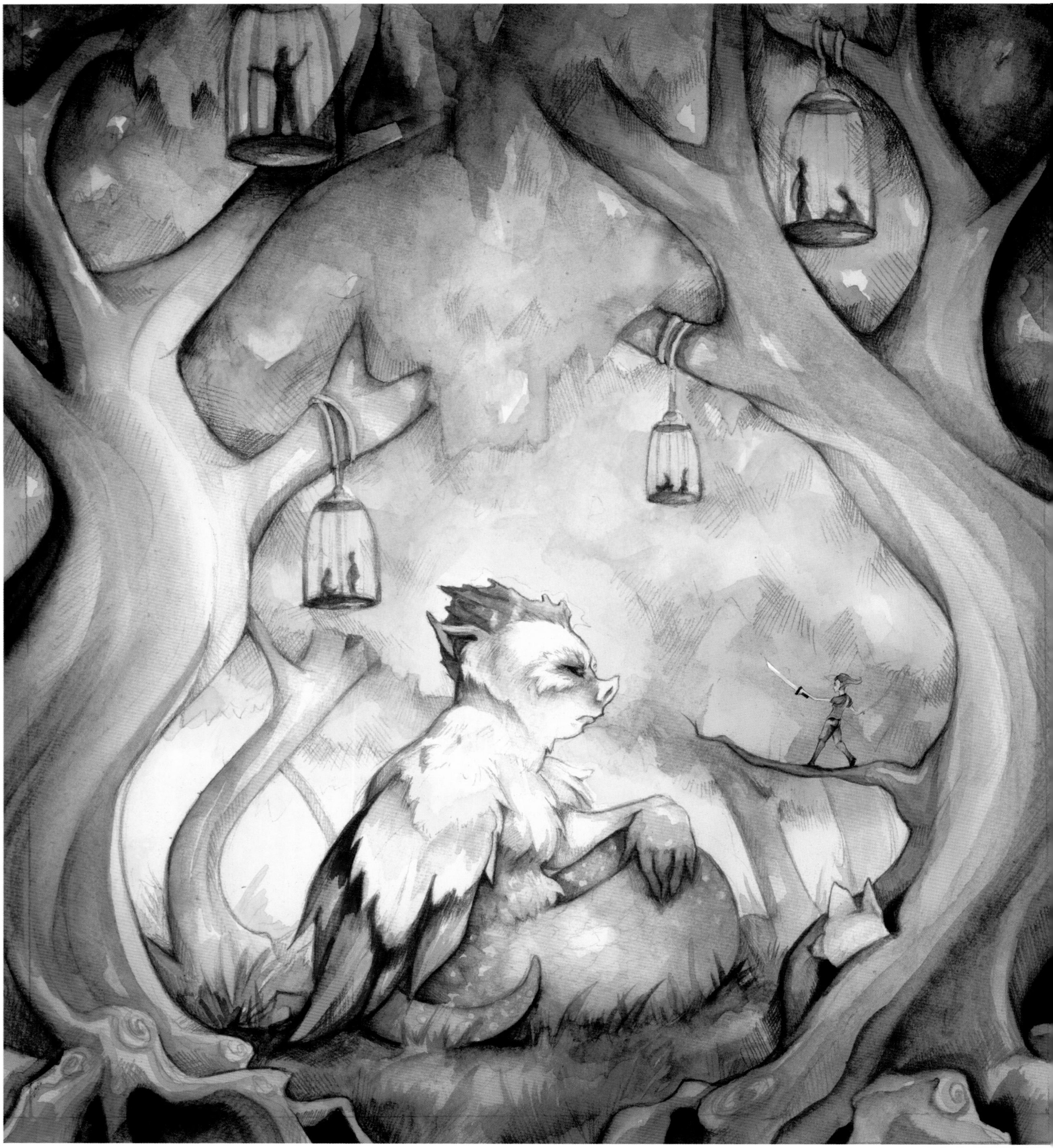

☆☆☆

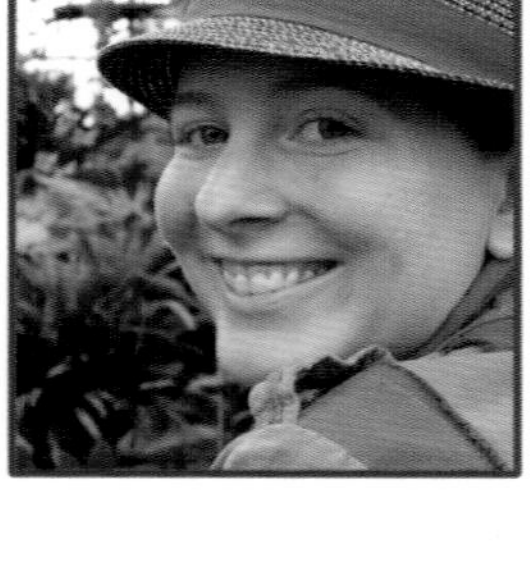

Ashley Keene

SKILLS: Penciller, Colorist, Pinup Artist
LOCATION: Tucson, AZ
FUN FACT: When I was little, I got to tour the NASA control room in Florida!

http://www.umbertheprussianblue.com

Portfolio
by Jessica Hickman

PRO TIP

"CATER YOUR PORTFOLIO TO WHAT YOU WANT TO WORK IN. DO NOT ADD A LITTLE BIT OF EVERYTHING. IF YOU WANT TO BE A PENCILLER THEN PRESENT PENCILING SAMPLES. COLORIST? SHOW COLORING SAMPLES. WRITING? WRITING SAMPLES, ETC. MOST SUBMISSION INSTRUCTIONS STATE THIS. NOT FOLLOWING THESE DIRECTIONS BEFORE YOU PRESENT YOUR PORTFOLIO CAN REFLECT NEGATIVELY ON YOU. A PERSONAL PORTFOLIO REVIEW IS ALSO A TYPE OF JOB INTERVIEW. PRESENT YOURSELF IN A RESPECTFUL AND PROFESSIONAL MANNER. SHOW ONLY YOUR BEST WORK. DON'T CRAM YOUR ARTWORK INTO A FLIMSY FOLDER. PROVIDE A RESUME. BE POLITE."

PART FOUR

TEAM SUZANNAH

☆ ☆ ☆ For each section of *Womanthology* a different lady took on the role of editor over the writers, pencillers, inkers, colorists, and letterers for their stories or pinups. They were in charge of making sure the creators worked as a team, had all the info they needed, and that all stories and pinups were turned in on time. This section is Suzannah Rowntree's.

EDITOR - SUZANNAH ROWNTREE
Location: Westchester, NY
Day Job: Features Editor for *Life With Archie* Magazine, Archie Comics

A little about yourself: Born in upstate NY to a British ex-pat and third-generation Italian-German immigrant, I only lived in the USA for three years before we moved to England and stayed there until I was 18 years old. I have been described as a cross between Simon Cowell and Mary Poppins. I like David Bowie, the Muppets, comic books, and cartoons. I love to bake, and inflict my experiments (such as Dr. Pepper or Bacon cupcakes) on my co-workers at Archie Comics with frightening regularity.

What does *Womanthology* mean to you? When I was a kid, I felt a lot of the time like I was the only girl reading comic books. Boys were, but they totally didn't want to talk to girls at that time, whether they were doing cool things like reading about Spider-Man or not! Projects like this really help to foster a sense of community, whether you're an industry veteran or an up-and-comer still in school. That's always going to be something I want to be involved in. I'm glad that I did—I've learned at least as much from the experience and my team as I'm sure that I've taught!

Funny fact: I have a cat that thinks he's a dog. Seriously. He'll play fetch with me.

☆ ☆ ☆

SOCIAL NETWORKING TEAM		ORGANIZATIONAL ASSISTANCE	
Tatiana Christian	Nicole Sixx	Rachel Deering	Katie Shanahan
Jennifer Weber	Renae De Liz	Tara-Lea Aleszczyk	Amanda Deibert
Jennifer Doudney	Jessica Hickman	Tanja Wooten	Meli Glover

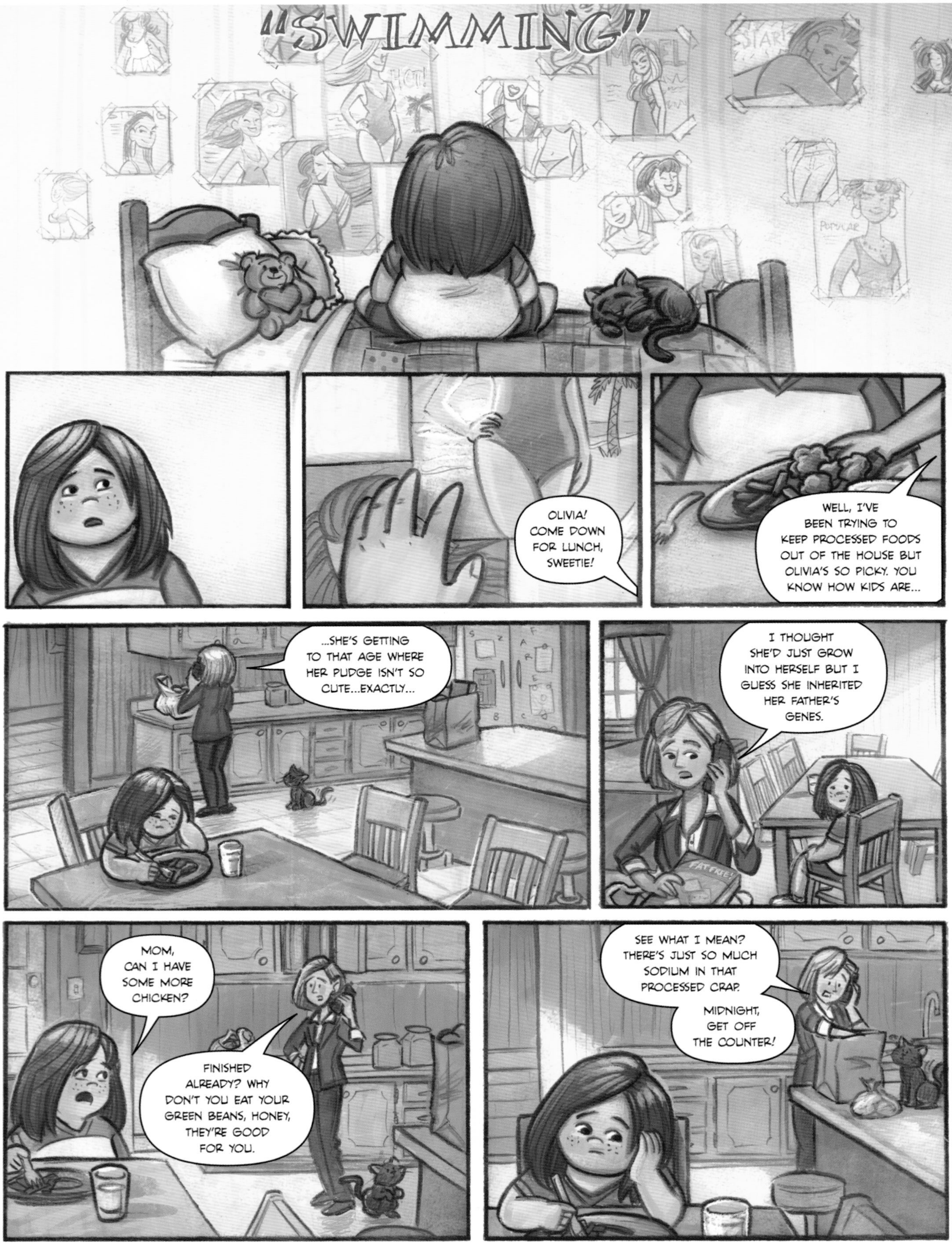
"SWIMMING"
OLIVIA! COME DOWN FOR LUNCH, SWEETIE!
WELL, I'VE BEEN TRYING TO KEEP PROCESSED FOODS OUT OF THE HOUSE BUT OLIVIA'S SO PICKY. YOU KNOW HOW KIDS ARE...
...SHE'S GETTING TO THAT AGE WHERE HER PUDGE ISN'T SO CUTE...EXACTLY...
I THOUGHT SHE'D JUST GROW INTO HERSELF BUT I GUESS SHE INHERITED HER FATHER'S GENES.
FAT FREE!
MOM, CAN I HAVE SOME MORE CHICKEN?
FINISHED ALREADY? WHY DON'T YOU EAT YOUR GREEN BEANS, HONEY, THEY'RE GOOD FOR YOU.
SEE WHAT I MEAN? THERE'S JUST SO MUCH SODIUM IN THAT PROCESSED CRAP.
MIDNIGHT, GET OFF THE COUNTER!

WRITER: ASHLEY AVARD   ARTIST: DANI JONES   LETTERING: RACHEL DEERING

☆☆☆

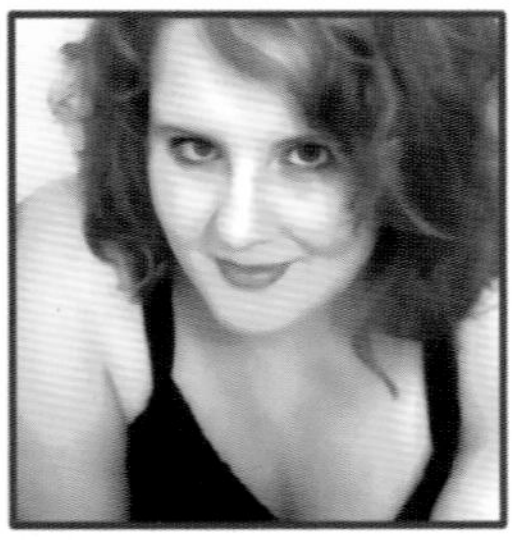

ASHLEY AVARD

SKILLS: Writer
LOCATION: Pennsylvania
FUN FACT: Addicted to horror movies, gender theory, activism, and the color green.

http://mendthiscrack.wordpress.com/

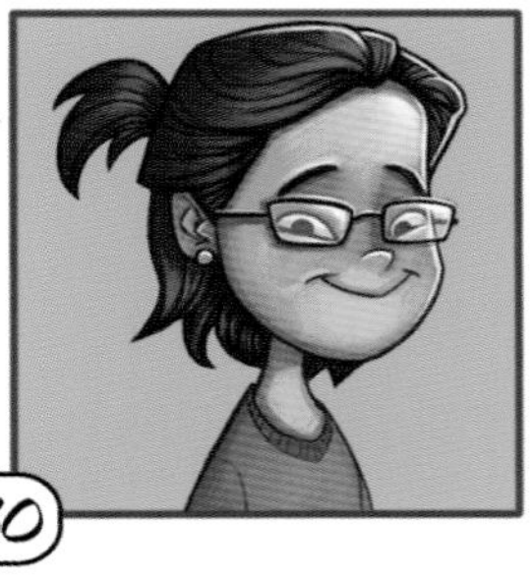

DANI JONES

SKILLS: Penciller, Colorist
LOCATION: New Hampshire
FUN FACT: I am a triplet! If you meet a girl and she looks like me, there is a 2 in 3 chance she is not me.

http://danidraws.com

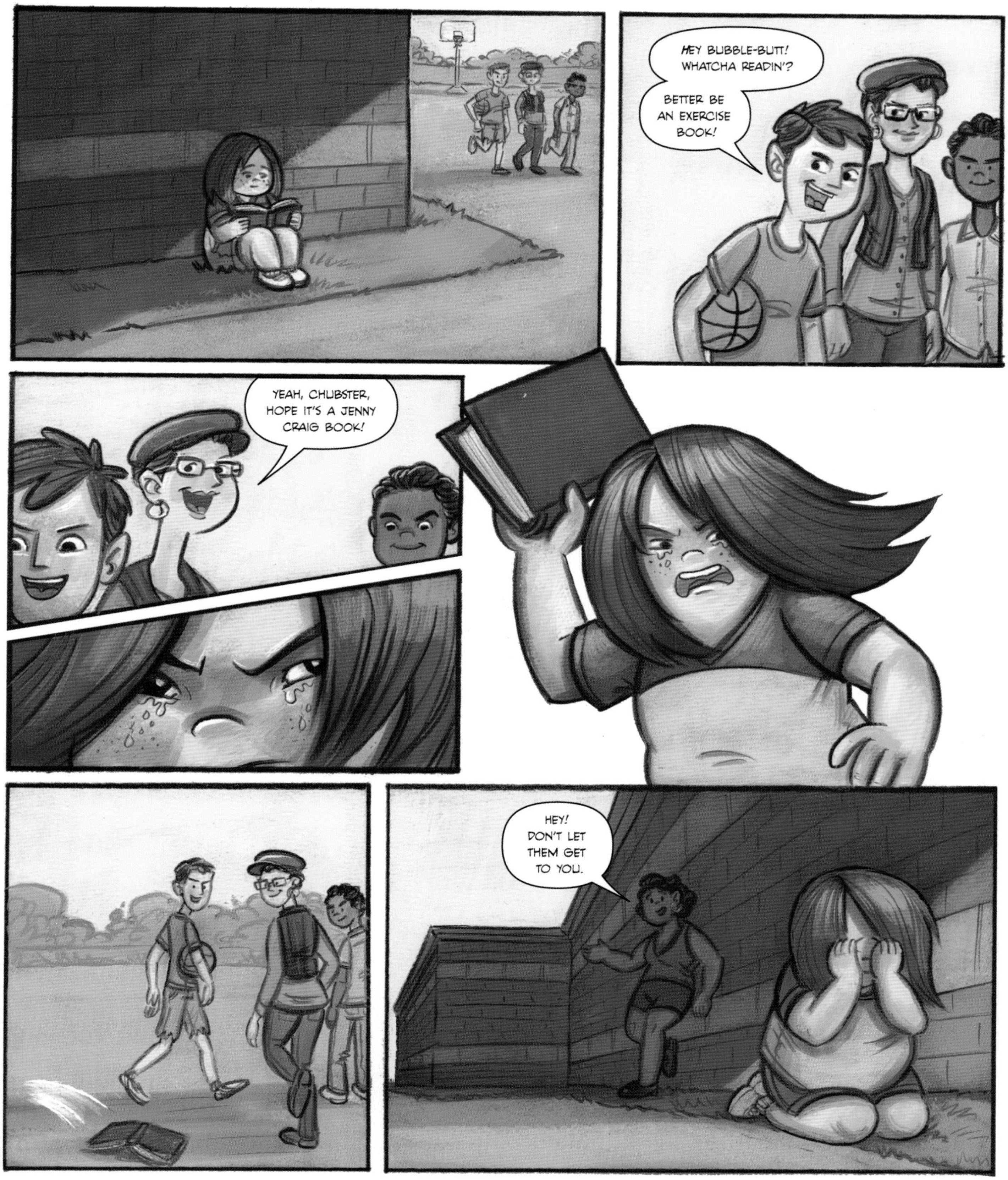
HEY BUBBLE-BUTT! WHATCHA READIN'?
BETTER BE AN EXERCISE BOOK!
YEAH, CHUBSTER, HOPE IT'S A JENNY CRAIG BOOK!
HEY! DON'T LET THEM GET TO YOU.

☆ ☆ ☆

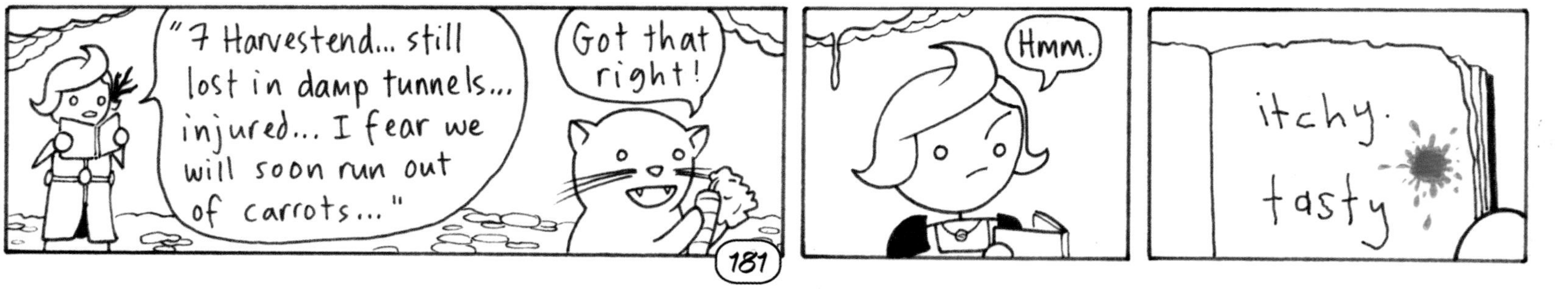
"7 Harvestend... still lost in damp tunnels... injured... I fear we will soon run out of carrots..."
Got that right!
Hmm.
itchy.
tasty

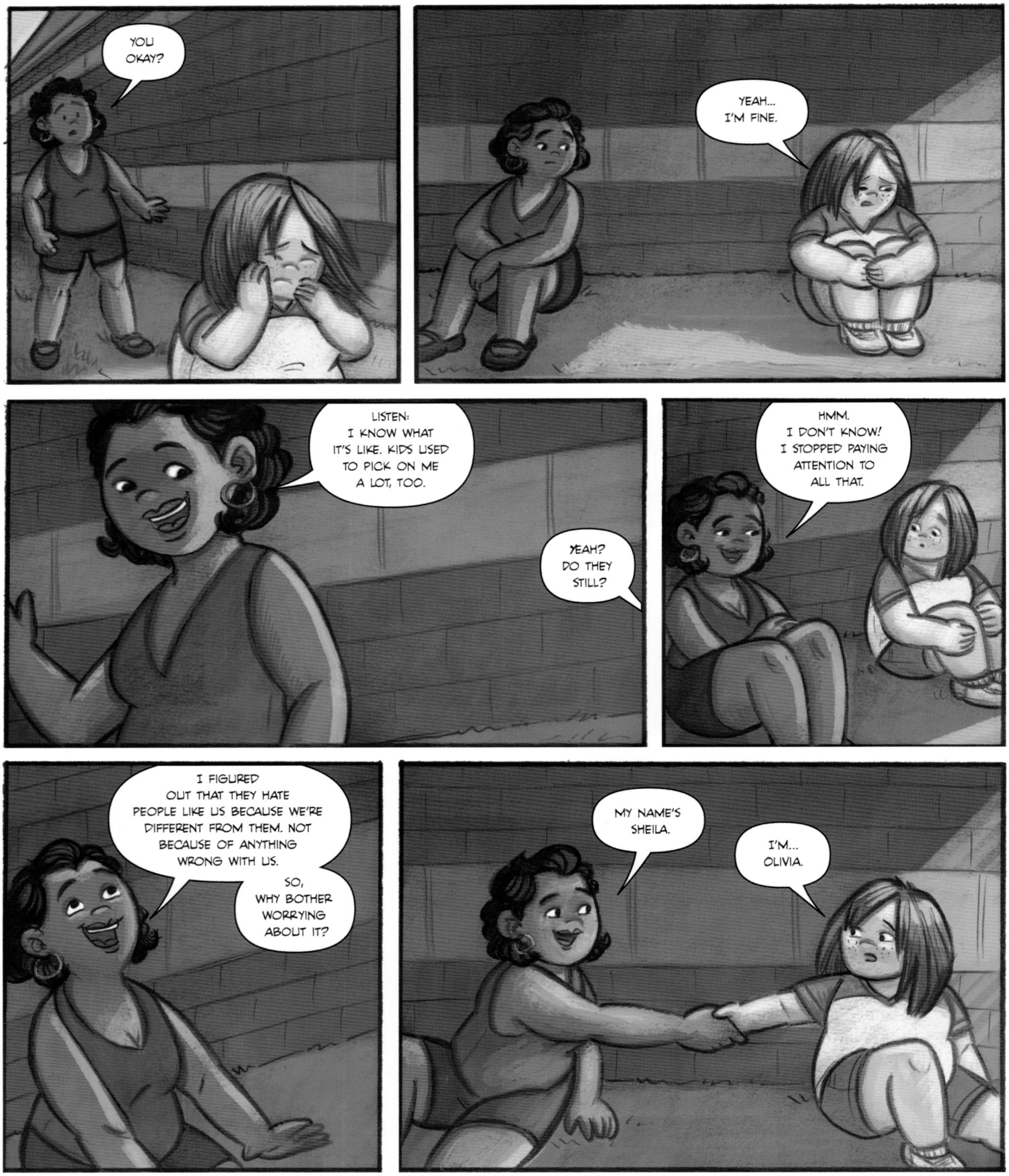
YOU OKAY?
YEAH... I'M FINE.
LISTEN: I KNOW WHAT IT'S LIKE. KIDS USED TO PICK ON ME A LOT, TOO.
YEAH? DO THEY STILL?
HMM. I DON'T KNOW! I STOPPED PAYING ATTENTION TO ALL THAT.
I FIGURED OUT THAT THEY HATE PEOPLE LIKE US BECAUSE WE'RE DIFFERENT FROM THEM. NOT BECAUSE OF ANYTHING WRONG WITH US.
SO, WHY BOTHER WORRYING ABOUT IT?
MY NAME'S SHEILA.
I'M... OLIVIA.

☆ ☆ ☆

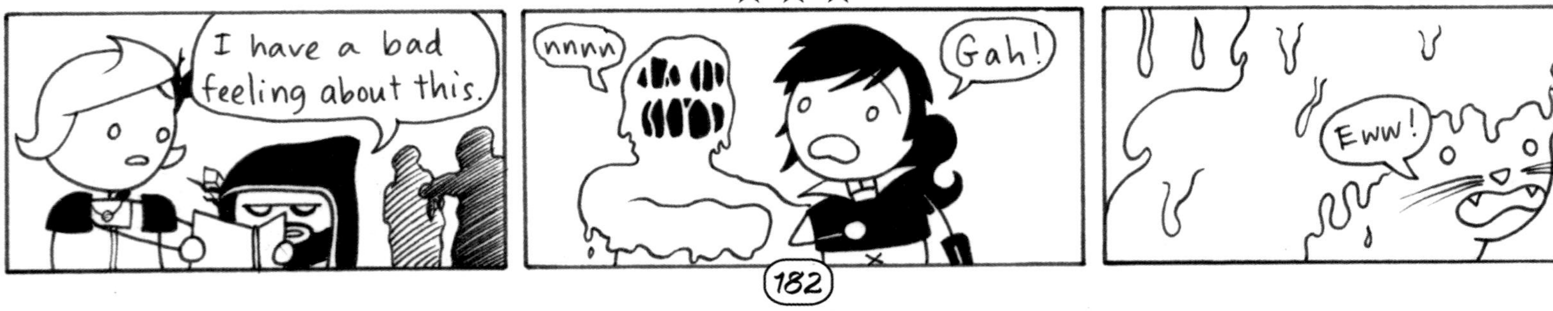
I have a bad feeling about this.
nnnn
Gah!
Eww!

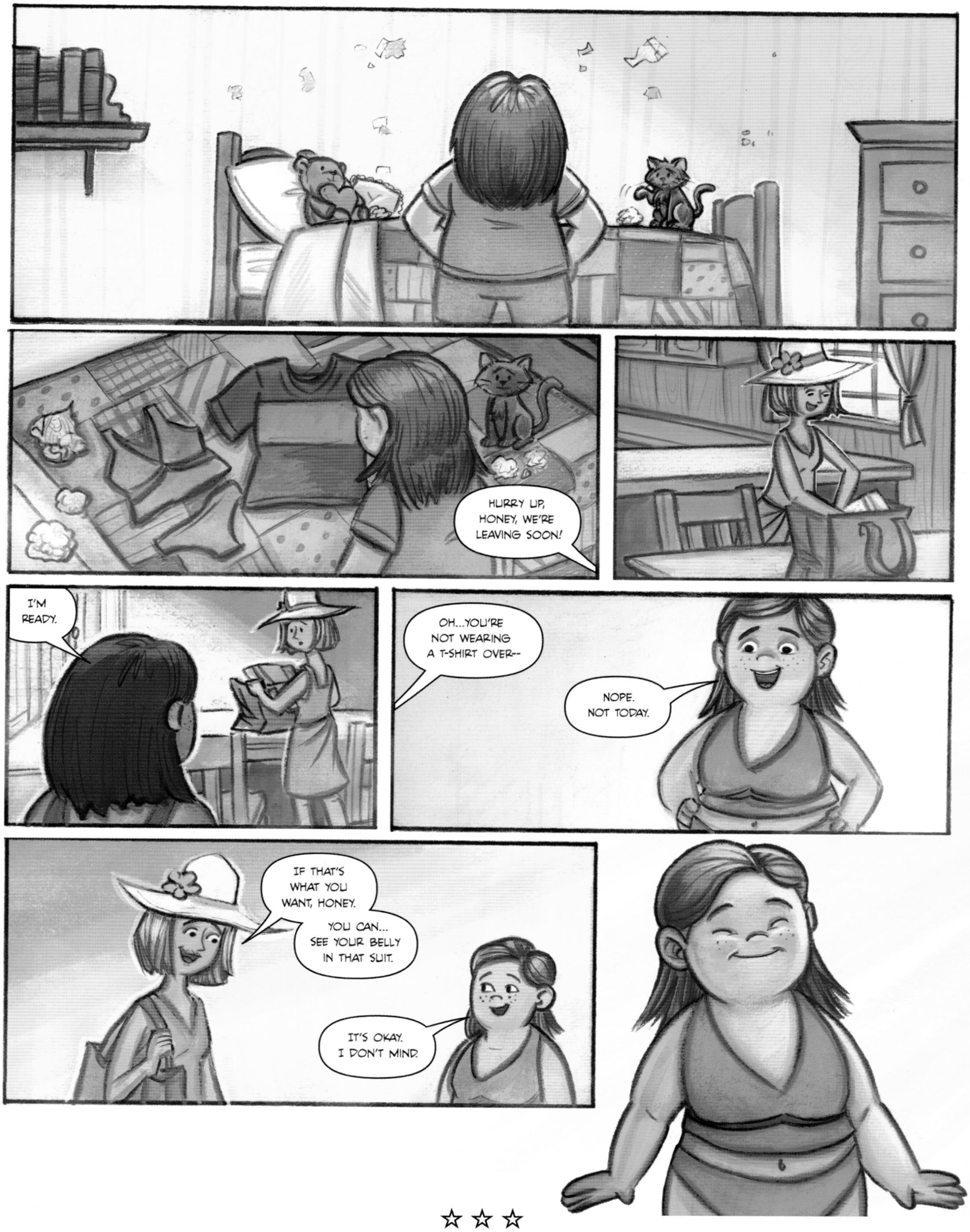
HURRY UP, HONEY, WE'RE LEAVING SOON!
I'M READY.
OH...YOU'RE NOT WEARING A T-SHIRT OVER--
NOPE. NOT TODAY.
IF THAT'S WHAT YOU WANT, HONEY.
YOU CAN... SEE YOUR BELLY IN THAT SUIT.
IT'S OKAY. I DON'T MIND.

☆ ☆ ☆

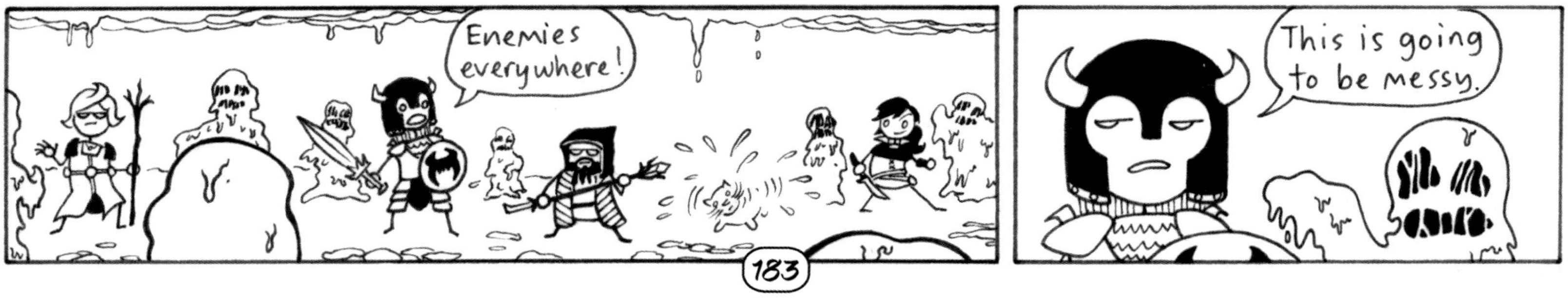
Enemies everywhere!
This is going to be messy.

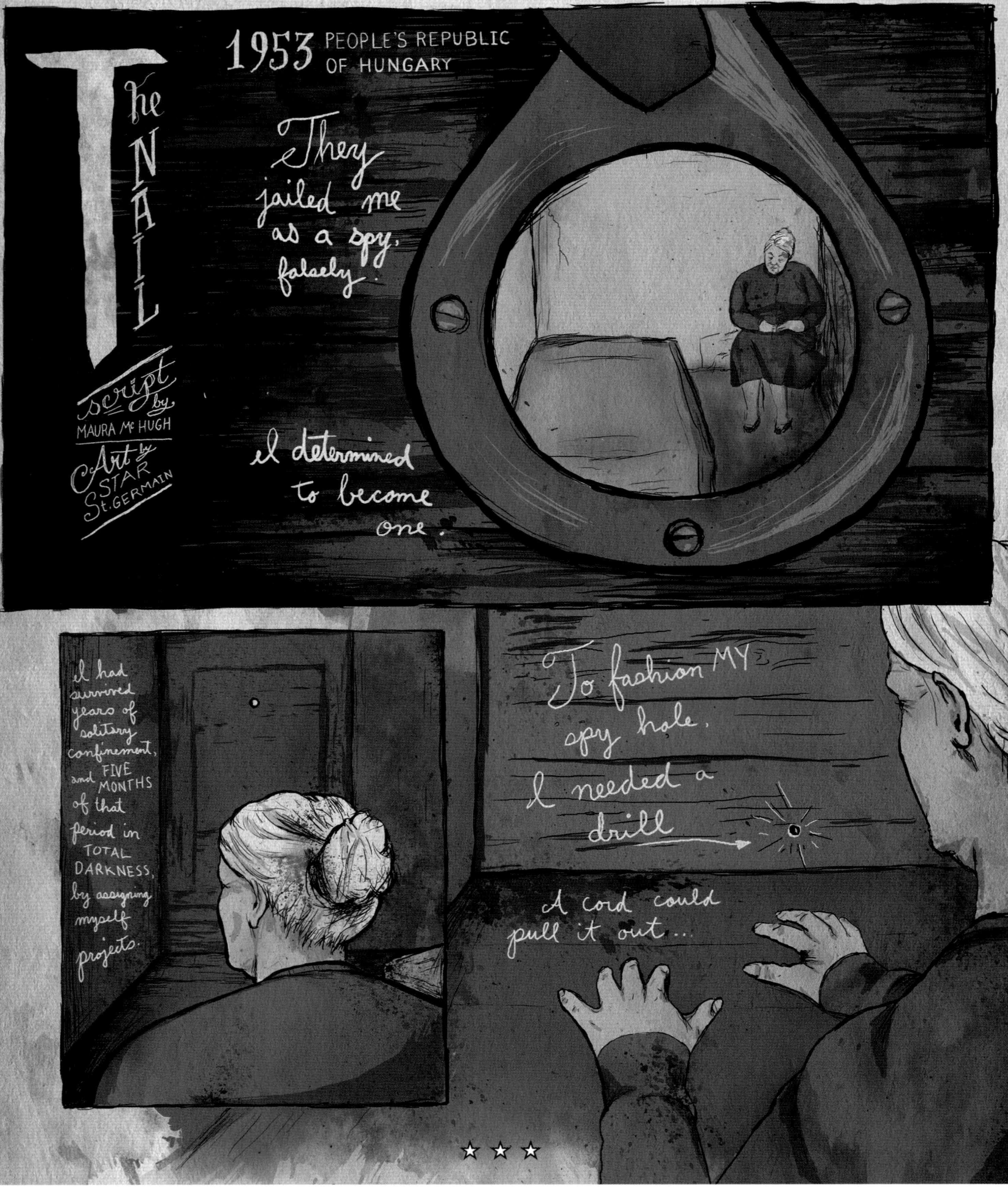
The NAIL
script by MAURA McHUGH
Art by STAR St.GERMAIN
1953 PEOPLE'S REPUBLIC OF HUNGARY
They jailed me as a spy, falsely.
I determined to become one.
I had survived years of solitary confinement, and FIVE MONTHS of that period in TOTAL DARKNESS, by assigning myself projects.
To fashion MY spy hole, I needed a drill
A cord could pull it out...

☆ ☆ ☆

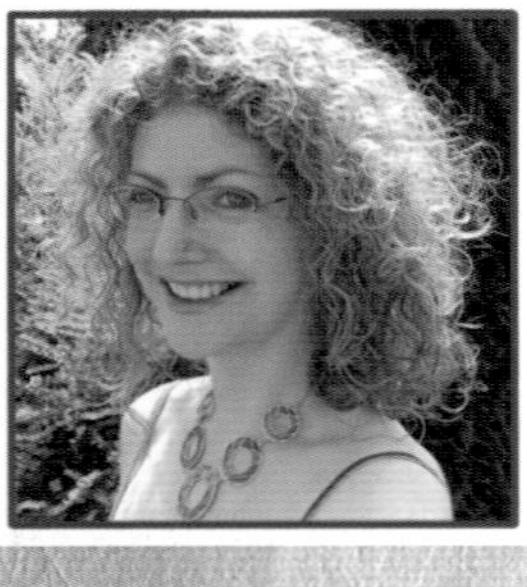

MAURA MCHUGH

SKILLS: Writer
LOCATION: Galway, Ireland
FUN FACT: I used to buy my brothers' comics so I could read them.

http://splinister.com/

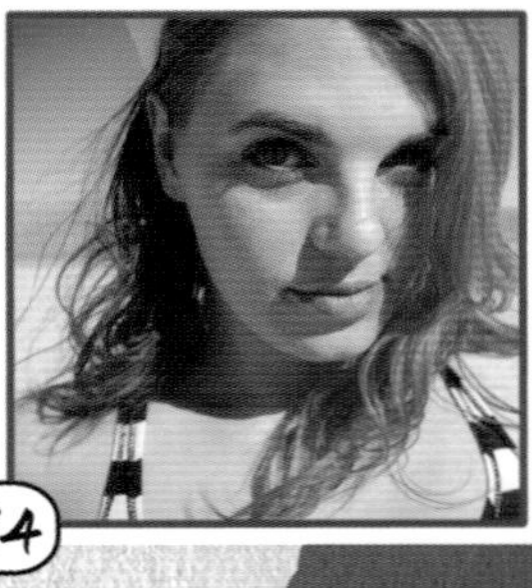

STAR ST.GERMAIN

SKILLS: Penciller, Inker, Colorist, Letterer
LOCATION: San Francisco, CA
FUN FACT: I wear red every day and can clap with one hand.

thisisstar.com

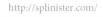

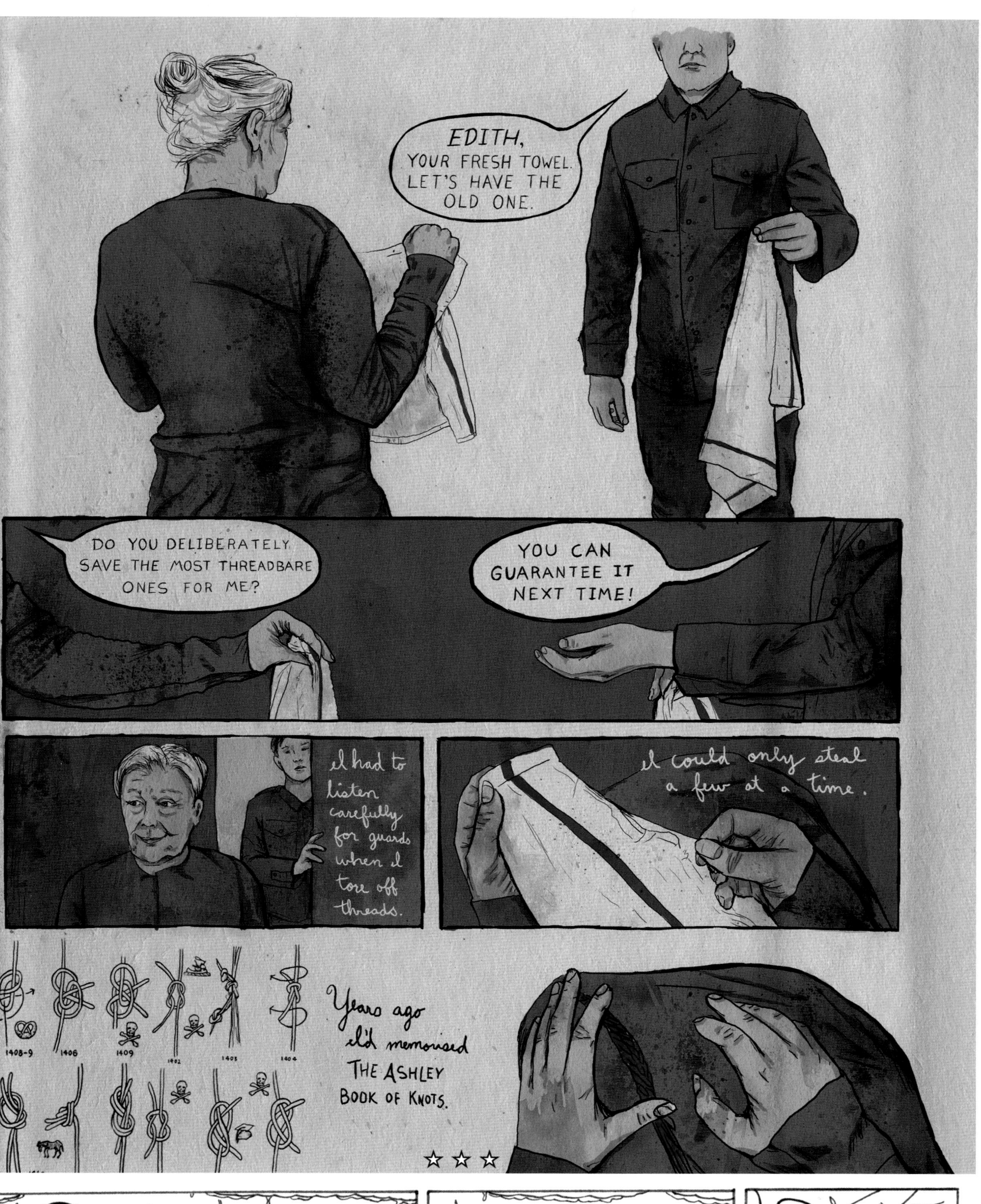
EDITH, YOUR FRESH TOWEL. LET'S HAVE THE OLD ONE.
DO YOU DELIBERATELY SAVE THE MOST THREADBARE ONES FOR ME?
YOU CAN GUARANTEE IT NEXT TIME!
I had to listen carefully for guards when I tore off threads.
I could only steal a few at a time.
Years ago I'd memorised THE ASHLEY BOOK OF KNOTS.

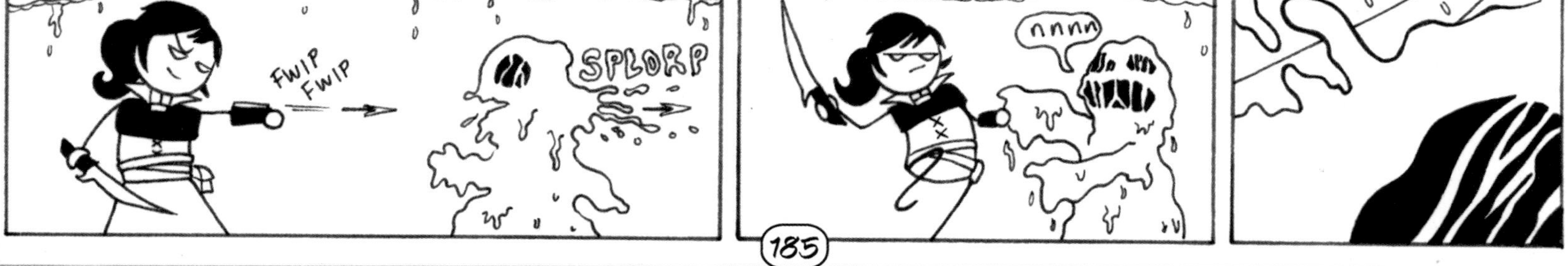
FWIP FWIP
SPLORP
nnnn

ONLY THE BEST FOR YOU, DOCTOR.

BLESS YOU.

US IMPERIALIST EXPLOITERS DO APPRECIATE A FINE LAUNDRY SERVICE.

I got a fresh towel every two weeks.

It took over TWO MONTHS to steal 32 threads.

I was never told the length of my jail sentence, or if I would ever be released. Prison schooled me in patience.

I plaited a strong cord.

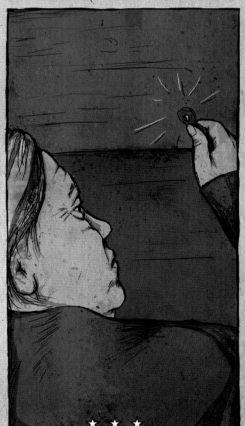

It wouldn't budge.

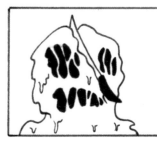

nnnn

Interesting.

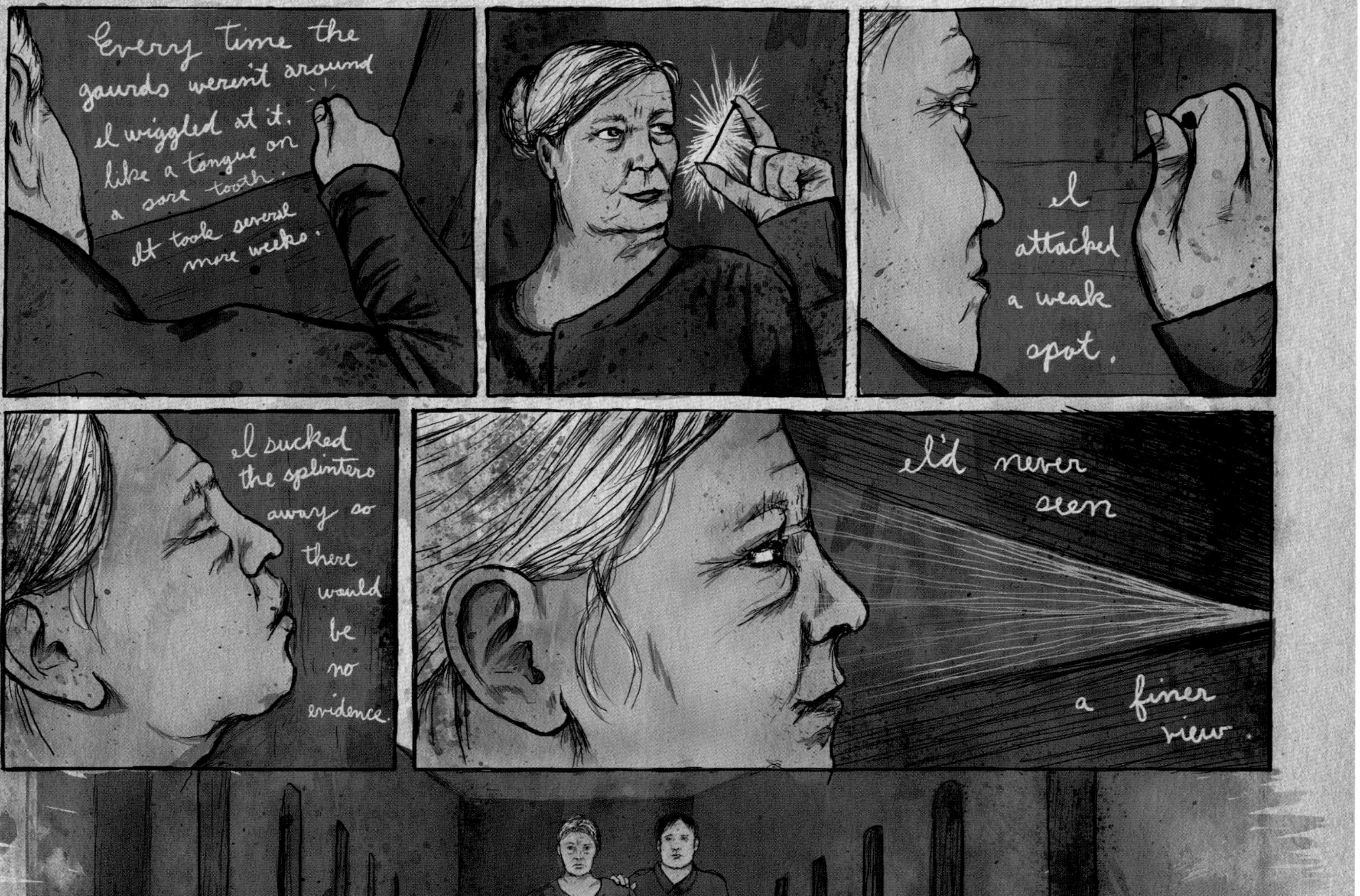
Every time the gaurds weren't around I wiggled at it, like a tongue on a sore tooth.
It took several more weeks.
I attacked a weak spot.
I sucked the splinters away so there would be no evidence.
I'd never seen
a finer view.
They transferred me to another gaol eventually
but they never discovered my true spycraft.
DR. EDITH BONE (1889-1975) SURVIVED 7 YEARS IN SOLITARY CONFINEMENT BY OCCUPYING HER MIND WITH PUZZLES, POETRY, AND STRATAGEMS. SHE WAS FINALLY RELEASED, UNDEFEATED AND SANE, DURING THE HUNGARIAN REVOLUTION OF 1956.

☆ ☆ ☆

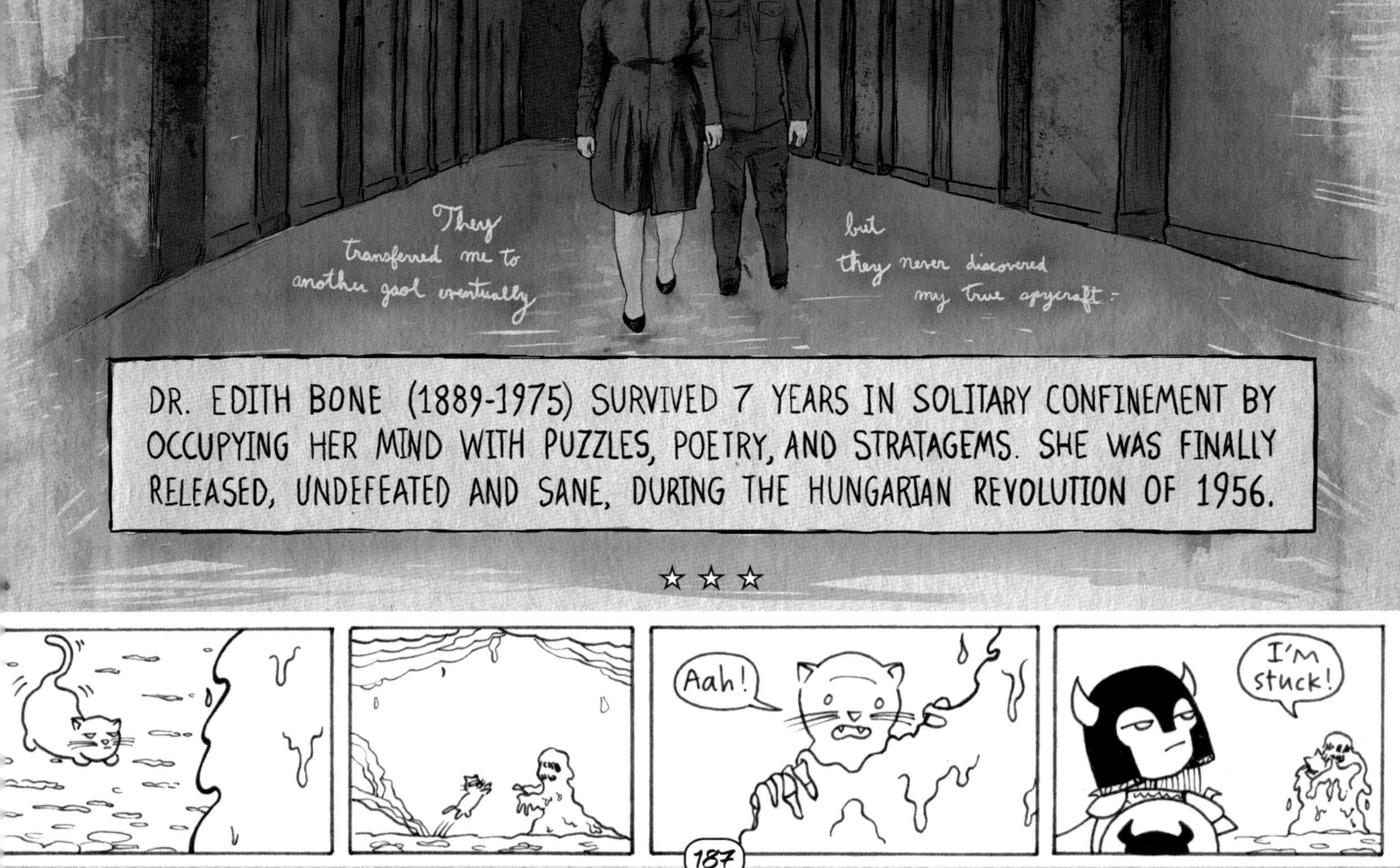
Aah!
I'M stuck!

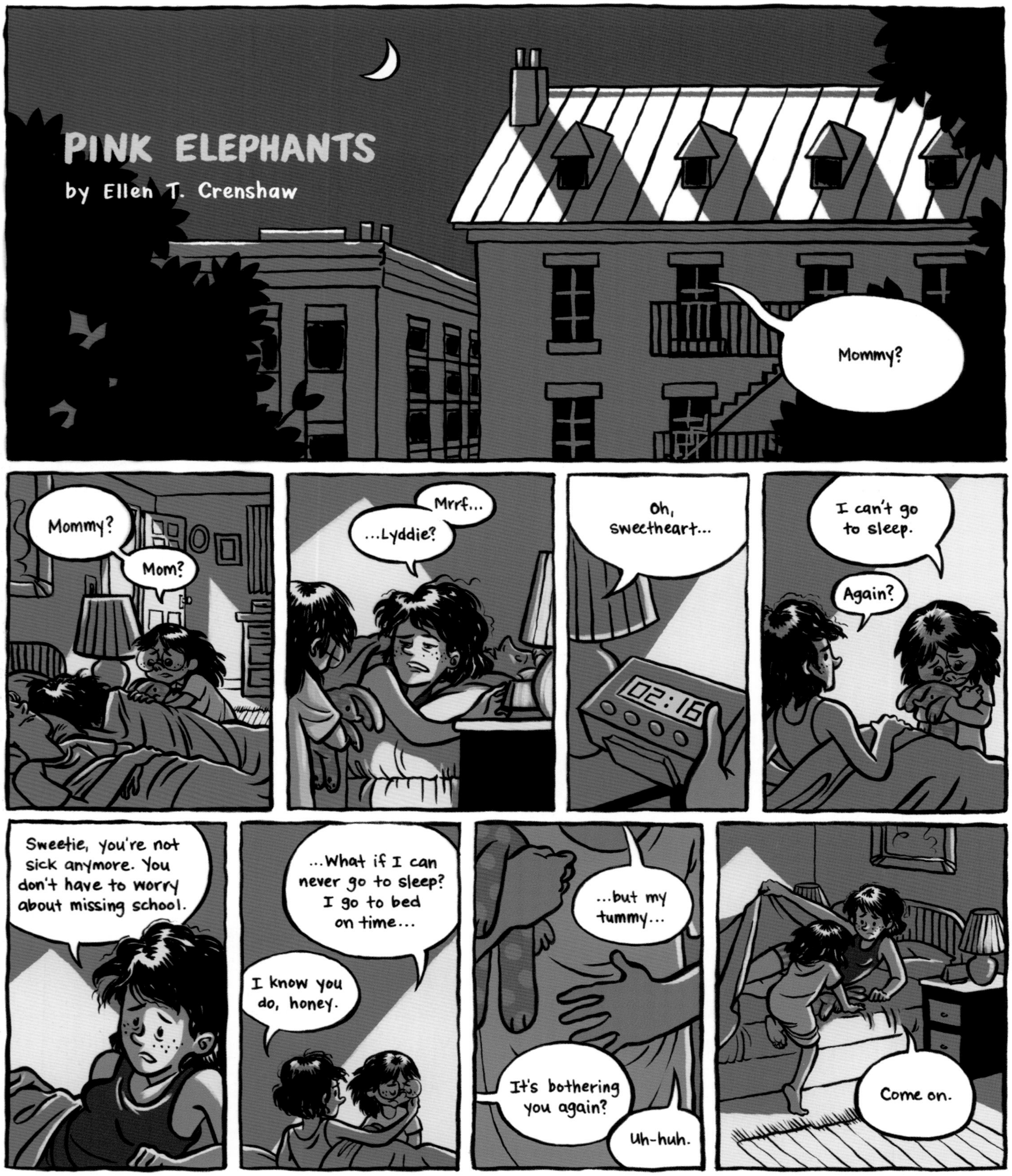
PINK ELEPHANTS
by Ellen T. Crenshaw
Mommy?
Mommy?
Mom?
Mrrf...
...Lyddie?
Oh, sweetheart...
02:16
I can't go to sleep.
Again?
Sweetie, you're not sick anymore. You don't have to worry about missing school.
...What if I can never go to sleep? I go to bed on time...
I know you do, honey.
...but my tummy...
It's bothering you again?
Uh-huh.
Come on.

☆☆☆

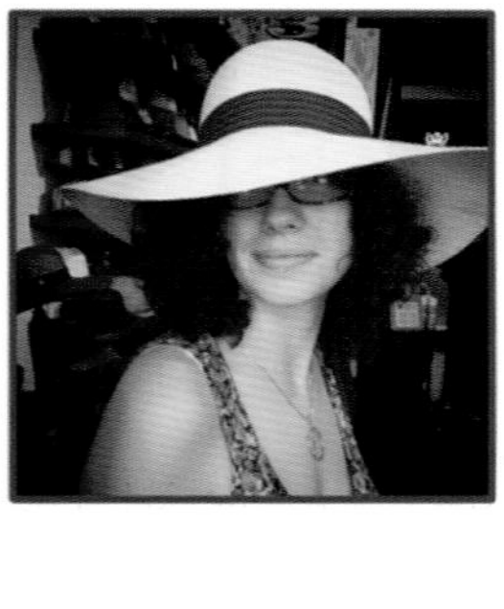

ELLEN T. CRENSHAW

SKILLS: Writer, Penciller, Inker, Colorist, Letterer
LOCATION: Boston, MA
FUN FACT: I know the lyrics to nearly every *Animaniacs* song.

etcillustration.com

PRO TIP

SELF-EMPLOYED
BY DEVIN GRAYSON

"ALMOST ALL COMIC CREATORS ARE INDEPENDENT CONTRACTORS. THAT MEANS YOU'RE GOING TO BE SELF-EMPLOYED AND YOU'RE GOING TO HAVE TO LEARN TO MARKET YOURSELF AND NEGOTIATE CONTRACTS WITH INDIVIDUAL COMPANIES. BUT IT ALSO MEANS YOU CAN WORK FOR AS MANY DIFFERENT PUBLISHERS AS YOU LIKE!"

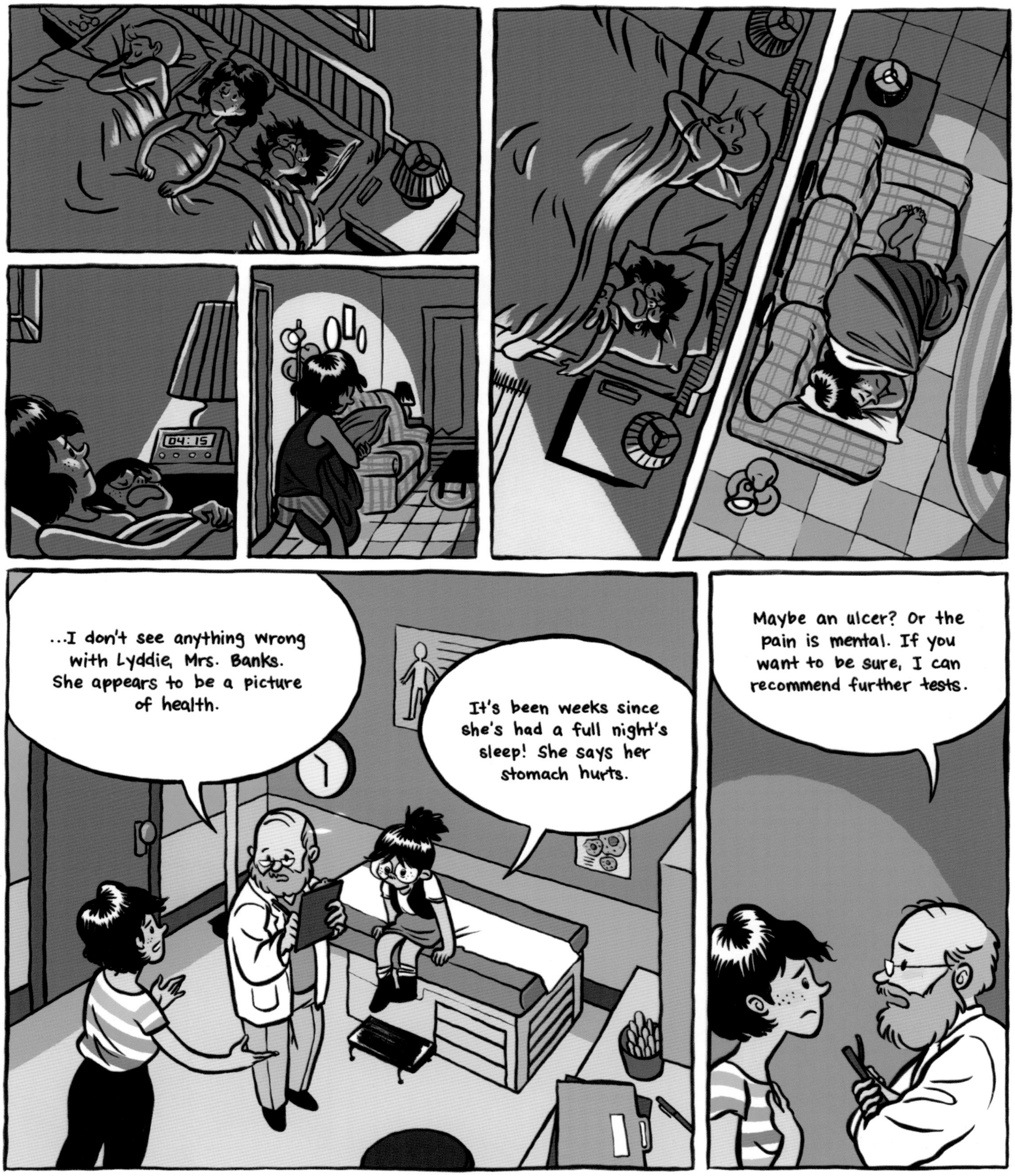
...I don't see anything wrong with Lyddie, Mrs. Banks. She appears to be a picture of health.
It's been weeks since she's had a full night's sleep! She says her stomach hurts.
Maybe an ulcer? Or the pain is mental. If you want to be sure, I can recommend further tests.

☆ ☆ ☆

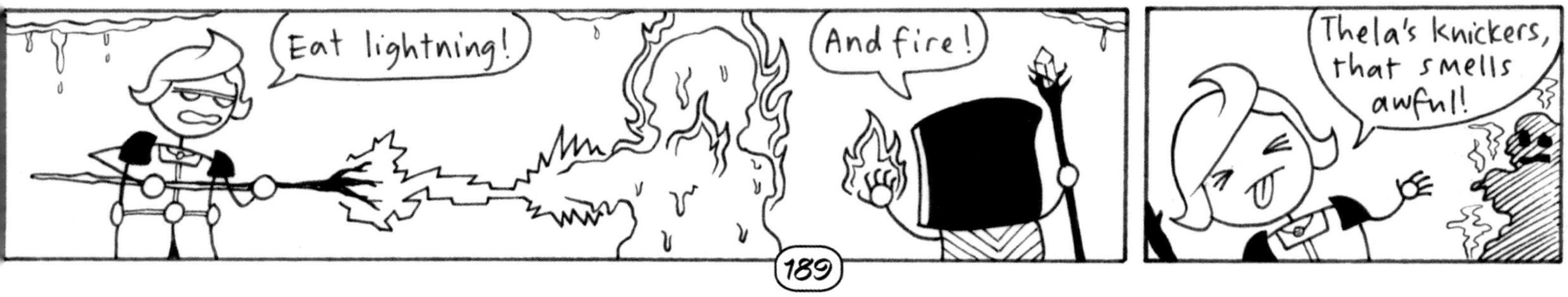
Eat lightning!
And fire!
Thela's knickers, that smells awful!

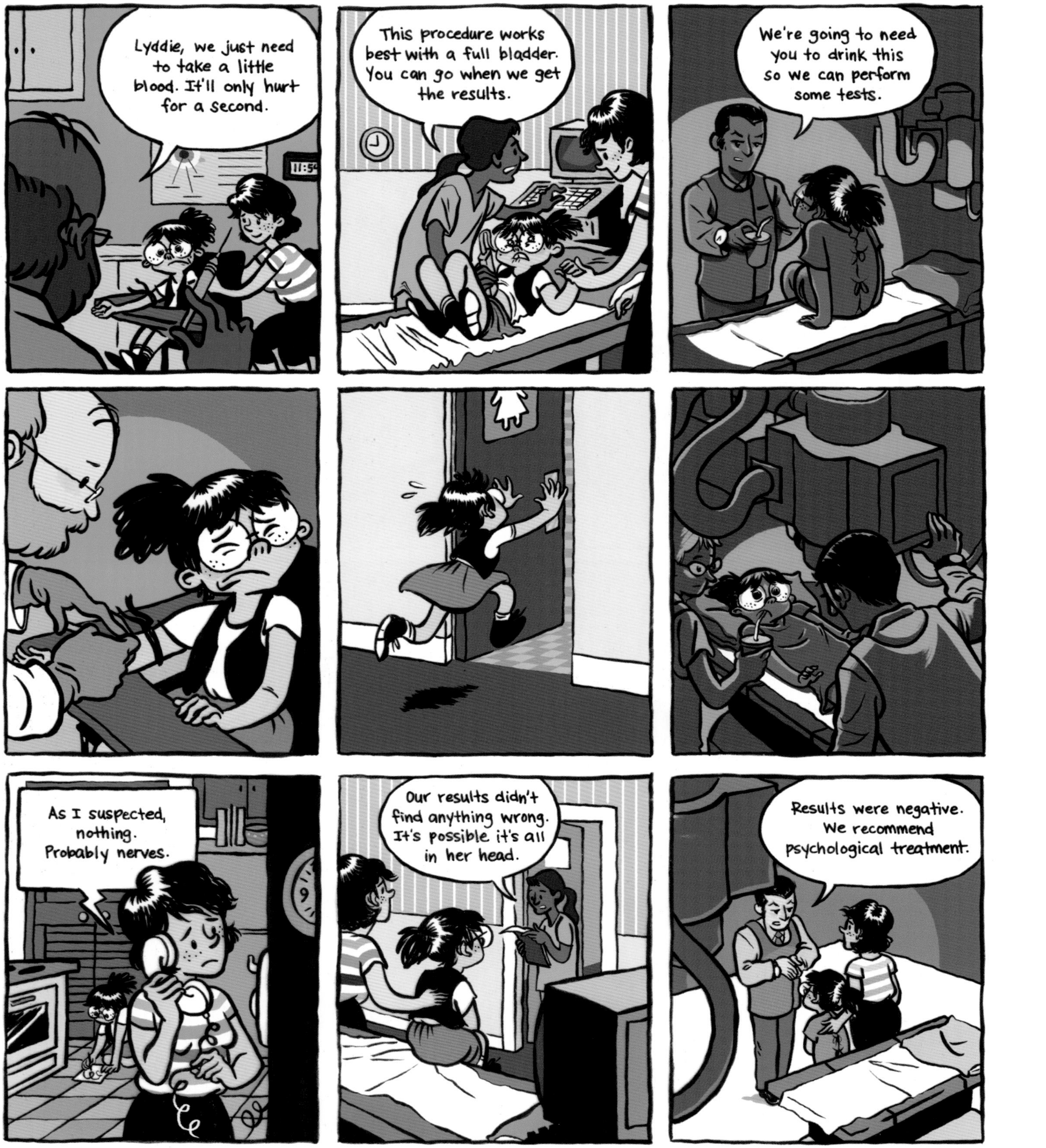
Lyddie, we just need to take a little blood. It'll only hurt for a second.
This procedure works best with a full bladder. You can go when we get the results.
We're going to need you to drink this so we can perform some tests.
As I suspected, nothing. Probably nerves.
Our results didn't find anything wrong. It's possible it's all in her head.
Results were negative. We recommend psychological treatment.

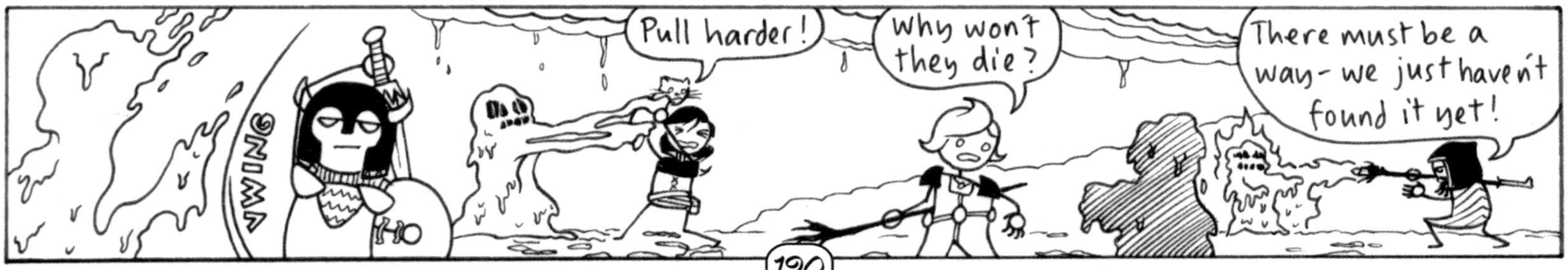
Pull harder!
Why won't they die?
There must be a way- we just haven't found it yet!

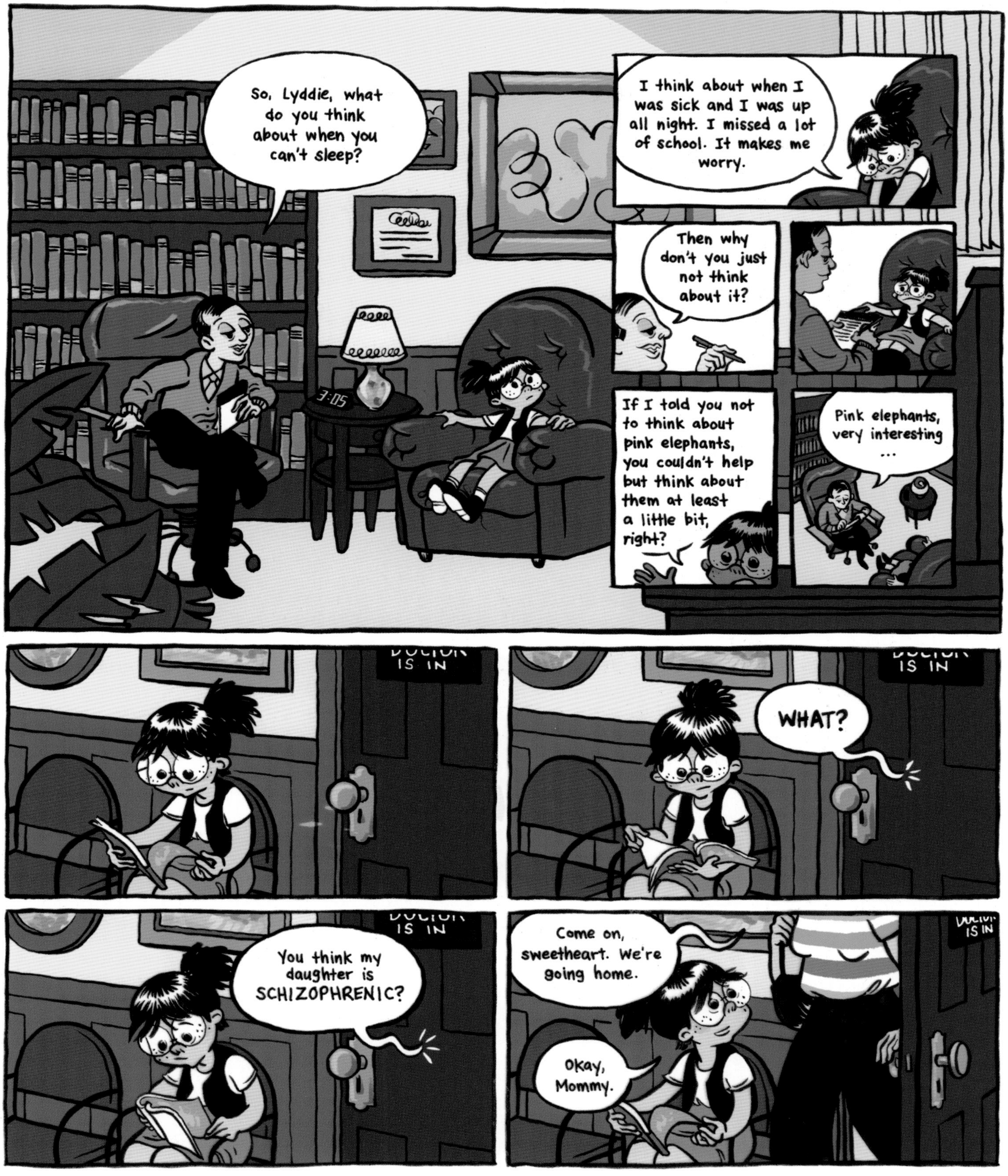
So, Lyddie, what do you think about when you can't sleep?
3:05
I think about when I was sick and I was up all night. I missed a lot of school. It makes me worry.
Then why don't you just not think about it?
If I told you not to think about pink elephants, you couldn't help but think about them at least a little bit, right?
Pink elephants, very interesting ...
IS IN
IS IN
WHAT?
IS IN
You think my daughter is SCHIZOPHRENIC?
IS IN
Come on, sweetheart. We're going home.
Okay, Mommy.

☆ ☆ ☆

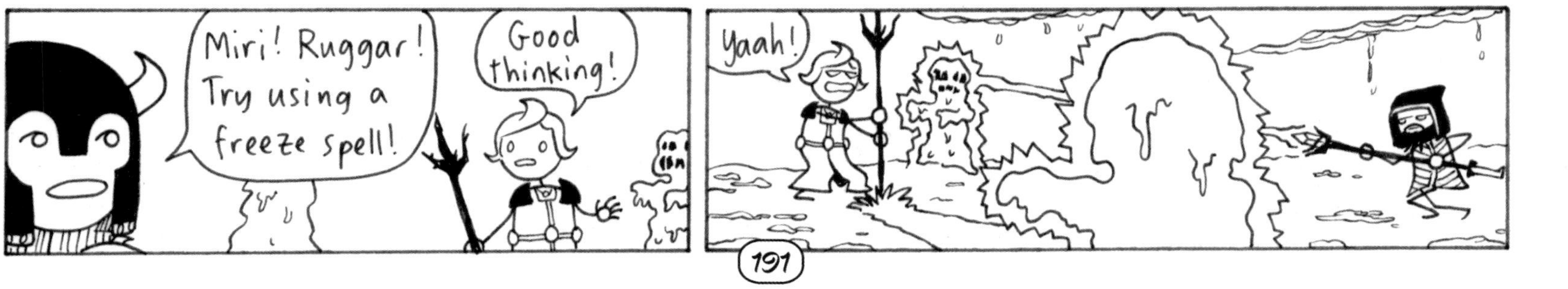
Miri! Ruggar! Try using a freeze spell!
Good thinking!
Yaah!

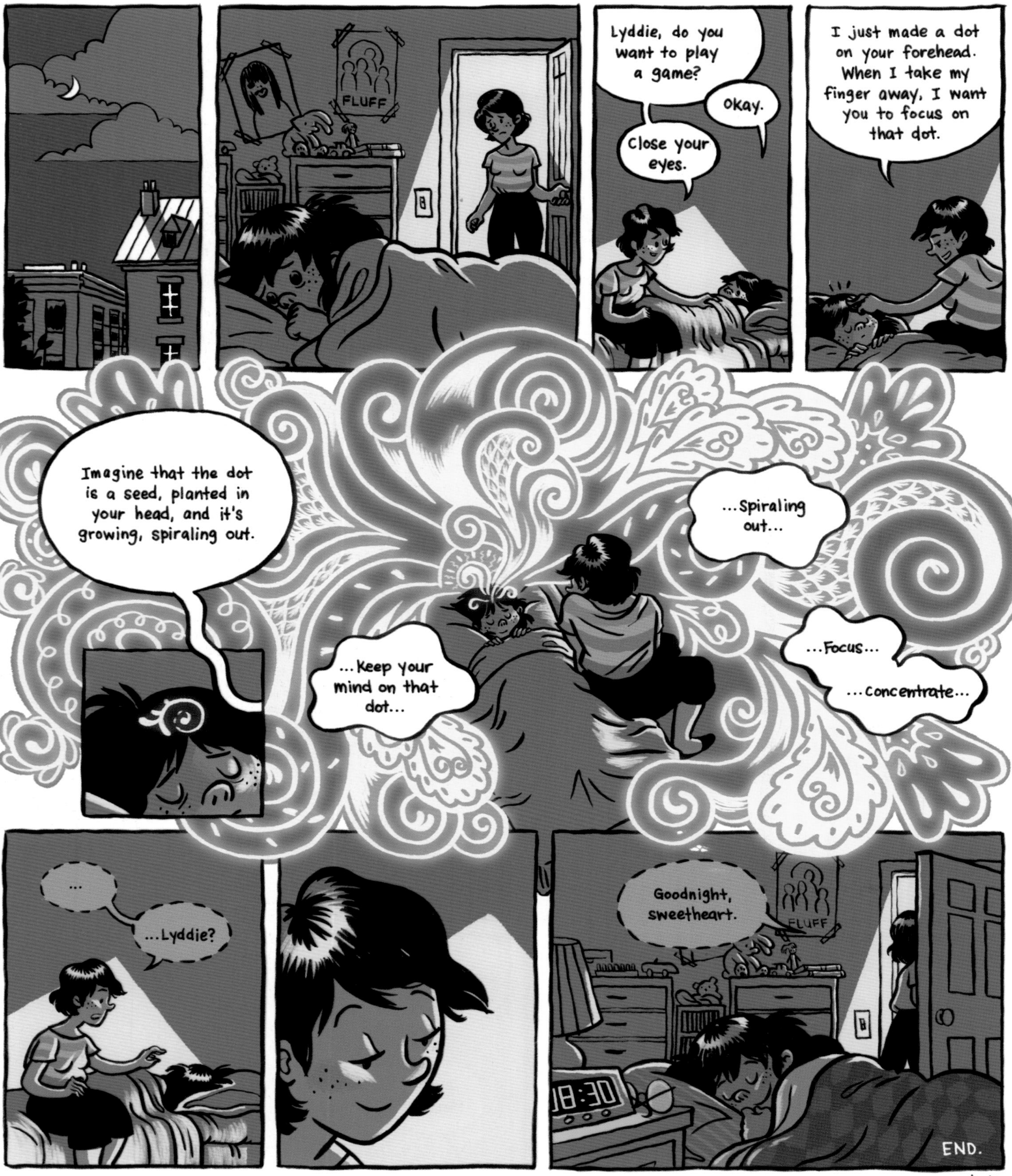
Lyddie, do you want to play a game?
Okay.
Close your eyes.
I just made a dot on your forehead. When I take my finger away, I want you to focus on that dot.
Imagine that the dot is a seed, planted in your head, and it's growing, spiraling out.
...Keep your mind on that dot...
...Spiraling out...
...Focus...
...Concentrate...
...
...Lyddie?
FLUFF
Goodnight, sweetheart.
END.
etc '11

☆ ☆ ☆

PRO TIP

TOOLS

BY RENAE DE LIZ

"IT'S NOT THE TOOL THAT MAKES THE ARTIST. YOU CAN CREATE ART, YOU CAN DEVELOP YOUR SKILLS, AND YOU CAN EVEN MAKE A LIVING WITH A SIMPLE PENCIL AND PIECE OF PAPER. SO DON'T WORRY IF YOU DON'T HAVE THE TOP OF THE LINE COMPUTER AND TABLET OR EXPENSIVE MARKERS OR PAINTS AND CANVAS. START WHERE YOU CAN AND BUILD FROM THERE!"

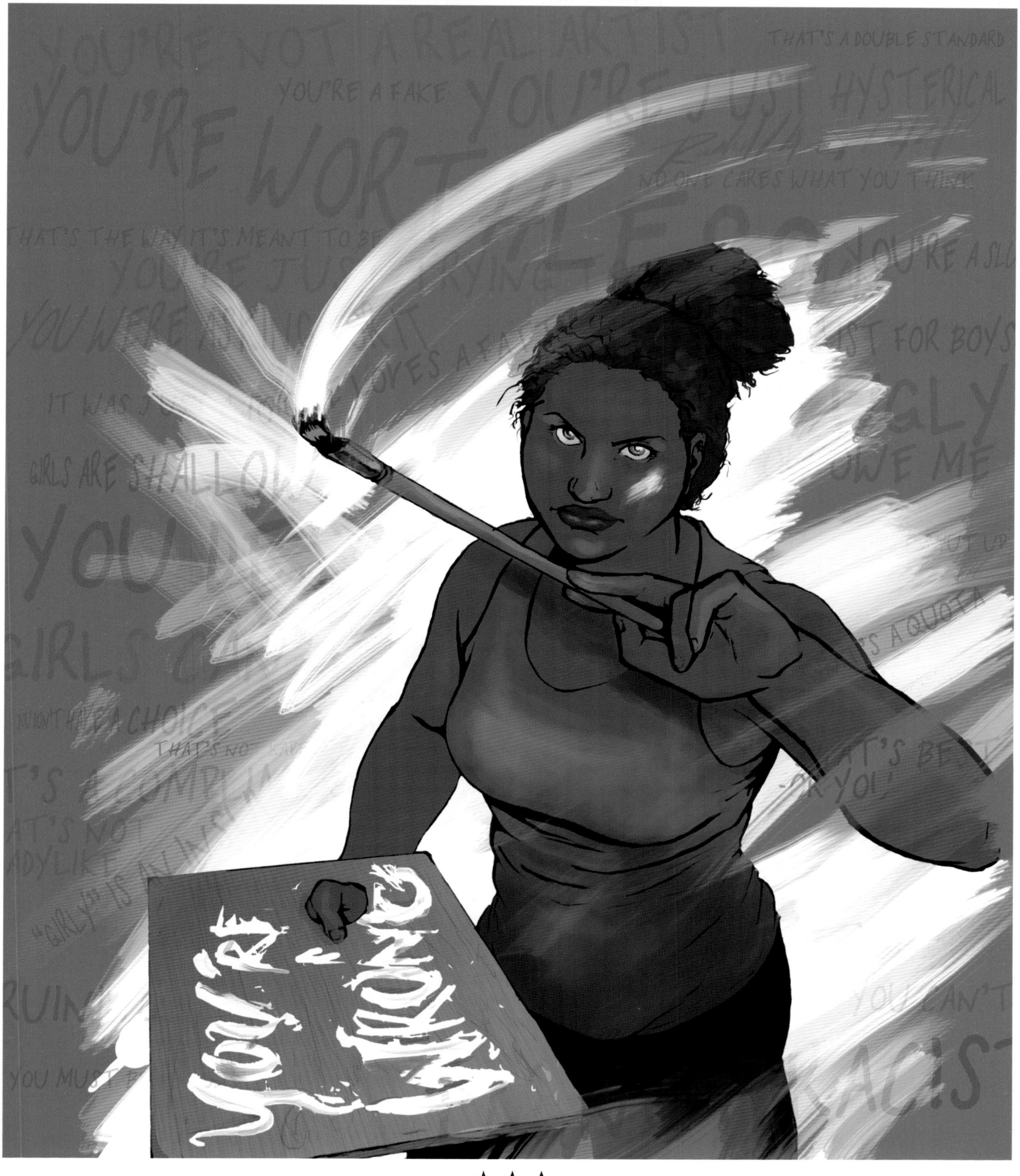
YOU'RE NOT A REAL ARTIST
THAT'S A DOUBLE STANDARD
YOU'RE A FAKE
YOU'RE JUST HYSTERICAL
YOU'RE WRONG

☆☆☆

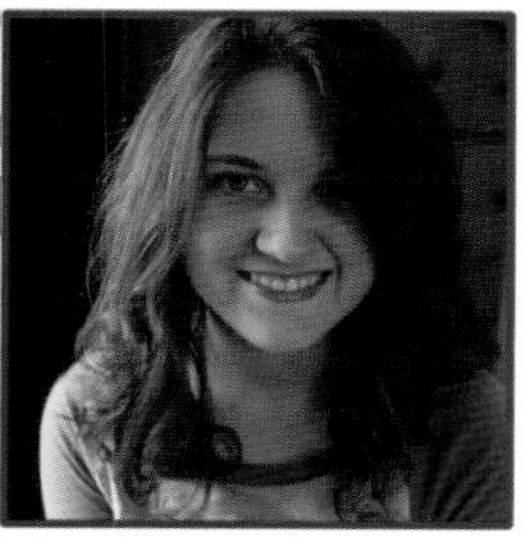

RACHEL MOIR

SKILLS: Penciller, Inker, Colorist
LOCATION: Ann Arbor, MI
FUN FACT: Thinks all the best stories have a dose of fairy tale.

rjmart.com

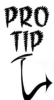

PRO TIP

INKING PORTFOLIO
BY STACIE PONDER

"YOUR INKING PORTFOLIO SHOULD ALWAYS INCLUDE A COPY OF THE ORIGINAL PENCILS SO THE REVIEWER CAN SEE WHAT YOU'VE ADDED TO THE ARTWORK IN TERMS OF LINE WEIGHT, TEXTURE, AND THE SUCH."

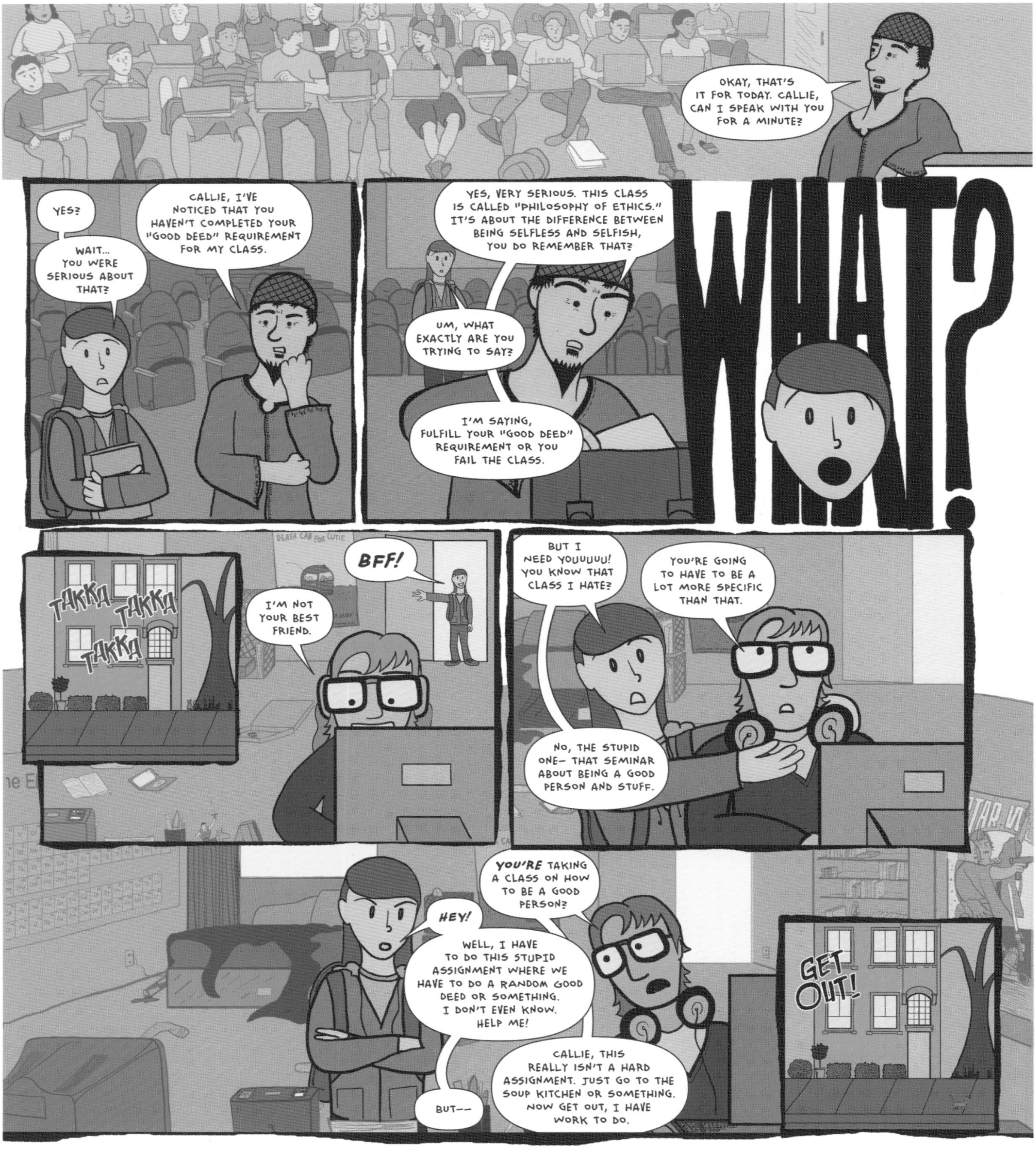
OKAY, THAT'S IT FOR TODAY. CALLIE, CAN I SPEAK WITH YOU FOR A MINUTE?
YES?
CALLIE, I'VE NOTICED THAT YOU HAVEN'T COMPLETED YOUR "GOOD DEED" REQUIREMENT FOR MY CLASS.
WAIT... YOU WERE SERIOUS ABOUT THAT?
YES, VERY SERIOUS. THIS CLASS IS CALLED "PHILOSOPHY OF ETHICS." IT'S ABOUT THE DIFFERENCE BETWEEN BEING SELFLESS AND SELFISH, YOU DO REMEMBER THAT?
UM, WHAT EXACTLY ARE YOU TRYING TO SAY?
I'M SAYING, FULFILL YOUR "GOOD DEED" REQUIREMENT OR YOU FAIL THE CLASS.
WHAT?
TAKKA TAKKA TAKKA
DEATH CAB FOR CUTIE
BFF!
I'M NOT YOUR BEST FRIEND.
BUT I NEED YOUUUUU! YOU KNOW THAT CLASS I HATE?
YOU'RE GOING TO HAVE TO BE A LOT MORE SPECIFIC THAN THAT.
NO, THE STUPID ONE- THAT SEMINAR ABOUT BEING A GOOD PERSON AND STUFF.
YOU'RE TAKING A CLASS ON HOW TO BE A GOOD PERSON?
HEY!
WELL, I HAVE TO DO THIS STUPID ASSIGNMENT WHERE WE HAVE TO DO A RANDOM GOOD DEED OR SOMETHING. I DON'T EVEN KNOW. HELP ME!
CALLIE, THIS REALLY ISN'T A HARD ASSIGNMENT. JUST GO TO THE SOUP KITCHEN OR SOMETHING. NOW GET OUT, I HAVE WORK TO DO.
BUT--
GET OUT!

WRITER: KAYLA BANKS ARTIST: BRENDA KIRK COLORIST: JORDIE BELLAIRE LETTERER: RACHEL DEERING

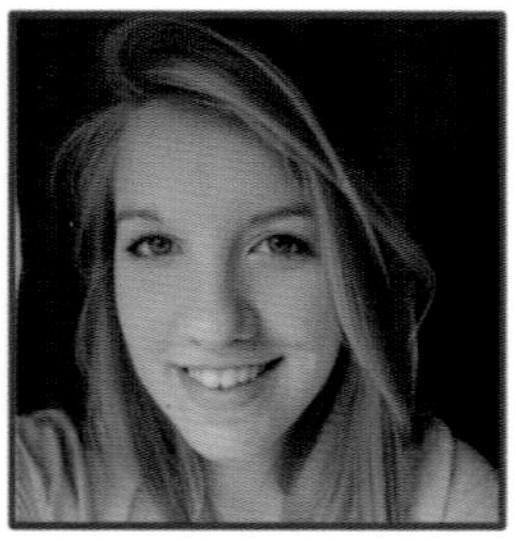

KAYLA BANKS

SKILLS: Writer
LOCATION: Connecticut
FUN FACT: I occasionally have pink hair.

http://twitter.com/#!/SouthernOcean29

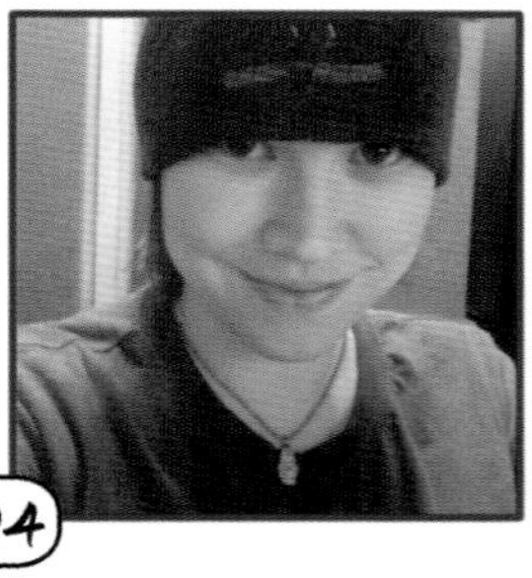

BRENDA KIRK

SKILLS: Penciller, Inker
LOCATION: Columbus, OH
FUN FACT: I am an ordained Dudeist priest.

http://www.geektress.com
http://www.brain-confetti.com

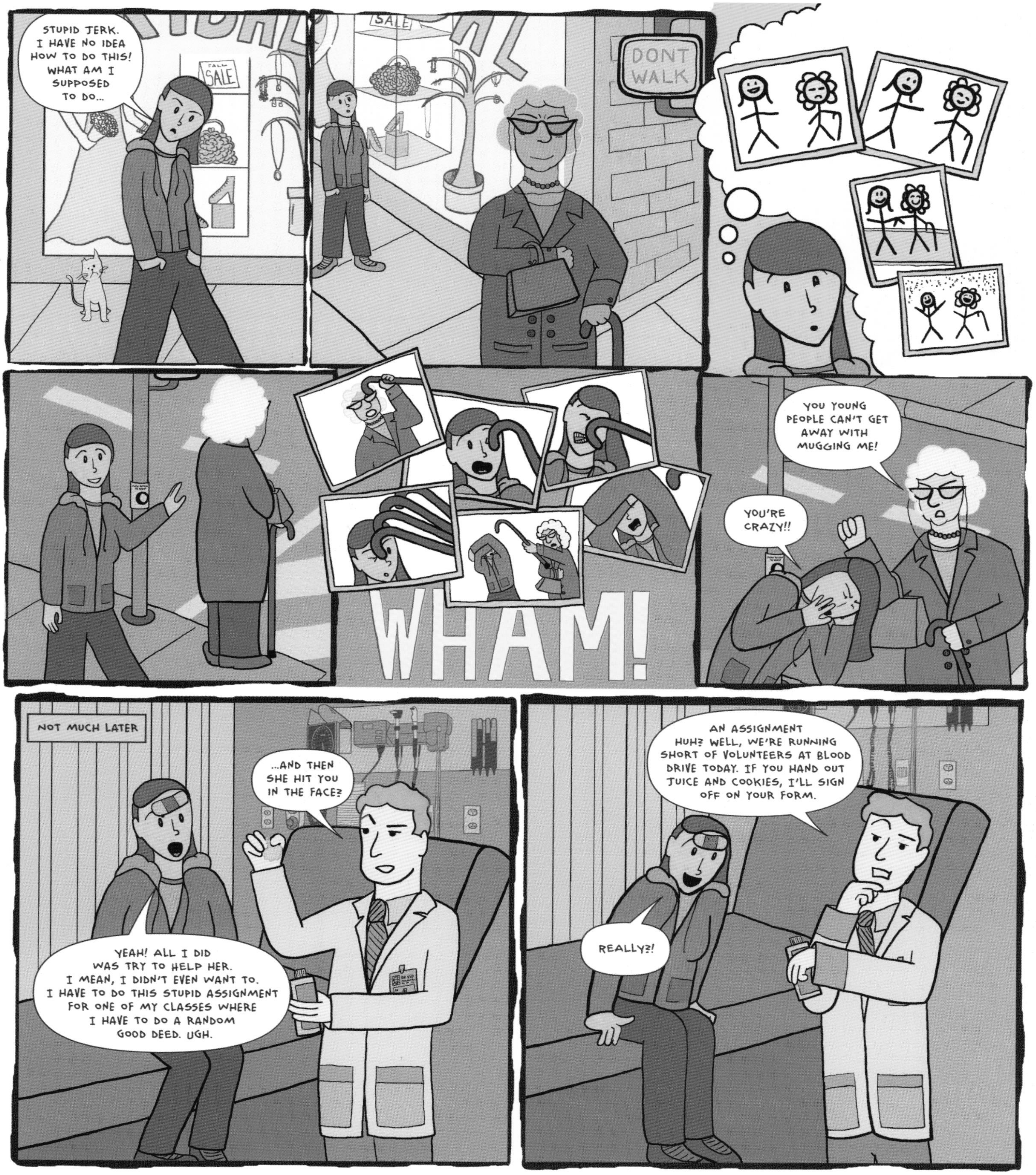
STUPID JERK. I HAVE NO IDEA HOW TO DO THIS! WHAT AM I SUPPOSED TO DO...
FALL SALE
SALE
DONT WALK
WHAM!
YOU YOUNG PEOPLE CAN'T GET AWAY WITH MUGGING ME!
YOU'RE CRAZY!!
NOT MUCH LATER
...AND THEN SHE HIT YOU IN THE FACE?
YEAH! ALL I DID WAS TRY TO HELP HER. I MEAN, I DIDN'T EVEN WANT TO. I HAVE TO DO THIS STUPID ASSIGNMENT FOR ONE OF MY CLASSES WHERE I HAVE TO DO A RANDOM GOOD DEED. UGH.
AN ASSIGNMENT HUH? WELL, WE'RE RUNNING SHORT OF VOLUNTEERS AT BLOOD DRIVE TODAY. IF YOU HAND OUT JUICE AND COOKIES, I'LL SIGN OFF ON YOUR FORM.
REALLY?!

☆ ☆ ☆

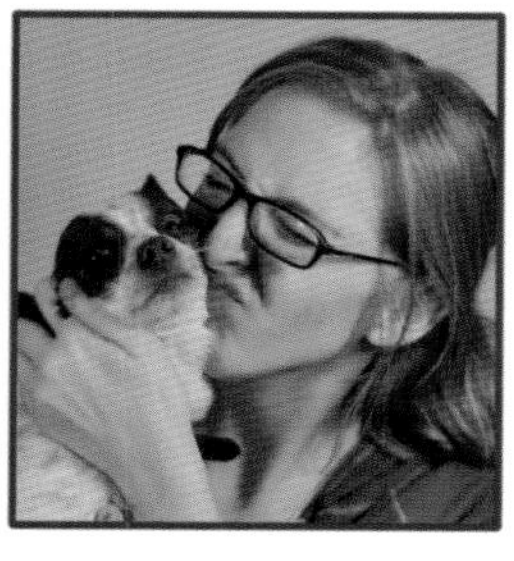

JORDIE BELLAIRE

SKILLS: Colorist
LOCATION: Brooklyn or Dublin
FUN FACT: Cappuccino admirer.

http://jordiecolorsthings.tumblr.com

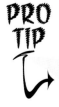

PRO TIP

DRESS
BY BARBARA KAALBERG

"WHEN MEETING A POSSIBLE EMPLOYER FOR AN INTERVIEW AT A CONVENTION, DRESS APPROPRIATELY. DO NOT DRESS IN COS-PLAY. DO NOT WEAR A TEE SHIRT ADVERTISING FROM A RIVAL COMPANY. DRESS CASUALLY BUT SMARTLY."

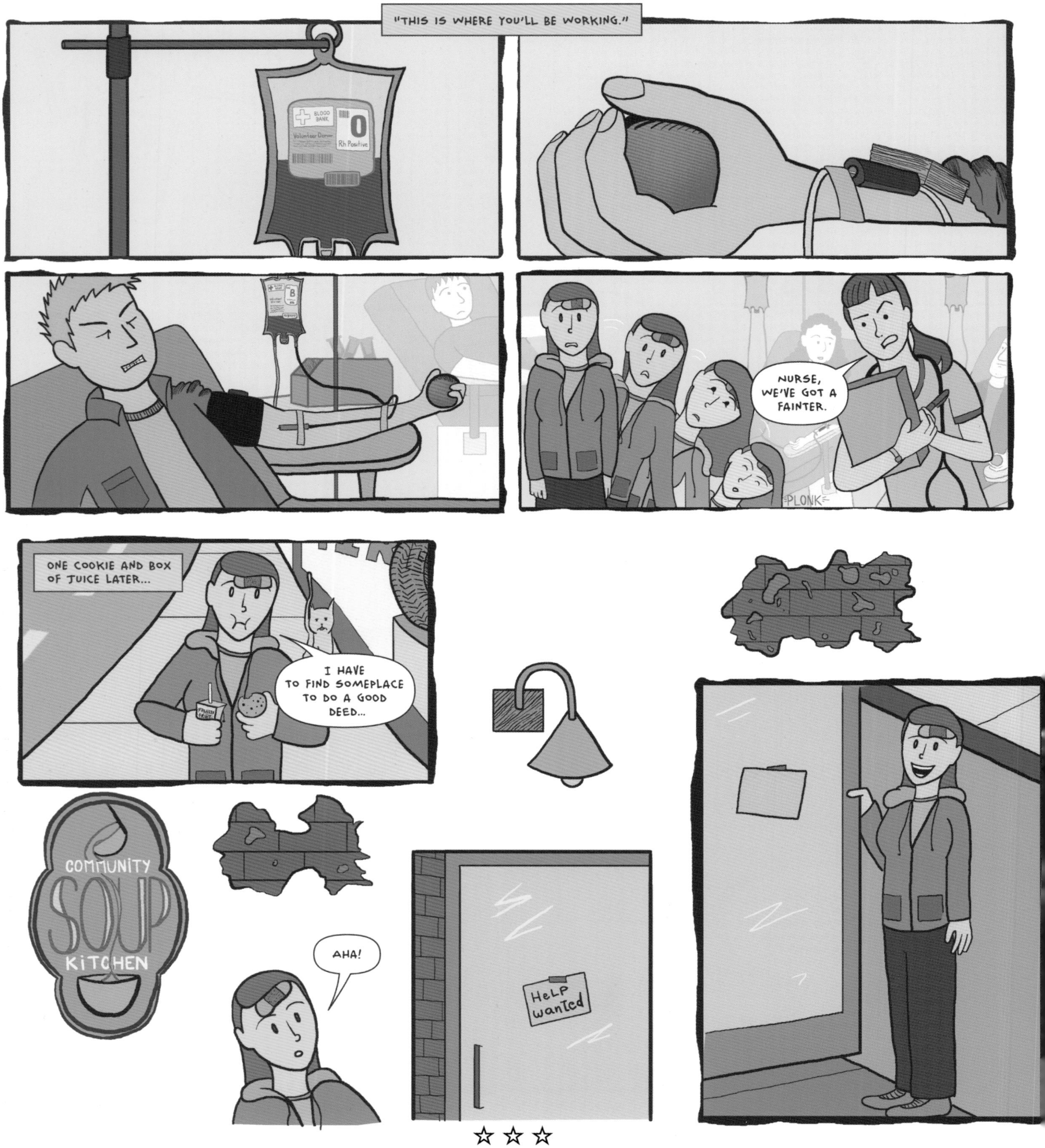
"THIS IS WHERE YOU'LL BE WORKING."
BLOOD BANK
0
Volunteer Donor
Rh Positive
NURSE, WE'VE GOT A FAINTER.
PLONK
ONE COOKIE AND BOX OF JUICE LATER...
I HAVE TO FIND SOMEPLACE TO DO A GOOD DEED...
COMMUNITY SOUP KITCHEN
AHA!
HeLP wanted

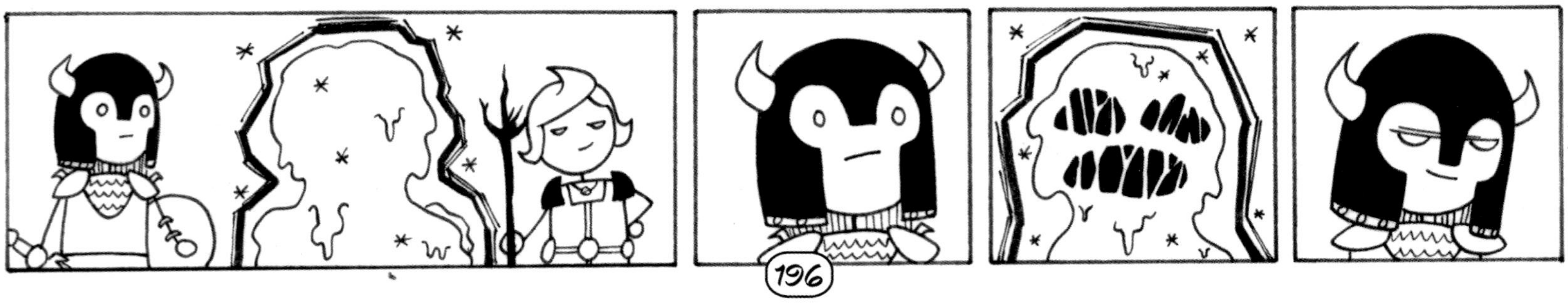

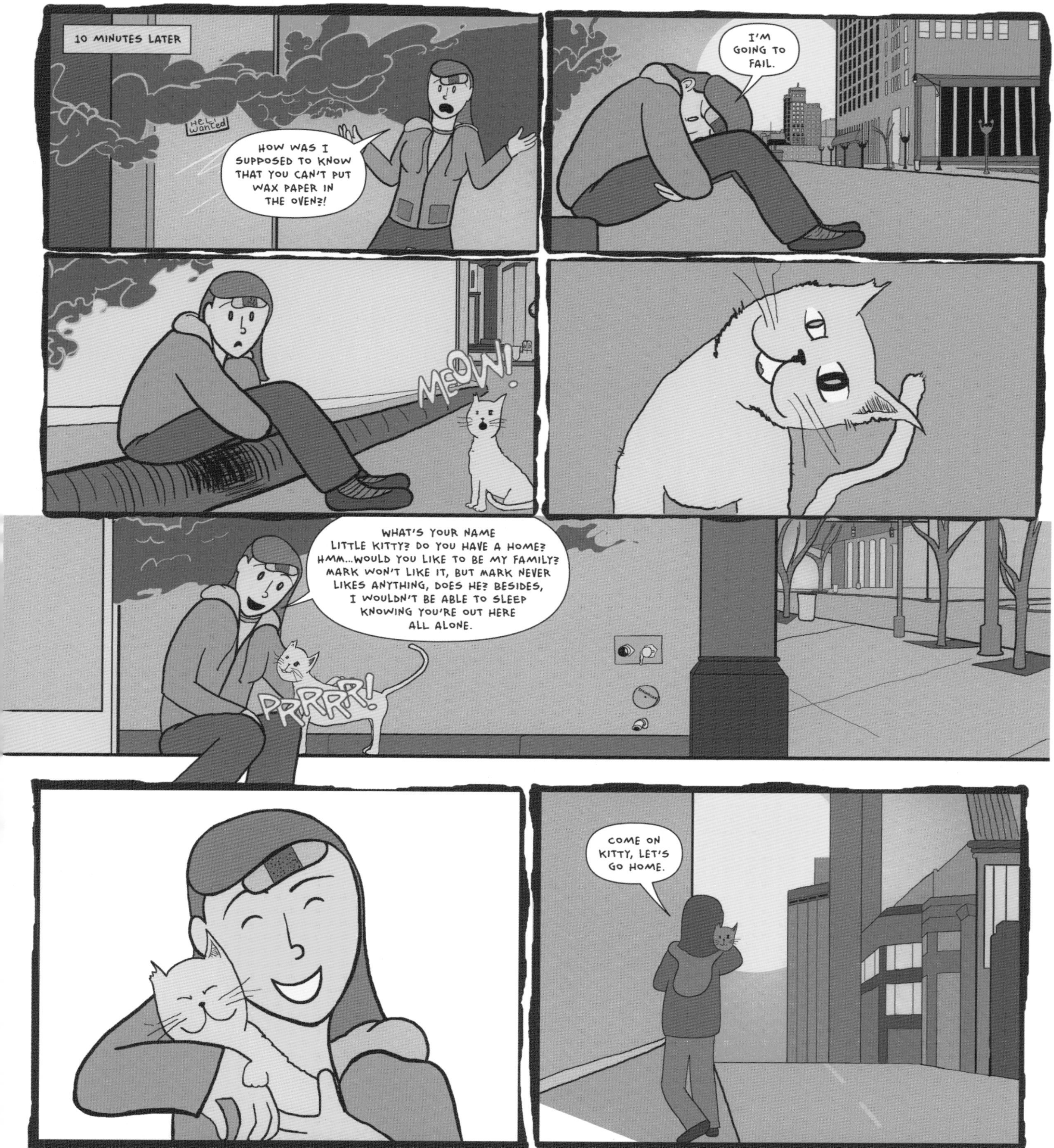
10 MINUTES LATER
HOW WAS I SUPPOSED TO KNOW THAT YOU CAN'T PUT WAX PAPER IN THE OVEN?!
I'M GOING TO FAIL.
MEOW!
WHAT'S YOUR NAME LITTLE KITTY? DO YOU HAVE A HOME? HMM...WOULD YOU LIKE TO BE MY FAMILY? MARK WON'T LIKE IT, BUT MARK NEVER LIKES ANYTHING, DOES HE? BESIDES, I WOULDN'T BE ABLE TO SLEEP KNOWING YOU'RE OUT HERE ALL ALONE.
PRRRR!
COME ON KITTY, LET'S GO HOME.

☆ ☆ ☆

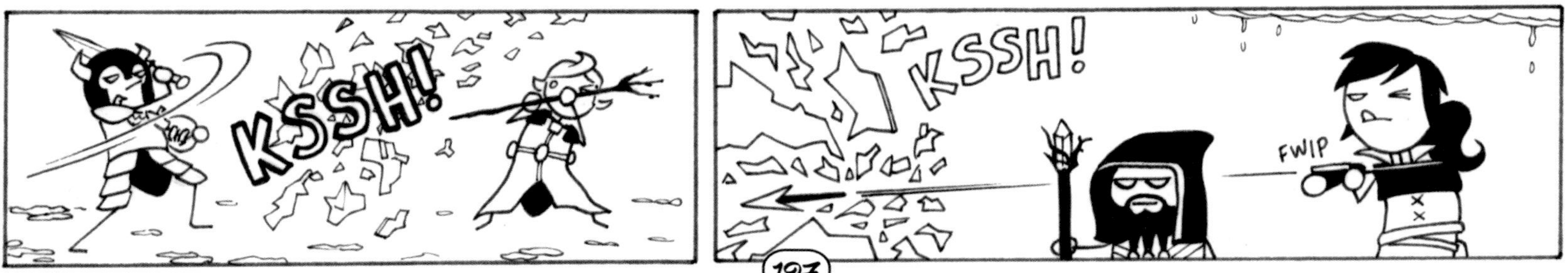
KSSH!
KSSH!
FWIP

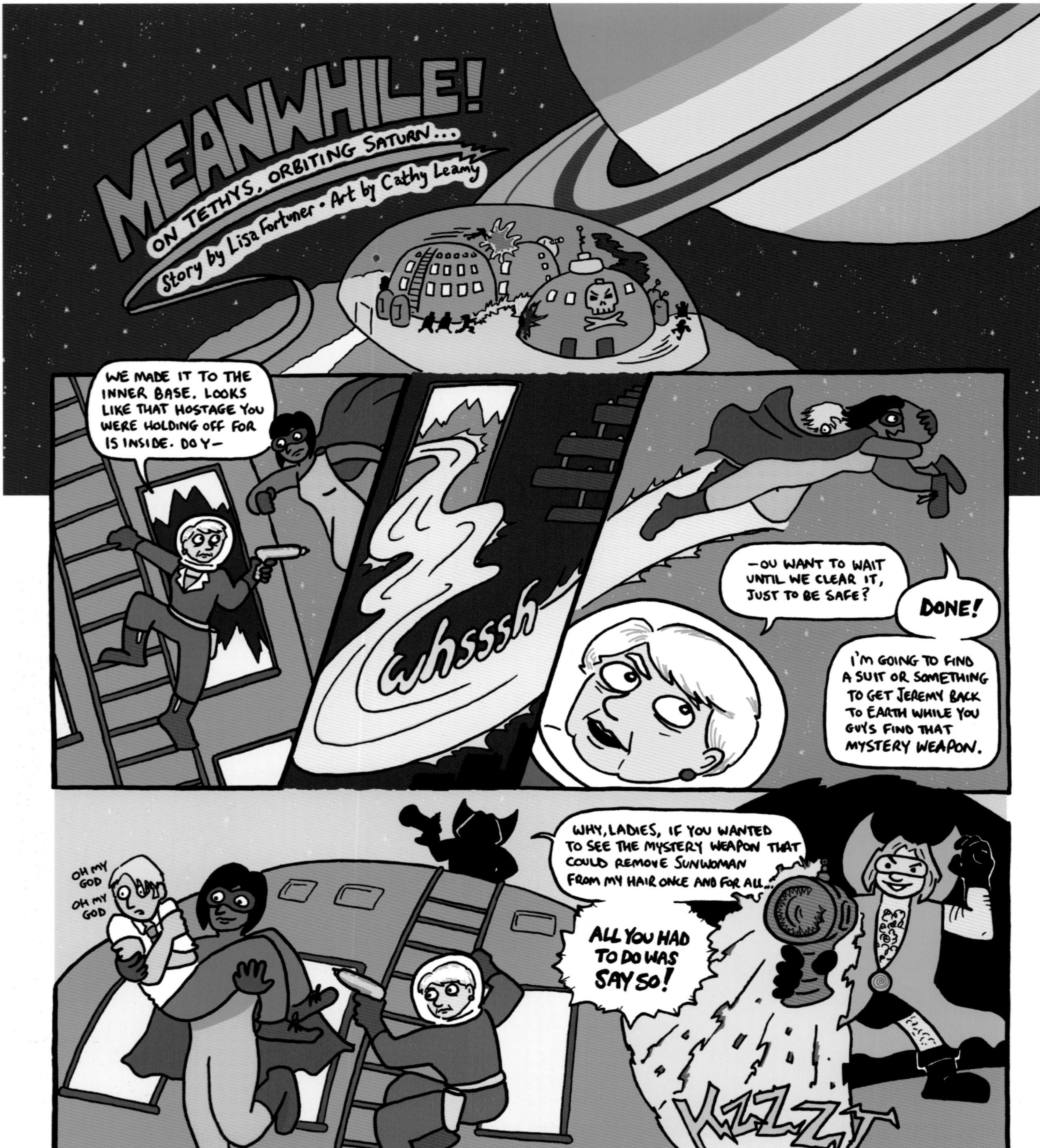

MEANWHILE!
ON TETHYS, ORBITING SATURN...
Story by Lisa Fortuner • Art by Cathy Leamy
WE MADE IT TO THE INNER BASE. LOOKS LIKE THAT HOSTAGE YOU WERE HOLDING OFF FOR IS INSIDE. DO Y—
whssssh
—OU WANT TO WAIT UNTIL WE CLEAR IT, JUST TO BE SAFE?
DONE!
I'M GOING TO FIND A SUIT OR SOMETHING TO GET JEREMY BACK TO EARTH WHILE YOU GUYS FIND THAT MYSTERY WEAPON.
OH MY GOD
OH MY GOD
WHY, LADIES, IF YOU WANTED TO SEE THE MYSTERY WEAPON THAT COULD REMOVE SUNWOMAN FROM MY HAIR ONCE AND FOR ALL...
ALL YOU HAD TO DO WAS SAY SO!
KZZZT

☆☆☆

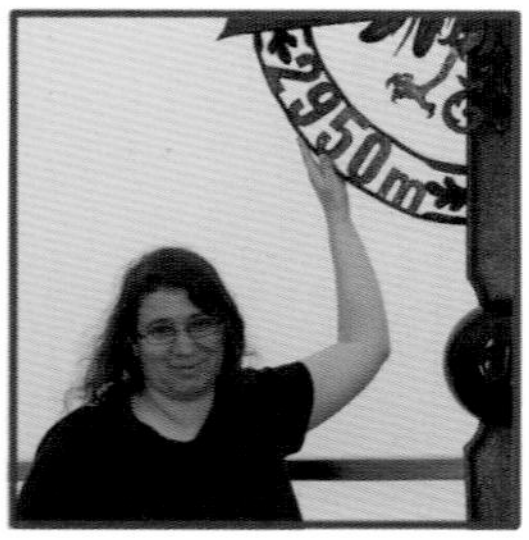

LISA FORTUNER

SKILLS: Writer
LOCATION: Kaiserslautern, Germany
FUN FACT: I can honestly say that I am more afraid to be caught inappropriately dressed than to be shot.

http://ragnell.blogspot.com

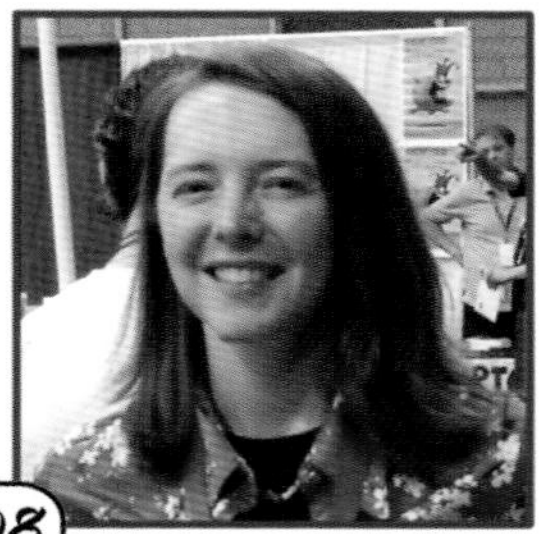

CATHY LEAMY

SKILLS: Artist
LOCATION: Boston, Massachusetts
FUN FACT: I can fox trot till the break of dawn!

http://www.metrokitty.com

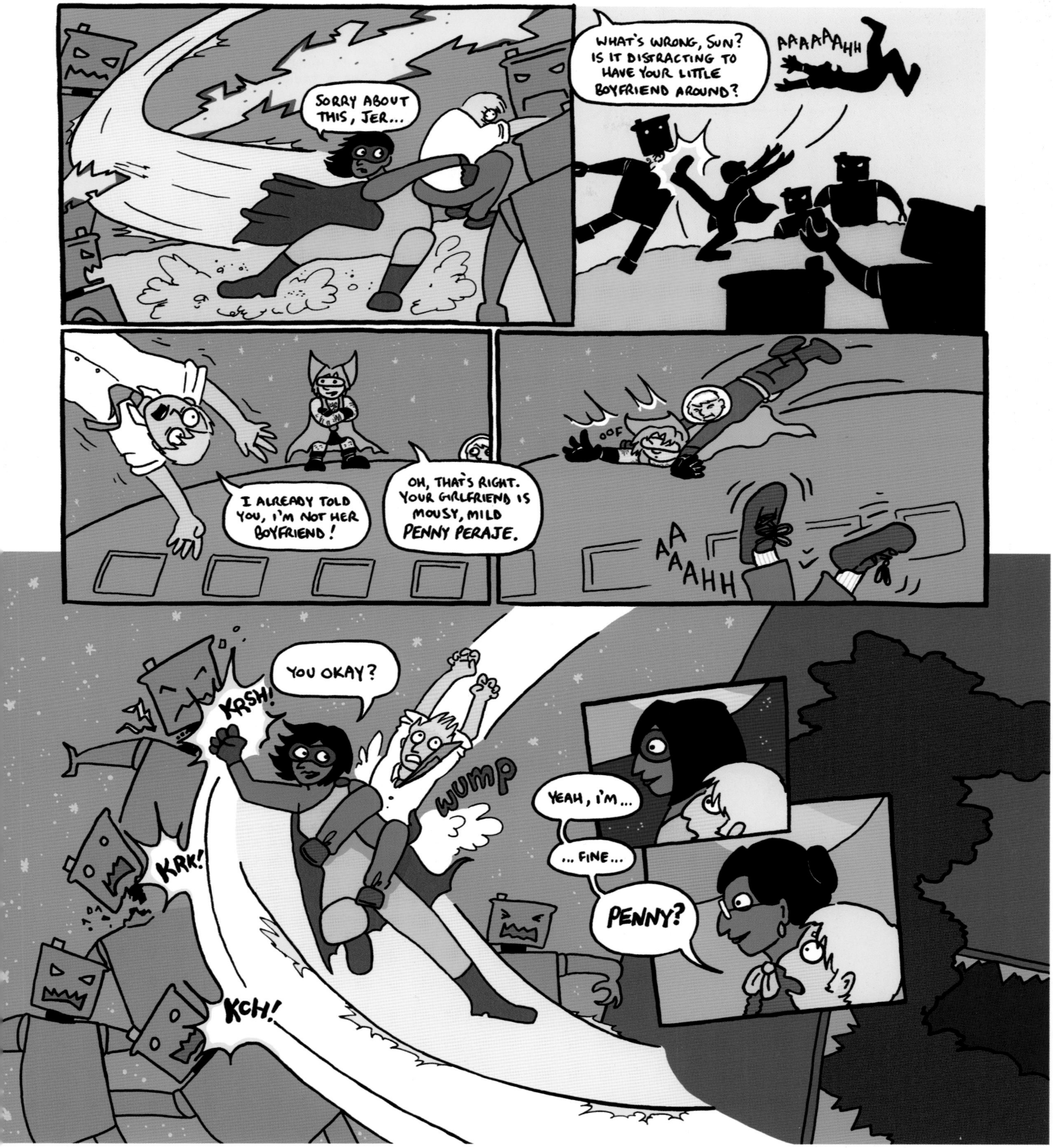
SORRY ABOUT THIS, JER...
WHAT'S WRONG, SUN? IS IT DISTRACTING TO HAVE YOUR LITTLE BOYFRIEND AROUND?
AAAAAAHH
I ALREADY TOLD YOU, I'M NOT HER BOYFRIEND!
OH, THAT'S RIGHT. YOUR GIRLFRIEND IS MOUSY, MILD PENNY PERAJE.
OOF
AAAAHH
YOU OKAY?
KRSH!
WUMP
KRK!
KCH!
YEAH, I'M...
... FINE...
PENNY?

☆ ☆ ☆

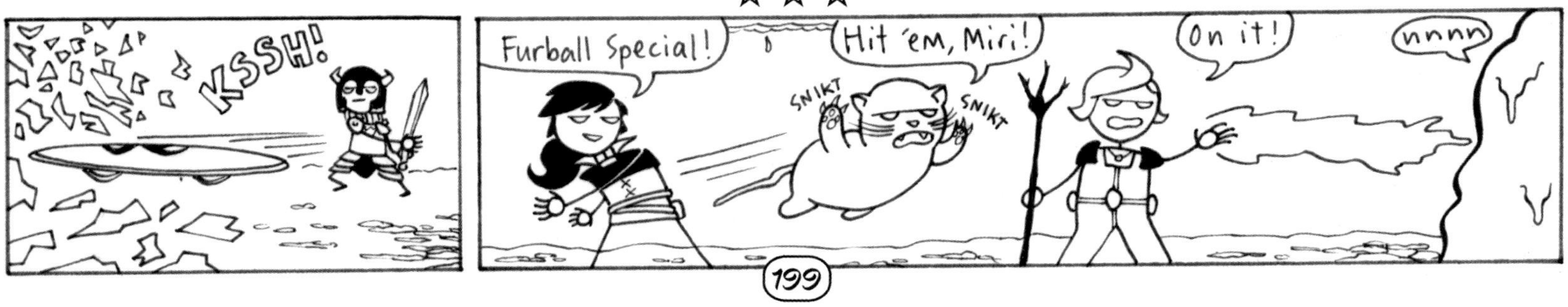
KSSH!
Furball Special!
Hit 'em, Miri!
SNIKT
SNIKT
On it!
nnnn

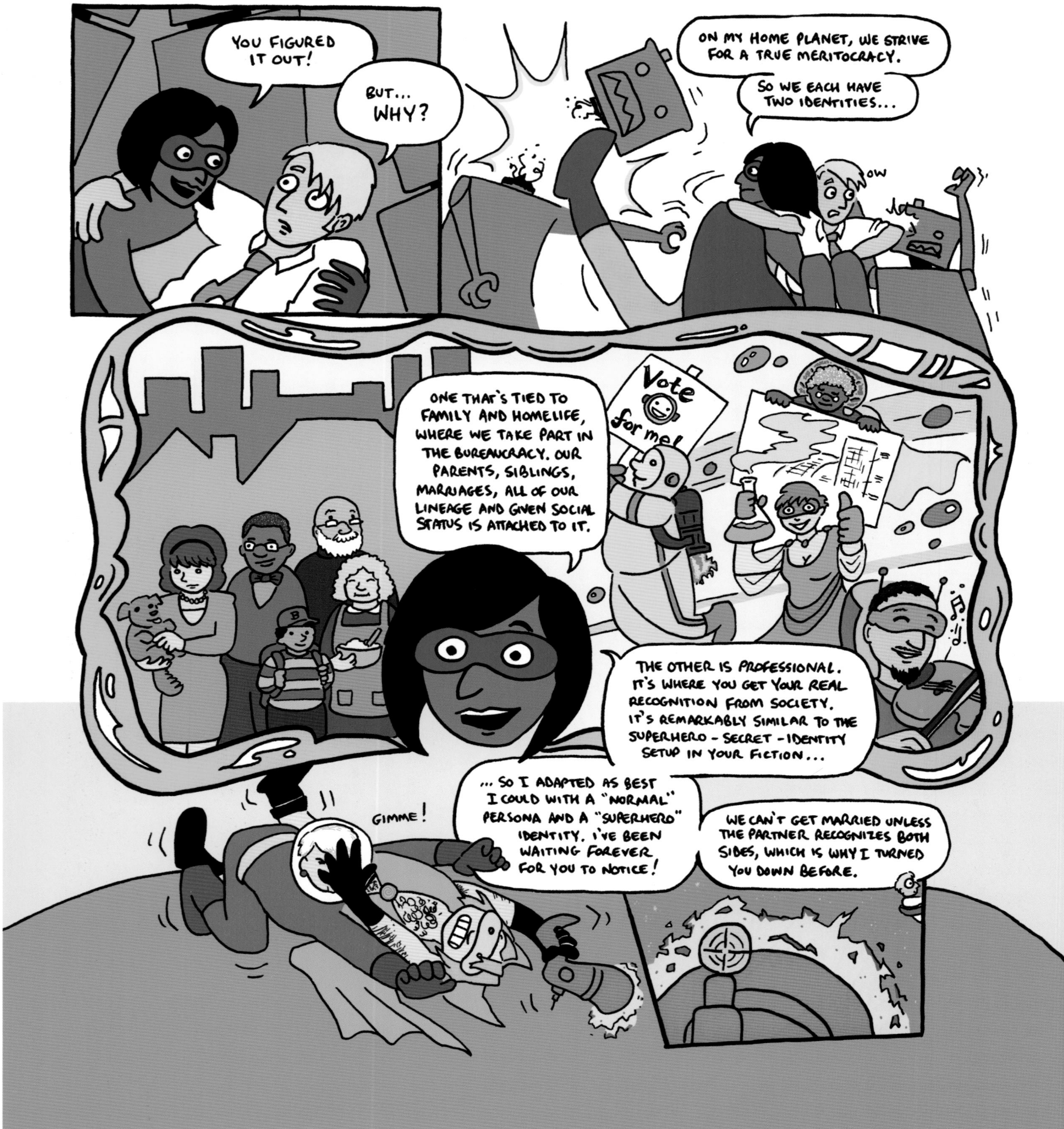
YOU FIGURED IT OUT!
BUT... WHY?
ON MY HOME PLANET, WE STRIVE FOR A TRUE MERITOCRACY.
SO WE EACH HAVE TWO IDENTITIES...
OW
Vote for me!
ONE THAT'S TIED TO FAMILY AND HOMELIFE, WHERE WE TAKE PART IN THE BUREAUCRACY. OUR PARENTS, SIBLINGS, MARRIAGES, ALL OF OUR LINEAGE AND GIVEN SOCIAL STATUS IS ATTACHED TO IT.
THE OTHER IS *PROFESSIONAL*. IT'S WHERE YOU GET YOUR REAL RECOGNITION FROM SOCIETY. IT'S REMARKABLY SIMILAR TO THE SUPERHERO - SECRET - IDENTITY SETUP IN YOUR FICTION...
... SO I ADAPTED AS BEST I COULD WITH A "NORMAL" PERSONA AND A "SUPERHERO" IDENTITY. I'VE BEEN WAITING FOREVER FOR YOU TO NOTICE!
GIMME!
WE CAN'T GET MARRIED UNLESS THE PARTNER RECOGNIZES BOTH SIDES, WHICH IS WHY I TURNED YOU DOWN BEFORE.

☆ ☆ ☆

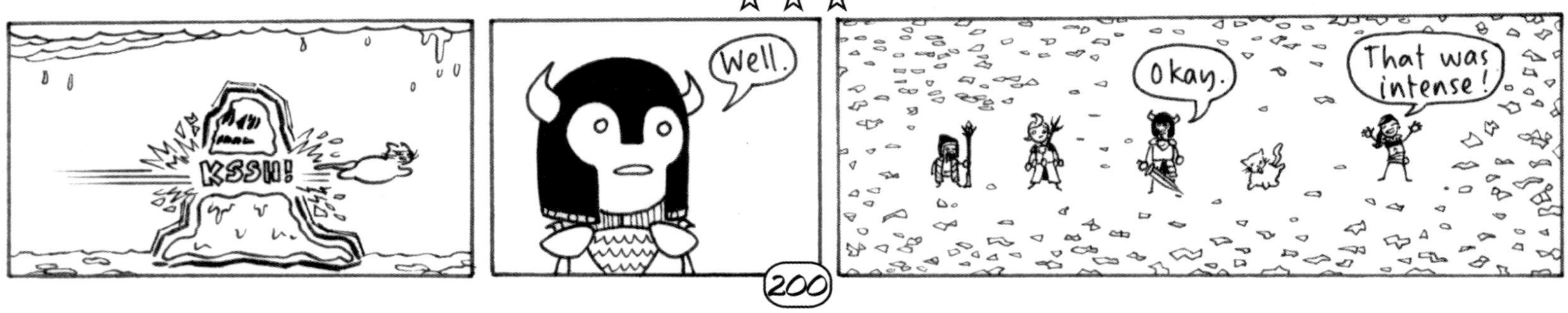
KSSH!
Well.
Okay.
That was intense!

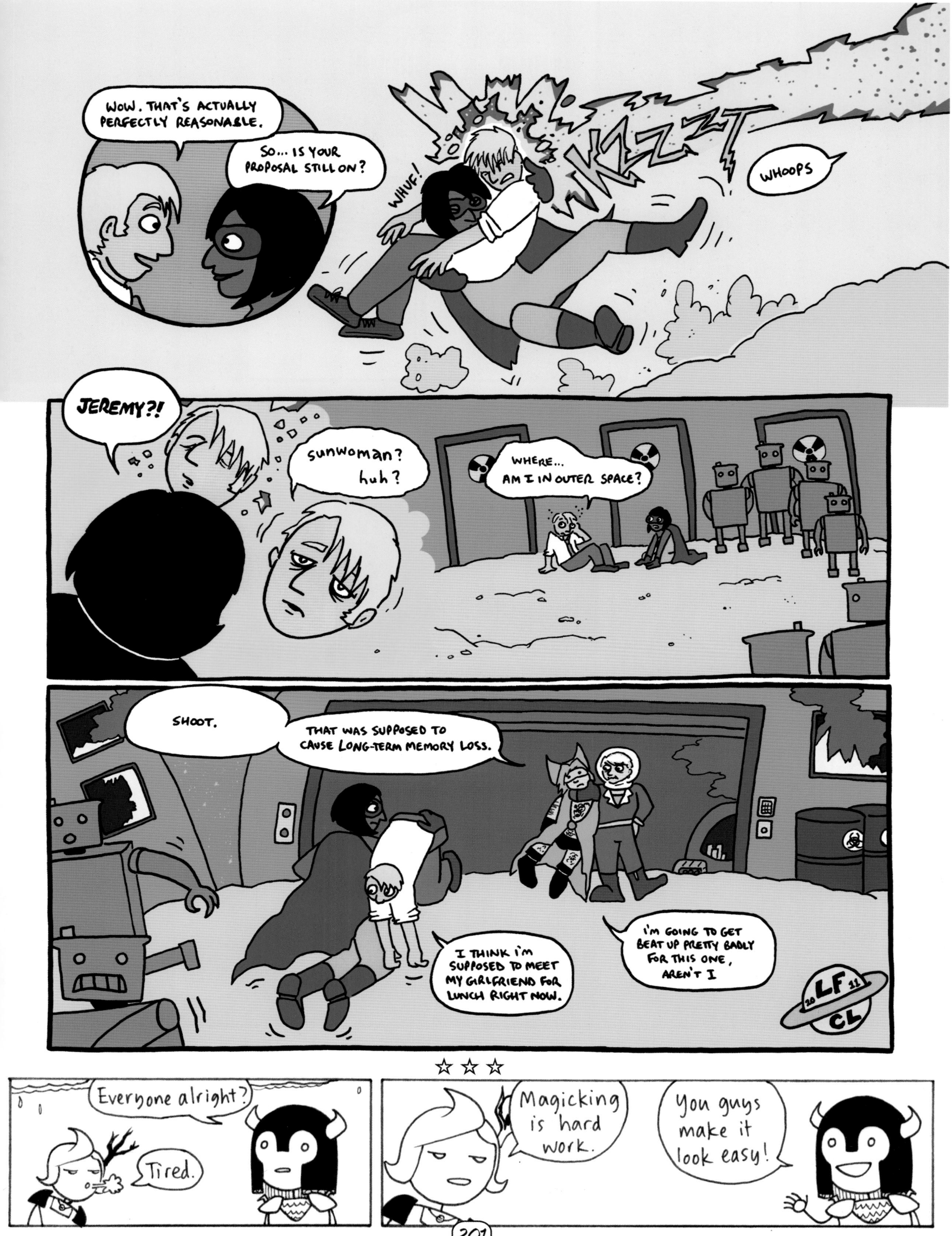
WOW. THAT'S ACTUALLY PERFECTLY REASONABLE.
SO... IS YOUR PROPOSAL STILL ON?
WHUF!
KZZZT
WHOOPS
JEREMY?!
sunwoman? huh?
WHERE... AM I IN OUTER SPACE?
SHOOT.
THAT WAS SUPPOSED TO CAUSE LONG-TERM MEMORY LOSS.
I THINK I'M SUPPOSED TO MEET MY GIRLFRIEND FOR LUNCH RIGHT NOW.
I'M GOING TO GET BEAT UP PRETTY BADLY FOR THIS ONE, AREN'T I
20 LF 11 CL
☆ ☆ ☆
Everyone alright?
Tired.
Magicking is hard work.
You guys make it look easy!

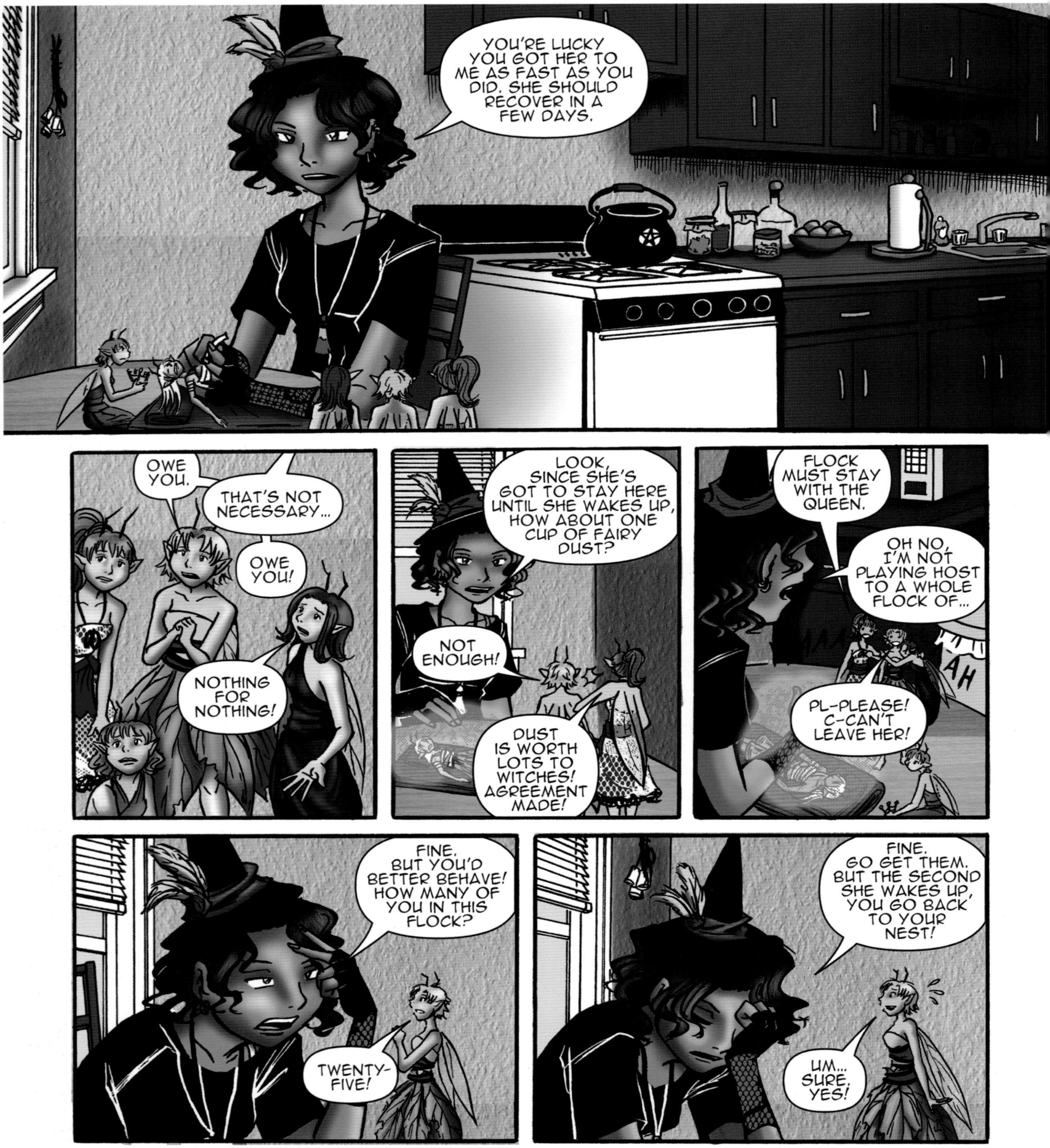

YOU'RE LUCKY YOU GOT HER TO ME AS FAST AS YOU DID. SHE SHOULD RECOVER IN A FEW DAYS.
OWE YOU.
THAT'S NOT NECESSARY...
OWE YOU!
NOTHING FOR NOTHING!
LOOK, SINCE SHE'S GOT TO STAY HERE UNTIL SHE WAKES UP, HOW ABOUT ONE CUP OF FAIRY DUST?
NOT ENOUGH!
DUST IS WORTH LOTS TO WITCHES! AGREEMENT MADE!
FLOCK MUST STAY WITH THE QUEEN.
OH NO, I'M NOT PLAYING HOST TO A WHOLE FLOCK OF...
AH
PL-PLEASE! C-CAN'T LEAVE HER!
FINE. BUT YOU'D BETTER BEHAVE! HOW MANY OF YOU IN THIS FLOCK?
TWENTY-FIVE!
FINE. GO GET THEM. BUT THE SECOND SHE WAKES UP, YOU GO BACK TO YOUR NEST!
UM... SURE, YES!

WRITER: KENDRA PAPE-GREEN   ARTIST: VANESSA SATONE   COLORIST: KIMBERLY ANN BLACK   LETTERER: RACHEL DEERING

☆ ☆ ☆

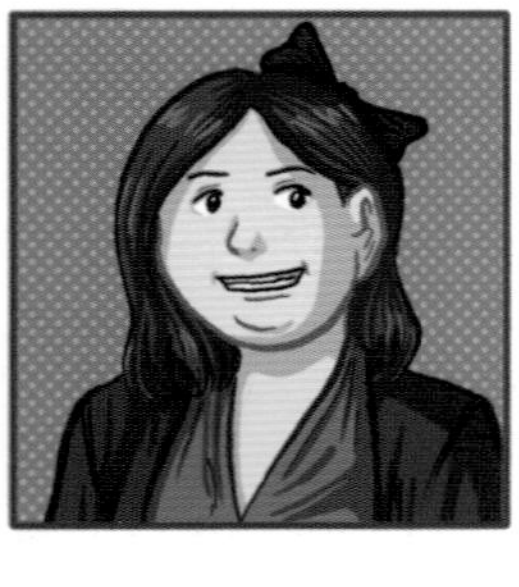

KENDRA PAPE-GREEN

SKILLS: Writer
LOCATION: Ontario
FUN FACT: I usually talk too much, and a bit too fast. But I always try and have interesting things to say!

www.popcornpatter.blogspot.com

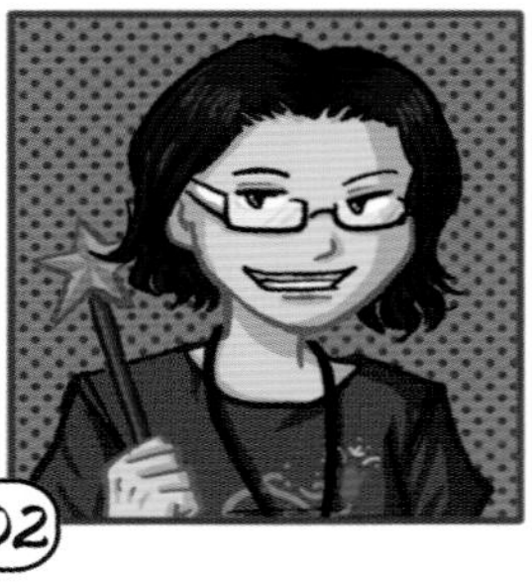

VANESSA SATONE

SKILLS: Penciller, Inker
LOCATION: Brooklyn, NY
FUN FACT: I have self-published four graphic novels and several mini comics.

http://visforvacant.com

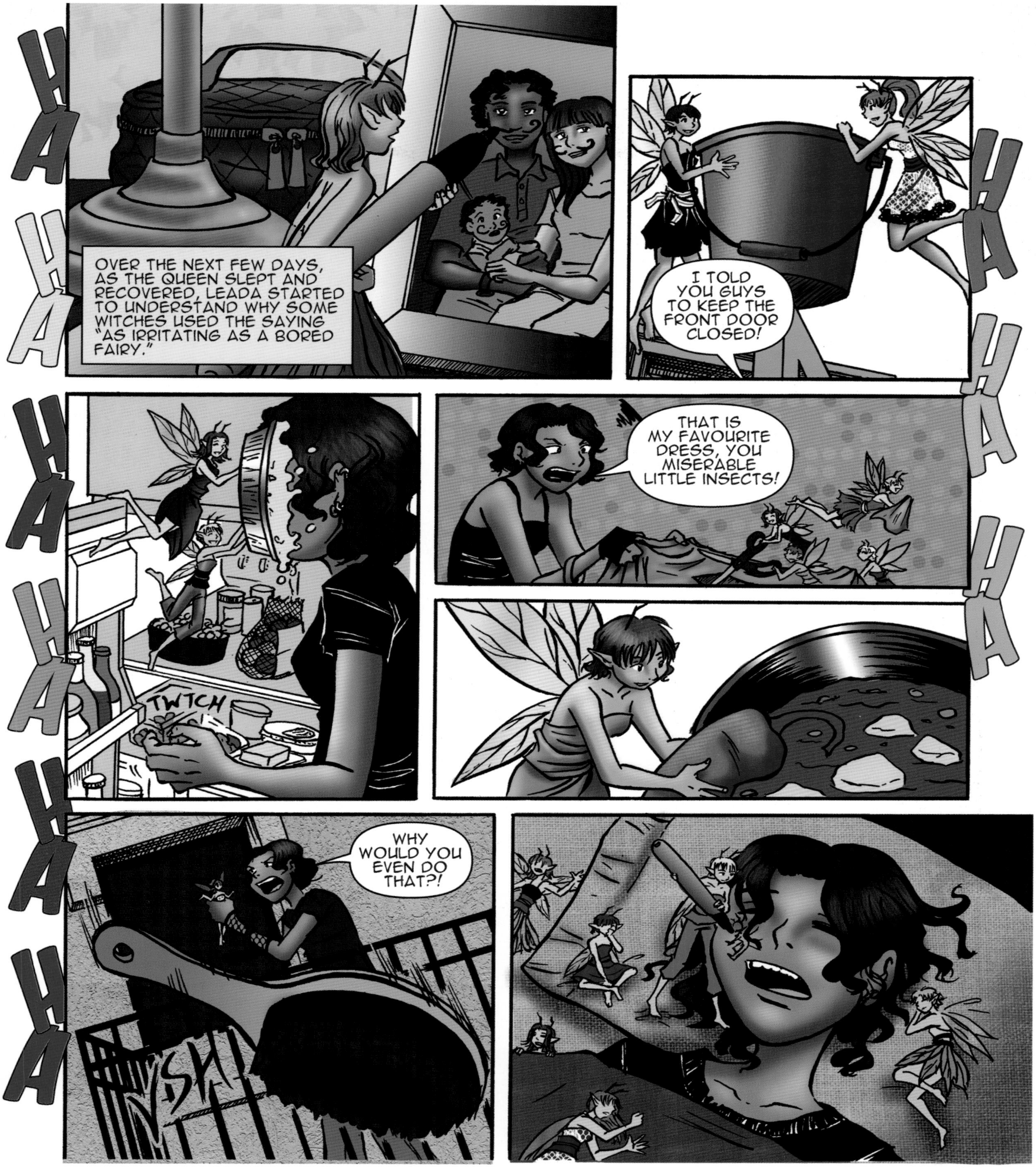
HAHAHA
OVER THE NEXT FEW DAYS, AS THE QUEEN SLEPT AND RECOVERED, LEADA STARTED TO UNDERSTAND WHY SOME WITCHES USED THE SAYING "AS IRRITATING AS A BORED FAIRY."
I TOLD YOU GUYS TO KEEP THE FRONT DOOR CLOSED!
HAHAHA
HAHAHAHAHA
TWTCH
THAT IS MY FAVOURITE DRESS, YOU MISERABLE LITTLE INSECTS!
HAHAHA
WHY WOULD YOU EVEN DO THAT?!
SH

☆☆☆

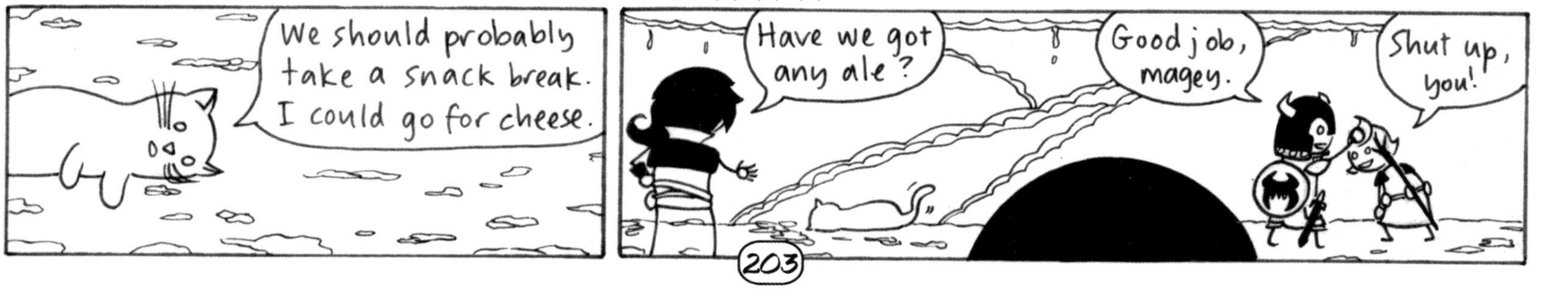
We should probably take a snack break. I could go for cheese.
Have we got any ale?
Good job, magey.
Shut up, you!

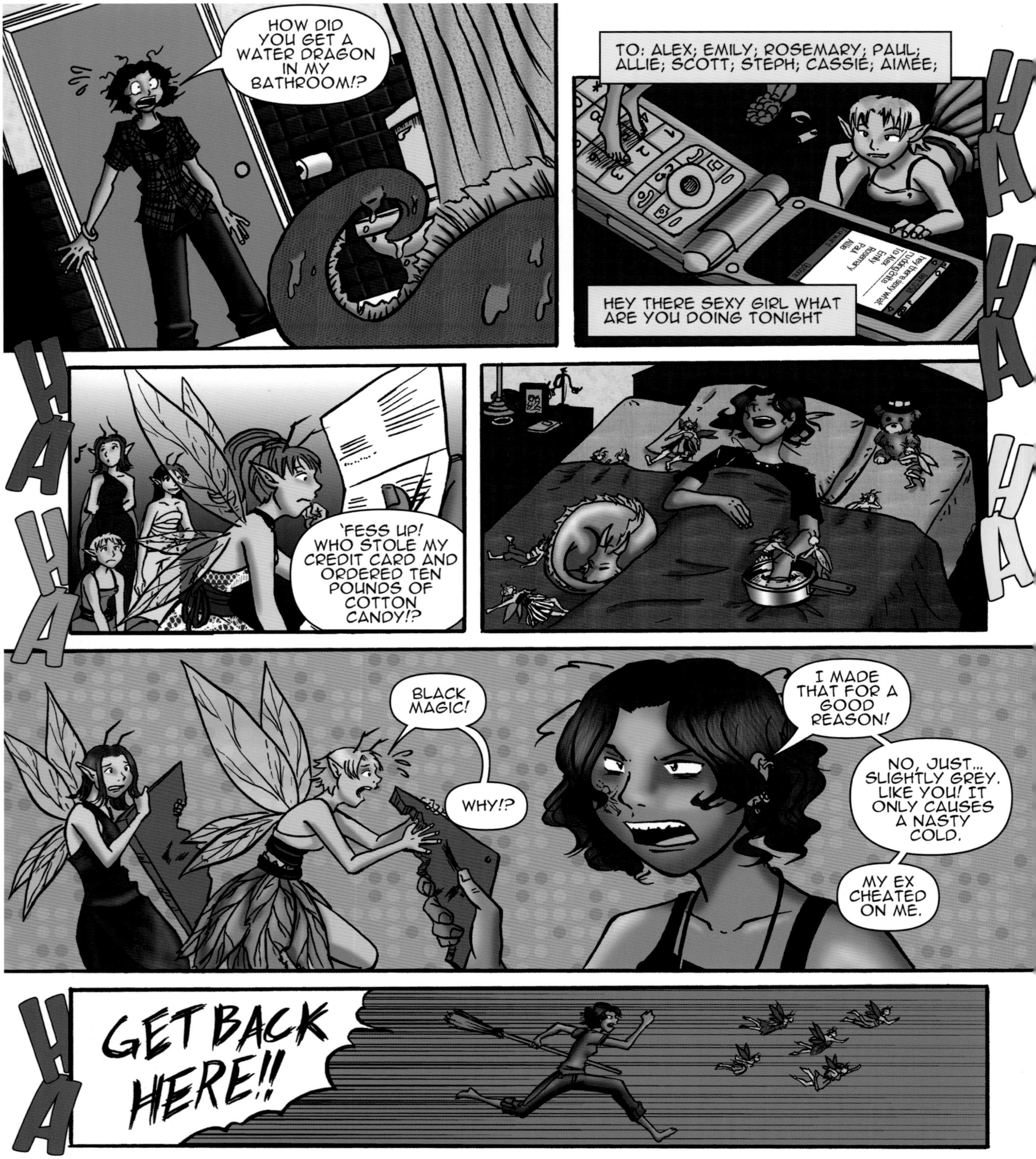
HOW DID YOU GET A WATER DRAGON IN MY BATHROOM!?
TO: ALEX; EMILY; ROSEMARY; PAUL; ALLIE; SCOTT; STEPH; CASSIE; AIMÉE;
HEY THERE SEXY GIRL WHAT ARE YOU DOING TONIGHT
HAHAHA
HAHAHA
'FESS UP! WHO STOLE MY CREDIT CARD AND ORDERED TEN POUNDS OF COTTON CANDY!?
BLACK MAGIC!
WHY!?
I MADE THAT FOR A GOOD REASON!
NO, JUST... SLIGHTLY GREY. LIKE YOU! IT ONLY CAUSES A NASTY COLD.
MY EX CHEATED ON ME.
HA
GET BACK HERE!!

☆ ☆ ☆

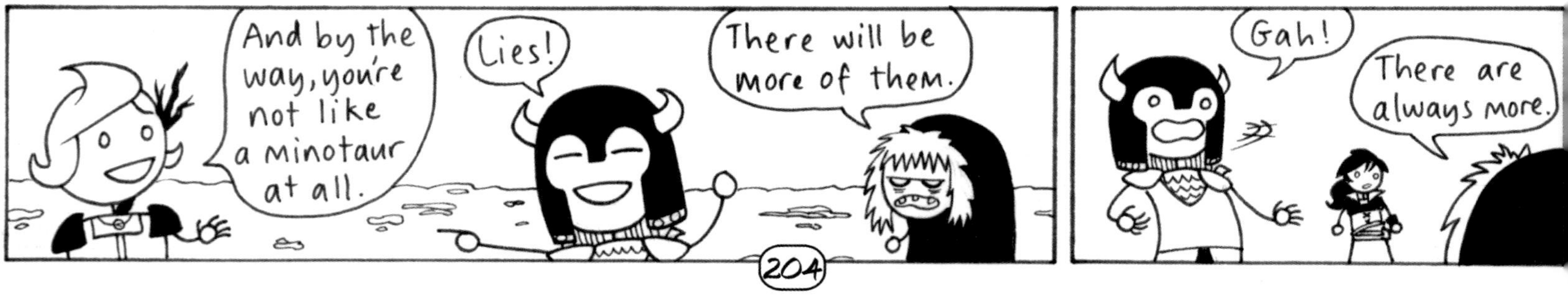
And by the way, you're not like a minotaur at all.
Lies!
There will be more of them.
Gah!
There are always more.

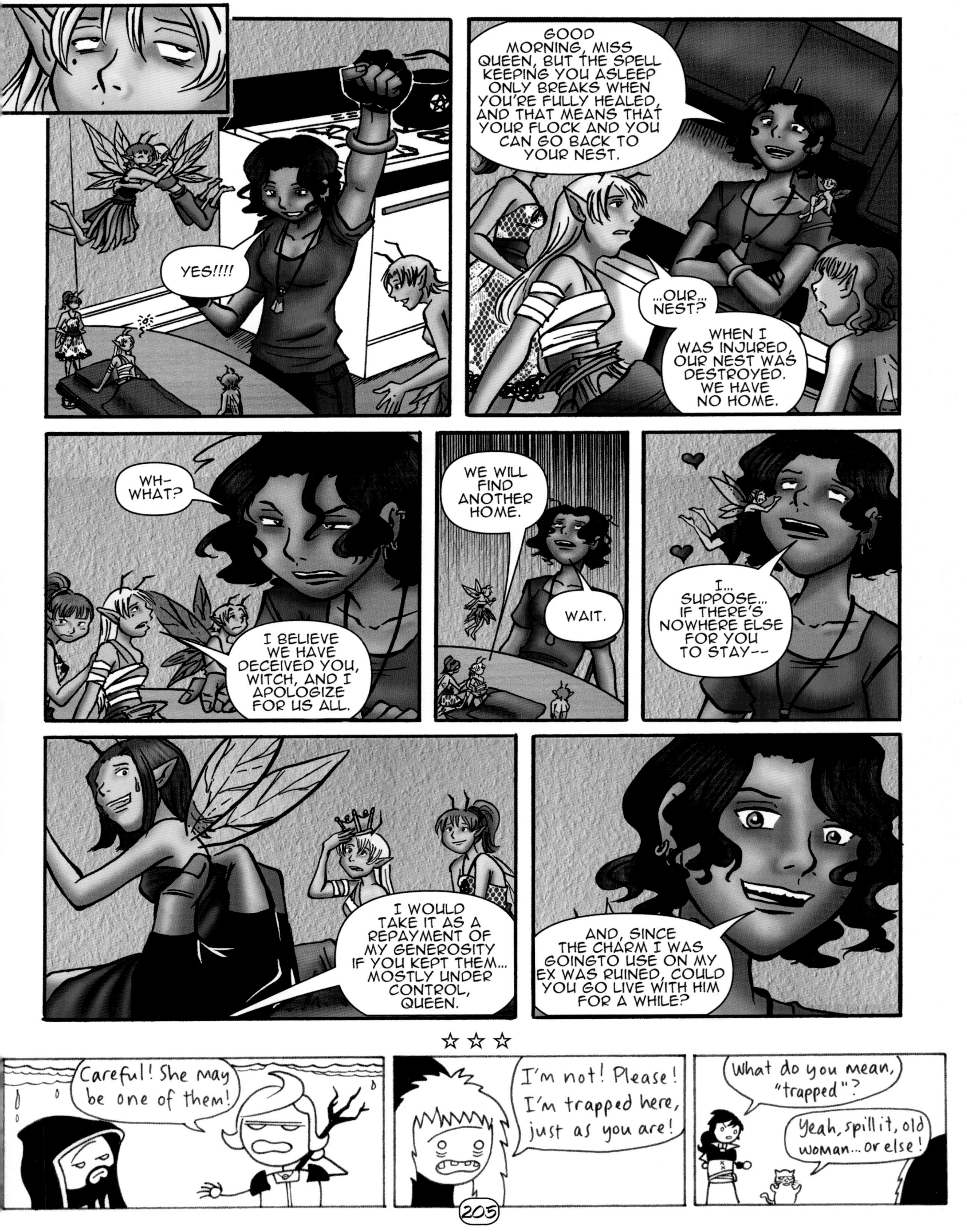
YES!!!!
GOOD MORNING, MISS QUEEN, BUT THE SPELL KEEPING YOU ASLEEP ONLY BREAKS WHEN YOU'RE FULLY HEALED, AND THAT MEANS THAT YOUR FLOCK AND YOU CAN GO BACK TO YOUR NEST.
...OUR... NEST?
WHEN I WAS INJURED, OUR NEST WAS DESTROYED. WE HAVE NO HOME.
WH-WHAT?
I BELIEVE WE HAVE DECEIVED YOU, WITCH, AND I APOLOGIZE FOR US ALL.
WE WILL FIND ANOTHER HOME.
WAIT.
I... SUPPOSE... IF THERE'S NOWHERE ELSE FOR YOU TO STAY--
I WOULD TAKE IT AS A REPAYMENT OF MY GENEROSITY IF YOU KEPT THEM... MOSTLY UNDER CONTROL, QUEEN.
AND, SINCE THE CHARM I WAS GOINGTO USE ON MY EX WAS RUINED, COULD YOU GO LIVE WITH HIM FOR A WHILE?
☆ ☆ ☆
Careful! She may be one of them!
I'm not! Please! I'm trapped here, just as you are!
What do you mean, "trapped"?
Yeah, spill it, old woman... or else!

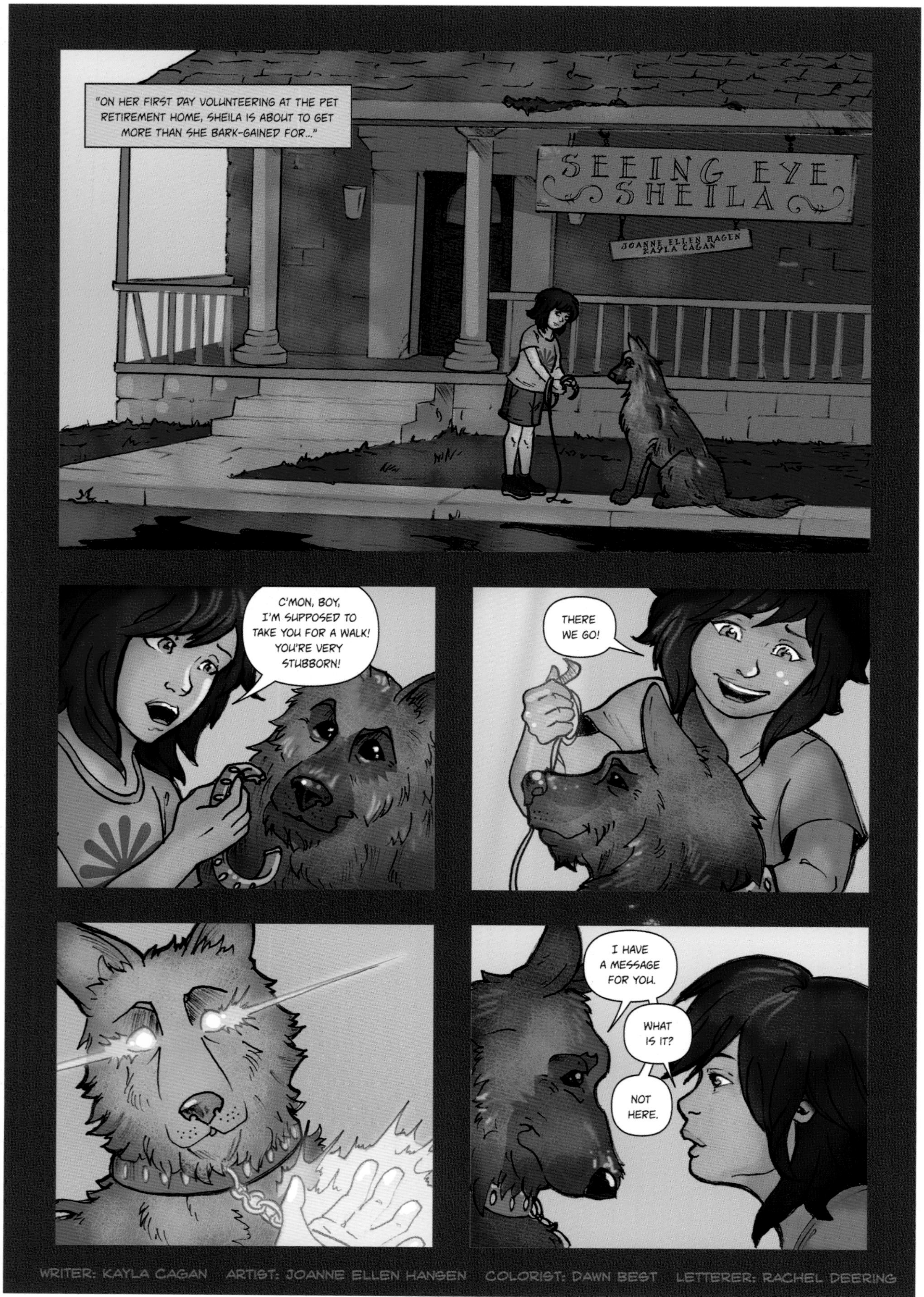
"ON HER FIRST DAY VOLUNTEERING AT THE PET RETIREMENT HOME, SHEILA IS ABOUT TO GET MORE THAN SHE BARK-GAINED FOR..."
SEEING EYE SHEILA
JOANNE ELLEN HAGEN KAYLA CAGAN
C'MON, BOY, I'M SUPPOSED TO TAKE YOU FOR A WALK! YOU'RE VERY STUBBORN!
THERE WE GO!
I HAVE A MESSAGE FOR YOU.
WHAT IS IT?
NOT HERE.
WRITER: KAYLA CAGAN ARTIST: JOANNE ELLEN HANSEN COLORIST: DAWN BEST LETTERER: RACHEL DEERING

☆☆☆

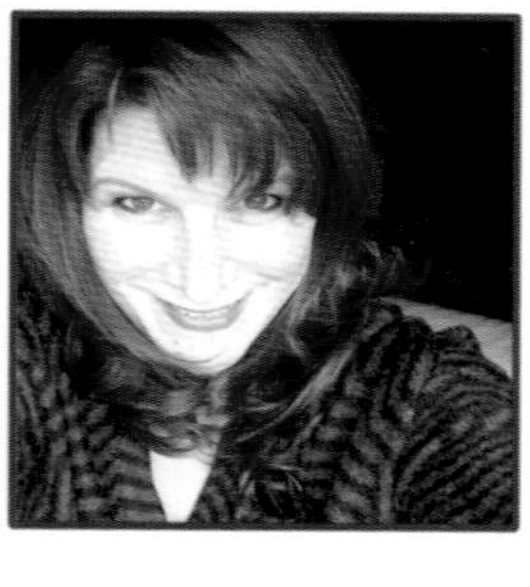

KAYLA CAGAN

SKILLS: Writer
LOCATION: Los Angeles, CA
FUN FACT: I have never baked a cake from scratch.

http://about.me/kaylacagan

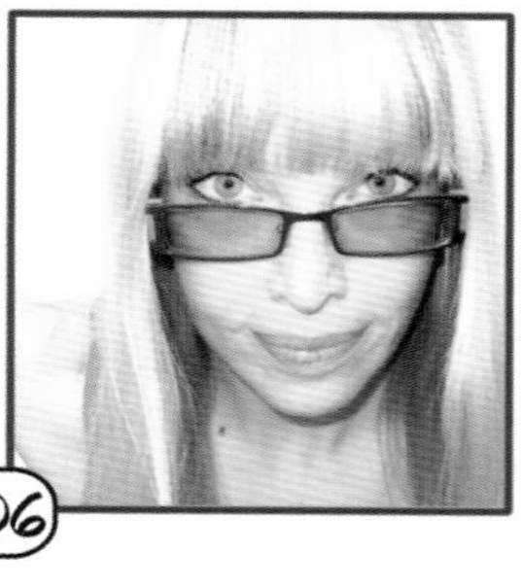

JOANNE ELLEN HANSEN

SKILLS: Penciller
LOCATION: Ontario, Canada
FUN FACT: I am a Personal Trainer Specialist by trade, but have published four independant comic books and created the covers for many more.

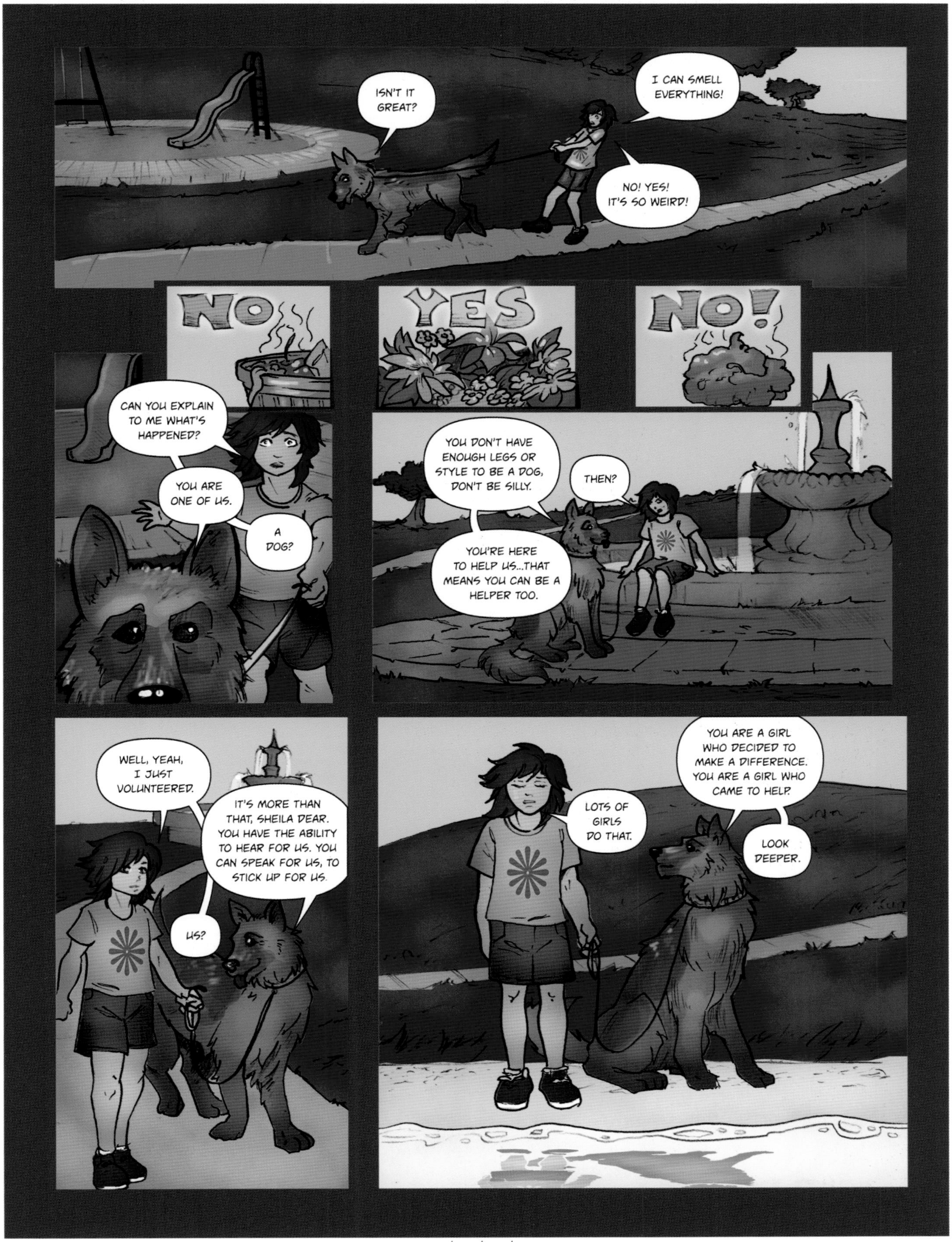
ISN'T IT GREAT?
I CAN SMELL EVERYTHING!
NO! YES! IT'S SO WEIRD!
NO
YES
NO!
CAN YOU EXPLAIN TO ME WHAT'S HAPPENED?
YOU ARE ONE OF US.
A DOG?
YOU DON'T HAVE ENOUGH LEGS OR STYLE TO BE A DOG, DON'T BE SILLY.
THEN?
YOU'RE HERE TO HELP US...THAT MEANS YOU CAN BE A HELPER TOO.
WELL, YEAH, I JUST VOLUNTEERED.
IT'S MORE THAN THAT, SHEILA DEAR. YOU HAVE THE ABILITY TO HEAR FOR US. YOU CAN SPEAK FOR US, TO STICK UP FOR US.
US?
LOTS OF GIRLS DO THAT.
YOU ARE A GIRL WHO DECIDED TO MAKE A DIFFERENCE. YOU ARE A GIRL WHO CAME TO HELP.
LOOK DEEPER.

☆☆☆

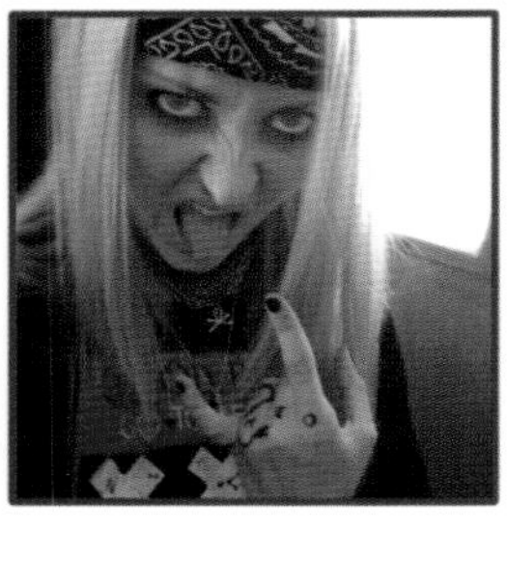

DAWN BEST

SKILLS: Inker, Colorist
LOCATION: Columbus, OH
FUN FACT: Not the best artist in the world - just the busiest!

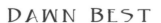

http://www.dawnbest.com

PRO TIP

CRITICISM
BY STACIE PONDER

"REMEMBER THAT CRITICISM IS ABOUT THE WORK, NOT ABOUT YOU PERSONALLY. THERE'S ALWAYS ROOM FOR IMPROVEMENT."

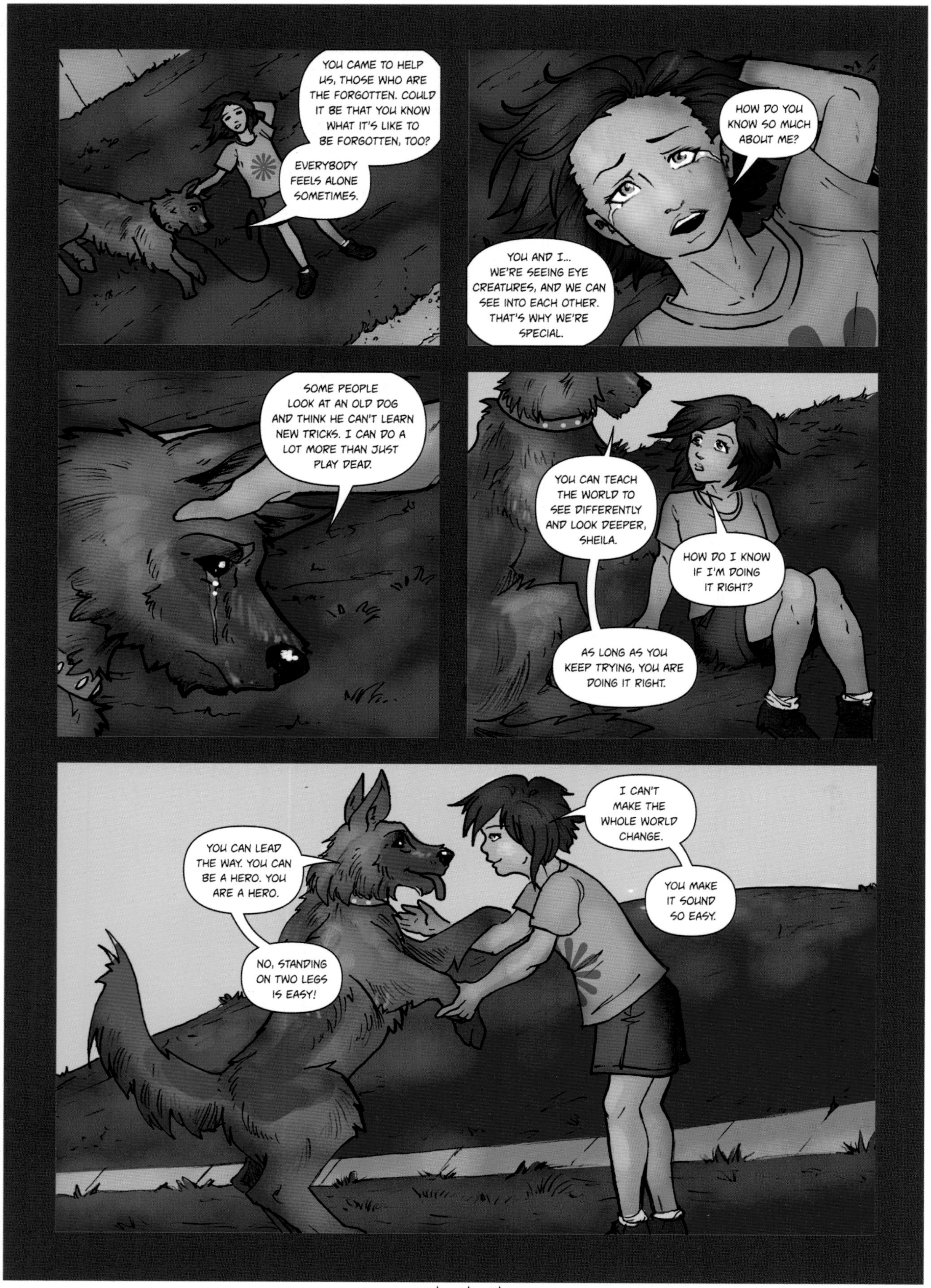
YOU CAME TO HELP US, THOSE WHO ARE THE FORGOTTEN. COULD IT BE THAT YOU KNOW WHAT IT'S LIKE TO BE FORGOTTEN, TOO?
EVERYBODY FEELS ALONE SOMETIMES.
HOW DO YOU KNOW SO MUCH ABOUT ME?
YOU AND I... WE'RE SEEING EYE CREATURES, AND WE CAN SEE INTO EACH OTHER. THAT'S WHY WE'RE SPECIAL.
SOME PEOPLE LOOK AT AN OLD DOG AND THINK HE CAN'T LEARN NEW TRICKS. I CAN DO A LOT MORE THAN JUST PLAY DEAD.
YOU CAN TEACH THE WORLD TO SEE DIFFERENTLY AND LOOK DEEPER, SHEILA.
HOW DO I KNOW IF I'M DOING IT RIGHT?
AS LONG AS YOU KEEP TRYING, YOU ARE DOING IT RIGHT.
I CAN'T MAKE THE WHOLE WORLD CHANGE.
YOU MAKE IT SOUND SO EASY.
YOU CAN LEAD THE WAY. YOU CAN BE A HERO. YOU ARE A HERO.
NO, STANDING ON TWO LEGS IS EASY!

☆ ☆ ☆

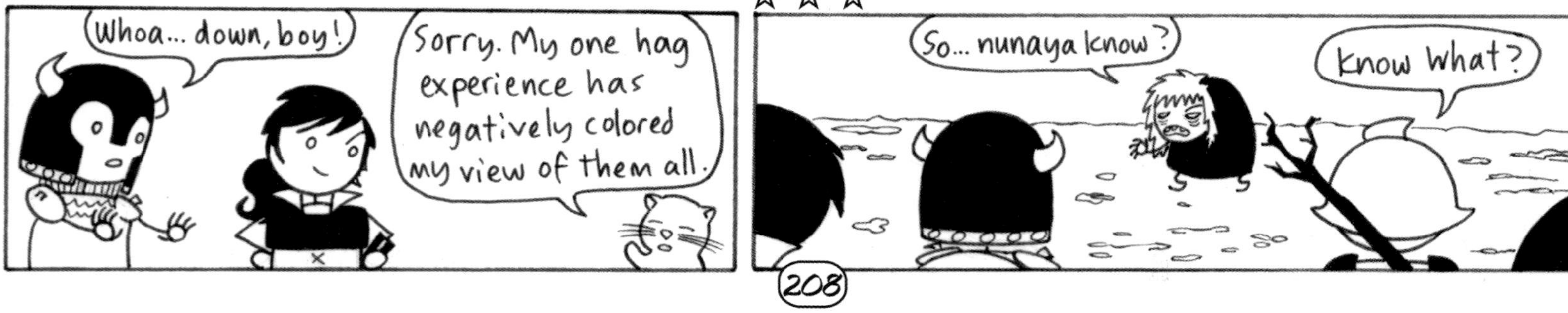
Whoa... down, boy!
Sorry. My one hag experience has negatively colored my view of them all.
So... nunaya know?
Know What?

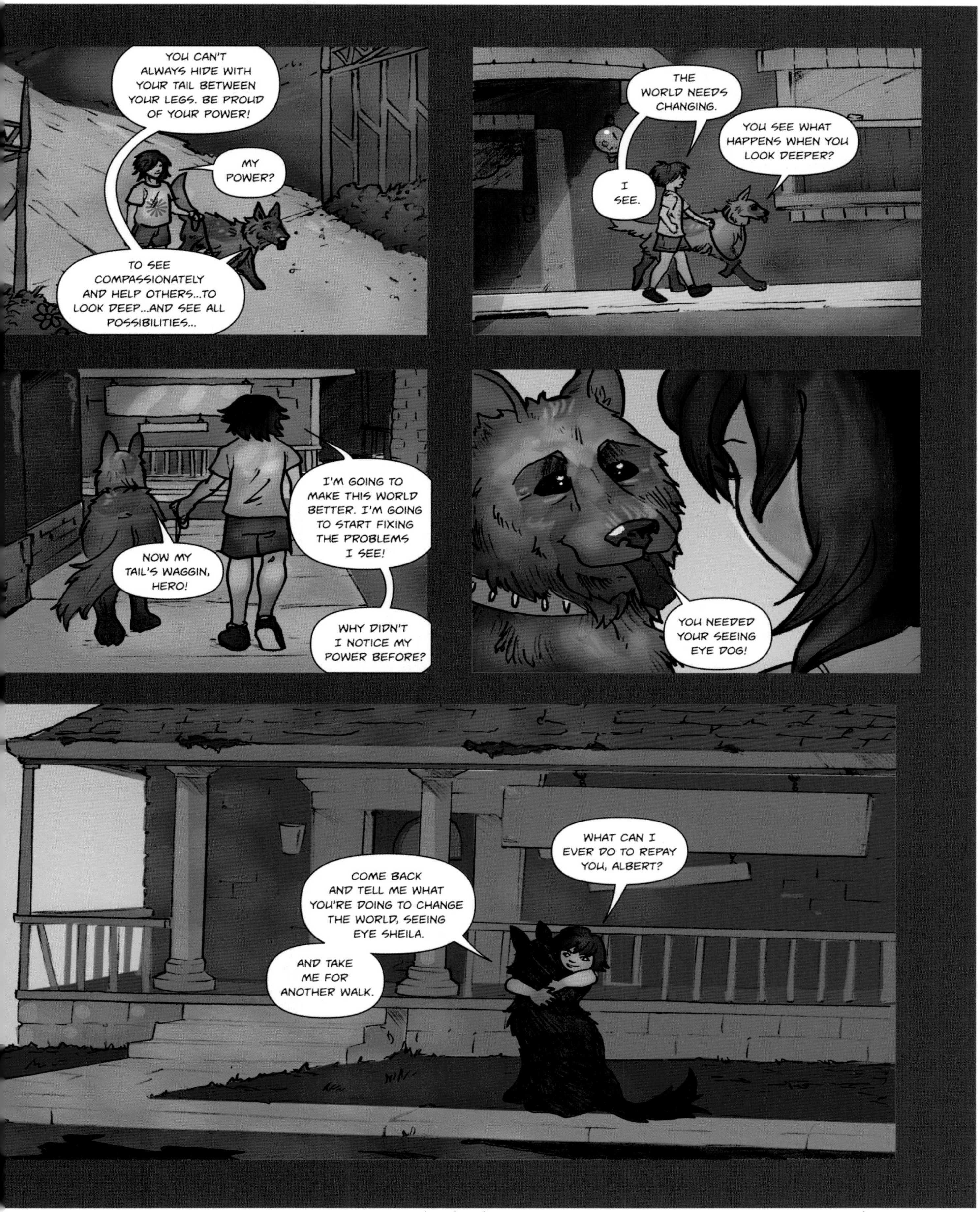
YOU CAN'T ALWAYS HIDE WITH YOUR TAIL BETWEEN YOUR LEGS. BE PROUD OF YOUR POWER!
MY POWER?
TO SEE COMPASSIONATELY AND HELP OTHERS...TO LOOK DEEP...AND SEE ALL POSSIBILITIES...
THE WORLD NEEDS CHANGING.
I SEE.
YOU SEE WHAT HAPPENS WHEN YOU LOOK DEEPER?
I'M GOING TO MAKE THIS WORLD BETTER. I'M GOING TO START FIXING THE PROBLEMS I SEE!
NOW MY TAIL'S WAGGIN, HERO!
WHY DIDN'T I NOTICE MY POWER BEFORE?
YOU NEEDED YOUR SEEING EYE DOG!
WHAT CAN I EVER DO TO REPAY YOU, ALBERT?
COME BACK AND TELL ME WHAT YOU'RE DOING TO CHANGE THE WORLD, SEEING EYE SHEILA.
AND TAKE ME FOR ANOTHER WALK.

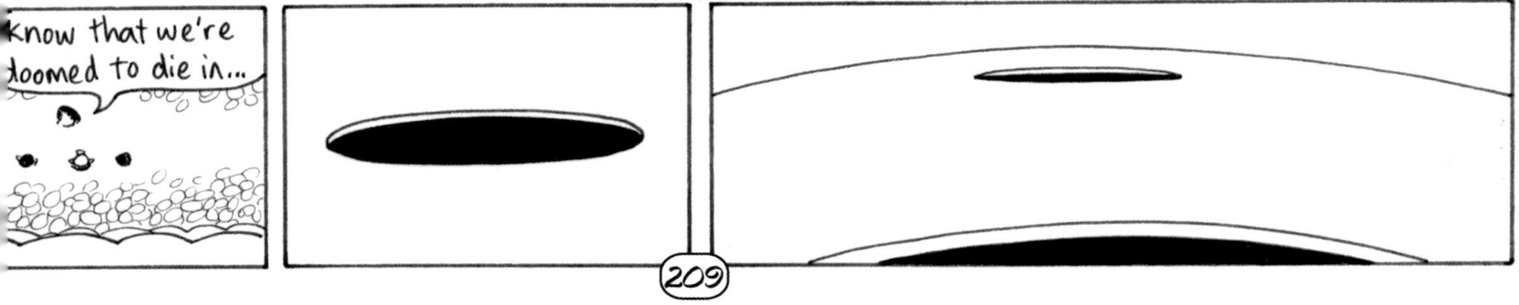
know that we're doomed to die in...

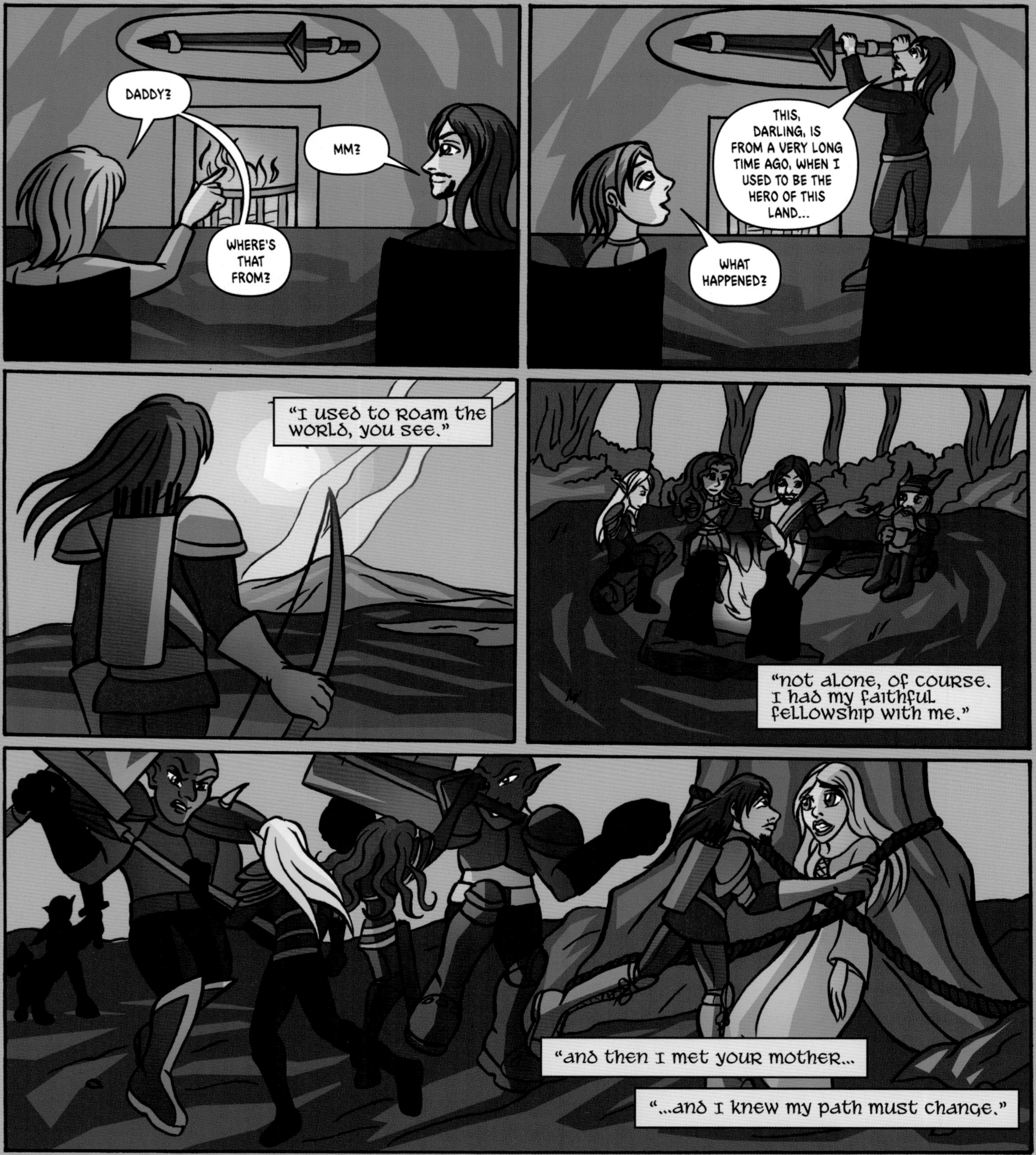
DADDY?
MM?
WHERE'S THAT FROM?
THIS, DARLING, IS FROM A VERY LONG TIME AGO, WHEN I USED TO BE THE HERO OF THIS LAND...
WHAT HAPPENED?
"I used to roam the world, you see."
"not alone, of course. I had my faithful fellowship with me."
"and then I met your mother...
"...and I knew my path must change."

WRITER: JENNI GOODCHILD ARTIST: SHERRI ROSE INKER: NICOLE GOFF COLORIST: DAWN BEST LETTERER: RACHEL DEERING

☆☆☆

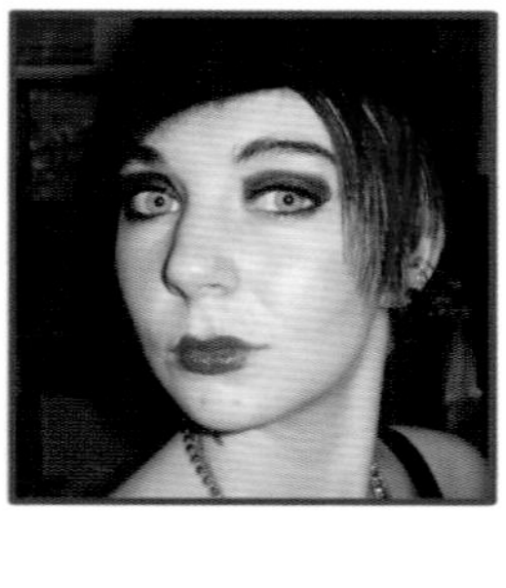

JENNI GOODCHILD

SKILLS: Writer
LOCATION: Oxford, UK
FUN FACT: I have rainbow hair!

www.theoxfordpixie.tumblr.com

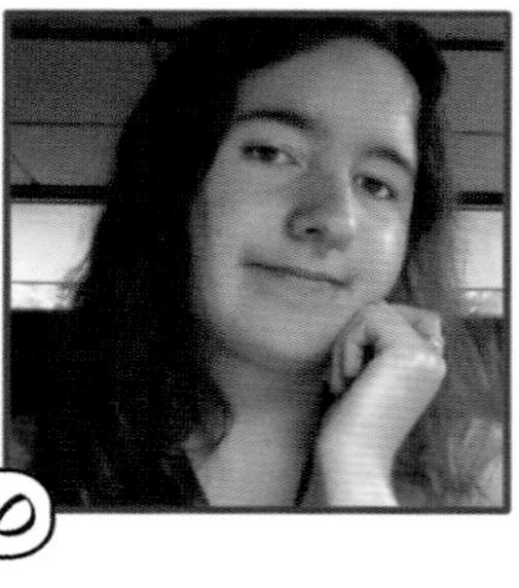

SHERRI ROSE

SKILLS: Penciller
LOCATION: Florida
FUN FACT: Most famous for drawing ponies.

http://sherridrawsstuff.blogspot.com/

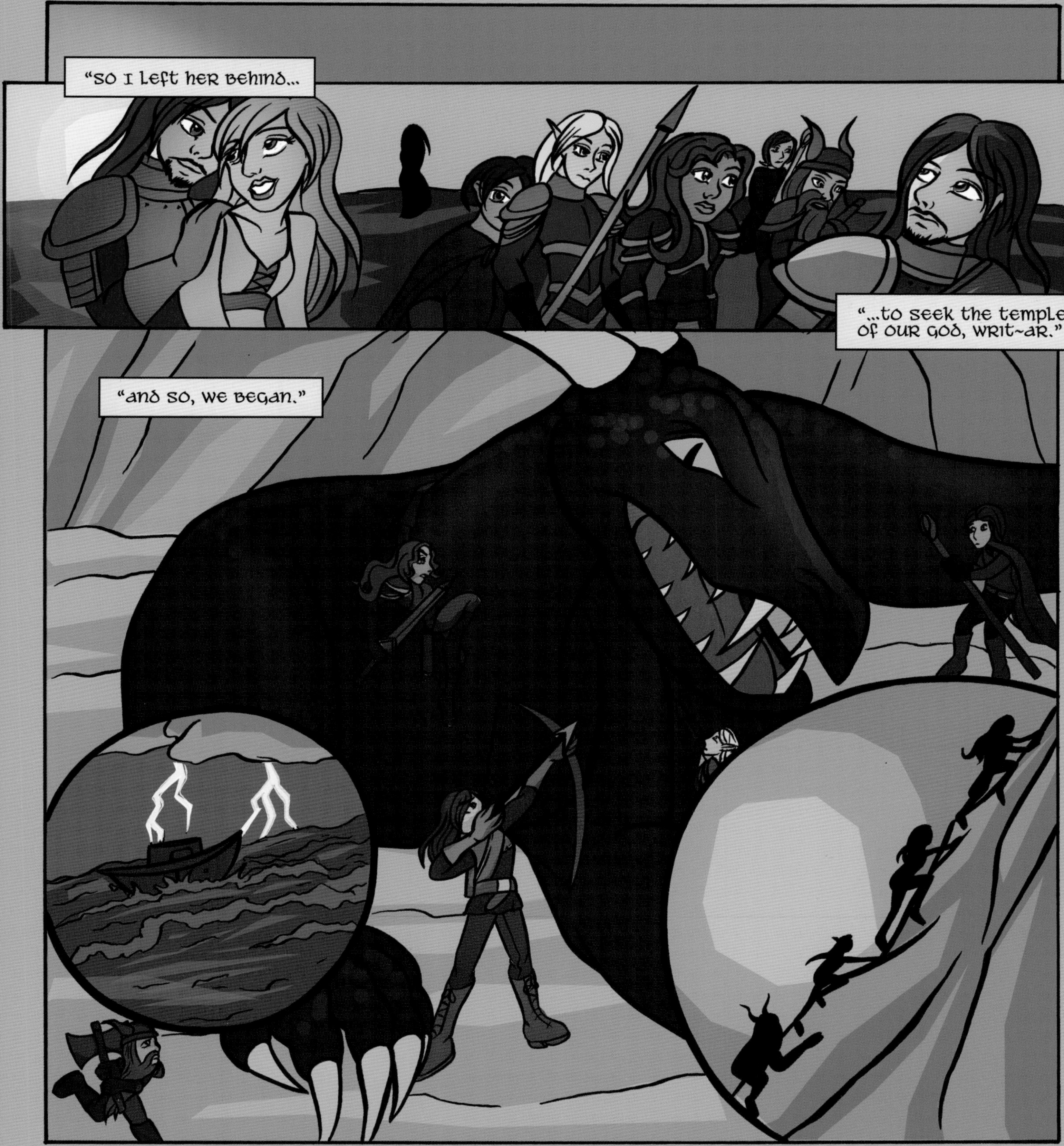
"SO I LEFT HER BEHIND...
"...TO SEEK THE TEMPLE OF OUR GOD, WRIT-AR."
"AND SO, WE BEGAN."

☆ ☆ ☆

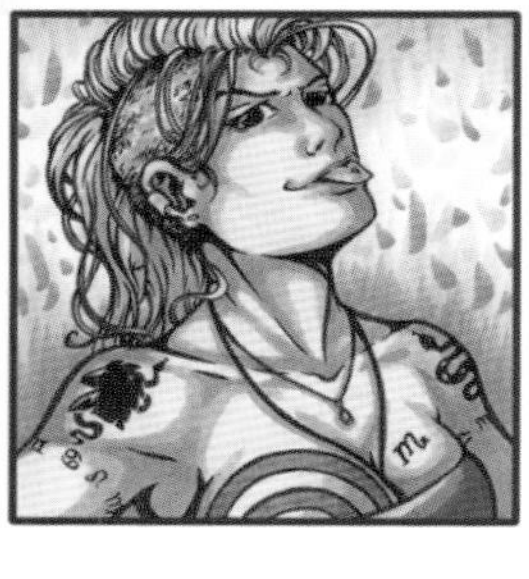

NICOLE GOFF

SKILLS: Inker
LOCATION: Virginia
FUN FACT: I did a solo motorcycle trip around the U.S., hitting all four corners of the country within 30 days.

www.NGoff.deviantart.com

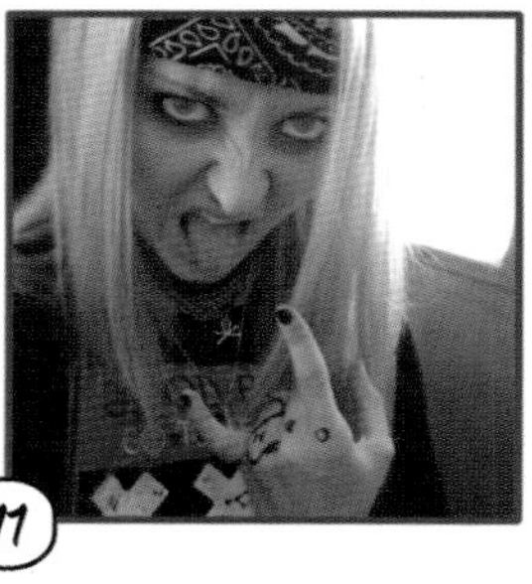

DAWN BEST

SKILLS: Inker, Colorist
LOCATION: Columbus, OH
FUN FACT: Not the best artist in the world - just the busiest!

http://www.dawnbest.com

"eventually, after many months, we came to the temple."

"and I begged for writ~ar to change my fate, to let me marry the woman I loved."

The land needs a hero.

You are that hero.

It cannot be changed.

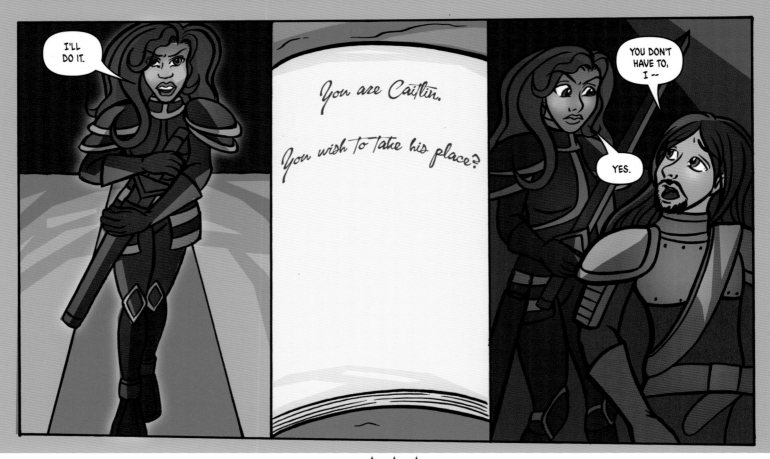

I'LL DO IT.

You are Caitlin.

You wish to take his place?

YOU DON'T HAVE TO, I --

YES.

☆ ☆ ☆

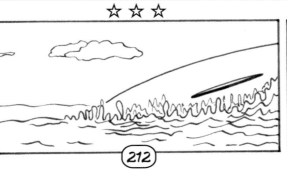

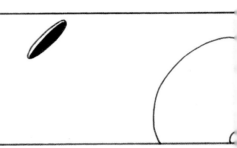

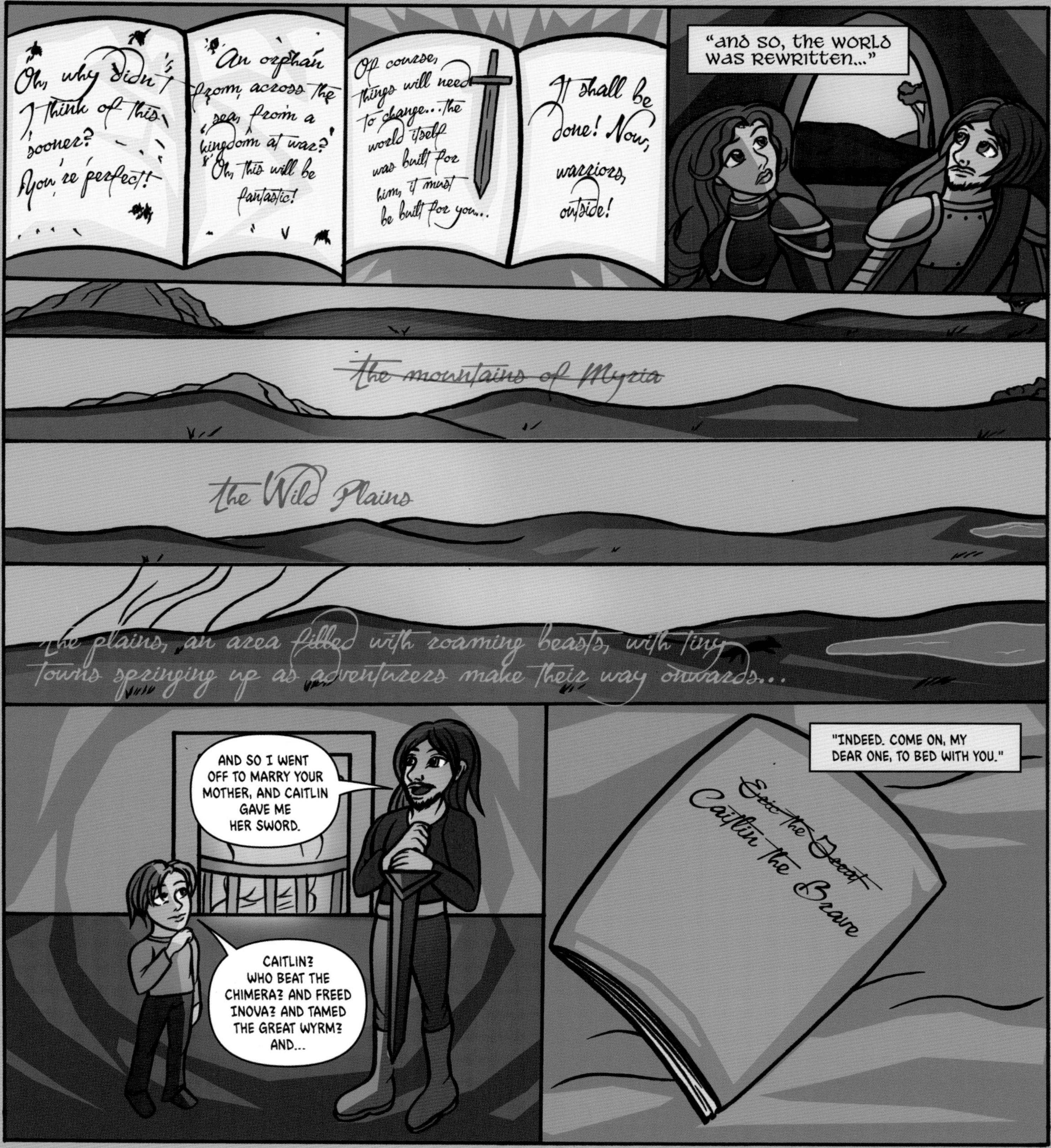
Oh, why didn't I think of this sooner? You're perfect!
An orphan from across the sea, from a kingdom at war? Oh, this will be fantastic!
Of course, things will need to change... the world itself was built for him, it must be built for you...
It shall be done! Now, warriors, outside!
"and so, the WORLD was REWRITTEN..."
The mountains of Myria
the Wild Plains
The plains, an area filled with roaming beasts, with tiny towns springing up as adventurers make their way onwards...
AND SO I WENT OFF TO MARRY YOUR MOTHER, AND CAITLIN GAVE ME HER SWORD.
CAITLIN? WHO BEAT THE CHIMERA? AND FREED INOVA? AND TAMED THE GREAT WYRM? AND...
"INDEED. COME ON, MY DEAR ONE, TO BED WITH YOU."
Eric the Great
Caitlin the Brave

☆ ☆ ☆

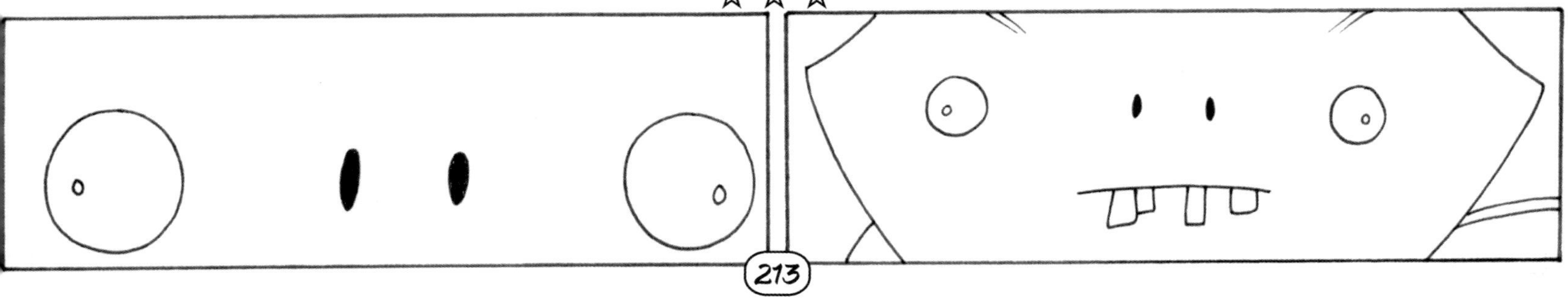

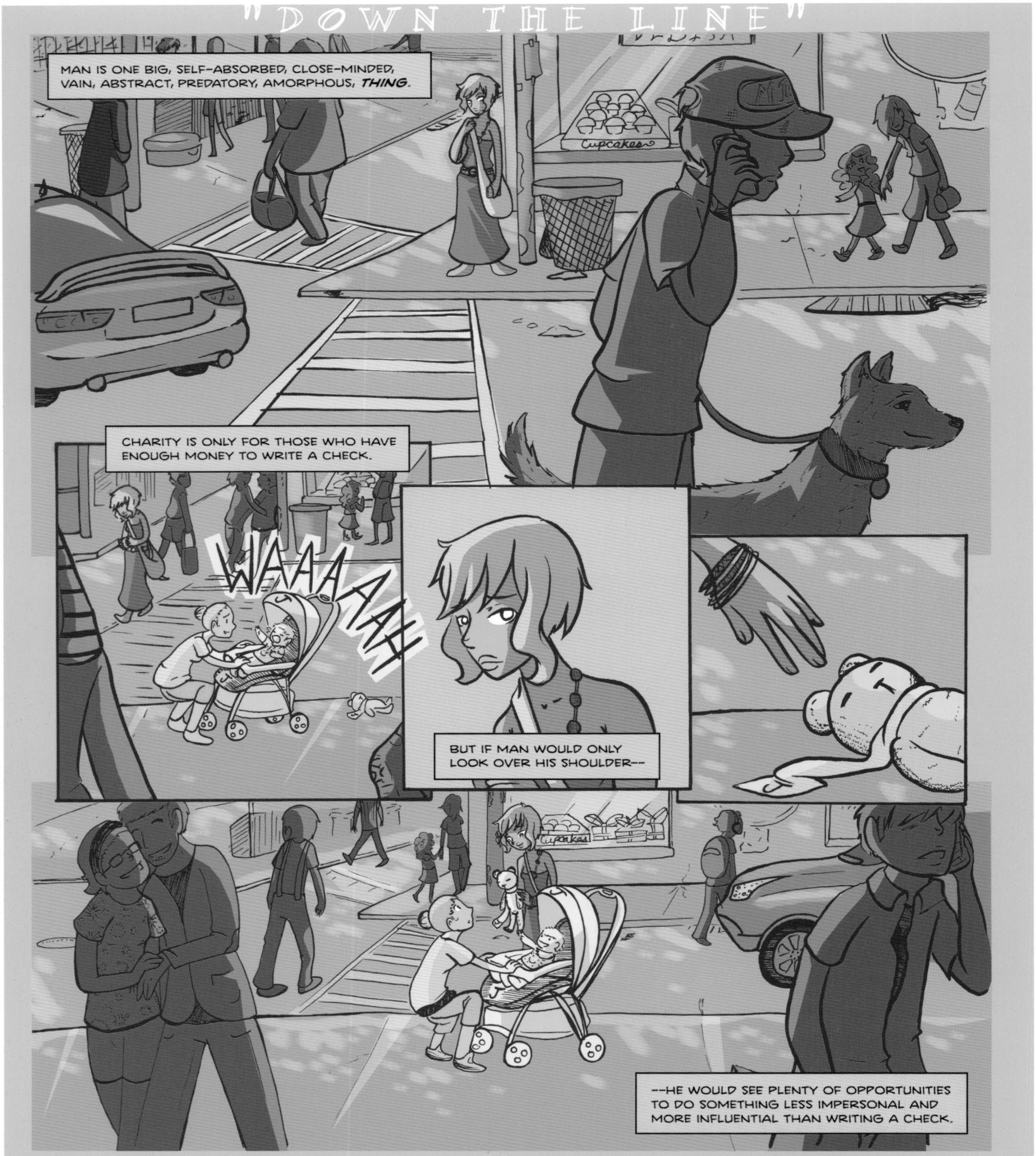
"DOWN THE LINE"
MAN IS ONE BIG, SELF-ABSORBED, CLOSE-MINDED, VAIN, ABSTRACT, PREDATORY, AMORPHOUS, *THING*.
Cupcakes
CHARITY IS ONLY FOR THOSE WHO HAVE ENOUGH MONEY TO WRITE A CHECK.
WAAAAAH
BUT IF MAN WOULD ONLY LOOK OVER HIS SHOULDER--
Cupcakes
--HE WOULD SEE PLENTY OF OPPORTUNITIES TO DO SOMETHING LESS IMPERSONAL AND MORE INFLUENTIAL THAN WRITING A CHECK.

WRITER: GEORGIE LEE ARTIST: BEATRIZ BRAVO COLORIST: DAWN BEST LETTERER: RACHEL DEERING

☆☆☆

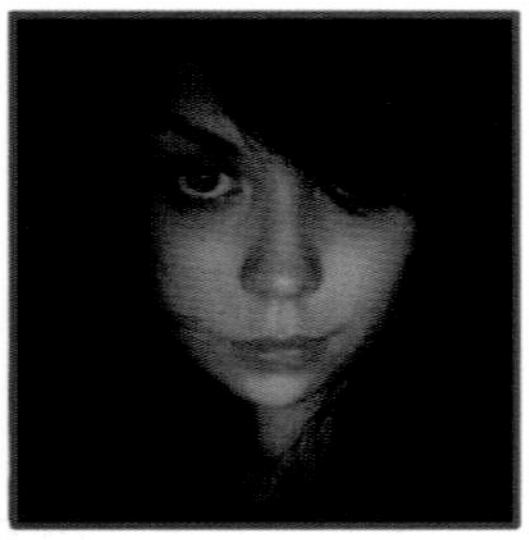

GEORGIE LEE

SKILLS: Writer
LOCATION: North Carolina
FUN FACT: My cat can say my name. Not lying. It's a fact. He also is allergic to himself, has asthma, and can understand English. He's pretty much awesome.

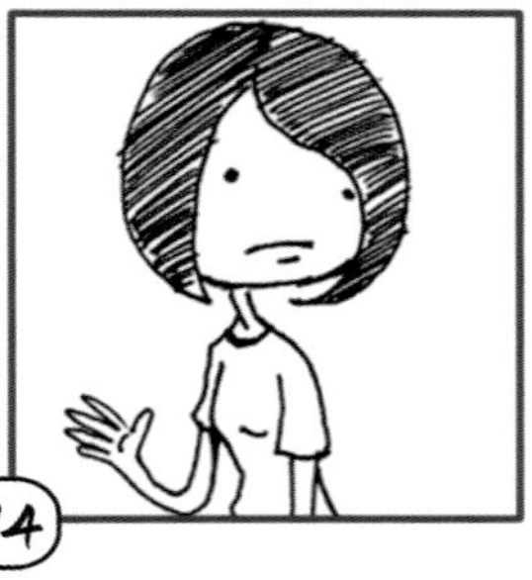

BEATRIZ BRAVO

SKILLS: Penciller, Inker
LOCATION: New Jersey
FUN FACT: Learned all my nerdy tendancies from my dad.

beabravo.tumblr.com

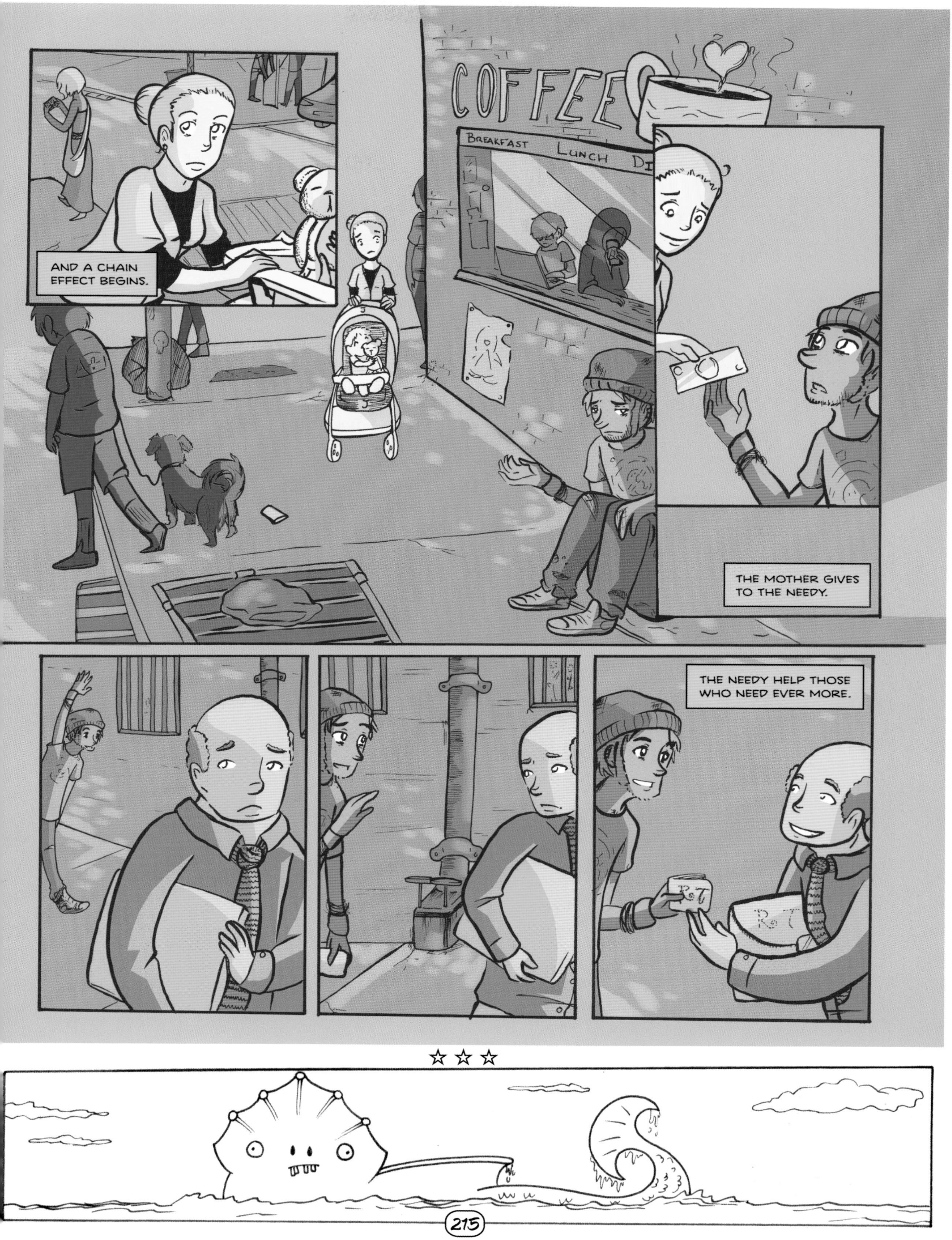
AND A CHAIN EFFECT BEGINS.
COFFEE
BREAKFAST LUNCH DI
THE MOTHER GIVES TO THE NEEDY.
THE NEEDY HELP THOSE WHO NEED EVER MORE.
☆ ☆ ☆

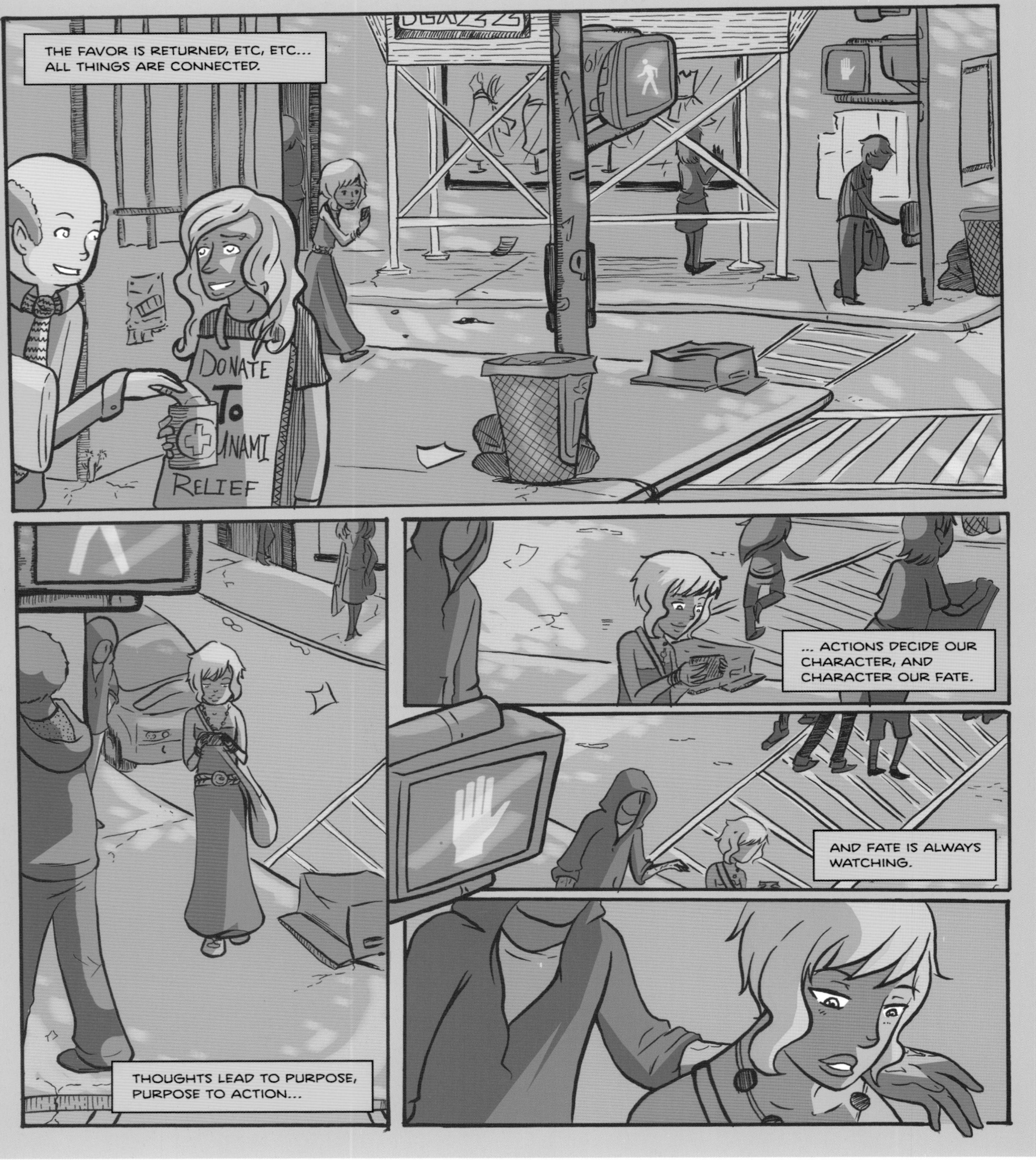
THE FAVOR IS RETURNED, ETC, ETC... ALL THINGS ARE CONNECTED.
DONATE
To
RELIEF
THOUGHTS LEAD TO PURPOSE, PURPOSE TO ACTION...
... ACTIONS DECIDE OUR CHARACTER, AND CHARACTER OUR FATE.
AND FATE IS ALWAYS WATCHING.

☆ ☆ ☆

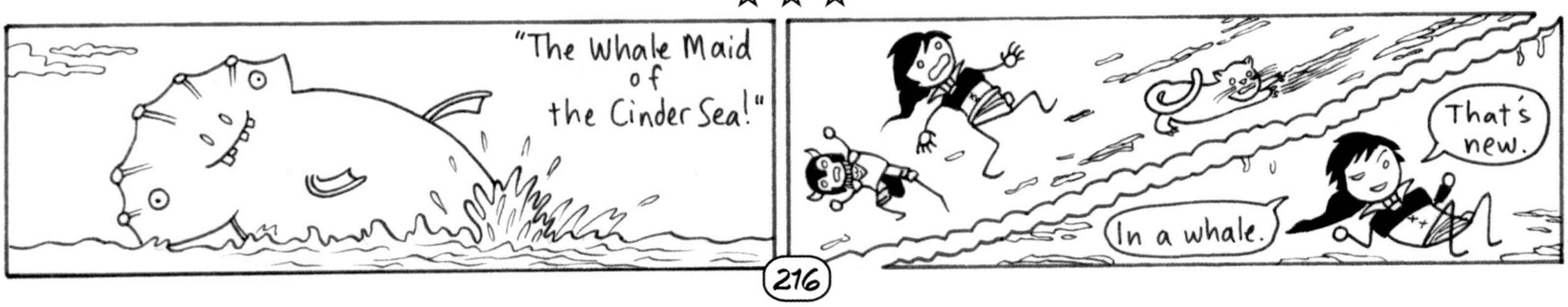
"The Whale Maid of the Cinder Sea!"
In a whale.
That's new.

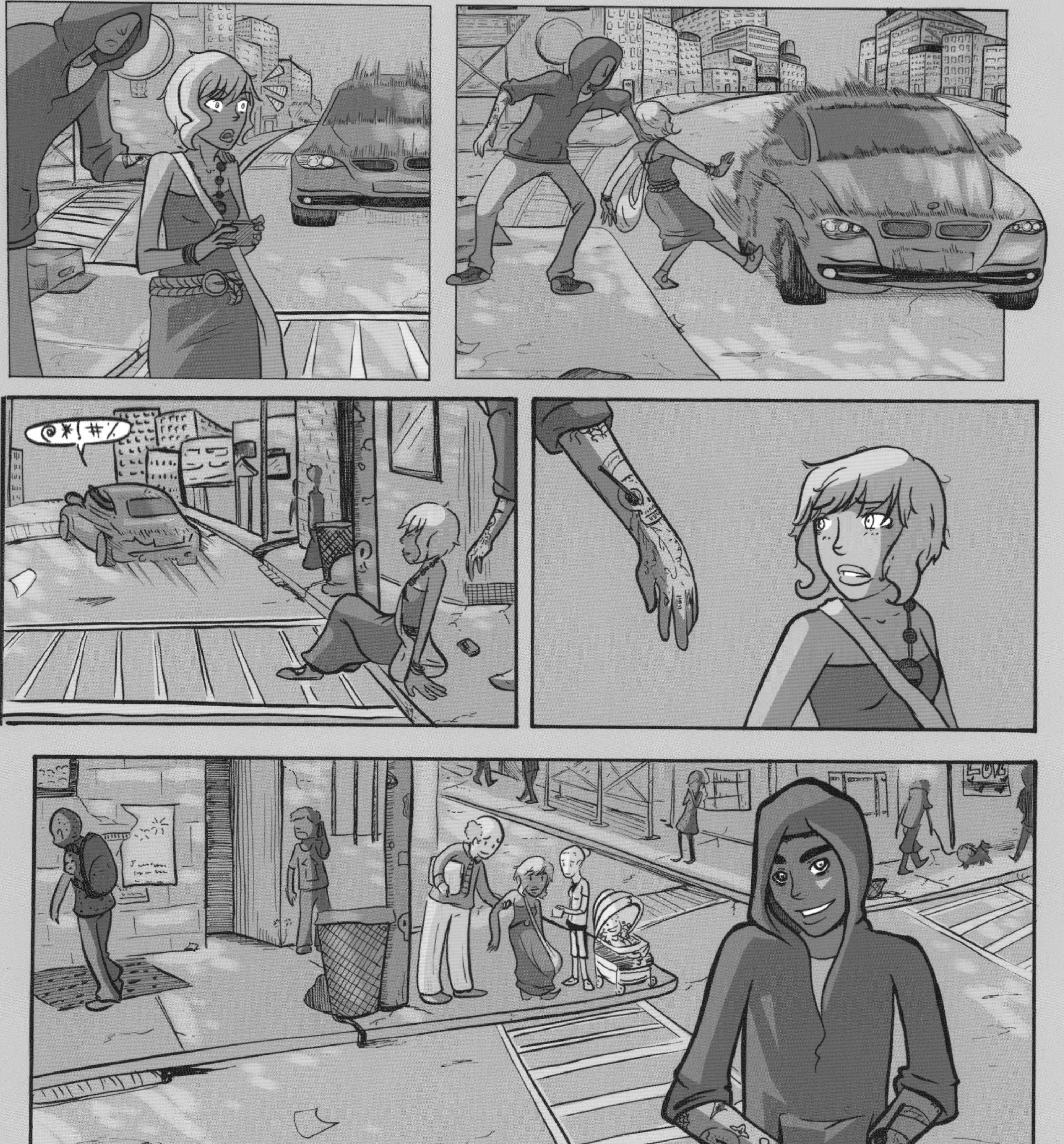
@*!#%
ALWAYS.

☆ ☆ ☆

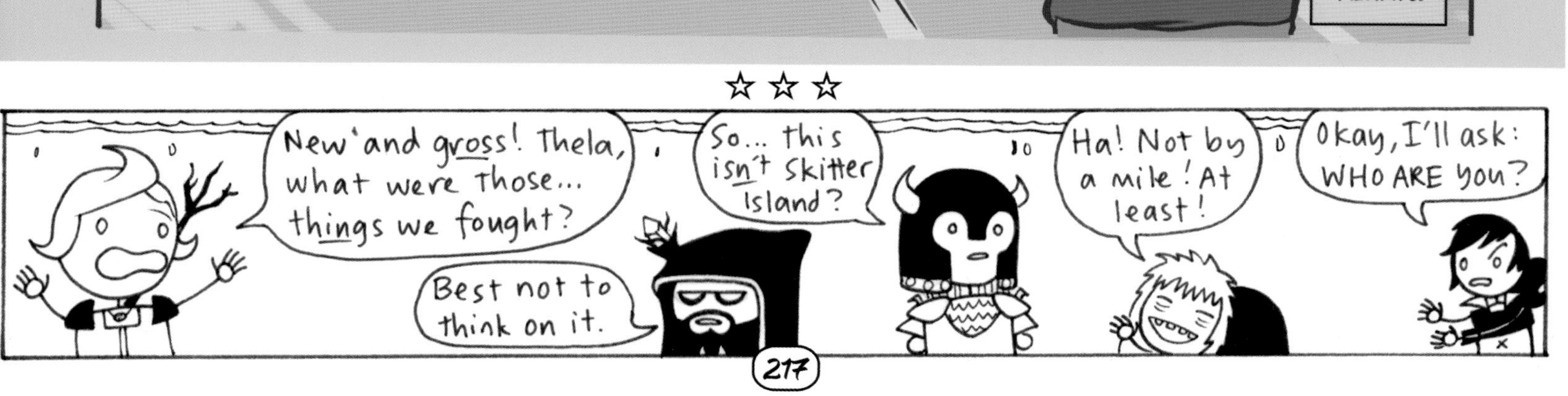
New'and gross! Thela, what were those... things we fought?
Best not to think on it.
So... this isn't Skitter Island?
Ha! Not by a mile! At least!
Okay, I'll ask: WHO ARE you?

Meet the
hero
that rescues
your heart
without even
trying...

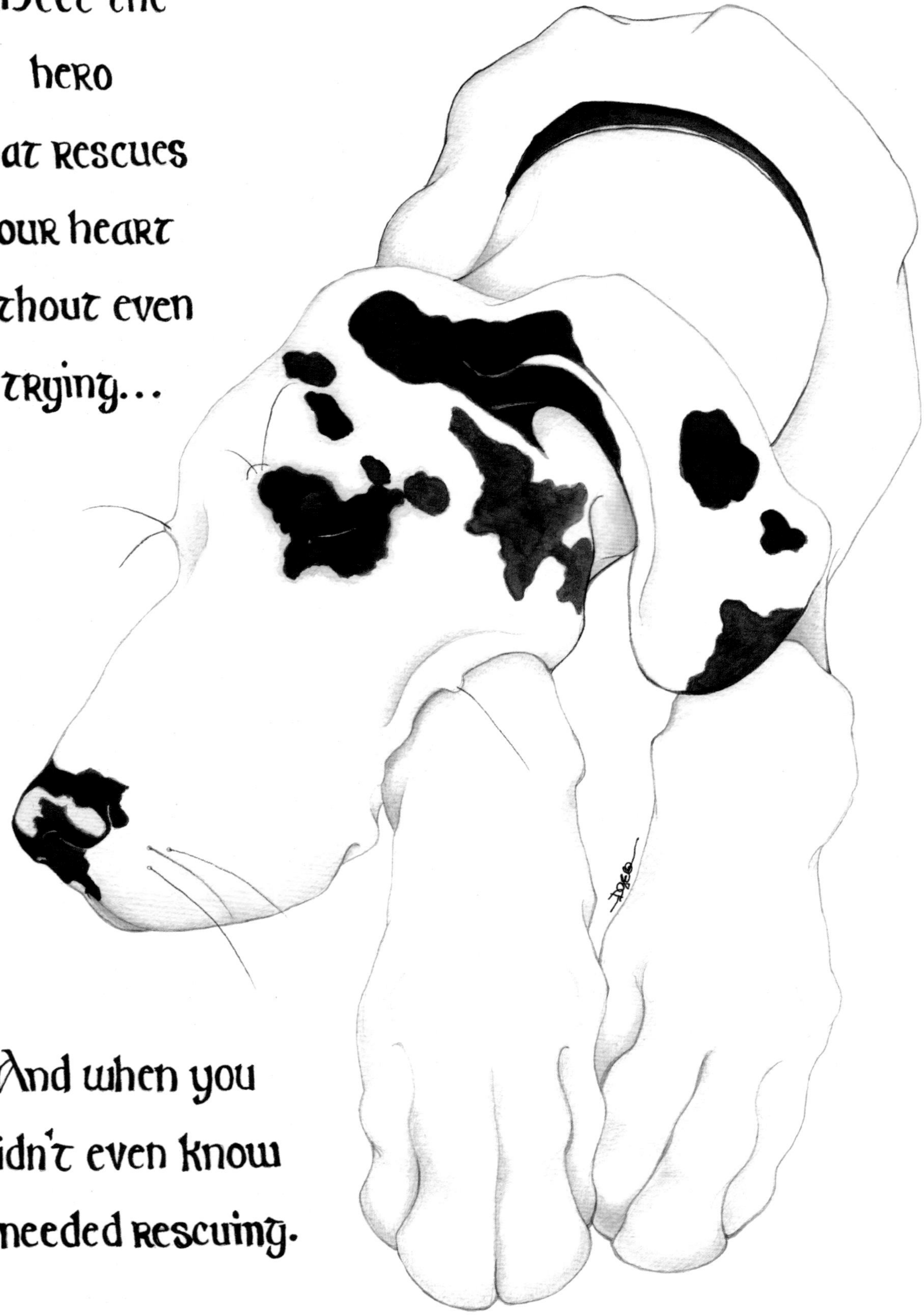

And when you
didn't even know
it needed rescuing.

☆☆☆

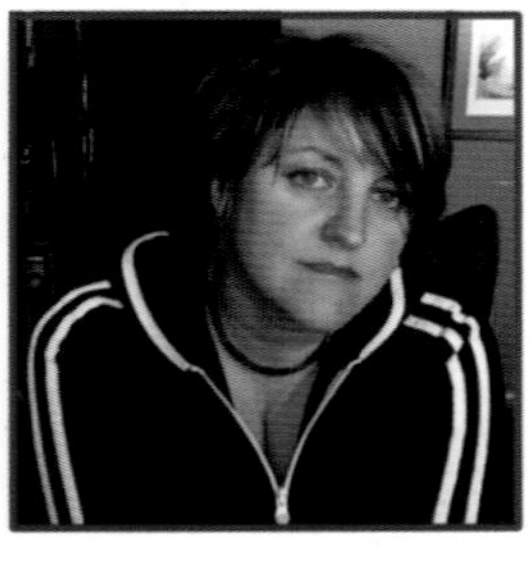

DARLA G. ECKLUND

SKILLS: Pencils, Watercolor, Inking, Writing
LOCATION: Columbia Heights, MN
FUN FACT: I could honestly survive on a diet made up entirely of buttered noodles.

http://darlaecklund.blogspot.com/

PRO TIP

KINDNESS

BY RENAE DE LIZ

"THERE IS NEVER A REASON TO BE UNFRIENDLY TO SOMEONE, ESPECIALLY TO A CO-WORKER, NO MATTER WHAT THEY DO OR SAY. SPEAKING OUT IN ANGER AND FRUSTRATION IS A SURE FIRE WAY TO CLOSE DOORS, WHILE COMPROMISE, KINDNESS, AND UNDERSTANDING KEEPS THEM OPEN."

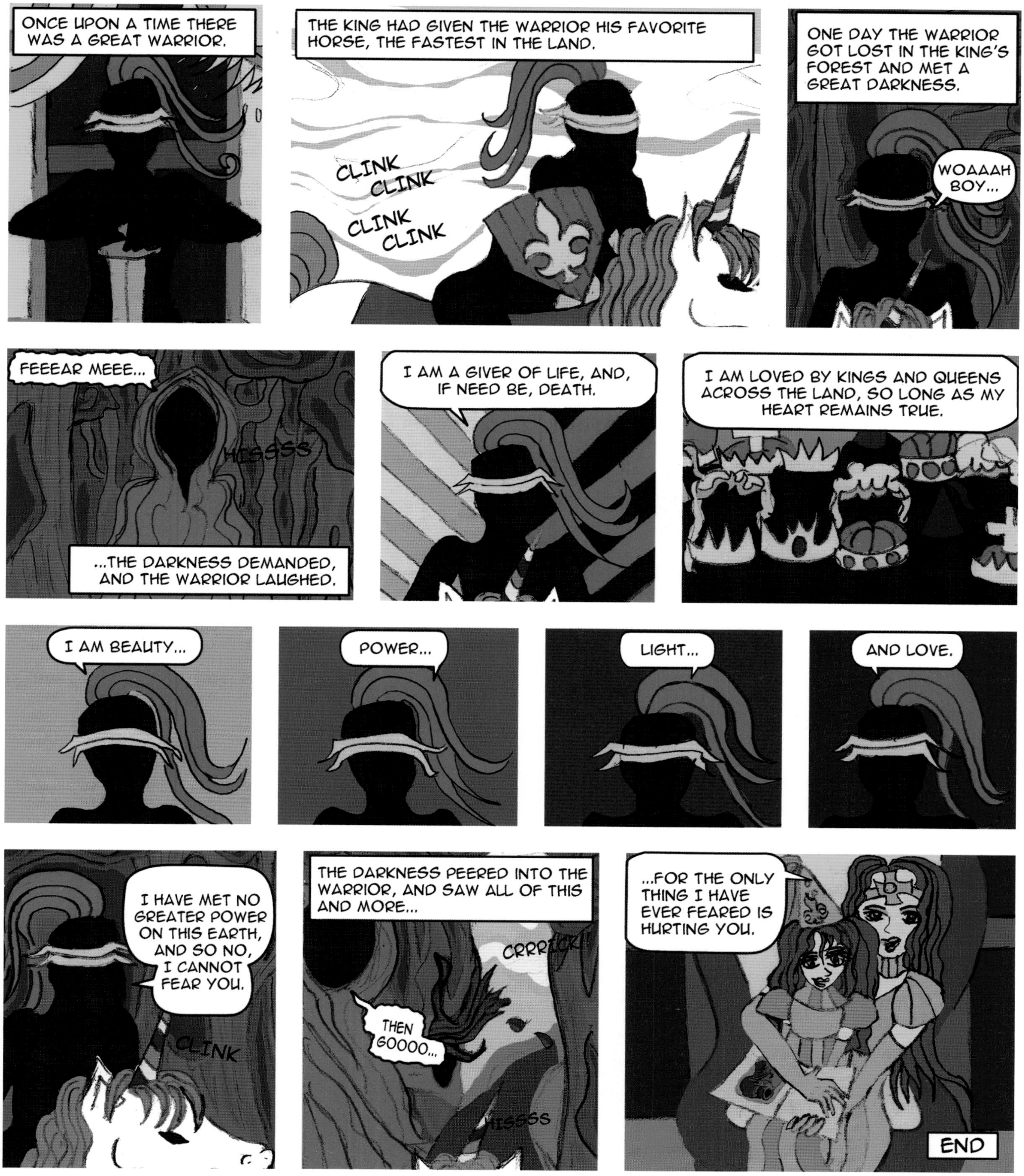

ONCE UPON A TIME THERE WAS A GREAT WARRIOR.
THE KING HAD GIVEN THE WARRIOR HIS FAVORITE HORSE, THE FASTEST IN THE LAND.
CLINK CLINK
CLINK CLINK
ONE DAY THE WARRIOR GOT LOST IN THE KING'S FOREST AND MET A GREAT DARKNESS.
WOAAAH BOY...
FEEEAR MEEE...
HISSSS
...THE DARKNESS DEMANDED, AND THE WARRIOR LAUGHED.
I AM A GIVER OF LIFE, AND, IF NEED BE, DEATH.
I AM LOVED BY KINGS AND QUEENS ACROSS THE LAND, SO LONG AS MY HEART REMAINS TRUE.
I AM BEAUTY...
POWER...
LIGHT...
AND LOVE.
I HAVE MET NO GREATER POWER ON THIS EARTH, AND SO NO, I CANNOT FEAR YOU.
CLINK
THE DARKNESS PEERED INTO THE WARRIOR, AND SAW ALL OF THIS AND MORE...
CRRRICK!
THEN GOOOO...
HISSSS
...FOR THE ONLY THING I HAVE EVER FEARED IS HURTING YOU.
END

☆ ☆ ☆

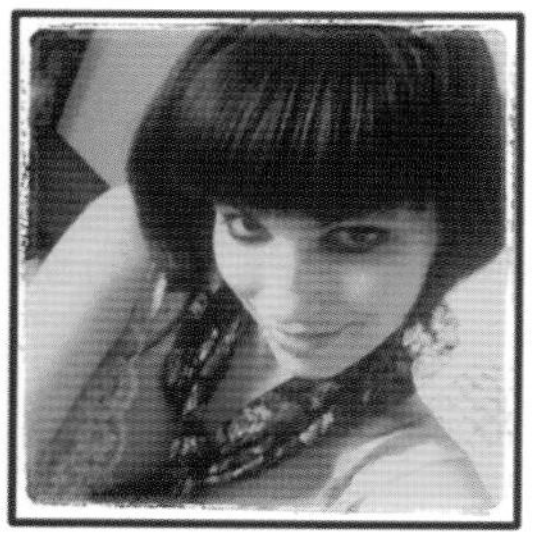

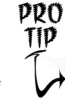

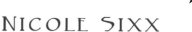

NICOLE SIXX

SKILLS: Penciler, Inker, Colorist, Letterer, Writer

LOCATION: Los Angeles

FUN FACT: My motto for life is the geekier the better!

http://twitter.com/nicolesixx_

PRO TIP

BLAH BLAH BLAH

BY ANNIE NOCENTI

"TALK BACK TO YOUR WRITER. WE WRITERS ARE FULL OF BLAH BLAH BLAH. SO MUCH BLAH BLAH THAT WE GIVE YOU TOO MUCH TO DRAW PER PAGE. TALK TO US! TELL US THAT YOU WANT TO TURN PANEL 12 INTO AN AWESOME SPLASH PAGE AND NEED 3 MORE PAGES TO DRAW FOR A SEQUENCE TO HAVE BREATH, AND LIFE, AND FLUID MOVEMENT. IT'S A COLLABORATION. THE WRITER GIVES YOU A BLUEPRINT, YEAH, BUT YOU'RE THE DIRECTOR, YOU'RE WHAT WE END UP SEEING. TALK BACK TO US!"

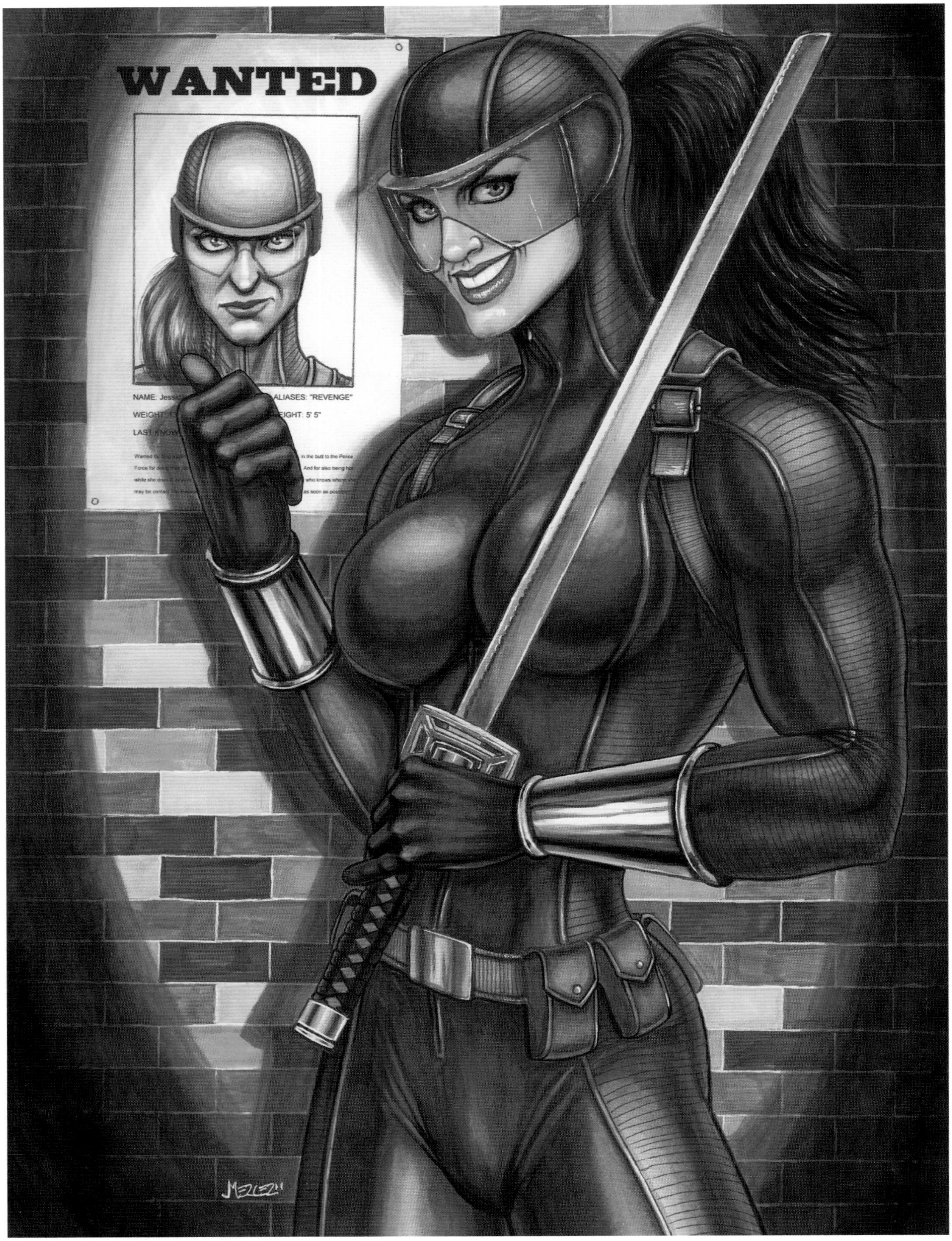

WANTED
ALIASES: "REVENGE"

☆☆☆

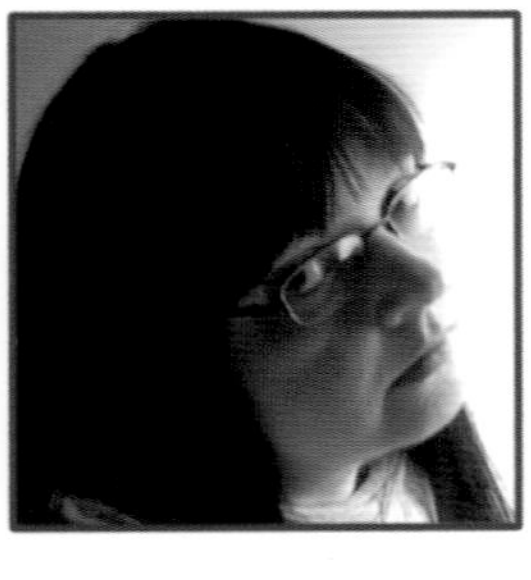

JENNIFER MERCER

SKILLS: Penciller, Inker, Colorist
LOCATION: Ocala, Florida
FUN FACT: I'm a 41-year-old martial arts and sci fi nerd and proud of it!

http://www.jenshome.com

PRO TIP

EDITING
BY BARBARA RANDALL KESEL

"IF YOU'RE EDITING BECAUSE YOU WANT TO BE A PENCILER OR WRITER, REMEMBER THAT YOU'RE NOT THE PENCILER OR WRITER. YOUR JOB IS TO INSPIRE, MOTIVATE, AND ENHANCE THEIR WORK, NOT SUBSTITUTE YOUR OWN."

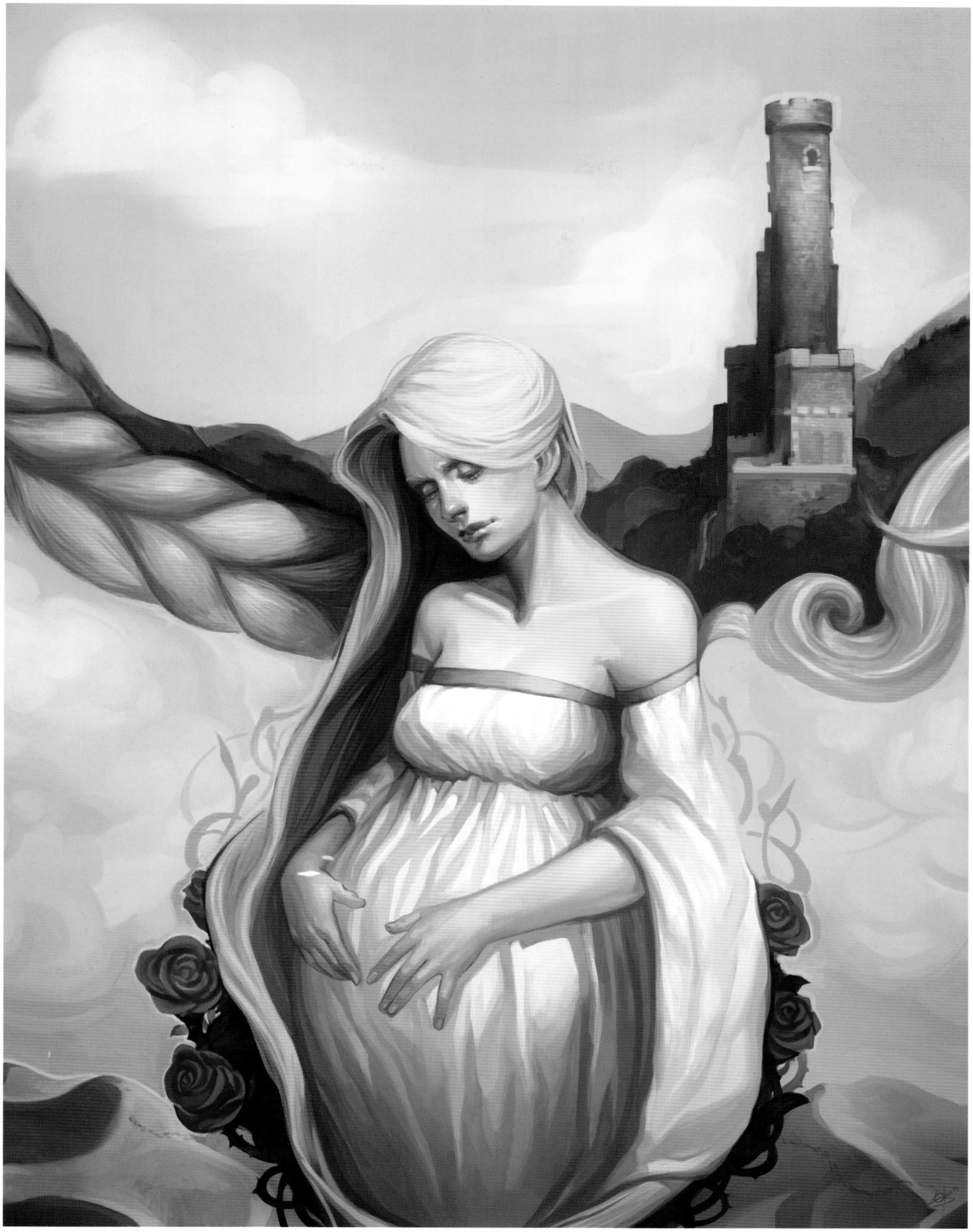

☆☆☆

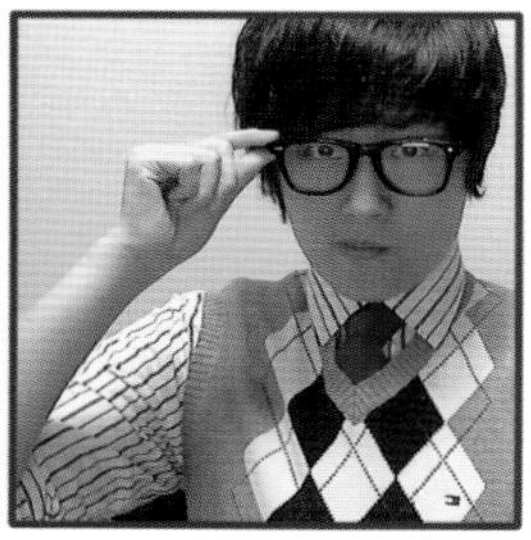

MENG TIAN ZHANG

SKILLS: Painter
LOCATION: Toronto, Canada
FUN FACT: I can pull off the most amazing sturgeon face.

http://mengtzhang.com

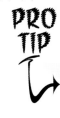

PRO TIP

PORTFOLIO

BY NICOLE FALK

"HAVE A CLEAN, SIMPLE PORTFOLIO WITH YOUR AWESOME WORK. ALWAYS BE PROUD OF YOUR WORK, ESPECIALLY WHEN YOU ARE TRYING TO GET A JOB WITH IT! DON'T EVER INSULT YOURSELF OR YOUR WORK IN FRONT OF SOMEONE YOU ARE ASKING TO HIRE YOU. THEY CAN ONLY BELIEVE IN YOU AS MUCH AS YOU BELIEVE IN YOURSELF! (NO MATTER HOW CHEESY THAT SOUNDS)"

WE CAN BE HEROES by Rori!

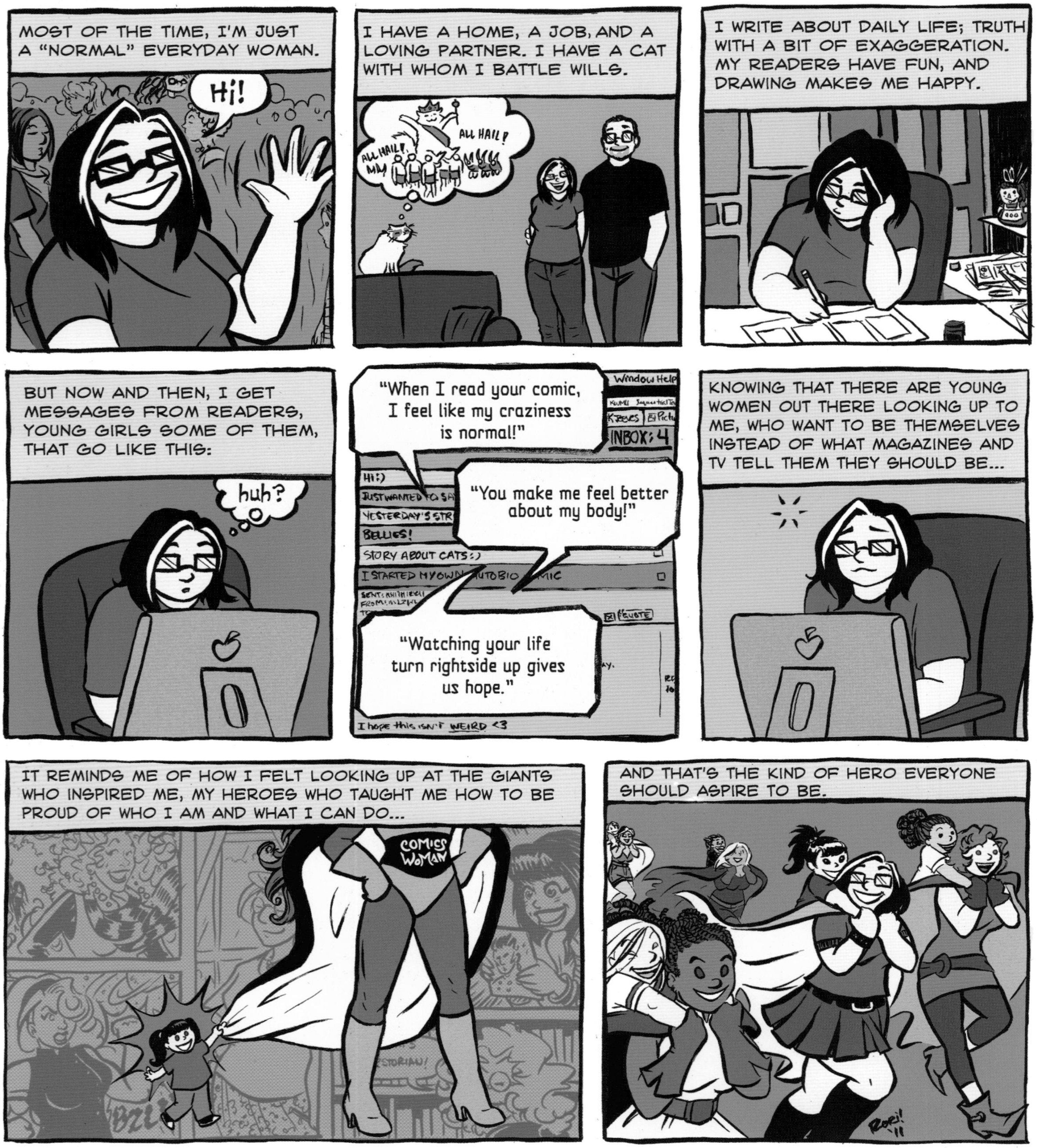
MOST OF THE TIME, I'M JUST A "NORMAL" EVERYDAY WOMAN.
Hi!
I HAVE A HOME, A JOB, AND A LOVING PARTNER. I HAVE A CAT WITH WHOM I BATTLE WILLS.
ALL HAIL!
ALL HAIL!
I WRITE ABOUT DAILY LIFE; TRUTH WITH A BIT OF EXAGGERATION. MY READERS HAVE FUN, AND DRAWING MAKES ME HAPPY.
BUT NOW AND THEN, I GET MESSAGES FROM READERS, YOUNG GIRLS SOME OF THEM, THAT GO LIKE THIS:
huh?
Window Help
INBOX: 4
"When I read your comic, I feel like my craziness is normal!"
HI:)
"You make me feel better about my body!"
BELLIES!
STORY ABOUT CATS :)
"Watching your life turn rightside up gives us hope."
I hope this isn't WEIRD <3
KNOWING THAT THERE ARE YOUNG WOMEN OUT THERE LOOKING UP TO ME, WHO WANT TO BE THEMSELVES INSTEAD OF WHAT MAGAZINES AND TV TELL THEM THEY SHOULD BE...
IT REMINDS ME OF HOW I FELT LOOKING UP AT THE GIANTS WHO INSPIRED ME, MY HEROES WHO TAUGHT ME HOW TO BE PROUD OF WHO I AM AND WHAT I CAN DO...
COMICS WOMAN
AND THAT'S THE KIND OF HERO EVERYONE SHOULD ASPIRE TO BE.
RORI! '11

☆ ☆ ☆

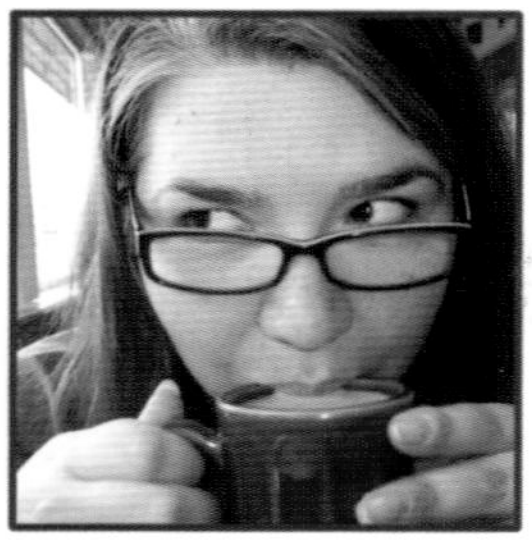

RORI

SKILLS: Writer, Artist, Letterer (everything)
LOCATION: St. Louis
FUN FACT: I got married to my comic-making husband at a comic book shop on Free Comic Book Day.

http://www.tinypinkrobots.com

PRO TIP

RUTS
BY KIMBERLY DE LIZ

"AVOID RUTS. MIX UP YOUR MEDIA AND TRY NEW TECHNIQUES."

PART FIVE

TEAM NICOLE

☆ ☆ ☆ For each section of *Womanthology* a different lady took on the role of editor over the writers, pencillers, inkers, colorists, and letterers for their stories or pinups. They were in charge of making sure the creators worked as a team, had all the info they needed, and that all stories and pinups were turned in on time. This section is Nicole Falk's.

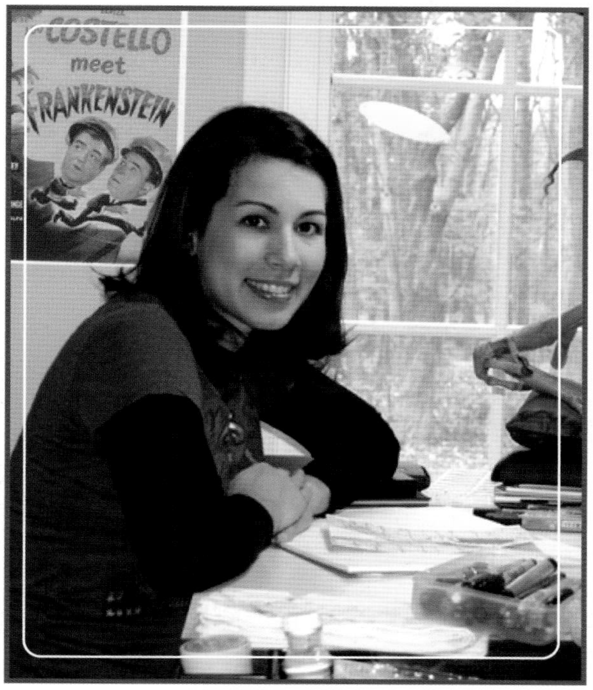

COSTELLO
meet
FRANKENSTEIN

EDITOR - NICOLE FALK

Location: New Jersey

Day Job: Art Director - Photography and Figural Package Design for a Toy Manufacturer, and Mommy to an insanely amazing little girl named Penelope Coraline.

A little about yourself: I'm a middle child, so I'm loud, independent, jokey (some might say lightly sarcastic), and super friendly. I graduated with a Fine Arts degree from Mason Gross School of the Arts at Rutgers University. I became a professional photojournalist, which then led me to N.E.C.A., a collectible toy company, where I found my career and my husband. I worked for 8 years as the head photographer and lead package designer. I worked side by side with my husband creating awesome toys, until we had our daughter, and I decided to stay home to hang out with her and our pug. I love movies, comics, toys, video games, drawing, and crafts. Oh, and of course anything related to Halloween, Fall, or remotely spooky things.

What does *Womanthology* mean to you? As soon as Renae had sent out that one (groundbreaking) inquiring little tweet, I was on board! I knew right away this was going to be something monumental, and I wanted to be a part of it. I was so excited at the thought of my own little comic, I started writing and drawing right away. Once I was asked to become an editor, I just about flipped out! I was thrilled to be an even bigger and more integral part of the book, I just couldn't wait to get started. Creating my own comic was just as awesome as I thought it would be, and I plan to try and continue creating more. However, being an editor was one of the most rewarding experiences I've ever encountered, and I really hope I can venture into that work again. Besides patience and professionalism, from working on this anthology I have learned to really believe in my own abilities and trust my opinions. I cannot thank Renae enough for giving me this chance, and I am proud and honored to be a part of this extraordinary body of work.

Funny fact: Over the past decade I've been fortunate enough to make my living helping to create consumer products from some of my favorite properties. Licenses that I have loved since my childhood which include *Nightmare on Elm Street, Halloween, Ghostbusters, Evil Dead, Gremlins,* and *The Nightmare Before Christmas*. I was very lucky that the new company needed a female designer at the time to help add a female perspective to their product lines. They just didn't know I was more excited designing for *Hellraiser* than I was for *My Little Pony*.

☆ ☆ ☆

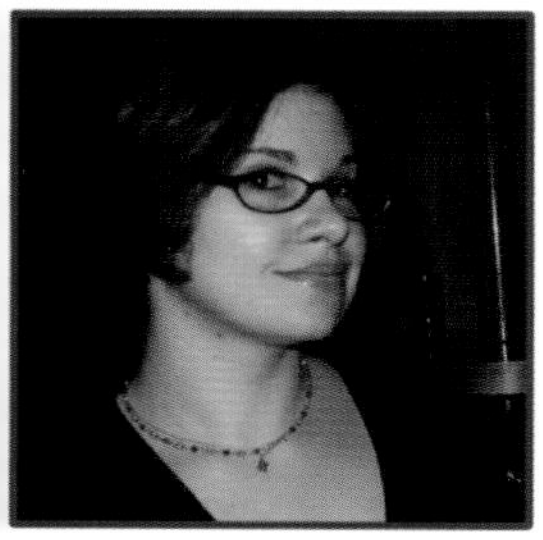

SARAH LITT

SKILLS: Consultant
LOCATION: California
FUN FACT: I LOVE cookies!

www.artandcookies.tumblr.com

SARAH LITT HELPED WITH ORGANIZATIONAL AND EDITORIAL DUTIES EARLY ON IN THE PROCESS OF DEVELOPING WOMANTHOLOGY.

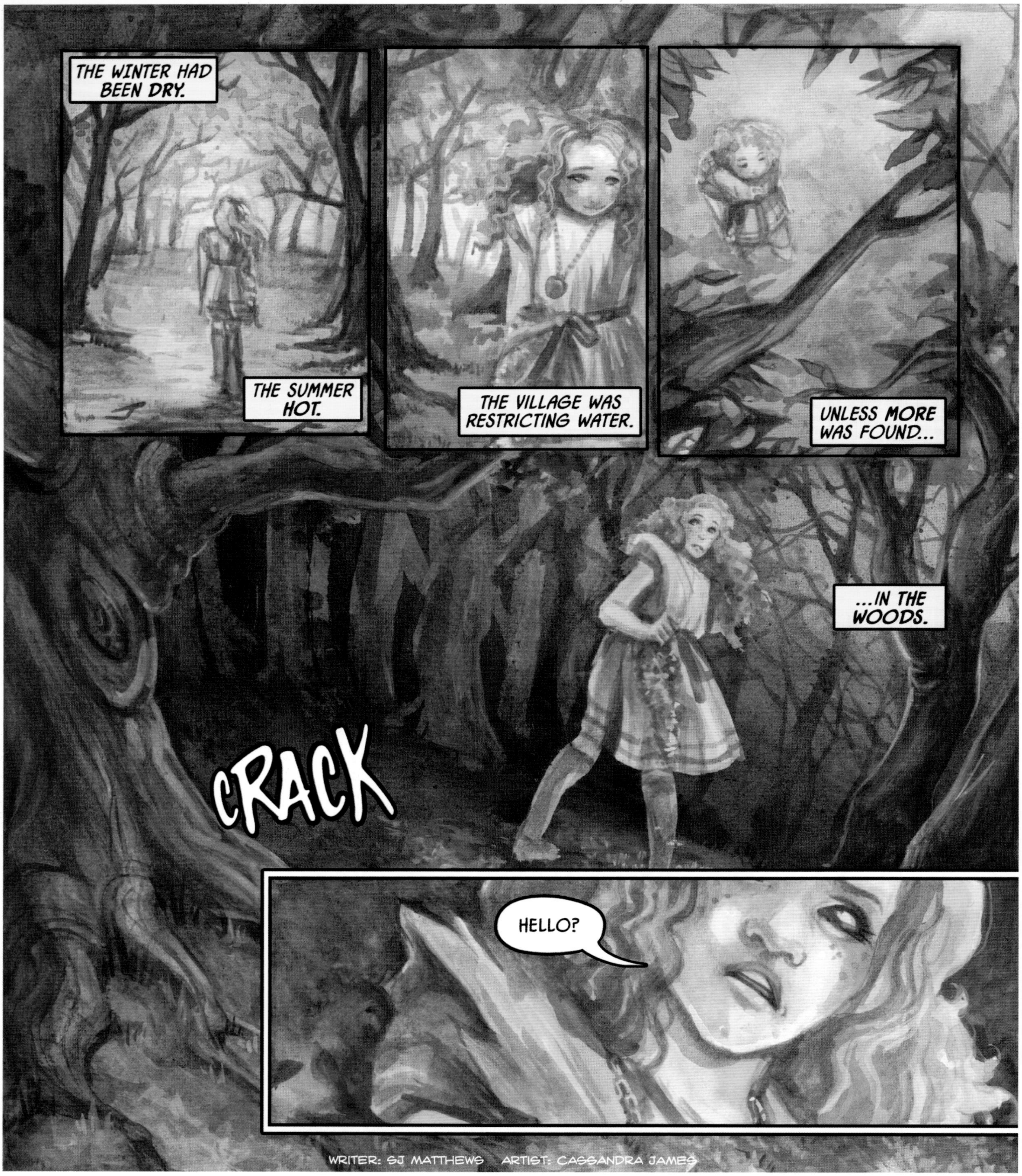
THE WINTER HAD BEEN DRY.
THE SUMMER HOT.
THE VILLAGE WAS RESTRICTING WATER.
UNLESS MORE WAS FOUND...
...IN THE WOODS.
CRACK
HELLO?
WRITER: SJ MATTHEWS ARTIST: CASSANDRA JAMES

☆ ☆ ☆

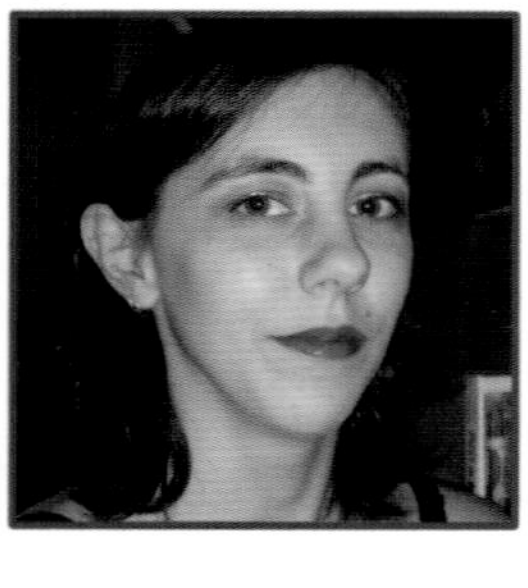

SJ MATTHEWS

SKILLS: Writer
LOCATION: Adelaide, Australia
FUN FACT: I think it would be interesting to be a fungi. Or a cephalopod.

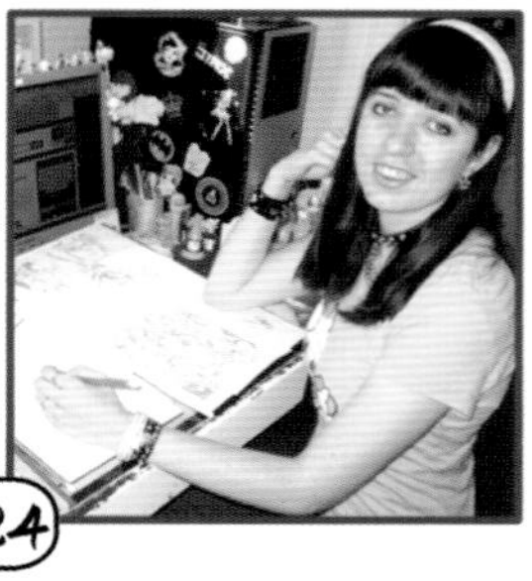

CASSANDRA JAMES

SKILLS: Art, Letters
LOCATION: Australia
FUN FACT: I still sleep with a plush toy, a monkey named Winston.

www.cassubeans.com

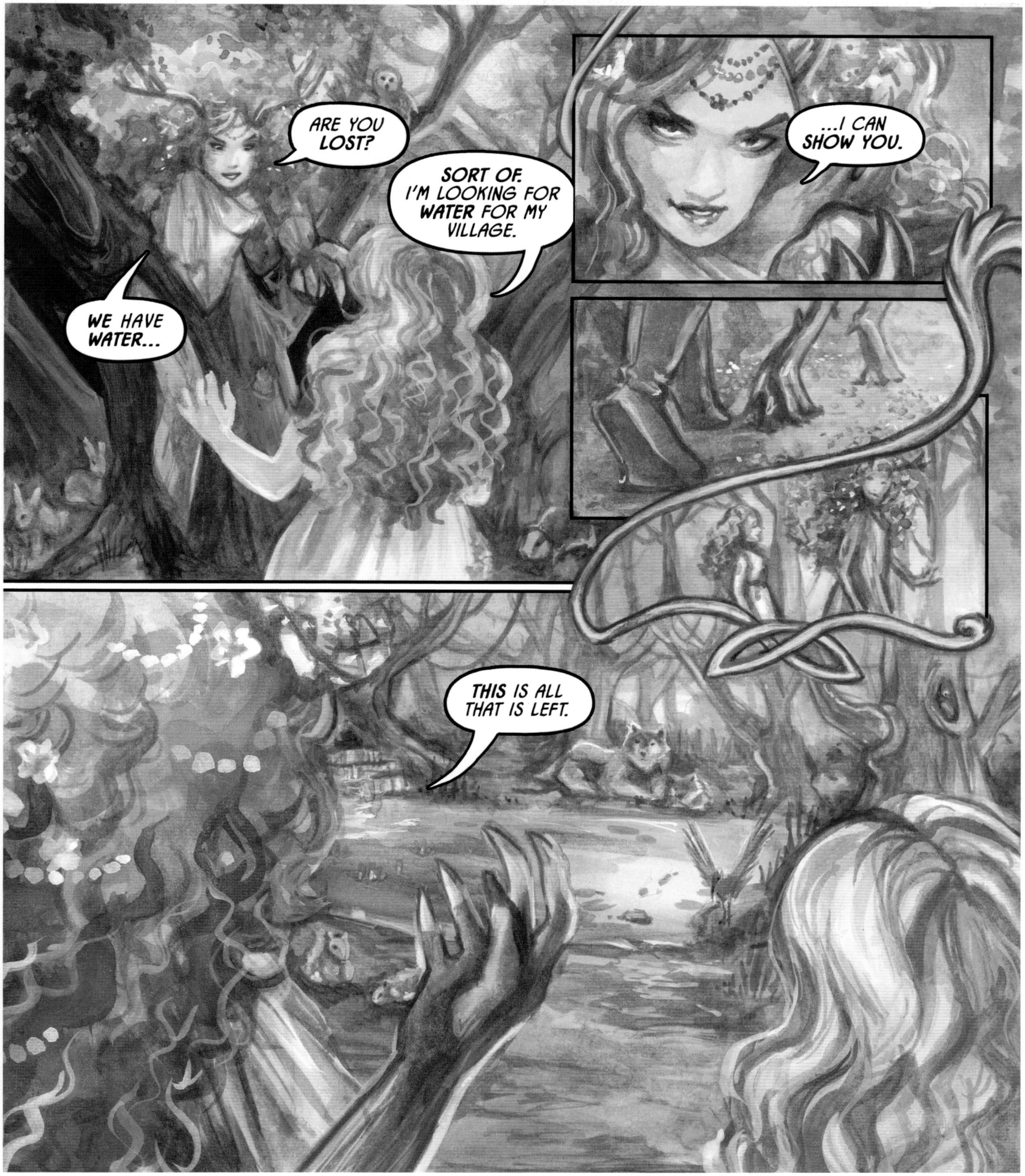
ARE YOU LOST?
SORT OF. I'M LOOKING FOR WATER FOR MY VILLAGE.
WE HAVE WATER...
...I CAN SHOW YOU.
THIS IS ALL THAT IS LEFT.

☆☆☆

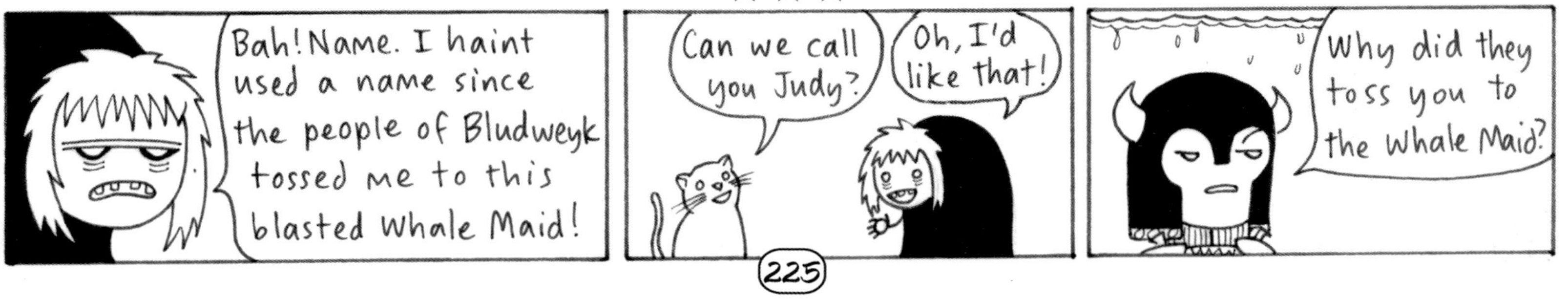
Bah! Name. I haint used a name since the people of Bludweyk tossed me to this blasted Whale Maid!
Can we call you Judy?
Oh, I'd like that!
Why did they toss you to the Whale Maid?

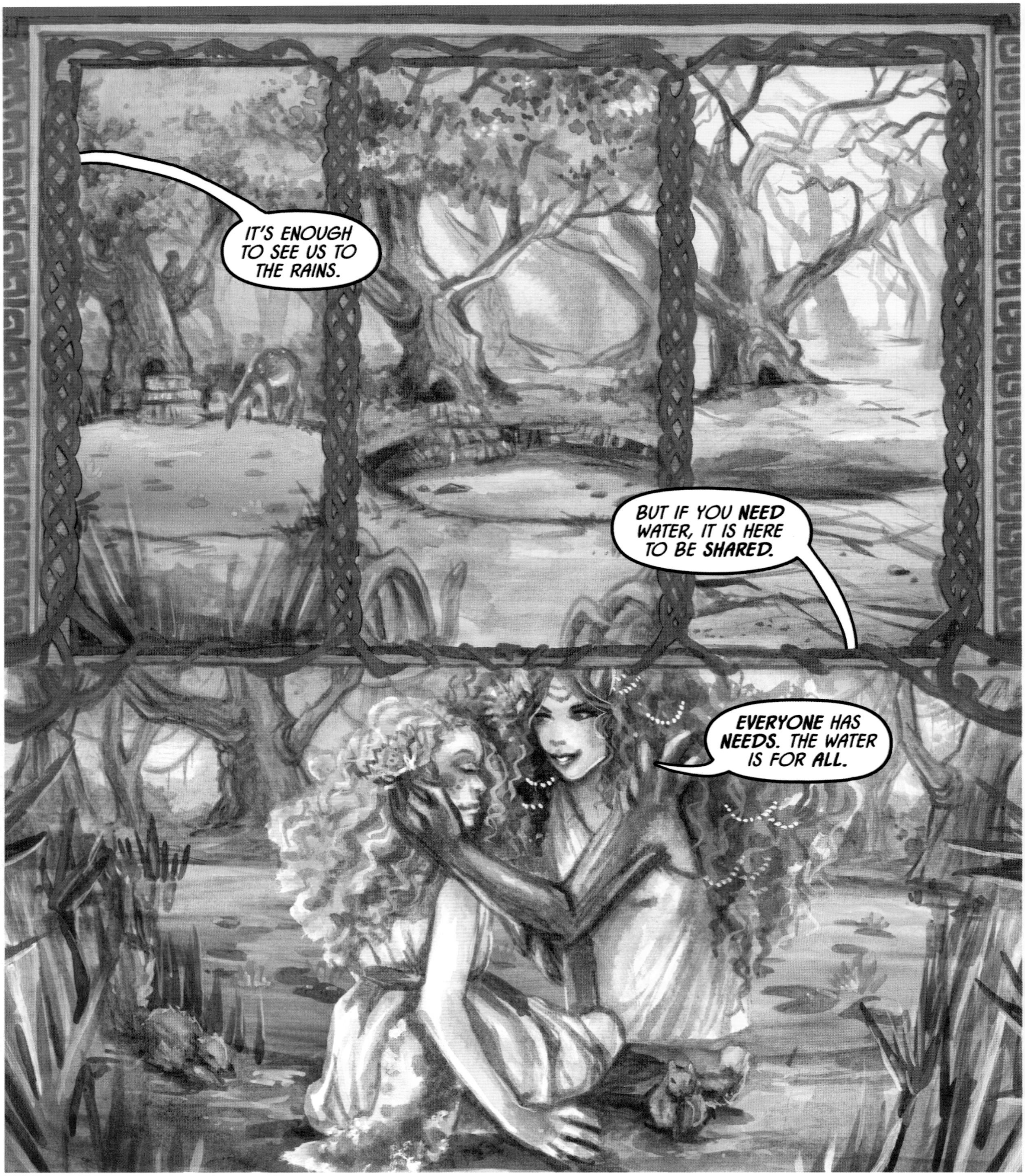
IT'S ENOUGH TO SEE US TO THE RAINS.
BUT IF YOU **NEED** WATER, IT IS HERE TO BE **SHARED.**
EVERYONE HAS **NEEDS.** THE WATER IS FOR **ALL.**

☆☆☆

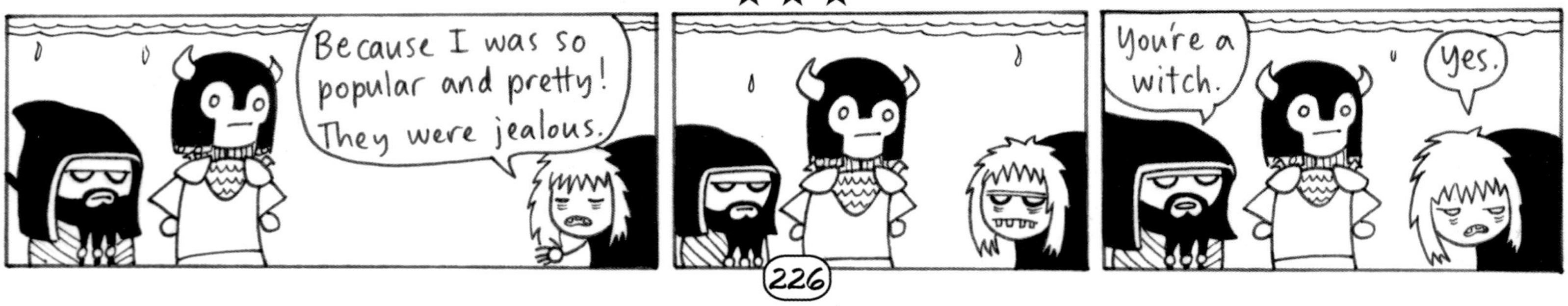
Because I was so popular and pretty! They were jealous.
You're a witch.
Yes.

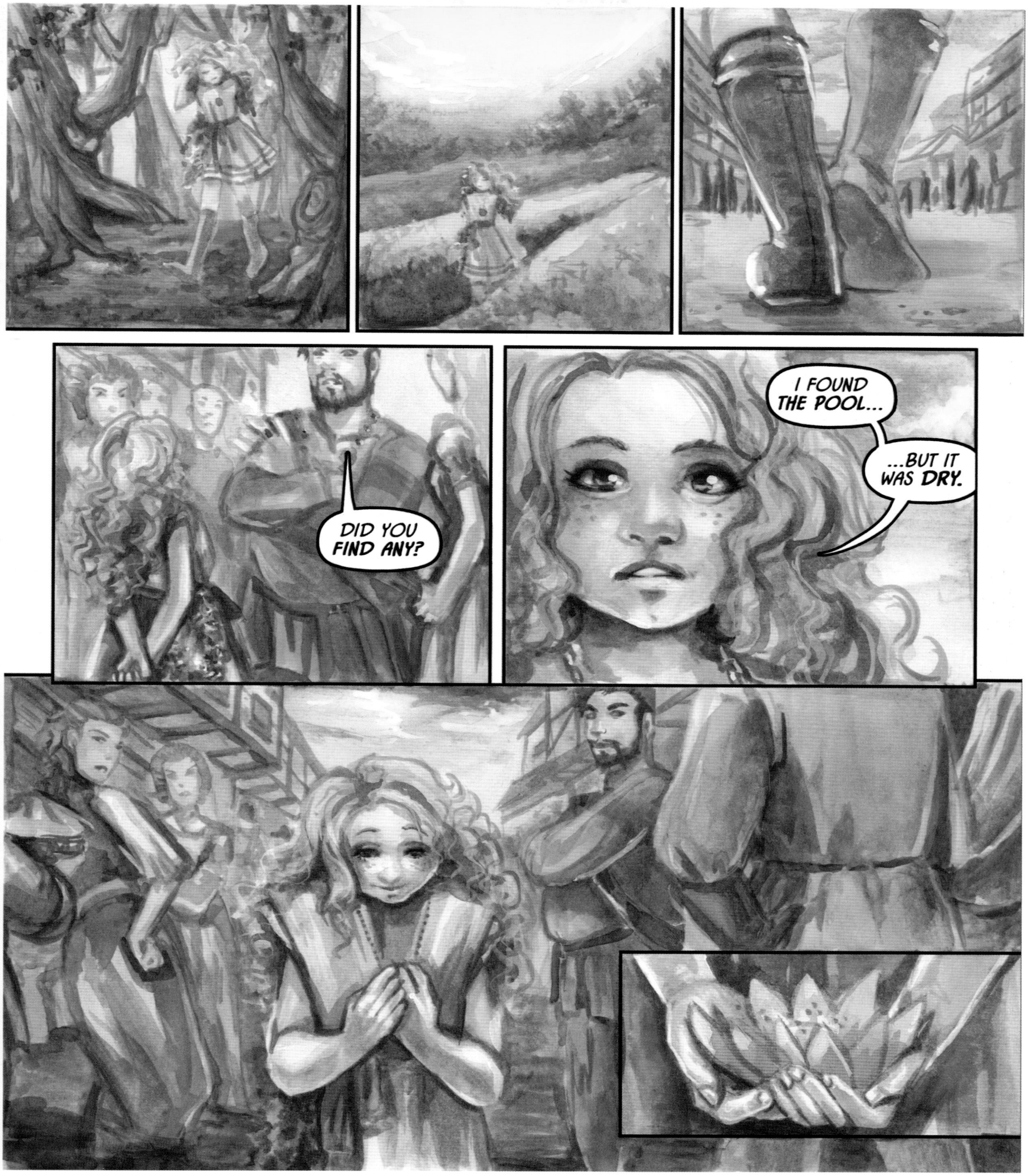
DID YOU FIND ANY?
I FOUND THE POOL...
...BUT IT WAS DRY.

☆ ☆ ☆

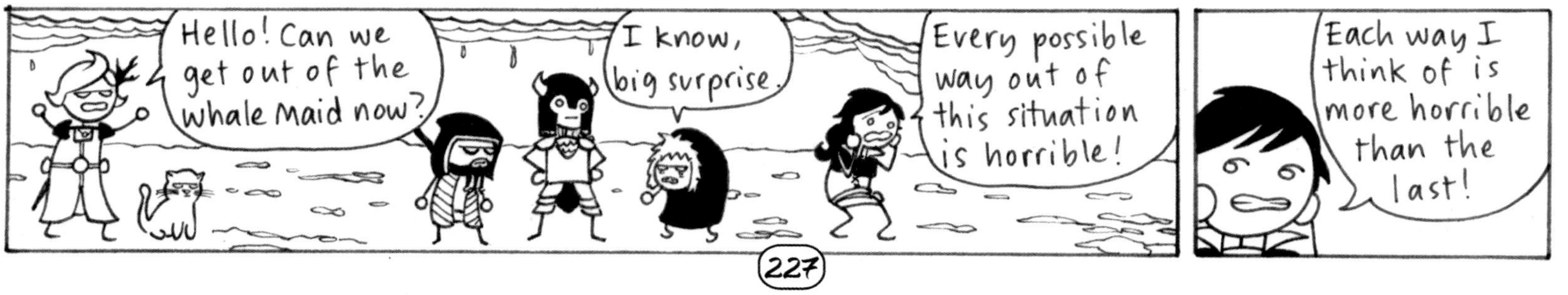
Hello! Can we get out of the whale Maid now?
I know, big surprise.
Every possible way out of this situation is horrible!
Each way I think of is more horrible than the last!

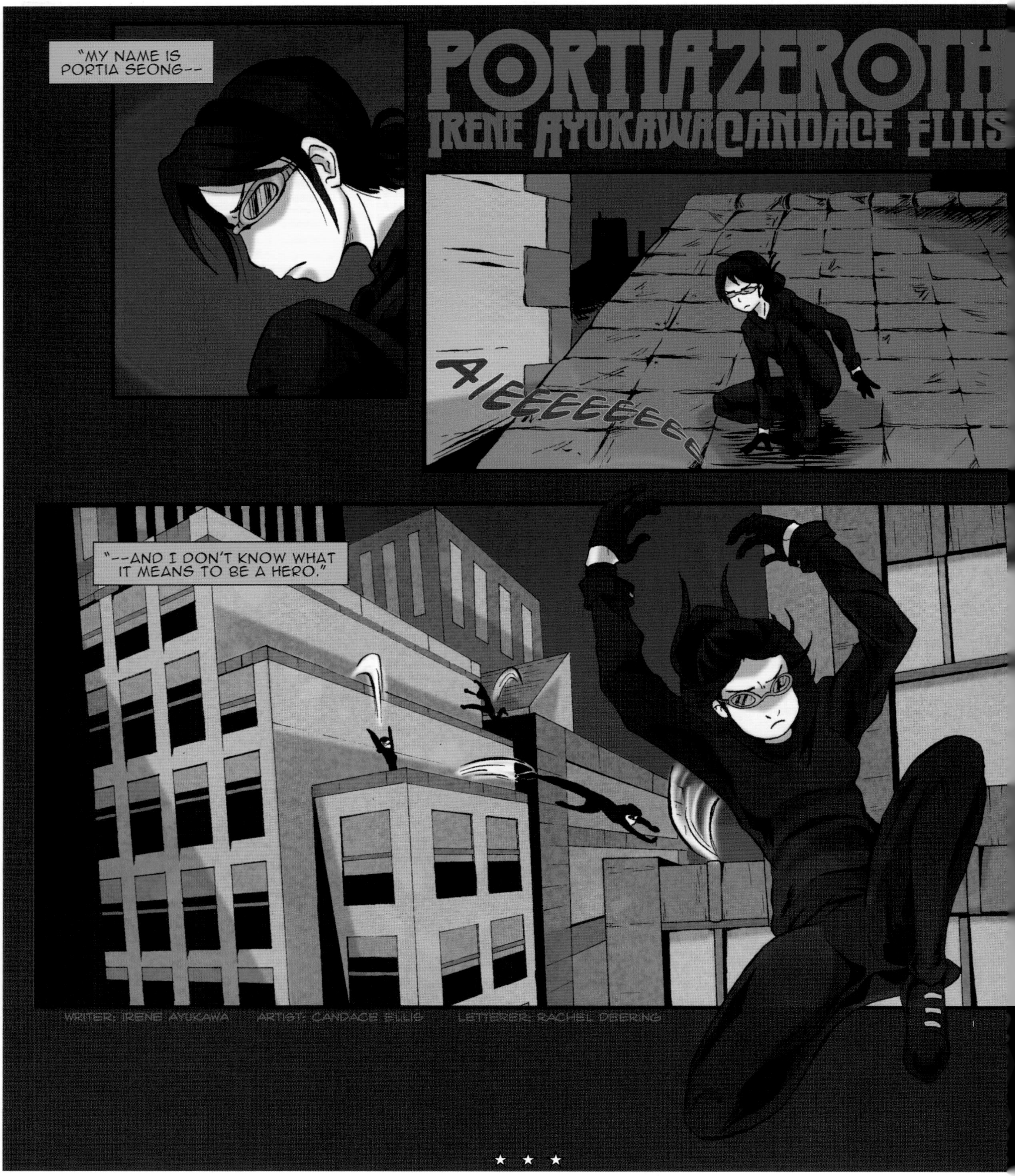
PORTIAZEROTH
IRENE AYUKAWA
CANDACE ELLIS
"MY NAME IS PORTIA SEONG--
AIEEEEEEEEE
"--AND I DON'T KNOW WHAT IT MEANS TO BE A HERO."
WRITER: IRENE AYUKAWA ARTIST: CANDACE ELLIS LETTERER: RACHEL DEERING

★ ★ ★

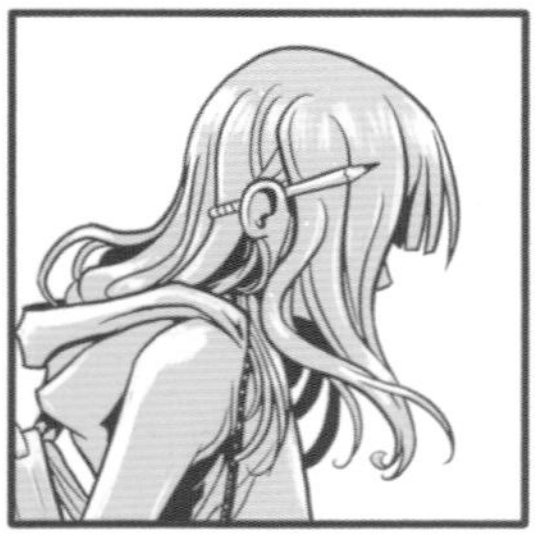

IRENE AYUKAWA

SKILLS: Writer
LOCATION: Ottawa, ON, Canada
FUN FACT: My love of nail polish will be the end of me. Want to see my new colours?

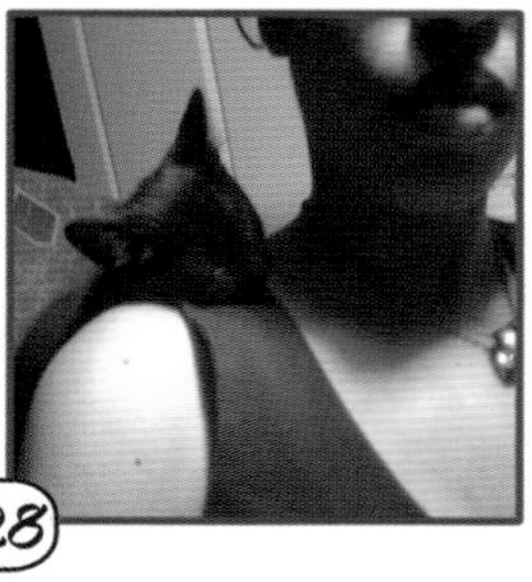

CANDACE ELLIS

SKILLS: Penciller, Inker, Colorist
LOCATION: SF Bay Area
FUN FACT: I was a mermaid in a past life.

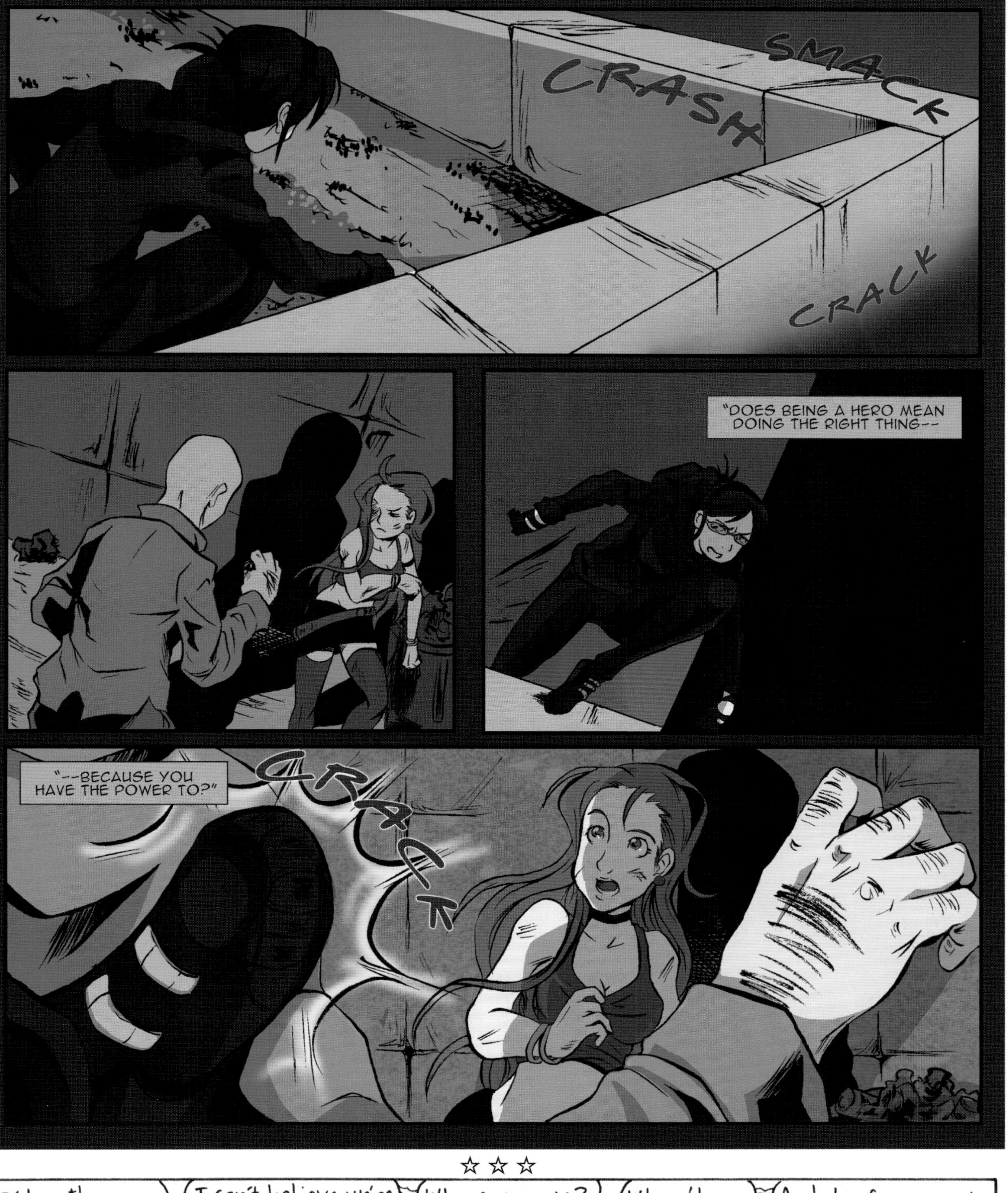
CRASH
SMACK
CRACK
"DOES BEING A HERO MEAN DOING THE RIGHT THING--
"--BECAUSE YOU HAVE THE POWER TO?"
CRACK

☆ ☆ ☆

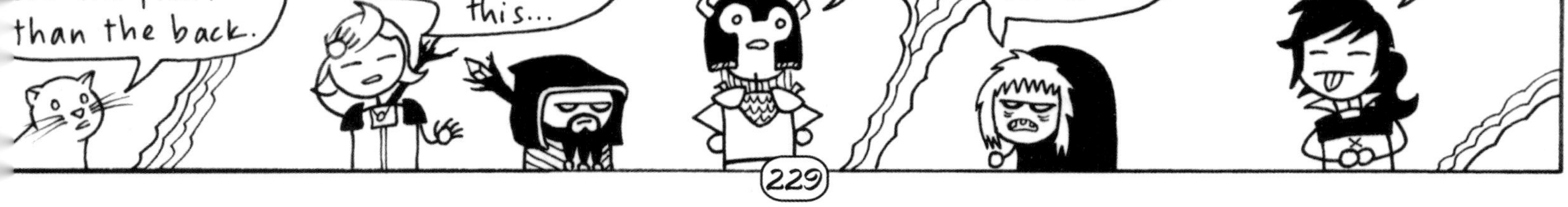
I'd rather go out the front than the back.
I can't believe we're even talking about this...
Where are we?
Where'd you come in?
A... hole of some sort.

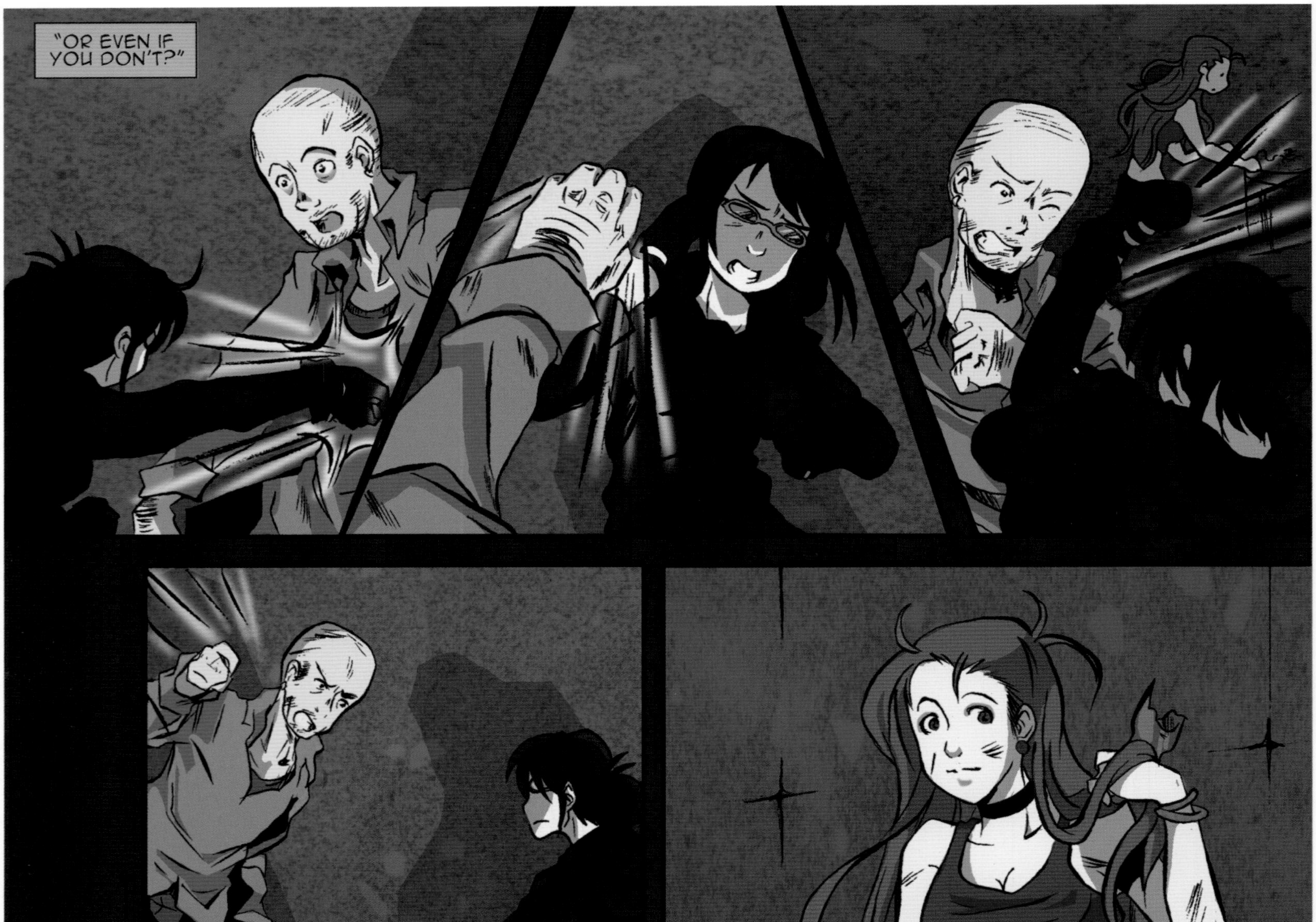
"OR EVEN IF YOU DON'T?"
CRASSHH
"MAYBE IT'S BEING IN THE RIGHT PLACE AT THE RIGHT TIME."

☆ ☆ ☆

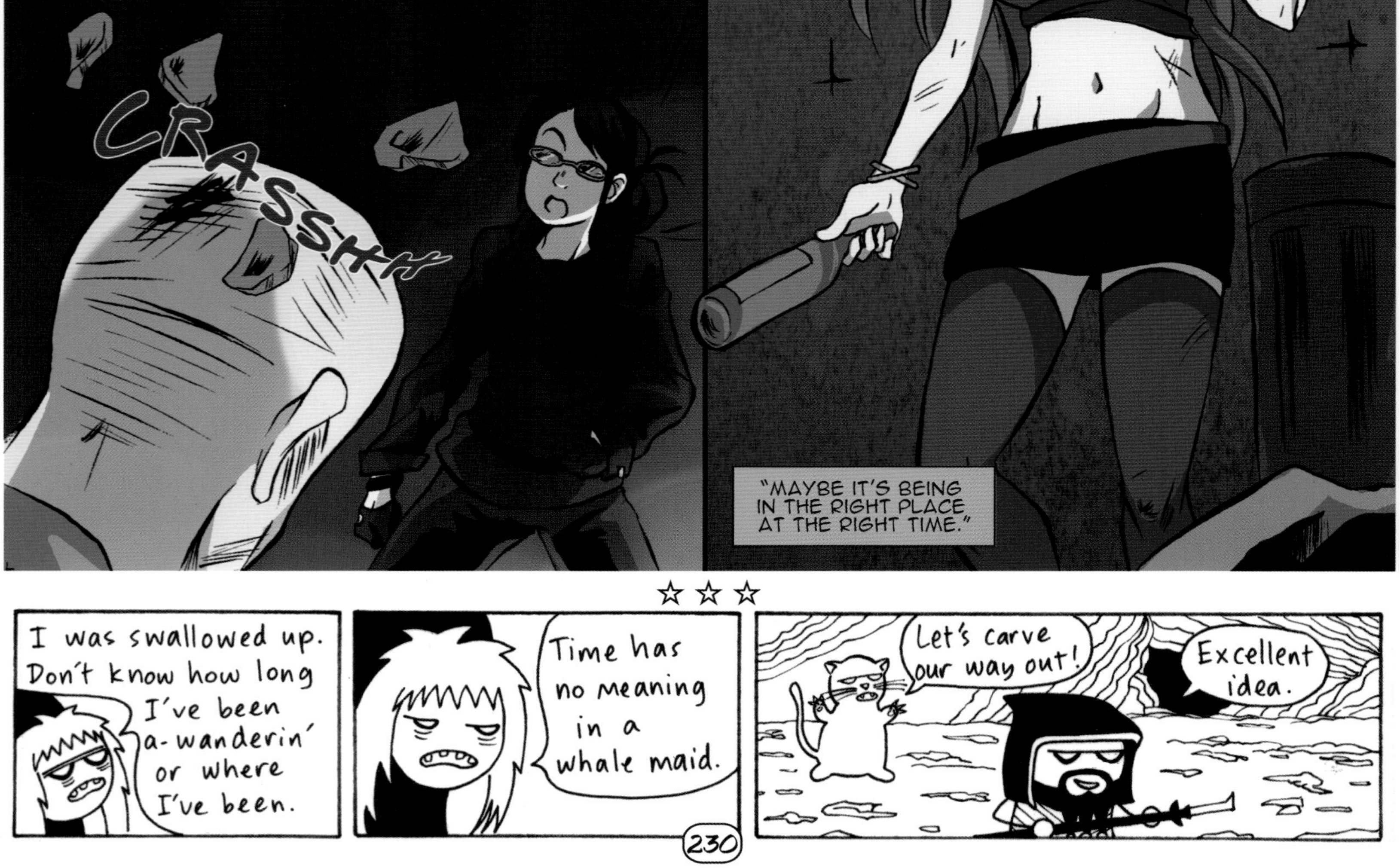
I was swallowed up. Don't know how long
I've been a-wanderin' or where I've been.
Time has no meaning in a whale maid.
Let's carve our way out!
Excellent idea.

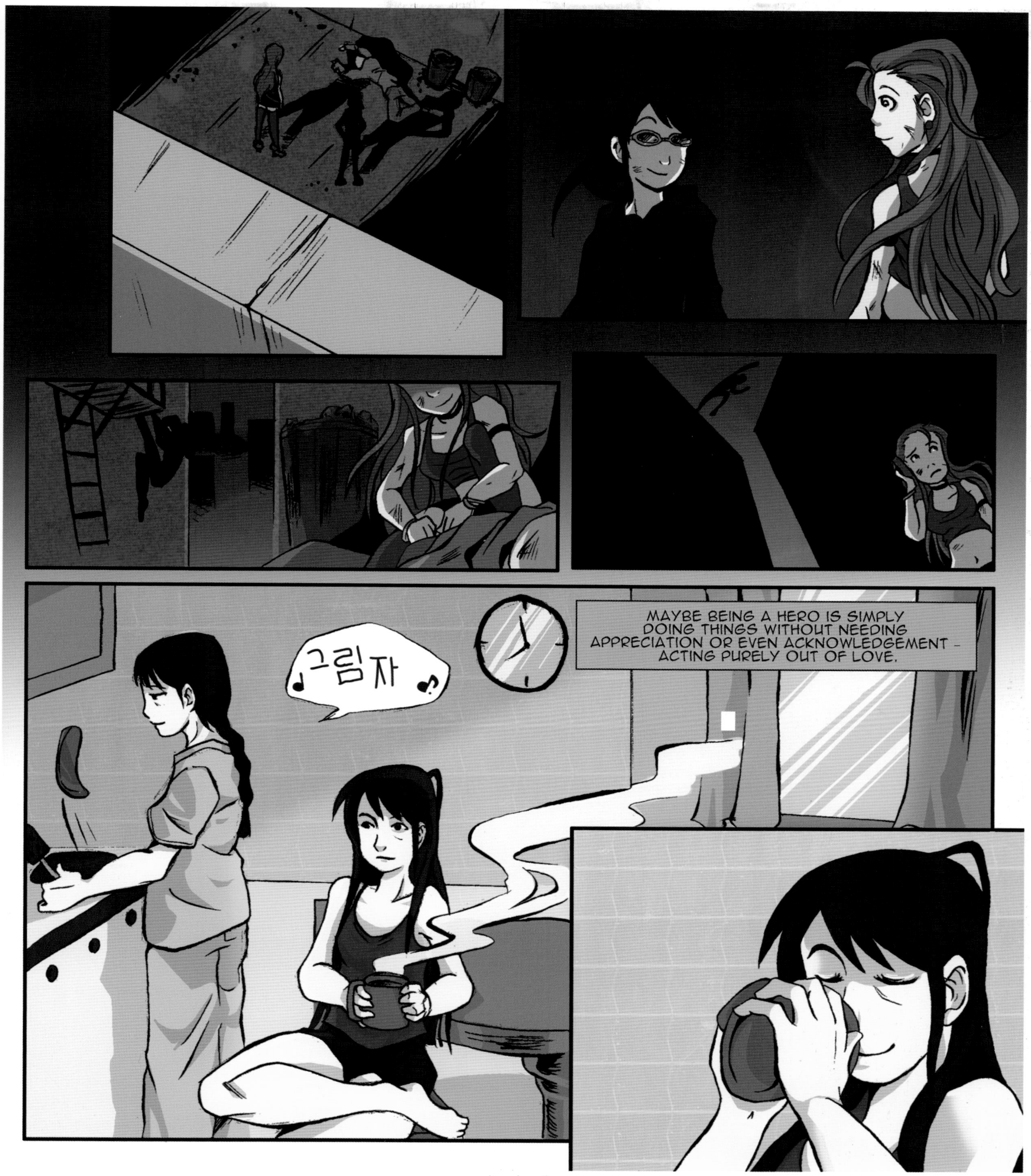

그림자
MAYBE BEING A HERO IS SIMPLY DOING THINGS WITHOUT NEEDING APPRECIATION OR EVEN ACKNOWLEDGEMENT – ACTING PURELY OUT OF LOVE.

☆ ☆ ☆

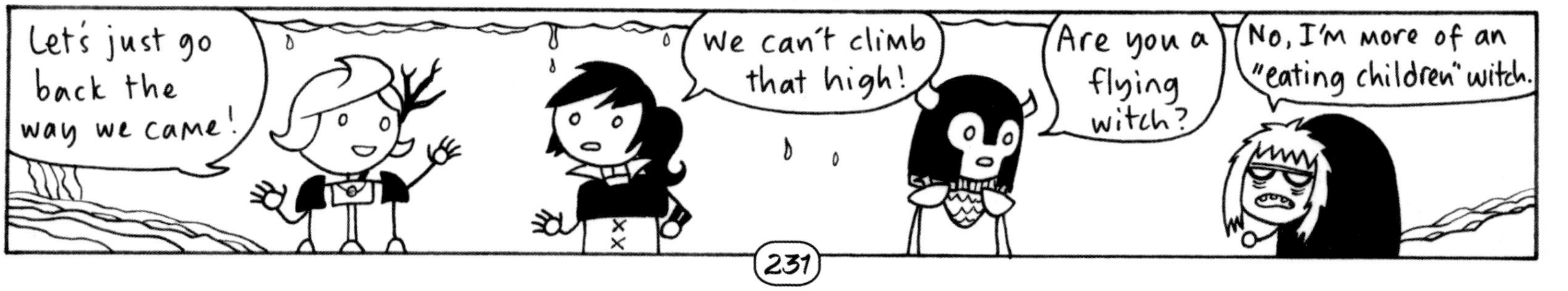

Let's just go back the way we came!
We can't climb that high!
Are you a flying witch?
No, I'm more of an "eating children" witch.

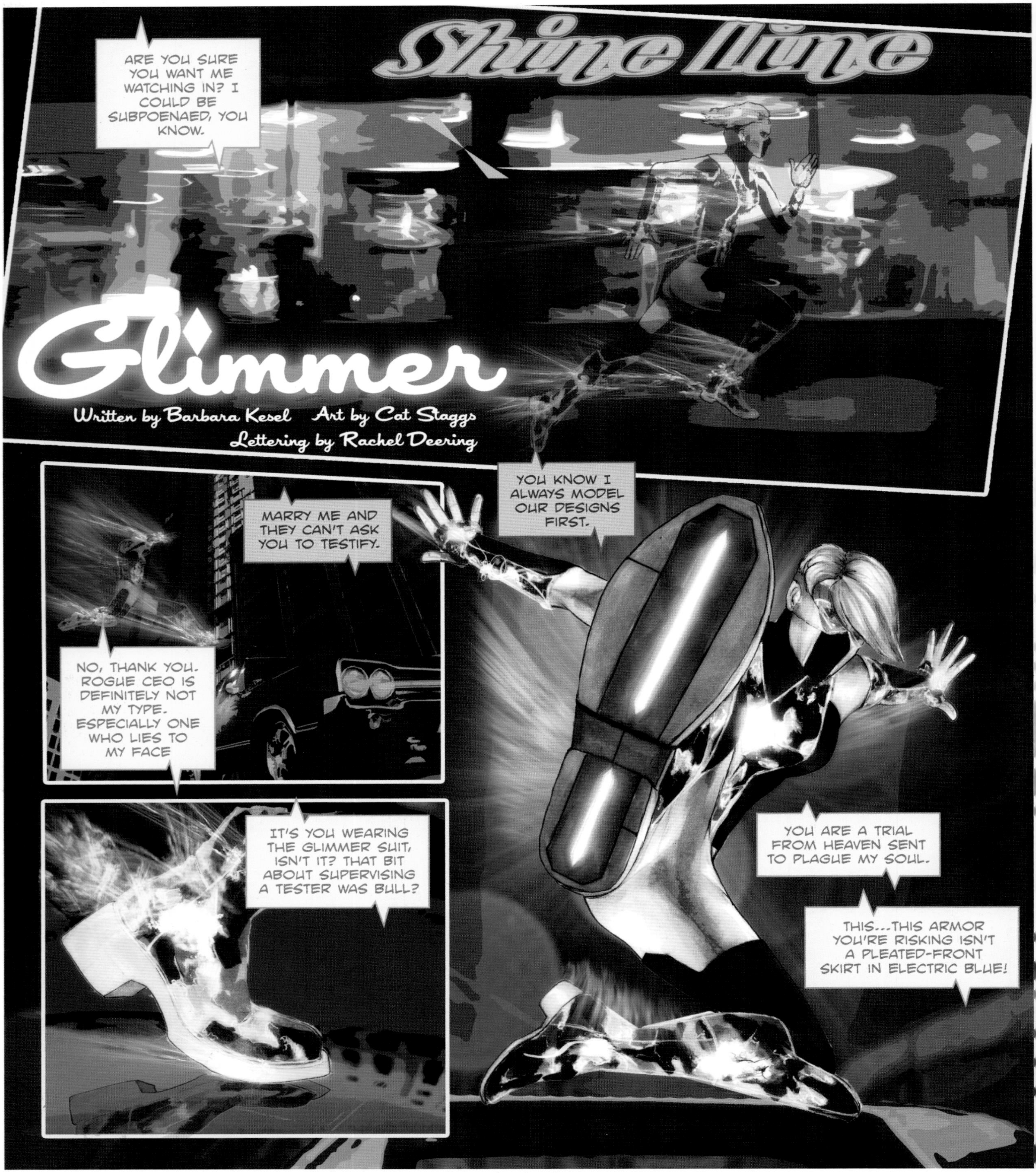

Shine Line
ARE YOU SURE YOU WANT ME WATCHING IN? I COULD BE SUBPOENAED, YOU KNOW.
Glimmer
Written by Barbara Kesel Art by Cat Staggs
Lettering by Rachel Deering
YOU KNOW I ALWAYS MODEL OUR DESIGNS FIRST.
MARRY ME AND THEY CAN'T ASK YOU TO TESTIFY.
NO, THANK YOU. ROGUE CEO IS DEFINITELY NOT MY TYPE. ESPECIALLY ONE WHO LIES TO MY FACE
IT'S YOU WEARING THE GLIMMER SUIT, ISN'T IT? THAT BIT ABOUT SUPERVISING A TESTER WAS BULL?
YOU ARE A TRIAL FROM HEAVEN SENT TO PLAGUE MY SOUL.
THIS...THIS ARMOR YOU'RE RISKING ISN'T A PLEATED-FRONT SKIRT IN ELECTRIC BLUE!

☆ ☆ ☆

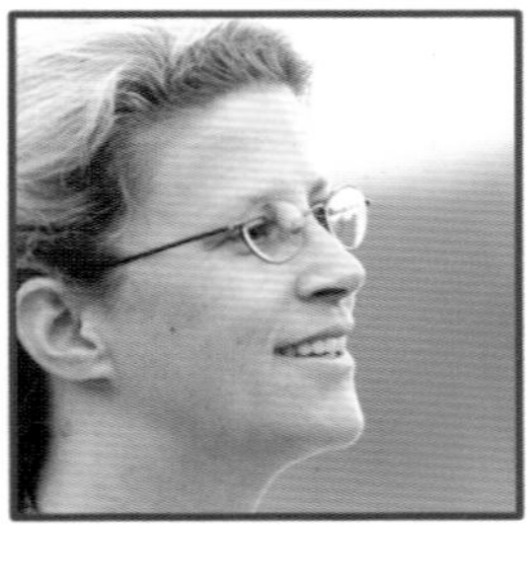

BARBARA RANDALL KESEL

SKILLS: Writer
LOCATION: Diamond Bar, CA
FUN FACT: Ambidextrous, double-jointed Libra: I wobble both literally and figuratively.

barbararandallkesel.com

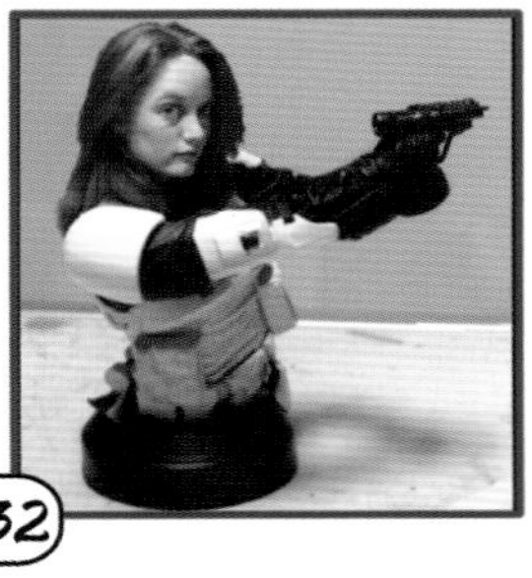

CAT STAGGS

SKILLS: Penciller, Painter
LOCATION: Los Angeles, CA
FUN FACT: I unironically love *Xanadu*.

www.catstaggs.com

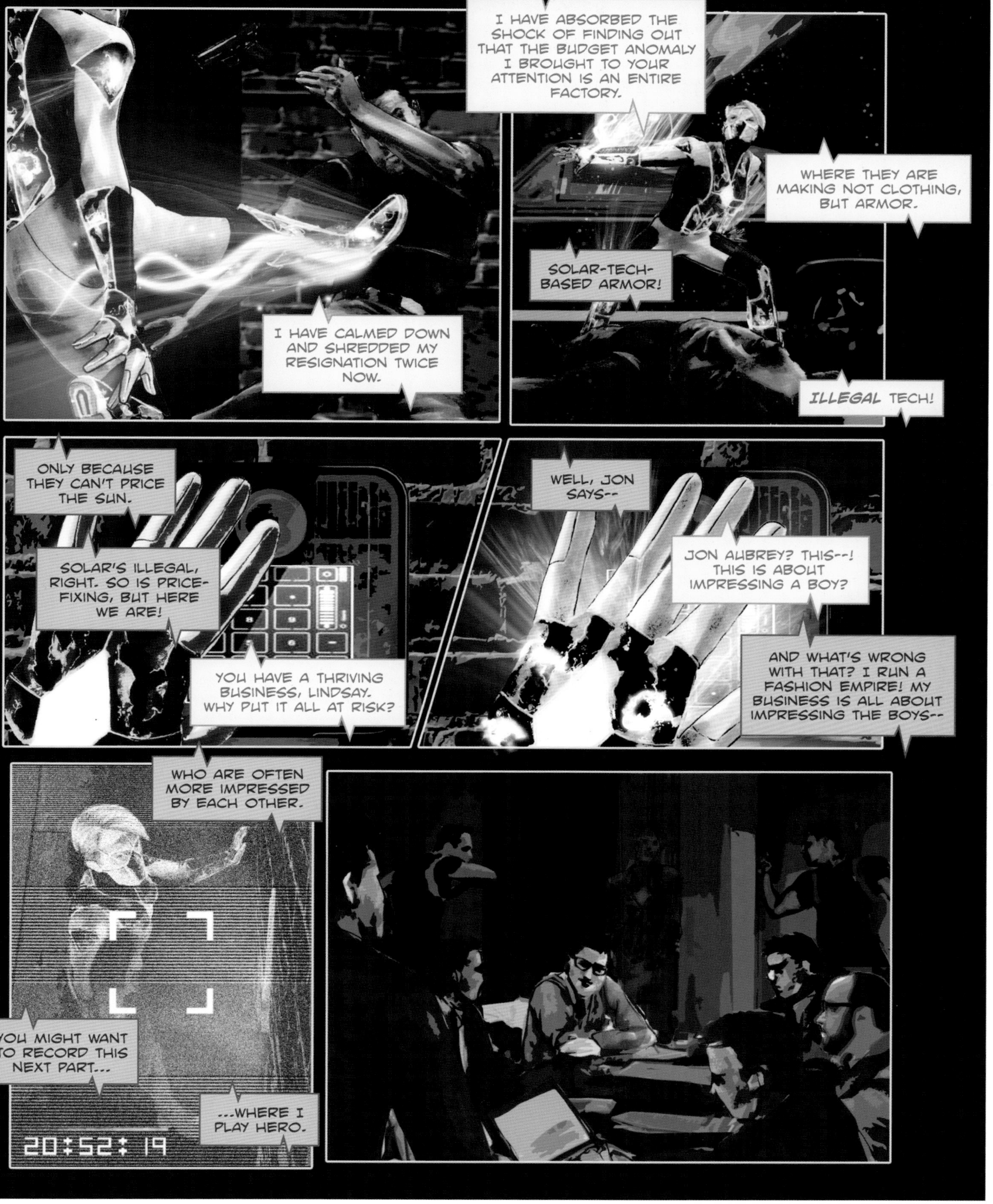
I HAVE CALMED DOWN AND SHREDDED MY RESIGNATION TWICE NOW.
I HAVE ABSORBED THE SHOCK OF FINDING OUT THAT THE BUDGET ANOMALY I BROUGHT TO YOUR ATTENTION IS AN ENTIRE FACTORY.
WHERE THEY ARE MAKING NOT CLOTHING, BUT ARMOR.
SOLAR-TECH-BASED ARMOR!
ILLEGAL TECH!
ONLY BECAUSE THEY CAN'T PRICE THE SUN.
SOLAR'S ILLEGAL, RIGHT. SO IS PRICE-FIXING, BUT HERE WE ARE!
YOU HAVE A THRIVING BUSINESS, LINDSAY. WHY PUT IT ALL AT RISK?
WELL, JON SAYS--
JON AUBREY? THIS--! THIS IS ABOUT IMPRESSING A BOY?
AND WHAT'S WRONG WITH THAT? I RUN A FASHION EMPIRE! MY BUSINESS IS ALL ABOUT IMPRESSING THE BOYS--
WHO ARE OFTEN MORE IMPRESSED BY EACH OTHER.
YOU MIGHT WANT TO RECORD THIS NEXT PART...
...WHERE I PLAY HERO.
20:52:19

☆ ☆ ☆

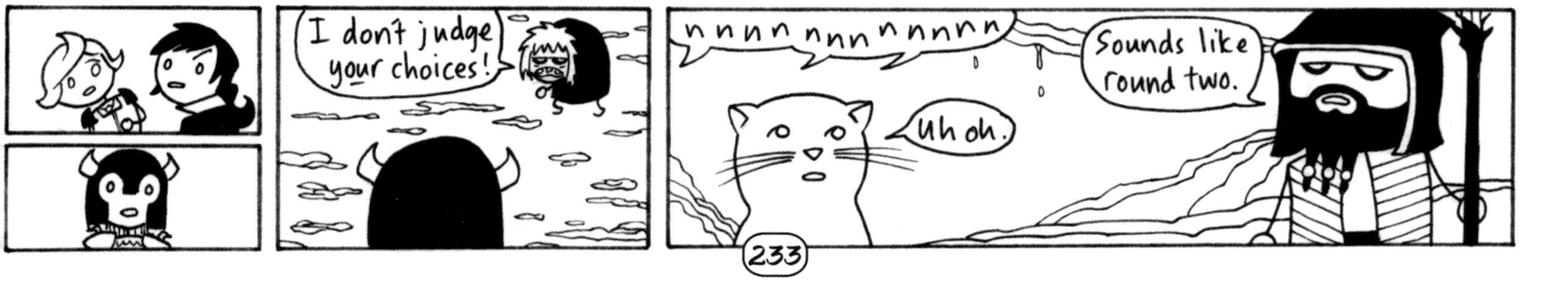
I don't judge your choices!
nnnnnnnnnnnn
Sounds like round two.
Uh oh.

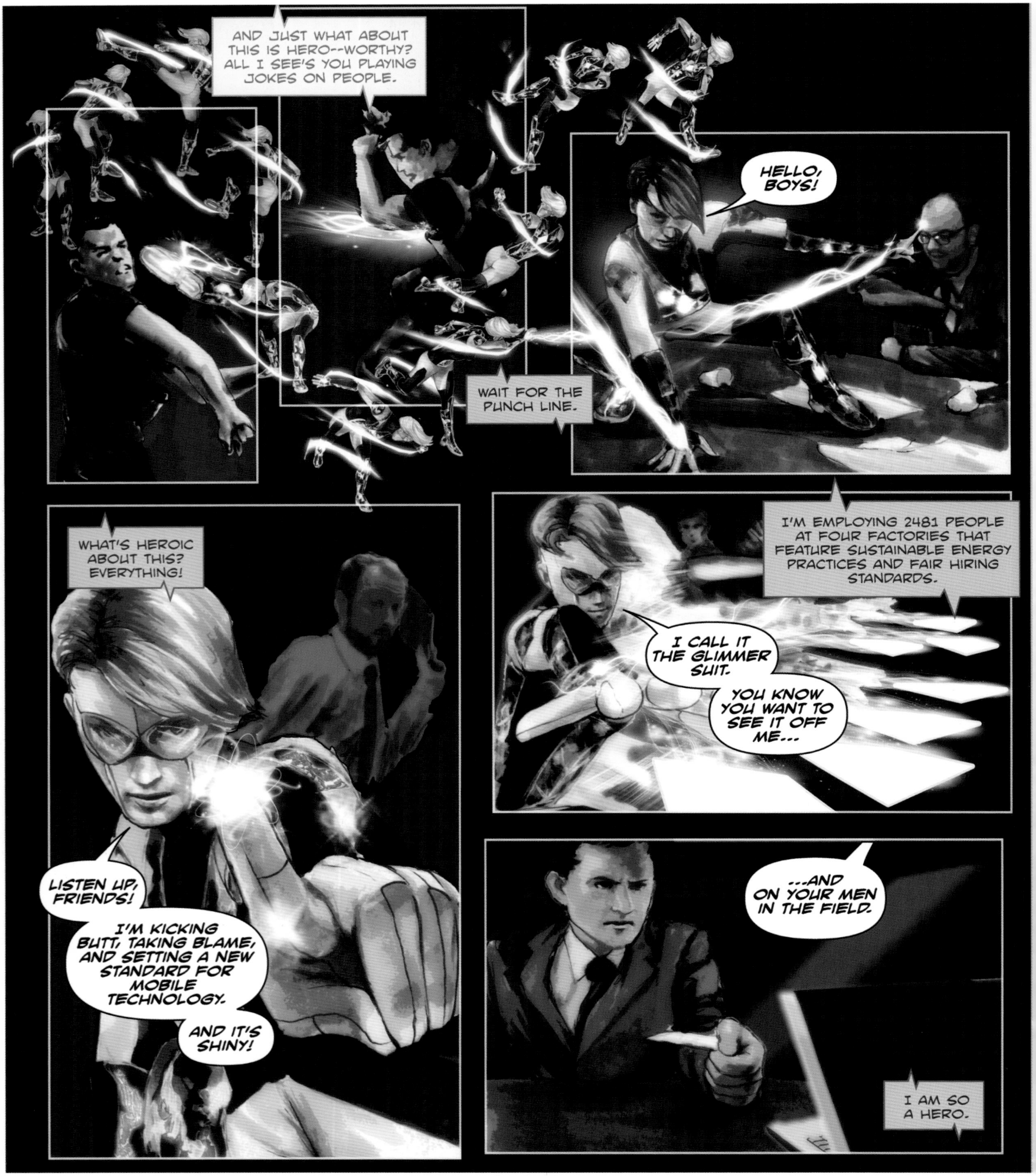
AND JUST WHAT ABOUT THIS IS HERO--WORTHY? ALL I SEE'S YOU PLAYING JOKES ON PEOPLE.
WAIT FOR THE PUNCH LINE.
HELLO, BOYS!
WHAT'S HEROIC ABOUT THIS? EVERYTHING!
LISTEN UP, FRIENDS!
I'M KICKING BUTT, TAKING BLAME, AND SETTING A NEW STANDARD FOR MOBILE TECHNOLOGY.
AND IT'S SHINY!
I'M EMPLOYING 2481 PEOPLE AT FOUR FACTORIES THAT FEATURE SUSTAINABLE ENERGY PRACTICES AND FAIR HIRING STANDARDS.
I CALL IT THE GLIMMER SUIT.
YOU KNOW YOU WANT TO SEE IT OFF ME...
...AND ON YOUR MEN IN THE FIELD.
I AM SO A HERO.

☆ ☆ ☆

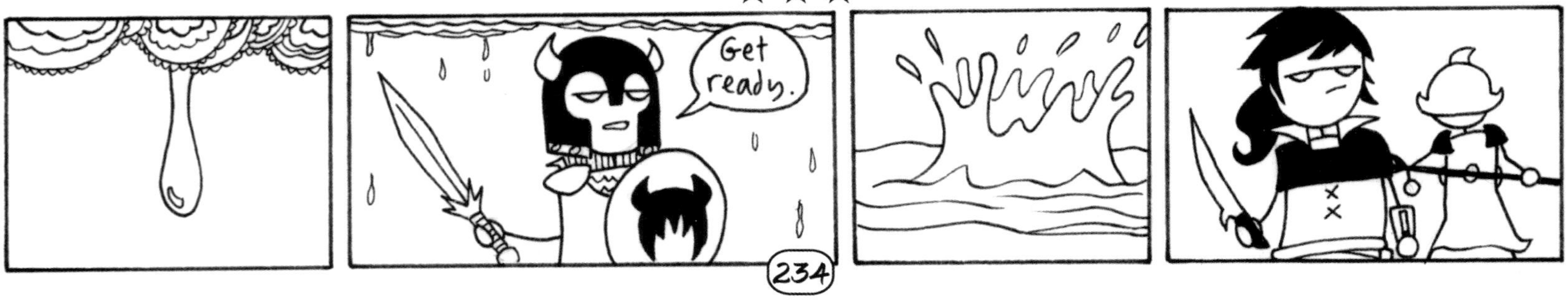
Get ready.

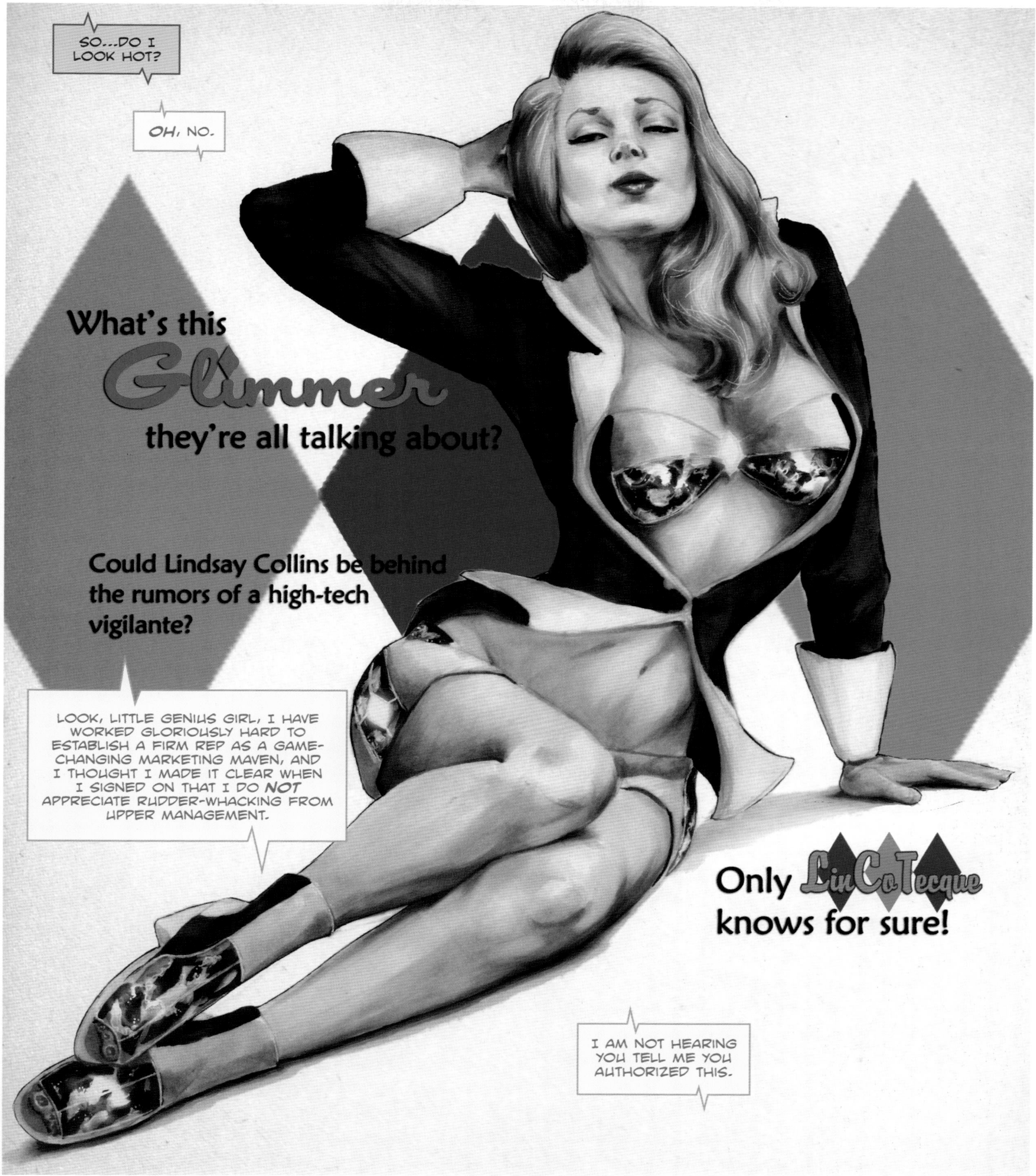
SO...DO I LOOK HOT?
OH, NO.
What's this Glimmer they're all talking about?
Could Lindsay Collins be behind the rumors of a high-tech vigilante?
LOOK, LITTLE GENIUS GIRL, I HAVE WORKED GLORIOUSLY HARD TO ESTABLISH A FIRM REP AS A GAME-CHANGING MARKETING MAVEN, AND I THOUGHT I MADE IT CLEAR WHEN I SIGNED ON THAT I DO NOT APPRECIATE RUDDER-WHACKING FROM UPPER MANAGEMENT.
Only LinCoTecque knows for sure!
I AM NOT HEARING YOU TELL ME YOU AUTHORIZED THIS.

☆ ☆ ☆

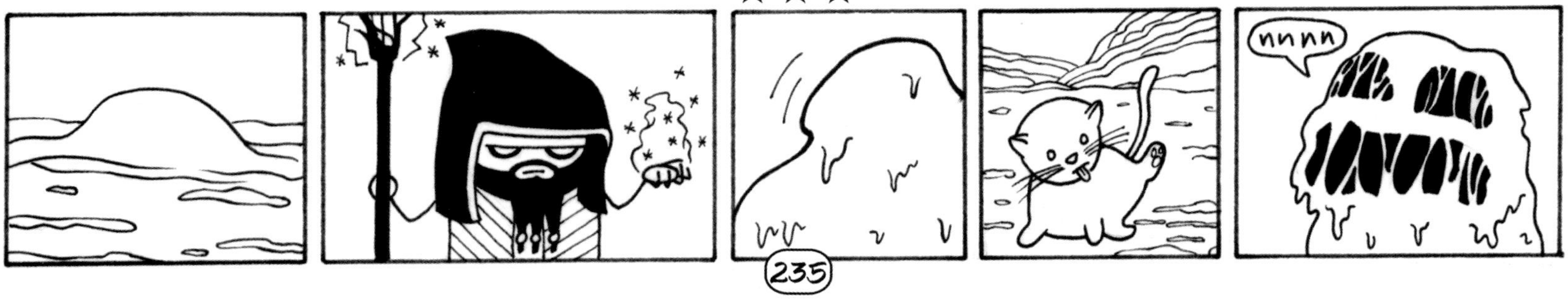
nnnn

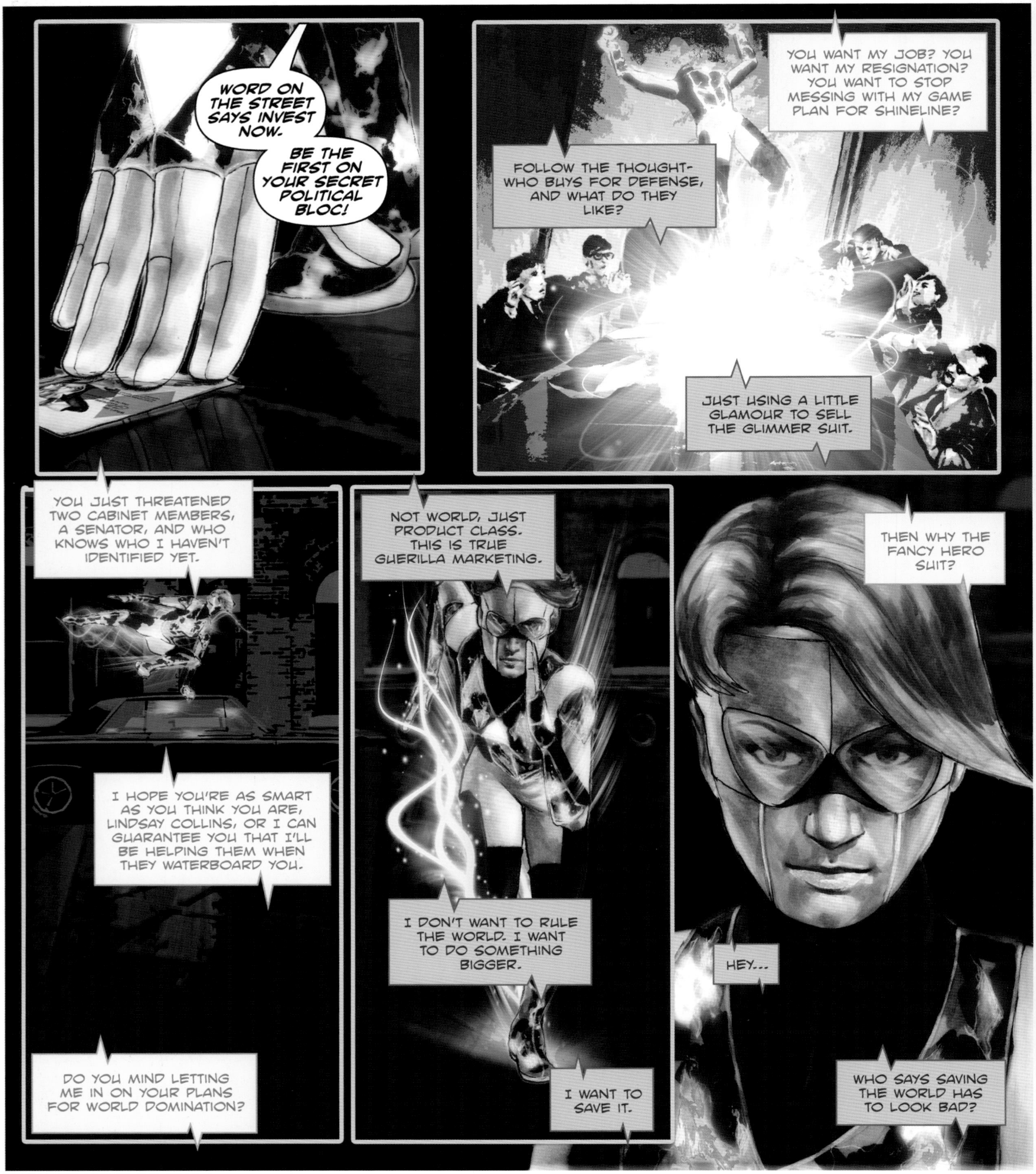
WORD ON THE STREET SAYS INVEST NOW.
BE THE FIRST ON YOUR SECRET POLITICAL BLOC!
YOU WANT MY JOB? YOU WANT MY RESIGNATION? YOU WANT TO STOP MESSING WITH MY GAME PLAN FOR SHINELINE?
FOLLOW THE THOUGHT- WHO BUYS FOR DEFENSE, AND WHAT DO THEY LIKE?
JUST USING A LITTLE GLAMOUR TO SELL THE GLIMMER SUIT.
YOU JUST THREATENED TWO CABINET MEMBERS, A SENATOR, AND WHO KNOWS WHO I HAVEN'T IDENTIFIED YET.
I HOPE YOU'RE AS SMART AS YOU THINK YOU ARE, LINDSAY COLLINS, OR I CAN GUARANTEE YOU THAT I'LL BE HELPING THEM WHEN THEY WATERBOARD YOU.
DO YOU MIND LETTING ME IN ON YOUR PLANS FOR WORLD DOMINATION?
NOT WORLD, JUST PRODUCT CLASS. THIS IS TRUE GUERILLA MARKETING.
I DON'T WANT TO RULE THE WORLD. I WANT TO DO SOMETHING BIGGER.
I WANT TO SAVE IT.
THEN WHY THE FANCY HERO SUIT?
HEY...
WHO SAYS SAVING THE WORLD HAS TO LOOK BAD?

☆ ☆ ☆

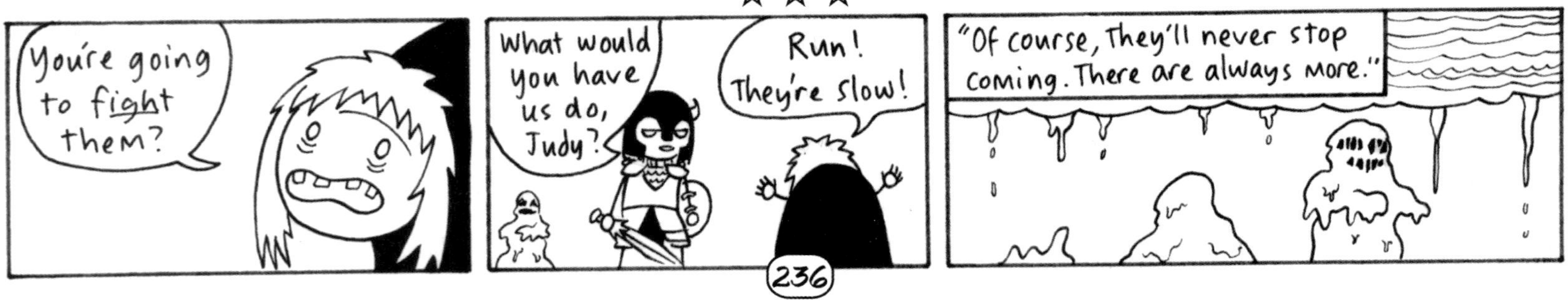
You're going to fight them?
What would you have us do, Judy?
Run! They're slow!
"Of course, They'll never stop coming. There are always more."

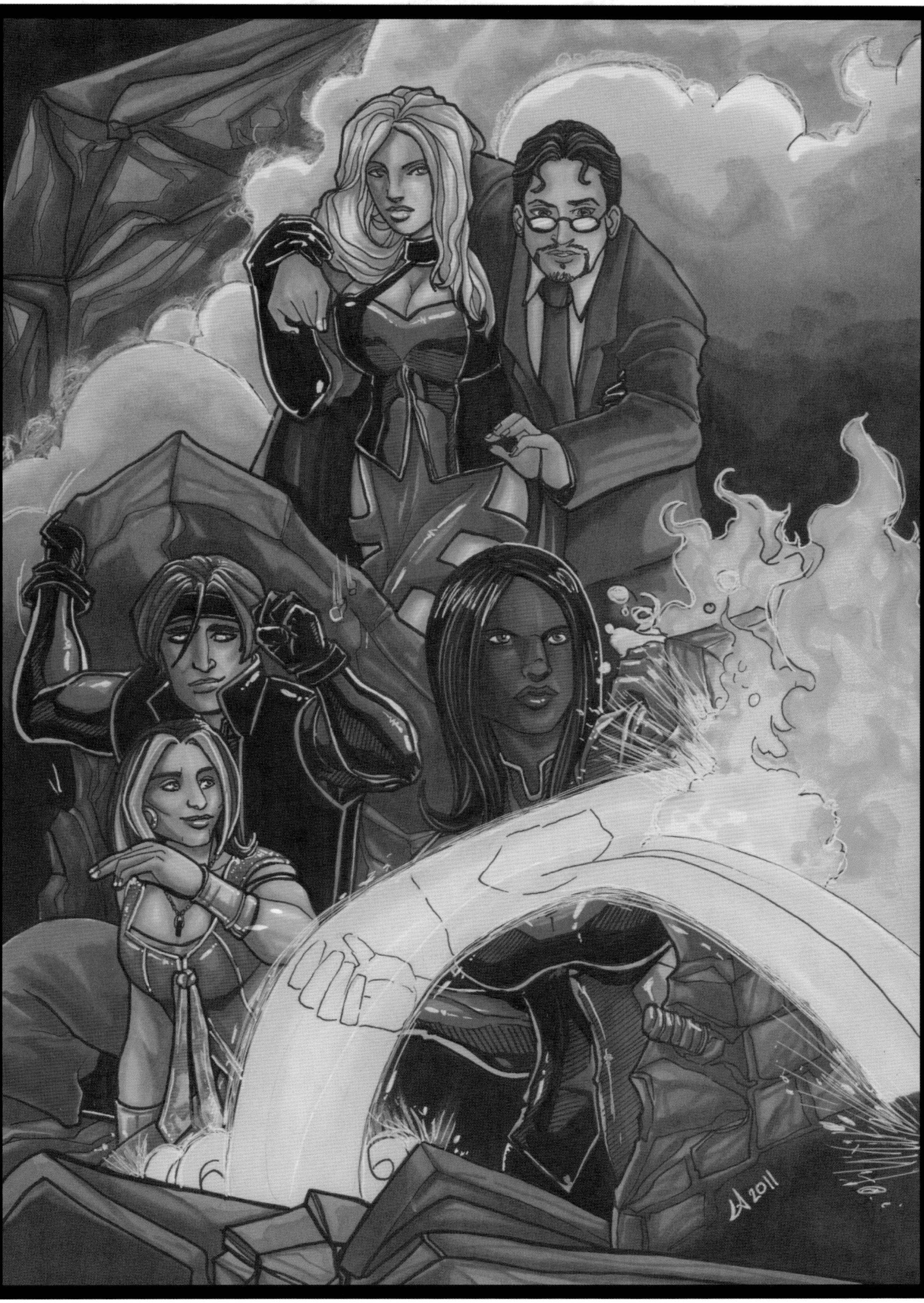

☆☆☆

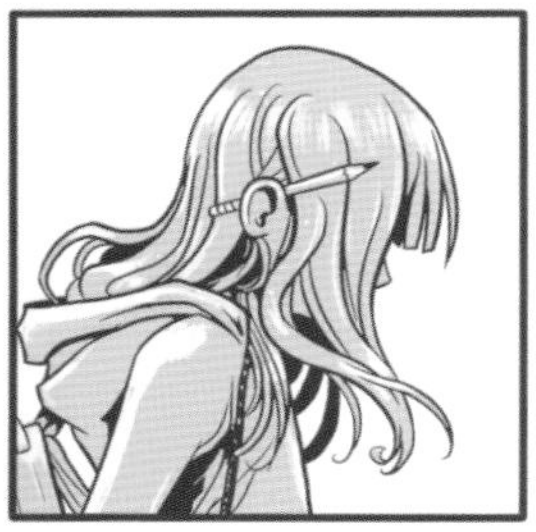

LYNNE ANDERSON

SKILLS: Pinup Artist (all three chores required)
LOCATION: Colorado
FUN FACT: It's interesting that I can't ever think of anything interesting about myself ;)

www.chaoticharmony.com

PRO TIP

WRITING LESS
BY LAURA MORLEY

"DON'T MAKE YOUR SCRIPTS TOO VERBOSE. FIRSTLY, RAMBLING PANEL DESCRIPTIONS CAN DISTRACT, BORE, OR OVERWHELM YOUR ARTIST. SECONDLY, YOU'LL ALMOST ALWAYS MAKE A BETTER COMIC IF YOUR ARTIST'S INVOLVED IN THE VISUAL STORYTELLING TOO."

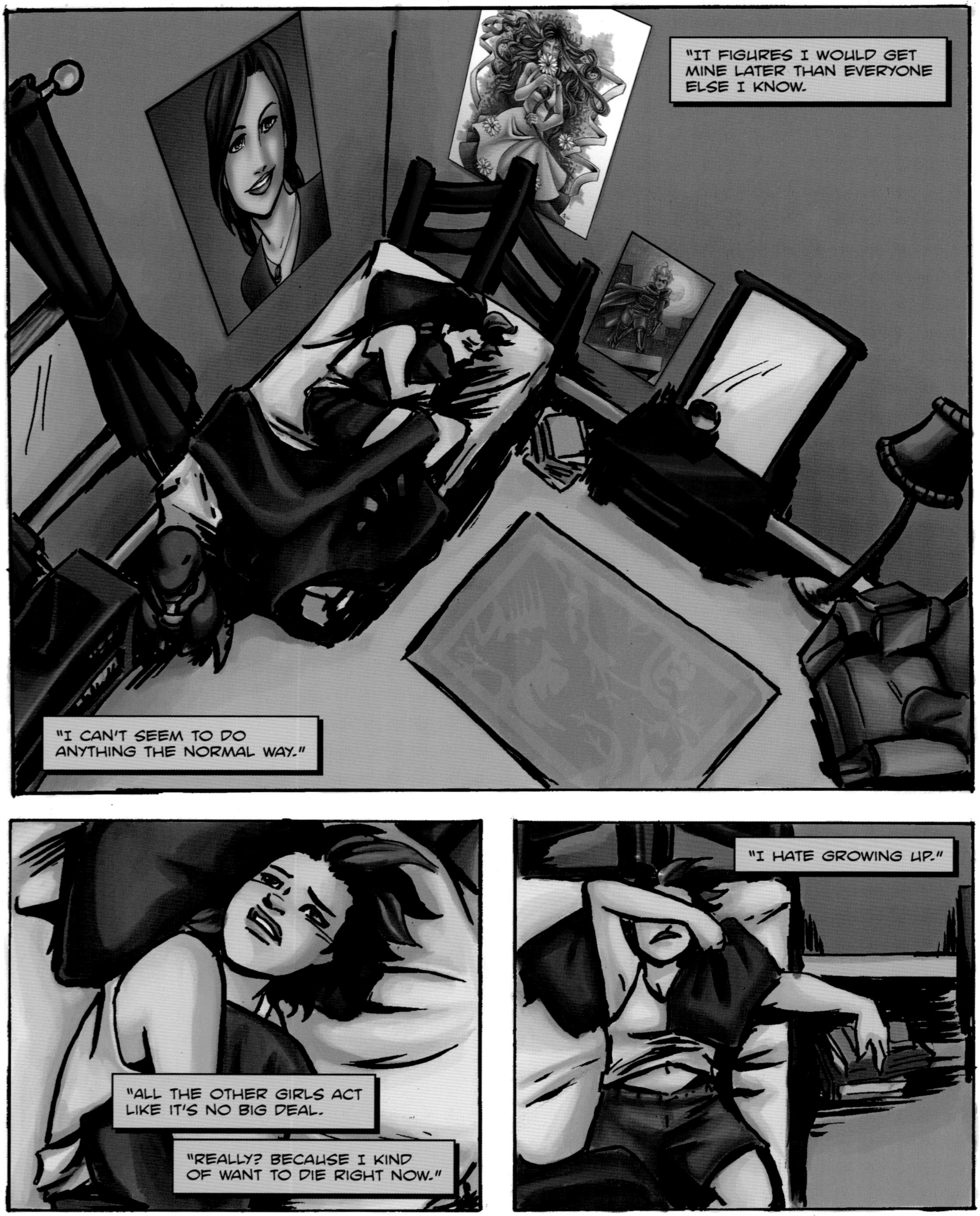
"IT FIGURES I WOULD GET MINE LATER THAN EVERYONE ELSE I KNOW.
"I CAN'T SEEM TO DO ANYTHING THE NORMAL WAY."
"ALL THE OTHER GIRLS ACT LIKE IT'S NO BIG DEAL.
"REALLY? BECAUSE I KIND OF WANT TO DIE RIGHT NOW."
"I HATE GROWING UP."

WRITER: MARIAH MCCOURT ARTIST: CK RUSSELL COLORIST: THALIA DE LA TORRE LETTERER: RACHEL DEERING

☆☆☆

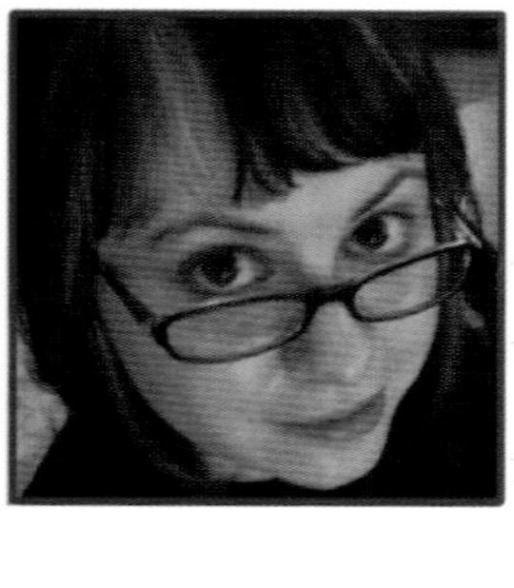

MARIAH MCCOURT

SKILLS: Writer, Artist, Editor
LOCATION: San Francisco
FUN FACT: Stories are my life.

squidygirl.blogspot.com

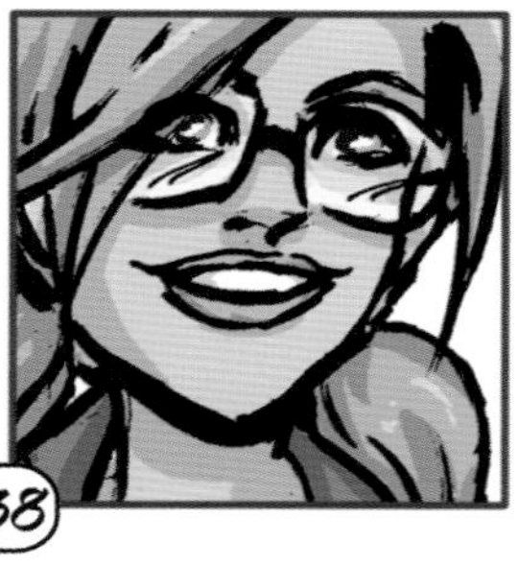

CK RUSSELL

SKILLS: Penciller, Inker
LOCATION: Prince Edward Island, Canada
FUN FACT: I started drawing to fund my comic habit. Two great tastes that taste better together!

http://ckrussell.com

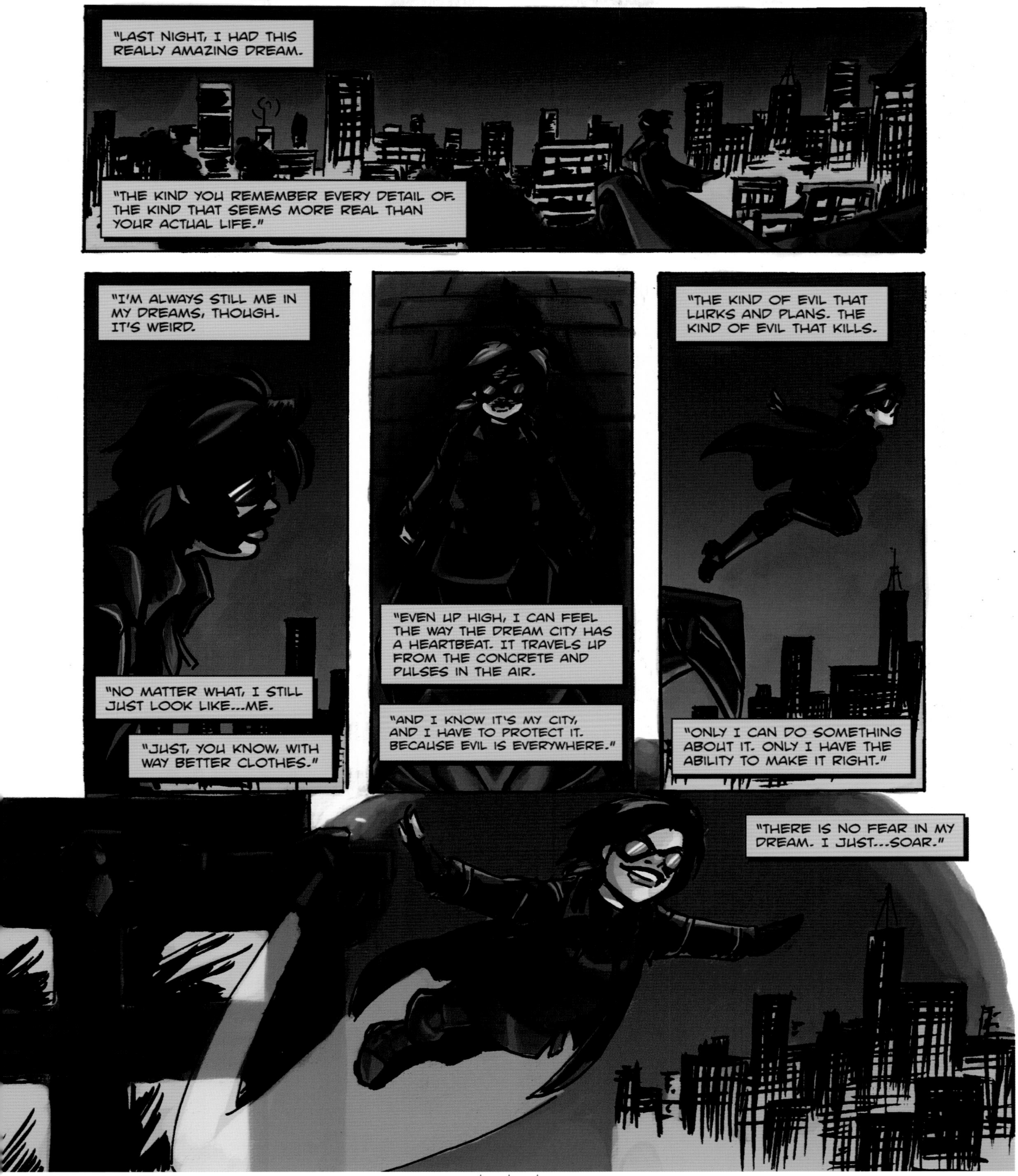
"LAST NIGHT, I HAD THIS REALLY AMAZING DREAM.
"THE KIND YOU REMEMBER EVERY DETAIL OF. THE KIND THAT SEEMS MORE REAL THAN YOUR ACTUAL LIFE."
"I'M ALWAYS STILL ME IN MY DREAMS, THOUGH. IT'S WEIRD.
"NO MATTER WHAT, I STILL JUST LOOK LIKE...ME.
"JUST, YOU KNOW, WITH WAY BETTER CLOTHES."
"EVEN UP HIGH, I CAN FEEL THE WAY THE DREAM CITY HAS A HEARTBEAT. IT TRAVELS UP FROM THE CONCRETE AND PULSES IN THE AIR.
"AND I KNOW IT'S MY CITY, AND I HAVE TO PROTECT IT. BECAUSE EVIL IS EVERYWHERE."
"THE KIND OF EVIL THAT LURKS AND PLANS. THE KIND OF EVIL THAT KILLS.
"ONLY I CAN DO SOMETHING ABOUT IT. ONLY I HAVE THE ABILITY TO MAKE IT RIGHT."
"THERE IS NO FEAR IN MY DREAM. I JUST...SOAR."

☆☆☆

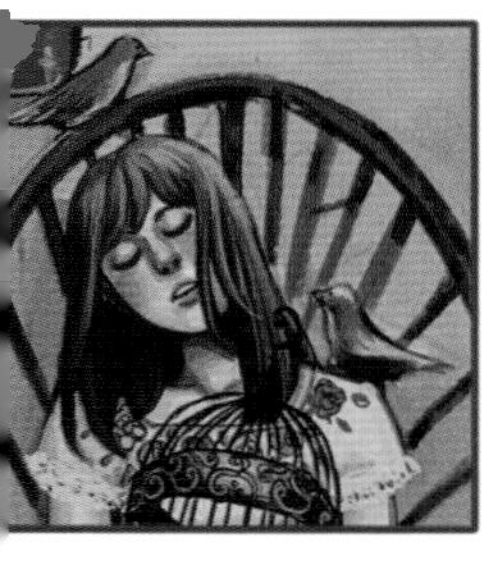

THALIA DE LA TORRE

SKILLS: Artist
LOCATION: Mexico City
FUN FACT: I can bend my arms 360 degrees! :D

http://belivac.blogspot.com

PRO TIP

EDITORS

BY MARIAH MCCOURT

"NOT MANY PEOPLE WANT TO BE EDITORS, BUT IF YOU DO, IT REALLY IS A SKILL THAT NEEDS REFINING AND CRAFTING. YOU'RE HELPING OTHER PEOPLE TELL THEIR STORIES AND YOU MUST NEVER, EVER, FORGET THAT. IT'S NOT ABOUT YOU, IT'S NOT ABOUT WHAT YOU WOULD DO, IT'S ABOUT FINDING THE CORE OF WHAT THE WRITER IS TRYING TO EXPRESS AND HELPING THEM ACHIEVE IT. BE CLEAR ABOUT WHAT DOES AND DOES NOT WORK, GIVE THOUGHTFUL, REASONABLE SUGGESTIONS. EXPLAIN YOURSELF, DON'T LECTURE."

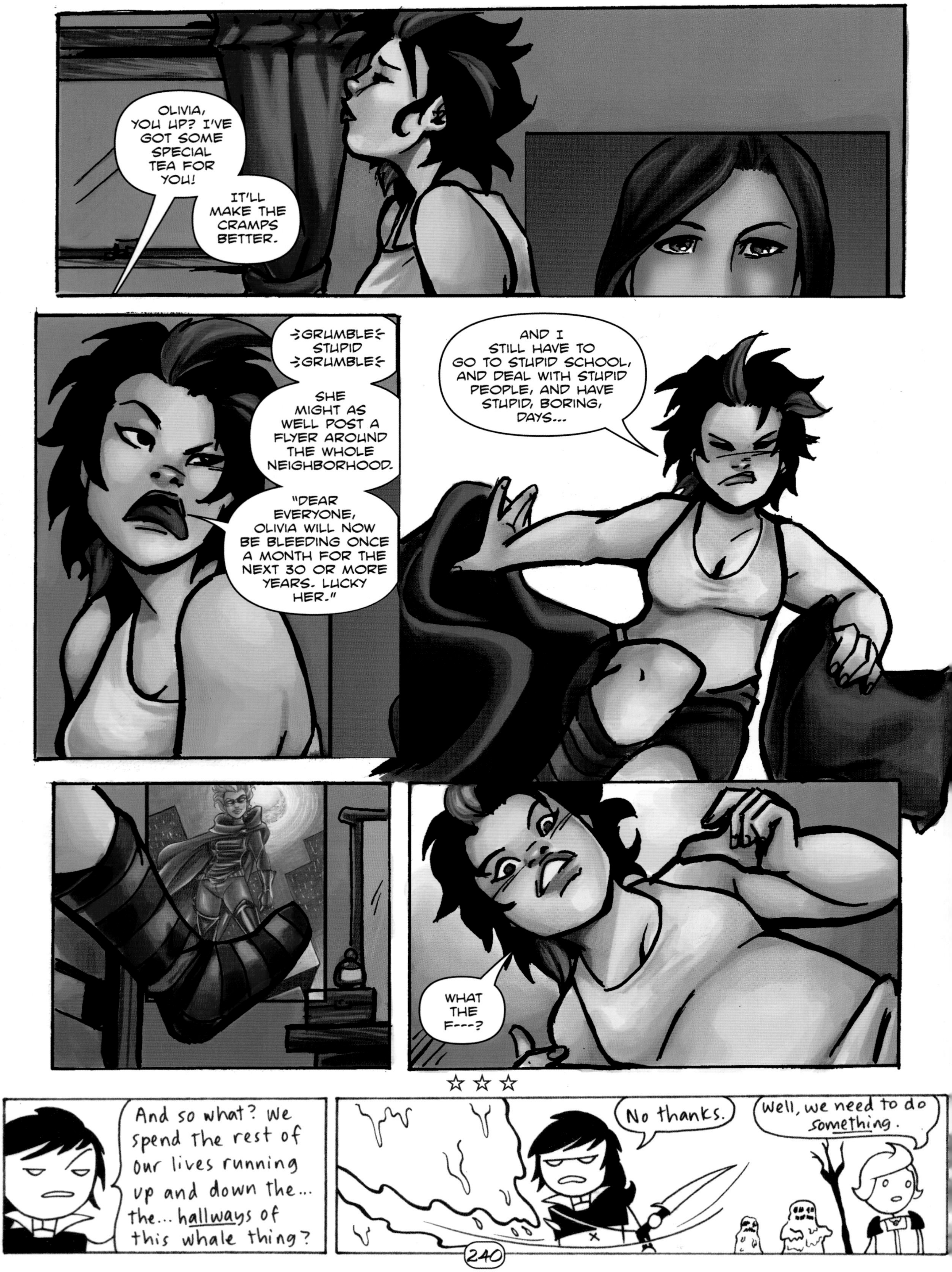
OLIVIA, YOU UP? I'VE GOT SOME SPECIAL TEA FOR YOU!
IT'LL MAKE THE CRAMPS BETTER.
-GRUMBLE- STUPID -GRUMBLE-
SHE MIGHT AS WELL POST A FLYER AROUND THE WHOLE NEIGHBORHOOD.
"DEAR EVERYONE, OLIVIA WILL NOW BE BLEEDING ONCE A MONTH FOR THE NEXT 30 OR MORE YEARS. LUCKY HER."
AND I STILL HAVE TO GO TO STUPID SCHOOL, AND DEAL WITH STUPID PEOPLE, AND HAVE STUPID, BORING, DAYS...
WHAT THE F---?
☆ ☆ ☆
And so what? We spend the rest of our lives running up and down the... the... hallways of this whale thing?
No thanks.
Well, we need to do something.

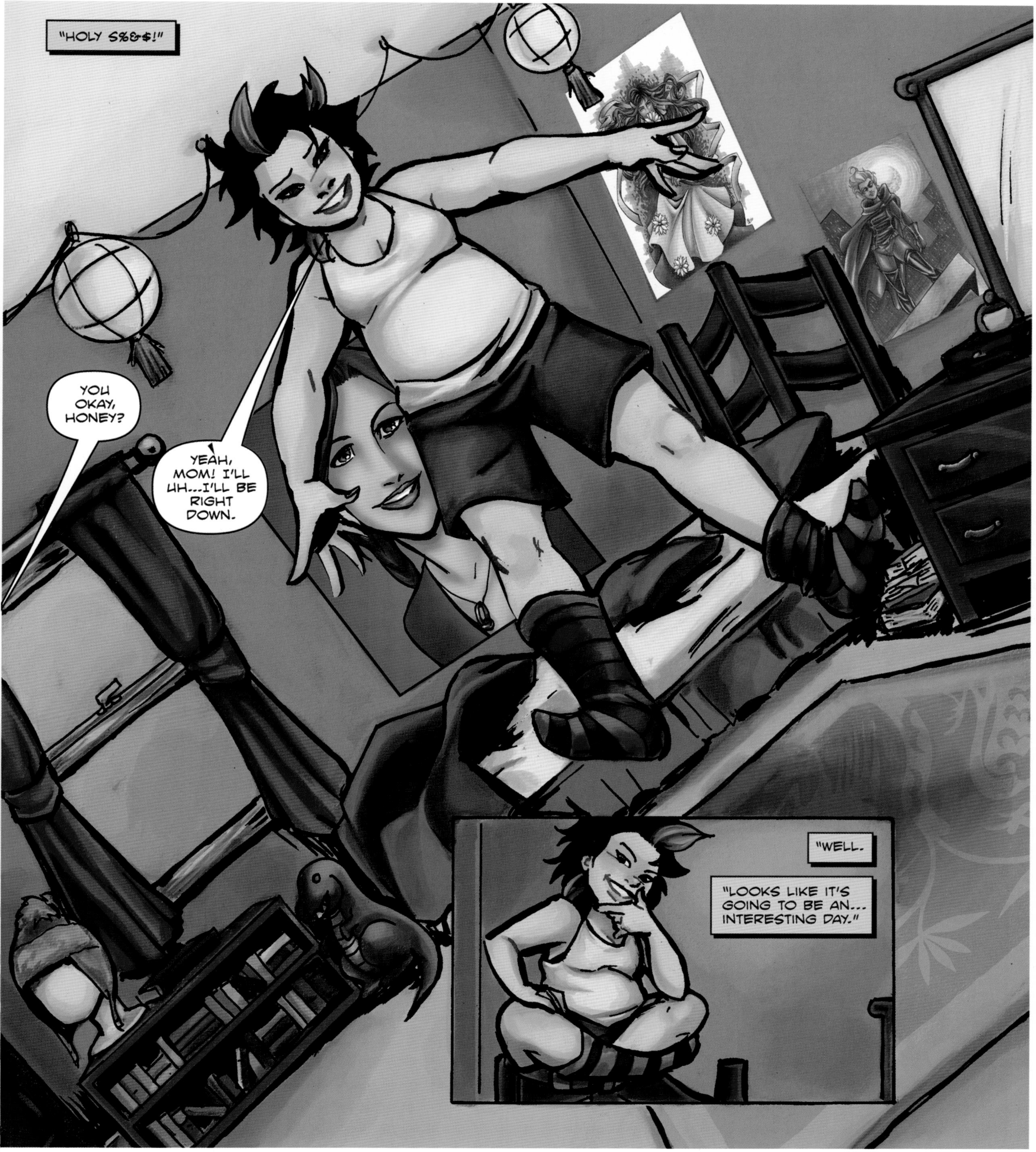
"HOLY $%&$!"
YOU OKAY, HONEY?
YEAH, MOM! I'LL UH...I'LL BE RIGHT DOWN.
"WELL.
"LOOKS LIKE IT'S GOING TO BE AN... INTERESTING DAY."

☆ ☆ ☆

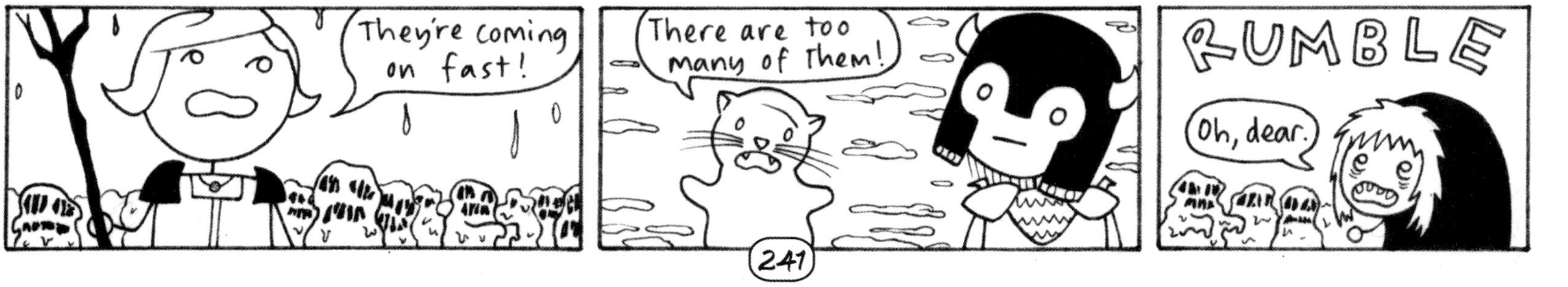
They're coming on fast!
There are too many of them!
RUMBLE
Oh, dear.

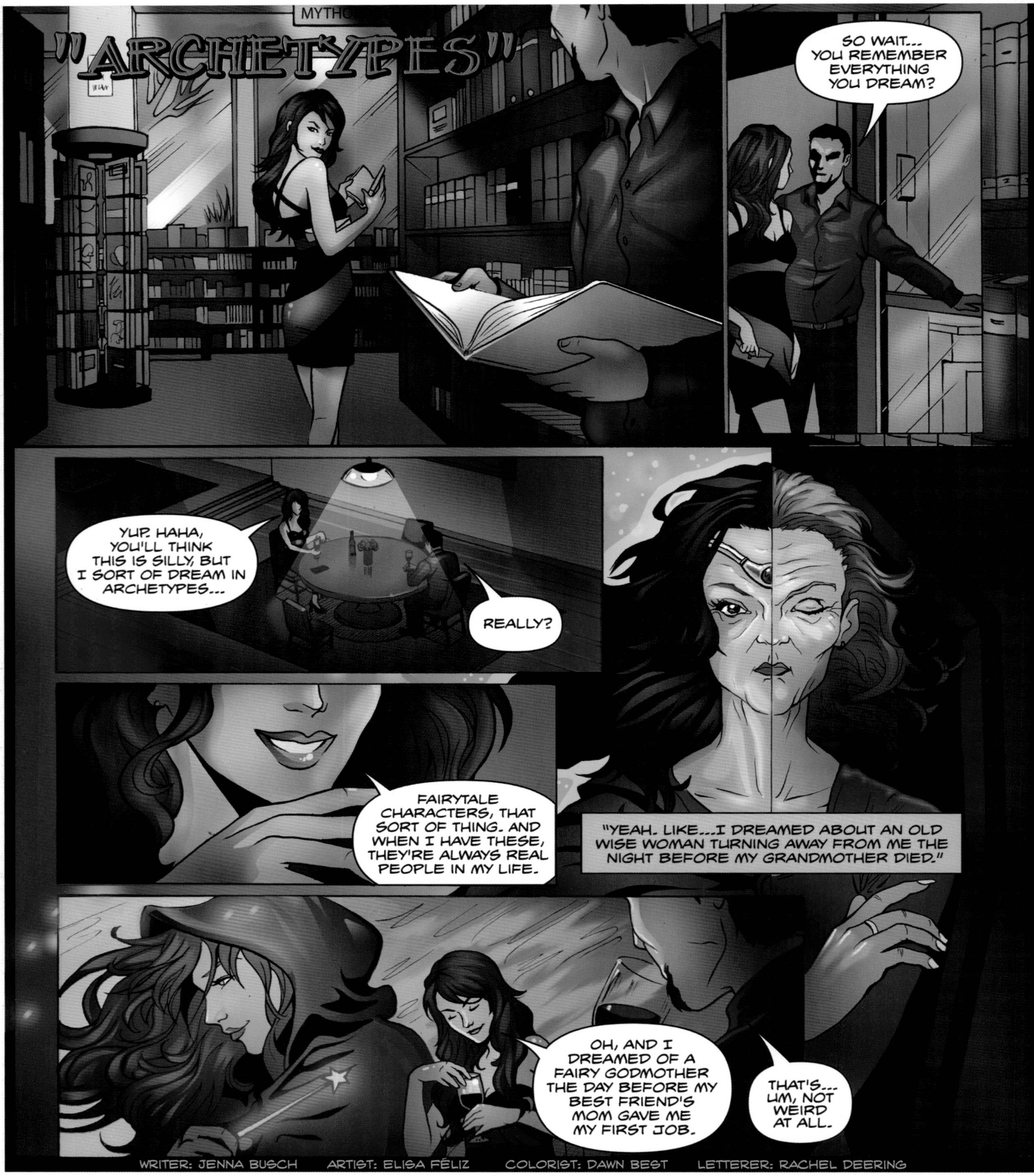
"ARCHETYPES"
SO WAIT... YOU REMEMBER EVERYTHING YOU DREAM?
YUP. HAHA, YOU'LL THINK THIS IS SILLY, BUT I SORT OF DREAM IN ARCHETYPES...
REALLY?
FAIRYTALE CHARACTERS, THAT SORT OF THING. AND WHEN I HAVE THESE, THEY'RE ALWAYS REAL PEOPLE IN MY LIFE.
"YEAH. LIKE...I DREAMED ABOUT AN OLD WISE WOMAN TURNING AWAY FROM ME THE NIGHT BEFORE MY GRANDMOTHER DIED."
OH, AND I DREAMED OF A FAIRY GODMOTHER THE DAY BEFORE MY BEST FRIEND'S MOM GAVE ME MY FIRST JOB.
THAT'S... UM, NOT WEIRD AT ALL.
WRITER: JENNA BUSCH ARTIST: ELISA FÉLIZ COLORIST: DAWN BEST LETTERER: RACHEL DEERING

☆☆☆

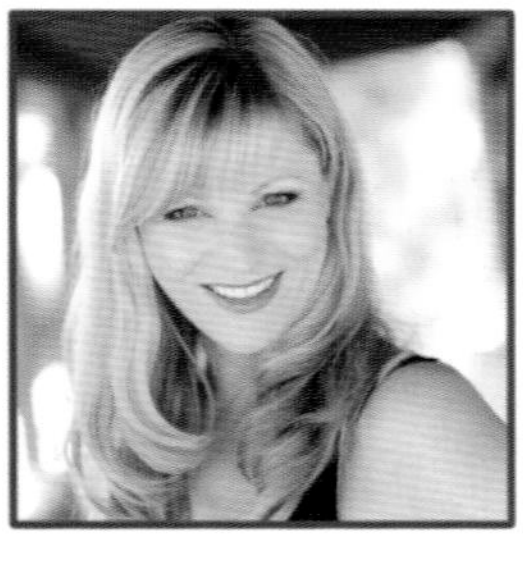

JENNA BUSCH

SKILLS: Writer-"Archetypes," Co-writer-"Ladybird"
LOCATION: Los Angeles, CA
FUN FACT: I've been a musical theater actress, a makeup artist, an entertainment journalist...and I speak a little Gaelic!

http://girlmeetslightsaber.blogspot.com/

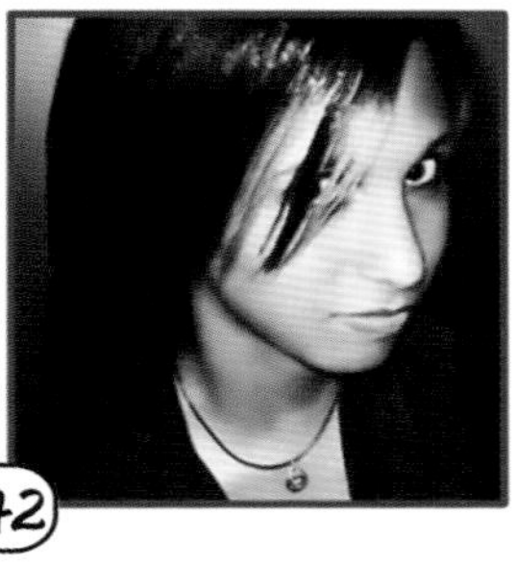

ELISA FéLIZ

SKILLS: Penciller, Inker
LOCATION: Santo Domingo, Dominican Republic
FUN FACT: Designed a third of my wardrobe.

www.elisafeliz.com

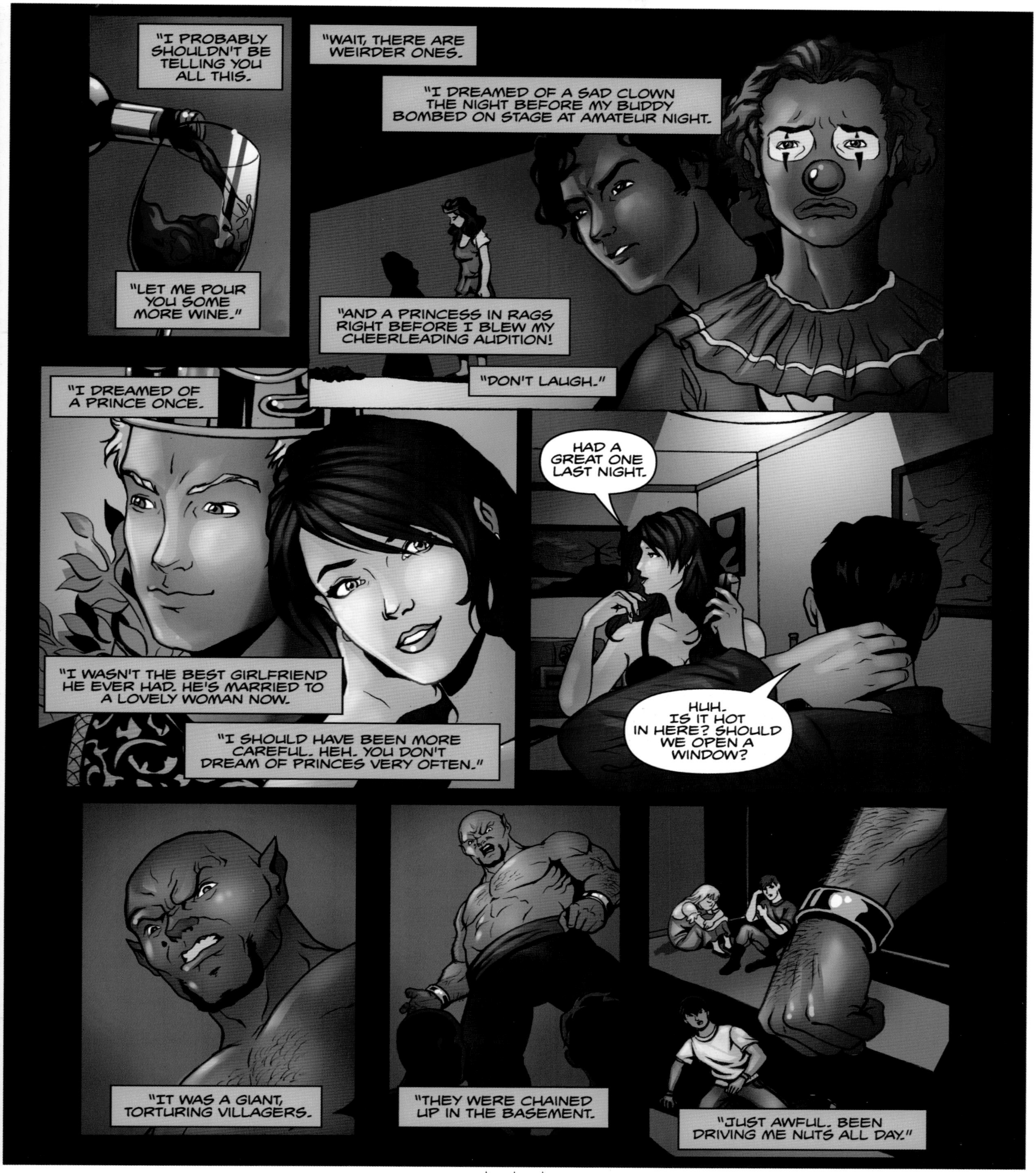
"I PROBABLY SHOULDN'T BE TELLING YOU ALL THIS.
"LET ME POUR YOU SOME MORE WINE."
"WAIT, THERE ARE WEIRDER ONES.
"I DREAMED OF A SAD CLOWN THE NIGHT BEFORE MY BUDDY BOMBED ON STAGE AT AMATEUR NIGHT.
"AND A PRINCESS IN RAGS RIGHT BEFORE I BLEW MY CHEERLEADING AUDITION!
"DON'T LAUGH."
"I DREAMED OF A PRINCE ONCE.
"I WASN'T THE BEST GIRLFRIEND HE EVER HAD. HE'S MARRIED TO A LOVELY WOMAN NOW.
"I SHOULD HAVE BEEN MORE CAREFUL. HEH. YOU DON'T DREAM OF PRINCES VERY OFTEN."
HAD A GREAT ONE LAST NIGHT.
HUH. IS IT HOT IN HERE? SHOULD WE OPEN A WINDOW?
"IT WAS A GIANT, TORTURING VILLAGERS.
"THEY WERE CHAINED UP IN THE BASEMENT.
"JUST AWFUL. BEEN DRIVING ME NUTS ALL DAY."

☆ ☆ ☆

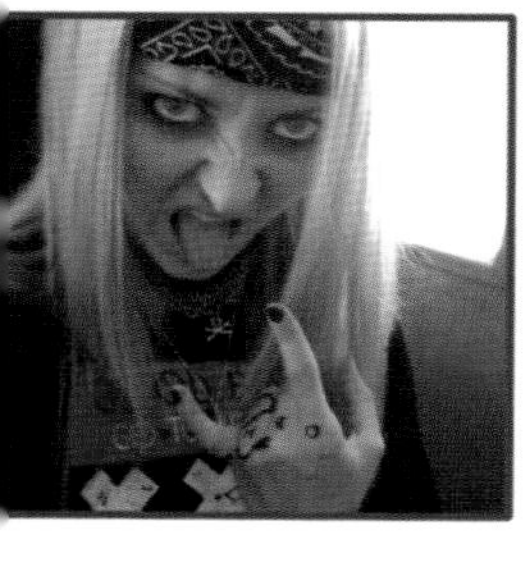

DAWN BEST

SKILLS: Inker, Colorist
LOCATION: Columbus, OH
FUN FACT: Not the best artist in the world - just the busiest!

http://www.dawnbest.com

PRO TIP

CONCEPT

BY LAURA MORLEY

"SOMETIMES A CONCEPT ('IMAGINE SOMEONE DEVELOPS A SERUM FOR ETERNAL LIFE!') COMES TO YOU LONG BEFORE THE ACTUAL PLOT. A GOOD FAST-TRACK TO TURNING THAT BIG CONCEPT INTO AN ACTUAL STORY IS TO ASK YOURSELF 'IF THIS THING WERE REAL, WHO'D HAVE THE MOST TO LOSE? HOW WOULD THEY FIGHT IT?' (MAYBE OUR SERUM-INVENTOR GAINS A MERCENARY FUNERAL DIRECTOR AS A NEMESIS...)"

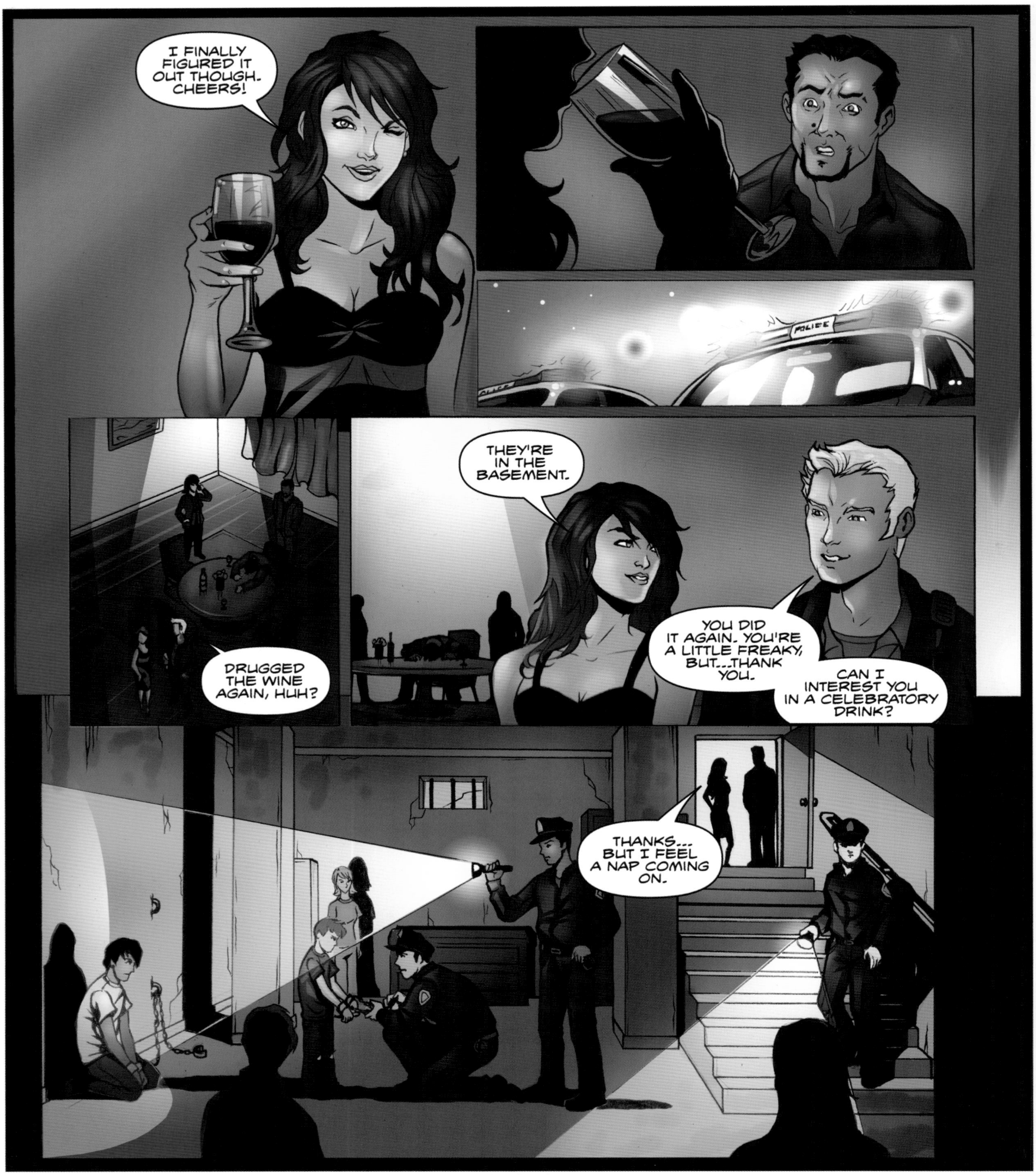
I FINALLY FIGURED IT OUT THOUGH. CHEERS!
POLICE
THEY'RE IN THE BASEMENT.
DRUGGED THE WINE AGAIN, HUH?
YOU DID IT AGAIN. YOU'RE A LITTLE FREAKY, BUT...THANK YOU.
CAN I INTEREST YOU IN A CELEBRATORY DRINK?
THANKS... BUT I FEEL A NAP COMING ON.

☆☆☆

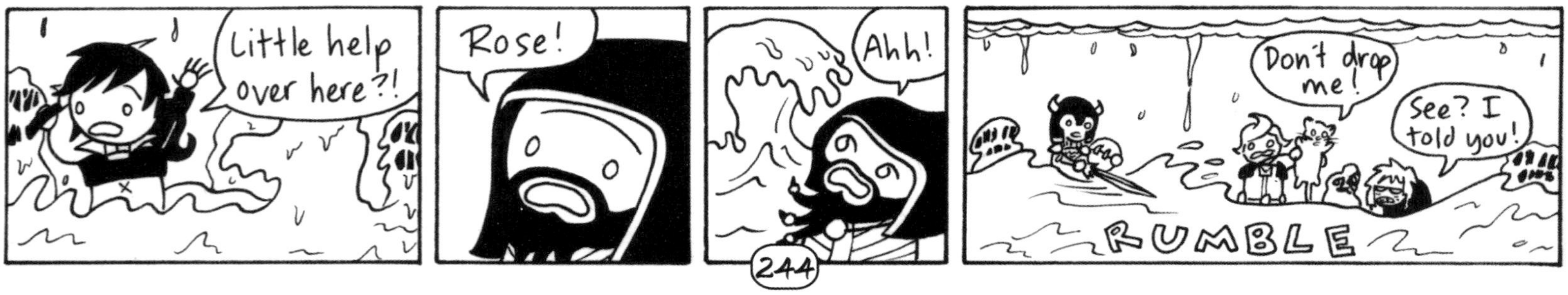
Little help over here?!
Rose!
Ahh!
Don't drop me!
See? I told you!
RUMBLE

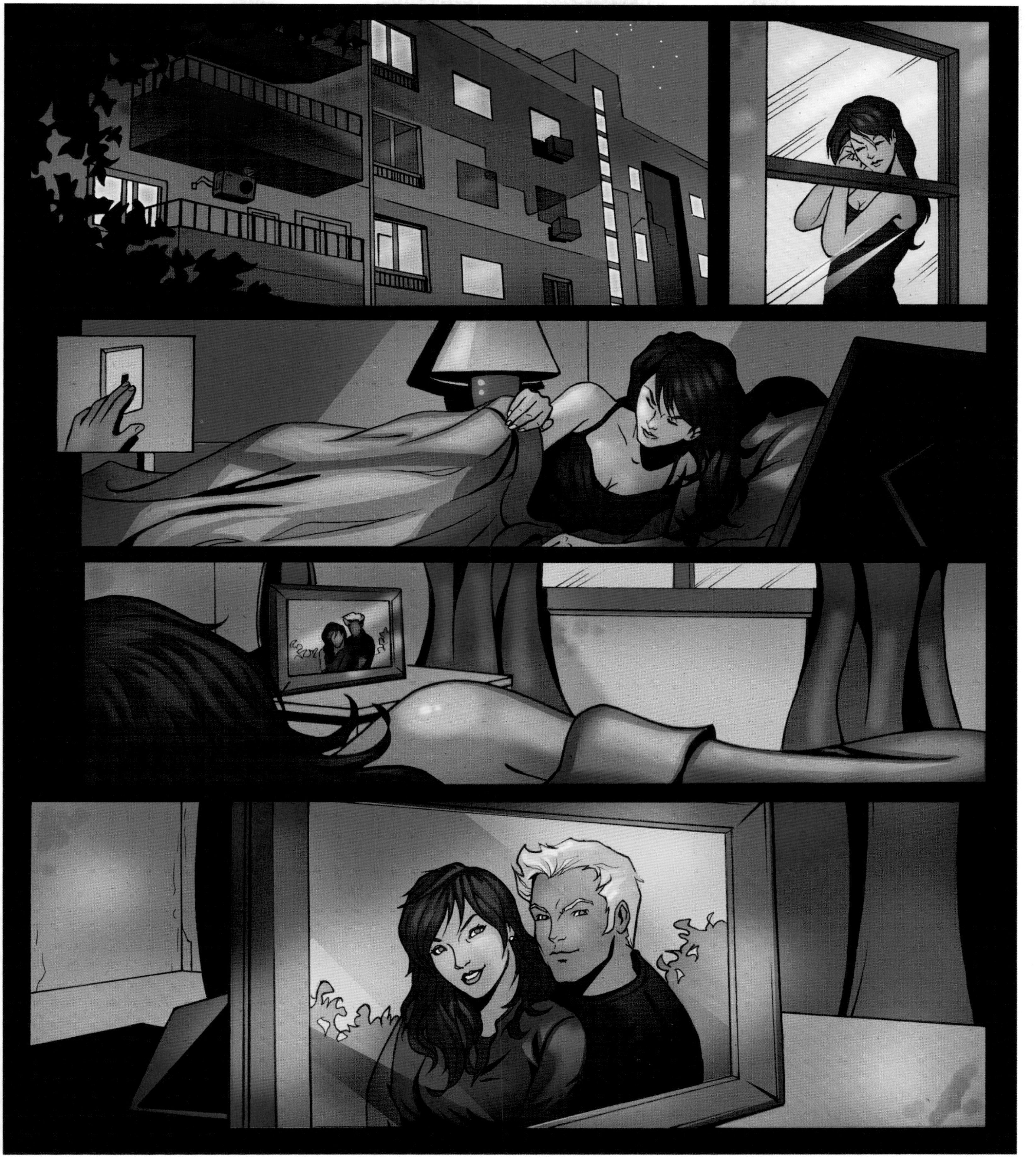

☆ ☆ ☆

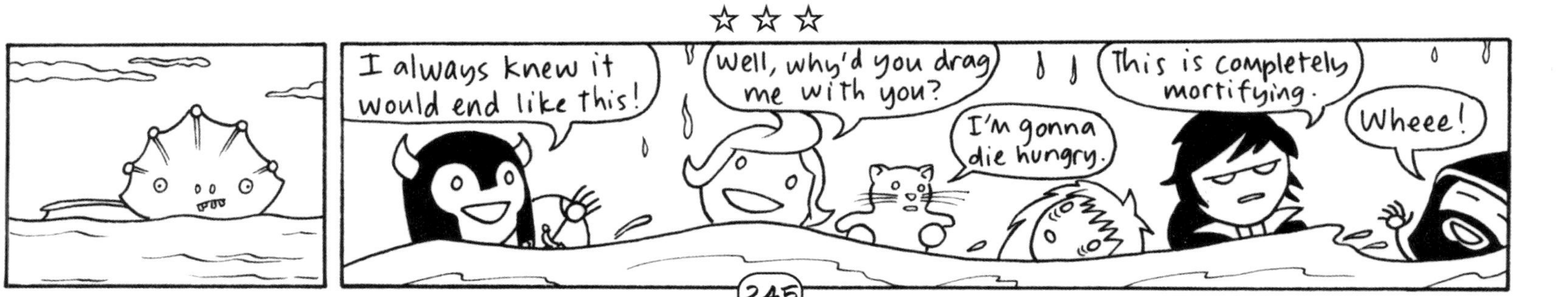
I always knew it would end like this!
Well, why'd you drag me with you?
I'm gonna die hungry.
This is completely mortifying.
Wheee!

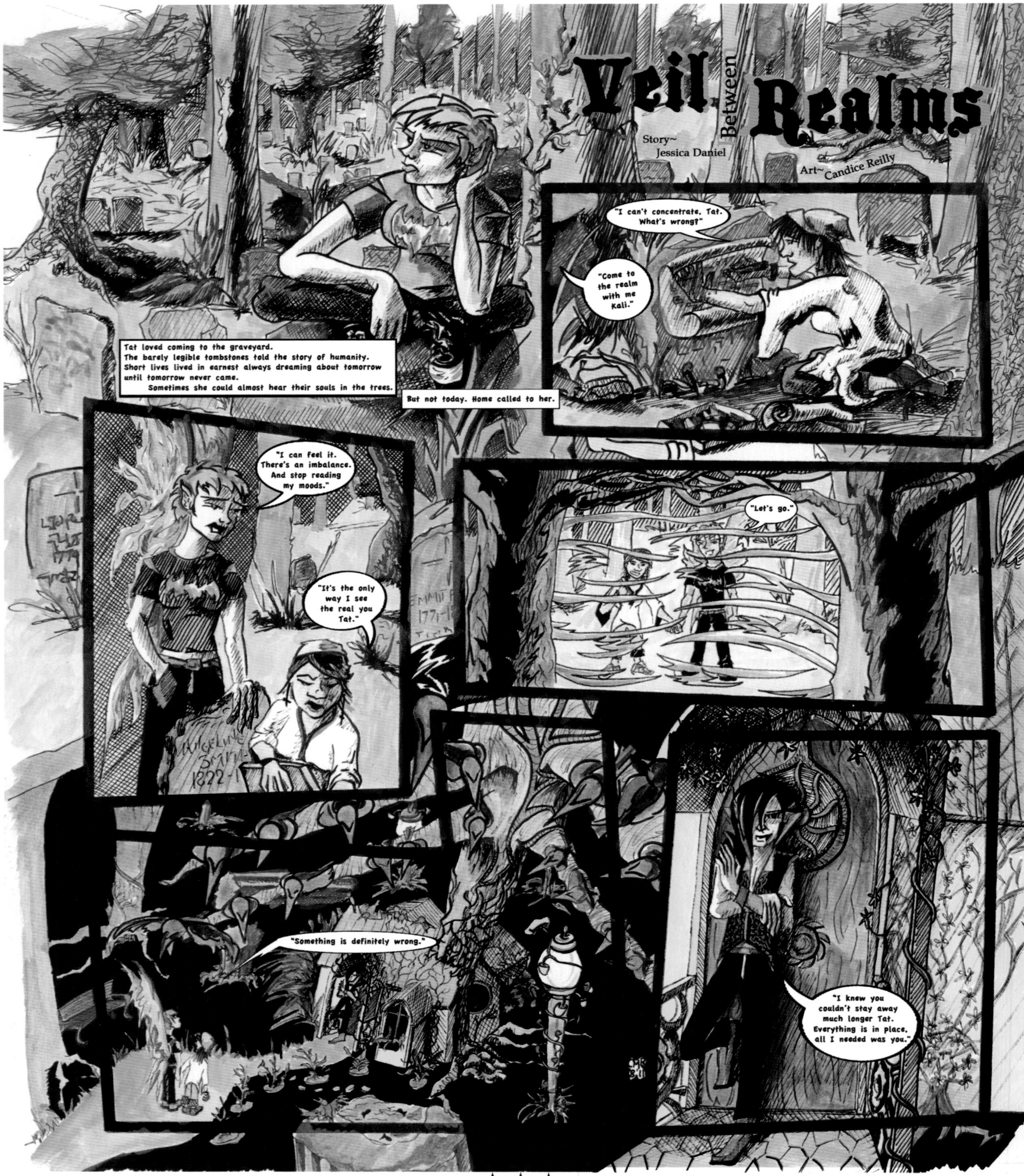
Veil Between Realms
Story~ Jessica Daniel
Art~ Candice Reilly
Tat loved coming to the graveyard.
The barely legible tombstones told the story of humanity.
Short lives lived in earnest always dreaming about tomorrow until tomorrow never came.
Sometimes she could almost hear their souls in the trees.
But not today. Home called to her.
"I can't concentrate, Tat. What's wrong?"
"Come to the realm with me Kali."
"I can feel it. There's an imbalance. And stop reading my moods."
"It's the only way I see the real you Tat."
"Let's go."
"Something is definitely wrong."
"I knew you couldn't stay away much longer Tat. Everything is in place, all I needed was you."

☆ ☆ ☆

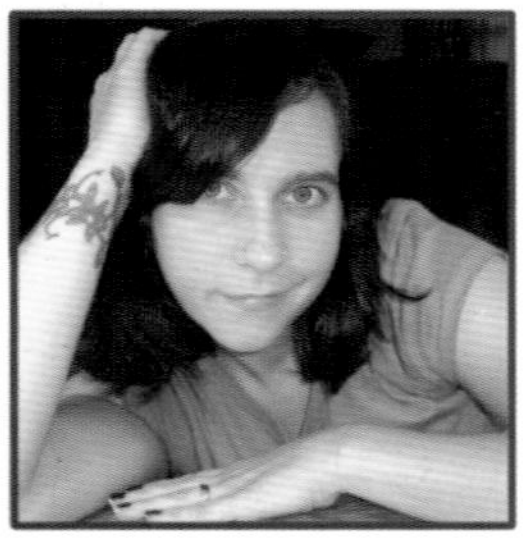

JESSICA DANIEL

SKILLS: Writer
LOCATION: Blue Island, IL
FUN FACT: My interests may wander into the eclectic —strange, even— but at heart it is my passion for my family and the story of each moment that are the ink on my page.

http://suchnonesuch.wordpress.com/

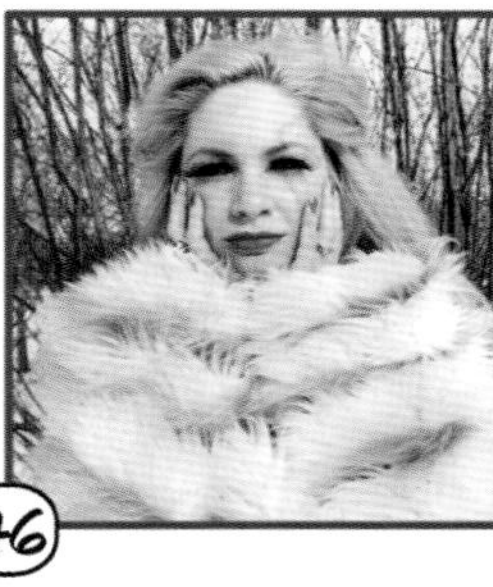

CANDICE REILLY

SKILLS: Penciller, Inker, Colorist, Letterer
LOCATION: Chicago, Illinois
FUN FACT: I am known by many names, but you can call me T-Rex!

www.smrtart.com

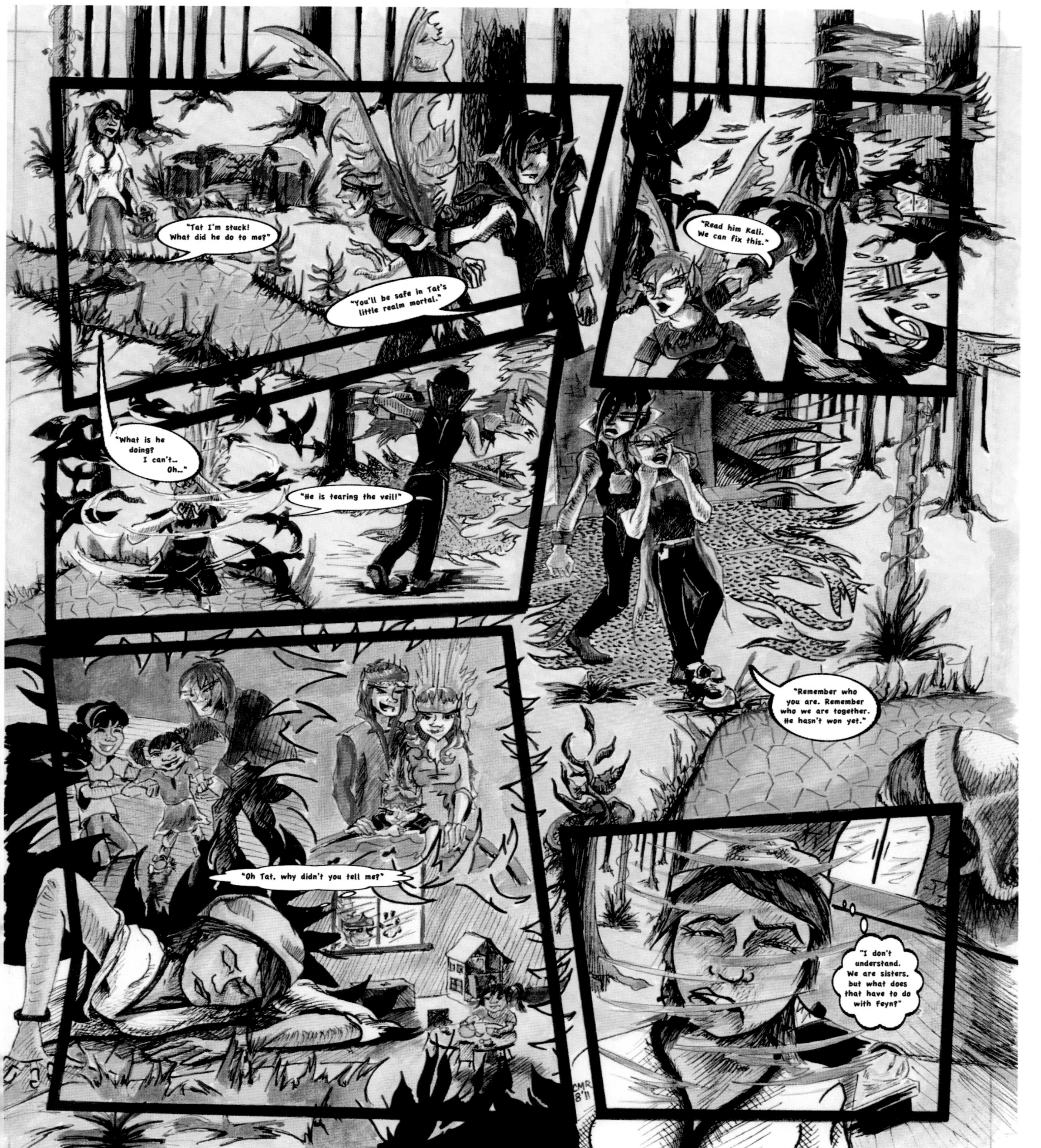
"Tat I'm stuck! What did he do to me?"
"You'll be safe in Tat's little realm mortal."
"Read him Kali. We can fix this."
"What is he doing? I can't... Oh..."
"He is tearing the veil!"
"Remember who you are. Remember who we are together. He hasn't won yet."
"Oh Tat, why didn't you tell me?"
"I don't understand. We are sisters, but what does that have to do with Feyn?"
CMR 8'11

☆☆☆

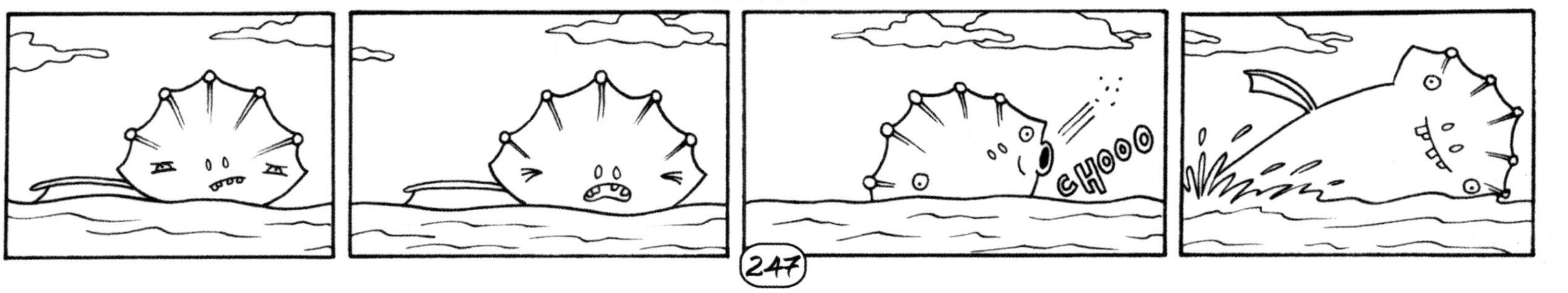
CHOOO

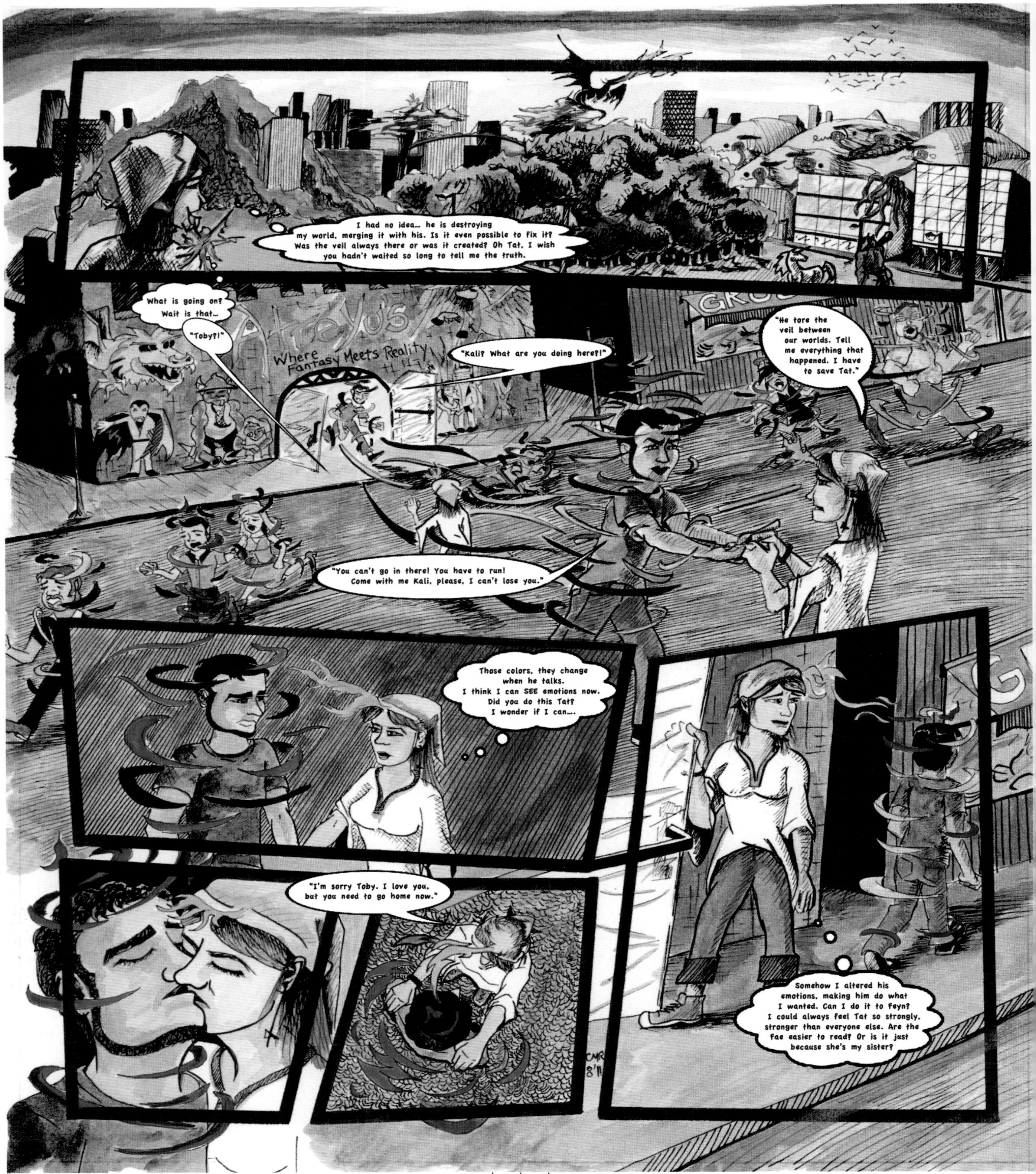
I had no idea... he is destroying my world, merging it with his. Is it even possible to fix it? Was the veil always there or was it created? Oh Tat, I wish you hadn't waited so long to tell me the truth.
What is going on? Wait is that...
"Toby?!"
Atreyu's
Where Fantasy Meets Reality
"Kali? What are you doing here?!"
"He tore the veil between our worlds. Tell me everything that happened. I have to save Tat."
"You can't go in there! You have to run! Come with me Kali, please, I can't lose you."
Those colors, they change when he talks. I think I can SEE emotions now. Did you do this Tat? I wonder if I can....
"I'm sorry Toby. I love you, but you need to go home now."
Somehow I altered his emotions, making him do what I wanted. Can I do it to Feyn? I could always feel Tat so strongly, stronger than everyone else. Are the Fae easier to read? Or is it just because she's my sister?
CMR 8'11

☆ ☆ ☆

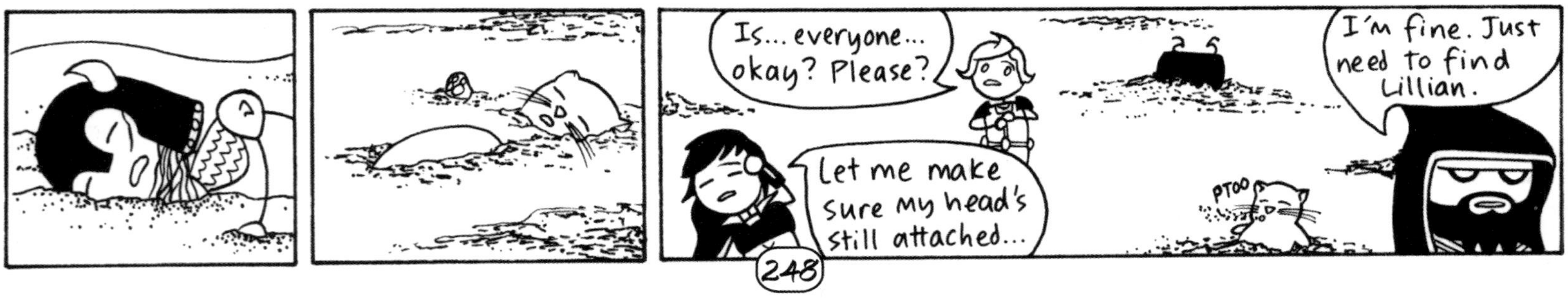
Is... everyone... okay? Please?
I'm fine. Just need to find Lillian.
Let me make sure my head's still attached...
PTOO

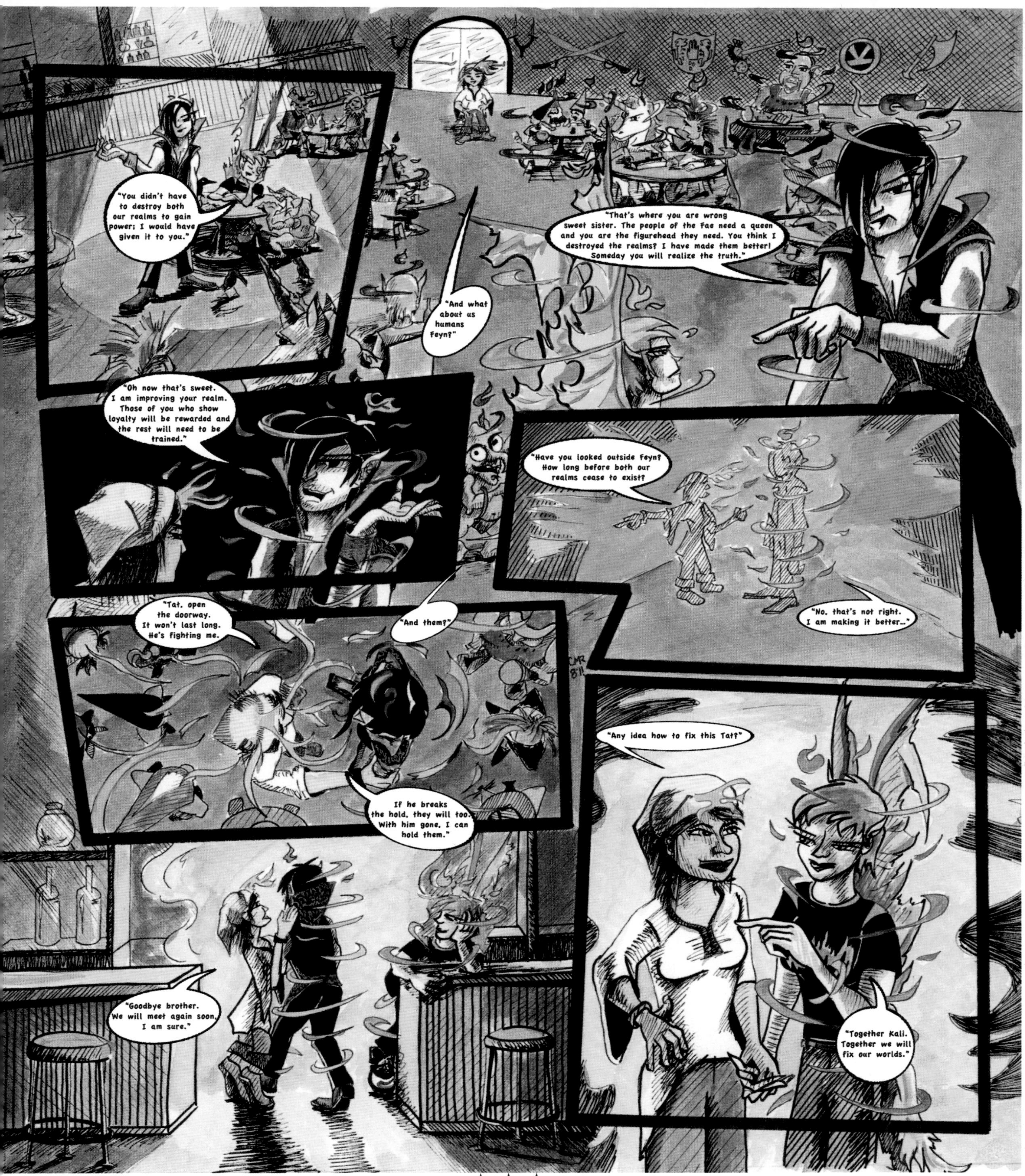
"You didn't have to destroy both our realms to gain power; I would have given it to you."
"That's where you are wrong sweet sister. The people of the Fae need a queen and you are the figurehead they need. You think I destroyed the realms? I have made them better! Someday you will realize the truth."
"And what about us humans Feyn?"
"Oh now that's sweet. I am improving your realm. Those of you who show loyalty will be rewarded and the rest will need to be trained."
"Have you looked outside Feyn? How long before both our realms cease to exist?"
"No, that's not right. I am making it better..."
"Tat, open the doorway. It won't last long. He's fighting me."
"And them?"
If he breaks the hold, they will too. With him gone, I can hold them."
"Goodbye brother. We will meet again soon, I am sure."
"Any idea how to fix this Tat?"
"Together Kali. Together we will fix our worlds."

☆ ☆ ☆

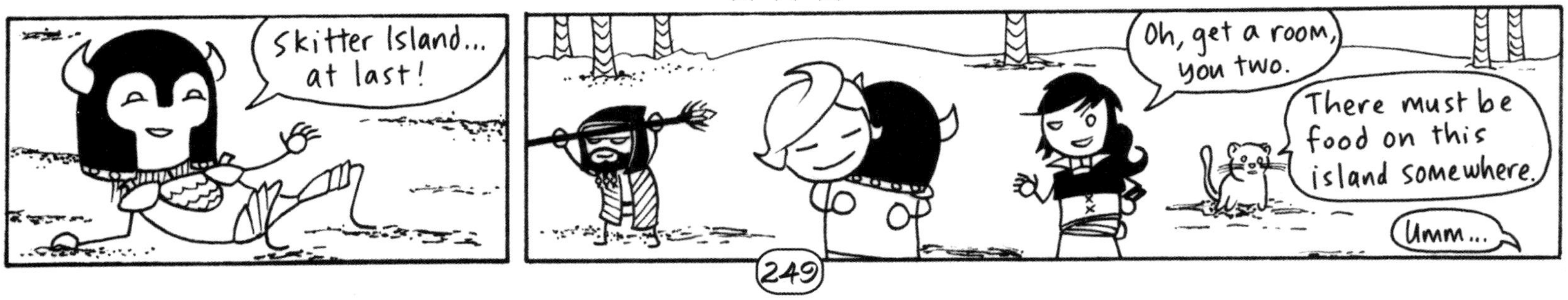
Skitter Island... at last!
Oh, get a room, you two.
There must be food on this island somewhere.
Umm...

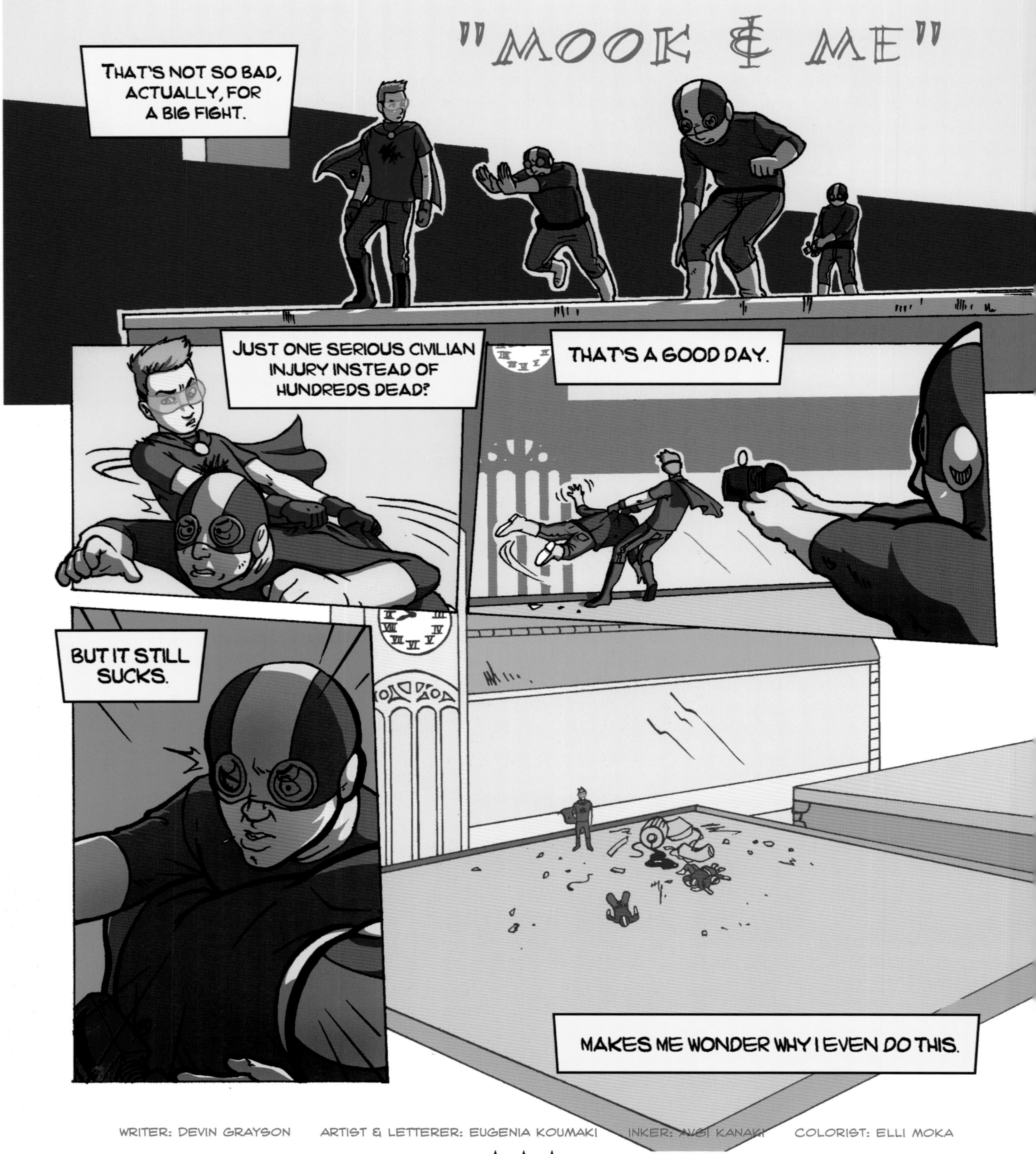
"MOOK & ME"
THAT'S NOT SO BAD, ACTUALLY, FOR A BIG FIGHT.
JUST ONE SERIOUS CIVILIAN INJURY INSTEAD OF HUNDREDS DEAD?
THAT'S A GOOD DAY.
BUT IT STILL SUCKS.
MAKES ME WONDER WHY I EVEN DO THIS.

WRITER: DEVIN GRAYSON   ARTIST & LETTERER: EUGENIA KOUMAKI   INKER: AVGI KANAKI   COLORIST: ELLI MOKA

☆☆☆

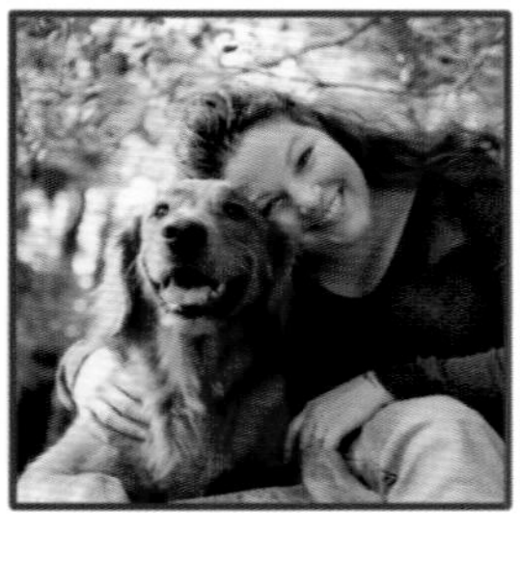

DEVIN GRAYSON

SKILLS: Writer
LOCATION: Hayward, CA
FUN FACT: Some of my best friends are fictional.

www.devingrayson.com

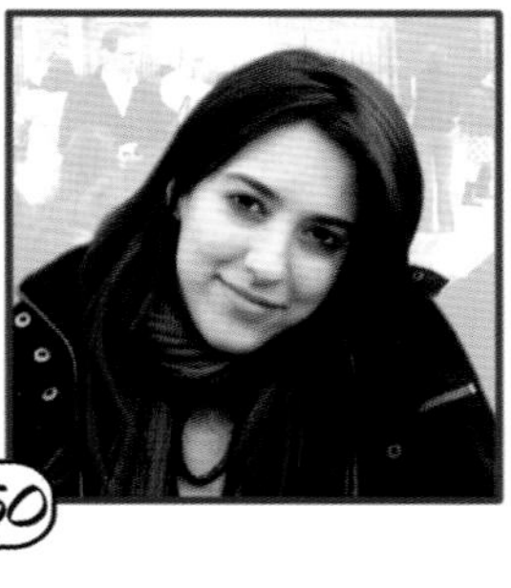

EUGENIA KOUMAKI

SKILLS: Penciller, Letterer
LOCATION: Athens, Greece
FUN FACT: I eat all my food, fix teeth, and draw comics.

koumaki.blogspot.com

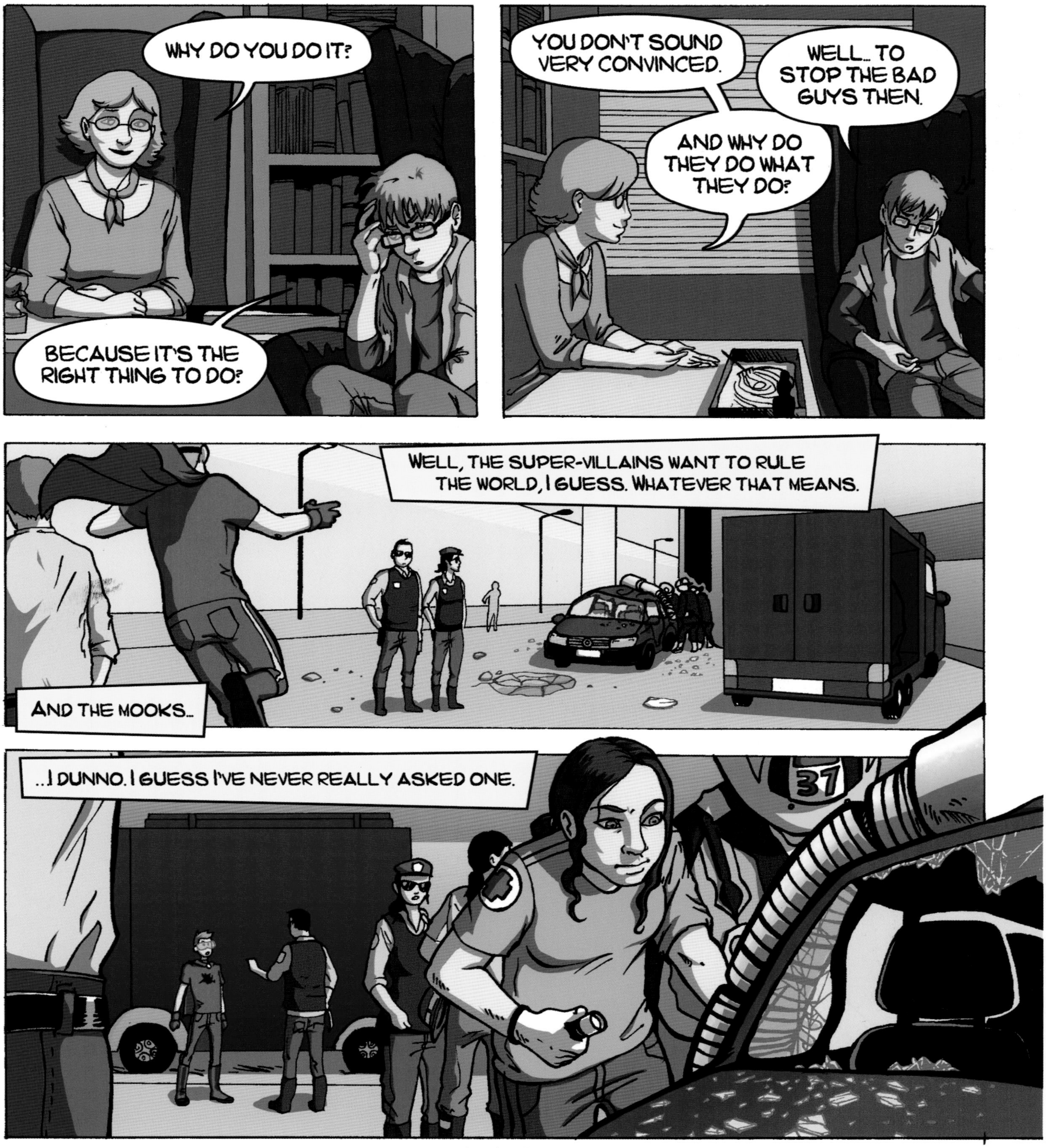
WHY DO YOU DO IT?
BECAUSE IT'S THE RIGHT THING TO DO?
YOU DON'T SOUND VERY CONVINCED.
WELL... TO STOP THE BAD GUYS THEN.
AND WHY DO THEY DO WHAT THEY DO?
WELL, THE SUPER-VILLAINS WANT TO RULE THE WORLD, I GUESS. WHATEVER THAT MEANS.
AND THE MOOKS...
...I DUNNO. I GUESS I'VE NEVER REALLY ASKED ONE.
37

☆ ☆ ☆

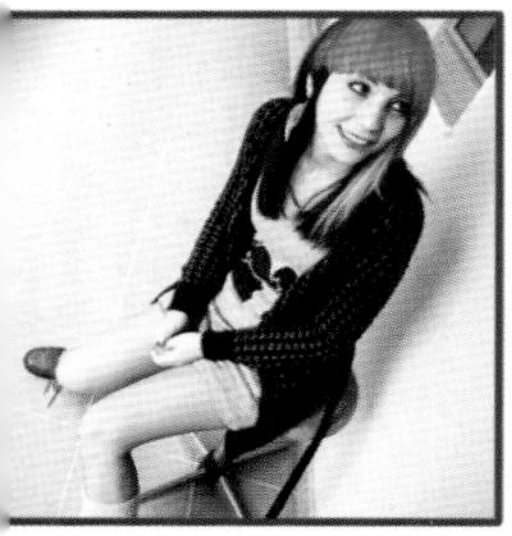

AVGI KANAKI

SKILLS: Inker
LOCATION: Athens, Greece
FUN FACT: I really love cinnamon! And butter cookies.

http://clockworkdollhouse.deviantart.com/

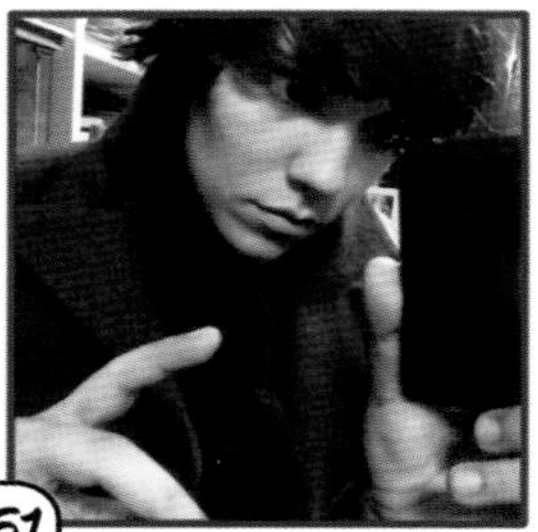

ELLI "HARRY" MOKA

SKILLS: Colorist
LOCATION: Piraeus, Greece
FUN FACT: I am a Chamelion Arched Time Lord.

http://asaph.deviantart.com/

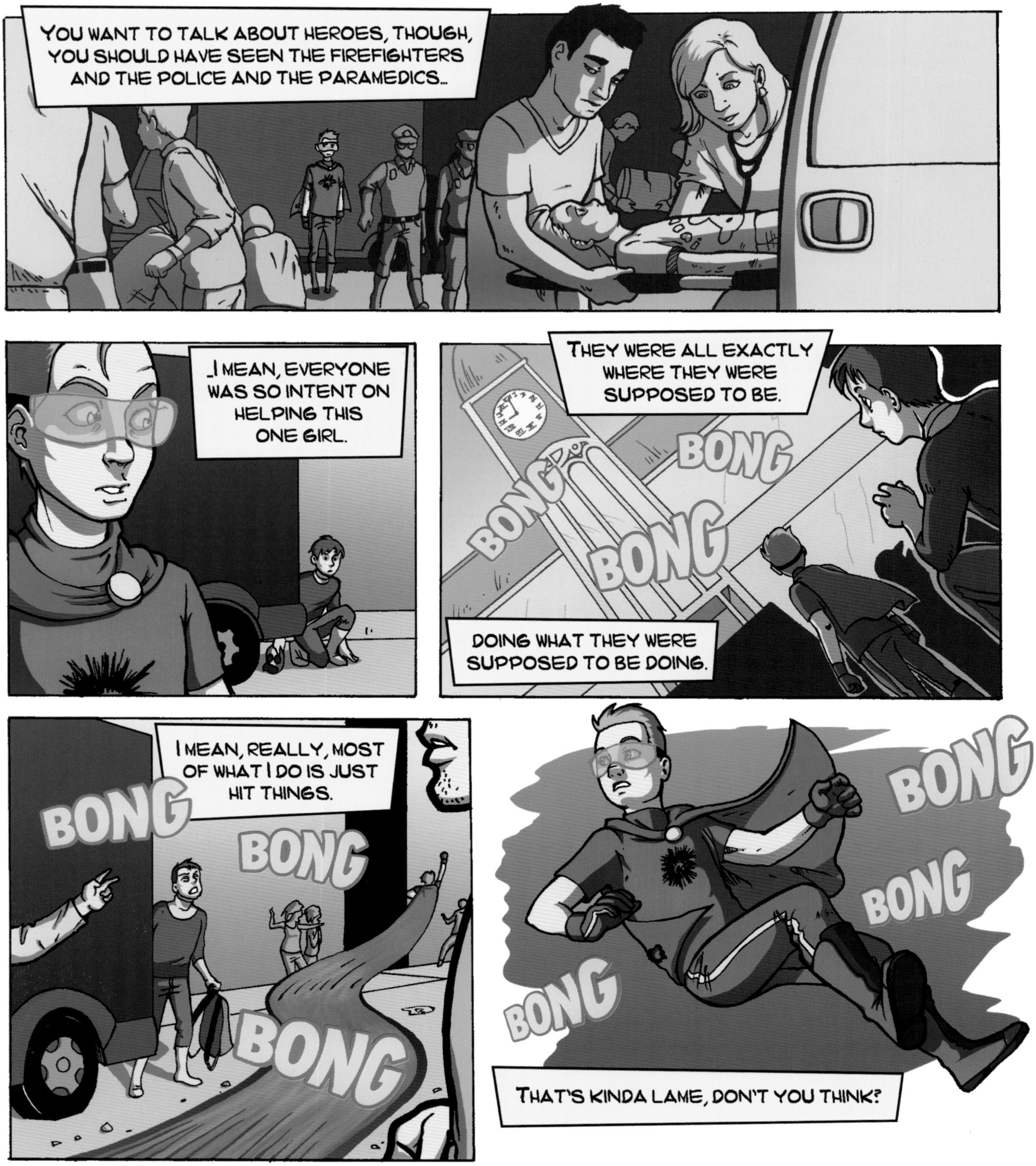
YOU WANT TO TALK ABOUT HEROES, THOUGH, YOU SHOULD HAVE SEEN THE FIREFIGHTERS AND THE POLICE AND THE PARAMEDICS...
...I MEAN, EVERYONE WAS SO INTENT ON HELPING THIS ONE GIRL.
THEY WERE ALL EXACTLY WHERE THEY WERE SUPPOSED TO BE.
BONG
BONG
BONG
DOING WHAT THEY WERE SUPPOSED TO BE DOING.
I MEAN, REALLY, MOST OF WHAT I DO IS JUST HIT THINGS.
BONG
BONG
BONG
BONG
BONG
BONG
THAT'S KINDA LAME, DON'T YOU THINK?

☆ ☆ ☆

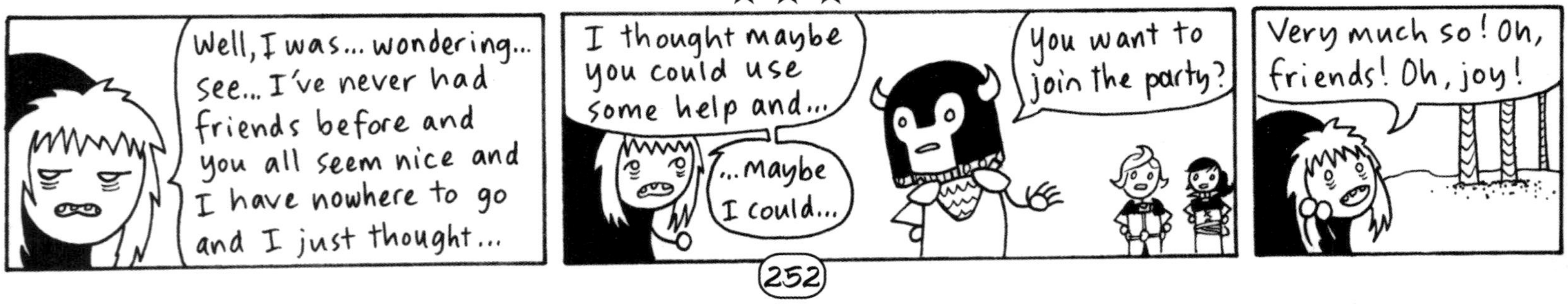
Well, I was... wondering... see... I've never had friends before and you all seem nice and I have nowhere to go and I just thought...
I thought maybe you could use some help and...
...Maybe I could...
You want to join the party?
Very much so! Oh, friends! Oh, joy!

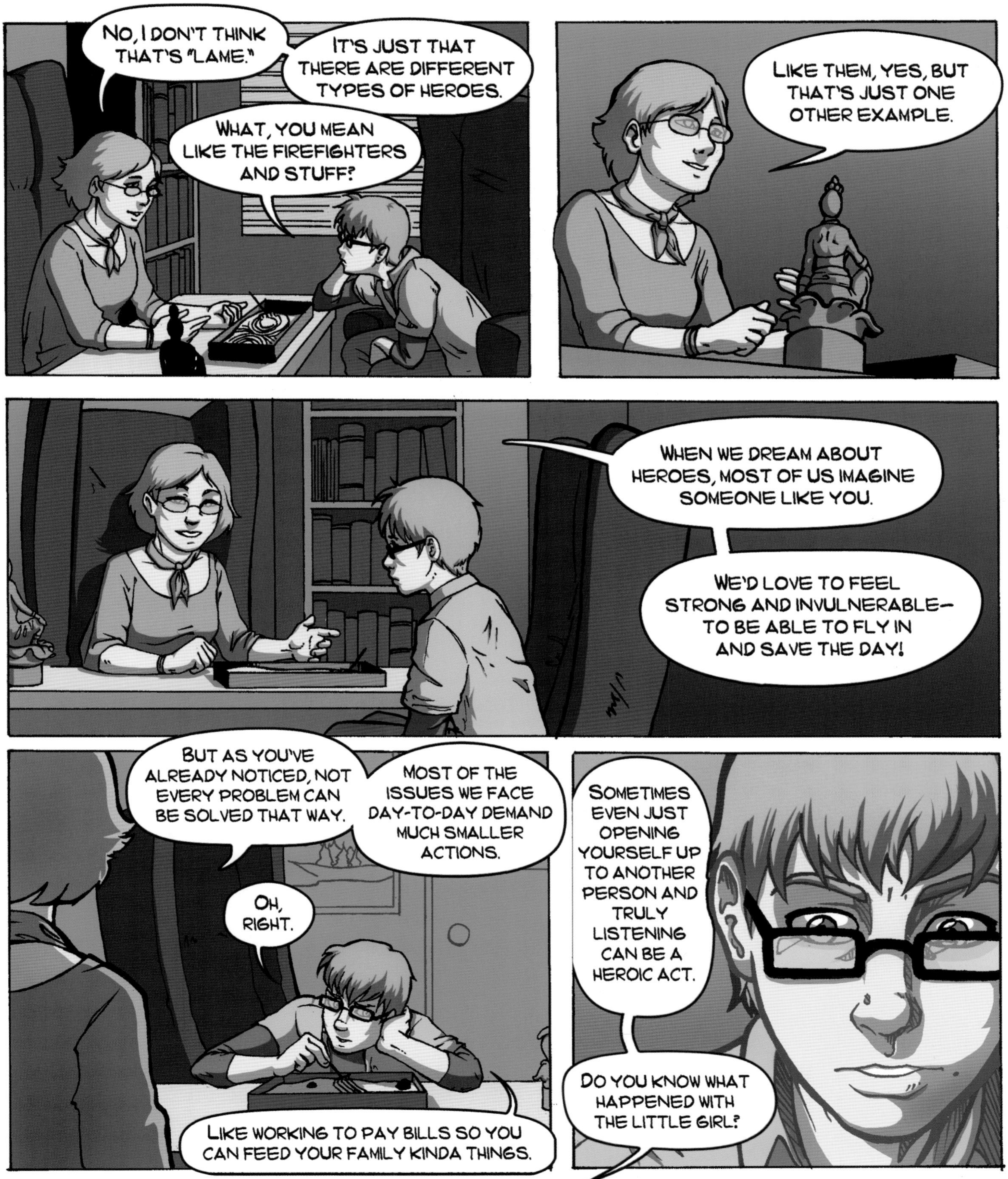

NO, I DON'T THINK THAT'S "LAME."
IT'S JUST THAT THERE ARE DIFFERENT TYPES OF HEROES.
WHAT, YOU MEAN LIKE THE FIREFIGHTERS AND STUFF?
LIKE THEM, YES, BUT THAT'S JUST ONE OTHER EXAMPLE.
WHEN WE DREAM ABOUT HEROES, MOST OF US IMAGINE SOMEONE LIKE YOU.
WE'D LOVE TO FEEL STRONG AND INVULNERABLE— TO BE ABLE TO FLY IN AND SAVE THE DAY!
BUT AS YOU'VE ALREADY NOTICED, NOT EVERY PROBLEM CAN BE SOLVED THAT WAY.
MOST OF THE ISSUES WE FACE DAY-TO-DAY DEMAND MUCH SMALLER ACTIONS.
OH, RIGHT.
LIKE WORKING TO PAY BILLS SO YOU CAN FEED YOUR FAMILY KINDA THINGS.
SOMETIMES EVEN JUST OPENING YOURSELF UP TO ANOTHER PERSON AND TRULY LISTENING CAN BE A HEROIC ACT.
DO YOU KNOW WHAT HAPPENED WITH THE LITTLE GIRL?

☆ ☆ ☆

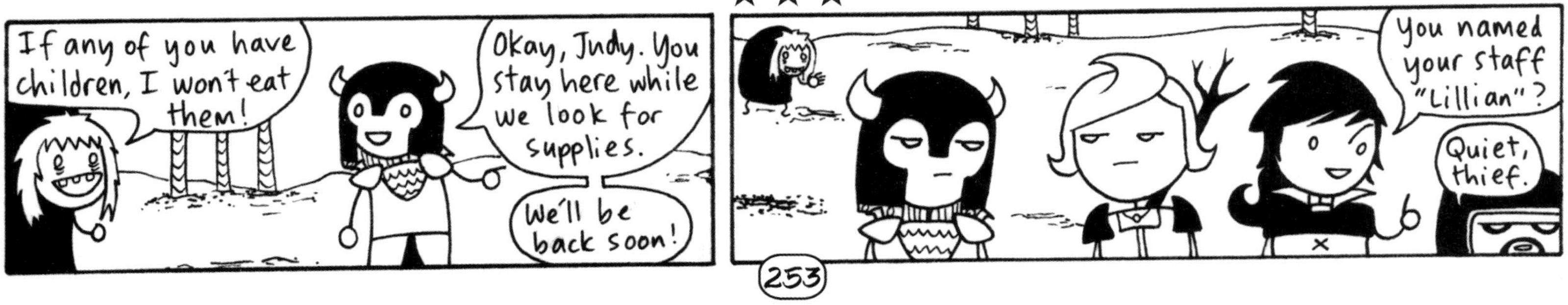

If any of you have children, I won't eat them!
Okay, Judy. You stay here while we look for supplies.
We'll be back soon!
You named your staff "Lillian"?
Quiet, thief.

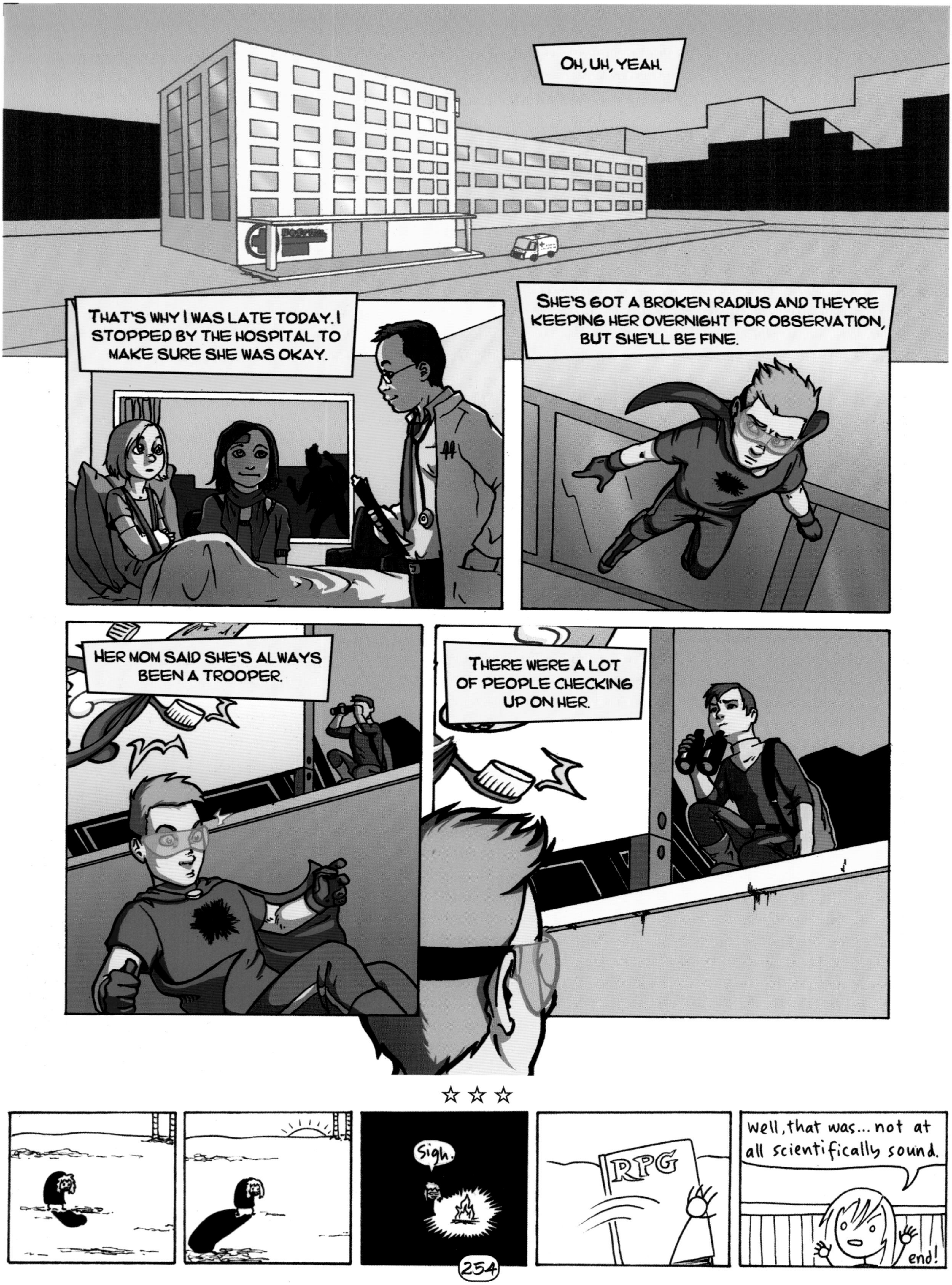
OH, UH, YEAH.
THAT'S WHY I WAS LATE TODAY. I STOPPED BY THE HOSPITAL TO MAKE SURE SHE WAS OKAY.
SHE'S GOT A BROKEN RADIUS AND THEY'RE KEEPING HER OVERNIGHT FOR OBSERVATION, BUT SHE'LL BE FINE.
HER MOM SAID SHE'S ALWAYS BEEN A TROOPER.
THERE WERE A LOT OF PEOPLE CHECKING UP ON HER.
☆ ☆ ☆
Sigh.
RPG
Well, that was... not at all scientifically sound.
end!

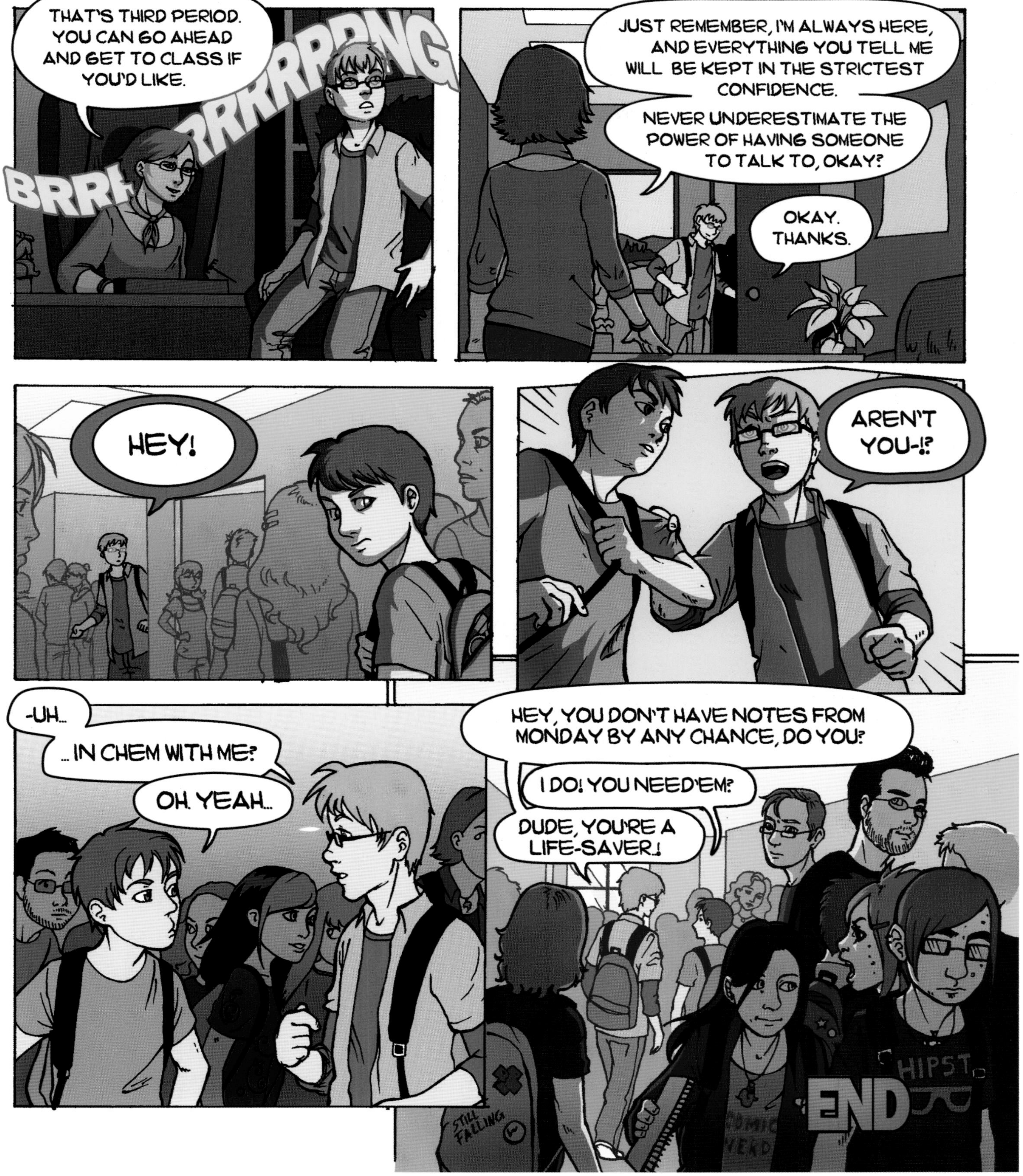
THAT'S THIRD PERIOD. YOU CAN GO AHEAD AND GET TO CLASS IF YOU'D LIKE.
BRRRRRRRRRRRRRRRRNG!
JUST REMEMBER, I'M ALWAYS HERE, AND EVERYTHING YOU TELL ME WILL BE KEPT IN THE STRICTEST CONFIDENCE.
NEVER UNDERESTIMATE THE POWER OF HAVING SOMEONE TO TALK TO, OKAY?
OKAY. THANKS.
HEY!
AREN'T YOU-!?
-UH...
...IN CHEM WITH ME?
OH. YEAH...
HEY, YOU DON'T HAVE NOTES FROM MONDAY BY ANY CHANCE, DO YOU?
I DO! YOU NEED 'EM?
DUDE, YOU'RE A LIFE-SAVER.!
HIPST
STILL FALLING
END

☆☆☆

SURPRISE!

BY BARBARA RANDALL KESEL

PRO TIP

"SURPRISE! WANT TO GET SOME SHOCK INTO YOUR STORY? ASSUMING THAT YOUR STORY READS LIKE A CONVENTIONAL COMIC, WHERE PAGES ARE TURNED BY HAND AND NOT DISPLAYED IN SEQUENCE ON A COMPUTER SCREEN, REMEMBER THAT YOU CAN ONLY SURPRISE THE READER ON A LEFT-HAND PAGE. THE EYE SCANS IMAGES SO QUICKLY THAT THE BRAIN CAN TAKE IN THE GENERAL IMAGES ON TWO PAGES MUCH FASTER THAN IT CAN DECODE AND READ THE WORDS. EVEN THOUGH WE BREAK THE PACING DOWN INTO PANEL UNITS, THE READER SEES IT ALL AT ONCE, THEN GOES SLOWLY OVER EACH IMAGE TO GET THE FINE DETAILS. SO, IF YOU WANT THAT NEW COSTUME, SUDDEN EXPLOSION, SPECIAL GUEST STAR OR UNEXPECTED VISTA TO HAVE THE MOST IMPACT, REMEMBER TO PACE OUT YOUR STORY SO IT FALLS ON A LEFT-HAND PAGE."

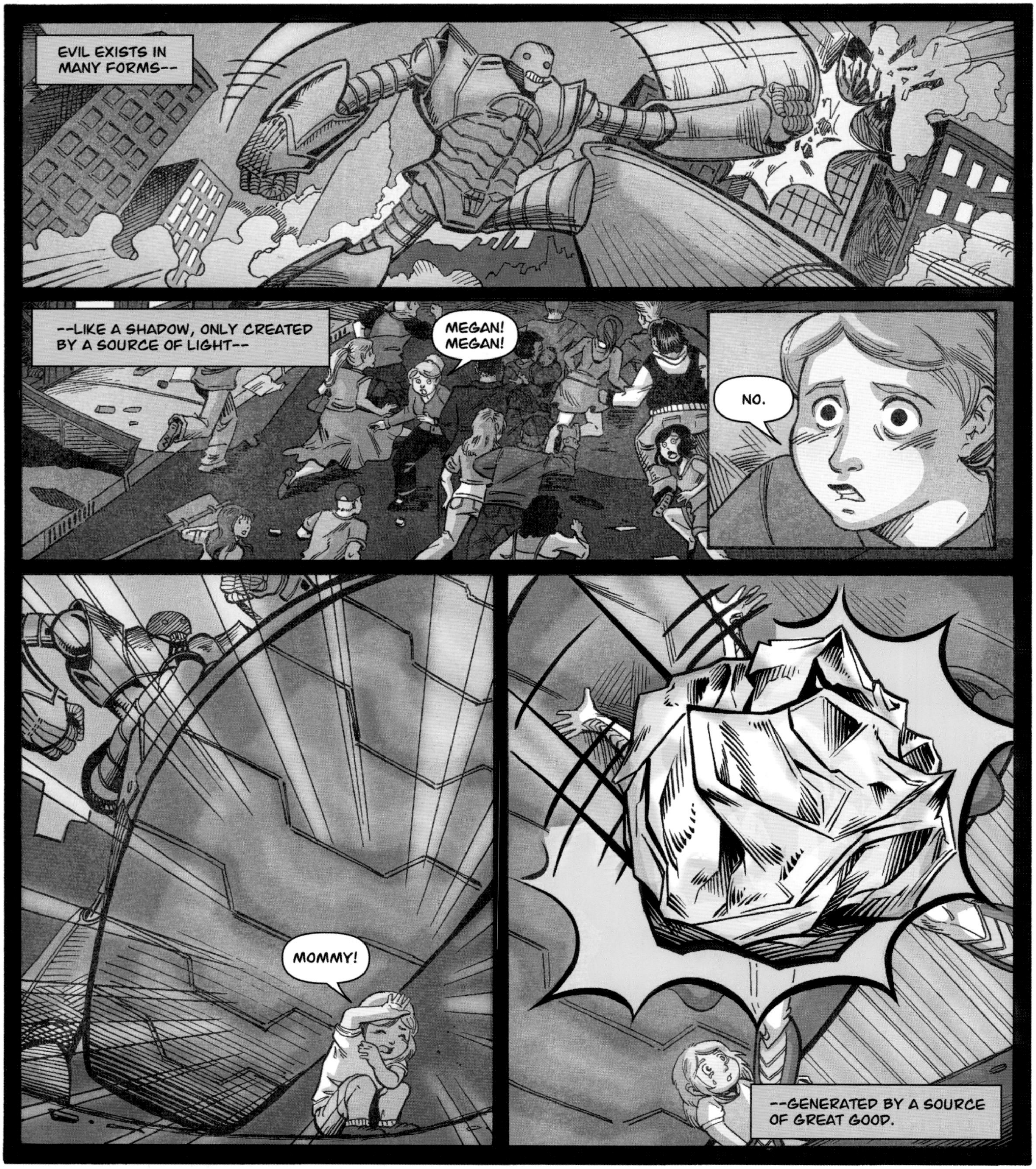
EVIL EXISTS IN MANY FORMS--
--LIKE A SHADOW, ONLY CREATED BY A SOURCE OF LIGHT--
MEGAN! MEGAN!
NO.
MOMMY!
--GENERATED BY A SOURCE OF GREAT GOOD.

WRITER: KATIE BERNARD ARTIST: HEIDI ARNHOLD INKER: BARBARA KAALBERG COLORIST: MARY BELLAMY LETTERER: RACHEL DEERING

☆☆☆

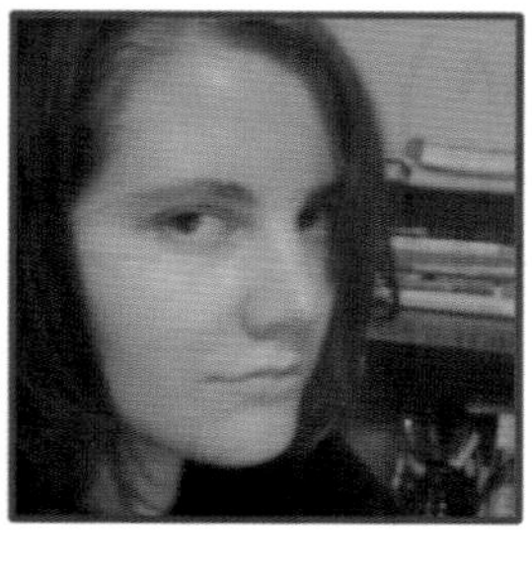

KATIE BERNARD

SKILLS: Writer
LOCATION: Phoenix, AZ
FUN FACT: Spent most of my life working toward being a comic book artist. Found writing to be more cathartic. Go figure.

katiebernard.tumblr.com

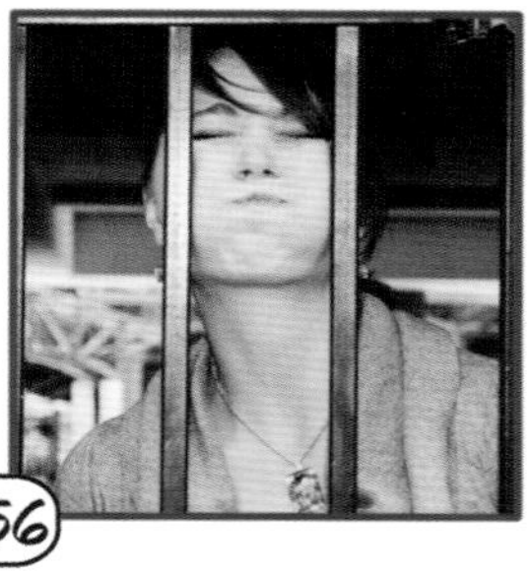

HEIDI ARNHOLD

SKILLS: Penciller
LOCATION: Atlanta, GA
FUN FACT: I only see the sun about twice a week, and I speak bunny language.

www.heidiarnhold.com

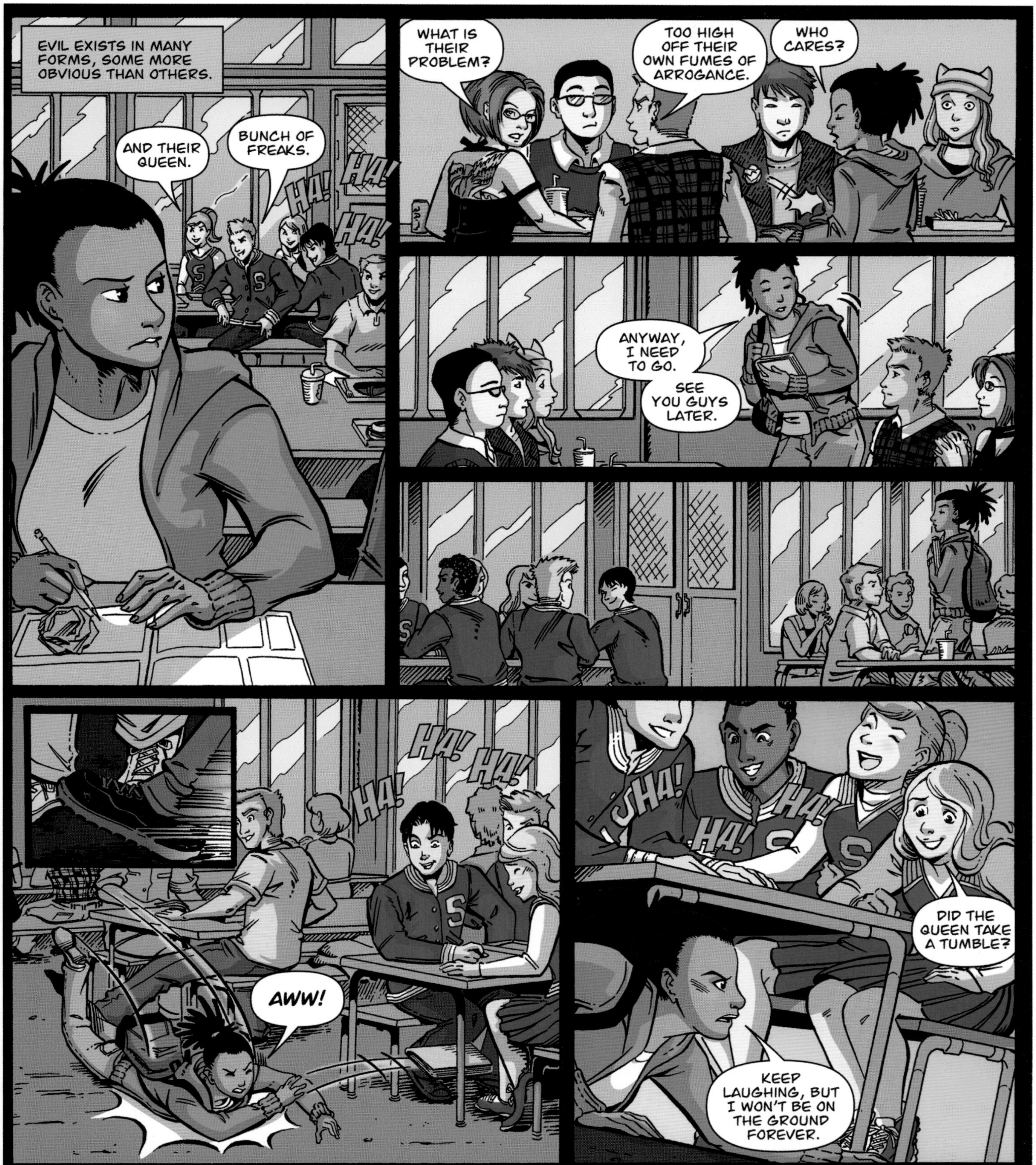
EVIL EXISTS IN MANY FORMS, SOME MORE OBVIOUS THAN OTHERS.
AND THEIR QUEEN.
BUNCH OF FREAKS.
HA!
HA!
HA!
WHAT IS THEIR PROBLEM?
TOO HIGH OFF THEIR OWN FUMES OF ARROGANCE.
WHO CARES?
ANYWAY, I NEED TO GO.
SEE YOU GUYS LATER.
HA!
HA!
HA!
AWW!
HA!
HA!
HA!
DID THE QUEEN TAKE A TUMBLE?
KEEP LAUGHING, BUT I WON'T BE ON THE GROUND FOREVER.

☆ ☆ ☆

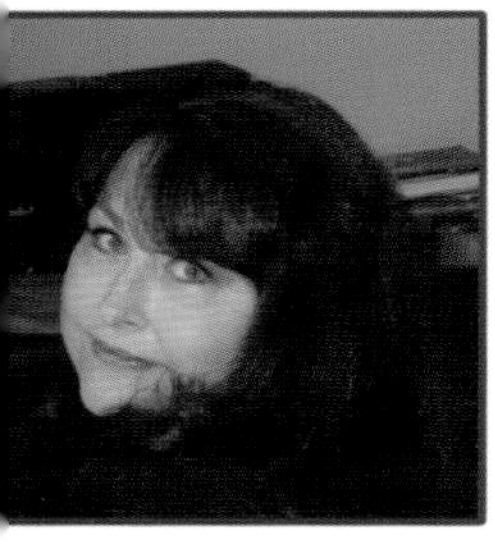

BARBARA KAALBERG

SKILLS: Inker
LOCATION: Madison, WI
FUN FACT: I started out as a fantasy painter before switching to inking.

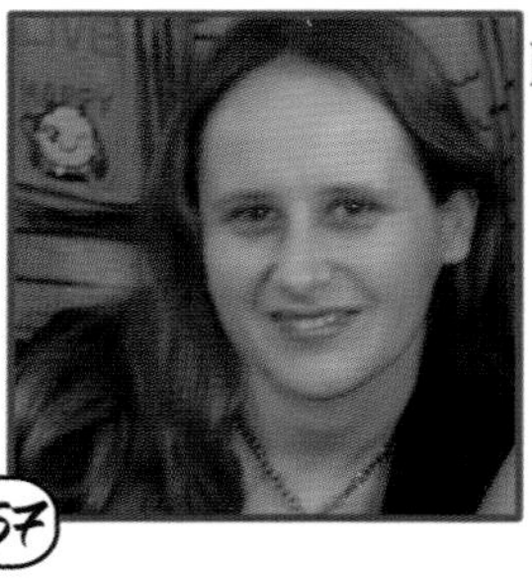

MARY "ZORILITA" BELLAMY

SKILLS: Illustrator, Colorist
LOCATION: Los Angeles, CA
FUN FACT: I am strangely good at home repair.

http://www.marybellamy.com

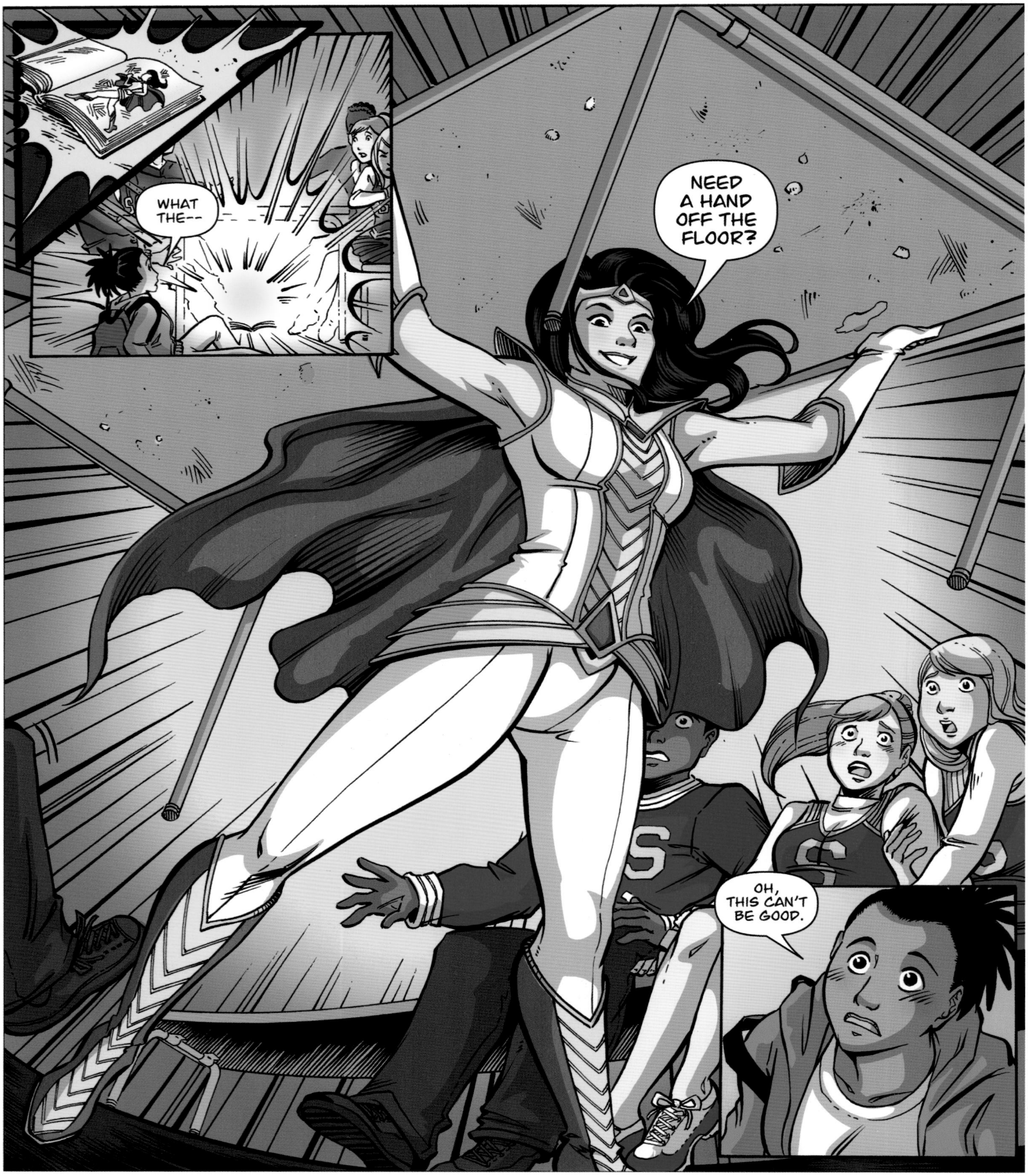
WHAT THE--
NEED A HAND OFF THE FLOOR?
OH, THIS CAN'T BE GOOD.

☆☆☆

PRO TIP

SPEAKING ORDER

BY RACHEL DEERING

"WHEN ILLUSTRATING FROM ANOTHER PERSON'S SCRIPT, ALWAYS TAKE NOTE OF THE SPEAKING ORDER OF THE CHARACTERS. TRY TO PLACE THE CHARACTER WHO SPEAKS FIRST ON THE LEFT SIDE OF THE PANEL, SO THAT DIALOGUE FLOWS NATURALLY."

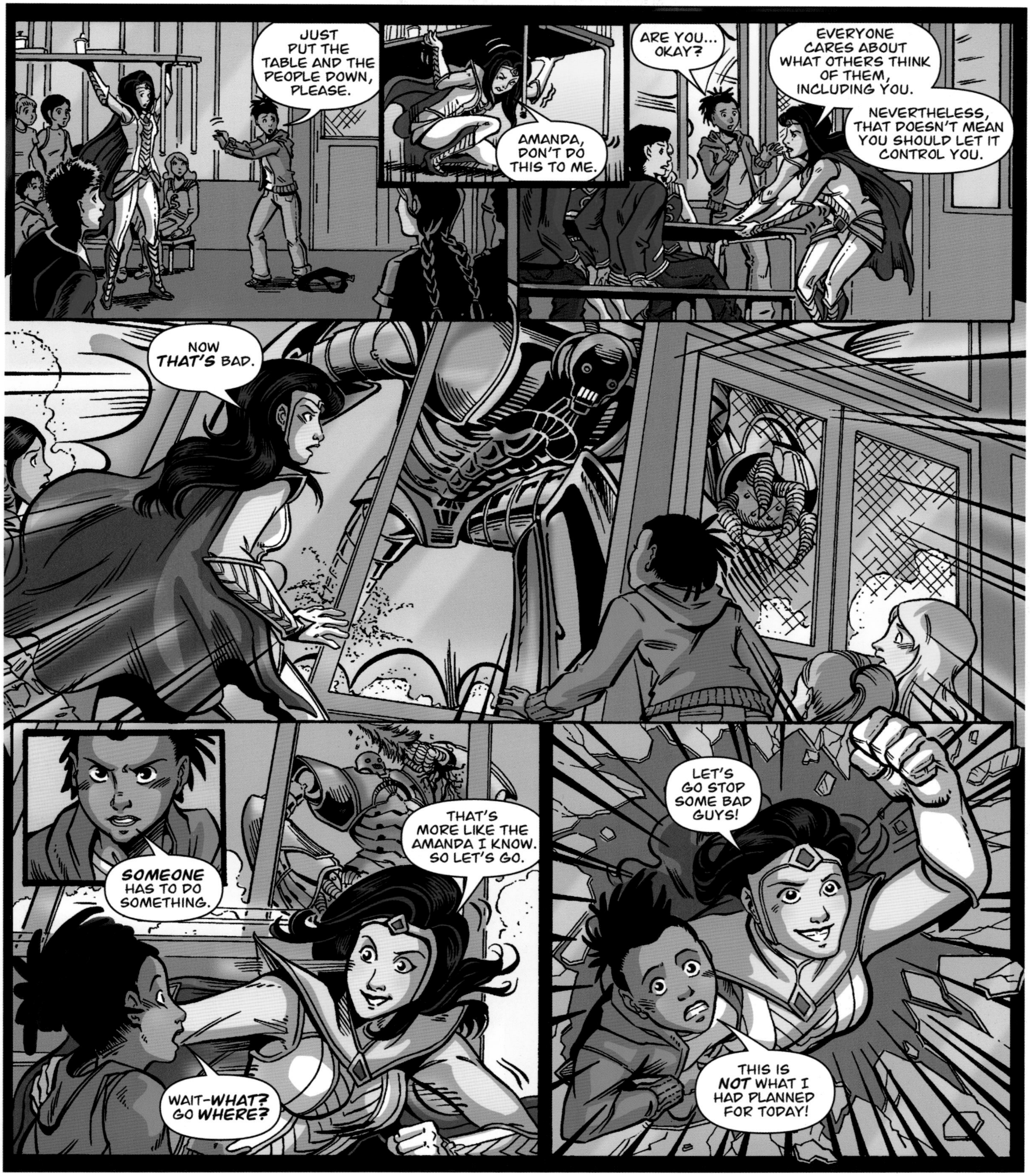
JUST PUT THE TABLE AND THE PEOPLE DOWN, PLEASE.
AMANDA, DON'T DO THIS TO ME.
ARE YOU... OKAY?
EVERYONE CARES ABOUT WHAT OTHERS THINK OF THEM, INCLUDING YOU.
NEVERTHELESS, THAT DOESN'T MEAN YOU SHOULD LET IT CONTROL YOU.
NOW THAT'S BAD.
SOMEONE HAS TO DO SOMETHING.
THAT'S MORE LIKE THE AMANDA I KNOW. SO LET'S GO.
WAIT-WHAT? GO WHERE?
LET'S GO STOP SOME BAD GUYS!
THIS IS NOT WHAT I HAD PLANNED FOR TODAY!

☆☆☆

PRO TIP

BE YOURSELF!

BY BARBARA RANDALL KESEL

"BE AUDACIOUSLY YOURSELF! COMICS IS A MEDIUM THAT'S OPEN TO AN INFINITE NUMBER OF CREATIVE VOICES. BE SURE TO FIND YOURS BY USING YOUR OWN THOUGHTS, QUESTIONS, EXPERIENCES, OR OBSERVATIONS AS THE BASIS FOR A STORY. SURE, A LOT OF STORIES HAVE UNIVERSAL CORES (AND THE ARGUMENT IS MADE THAT THERE ARE ONLY FIVE OR SO BASIC STORIES AND EVERYTHING ELSE IS JUST DETAILS OR STYLE ADDED ON), BUT TRY TO MAKE YOUR WORKS UNIQUELY AND COMPLETELY YOURS."

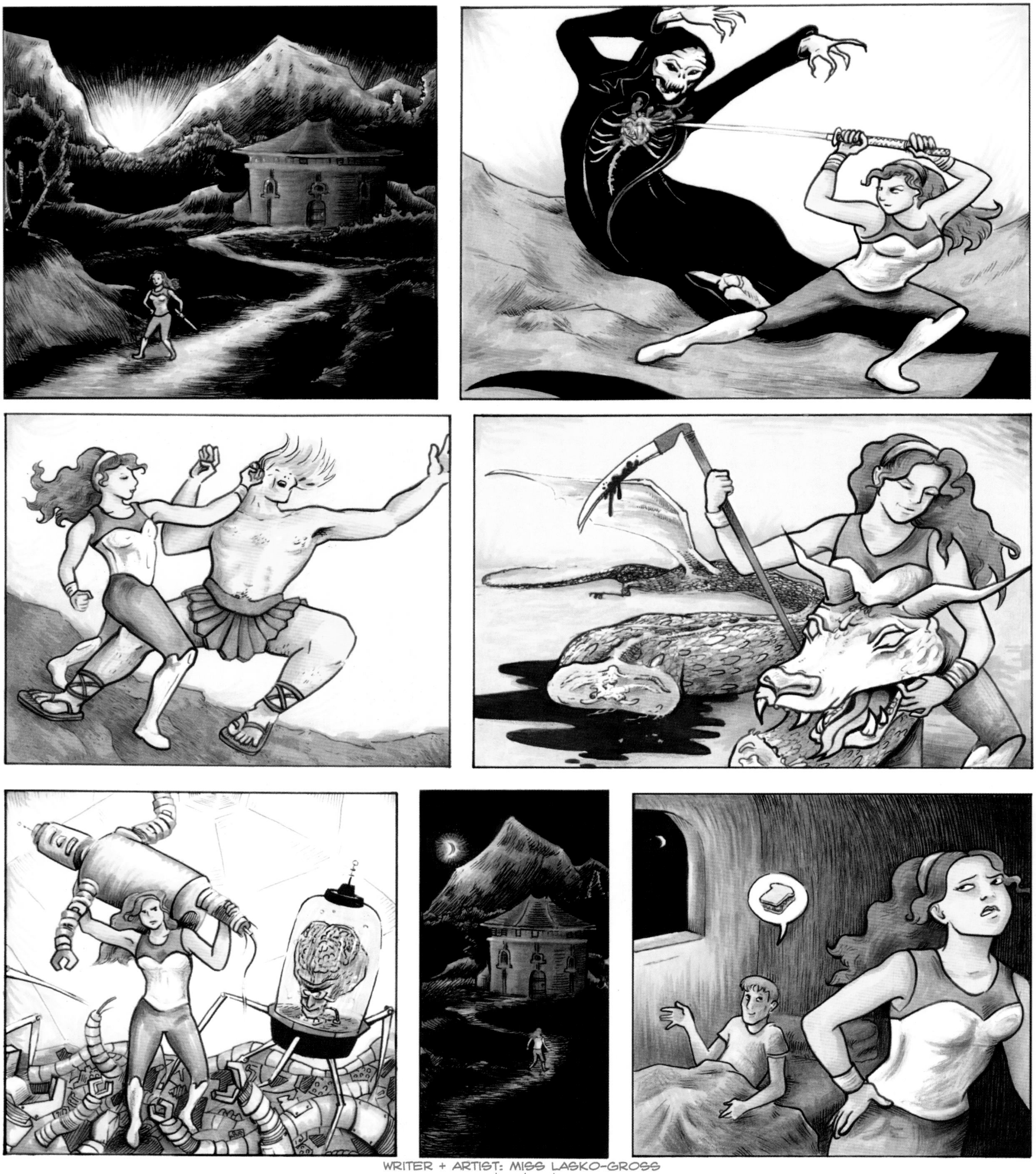

WRITER + ARTIST: MISS LASKO-GROSS

☆☆☆

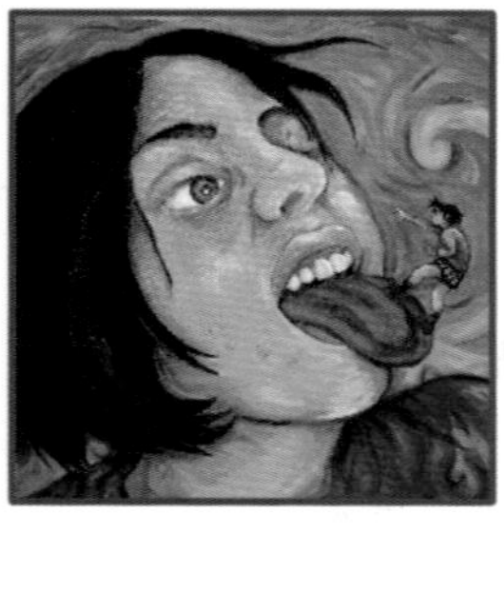

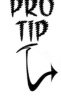

MISS LASKO-GROSS

SKILLS: Artist, Writer
LOCATION: New York City
FUN FACT: I'm the author and illustrator of Fantagraphics Books' *A Mess Of Everything*.

http://www.writershouseart.com/miss-lasko-gross/

PRO TIP

DIALOGUE
BY RACHEL DEERING

"WHEN SCRIPTING YOUR STORY, TRY TO KEEP THE AMOUNT OF COPY AT OR BELOW 35 WORDS IN A SINGLE PANEL. IF A CHARACTER IS TO DELIVER A LOT OF DIALOGUE, OR A GREAT DEAL OF EXPOSITION IS TO BE DONE IN A CAPTION BOX, CONSIDER BREAKING IT UP INTO SEVERAL PANELS."

Sir Real's Calamitous Caper

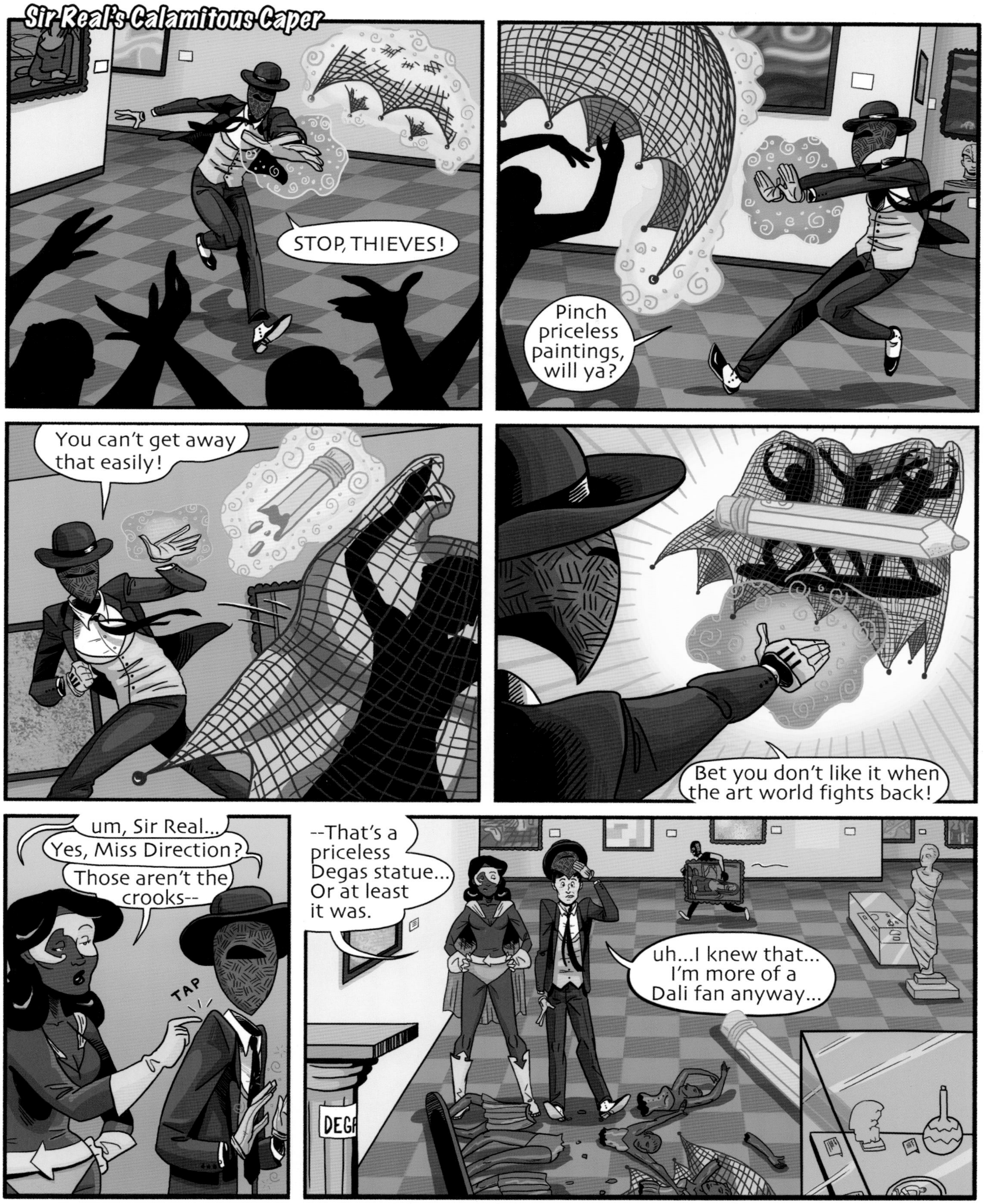
STOP, THIEVES!
Pinch priceless paintings, will ya?
You can't get away that easily!
Bet you don't like it when the art world fights back!
um, Sir Real...
Yes, Miss Direction?
Those aren't the crooks--
TAP
--That's a priceless Degas statue... Or at least it was.
uh...I knew that... I'm more of a Dali fan anyway...
DEGA

WRITER + ARTIST: JANNA BROWER

☆☆☆

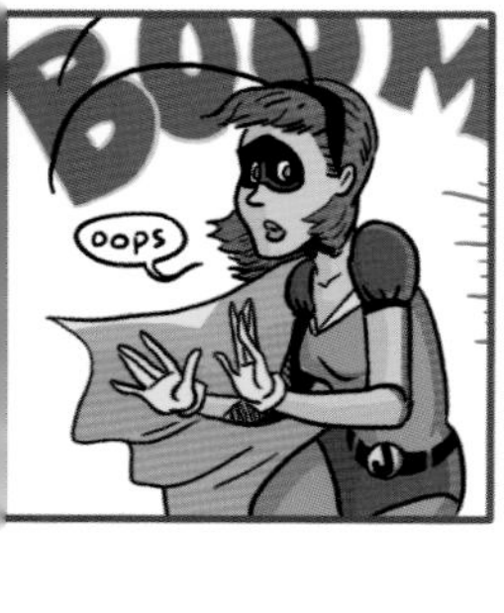
BOOM
OOPS

JANNA BROWER

SKILLS: Writer, Artist

LOCATION: New Jersey

FUN FACT: I'm kind of a klutz!

www.wix.com/jbrower3/portfolio

PRO TIP

YOUNG

BY LAURA MORLEY

"DON'T FEEL THAT JUST BECAUSE YOU'RE YOUNG, YOU DON'T KNOW ENOUGH TO TELL STORIES. THINK ABOUT WHAT YOU FIND SCARY, WHAT YOU FIND EXCITING, WHAT YOU WISH COULD EXIST IN THE WORLD. THINK UP AN IDEA, THEN ASK YOURSELF: WHAT WOULD MAKE IT BIGGER? WHAT WOULD MAKE IT STRANGER? WHAT WOULD MAKE IT LESS ORDINARY? YOU'LL FIND A STORY BEFORE YOU KNOW IT."

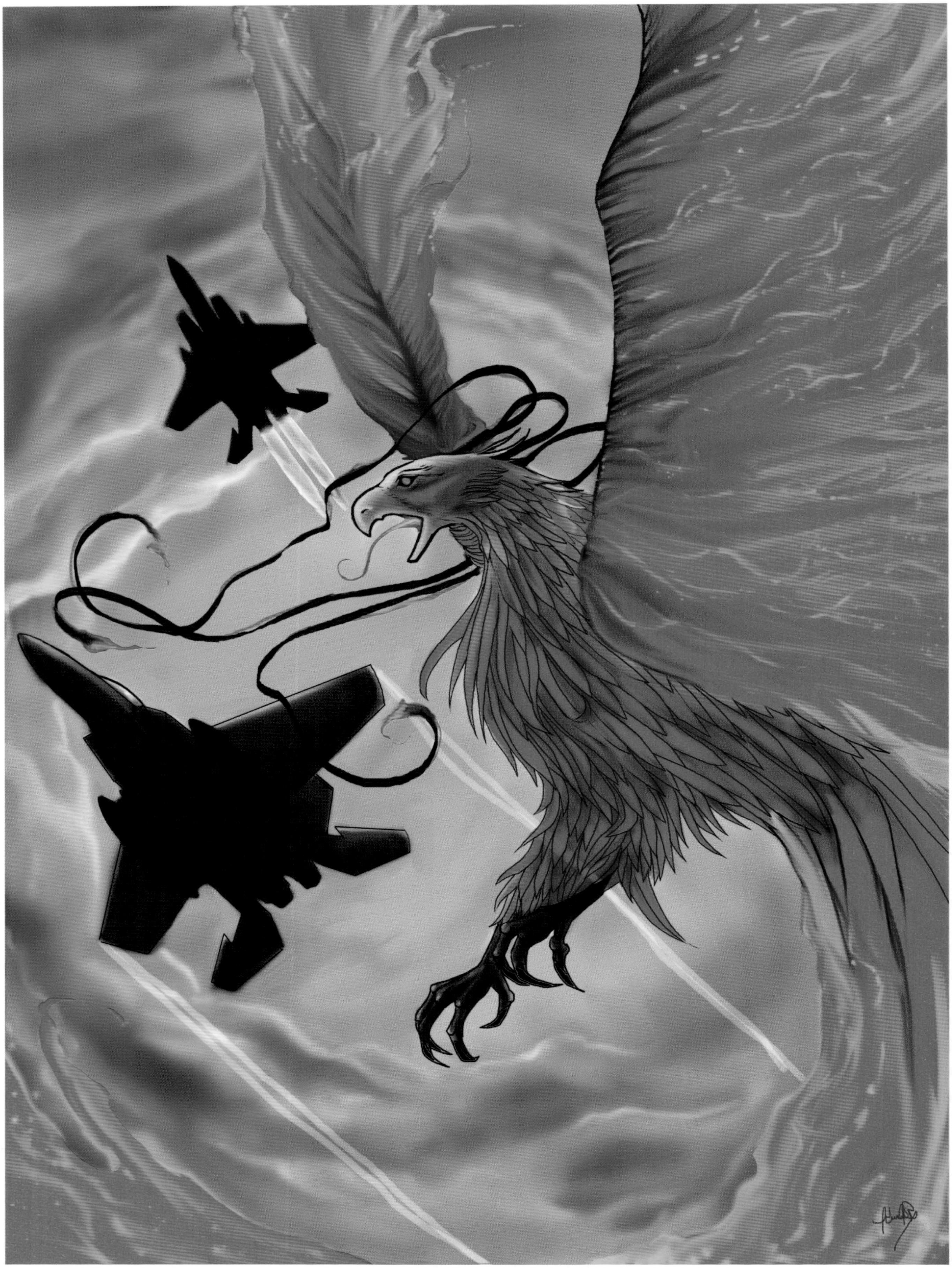

☆ ☆ ☆

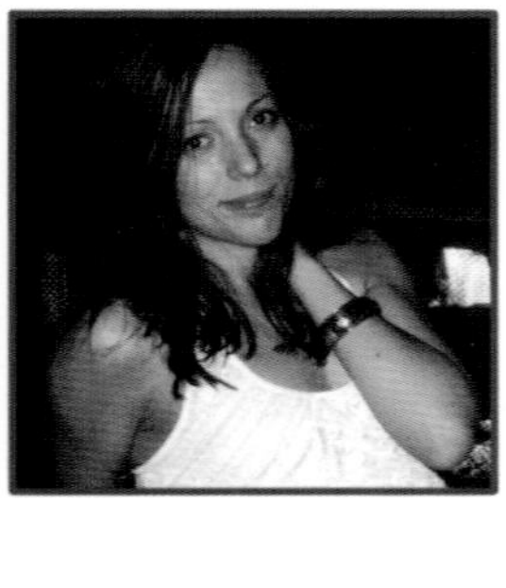

KIMBERLY DE LIZ

SKILLS: Penciller, Inker, Colorist
LOCATION: Omaha, NE
FUN FACT: Single mother on active duty in the USAF.

http://kdeliz.deviantart.com/

PRO TIP

CONFIDENCE

BY RACHEL DEERING

"HAVING CONFIDENCE IN YOUR WORK IS A WONDERFUL THING, BUT TAKE CARE THAT IT DOESN'T COME OFF AS HUBRIS."

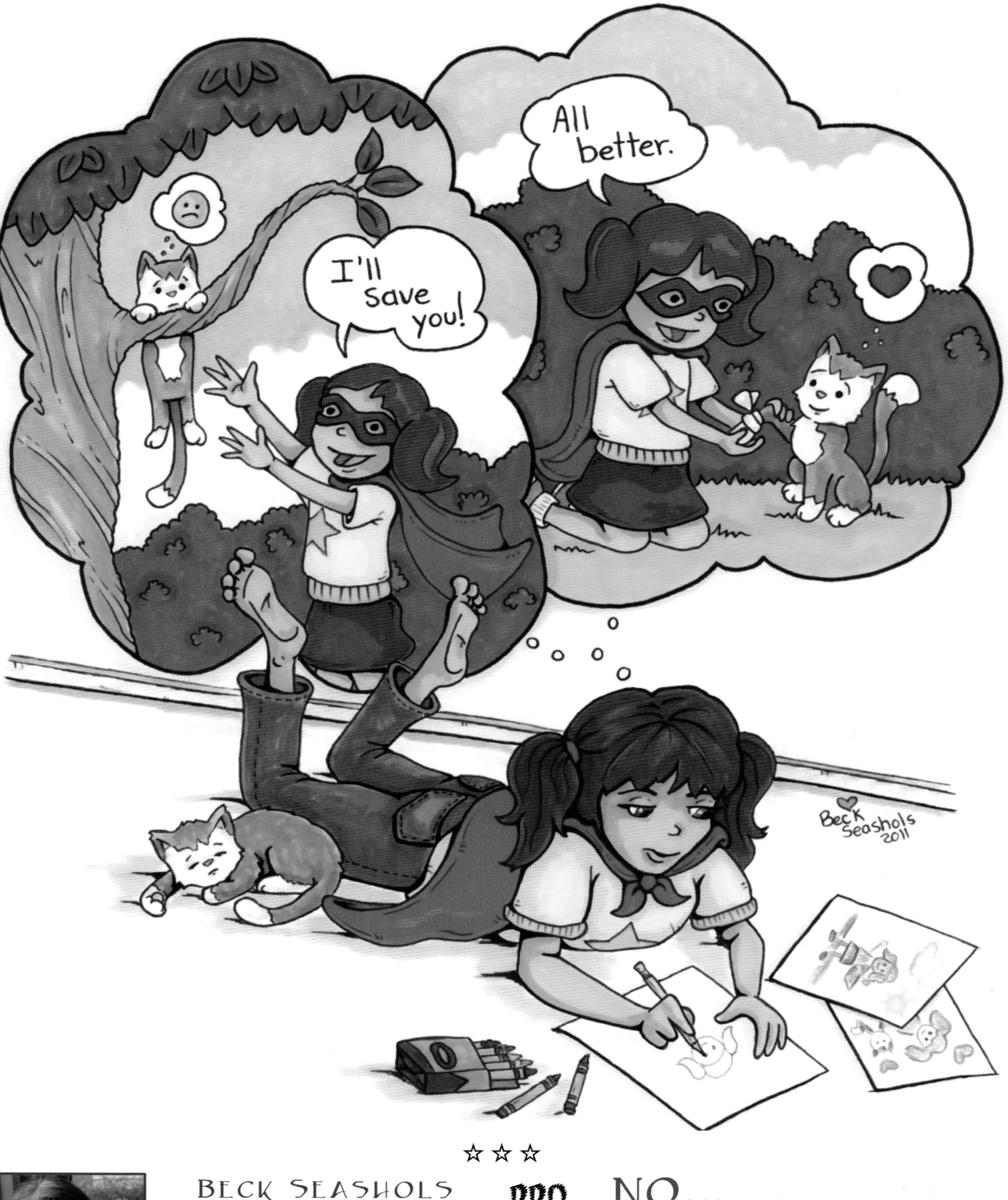
I'll save you!
All better.
Beck Seashols 2011

☆☆☆

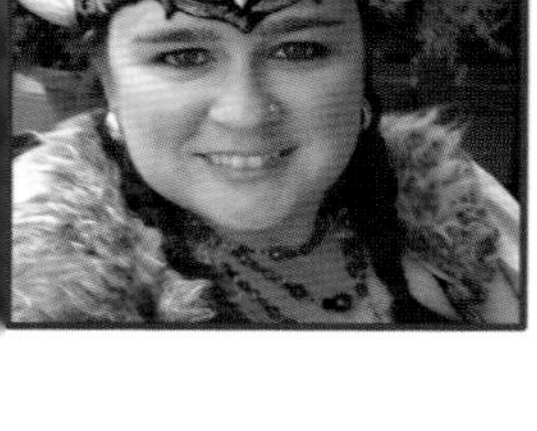

BECK SEASHOLS

SKILLS: Penciller, Inker, Colorist
LOCATION: Roanoke, Virginia USA
FUN FACT: Queen of Glitter

www.Beckadoodles.com

PRO TIP

NO...

BY STEPHANIE HANS

"PLEASE DON'T TAKE IT PERSONALLY WHEN AN EDITOR SAYS 'NO.' YOU WILL NOT BE PUBLISHED FOR ANY OTHER REASON THAN BEING THE RIGHT PERSON FOR THE RIGHT PROJECT. DO NOT ARGUE AND PLEASE, DO NOT BEG. YOUR ARTWORKS SHOULD DO THE TALKING FOR YOU."

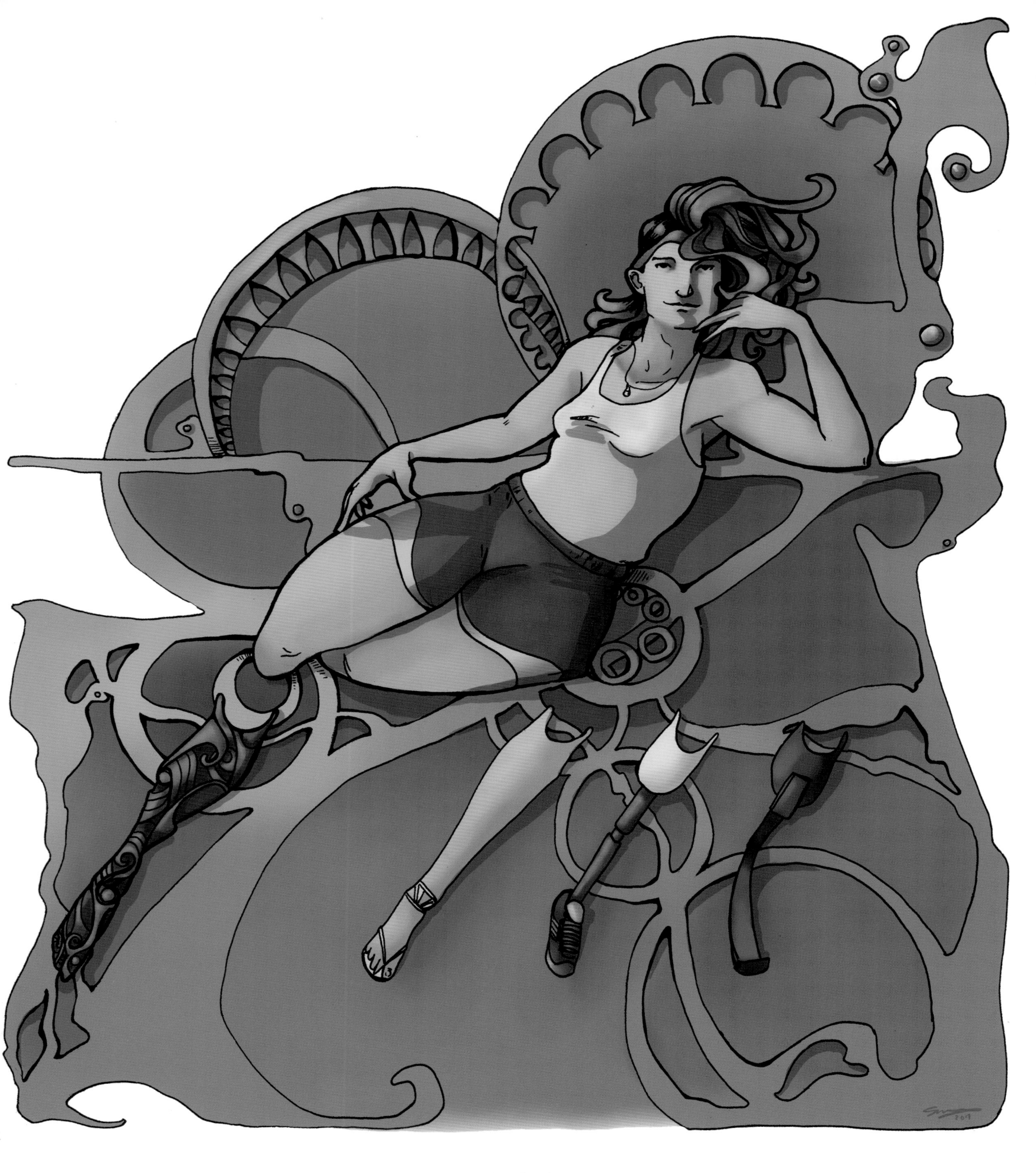

☆☆☆

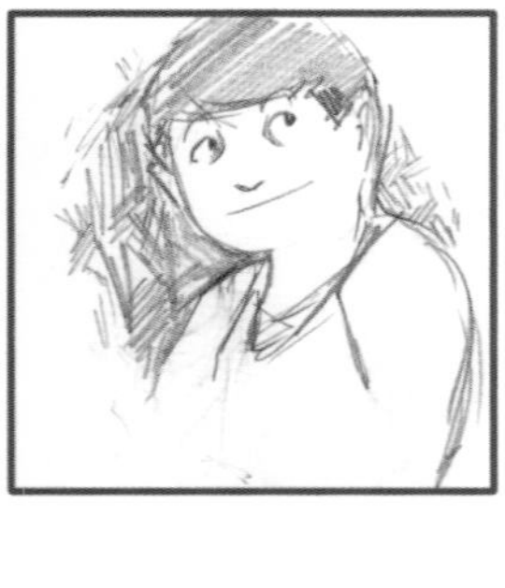

BETH SPARKS

SKILLS: Penciller, Colorist, Inker
LOCATION: East Lansing, Michigan
FUN FACT: I am slowly gathering an elaborate collection of tools in the name of self-sufficiency and justice.

solid-state-studios.blogspot.com

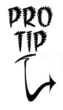

PRO TIP

HONEST

BY STEPHANIE HANS

"DO NOT TRY TO BECOME WHAT YOU THINK PUBLISHERS ARE AWAITING FROM YOU. BE HONEST WITH WHAT YOU WANT TO DO AND WHAT YOU SHOW BECAUSE THIS IS WHAT THEY WILL ASK YOU TO DO."

KIDS
&
TEENS

★ ★ ★

FEATURING THE ART OF
THE NEXT GENERATION OF COMICS
PLUS: TIPS ON HOW TO BUILD A CAREER
AS A PROFESSIONAL ARTIST!

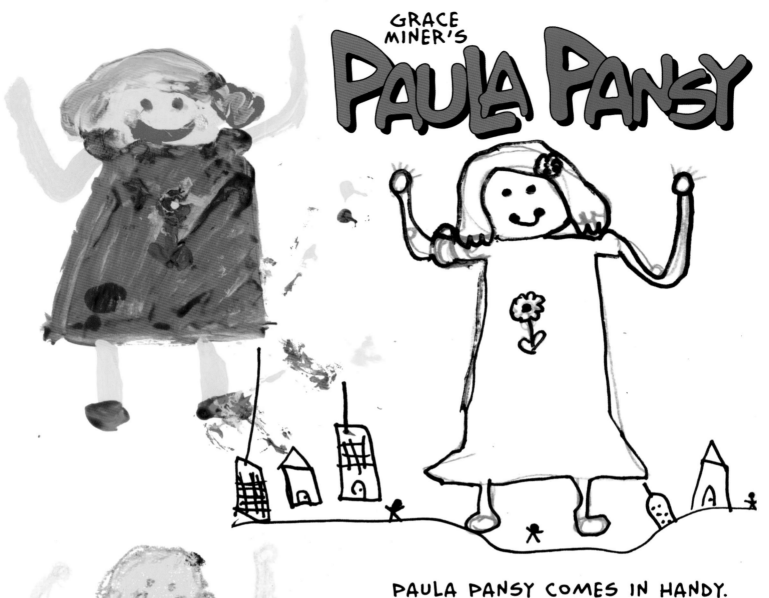

GRACE MINER'S

PAULA PANSY

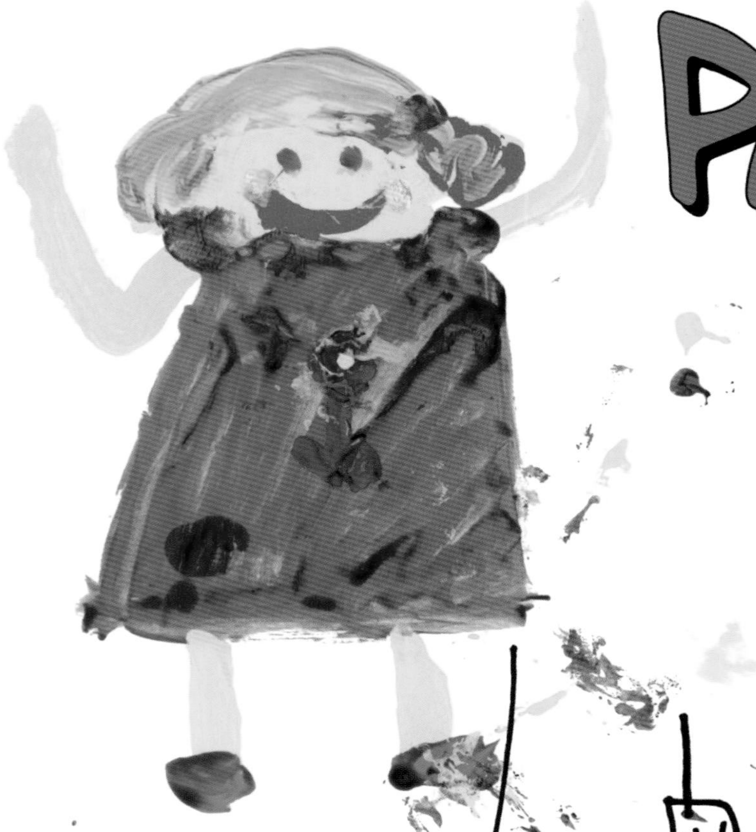

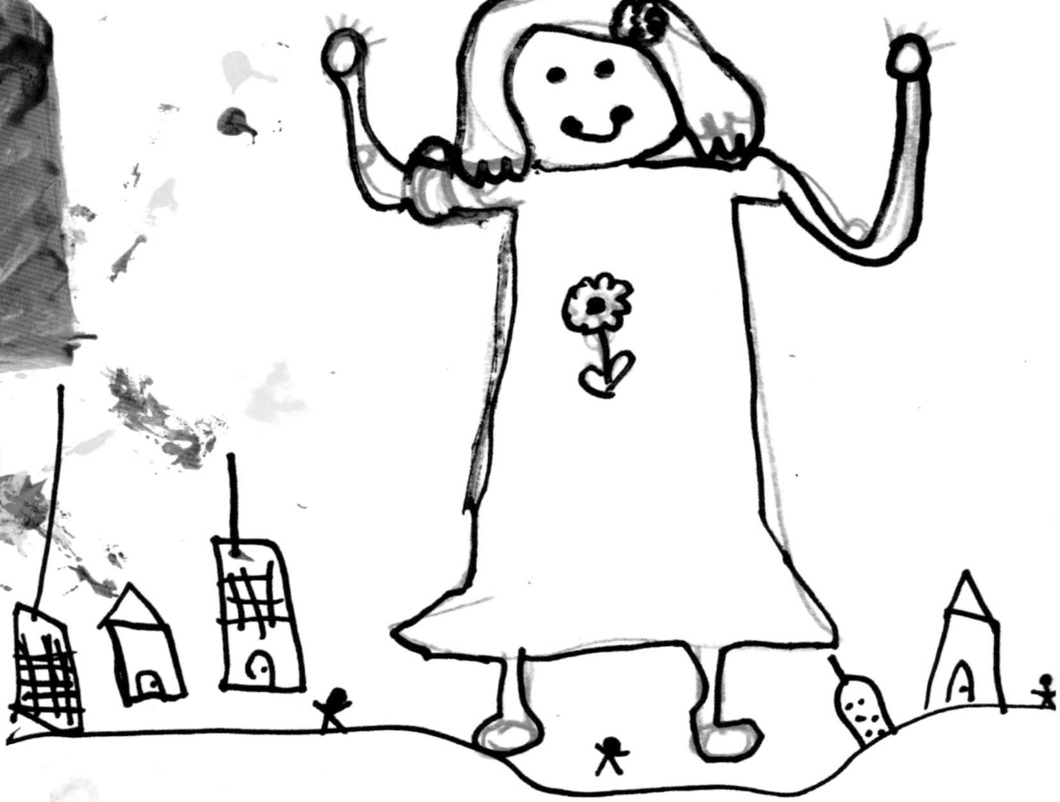

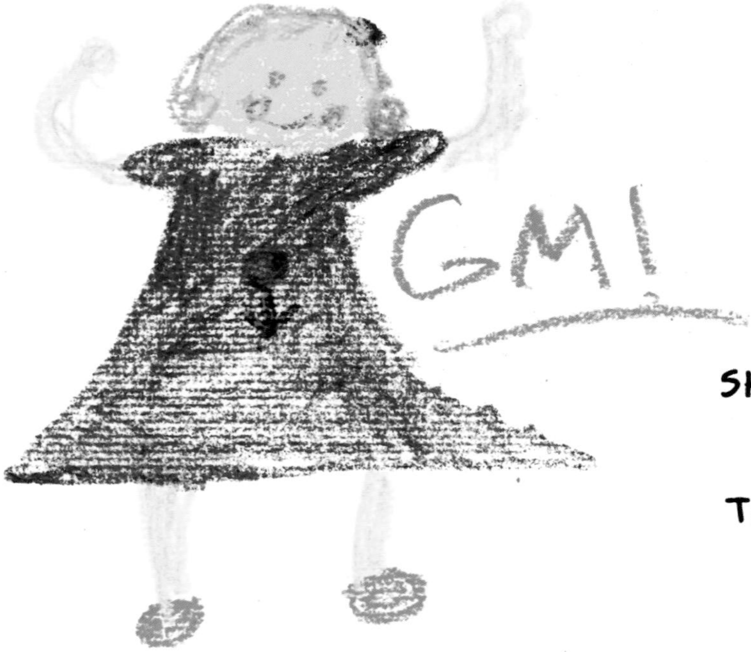
GMI

PAULA PANSY COMES IN HANDY.
PAULA PANSY, SHE ALSO
LOVES CANDY.
WHEN THE BAD GUYS PUSH
HER DOWN,
SHE GROWS UP TALL AND STOMPS
AROUND (ON BAD GUYS).
THEN SHE GROWS SMALL HAPPILY.

PAULA PANSY.

☆ ☆ ☆

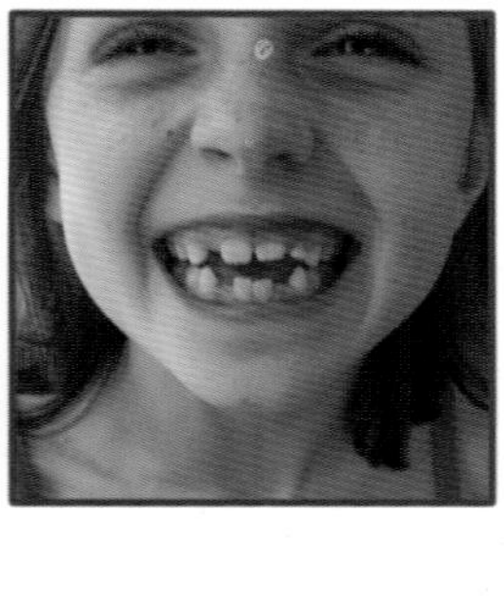

GRACE MINER

SKILLS: Writer, Illustrator
LOCATION: North Carolina
FUN FACT: Grace has sketched with artists from around the world since she was 6. And she's a bit put out that she can't just hop in the car and visit them all. She is aided and abetted by her sister Cate.

www.5MinuteMarvels.com

Tips for Kids! Practice!

by Nicole Falk

"PRACTICE, PRACTICE, PRACTICE! ARTISTS WORKING WEREN'T JUST BORN WITH THE TALENT TO DRAW BRILLIANTLY. THEY WORK REALLY HARD, DRAWING & PRACTICING EVERY DAY FOR YEARS!"

Heroic! by Morgan Denham

Heroic is your teacher teaching you new stuff in class

Heroic is a policeman strong and loyal

Heroic is a fireman rushing to the rescue

Heroic is your best friend always there when you need them

Heroic is my Mommy's cooking when we are hungry

Heroic feels like my family's love

Heroic can be as simple as waking to a beautiful warm day

Heroic can be as complex as a Greek Myth

Heroic can be anything or anyone, even you!

☆ ☆ ☆

MORGAN DENHAM

SKILLS: Cartoonist
LOCATION: Olympus
FUN FACT: I love archaeology, mythology, art, writing, and poetry. I yell to Poseidon when visiting the beach.

BrianDenham.com

Tips for Kids!

267

Little Things
by Renae De Liz

"I GREW UP LEARNING TO DRAW BY OBSERVING ALL THE LITTLE THINGS AROUND ME. HOW MY CAT WALKED, HOW MY SISTER'S HAIR MOVED, HOW THE WIND BLEW LEAVES AROUND, HOW PEOPLE'S EYES SQUINTED WHEN THEY SMILED. WATCH HOW THE WORLD MOVES AROUND YOU AND APPLY IT TO YOUR DRAWING. YOUR ARTWORK STYLE WILL GROW WITH A LIFE AND NATURAL EASE THAT IS INCREDIBLY DIFFICULT TO LEARN AS AN ADULT."

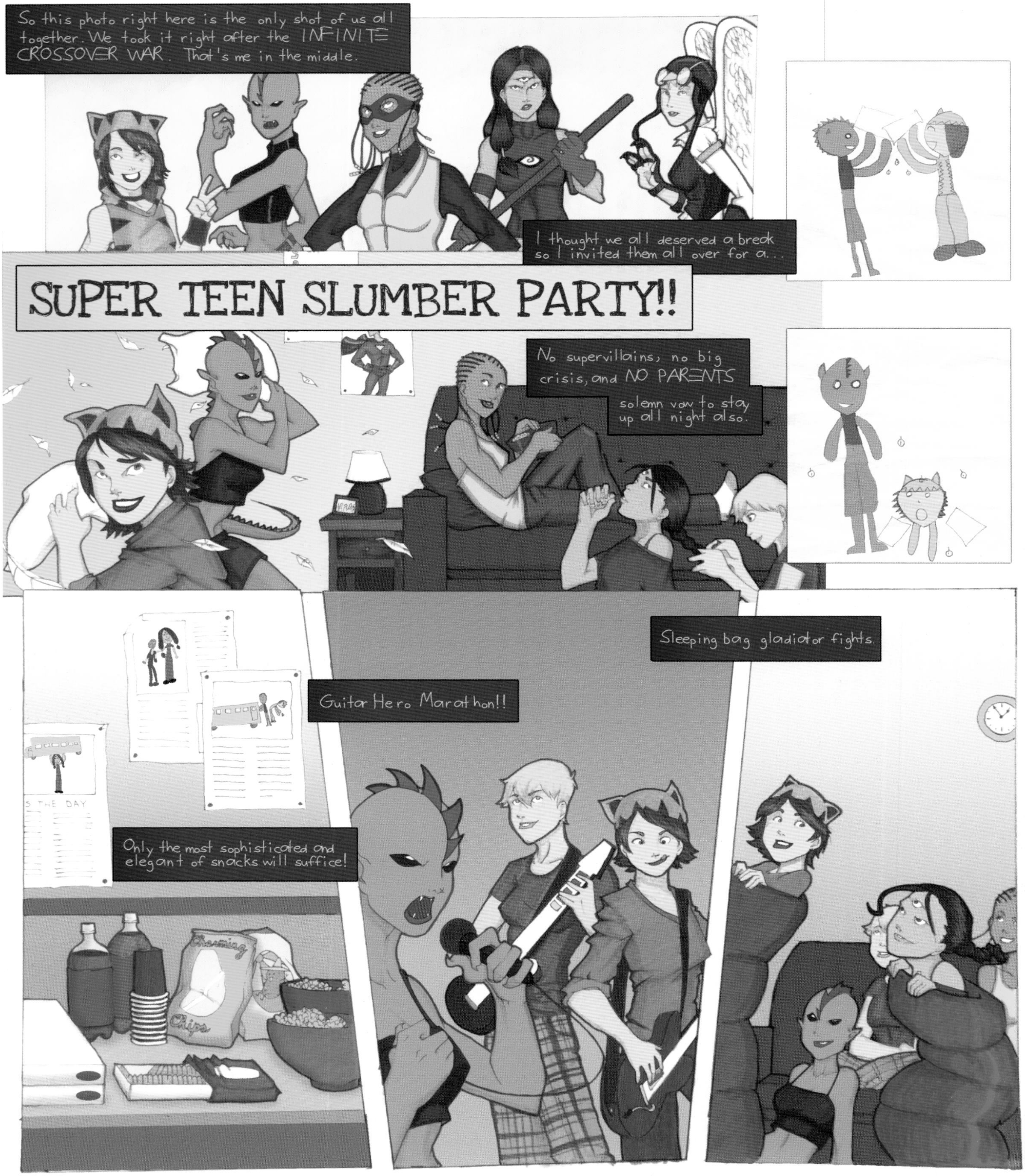
So this photo right here is the only shot of us all together. We took it right after the INFINITE CROSSOVER WAR. That's me in the middle.
I thought we all deserved a break so I invited them all over for a...
SUPER TEEN SLUMBER PARTY!!
No supervillains, no big crisis, and NO PARENTS
solemn vow to stay up all night also.
Only the most sophisticated and elegant of snacks will suffice!
Chips
Guitar Hero Marathon!!
Sleeping bag gladiator fights.

WRITER: GAIL SIMONE ARTISTS: ELENI LADD, KELSIE LADD, KALYSSA LADD, SAMARA LADD COLORIST: MARY BELLAMY LETTERER: ELENI LADD

☆ ☆ ☆

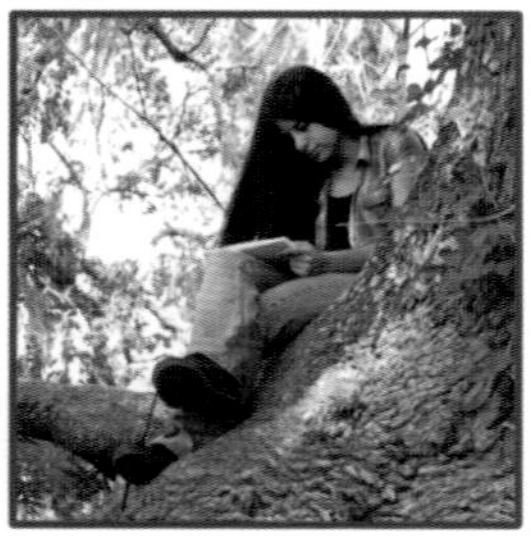

ELENI LADD

SKILLS: Penciller
LOCATION: South Carolina
FUN FACT: When I was really little my first drawings were roadmaps for my Micro Machines to drive on, using any paper I could get ahold of.

youngtitan213.tumblr.com/

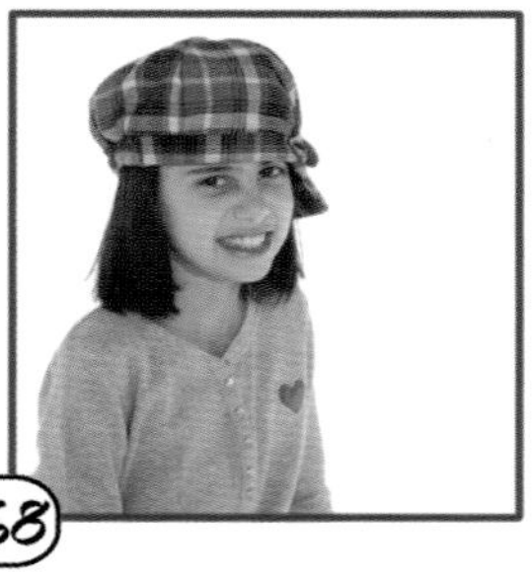

KALYSSA LADD

SKILLS: Penciller
LOCATION: South Carolina
FUN FACT: I can eat a whole lemon without squinting.

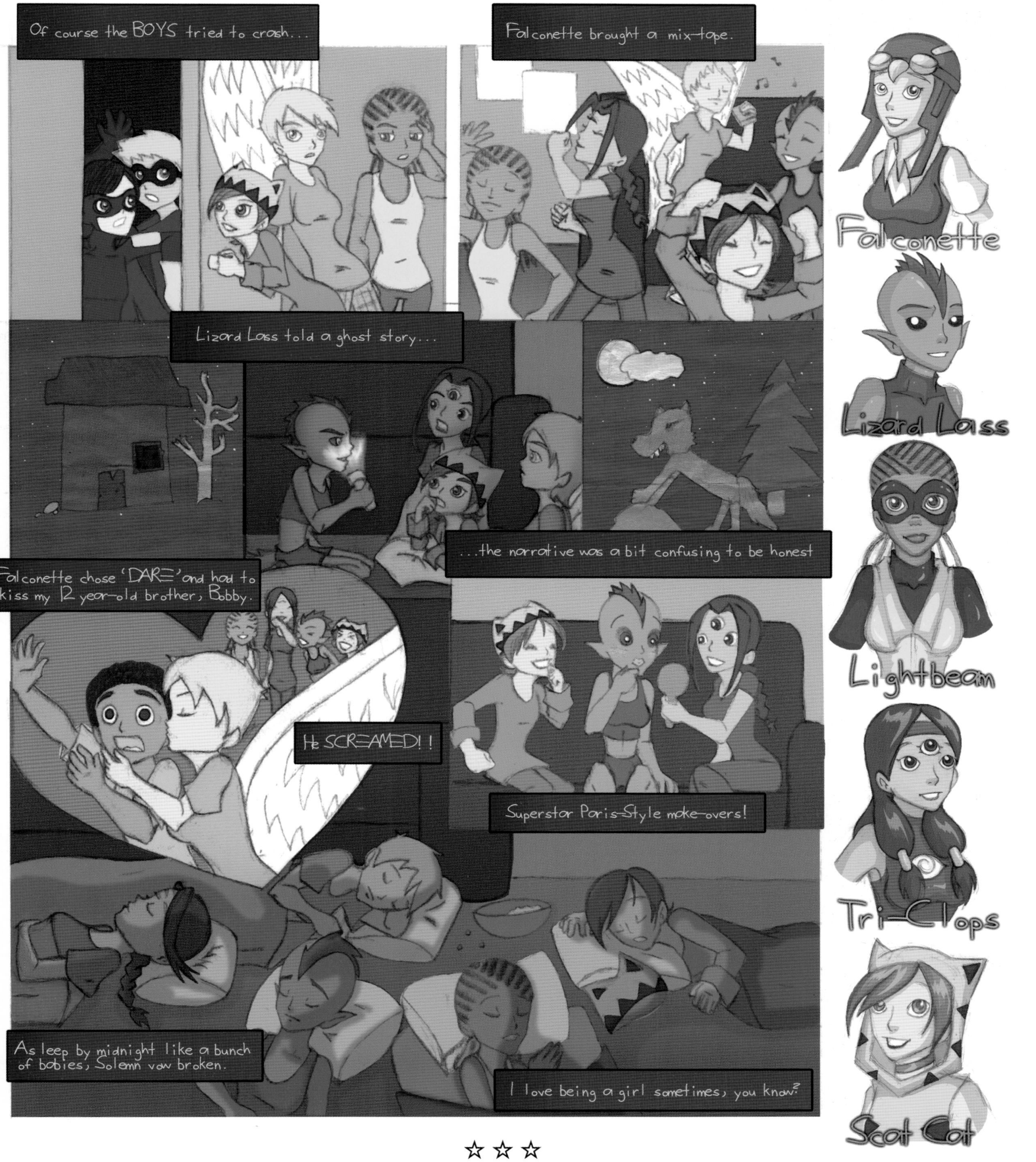

Of course the BOYS tried to crash...
Falconette brought a mix-tape.
Lizard Lass told a ghost story...
...the narrative was a bit confusing to be honest
Falconette chose 'DARE' and had to kiss my 12 year-old brother, Bobby.
He SCREAMED!!
Superstar Paris-Style make-overs!
Asleep by midnight like a bunch of babies, Solemn vow broken.
I love being a girl sometimes, you know?
Falconette
Lizard Lass
Lightbeam
Tri-Clops
Scat Cat

☆☆☆

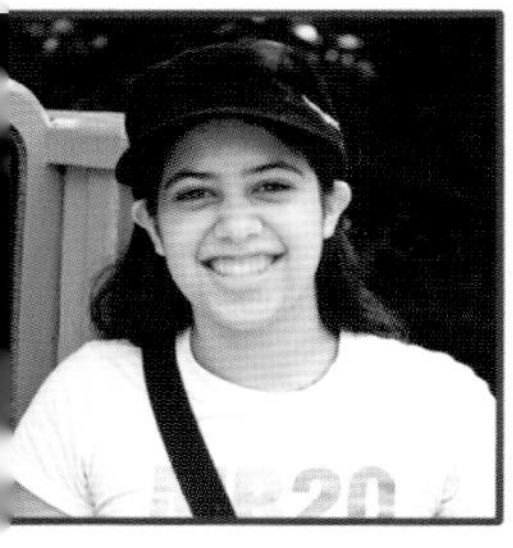

KELSIE LADD

SKILLS: Penciller
LOCATION: South Carolina
FUN FACT: I have the uncanny ability to find any lost item.

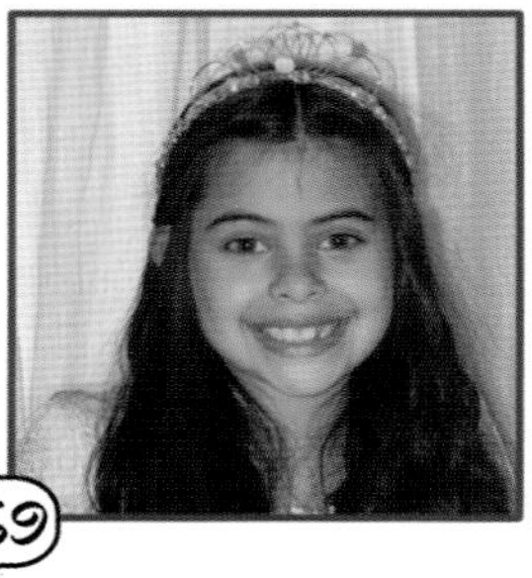

SAMARA LADD

SKILLS: Penciller
LOCATION: South Carolina
FUN FACT: An actual superpower: the ability to increase my density!!

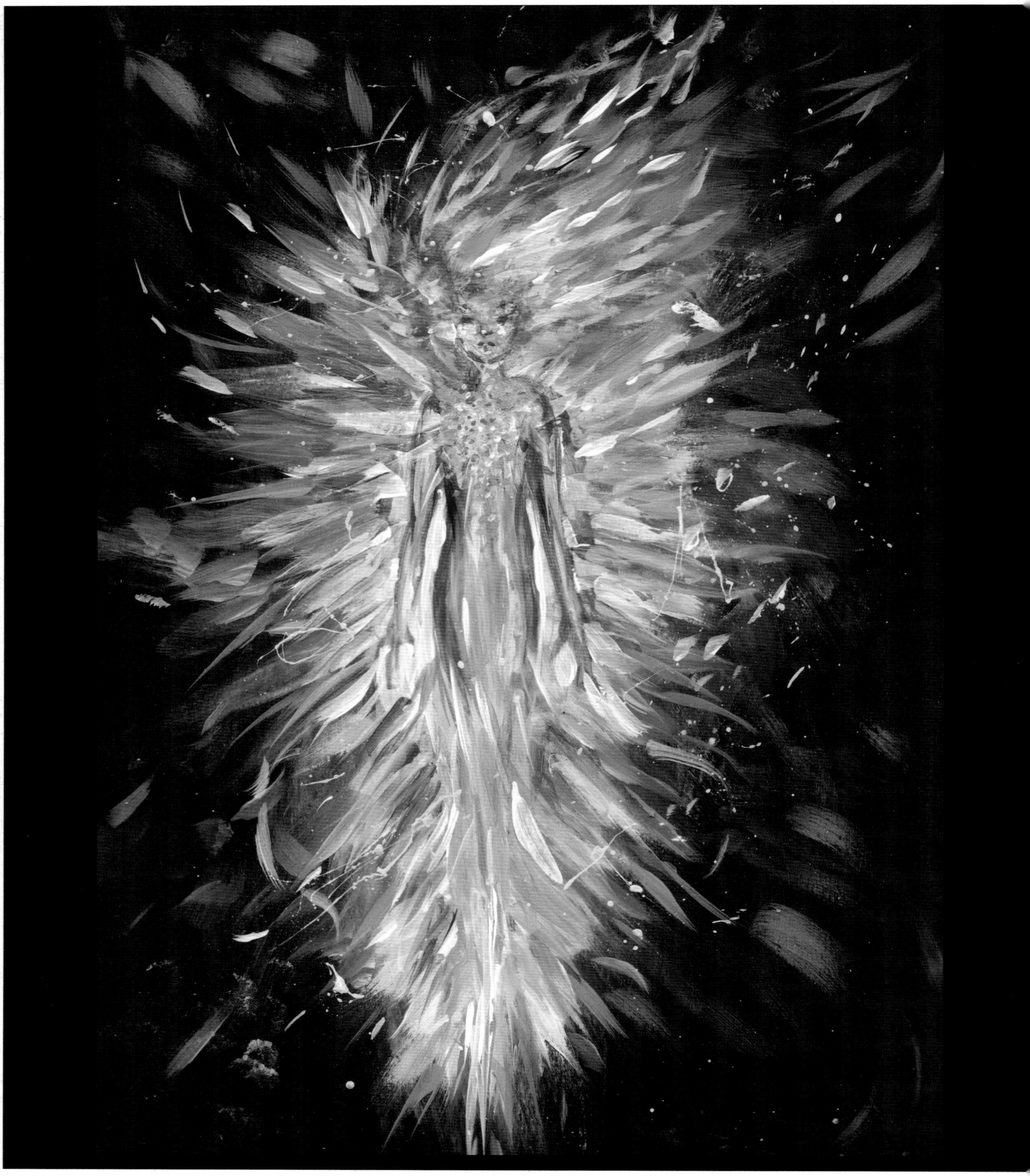

☆☆☆

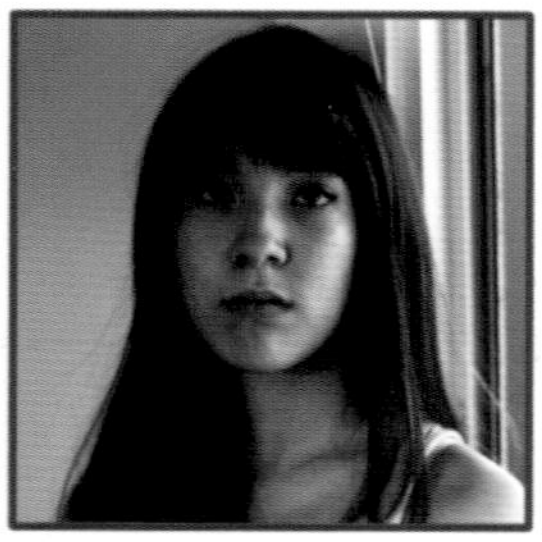

KELSEY LEE

SKILLS: Painter
LOCATION: San Diego, CA
FUN FACT: I'm sixteen and I speak four different languages.

Tips for Kids!

Too Young

by Jessica Hickman

"YOU'RE NEVER TOO YOUNG TO START CREATING BOOKS! GRAB SOME PAPER, PENCILS, MARKERS AND MAKE YOURSELF A COMIC. SHOW IT TO FAMILY AND FRIENDS AND GET THEIR FEEDBACK."

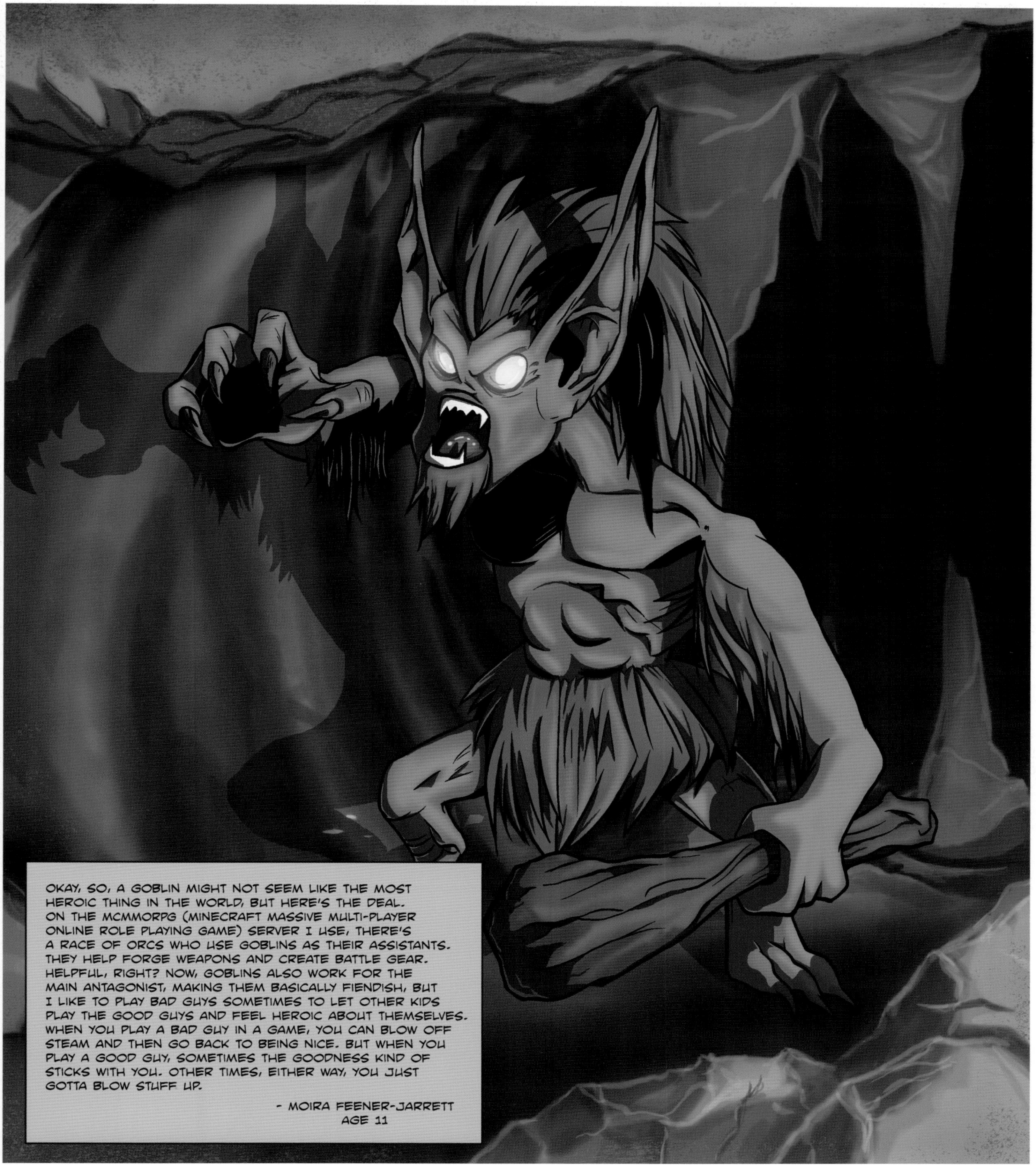
OKAY, SO, A GOBLIN MIGHT NOT SEEM LIKE THE MOST HEROIC THING IN THE WORLD, BUT HERE'S THE DEAL. ON THE MCMMORPG (MINECRAFT MASSIVE MULTI-PLAYER ONLINE ROLE PLAYING GAME) SERVER I USE, THERE'S A RACE OF ORCS WHO USE GOBLINS AS THEIR ASSISTANTS. THEY HELP FORGE WEAPONS AND CREATE BATTLE GEAR. HELPFUL, RIGHT? NOW, GOBLINS ALSO WORK FOR THE MAIN ANTAGONIST, MAKING THEM BASICALLY FIENDISH, BUT I LIKE TO PLAY BAD GUYS SOMETIMES TO LET OTHER KIDS PLAY THE GOOD GUYS AND FEEL HEROIC ABOUT THEMSELVES. WHEN YOU PLAY A BAD GUY IN A GAME, YOU CAN BLOW OFF STEAM AND THEN GO BACK TO BEING NICE. BUT WHEN YOU PLAY A GOOD GUY, SOMETIMES THE GOODNESS KIND OF STICKS WITH YOU. OTHER TIMES, EITHER WAY, YOU JUST GOTTA BLOW STUFF UP.
- MOIRA FEENER-JARRETT
AGE 11

☆ ☆ ☆

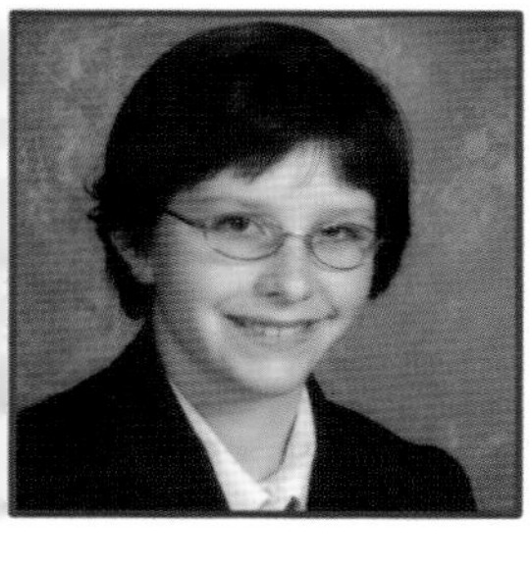

MOIRA FEENER-JARRETT

SKILLS: Penciller
LOCATION: Hayward, CA
FUN FACT: Believes the cake is a tasty lie.

Tips for Kids!

Everyday

by Suzannah Rowntree

"DRAW SOMETHING THAT YOU SEE ONCE EVERYDAY, LITTLE THINGS LIKE PENS AND SHOELACES ARE OKAY."

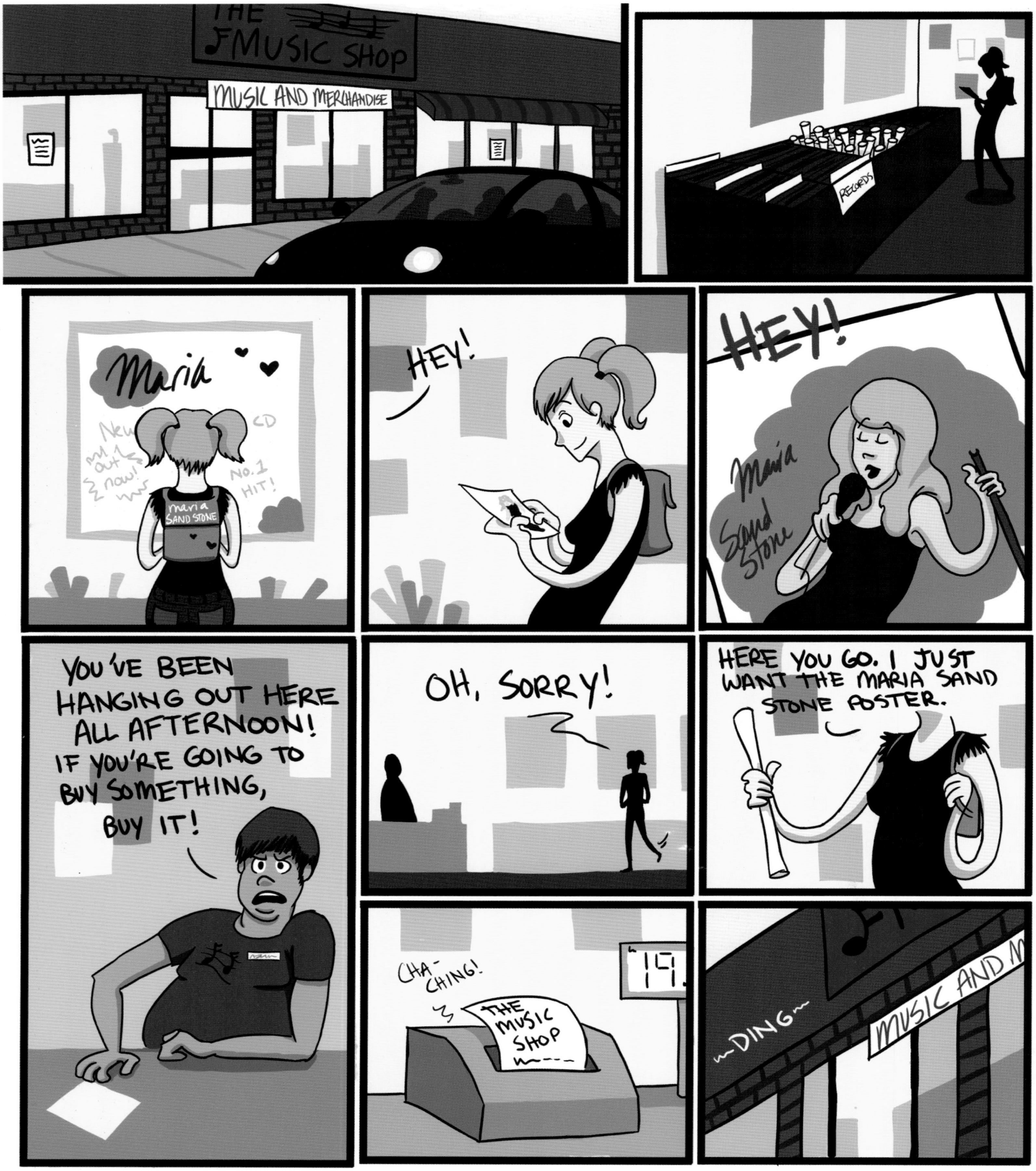
THE MUSIC SHOP
MUSIC AND MERCHANDISE
RECORDS
Maria
New CD out now!
No. 1 HIT!
maria SAND STONE
HEY!
HEY!
Maria Sand Stone
YOU'VE BEEN HANGING OUT HERE ALL AFTERNOON! IF YOU'RE GOING TO BUY SOMETHING, BUY IT!
OH, SORRY!
HERE YOU GO. I JUST WANT THE MARIA SAND STONE POSTER.
CHA-CHING!
THE MUSIC SHOP
14.
~DING~
MUSIC AND M

☆☆☆

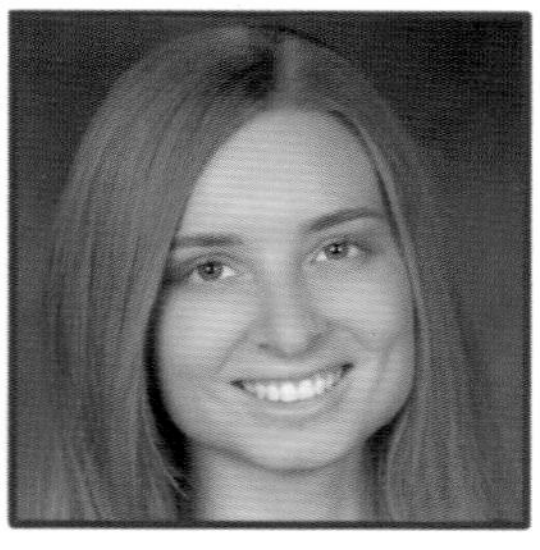

NICOLE PANNEBAKER

SKILLS: Penciling, Coloring, Inking

LOCATION: Orange County, CA

FUN FACT: I love U.S. history and the old west!

http://plaidsheep.deviantart.com

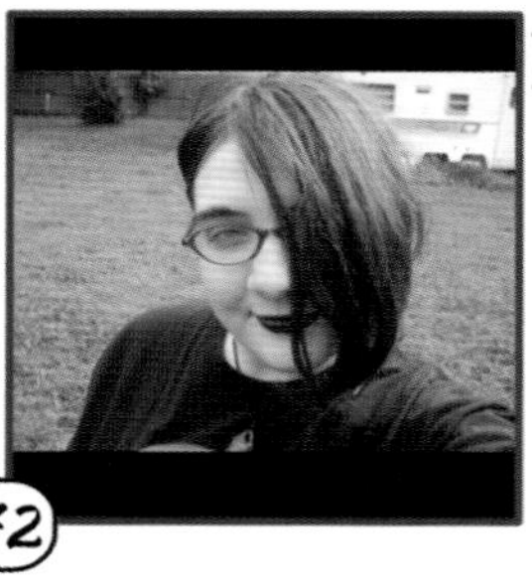

BRITTANY BATTIST

SKILLS: Writer

FUN FACT: I'm a huge geek when it comes to comic books, novels, anime, and video games.

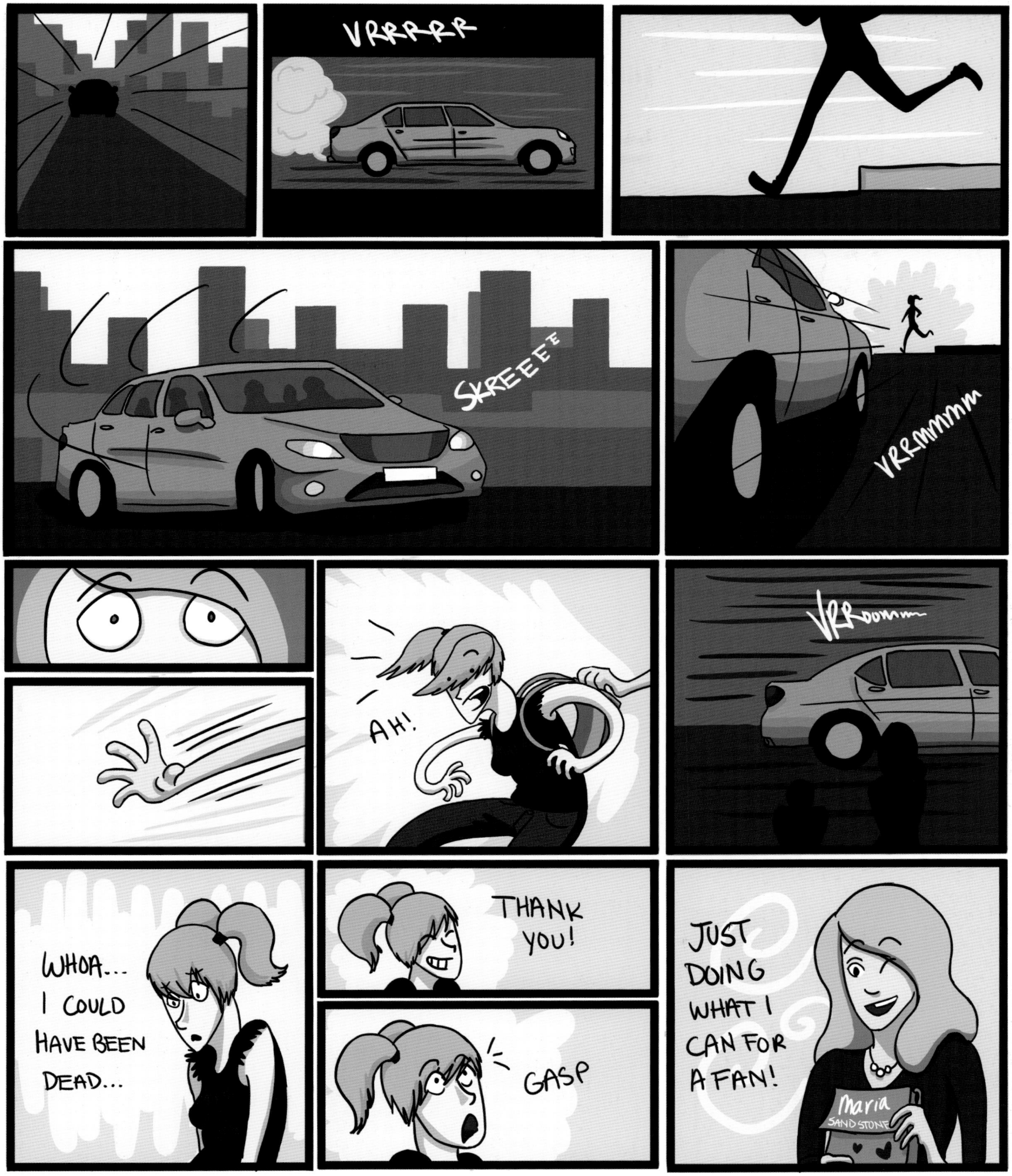
VRRRRR
SKREEEE
VRRMMMMM
AH!
VRRoomm
WHOA... I COULD HAVE BEEN DEAD...
THANK YOU!
GASP
JUST DOING WHAT I CAN FOR A FAN!
Maria SANDSTONE

☆☆☆

Tips for Kids!

Ask Yourself

by Laura Morley

"DON'T FEEL THAT JUST BECAUSE YOU'RE YOUNG, YOU DON'T KNOW ENOUGH TO TELL STORIES. THINK ABOUT WHAT YOU FIND SCARY, WHAT YOU FIND EXCITING, WHAT YOU WISH YOU COULD EXIST IN THE WORLD. THINK UP AN IDEA, THEN ASK YOURSELF: WHAT WOULD MAKE IT BIGGER? WHAT WOULD MAKE IT STRANGER? WHAT WOULD MAKE IT LESS ORDINARY? YOU'LL FIND A STORY BEFORE YOU KNOW IT."

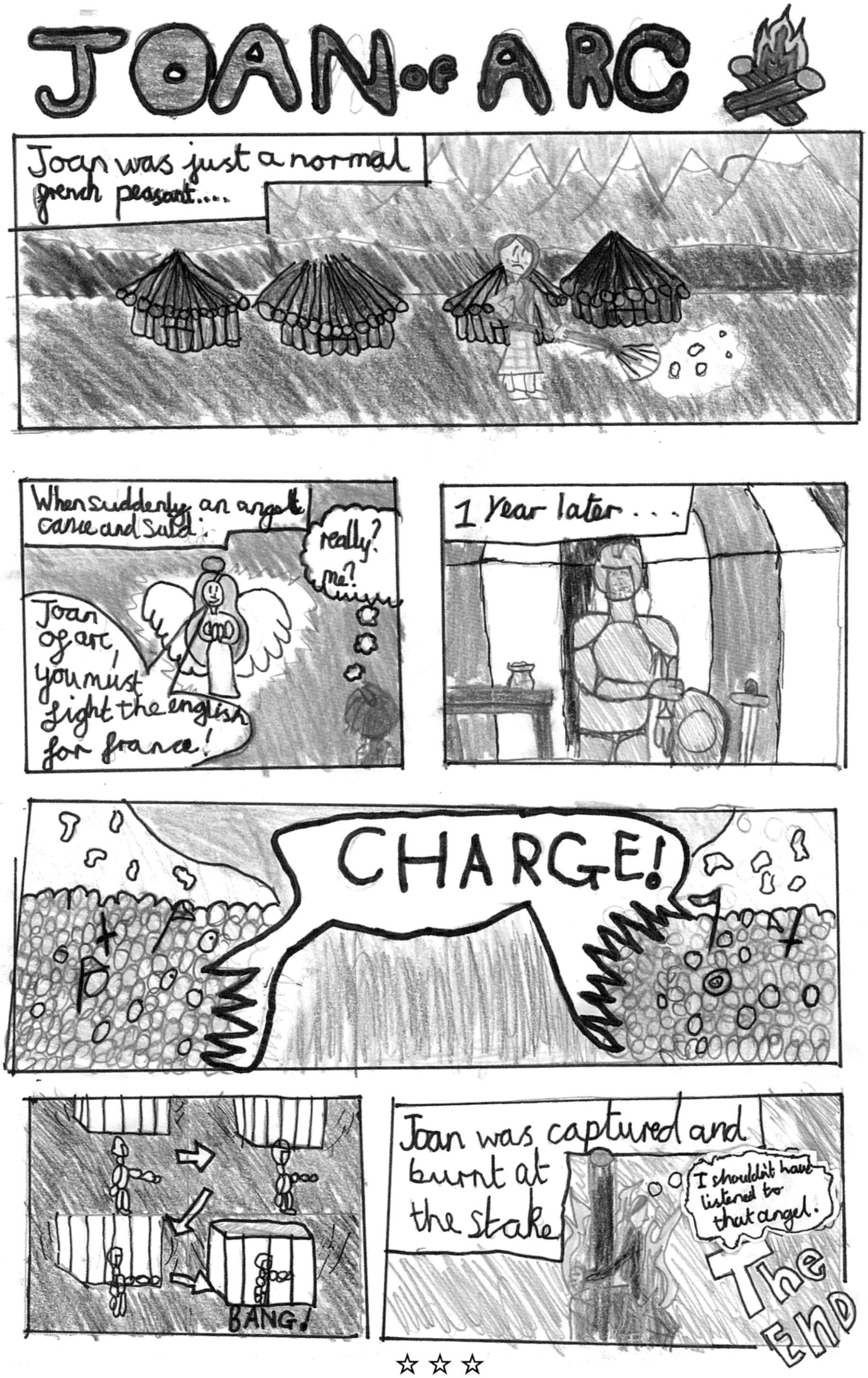
JOAN of ARC
Joan was just a normal french peasant....
When suddenly an angel came and said:
Joan of arc, you must fight the english for france!
really? me?
1 Year later . . .
CHARGE!
BANG!
Joan was captured and burnt at the stake
I shouldn't have listened to that angel.
The End

☆ ☆ ☆

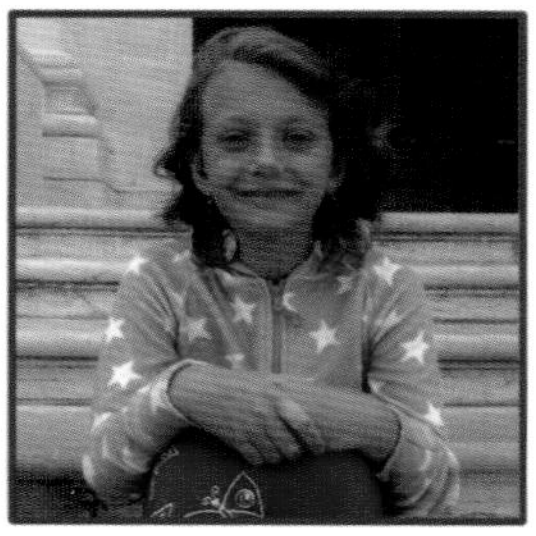

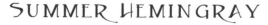

SUMMER HEMINGRAY

SKILLS: Artist
LOCATION: Brighton
FUN FACT: It's my ambition to watch every episode of the *The Simpsons* ever made. Even the new ones make me laugh.

Tips for Kids!

Library comics!

by Jessica Hickman

"LIBRARIES HAVE SOME COMIC BOOKS AND GRAPHIC NOVELS TOO. YOU CAN CHECK THEM OUT, TAKE THEM HOME TO LOOK OVER, THEN RETURN THEM WHEN YOU'RE DONE!"

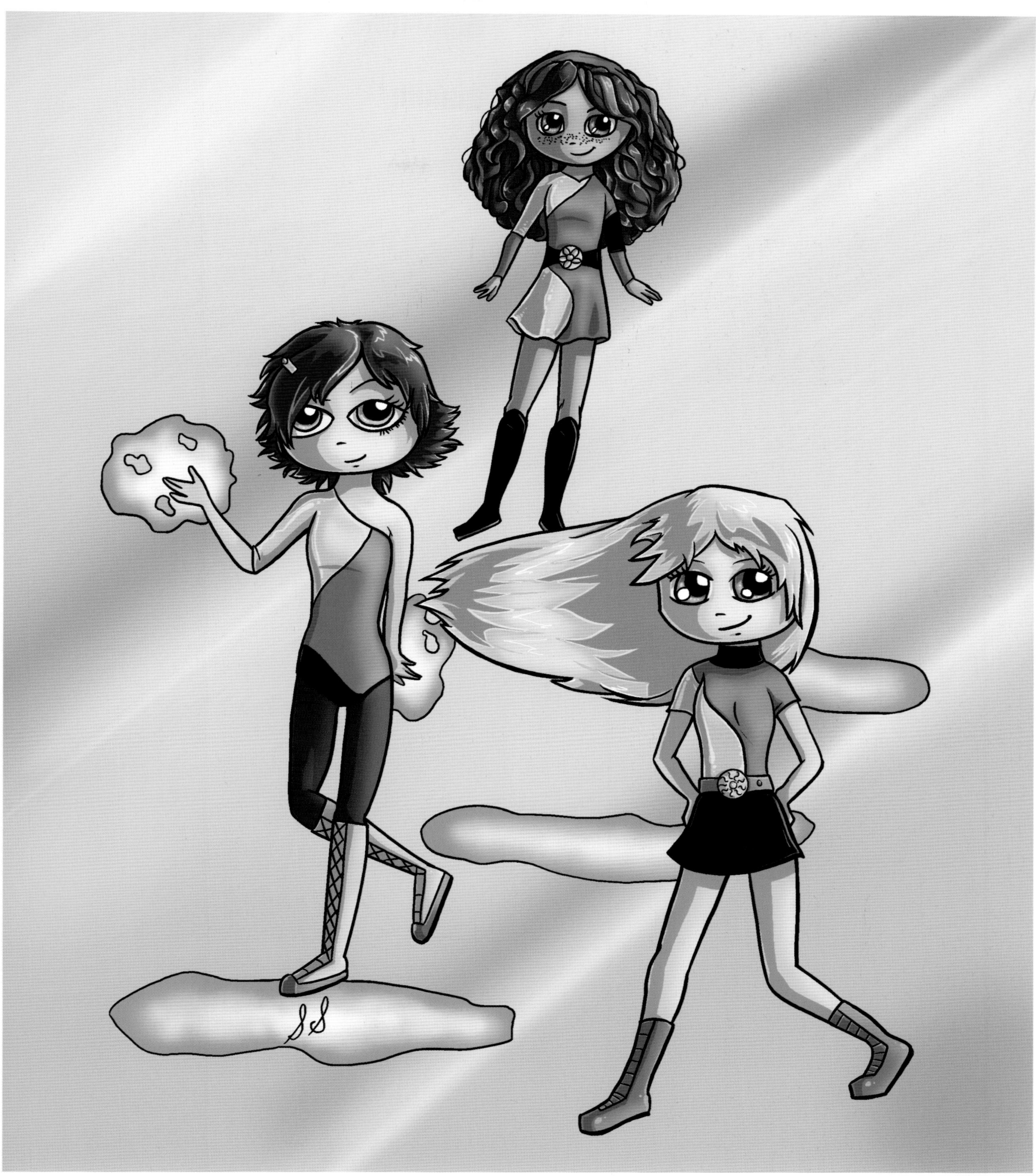
SS

☆ ☆ ☆

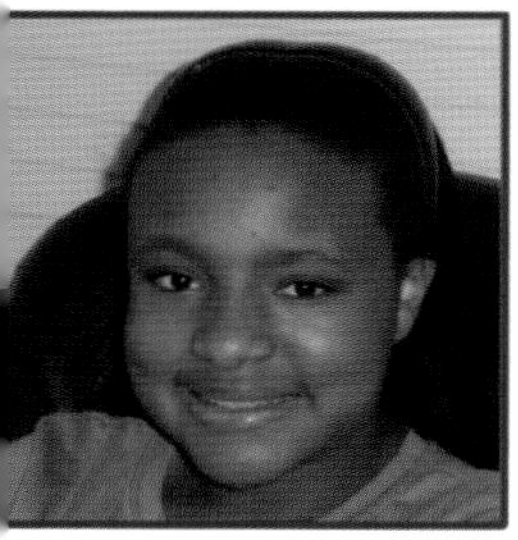

SHAYLA SIMONS

SKILLS: Penciling, Coloring, Inking

LOCATION: Greensboro, NC

FUN FACT: I'm addicted to Deviantart!!

Tips for Kids!

Don't Give Up!

by Laura Morley

"DON'T GIVE UP. EVERYONE WHO CAN DRAW BEAUTIFULLY NOW WAS A BEGINNER ONCE. AND DON'T GET FRUSTRATED IF YOUR WORK DOESN'T YET LOOK THE WAY YOU WANT IT TO: PERSEVERANCE IS THE MOST IMPORTANT SKILL YOU'LL NEED, AND IT'S ONE YOU CAN START USING RIGHT NOW."

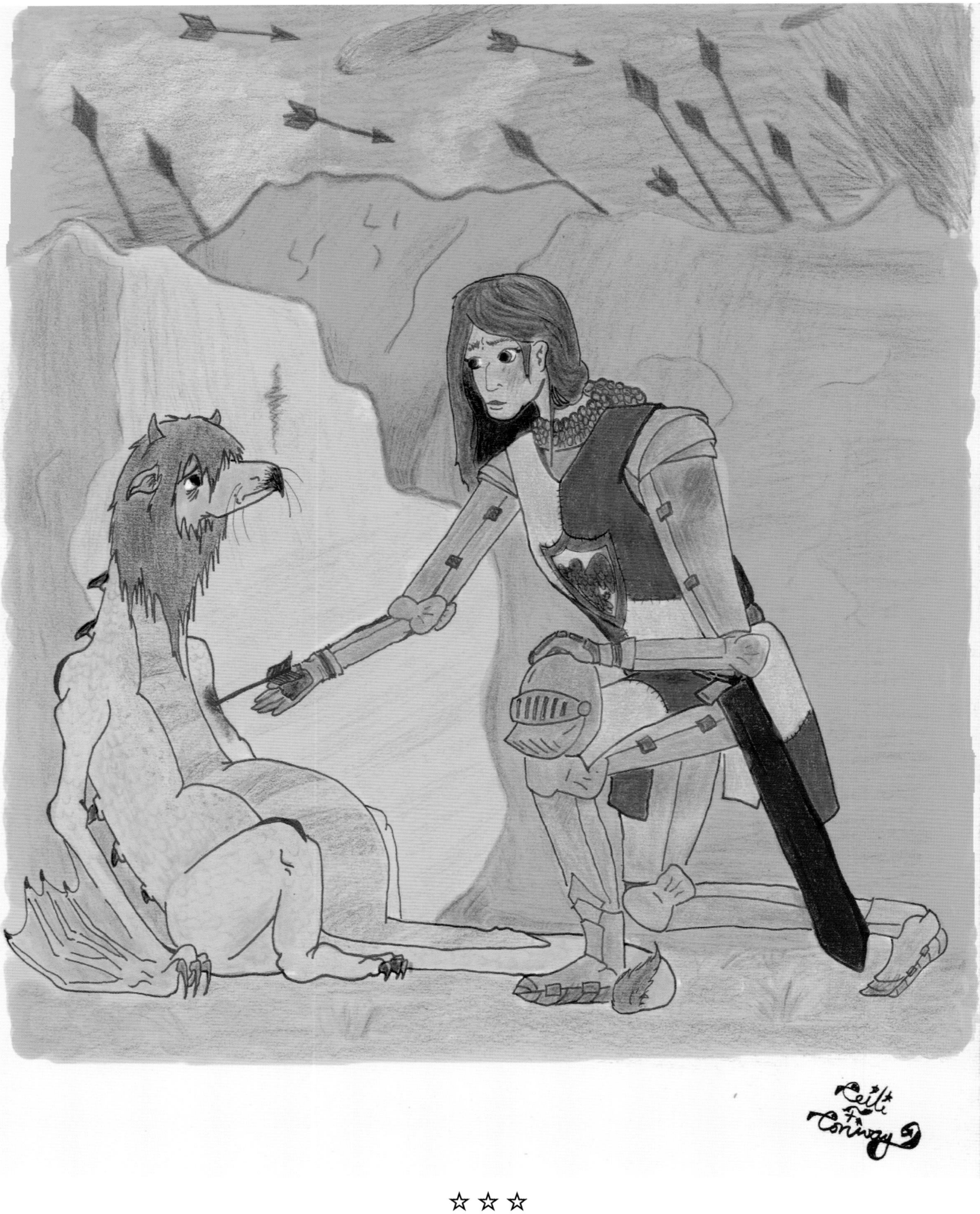
Ceili Conway

☆ ☆ ☆

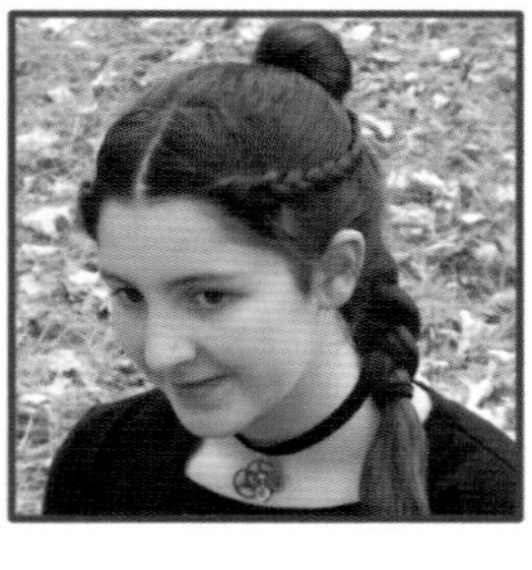

CEILI CONWAY

SKILLS: Penciller, Inker
LOCATION: Delmar, NY
FUN FACT: I like to sort books during power outages.

www.the-world-inside-my-head.webs.com

Tips for Kids! Challenge Yourself!

by Renae De Liz

"DON'T BE AFRAID TO DRAW THINGS THAT DO NOT COME EASY TO YOU, LIKE A DIFFICULT ANGLE, OR BODY TYPE. IT MAY NOT LOOK RIGHT THE FIRST TIME, BUT YOU CAN BET THE NEXT TIME IT WILL BE BETTER, AND THE NEXT EVEN BETTER. EACH NEW THING YOU TRY TO DRAW IS YOU FLEXING YOUR ARTISTIC MUSCLES, AND SOMETIMES IT TAKES A LOT OF WORK TO BUILD THEM!"

HOW TO CREATE COMICS!

☆ ☆ ☆

IN-DEPTH ARTICLES
TEACHING YOU THE INS
AND OUTS OF CREATING
COMIC BOOKS!

EDITED BY RACHEL DEERING

HOW TO... WRITE COMICS!

BY BARBARA KESEL

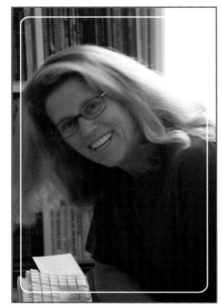

"Do you put the words inside the little balloons?" If you write for comics, it's a question that comes up a lot from readers. What does the writer do? Well, we DO write the words that go into the little balloons, but that's just part of the job. We also (and many of these steps can be done in collaboration with the artist and sometimes the writer IS the artist) come up with the original idea, describe what the artist can draw to bring that idea to life, and write the words that go onto the final page as words and not pictures.

All writing starts with an IDEA. In the case of "Glimmer Suit," I met with Cat Staggs to find out what kind of story she'd like to draw, and what aspects of her work she wanted to spotlight. Cat wanted to do something in the classic comics style, something a little "superhero." In reviewing her work, I'd noticed that she does AWESOME fake covers, so I wanted to bring that advertising art idea into the story, but still have a story. As we talked, I jotted down some key ideas:

CAT STAGGS
4-PAGE WITH "MAGAZINE"/"POSTER" REVEAL
TONGUE IN CHEEK
5 pgs?
SUPERHERO
DIFFERENCE BETWEEN HEROISM +
SUPERHERO ACTION SPLASH
CONTRAST BETWEEN REALITY + IMAGE
SHE FIGHTS : COURAGE IS SEXY
CRIME/NOIR NERD

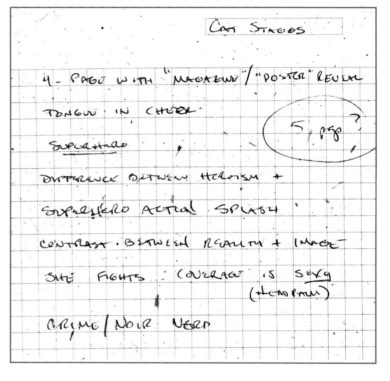

If you've read the story, you'll notice that the idea went from having the lead character reacting to the glamour shot to the lead character generating the glamour shot. I knew that I wanted a pinup page for Cat, and that I wanted the story to incorporate the lead character's reaction to it.

Next I wrote up a short SERIES BIBLE. The "series" may only consist of one five-page story, but putting some time into world-building for any idea is never a bad thing.

"GLIMMER SUIT" - CHARACTERS

LINDSEY COLLINS: The original girl with the long hair and short jacket, Lindsey's gotten more serious now that she's hit 30. Fashionistas are atwitter at Lindsey's new gamine profile: the former long locks sacrificed for an Audrey Hepburn efficiency do, the fashion-forward wild stylista seems to be turning yoga-girl subdued. What the world knows is that LinCoTecque, the company child genius Lindsay founded at 14, is now a worldwide brand. What they don't know is that a new relationship with an outspoken ecologist has sparked Lindsay's moral core and made her determined to save the world. After all, this relationship might be serious, so she might want to have children with him, so the world they live is has got to be healthy enough. She's focusing her entire scientific and marketing genius on the problem and thinks she's on the road to real change. Now she just has to sell an unwelcome idea.

Hardly a problem for the woman who made "SmartSocks" a household name.

This world is slightly more advanced than our own, a little faster, sleeker, darker; the love child of *Blade Runner* and *Tron*. Retro touches are everywhere, from the noir fashions to the Streamline architecture, but the one-handed cellphone stride and the grunting traffic jams still make it feel like now. The economy's been bad for years now—every third light is out and half the storefronts are empty.

People are scared, and bad people do bad things.

Solar technology exists in a shady place: made illegal by gas industry lobbyists and un-American by their biggest political handmaiden (a young Congresswoman everyone expects is on a fast track to higher glory), it has spawned a renegade underground of scientists and tinkerers who want to see the light again through the murk.

"GLIMMER SUIT" - CHARACTERS (CONT'D)

One driven young inventor goes even further: she's developed a wearable form of stored power. Because of the illegal nature of experimentation, she's worked her discoveries into a fashionable mobile armor that refracts, reflects, focuses, and magnifies the power of light.

She calls it the GLIMMER SUIT.

It's a statement. It's a weapon. It's a business plan.

Because the best way to turn illegal tech into tomorrow's safeguard is to make it absolutely irresistible.

Sell a hero. Save the world.

Give 'em a little GLIMMER of hope.

Now, if this was a new series I was pitching to a comics company, I'd do up a PITCH document that would include the series intro, a story synopsis, short character descriptions, and some sample art if I had already put together a team. You can find information on company websites describing if they do or don't accept submissions and the forms or releases you have to include. If you are new to the company or the field, you'd also want to include a little bio of yourself and while you don't need to include a marketing report, some idea of the potential audience is helpful. If you happen to have a blog with 20,000 followers, mention that!

[It can be difficult for new writers to get their work read. It takes seconds to scan art and see if it's good or bad; it takes minutes or hours to read a script sample. It's always easier to get editors or readers to read a comics story. If you're not your own artist, team up with one or hire one and produce your own mini-comic or web comic. You can find a comics artist in artists' alley at a con, or on art-portfolio websites.]

Next comes the SCRIPT. The script isn't just the "words in the little balloons." It's the architectural blueprint for the story, with descriptions to the artist indicating what goes on each page, panel by panel, AND the script for what goes in the balloons, in the captions, on the signs, and sound effects. (Some writers work plot style, where the story is sketched out in a PLOT and DIALOGUE is added after the art is drawn.) There is no one standard script format—you can get a different sample from pretty much every working writer—but the necessary parts include panel descriptions and all words that need to be lettered.

PANEL ONE: Night. An urban street with multiple stylish storefronts. The GLIMMER SUIT catches the light thrown off by a fashion store window as LINDSAY COLLINS races by while wearing it, pounding the pavement with the deliberate bounce-crouch of a free runner. (See GLIMMER SUIT doc for suit description.) The Glimmer Suit reflects the chaos of colors thrown off by the window display of the newest colorglow ShineLine fabric apparel. (Imagine a techno-hipster cool "Urban Outfitters" display.)

[LETTERING NOTE: Two voices appear in electronic form here: GEO ELECT and GLIM ELECT. This is a private conversation between Georgia at the main office and Lindsay/Glimmer in the field. I'd like these to be tail-less squared-off balloons, a hybrid of captions and electronic communication.]

GEO ELECT:	ARE YOU SURE YOU WANT ME WATCHING IN? I COULD BE SUBPOENAED, YOU KNOW.
SIGN TEXT: (ad style):	Go with the glow—SHINELINE™ available here!

That script then goes off to the letterer and digital type is laid over the art pages. The composited page leaps through the internet to the printer and then shows up in the shops as a finished comic (or graphic novel). Just like magic.

- BARBARA RANDALL KESEL

HOW TO... DRAW IN INK!

BY MING DOYLE

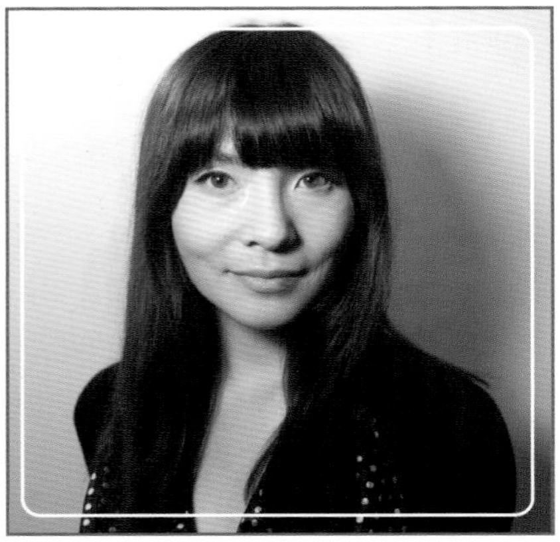

Hey all! I'm Ming Doyle, a Boston-based freelance illustrator and comic book artist. I've had the pleasure of handling writing and art duties on "The Spinster," a two-page retro-styled adventure yarn for the *Womanthology* project, with colors being handled by the immensely talented and stylish Jordie Bellaire. Here's a brief, behind-the-scenes look at my inking process.

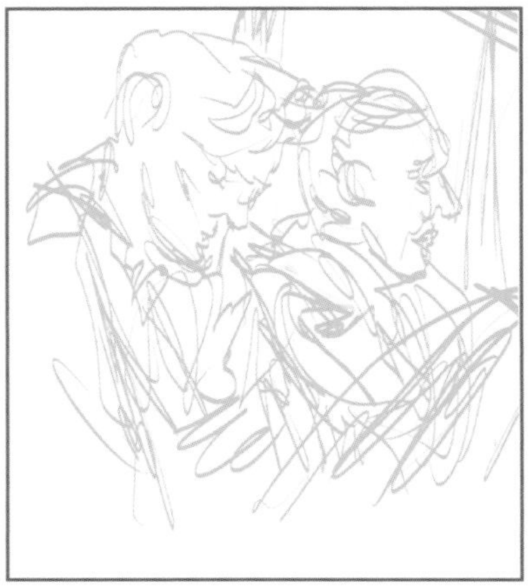

Since I do my own inking, I usually tend to jump straight from the rough thumbnail stage into finished line art. This is an approach that probably doesn't work for everybody, and it's true that I've ended up cursing myself for my lack of forethought and precision in the preliminary stages on more than one occasion. However, the thing I enjoy most about blocking things out with such loose scribbles is the extra room to consider composition without locking myself in to one initial thought before moving into inks. And sometimes stray lines turn into details I didn't realize the picture might even be missing! Call it looking for faces in clouds.

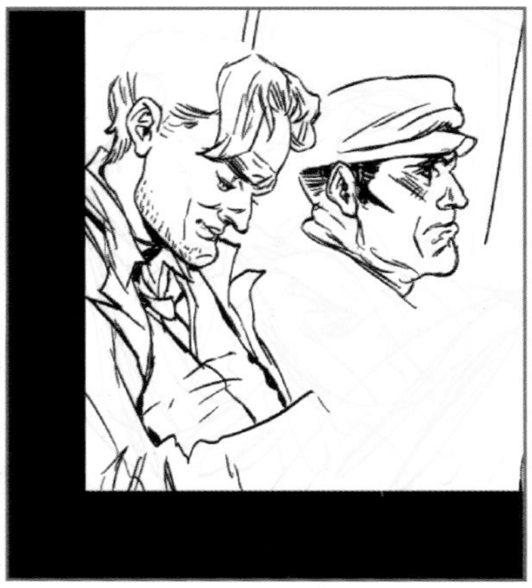

I decided to digitally ink "The Spinster" because I wanted a bit more precision than I'm usually able to achieve with traditional media. But whether I ink in Photoshop or on paper, the process remains the same. I lay my lines down over a very low-opacity version of my original thumbnails and make liberal use of the eraser tool or a Wite-Out pen, depending.

And here's the finished section! Even when working digitally, I like to preserve some of the small idiosyncrasies and "mistakes" I may make. I'm always striving to better my anatomy, perspective, and composition skills, but I do try not to lose sight of my vision even with all those academic concerns.

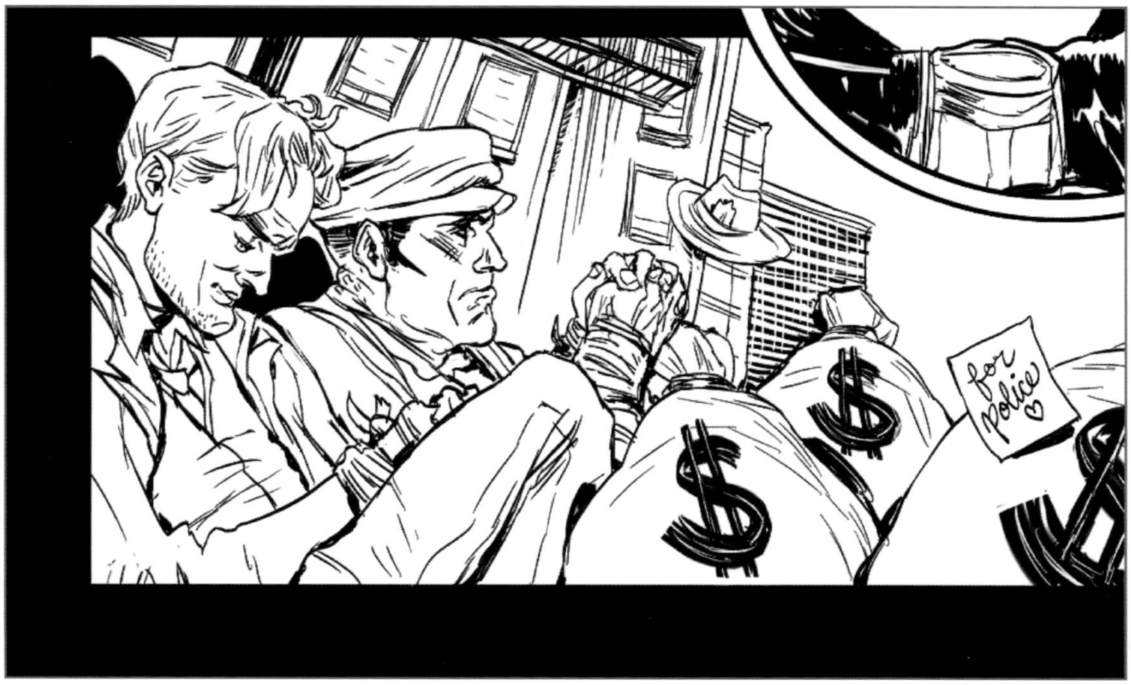
for police

Lastly, here are some comparison shots of my thumbnails and my finished inks. Phew!

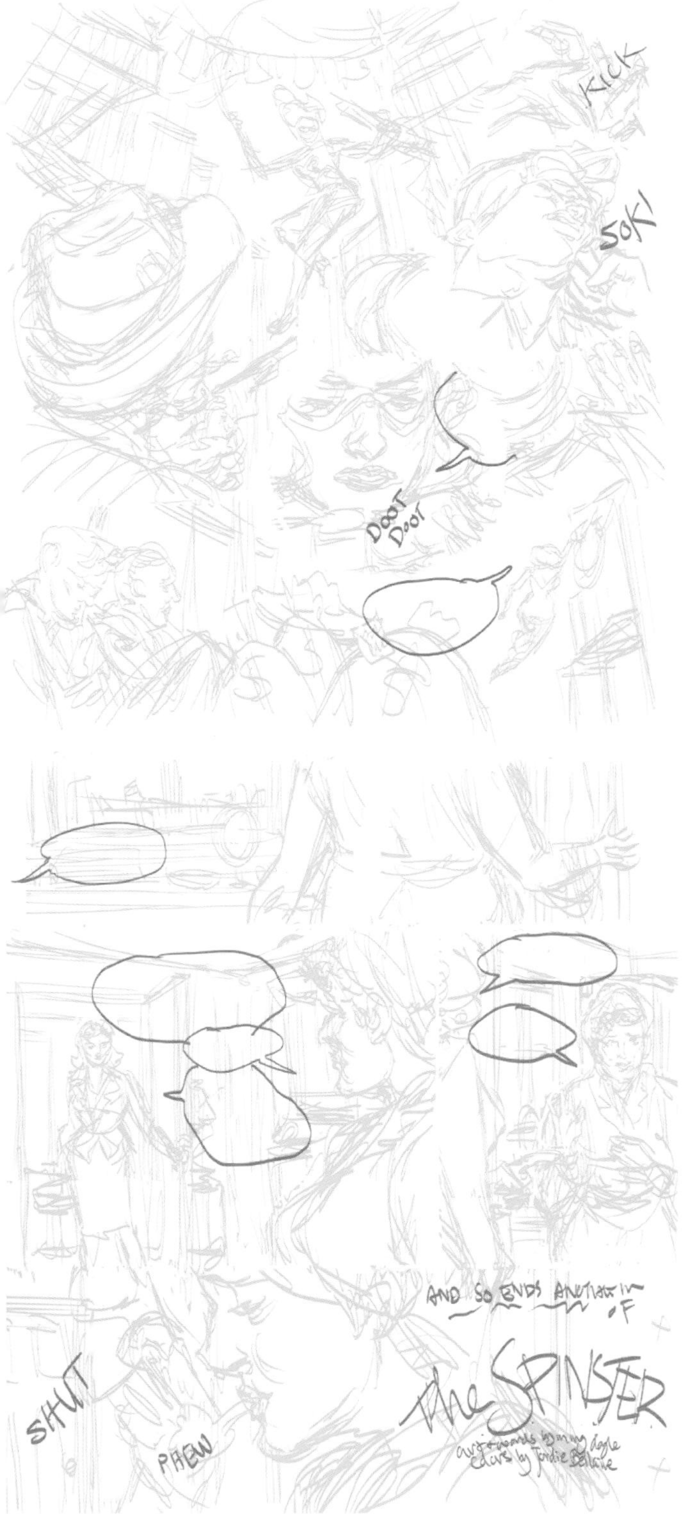
KICK
SOK!
DOOT DOOT
AND SO ENDS ANOTHER OF
The SPINSTER
SHUT
PHEW

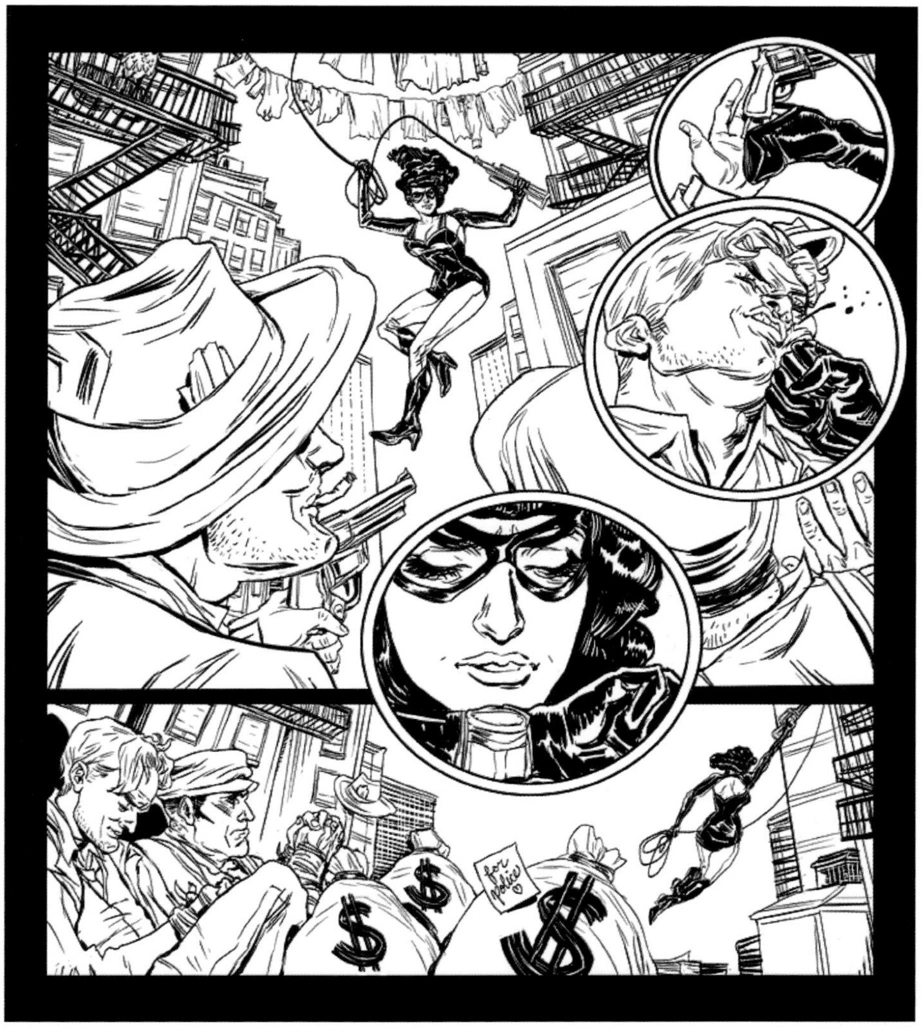

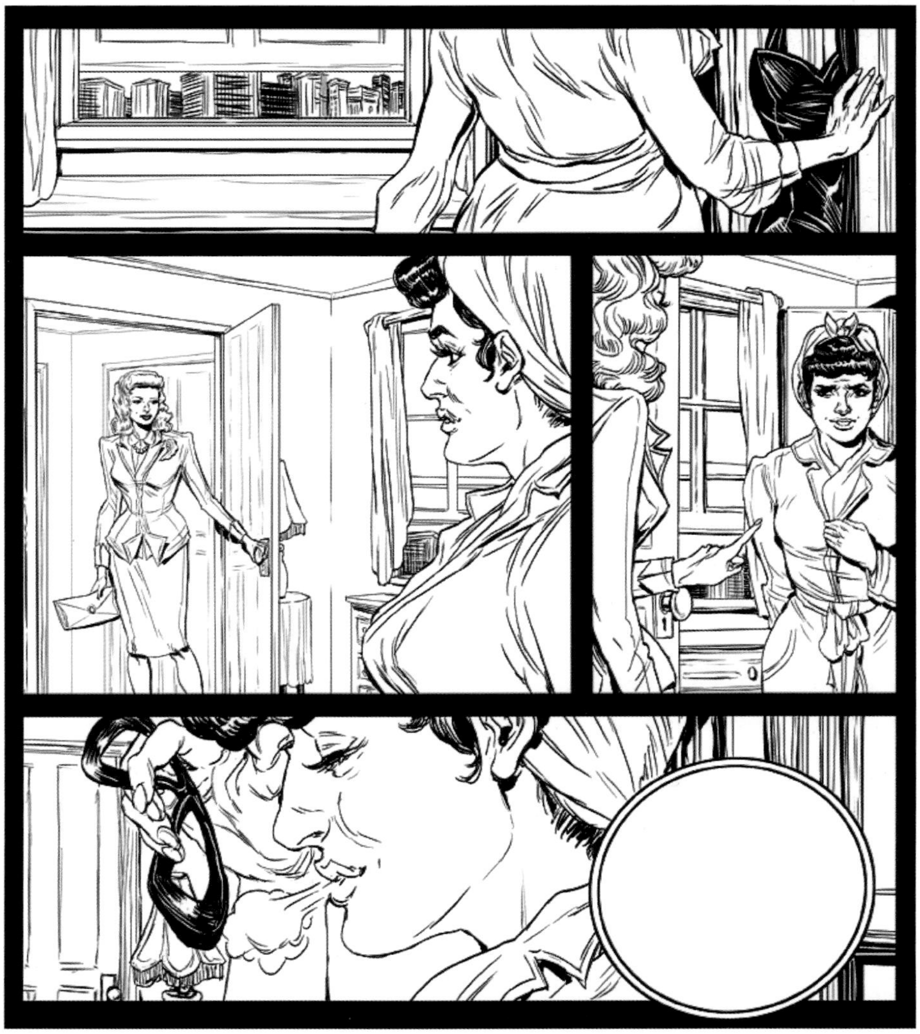

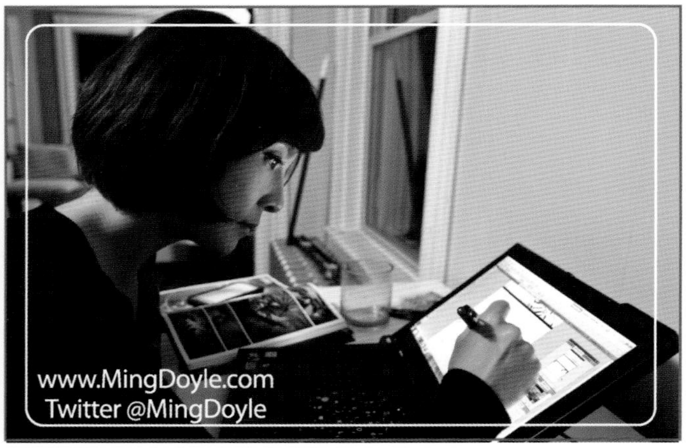
www.MingDoyle.com
Twitter @MingDoyle

HOW TO... INK COMICS!
BY BARBARA KAALBERG

Inking is the final step in an amalgamation of creative visions between the writer, penciller, and inker in the design of a comic book. Sometimes known as a "finisher" or "embellisher," an inker's job is to interpret the lines of the pencilled page into a finished product. Depending on how tight (very detailed) or loose (very sketchy) the pencils are, the inks can either hold very close to the penciller's vision with only minor

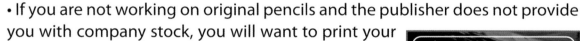

adjustments or become highly influenced by the inker's own art. Inkers correct mistakes, add depth, definition, weight, shading, and texture. Inks make the art "pop" or jump off the page, adding clarity, atmosphere, and drama to the finished piece.

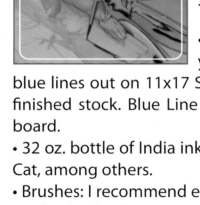

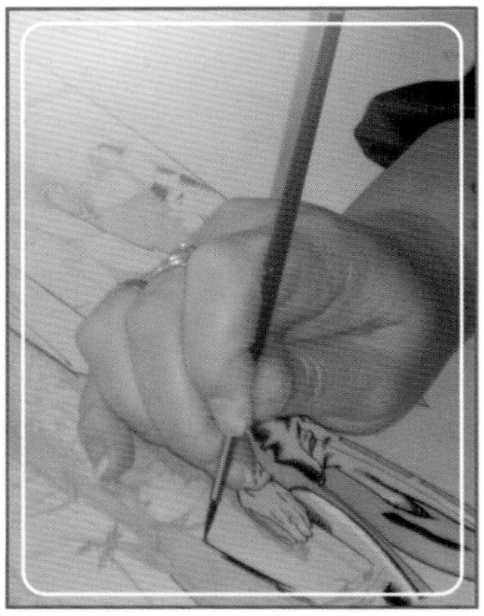

The basic tools of an inker can be widely varied and depend a lot on personal preference. It is essential to start with a good light source, a drawing board, and an ergonomically comfortable chair. A scanner/copier that will handle 11x17 art board is incredibly handy. I recommend the Brother Professional Series MFC-J67 10DW. Following that, your tools should include the following:

• If you are not working on original pencils and the publisher does not provide you with company stock, you will want to print your blue lines out on 11x17 Strathmore 400 or 500 pound, cold pressed, smooth finished stock. Blue Line Pro also carries a line of pre-ruled comic book art board.

• 32 oz. bottle of India ink. Brands include Higgins, Speedball, and Blick Black Cat, among others.

• Brushes: I recommend either the Windsor & Newton series 7, sizes 2 or 3 and Raphael Kolinsky 8404's, sizes 2 or 3.

• Pens with nibs: A good starter set would include the quintessential size 102

Crow quill (springy and semi-flexible), the 107 Hawk quill (very stiff and fine) and the 103 (very flexible).

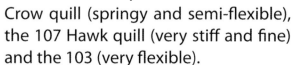

• Pens & pencils: Tech pens (various sizes), Faber Castell Pitt Pens (various sizes), #2 pencil or tech pencil and a blue line pencil

• Circle and oval templates, french curves, ruler, T-square (all with beveled edges), kneaded eraser, exacto knife (for scraping nibs), and white out (I use simple, white, acrylic craft paint). Most art supplies can be found at Dick Blick Art Supply.

Steps in Inking

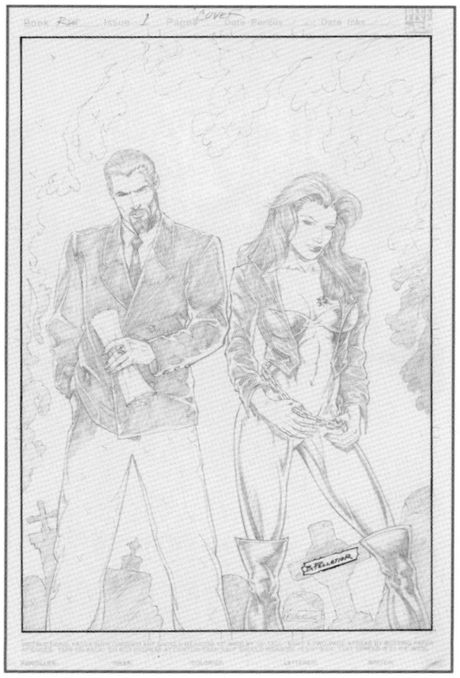

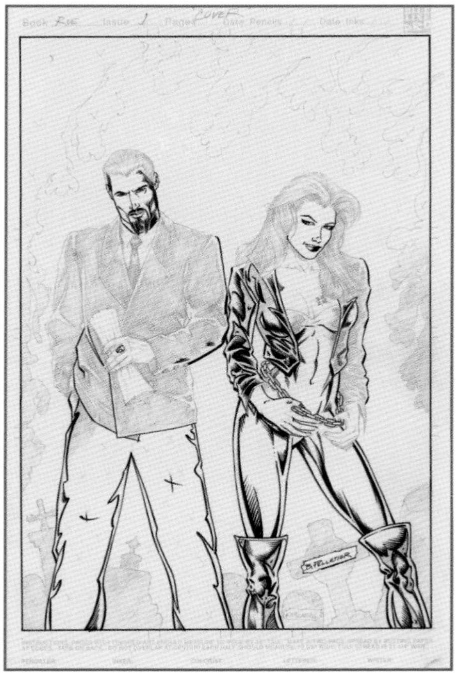

1. Make or download a copy of the original pencils before starting. You will need this both for reference and for your portfolio (ask pencillers on social media sites like Facebook or at conventions if you can have copies of their pencils to practice on).

2. If you are working with an email download and not on originals, convert the pencils to blue lines and print out by opening the jpg in Photoshop. Go to Image > Mode > CMYK color. Go to Image > Adjustment > Hue/Saturation. Click the "Colorize" button in the lower right corner of the box, enter Hue 193 - Saturation 67 - Lightness 79 and click OK. Print!

3. Rule your borders and begin inking. Everyone has a different approach. Some like to fill in the big, black areas first to get a sense of balance, some like to do the faces first, most ink from the top left and work their way to the bottom right. I do just the opposite when working on original pencils to preserve the integrity of the pencils. Do not rest your brush or pen against the skin between thumb and forefinger, but hold it in a more upright position and use your pinky finger as a stabilizer.

4. Determine which way the light source is coming from. The lines facing the light source should be thinner than the lines away from the light source. Give weight and proximity to items by defining line thickness. For instance, to indicate three dimensionality, the lines on top of an arm should be thinner than the lines on the underside of an arm (take into account light source variables) and items in the foreground will have a heavier line weight than those in the background. Pencils can have many shaded subtleties. It is the inker's job to determine if those areas would be better served by filling them in as a solid black or texturing them with one of many hatching or crosshatching styles. Study the effects, line weights, and texturing of some of the greats like Joe Sinnott, Bob McLeod, Wendy Pini, and especially Wally Wood, amongst many others.

Now, put together your portfolio. Choose just 6 to 8 examples on 11x17 copies, both before and after pages. Select a good sampling of your best work that includes both pin-ups and sequential art. Editors will not comb through a lot of stuff and they quickly get an idea of what you are capable of. Be prepared to take harsh critiques. They are not personal attacks. Those editors are telling you what they are looking for in an inker. Listen, learn, thank them for their time, then try again, if necessary. Persistence pays off. Good Luck!

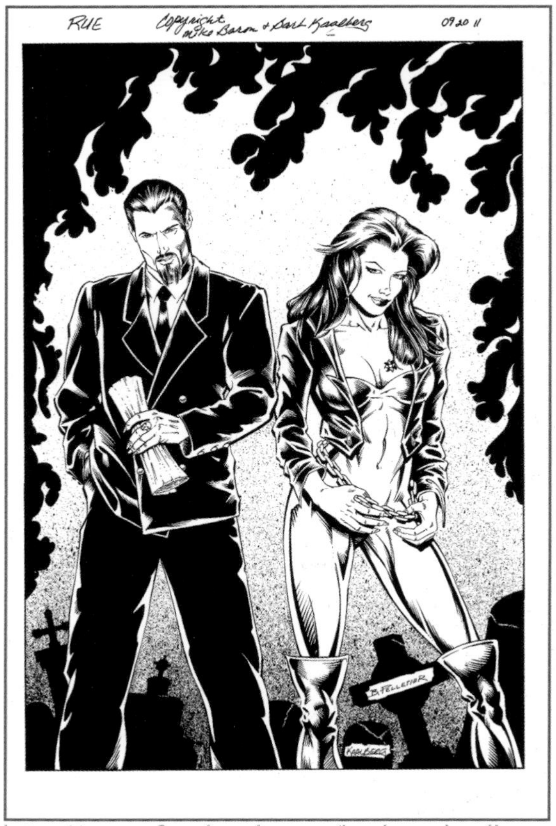

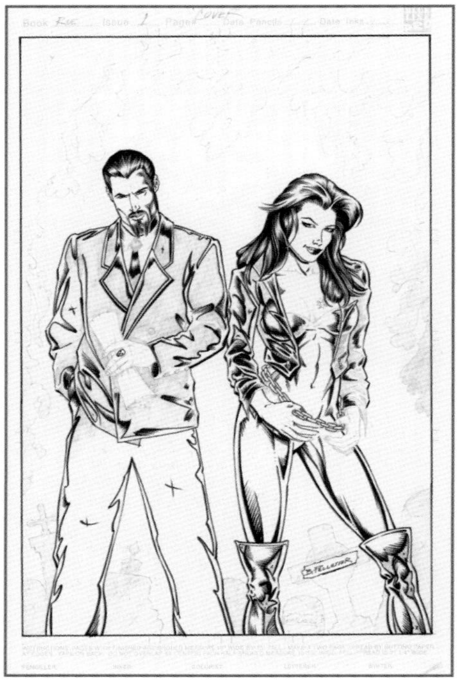

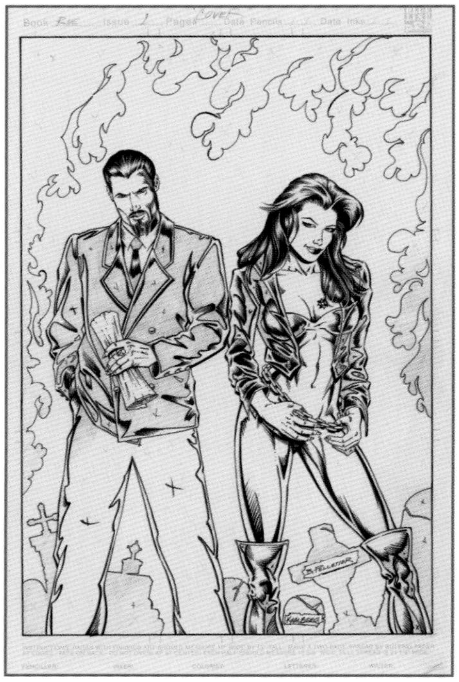

http://www.facebook.com/barbara.kaalberg

HOW TO... COLOR COMICS!

BY NEI RUFFINO

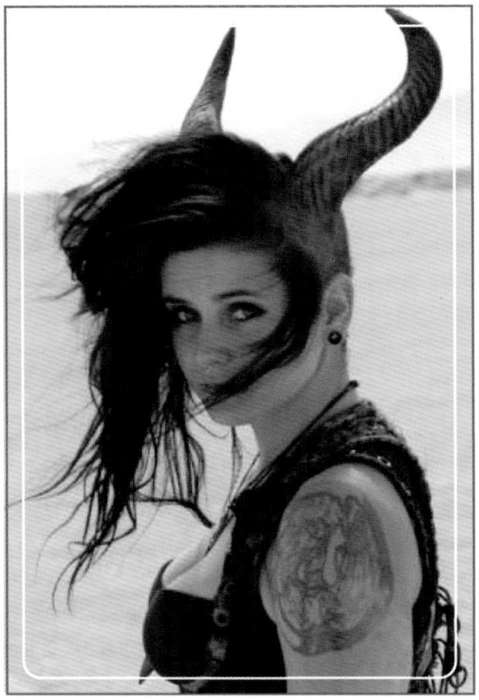

Step 1: Flats.

I lay down colors dark enough to build highlights off of. I don't use a set palette for this, just basing it off instinct and intent. I've used the lasso tool to trace and bucket to fill the colors. You can use just one layer for this process, as tapping the bucket will only change the color you tap, and not cover any of the area you've already filled. Not only does using fewer layers for your page keep them more organized, it saves time and, most of all, keeps the file size smaller. You can also hold alt while you use your lasso to alternate between free form and polygonal lasso tools. Make sure anti-aliasing is turned off on your lasso to make sure you can go back in and select these areas later.

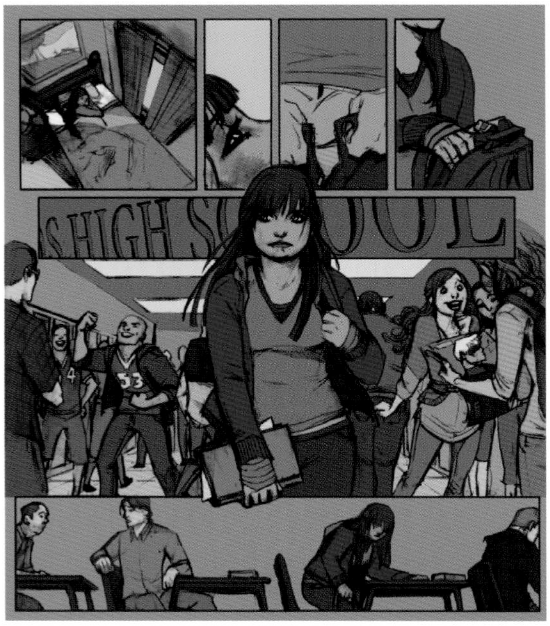

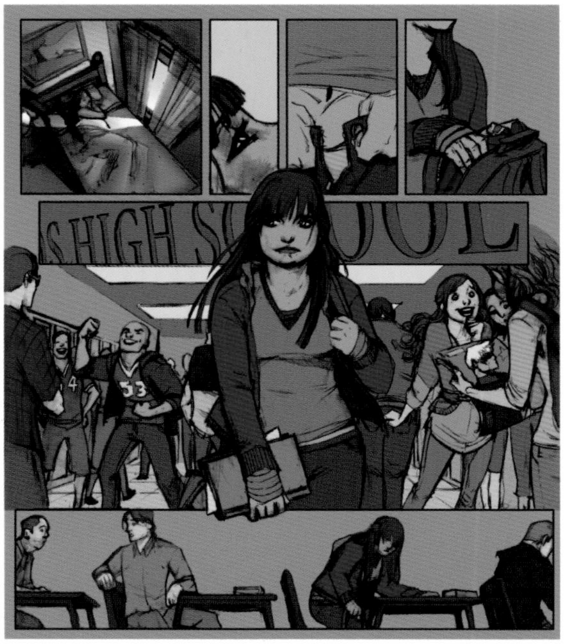

Step 2: Rendering, mood setting, and following light sources.

You want to start by establishing your light sources. It's good to use pages or pinups with backgrounds most for practicing this, staying away from white. The first panel shows our hero waking, so you want to give her room an early morning effect and keep it simple with detail on the focus. In this panel that is time of day, and our hero.

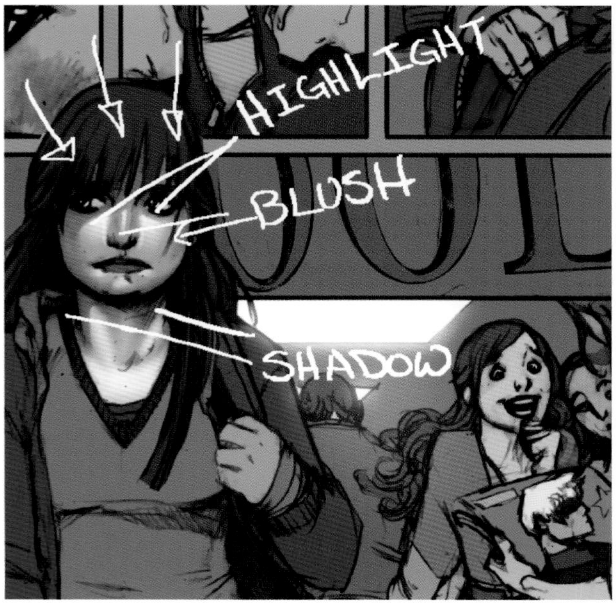
HIGHLIGHT
BLUSH
SHADOW

2.2: Follow the light source!

My brushes are the basic set of rounds that come with Photoshop. Soft and hard edged brushes used together can give a sense of the color being blended, but sharp where they need to be. Also mixed opacity and flow help to hide the appearance of brush strokes.

2.3: Continue with that direction on the rest of the character.

Second panel is where we really get a chance to play with some lighting and planes of her figure. We want to pop her out and push everything back but we don't want to hide the lines. To do this, I use a mix of saturation and color temperature. Warmth brings our main character forward while the cooler de-saturated colors of the background naturally push it back.

Step 3: Adjustments.

•I use levels here to adjust the values in the crowd so that they fall back even a little bit more and add a little more mood.

• Here are some adjustments made to the color of her hoodie. I wanted to warm it up to better fit in with her current scheme of warmer = pops more. The purple was a bit too cool.

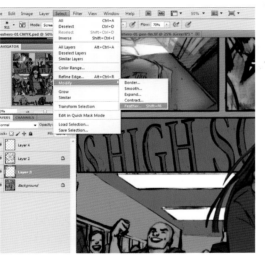

• A final brightness adjustment just above my flats and below my rendering. All this will affect is my darkest colors, the flats. I use this trick only to help my pages to print better in the final product.

Step 4: Special effects.

If you want to add glows to your page, you can use this method. Use your wand to select the flats and then go to Select > Modify > Feather. I choose about 10-20 pixels, but do what feels right. Then you make a new normal mode layer above the lines, and brush in your color. I've also added a little extra glow without a selection to give it a bit more mood.

Afterword:

These are the basic techniques that I use for my coloring, but there are a wealth of tricks and tips that you can find all over the web. I'm "self-taught" but that doesn't mean I learned all of this by experimenting. A great deal of it was found in online communities through asking and receiving advice and critiques, and seeking the help of established professionals. From educating myself with the available information and being quite observant of the colors around me as well as paying attention to lighting in photos, I've been able to learn the vast majority of what I use every day when I color. I encourage that sort of thing, and always try to help when I can. One thing for you to keep in mind when seeking advice from a professional is being precise on your questions. Also, not asking too much of them at one time. Good luck!

NEI

http://www.bakanekonei.deviantart.com

HOW TO... LETTER COMICS!

BY RACHEL DEERING

So you'd like to try your hand at lettering a comic? Understandable. We are the least paid and most overlooked member of the creative team. Wait. What did I just say? Least paid and most overlooked?! Why would anyone want to be a letterer?! Because it's fun, relatively fast once you get the hang of it, and not a lot of people out there are doing it, so you stand a good chance of working on a lot of books! Still with me? All right, let's learn something!

The first thing you want to do before attempting to letter a story is build up a font bank. There are several sites out there that offer amazing fonts at affordable prices. All of the fonts I used in *Womanthology* came from Nate Piekos at www.blambot.com. Check it out!

PRO TIP: *Please, for the love of all that is printed, do NOT use Comic Sans! That's a surefire way to become the subject of ridicule.*

Okay, so you've got a few dialogue fonts, some for sound effects, and one or two for design. Now, you need a program in which to use them! I use Adobe Illustrator, but use whatever vector program you like.

THOSE
WHO RESTRAIN
DESIRE DO SO
BECAUSE THEIRS
IS WEAK
ENOUGH TO BE
RESTRAINED.
-BLAKE

LAYERS
ARTBOARDS
SFX
Dialogue
Balloons
1 Image
Create New Layer
4 Layers

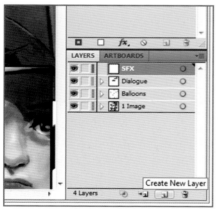

PRO TIP: *Lettering with non-vector (rasterized) fonts will sometimes make your dialogue appear blurry in print.*

THOSE
WHO RESTRAIN
DESIRE DO SO
BECAUSE THEIRS
IS WEAK
ENOUGH TO BE
RESTRAINED.
-BLAKE

Now you've got the fonts under control, and your vector graphics program is all fired up. You're ready to start slinging letters. Almost. I letter my pages at print size and at least 300 DPI, so make sure your art files meet these standards. Import the art and set it as the bottom layer. Create a new layer above your art and label it "Balloons". Create two more layers above that for "Dialogue" and "SFX." Finally, you're ready to rock!

THOSE
WHO RESTRAIN
DESIRE DO SO
BECAUSE THEIRS
IS WEAK
ENOUGH TO BE
RESTRAINED.
-BLAKE
1
2
3

Copy the text from your script into the "Dialogue" layer. Make sure it is center aligning, and break the dialogue down into lines of a few words each. The idea is to make the text look circular, so that it fits well inside your word balloon. If you're lettering a caption, you'll want a more square form for your text.

PRO TIP: *It's okay to have a line with only one or two words. Sometimes it's necessary.*

KABLOOMER

All right, you've got your dialogue laid out into a circle. Now, we're ready to stick it into a word balloon. Select the "Balloons" layer, choose the circle or ellipse tool, and draw a circle around your dialogue. There are four points on the balloon that allow you to tweak the size and shape to suit your dialogue. After you have perfected the balloon, select the pen tool. Use this to make the tail for the balloon. Click a point inside your balloon where you want the tail to begin. Then click the point where you want the tail to end, but hold the mouse button. Move the cursor to get a nice curve to your tail. When you get the curve you want, release the mouse button and click the point at the tip of the tail. This will convert the point to an anchor. Click one last point inside the balloon, opposite the first point, holding the mouse button again. Drag this line to mirror the curve of the first. Select the tail and the balloon, and merge them. Now you can set the thickness and color of the stroke. I recommend either .75 or 1 for the stroke thickness.

PRO TIP: *You can create a template with various styles of balloons and tails for later use. This saves a LOT of time down the road.*

Now that you've mastered dialogue shaping and creating word balloons, you're going to need some cool-looking sound effects! Begin by selecting an SFX font and typing the sound in a larger point size on the SFX layer. Now, you've got a straight line of text. That might look cool, but you want to add some real character to that punch or explosion. Use the arrow tool to select your sound effect and press CTRL+SHIFT+O. This converts your text to outlines. Now press CTRL+SHIFT+G to ungroup the letters. You can now manipulate each individual letter! Vary the sizes and angles of the letters, making sure to overlap them just a little. Select each letter, starting from the left, and press CTRL+SHIFT+[. This will make sure that each letter is above the one to its right, creating a more natural look. Now select all of the letters and press CTRL+G to regroup them. You can now set the color and stroke for the sound effect.

KABLOOMER

KABLOOMER

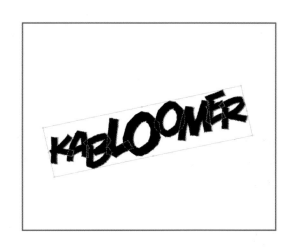

PRO TIP: *Always color sound effects from the palette of the panel in which you're working. Sound effects that don't match the art stand out too much and take the reader out of the story.*

Follow these steps and you'll have the basics down in no time. For more detailed tutorials, check out www.blambot.com and www.balloontales.com.

To build your lettering portfolio, have at least 5-8 pages of sequentials (with permission from the artist) that show a wide range of balloon styles, sound effects, and fonts. Make sure you have examples of bold and italic words. You also want examples of various styles of titles and logos. Good luck!

HOW TO... DRAW MONSTERS!

BY FIONA STAPLES

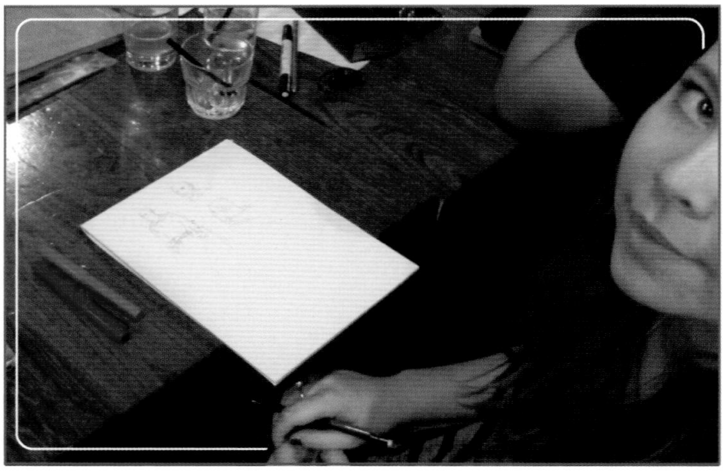

HOW TO DRAW MONSTERS

1. Monsters, dragons, and other fantasy creatures may be imaginary, but you can make the ones you draw much more believable if you base them on real animals. Even if the creature you design is something totally crazy, understanding a few things about anatomy will make the monster look plausible and authentic!

Do some research—go to the zoo or flip through a *National Geographic*, and practice sketching different animals. Your sketches don't have to be detailed, but pay attention to things like the animals' basic shapes, the way they stand and the way they move, where their skin or fur wrinkles, and how their weight is distributed.

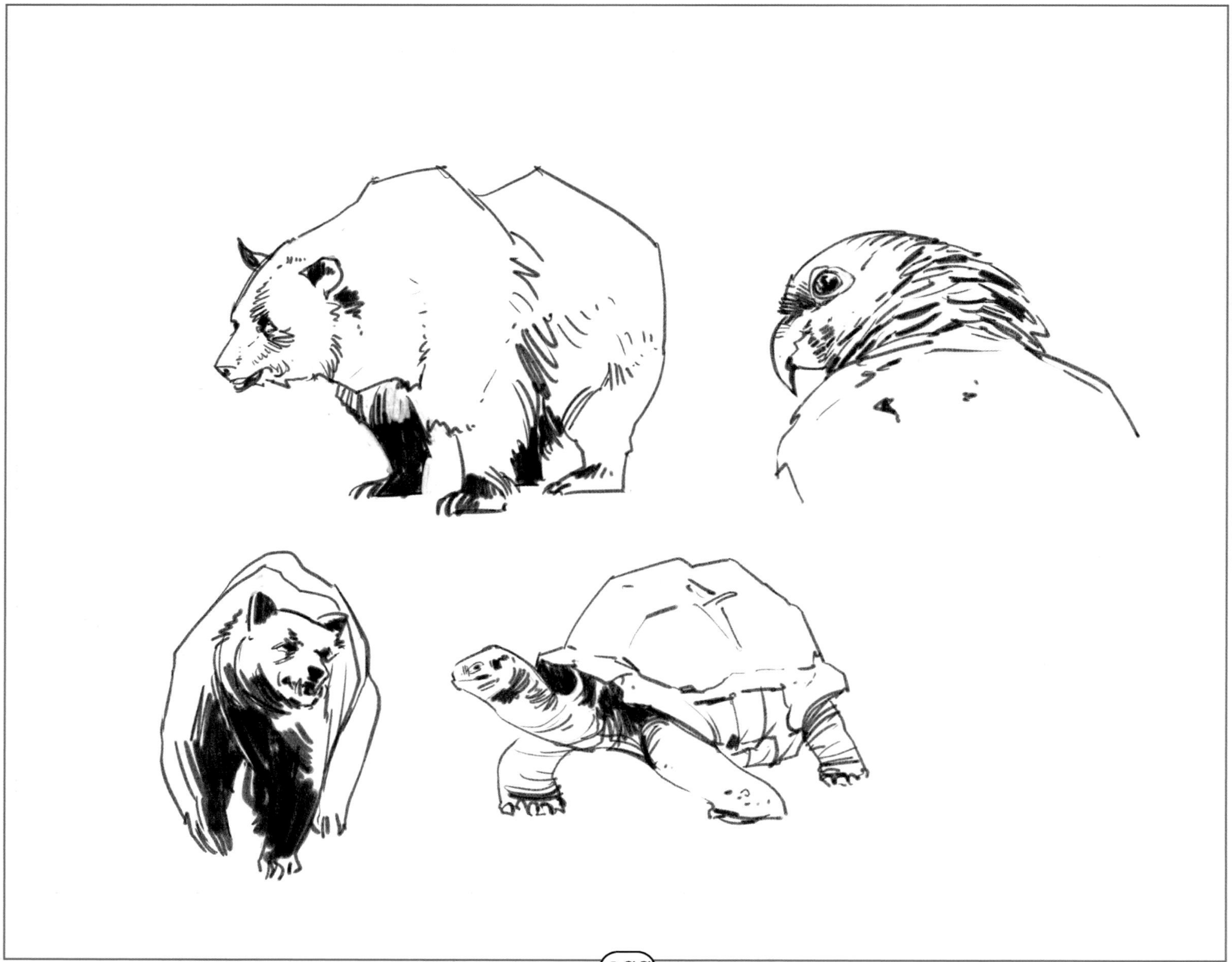

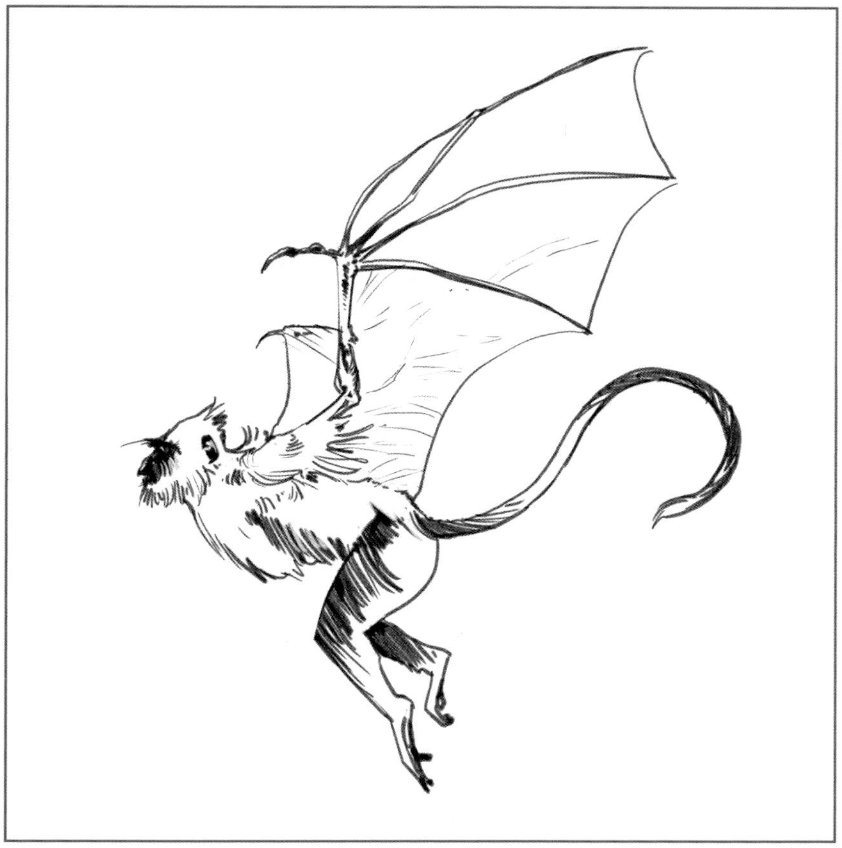

2. A fun exercise is combining two or more animals into one. It makes you think about the animals' musculature and skeletal structure, and how they're put together. If you figure out how the creature you're drawing works, it'll look like it might be able to function in real life.

3. For the serpent in "Everwell," the writer, Jody, gave me everything I needed to know. She described it simply as part snake, part cat, with horns! I based the head on a tiger.

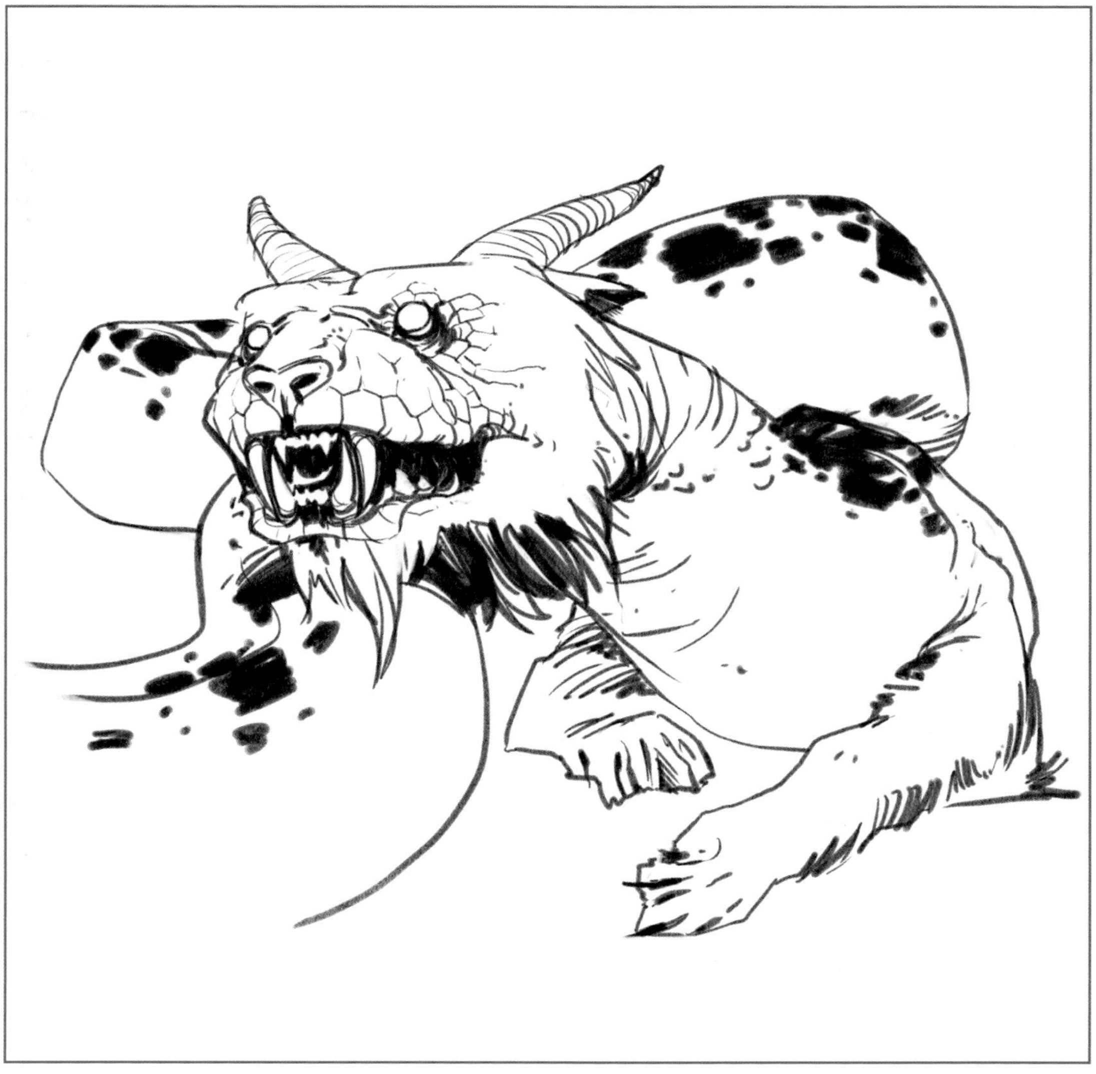

HOW TO... COLOR WITH MARKERS!
BY JESSICA HICKMAN

COLORING WITH MARKERS

Hello, everyone! What follows are some quick tips I use when I am doing an illustration with markers. Feel free to take what you will from my examples!

1. First off, I draw on a type of paper that will work well with markers. Usually a brand that states it can be used with any wet media (marker, inks, acrylic, etc.). For this example, of course, we will be using markers.

2. Once I am finished with the drawing, I then decide where the light source will be. Depending on what I want the final piece to look like I will use "warm" colored markers (for flesh tones, reds, browns, oranges, etc.) and "cold" colors (for blues, greens, etc.). Those are basically my "background" colors, which I lay down first.

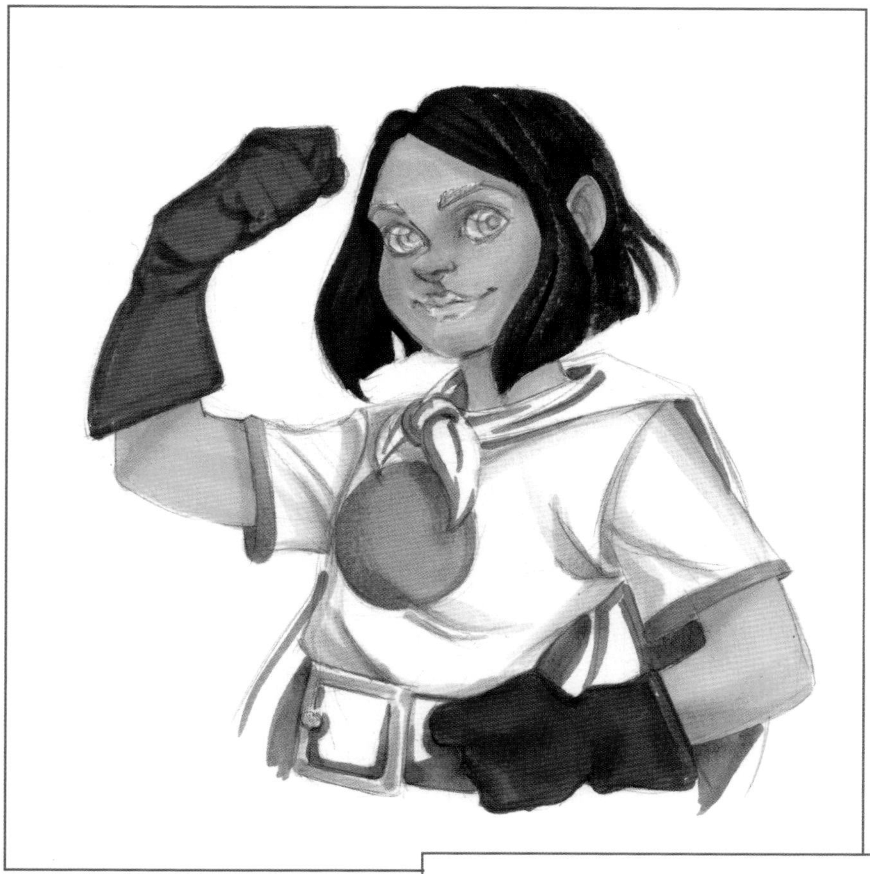

3. Then, I will color over those "background" colors. For this illustration I am using flesh-tone markers for the skin, red for the cape, brown for the gloves, and a darker brown for the hair. I also use different types of greens for her eyes and t-shirt. The background colors I put down first show through underneath the colors and they give a nice "shadow" effect.

4. I like to do several layers with my markers so they blend together. This is another reason why using paper made for wet media works well...the more marker layers you use the wetter the paper can get. To get the markers to blend well, I will go over and over an area quickly—before the layers of marker get a chance to dry.
Once I am happy with the overall look of the drawing, I will then ink over it. I personally save the inking for last because I don't want to take the chance of inking first, then coloring over the ink lines with markers and having the inks "bleed" into the marker colors. Some people prefer to ink first. After I ink, I then put some white dots (for eye highlights, etc.) and then I'm done!

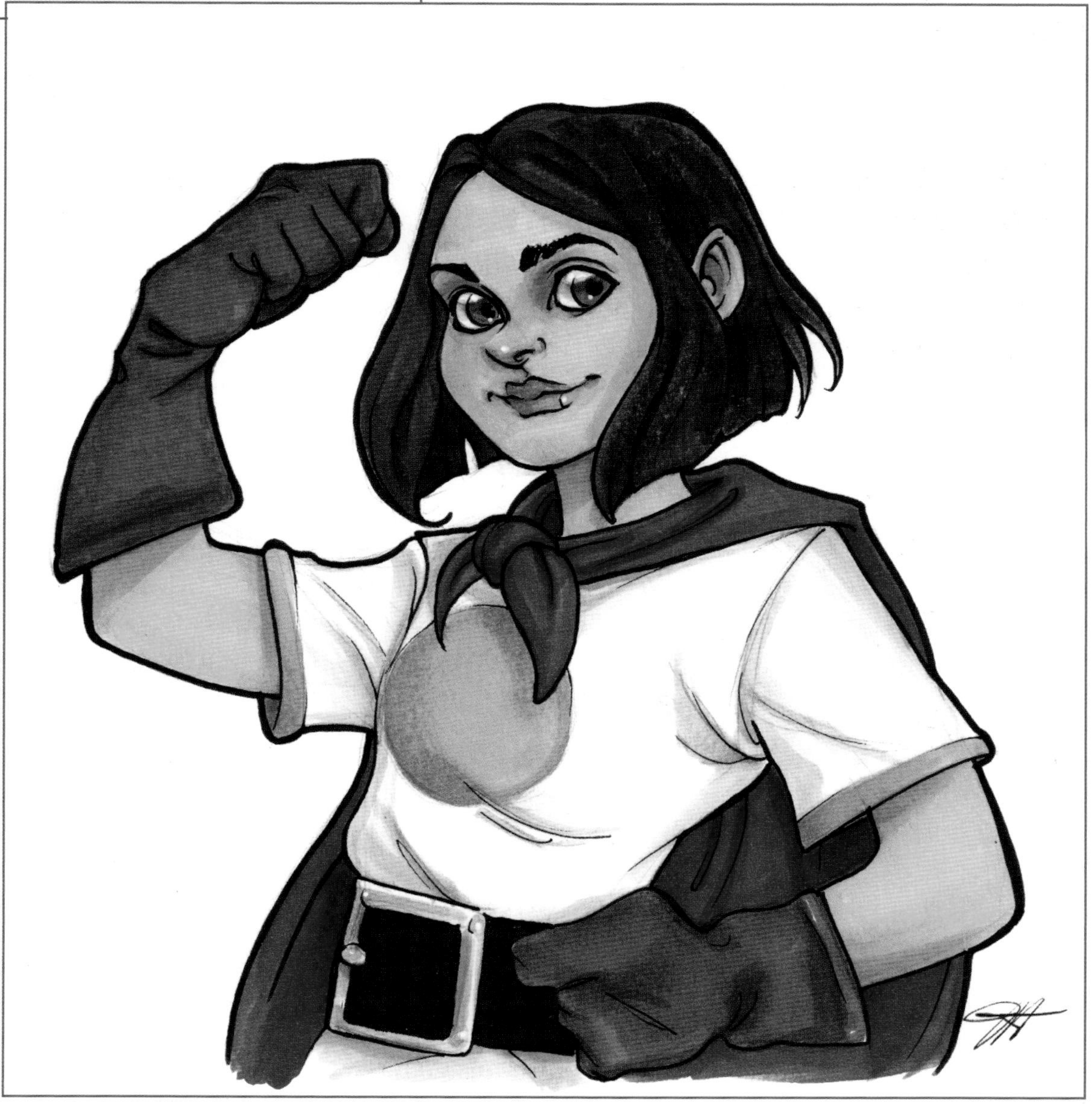

HOW TO... COLOR DIGITALLY!

BY ALICIA FERNANDEZ

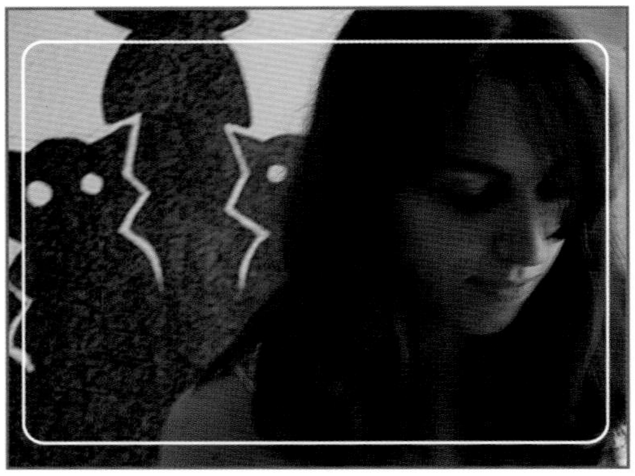

I start with a low-resolution version of the page (72dpi) and use greyscale to separate elements, define contrast, and focus interest. (Image 1)

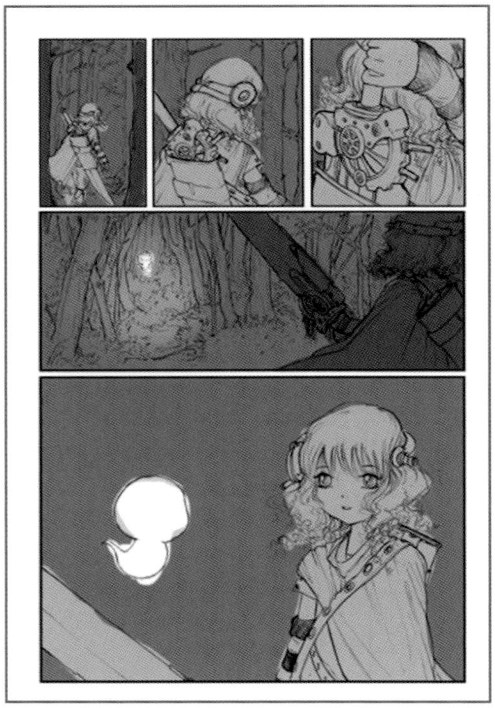

IMAGE 1

TIP: *Make sure that relevant elements, such as the main characters, are easy to see and follow along the panels. Use highlights.* *(Image 1a)*

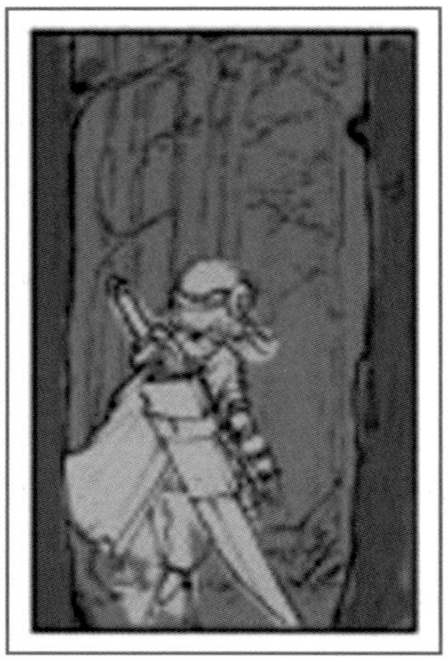

IMAGE 1a

And darker shadows to direct the viewer's attention. *(Image 1b)*

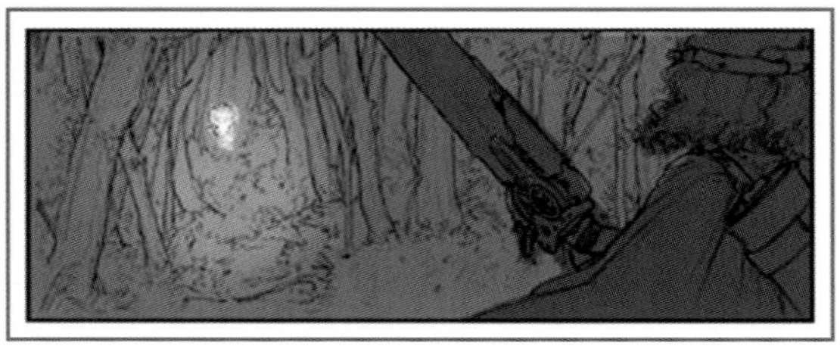

IMAGE 1b

Next, it's time to start messing around with colors in order to find the color palette that best suits the page. Take your time at this point until you feel satisfied. There are no rules for this, it is all about your personal taste and the mood of the story. Also, keep the contrast you decided upon in the previous step. *(Image 2)*

TIP: *It is important that the color test is created at a low resolution, in order to focus on the overall look of the page and not the details.*

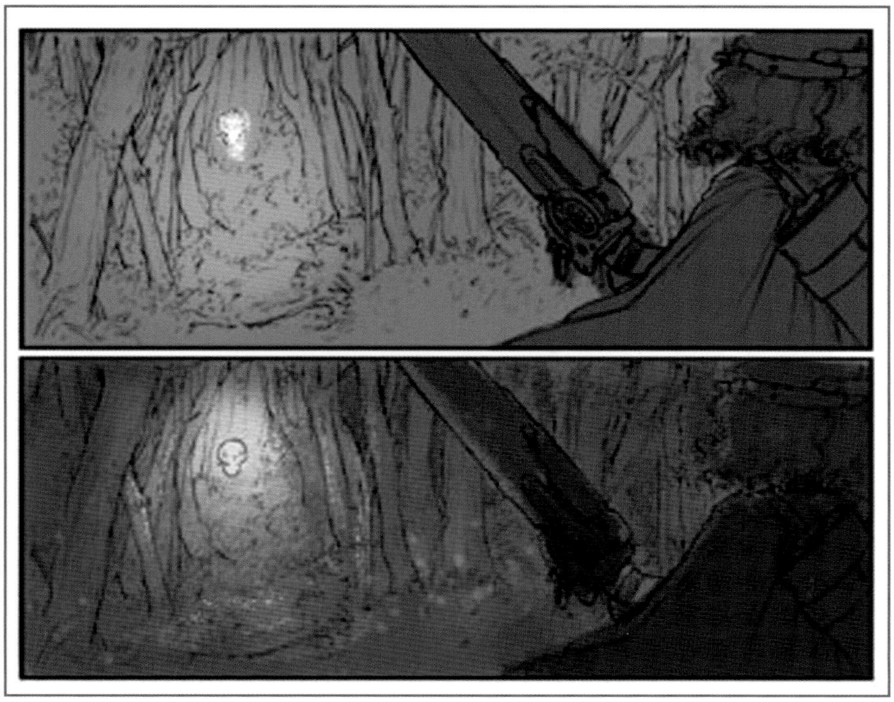

IMAGE 2

After carefully selecting the color palette, I start painting the page for real, picking colors from the color test. (Image 2) If your final image will be for print, make sure your document is at least 300 DPI resolution. I keep the lineart layer on top, and set the layer mode to multiply. Then, I start painting separate elements on different layers below the lineart, with a simple round brush, set to 100% opacity. The result is a color base. (Image 3)

TIP: *Keep the layer count to a minimum, but having elements such as backgrounds, characters, and main elements on different layers will make life much easier.*

IMAGE 3

IMAGE 4

If you like using textures, whether painted or overlayed, this is the time to apply them. I use a chalk-like brush to texturize areas as vegetation, fur, clothes, etc. Block the transparency of your previous set layers to paint the textures directly, or use new layers set as clipping masks.

The next step is shading. Set as many layers as you need to multiply mode, but try to be logical and simple. Whatever you do, never, NEVER use black for shading. Use complementary colors, violets, dark blues instead. (Image 4)

TIP: *To keep track of the contrast, fill a layer with 50% grey (#818080) and set it on top at 100% opacity and set the layer mode to "color." Lock and unlock visibility to make sure you are not losing the contrast as your colors progress.*

Finally, highlights and minor details. I use overlay mode layers with soft colors such as pale blue or yellow, and some minor white details. (Image 5) Be consistent with the decided light sources, and add some secondary sources, if necessary, to avoid over-darkened areas.

TIP: *Light is not about adding white to an image. Light is about contrast. If you want some elements to appear bright, make sure they have dark shadows projected around them.* (Image 5a)

That's all! Have fun!

IMAGE 5a

IMAGE 5

HOW TO... DRAW HANDS!
BY QING HAN

I find that sketching constantly in your sketchbook helps a lot to get the creative juices flowing, not to mention it just helps with skill raising in general. Show your artwork whenever you can; don't go out of your way to hide it like some of the people I know. The more your artwork gets seen, the better chances of getting known. Just keep drawing! :)

Tutorial and tips on drawing the Hand

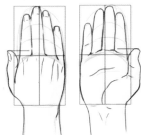

General Proportions of the Hand tip:

The size of the palm is around the same length as the longest finger (middle finger). The thumb reaches the middle of the first ridge, of the index finger.

Different people have different types of thumbs and fingers. Men tend to have larger knuckles and joints, with more veins showing, whereas women have smoother hands.

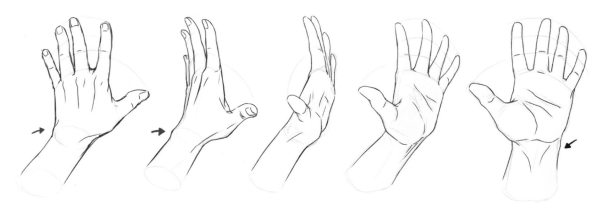

Don't forget to draw the ulna! It's the round bone that sticks out and is on the same side as your pinky. It shows up on chubbier people too.

Male vs Female hands:

As mentioned before, manlier hands tend to have bigger joints and flatter finger tips. The knuckles are also bigger, whereas the female hand is softer, with fingertips smaller and more refined looking. This is a good thing to keep in mind when drawing female versus male characters.

Try to be more dynamic when posing the hand.

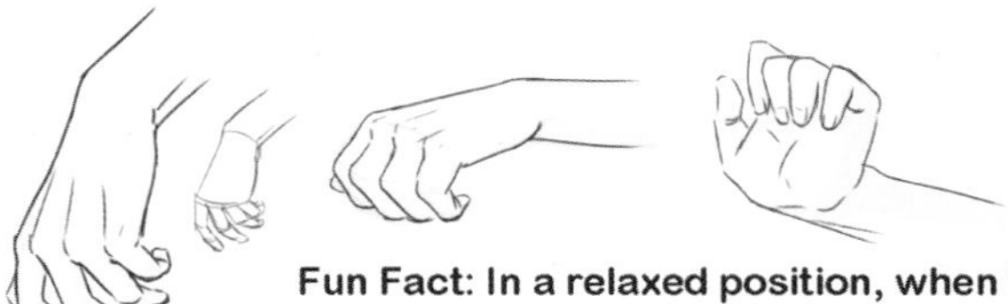

Fun Fact: In a relaxed position, when the hand is left lower than the wrist, the fingers are uncurled. The higher the hand is raised above the wrist, the more it curles into a fist-like position. For the same reason, it's harder to extend your fingers out when your hand is lifted at 90 angle to your forearm.

hand references

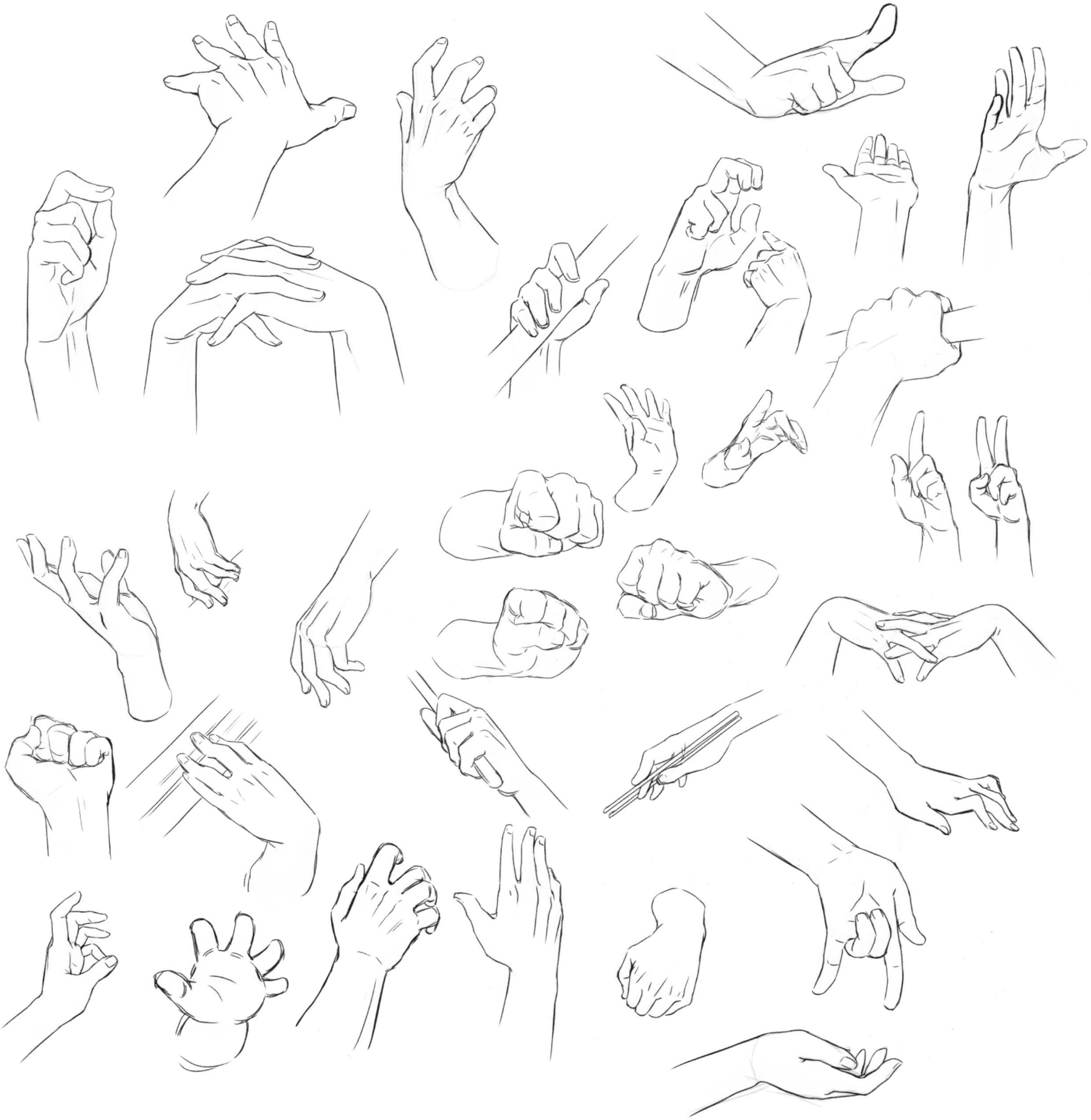

Tip 1: You should never try to hide the hands when drawing a picture; after all, forcing yourself to draw them on a body is the best way to practice.

Tip 2: Never be afraid of using references. Use your own hands if you must, or take pictures of other people's hands (with their permission, perhaps). Imagination and memory can only take you so far technical-wise, so you have to master the basics before veering off to do your own thing.

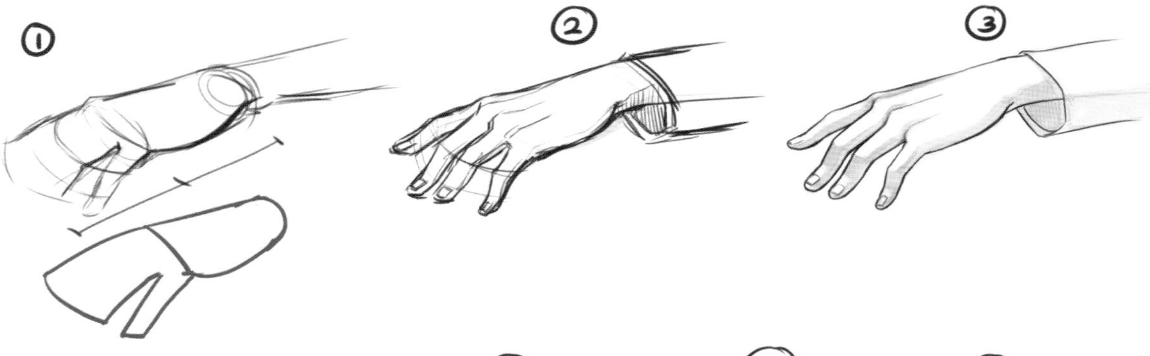
1
2
3

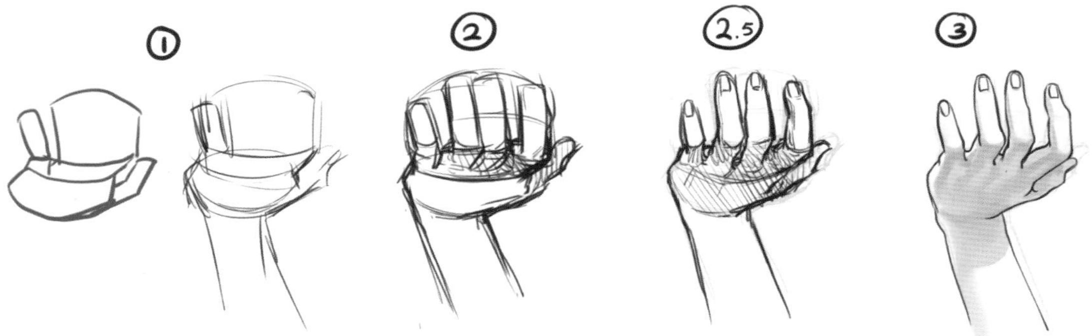
1
2
2.5
3

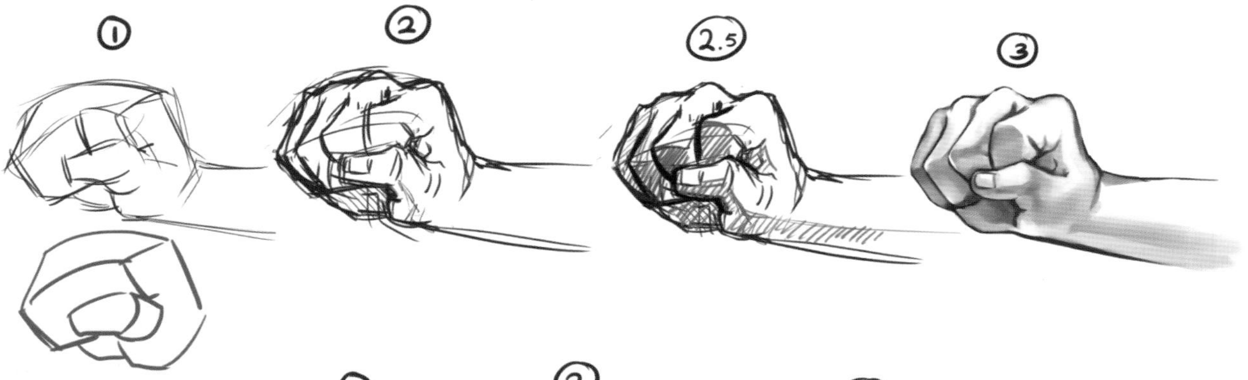
1
2
2.5
3

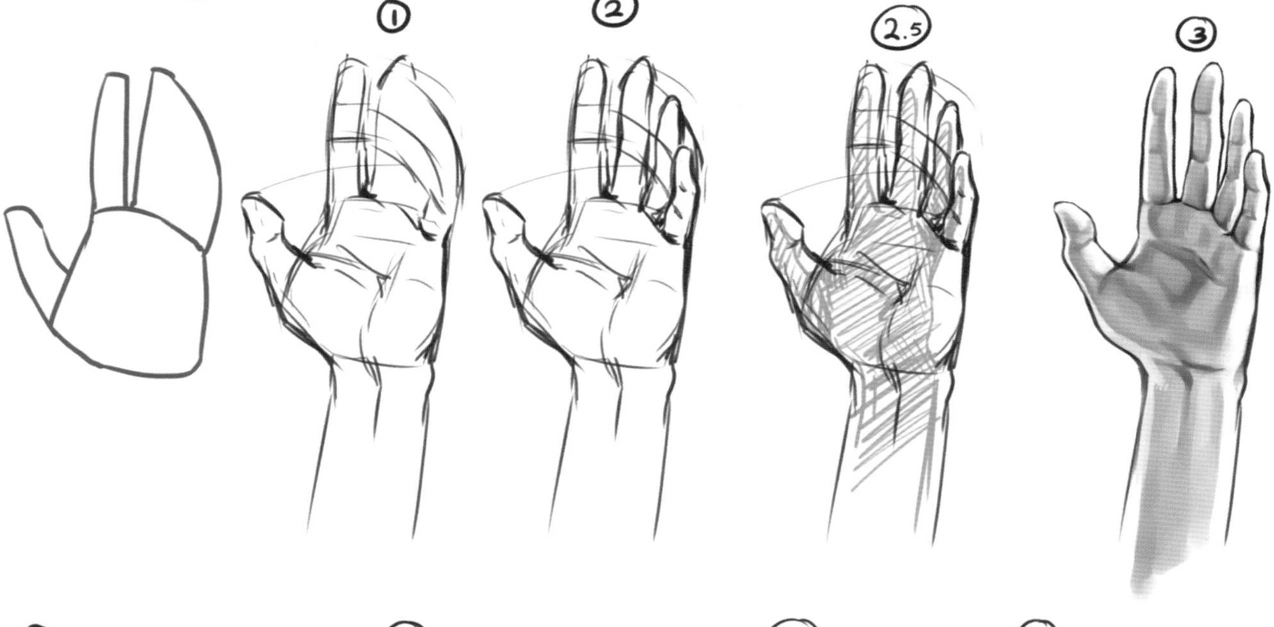
1
2
2.5
3

(1)

When drawing hands, it's best to keep in mind the most basic structure of the hand, which is broken down to the palm, the fingers, and the thumb. You don't have to neccesarily draw out the red structure, but keep it in mind when starting the quick sketch of the hand.

(2)

Shape out the fingers the way they should be shaped, keeping in mind the anatomy of the hand. It doesn't have to match the initial sketch exactly, and can be adjusted until it looks right.

(2.5)

I don't usually draw this step out, but it does help establishing the light source and approximately where the shadows would fall.

(3)

Here, I drew two types of hand, one lined and done in two layers, the other more realistic and done in one layer. The starting step is all the same. You clean up the sketch so it looks like a presentable hand. Each finger is more rectangular in shape rather than cylinder, so shade accordingly.

ps. Don't be afraid to use your own hand as reference.

HOW TO... BUILD ON A SKETCH!

BY KATIE SHANAHAN

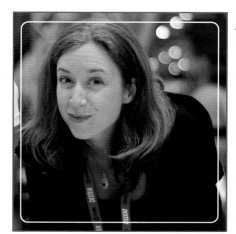

Hey there! I'm Katie, a cartoonist and storyboard artist from Toronto, Canada. I've put together this tutorial to show how I take an image from a rough scribbly sketch to an inked illustration. This is more of a technical guide explaining my process rather than a "how to draw such-and-such," and hopefully you'll find it helpful. It's a condensed version of a larger tutorial that you can read on my website: http://ktshy.blogspot.com/p/tutorials.html

VOLUME

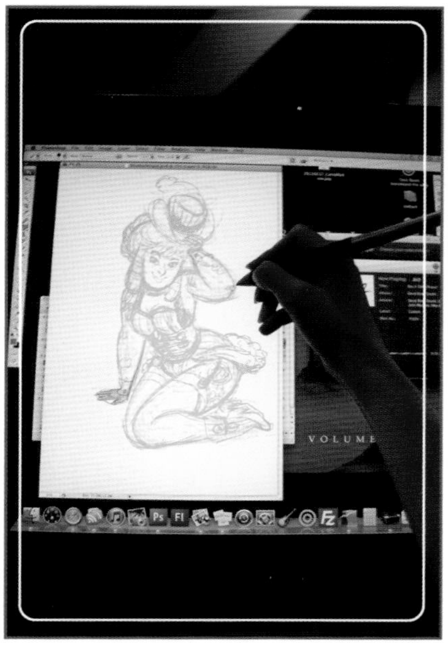

When I pencil, I tend to do it digitally in Photoshop CS3, on a Wacom Cintiq monitor which lets me draw right on the screen. Why work digitally? I like being able to make fast fixes on the fly. (Messed up the angle of an arm? No prob! Just rotate it. Foot too big? Shrink that sucker!) I work in red tones so that after I ink I can hide the red channel which will make all my pencils disappear (if you have no idea what I'm talking about don't worry, I'll be describing it in detail when we get to that step).

Strathmore
Windpower
smooth Bristol
smooth finish
acid free

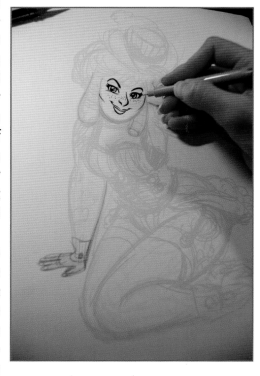

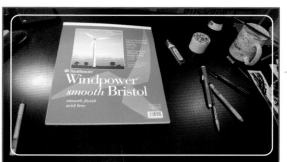

After the pencils are done it's on to inks. Some artists like to ink digitally; I prefer inking traditionally with fine-line markers and a brush. Here are my tools. I start by printing my finished red digital-sketch onto smooth bristol paper (don't print too dark!))

The most important part of a drawing is the face, especially the eyes, so ink that first to make sure you've got the expression and character down in a way you're happy with. My preferred inking method is with a brush, but because brush-work is still fairly new to me I don't have a lot of control with it in tight areas, so I use a fine line marker to ink the face (Micron pigma pens alternating between a size 005 and a 01). I've been inking my drawings since I was 14 and have built up a lot of confidence and skill that just comes with years of practice. So if you're a little wobbly with your inking, keep at it! Doing it over and over is what will make you better.

SUPER BLACK
Series 7 · Finest Sable · Winsor & Newton

With the small details done I switch over to the brush. I use a Windsor & Newton series 7 sable brush in size 01. If you're new to inking, I recommend not forking over the cash on a sable brush just yet: look into less expensive synthetic brushes, like Windsor & Newton's University series 233 (they have red handles). For ink I use Speedball's Superblack India Ink straight from the bottle (don't add water).

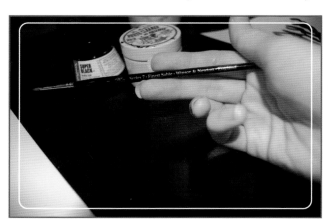

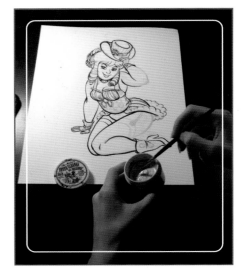

Inking! (I forgot to snap a photo while doing so, so here's me cleaning the brush afterwards.)

A good tip for inking long, broad lines is to push the lines away from your body rather than pulling them towards you. Try having your control be in your elbow and shoulder rather than twisting your wrist around, as too much of this can lead to strain (think of it like drawing with a cast on from hand to elbow, keeping your wrist locked). Be sure to rotate the paper as needed so you're inking comfortably. You want to take good care of your arms so you can draw for a long time! Once you're finished, rinse the brush in warm water (I use "The Master's Brush Cleaner and Preserver" to give my brushes a good shampoo.)

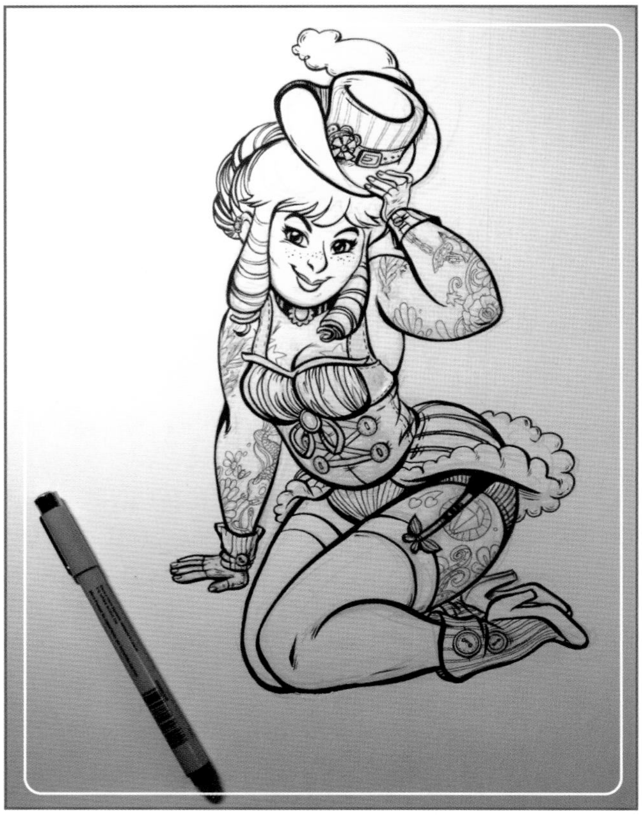

Inks are done! But now I want to get rid of the red pencils underneath.

tattoopinup.psd @ 25% (RGB/8)
Layers
Channels
Tool Presets
RGB
Red
Green
Blue
CLICK!
CLICK

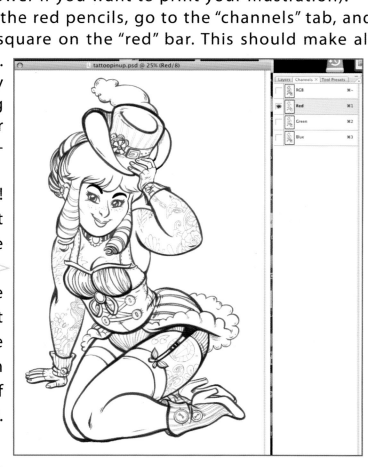

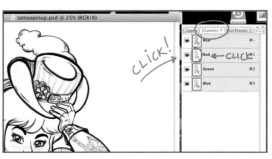

Do this by going back into the computer and scanning the image into Photoshop at 300 dpi resolution (no lower if you want to print your illustration).

To erase the red pencils, go to the "channels" tab, and click the white square on the "red" bar. This should make all the red colouring disappear from your drawing. If the channels tab is missing, you can find it by going up to your menu bar and selecting Windows> Channels. NOTE: This works for other coloured pencils as well: if you made your pencils blue, click the blue channel instead.

tattoopinup.psd @ 25% (Red/8)
Layers
Channels
Tool Presets
RGB
Red
Green
Blue

Now only the black inked lines are visible... but wait! Some of my darkest pencil lines are still there as light grey lines. CURSES! We must vanquish them!

Image
Layer
Select
Filter
Analysis
View
Mode
Adjustments
Duplicate...
Apply Image...
Calculations...
Image Size...
Canvas Size...
Pixel Aspect Ratio
Rotate Canvas
Crop
Trim...
Reveal All
Variables
Apply Data Set...
Trap...
Bitmap...
Grayscale
Duotone
Indexed Color...
RGB Color
CMYK Color
Lab Color
Multichannel
8 Bits/Channel
16 Bits/Channel
32 Bits/Channel
Color Table...

First I make the image "greyscale" so that the red channel is gone for good (it's only hidden right now; if you click off of it all the reds will reappear).

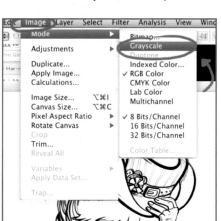

I clean up the drawing by tweaking the levels and pumping up the black and white contrast:

Image> Adjustment > Levels.

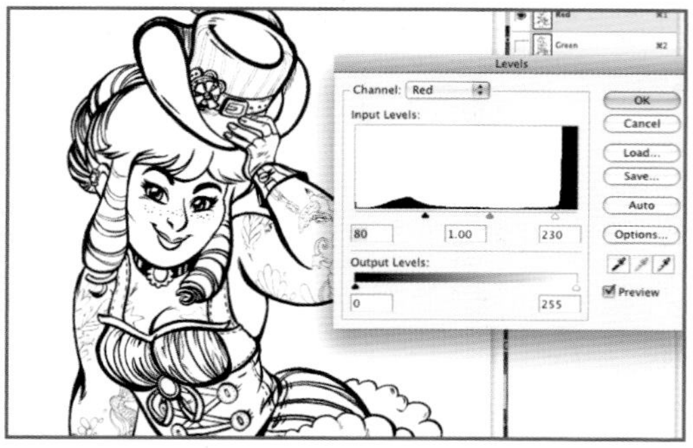
Levels
Channel: Red
Input Levels:
80
1.00
230
Output Levels:
0
255
OK
Cancel
Load...
Save...
Auto
Options...
Preview

DONE!

One piece of advice I like to give for displaying your work is to always put your best pieces first. Prospective clients are looking at so many portfolios you need to WOW them from the start, and make them want to keep flipping pages. A good idea is to keep some of your second-best stuff for last so that you have consistent quality throughout and the viewers leave on a high note when they finish viewing your portfolio. Also? Get your art online! It's the fastest and easiest way to get your artwork in front of eyeballs!

Hope you found that helpful! If you'd like to see how I go from here to colour, check out the full tutorial on my website:
http://ktshy.blogspot.com/p/tutorials.html

Cheers!
KATIE

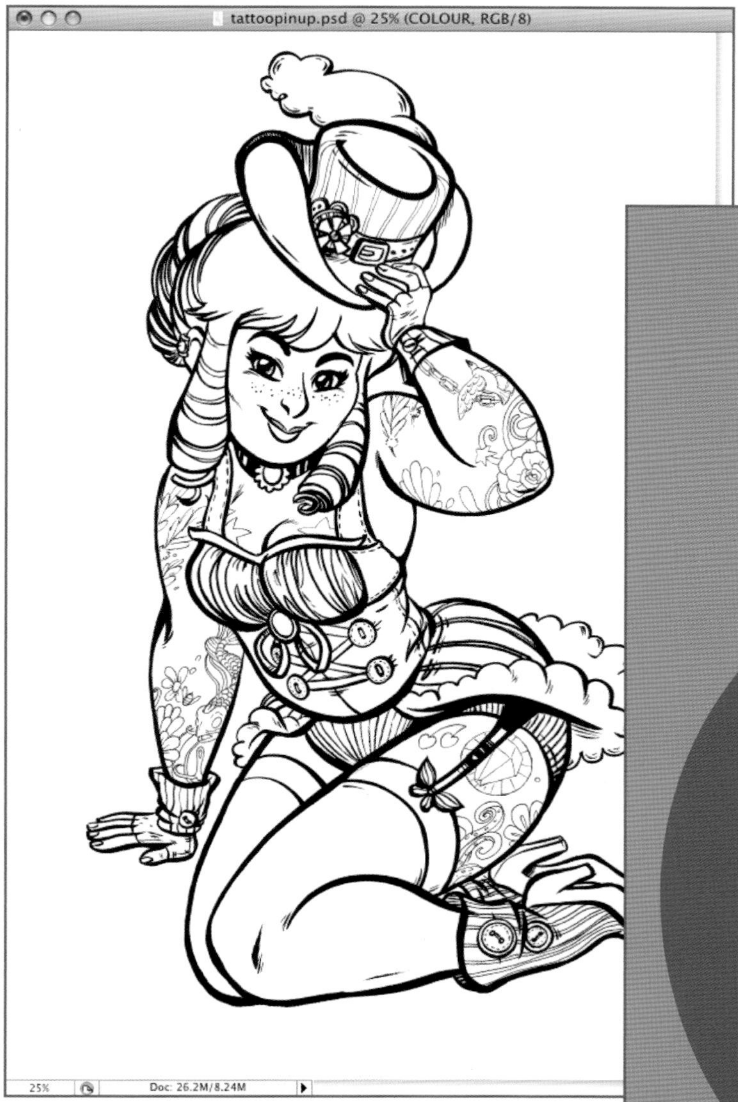
tattoopinup.psd @ 25% (COLOUR, RGB/8)
25%
Doc: 26.2M/8.24M

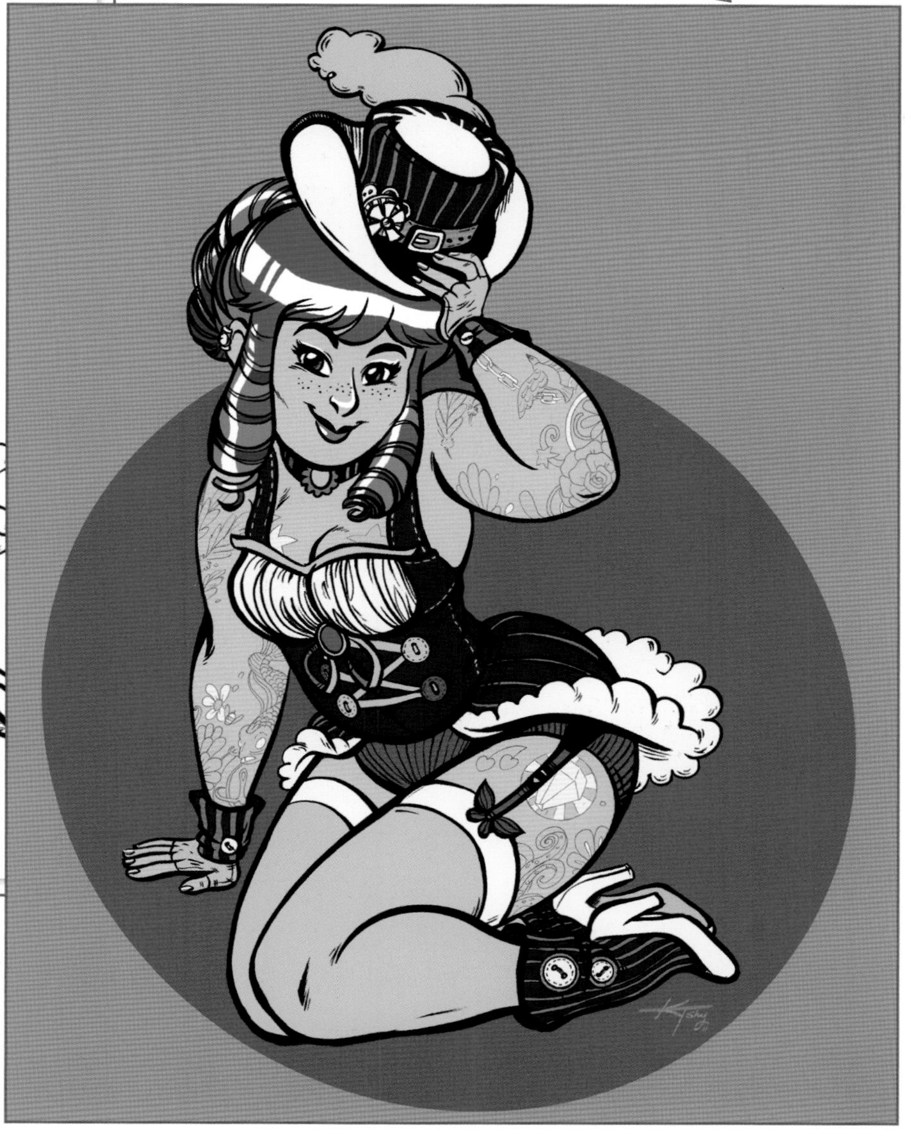

CREATOR INTERVIEWS

★ ★ ☆

IN-DEPTH
INTERVIEWS WITH
PROFESSIONAL WOMEN
IN THE COMIC BOOK
INDUSTRY.

EDITED BY JENNIFER DOUDNEY

☆ ☆ ☆ CREATOR INTERVIEW ☆ ☆ ☆

COLLEEN DORAN

How did you discover comics, and when (and why) did you start taking comics seriously as a career choice?

I'd been interested in comics since I was a little girl. I wanted to be an animator for Disney, but when I was twelve, I got holed up sick with a box of comic books, and changed my mind.

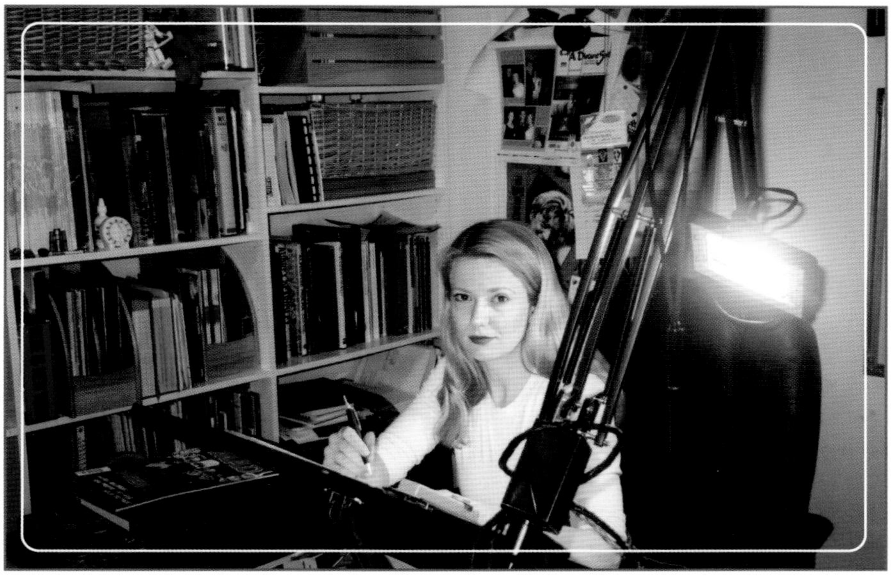

How and when did you first "break in" to comics?

I got my first job working for an advertising agency when I was fifteen years old, and then got tapped when I was sixteen to do a comic book for a man named Tom Long, who is credited with giving first work to Mike Kaluta and Steve Hickman. The book was too adult for me, and I quit. I don't think he realized how young I was. But it was my first paying gig.

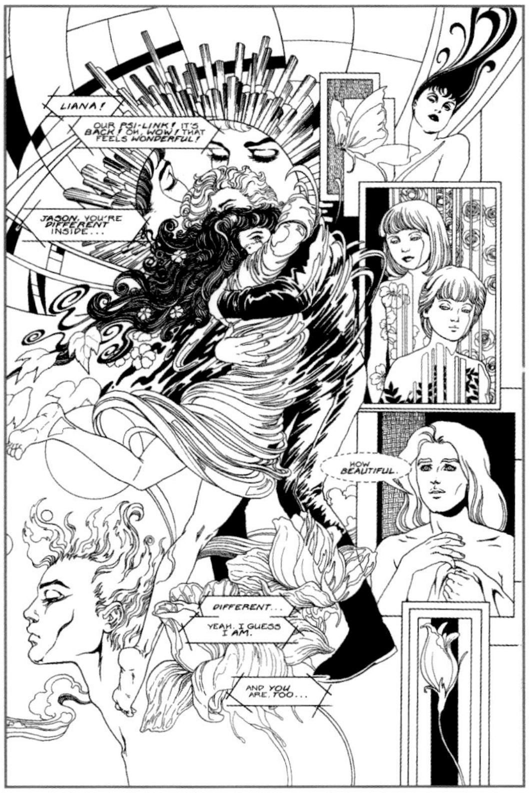

LIANA!
OUR PSI-LINK! IT'S BACK! OH, WOW! THAT FEELS WONDERFUL!
JASON, YOU'RE DIFFERENT INSIDE...
HOW BEAUTIFUL.
DIFFERENT...
YEAH, I GUESS I AM.
AND YOU ARE, TOO...

What is the best advice you've ever heard, concerning working in comics, and what is the best advice you would personally give to an aspiring creator/someone who wants to work in comics?

Don't try to be famous, try to be good.

What's an interesting/funny fact about yourself?

I'm blind as a bat, which makes my accomplishments making pictures a freaking miracle.

Considering your success with *A Distant Soil* online, would you recommend self-publishing online to fellow creators? Why or why not?

Yes, of course, but most people who find success online tend to exaggerate the level of that success, and I think it gives aspiring artists a false impression of what to expect. The odd thing about *A Distant Soil* is that it is basically a reprint of published material, but it makes more money than most original work online. The great advantage being that the original art is worth something, and a lot of online artists are digital. I have a printed catalogue of work I sell, and physical art. I do not make money the way everyone says you make money online: t-shirts, coffee mugs, that sort of thing. I make almost nothing going that route. All the advice I ever got about webcomics did not work for me. I had to forge my own path. I think most of the advice you will ever see about webcomics is lousy, actually, unless that advice is go your own way, because what works for one person will not work for the next. Every book is different, every audience is different. We're not dealing with data, we're dealing with people.

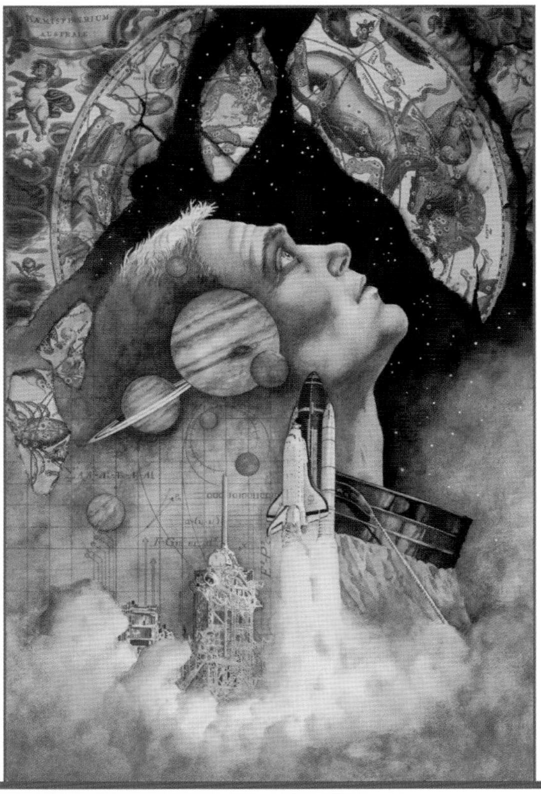

What is your favorite food?

Coney Island hot dogs.

What is your favorite thing to do in your spare time?

Gardening.

www.ColleenDoran.com
www.ADistantSoil.com
Twitter @ColleenDoran

☆ ☆ ☆ CREATOR INTERVIEW ☆ ☆ ☆

DEVIN GRAYSON

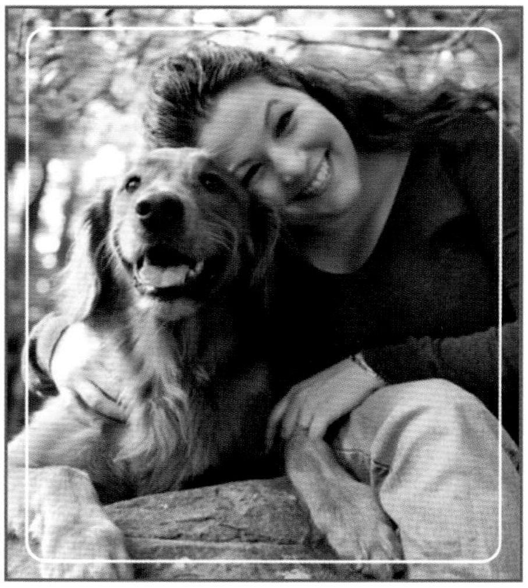

How did you discover comics, and when (and why) did you start taking comics seriously as a career choice?

I grew up in very literary, hippy households and there just weren't any comic books around. I discovered the medium in my early twenties, right after college. I was channel surfing in a tiny studio apartment in San Francisco when I ran across an early episode of *Batman: The Animated Series*. Although it was a cartoon it was very sophisticated and alluring, and to say I got sucked in would be an understatement. There was a scene with Batman and Robin in the Batmobile, and Robin has his feet up on the dashboard, visual storytelling at its best. I was immediately fascinated with the idea that Batman had, in essence, raised a kid. My then friend and the current love of my life was working in a comic book store in the city at the time. He hooked me up with armfuls of Alan Moore comics and Neil Gaiman's *Sandman* series, a gazillion random *Teen Titans* issues and Scott McCloud's wonderful *Understanding Comics*, the book that really sold me on the medium. McCloud discussed comics the way my dad talked about jazz—sophisticated and filled with possibilities for growth and reinvention. Later I also came to appreciate how communal working in comics is; writing can be a very lonely discipline, but with comics you have this amazing team working with you to bring the story to life visually. I still love the explorative elements of the medium and the camaraderie of the industry.

How and when did you first "break in" to comics?

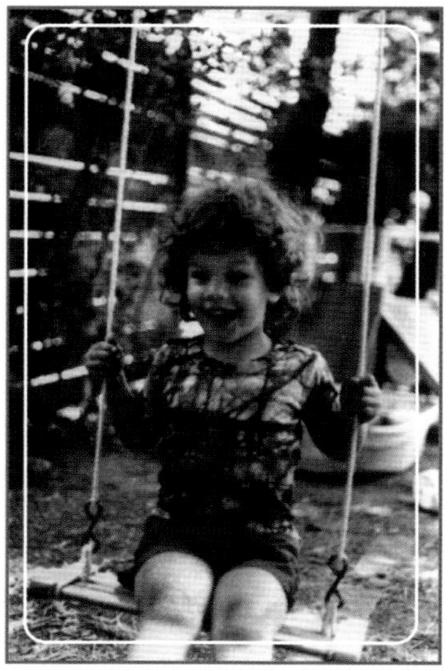

It was around 1995 when I cold-called DC Comics. I found a phone number online for DC Comics' reception. I asked to speak to "whoever was in charge of *Batman*," and without a moment's hesitation (could this possibly still happen today!?) the woman at the front desk put me through to Denny O'Neil. Since I was too ignorant about the industry to understand who I was talking to at the time, I just blurted out that I was a writing student in the Bay Area, but I didn't know much about comic books and wanted to learn so that I could write *Batman*. He was quiet for a moment and then he started to laugh. He told me that he received literally hundreds of calls a week from people who had read every comic book ever written but didn't know the first thing about writing, and that there really wasn't much he could do for them. But if I already had the writing part down, then sure—teaching me about comics would be a pleasure. He directed me to send writing samples to his second-in-command, editor Scott Peterson, and a kind of long-distance tutelage was born. I cyber-stalked Scott when he did online chats for the Bat-books and sent him letters with S.A.S. postcards included, spoke with editor Darren Vincenzo at 6 am PST about script formatting, and exchanged emails with editor Jordan Gorfinkel about the characters and their histories. Eventually Darren called and asked if I felt ready to try my hand at a short script—that became "Like Riding a Bike" with artist Rodolfo Damaggio in *The Batman Chronicles* #7. Eventually Denny-san offered me the *Catwoman* monthly with artist Jim Balent. I giddily quit my job and soon after moved to New York so I could finally meet my four editor-heroes, and I've been working as a professional writer one way or another ever since.

What is the best advice you've ever heard, concerning working in comics, and what is the best advice you would personally give to an aspiring creator/ someone who wants to work in comics?

I've received so much priceless advice from so many amazing people over the years, but one thing that's really stuck with me came from Mark Waid, who told me that writer's block is your subconscious' way of telling you that there's something structurally wrong with your story. Take a step back, kill your darlings, and redo the pages that lead up to the block. Following that advice has worked for me every time.

My best advice to an aspiring writer is to figure out what you love writing about—not who or what or which medium you want to write in, but the thematic material that has the most resonance for you—and direct your attention back to that when you're blocking out your stories or pitches. You'll always find your voice there, and your unique voice as a writer is pretty much the only thing that can set you apart from the pack.

What's an interesting/funny fact about yourself?

I never write anything without making a music soundtrack/playlist for it first. As a writer, I focus a lot on lyrics, but I'm an avid music fan too with a very eclectic and constantly growing collection of songs, almost all of which make me think of a fictional character I've written or am in the process of writing.

What is your favorite food?

Sushi! Only in places near large bodies of water, though. If I'm landlocked, it's tofu.

What is your favorite thing to do in your spare time?

I'm an RPG addict. Good, old-fashioned pencils, character sheets, and dice. And smart phones with photos of actors cast as the characters and their corresponding playlists, of course. ;-P

www.DevinGrayson.com Twitter @Gothamette

☆ ☆ ☆ CREATOR INTERVIEW ☆ ☆ ☆

JUNE BRIGMAN

10.31.06
To June (THE MODEL)

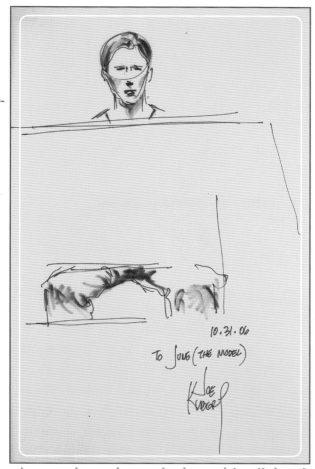

June as drawn by comics legend Joe Kubert!

How did you discover comics, and when (and why) did you start taking comics seriously as a career choice?

I'd never looked at a comic until my boyfriend, now husband, Roy Richardson showed me some books from his collection. I was 18 years old, and he had to teach me how to read them, left right and down. I loved Jack Kirby's *New Gods* and Joe Kubert's *Tarzan*. I didn't consider comics as a career until I went to my first convention. I met Gil Kane and watched him do these amazing drawings on the spot, no model, no photo reference. I didn't know that was possible. I was majoring in art at the University of Georgia, but didn't know what direction to go in. I'd loved drawing since I was a child. Comics require very strong drawing skills, and that appealed to me.

How and when did you first "break in" to comics?

My first paying work was for Bill Black, who had a small company based in Florida, Americomics. My first mainstream work was in DC's *New Talent* book. After that, Larry Hama gave me a small back up job in *Conan*. But my big break came when I met Louise Simonson. She was looking for an artist who could draw children. There weren't many artists who could do that, but I'd had some experience from doing children's portraits. We put together a proposal for a comic book series about siblings who get superpowers, which became *Power Pack*. It had a small but devoted following. Almost thirty years later, I still get fan mail for my work on the series.

What is the best advice you've ever heard, concerning working in comics, and what is the best advice you would personally give to an aspiring creator/someone who wants to work in comics?

Probably the best advice I've heard was from Bob McLeod, my teacher, who advised me to take another career path. While I have no regrets about my choice of career, the life of a freelance cartoonist isn't easy. If you want to get rich, become an investment banker. But if you're determined to become a cartoonist, then the best advice I can give is: stay focused. Sign off from Facebook. Put down the iPhone. Say no to invitations from family and friends. They'll eventually forget about you. Then you can really get some work done.

What's an interesting/funny fact about yourself?

If I hadn't become an artist, I would have been a jockey.

As a teacher at Savannah College of Art and Design, what is a lecture or topic you look forward to sharing with your students each year?

I love talking about anything concerning drawing comics. I especially love teaching figure drawing. The human body always fascinates me. Landscapes, not so much.

What is your favorite food?

Right now, it's Chick-Fil-A peach milkshakes.

What is your favorite thing to do in your spare time?

Go riding. I lease a beautiful, talented mare that can jump, do dressage, or just take me on a nice trail ride. I was one of those horse-crazy girls. If I live long enough, I'll be a horse-crazy old lady.

☆ ☆ ☆ CREATOR INTERVIEW ☆ ☆ ☆

LOUISE SIMONSON

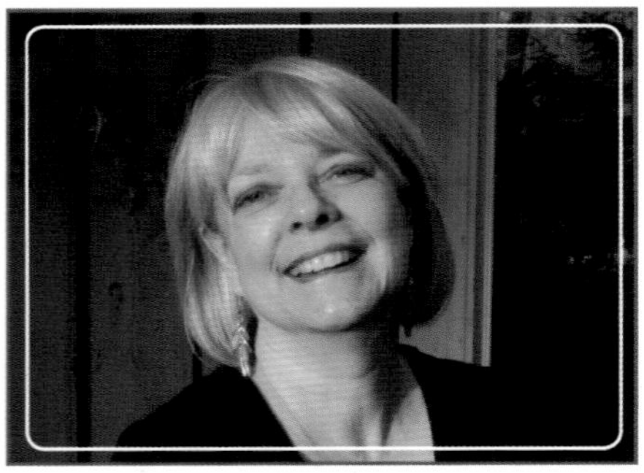

How did you discover comics, and when (and why) did you start taking comics seriously as a career choice?

I read comics as a small kid—*Little Lulu, Sugar & Spike*, the *Archies*. Found those on the newsstand. Had a subscription to the *Duck* comics. But I also sometimes read adventure comics like *Lone Ranger* and *Superman*. (The '50s Lois did annoy me, though! She was a reporter, for Pete's sake! Didn't she have better things to do than try to cut Clark's hair to prove he was Superman?!) Loved the EC sci-fi and horror comics but they were hard to find, so I didn't see them very often.

As I grew older, I loved writing and loved art, but saved my tiny allowance for other purchases and read library books.

How and when did you first "break in" to comics?

During the early 1970s, I was living in New York, working in advertising-promotion for a magazine publisher. I read the Warren black and white horror comics and had a lot of friends who worked in comics.

A friend who worked at Warren Publishing told me there was a job opening in their production department that paid more than my job at McFadden. I applied for it and got it. As simple as that.

Once I was there, and saw how comics worked from the inside, I began to seriously love everything about it.

Warren was a small company and the people who worked there could fill a lot of roles, if they chose. I volunteered to write ad copy for Warren's Captain Company and letters pages, in addition to my production work. My answer to any "Can anyone do—" question was, "I can!" whether I'd ever done it before or not. In a couple of months, Warren created an assistant editor position, and slotted me into it. By that time, I was hooked on making comics. A few years later, when the editor DuBay left, Warren was looking around outside the company for a new editor for the line.

I talked him into giving me the position.

What is the best advice you've ever heard, concerning working in comics, and what is the best advice you would personally give to an aspiring creator/ someone who wants to work in comics?

The best advice for ANY working life that I ever heard is find out what you love, then do it, to the best of your ability, every time.

My advice beyond that is:

- Every editor is a walking opinion, and opinions will differ. Show your work to many editors. Be brave. Don't get discouraged. "No" from one person doesn't mean "No" from everyone.
- Thank everyone who comments on your work, even if they've said something you don't want to hear.
- Nobody likes to hear that there's room for improvement, but if someone suggests a way you might get better, think about it. Try not to get huffy or defensive. Maybe give it a try. If two people give you similar advice, try doing it their way, as a test, even if you think they might be wrong. If you hear the same advice from three people, LISTEN AND DO!
- Keep an open mind. You might find something in another area that you love just as much and do better.
- Much of comics is a team business. Try to work and play well with others.
- See things in the most positive light. Think how any event might be a chance to learn and improve.
- Be as kind as possible to everyone you meet. Give help as well as receive it.
- Don't be afraid to ask questions. Really listen to the answers.
- Keep your eyes open to opportunities. If the chance arises, make your own luck.

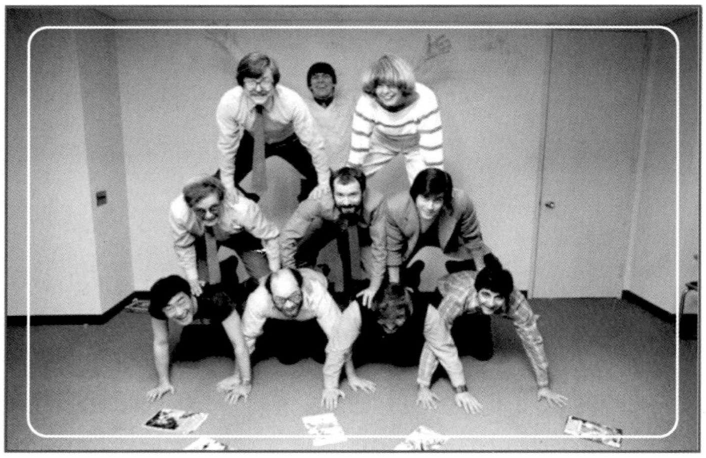

Marvel Comics editors triangle, 1980s

What's an interesting/funny fact about yourself?

I have three sisters, a daughter, two granddaughters, and nine nieces who are smart, funny, and talented. I have one grandson, and two nephews. My family specializes in fabulous women! (And the guys we produce are choice, too!)

You've said you prefer traditional heroes to the current anti-hero trend. Why is that and did that influence the creation of Steel?

I'm a child of the '50s. I believe in good and evil. I think having a moral code is a good thing. I applaud ethical behavior. I believe in personal responsibility. My hero is the embodiment of a responsible, decent person in an imperfect world. He (or she) is trying to do the right thing and make the world a better place. The old "with great powers" concept. Except that, in the modern world, it's sometimes hard to tell where right stops and wrong begins.

A traditional story is about conflict. For me, in a story, having a hero who is struggling to make moral choices in a world that is careening out of control adds to the dynamic tension. He's facing not just his own demons (and everyone has them!) but also the myriad demons—both solid and abstract—of his world. My heroes are intelligent. They're aware of the forces that shape their environment and that there are no easy answers. But they're doing their best.

Steel was one of the "heroes" who arrived in Metropolis after the death of Superman back in the early '90s. At the Superman summit, we sort of divided up the aspects of Superman. Other teams grabbed other parts, but Jon Bogdanove and I grabbed Superman's soul.

We wanted to create a character with that same sense of responsibility that Superman has. So yep, we deliberately created Steel as a traditional hero, though Steel wouldn't have seen himself that way. Humility seems to be another aspect of real-life heroes that we wanted to emulate.

What is your favorite food?

You mean I have to name just one? Um...baked sweet potatoes with lots of butter. But really dark organic chocolate is good, too!

What is your favorite thing to do in your spare time?

Read.

☆ ☆ ☆ CREATOR INTERVIEW ☆ ☆ ☆

NICOLA SCOTT

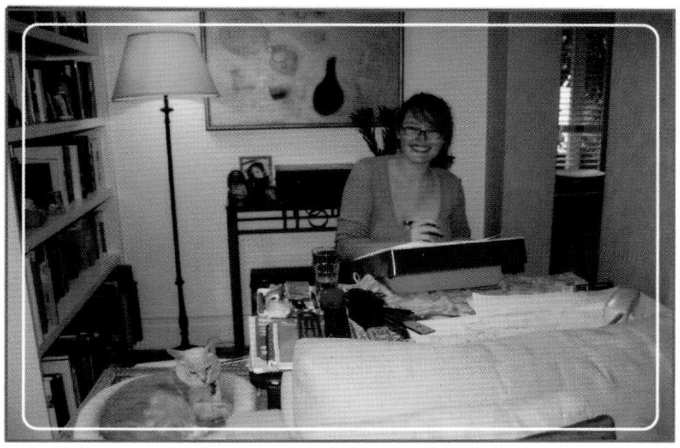

How did you discover comics, and when (and why) did you start taking comics seriously as a career choice?

Very rarely did I see comics around when I was a kid. I was into superheroes in a big way but they were all from TV and film, like Wonder Woman, Electra Woman, Isis, Superman, and Batman. The comics that I did see, even when they included these characters, were so different from what I was used to that I thought they (the comics makers) had got it wrong. I didn't realize that this was where they had come from.

I got my first real understanding of comics, and their stature as the source material, when I was in my late teens. I was introduced to George Perez's *Wonder Woman* and it completely blew my mind. I read a few books regularly for a couple of years but didn't really have anyone to share the interest with. I've always been drawing and painting, coming from an artistic family, and I often drew superheroes for fun. It was probably in my teens that I briefly flirted with the dream that I might draw them for real one day. It seemed logical but I wasn't really thinking particularly seriously about my future life and when I did it was to chase all kinds of other fantasies first.

It was not too long before my thirtieth birthday that I decided to draw comics, and the idea struck like lightning. I was going through a few days of wondering what the hell I was doing with my life and thinking that it was time to get serious about something. I knew it had to be creative and so I broke it down to the things I could do well (act, sew, draw) and how one might make a living from those things. After careful consideration I was down to just drawing, and in a moment of thinking "what would I be happy drawing if I had to draw every day" the light bulb dinged. Wonder Woman. I'd be really happy if I could draw Wonder Woman all day every day, and right now, somewhere in the world, someone actually had that very job. That was the job I wanted and it meant drawing comics!

How and when did you first "break in" to comics?

Right after that moment, straight away, I went to a comic book store and started buying books. Anything I liked the art in. I started chatting to the guy who worked there, stared going to conventions and chatting to people there, too. I started drawing constantly (I hadn't drawn much for a long time), setting myself rules and asking lots of questions.

It was only about nine months later that I went to my first San Diego Comic Con, with no idea what I was doing, but I came away from that experience with some firm direction, a greater sense of what I wanted and how to get there. Along the way I found myself drawing lots of sci-fi and horror books, taking on anything that was likely to see print—and if it paid, all the better—and learning on the go. It was four years before I got my first monthly at DC Comics.

What is the best advice you've ever heard, concerning working in comics, and what is the best advice you would personally give to an aspiring creator/someone who wants to work in comics?

Early on I heard a big-time pro say that there were three things you can be that could help get you work. Be good, make deadlines, be fun to hang out with. Any two could get you work but all three could keep you in work. Go for all three.

For me, it was about working out exactly what I wanted to do and where that job is. I had the saying in my head "If you want to be a fisherman, go where the fish are", i.e.; don't sit around waiting for it to happen. Work out what you want and plot a path to get there. After my first SDCC I knew I wanted to go for interior work on superhero books. Straight away that told me the skills I needed to pick up and the companies I need to go for.

What's an interesting/funny fact about yourself?

In 1998, when I was in my mid-twenties and still attempting to get my acting career off the ground (doing all the wrong things, BTW), I found myself auditioning for a new *Wonder Woman* TV show that was being developed. I went through a couple of screen tests and was given the impression that it was down to me, a chick from *Baywatch* and someone else. Pre-production halted before anyone was cast but I did get some photos of me in the costume. It was after that bummer that I quit acting.

Being a Wonder Woman fan yourself, what do you believe has allowed Wonder Woman to stand the test of time? What can up-and-coming creators learn from her achievements and shortcomings as a character?

Wonder Woman was so iconic, visually and conceptually, from the get-go that she was able to capture her status as the premier superheroine immediately. When social norms changed, Wonder Woman was able to evolve with it, becoming a face of the feminist movement. At her best she's nurturing and gracious to all, protective and capable, strong but not really aggressive and always a little incidentally glamorous. She's the very best of all the feminine aspects.

What is your favorite food?

You're kidding, right? I have to choose just one? Bacon.

What is your favorite thing to do in your spare time?

I don't get much of that. Time with friends and family. Going to the movies with my husband. Cuddling my cat. Looking at real estate.

☆ ☆ ☆ CREATOR INTERVIEW ☆ ☆ ☆

ROBIN FURTH

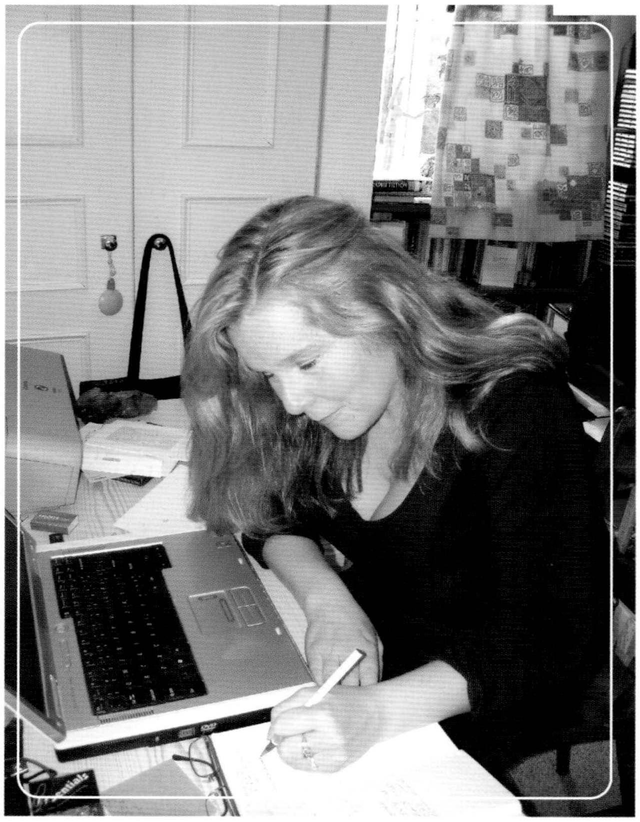

How did you discover comics, and when (and why) did you start taking comics seriously as a career choice?

I have always loved illustrated tales of all kinds. In fact, one of my earliest and most important creative inspirations was Ivan Bilibin, the famous late-nineteenth-century Russian illustrator. I spent hours looking at his work, and it formed a huge part of my dream life. (In fact, here's an image of his character Vasilisa, just as she is escaping the Baba Yaga's house. In some secret part of my soul, I always identified with Vasilisa . . .)

I was a huge fan of the Archie comics, and of the Sunday funnies. (I sometimes wonder how many kids fall in love with comics because of the Sunday funnies!) When I was young I loved to draw, but on the whole my art teachers weren't very supportive. In a couple of instances, my art work was mocked by older kids (for about a year I drew people with beaks instead of noses!) and the self-consciousness stuck. So my focus turned to fantasy novels and science fiction. Even that was challenged at school by teachers who meant well. I was a good student, so they really wanted me to read "serious" books—ones that would get me into college! But still, the love of magical stories, and of the illustrated tale, remained.

Words and images together are incredibly powerful. When I was at college, we read William Blake's Songs of Innocence and Experience without their accompanying art. When I finally read the poems as William Blake meant them to be seen—as art pieces, where words and images go together, you could even call them early comics—I was amazed. It was magic.

I have always wanted to be a writer, and I have always had tremendous respect for comic book artists, but I never dreamed that I could write comics even though I couldn't draw the panels myself! My husband collected *Fat Freddy's Cat*, the *Fabulous Furry Freak Brothers*, and early *Viz*. I loved gothic comics, and also the work of Robert Crumb and his wife, Aline Kominsky-Crumb. But as I said, I never thought I'd be able to work with artists in the incredible collaborations that I have since experienced.

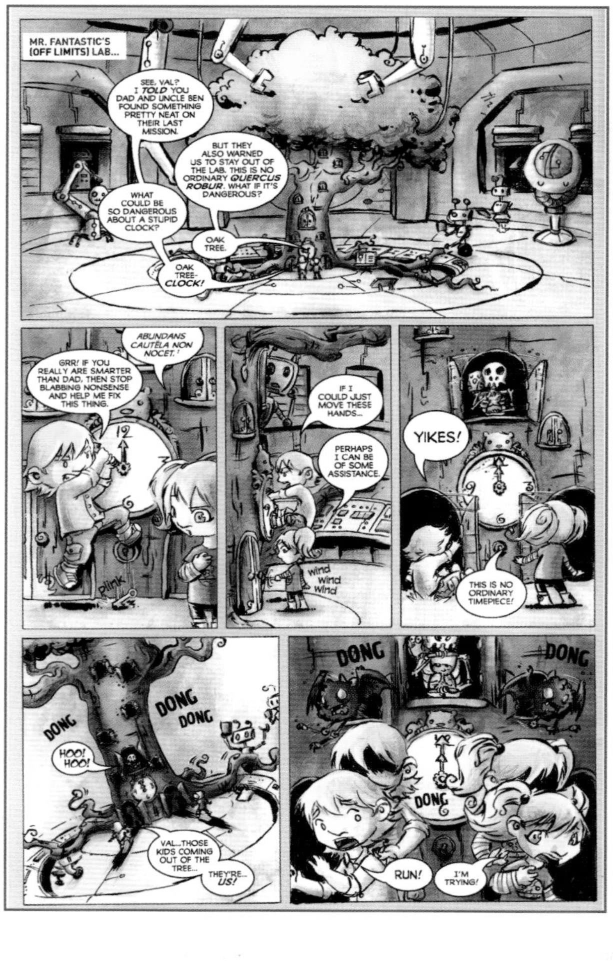

MR. FANTASTIC'S (OFF LIMITS) LAB...
SEE, VAL? I TOLD YOU DAD AND UNCLE BEN FOUND SOMETHING PRETTY NEAT ON THEIR LAST MISSION.
BUT THEY ALSO WARNED US TO STAY OUT OF THE LAB. THIS IS NO ORDINARY QUERCUS ROBUR. WHAT IF IT'S DANGEROUS?
WHAT COULD BE SO DANGEROUS ABOUT A STUPID CLOCK?
OAK TREE.
OAK TREE-CLOCK!
GRR! IF YOU REALLY ARE SMARTER THAN DAD, THEN STOP BLABBING NONSENSE AND HELP ME FIX THIS THING.
ABUNDANS CAUTĒLA NON NOCET.
plink
IF I COULD JUST MOVE THESE HANDS...
PERHAPS I CAN BE OF SOME ASSISTANCE.
wind wind wind
YIKES!
THIS IS NO ORDINARY TIMEPIECE!
DONG
DONG DONG
HOO! HOO!
VAL...THOSE KIDS COMING OUT OF THE TREE...
THEY'RE... US!
DONG
DONG
DONG
RUN!
I'M TRYING!

How and when did you first "break in" to comics?

I was extremely lucky since comics found me. While Stephen King was working on the last three *Dark Tower* novels I was his research assistant. I created the *DARK TOWER CONCORDANCE*, which gives detailed entries about all the characters, places, languages, etc. that appear in the novels. Because of this, I knew the books as well as Steve did, so when Marvel Comics decided to adapt the series to comics, Steve wanted me to be involved. Originally I was only going to be a consultant, but I ended up plotting the stories as well. Since then, I've had the chance to plot and script a variety of comics, and to work with really wonderful artists.

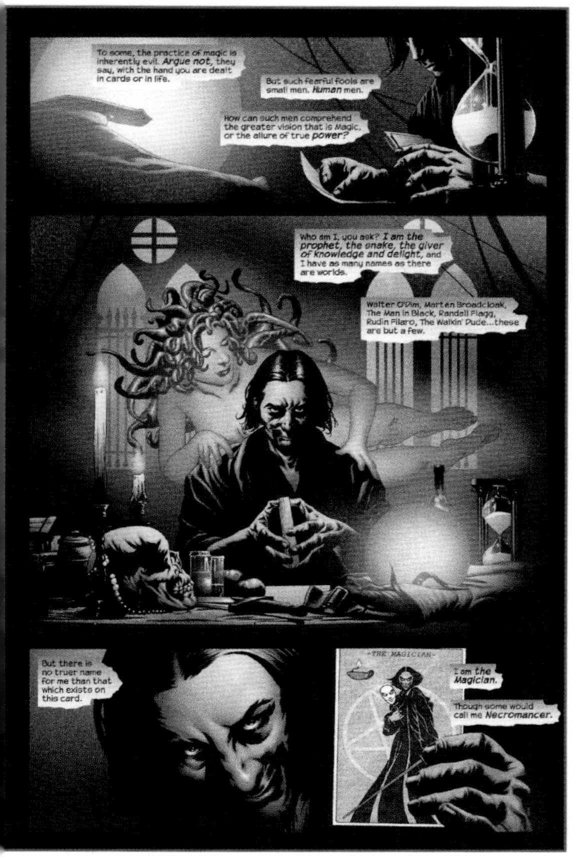
To some, the practice of magic is inherently evil. *Argue not*, they say, with the hand you are dealt in cards or in life.
But such fearful fools are small men. *Human* men.
How can such men comprehend the greater vision that is *Magic*, or the allure of true *power?*
Who am I, you ask? *I am the prophet, the snake, the giver of knowledge and delight,* and I have as many names as there are worlds.
Walter O'Dim, Marten Broadcloak, The Man in Black, Randall Flagg, Rudin Filaro, The Walkin' Dude...these are but a few.
But there is no truer name for me than that which exists on this card.
-THE MAGICIAN-
I am *the Magician.*
Though some would call me *Necromancer.*

When I first started working in comics the learning curve was VERY steep, but everybody involved was incredibly helpful. At first I was extremely self-conscious because I came from a literary background, not a comic book background, but Ralph Macchio (one of the senior editors at Marvel) was really supportive. He told me that my background would bring something new to the stories. I can only hope that it has. I have had the wonderful luck to co-write with Peter David, and to work with fantastically talented artists. Being Stephen King's representative helped me incredibly, and I will always be in Steve's debt.

What's the best advice you've heard about working as a writer or artist? Is there any advice you'd give to an aspiring creator?

A good editor is worth his or her weight in gold. She can see aspects of your story that you can't see, since you are too close to it. Ralph Macchio once told me not to look at reviews, since bad reviews are really devastating. In my experience, one bad review can outweigh five good reviews! Sometimes it takes readers a little while to know where you are coming from. What you do is new, so it might take a little while to find an audience. And finally, meet other comic book writers and artists. Pair up, talk about the work. Support each other. Collaboration is a magical experience. Whenever I hand a script to an artist, I am amazed by the beauty of what they create. It's like two imaginations work together to create this fantastic new piece. It is fantastic!

How did researching for Stephen King strengthen your work as a writer?

Watching Steve King work is absolutely amazing. I would often get early drafts of the *Dark Tower* novels, and those manuscripts were CLEAN! The writing was beautiful and the characterization and setting was complete. He did some revisions, but the stories flowed right out of him. I don't think many writers can do that.

What is your favorite food?

Beetroot pesto, basil pesto, Thai food. I'm vegetarian, so I love fruit and veg!

What is your favorite thing to do in your spare time?

I love to write, read, dream, and to spend time with my husband Mark!

What's an interesting/funny fact about yourself?

I've lived for ten years in Mid-World!

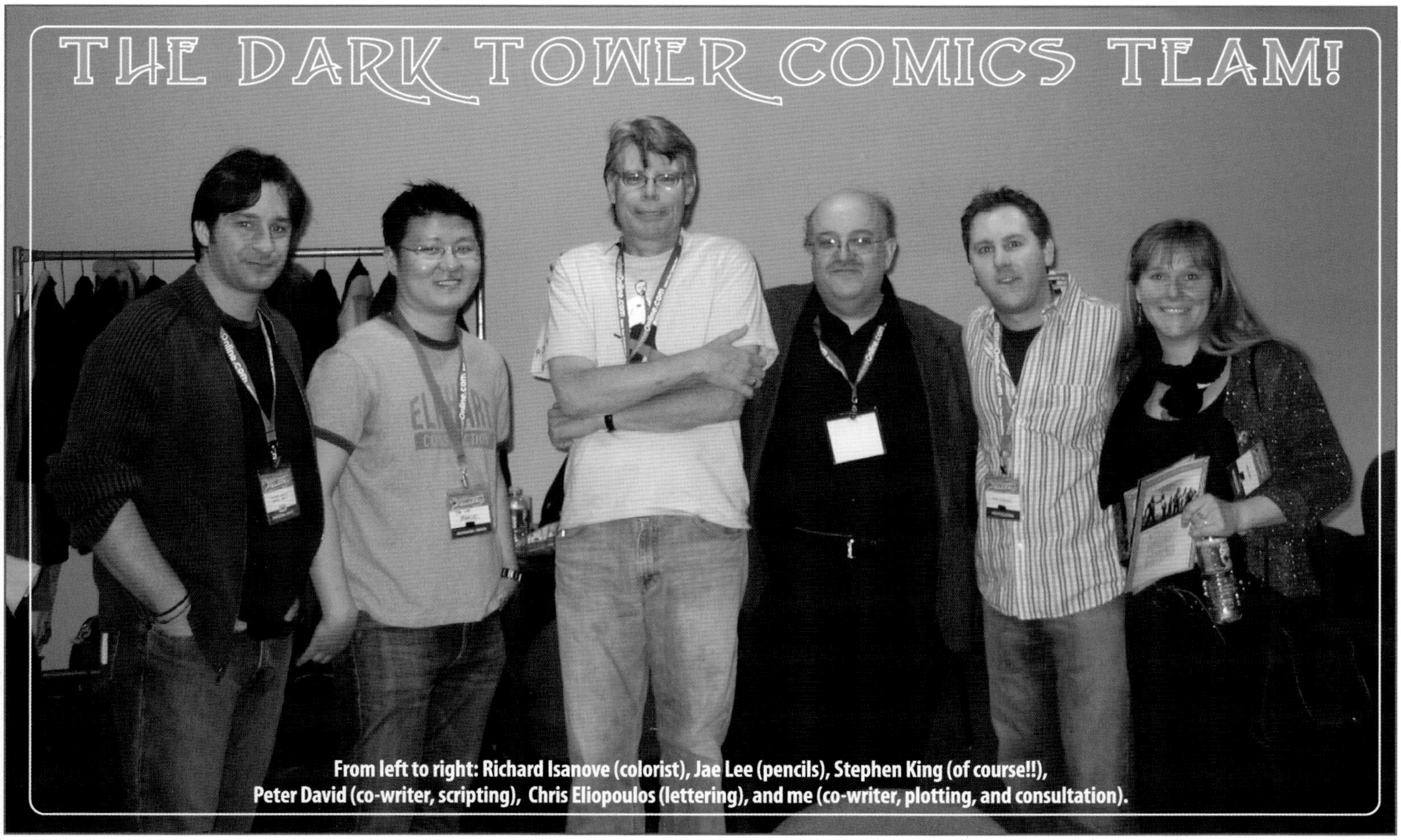
THE DARK TOWER COMICS TEAM!

From left to right: Richard Isanove (colorist), Jae Lee (pencils), Stephen King (of course!!), Peter David (co-writer, scripting), Chris Eliopoulos (lettering), and me (co-writer, plotting, and consultation).

☆ ☆ ☆ CREATOR INTERVIEW ☆ ☆ ☆

WENDY PINI

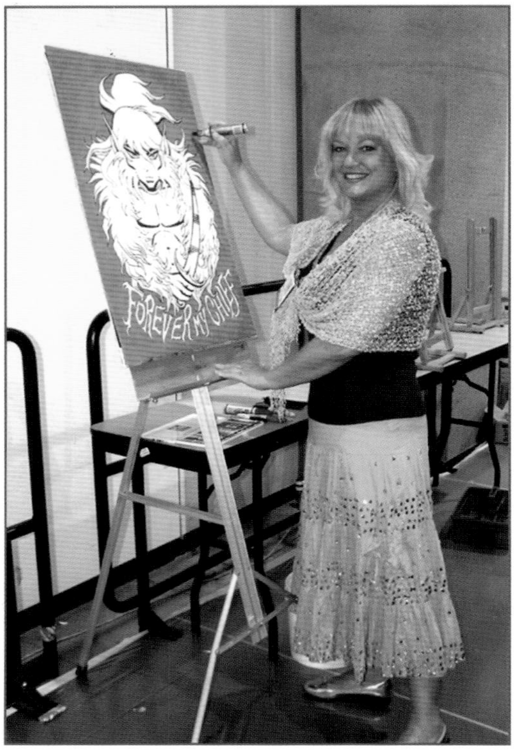

Considering your experiences with self-publishing, would you recommend it to any up-and-coming creators? Why or why not?

My experiences in self-publishing, good and bad, are something I wouldn't trade for the world. It's been a long journey…more than three decades. *Elfquest*, along with *Cerebus the Aardvark*, *Star Reach*, and a couple of other bw titles, started the Independent Comics Movement back in the mid '70s. When Richard and I began the quest it was practically an open playing field. The time was right for an epic fantasy saga like *Elfquest* and, no matter the mistakes we made as tyro publishers, it seemed nothing could get in the way of the elves' success. Which only proves timing is everything. In 2011, conditions are extremely different. The stars will never align for independent publishing like that again.

That said, there's a bright spot for visionary women creators who aren't attracted to the idea of working for the mainstream or even smaller established comics companies: the Internet. On the web, as I type, there is an exuberant spirit, much like in the mid '70s, fueling tons of new comics material by independent artists and writers. It's a fantastic, instant-gratification way to get your work out there—in full color, if you want—and seen by the masses. With the print publishing industry in total turmoil and the sales of regular comics still dropping, opportunities in that arena are scarce and the competition is fierce—I mean piranha fierce!

Some words of caution, though: self-publishing on the Internet takes technical know-how. You need to network with experienced others to learn the ropes. And only a very few web comics manage to turn a profit. In the end, to make any kind of a living, you have to find a regular publisher who will get it out there as a graphic novel—or do it yourself.

What are some of the more common weaknesses in comic storylines today and how can new creators avoid them?

What a great question! Generally speaking, I think anything goes. Tried-and-true storytelling rules have broken down in the larger media, producing incredibly mediocre pop mythology—a lot by women!—that, nevertheless, makes billions (witness *Twilight*). So who's to say what works and doesn't work anymore? Some years ago I used to be highly critical of what I perceived as sloppy, pointless, trite and overblown writing in comics—mostly in the superhero genre. But having occasionally been accused of those crimes myself, I know that all criticism is subjective and whatever works for the fans works, regardless of its relative merit.

What I would say to today's young women storytellers who want to break into comics is: whatever genre you choose, fantasy, horror, humor, social commentary, erotica, etc., your story needs a point of view and it needs structure. Above all, solid structure is what seems to elude many aspiring female creators in both their artwork and writing. Telling a tale with a proper beginning, middle, and end—in other words following the steps of the classic Hero's Journey—requires focus. For a main character to go through an arc that rewards an audience's participation and interest, there has to be some semblance of purpose…some transformation realized by journey's end.

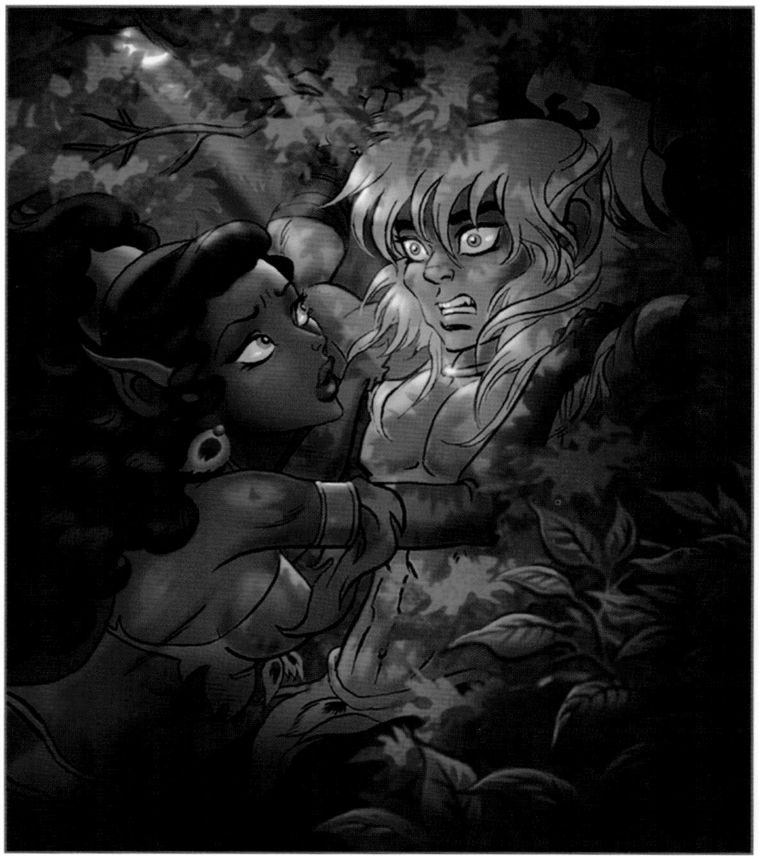

What is the best advice you've ever heard, concerning working in comics, and what is the best advice you would personally give to an aspiring creator/ someone who wants to work in comics?

This isn't something I heard…it's just something I know. If there's a story inside you that wants to come out, find a way to tell it, no matter how many hills you have to climb or how many doors you have to beat down. If you're a comics writer who can't draw, pore over the offerings at websites such as DeviantArt or haunt the corridors of art schools and make a connection. Don't give up, because good stories are pan-cultural, bringing humankind together in one spirit. Good stories heal and transform people's lives, release laughter and tears, and inspire growth. You are very lucky, indeed, if you have a story inside you (and most people do). Don't ever make the mistake of thinking it's trivial and unimportant and that you're not worthy of being heard. Just find a way to tell your tale as you want to tell it and watch what happens.

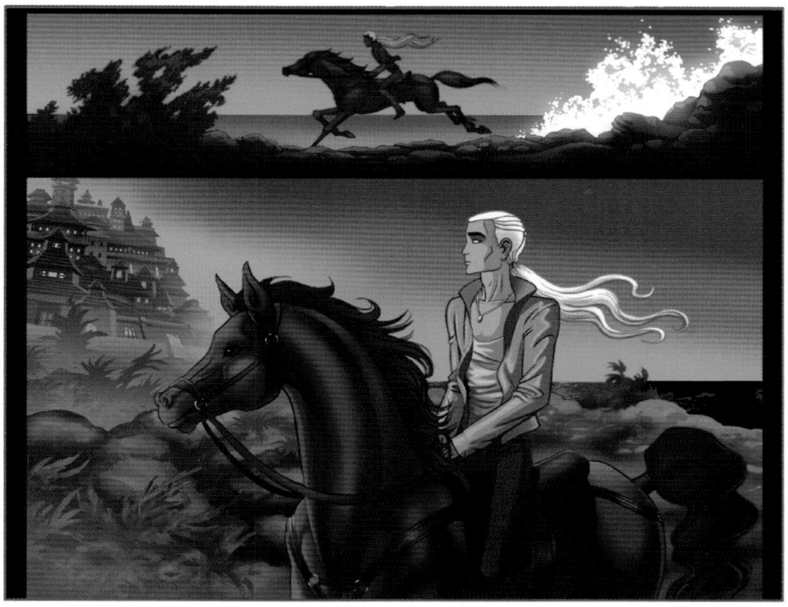

How did you discover comics, and when (and why) did you start taking comics seriously as a career choice?

From *Sequential Tart* Interview by Dani Fletcher, 2001: Comics have always been part of my life in one form or another, just as the ability to create in different mediums always has. As a very little girl, I used to love reading *Casper* and *Wendy the Good Little Witch* and practice drawing the characters. In grade school I graduated to *Superboy* and went on to collect certain Marvel comics in high school.

Was I an avid comics fan for comics' sake? No. To me, they were movies on paper—my imagination filled in the movement that was missing. My real childhood passion was for animation, from Disney to Hanna Barbera to Warner Bros. I thought nothing could top them. Then, at age ten, I discovered anime in the form of Osamu Tezuka's *Astro Boy*, *Kimba the White Lion*, *Marine Boy* and *Speed Racer* and full-length features like *Alakazam the Great*, *Magic Boy* and *The Littlest Warrior* taught me a new way to think of animation as a medium for darkly dramatic, emotionally powerful storytelling. That changed my attitude toward comics as well.

I loved the sense of "otherness" achieved by manga artists. Their heroes, heroines, and, frequently, their villains have an idealized, mask-like, androgynous beauty—much like elves. Almost all manga artists, men and women, have a strong feminine sensibility in their work. It shows up in their eloquent use of line. Entertainment laced with sexual ambiguity goes way, way back in oriental culture. I still find it mysterious and compelling. (Note: *Elfquest* actually has the distinction of being the first ongoing anime/manga-influenced comic series in America.)

What's an interesting/funny fact about yourself?

Well, I'm very good at writing and drawing credible male characters. It's my forte. The way I get into it, particularly for *Elfquest*, which is full of action characters, is to act out the parts physically. In other words, if I'm doing a scene for Cutter, I warm up by standing the way he stands with chest thrust out and feet firmly planted. Then I throw a few punches or pretend to sweep a sword around, just to feel what it's like to be in his powerful, little body. I've done this in the privacy of my own studio for as long as I can remember and I'm still doing it at age 60 as I work on *Elfquest: The Final Quest*. Fortunately, Richard has yet to catch me on film.

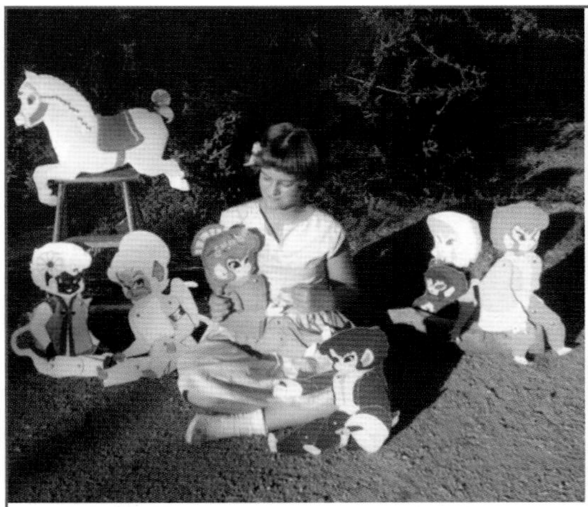

WENDY FLETCHER CIRCA 1963 WITH HANDMADE CARDBOARD MONKEY TRIBE INSPIRED BY DIRECTOR OSAMU TEZUKA'S "ALAKAZAM THE GREAT."

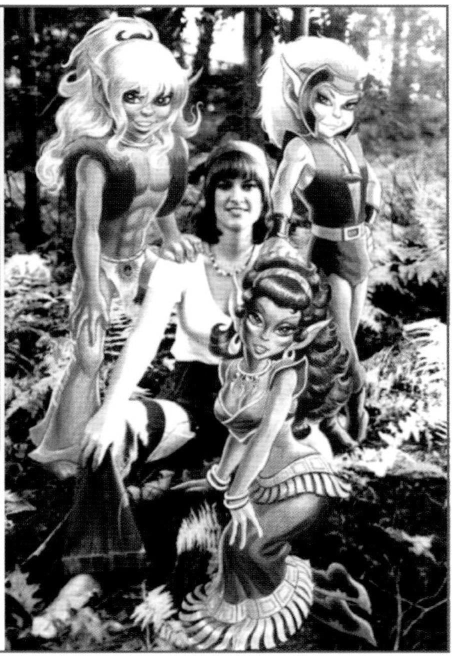

WENDY PINI 1979 WITH ELFQUEST'S CUTTER, LEETAH AND SKYWISE -- SOME THINGS NEVER CHANGE.

What is your favorite thing to do in your spare time?

I love to take drives to nowhere with Richard and our pomeranian Angel. Maybe we have a destination in mind, maybe not. Just being free and loose with no obligations, for a while, is a great way to recharge.

What is your favorite food?

Sushi...specifically a magnificently prepared bowl of chirashi sushi. Heaven!

☆ ☆ ☆ CREATOR INTERVIEW ☆ ☆ ☆

POSY SIMMONDS

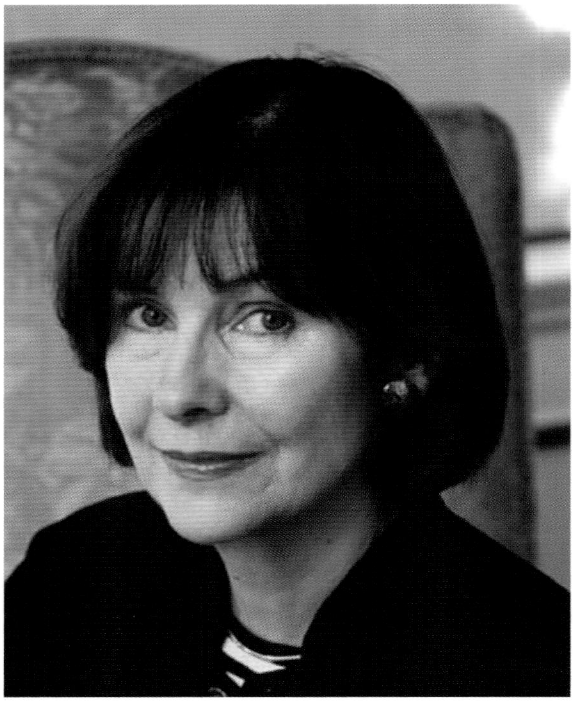

How did you discover comics, and when (and why) did you start taking comics seriously as a career choice?

I had English comics as a child (e.g., *Beano, Dandy, Eagle*), and also US comics, which American children living in the village would pass on to me (e.g., *Superman, Sad Sack, Blondie & Dagwood, Casper The Ghost, Little Nancy*). A madeleine took Proust on a nostalgic journey—for me, it would be the smell of an inky American comic from the 1950s.

From the age of eight I made my own comics, but my ambition was to go to art school and become a painter. Then I went to art school and discovered I much preferred the combination of words and pictures.

How and when did you first "break in" to comics?

When I left art college, work began slowly—the odd drawing/cartoon here and there (*The Times, New Society, Reader's Digest*). In 1969 I began doing a daily panel for *The Sun* and then moved to *The Guardian*, where I illustrated articles, or wherever a drawing was needed. These drawings were usually done at speed to meet a 4 pm deadline. The big break came in 1977, when the paper asked me to do a weekly strip for their Women's page. It was a biggish space (270mm x 190mm) and the strip ran until 1987, when I wanted a change.

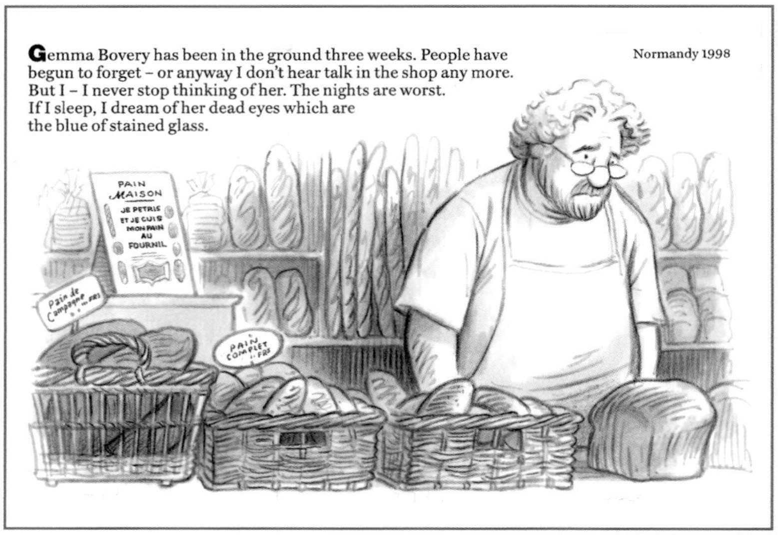
Gemma Bovery has been in the ground three weeks. People have begun to forget – or anyway I don't hear talk in the shop any more. But I – I never stop thinking of her. The nights are worst. If I sleep, I dream of her dead eyes which are the blue of stained glass.
Normandy 1998
PAIN MAISON
JE PETRIS ET JE CUIS MON PAIN AU FOURNIL
Pain de Campagne
PAIN COMPLET

What's been your most satisfying work?

Probably *Gemma Bovery*, because it was difficult and the research and planning were so lengthy. The story appeared in *The Guardian* in daily episodes. The serial was half-completed when it started running, and towards the end I was only three or four episodes ahead, making for a hair-raising ride. But there was something about being on this live, hatching thing, which stimulated the imagination like nothing else I know.

What do you think is distinct about the UK's comics and cartooning culture, as compared with traditions in continental Europe and the US?

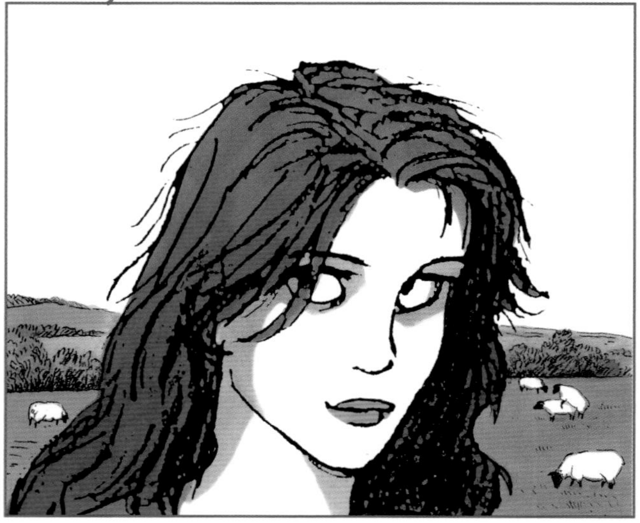

Having always worked for newspapers, I only met the comic world relatively recently. Britain has certainly lagged behind France and Belgium, but for more than a decade there's been a huge explosion over here, of interest and production of every genre of comic. Bande Dessinée isn't the 9th Art here, as it is in France....but, who knows, it may yet happen.

When I grew up in the 1950s, comics were thought to be for children, things you were supposed to grow out of. Adults had cartoons, political or funny, in newspapers and magazines like *Punch* and *Private Eye*. One of Britain's strengths has been its tradition of political cartoons, from the 18th century onwards; artists like Hogarth, Rowlandson, Cruikshank, and Gillray were among my heroes when growing up. Still are.

What's the best advice you've heard about working as a writer or artist? Is there any advice you'd give to an aspiring creator?

Carry a notebook. Draw every day. Write every day.

WOMEN of the PAST

☆☆☆

LIFE STORIES
AND ARTWORK BY
THE WOMEN OF
COMICS HISTORY!

EDITED BY LAURA MORLEY

☆ ☆ ☆ WOMEN OF THE PAST! ☆ ☆ ☆

TARPE MILLS

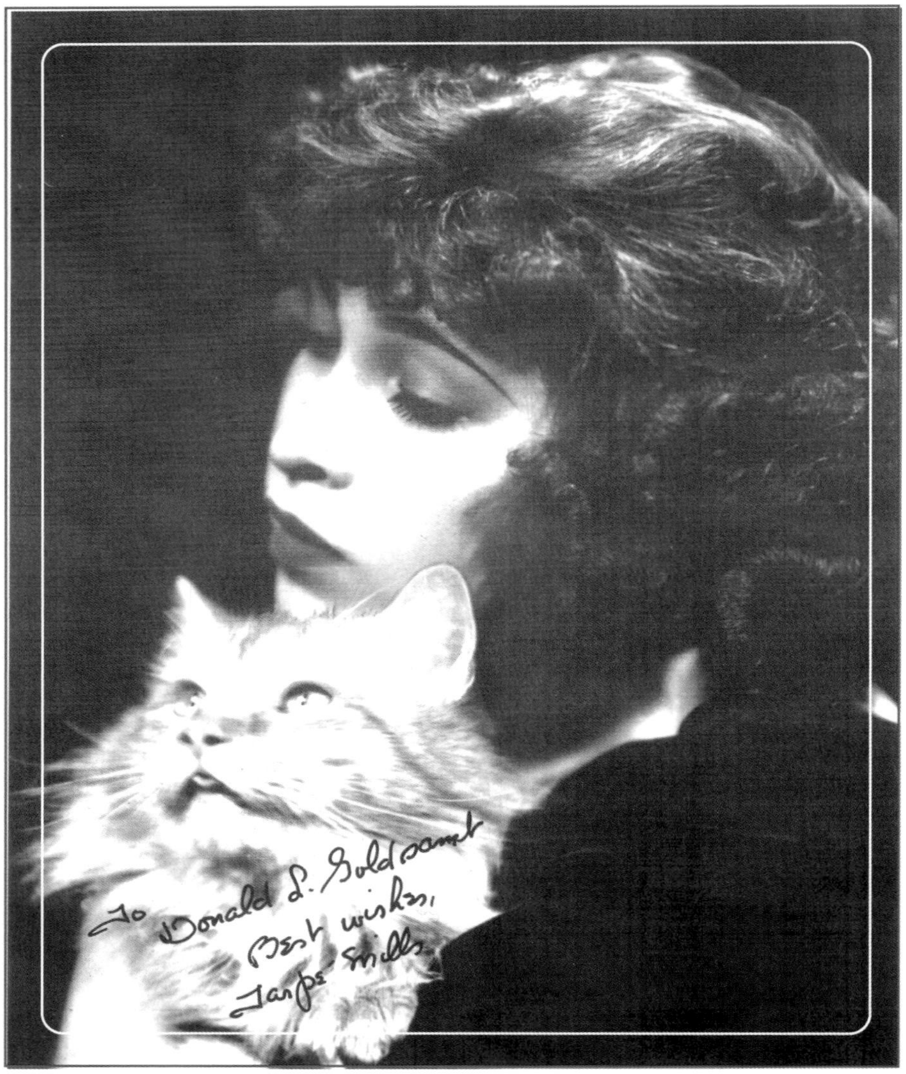
To Donald
Best wishes,
Tarpe Mills

Tarpe Mills and Miss Fury

By Trina Robbins ©2011

June Tarpe Mills (1912-1988) had already been contributing to comic books for a few years with comics the likes of *The Purple Zombie* and *Daredevil Barry Finn* when in 1941, beating *Wonder Woman* to the punch by six months, she debuted *Miss Fury*, the first major costumed action heroine in comics, in the pages of America's newspapers. Originally a sculpture major at Pratt Institute, she had turned to comics while temporarily laid low with a foot injury. In an interview, Mills said that she had changed her first name to the more sexually ambiguous family name, Tarpe, when drawing for comic books, because "It would have been a major let-down to the kids if they found out that the author of such virile and awesome characters was a gal."

But once her newspaper strip debuted, the secret was out. Newspaper artcles with such titles as "Meet the Real Miss Fury—It's All Done With Mirrors," pointed out that not only was Tarpe Mills a woman, but that she had based her comic strip heroine's looks on her own.

Not only did Mills put herself into the strip as Miss Fury, she also put in her own white Persian cat, Peri-Purr, giving the heroine a white Persian cat of the same name. Peri-Purr is not just another pretty face, either. Twice he saves the heroine by jumping on a guy who's about to shoot her, and in one story arc, when the heroine is kidnapped and a double takes her place, everyone—even the heroine's boyfriend—is fooled, except Peri-Purr, who knows with his cat second sense that this stranger is not his beloved mistress. He follows the imposter around the house, hissing and spitting at her.

Throughout the 1940s newspaper comics pages featured film noiresque strips such as *Johnny Hazard*, *Kerry Drake*, and *Bruce Gentry*, all influenced by Milton Caniff's *Terry and the Pirates*, starring hard-boiled heroes who usually fought bad guys from the Axis, but of that genre only *Miss Fury* was created by a woman. And the strip's hero is Marla, not Johnny or Kerry or Bruce. While the women in those other strips usually exist as decoration or victims to be rescued by the hero, Marla, though just as decorative, could take care of herself in a tight spot. In the page before you, Marla had been kidnapped and a double had taken her place. Here Marla has escaped and confronts her double on one of the pages that have inspired me to dub Tarpe Mills "Queen of the Cat Fights."

As her alter ego, Miss Fury, Marla Drake wore a form-fitting panther skin, but she just as often had her adventures while wearing the stylish fashions of the 1940s.

Just as intriguing as the strip's heroine are some of the best villains in comics, and on the other page you can meet Marla's nemesis, the Baroness Erica Von Kampf, the villainess you love to hate. (In a 1944 interview, Mills said that at one time the Baroness pulled in more fan mail than the heroine.) On this rather risqué page (Can you imagine a strip like this in today's newspapers?) the Baroness fills the reader in on the strip's past: she had stolen Marla's weak-willed fiancé and tricked him into a marriage which he annulled upon learning of her Nazi affiliations. But he never learned that he had a son! Later in this story arc, Marla rescues the boy from a mad scientist and adopts him, never knowing he is the child of her ex-fiancé and the Baroness. Wow!

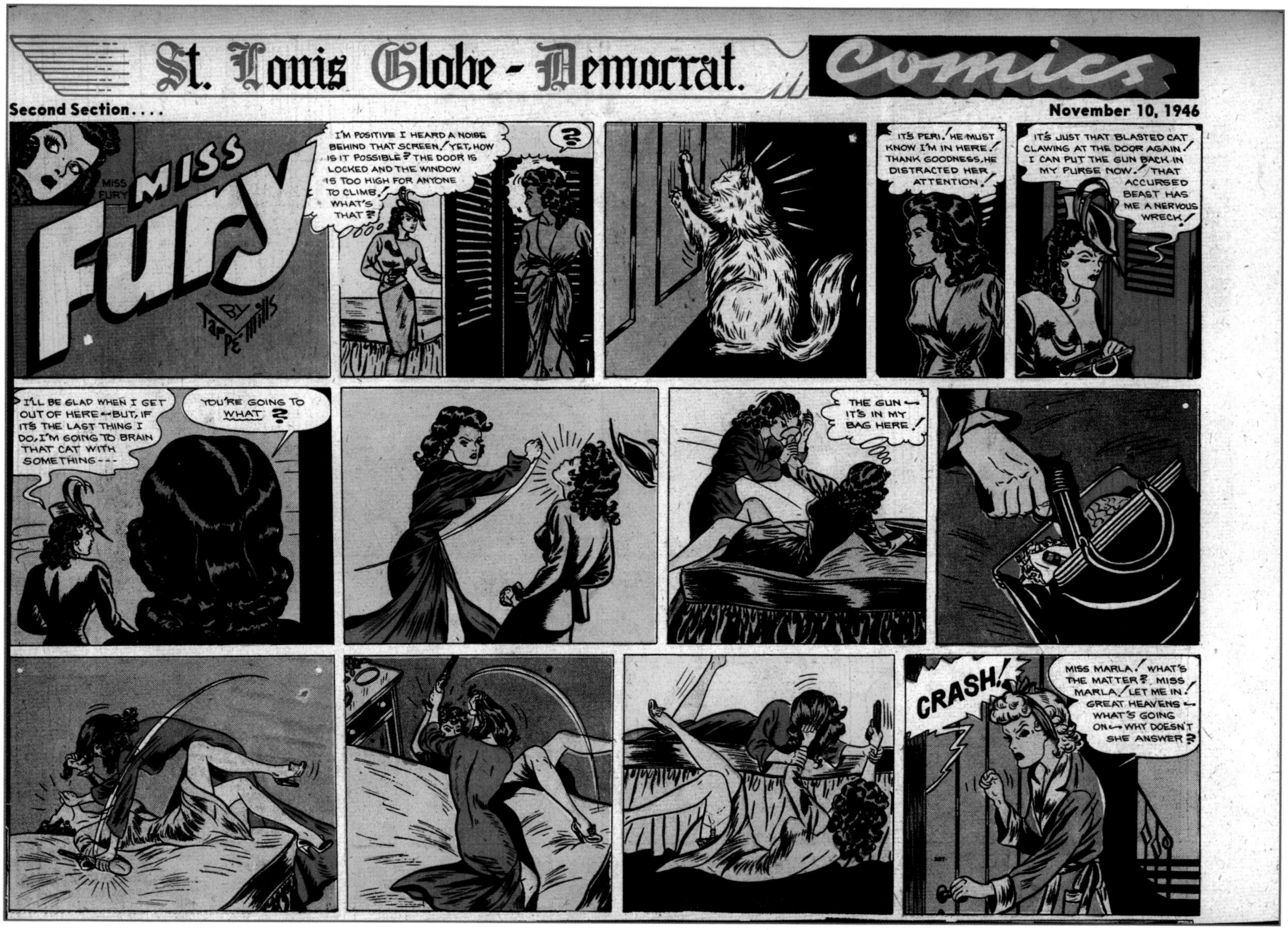
St. Louis Globe-Democrat.
Comics
Second Section....
November 10, 1946
MISS FURY
BY TARPE MILLS
I'M POSITIVE I HEARD A NOISE BEHIND THAT SCREEN! YET, HOW IS IT POSSIBLE? THE DOOR IS LOCKED AND THE WINDOW IS TOO HIGH FOR ANYONE TO CLIMB! WHAT'S THAT?
?
IT'S PERI! HE MUST KNOW I'M IN HERE! THANK GOODNESS, HE DISTRACTED HER ATTENTION!
IT'S JUST THAT BLASTED CAT CLAWING AT THE DOOR AGAIN! I CAN PUT THE GUN BACK IN MY PURSE NOW! THAT ACCURSED BEAST HAS ME A NERVOUS WRECK!
I'LL BE GLAD WHEN I GET OUT OF HERE—BUT, IF IT'S THE LAST THING I DO, I'M GOING TO BRAIN THAT CAT WITH SOMETHING---
YOU'RE GOING TO WHAT?
THE GUN— IT'S IN MY BAG HERE!
CRASH!
MISS MARLA! WHAT'S THE MATTER? MISS MARLA! LET ME IN! GREAT HEAVENS— WHAT'S GOING ON— WHY DOESN'T SHE ANSWER?

☆ ☆ ☆ WOMEN OF THE PAST! ☆ ☆ ☆

NELL BRINKLEY

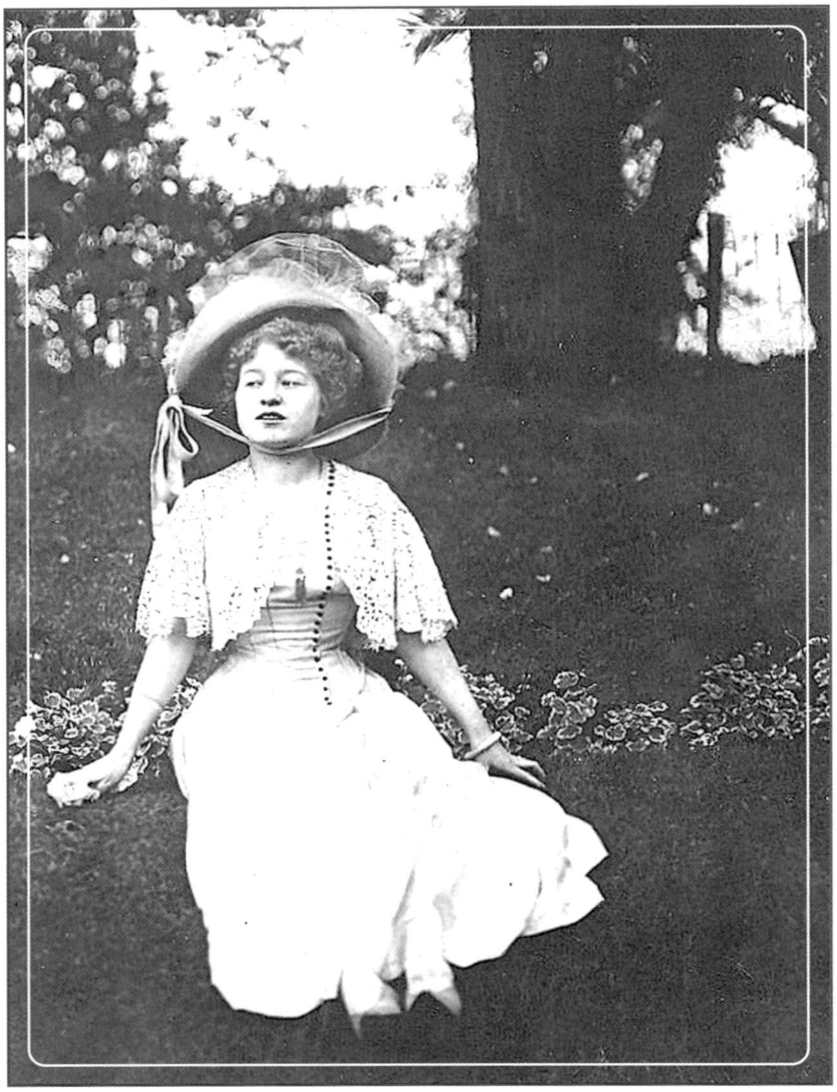

Nell Brinkley

By Trina Robbins ©2011

Nell Brinkley (1886-1944) arrived in New York in 1907 at the tender age of 21, to draw for the Hearst newspaper syndicate.

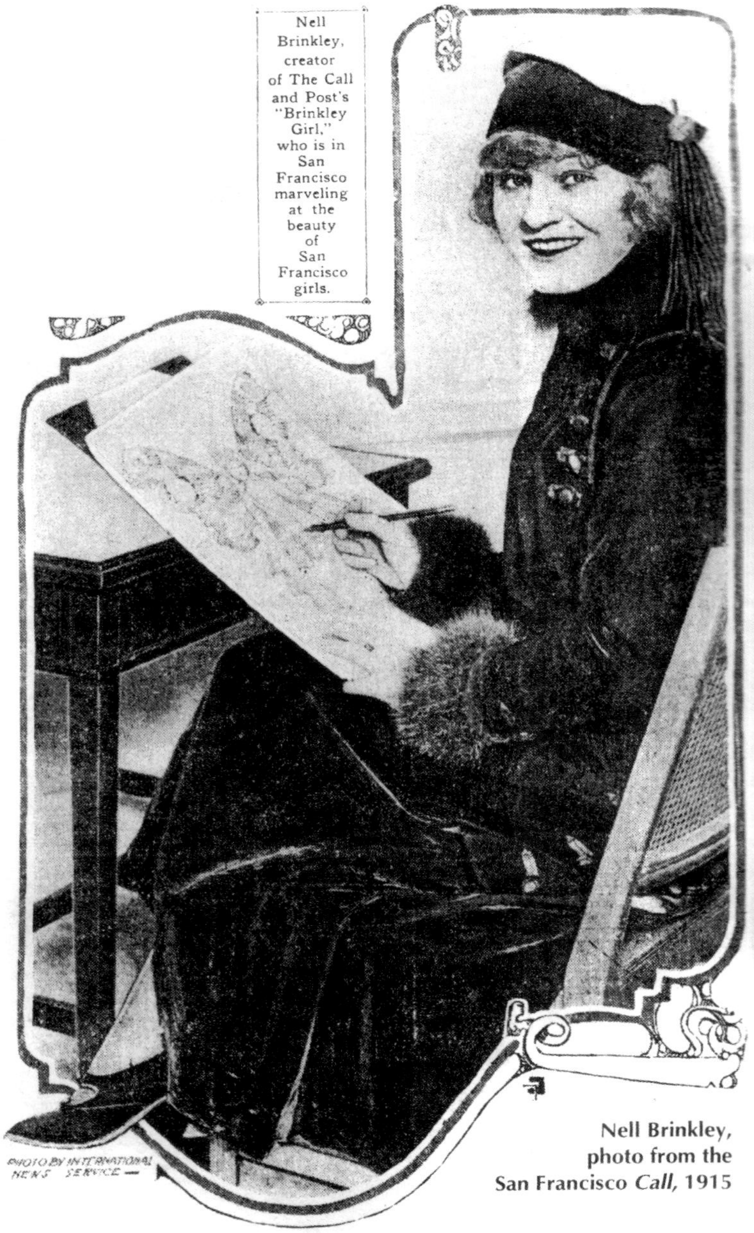
Nell Brinkley, creator of The Call and Post's "Brinkley Girl," who is in San Francisco marveling at the beauty of San Francisco girls.
PHOTO BY INTERNATIONAL NEWS SERVICE

Nell Brinkley, photo from the San Francisco *Call*, 1915

It didn't take long for her delicately drawn art nouveau "Brinkley Girls" to catch on, and soon she and her stylish girls were the subject of popular songs, and her daily and Sunday pages were being saved and collected by countless fans, most of them young women.

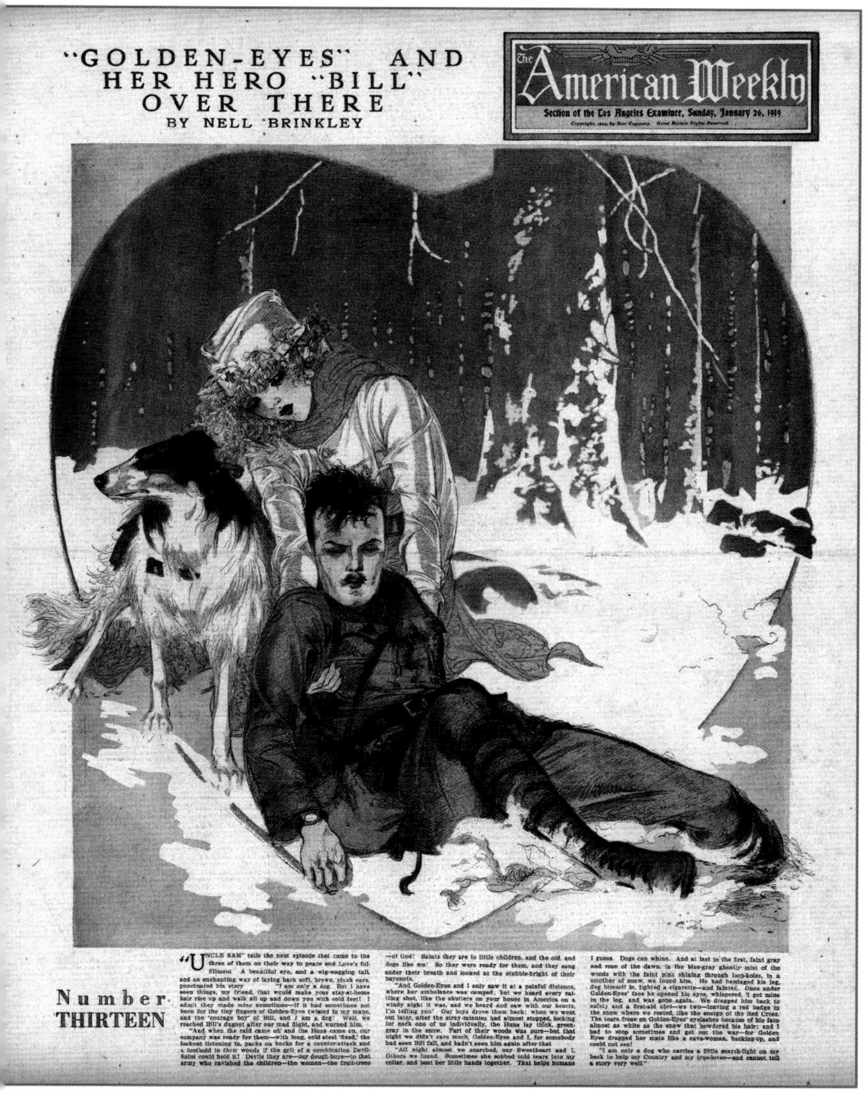

"GOLDEN-EYES" AND HER HERO "BILL" OVER THERE
BY NELL BRINKLEY
The American Weekly
Section of the Los Angeles Examiner, Sunday, January 26, 1919
Number THIRTEEN
"UNCLE SAM" tells the next episode that came to the three of them on their way to peace and Love's fulfillment A beautiful eye, and a wig-wagging tail, and an enchanting way of laying back soft, brown, plush ears, punctuated his story "I am only a dog. But I have seen things, my friend, that would make your stay-at-home hair rise up and walk all up and down you with cold feet! I admit they made mine sometimes—if it had sometimes not been for the tiny fingers of Golden-Eyes twisted in my mane, and the 'courage boy' of Bill, and I am a dog! Well, we reached Bill's dugout after our mad flight, and warned him.
"And when the raid came off and the Huns came on, our company was ready for them—with long, cold steel 'fixed,' the lookout listening in, packs on backs for a counter-attack and a foothold in their woods if the grit of a combination Devil-Saint could hold it! Devils they are—our dough-boys—to that army who ravished the children—the women—the fruit-trees—of God! Saints they are to little children, and the old, and dogs like me! So they were ready for them, and they sang under their breath and looked at the stubble-bright of their bayonets.
"And Golden-Eyes and I only saw it at a painful distance, where her ambulance was camped; but we heard every rattling shot, like the shutters on your house in America on a windy night it was, and we heard and saw with our hearts, I'm telling you! Our boys drove them back; when we went out later, after the stray-minnies had almost stopped, looking for each one of us individually, the Huns lay thick, green-gray in the snow. Part of their woods was ours—but that night we didn't care much, Golden-Eyes and I, for somebody had seen Bill fall, and hadn't seen him again after that
"All night almost we searched, our Sweetheart and I. Others we found. Sometimes she sobbed cold tears into my collar, and beat her little hands together. That helps humans I guess. Dogs can whine. And at last in the first, faint gray and rose of the dawn, in the blue-gray ghostly mist of the woods with the faint pink shining through loop-holes, in a smother of snow, we found him. He had bandaged his leg, dug himself in, lighted a cigarette—and fainted. Once under Golden-Eyes' face he opened his eyes, whispered, 'I got mine in the leg, and was gone again. We dragged him back to safety and a first-aid shri—we two—leaving a red badge in the snow where we rested, like the ensign of the Red Cross. The tears froze on Golden-Eyes' eyelashes because of his face almost as white as the snow that powdered his hair; and I had to stop sometimes and get out the way—for Golden Eyes dragged her mate like a cave-woman, backing-up, and could not see!
"I am only a dog who carries a little search-light on my back to help my Country and my true-loves—and cannot tell a story very well."

She even sold product; you could buy Nell Brinkley Hair Curlers for ten cents a card!

Nell was compared to Charles Dana Gibson and his popular "Gibson Girls," but her serialized stories and later proto-comics often exhibited an early feminism that was completely lacking in Gibson's bland and passive girls. In her first serialized drama, *Golden Eyes and her hero, Bill,* drawn during World War I, Golden Eyes, with the aid of her plucky collie, "Uncle Sam," finds her boyfriend wounded on the field of battle and drags him to safety.

By the 1920s, Nell was drawing an early form of comics, though without panel borders or speech balloons. In her 1928 *Dimples' Day Dreams*, Dimples imagines herself running for President of the United States, dressed in a to-die-for pant-suit. "Why not even be president?" she thinks, "A gal where Cal (Coolidge) is now!"

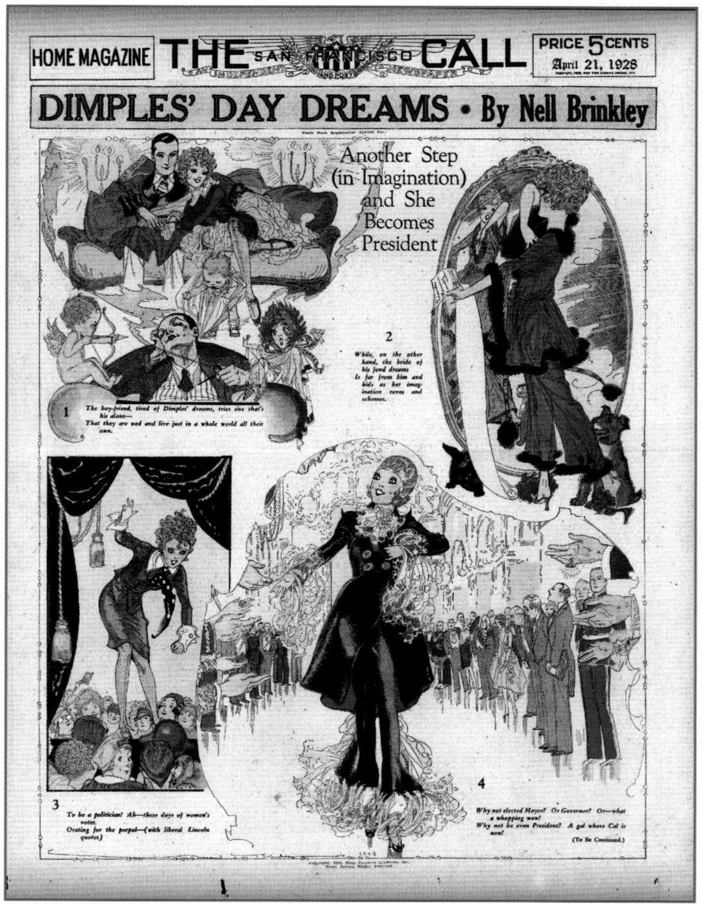

HOME MAGAZINE
THE SAN FRANCISCO CALL
PRICE 5 CENTS
April 21, 1928
DIMPLES' DAY DREAMS • By Nell Brinkley
Another Step (in Imagination) and She Becomes President
1
The boy-friend, tired of Dimples' dreams, tries one that's his alone—
That they are wed and live just in a whole world all their own.
2
While, on the other hand, the bride of his fond dreams
Is far from him and kids as her imagination roves and schemes.
3
To be a politician! Ah—these days of women's votes.
Orating for the peepul—(with liberal Lincoln quotes)
4
Why not elected Mayor? Or Governor? Or—what a whopping wow!
Why not be even President? A gal where Cal is now!
(To Be Continued.)

☆ ☆ ☆ WOMEN OF THE PAST! ☆ ☆ ☆

ROSE O'NEILL

By Colleen Doran ©2011

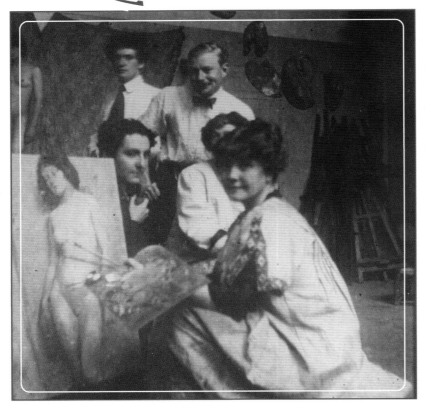

Rose O'Neill is largely ignored by modern histories of comics. However, Rose O'Neill is distinguished not only for her incredible body of work, and the multi-million-dollar franchise she created around it, her accomplishments are made even more remarkable as she did it all before women had the right to vote.

Born in 1874 in Wilkes Barre, Pennsylvania, Rose was a beautiful, precocious girl. She spent many hours teaching herself to draw by copying masterpiece engravings. Her good looks, outgoing personality, and intelligence won for her a brief stage career as a child actress.

At the age of 14, she entered an art contest sponsored by the *Omaha World Herald*. Her drawing skills were so advanced that the judges were unable to believe the winning entry was the work of a girl with no formal training. She was required to demonstrate her skills in the judge's presence before they awarded her first prize. Rose, who had not entirely enjoyed her foray onto the stage, now turned her entire attention to art.

In a few short years, Rose was a full-time professional illustrator with clients nationwide. At eighteen, she was on her way to New York. Rose roomed with the Sisters of St. Regis, who accompanied her on professional forays. She scored assignments with many major publications, including *Life Magazine*, *Harper's Bazaar*, and *Colliers*.

In addition to commercial illustration, Rose drew many clever and beautiful cartoons satirizing family life, fashionable girls, and social foibles in a beaux arts style that reflected the graphic sensibilities of European poster art. Eventually, she was hired to be the first woman staff artist at prestigious *Puck* magazine.

In 1896, she married movie-idol-handsome Gray Latham who, together with his brother and father, invented early film technology, created the first public showing of film on a screen, and shot groundbreaking movie footage of extended action scenes. However, the Latham family's fortunes were diminished in a lengthy court battle with the voracious, invention-claim-jumping Thomas Edison. Gray exploited popular, wage-earning Rose, often showing up at her publishers to collect her money and run off with it before she could. The marriage ended in an acrimonious divorce.

PUCK
O'Neill

EVIDENTLY.

THE AMATEUR.—Sometimes I think I have artistic talent and sometimes I think not.
HER FRIEND.—Well—er—you can't be mistaken all the time!

Rose was deeply troubled by the split, but rebounded by marrying her colleague at *Puck*, the distinguished literary editor Harry Leon. While this marriage wasn't a particularly happy one either, it heralded a highly successful creative period for O'Neill. She wrote and illustrated novels, and was elected to the Paris Societe des Beaux Arts, where she enjoyed the first European exhibit of her art.

PUCK

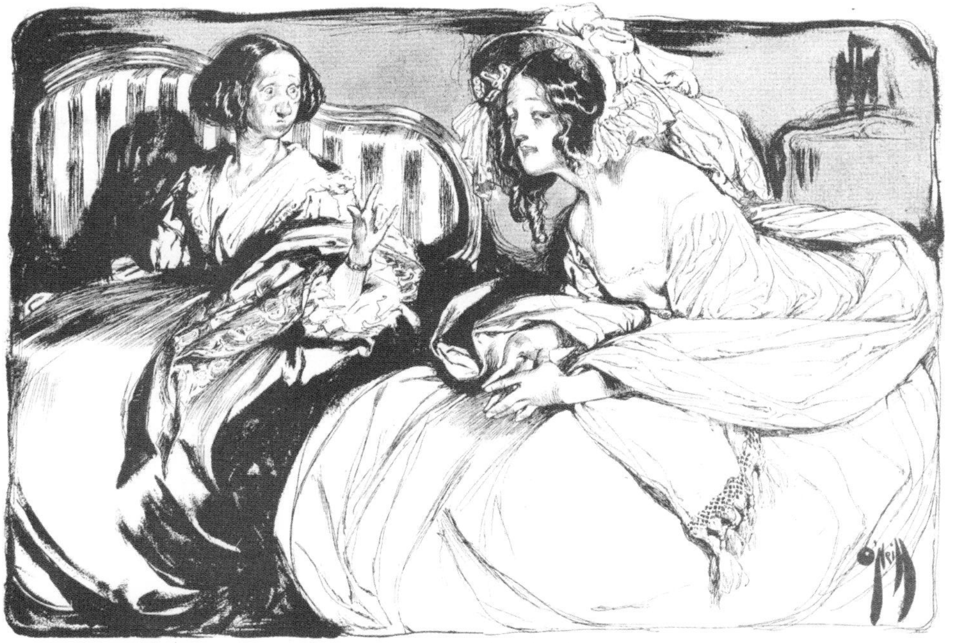

O'Neill

AT A DISADVANTAGE.

"If you 'd let *me* advise you in this love affair —"
"Well, you see, Auntie, though you 're a good deal older than I am, you have n't had so much experience."

Rose divorced her sullen, serious husband, and went on to create the Kewpies in 1909. Exuberant, cuddly, and bubbly like Rose herself, the babyish, cupid-like characters were a worldwide sensation. Appearing in *The Ladies Home Journal, Good Housekeeping,* and *Women's Home Companion* for nearly three decades, the Kewpies spawned a multi-million-dollar merchandising empire that made Rose O'Neill one of the wealthiest artists in the world.

The Kewpies gave the extravagant Rose the ability to live as extravagantly as her imagination allowed. She acquired multiple homes from Capri to Connecticut, gifting the Mediterranean villa to painter Charles Caryl Coleman. Rose O'Neill was the primary support for her extended family, and provided for them amply, financing their large Ozark, Missouri, home, Bonniebrook. She socialized with prominent artists and writers such as Thomas Hart Benton, James Montgomery Flagg, and Booth Tarkington.

She was strongly supported in her fine arts aspirations by sculptor Auguste Rodin, who was deeply impressed by the body of her personal work, the "Sweet Monsters." The strange, mysterious, almost primordial drawings are sensual and mythic in nature, a great—and some thought, shocking—departure from her popular Kewpies. "Sweet Monsters" were exhibited to great reviews in 1921 at the Galerie Devambez in Paris, and at the Wildenstein Gallery in New York the following year.

O'Neill was also a prominent suffragette, who lent the images of her cartoon Kewpies to the movement, winged babies marching with banners that read "Votes for Our Mothers." Together with her sister Callista, Rose appeared in public rallies. Both women adopted modern, loose garb and eschewed the constraining corset fashions of the day. To *The New York Press* in 1915, she said: "The first step is to free women from the yoke of modern fashions and modern dress. How can they hope to compete with men when they are boxed up tight in the clothes that are worn today?"

O'Neill lent her art to many worthy charities such as The Red Cross and The National Tuberculosis Society. She worked tirelessly on numerous committees for social causes.

She was a workaholic, driven to express herself as a writer, sculptor, cartoonist, poet, never resting even after she accumulated her millions.

However, Rose O'Neill's lavish living and extremely generous nature eventually drained her financial resources. The Great Depression's descent in 1930s America killed the Kewpie money machine. O'Neill faced ruin. In a magazine market that turned to photographs, many prominent illustrators found work difficult to secure. Rose was forced to sell most of her property.

Unfortunate timing struck her next venture: she created a Buddha character called Ho-Ho. Just in time for Pearl Harbor. The product did not catch on.

Rose O'Neill passed away in 1944 after a series of strokes, most of her estate impoverished. However, she left behind an extraordinary legacy in her catalogue of over 5,000 works.

Shortly after her death, her family home burned down, which destroyed most of her possessions and memorabilia. Fortunately, she donated a large body of her original art to the School of the Ozarks. The works were removed only two days before the fire.

The O'Neill home in Bonniebrook was rebuilt and is now a museum dedicated to Rose, the work of Missouri artists, and women artists in general. After a major renovation and gallery expansion, the site hosts an annual Kewpiesta festival dedicated to Rose and her kewpies, and a Rose O'Neill Faerie Gathering, as well as multiple art exhibits featuring the work of notables such as Thomas Hart Benton. The website www.roseoneill.org has extensive biographical information and many scans of her art. To find out more about the Faerie Festival, go to www.oneillfaeries.org. Her museum blog is at www.discoveringroseoneill.blogspot.com.

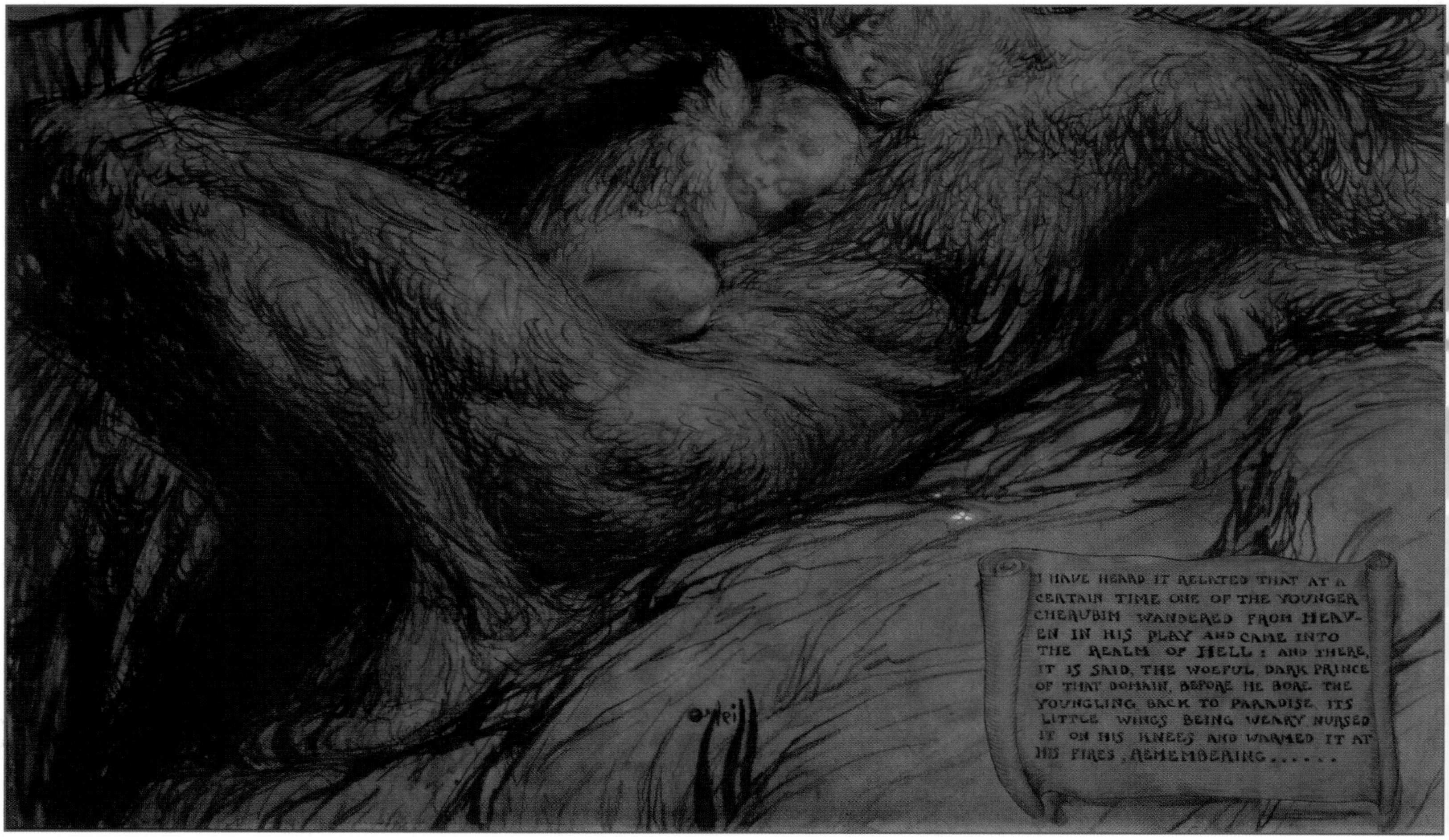
I HAVE HEARD IT RELATED THAT AT A
CERTAIN TIME ONE OF THE YOUNGER
CHERUBIM WANDERED FROM HEAV-
EN IN HIS PLAY AND CAME INTO
THE REALM OF HELL : AND THERE,
IT IS SAID, THE WOEFUL, DARK PRINCE
OF THAT DOMAIN, BEFORE HE BORE THE
YOUNGLING BACK TO PARADISE, ITS
LITTLE WINGS BEING WEARY, NURSED
IT ON HIS KNEES AND WARMED IT AT
HIS FIRES, REMEMBERING......
O'Neill

With sincere thanks to Martha Melton of the Bonniebrook Gallery and Museum. All art reproduced here directly from the originals.

☆ ☆ ☆ WOMEN OF THE PAST! ☆ ☆ ☆

ETHEL HAYS

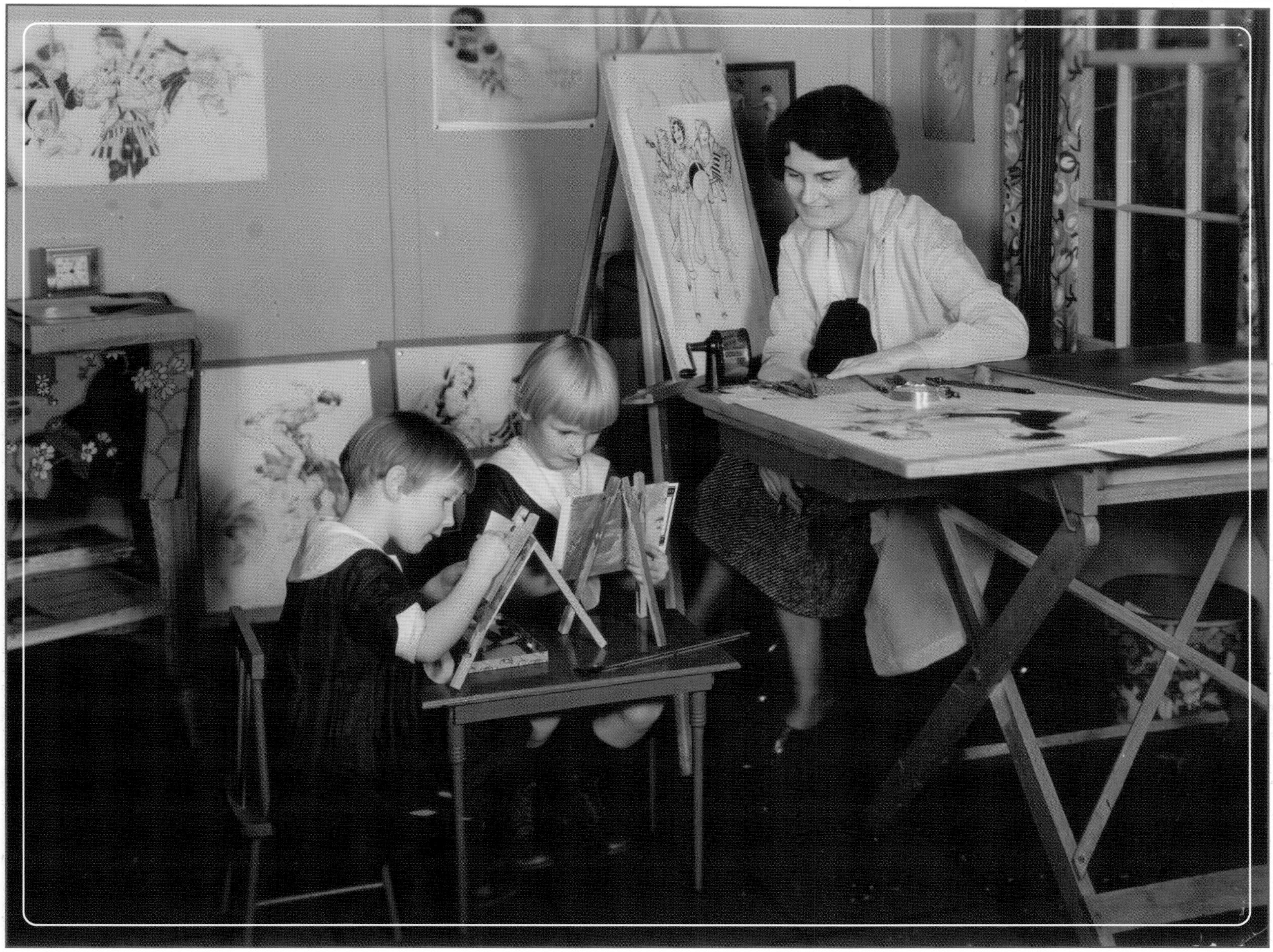

Ethel Hays

By Colleen Doran ©2011

Images courteousy of Trina Robbins

ETHEL: Goat Getters

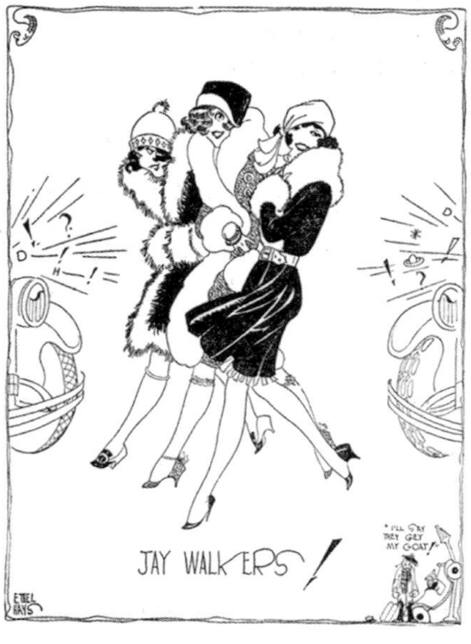
JAY WALKERS
ETHEL HAYS

Born in 1892 in Billings, Montana, Ethel Hays was a classically trained artist who attended The Los Angeles School of Design, before achieving a scholarship at the Arts League in New York. She earned another scholarship to the Academie Julian in Paris, but was forced home at the start of World War I.

Hays turned her fine artistic abilities into therapy for convalescing soldiers in US Army hospitals, where the enthusiastic troops introduced her to cartooning. Hays learned to love this medium as well, entering the Landon School of Illustration and

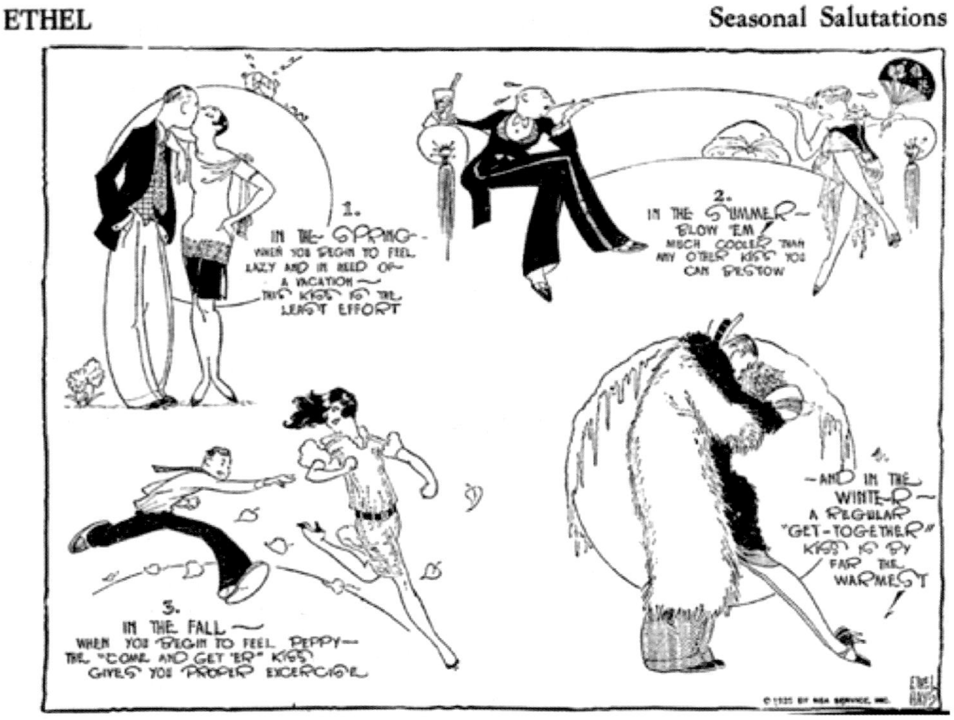
ETHEL
Seasonal Salutations
1.
IN THE SPRING - WHEN YOU BEGIN TO FEEL LAZY AND IN NEED OF - A VACATION ~ THIS KISS IS THE LEAST EFFORT
2.
IN THE SUMMER - BLOW 'EM! MUCH COOLER THAN ANY OTHER KISS YOU CAN BESTOW
3.
IN THE FALL ~ WHEN YOU BEGIN TO FEEL PEPPY - THE "COME AND GET 'ER" KISS GIVES YOU PROPER EXCERCISE
4.
- AND IN THE WINTER - A REGULAR "GET-TOGETHER" KISS IS BY FAR THE WARMEST!
ETHEL HAYS

Cartooning to pursue comics as a career. Her advanced skills landed her a gig as a student teacher and, before long, Hays became a professional at The Cleveland Press, penning the cartoon feature *Vic and Ethel* in 1923, written by Victoria Benham.

When Benham left the newspaper to get married, Hays continued solo, and the *Vic and Ethel* strip morphed into *Ethel*.

After years of war, the American public clamored for optimistic, light-hearted entertainment. Ethel Hays captured this spirit with her drawings of young, liberated American girls. The Hays heroines were sleek, well-dressed, athletic, exuberant flappers. Her peerless draughtsmanship and elegant linework, combined with her penchant for pretty girls, made Hays one of the most popular cartoonists of the time.

In 1925, Hays supplemented her thrice-weekly feature *Ethel* with the weekly one-panel gag *Flapper Fanny Says*, another work in her signature "pretty-girls and glamour" style. Enormously successful, it was featured in 500 newspapers in its first year alone. The strip spawned an array of coloring books and paper dolls, and was widely imitated in strips such as *Flapper Filosofy* by Faith Burrows.

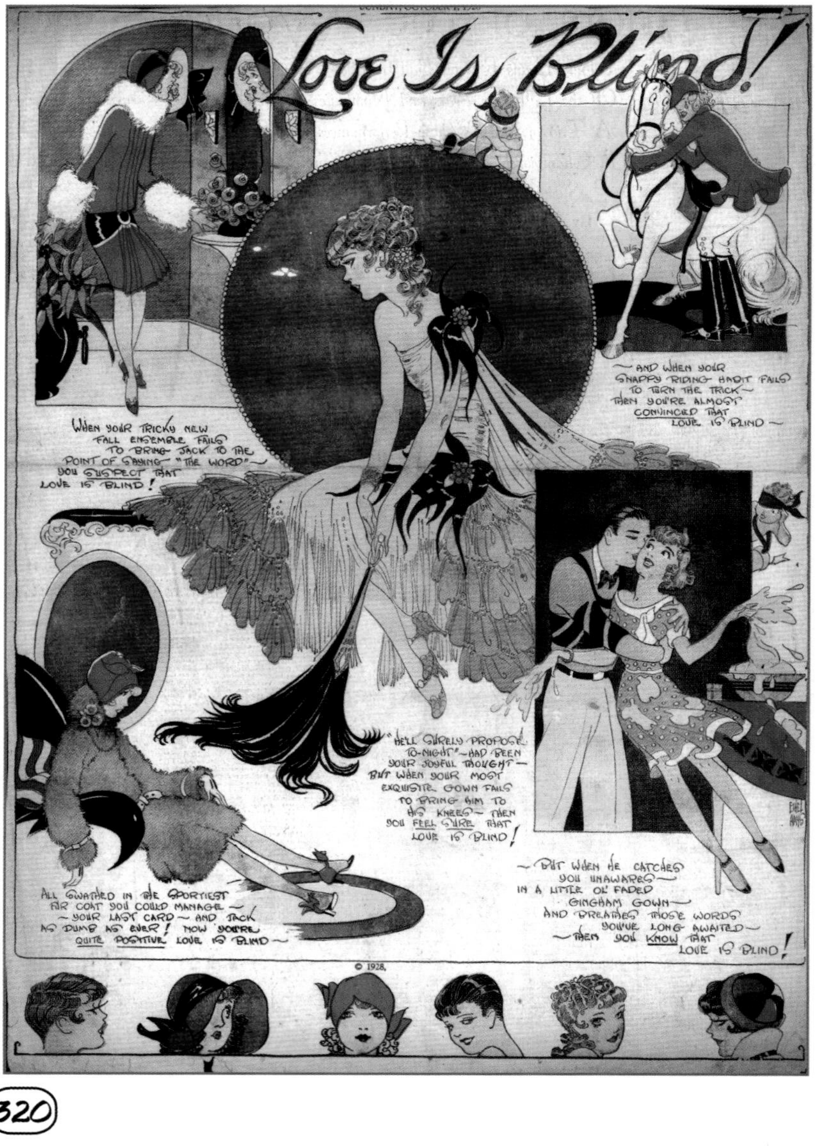
Love Is Blind!
WHEN YOUR TRICKY NEW FALL ENSEMBLE FAILS TO BRING JACK TO THE POINT OF SAYING "THE WORD" ~ YOU SUSPECT THAT LOVE IS BLIND!
~ AND WHEN YOUR SNAPPY RIDING HABIT FAILS TO TURN THE TRICK ~ THEN YOU'RE ALMOST CONVINCED THAT LOVE IS BLIND ~
"HE'LL SURELY PROPOSE TO-NIGHT" ~ HAD BEEN YOUR JOYFUL THOUGHT ~ BUT WHEN YOUR MOST EXQUISITE GOWN FAILS TO BRING HIM TO HIS KNEES ~ THEN YOU FEEL SURE THAT LOVE IS BLIND!
ALL SWATHED IN THE SPORTIEST FUR COAT YOU COULD MANAGE ~ ~ YOUR LAST CARD ~ AND JACK AS DUMB AS EVER! NOW YOU'RE QUITE POSITIVE LOVE IS BLIND ~
~ BUT WHEN HE CATCHES YOU UNAWARES ~ IN A LITTLE OL' FADED GINGHAM GOWN ~ AND BREATHES THOSE WORDS YOU'VE LONG AWAITED ~ ~ THEN YOU KNOW THAT LOVE IS BLIND!
ETHEL HAYS
© 1928.

By 1930, the workload wore on the productive Hays, who was by then married with two small children. She turned over her art chores on *Flapper Fanny* to promising young cartoonist Gladys Parker, who continued the strip into the 1940s.

Despite her intent to cut back on art and care for her family, Hays took on illustration chores for a variety of newspaper features. She was at her best on the full-page wonders, like *Great Loves of Literature*, that were syndicated in Sunday newspaper supplement *Every Week*.

Measuring a substantial 15″x22″, these eye-popping, gorgeously rendered, romantic pictures are a treat for the cartoon collector.

Hays then moved on to yet another strip about carefree young women, *Marianne*. Like all her work, *Marianne* was beautifully drawn, but Hays lost interest in short order, turning the art chores over to Virginia Krausmann in 1936. Hays also produced a series of cartoons for the *Christian Science Monitor* strip *Manly Manners*.

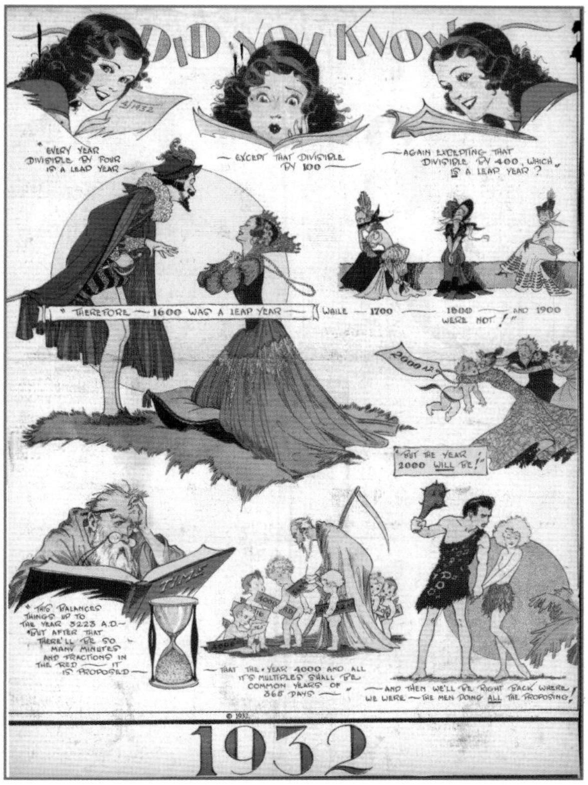
DID YOU KNOW
"EVERY YEAR DIVISIBLE BY FOUR IS A LEAP YEAR —
— EXCEPT THAT DIVISIBLE BY 100 —
— AGAIN EXCEPTING THAT DIVISIBLE BY 400, WHICH IS A LEAP YEAR?
" THEREFORE — 1600 WAS A LEAP YEAR —
WHILE — 1700 — 1800 — AND 1900 WERE NOT!"
2000 A.D.
"BUT THE YEAR 2000 WILL BE!"
" THIS BALANCES THINGS UP TO THE YEAR 3223 A.D. — BUT AFTER THAT THERE'LL BE SO MANY MINUTES AND FRACTIONS IN THE RED — IT IS PROPOSED —
— THAT THE YEAR 4000 AND ALL IT'S MULTIPLES SHALL BE COMMON YEARS OF 365 DAYS —"
— AND THEN WE'LL BE RIGHT BACK WHERE WE WERE — THE MEN DOING ALL THE PROPOSING!
TIME
© 1932
1932

In a few years, Ethel Hays would abandon cartooning entirely in favor of a focus on children's books. For several decades, Hays produced many successful works on a wide variety of projects, including *Raggedy Ann and Andy*, a widely licensed work for which she was the primary artist. Her art appeared on paper dolls, coloring books, and countless other products.

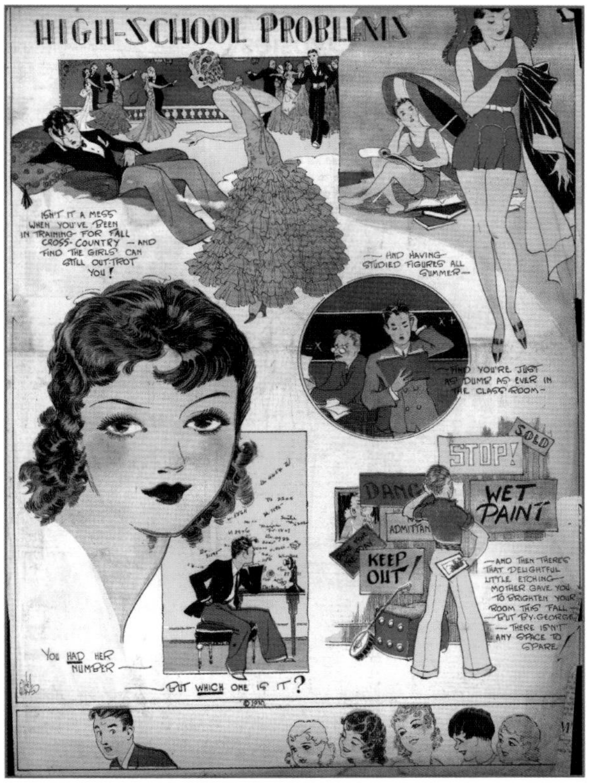
HIGH-SCHOOL PROBLEMS
ISN'T IT A MESS WHEN YOU'VE BEEN IN TRAINING FOR FALL CROSS-COUNTRY — AND FIND THE GIRLS CAN STILL OUT-TROT YOU!
— AND HAVING STUDIED FIGURES ALL SUMMER —
— AND YOU'RE JUST AS DUMB AS EVER IN THE CLASS ROOM —
SOLD
STOP!
WET PAINT
ADMITTANCE
KEEP OUT!
— AND THEN THERE'S THAT DELIGHTFUL LITTLE ETCHING — MOTHER GAVE YOU TO BRIGHTEN YOUR ROOM THIS FALL — BUT BY GEORGE — THERE ISN'T ANY SPACE TO SPARE!
YOU HAD HER NUMBER —
— BUT WHICH ONE IS IT?

Among her extensive credits were *The Town Mouse and the Country Mouse, The Little Red Hen*, and the now-controversial *Little Black Sambo*.

Ethel Hays remained a productive artist into the 1960s. She died in New Mexico in 1989.

Most of Hays's catalogue of cartoon work is in the public domain and widely available online. Largely ignored by modern fans, her original cartoons can be had for a song. Her children's books are also easy to find and very affordable via online auction sources.

The underrated and underappreciated Hays is yet another example of a woman cartoonist of outstanding ability left behind by comics history. Hays not only produced a beautiful catalogue of work, but supported and encouraged the careers of other young women cartoonists. While biographical information about Hays is sketchy, her work speaks for itself. She was an exceptional cartoonist who deserves to be remembered.

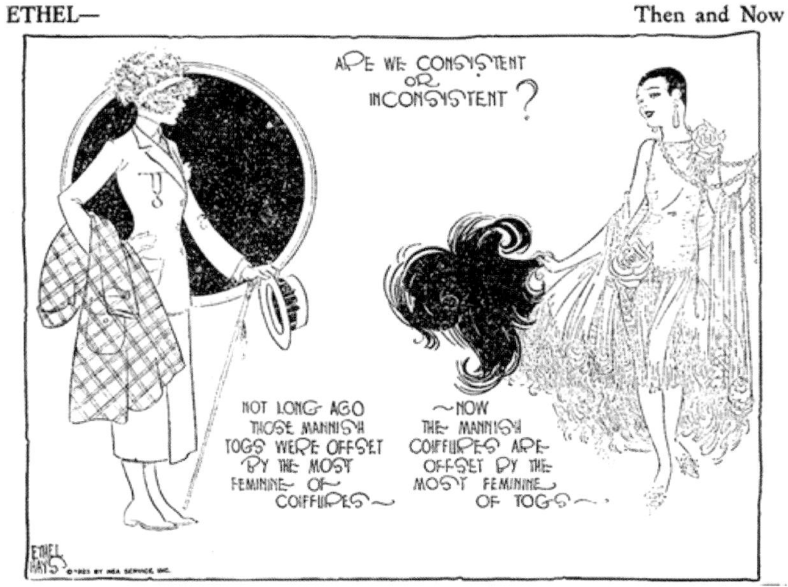
ETHEL—
Then and Now
ARE WE CONSISTENT OR INCONSISTENT?
NOT LONG AGO THOSE MANNISH TOGS WERE OFFSET BY THE MOST FEMININE OF COIFFURES —
— NOW THE MANNISH COIFFURES ARE OFFSET BY THE MOST FEMININE OF TOGS —
ETHEL HAYS

SPONSORS

★ ★ ★

AMAZING PEOPLE
WHO HELPED MAKE
WOMANTHOLOGY A
REALITY IN BIG WAYS!

THANK YOU!

Sometimes being a woman means reinventing yourself into the heroine that they deserve. It also means watching pieces of yourself unravel, only to be woven into a richer fabric.

A candid letter to my girls, Gwyn and Elie.

May I as a mom always remember that I am the model for which you base your ideals.

On that note, I hope you turn a blind eye to the times, I've forgotten to be a lady in public. You need to ignore the times that I've yelled at slow traffic, complained about other people or sworn that I was going to change my name and become a forest ranger.

I hope that you do remember: You should always be nice to the janitor. Even if someone seems perfect on the outside, there are always things that people are scared of, worry about or flat out don't like about themselves. Singing in the car can cure most bad moods. Always do your best, but even if it is an off day, know that even your "so-so" is better than most other people's best. Life is a journey, so pick people you like to travel with and pack a snack. Work hard everyday, but make time to play hard and love endlessly. Smile- it costs nothing, but can be worth a million dollars. Care about others, even the friends you haven't met yet, they are somebody's someone. Laugh often. Try to learn something new everyday. You can save the world if you are wearing a cape and tiara or overalls and flip flops.

But most of all, know that you are beautiful and strong each in your own way. And for that you are treasured and LOVED always!

Love,
The not so perfect role model that hopes she hasn't screwed up too badly, known as Momma

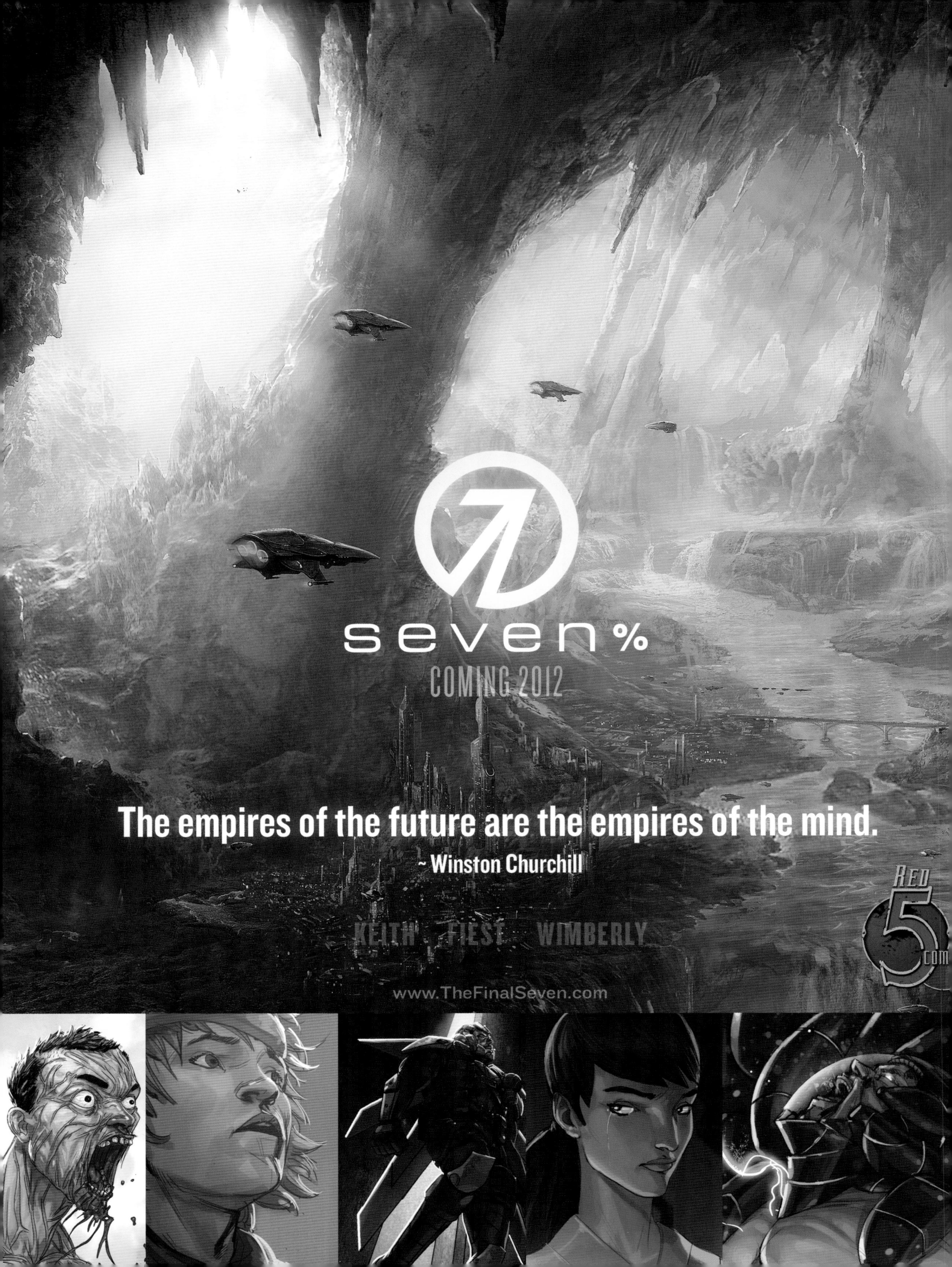

seven%
COMING 2012
The empires of the future are the empires of the mind.
~ Winston Churchill
KEITH FIEST WIMBERLY
RED 5 COM
www.TheFinalSeven.com

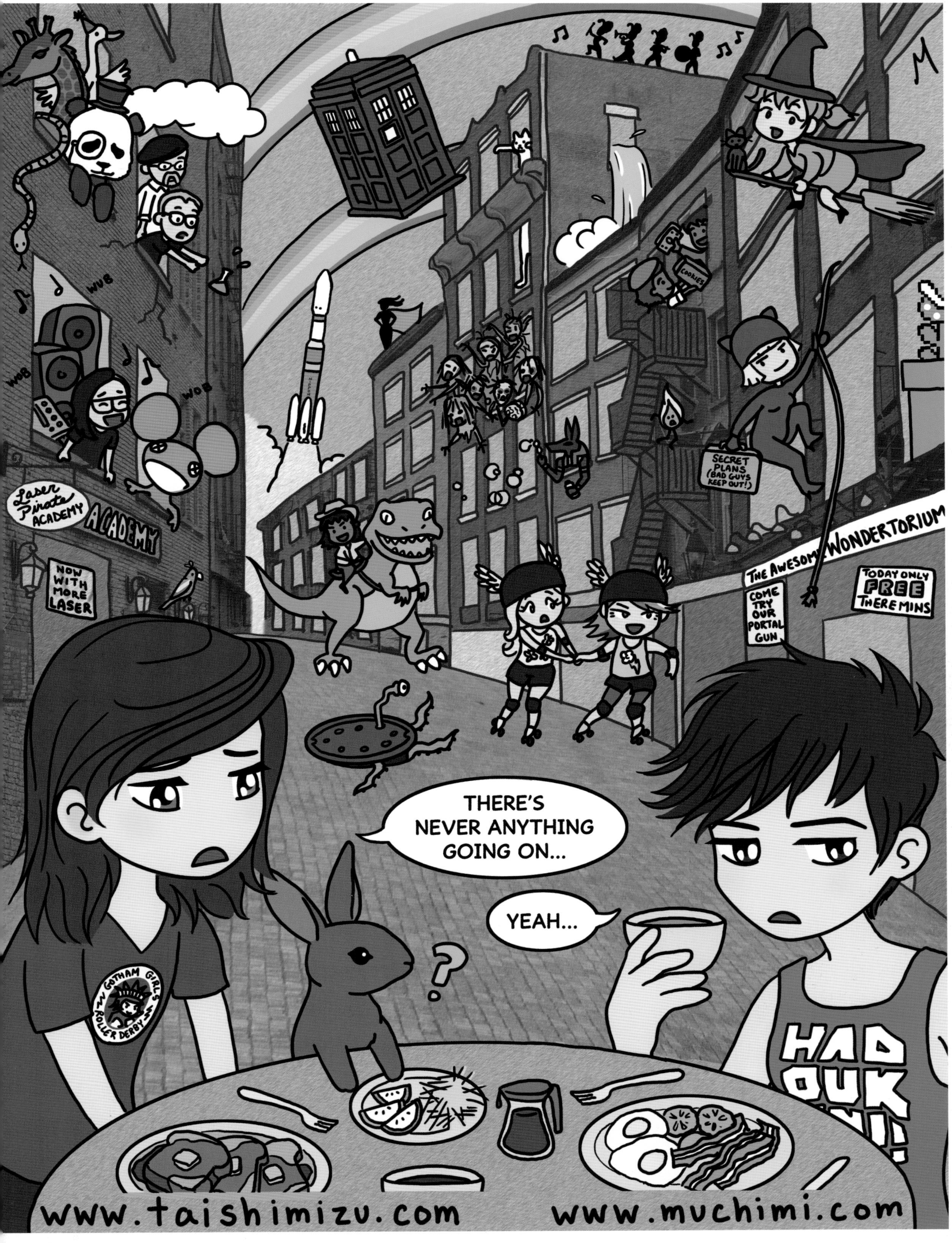
Laser Pirate ACADEMY
ACADEMY
NOW WITH MORE LASER
WUB
SECRET PLANS (BAD GUYS KEEP OUT!)
COOKIES
THE AWESOME WONDERTORIUM
COME TRY OUR PORTAL GUN
TODAY ONLY FREE THEREMINS
THERE'S NEVER ANYTHING GOING ON...
YEAH...
?
GOTHAM GIRLS ROLLER DERBY
HADOUK
www.taishimizu.com
www.muchimi.com

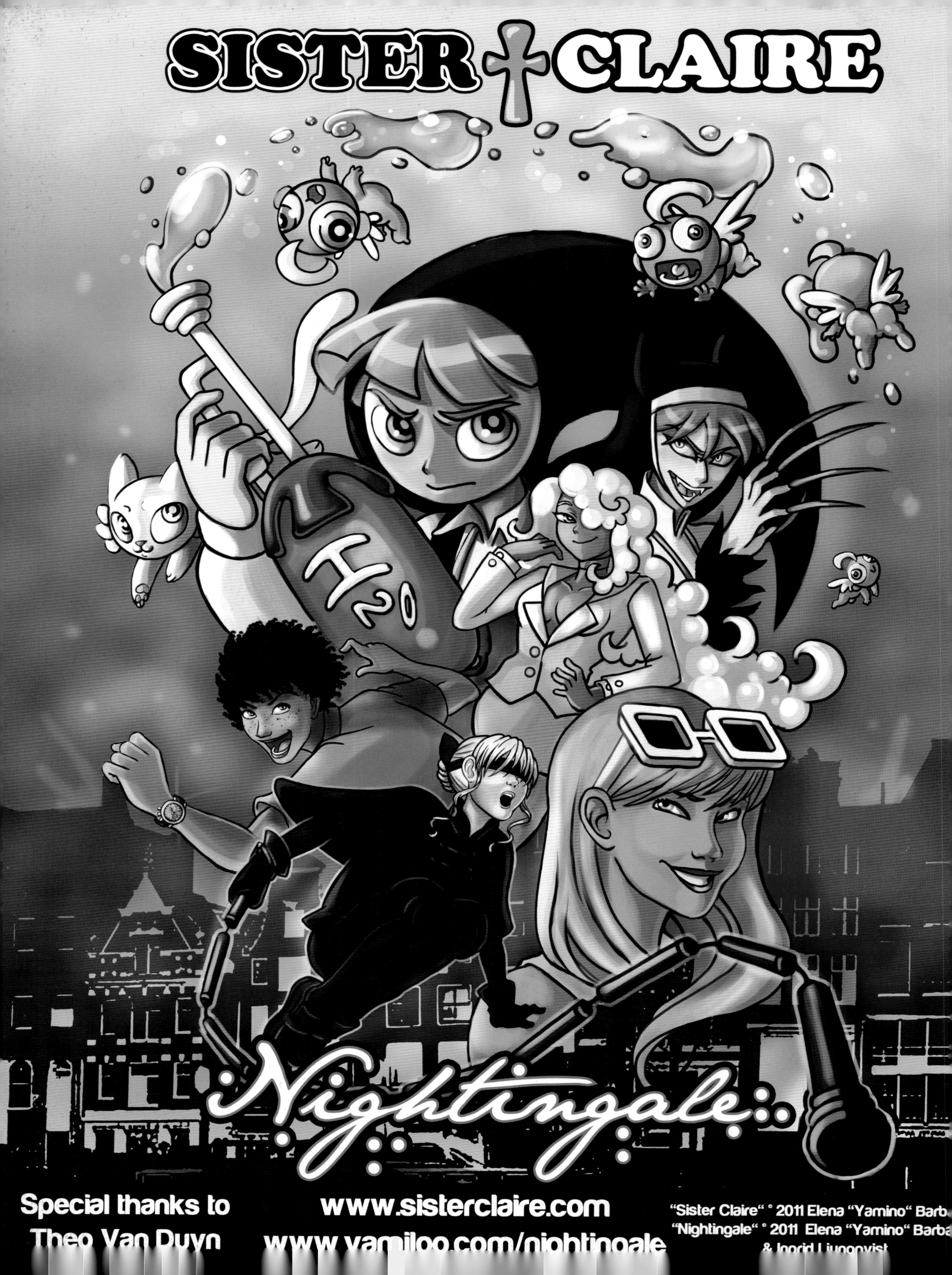
SISTER CLAIRE
H2O
Nightingale
Special thanks to
Theo Van Duyn
www.sisterclaire.com
www.yamiloo.com/nightingale
"Sister Claire" © 2011 Elena "Yamino" Barba
"Nightingale" © 2011 Elena "Yamino" Barba
& Ingrid Ljungqvist

You don't have to be a superhero to save the world.

Spandex optional.
Love required.

On GlobalGiving.org you can support grassroots organizations that are educating children, feeding the hungry, building houses, training women (and men) with job skills, and doing hundreds of other amazing things. (Like training giant rats to sniff out landmines!) Simply fly, teleport, dash, sling, disapparate, or point your browser to globalgiving.org and help us change the world one project at a time.

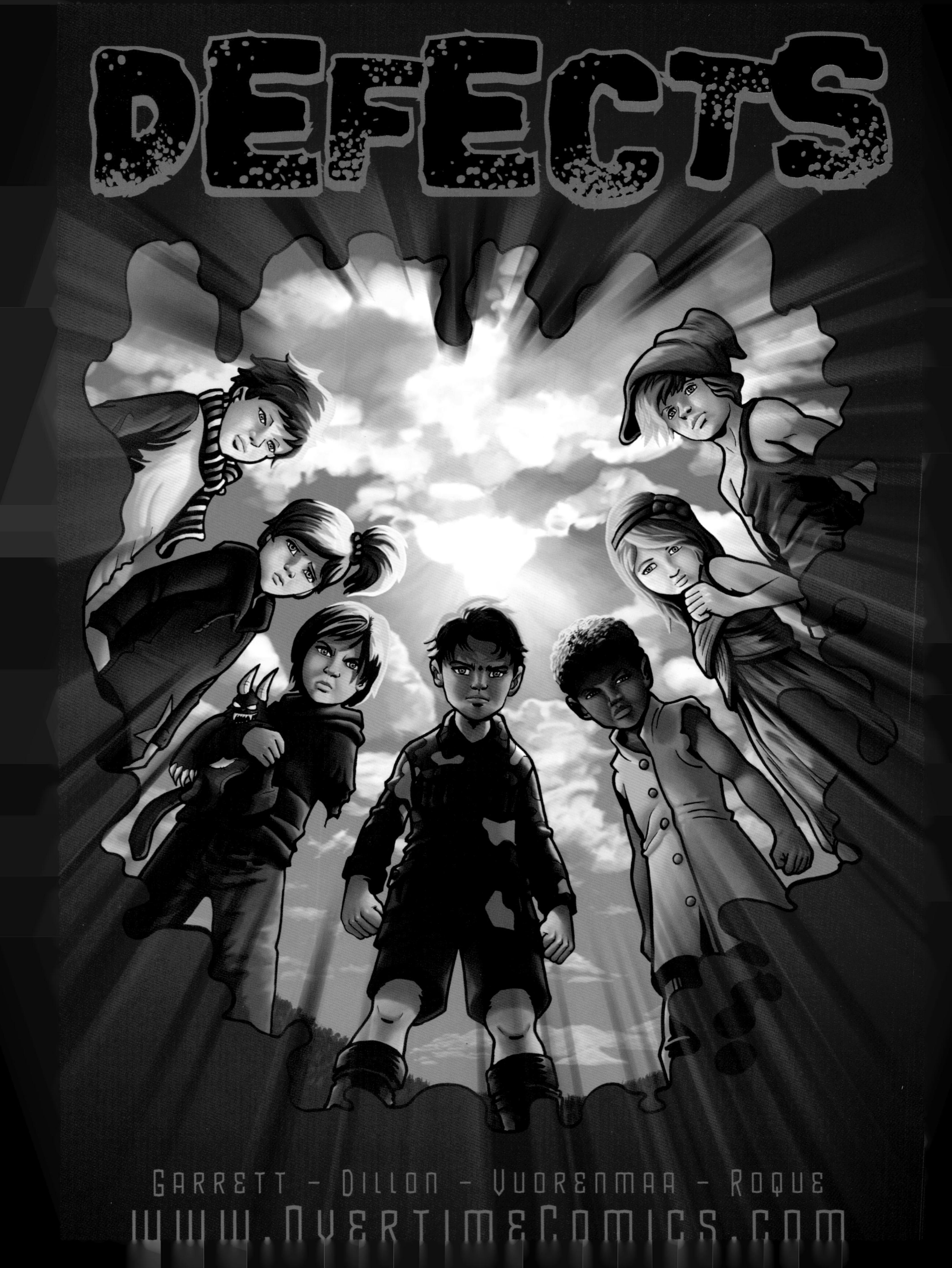
DEFECTS
GARRETT - DILLON - VUORENMAA - ROQUE
WWW.OVERTIMECOMICS.COM

FROM WRITER G.VON STODDARD COMES A SUPERNATURAL COMING OF AGE ADVENTURE
WITH ART BY WOMANTHOLOGY CONTRIBUTOR , CANDACE ELLIS

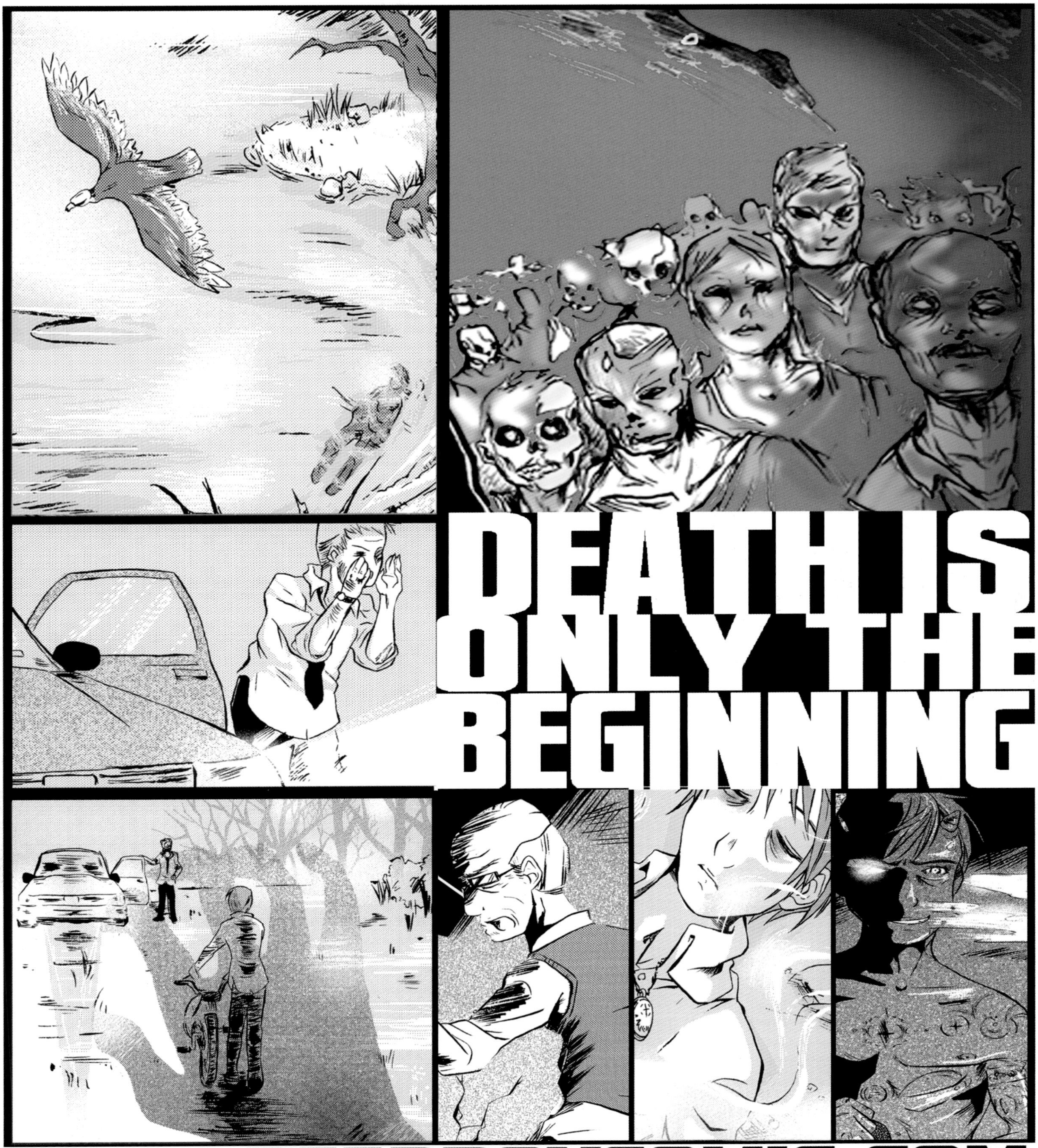

DEATH IS ONLY THE BEGINNING

WWW.DEADBOYCOMIC.COM

THANK YOU ALL FOR YOUR SUPPORT!

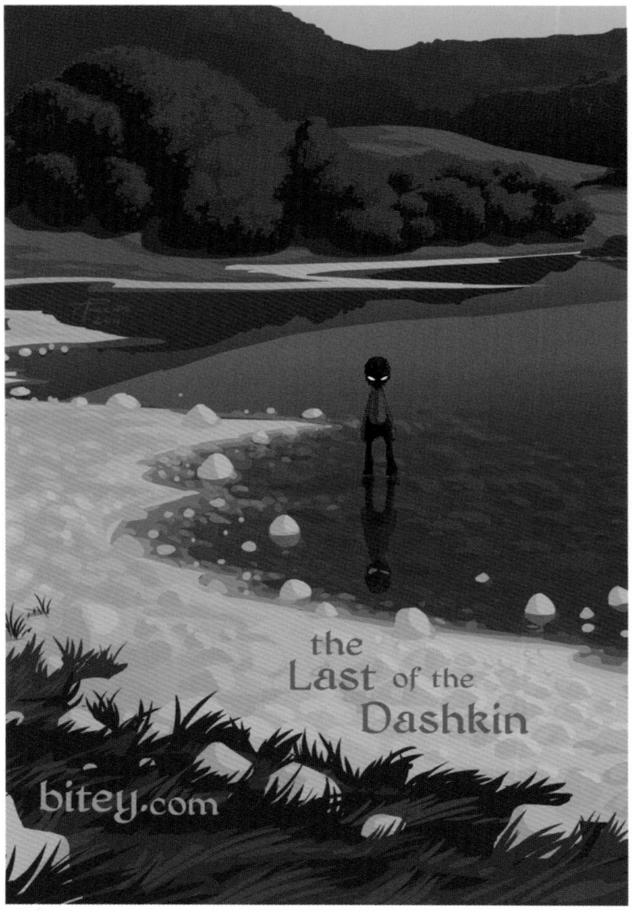
the Last of the Dashkin
bitey.com

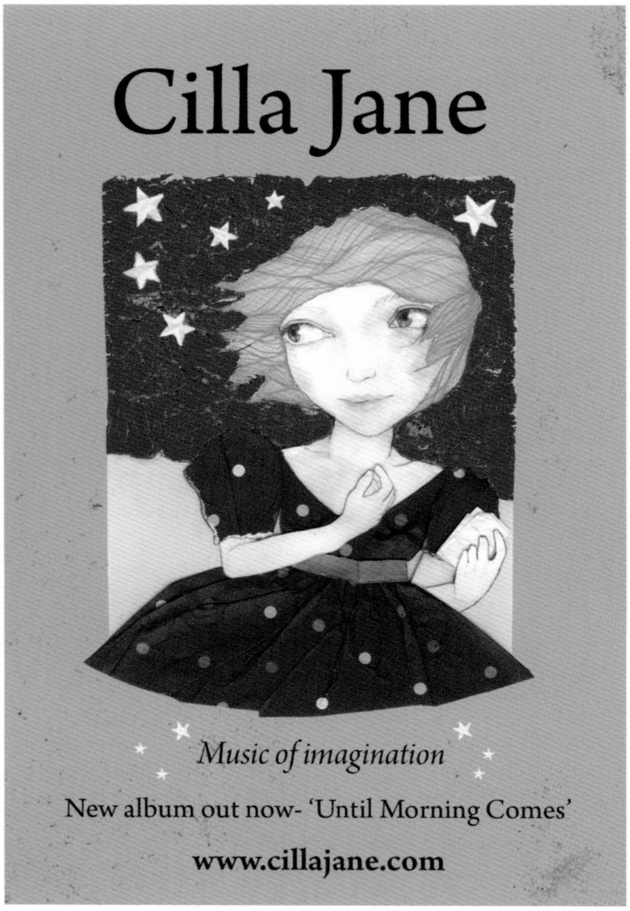
Cilla Jane
Music of imagination
New album out now- 'Until Morning Comes'
www.cillajane.com

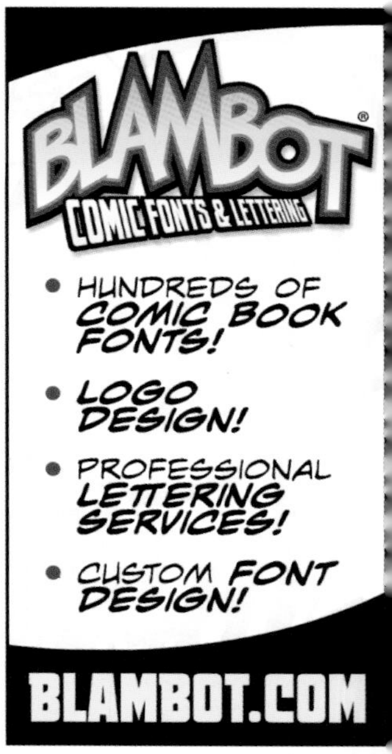
BLAMBOT®
COMIC FONTS & LETTERING
• HUNDREDS OF COMIC BOOK FONTS!
• LOGO DESIGN!
• PROFESSIONAL LETTERING SERVICES!
• CUSTOM FONT DESIGN!
BLAMBOT.COM

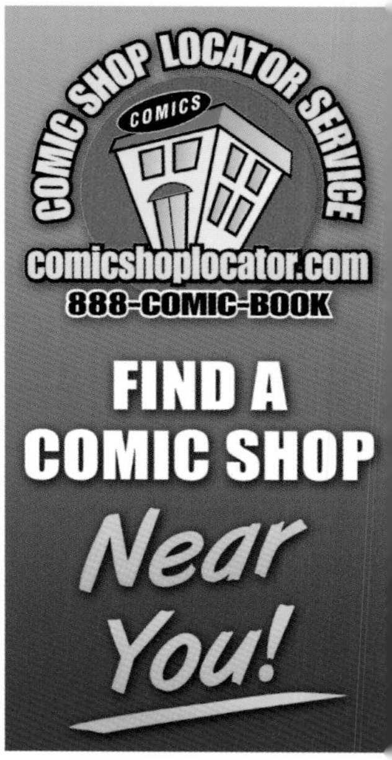
COMIC SHOP LOCATOR SERVICE
COMICS
comicshoplocator.com
888-COMIC-BOOK
FIND A COMIC SHOP
Near You!

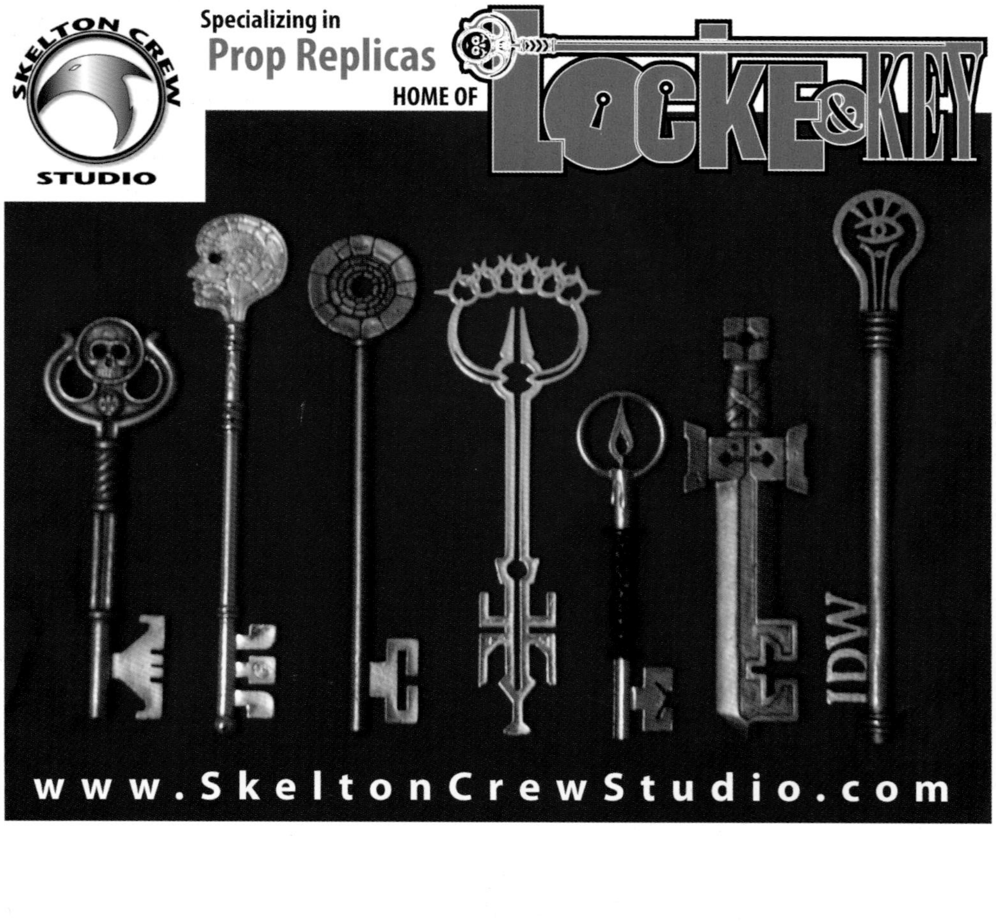
SKELTON CREW STUDIO
Specializing in
Prop Replicas
HOME OF
LOCKE & KEY
IDW
www.SkeltonCrewStudio.com

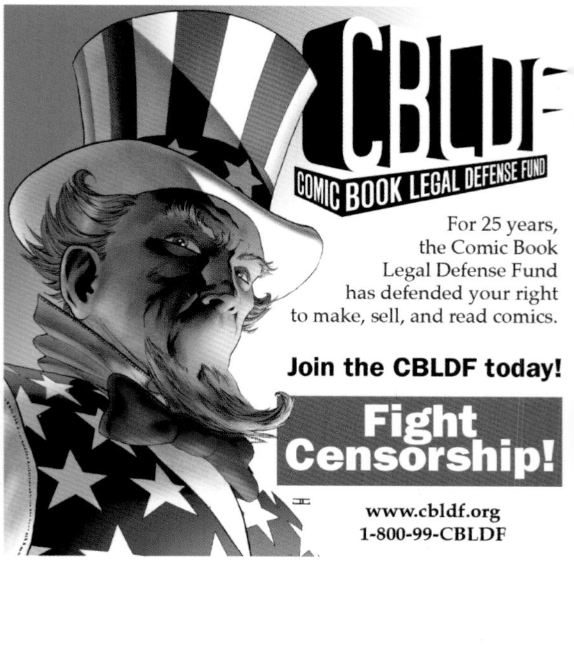
CBLDF
COMIC BOOK LEGAL DEFENSE FUND
For 25 years,
the Comic Book
Legal Defense Fund
has defended your right
to make, sell, and read comics.
Join the CBLDF today!
Fight Censorship!
www.cbldf.org
1-800-99-CBLDF

Comics and Illustrations
from LOCKE & KEY artist
and co-creator...
DeviantArt
http://gabrielrodriguez.deviantart.com
Blog
http://www.gr.cl
GaBRieL RoDRiGueZ
COMIC & ILLUSTRATION

A thank you!

Womanthology has been one of the best experiences in my professional career thus far. So many wonderful and encouraging women who worked to make the coolest book possible!
This project has also reignited my love of storytelling. It's been a hugely inspiring experience, I hope it shows and in turn inspires others.
Thanks to IDW, Renae, Jessica, Bonnie, Laura, Mariah, Nicole, Suzannah, the talented artists, writers, and the amazing people who donated to make this project possible.

THANKS!

Sarah Wilkinson
www.sarahwilkinson.net
Artist of trading cards, comics, and books for properties such as Star Wars, Lord Of The Rings, Star Trek and many more.

Annie
Nocenti's
Haiti tales
"Goudou
Goudou"
at
HiLobrow.com

SAMANTHA NEWARK

WHAT A DELICIOUS EXPERIENCE THIS HAS BEEN BEING INVITED INTO THE WOMB OF WOMANTHOLOGY. HAVING MY SONG 'BLUE SEA' FROM MY ALBUM ADAPTED FOR THE BOOK BY SUCH TALENTED WOMEN IS A TREAT BEYOND MEASURE.

MY ROLE AS JEM/JERRICA IN THE CARTOON SERIES 'JEM AND THE HOLOGRAMS' IS ALL ABOUT GIRL POWER AND MENTORING AND BEING GENEROUS AND SUPPORTIVE OF EACH OTHERS DREAMS. RENAE AND ALL INVOLVED ARE TRUE JEMGIRLS AND WOMANTHOLOGY IS TRULY OUTRAGEOUS!
WWW.SAMANTHANEWARK.COM

CAMILLA d'ERRICO camilladerrico.com
HELMETGIRLS helmetgirls.com
tanpopo tanpopoandkuro.com

CHECK OUT THE HILLARIOUS WEEKLY WEBSTRIP

HOW MANY CALORIES DO YOU THINK A BOTTLE OF WINE A DAY ADDS?

HOT MESS
BY AMANDA DEIBERT AND CAT STAGGS
COMEDIVA
WWW.COMEDIVA.COM where the funnygirls are
WWW.AMANDADEIBERT.COM
WWW.CATSTAGGS.COM

I would like to use this space to thank some of the more important women in my life:

My mother, Casi
my step-mother, Linda
my auntie Bree
my sister, Jessi
my dearest Moira
and my friend Carol Edwards, whose work at Early Alert Canines is part of what keeps me well enough to write and run around the world finding new things to write about.

For more information on her heroic nonprofit, and to donate if you can, please visit:

www.earlyalertcanines.org
Early Alert Canines

Thank you!
~ Devin Grayson

HEROIC

B. Clay Moore

Co-creator of Hawaiian Dick, Jackie Karma and Battle Hymn (Image Comics), The Leading Man and Billy Smoke (Oni Press), writer for DC Comics, Marvel Comics, and most major publishers.

bclaymoore.wordpress.com

kellysheroes.webs.com
STEAMPUNK GEAR
I WANT YOU
GADGETS, GOGGLES, GIZMOS, AND GEAR FOR THE STEAMPUNK ENTHUSIAST!

SUFFERING FROM WRITER'S BLOCK... AGAIN?

We've all experienced them-those moments of peralyzing self-doubt, or even rage, when all of our work seems pointless or downright terrible. Why bother? We ask ourselves. Nobody will read this anyway...

The poet Ted Hughes maintained that every writer has an internal policeman who is determined to stop him or her from writing. And that goes for all writers, not just new or unpublished ones.
Remember, James Joyce threw the first manuscript of Portrait of the Artist onto the fire, and Stephen King tossed the first pages of Carrie into the trashcan. We all face self-doubt. The trick is taking up the pen despite the fear.

GOOD LUCK!
Robin Furth

Quirk says:
"BARK BARK, BARK BARK, BARK BARK!*"

*Which means either:
"Congratulations, everybody!"
or
"Grab the leash, and take me for a walk!"

Love from Quirk and Barbara RK.

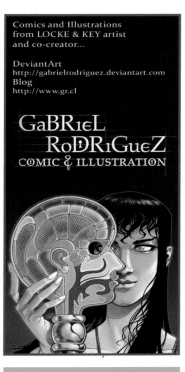

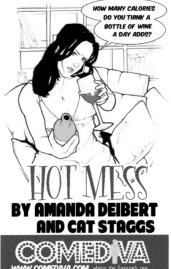

TO THE BACKERS OF WOMANTHOLOGY

★ ★ ★ **THANK YOU!** ★ ★ ★

TAI SHIMIZU   JACQUELINE URICK
KEVIN CHIOU   GEOFF LATULIPPE
GAVIN ap'MORRYGAN

@bluecanarykit
@euphoriafish
Aaron Duran
Aaron Hunter
Aaron J Shay
Abby Berendt Lavoi: TeamJADED Productions
Abby Dawn Marie Pape-Green
Abigail Luthmann
Adrienne 'EvilBob' Keith
Alex & Nicole Violette
Ali Hall
Amanda Garrett
Amanda Perez
Amy Michelle Stone
Anastasia Glass
Andrew Keene (Hi Ashley!)
Anna "Dynamite" McKibben
Argentina Arias Gómez
Ashley Guy Watson
Ashley Hay
Brian Knippenberg
Brian Zastoupil
Bryant Durrell
Bryden Easton
Cal Slayton
Carol Borden
Carol Connolly
Caroline Standish
Carolyn Belefski
Carter McKendry
Caryn Humphreys
Catherine Sarratt
Cathy Matusiak
Charles Boylan
Chelsea Novak
Cheryl Harris
Chris Murrin
Christian Sager

Christine Altese
Christine E Taylor
Clair Louise Kruskamp
Clare Bayley
Cliff Chiang
Clydene Nee
Comfort Love and Adam Withers
Committed Comics
Cordelia Donovan
Dane Minich
Denitt Perez
Desirée Autumn Ikeler
Devin Grayson
DiRT - Pop Culture Network
Dominique Brooks
Don Roff
Edward V. Lopez
Eileenica Morager
Elaine Lee
Elayne Riggs
Elliott Marshal Brown
Elliott Salinas
Erica Friedman
Erik Smith
Erin Kys
Felipe Sobreiro
G. Brett Williams
Gab Contreras
Galen Lim
GamingAngels.com
Gavin ap' Morrygan
Gillian "Giddy!" Mann
Giulietta Speziani
G-Mart Comics
Harry Murfitt
Helen Schreiner
Holly Harrop
Ian Brill
India Allen
J.K. Woodward
Jaelin Nemain
Jamal Y. Igle

James F. Wright aka Chuck Spear
James Garnham
Jan Roger Henden
Jeanine Schaefer
Jenn McCreary
Jennifer R. Parker
Jeremy THE AWESOME Fiest
Jessica Johnson
Jonathon Myers
Jorge Cuaik
Josh Crawley
Julie Benson
JustinChung.com
Kanghyun Chu
Kate Marie Hill
Kathleen R. Carbone
Kathy Flynn
Kevin Clark
Kim Brown
Kitamu Latham-Sampier
Lacey Nogueira
Len O'Grady
Liam Dunlop
Lisa & Maggie Bacallao
Madison, Patrick & Ebony Strange
Marc Hammond
Maria Lima
Mark Sable
Marty Todd
Mat Nixon
Matthew Borgatti
Mia Kalogjera
Michael "Karizma" M
Michael Perridge
Molly Jane Kremer
Monique Poirier
Natasha Adeline Malia
Nate Piekos
Nicole Denise Lewandowski

Nix Comics Quarterly
Noel Anthony Haughey
Oliver Mertz
Pamela Shaw
Patricia Mulvihill
Paul Allor
Paul Bines
Paul 'n Pippa L-T
Phineas Hodson
Pornokitsch
R. Thomas Riley
Rachel Kiri Walker
Rich Johnston
Rico Renzi
Robert & Judith Cock
Robert Lee Mayers
Roxanne Earnest
Sara Amor
Sarah Wilkinson
Sasha Perl-Raver
Sean Becker
Sean Hackett
Sean Hillman
Shannon Watters
Shaun Kronenfeld
Shauna J. Grant
Sophie Powell
Stellalune
Sue Coombes
Talmai Mathis
Tammy and Jim Garrison
Tasha Zimich
The Mean Geek Podcast-Bill and AJ
Tom Stidman
Tracey van Zaanen
Umar Ditta
Vanessa C. Pais
Widgett Walls
Worst Webcomic
Yasmin Liang
Zachary Cole

wyatt_e, [insertgeekhere], 15paintedcups, 54321dd, A. David Lewis, A.j. Michel, Aaron Duran, Aaron Hunter, Aaron J Shay, Aaron Kessel, Aaron aggart, Abby Berendt Lavoi, Abi Braceros, Abigail Luthmann, Adam, Adam B Kaufman, Adam Blomquist, Adam Borden, Adam J. Monetta, Adam olicoeur, Adam Lipkin, Adam Phillips, Adam Steen, Adam Stone, Adam Talley, ADAM TALLEY, Adam W, Adele Fergus- O'Brien, adeleshakal, delmira Sanchez, Adisakdi Tantimedh, Aditya Patel, adrian hunter, Adriano Antonini, Adrienne E. Keith, Adrienne Travis, afrofrench, Agnes arbowska, Aida, Aimee Hudson, Ainah, Aja Moore, Alan Alvarez, Alan Hom, Alan Irwin, Alan Ralph, Alan Velasquez, Alanna, Aldous Russell, lejandra Garcia, Alex Breen, Alex Chung, Alex Johnson, Alex Koti, Alex manglis, Alex Raymond, Alex Violette, Alex Wilson, Alexa Dickman, Alexa Morrow, Alexander Hoffman, Alexander Moore, Alexandra Edwards, Alexandra H, Alexandria Brown, Alexis Hernadez, Alfred Austria, Alfred Moscola, Alica, Alice, Alice Chen, Alice Thomsen, Alicia, Alicia C, Alicia Cunningham, Alisa Krasnostein, Alisha Christine, Alisha Vargas, Alison Hall, ison sampson, Alix Clinkingbeard, Allan Harvey, Alli Gonding, Allison, Allison Pang, Alvin Chong, Alvin Robles, Alyssa, Alyssa Michek, Amanda, manda (Floor to Ceiling Books), Amanda Deibert, Amanda Hubik Anzaldua, Amanda L Marron, Amanda Lees, Amanda Perez, Amanda Powter, manda Rutter, Amanda Wyss, Amaquieria, Amber, Amber Lanagan, Amber Tidd-Hiebert, Amelia Altavena, Amelia Seyruun, Aminuddin Abdollah, my Archambault, amy chu, Amy Dallen, Amy Huang, Amy Ratcliffe, Amy Sasso, Amy Stone, Amy Swank, Ana Cerro, anaditae, Anastasia Glass, nde Parks, Andre Dixon, Andre Moreira Forni, Andrea Blythe, Andrea Futrelle, Andrea Gonzales, Andrea Maclam, Andrea Speed, AndreaBall, ndreas, andrew burchell, Andrew C, Andrew Daniel, Andrew J. Williams, Andrew Keene, Andrew Mitchell, Andrew Paulson, Andrew Radke, ndrew Sanford, Andrew Seymour, Andrew Williams, Andrew Wilson, Andy Bartalone, Andy Beger, Andy Thorington, Andy Thorington, Angela, ngela Graham, Angela Paman, Angelia Pitman, Angelica Gonzalez, Angelina Geisler Starks, Angelique, angelsfool, Angie Light, Angie Olson, ngkarn Vibulakaopun, animachina, anna, Anna Daniell, Anna Neatrour, Annabelle, Annalisa Oswald, Anne Bean, Anne Smith Saunders, Annie, nthony, Anthony Matthews, argentina, Arianne Limbrick, Arnaud de Vallois, Arnoldo Rivas, Arran, ascasc, ashlee hayes, Ashleigh Popplewell, shley, Ashley Clark, Ashley Hay, Ashley Peebles, Ashley Watson, Auburn Slavec, Autumn Crossman-Serb, Avigayil Morris, Ayal Pinkus, Aziz, Bailey hoemaker Richards, Bananamanager, Barbara Crampton, Barbara Griffin, Barbara Haveron, Barry Lyga, Barry Seawright, beabravo, Becca Hillburn, eck Seashols, Becky, beepuke, Belinda Fernandez, Ben DeFeo, Ben Kraus, Ben Trigg, Ben Whittenbury, Benazeer Noorani, Benjamin Bailey, Benja- in Russell, Benjamin Truman, Benson Peacock, Berit Andrea Sletten, Beth Beinke, Betty Felon, Bill Boehmer, Bill Nichols, bill thurman, Bill Yu, Billy eynolds, Blair Campbell, BlueJeanius, Bob Holt, Bob Shaw, Bobby, Bobby Kokrda, bodlon, Bonnie Burton, Bonnie L. Norman, Brad Backofen, Brad enby, Brad Richardson, Bradley Duncan, Bradley Hatfield, Brandon Eaker, Brandon J. Carr, Brandon Kunc, Brandon Nieves, Brandon Ramsey, randon Thomas, Brandon Watkins, Branwyn Bigglestone, brea, Bree Rees, Bree Smith, brenda, Brenda Kirk, Brendan Burke, Brendan Darling, rendan McGuigan, Brendan Tihane, Brent Spencer, Brenton, Brett Danalake, Brett DaSilva, Brett Schenker, Brian, Brian Ashmore, Brian Bubonic, rian Christensen, Brian Holguin, Brian Houser, Brian Knippenberg, brian lynch, BRian Marino, Brian McFadden, Brian Shiroyama, brian smith, rian tudor, Brian Zastoupil, BriAnna Olson, Brianna Roberts, Brianne Christiansen, Brianne Melnyk, Brice Bridges, Bridget Tice, Britt Hammerberg, ryan, Bryan Gough, BRYAN HISSONG, Bryan Young, Bryant Durrell, Bryce Holland, Bryden Easton, C Walker, cainofdreaming, Caitlin, Caitlin Bray, aitlin Eve Rosendorn, Caitlin Rose Boyle, Caitlin Shaw, Cal Slayton, Calliope, Calum Johnston, Cameron, Cameron Davison, Cameron Rice, ameron Stewart, Camilla Zhang, Candace, Candace Foy, candace powell, Candice Reilly, candoh, candra, Canon, Canvas, Cara, Cara Mumford, ara Wynn-Jones, Caracolquiscol, Carl Mageski, Carl Rigney, Carl Towns, Carla Coupe, Carla Hall, Carlos Padilla, Carlos Salinas, Carly Sheil, Carol onnolly, Caroline Gilroy, Caroline Standish, CarolineEAnd, Carolyn Belefski, Carrie Kirkland, Carter McKendry, Caryn Cameron, Caryn Humphreys, assie, Cassie Grossman, Cassie Harris, Cat Davidson-Hall, Cat Peters, Cat WIlson, CatFord, Catharine, Catherine Braiding, Catherine Kincannon, atherine S, Cathy, Cathy Hart, Cathy Matusiak, Cathy Sullivan, cattawampus, Caytlin Vilbrandt, CE Murphy, Cecilia Hillway, Chameleongirl, Chan- ler Paul Poling, Chandra Jenkins, Chandra Reyer, Chantay Legacy Leonard, Chaotic Geek, Charity A. Petrov, Charles Boylan, Charles Piner, Charles arratt, Charles Shields, charlie caliano, Charlotte Catalano, charlotte lai, Chaunacey Dunklee, Chelsea Novak, Chelsea Sundher, Cheri Schmitt, heryl Harris, Cheryl Trooskin-Zoller, Chiz, Chris, Chris Buchner, Chris Casos, Chris D'Angelo, Chris Duck, Chris Garrett, Chris Hansbrough, Chris argett, Chris Murrin, Chris Poynter, Chris Romer, chris ryall, Chris Samnee, Chris Stevens, Chris Vincent, Chris Walsh, Christian Fisher, Christian Marra, Christian Otholm, Christian Sager, Christianne Benedict, christieanne, Christina Castillo, Christina Crenshaw, Christina S, Christina Tran, hristine, Christine Altese, Christine Black, Christine E. Taylor, Christine Lawrence, Christine Makepeace, Christopher Cole, Christopher Daley, hristopher Flocco, Christopher James Palafox, Christopher Kelley, Christopher M. Lopez, Christopher Sarnowski, Christopher Whitfield, christyrm, HUNK, Cindy Au, cinik, Citten, Clair Louise Kruskamp, Claire Black, Claire Van Der Loo, Clare Bayley, Claudia Barillas, Cliff Chiang, ClinkingDog, lmcshane, clydene nee, Colin Carley, Colin Eggers, Colin Fredericks, Colin M Orr, Colin Solan, Colton Steadman, Comfort Love, Comikaze Expo, ommitted Comics, coolbeanjeans, Cordelia Donovan, Corey Scott, Corrie Pikul, Corvus Elrod, Cougar, Courtney Abbott, Coyotzin, Craig Polkow, RAMOISAN, Crystal Kay Knispel, Crystal Rotz, Cuculine, Cullen, Cully Hamner, Curtis Fletcher, cwena, CYNTHIA SEABERG, Cynthia von Buhler, D Valther, D.L. Whitted, d2frma2, Dalia Tebechrani, dan edwards, dan parriott, Dan Ponce, Dan Rivera, Dan Standing, dan_eyer, Dana Altenburger, ana Longley, Dana Rae, Dani, Dani Jones, Dani Perea, DaniBrown, Danie West, Daniel A. Campisi, Daniel Flores, Daniel He, Daniel L. Emmons, aniel Luke, Daniel Purcell, Daniel Queiroz Porto, Daniel Roth, Daniel Schulz, Daniel Snoke, Daniel Solis, Danielle Lewon, dannfuller, DanSai, Dante uccieri, Dante Tumminello, danvena, Dara, Daria Brooks, Dark, darkhavens, darrellferguson, Darryl Clarke, Darwin Pierce, Darwyn & Marsha, aryn Tsuji, Dave Garber, Dave Garber, Dave Michalak, Dave Punk, David, David & Nancy Fry, David Atchison, David Benton, David Bolick, David rami, David Claiborne, David Dingman, David Dou, David Grassi, David Grassi McDaniels, David Jackson, David Jacobs, David Jafra, David Joyce, avid M Ronzone, David Meikis, David Priere, David Sherman, David Snider, David Tai. David Travis. Dawn Lahey, Dean Hacker. Debbie Cerda, eborah, Deborah Grech, Deborah J. Brannon, Deborah Moore, dechanique, Delores Jeffrey, Dembol, Demelza Jean, Denise Pirko, Denitt Perez, ennis Imoto, Derek Yee, Deron Bennett, Desiree Ikeler, deVidiax, Devin Bruce , Devin Grayson, Diana McQueen, Dianne 'Dawn' Garcia, Dina Kamp- neyer, Dirk Manning, DiRT, Domenique White, Dominique Brooks, Dominique Rodier, Don Alsafi, Don Brown, Don Flinspach, Don Roff, Don Wood, onald Reynolds, Dorene Grover, Doris Cacoilo, Dorothy Harrison, Doug Bissell, Doug Dorr, Doug Greer , Doug Smith, Douglas Hill, Douglas Sturk r, dougty, Dr. Kara, DrBravo2, dreamer, Drew Coombs, drgnldy71, Duane Watson, DumpyLittleRobot, Dzenita, E. Chris Lynch, Ed Watson, Eddie A. an Dijk, Eddie Lopez, Edgar Dapremont, Edie Cougar, Edward Harris, Edwyn Tiong Yung Ron, eggdropsoap, egrissom, Eileen McLain, eincomicle- en, Elaine Lee, Elayne Riggs, Eleanor Cove, Elena Fried, Elena Murphy, Elisa McCausland, Elisabeth Beinke, Eliza Bowen, Elizabeth, Elizabeth arrial, Elizabeth Breitweiser, Elizabeth Chen, Elizabeth G, Elizabeth Posadas, Elizabeth Woolley, Elle Sciocchetti, Elliot Blake, Elliott Alexander alinas, Elliott Brown, Ellise Heiskell, Emilio Torres Jr., Emily, Emily Braun, Emily Corrado, Emily Corrado, Emily Earl, Emily Langton, Emily Shuttle- worth, Emily Stothard, Emily Taylor, emjstone, Emma Conner, Emma Grogan, Emma Murray, Emma Pomes, Emma-Jean Stewart, EmmaVox, Emme- ine Pui Ling Dobson, enandrews, Eric Detweiler, eric knight, Eric McLeod, eric orchard, Erica Friedman, Erica Heflin, Erica Mederos, Erica Simon, rica Soileau, Erik Parker, Erik Rinard, Erik Smith, Erika Cervantes, Erika H. Ruhl, Erika Homan, Erin and Marc, Erin Dukarski, Erin Gowdy, Erin Kelly, rin Kys, Erin Montemurro, Erin Subramanian, Erin Tapken, Erin Victor, Ernesto Bravo Jr., Ernst Riemer, Esmee & Andre, Esmond Chong, España heriff, esther m palmer, Evan, Evan Huntoon, Evan Pivazyan, Evey Wong, F. Cinquacento, fabianran, faintdreams, FaolchuDonn, fawn, Felicia Day

☆ ☆ ☆ ☆ ☆ ☆

Felipe Sobreiro, fernando x fuentes, Fiona Robertson, Fionnuala Murphy, Fiorella Santana, Florence Chai, Flynt, Forest, forgecat, foulness, Frances Frank A. Kadar, Frankie B Washington, Frankie Gray, frazer irving, Fred Flores, Fred Hicks / Evil Hat Productions, Frederick Hurley, Gab Contreras Gabriela Datterati, Gaby F, Gail Courtney, Gail Kwak, Galen Lim, Garrett Jones, Garth Matthams, Gary, Gary Arkell, Gary Chun, Gary Colletti, Gary D Simmons, Gary Dominguez, Gary Fuhr, Gary Makries, Gary S. Arkell, Gavin ap' Morrygan, Gavin Thomson, Geek Girl Diva, gem2niki, Geof LaTulippe, Geoffrey Brett Williams, George Gatewood, George Lentino, George Middeton, George Shea, George Wright, Gerald Von Stoddard Gibran Graham, Gillian Gilbert Ybabez, Gillian Mann, Gillian Smith, Gina, Gina Gallego, Glen Ivey, Glenn Arseneau, gloria sanchez, G-Mart Comics GnomeGirl, Gordon McAlpin, grace, Grace Fong, Grace Goff, Grace Vanness, Grant Alter, Greg Evans, Greg Muciño, Greg Pak, Greg Riedesel, Gregg Yasukochi, Gretchen Gueguen, Gretchen S., GriffinFire, GWC Audra, Gyrfalcon2138, H.D., HachiHelen, Hadley Andersen, Hannah Genslinge Hannah Moore, Harry Vetter, Haviva Avirom, hayley roberts, Heather Creely, Heather Martin, Heather Myers, Heather Royston, Heidi Berthiaume Helen Kaelin, Helen Schreiner, Helen Wortham, Helena, helia phoenix, Herman Louw, hetchkay, Hilary, Hive Mind Comics, Holly Bird, Holly DePatie Holly Harrop, Holly Sewell, Honami Kyozuka, honorless, Hooper Triplett, hr doran, hysteriq, Ian Brill, Ian Ng, Ian Struckhoff, ignacia, Incredible Ink India Allen, Indigo Buchanan, Industrial Scribe, Irma Ahmed, Isabel, Isabelle, Isabelle Hurteau, Israel Skelton, Ivy Tsai, J Rangel, J Schwalbach-Smith J.K.Woodward, J.R. Deans, JABenson, Jac Ting Lim, Jack, Jack Chiu, Jack Teague, JackFractal, jackie, Jaclyn Duhe, Jacob Smith, Jacqueline Urick Jacquelyn Erdman, Jad Hindy, jade, Jade Groot, Jae Nemain, Jai Nitz, jaime kimbrel, Jaime Wurth, Jake Brooks, Jamal Igle, James, James A. Stewart James Andrewson, James Chan, James Daily, James D'Elia, James Garnham, James Gilmore, James Kwak, James Leask, James P. McNamara, James Parrish, James Tuttle, Jamey Barlow, Jamie Gambell, Jamie Jeans, Jamie Macfarlane, Jamie Roberts, Jamie Sperry, Jamie Stubbs, Jan Roger Henden Jane Lee, Jane Nolan, jane ormerod-wilkinson, Janelle Asselin, Janice, Janine F, Janine Macbeth, Janna Hochberg, Janna O'Shea, Jared Shurin Jarod West, Jarrod Abel, Jarrod Farquhar-Nicol, Jason Arthur, Jason Bickings, Jason Dougherty, Jason Fedorchuk, Jason Porath, Jason Smith, Jason Tippitt, Jason W. Gavin, Jasper Dodge, Jaypaul barrow, Jazmine, Jazmine Rodriguez, JC Cohen, Jean Egdorf, Jean Fischer, Jeanine Schaefer, Je Kaplan, Jeff Barbanell, Jeff Orgill, Jeff Petersen, Jeff Pollet, Jeff Schultz, Jeff Stolarcyk, Jeff Whitnack, Jeffrey Hardy Quah, Jeffrey J. Ellen, Jeffrey Lamar, Jeliza Patterson, Jen Bolton, Jen Peters, Jen Ramirez, Jen Rose, Jen Sparenberg, Jenn, Jenn McCreary, Jenna Busch, Jenni Goodchild, Jenn Kirkruff, Jennifer, Jennifer Cohen, Jennifer Doudney, Jennifer Farrens, Jennifer Hite, Jennifer Jeon, Jennifer K. Stuller, Jennifer Kye, Jennifer Landa Jennifer McGee, Jennifer Parker, Jennifer Parsons, Jennifer Proch, Jennifer Reeves, Jennifer Renata Mendieta, Jennifer Sparkman, Jennifer Thorpe-Moscon, Jeprox, Jerel Parenton, Jeremy, Jeremy Byrge, Jeremy Canceko, Jeremy Fiest, Jeremy Melloul, Jeremy Reppy, Jeremy Treece, JeremyCoatney, Jerzy Drozd, Jess, Jesse Lee Porter, Jesse Porter, Jessica, Jessica Browder, Jessica Cantlope, Jessica Daniel, Jessica Doyle, Jessica Fure, Jessica Hickman, Jessica Hood, Jessica Johnson, Jessica L. Wilkie, Jessica Moran, Jessica West, Jessica Wilkie, Jhenne Tyler Beauford, Jill Fogarty, Jill Friedman, Jill Pantozzi, Jillanne Marie Martin, Jim Lee, Jim Lesniak, Jimmy Dunn, JIMMY PALMIOTTI, jiwasz, JL STRAW, Joamette Gil, Joanna Freeman Joanna Rosalie Doherty-Bailey, Joanna Stone, Joanna Wanfried, Joda01, jodi, Jody Collins, Jody H, Jody Houser, Joe Hill, Joe Keatinge, Joe Rubinstein, Joe White, joe768, Joel Becker, Joey Lindsey, Joey Nazzari, John, John Ayliff, John Braun, John Chambers, John Cohen, John Craig, John Hague, John Harrison, John J. Beach, John LaTemple, John Mundt, Esq., John Nacinovich, John Nordlinger, John Parkin, John Wimmer, John Yap Johnny Hsu, Jon Stern aka Wee Heavy, Jonah Stachura, Jonathan Goff, Jonathan Dibblee, Jonathan Gelatt, Jonathan H. Liu, Jonathan Hudgens Jonathan Huth, Jonathan JayLando Dipratna, Jonathan Petersen, Jonathan Wallace, Jonathon Benefield, Jonathon Myers, Jorby, Jordan Liv Jordan T. Neves, Jorge Cuaik, Jorge Guzman, Joseph Brennan, Joseph Fernandes, Joseph Hatton, Joseph Soonsin Lee, Josephine Narvais, Josh A Cagan, Josh Crawley, Josh Elder, Josh Maher, Joshua Beale, Joshua Goldfond, Joshua Levitsky, Joshua Levitsky, Joshua Robertson, Joshua Shapel Joshua Simpson, Joshua Stone, Joumana Medlej, JT Molloy, Juan Mario Cardenas, Juan Mauricio Muñoz Lievana, Juju Mendivil, Jules Beulen, Julia Julia Frizzell, Julia Piatt, Julian Orr, Juliana Xavier, Julie Benson, Julie Delliquanti, Julie Faulkner, June Ashley, Justin Cantelo, justin molinari, Justin Shimp, JustinChung.com, Justine, K. D. Bryan, Kaan Evren Basaran, Kameron Gates, Kanghyun Chu, Kara Cipolloni, Karen Burrows, Karen Cheung Karen Lam, Karen Lee, Karen Mahoney, Karen Whatchamacallister, kari eidnes, Karine, Karizma, Karol Callaway, Kat Kan, Kat Kosmala, kat laurange Kat Perdock, Kat Vassar, Katanyna, Kate Dollarhyde, Kate Edwards, Kate Hill, Kate Jeal, Kate Larking, Kate MacNeil, Kate MacQueen, Kate Marie Hill Kate Morrison, Kate Stewart, kateison, Katelyn Sweigart, Katharyn Emmert, Katherine, Katherine Carlson, Katherine Hernandez, Katherine Raines Kathleen Brennan, Kathleen R. Carbone, Kathryn Sullivan, Kathryn Todd, Kathryn Whiteford, Kathy Altice, Kathy Flynn, Katie, Katie Cunningham Katie Doyle, Katie Narduzzo, Katie O'Neal, Katie Scott-Cornell, Katie Sheahan, Katkat, Katrina Lehto, Katrina Salumbides, Katy, Kay Lunkenheimer Kayla, Kayla Banks, KC Kupperman, KCFS, Keidy Zuniga, Keith Chow, Kel Nuttall, Kelly, Kelly Frederick, Kelly Gerlach, Kelly Gerlach, Kelly Thompson Kelsey Hvorecny, Ken Arthur, Ken Eppstein, Ken Ograyensek, Kenny Mak, keri willson, Kerry Jane, Kevin Bates, Kevin Chiou, Kevin Church, Kevin Clark, Kevin D. Bond, Kevin Freeman, Kevin Gemser, Kevin H., Kevin J. Maroney, Kevin Kiniry, Kevin Leddy, Kevin McAninch, Kevin Walker, Kik Williams, Kim Blessing, Kim Brown, Kim Dancy, Kim McLoren, Kim Pham, Kim S., Kimberley, kimberly, Kimberly Barry, Kimberly Bradshaw, Kimberly Burgess, Kimberly Komatsu, Kin Wong, Kind Of Strange, Kirby Krueger, Kircee, Kirk Anderson, Kirsten Jacobsen, Kirsten Thompson, Kit White Kitamu Latham-Sampier, K-Lub R. Hall, Kolter Kiess, Komainu, kopiikat, Kourtnie McKenzie, Kris Miranda, Kris Rudin, Krista Thorson, Kristen, Kristen Van Dam, Kristi, Kristie Semmel, Kristin, Kristin Brroks, Kristin Burns, Kristin Driggers, Kristin Lear, Kristin Taylor, Kristina Knight, Kristine, Kristine Roper, Kristopher Kersey, Krystal Lynn Bittner, Krystal V. Weber, Kyle Hendricks, L Fayth, L Leist, Lacey Nogueira, Lance Curran, Lanora Melilo, La deSouza, Lara Eakins, Larry Lambert, LarryKing, lauke, Laura, Laura Angell, Laura Ewing, Laura Frank, Laura Fritsch, laura gramlich, Laura Hall, Laura Kinnaman, Laura M., Laura Martin, Laura Miello, Laura Truxillo, Laura Wilson, Laura Zinger, Lauren, Lauren Burke, Lauren Pottinger, Laurie Vilbrandt Laurie Wielenga, Lawrence Chu, Lawrence McClurkin, lazendar, LBCM, Le Guidon, Leading Edge, Leah, Leigh Pfeffer, Leigh Tyberg, Lene Taylor, Leo Lingas, Leo Ngo, Leonard O'Grady, Leonardo Olea, Leslie Flynn, Leslie S Klinger, Leticia Medina, lex naka, Liam Dunlop, Lianne Mc Intosh, Libby Rich, lilacsigil, lillerina, Limae, Lin Workman, Linda Lindsey, Linda M. Najera, Linda Whittelsey, Linda Wilmsen-Boulay, Lindsay Christopherson Lindsay Mays, Lindsay Voytek, Lindsey Ouimet, line langsaeter, Lisa, Lisa Bacallao, Lisa Coxson, Lisa Fortuner, Lisa Manglass, Lisa McCarty, Lisa Treece, Liz Burns, Liz McDonough, Liz Smith, Liz Westlake, Liz Wrightson, Liza P, liznugent, llamaslovedrama, Llexi Leon, Llinos Cathryn Thomas Logan Riley, Lorelei Bunjes, Lori Sanders, Lou Srygley, Lou Valenti, Louise Morgan, Luce, Lucy Venetsky, Lukas Myhan, LukasM, Luke Brown, Lutz Albers, Lydia Liao, Lynette Young, Lynn Gottshall, Lynne Anderson, M. C. Matz, m. Cruickshank, M. Sweeney Lawless, M. Zehr, m0oka, M3 Sweatt Ma'at Crook, Maddy B, Madeline Z., Maeghan Kearney, Maggie Bree, Maggie Bree Sidlinger, mamath, MAnderson, Mandy Bulat, MAPendragon Marc Green, Marc Hammond, Marc Mason, marcela, Marcia Ortiz, Marcus Ervin, Margaret, Margaret Dunlap, Margaret E Galbraith, Margaret Hogg margaret liss, Margaret Richter, Margie, Maria, Maria Kirchner, Maria Lima, Maria Perr, Mariann Foster, Marianna Pollock, MARIE BURR, Marie Dalby Mariko Shewmake, Marina Handwerk, Mario Armando Gonzalez, Mario Boon, Marisa, Marisa Ortiz, Marisol Eggleton, Marissa Black, Marissa Nolan-Layman, Mariya Krutova, Marjory wallace, Mark Katzoff, Mark R Stegbauer, Mark Sable, Mark Truman, Marly, Martin Bignell, Martin Grider Marty Todd, marvin Ruffin, Mary, Mary Agner, Mary Canada, Mary Compeau, MatFunwithmarkers, Mathew Quitney, Mathieu Doublet, Mathilde Sachiko Bouhon, Matias Christensen, Matias Duarte, Mato Delgado, Matt Carroll, Matt Daniel, Matt Lennon, Matt M McElroy, Matt McDaniel, Matt Riggsby, Matt Thorn, Matthew Ashcraft, Matthew Borgatti, Matthew Cahill, Matthew Duda, Matthew Fabb, Matthew Ferrell, Matthew Hall,

☆ ☆ ☆ ☆ ☆ ☆

Matthew Johnston, Matthew Lemmon, Matthew O'Malley, Matthew Swift, MattMoore, Maura McHugh, maurice gaston, Mauricio Moura, Mauricio, Muñoz Liévana, Max Beckman, Maya, Maya Keshavan, mazyloron, MC Alcock, McHenry Keith, Meagan L. Healy, meg gandy, Megan, Megan Fortner, Megan Koepsell, Megan Lavey-Heaton, Megan Metzger, Megan Rose, Megan Skogland, Meghan Augusta, Meghan Callahan, Meghan K., Callahan, Meghan Sullivan, Mel.N., Melanie D'Arcy, Melanie Snyder, Melanie T. D'Arcy, Melinda Hill, Melinda Wilson, Melissa, Melissa Guillet, Melissa Kay, Melissa Spencer, Melissa Walsh, Mell Scalzi, Melmoth, meowiris, mercurious, Merrick M, Micah Baldwin, Micah Griffin-Lundy, Micha Savelsbergh, Michael & Bendy Wyatt, Michael Brassell, Michael Colford, Michael Farrah, Michael Howard, Michael Lynn Wherley, Michael Mann, Michael Perridge, Michael Stum, Michael Suarez, Michael Takahara, Michael Thornton, Michael Volovar, Michael Wirth, Michael Woods, Michael Wyatt, Michal Bluma, Michele, Michele Tepper, Michelle, Michelle Flamm, Michelle Ikemoto, Michelle Manning, Michelle Starry, Michelle Watkins, Mike Aragona, Mike Campbell, Mike Exner, Mike Lunsford, Mike Madrid, Mike Maihack, Mikito Kawasaki, milan, Mimi, Miriam Barberena, Miriam Kim, MisfitsTamara, MJ00, Mollie Ann Roaden, Molly Hayden, Molly Jane Kremer, Monica Loren, Monica Richards, Monique Pihl, Monique Poirier, Monkmunk, Montse Portella, Moonie Garcia, Morgan Dambergs, Morgan Dodge, Morgan Stonebraker, mrmikeex3, Ms. Alicia Bianca Cline, Ms. Alicia Cline, Mur Lafferty, Musictwig, Mytana, N Koeppen, Nadia Attlee, Nafmi Sanichar-van Herwijnen, Nancy, Nancy Fry, Nancy Martira, Naomi Bosch, Naomi Clark, Naomi Petrash, Natalie Ebnet, Natalie Hasell, Natalie Stachowski, Natalye Tate, Natasha, Natasha-zimich, Nate Bunnyfield, Nate Helmkamp, Nateal Erickson, Nathan Schreiber, nattherat, Neil Aitken, nicci, Nicholas Favorito, Nicholle Owens, Nick, Nick Mockoviak, nick.anello1, Nicki France, Nicki Howe, Nicole, Nicole Falk, Nicole Lewandowski, nicole maniez, nicole meiring, Nicole Osier, Nicole Rich, Nicole Sixx, Nicole Teixeira, Nida Zada, niki carlson, Nikka Aberman, Nikki H, Nikki Jeske, Nikki Orvis, Nikki St Pierre, Nikos, Nina Raoof, Niphridell, Niraj Patil, Nishan Patel, Nissa Campbell, nkkingston, nobuko cobi narita, Noel Anthony Haughey, Nolan T, Norbert Wellmann, Noreen E Murphy, Noriko Shoji, Norm Walsh, Nova Bridges, Nyssa Gilkey, Ola Eriksson, Oliver Mertz, Olivia Desormeaux, Omar Yanez, Ona Loots, Optimystical Studios, P.J.Mendoza, Pablo S. Maggi, Paige Pumphrey, Pam Keene, Pamela Shaw, Paola Kathuria, Paolo Belfiore, Pat Loika, Pat Shores, Patricia Hallstein, Patricia Mulvihill, Patrick Farley, Patrick Lee, Patrick Michael Strange, Patrick Suin, Patrick Sun, PatrickAT, Paul & Pippa, Paul Allor, Paul Bernard, Paul Bines, Paul Braidford, Paul Cornell, Paul Handley, Paul J Mendoza, Paul Johnston, Paul Lopez-Wood, Paul O'Regan, Paula Knudsen, Paul-Gabriel Wiener, Peggy, Peggy Neumeier, penguinpaladin, Perazza, Peter Beck, Peter Lange, Peter O'Brien, Peter Vervloet, Petra de Jong, PharaohKatt, Pharoah Bolding, Phil Hester, Phil Jackson, Phillip Suttkus, Phyllis Novin, pi8you, picassowary, Pierre Oleo, Pkad, poetactics, Polia Giannoulidis, pomfelo, Priscilla Lam, Priscilla Spencer, Purple Duck Games, R Thomas Riley, R. Francis Smith, rachaar, Rachael Derrick, Rachel, Rachel Aavang, Rachel Huntress, Rachel Kiri Walker, Rachel Lunt, Rachel Smythe, rachel walker, Rachelle Berry, Rae Grimm, Rafia Mirza, Ralph Contreras, Randy, Randy Eng, Randy Ma, Rangaprabhu Parthasarathy, ranti junus, Raul Marengo, Raven Moore, Rawnzilla, Ray Cornwall, Ray Hill, Ray Wegner, RDL Collector, Rebecca Brown, Rebecca Coffey, Rebecca Mansfield, Rebecca Schneider, Rebekah Meyer, Redsonja1313, Reed Olsen, Relena Belnades, Renaud Mathieu, Renee Kurilla, Renée Marie, Reynardin, RFlovin, Rian Fike, Ricardo Amaral Filho, rich douek, Rich Johnston, Richard Christopher, Richard cox, Richard DeDominicis, Richard Morgan, Richard Oh, Richard Rockwood, Rick Lowell, Rick Spears, rick starczewski, Rico Renzi, Risa Cho, Ritchie, Tiongson, rivenrock, Rob Berardino, ROB BROWNING, Rob Casteel, Rob Kaas, Rob McMonigal, Rob Stenzinger, Robbie Boerner, Robbie Th'ng, Robert, Robert Harrington, Robert Loper, Robert Muhlig, Robert Simon, Robert Smith, robert stradley, Robert Stutts, Robert T. Bakie, Robert Yocum, Robin, Robin Sheasley, Robyn Bremner, Robyn Cobham, Rochelle Mantanona, rod espinosa, Rodrigo Ortiz Vinholo, Ron Phillips, Ron Vink, ronald curell, Ronald Montgomery, Ronald Smith, Ronda Pattison, Roni Callahan, Rosanna, Rose Levy, Rosemary Cheetham, Ross Campbell, Roxanne, Roxanne Lenzo, Roy Swan, Rupert, Rus Wooton, Rusty Rowley, Ruth, Ruth Adams, Ruth Anne Arnold, RWOS, Ryan, Ryan Calimlim, Ryan Closs, Ryan Cracknell, Ryan Fedon, Ryan Fehr, Ryan Havers, Ryan Kimber, Ryan Mogge, Ryan Perkins, Ryan Poole, Ryan Schrodt, Ryvre Hardrick, S Halud, S Segal, safyrejet, Saiful Remy Mokhtar, sallysaurus rex, Sam Meier, Samantha, Samanda b Jeude, Samantha Newark, samanthaleigh, Samara Drewe, sami, samiagraphe, san.patricio, Sandra, Sandra Acevedo Cala, Sandra Hirschmann, Santiago Bourges Waldegg, Saoirse Delaney, Sara, Sara Amor, Sara Eileen, Sara Jeska, Sara Palazzo, Sara Richard, Sarah, Sarah Ann Nelson, Sarah C Frigon, Sarah Clark, Sarah Coldheart, Sarah Elkins, Sarah Elliott, Sarah Fogg, sarah gaydos, Sarah Kremen-Hicks, Sarah Romig, Sarah Schanze, Sarah Stewart, Sarah Timberlake Taylor, Sarah W., Sarah Wilkinson, sarisa, Sasha, Sasha Perl-Raver, Satyajit Chetri, Savanna Reardon-Cannaday, Savannah, scarlett, Schleproque, Scott, Scott "Young Scott" Cameron, Scott Bachmann, Scott Cameron, Scott D.M. Simmons, Scott Edgar, Scott Fogg, Scott Gable, Scott Henricks, Scott Morrison, Scott Ng, Scott Parsons, Scott Puckett, Scott Robertson, Scott Rubin, Scott Santos, ScottDMSimmons, Sean Becker, Sean Dulaney, Sean Francis, Sean Hackett, Sean Hillman, Sean Hopkins, Sean Jurgens, Sean McCabe, Sean P. Aune, Sean Whelan, Sean Williams, Seana Miller, seanrabin, Sebastian S., Secret Agent, SeeDCOrr, Serge Ladd, Seth Rosenblatt, shadowpro3, shane grant, Shaneyah, Shanna Mandell, Shannon, Shannon Dockter, Shannon W., Shannon Weathers, SharoninaVolvo, Sharron Hawthorne, Shaun, Shaun Kronenfeld, Shaun Manning, Shaun O'Kelley, Shauna J. Grant, Shawn Demumbrum, Shawn Tyson, Shel Kennon, Shelby Norris, Shing Yin Khor, Shiny Rosie, Sian Harrop, Signal Watch, Sigrid Ellis, SilverLocust, Simon Hamelin, Simon Tam, SitaRaine, SJ Matthews, SJ Mueller, Skaja Wills, Skullcat, slnaeole, Slnsalim, SmithingChick, Snappop, Sonia Harris, Sophie Powell, Soyini, Spenser Anderson, Spidersaiyan, squarerootofpi, Stacey Leigh Brooks, Stacy Flores, Stacy Head, stacy metzger, starringbuttons, Stefan Grosse, Stellalune, Steph Stokes, Stephanie, Stephanie Duchin, Stephanie Lippitt, Stephanie Noell, Stephanie Phillips, Stephanie Tennison, Stephanie Wooten, Stephen, Stephen R, stephen spotswood, Stephen Struharik, Stephen Vale, Steve, Steve Brezenoff, Steve Horton, Steve Niles, Steve Salomon, Steve VanHorn, Steve Watkinson, Steven, Steven King, Steven Mangold, Steven Sifert, Stew Fyfe, Stuart Chaplin, Stuart Gunn, Sue Coombes, Susan, Susan Broman, Susan Esparza, Susan Holland, susan rubin, Susanna Modjallal, Susannah Paletz, Susie Tsang, suzanne, Suzanne Scott, Suzo, Sveta, Svetlana, Sydnie Jimerson, T. L. Mason, T.J. Fuller, Jr., Tabitha James, Tai Shimizu, Talendra, Talmai Mathis, Tami Brouillette, Tammy Graham, Tammy Lynn Garrison, Tania Burgos-Lucero, Tanja Wooten, Tanya, Tara, Tara Abbamondi, Tara Gariepy, tartarus, Taryn O'Neill, taterpie, Tawnly Pranger, Taylor, Ted Adams, Ted Van Duyn, Teez, Tehani Wessely, Telza, Teresa D. Lee, TERRENCE P J MICHEAU, Terry Maltos, Terry Read, Thanun Khowdee, The Comic Book Shop, The Girl with The Wandering Eye, The Pandas, The Patterson's, thegrumpygoldfish, Theo, Theodore Cullen, ThePinkNinja, Theresa Wollenstein, Therese Magnani, thisismymirror.com, Thomas Barnes, Thomas Branch, Thomas Eit, Thomas Hahn, Thomas Heaton, Thomas Kwok, Thomas Stidman, Thomas Swingler, Thomas Walmsley, Tiarra Wantz, Ticklefist, Tiff Hudson, Tihleigh Roach, Tihleigh Roach, Tim Beedle, Tim D'Allaird, Tim Geraghty, Tim Goldenburg, Tim Hanley, Tim Kirk, Tim Kretzer, Tim Miner, Tim Roller, Timothy Gula, Timothy Nakayama, Timothy Shiner, Tisha Woods, Todd DuBois, Todd Farmer, todd piken, Tom Hodges, Tom Rafferty, Tom Regan, Tom Stillwell, Tom Zimmermann, tomc, tommythewolfboy, Tony Deliz, Tony Lee, TotusMel, TQ Broens, Tracey Brighton, Tracey Van Zaanen, Tracy Grogan, tragic_antihero, Travis Hardiman, Trevor Thompson, trevstor, Trin Miller, Trina Finton, Tristan Frodelius, Tristan Thomas, Tsutako, Turdle, Tyler & Wendy Chin-Tanner, Umar Ditta, Unika, upekha bandaranayake, Uthor, Valerie Reilly, valium, Valya, Vanessa Cox, Vanessa Satone, vcky, Vee C Pais, Veronica, Verónica Muñiz-Soto, veronika, Veronika Hurbis, Veronika von Volkova, Vic Donnelly, Vicki Burklund, victoria collinson, Vincent McBride, Virginia Cubillos Alvarez, Vroooom, Wallace Polsom, Wallace Sellars, Walter Herz, Walter Mitchell, Walter Ostlie, Wei-yi Huang, Wendi Freeman, Whitney Johnson, Widgett Walls, Will Turcan, William, William Beisswanger, William Chrapcynski http://www.bsodcomic.net, William Elliott, William Gatevackes, William Mincy, William Schlote, Winston Yuan, wonderali, Woodrow Jarvis Hill, worstwebcomic, Worthy Glover, Y. Penders, Yasmin Liang, Yvonne Knapp, Zabet Stewart, Zach, Zach Wilson, Zachary Brown, Zachary Cole, Zachary Kelsey, Zack Rosenberg, Zack Turner, Zapatos, Zoe River Roaden, Zoe Wadsworth

☆ ☆ ☆

WOMANTHOLOGY

☆☆☆

HEROIC

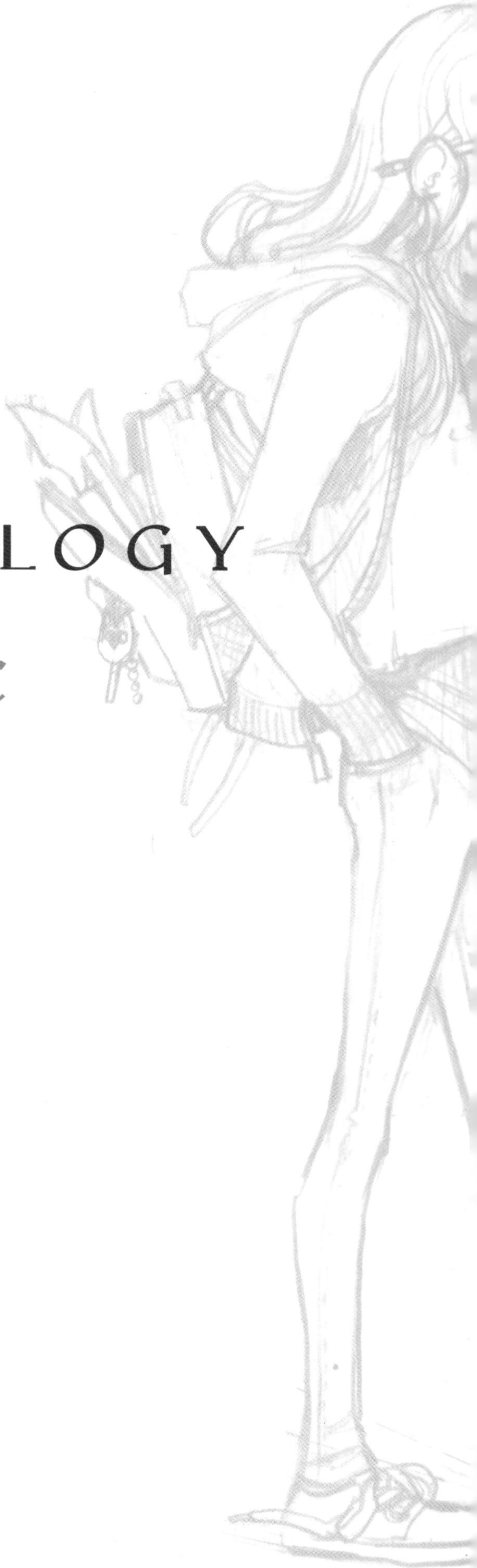